Atlas of WORLD HISTORY

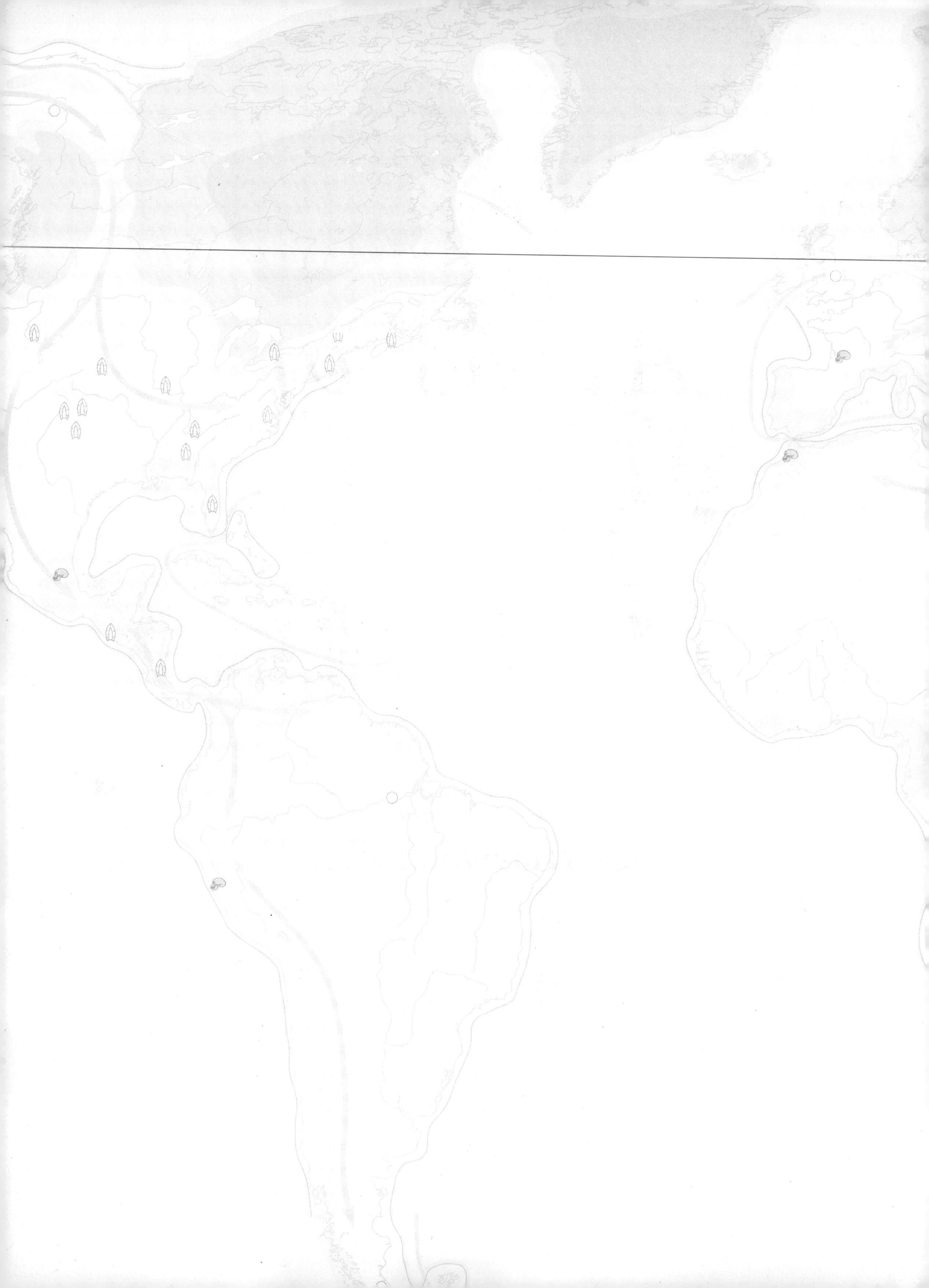

Atlas of
WORLD HISTORY

John Haywood, Ph. D.
Honorary Teaching Fellow, Lancaster University, UK

with

Brian Catchpole, M.A. • **Simon Hall,** M.A.
Edward Barratt, M.A.

FALL
RIVER
PRESS

Project director Peter Furtado

Cartographic manager Richard Watts

Advisory editors

Jeremy Black
Professor of History, University of Exeter, UK

K.M. Chaudhuri
Vasco da Gama Professor of European Exploration, European University Institute, Florence, Italy

Barry Cunliffe
Professor of European Archaeology, University of Oxford, UK

Brian M. Fagan
Professor of Anthropology, University of California, Santa Barbara, USA

J.E. Spence
Associate Fellow, Royal Institute of International Affairs, UK

Academic advisors

J.I. Catto
Oriel College, University of Oxford, UK

Professor Robin Cohen
University of Warwick, UK

Professor J.H. Elliott
Regius Professor of Modern History, University of Oxford, UK

Professor Harold James
Princeton University, New Jersey, USA

Professor Maldwyn A. Jones
University of London, UK

Dr Stewart Lone
Australian Defence Force Academy

Dr Oswyn Murray
Balliol College, University of Oxford, UK

Professor A.J.S. Reid
The Australian National University

Professor Francis Robinson
Royal Holloway, University of London, UK

Dr Kate Spence
Christ's College, University of Cambridge, UK

Professor John K. Thornton
Millersville University, Pennsylvania, USA

This page:
Ottoman janissaries, c.AD 1820

Opposite above:
Chinese bronze horse, c.AD 200

Opposite below:
Mughal Indian rug design, c.1550

Following page:
Above: French revolutionary caricature, c.1789
Below: Russian revolutionary poster, c.1920

Art director Ayala Kingsley
Art editor Martin Anderson
Cartographic editor Tim Williams
Editors Susan Kennedy, Peter Lewis, Clive Carpenter, Irene Lyford
Cartographer Nathalie Johns
Picture researcher Claire Turner
Production Clive Sparling
Editorial assistant Marian Dreier
Typesetter Brian Blackmore
Illustrations Charles Raymond
Proofreader Lynne Elson
Indexer Ann Barrett

This 2009 edition published by the Fall River Press, by arrangement with The Brown Reference Group Ltd

Fall River Press
122 Fifth Avenue
New York, NY 10011

ISBN 978–1-4351-1548-4

Printed and bound in Malaysia

10 9 8 7 6 5 4 3 2 1

Produced and prepared by
The Brown Reference Group Ltd
(incorporating Andromeda Oxford Ltd)

Contents

Part 1
The Ancient World
(4,000,000 – 500 BC)

Part 2
The Classical World
(500 BC – AD 600)

Part 3
The Medieval World
(AD 600 – 1492)

Part 4
From Columbus to American Independence
(AD 1492 – 1783)

Contents

FOREWORD

Time is a surprisingly difficult concept to grasp, and yet in the modern world we are obsessed by it. Ask someone in Britain how far away Australia is, and the chances are, if they know at all, they will reply not in terms of distance but of time: "about 18 hours". But how many of us, even professional archeologists, can conceive of the span of four million years that humans have inhabited the Earth? At best we can feel our way back, steadying ourselves on familiar fixed points provided by known historical dates. One of our most commonly remembered dates is 1492, the year of the first voyage of Christopher Columbus and the earliest confrontation between Europe and the Americas. But its familiarity reveals how blinkered our western-centered vision is. A lifetime earlier, in 1415, a giraffe from Kenya was taken to Beijing and presented to the incredulous Ming emperor. This gift was a result of the voyages of trade and exploration by the Chinese sailor Zheng He. Columbus had a mere three ships at his disposal, Zheng He was accompanied by 62 galleons and more than a hundred support vessels. In the fifteenth century , the histories of different parts of the globe started to come together: the world began to shrink into a single global system.

This was a process that had started much earlier. A family of Venetian jewel merchants, of whom the best known was Marco Polo, traveled extensively in Asia, reaching Beijing in the late thirteenth century. Eleven centuries earlier, a not dissimilar journey had been made. The Chinese Han Annals record a visit from ambassadors of An-dun, king of Da-jin – the Roman emperor Marcus Aurelius. They note with regret the absence of jewels among the gifts he offered.

ABOVE A British soldier in India in the early 19th century adopts the traditional means of transport for dignitaries.

LEFT A Roman trading vessel. The Romans regularly sailed to southern India from the 1st century AD.

These historical anecdotes are vivid reminders both of the passage of time and of worlds in contact – and potential collision. They have in common one thing: they are all the products of cultures at moments of maximum innovation – Columbus during Renaissance and the first emergence of the nation-state; Zheng He at the flowering of the Ming dynasty; Marcus Aurelius at the peak of the Roman empire, before it was ground down by the incursions of barbarian tribes. Historians – and, for that matter, prehistorians – tend to focus on societies that are innovative, and on periods of maximum change. Those large areas of the world where societies that choose to conserve rather than innovate have survived, often over immense periods of time, commonly suffer a relative neglect in the historical story. At last, however, in the *Cassell Atlas of World History* this imbalance has been redressed for the general reader and student.

The *Atlas* is a genuinely global atlas of human history. It provides detailed insights into the major events and periods of dramatic change, while at the same time standing back to offer successive visions of the world in perspective. Above all, insofar as the available evidence allows, all regions of the world are given even-handed treatment. In this one book scholarship and graphics combine to present the entire story of humankind with a balance never before achieved. It is a stunning achievement and one which cannot fail to open the minds of us all.

Barry Cunliffe
Institute of Archaeology, University of Oxford

USING THIS ATLAS

This book has a consistent organization and, wherever possible, a standard presentation, to help the reader understand the information shown on each map, and to trace a particular story from region to region, or from period to period. The book is arranged in six chronological Parts, and the maps are numbered according to the Part within which they appear, followed by the number of the map within that Part. Thus, map number 4.23 is map 23 in Part 4.

TYPOGRAPHICAL CONVENTIONS

World maps

FRANCE	state or empire
Belgian Congo	dependency or territory
Mongols	tribe, chiefdom or people
Anasazi culture	cultural group

Regional maps

HUNGARY	state or empire
Bohemia	dependency or territory
Slavs	tribe, chiefdom or people
ANATOLIA	geographical region
⚔	battle
•	site or town

OUTLINE OF WORLD HISTORY AND REGIONAL MAPS

Every Part begins with a global outline. A series of snapshot maps, each at a named date, give a portrait of world history.

World map spreads show the level of political or social complexity in standard categories from earliest times to the present. States and empires are shown in capital letters, dependencies or territories in upper-and-lower case. Societies or peoples which have not yet developed into states are shown in bold upper-and-lower-case type; the colors indicate their level of social organization.

World map spreads carry timecharts which are organized region by region. The text on these spreads includes many crossreferences to relevant spreads elsewhere in the Atlas.

Regional map spreads provide a survey of a part of the world between the dates shown in the map title. The maps in each Part for a continent or major region are arranged together in a section, named in the heading on the right-hand side of the spread. These sections are also shown in the Contents page.

Maps are shown in true cartographic projections, each one chosen for the best presentation of the information on the map. North is generally at the top of the page. Some degree of distortion may be found in the case of some maps, such as those of the whole of Asia, which cover a very large section of the world.Where necessary location maps have been included.

Every regional map spread includes standard features: the maps follow similar typographical conventions to the world maps; thick grey lines are used for major borders, thin grey lines for internal borders.

Campaigns or journeys are indicated by lines with arrowheads; thicker grey arrows are used for migrations or movements of large numbers of people. Trade routes are thinner lines, with arrowheads when the trade is specifically one-way.

Each item shown in the map key is referred to in the text at some point on the spread. The main text on each spread explains and amplifies the information drawn on the map.

The spread also carries a timeline, arranged in geographical or thematic sections. Extended events such as wars or dynasties are shown with colored bands; historical periods (such as "Bronze Age") are indicated with grey bands. Every regional map also carries between five and nine numbered "pointers". These refer to the captions elsewhere on the page, which offer additional historical detail about the places indicated.

Cross-references are provided in the panel on the bottom right; these list the numbers of other maps with related information, together with a suggestion of the relevant themes.

The volume index provides detailed references to the text, timelines, numbered captions and map keys. For reasons of space it has not been possible to index every location on the maps themselves.

Part 1

THE ANCIENT

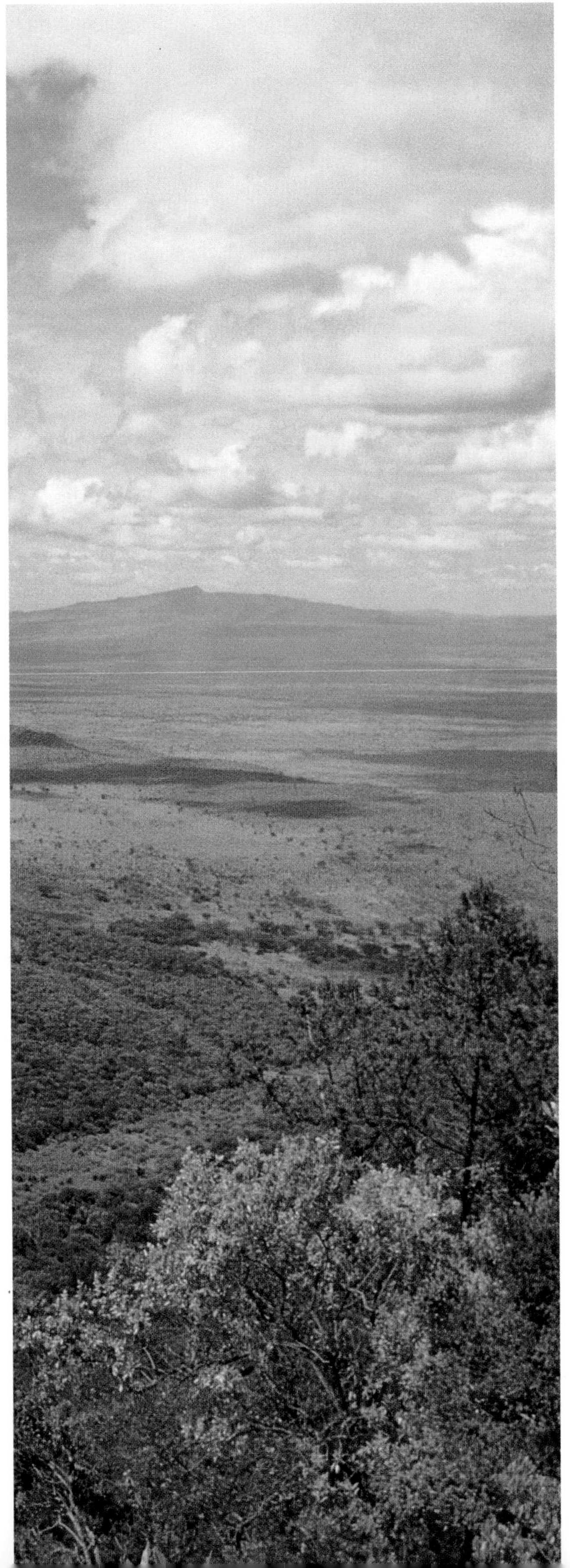

Four million years of biological and cultural evolution took place before the beginning of what is considered history proper, the moment when literacy developed and written records appeared, a little over five thousand years ago. The remarkable story of human prehistory ranges from the origins of humankind on the African savanna to the emergence of the first civilizations and empires. Our knowledge of prehistory is the product of research in many academic disciplines – evolutionary biology, geology, paleontology, and zoology. But the central thread comes from thousands of archeological excavations, of inconspicuous scatters of stone tools and animal bones, hunting camps and farming villages as well as large towns and spectacular cities.

Archeology, alone among the sciences and humanities, can study and explain changes in societies, indeed in humanity itself, over immensely long periods of time. The British archeologist Stuart Piggott once described archeology as the science of rubbish. Archeologists do, indeed, study the abandoned sites, artifacts and food remains of ancient societies, but they go beyond mere description and have sophisticated explanations of why human cultures have changed. Why, for example, did some societies acquire the farming skills that were to revolutionize human life? And how and why did humans cross from Siberia into Alaska and colonize the Americas some 15,000 years ago? The archeologist tries to account for these and other such developments in terms of social organization, as well as in practical terms of technology and environmental change.

The most enduring intellectual framework for our most distant past derives from the evolutionary theories of Charles Darwin, formulated in *The Origin of Species* in 1859. Another great Victorian biologist, Thomas Henry Huxley, called human origins "the question of questions" and boldly compared a

WORLD

4,000,000 – 500 BC

beetle-browed Neanderthal skull recently discovered in Germany to that of a chimpanzee. The theory of evolution by natural selection made it possible to imagine a vast antiquity, a blank timescape for human evolution to unfold over hundreds of thousands, if not millions, of years.

The measuring and peopling of this once empty timescape is one of the great scientific achievements of the 20th century. Darwin and Huxley could only guess at the evolution of humanity. Today, study of the DNA in our body cells tells us that the hominid line – of which *Homo sapiens sapiens*, the anatomically modern species of humankind, is the culmination – separated from the other apes between four and five million years ago. Today, archeology tells us that our human ancestors appeared in Africa and moved out to populate the rest of the world almost two million years ago, and that modern humans may also have originated in Africa. Thanks to archeology, we can not only wonder at the artistic traditions of 30,000 years ago, but also build up sophisticated chronologies based on scientific analysis as well as on techniques of stylistic comparison. Archeology continually presents challenges for new interpretation – as with the accelerator mass spectrometers for radiocarbon dating tiny samples, which caused the accepted dates for the earliest agriculture around the world to be revised in the 1990s. From archeology, again, we know that literate civilizations developed in many places independently throughout the world. Historians using written sources, and archeologists using material remains, can then collaborate in piecing together a narrative of these civilizations.

Modern scholars sometimes think of natural evolution like the branches of a tree, with new species emerging as the endlessly proliferating limbs and twigs, which derive from a trunk of remote common ancestors. Human societies too have evolved in many ways, dictated in part by the varied natural environments. But there are similarities, especially in social and political organization and in the ways in which people make their livings. A flexible classification of human societies into "prestate societies" and "state-organized societies" was made by the American anthropologist Elman Service.

The simplest prestate societies were small family bands, egalitarian groups with communal leadership based on experience. Usually hunters and gatherers of plant foods, band societies prevailed for an immensely long time, until the beginnings of farming. Some, such as the Canadian Inuit and the San of southern Africa, have survived to modern times.

Early farmers lived in permanent villages, and needed new social institutions to settle quarrels and establish land ownership. Many village societies were "tribes" or egalitarian groups with kin-based organization to regulate land ownership and undertake communal tasks. "Chiefdoms" were an elaboration of tribes; they were still kin-based, but power lay in the hands of a few people who controlled long-distance trade and accumulated considerable wealth.

"State-organized societies" or civilizations operated on a far larger scale than chiefdoms. They often involved cities and saw the development of some kind of writing system to keep complex records. Early civilizations had centralized political and economic organization, with power in the hands of a supreme ruler at the pinnacle of a socially stratified society.

Four major themes dominate the long early chapter of our history: the origins of humanity, the evolution and spread of humans throughout the globe, the beginnings of agriculture, and the emergence of civilizations. All of these are bound up with the ways in which food has been secured. For 99 percent of all human history, people lived by hunting and gathering. It may seem that hunting is as old as humanity itself, but that may not in fact be the case. Our earliest ancestors probably

AFRICA was the birthplace of humankind. Here, in the Rift Valley of east Africa, the human ancestors acquired skills of toolmaking, hunting and the use of fire. Not only modern humans, but all the hominid precursors to humans, emerged in this region.

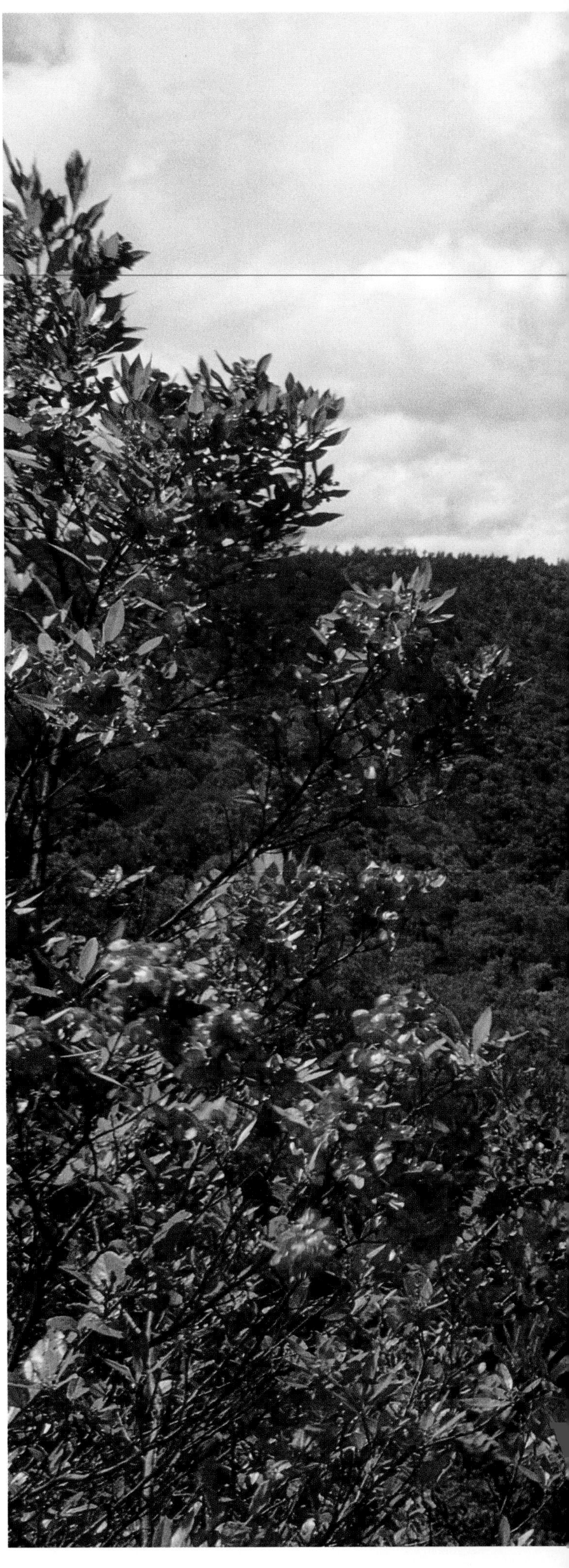

used fleetness of foot and opportunism to scavenge their meat from lion and leopard kills. Exactly when hunting began is doubtful, for ancient weaponry consisted of little more than sharpened and fire-hardened sticks. The appearance of modern humans may have been the moment when animals large and small were first hunted. Stone-tipped spears, then barbed antler projectiles, and special sticks known as spear-throwers soon allowed the hunters to shoot game from a safe distance. When the bow-and-arrow came into use some 10,000 years ago, humans became efficient hunters of animals of every size and birds on the wing. And as the ice sheets retreated at this time, people intensified the quest for food; sea mammals and fish were exploited, and permanent settlements began to emerge at some favored sites.

Hunting is often seen as the glamorous part of foraging, but edible plant foods formed the essential diet of humanity for four million years. Our ancestors possessed an encyclopedic knowledge of plants, knowing which species to eat as staples, and which to fall back on in lean times. It was only when human populations rose sharply at the end of the Ice Age that people began to plant wild grasses and tubers deliberately, to extend the range of wild forms that had been gathered for millennia. And, in a remarkably short time – perhaps three thousand years – the growing of crops and the domestication of animals spread very widely.

With the beginnings of farming, the pace of cultural change accelerated. At first, civilizations like those of the Egyptians, the Shang in China, and the Sumerians in Mesopotamia were independent entities with little or no contact with one another. Gradually trade in precious objects and useful raw materials developed and states became more reliant on each other. By 500 BC, the first chapter of human history had given way to a world in which much larger political and economic entities, known as empires, played a leading role. But the first four million years had already created human biological and cultural diversity and laid the foundations of our own world ■

1.01 HUMAN ORIGINS • 4,000,000 – 100,000 YEARS AGO •

Human evolution began as the Earth's climate started to cool during the Miocene epoch (25–5 million years ago), and culminated about one million years ago in the Pleistocene Ice Age. During the early Miocene the global climate was warmer than today. Widespread tropical forests in Africa and Eurasia supported diverse populations of early hominoid apes, including a common ancestor of gorillas, chimpanzees and humans.

By the end of the Miocene ice caps had formed at the Poles, and drier conditions in Africa caused tropical forests to shrink. In east Africa, probably the birthplace of the hominids, this was exacerbated by geological movements that led to the uplift of the East African plateau and the formation of the Rift Valley. The ancestral hominids were confined to shrinking "islands" of forest surrounded by open woodland and savanna. As a result they learned to walk on two legs, allowing them to cover long distances on the ground.

The oldest known hominid, 4.4-million-year-old *Ardipithecus ramidus*, was probably bipedal, and the slightly later species *Australopithecus afarensis* certainly was, although (like later australopithecines) it retained a good tree-climbing ability. By 3 million years ago the australopithecines had evolved into two types, known as robusts and graciles. The robusts (named for their massive jaws and teeth) were not human ancestors. The gracile *Australopithecus africanus* had smaller teeth and jaws, and lived on plant foods and meat scavenged from the carcasses of the savanna's herd animals. The first hominid to be considered human, *Homo habilis*, appeared about 2.4 million years ago. This lived in a similar way to the gracile australopithecines, but had a larger brain – almost half the size of a modern human's, compared with a third, for australopithecines and chimpanzees. Whereas the australopithecines used simple tools such as stones and sticks, *Homo habilis* made sharp flakes and chipped pebble tools for butchering large animals. This simple toolmaking culture is known as the Oldowan, for the early hominid fossil site of Olduvai Gorge in the Rift Valley.

About 1.9 million years ago *Homo habilis* was replaced by *Homo erectus*, with a brain size about two-thirds that of modern humans. Over the next million years this proportion grew to three-quarters, the brain evolving rapidly as the climate fluctuated from dry glacial periods to moister, warmer interglacial periods. There was little time to adapt physically to new conditions, and intelligent animals that could cope by modifying their

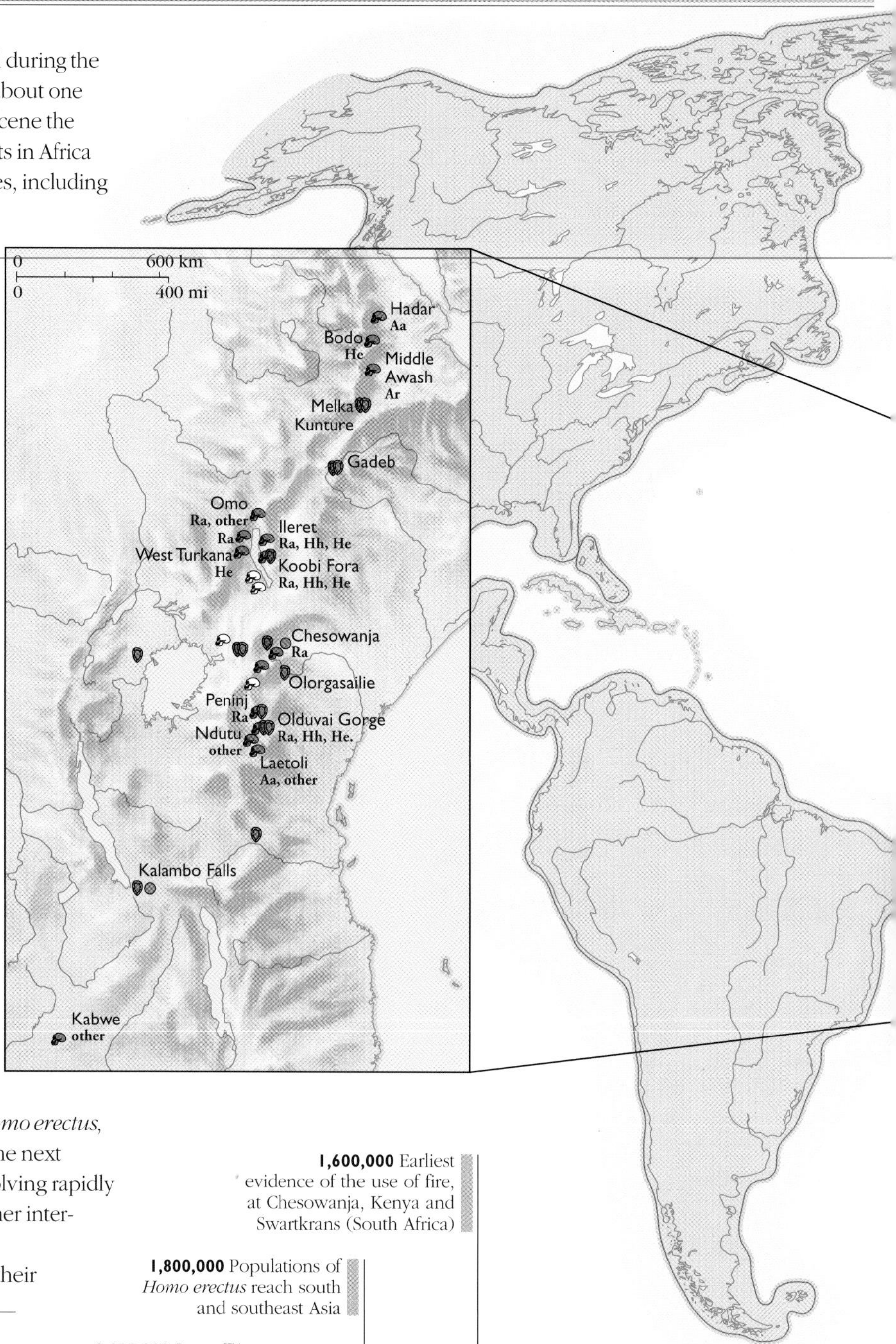

0 600 km
0 400 mi
Hadar Aa
Bodo He
Middle Awash Ar
Melka Kunture
Gadeb
Omo Ra, other
Ra
West Turkana He
Ileret Ra, Hh, He
Koobi Fora Ra, Hh, He
Chesowanja Ra
Olorgasailie
Peninj Ra
Ndutu other
Olduvai Gorge Ra, Hh, He.
Laetoli Aa, other
Kalambo Falls
Kabwe other

c.3,600,000 Hominid bipedal footsteps from this date have been found at Laetoli, Tanzania

c.3,500,000 "Lucy", the most complete *Australopithecus afarensis* found, lives at Hadar, Ethiopia

c.2,400,000 Date of the oldest known stone tools, from Hadar, Ethiopia and the start of the African Lower Paleolithic

c.2,000,000 Stone choppers, from Olduvai Gorge, Tanzania, initiate the Oldowan culture

1,800,000 Populations of *Homo erectus* reach south and southeast Asia

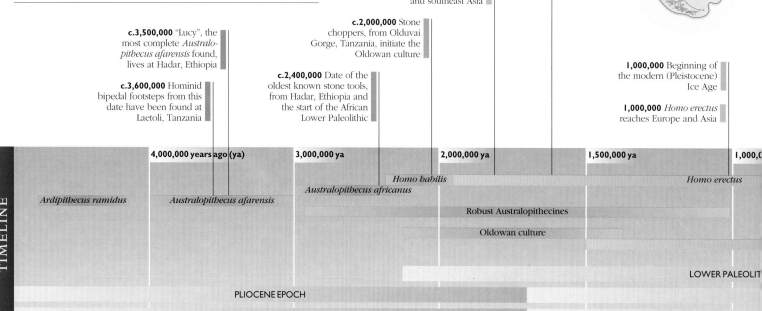

1,600,000 Earliest evidence of the use of fire, at Chesowanja, Kenya and Swartkrans (South Africa)

1,000,000 Beginning of the modern (Pleistocene) Ice Age

1,000,000 *Homo erectus* reaches Europe and Asia

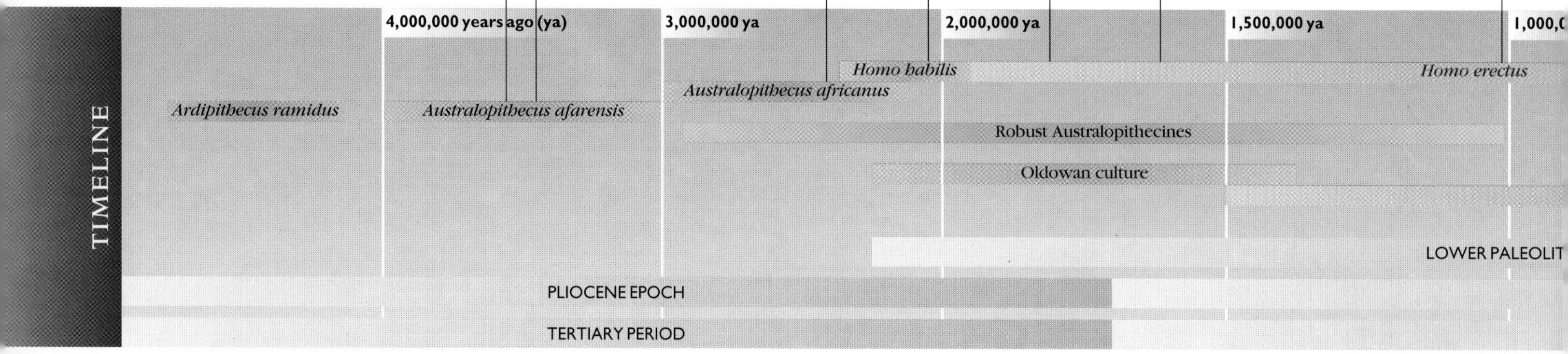

TIMELINE

4,000,000 years ago (ya) | **3,000,000 ya** | **2,000,000 ya** | **1,500,000 ya** | **1,000,0**

Ardipithecus ramidus
Australopithecus afarensis
Australopithecus africanus
Homo habilis
Homo erectus
Robust Australopithecines
Oldowan culture
LOWER PALEOLIT
PLIOCENE EPOCH
TERTIARY PERIOD

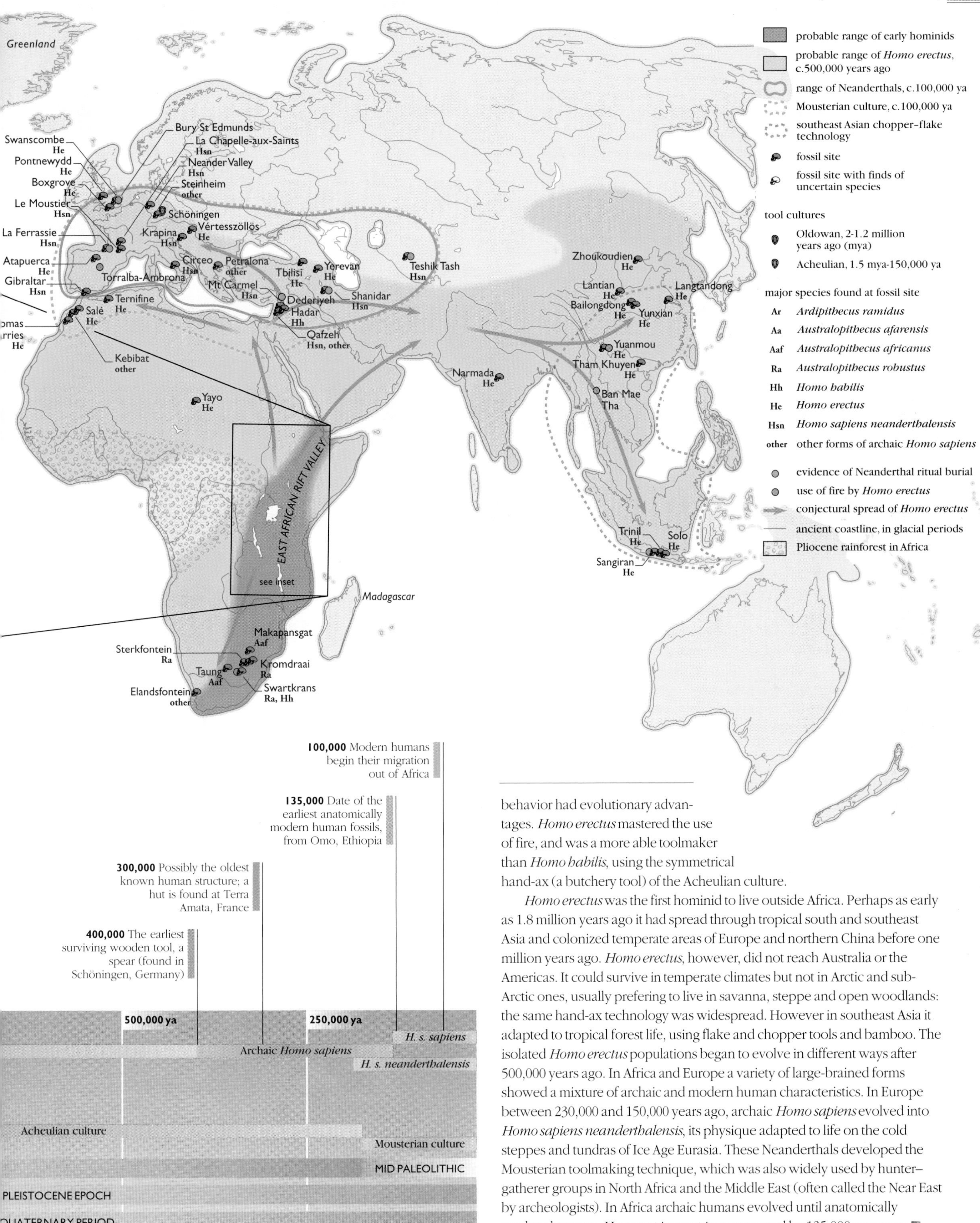
Greenland
Swanscombe He
Pontnewydd He
Boxgrove He
Le Moustier Hsn
La Ferrassie Hsn
Atapuerca He
Gibraltar Hsn
Salé He
Kebibat other
Bury St Edmunds
La Chapelle-aux-Saints Hsn
Neander Valley Hsn
Steinheim other
Schöningen
Vértesszöllös He
Krapina Hsn
Circeo Hsn
Petralona other
Torralba-Ambrona
Ternifine He
Tbilisi He
Yerevan He
Mt Carmel Hsn
Dederiyeh
Hadar Hh
Shanidar Hsn
Qafzeh Hsn, other
Teshik Tash Hsn
Yayo He
EAST AFRICAN RIFT VALLEY
see inset
Madagascar
Makapansgat Aaf
Sterkfontein Ra
Kromdraai Ra
Taung Aaf
Swartkrans Ra, Hh
Elandsfontein other
Zhoukoudien He
Lantian He
Bailongdong He
Yunxian He
Langtandong He
Yuanmou He
Tham Khuyen He
Narmada He
Ban Mae Tha
Trinil He
Solo He
Sangiran He
probable range of early hominids
probable range of Homo erectus, c.500,000 years ago
range of Neanderthals, c.100,000 ya
Mousterian culture, c.100,000 ya
southeast Asian chopper-flake technology
fossil site
fossil site with finds of uncertain species
tool cultures
Oldowan, 2-1.2 million years ago (mya)
Acheulian, 1.5 mya-150,000 ya
major species found at fossil site
Ar Ardipithecus ramidus
Aa Australopithecus afarensis
Aaf Australopithecus africanus
Ra Australopithecus robustus
Hh Homo habilis
He Homo erectus
Hsn Homo sapiens neanderthalensis
other other forms of archaic Homo sapiens
evidence of Neanderthal ritual burial
use of fire by Homo erectus
conjectural spread of Homo erectus
ancient coastline, in glacial periods
Pliocene rainforest in Africa
100,000 Modern humans begin their migration out of Africa
135,000 Date of the earliest anatomically modern human fossils, from Omo, Ethiopia
300,000 Possibly the oldest known human structure; a hut is found at Terra Amata, France
400,000 The earliest surviving wooden tool, a spear (found in Schöningen, Germany)
500,000 ya
250,000 ya
H. s. sapiens
Archaic Homo sapiens
H. s. neanderthalensis
Acheulian culture
Mousterian culture
MID PALEOLITHIC
PLEISTOCENE EPOCH
QUATERNARY PERIOD

behavior had evolutionary advantages. *Homo erectus* mastered the use of fire, and was a more able toolmaker than *Homo habilis*, using the symmetrical hand-ax (a butchery tool) of the Acheulian culture.

Homo erectus was the first hominid to live outside Africa. Perhaps as early as 1.8 million years ago it had spread through tropical south and southeast Asia and colonized temperate areas of Europe and northern China before one million years ago. *Homo erectus*, however, did not reach Australia or the Americas. It could survive in temperate climates but not in Arctic and sub-Arctic ones, usually prefering to live in savanna, steppe and open woodlands: the same hand-ax technology was widespread. However in southeast Asia it adapted to tropical forest life, using flake and chopper tools and bamboo. The isolated *Homo erectus* populations began to evolve in different ways after 500,000 years ago. In Africa and Europe a variety of large-brained forms showed a mixture of archaic and modern human characteristics. In Europe between 230,000 and 150,000 years ago, archaic *Homo sapiens* evolved into *Homo sapiens neanderthalensis*, its physique adapted to life on the cold steppes and tundras of Ice Age Eurasia. These Neanderthals developed the Mousterian toolmaking technique, which was also widely used by hunter–gatherer groups in North Africa and the Middle East (often called the Near East by archeologists). In Africa archaic humans evolved until anatomically modern humans, *Homo sapiens sapiens*, appeared by 135,000 years ago ■

1.02 Peopling the Earth • 100,000 – 10,000 YEARS AGO •

The earliest known anatomically modern *Homo sapiens sapiens* had appeared in Africa by 135,000 years ago (ya). By 90,000 years ago anatomically modern humans existed in the Middle East; by 75,000 years ago they were in east Asia and by 40,000 in Europe and Australia. By the end of the Ice Age 10,000 years ago, only some oceanic islands, Antarctica and some parts of the high Arctic remained completely uninhabited.

Two rival explanations have been offered for these facts. One argues that the modern human races developed directly from the regional *Homo erectus* populations: modern Africans evolved from *Homo erectus* via African archaic *Homo sapiens*; modern Europeans from *Homo erectus* via European archaic *Homo sapiens* and Neanderthals and so on. Critics point out that parallel evolution of this sort over such a wide area is implausible and that there is no supporting fossil evidence. The second explanation, known as the single-origins or "out of Africa" model, is supported by genetic evidence suggesting that all modern humans derive from African ancestors who lived between about 285,000 and 150,000 years ago, and that all modern non-African humans are descendants of a single group of this ancestral population that migrated out of Africa around 100,000 years ago. According to this model, the descendants of this group spread across Eurasia. The anatomically modern humans had better developed speech abilities than the archaic natives, who could not compete with the newcomers and gradually became extinct.

This model is more compatible with the fossil and archeological evidence than the first. Between 120,000 and 90,000 years ago the African climate was more moist than it is today and bands of hunters and gatherers could have crossed the Sahara. The earliest known fossils of modern humans outside Africa date to about 90,000 years ago and were found in Israel – just the place and date predicted by the single-origins theory. Only in Africa have forms intermediate between archaic and modern humans been found. In Europe, the Neanderthals and early modern humans formed distinct populations that coexisted for over 10,000 years: the Neanderthals did not evolve into modern humans. In east and southeast Asia, the *Homo erectus* populations were replaced by modern humans with no trace of intermediate forms.

When the first modern humans reached the Middle East, the global climate was beginning to enter one of the most severe glacial periods of the Ice Age. Human technology was probably inadequate for survival in the arctic climates of Europe and central Asia, and these areas were left to the hardier Neanderthals. Instead the moderns moved east, reaching China and southeast Asia around 75,000 years ago. Here they developed boat- or raft-building skills and

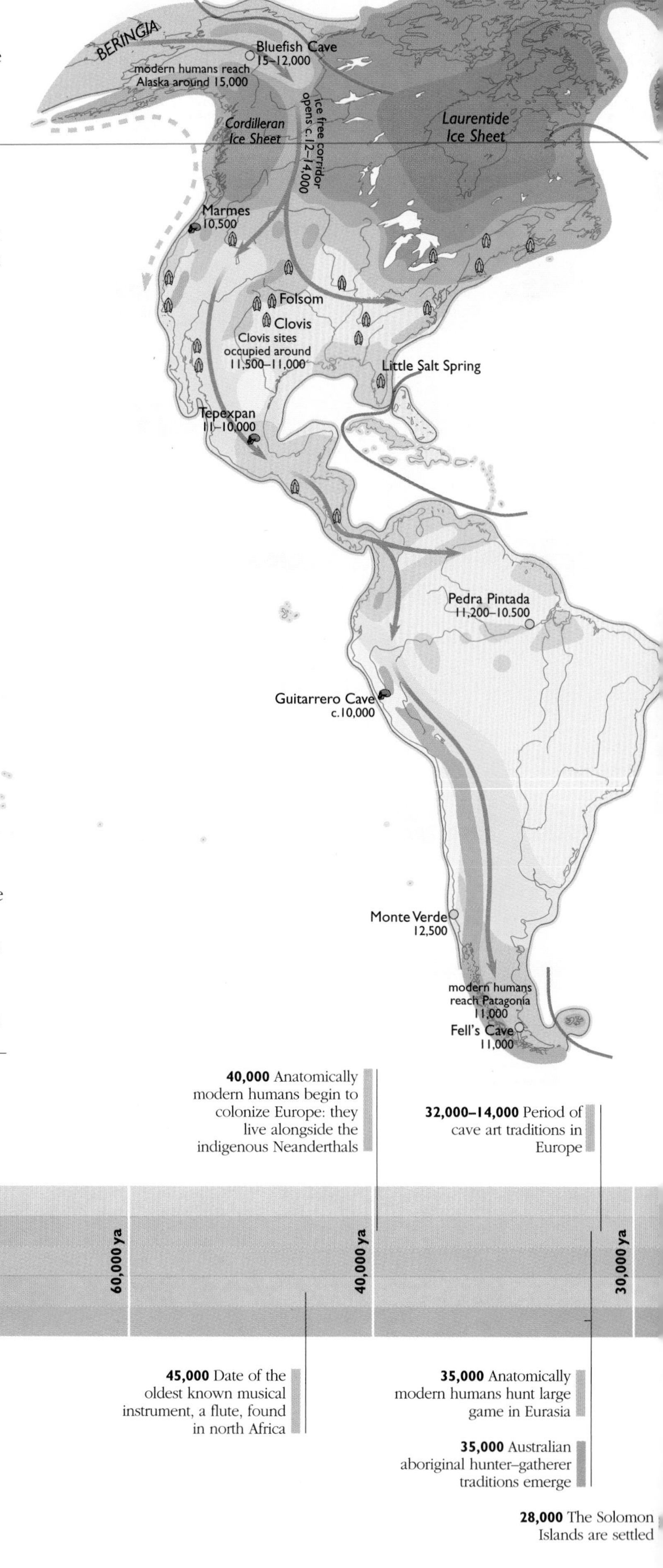

BERINGIA
Bluefish Cave
15–12,000
modern humans reach
Alaska around 15,000
ice free corridor
opens c.12–14,000
Cordilleran
Ice Sheet
Laurentide
Ice Sheet
Marmes
10,500
Folsom
Clovis
Clovis sites
occupied around
11,500–11,000
Little Salt Spring
Tepexpan
11–10,000
Pedra Pintada
11,200–10.500
Guitarrero Cave
c.10,000
Monte Verde
12,500
modern humans
reach Patagonia
11,000
Fell's Cave
11,000

TIMELINE

The Americas | Europe | Middle East | Africa | East and South Asia

100,000 years ago | 80,000 ya | 60,000 ya | 40,000 ya | 30,000 ya

115,000 Onset of the last glaciation of the (Pleistocene) Ice Age

90,000 Anatomically modern humans living at Qafzeh, Israel

40,000 Anatomically modern humans begin to colonize Europe: they live alongside the indigenous Neanderthals

32,000–14,000 Period of cave art traditions in Europe

c.120,000 Middle Stone Age flake-tool technology is well established in tropical Africa

120,000–90,000 Periods of higher rainfall make the Sahara habitable by humans

c.75,000 Glaciation causes Africa to become arid: the Sahara becomes impassable by humans

75,000 Anatomically modern humans inhabit China and southeast Asia

45,000 Date of the oldest known musical instrument, a flute, found in north Africa

35,000 Anatomically modern humans hunt large game in Eurasia

35,000 Australian aboriginal hunter–gatherer traditions emerge

28,000 The Solomon Islands are settled

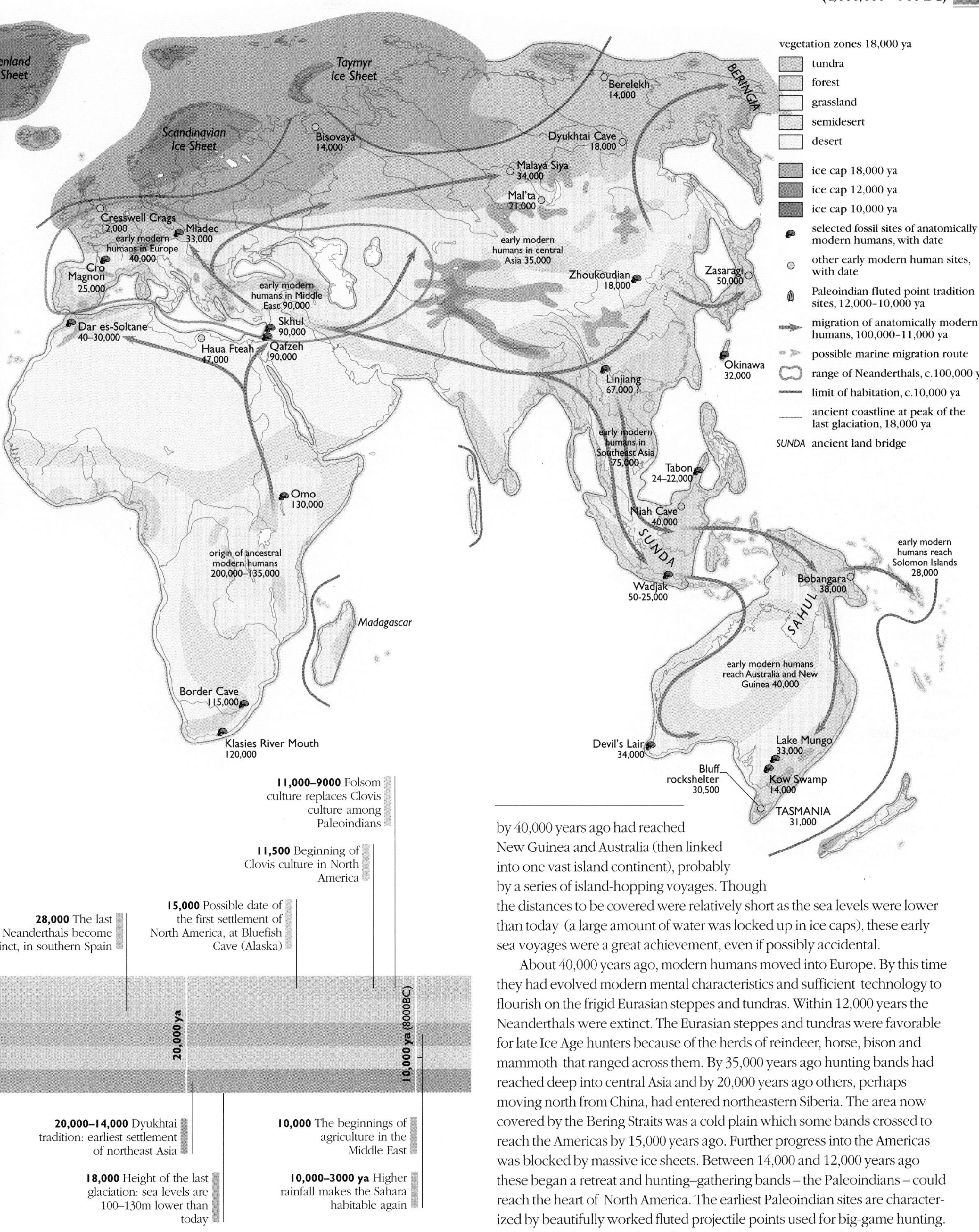

vegetation zones 18,000 ya
tundra
forest
grassland
semidesert
desert
ice cap 18,000 ya
ice cap 12,000 ya
ice cap 10,000 ya
selected fossil sites of anatomically modern humans, with date
other early modern human sites, with date
Paleoindian fluted point tradition sites, 12,000–10,000 ya
migration of anatomically modern humans, 100,000–11,000 ya
possible marine migration route
range of Neanderthals, c.100,000 ya
limit of habitation, c.10,000 ya
ancient coastline at peak of the last glaciation, 18,000 ya
SUNDA ancient land bridge
enland Sheet
Taymyr Ice Sheet
Scandinavian Ice Sheet
Berelekh 14,000
BERINGIA
Bisovaya 14,000
Dyukhtai Cave 18,000
Malaya Siya 34,000
Mal'ta 21,000
Cresswell Crags 12,000
Mladec 33,000
early modern humans in Europe 40,000
Cro Magnon 25,000
early modern humans in central Asia 35,000
early modern humans in Middle East 90,000
Zhoukoudian 18,000
Zasaragi 50,000
Dar es-Soltane 40–30,000
Skhul 90,000
Haua Fteah 47,000
Qafzeh 90,000
Okinawa 32,000
Linjiang 67,000 ?
early modern humans in Southeast Asia 75,000
Tabon 24–22,000
Omo 130,000
Niah Cave 40,000
SUNDA
origin of ancestral modern humans 200,000–135,000
early modern humans reach Solomon Islands 28,000
Bobangara 38,000
Wadjak 50-25,000
SAHUL
Madagascar
early modern humans reach Australia and New Guinea 40,000
Border Cave 115,000
Klasies River Mouth 120,000
Devil's Lair 34,000
Lake Mungo 33,000
Bluff rockshelter 30,500
Kow Swamp 14,000
TASMANIA 31,000
11,000–9000 Folsom culture replaces Clovis culture among Paleoindians
11,500 Beginning of Clovis culture in North America
28,000 The last Neanderthals become extinct, in southern Spain
15,000 Possible date of the first settlement of North America, at Bluefish Cave (Alaska)
20,000 ya
10,000 ya (8000BC)
20,000–14,000 Dyukhtai tradition: earliest settlement of northeast Asia
10,000 The beginnings of agriculture in the Middle East
18,000 Height of the last glaciation: sea levels are 100–130m lower than today
10,000–3000 ya Higher rainfall makes the Sahara habitable again

by 40,000 years ago had reached New Guinea and Australia (then linked into one vast island continent), probably by a series of island-hopping voyages. Though the distances to be covered were relatively short as the sea levels were lower than today (a large amount of water was locked up in ice caps), these early sea voyages were a great achievement, even if possibly accidental.

About 40,000 years ago, modern humans moved into Europe. By this time they had evolved modern mental characteristics and sufficient technology to flourish on the frigid Eurasian steppes and tundras. Within 12,000 years the Neanderthals were extinct. The Eurasian steppes and tundras were favorable for late Ice Age hunters because of the herds of reindeer, horse, bison and mammoth that ranged across them. By 35,000 years ago hunting bands had reached deep into central Asia and by 20,000 years ago others, perhaps moving north from China, had entered northeastern Siberia. The area now covered by the Bering Straits was a cold plain which some bands crossed to reach the Americas by 15,000 years ago. Further progress into the Americas was blocked by massive ice sheets. Between 14,000 and 12,000 years ago these began a retreat and hunting–gathering bands – the Paleoindians – could reach the heart of North America. The earliest Paleoindian sites are characterized by beautifully worked fluted projectile points used for big-game hunting. The Paleoindians spread rapidly through the Americas and had reached Patagonia in South America by 11,000 years ago ■

1.03 The rise of agriculture • 10,000 – 500 BC •

Farming communities arose independently in many parts of the world between 10,000 and 5000 BC as a response to the environmental changes that followed the end of the Ice Age. The warmer climate was a mixed blessing: sea levels rose as the ice sheets melted, flooding huge areas of lowland hunting grounds. The savannas, steppes and tundras, all abundant in big game, shrank as the forests advanced.

In many areas, hunter–gatherers began to exploit small game birds, fish and plants to a greater extent than before. It was among these communities that agriculture first arose. Probably the first stage was planting the seeds of favored wild plant foods to guarantee their continuing availability. Next was the domestication of food plants by breeding strains with desirable characteristics. Because their seeds had a high carbohydrate content and were easy to store, the most important domesticated plant foods were strains of the cereals – wheat, barley, oats, rice, millet and maize – that still form the staple food crops today. Relatively few animal species have been domesticated; most of those have been herd animals, whose tendency to "follow the leader" makes them easier to manage. Animal domestication began with the management and selective culling of wild herds. Penning the animals followed, then selective breeding for desirable qualities. Most early centers of agriculture were rich in wild plants and animals suitable for domestication. Elsewhere agriculture relied on the introduction of crops and livestock from established farming areas.

Some communities of hunter–gatherers moved from casual cultivation of wild plants (incipient agriculture) to a full farming economy far more quickly than others. Farmers have to work harder than hunter–gatherers, and few made the transition willingly. Rising populations probably forced many to adopt cultivation to supplement wild food supplies. In the Fertile Crescent of the Middle East, where farming first developed, (▷ *1.08*) the transition from incipient agriculture to dependence on domesticated cereals took only three centuries, 8000–7700 BC, and domesticated animals replaced hunted wild animals a millennium later. In Mesoamerica a full farming way of life developed within a few centuries of the domestication of maize (▷ *1.28*). In eastern North America hunting and gathering remained the main source of food for some three millennia after the first cultivation of domesticated food around 2500 BC. Even farmers who grew most of their food still exploited wild food sources.

Agriculture led to far-reaching technological developments. Most hunter–gatherers had to carry everything from camp to camp: farmers were sedentary, so weight became less critical. New tools, such as polished stone

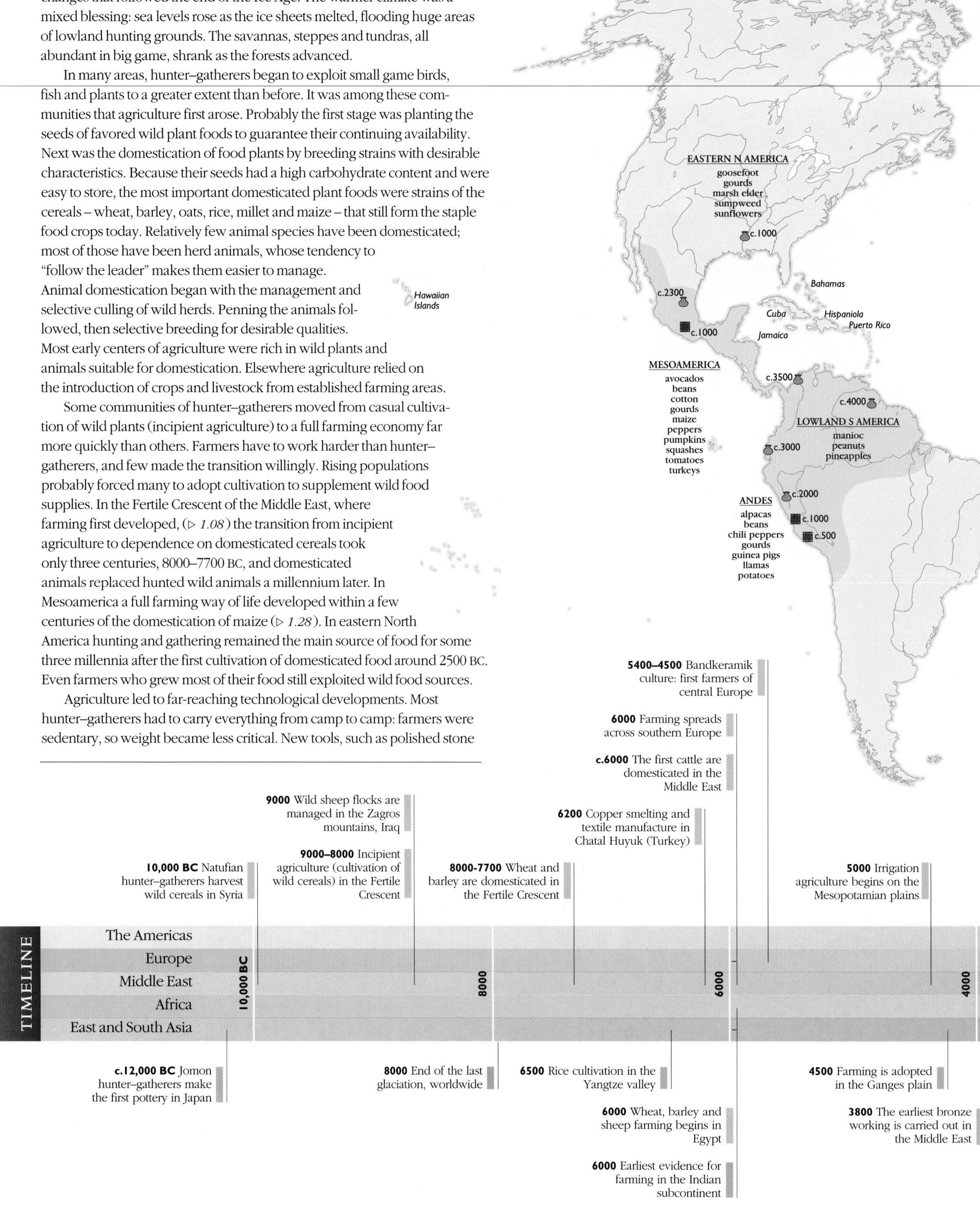

EASTERN N AMERICA
goosefoot
gourds
marsh elder
sumpweed
sunflowers
c.1000
Bahamas
Hawaiian Islands
c.2300
Cuba
Hispaniola
Puerto Rico
c.1000
Jamaica
MESOAMERICA
avocados
beans
cotton
gourds
maize
peppers
pumpkins
squashes
tomatoes
turkeys
c.3500
c.4000
LOWLAND S AMERICA
manioc
peanuts
pineapples
c.3000
c.2000
ANDES
alpacas
beans
chili peppers
gourds
guinea pigs
llamas
potatoes
c.1000
c.500
TIMELINE
The Americas
Europe
Middle East
Africa
East and South Asia
10,000 BC
8000
6000
4000
c.12,000 BC Jomon hunter–gatherers make the first pottery in Japan
10,000 BC Natufian hunter–gatherers harvest wild cereals in Syria
9000 Wild sheep flocks are managed in the Zagros mountains, Iraq
9000–8000 Incipient agriculture (cultivation of wild cereals) in the Fertile Crescent
8000 End of the last glaciation, worldwide
8000-7700 Wheat and barley are domesticated in the Fertile Crescent
6500 Rice cultivation in the Yangtze valley
6200 Copper smelting and textile manufacture in Chatal Huyuk (Turkey)
c.6000 The first cattle are domesticated in the Middle East
6000 Farming spreads across southern Europe
6000 Wheat, barley and sheep farming begins in Egypt
6000 Earliest evidence for farming in the Indian subcontinent
5400–4500 Bandkeramik culture: first farmers of central Europe
5000 Irrigation agriculture begins on the Mesopotamian plains
4500 Farming is adopted in the Ganges plain
3800 The earliest bronze working is carried out in the Middle East

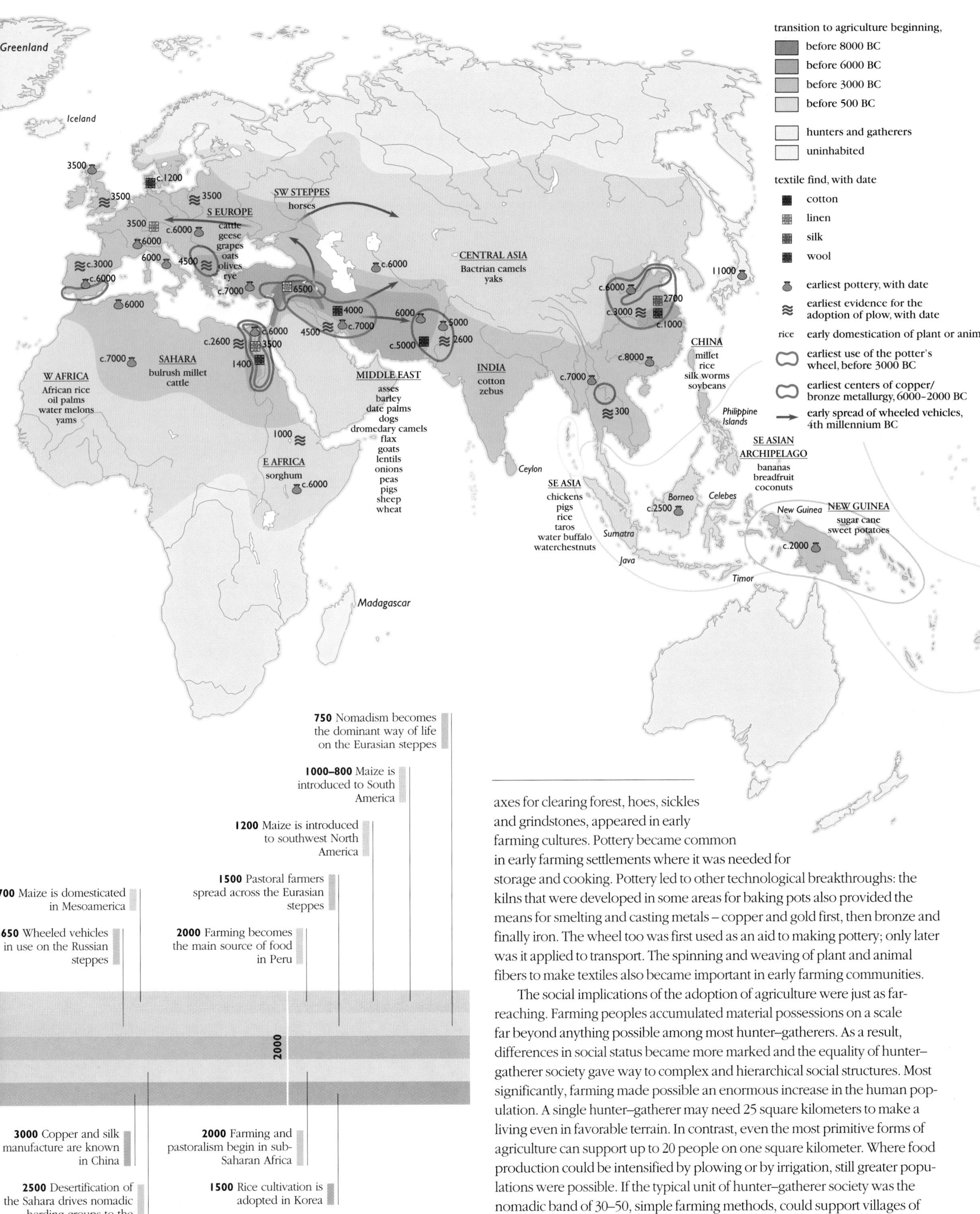

transition to agriculture beginning,
before 8000 BC
before 6000 BC
before 3000 BC
before 500 BC
hunters and gatherers
uninhabited
textile find, with date
cotton
linen
silk
wool
earliest pottery, with date
earliest evidence for the adoption of plow, with date
rice early domestication of plant or animal
earliest use of the potter's wheel, before 3000 BC
earliest centers of copper/ bronze metallurgy, 6000–2000 BC
early spread of wheeled vehicles, 4th millennium BC
Greenland
Iceland
SW STEPPES
horses
S EUROPE
cattle
geese
grapes
oats
olives
rye
CENTRAL ASIA
Bactrian camels
yaks
W AFRICA
African rice
oil palms
water melons
yams
SAHARA
bulrush millet
cattle
MIDDLE EAST
asses
barley
date palms
dogs
dromedary camels
flax
goats
lentils
onions
peas
pigs
sheep
wheat
E AFRICA
sorghum
INDIA
cotton
zebus
CHINA
millet
rice
silk worms
soybeans
Philippine Islands
SE ASIAN ARCHIPELAGO
bananas
breadfruit
coconuts
Ceylon
SE ASIA
chickens
pigs
rice
taros
water buffalo
waterchestnuts
Borneo
Celebes
Sumatra
Java
Timor
New Guinea
NEW GUINEA
sugar cane
sweet potatoes
Madagascar
750 Nomadism becomes the dominant way of life on the Eurasian steppes
1000–800 Maize is introduced to South America
1200 Maize is introduced to southwest North America
1500 Pastoral farmers spread across the Eurasian steppes
700 Maize is domesticated in Mesoamerica
650 Wheeled vehicles in use on the Russian steppes
2000 Farming becomes the main source of food in Peru
2000
3000 Copper and silk manufacture are known in China
2000 Farming and pastoralism begin in sub-Saharan Africa
2500 Desertification of the Sahara drives nomadic herding groups to the edges of the desert
1500 Rice cultivation is adopted in Korea

axes for clearing forest, hoes, sickles and grindstones, appeared in early farming cultures. Pottery became common in early farming settlements where it was needed for storage and cooking. Pottery led to other technological breakthroughs: the kilns that were developed in some areas for baking pots also provided the means for smelting and casting metals – copper and gold first, then bronze and finally iron. The wheel too was first used as an aid to making pottery; only later was it applied to transport. The spinning and weaving of plant and animal fibers to make textiles also became important in early farming communities.

The social implications of the adoption of agriculture were just as far-reaching. Farming peoples accumulated material possessions on a scale far beyond anything possible among most hunter–gatherers. As a result, differences in social status became more marked and the equality of hunter–gatherer society gave way to complex and hierarchical social structures. Most significantly, farming made possible an enormous increase in the human population. A single hunter–gatherer may need 25 square kilometers to make a living even in favorable terrain. In contrast, even the most primitive forms of agriculture can support up to 20 people on one square kilometer. Where food production could be intensified by plowing or by irrigation, still greater populations were possible. If the typical unit of hunter–gatherer society was the nomadic band of 30–50, simple farming methods, could support villages of hundreds of people, and intensive methods, towns of thousands of people ■

By 2000 BC the revolutionary impact of agriculture had become clear. Farming was practiced on every continent and would overtake hunting and gathering as the way of life of most people well before the Christian era.

Not all early farming societies developed the same level of complexity. Poor soil, climate, endemic diseases of humans or livestock or a lack of suitable crops limited development in many areas. The greater the resources possessed by a society, the more complex it could become; in a few favorable environments (such as the northwest of North America), hunter-gatherer societies too achieved greater levels of social complexity.

Most early farming societies were kinship-based tribes of hundreds or a few thousand people living in villages or dispersed homesteads. Although they recognized ties of kinship, religion or language with others, each tribe was essentially independent. Differences of rank and status existed but leaders could rarely exercise coercive power over other tribes' people. Archeologically, such societies (known to anthropologists as "segmentary societies") can be recognized by communal burial practices, the remains of permanent homesteads and villages and communal works such as the megalithic tombs of prehistoric western Europe. In 2000 BC segmentary farming societies were dominant in south and southeast Asia, New Guinea, north Africa, northern Europe and parts of Mesoamerica and South America.

Where intensive agricultural techniques could be used, largescale hierarchical communities of up to 20,000 people, known as "chiefdoms", could develop. Rank and status were linked to lineage: the senior person of the senior lineage was the chief, who was thereby the ruler of the whole community. Chieftains could exercise coercive power, often through a warrior class, and support specialist craftsmen. Archeologically, chiefdoms show major construction projects requiring large resources of labor and wealth, such as Stonehenge in southern Britain (▷ *1.20*). In chiefdoms the quantity and quality of grave goods placed with burials indicate the rank and status of the individual and a few burials are lavishly furnished. Chiefdoms commonly had a dominant central site such as a stronghold or ceremonial center, and smaller satellite settlements. In 2000 BC chiefdoms were established in the Middle East and southwest central Europe, in China and the Andes. In western Europe segmentary farming societies were giving way to chiefdoms at this time.

Arctic marine mammal hunters
Aleuts
Archaic Amerindian hunter-gatherers
Hawaiian Islands
Bahamas
Cuba
Hispaniola
Puerto Rico
Jamaica
maize farming replacing hunting and gathering
Valdivia tradition
Aspero tradition
Chinchoros tradition
Archaic Amerindian hunter-gatherers

TIMELINE

The Americas | Europe | Middle East | Africa | East and South Asia

4500 BC — 4000 — 3500 — 3000

c.4300 The first megalithic tombs are built in western Europe

5000–2000 Hunting cultures spread across Arctic North America to Greenland

4300–3100 Uruk period in Mesopotamia. The first cities are built.

3800 Bronze casting techniques employed for the first time in the Middle East

4000 Pottery first comes into use in the Americas (Guyana)

3400 Earliest writing appears in Uruk (Iraq). City-states emerge in Sumeria (southern Mesopotamia)

3500 Permanent fishing village settlements are inhabited in Peru

3500 Farming is established throughout Europe

3200–1800 Chinese Longshan advanced farming cultures; first towns are built in China

c.3000 Foundation of the Egyptian state

3000 Ancestral Austronesians migrate from Taiwan to the Philippines

3000–1700 Pastoral farming is established on the central Asian steppes (Afanasevo culture)

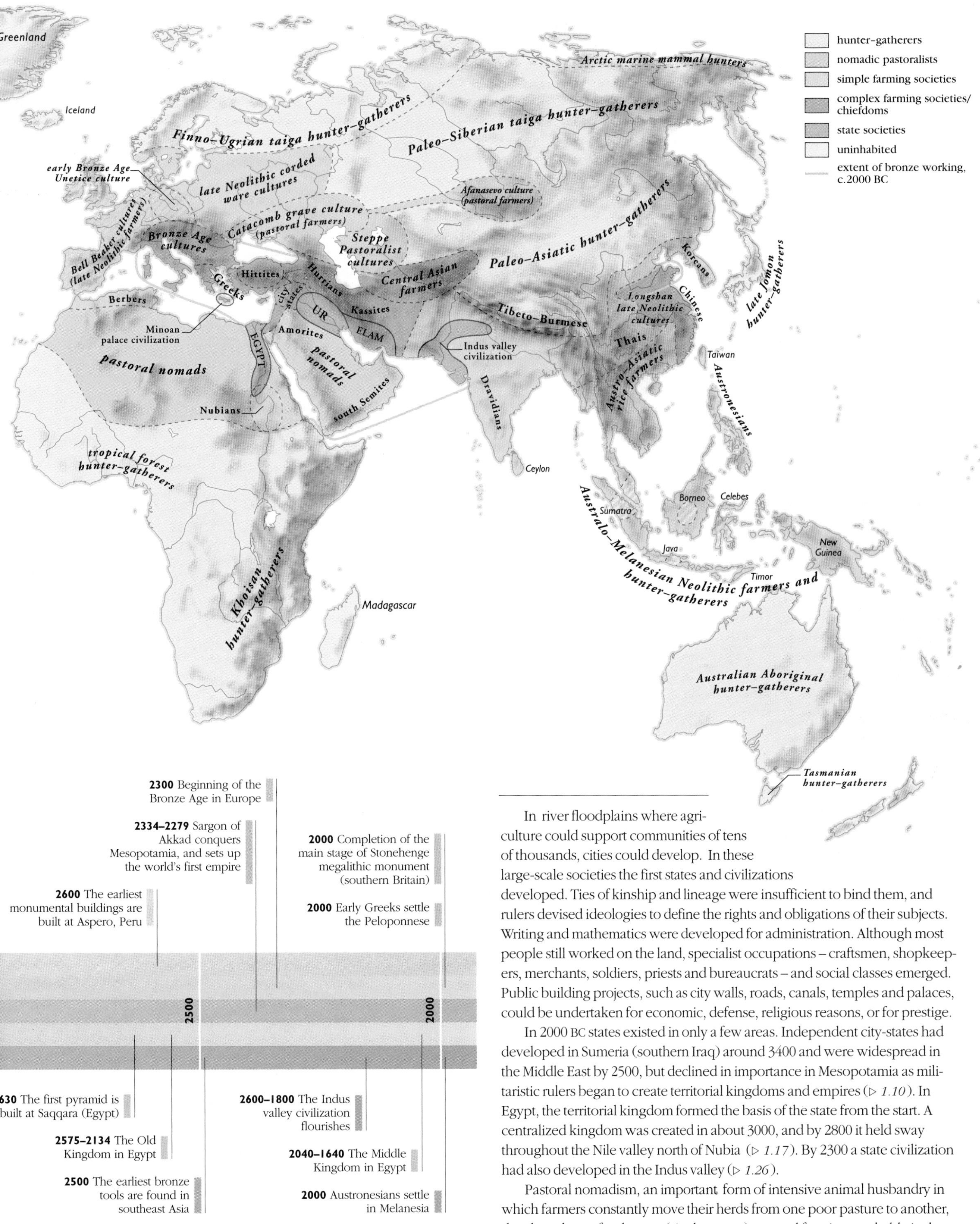
hunter-gatherers
nomadic pastoralists
simple farming societies
complex farming societies/ chiefdoms
state societies
uninhabited
extent of bronze working, c.2000 BC
Greenland
Iceland
Arctic marine mammal hunters
Finno-Ugrian taiga hunter-gatherers
Paleo-Siberian taiga hunter-gatherers
early Bronze Age Unetice culture
late Neolithic corded ware cultures
Afanasevo culture (pastoral farmers)
Catacomb grave culture (pastoral farmers)
Bell Beaker cultures (late Neolithic farmers)
Bronze Age cultures
Steppe Pastoralist cultures
Paleo-Asiatic hunter-gatherers
Koreans
late Jomon hunter-gatherers
Hittites
Hurrians
Central Asian farmers
Greeks
city states
Berbers
UR
Kassites
Tibeto-Burmese
Longshan late Neolithic cultures
Chinese
Minoan palace civilization
Amorites
ELAM
Thais
Indus valley civilization
Taiwan
EGYPT
pastoral nomads
Austro-Asiatic rice farmers
Pastoral nomads
Dravidians
Austronesians
Nubians
south Semites
tropical forest hunter-gatherers
Ceylon
Borneo
Celebes
Sumatra
Australo-Melanesian Neolithic farmers and hunter-gatherers
Java
New Guinea
Timor
Khoisan hunter-gatherers
Madagascar
Australian Aboriginal hunter-gatherers
Tasmanian hunter-gatherers
2300 Beginning of the Bronze Age in Europe
2334–2279 Sargon of Akkad conquers Mesopotamia, and sets up the world's first empire
2000 Completion of the main stage of Stonehenge megalithic monument (southern Britain)
2600 The earliest monumental buildings are built at Aspero, Peru
2000 Early Greeks settle the Peloponnese
2500
2000
2630 The first pyramid is built at Saqqara (Egypt)
2600–1800 The Indus valley civilization flourishes
2575–2134 The Old Kingdom in Egypt
2040–1640 The Middle Kingdom in Egypt
2500 The earliest bronze tools are found in southeast Asia
2000 Austronesians settle in Melanesia

In river floodplains where agriculture could support communities of tens of thousands, cities could develop. In these large-scale societies the first states and civilizations developed. Ties of kinship and lineage were insufficient to bind them, and rulers devised ideologies to define the rights and obligations of their subjects. Writing and mathematics were developed for administration. Although most people still worked on the land, specialist occupations – craftsmen, shopkeepers, merchants, soldiers, priests and bureaucrats – and social classes emerged. Public building projects, such as city walls, roads, canals, temples and palaces, could be undertaken for economic, defense, religious reasons, or for prestige.

In 2000 BC states existed in only a few areas. Independent city-states had developed in Sumeria (southern Iraq) around 3400 and were widespread in the Middle East by 2500, but declined in importance in Mesopotamia as militaristic rulers began to create territorial kingdoms and empires (▷ *1.10*). In Egypt, the territorial kingdom formed the basis of the state from the start. A centralized kingdom was created in about 3000, and by 2800 it held sway throughout the Nile valley north of Nubia (▷ *1.17*). By 2300 a state civilization had also developed in the Indus valley (▷ *1.26*).

Pastoral nomadism, an important form of intensive animal husbandry in which farmers constantly move their herds from one poor pasture to another, developed out of sedentary (single-center) pastoral farming, probably in the Sahara where desertification spread after 3000 BC ■

The fragility of the first civilizations was evident during the second millennium BC. Sumeria had vanished as a political entity shortly before 2000 BC, though its achievements were built upon by the Babylonian and Assyrian states which arose in the early second millennium (▷ *1.11*). The rivalry between these two states was to endure until the middle of the first millennium. The other major power of the Middle East was the Hittite kingdom of Anatolia. One of the secrets of Hittite success is thought to have been their early mastery of iron working, in about 1500 BC. Meanwhile, Egypt expanded far south into Nubia and north into the Levant (▷ *1.18*). In the eastern Mediterranean, the Minoans of Crete were replaced by the Mycenaean civilization that emerged on the Greek mainland around 1600. Around 1400 the Mycenaeans conquered Crete and introduced the Greek language; they also settled on Cyprus and in Anatolia (▷ *1.22*).

This civilized world was thrown into chaos about 1200 by a wave of invasions. Mycenae was destroyed by invaders from the north, plunging Greece into a 400-year-long "dark age". Thracians, Phrygians and Anatolian Luvians overthrew the Hittite empire and nomadic Aramaeans occupied much of Mesopotamia. Egypt was invaded by mysterious Sea Peoples. Their fleets were driven from the Nile, but they settled in the Levant where they were known as the Philistines.

By 1000 stability was returning. The Hittites survived though as a shadow of their former selves. The Aramaeans had settled and were assimilating with the urbanized peoples of the conquered territories: their language became the common tongue of the Middle East for the next millennium. Assyria and Babylon were beginning to recover (▷ *1.12*). The Levant was a mosaic of tiny states: of these, the Phoenician city-states and Israel acquired a historical importance out of all proportion to their size (▷ *1.14*). Egyptian power was in decline and the Nubians, after a millennium of Egyptian domination, set up the kingdom of Kush. In sub-Saharan Africa, the transition to a farming way of life was beginning.

In Asia, the Indus valley civilization had collapsed around 1700; about 200 years later the Aryans, an Indo-European pastoralist people, migrated into India. In northern China the Neolithic Longshan cultures developed into the urbanized Shang state around 1766, marking the start of Chinese civilization. Around 1122 the Shang dynasty was ousted by the ruler of the Zhou sub-kingdom (▷ *1.27*).

The Austronesian farming peoples continued to colonize the southeast Asian archipelagoes; by 2000 they had bypassed New Guinea and settled the western Pacific Bismarck archipelago around 1500 BC. The Lapita culture,

Arctic marine mammal hunters
Aleuts
sub-Arctic forest hunter-gatherers
west coast foraging, hunting and fishing peoples
plateau fishers and hunter-gatherers
desert hunter-gatherers
plains bison hunters
east woodlands hunter-gatherers
Poverty Point culture
Bahamas
Hawaiian Islands
Cuba
Hispaniola
Jamaica
Puerto Rico
Caribbean hunter-gatherers
Olmec culture
maize farmers
manioc farmers (replacing hunter-gatherers)
Chorrera culture
Amazonian forest hunter-gatherers
El Paraiso culture
Chiripa culture
Chinchoros tradition
savanna hunter-gatherers
shellfish gatherers
Andean hunter-gatherers
pampas hunter-gatherers
shellfish gatherers and marine mammal hunters

TIMELINE

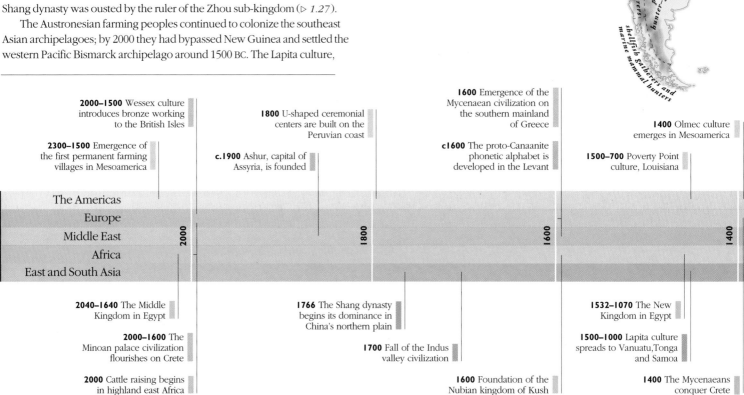

The Americas / Europe / Middle East / Africa / East and South Asia

2000 — 1800 — 1600 — 1400

2000–1500 Wessex culture introduces bronze working to the British Isles

2300–1500 Emergence of the first permanent farming villages in Mesoamerica

1800 U-shaped ceremonial centers are built on the Peruvian coast

c.1900 Ashur, capital of Assyria, is founded

1600 Emergence of the Mycenaean civilization on the southern mainland of Greece

c1600 The proto-Canaanite phonetic alphabet is developed in the Levant

1400 Olmec culture emerges in Mesoamerica

1500–700 Poverty Point culture, Louisiana

2040–1640 The Middle Kingdom in Egypt

2000–1600 The Minoan palace civilization flourishes on Crete

2000 Cattle raising begins in highland east Africa

1766 The Shang dynasty begins its dominance in China's northern plain

1700 Fall of the Indus valley civilization

1600 Foundation of the Nubian kingdom of Kush

1532–1070 The New Kingdom in Egypt

1500–1000 Lapita culture spreads to Vanuatu,Tonga and Samoa

1400 The Mycenaeans conquer Crete

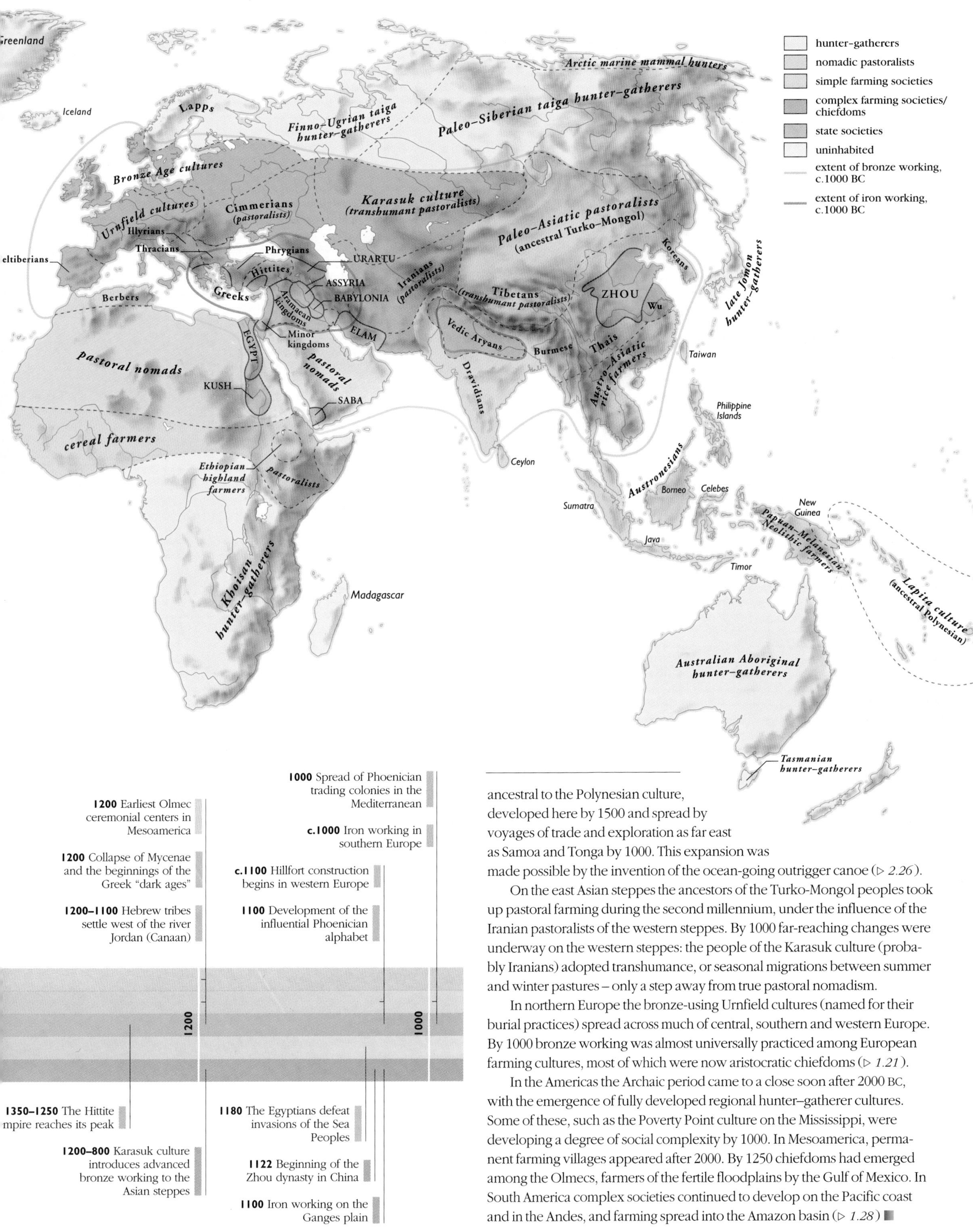
hunter-gatherers
nomadic pastoralists
simple farming societies
complex farming societies/ chiefdoms
state societies
uninhabited
extent of bronze working, c.1000 BC
extent of iron working, c.1000 BC
Iceland
Lapps
Finno-Ugrian taiga hunter-gatherers
Arctic marine mammal hunters
Paleo-Siberian taiga hunter-gatherers
Bronze Age cultures
Urnfield cultures
Cimmerians (pastoralists)
Karasuk culture (transhumant pastoralists)
Paleo-Asiatic pastoralists (ancestral Turko-Mongol)
Illyrians
Thracians
Phrygians
URARTU
Hittites
ASSYRIA
BABYLONIA
Iranians (pastoralists)
Greeks
Aramaean kingdoms
Berbers
Minor kingdoms
ELAM
EGYPT
Tibetans (transhumant pastoralists)
ZHOU
Wu
Koreans
late Jomon hunter-gatherers
Vedic Aryans
Burmese
Thais
Taiwan
pastoral nomads
pastoral nomads
KUSH
SABA
Dravidians
Austro-Asiatic rice farmers
Philippine Islands
cereal farmers
Ethiopian highland farmers
pastoralists
Ceylon
Austronesians
Borneo
Celebes
Sumatra
New Guinea
Papuan-Melanesian Neolithic farmers
Java
Timor
Khoisan hunter-gatherers
Madagascar
Lapita culture (ancestral Polynesian)
Australian Aboriginal hunter-gatherers
Tasmanian hunter-gatherers
1200
1000

1200 Earliest Olmec ceremonial centers in Mesoamerica

1200 Collapse of Mycenae and the beginnings of the Greek "dark ages"

1200–1100 Hebrew tribes settle west of the river Jordan (Canaan)

1000 Spread of Phoenician trading colonies in the Mediterranean

c.1000 Iron working in southern Europe

c.1100 Hillfort construction begins in western Europe

1100 Development of the influential Phoenician alphabet

1350–1250 The Hittite empire reaches its peak

1200–800 Karasuk culture introduces advanced bronze working to the Asian steppes

1180 The Egyptians defeat invasions of the Sea Peoples

1122 Beginning of the Zhou dynasty in China

1100 Iron working on the Ganges plain

ancestral to the Polynesian culture, developed here by 1500 and spread by voyages of trade and exploration as far east as Samoa and Tonga by 1000. This expansion was made possible by the invention of the ocean-going outrigger canoe (▷ *2.26*).

On the east Asian steppes the ancestors of the Turko-Mongol peoples took up pastoral farming during the second millennium, under the influence of the Iranian pastoralists of the western steppes. By 1000 far-reaching changes were underway on the western steppes: the people of the Karasuk culture (probably Iranians) adopted transhumance, or seasonal migrations between summer and winter pastures – only a step away from true pastoral nomadism.

In northern Europe the bronze-using Urnfield cultures (named for their burial practices) spread across much of central, southern and western Europe. By 1000 bronze working was almost universally practiced among European farming cultures, most of which were now aristocratic chiefdoms (▷ *1.21*).

In the Americas the Archaic period came to a close soon after 2000 BC, with the emergence of fully developed regional hunter–gatherer cultures. Some of these, such as the Poverty Point culture on the Mississippi, were developing a degree of social complexity by 1000. In Mesoamerica, permanent farming villages appeared after 2000. By 1250 chiefdoms had emerged among the Olmecs, farmers of the fertile floodplains by the Gulf of Mexico. In South America complex societies continued to develop on the Pacific coast and in the Andes, and farming spread into the Amazon basin (▷ *1.28*) ■

1.06 THE WORLD • 500 BC •

The number and size of organized states in the Middle East, India and the Mediterranean rose sharply between 1000 and 500 BC. A succession of empires dominated the Middle East. The first was the Assyrian empire which stretched from the Zagros mountains to Egypt by the 7th century. Assyrian rule was harsh and in 625 the Babylonians rebelled and seized most of the empire for themselves (▷ *1.13*). Then the Iranian Medes pushed west, conquering the Caucasus and eastern Anatolia. In 550 Cyrus II "the Great", an Iranian king, seized the Median kingdom and founded the Persian empire. He then took western Anatolia and the Babylonian empire. By 500 the Persian empire extended from Egypt to the Indus (▷ *1.15*).

State-organized societies had also spread throughout the Mediterranean world. By 700 Greece was a patchwork of independent city-states: by 500 these cities, and Athens in particular, entered a period of intellectual creativity unparalleled in world history (▷ *1.24*). The Greeks and Phoenicians also founded trading colonies throughout the Mediterranean. Although the Phoenicians lost their independence by 500, Carthage, their colony in north Africa, was the leading power of the western Mediterranean. The Greek cities of Sicily and southern Italy had a powerful influence, notably on the Etruscans who dominated northern Italy by 500. North of the Alps the Urnfield cultures of central Europe were replaced by the aristocratic iron-using Celtic Hallstatt culture c.600 (▷ *1.25*).

States reappeared in the Indian subcontinent in the 9th century. The focus this time was the Ganges plain where Vedic Aryan chiefdoms began to coalesce into kingdoms and republics. By 500 the largest was the kingdom of Magadha. At the same time the Aryans extended southward, conquering the Dravidians and imposing Hindu religion on them (▷ *1.26*). The Chinese Zhou kingdom expanded to the southeast after 1000, but what it gained in area it lost in internal cohesion. The Zhou kingdom was a decentralized feudal state and by the 8th century the powerful warlords had so undermined the power of the monarchy that it was powerless to prevent the kingdom from breaking up (▷ *1.27*). Meanwhile the first chiefdoms emerged around 500 in Korea and in Van Lang in southeast Asia.

One far-reaching development of the early first millennium was the change in lifestyle of the Iranian peoples (Scythians, Sarmatians, Sakas and Yue Qi) of the Eurasian steppes from transhumant (seasonal) pastoralism to nomadic pastoralism. The steppe peoples had been pioneers in the use of horses: they had domesticated them for their meat around 4000 BC, they had harnessed them to wagons (4th millennium) and war chariots (2nd millennium) and by 1000 BC they had mastered

TIMELINE

The Americas / Europe / Middle East / Africa / East and South Asia

1000 · 900 · 800 · 700 · 600

1000 Emergence of the kingdom of Israel

1000–500 Formative period of Hinduism

900–700 Nomadism becomes the dominant way of life on the Eurasian steppes

900 The first states emerge on the Ganges plain

800 Zapotecs develop hieroglyphic script in Mesoamerica

800–500 Greek colonization of the Mediterranean and Black Sea

800 Emergence of the Etruscan civilization in Italy

814 Foundation of the Phoenician colony of Carthage

800 The Aryans expand into southern India

770–481 The "Springs and Autumns" period in China: the Zhou kingdom breaks up into minor states

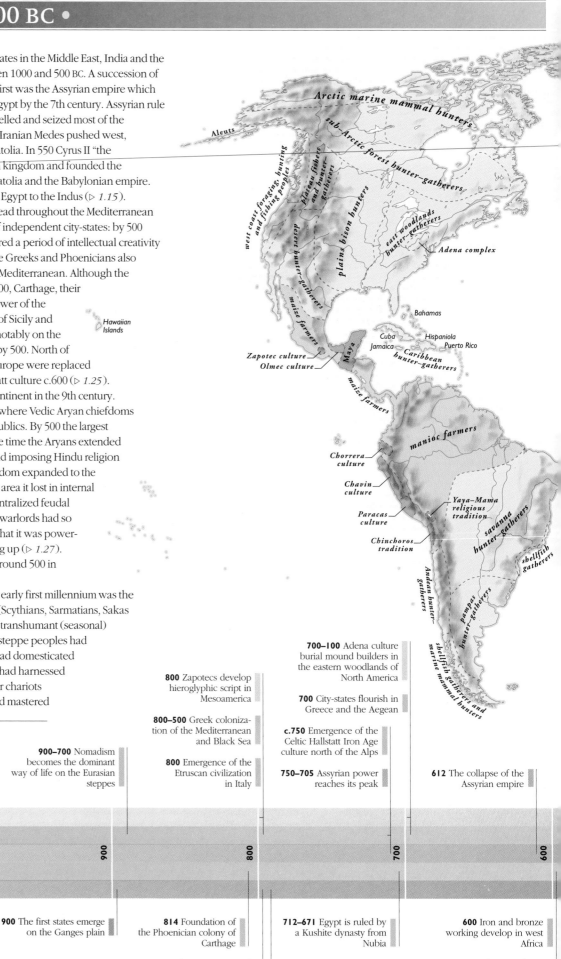

700–100 Adena culture burial mound builders in the eastern woodlands of North America

700 City-states flourish in Greece and the Aegean

c.750 Emergence of the Celtic Hallstatt Iron Age culture north of the Alps

750–705 Assyrian power reaches its peak

712–671 Egypt is ruled by a Kushite dynasty from Nubia

612 The collapse of the Assyrian empire

600 Iron and bronze working develop in west Africa

600 Introduction of iron working into China

c.590 The Nubian capital established at Meroë

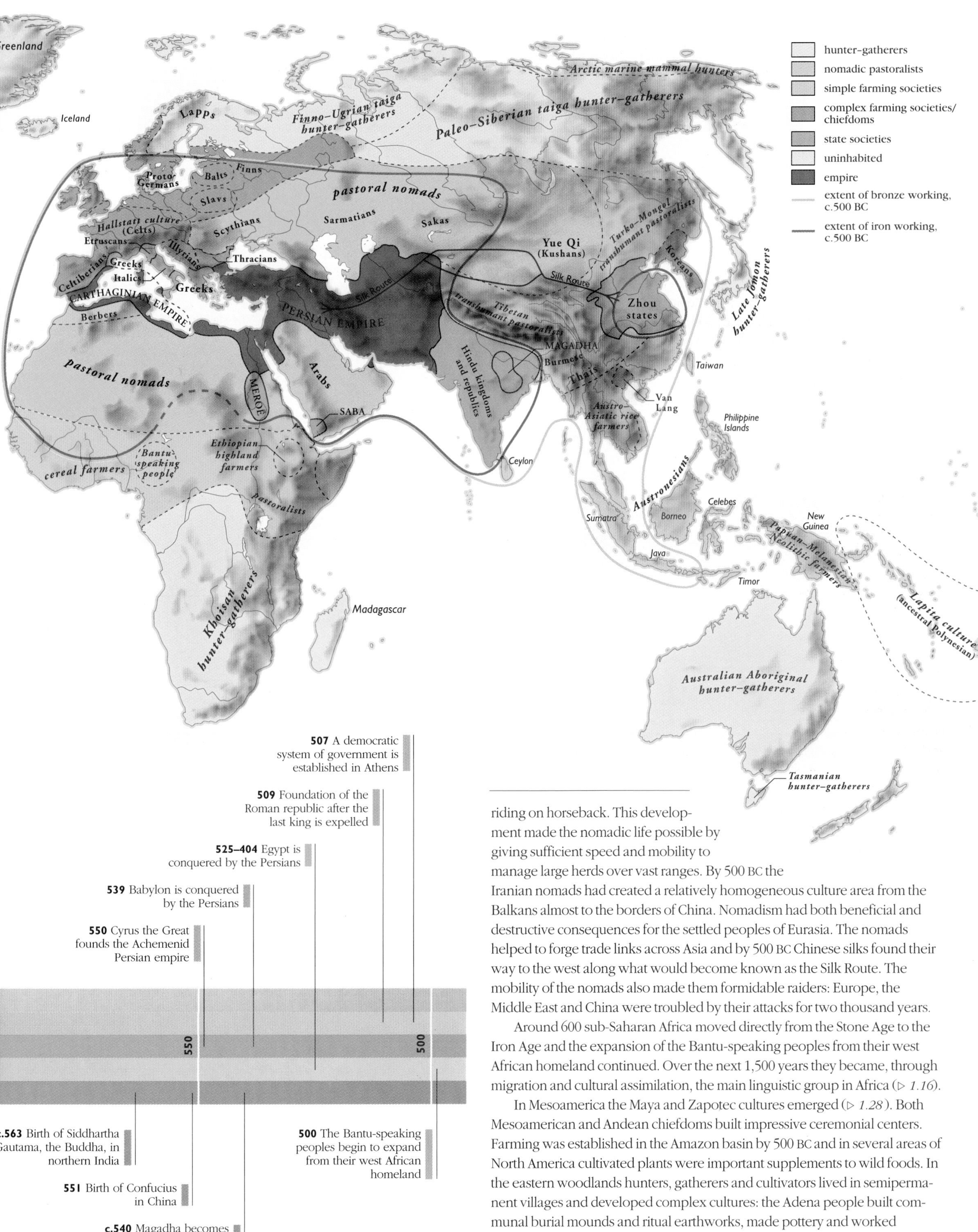
hunter-gatherers
nomadic pastoralists
simple farming societies
complex farming societies/ chiefdoms
state societies
uninhabited
empire
extent of bronze working, c.500 BC
extent of iron working, c.500 BC
Greenland
Iceland
Lapps
Finno-Ugrian taiga hunter-gatherers
Arctic marine mammal hunters
Paleo-Siberian taiga hunter-gatherers
Proto-Germans
Balts
Finns
Slavs
pastoral nomads
Hallstatt culture (Celts)
Scythians
Sarmatians
Sakas
Etruscans
Celtiberians
Greeks
Italics
Illyrians
Thracians
Greeks
CARTHAGINIAN EMPIRE
Berbers
Silk Route
PERSIAN EMPIRE
Yue Qi (Kushans)
Turko-Mongol transhumant pastoralists
Koreans
Silk Route
Tibetan transhumant pastoralists
Zhou states
Late Jomon hunter-gatherers
MAGADHA
Burmese
Thais
Hindu kingdoms and republics
Arabs
pastoral nomads
MEROË
SABA
Taiwan
Van Lang
Austro-Asiatic rice farmers
Philippine Islands
Ethiopian highland farmers
Bantu-speaking people
cereal farmers
Ceylon
Austronesians
Pastoralists
Celebes
Sumatra
Borneo
New Guinea
Papuan–Melanesian Neolithic farmers
Java
Timor
Madagascar
Lapita culture (ancestral Polynesian)
Khoisan hunter-gatherers
Australian Aboriginal hunter-gatherers
Tasmanian hunter-gatherers

507 A democratic system of government is established in Athens

509 Foundation of the Roman republic after the last king is expelled

525–404 Egypt is conquered by the Persians

539 Babylon is conquered by the Persians

550 Cyrus the Great founds the Achemenid Persian empire

550

500

c.563 Birth of Siddhartha Gautama, the Buddha, in northern India

551 Birth of Confucius in China

c.540 Magadha becomes the dominant kingdom in the Indian subcontinent

500 The Bantu-speaking peoples begin to expand from their west African homeland

riding on horseback. This development made the nomadic life possible by giving sufficient speed and mobility to manage large herds over vast ranges. By 500 BC the Iranian nomads had created a relatively homogeneous culture area from the Balkans almost to the borders of China. Nomadism had both beneficial and destructive consequences for the settled peoples of Eurasia. The nomads helped to forge trade links across Asia and by 500 BC Chinese silks found their way to the west along what would become known as the Silk Route. The mobility of the nomads also made them formidable raiders: Europe, the Middle East and China were troubled by their attacks for two thousand years.

Around 600 sub-Saharan Africa moved directly from the Stone Age to the Iron Age and the expansion of the Bantu-speaking peoples from their west African homeland continued. Over the next 1,500 years they became, through migration and cultural assimilation, the main linguistic group in Africa (▷ *1.16*).

In Mesoamerica the Maya and Zapotec cultures emerged (▷ *1.28*). Both Mesoamerican and Andean chiefdoms built impressive ceremonial centers. Farming was established in the Amazon basin by 500 BC and in several areas of North America cultivated plants were important supplements to wild foods. In the eastern woodlands hunters, gatherers and cultivators lived in semipermanent villages and developed complex cultures: the Adena people built communal burial mounds and ritual earthworks, made pottery and worked copper. Full farming economies, though, did not appear for many centuries ■

Writing was invented as an aid to administration in communities that had grown so complex that human memory could no longer store all the information needed for efficient government. The earliest known writing has been found on clay tablets from the Sumerian city of Uruk (in modern Iraq), from about 3400 BC but, as this was already a complete system with over seven hundred signs, development must have begun much earlier.

The earliest Sumerian signs are pictographs – for example the sign for barley is a simplified picture of an ear of barley. More complex ideas were expressed by combining signs: thus a head and a bowl together meant "to eat". The signs were inscribed on wet clay tablets which were then dried. This proved to be a very durable medium and many thousands of clay tablets have survived (▷ *1.10*). After about 2900 BC the signs were gradually simplified and inscribed with a rectangular-ended reed stylus. This left wedge-shaped strokes from which this script derives its name (cuneiform, from the Latin *cuneus*, "wedge").

Cuneiform was gradually refined so that a sign could also stand for the phonetic value of the word: if this system were used for modern English, the sign for "man" could also be used in combination with another sign, such as that for "age", to make another word, "manage". Syllable signs were also introduced, enabling cuneiform to record accurately all elements of human speech. Most early Sumerian documents were accounts and records of transactions. It was not until about 2400 that writing was used to record law codes, letters, chronicles, religious beliefs or for literature.

The Sumerian writing systems were widely adapted to other languages. Elamite and Indus valley pictographic derive from Sumerian pictographic (▷ *1.26*) and although Egyptian hieroglyphic writing (a system that is almost as old as the Sumerian) was unique, the idea was probably based on Sumerian pictographs (▷ *1.17*). Cuneiform was adapted successfully to the Akkadian, Assyrian, Babylonian, Elamite, Hittite, Hurrian and Urartian languages among others. Nevertheless, hundreds of different signs had to be learned, and scribes needed several years to master cuneiform and hieroglyphic scripts; as a result literacy remained the preserve of a tiny minority of specialists, and the cultural impact of its introduction was limited.

In the early 16th century BC the much simpler proto-Canaanite phonetic alphabet, with only 28 letters that stood for syllables which could be combined to spell out the sound of a word, was developed in the Levant or eastern Mediterranean coastal region (▷ *1.12*). The letters were based on Egyptian hieroglyphs. By 1000 BC many variants of the proto-Canaanite script had developed, most important among them the Phoenician, Aramaic and the Arabian Sabean and Nabatean alphabets. The Aramaic alphabet was adopted by the Assyrians by the 8th century and replaced cuneiform as the main script of the Middle East. Adaptations of Aramaic were introduced into India in the 7th century and became the basis of modern Indian scripts and, ultimately, of the Indian-derived scripts of southeast and central Asia. Nabatean developed into the Arabic script in the 7th century AD while Sabean crossed the Red Sea to form the basis of Ethiopic, which was the only independent script to emerge in sub-Saharan Africa.

The Phoenician alphabet was the basis of the Old Hebrew and Greek alphabets. The Greeks adapted the Phoenician alphabet in the 8th century by introducing separate letters for consonant and vowel sounds (▷ *1.23*). This was more precise than any syllabic alphabet. The Greek alphabet was in turn adapted to form new scripts by the peoples of Anatolia, the Balkans and Italy, including the Etruscans whose script was developed by the Romans into the Latin alphabet. Alphabetic scripts were easier to learn and use and they permitted literacy to become a widespread accomplishment, rather than just the preserve of professional scribes and administrators.

China, Mesoamerica and Polynesia each saw the independent development of writing. In Shang Dynasty China, a script with both pictographic and phonetic elements appeared around 1600 BC. Most early examples record the results of divinations on animal bones, but the script was also used for record-keeping (▷ *1.27*). This script was constantly refined and standardized over the centuries, and the modern Chinese writing system is still based on its principles. The Chinese script became the basis of Japanese and Korean scripts (though the Koreans later adopted an alphabetic script).

Hawaiian Islands
Zapotec hieroglyphic
Mixtec
Maya
Jamaica
Hispaniola
Puerto Rico
Easter Island
Rongorongo

In Mesoamerica the Zapotecs began to develop a hieroglyphic script about 800 BC, from which the later Mesoamerican scripts derive (▷ *1.28*). Of these, only the Mayan was a fully developed literary language capable of expressing all aspects of spoken language. Writing did not develop in the Andean civilizations although the Inca *quipu*, a mnemonic device made of knotted strings, fulfilled some of the functions of a simple script. Colored strings symbolized different commodities or services while the number of knots represented quantities held or required.

Another script to arise independently of any other was the hieroglyphic script developed in the Polynesian chiefdoms of Easter Island about AD 1500. Known as Rongorongo, it fell out of use before Europeans reached Easter Island and has not been deciphered ■

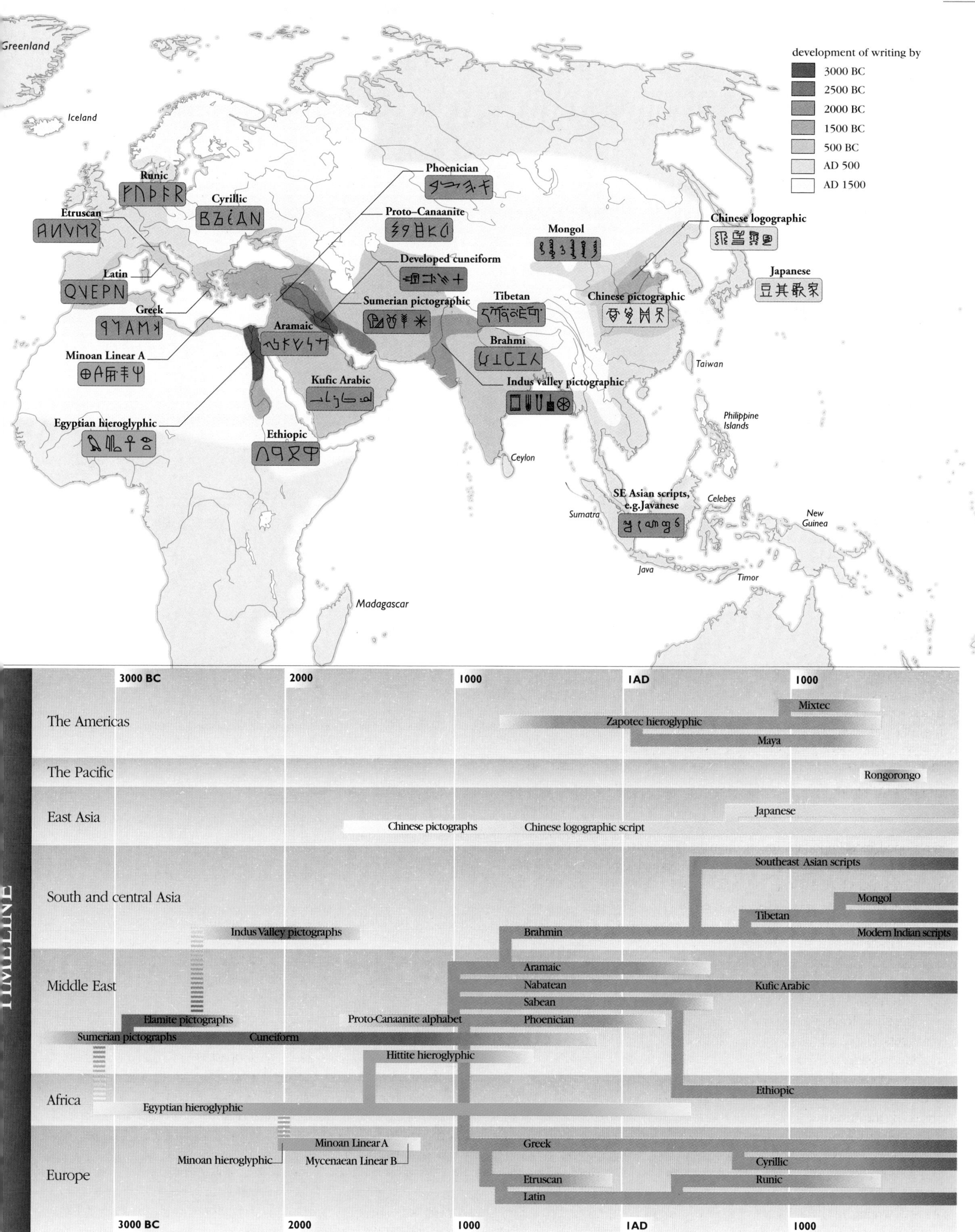
development of writing by
3000 BC
2500 BC
2000 BC
1500 BC
500 BC
AD 500
AD 1500
Greenland
Iceland
Runic
Cyrillic
Etruscan
Latin
Greek
Minoan Linear A
Egyptian hieroglyphic
Phoenician
Proto–Canaanite
Developed cuneiform
Sumerian pictographic
Aramaic
Kufic Arabic
Ethiopic
Mongol
Tibetan
Brahmi
Indus valley pictographic
Chinese logographic
Chinese pictographic
Japanese
Taiwan
Philippine Islands
Ceylon
SE Asian scripts, e.g. Javanese
Sumatra
Celebes
New Guinea
Java
Timor
Madagascar
TIMELINE
3000 BC
2000
1000
1AD
1000
The Americas
Mixtec
Zapotec hieroglyphic
Maya
The Pacific
Rongorongo
East Asia
Japanese
Chinese pictographs
Chinese logographic script
South and central Asia
Southeast Asian scripts
Mongol
Tibetan
Indus Valley pictographs
Brahmin
Modern Indian scripts
Middle East
Aramaic
Nabatean
Kufic Arabic
Sabean
Elamite pictographs
Proto-Canaanite alphabet
Phoenician
Sumerian pictographs
Cuneiform
Hittite hieroglyphic
Africa
Ethiopic
Egyptian hieroglyphic
Europe
Minoan Linear A
Minoan hieroglyphic
Mycenaean Linear B
Greek
Cyrillic
Etruscan
Runic
Latin
3000 BC
2000
1000
1AD
1000

1.08 The first farmers of the Middle East • 10,000 – 6000 BC •

The earliest communities to rely on farming for most of their food grew up in the area known as the Fertile Crescent. This region of good soils and light but reliable rainfall extends in an arc from the foothills of Iraq's Zagros mountains, through south Turkey to western Syria, the Lebanon and Israel. Toward the end of the Ice Age it was colonized by plants such as wild emmer and einkorn wheat, wild barley, wild pulses, and almond, oak and pistachio trees. The supply of cereals and nuts was so rich that in some areas the hunter–gatherer population could settle in semi-permanent villages.

Among these sedentary hunter–gatherers were the Natufians of the Levant, whose way of life developed about 10,500 BC. Except for short stays at seasonal camps, the Natufians lived in villages of substantial wooden huts with stone foundations. They hunted gazelle intensively but their staple food was wild cereals, which they harvested with bone-handled reaping knives, stored in stone jars and processed with querns, grindstones, and mortars and pestles. Settled living and abundant food led them to abandon the egalitarianism of the nomadic hunter–gatherer band. A wide variation in the range and quality of goods found in individual burials points to the existence of social ranking.

During the 9th millennium they began to cultivate wild cereals close to their settlements. In some places, such as at Tell Mureybet in Syria, wild cereals may even have been introduced to areas where they did not naturally occur. The climate was changing and the natural range of wild cereals was shrinking, so these developments were probably an attempt to secure the food supply. Around 8000 BC these early farmers learned to breed wild cereals selectively for characteristics that increased the yield and made them easier to harvest. Within a few centuries domesticated strains of barley, emmer and einkorn wheat had appeared. Although cultivated plants were important to the economies of these transitional, or "proto-Neolithic", farmers, hunting and gathering continued to be crucial sources of food. As the population began to outstrip the environment's capacity to support the old lifestyle, the dependence on farming increased. By about 7500 BC communities with a full farming economy had developed, marking the proper beginning of the Neolithic or "New Stone Age" (the period between the adoption of agriculture and that of metal working).

One of the most impressive proto-Neolithic sites is at Jericho, where a walled settlement of 1,500 people had grown up near a permanent spring by about 8000 BC. Domesticated barley and emmer wheat, pulses and figs were cultivated, but wild animals – gazelle and wild sheep and goats – were also important food sources. The people lived in huts built of sun-dried mud bricks, the earliest known use of what became the most important building material of the Middle East. Mud brick was easy to produce; when a house fell into disrepair it was simply knocked down and replaced by a new one. Over the centuries, successive rebuildings on the same site produced a high mound of debris,

7

spread of domesticated emmer wheat and barley to southeast Europe, 7th millennium

Aegean Sea

Ashikli Huyu

Hacilar

Suberde

Can

TAURU

Cyprus

Khiro

Mediterranean Sea

- wild strains of einkorn wheat only
- wild strains of emmer and einkorn wheat, and barley
- distribution of wild sheep and goats
- southeastern limit of range of aurochs
- southern limit of dry farming
- area of Epipaleolithic Natufian sites, 10,500–8500
- proto-Neolithic settlement, 8500–7500
- aceramic Neolithic farming village, 7500–6500
- aceramic site with population of over 1000
- obsidian source
- distribution of Armenian obsidian
- distribution of Anatolian obsidian
- modern coastline and drainage where altered

0 300 km
0 200 mi

TIMELINE

Zagros/Taurus mts

- **11,000** Dogs are the first animals to be domesticated
- **9000** Management of wild sheep herds
- **8000–7700** Barley, emmer and einkhorn wheat are domesticated
- **7000** Native copper is worked by cold hammering
- **7000** Goats are domesticated.
- **6700** Sheep are domesticated
- **6500** Pigs are domesticated
- **6000** Cattle are domesticated
- **6000** Development of irrigation in the Zagros foothills

Levant

- Natufian hunter-gatherers
- **10,500** Natufians harvest wild cereals, using stone sickles
- **10,000** Buildings with stone foundations and semi-permanent settlements
- **8000** Mud brick is used for building
- **8000** Emergence of the first farming communities
- **7500** First use of flax for textiles

General

- **7500** Long-distance trade in obsidian begins
- **7000–6500** Permanent farming villages are widespread; lentils and peas are domesticated
- **6500** Pottery comes into general use

EPIPALEOLITHIC | PROTO-NEOLITHIC | ACERAMIC NEOLITHIC | NEOLITHIC

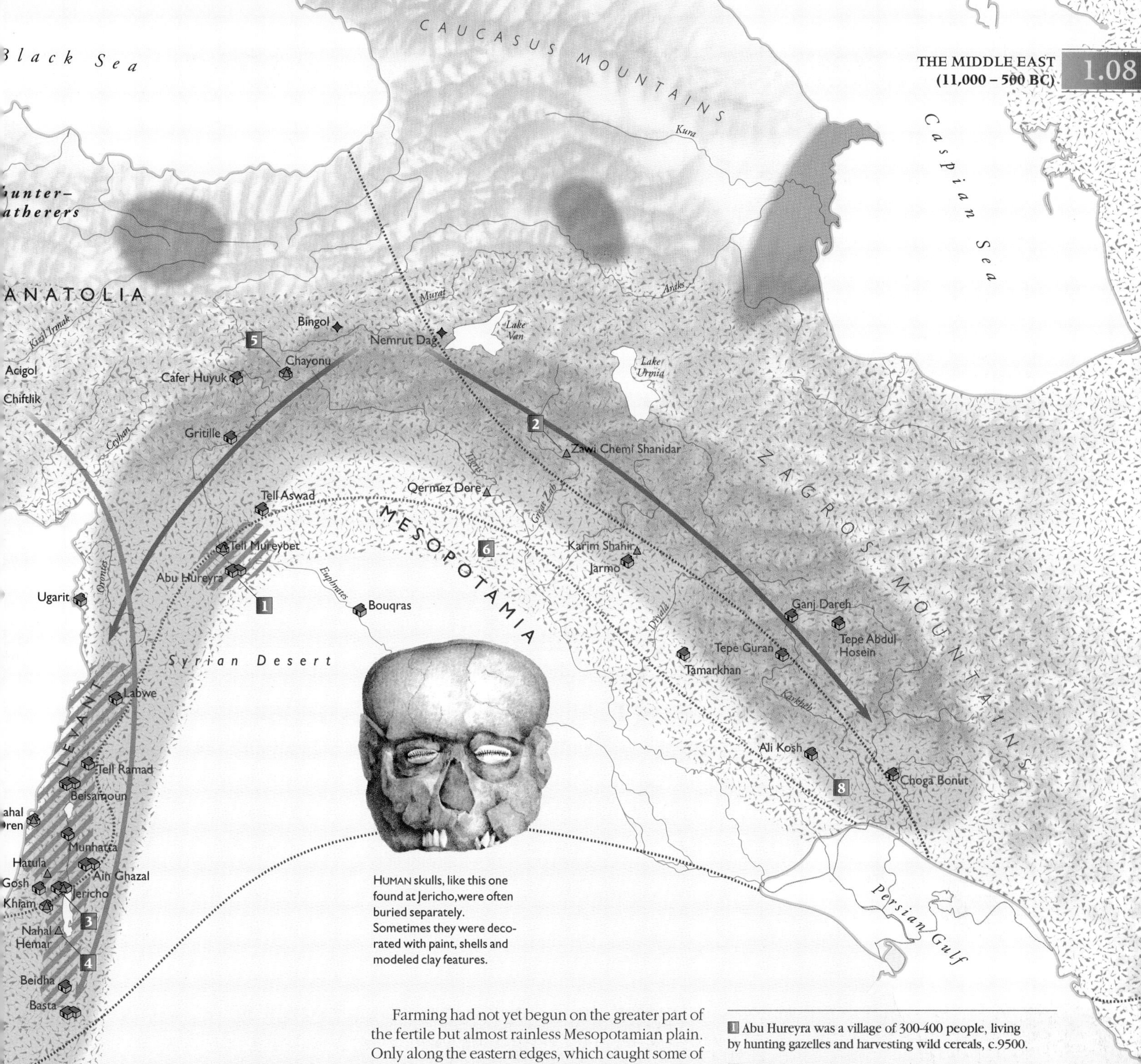
Black Sea
CAUCASUS MOUNTAINS
Kura
Caspian Sea
Hunter–gatherers
ANATOLIA
Murat
Araks
Kizil Irmak
Bingol
Nemrut Dag
Lake Van
Lake Urmia
Chayonu
Cafer Huyuk
Acigol
Chiftlik
Gritille
Ceyhan
Zawi Chemi Shanidar
ZAGROS MOUNTAINS
Tigris
Qermez Dere
Tell Aswad
MESOPOTAMIA
Great Zab
Tell Mureybet
Karim Shahir
Jarmo
Abu Hureyra
Euphrates
Orontes
Ugarit
Bouqras
Diyala
Ganj Dareh
Tepe Abdul Hosein
Tepe Guran
Tamarkhan
Syrian Desert
Labwe
LEVANT
Karkheh
Ali Kosh
Tell Ramad
Choga Bonut
Beisamoun
Munhatta
Hatula
Ain Ghazal
Gosh
Jericho
Khiam
Nahal Hemar
Beidha
Basta
Persian Gulf
1
2
3
4
5
6
8

HUMAN skulls, like this one found at Jericho, were often buried separately. Sometimes they were decorated with paint, shells and modeled clay features.

called a *tell* in Arabic, *huyuk* in Turkish and *tepe* in Persian. These settlement mounds are the most characteristic archeological sites of the region.

Farming also began to develop in southern Anatolia and the Zagros mountains. In the mountains hunter– gatherers intensified their management of flocks of wild sheep and goats. Animal bones from a settlement at Zawi Chemi Shanidar (9000 BC) show that the inhabitants killed mainly immature sheep. Since hunting would have resulted in a more random distribution of ages, the sheep had probably been penned and selectively culled. Pollen samples also suggest that wild cereals were cultivated at Zawi Chemi Shanidar. By the 7th millennium, domesticated sheep and goats were an important part of the economy of villages such as Chayonu (now in eastern Turkey).

Farming had not yet begun on the greater part of the fertile but almost rainless Mesopotamian plain. Only along the eastern edges, which caught some of the rainfall of the Zagros mountains, was farming possible before the development of irrigation and heat-resistant cereal strains in the 6th millennium.

The early farming communities had no pottery; this period of the Neolithic is known as the aceramic or prepottery Neolithic. The first pottery appeared by 7000 BC, but such was its usefulness for cooking and storage that its use had become widespread within five centuries. By this time bread wheat had also been developed, flax – the raw material of linen cloth – had been domesticated, as had the pig, and cattle were introduced from southeastern Europe where farming was just beginning.

The sedentary way of life meant that communities became less self-sufficient and long-distance trade, particularly in salt and toolmaking stone, became more important. The finest toolmaking stone, obsidian (volcanic glass), was traded over long distances. Obsidian from Anatolia has been found in early Neolithic sites almost as far south as the Red Sea, while obsidian from the region by Lake Van reached the Mediterranean and the Persian Gulf.

1 Abu Hureyra was a village of 300-400 people, living by hunting gazelles and harvesting wild cereals, c.9500.

2 Zawi Chemi Shanidar, a summer settlement c.9000, shows evidence for intensive management of wild sheep herds.

3 Jericho was a permanent settlement by 8500 BC, and was walled by 8000.

4 Nahal Hemar, an aceramic Neolithic site, has the earliest evidence for textile manufacture (flax).

5 At Chayonu, native copper was used 7300–6500 to make tools and ornaments.

6 Before 6000 BC Mesopotamia was only sparsely populated with hunter–gatherers.

7 Cultivation of emmer wheat and barley began in southeast Europe c.6000 BC, probably as a result of trade contacts with the Middle East.

8 Ali Kosh was one of the earliest farming communities on the Mesopotamian plain, founded 8000 BC.

See also 1.03 (rise of agriculture), 1.09 (MiddleEast), 1.16 (Africa)

1.09 Advanced farmers of the Middle East • 6500 – 4300 BC •

By the time that pottery came into widespread use in the Fertile Crescent, around 6500 BC, the densest concentration of farming settlements was still to be found in the uplands of the Levant, southern Anatolia and the Zagros mountains, where there was reliable rainfall. Most villages had no more than a few hundred inhabitants and had social structures with relatively little distinction between rich and poor; the simple subsistence economies were based on cereals and herds of sheep, goats or cattle.

An important exception was the town-sized settlement which grew up around 6700 BC at Chatal Huyuk in Turkey. This settlement of densely packed mud-brick houses is the largest Neolithic settlement yet found. Long-distance trade in obsidian from nearby volcanoes, and improved agricultural yields resulting from the adoption of simple irrigation techniques, may have played a role in the town's growth. Chatal Huyuk had rich artistic traditions of wall-painting and sculpture, and a great many elaborately decorated shrines have been found. Many other crafts were practiced, including weaving, basketry, copper working (the earliest known evidence of copper smelting has been found here), fine stone toolmaking and pottery. Chatal Huyuk, however, was a precocious development. The local environment could not sustain longterm urban growth: the site was abandoned after about a thousand years and the pattern of dispersed settlements, typical of the rest of Neolithic Anatolia, was resumed.

The conditions for sustainable urban growth were first achieved in Mesopotamia. Farming was still confined to the fringes of the Mesopotamian plain in 6500 BC but it had spread throughout the region by 5500. The expansion of farming settlement across the plain is reflected by a series of cultures, each of which can be identified by a distinctive pottery style. The first of these was the Hassuna culture (6500–6000), centered on northern Mesopotamia and mostly within the dry farming zone. The Hassuna people grew emmer, einkorn and barley, bred sheep, goats, pigs and cattle and hunted a little. There is evidence for copper and lead smelting and the Hassuna culture was the earliest to produce painted pottery and fire it in purpose-built kilns. Stamp seals, later used widely in Mesopotamia to indicate ownership, were also first used in the Hassuna culture.

The Hassuna culture was replaced around 6000 by the Halafian culture. A storehouse excavated at Arpachiyeh, containing a concentration of fine pottery, jewelry, sculpture and flint and obsidian tools, suggests that the Halafians were ruled by chiefs who amassed considerable personal wealth and controlled the community's trade contacts. The influence of the Halafian culture was confined almost entirely to the dry farming zone but the same was not true of the contemporary, and overlapping,

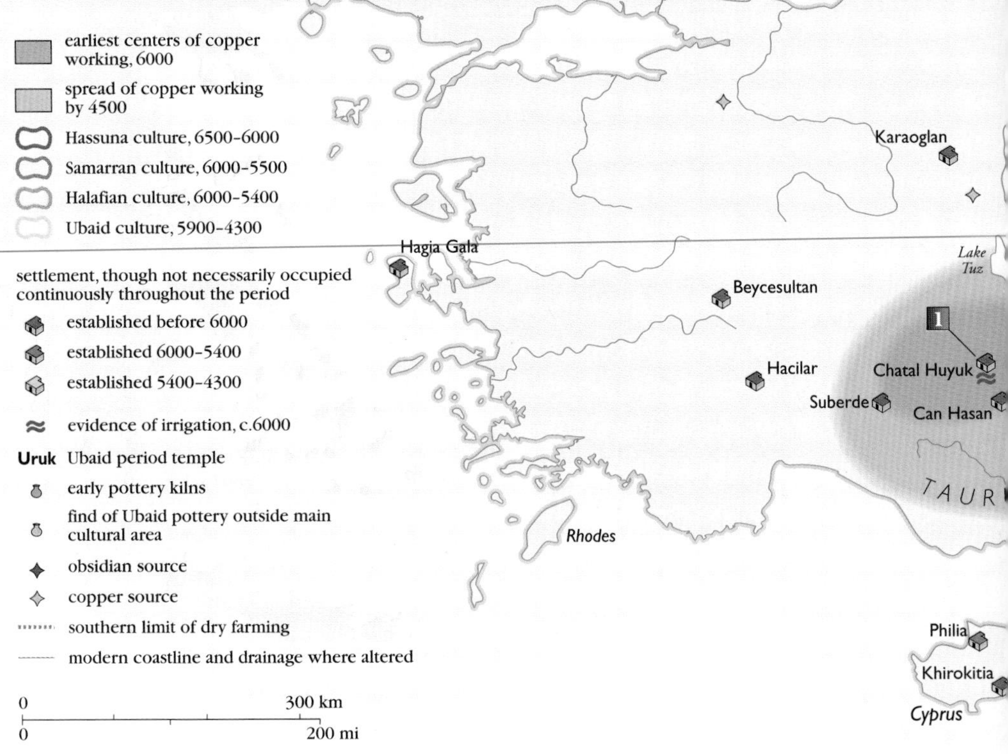

earliest centers of copper working, 6000
spread of copper working by 4500
Hassuna culture, 6500–6000
Samarran culture, 6000–5500
Halafian culture, 6000–5400
Ubaid culture, 5900–4300
settlement, though not necessarily occupied continuously throughout the period
established before 6000
established 6000–5400
established 5400–4300
evidence of irrigation, c.6000
Uruk Ubaid period temple
early pottery kilns
find of Ubaid pottery outside main cultural area
obsidian source
copper source
southern limit of dry farming
modern coastline and drainage where altered
0
300 km
0
200 mi
Karaoglan
Hagia Gala
Lake Tuz
Beycesultan
1
Hacilar
Chatal Huyuk
Suberde
Can Hasan
TAUR
Rhodes
Philia
Khirokitia
Cyprus

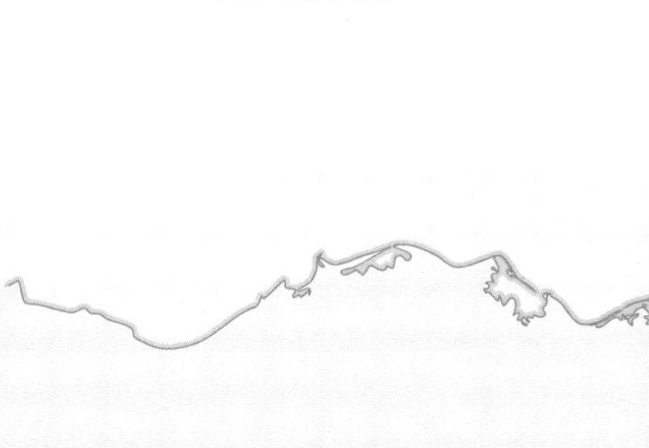

Mediterranean Sea

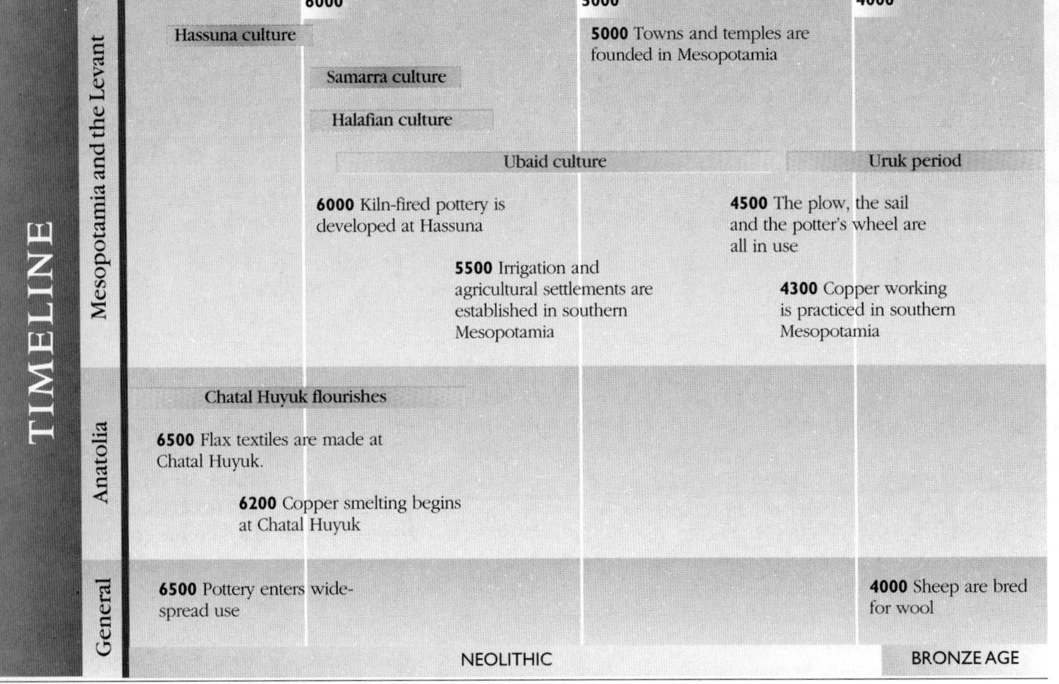

TIMELINE
Mesopotamia and the Levant
6000
5000
4000
Hassuna culture
5000 Towns and temples are founded in Mesopotamia
Samarra culture
Halafian culture
Ubaid culture
Uruk period
6000 Kiln-fired pottery is developed at Hassuna
4500 The plow, the sail and the potter's wheel are all in use
5500 Irrigation and agricultural settlements are established in southern Mesopotamia
4300 Copper working is practiced in southern Mesopotamia
Anatolia
Chatal Huyuk flourishes
6500 Flax textiles are made at Chatal Huyuk.
6200 Copper smelting begins at Chatal Huyuk
General
6500 Pottery enters widespread use
4000 Sheep are bred for wool
NEOLITHIC
BRONZE AGE

1 Chatal Huyuk had a population of about 6000 people, mainly farmers, between 6700–5700 BC.

2 Tell Umm Dabaghiyeh was a permanent hunter settlement c.6000, trading hides for grain with the northern farmers.

3 Choga Mami is the site of the earliest known irrigation canals; 5500 BC.

4 The fertile but rainless south Mesopotamia plain was colonized by farmers after the development of irrigation c.5500 BC.

5 Kilns were first used for firing pottery in Hassuna c.6000 BC.

6 The Ubaid settlement of Tell Awayli had a grain storehouse with a total area of 200 square meters.

7 Eridu was the oldest town in southern Mesopotamia. It had a large temple and a population of five thousand by the end of the Ubaid period.

8 Ubaid pottery from Ur found here indicates trade links between Mesopotamia and Arabia.

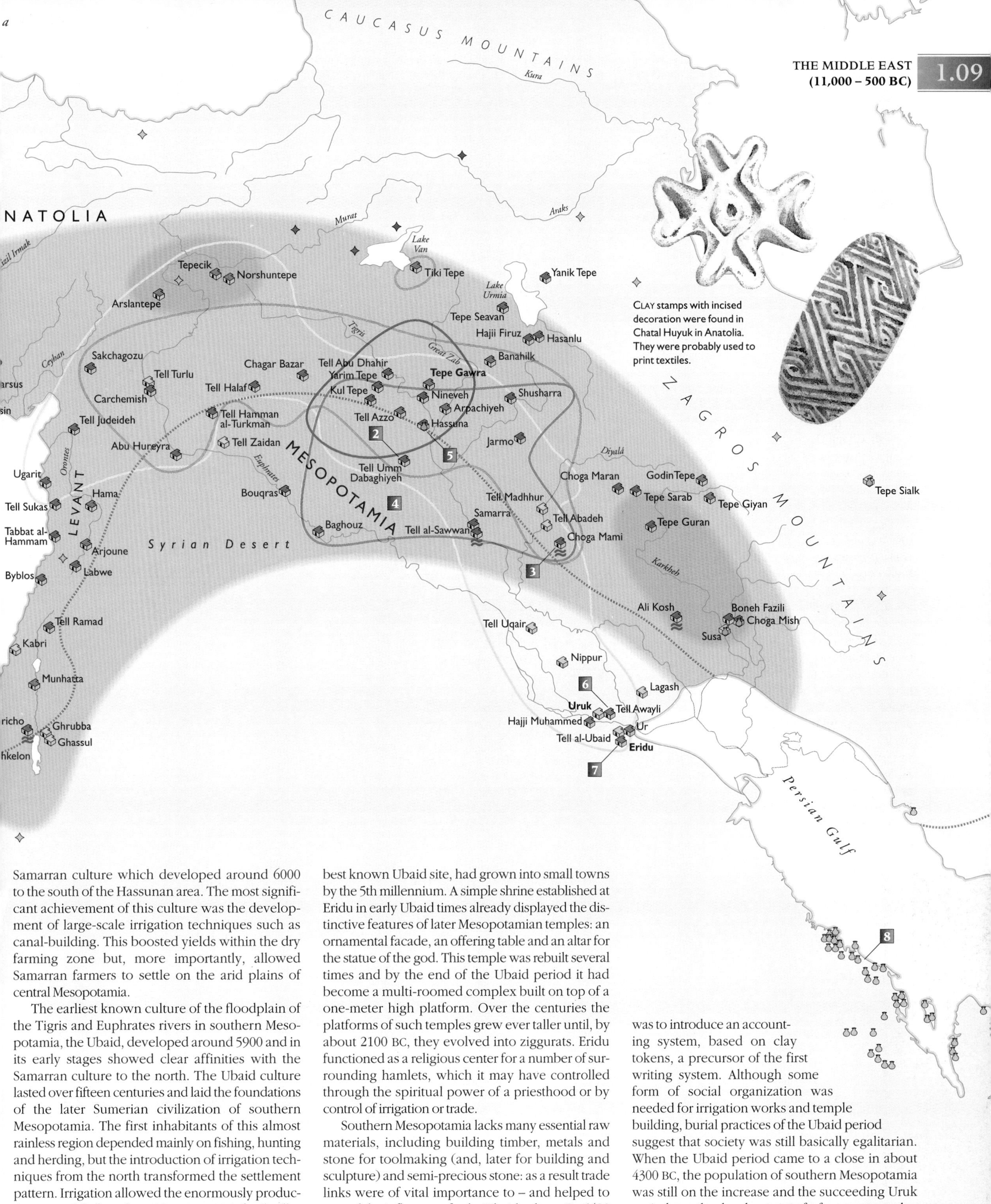
CAUCASUS MOUNTAINS
Kura
ANATOLIA
Murat
Lake Van
Araks
Tepecik
Norshuntepe
Arslantepe
Tiki Tepe
Lake Urmia
Yanik Tepe
Tepe Seavan
Hajii Firuz
Hasanlu
Tigris
Great Zab
Banahilk
Ceyhan
Sakchagozu
Tell Turlu
Chagar Bazar
Tell Abu Dhahir
Yarim Tepe
Tepe Gawra
Tell Halaf
Kul Tepe
Nineveh
Shusharra
Carchemish
Arpachiyeh
Tell Hamman al-Turkman
Tell Azzo
Hassuna
Tell Judeideh
Jarmo
Abu Hureyra
Tell Zaidan
MESOPOTAMIA
Orontes
Euphrates
Diyala
Ugarit
Tell Umm Dabaghiyeh
Choga Maran
Godin Tepe
Tepe Sialk
LEVANT
Hama
Bouqras
Tell Madhhur
Tepe Sarab
Tepe Giyan
Tell Sukas
Samarra
Tell Abadeh
Tabbat al-Hammam
Baghouz
Tell al-Sawwan
Tepe Guran
Syrian Desert
Choga Mami
Arjoune
Labwe
Byblos
ZAGROS MOUNTAINS
Karkheh
Ali Kosh
Boneh Fazili
Choga Mish
Tell Ramad
Tell Uqair
Susa
Kabri
Nippur
Munhatta
Lagash
Uruk
Tell Awayli
Hajji Muhammed
Ur
Tell al-Ubaid
Eridu
Ghrubba
Ghassul
Persian Gulf
2
3
4
5
6
7
8

CLAY stamps with incised decoration were found in Chatal Huyuk in Anatolia. They were probably used to print textiles.

Samarran culture which developed around 6000 to the south of the Hassunan area. The most significant achievement of this culture was the development of large-scale irrigation techniques such as canal-building. This boosted yields within the dry farming zone but, more importantly, allowed Samarran farmers to settle on the arid plains of central Mesopotamia.

The earliest known culture of the floodplain of the Tigris and Euphrates rivers in southern Mesopotamia, the Ubaid, developed around 5900 and in its early stages showed clear affinities with the Samarran culture to the north. The Ubaid culture lasted over fifteen centuries and laid the foundations of the later Sumerian civilization of southern Mesopotamia. The first inhabitants of this almost rainless region depended mainly on fishing, hunting and herding, but the introduction of irrigation techniques from the north transformed the settlement pattern. Irrigation allowed the enormously productive potential of southern Mesopotamia's fertile alluvial soils to be realized. Productivity received another boost in the 5th millennium with the invention of the plow. Intensive agriculture meant that the population rose rapidly and many new farming villages were founded. Some of these, like Eridu, the best known Ubaid site, had grown into small towns by the 5th millennium. A simple shrine established at Eridu in early Ubaid times already displayed the distinctive features of later Mesopotamian temples: an ornamental facade, an offering table and an altar for the statue of the god. This temple was rebuilt several times and by the end of the Ubaid period it had become a multi-roomed complex built on top of a one-meter high platform. Over the centuries the platforms of such temples grew ever taller until, by about 2100 BC, they evolved into ziggurats. Eridu functioned as a religious center for a number of surrounding hamlets, which it may have controlled through the spiritual power of a priesthood or by control of irrigation or trade.

Southern Mesopotamia lacks many essential raw materials, including building timber, metals and stone for toolmaking (and, later for building and sculpture) and semi-precious stone: as a result trade links were of vital importance to – and helped to spread the influence of – the Ubaid culture. By 5400 the Ubaid culture had replaced the Halafian culture in northern Mesopotamia while Ubaid pottery manufactured around Ur has been found throughout the Persian Gulf region.

An important innovation of the Ubaid culture was to introduce an accounting system, based on clay tokens, a precursor of the first writing system. Although some form of social organization was needed for irrigation works and temple building, burial practices of the Ubaid period suggest that society was still basically egalitarian. When the Ubaid period came to a close in about 4300 BC, the population of southern Mesopotamia was still on the increase and the succeeding Uruk period saw the development of a far more complex and hierarchical society.

See also 1.03 (the rise of agriculture), 1.10 (earliest cities), 1.20 (southeast Europe)

1.10 The first cities of Mesopotamia • 4300 – 2334 BC •

The world's first cities and states emerged in the region of Sumeria in southern Mesopotamia in the Uruk period (4300–3100), named for the oldest and largest Sumerian city. States, with their social classes, centralized government and well-organized trade, became important mechanisms for coordinating flood control (important in this region) and other public works. Early Sumerian cities were dominated by temple complexes, and the priesthood probably took the lead in this organization. The Tigris and Euphrates rivers are subject to violent floods and unpredictable changes of course, events which must have seemed like the acts of capricious gods (the biblical story of the flood is of Sumerian origin). The priests claimed to be able to propitiate the gods, and this may have given them the authority to be accepted as rulers of their cities.

Most Sumerian cities of the Uruk period had a population between two and eight thousand people, although Uruk itself, the largest, had over 10,000; by 2700 BC this had risen to about 50,000. Most of these were farmers who traveled out each day to the surrounding fields. However, the food surpluses they produced were great and Sumerian society became the first to have the resources to support large numbers of people in specialist occupations: sculptors, potters, bronze-casters, stonemasons, bakers, brewers and weavers.

The temples became centers of redistribution where the surplus food of the countryside and craft products were gathered to be given out as rations, or traded abroad for raw materials that could not be found locally. These trade links ranged from India and Afghanistan to Egypt, and played an important part in spreading the influence of Sumerian civilization throughout the Middle East. It was a complex task to manage the redistribution of produce. Keeping track of all the transactions was beyond the ability of unaided memory and by around 3400 a system of pictographic writing, probably derived from an earlier token system, had been developed.

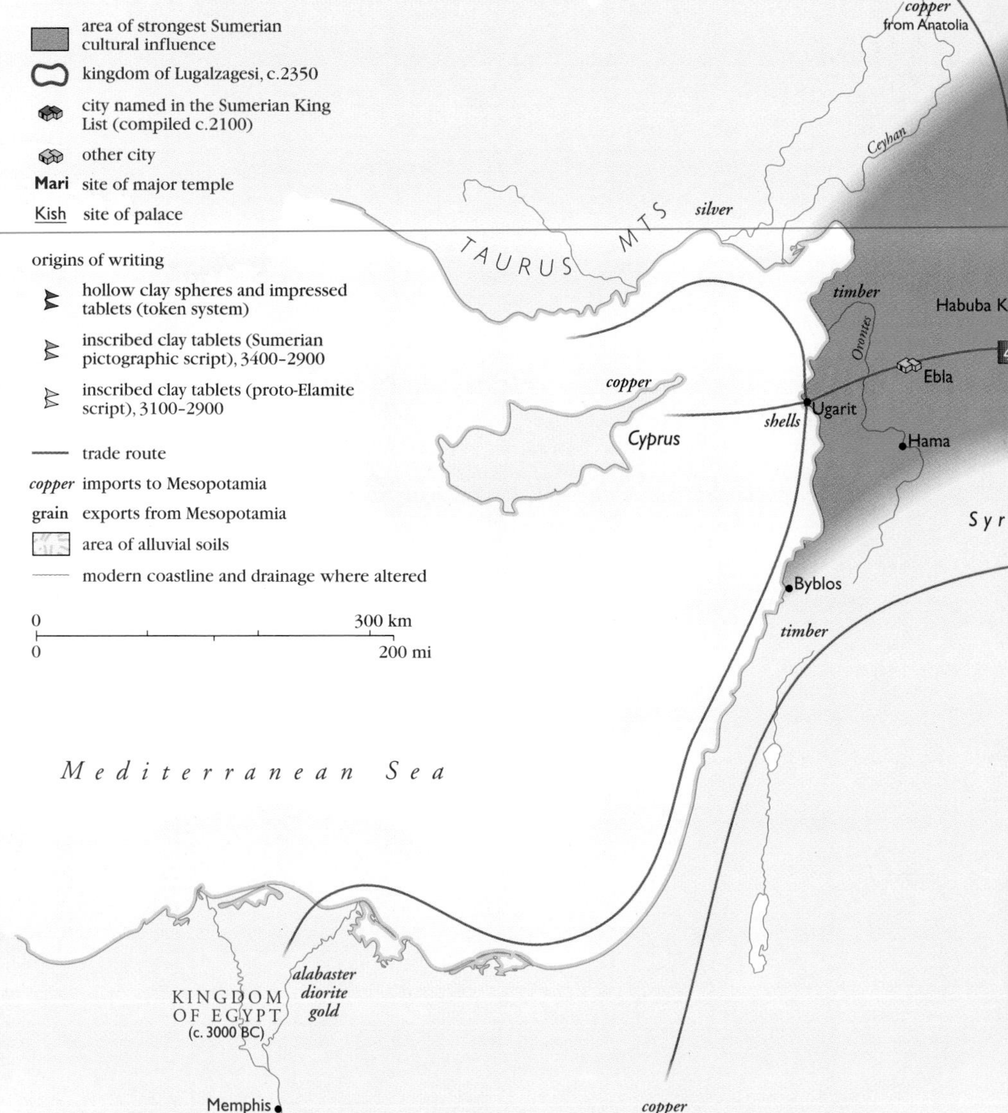

area of strongest Sumerian cultural influence
kingdom of Lugalzagesi, c.2350
city named in the Sumerian King List (compiled c.2100)
other city
Mari site of major temple
Kish site of palace
origins of writing
hollow clay spheres and impressed tablets (token system)
inscribed clay tablets (Sumerian pictographic script), 3400–2900
inscribed clay tablets (proto-Elamite script), 3100–2900
trade route
copper imports to Mesopotamia
grain exports from Mesopotamia
area of alluvial soils
modern coastline and drainage where altered
0
300 km
0
200 mi
copper from Anatolia
Ceyhan
silver
TAURUS MTS
timber
Habuba Kabira
Orontes
Ebla
copper
Ugarit
shells
Cyprus
Hama
Syria
Byblos
timber
Mediterranean Sea
alabaster
diorite
gold
KINGDOM OF EGYPT (c. 3000 BC)
Memphis
copper

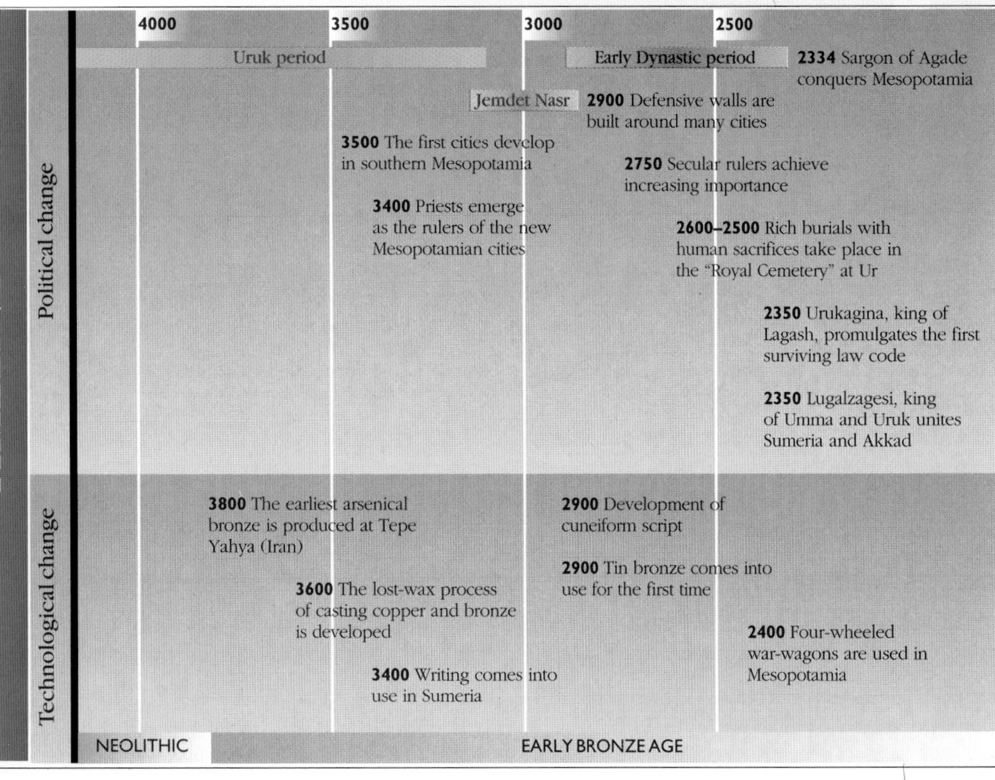

TIMELINE
Political change
Technological change
4000
3500
3000
2500
Uruk period
Early Dynastic period
Jemdet Nasr
2334 Sargon of Agade conquers Mesopotamia
2900 Defensive walls are built around many cities
3500 The first cities develop in southern Mesopotamia
2750 Secular rulers achieve increasing importance
3400 Priests emerge as the rulers of the new Mesopotamian cities
2600–2500 Rich burials with human sacrifices take place in the "Royal Cemetery" at Ur
2350 Urukagina, king of Lagash, promulgates the first surviving law code
2350 Lugalzagesi, king of Umma and Uruk unites Sumeria and Akkad
3800 The earliest arsenical bronze is produced at Tepe Yahya (Iran)
2900 Development of cuneiform script
2900 Tin bronze comes into use for the first time
3600 The lost-wax process of casting copper and bronze is developed
2400 Four-wheeled war-wagons are used in Mesopotamia
3400 Writing comes into use in Sumeria
NEOLITHIC
EARLY BRONZE AGE

Sumerian civilization entered a new and troubled phase in the Early Dynastic period (2900–2334 BC). Massive defensive walls were built around the cities, bronze weapons were produced in increasing quantities and war begins to feature prominently as a subject of official art with rulers often being shown trampling on their enemies. This period also saw writing applied to purposes other than administration, as rulers began to record their glorious deeds to ensure their posthumous reputations. The gap between rich and poor widened and slavery appears in the records for the first time. Secular leaders now appear alongside the priest-kings. Some had the title *sangu* (accountant), suggesting that bureaucrats had achieved equal status with the priests. Others were called *lugal* (literally "big man"): these may have been war leaders, elected in times of emergency in the past, who had succeeded in making their power permanent. To show that their rule had divine approval these secular rulers built palaces next to the temple precincts, where they lived in opulence. In death they were given rich burials, such as those excavated at the Royal Cemetery at Ur, accompanied by the luxuries of their everyday lives and even their sacrificed retainers. Lacking the spiritual authority of the priesthood, the new secular rulers established their authority through law codes,

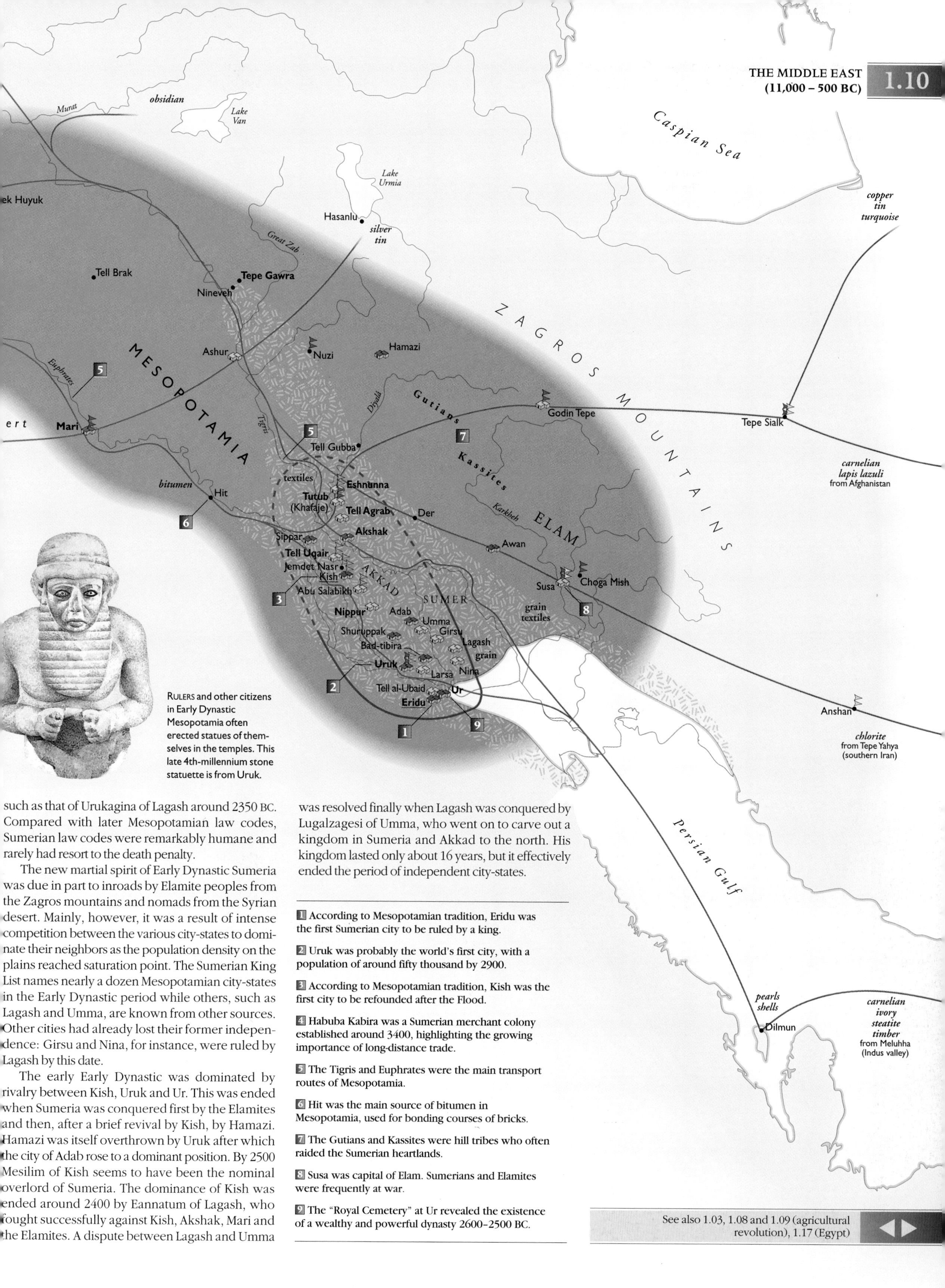

Murat
obsidian
Lake Van
Caspian Sea
Lake Urmia
ek Huyuk
Hasanlu
silver tin
copper tin turquoise
Great Zab
Tell Brak
Tepe Gawra
Nineveh
ZAGROS MOUNTAINS
MESOPOTAMIA
Ashur
Nuzi
Hamazi
Euphrates
5
Diyala
Gutians
Godin Tepe
Tepe Sialk
ert
Mari
Tigris
5
7
Tell Gubba
Kassites
carnelian lapis lazuli from Afghanistan
bitumen
Hit
textiles
Eshnunna
Tutub (Khafaje)
Tell Agrab
Der
6
Karkheh
ELAM
Akshak
Sippar
Awan
Tell Uqair
Jemdet Nasr
Kish
AKKAD
Susa
Choga Mish
3
Abu Salabikh
SUMER
8
Nippur
Adab
grain textiles
Umma
Shuruppak
Girsu
Bad-tibira
Lagash
grain
Uruk
Larsa
Nina
2
Tell al-Ubaid
Ur
Eridu
Anshan
9
1
chlorite from Tepe Yahya (southern Iran)
Persian Gulf
pearls shells
Dilmun
carnelian ivory steatite timber from Meluhha (Indus valley)

RULERS and other citizens in Early Dynastic Mesopotamia often erected statues of themselves in the temples. This late 4th-millennium stone statuette is from Uruk.

such as that of Urukagina of Lagash around 2350 BC. Compared with later Mesopotamian law codes, Sumerian law codes were remarkably humane and rarely had resort to the death penalty.

The new martial spirit of Early Dynastic Sumeria was due in part to inroads by Elamite peoples from the Zagros mountains and nomads from the Syrian desert. Mainly, however, it was a result of intense competition between the various city-states to dominate their neighbors as the population density on the plains reached saturation point. The Sumerian King List names nearly a dozen Mesopotamian city-states in the Early Dynastic period while others, such as Lagash and Umma, are known from other sources. Other cities had already lost their former independence: Girsu and Nina, for instance, were ruled by Lagash by this date.

The early Early Dynastic was dominated by rivalry between Kish, Uruk and Ur. This was ended when Sumeria was conquered first by the Elamites and then, after a brief revival by Kish, by Hamazi. Hamazi was itself overthrown by Uruk after which the city of Adab rose to a dominant position. By 2500 Mesilim of Kish seems to have been the nominal overlord of Sumeria. The dominance of Kish was ended around 2400 by Eannatum of Lagash, who fought successfully against Kish, Akshak, Mari and the Elamites. A dispute between Lagash and Umma was resolved finally when Lagash was conquered by Lugalzagesi of Umma, who went on to carve out a kingdom in Sumeria and Akkad to the north. His kingdom lasted only about 16 years, but it effectively ended the period of independent city-states.

1 According to Mesopotamian tradition, Eridu was the first Sumerian city to be ruled by a king.

2 Uruk was probably the world's first city, with a population of around fifty thousand by 2900.

3 According to Mesopotamian tradition, Kish was the first city to be refounded after the Flood.

4 Habuba Kabira was a Sumerian merchant colony established around 3400, highlighting the growing importance of long-distance trade.

5 The Tigris and Euphrates were the main transport routes of Mesopotamia.

6 Hit was the main source of bitumen in Mesopotamia, used for bonding courses of bricks.

7 The Gutians and Kassites were hill tribes who often raided the Sumerian heartlands.

8 Susa was capital of Elam. Sumerians and Elamites were frequently at war.

9 The "Royal Cemetery" at Ur revealed the existence of a wealthy and powerful dynasty 2600–2500 BC.

See also 1.03, 1.08 and 1.09 (agricultural revolution), 1.17 (Egypt)

1.11 The first empires • 2334 – 1595 BC •

By the end of the Early Dynastic period Sumeria, though still wealthy and populous, was being overtaken by Akkad as the leading center of Mesopotamian civilization. The rise of Akkad is reflected in the career of the first great conqueror known to history, Sargon "the Great" of Agade (r.2334–2279). Sargon's origins are obscure. He claimed that his father had been a date-grower and that he himself had been an official to the king of the Akkadian city of Kish. How he came to power is unknown but he may have staged a coup against his employer to become king of Kish. Sargon's first task was to eliminate the most powerful ruler in Mesopotamia, Lugalzagesi of Umma and Uruk, which he did in three hard-fought battles. He went on to conquer the rest of Sumeria, Akkad and Elam before pushing west to the Mediterranean and Anatolia. The island of Dilmun (Bahrain) and parts of Iran may also have been conquered. Sargon united peoples of many different ethnic and cultural identities to create an entirely new kind of state, an empire. To celebrate his conquests he founded the city of Agade, which has yet to be located. His empire reached its peak of power under his grandson Naram-Sin (r.2254–2218) but thereafter declined and collapsed about 2193, probably as a result of invasions by the Gutians and Amorites. For eighty years the old pattern of competing city-states returned until a Sumerian revival occurred.

Using diplomacy as much as force, Ur-Nammu (r.2112–2095), the first king of the Third Dynasty of Ur, built a new empire stretching as far north as Assyria. Ur-Nammu's reign saw the construction of the first ziggurats, the high temple platforms that are Mesopotamia's most distinctive monuments. About 2034 the empire of the Third Dynasty came under pressure from the nomadic Amorites of the Syrian desert but it was a knockout blow from the Elamites, who sacked Ur in 2004, that led to the fall of the empire. Sumeria never regained its preeminence.

The two centuries following the fall of the Third Dynasty are a confusion of minor states and of inroads by the Amorites. The Amorites were a strong influence in the rise of the two states that were to dominate the next one and a half millennia of Mesopotamian history: Assyria and Babylon. Assyria emerged as an important trading power in the 19th century BC but it was only after the Amorite Shamshi-Adad tookthe capital Ashur, along with most of northern Mesopotamia, in about 1813 that it became a major territorial power. An Amorite dynasty had also set up at Babylon around 1894 and when Hammurabi came to the throne in 1792 Babylon controlled most of Akkad (subsequently known as Babylonia). Five years later Hammurabi marched south and conquered Sumeria. In 1781 Shamshi-Adad died and, weakened by attacks from Eshnunna and the Elamites, most of his kingdom was under Hammurabi's control by 1757. Two years later Hammurabi conquered the last Mesopotamian power, Eshnunna. Babylon now became the religious and cultural center of Mesopotamia.

In the 17th century BC new and threatening powers began to gather on the borders of Mesopotamia. The most important of these were the Hurrians and the Hittites. The Hurrians were a tribal people from Armenia who overran Assyria around 1680. The Hittites were an Indo-European people who had invaded Anatolia from Thrace about 1800 and had emergedas a powerful kingdom by 1650.

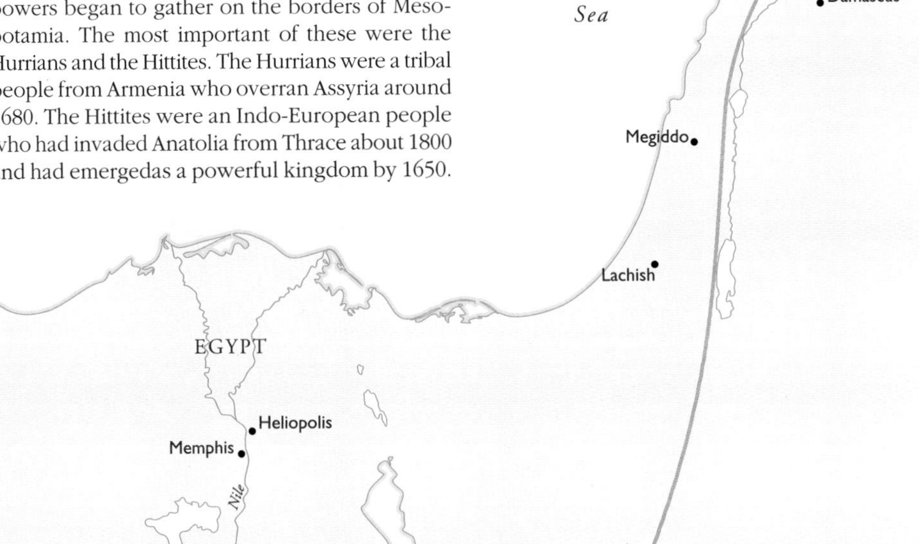
Hittites
Hattusas
(Boghazkoy)
Lake
Tuz
Puruskhanda
Kultepe
(Kanesh)
3
Ceyhan
TAURUS MTS
Orontes
Ebla
Ugarit
Cyprus
LEVANT
Qatna
Byblos
Mediterranean
Sea
Damascus
Megiddo
Lachish
EGYPT
Heliopolis
Memphis
Nile

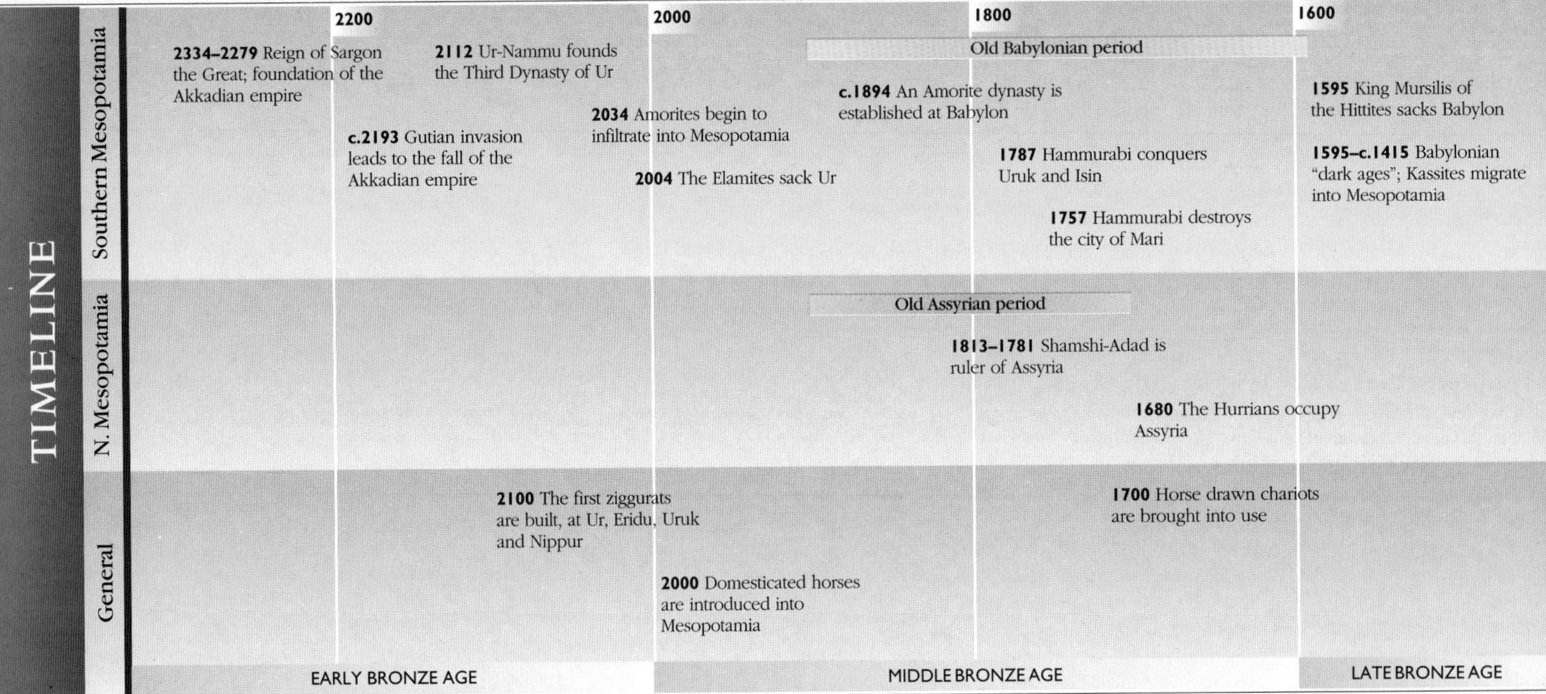
TIMELINE
Southern Mesopotamia
N. Mesopotamia
General
2200
2000
1800
1600
2334–2279 Reign of Sargon the Great; foundation of the Akkadian empire
2112 Ur-Nammu founds the Third Dynasty of Ur
Old Babylonian period
c.2193 Gutian invasion leads to the fall of the Akkadian empire
2034 Amorites begin to infiltrate into Mesopotamia
2004 The Elamites sack Ur
c.1894 An Amorite dynasty is established at Babylon
1787 Hammurabi conquers Uruk and Isin
1757 Hammurabi destroys the city of Mari
1595 King Mursilis of the Hittites sacks Babylon
1595–c.1415 Babylonian "dark ages"; Kassites migrate into Mesopotamia
Old Assyrian period
1813–1781 Shamshi-Adad is ruler of Assyria
1680 The Hurrians occupy Assyria
2100 The first ziggurats are built, at Ur, Eridu, Uruk and Nippur
2000 Domesticated horses are introduced into Mesopotamia
1700 Horse drawn chariots are brought into use
EARLY BRONZE AGE
MIDDLE BRONZE AGE
LATE BRONZE AGE

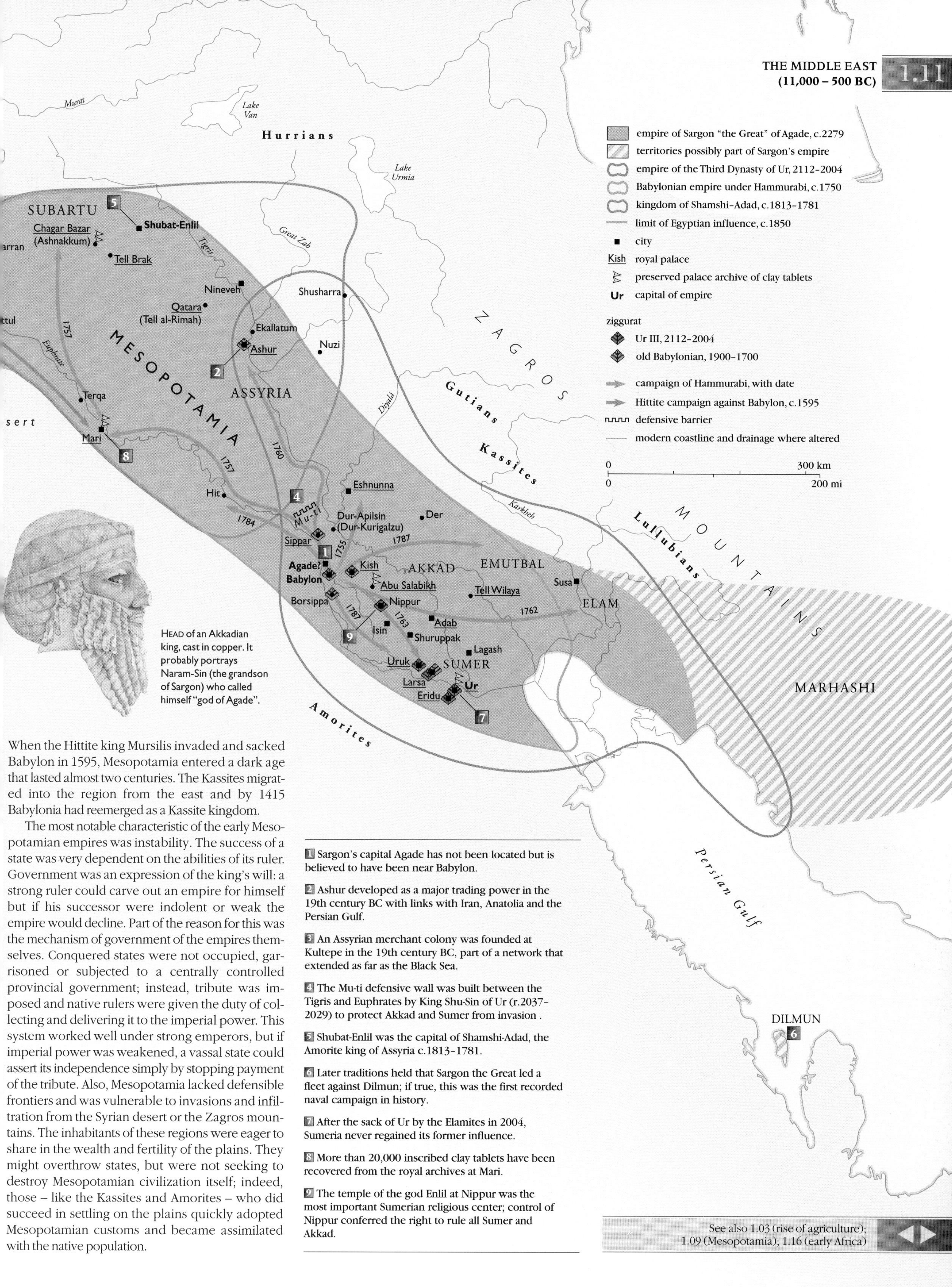
empire of Sargon "the Great" of Agade, c.2279
territories possibly part of Sargon's empire
empire of the Third Dynasty of Ur, 2112–2004
Babylonian empire under Hammurabi, c.1750
kingdom of Shamshi-Adad, c.1813–1781
limit of Egyptian influence, c.1850
city
Kish royal palace
preserved palace archive of clay tablets
Ur capital of empire
ziggurat
Ur III, 2112–2004
old Babylonian, 1900–1700
campaign of Hammurabi, with date
Hittite campaign against Babylon, c.1595
defensive barrier
modern coastline and drainage where altered
0 300 km
0 200 mi
Murat
Lake Van
Hurrians
Lake Urmia
SUBARTU
Chagar Bazar (Ashnakkum)
Shubat-Enlil
Tell Brak
Tigris
Great Zab
Nineveh
Shusharra
Qatara (Tell al-Rimah)
Ekallatum
Ashur
Nuzi
MESOPOTAMIA
ASSYRIA
ZAGROS
Euphrates
Terqa
Mari
Gutians
Diyala
Kassites
Hit
Eshnunna
Mu-ti
Dur-Apilsin (Dur-Kurigalzu)
Der
Sippar
Agade?
Babylon
Kish
AKKAD
EMUTBAL
Abu Salabikh
Tell Wilaya
Susa
ELAM
Borsippa
Nippur
Isin
Adab
Shuruppak
Lagash
Uruk
SUMER
Larsa
Eridu
Ur
Karkheh
Lullubians
MOUNTAINS
MARHASHI
Amorites
Persian Gulf
DILMUN
1784
1755
1787
1762
1763
1757
1760

HEAD of an Akkadian king, cast in copper. It probably portrays Naram-Sin (the grandson of Sargon) who called himself "god of Agade".

When the Hittite king Mursilis invaded and sacked Babylon in 1595, Mesopotamia entered a dark age that lasted almost two centuries. The Kassites migrated into the region from the east and by 1415 Babylonia had reemerged as a Kassite kingdom.

The most notable characteristic of the early Mesopotamian empires was instability. The success of a state was very dependent on the abilities of its ruler. Government was an expression of the king's will: a strong ruler could carve out an empire for himself but if his successor were indolent or weak the empire would decline. Part of the reason for this was the mechanism of government of the empires themselves. Conquered states were not occupied, garrisoned or subjected to a centrally controlled provincial government; instead, tribute was imposed and native rulers were given the duty of collecting and delivering it to the imperial power. This system worked well under strong emperors, but if imperial power was weakened, a vassal state could assert its independence simply by stopping payment of the tribute. Also, Mesopotamia lacked defensible frontiers and was vulnerable to invasions and infiltration from the Syrian desert or the Zagros mountains. The inhabitants of these regions were eager to share in the wealth and fertility of the plains. They might overthrow states, but were not seeking to destroy Mesopotamian civilization itself; indeed, those – like the Kassites and Amorites – who did succeed in settling on the plains quickly adopted Mesopotamian customs and became assimilated with the native population.

1 Sargon's capital Agade has not been located but is believed to have been near Babylon.

2 Ashur developed as a major trading power in the 19th century BC with links with Iran, Anatolia and the Persian Gulf.

3 An Assyrian merchant colony was founded at Kultepe in the 19th century BC, part of a network that extended as far as the Black Sea.

4 The Mu-ti defensive wall was built between the Tigris and Euphrates by King Shu-Sin of Ur (r.2037–2029) to protect Akkad and Sumer from invasion .

5 Shubat-Enlil was the capital of Shamshi-Adad, the Amorite king of Assyria c.1813–1781.

6 Later traditions held that Sargon the Great led a fleet against Dilmun; if true, this was the first recorded naval campaign in history.

7 After the sack of Ur by the Elamites in 2004, Sumeria never regained its former influence.

8 More than 20,000 inscribed clay tablets have been recovered from the royal archives at Mari.

9 The temple of the god Enlil at Nippur was the most important Sumerian religious center; control of Nippur conferred the right to rule all Sumer and Akkad.

See also 1.03 (rise of agriculture); 1.09 (Mesopotamia); 1.16 (early Africa)

1.12 The Hittite and Assyrian empires • 1595 – 1000 BC •

In the two centuries following the Hittite sack of Babylon in 1595, the kingdom of Mittani controlled most of northern Mesopotamia and, at its peak, southern Anatolia. Mittani was founded about 1550 by the Hurrians, who had begun to encroach on northern Mesopotamia early in the previous century. As its power spread west into the Levant (the part of the Fertile Crescent bordering the Mediterranean), Mittani came into conflict with the Egyptians. Under Tuthmosis I (r.1504–1492), Egypt controlled all of the Levant and established a frontier on the Euphrates.

The Egyptians were unable to maintain this frontier and over the next century Mittani regained control over the northern Levant and pushed the Egyptians south of the Orontes river. Then, during the reign of Tuthmosis IV (r.1401–1391) Egypt and Mittani formed an alliance. The peace initiative probably came from Mittani which was faced with a revival of Hittite power in the north, while in the east the Assyrians had won back their independence. When Egypt became preoccupied with internal affairs during the reign of Akhenaten (r.1353–1335), Mittani was left exposed.

The Hittite king Suppiluliumas (r.1344–1322) spent the early part of his reign establishing Hittite dominance in Anatolia, and then in about 1340 sacked Washukanni, Mittani's capital, before sweeping on into the Levant. Mittani began to crumble and when he launched a second campaign around 1328 (or 1323) the western half of the kingdom fell. Suppiluliumas established a puppet ruler at Washukanni, intending western Mittani to become a buffer state against Assyria. As such it was a failure, and fell to the Assyrians by 1300.

The Hittites, who now held the same commanding position in the Levant that Mittani had held in the 15th century, incurred the enmity of Egypt, where a new dynasty had come to power in 1307, eager to reestablish Egypt's position in the Levant. By 1290 the Egyptians had recovered Canaan, which had become independent under Akhenaten, and in 1285 pharaoh Ramesses II (r.1290–1224) launched a major invasion of Hittite territory. The Hittite king Muwatallis II (r.1295–1271) was prepared and, in a battle between two fleets of chariots at Qadesh, Ramesses was defeated (though he claimed a great victory). The Egyptians withdrew and Hittite control was extended as far south as Damascus. Relations between the two empires remained difficult until 1258 when they agreed an alliance, as the Hittites were alarmed at the growth of Assyrian power.

Assyrian expansion had begun under Ashur-uballit I (r.1363–1328), who seized Nineveh from the crumbling Mittanian kingdom in about 1330, and was continued in the 13th century. Tukulti-Ninurta I (r.1243–1207) waged campaigns against the Hittites and the Kassite kingdom of Babylonia and built an empire that stretched from the upper Euphrates to the Persian Gulf. However, the empire fell apart after he was murdered by discontented nobles.

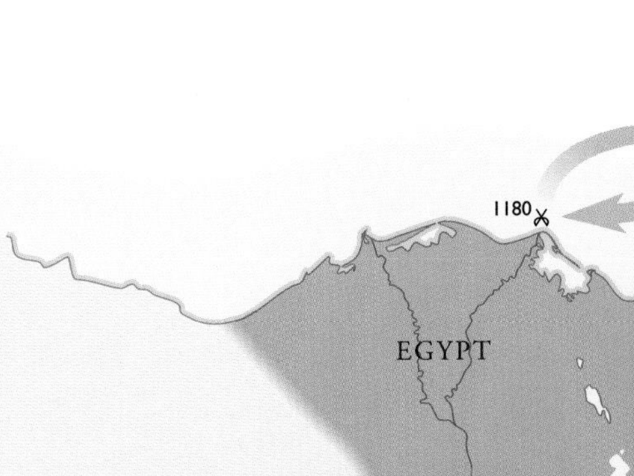
1180
EGYPT

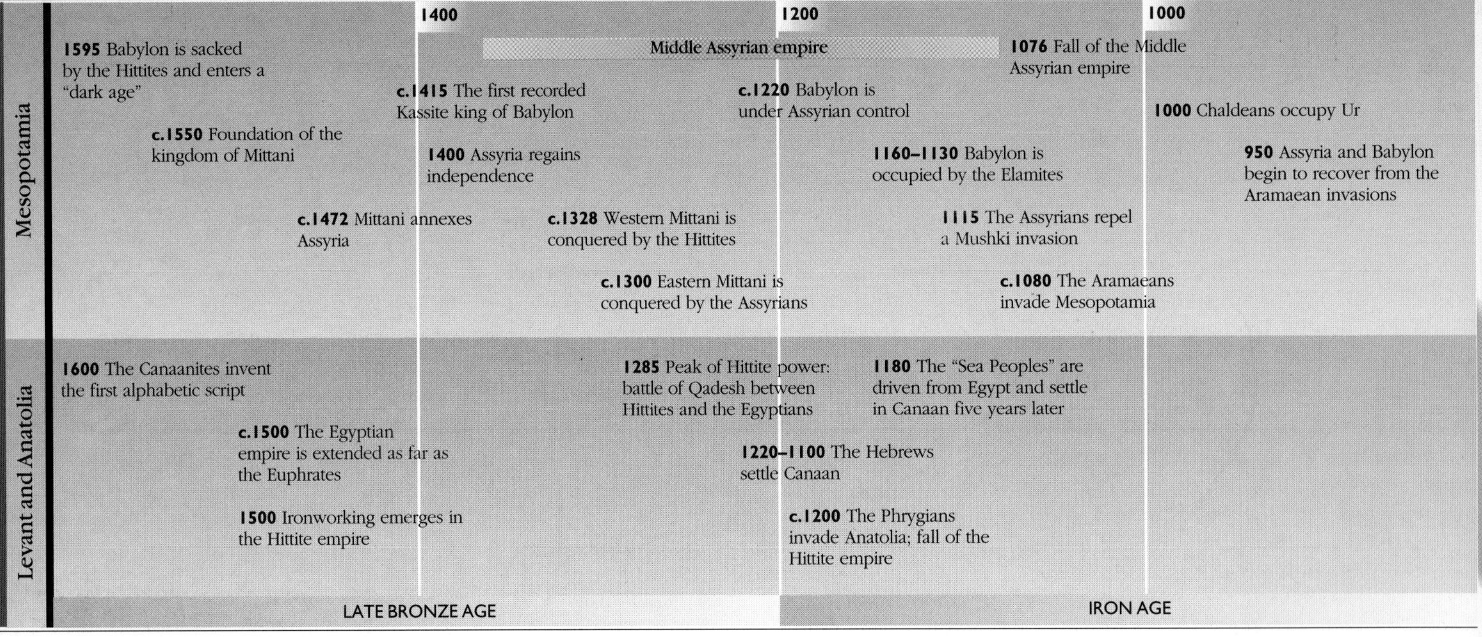
TIMELINE
Mesopotamia
1400
1200
1000
1595 Babylon is sacked by the Hittites and enters a "dark age"
Middle Assyrian empire
1076 Fall of the Middle Assyrian empire
c.1415 The first recorded Kassite king of Babylon
c.1220 Babylon is under Assyrian control
1000 Chaldeans occupy Ur
c.1550 Foundation of the kingdom of Mittani
1400 Assyria regains independence
1160–1130 Babylon is occupied by the Elamites
950 Assyria and Babylon begin to recover from the Aramaean invasions
c.1472 Mittani annexes Assyria
c.1328 Western Mittani is conquered by the Hittites
1115 The Assyrians repel a Mushki invasion
c.1300 Eastern Mittani is conquered by the Assyrians
c.1080 The Aramaeans invade Mesopotamia
Levant and Anatolia
1600 The Canaanites invent the first alphabetic script
1285 Peak of Hittite power: battle of Qadesh between Hittites and the Egyptians
1180 The "Sea Peoples" are driven from Egypt and settle in Canaan five years later
c.1500 The Egyptian empire is extended as far as the Euphrates
1220–1100 The Hebrews settle Canaan
1500 Ironworking emerges in the Hittite empire
c.1200 The Phrygians invade Anatolia; fall of the Hittite empire
LATE BRONZE AGE
IRON AGE

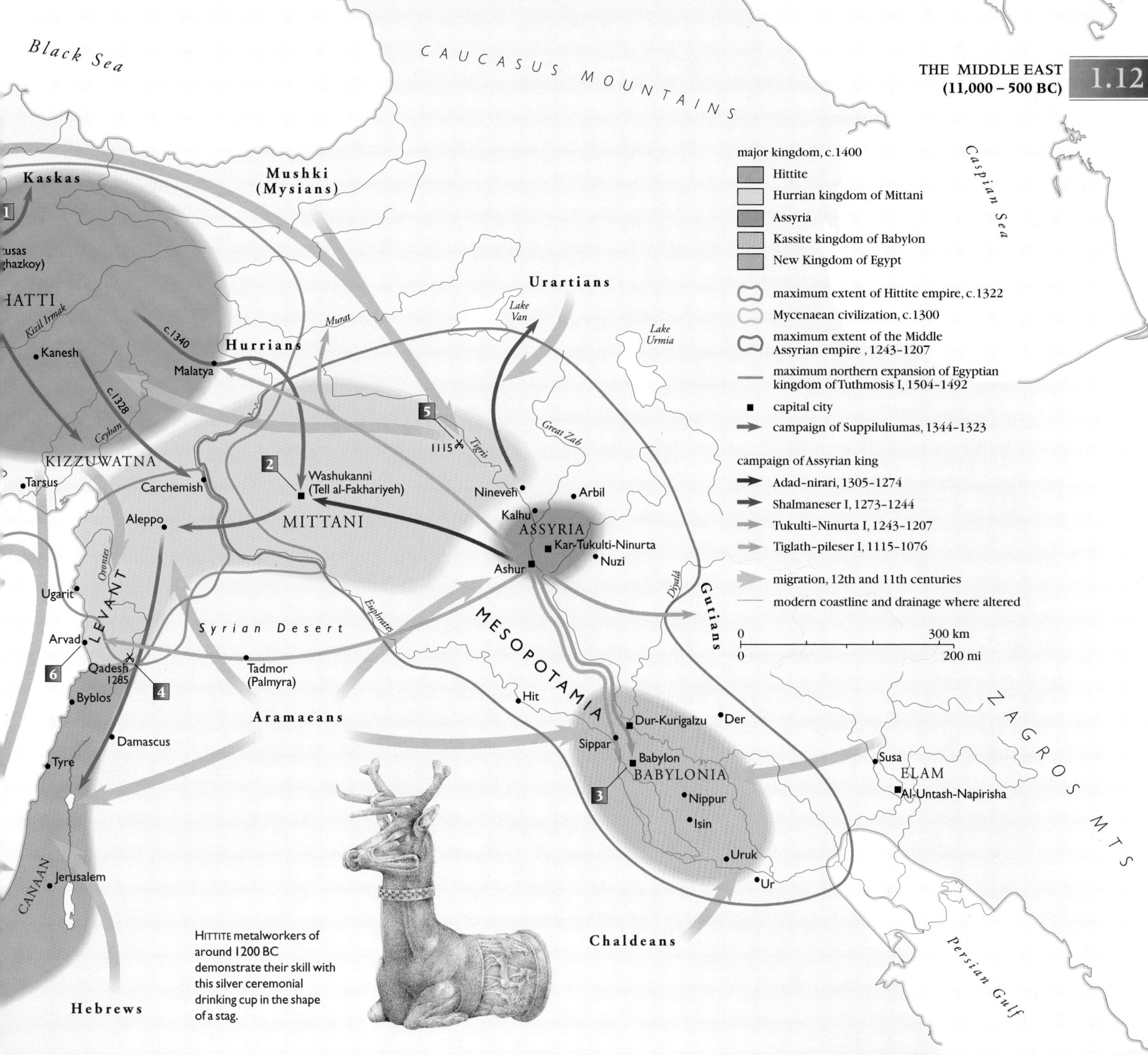
Black Sea
CAUCASUS MOUNTAINS
Caspian Sea
major kingdom, c.1400
Hittite
Hurrian kingdom of Mittani
Assyria
Kassite kingdom of Babylon
New Kingdom of Egypt
maximum extent of Hittite empire, c.1322
Mycenaean civilization, c.1300
maximum extent of the Middle Assyrian empire, 1243–1207
maximum northern expansion of Egyptian kingdom of Tuthmosis I, 1504–1492
capital city
campaign of Suppiluliumas, 1344–1323
campaign of Assyrian king
Adad-nirari, 1305–1274
Shalmaneser I, 1273–1244
Tukulti-Ninurta I, 1243–1207
Tiglath-pileser I, 1115–1076
migration, 12th and 11th centuries
modern coastline and drainage where altered
0 300 km
0 200 mi
Kaskas
Mushki (Mysians)
HATTI
Kizil Irmak
Kanesh
Malatya
Hurrians
Murat
Urartians
Lake Van
Lake Urmia
c.1340
c.1328
Ceyhan
KIZZUWATNA
Tarsus
Carchemish
Washukanni (Tell al-Fakhariyeh)
MITTANI
Aleppo
1115
Tigris
Great Zab
Nineveh
Arbil
Kalhu
ASSYRIA
Kar-Tukulti-Ninurta
Nuzi
Ashur
Orontes
LEVANT
Ugarit
Arvad
Qadesh 1285
Byblos
Syrian Desert
Tadmor (Palmyra)
Euphrates
MESOPOTAMIA
Diyala
Gutians
Aramaeans
Damascus
Tyre
Hit
Dur-Kurigalzu
Der
Sippar
Babylon
BABYLONIA
Nippur
Isin
Uruk
Ur
Susa
ELAM
Al-Untash-Napirisha
ZAGROS MTS
Persian Gulf
Chaldeans
CANAAN
Jerusalem
Hebrews

HITTITE metalworkers of around 1200 BC demonstrate their skill with this silver ceremonial drinking cup in the shape of a stag.

Around 1200 new waves of migrations brought chaos to the region. Shortly after 1205 the Hittite kingdom collapsed, destroyed by the Phrygians, who had entered Anatolia from Thrace. At the same time Egypt came under attack from a group known to the Egyptians as the Sea Peoples. Their origin is uncertain. Some may have come from the Aegean islands and Anatolian coast but they were joined by others already settled in the Levant and Libya. The Sea Peoples were driven from Egypt in 1180 but settled in Canaan where they became known as the Philistines. Nomadic Hebrew tribes, related to the Aramaeans, were also moving into Canaan.

At the end of the 12th century Assyria was attacked by a confederation of Mushki (probably Mysians – relatives of the Phrygians) and native Anatolian peoples including the Kaskas and Hurrians. The new Assyrian king Tiglath-pileser I (r.1115–1076), forced the invaders to retreat into Anatolia, but he had less success against the nomadic Aramaeans who, despite 28 campaigns against them, had made considerable settlements in Assyria before his death. Tiglath-pileser's successors failed to contain the Aramaeans and by 1000 Assyria was reduced to its heartland around Ashur and Nineveh.

Babylonia's main problem from the 14th to 12th centuries was the kingdom of Elam. Devastating Elamite invasions of Babylon in the mid 12th century led to the fall of the Kassite dynasty. Babylon recovered under a native dynasty around 1130 and defeated the Elamites so thoroughly that they disappeared from history for 300 years. Then, in the 11th century Babylonia, like Assyria, had problems with migrating nomads – Aramaeans in the north, Chaldeans in the south – and, also like Assyria, was unable to do much about them. The nomads' tribal structures provided no central authority to destroy or negotiate with, and they had no cities that could be taken nor crops to be burned. The powerful Assyrian and Babylonian armies had no target to attack.

The period saw key technological advances, glass, glazed pottery and bricks and iron-smelting all appearing for the first time. Iron did not supplant bronze as the main metal for tools and weapons until around 900, but its use was widespread by 1200, the date accepted as the start of the Iron Age.

1 Hattusas became the Hittite capital in about 1650, and was destroyed about 1200, probably by Phrygian invaders.

2 Tell al-Fakhariyeh is the likely site of Washukanni, capital of Mittani, sacked by the Hittites in 1340 and the Assyrians c.1304–1274.

3 Babylon was sacked by the Hittites in 1595, and was under Kassite rule by 1415, held by the Assyrians 1220–1213 and the Elamites 1160–1130.

4 The Egyptians and Hittites clashed at Qadesh over control of Syria; this is the first battle in history well enough recorded for historians to reconstruct its course.

5 Tiglath-pileser I defeated an invading army of 20,000 Mushki in the upper Tigris valley.

6 On reaching the Mediterranean, Tiglath-pileser I went sailing and claimed to have harpooned a whale.

See also 1.13 (later Assyria); 1.14 (Bible lands); 1.18 (Egypt)

The Assyrian and Babylonian empires • 1000 – 539 BC •

By the 10th century the Aramaeans had begun to abandon their nomadic lifestyle and to settle in city-states across a wide area of the Levant and northern Mesopotamia. Simultaneously the Chaldeans were undergoing the same process in southern Mesopotamia. By settling down, the Aramaeans and Chaldeans lost most of the advantages that their loose nomadic organization had given them over the old military powers, and these now began to revive.

Like the Amorites a millennium earlier, the Aramaeans and Chaldeans adopted Mesopotamian culture but the Aramaeans, at least, kept their identity; their language and alphabet was the common tongue of the region by 500 BC. Mesopotamia experienced no further immigrations in this period but Anatolia and Iran saw the arrival of several waves of Iranian peoples, including the Medes and the Persians, who had both formed powerful kingdoms by the 6th century.

Of the Hittites, Assyria and Babylon, the three powers who had dominated the region before 1200, the Hittites made the least impressive recovery. With their heartland lost to the Phrygians, the Neo-Hittites (as they are now called) formed a number of small states in southern Anatolia, of which the most successful were Carchemish, Kummukhu (Commagene) and Khilakku (Cilicia). The Neo-Hittites were conquered by Assyria in the 8th century after which their identity became lost.

The Assyrian heartland around Ashur and Nineveh had survived the Aramaean invasions relatively unscathed and formed a strong base for recovery. The old pattern, established during the Middle Assyrian period, of expansion under able warrior kings followed by contraction under weak kings was continued in the new Assyrian empire. Expansion began again in the reign of Adad-nirari II (r.911–891) and by the reign of Ashurnasirpal II (r.883–859) the empire dominated northern Mesopotamia and received tribute from the Levant as far south as Tyre. During Ashurnasirpal's reign Ashur, Assyria's ancient capital, declined in importance and was superseded by a new purpose-built capital at Kalhu.

In 854 a coalition of Levantine states tried to halt the expansion of Assyrian power in the region. The coalition met Shalmaneser III (r.858–824) in battle at Qarqar on the Orontes and, though Shalmaneser claimed complete victory, Assyrian power in the Levant did suffer a setback. Relations between Assyria and Babylon had been good since about 911 when the two states became allies. Shalmaneser gave military support to the Babylonians against the Chaldeans and also gave them assistance against internal enemies.

After Shalmaneser's reign Assyria was crippled by internal problems and went into decline for sixty years. Recovery and expansion began again in the reign of Tiglath-pileser III (r.744–727), who assumed overlordship over Babylon, reconquered the Levant and exacted tribute from Israel and Judah. Tiglath-pileser was responsible for a complete overhaul of the administration of the empire to assert central power. Hereditary provincial governors in the Assyrian heartlands were replaced by a hierarchy of officials under direct royal control. Traveling inspectors were sent out to examine the performance of local officials. A post system was introduced and officials were required to send regular reports to the capital. Representatives were appointed to the courts of vassal states to safeguard the interests of Assyria. Large numbers of subject peoples were resettled to prevent local opposition. Finally, in perhaps the greatest break with the imperial traditions of the past, rebellious vassal states lost their nominal independence and were reorganized as provinces of Assyria, directly ruled by officials appointed by the king.

Under Sargon II (r.721–705) Assyrian power reached its zenith. Sargon broke the power of the Armenian kingdom of Urartu and expanded Assyrian dominions with campaigns against the Chaldeans (who had seized Babylon), Elamites and Hebrews. Sargon's last campaign ended in defeat, however, and he was killed in battle in Anatolia in 705. Sargon's successor Sennacherib (r.704–681) was preoccupied with rebellions in Judah, with Babylon

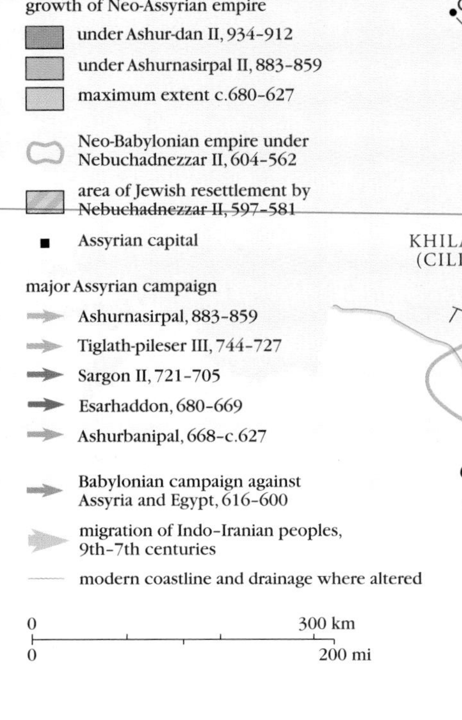
growth of Neo-Assyrian empire
under Ashur-dan II, 934–912
under Ashurnasirpal II, 883–859
maximum extent c.680–627
Neo-Babylonian empire under Nebuchadnezzar II, 604–562
area of Jewish resettlement by Nebuchadnezzar II, 597–581
Assyrian capital
major Assyrian campaign
Ashurnasirpal, 883–859
Tiglath-pileser III, 744–727
Sargon II, 721–705
Esarhaddon, 680–669
Ashurbanipal, 668–c.627
Babylonian campaign against Assyria and Egypt, 616–600
migration of Indo-Iranian peoples, 9th–7th centuries
modern coastline and drainage where altered
0 300 km
0 200 mi
Gordio
5
KHILAKKU (CILICIA)
TAU
Cyprus
Mediterranean Sea
675–6
Memphis
EGYPT
663
Nile

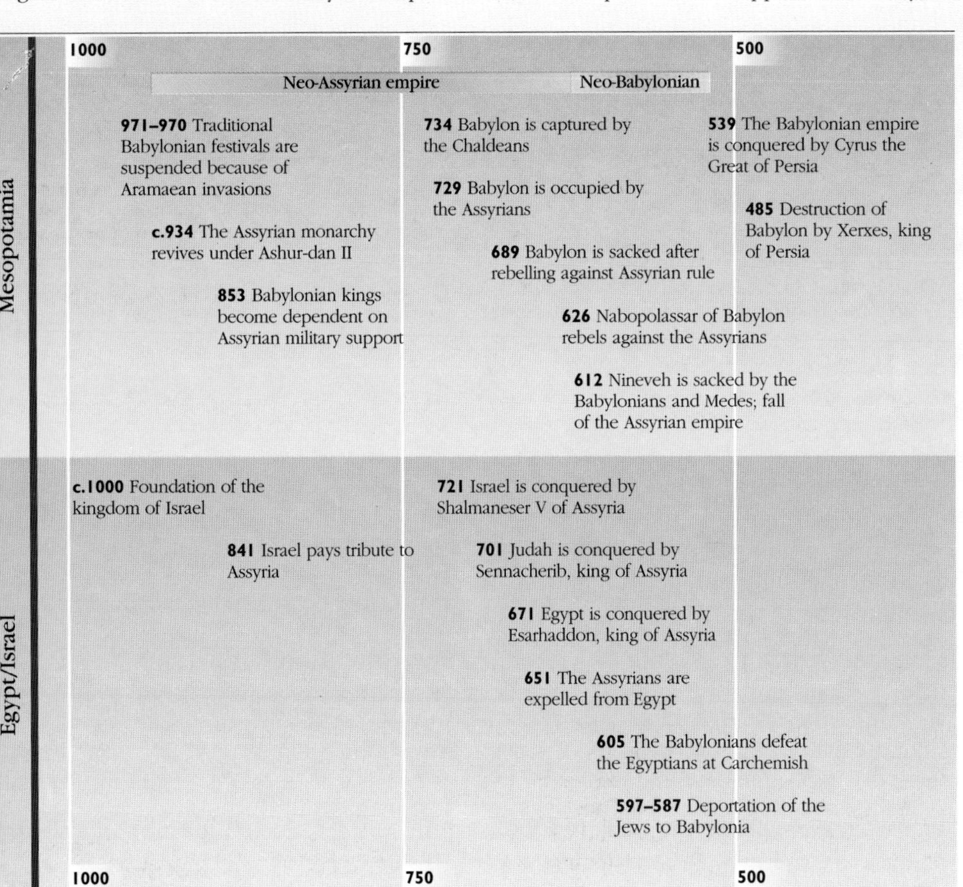
TIMELINE
1000
750
500
Neo-Assyrian empire
Neo-Babylonian
Mesopotamia
971–970 Traditional Babylonian festivals are suspended because of Aramaean invasions
c.934 The Assyrian monarchy revives under Ashur-dan II
853 Babylonian kings become dependent on Assyrian military support
734 Babylon is captured by the Chaldeans
729 Babylon is occupied by the Assyrians
689 Babylon is sacked after rebelling against Assyrian rule
626 Nabopolassar of Babylon rebels against the Assyrians
612 Nineveh is sacked by the Babylonians and Medes; fall of the Assyrian empire
539 The Babylonian empire is conquered by Cyrus the Great of Persia
485 Destruction of Babylon by Xerxes, king of Persia
Egypt/Israel
c.1000 Foundation of the kingdom of Israel
841 Israel pays tribute to Assyria
721 Israel is conquered by Shalmaneser V of Assyria
701 Judah is conquered by Sennacherib, king of Assyria
671 Egypt is conquered by Esarhaddon, king of Assyria
651 The Assyrians are expelled from Egypt
605 The Babylonians defeat the Egyptians at Carchemish
597–587 Deportation of the Jews to Babylonia
1000
750
500

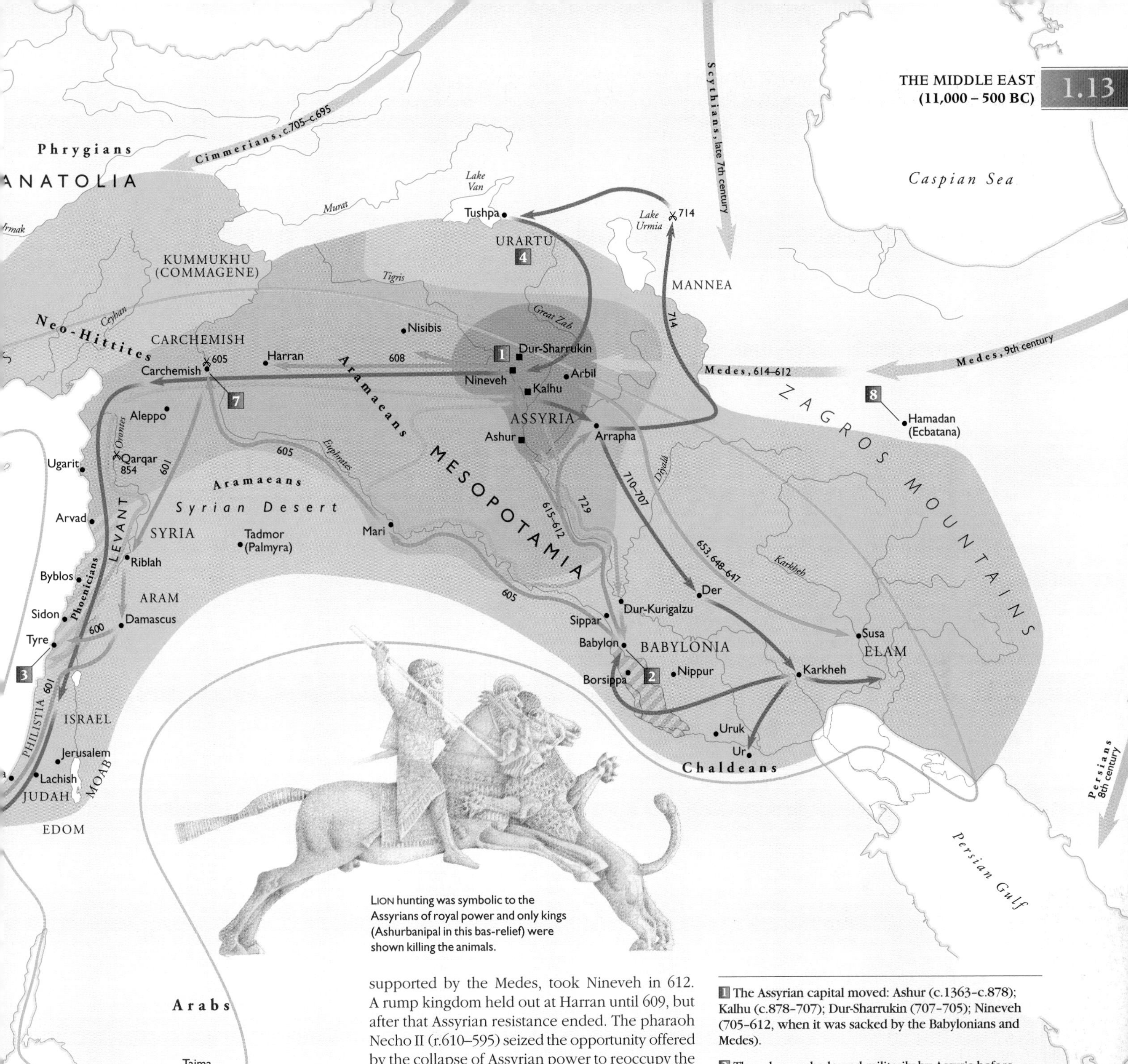
Phrygians
ANATOLIA
Cimmerians, c.705–c.695
Scythians, late 7th century
Caspian Sea
Lake Van
Tushpa
Lake Urmia
714
Murat
URARTU
4
KUMMUKHU (COMMAGENE)
Tigris
MANNEA
Ceyhan
Neo-Hittites
CARCHEMISH
Great Zab
Nisibis
Harran
605
Carchemish
608
1
Dur-Sharrukin
Nineveh
Arbil
Kalhu
Medes, 614–612
Medes, 9th century
Aramaeans
7
ZAGROS MOUNTAINS
8
Hamadan (Ecbatana)
Aleppo
ASSYRIA
Ashur
Arrapha
Orontes
Qarqar 854
605
601
Euphrates
MESOPOTAMIA
Ugarit
Aramaeans
Syrian Desert
Diyala
710–707
Arvad
LEVANT
SYRIA
Tadmor (Palmyra)
Mari
615–612
729
Riblah
653, 648–647
Karkheh
Byblos
Phoenicians
ARAM
605
Der
Sidon
Damascus
Dur-Kurigalzu
600
Sippar
Tyre
Babylon
BABYLONIA
Susa
ELAM
3
Borsippa
2
Nippur
Karkheh
601
PHILISTIA
ISRAEL
Uruk
Jerusalem
Ur
Lachish
Chaldeans
JUDAH
MOAB
EDOM
Persians 8th century
Persian Gulf
Arabs
Taima
Red Sea

LION hunting was symbolic to the Assyrians of royal power and only kings (Ashurbanipal in this bas-relief) were shown killing the animals.

and with Chaldean and Elamite attacks in the south. Assyrian expansion was renewed under Esarhaddon (r.680–669), who began the conquest of Egypt, and Ashurbanipal (r.668–c.627), who completed it and took great stores of booty back to Nineveh. This last conquest, however, succeeded only in over-extending the empire while Ashurbanipal's increasingly tyrannical rule spread discontent everywhere. Egypt regained its independence by 651 and, despite his subsequent conquest of Elam in 648, Ashurbanipal's reign ended in chaos. The Babylonian king Nabopolassar (626–605) rebelled against Assyrian rule and after ten years of fighting drove the Assyrians from Babylon.

In 615 Nabopolassar took the offensive and, supported by the Medes, took Nineveh in 612. A rump kingdom held out at Harran until 609, but after that Assyrian resistance ended. The pharaoh Necho II (r.610–595) seized the opportunity offered by the collapse of Assyrian power to reoccupy the Levant but was defeated by the Babylonian crown prince Nebuchadnezzar at Carchemish in 605. The Babylonians followed up their victory by occupying virtually all of the territory previously held by Assyria. Nebuchadnezzar came to the throne in the following year and spent his reign (r.604–562) consolidating his empire, rebuilding the city of Babylon in imperial splendor and ruling very much within the Assyrian tradition.

Nebuchadnezzar's dynasty lasted only until 556 when it was overthrown in a palace coup. An official, Nabonidus (r.555–539), was chosen as king but his religious unorthodoxy soon made him unpopular in the Babylonian heartland. When the Persian king Cyrus the Great invaded in 539, Babylon surrendered without a fight, bringing to a quiet end an imperial tradition that was almost two thousand years old. Mesopotamian civilization survived for some centuries but gradually declined under the influence of Persian, and subsequently Hellenistic, culture, and had died out by the beginning of the Christian era.

1 The Assyrian capital moved: Ashur (c.1363–c.878); Kalhu (c.878–707); Dur-Sharrukin (707–705); Nineveh (705–612, when it was sacked by the Babylonians and Medes).

2 Though overshadowed militarily by Assyria before 626, Babylon was the dominant religious and cultural center of Mesopotamia.

3 Tyre was the leading Phoenician city; in the 9th century the Phoenicians established trade routes to the western Mediterranean.

4 Urartu developed as a rival to Assyria in the 8th century; its power was broken by Sargon II in 714.

5 Gordion was the capital of the Phrygians; its last king Mitas (Midas) killed himself after being conquered by the Cimmerians around 695.

6 Thebes, the most southerly point reached by the Assyrians, was sacked by Ashurbanipal in 663.

7 Pharaoh Necho II's attempt to seize the Levant was ended by the Babylonians at Carchemish.

8 Hamadan became the capital of a powerful Median empire after the fall of Assyria.

See also 1.12 (Early Assyria and Babylon); 1.14 (Bible lands); 1.15 (Persians); 1.18 (Egypt)

1.14 The Bible lands • 1000 – 587 BC •

The Hebrew kingdoms of the Bible lands were dwarfed in scale and longevity by the great empires of the Middle East, yet their significance in world history is at least as great. The period of the independent monarchy, from the time of David to the Babylonian conquest in 587, was a formative time for Judaism and gave Jews a sense of historical destiny, driving them to preserve their religion and identity through centuries of foreign rule, exile and worldwide dispersal. Christianity and Islam both owe so much to Judaism that neither religion would have its present form had Judaism not survived.

The Hebrews migrated into Canaan in the early 12th century BC, a time when the great powers of the region were neutralized by troubles of various kinds. In their initial attacks under Joshua, the Hebrews occupied most of Canaan, which they settled in tribal units under chieftains (the "judges" of the biblical Book of Judges). However, many Canaanite enclaves remained and Hebrew expansion to the southwest was blocked by the Philistines who had settled in the area after being repulsed from Egypt in 1180. Most of the Canaanite enclaves were mopped up in the 11th century, but the Hebrews began to lose ground in the southwest to the Philistines.

The need for effective defense against the Philistines led the Hebrew tribes to unite under a monarchy. According to the Bible, the first king of the Hebrews was Saul (r.c.1020–c.1006), but it was his successor David who was responsible for consolidating the monarchy and creating the first Hebrew state. David conquered the Philistines, Ammonites, Moabites and Edomites and forced several of the Aramaean tribes of the Levant to accept his overlordship. These were great achievements, but he was aided by the temporary impotence of the powers who might otherwise have intervened. It was also to his advantage that the Aramaeans of the Levant (who had moved into the area after the fall of the Hittite empire) had settled in urban communities by 1000, and so were more vulnerable to attack than the still-nomadic Mesopotamian Aramaeans. Perhaps the most important event of David's reign was his capture of Jerusalem from the Canaanite Jebusites. By making Jerusalem his capital David ensured its lasting importance as a religious center.

David was succeeded by his son Solomon. Solomon's reign was largely peaceful, but maintaining his splendid court life and ambitious building projects, including the temple at Jerusalem, proved burdensome to his people. Some Hebrews were used as forced labor and territory was ceded to Tyre in return for supplying craftsmen and materials. He was criticized for tolerating the pagan religious practices of the many non-Hebrew wives he had acquired from diplomatic marriages. When his successor Rehoboam (r.928–911) dealt tactlessly with the economic complaints of the northern tribes, the kingdom split in two halves, Israel and Judah, and most of the non-Hebrew provinces fell away.

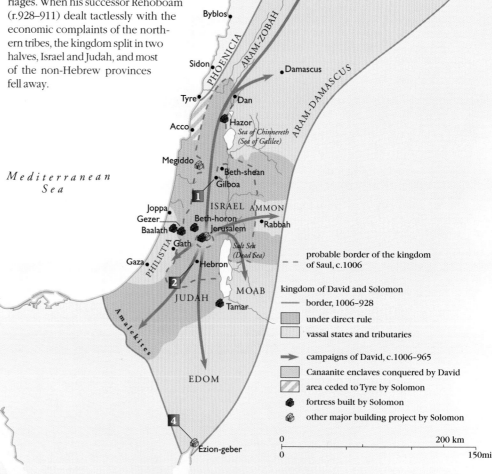

- - probable border of the kingdom of Saul, c.1006

kingdom of David and Solomon
— border, 1006–928
under direct rule
vassal states and tributaries

campaigns of David, c.1006–965
Canaanite enclaves conquered by David
area ceded to Tyre by Solomon
fortress built by Solomon
other major building project by Solomon

0 200 km
0 150mi

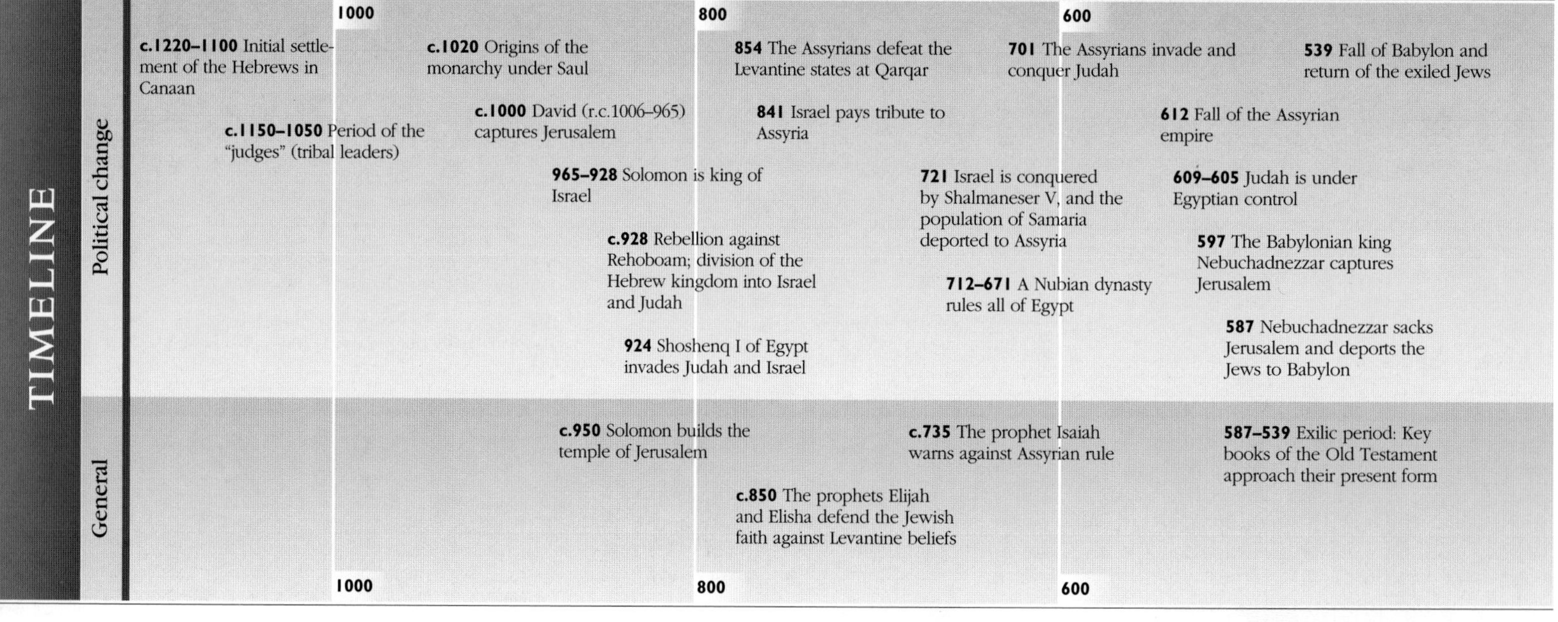
TIMELINE
Political change
1000
800
600
c.1220–1100 Initial settlement of the Hebrews in Canaan
c.1150–1050 Period of the "judges" (tribal leaders)
c.1020 Origins of the monarchy under Saul
c.1000 David (r.c.1006–965) captures Jerusalem
965–928 Solomon is king of Israel
c.928 Rebellion against Rehoboam; division of the Hebrew kingdom into Israel and Judah
924 Shoshenq I of Egypt invades Judah and Israel
854 The Assyrians defeat the Levantine states at Qarqar
841 Israel pays tribute to Assyria
721 Israel is conquered by Shalmaneser V, and the population of Samaria deported to Assyria
712–671 A Nubian dynasty rules all of Egypt
701 The Assyrians invade and conquer Judah
612 Fall of the Assyrian empire
609–605 Judah is under Egyptian control
597 The Babylonian king Nebuchadnezzar captures Jerusalem
587 Nebuchadnezzar sacks Jerusalem and deports the Jews to Babylon
539 Fall of Babylon and return of the exiled Jews
General
c.950 Solomon builds the temple of Jerusalem
c.850 The prophets Elijah and Elisha defend the Jewish faith against Levantine beliefs
c.735 The prophet Isaiah warns against Assyrian rule
587–539 Exilic period: Key books of the Old Testament approach their present form
1000
800
600

THE MIDDLE EAST (11,000 – 500 BC) 1.14

- border of former kingdom of Solomon
- greatest extent of kingdom of Israel
- greatest extent of kingdom of Judah
- border of state gaining independence from kingdoms of Israel or Judah
- kingdom of Egypt, 924
- Assyrian empire, 722
- Babylonian empire, 597

campaigns in Israel and Judah

- pharaoh Shoshenq I, 924
- Sennacherib, 701

0 150 km
0 100 mi

ASSYRIA
Aleppo
Euphrates
Orontes
6
Qarqar 854
Ugarit
Hamath
Syrian Desert
Cyprus
ARAM
Arvad
LEVANT
Tadmor
Riblah
Byblos
ARAM-ZOBAH
PHOENICIA
Sidon
Damascus
ARAM-DAMASCUS
Mediterranean Sea
Tyre
Dan
7
Acco
Hazor
Sea of Chinnereth (Sea of Galilee)
Megiddo
Beth-shean
8
Jordan
Samaria
Shechem
5
Joppa
AMMON
KINGDOM OF ISRAEL
Rabbah
9
Elteketh 701
Gezer
Jerusalem
Ashkelon
Bethlehem
MOAB independent of Israel, 843 BC
Gaza
Lachish
Arad
Salt Sea (Dead Sea)
PHILISTIA
KINGDOM OF JUDAH
EGYPT
EDOM independent of Judah, 843 BC
Ezion-geber

Disunity was a luxury the Hebrews could ill afford, as the power of both Egypt and Assyria was reviving. In 924 the pharaoh Shoshenq I (r.945–924) led a campaign through Philistia, Judah and Israel, sacking many cities and imposing tribute, although both kingdoms survived. In the 9th century relations between Israel and Judah was usually hostile and Israel often suffered attacks from Aram–Damascus, which was frequently allied to Judah. Under Omri and Ahab Israel became the most powerful kingdom in the region and played a leading role in attempts by the Levantine states to check the growing power of Assyria under Shalmaneser III. However, under Ahab's successor Jehu, Israel was forced to pay tribute to Assyria. In the early 8th century the kingdoms enjoyed relative peace and prosperity with Assyria in a period of decline, until Tiglath-pileser III (r.744–727) overran the Levant and forced vassal status on Israel and Judah. When Hoshea, king of Israel, rebelled against Assyria in 724 his capital Samaria was taken after a three-year siege and its population deported to Assyria. Despite receiving Egyptian support, a rebellion by Hezekiah, the king of Judah, was also put down by the Assyrians. As Assyrian power entered terminal decline in the 630s, Judah briefly regained independence under Josiah (r.640–609) who extended his authority over the old kingdom of Israel until he was killed in battle with the Egyptians at Megiddo. The Egyptians occupied the Levant but were defeated by the Babylonians at Carchemish in 605, after which Judah became a vassal state of Babylon.

In 597 Judah rebelled against Babylonian rule and was crushed by Nebuchadnezzar. Jerusalem was captured, the temple plundered and many of its citizens were deported to Babylonia. Ten years later Judah rebelled again but Jerusalem was taken after an eighteen-month siege. This was the end for independent Judah. Its last king Zedekiah was blinded and imprisoned with most of his nobles and more Hebrews were deported. Many others fled into exile in Egypt. Though a disaster in political terms, the Babylonian captivity was a creative period in Jewish history. Exile caused a great deal of religious reflection and it was the period when much of the Old Testament was written up in something close to its present form. Nor perhaps were the conditions of the exile extremely harsh. When Cyrus of Persia destroyed the Babylonian empire in 539 and gave the Jews leave to return home, thousands chose to remain where they were. Many others remained in Egypt. It was the beginning of the Diaspora.

HEBREW captives march into exile after the fall of Lachish in 701. Sennacherib commissioned this relief to record his triumph.

1 Saul was killed in battle against the Philistines at Gilboa c.1006.

2 Hebron was David's capital before his capture of Jerusalem from the Jebusite Canaanites c.1000.

3 The Aramaeans of Hamath submitted after David defeated the Aramaeans of Zobah and Damascus.

4 Solomon built a fleet at Ezion-geber to trade on the Red Sea with east Africa and Arabia.

5 Northern tribes rebelled against Rehoboam and formed the breakaway kingdom of Israel.

6 A coalition of Levantine states including Israel briefly checked Assyrian expansion at Qarqar, 854 BC.

7 Aram–Damascus emerged as a major rival to Israel in the 850s, but was conquered by Assyria in 732.

8 Samaria, the capital of Israel, was taken by the Assyrians in 721 after a three-year siege.

9 Jerusalem, capital of Judah, was sacked after the rebellion of 587, and its population deported to Babylon; they stayed until 539 when the victorious Achemenid Persians allowed them to return.

See also 1.07 (writing), 1.13 (Assyrians and Babylonians), 1.23 (eastern Mediterranean)

1.15 The Achemenid empire of Persia • 559 – 480 BC •

The Persians who took Babylon in 539 were comparative newcomers to the region. An Indo-Iranian people, the Persians had followed their close relations the Medes from central Asia to Iran in the 8th century. The founder of the Persian monarchy was Achemenes, who gave his name to the dynasty, but it is uncertain when he ruled. In 648, when Ashurbanipal destroyed the Elamite kingdom and occupied western Elam, the Persians seized the opportunity to take its eastern territories. Despite this Persia was overshadowed by, and often subject to, the powerful Median kingdom. It was in the reign of Cyrus the Great that Persia rose to empire.

Cyrus' career as a great conqueror started when his nominal overlord, the Median king Astyages, invaded Persia around 550 following a rebellion. Astyages was deserted by his army and captured when he met Cyrus in battle at Pasargadae. Cyrus followed up this easy victory by taking the Median capital at Hamadan (Ecbatana). Cyrus was now the most powerful ruler in the region. In 547 he repulsed an invasion of Media by King Croesus of Lydia, who withdrew to his capital Sardis and disbanded his army for the winter. Cyrus, however, had nothing against winter campaigns and, when he arrived unexpectedly, Sardis fell after a siege of only fourteen days. Leaving his generals to complete the conquest of Lydia and the Ionian Greeks, Cyrus marched east to push deep into central Asia. In 539 he crowned his career by conquering Babylonia. Discontent over the religious unorthodoxy of its king Nabonidus was rife and, by posing as a servant of the god Marduk and restorer of orthodoxy, he was even welcomed in Babylon.

In little more than a decade Cyrus had built the largest empire the world had yet seen, with remarkably little hard campaigning. Clearly the close relationship between the Medes and Persians aided in what was more of a dynastic takeover than a conquest, and in Mesopotamia the experience of incorporation in the Assyrian and Babylonian empires had long-since mixed cultures, weakened local identities and accustomed people to imperial rule. As a result there was little spirit of resistance to what amounted, in practice, to no more than the advent of a new imperial dynasty. Cyrus was diplomat as well as soldier and the consolidation of his empire owed much to his moderation. Demands for tribute were modest, he did not interfere with local customs, upheld the rights of the local priesthood and left local institutions of government intact.

Cyrus was killed in 530 on campaign against the Sakas in central Asia and was succeeded by his son Cambyses. Cambyses added Egypt and Libya to the empire before dying in mysterious circumstances,

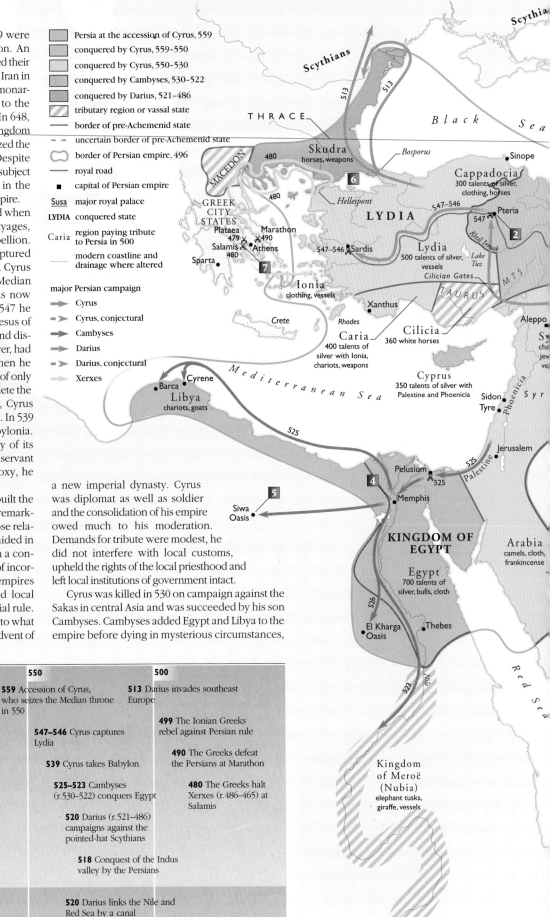

Persia at the accession of Cyrus, 559
conquered by Cyrus, 559-550
conquered by Cyrus, 550-530
conquered by Cambyses, 530-522
conquered by Darius, 521-486
tributary region or vassal state
border of pre-Achemenid state
uncertain border of pre-Achemenid state
border of Persian empire, 496
royal road
capital of Persian empire
Susa major royal palace
LYDIA conquered state
Caria region paying tribute to Persia in 500
modern coastline and drainage where altered
major Persian campaign
Cyrus
Cyrus, conjectural
Cambyses
Darius
Darius, conjectural
Xerxes

TIMELINE

Persian empire

c.850 The Medes migrate into Iran from central Asia.

c.750 The Persians migrate into southern Iran from central Asia

c.640 Persia becomes a vassal state of Media

c.630–553 Life of Zoroaster, the prophet of Iran and founder of the Parsee religion

559 Accession of Cyrus, who seizes the Median throne in 550

547–546 Cyrus captures Lydia

539 Cyrus takes Babylon

525–523 Cambyses (r.530–522) conquers Egypt

520 Darius (r.521–486) campaigns against the pointed-hat Scythians

518 Conquest of the Indus valley by the Persians

513 Darius invades southeast Europe

499 The Ionian Greeks rebel against Persian rule

490 The Greeks defeat the Persians at Marathon

480 The Greeks halt Xerxes (r.486–465) at Salamis

General

612 Fall of Nineveh and collapse of Assyria's empire

562 Decline of Babylon after the death of Nebuchadnezzar

520 Darius links the Nile and Red Sea by a canal

507 Kleisthenes lays the basis for democracy in Athens

GOLD bracelets like this were shown as part of the Lydians' tribute, depicted on reliefs at Persepolis

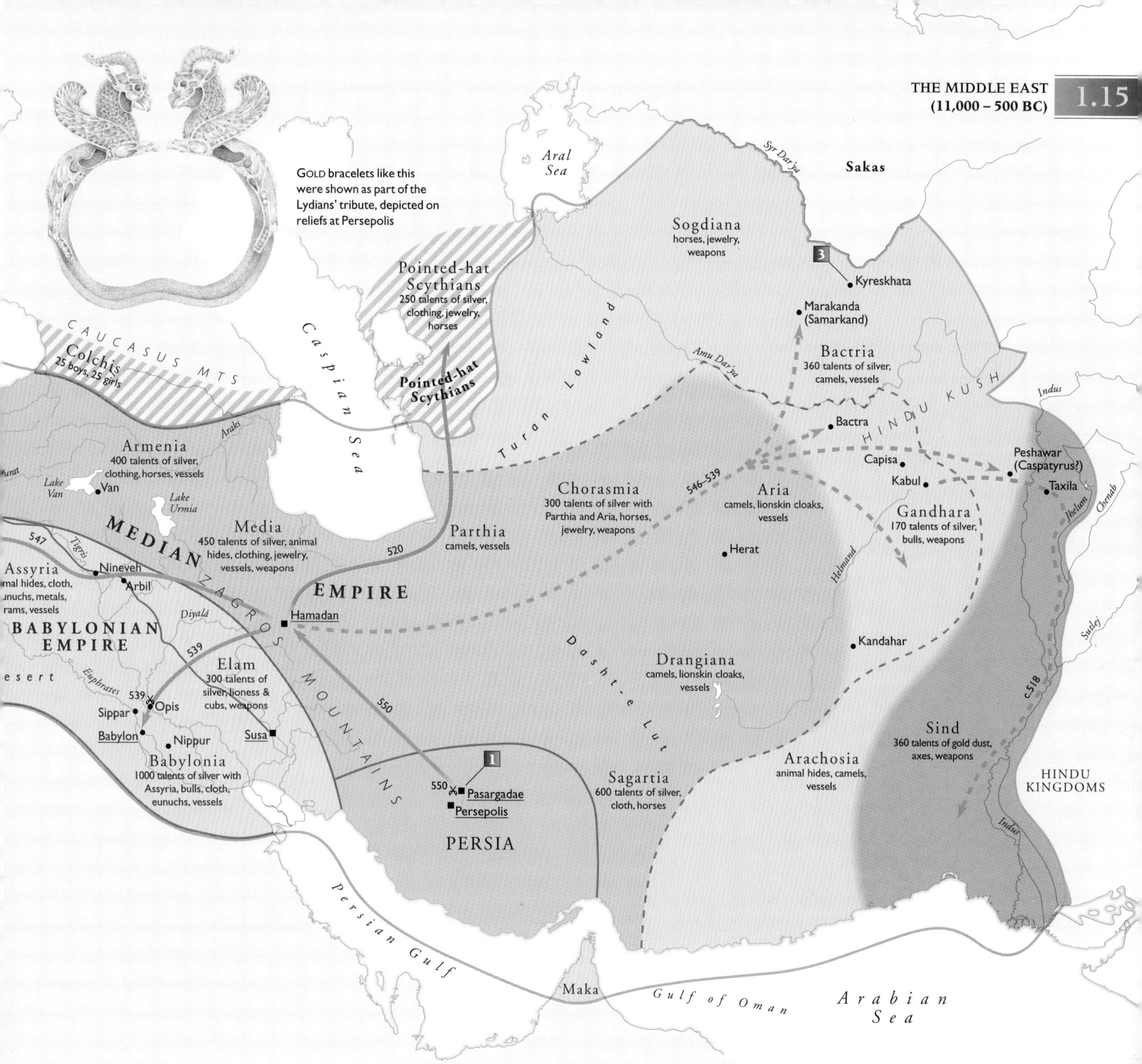

possibly murdered by his brother Smerdis. Smerdis was quickly overthrown and killed by Darius (r.521–486), a member of a junior Achemenid house. Darius faced rebellions from one end of the empire to the other but suppressed them all within a year. By 520 he was secure enough to campaign against the Caspian Scythians. In 518 he extended Persian control as far as, and possibly a little beyond, the Indus and in 513 he crossed into Europe; though he conquered Thrace, the expedition failed in its main objective of subduing the Black Sea Scythians. This failure encouraged a rebellion by the Ionian Greeks in 499. This was put down in 494 and Darius dispatched an expedition to punish the mainland Greeks for supporting the rebels. When this force was defeated by the Athenians at Marathon in 490, Darius began to plan for the conquest of Greece. The expedition was finally launched by his son Xerxes, but the decisive defeat of his fleet at Salamis in 480 and of his army at Plataea the following year brought the expansion of the empire to a halt.

Darius reorganized the empire into about twenty provinces under governors, or satraps, often relatives or close friends of the king. The system of taxation was regularized and fixed tributes, based on the wealth of each province, were introduced. Only Persia, which was not a conquered province, was exempt. The Assyrian imperial post system was expanded and the roads improved. Local garrison commanders remained directly responsible to the king. The official capital of the empire under Cyrus had been Pasargadae, but Hamadan was effectively the administrative capital. Darius moved the administrative capital to Susa and founded a new official capital at Persepolis. Under Darius the imperial administration used various local languages transcribed into cuneiform and written on clay tablets for documents, but his successors abandoned this system in favor of writing on parchment using the widespread Aramaic language and alphabet.

The Persian empire was a thoroughly cosmopolitan state which united elements of all the major civilizations of its time except the Chinese. By throwing together peoples from so many backgrounds, the empire promoted the diffusion and mixing of cultures and ended the isolation of the old civilizations.

1 Astyages, king of Media, was defeated by Cyrus at Pasargadae; Cyrus then took Hamadan and seized the Median throne.

2 Cyrus repulsed a Lydian invasion at Pteria, then captured the Lydian capital Sardis and King Croesus.

3 Kyreskhata was the strongest of a chain of forts built by Cyrus to protect the northern frontier.

4 After a hard-fought battle at Pelusium Cambyses captured Memphis (525) and took pharaoh Psammeticus III to Susa in chains.

5 A Persian force sent by Cambyses to capture Siwa vanished in the desert.

6 Darius built a bridge of boats over the Bosporus (513) to invade Europe; Xerxes did the same over the Hellespont in 480.

7 Persian expansion to the west was decisively halted by the Greeks at the naval battle of Salamis.

See also 1.14 (Babylon); 1.24 (Greece); 2.09 (Alexander); 2.07 (invasion of Greece)

1.16 Early farming in Africa • 7000 – 500 BC •

The end of the Ice Age, about 10,000 years ago, brought major climatic changes. Africa had been an arid continent during the last glaciation: rainforests were small and the Sahara desert formed a virtually impenetrable barrier between central and northern Africa. When the last glaciation ended rainfall increased over the whole continent, with most of the Sahara now able to support semi-arid grassland, diverse wildlife and large permanent lakes. Some 9,000 years ago hunter–gatherer bands lived in most of the area, exploiting game, lake-fish and wild plants of all kinds. Most groups became sedentary around favored watercourses or lakes and produced pottery decorated with a wavy-line motif while they exploited wild plants and hunted over the semi-arid neighborhood. They have yielded bone fishing harpoons, small stone tools and a pottery style decorated with wavy line patterns.

Some of Africa's earliest farming communities developed among these Saharan groups, perhaps as early as 6000 BC. Even though wetter than today, the Sahara suffered long drought cycles that affected the availability of both game and wild plant foods. One survival strategy was to supplement cereal grass yields by planting small gardens in areas where these wild grasses flourished. Over many centuries this resulted in a permanent dependence on crops such as bulrush millet, sorghum and African rice.

In the eastern Sahara, farming based on barley and wheat and domesticated indigenous wild cattle was established by 6500 BC. Farming probably began in the Nile valley soon after. A period of low Nile floods around this time probably reduced supplies of fish and other aquatic animals on which the local hunter–gatherers depended, and forced them to adopt farming. The fertile soils and reliable water supply of the Nile valley made it the richest and most densely populated farming area in Africa by the 4th millennium BC. Wheat and barley spread from Egypt throughout north Africa and to the Ethiopian highlands by about 500 BC, but they were unsuited to the climate of tropical Africa.

Another early center of agriculture in Africa was the Ethiopian highlands, where farming may have begun by 5000 BC based on teff, an indigenous Ethiopian cereal, and finger millet, a cereal of unknown origin. Other Ethiopian domesticates included noog, an oil plant, and ensete, a relative of the banana grown for its starchy root. Of these, only finger millet became important outside Ethiopia. Ethiopia's relative isolation meant that many food plants, including barley, flax, emmer wheat, peas and lentils, developed strains unique to the area.

Farming along the margins of the west African forest zone had begun by the 2nd millennium with indigenous plants such as yams, cowpeas and the oil palm. African rice, adapted to grow in flooded savanna waterholes, became a staple west of the Bandama river. Farmers spread using a technique of shifting agriculture in clearings cut or burned out of the forest.

The introduction of cattle, sheep and goats about 5000 BC revolutionized farming in the central Sahara. By the 4th millennium cattle- and sheep-herding and limited cultivation of cereals were widespread. The herders were seminomadic, and drove their animals between seasonal pastures. The Saharan herders left a vivid record of their way of life in thousands of naturalistic rock paintings found widely across the central Sahara. By about 3000 BC desertification intensified, perhaps in part because of overgrazing. The herders' response was to move out to the Sahel region of semi-arid savanna at its southern margins. South of the Sahara, cattle-herding was restricted by areas of dense rainforest and by the widespread tsetse fly. However, herder groups spread onto the east African highlands by 2000 BC and moved south.

Copper was worked in the southern Sahara in the 2nd millennium, but sub-Saharan Africa moved straight from the Stone Age to the Iron Age. Knowledge of iron working may have developed indigenously in the southern Sahara; alternatively it may have been introduced either down the Nile valley or from the Phoenician colonies in north Africa. Iron was being worked in the Nubian kingdom of Kush by about 600 BC, while it is attested in northern Nigeria at about the same time, where the Nok culture developed by the late 6th century.

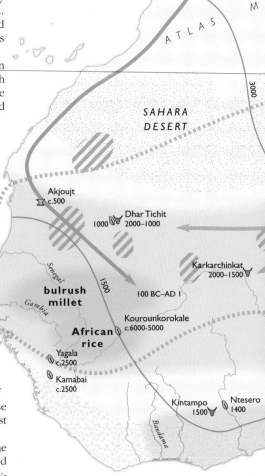

El Khril
5500
ATLAS
SAHARA
DESERT
3000
Akjoujt
c.500
Dhar Tichit
1000
2000–1000
Karkarchinkat
2000–1500
Senegal
bulrush
millet
1500
100 BC–AD 1
Gambia
Kourounkorokale
c.6000-5000
African
rice
Yagala
c.2500
Kamabai
c.2500
Kintampo
1500
Ntesero
1400
Bandama
ATLANTIC
OCEAN

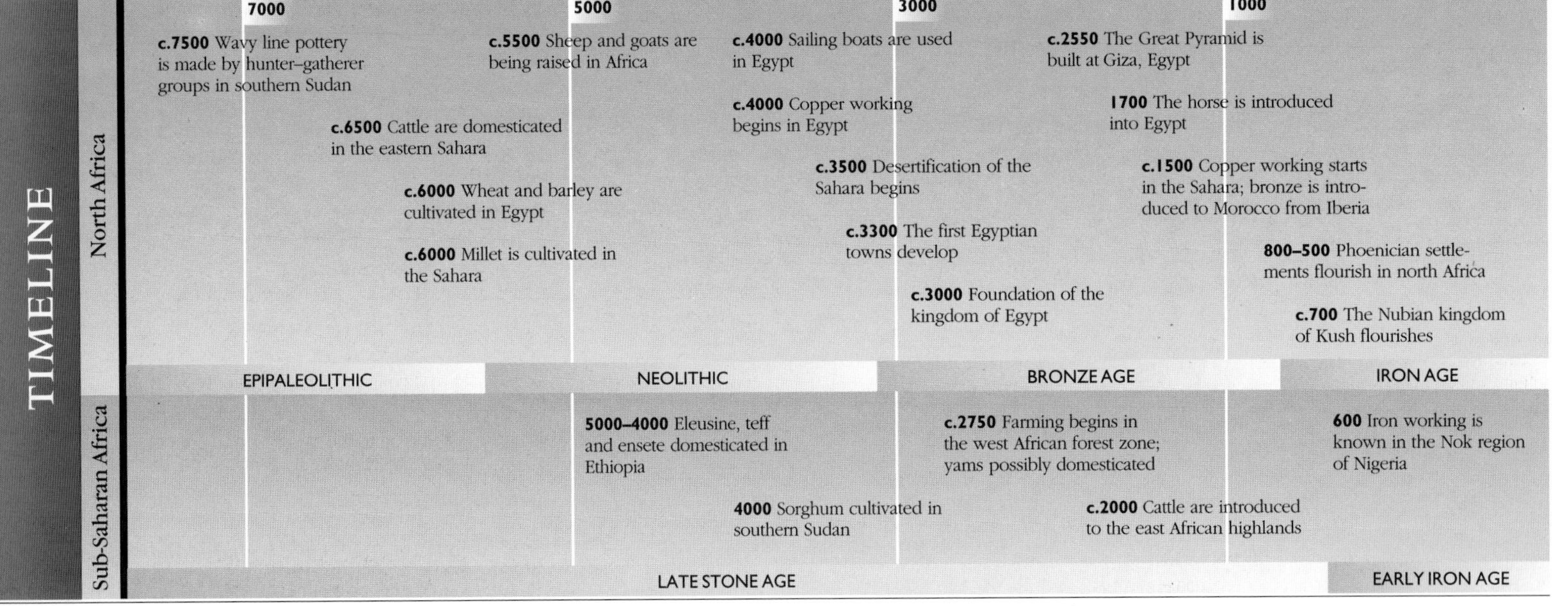
TIMELINE
North Africa
7000
5000
3000
1000
c.7500 Wavy line pottery is made by hunter–gatherer groups in southern Sudan
c.5500 Sheep and goats are being raised in Africa
c.4000 Sailing boats are used in Egypt
c.2550 The Great Pyramid is built at Giza, Egypt
c.4000 Copper working begins in Egypt
1700 The horse is introduced into Egypt
c.6500 Cattle are domesticated in the eastern Sahara
c.3500 Desertification of the Sahara begins
c.1500 Copper working starts in the Sahara; bronze is introduced to Morocco from Iberia
c.6000 Wheat and barley are cultivated in Egypt
c.3300 The first Egyptian towns develop
800–500 Phoenician settlements flourish in north Africa
c.6000 Millet is cultivated in the Sahara
c.3000 Foundation of the kingdom of Egypt
c.700 The Nubian kingdom of Kush flourishes
EPIPALEOLITHIC
NEOLITHIC
BRONZE AGE
IRON AGE
Sub-Saharan Africa
5000–4000 Eleusine, teff and ensete domesticated in Ethiopia
c.2750 Farming begins in the west African forest zone; yams possibly domesticated
600 Iron working is known in the Nok region of Nigeria
4000 Sorghum cultivated in southern Sudan
c.2000 Cattle are introduced to the east African highlands
LATE STONE AGE
EARLY IRON AGE

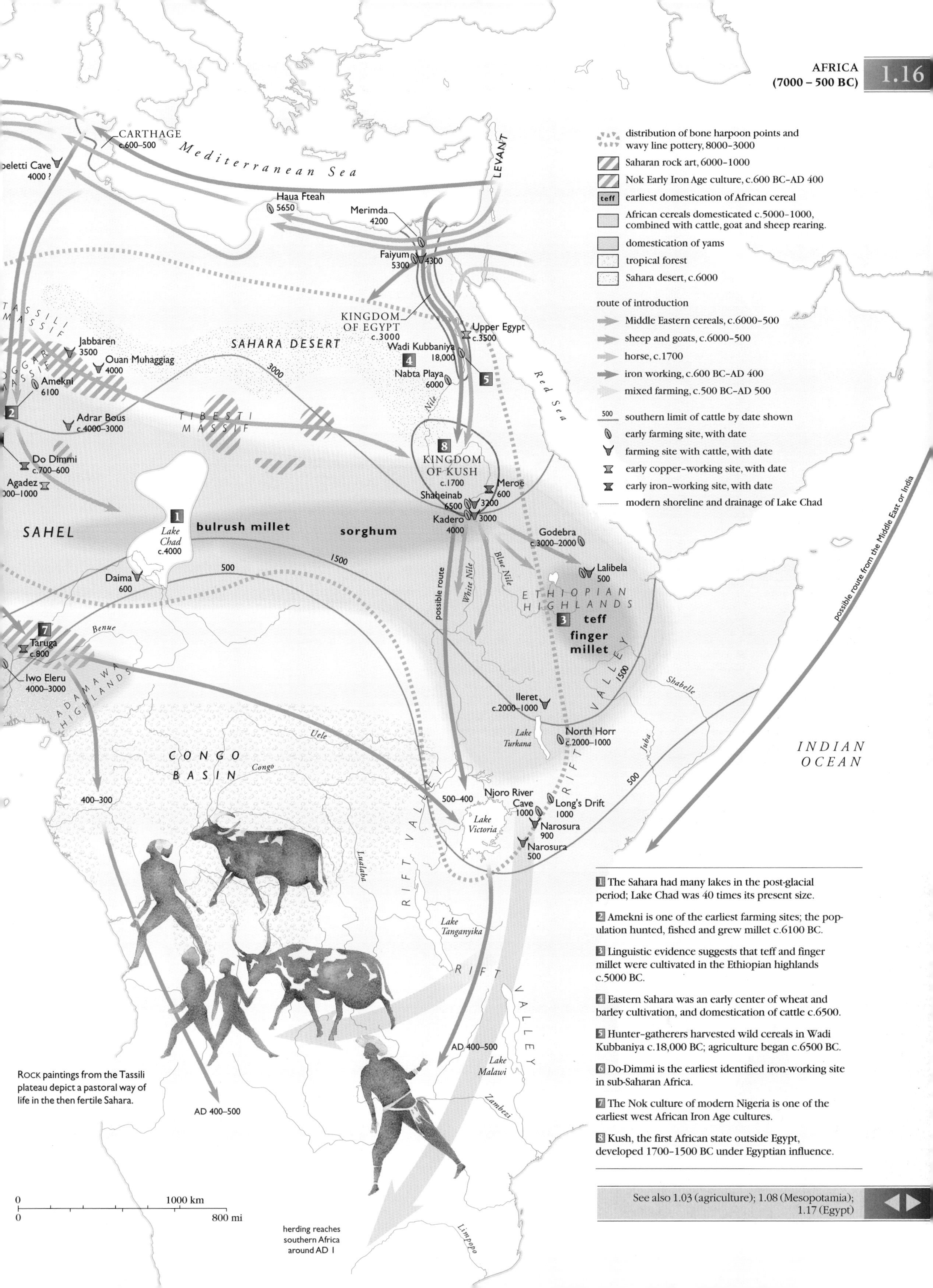

- distribution of bone harpoon points and wavy line pottery, 8000–3000
- Saharan rock art, 6000–1000
- Nok Early Iron Age culture, c.600 BC–AD 400
- teff — earliest domestication of African cereal
- African cereals domesticated c.5000–1000, combined with cattle, goat and sheep rearing.
- domestication of yams
- tropical forest
- Sahara desert, c.6000

route of introduction

- Middle Eastern cereals, c.6000–500
- sheep and goats, c.6000–500
- horse, c.1700
- iron working, c.600 BC–AD 400
- mixed farming, c.500 BC–AD 500
- 500 — southern limit of cattle by date shown
- early farming site, with date
- farming site with cattle, with date
- early copper-working site, with date
- early iron-working site, with date
- modern shoreline and drainage of Lake Chad

1 The Sahara had many lakes in the post-glacial period; Lake Chad was 40 times its present size.

2 Amekni is one of the earliest farming sites; the population hunted, fished and grew millet c.6100 BC.

3 Linguistic evidence suggests that teff and finger millet were cultivated in the Ethiopian highlands c.5000 BC.

4 Eastern Sahara was an early center of wheat and barley cultivation, and domestication of cattle c.6500.

5 Hunter-gatherers harvested wild cereals in Wadi Kubbaniya c.18,000 BC; agriculture began c.6500 BC.

6 Do-Dimmi is the earliest identified iron-working site in sub-Saharan Africa.

7 The Nok culture of modern Nigeria is one of the earliest west African Iron Age cultures.

8 Kush, the first African state outside Egypt, developed 1700–1500 BC under Egyptian influence.

ROCK paintings from the Tassili plateau depict a pastoral way of life in the then fertile Sahara.

0 — 1000 km
0 — 800 mi

See also 1.03 (agriculture); 1.08 (Mesopotamia); 1.17 (Egypt)

Ancient Egypt was totally dependent on the Nile. Below the First Cataract, the Nile flows through a narrow valley and, except where it broadens out into the Delta, its flood plain is nowhere more than a few kilometers wide, often less. The flood plain was probably the most favorable area for agriculture anywhere in the ancient world. The Nile flooded annually in the late summer, falling in the autumn and leaving the fields moist and fertilized with fresh silt ready for sowing. The crops grew through the warm Egyptian winter and were harvested in the spring before the next cycle of flooding. Egypt had little need of the complex irrigation systems and flood defenses of Mesopotamia, where the rivers flooded in spring, after the start of the growing season. Canals, however, were used to spread the floodwaters and increase the cultivable area. High yields were possible year after year: the farmers' surpluses were taken to state storehouses for distribution to administrators, craftsmen and priests, for trade or to build up reserves against the famine that would follow if the Nile flood failed. The Nile was also Egypt's main highway. The prevailing winds in Egypt blow north to south, enabling boats to travel upstream under sail and return downstream with the flow. Few settlements were far from the river, making it relatively easy to transport heavy loads of grain or stone over long distances. On either side of the narrow 800-kilometer (500-mile) fertile strip was the desert which isolated Egypt from the influence of other civilizations and protected it from invaders: Egyptian civilization was over 1,300 years old before it suffered its first major invasion.

Farming began in the Nile valley before 6000 BC and by 4000 BC it was densely populated by subsistence farmers. Chiefdoms and towns appeared by 3300. In the narrow confines of the valley competition was probably intense. Eventually, the chiefdoms amalgamated into two coalitions or kingdoms, centered respectively in Upper and Lower Egypt, which fought each other for supremacy. The first king known to have ruled all Egypt was Narmer, king of Upper Egypt who conquered Lower Egypt about 3000. This unification was consolidated by the foundation of Memphis as a new capital.

By the same date the hieroglyphic system of writing had appeared. The system worked on similar principles to the Sumerian pictographic script, but hieroglyphs were developed from symbolic motifs used to decorate pottery in Egypt's Predynastic period. Early hieroglyphs appear on slate palettes which Narmer had carved to commemorate his victories. These palettes show that the principle of theocratic kingship that would be the basis of the ancient Egyptian state was already well established. During the ensuing Early Dynastic period (2920–2575) the kings developed an efficient administration which made possible a dramatic increase in royal power at the beginning of the Old Kingdom (2575–2134), named for the kingdom ruled from Memphis by a succession of four dynasties.

The annual Nile flood was seen as a gift from the gods. The king claimed to be able to control the flood, but if the flood failed, his authority could be called into question. He was believed to be of divine descent and was held to be immortal. At his death immense effort was put into preserving his body and to providing it with a suitably regal tomb furnished with the luxuries of everyday life. Early royal tombs were built on platforms known as *mastabas*, but these were superseded by pyramids in the reign of King Djoser (r.2630–2611). Pyramid building climaxed in about 2550 with the 146-meter-high Great Pyramid, built for Khufu, and the slightly smaller pyramid of his son Khephren. These enormous buildings are impressive evidence of the power the kings exercised over their subjects. However the large pyramids strained the resources of the kingdom: later ones were more modest and none were built after the 17th century BC, by which time ideas of the afterlife had changed.

Egypt was governed by an efficient central and local bureaucracy. The kingdom was treated as the personal property of the king and the central bureaucracy was an extension of the royal household. The highest official was the vizier, who supervised the administration of justice and taxation. Below the vizier were chancellors, controllers of stores and other officials, supported by a staff of scribes trained in mathematics and writing. For the purposes of local government, Egypt was divided into provinces, or *nomes*, under governors selected from the royal or noble families.

During the 5th Dynasty (2465–2323) the monarchy was weakened by granting out lands as rewards and favors to the nobility. The provincial governorships became hereditary and drifted out of the control of the king. A period of low Nile floods then began around 2150, bringing famine and starvation, and the remaining royal authority crumbled. The Old Kingdom state collapsed and Egypt was divided between rival dynasties in Upper and Lower Egypt in what is known as the First Intermediate period.

THIS pottery lion, with a stylized mane resembling a headcloth, was found in the temple at Hierakonpolis. It dates from about the 3rd Dynasty.

Mediterranean Sea

to Libya

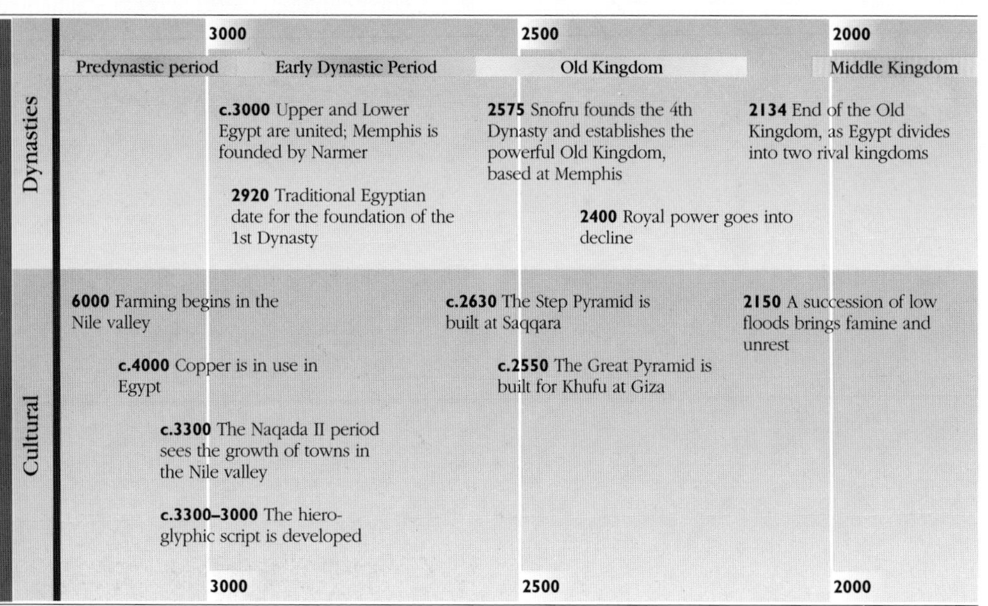

TIMELINE
Dynastics
Cultural
3000
2500
2000
Predynastic period
Early Dynastic Period
Old Kingdom
Middle Kingdom
c.3000 Upper and Lower Egypt are united; Memphis is founded by Narmer
2920 Traditional Egyptian date for the foundation of the 1st Dynasty
2575 Snofru founds the 4th Dynasty and establishes the powerful Old Kingdom, based at Memphis
2400 Royal power goes into decline
2134 End of the Old Kingdom, as Egypt divides into two rival kingdoms
6000 Farming begins in the Nile valley
c.4000 Copper is in use in Egypt
c.3300 The Naqada II period sees the growth of towns in the Nile valley
c.3300–3000 The hieroglyphic script is developed
c.2630 The Step Pyramid is built at Saqqara
c.2550 The Great Pyramid is built for Khufu at Giza
2150 A succession of low floods brings famine and unrest
3000
2500
2000

1 The First Cataract was the traditional southern frontier of Egypt through most of its history.

2 Hierakonpolis and Naqada were the first towns to develop in Egypt, c.3300. Narmer was probably king of Hierakonpolis.

3 Saqqara is the site of the oldest pyramid, the Step Pyramid, c.2630.

4 Giza is the site of the largest pyramids, including the Great Pyramid of Khufu.

5 The mountains of the Eastern Desert were the chief source of minerals.

6 Graffiti show that the Egyptians were exploiting Sinai's mineral wealth as early as the 3rd Dynasty (2649–2575).

7 The Egyptians maintained a trading post at Buhen in Nubia during the Old Kingdom.

8 Memphis was capital of Egypt for most of the Early Dynastic and Old Kingdom.

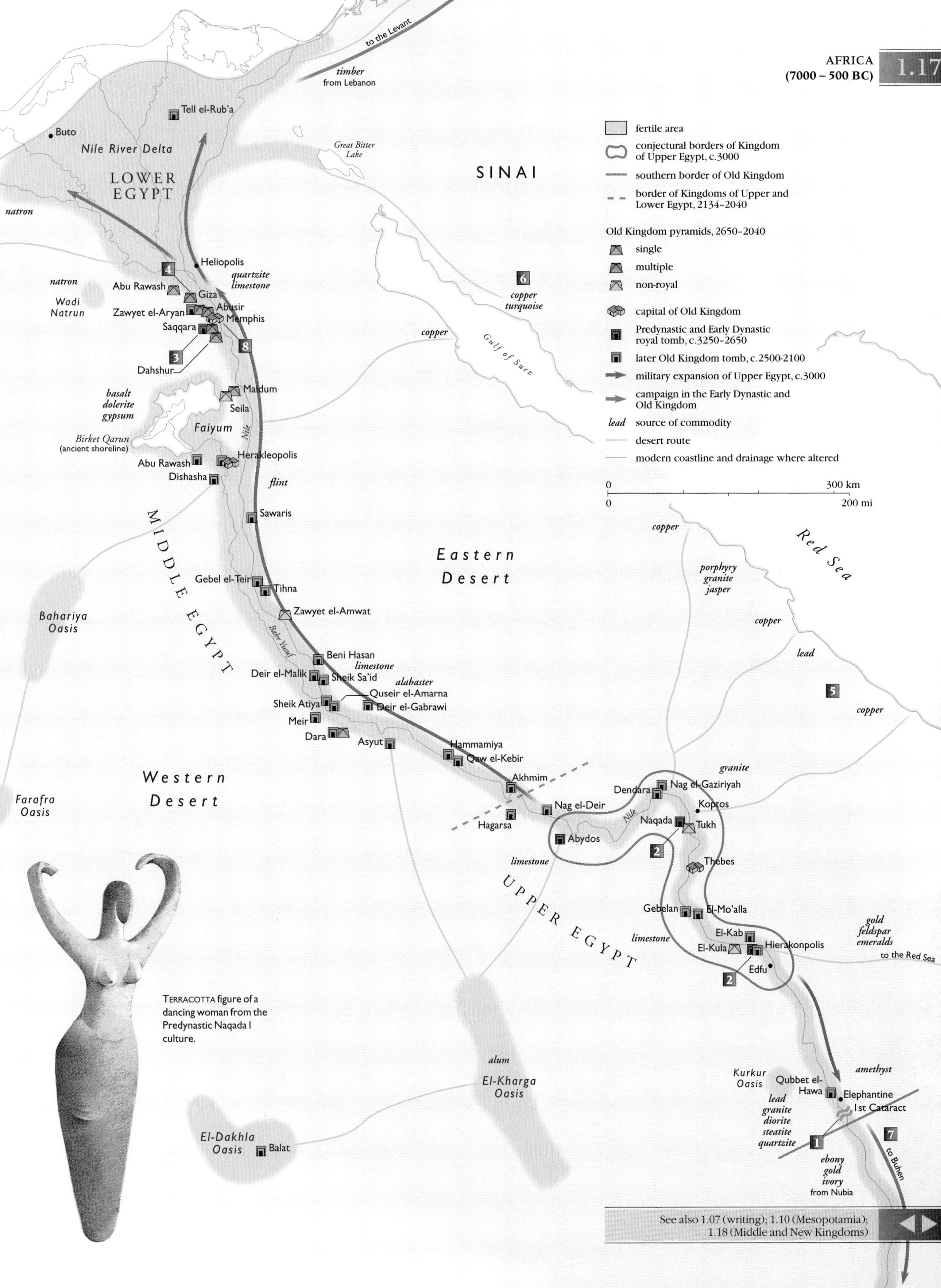
fertile area
conjectural borders of Kingdom of Upper Egypt, c.3000
southern border of Old Kingdom
border of Kingdoms of Upper and Lower Egypt, 2134–2040
Old Kingdom pyramids, 2650–2040
single
multiple
non-royal
capital of Old Kingdom
Predynastic and Early Dynastic royal tomb, c.3250–2650
later Old Kingdom tomb, c.2500-2100
military expansion of Upper Egypt, c.3000
campaign in the Early Dynastic and Old Kingdom
lead source of commodity
desert route
modern coastline and drainage where altered
0 300 km
0 200 mi
to the Levant
timber from Lebanon
Tell el-Rub'a
Buto
Nile River Delta
LOWER EGYPT
natron
Great Bitter Lake
SINAI
Heliopolis
quartzite limestone
Abu Rawash
Giza
Wadi Natrun
Zawyet el-Aryan
Abusir
Memphis
Saqqara
Dahshur
copper turquoise
copper
Gulf of Suez
basalt dolerite gypsum
Maidum
Seila
Faiyum
Nile
Birket Qarun (ancient shoreline)
Abu Rawash
Herakleopolis
Dishasha
flint
Sawaris
MIDDLE EGYPT
Eastern Desert
Red Sea
porphyry granite jasper
Gebel el-Teir
Tihna
Zawyet el-Amwat
Bahariya Oasis
Bahr Yusuf
Beni Hasan
limestone
Deir el-Malik
Sheik Sa'id
alabaster
Quseir el-Amarna
Sheik Atiya
Deir el-Gabrawi
Meir
Dara
Asyut
Hammamiya
Qaw el-Kebir
lead
Western Desert
Farafra Oasis
Akhmim
granite
Dendara
Nag el-Gaziriyah
Koptos
Nag el-Deir
Naqada
Tukh
Hagarsa
Abydos
limestone
Thebes
UPPER EGYPT
Gebelan
El-Mo'alla
gold feldspar emeralds
El-Kab
limestone
El-Kula
Hierakonpolis
to the Red Sea
Edfu
alum
El-Kharga Oasis
Kurkur Oasis
Qubbet el-Hawa
amethyst
Elephantine
1st Cataract
lead granite diorite steatite quartzite
El-Dakhla Oasis
Balat
ebony gold ivory from Nubia
to Buhen
1 2 3 4 5 6 7 8

TERRACOTTA figure of a dancing woman from the Predynastic Naqada I culture.

See also 1.07 (writing); 1.10 (Mesopotamia); 1.18 (Middle and New Kingdoms)

1.18 Middle and New Kingdom Egypt • 2040 – 332 BC •

The reunification of Egypt in 2040 BC by Mentuhotpe (r.2061–2010), of the Theban dynasty of Upper Egypt, marks the start of the Middle Kingdom. A few decades later royal authority and political stability had been restored and the power of the provincial governors reduced. To rebuild a loyal administration, the Middle Kingdom rulers promoted propagandist literature, while statuary presented the king as the care-worn "good shepherd" of his people. Pyramid building was revived, though more modestly than in the Old Kingdom.

Egypt's neighbors were now becoming organized in chiefdoms and petty kingdoms, and the Middle Kingdom rulers had to pursue a more aggressive foreign policy than their predecessors. Under Amenemhet I (r.1991–1962), Lower Nubia was conquered; the frontier at the Second Cataract was garrisoned and heavily fortified by his successors. Egyptian influence was extended over the Levant during the reign of Senwosret III (r.1878–1841) and local rulers were forced to become vassals of Egypt. During the 18th century the bureaucracy began to grow out of control and for much of the time the effective rulers of Egypt were the viziers. In the 17th century there was considerable immigration from the Levant into the Delta. Most immigrants were absorbed into the lower classes of Egyptian society but one, Khendjer, became king around 1745 BC.

Around 1640 Egypt was invaded by the Hyksos, a Semitic people from the Levant, who overran Lower Egypt, which they ruled from their capital at Avaris in the Delta. Upper Egypt remained independent under a vassal Theban dynasty but control over Lower Nubia was lost to the nascent kingdom of Kush. Hyksos rule, in what is known as the Second Intermediate period, made Egypt more open to foreign influences. Bronze came into widespread use, war chariots were introduced, as were weapons such as the composite bow and scale armor. New fashions in dress, musical instruments, domestic animals and crops were adopted through Hyksos influence. Otherwise, the Hyksos accepted Egyptian traditions and historical continuity was unbroken.

Under the Theban king Seqenenre II (died c.1555) the Egyptians began a long struggle to expel the Hyksos which was finally completed by Ahmose in 1532. This victory marks the beginning of the New Kingdom, under which the power and influence of ancient Egypt reached its peak. The Hyksos invasion had shown the Egyptians that their borders were no longer secure, and the New Kingdom was overtly militaristic and expansionist, reaching its greatest extent around 1500 under the warrior king Tuthmosis I. Tuthmosis conquered the entire Levant and established a frontier on the Euphrates. Lower Nubia was reconquered and Kush was overrun to beyond the Fourth Cataract. The primary motive of expansion into the Levant was to establish a buffer zone between Egypt and the aggressive powers of the Middle East; in Nubia, which had rich gold deposits, the motive was economic. In the Levant, local rulers were kept under the supervision of Egyptian officials and key cities were garrisoned. Nubia was subjected to full colonial government under a viceroy directly responsible to the king. Nubia was a great source of wealth to the New Kingdom, but the Egyptians faced a constant struggle to control the Levant, against local rebellions and expansionist powers such as the Hittite empire.

The power of Egypt declined after the reign of Amenophis IV (r.1353–1335). Amenophis, who changed his name to Akhenaten, was a radical religious reformer who attempted to replace Egypt's traditional polytheism with the monotheistic cult of the Aten, or sun disk. Akhenaten founded a new capital and promoted radically new art styles to symbolize the break with the past, but there was little popular enthusiasm for the new religion, which was abandoned after his death. In the ensuing period of political instability, Egypt lost control of the Levant to the Hittites. Campaigns by the kings (or pharaohs as they were now known) Sethos I (r.1305–1290) and Ramesses II "the Great" (r.1290–1224) to restore the Egyptian position were only partially successful and Ramesses eventually made peace with the Hittites.

Around 1200 the entire region was disrupted by

Middle Kingdom (12th Dynasty, 1991-1783)
- zone of direct control
- zone of dominance

Second Intermediate period
- Hyksos Kingdom (15th Dynasty, 1640-1532)
- Theban (17th Dynasty, 1646-1550)
- Kingdom of Kush
- maximum extent of New Kingdom under Tuthmosis I, 1504-1492
- royal capital, with dynasty
- city

royal tomb
- Middle Kingdom
- New Kingdom

fort or garrison
- Middle Kingdom
- New Kingdom

- sacked c.1200, probably by Sea Peoples
- Giza temple
- desert route used for communication between the Hyksos and Kushite allies
- gold deposit
- major migration
- modern coastline and drainage where altered

Libyan

0 300 km
0 200 mi

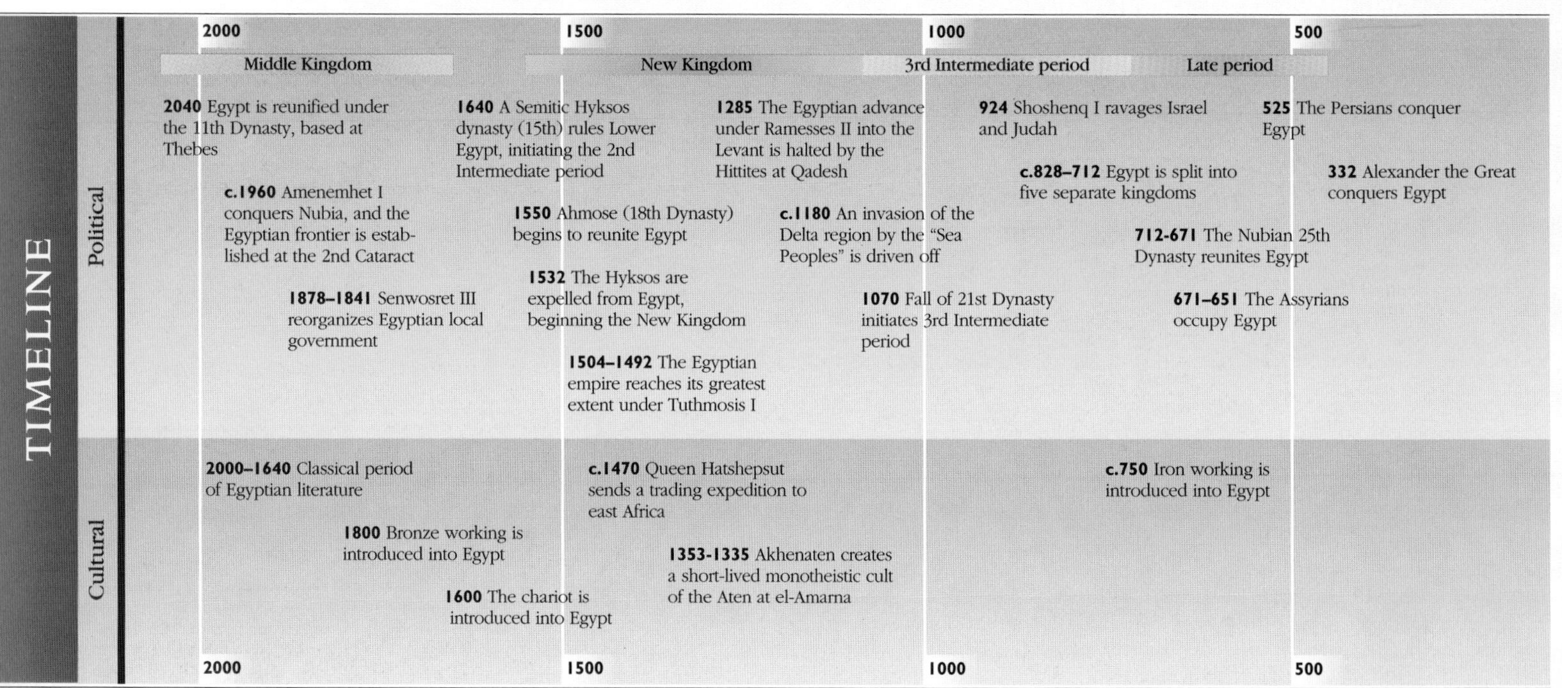
TIMELINE
Political
Cultural
2000
1500
1000
500
Middle Kingdom
New Kingdom
3rd Intermediate period
Late period
2040 Egypt is reunified under the 11th Dynasty, based at Thebes
c.1960 Amenemhet I conquers Nubia, and the Egyptian frontier is established at the 2nd Cataract
1878–1841 Senwosret III reorganizes Egyptian local government
1640 A Semitic Hyksos dynasty (15th) rules Lower Egypt, initiating the 2nd Intermediate period
1550 Ahmose (18th Dynasty) begins to reunite Egypt
1532 The Hyksos are expelled from Egypt, beginning the New Kingdom
1504–1492 The Egyptian empire reaches its greatest extent under Tuthmosis I
1285 The Egyptian advance under Ramesses II into the Levant is halted by the Hittites at Qadesh
c.1180 An invasion of the Delta region by the "Sea Peoples" is driven off
1070 Fall of 21st Dynasty initiates 3rd Intermediate period
924 Shoshenq I ravages Israel and Judah
c.828–712 Egypt is split into five separate kingdoms
712-671 The Nubian 25th Dynasty reunites Egypt
671–651 The Assyrians occupy Egypt
525 The Persians conquer Egypt
332 Alexander the Great conquers Egypt
2000–1640 Classical period of Egyptian literature
1800 Bronze working is introduced into Egypt
1600 The chariot is introduced into Egypt
c.1470 Queen Hatshepsut sends a trading expedition to east Africa
1353-1335 Akhenaten creates a short-lived monotheistic cult of the Aten at el-Amarna
c.750 Iron working is introduced into Egypt
2000
1500
1000
500

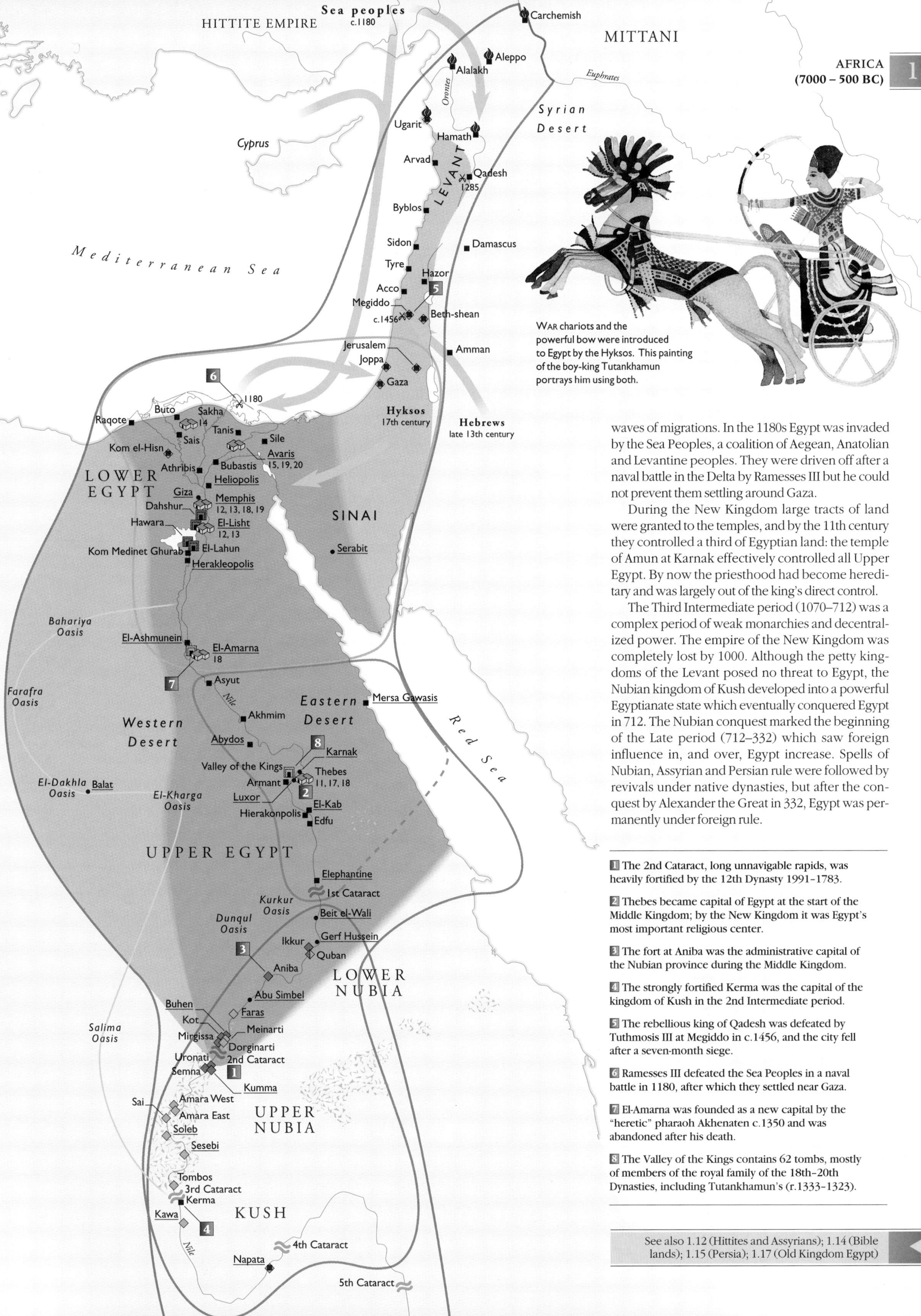
Sea peoples
c.1180
HITTITE EMPIRE
Carchemish
MITTANI
Aleppo
Alalakh
Euphrates
Orontes
Syrian
Desert
Ugarit
Hamath
Cyprus
Arvad
LEVANT
Qadesh
1285
Byblos
Sidon
Damascus
Mediterranean Sea
Tyre
Hazor
Acco
5
Megiddo
c.1456
Beth-shean
Jerusalem
Joppa
Amman
Gaza
6
1180
Hyksos
17th century
Hebrews
late 13th century
Buto
Sakha
14
Raqote
Tanis
Sais
Sile
Kom el-Hisn
Avaris
15, 19, 20
Athribis
Bubastis
LOWER EGYPT
Heliopolis
Giza
Memphis
12, 13, 18, 19
Dahshur
SINAI
Hawara
El-Lisht
12, 13
Kom Medinet Ghurab
El-Lahun
Serabit
Herakleopolis
Bahariya Oasis
El-Ashmunein
El-Amarna
18
7
Asyut
Farafra Oasis
Nile
Eastern Desert
Mersa Gawasis
Akhmim
Western Desert
Abydos
8
Karnak
Valley of the Kings
Thebes
11, 17, 18
Red Sea
El-Dakhla Oasis
Balat
Armant
El-Kharga Oasis
Luxor
2
El-Kab
Hierakonpolis
Edfu
UPPER EGYPT
Elephantine
1st Cataract
Kurkur Oasis
Beit el-Wali
Dunqul Oasis
Gerf Hussein
Ikkur
3
Quban
Aniba
LOWER NUBIA
Abu Simbel
Buhen
Faras
Kot
Meinarti
Salima Oasis
Mirgissa
Dorginarti
Uronati
2nd Cataract
Semna
1
Kumma
Amara West
Sai
Amara East
UPPER NUBIA
Soleb
Sesebi
Tombos
3rd Cataract
Kerma
KUSH
Kawa
4
Nile
4th Cataract
Napata
5th Cataract

WAR chariots and the powerful bow were introduced to Egypt by the Hyksos. This painting of the boy-king Tutankhamun portrays him using both.

waves of migrations. In the 1180s Egypt was invaded by the Sea Peoples, a coalition of Aegean, Anatolian and Levantine peoples. They were driven off after a naval battle in the Delta by Ramesses III but he could not prevent them settling around Gaza.

During the New Kingdom large tracts of land were granted to the temples, and by the 11th century they controlled a third of Egyptian land: the temple of Amun at Karnak effectively controlled all Upper Egypt. By now the priesthood had become hereditary and was largely out of the king's direct control.

The Third Intermediate period (1070–712) was a complex period of weak monarchies and decentralized power. The empire of the New Kingdom was completely lost by 1000. Although the petty kingdoms of the Levant posed no threat to Egypt, the Nubian kingdom of Kush developed into a powerful Egyptianate state which eventually conquered Egypt in 712. The Nubian conquest marked the beginning of the Late period (712–332) which saw foreign influence in, and over, Egypt increase. Spells of Nubian, Assyrian and Persian rule were followed by revivals under native dynasties, but after the conquest by Alexander the Great in 332, Egypt was permanently under foreign rule.

1 The 2nd Cataract, long unnavigable rapids, was heavily fortified by the 12th Dynasty 1991–1783.

2 Thebes became capital of Egypt at the start of the Middle Kingdom; by the New Kingdom it was Egypt's most important religious center.

3 The fort at Aniba was the administrative capital of the Nubian province during the Middle Kingdom.

4 The strongly fortified Kerma was the capital of the kingdom of Kush in the 2nd Intermediate period.

5 The rebellious king of Qadesh was defeated by Tuthmosis III at Megiddo in c.1456, and the city fell after a seven-month siege.

6 Ramesses III defeated the Sea Peoples in a naval battle in 1180, after which they settled near Gaza.

7 El-Amarna was founded as a new capital by the "heretic" pharaoh Akhenaten c.1350 and was abandoned after his death.

8 The Valley of the Kings contains 62 tombs, mostly of members of the royal family of the 18th–20th Dynasties, including Tutankhamun's (r.1333–1323).

See also 1.12 (Hittites and Assyrians); 1.14 (Bible lands); 1.15 (Persia); 1.17 (Old Kingdom Egypt)

1.19 Upper Paleolithic Europe • 35,000 YEARS AGO – 5000 BC •

Anatomically modern humans from Africa reached what is now the Middle East some 90,000 years ago, but it was not until the beginning of the Upper Paleolithic period, about 40,000 years ago, that they were able to move into Europe. Unlike the indigenous Neanderthals, who were physically adapted to the harsh Ice Age climate, the early anatomically modern humans were poorly equipped to survive in Europe until, some 50,000–40,000 years ago, they also acquired a fully modern human mental capacity. This enabled them to adapt to the cold climate through technological and social innovation, and compete on more than equal terms with the Neanderthals. The Neanderthals became extinct about 28,000 years ago. Whether it was as a result of a war of extermination or because superior modern human hunting techniques drove them into marginal environments is a subject of debate: current archeological opinion favors the latter.

Two parallel toolmaking traditions, the Châtelperronian and the Aurignacian, are found in Europe during the 10–12,000 years that modern humans and Neanderthals shared the continent. The Châtelperronian is apparently a development of the Mousterian tool culture and is thought to have been used by the Neanderthals. The Aurignacian has similarities with contemporary tool cultures in the Middle East and is therefore thought to have been introduced to Europe by anatomically modern humans. The Aurignacian and the succeeding Gravettian tool cultures both are fairly uniform over wide areas but later Upper Paleolithic tool cultures show greater variety between different regions. These variations are often in style rather than function and probably served as a way of expressing emerging ethnic identities. Typical Upper Paleolithic stone tools include scrapers, sharpened blades, burins – engraving tools used for antler harpoons – and bone points and needles were also used. The Solutrean culture introduced a sophisticated technique of pressure flaking which produced beautiful leaf shaped spear heads.

The most impressive characteristics of the Upper Paleolithic cultures are their art traditions, both decorated artifacts and cave-wall painting. The earliest Upper Paleolithic art dates from around 31,000 years ago but the traditions reached their peak in the Magdalenian (17,000–11,000 years ago), in the cave paintings of sites such as Lascaux and Altamira. The greatest concentration of Upper Paleolithic cave art is to be found in southwest France and northern Spain, an area with a particularly dense population at the time. The function of cave art is unknown but it is thought to have played a religious role. The most distinctive decorated artifacts are female "Venus" figurines made around 25,000 years ago. These have been found across Europe – evidence, perhaps, of a widespread religious cult.

Despite the cold, the tundras and steppes of Ice Age Europe were a very favorable environment for hunters, being filled with easily tracked herds of large grazing mammals. Upper Paleolithic hunters used a combination of semi-permanent base-camps – often sited at bottlenecks on animal migration routes, such as river crossings – and seasonal camps where particular game species were intensively exploited. Caves and south-facing rock shelters were favored camp sites, but in more exposed areas tents and huts were built.

The end of the last glaciation, around 10,000 years ago (8000 BC) marks the end of the Upper Paleolithic and the beginning of the Mesolithic

Upper Paleolithic, 40,000–10,000 years ago
- Levantine Aurignacian culture
- Aurignacian culture
- cave site
- cave site with painting
- open site
- open site with structure
- "Venus" figurine find

Mesolithic, 10,000–6000 ya (8000–4000 BC)
- major site
- site with shell midden

- maximum extent of ice sheet during last glaciation, c.18,000 ya
- extent of ice sheet, 7000 BC
- northern limit of deciduous woodland, c.18,000 ya
- northern limit of deciduous woodland, 7000 BC
- migration of anatomically modern humans from Middle East, c.40,000 ya
- ancient course of Thames/Rhine, 7000 BC
- modern coastline and drainage where altered

0 800 km
0 600 mi

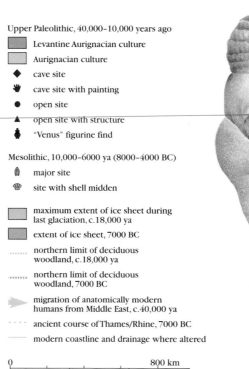

"VENUS" figurines with exaggerated sexual characteristics were a feature of the Gravettian culture and probably symbolized fertility. This example is from Willendorf in Austria.

ATLANTIC OCEAN

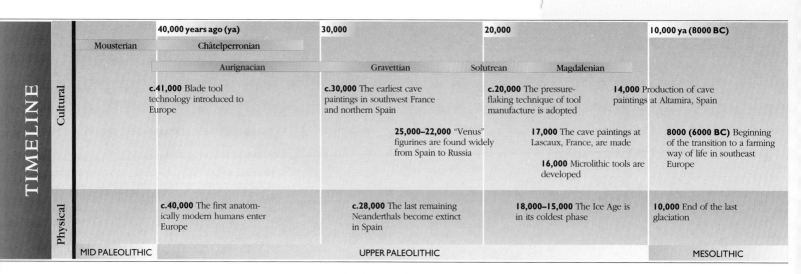

TIMELINE

	40,000 years ago (ya)	30,000	20,000	10,000 ya (8000 BC)
Cultures	Mousterian; Châtelperronian; Aurignacian	Gravettian	Solutrean; Magdalenian	
Cultural	**c.41,000** Blade tool technology introduced to Europe	**c.30,000** The earliest cave paintings in southwest France and northern Spain; **25,000–22,000** "Venus" figurines are found widely from Spain to Russia	**c.20,000** The pressure-flaking technique of tool manufacture is adopted; **17,000** The cave paintings at Lascaux, France, are made; **16,000** Microlithic tools are developed; **14,000** Production of cave paintings at Altamira, Spain	**8000 (6000 BC)** Beginning of the transition to a farming way of life in southeast Europe
Physical	**c.40,000** The first anatomically modern humans enter Europe	**c.28,000** The last remaining Neanderthals become extinct in Spain	**18,000–15,000** The Ice Age is in its coldest phase	**10,000** End of the last glaciation
	MID PALEOLITHIC	UPPER PALEOLITHIC		MESOLITHIC

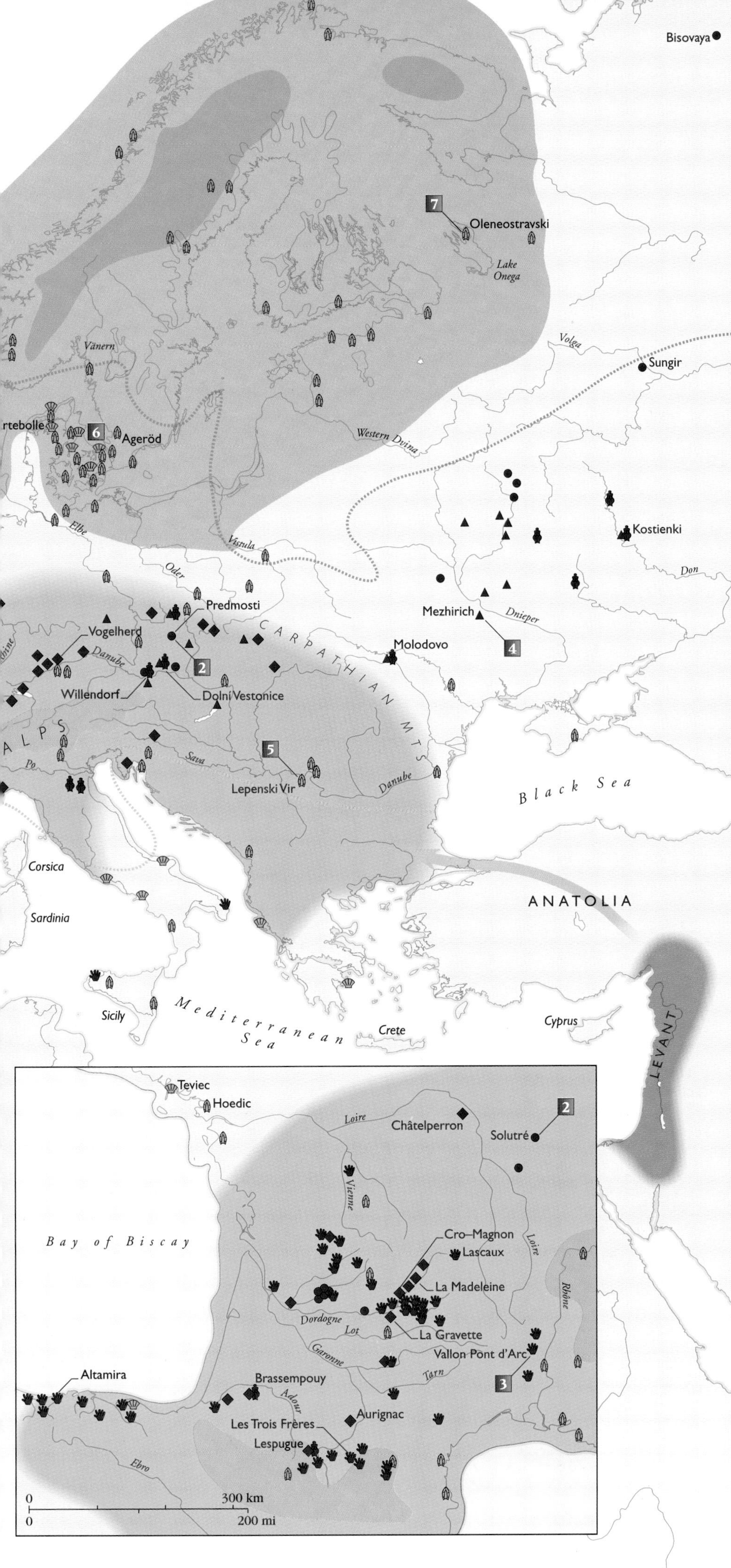
Bisovaya
7
Oleneostravski
Lake Onega
Vänern
Volga
Sungir
Western Dvina
rtebolle
6
Ageröd
Elbe
Vistula
Oder
Kostienki
Don
Predmosti
Vogelherd
Danube
Mezhirich
Dnieper
Molodovo
4
2
CARPATHIAN MTS
Willendorf
Dolni Vestonice
ALPS
Po
Sava
5
Lepenski Vir
Danube
Black Sea
Corsica
Sardinia
ANATOLIA
Sicily
Mediterranean Sea
Crete
Cyprus
LEVANT
Teviec
Hoedic
Loire
Châtelperron
Solutré
2
Vienne
Bay of Biscay
Cro-Magnon
Lascaux
Loire
La Madeleine
Rhône
Dordogne
Lot
La Gravette
Vallon Pont d'Arc
Garonne
Tarn
3
Altamira
Brassempouy
Adour
Aurignac
Les Trois Frères
Lespugue
Ebro
0
300 km
0
200 mi

period. As the climate became warmer, sea levels rose and dense forests advanced over most of Europe, bringing the big-game hunting way of life to an end. Large mammals were now fewer and more elusive, but a far greater diversity of plant foods, shellfish, fish, birds and small mammals was available. Mesolithic hunter–gatherers introduced many new devices to exploit these new food sources. The most important technological change was a reliance on microliths – small stone blades or flakes – used in combination to make composite tools such as knives, harpoons, fish spears and lightweight arrow heads. Nets, fish traps, shellfish scoops and dug-out canoes also came into widespread use for the first time in the Mesolithic.

Many areas of northern Europe which had previously been uninhabitable because of extreme cold or ice sheets received their first modern human inhabitants during the Mesolithic, while some which had been relatively densely populated, such as southwest France and the southwest steppes, became comparatively depopulated. The densest population moved to areas such as the Atlantic coast and southern Scandinavia. Hunter–gatherers here were able to adopt an increasingly sedentary way of life, making fewer and shorter migrations between camps. In southern Scandinavia and eastern Europe there were even permanent settlements occupied all year round. Task groups set out from these settlements to spend short periods at temporary seasonal camps to exploit locally abundant food resources.

The Mesolithic period came to an end with the adoption of the Neolithic farming way of life, a process which began about 6000 BC in southeast Europe and about two thousand years later in the British Isles and Scandinavia. In extreme northerly areas, an essentially Mesolithic way of life continued until the domestication of the reindeer early in the Christian era.

1 In the Upper Paleolithic, southwest France had light woodland for fuel, sheltered valleys with many caves, and lay across major animal migration routes; it was therefore Europe's most densely populated area.

2 Upper Paleolithic hunters used temporary camps to exploit particular game species. Solutré was a base for horse hunters, Predmosti for mammoth.

3 Cave paintings of woolly rhinoceros, horses and buffalo found at Vallon Pont d'Arc in 1994 are, at 30,000 years old, the oldest yet found.

4 On the treeless steppes, mammoth bones were used to build huts; a well-known example, c.18,000 years old, was found at Mezhirich.

5 The well-preserved Mesolithic settlement of Lepenski Vir includes many fish-head sculptures, perhaps indicating worship of a fish-deity.

6 Denmark, with marine, freshwater and terrestrial food sources in close proximity, was densely populated in the Mesolithic.

7 The first cemeteries, such as those at Cabeço da Arruda and Oleneostravski (about 170 burials each) date from the late Mesolithic (c.4250 BC).

8 Late Mesolithic hunter-gatherers (c.4000–3400 BC) visited Oronsay island several times a year for fish and shellfish.

See also 1.02 (peopling the earth); 1.08 (Middle East); 1.20 (Neolithic Europe)

1.20 Neolithic Europe • 5000 – 2000 BC •

The spread of agriculture through Europe was a complex process of small-scale migrations by farming peoples and the adoption of farming techniques by Mesolithic hunter–gatherers. It took time to develop crop strains suited to the colder and wetter climates of central, western and northern Europe. Hunter–gatherers readily adopted some aspects of the material culture of neighboring farmers, such as pottery and polished stone axes, but only adopted food production when natural food sources were in short supply. In many areas, Mesolithic hunter–gatherers were already semi-sedentary, so the transition to a settled farming way of life was probably easily made when it became necessary.

Farming, based on cereals, legumes, sheep, goats and cattle, first began in Europe in Greece and the Balkans around 6500 BC. This pattern of farming spread from the Balkans around the Mediterranean coasts to southern France and Spain by 5000. Whether the adoption of farming in Europe was an indigenous development or was influenced by the farming societies of the Middle East is doubtful. Southeastern Europe was within the range of wild einkorn wheat, cattle, pigs and sheep and farming may have developed as a result of experimentation with cultivation and animal husbandry by indigenous hunter–gatherers. Cattle may have been domesticated independently in southeast Europe but some crops, such as emmer wheat and barley, were certainly introduced from the Middle East.

The earliest farming culture of central Europe is the Bandkeramik or Linear Pottery culture. This originated in the northern Balkans around 5400 BC and over a few centuries spread north and west across the band of fertile and easily worked loess soils that extends across Europe from Romania to the Rhineland. When the population of a village became too large, a daughter settlement was simply founded a few kilometers away. The indigenous Mesolithic hunter–gatherer bands were not displaced by the Bandkeramik people, who settled on vacant lands between them, usually along rivers. However, the steady encroachment by the farmers placed pressure on the hunter–gatherers' resources and they were gradually forced to adopt farming too: gradually the two populations became assimilated. After a delay of several centuries, the farming way of life spread from central Europe into western Europe, then Britain and Scandinavia and the southwest steppes.

Farming in central and northern Europe was very different from that in the south. The cold winters led to spring sowing of crops (autumn sowing prevailed in southern Europe, the Middle East and north Africa) and there was greater emphasis on cattle and pigs, which were better suited to grazing in woodland than sheep and goats.

Neolithic settlements were generally small, with populations of only forty to sixty. The most common type of building was the wooden longhouse that accommodated both people and livestock. Except in treeless areas such as the Orkney Islands, where stone houses were built, settlements have left few traces; burials and ritual structures provide most evidence of the nature of Neolithic societies. In most of Europe the dead were buried in individual graves in cemeteries with offerings of stone tools, pottery and ornaments. There is little variation in the quantity and quality of grave goods, indicating that these communities were not divded between rich and poor. In many areas the dead were buried communally in megalithic tombs which remained in use for many generations. The tombs were usually covered with mounds of earth, and may have served as territorial markers as well as burial places, the presence of the community's ancestors legitimizing the ownership of the present generation. The Atlantic coast of western Europe, where the earliest megalithic tombs were built, was already relatively densely populated in Mesolithic times. Population pressure may have been felt after the introduction of agriculture, leading to a new concern with territoriality.

In the later Neolithic and the early Bronze Age, northwest Europe saw the construction of megalithic stone circles and circular earth structures known as henges. Some circles have astronomical alignments or form part of a complex ritual landscape but their exact functions are unknown. Some monuments are so large that they must have been built by chiefdoms able to command the resources

Ring of Brodgar
Skara Brae
Maes Howe
Orkney Islands
Callanish
Camster Long
Clava
Monamore
Ballynagilly
Castlerigg
Carrowmore
Long Meg & Daught
Great Langdale
Newgrange
The Knowth
Bryncelli Ddu
Lough Gur
Barclodiadd y Gawres
Derrynahinch
Belas Knap
Mynydd-bach
Rollright Stones
Ty Isaf
Avebury
Windmill Hill
Stonehenge
Merry Maidens
7
La Chaussée-Tirancourt
Les Fouaillages
Barnenez
La Hogue
Tressé
Liscuis
Carnac
Noisy
Gavrinis
Loire
ATLANTIC OCEAN
6
Cha
Puy de Paulhiac
La Halliade
St Michel-du-Touch
Pedra Coberta
PYRENEES
Pouey-Mayou
Perari
Artajona
Douro
Puig
Carapito
Tagus
Els Tudons
Furninha
Anta da Marquesa
Cabeço da Arruda
Balearic Islands
Poço da Gateira
Pedra Branca
Anta dos Gorgions
Nora Velha
Alcalá
Dolmen de Soto
Los Millares
Cueva de la Menga
Romeral
Romeral
El Barranquete
Los Murcielagos
Kristel-Jardins
Gar Cahal

TIMELINE

	6000	5000	4000	3000	2000
South, east & central Europe	**c.6500** Farming starts to appear in the Balkans; **c.6500** Cattle are domesticated in the Balkans; **c.6000** Farming spreads to Italy; **c.5400** The Bandkeramik farming culture of central Europe begins	**c.5000** Hierarchical societies emerge in southeast Europe; **c.4500** Copper smelting begins in the Balkans; **c.4500** The plow is in use in southeast Europe	**c.4000** The horse is domesticated on the southwestern steppes; **c.3300** Copper smelting begins in central Europe; **c.3200** Wheeled vehicles are in use in the Balkans and the southwestern steppes	**c.2500** Bronze is made in central Europe; **c.2300** Bronze is in use in southeast Europe	**c.2000** The Minoan palace civilization emerges in Crete
West and north Europe		**c.4500** Farming begins in western Europe; **c.4300** The first megalithic tombs are built, in Brittany	**c.4000** Farming is introduced into Britain and Scandinavia	**c.2900** Cord Impressed Pottery cultures appear in northern Europe; **c.2500** Bell Beaker cultures appear in western Europe; **c.2400** Copper is first in use in western Europe	**c.2000** The main stage of Stonehenge is completed in southern Britain

NEOLITHIC — BRONZE AGE

earliest farming cultures

- early Aegean and Anatolian Painted Ware cultures, 7000–6000
- Balkan Painted and Impressed Pottery cultures, 6500–4000
- Impressed Pottery cultures, 6000–4000
- Bandkeramik or Linear Pottery culture, 5400–4500
- Bowl cultures, 4500–3300
- Tripolye-Cucuteni cultures, 4200–3800
- Funnel-necked Beaker cultures, 4200–2800

- megalithic monument building, 4300–2000
- stone circle or alignment
- megalithic tomb
- excavation of early farming village
- other site
- spread of copper working by 4500
- spread of copper working by 3000
- general direction of the spread of farming, 6000–3000

0 600 km
0 400 mi

and populations of wide areas. The emergence of more hierarchical societies in the later Neolithic is also reflected in burial practices. In cultures such as the Cord Impressed Ware culture of eastern Europe and the Bell Beaker cultures in western Europe, variations in the quality and quantity of grave goods in burials indicate differences of wealth and status in farming societies. In many areas these changes are associated with the introduction of copper and gold metallurgy.

Metallurgy developed separately in the northern Balkans around 4800 BC and in southern Spain about fifteen centuries later. Both copper and gold were used to make small tools and ornaments. At first only native metals were used, cold-hammered into shape, but by 4500 copper ores were being mined in the Balkans for smelting. Copper was smelted in Spain, Italy and probably Britain by 2400. Copper tools had few advantages over stone ones, but the elites valued metal for display objects. Only in the Bronze Age did metal tools begin to replace stone tools in everyday use.

1 Starcevo was one of the earliest farming settlements in the Balkans, 6000–4000 BC. Hunting and gathering, cereals and cattle were all important.

2 Horses were domesticated in the Tripolye-Cucuteni cultures in the 4th millennium BC.

3 Incised clay tablets from Tartaria show that a simple system of notation had developed in the Balkans by 5000.

4 Copper ores were being mined at Rudna Glava in 4500 BC, the earliest known in the world.

5 A major stone temple complex was built at Tarxien c.3500–2400 BC.

6 Some three thousand standing stones aligned in multiple rows make Carnac one of the largest megalithic sites. Its purpose is unknown.

7 The stone circle at Stonehenge was built in several phases spanning the Neolithic and Bronze Age (c.3000–1500 BC).

8 An "ice man", whose body was found in 1991, froze to death in the Otztaler Alps c.3350–3120 BC.

BELL-BEAKER drinking cups with incised decoration have been found in graves all over western Europe. Pollen grains found in the bottom of some indicate that they had contained a mead-like drink.

See also 1.03 (spread of agriculture); 1.08 (Middle East); 1.19 (Mesolithic Europe)

1.21 Bronze Age Europe • 2000 – 500 BC •

The Bronze Age saw chiefdoms and warrior elites established across most of Europe. Beyond the Aegean, states were not formed until the Iron Age was well advanced and in northern and eastern Europe not until the early Middle Ages. The chiefdoms were competitive communities: fortifications were built in great numbers and new weapons such as swords and halberds were invented. Superb crafted display objects – ornaments, weapons, "parade-ground" armor, tableware, cult objects – made of bronze and precious metals, express the competitiveness of the period. Long-distance trade , particularly in tin and amber, arose to satisfy the demand for metals and other precious objects in areas where such resources were lacking. The increase in trade aided the spread of ideas and fashions and led to a high degree of cultural uniformity.

The earliest known use of bronze in Europe, in the Unetice culture in central Europe about 2500 BC, was probably an independent development and not the result of influence from the Middle East. Bronze came into use in southeast Europe, the Aegean and Italy two hundred years later, followed by Spain and, finally, the British Isles in about 1800. Scandinavia, with no workable deposits of copper or tin, continued in the Stone Age until the middle of the 2nd millennium BC. By this time bronze had entered Scandinavia, brought by traders in exchange for amber and, probably, furs.

Bronze technology led to a rapid increase in the use of metals. Bronze weapons and tools kept an edge better than stone or copper, could easily be resharpened and when broken could be melted down and recast. It was expensive, however, and its use was largely confined to the social elites in the early Bronze Age. Stone tools, sometimes copying the style of prestigious bronze tools, continued in everyday use. Large quantities of bronze artifacts, often of the highest quality, were buried or sunk in bogs as offerings to the gods.

The social distinctions of Bronze Age society are apparent in burial practices: a minority of burials being richly furnished with grave goods and the majority with few offerings. In the earlier Bronze Age three distinct burial practices are found. In southeast Europe the normal practice was burial of rich and poor alike in flat grave cemeteries. In most of eastern, northern and western Europe, the poor were buried in flat graves but the rich were buried under earth mounds known as barrows. Barrows required a communal effort to build and are evidence of the power of the elites. In some parts of western Europe Neolithic-style communal burials in megalithic tombs continued until about 1200 BC.

In southern and central Europe, large villages, often fortified, developed but in northern and western Europe the settlement pattern was one of dispersed homesteads. Population rose across Europe and agricultural settlers moved into many marginal upland areas. These were abandoned late in the Bronze Age, perhaps because of climatic deterioration or because the poor soils had been exhausted. As agricultural land rose in value, clear boundaries were laid out between communities in

early Bronze Age cultures, c.2300–1800
late megalithic cultures
Bell Beaker cultures
Nordic late Neolithic cultures
Cord Impressed Pottery cultures
Catacomb Grave cultures
Unetice culture
Danubian–Carpathian Bronze Age cultures
Balkan Bronze Age cultures
early Aegean Bronze Age cultures
North Italian Bronze Age cultures
South Italian Bronze Age cultures
spread of Urnfield cultures in late Bronze Age
by 14th century
by 12th century
by 9th century
early Bronze Age barrow burial
fortified site
late Bronze Age urnfield
metal hoard
shipwreck
settlement
other site
source of tin
source of copper
source of gold
source of amber
Mycenaean trade route
main amber trade route
0 600 km
0 400 mi
ATLANTIC OCEAN

TIMELINE

	2000	1500	1000
South and east Europe	**c.2500–1800** The Unetice culture appears in central Europe; **c.2300** Bronze working begins in southeast Europe; **c.2000** Hillforts are built in central Europe; **c.2000** The first European state emerges, in Crete; **c.2000** Trade routes across Europe appear for amber and metals	**c.1650** The Mycenaean civilization develops and traders are active in south Italy	**c.1350** The Urnfield culture appears in central Europe; **c.1200** Fall of the Mycenaean civilization; **c.1000** Iron comes into widespread use in Greece; **c.750** Beginning of the Hallstatt ("Celtic") Iron Age
West and north Europe	**c.2000** The Wessex culture flourishes in Britain, with rich barrow burials; **c.2000** The main stage of Stonehenge, in southern Britain, is completed		**1100** Hillforts are built in western Europe; **1000** Urnfield cultures spread to western Europe; **c.700** Iron in widespread use throughout Europe

NEOLITHIC — BRONZE AGE — IRON AGE

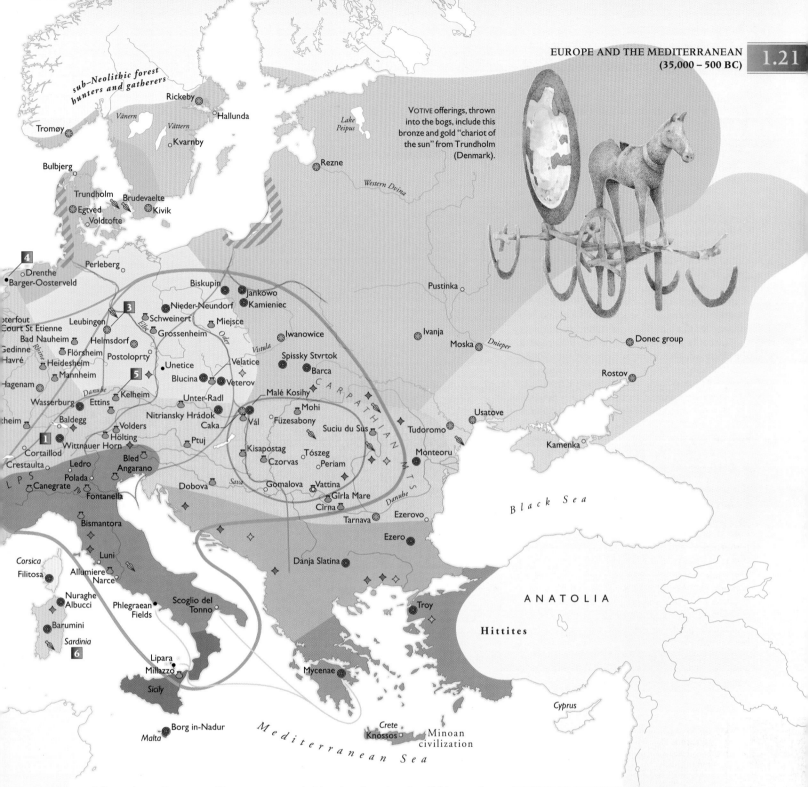

VOTIVE offerings, thrown into the bogs, include this bronze and gold "chariot of the sun" from Trundholm (Denmark).

many areas, especially northwest Europe, and farmland was enclosed into small fields that could be managed more intensively. Farmers benefited from the introduction of heavier plows, wheeled vehicles and horses. European wild oats were domesticated at this time, probably as horse fodder.

Around 1350 the Urnfield culture, named for its distinctive burial practices, appeared in Hungary. Bodies were cremated and the ashes buried in funerary urns in flat grave cemeteries of hundreds, even thousands, of graves. As with earlier Bronze Age burial customs, a minority of graves included rich offerings, weapons and armor. Some of these graves were covered with barrows, demonstrating a degree of continuity with the past, but this was by no means universal: the powers enjoyed by chieftains in the early Bronze Age may have been undermined to an extent by the emergence of a warrior class. By the 9th century Urnfield customs had spread over most of continental Europe. Except in the west where it was probably taken by migrating Celtic peoples, the Urnfield culture spread mainly as a result of the wide-ranging contacts on trade links. The later Bronze Age saw increased militarization, with extensive fortress building in western Europe and the introduction of the bronze slashing sword. Bronze armor was introduced, but probably for display only: it offers less protection than leather.

Small numbers of iron artifacts appeared in many areas about 1200. However, iron tools first became common only around 1000 in Greece and two hundred and fifty years later in northern Europe.

1 Bronze Age settlements along the northern fringes of the Alps were often built on islands in lakes for defense.

2 One of the last megalithic tombs to be used was at Island, in Ireland; it was still in use about 1200 BC about a millennium later than most megalithic tombs.

3 At Leubingen, an early Bronze Age barrow contains the remains of an elderly man accompanied by a girl, pottery, stone and bronze tools and weapons, and gold jewelry.

4 A late Bronze Age dismantled wooden "temple" was deliberately sunk into a peat bog at Barger-Oosterveld.

5 The Urnfield cemetery at Kelheim of 900–800 BC had more than 10,000 burials.

6 Defensive towers called *nuraghe* were built about 1800 BC in Sardinia; similar structures are found in Corsica and the Balearic islands.

7 A shipwreck from 800 BC off the southwest coast of Spain included more than 200 bronze weapons made in the Loire region.

See also1.20 (Neolithic Europe); 1.22 (Minoans and Mycenaeans); 2.18 (Celts)

1.22 The first civilizations of the Mediterranean • 2000 – 1100 BC •

Europe's first cities and states developed on the Aegean island of Crete around 2000 BC, where the Minoans developed a system of intensive agriculture based on wheat, olives and vines. Olives and vines grew well on rough hillsides and produced valuable commodities for long-distance trade, allowing good plowland to be kept for wheat production. Sheep were kept on Crete's mountain pastures and their wool supplied a textile industry that exported cloth to Egypt. Minoan pottery and metalwork was in demand throughout the eastern Mediterranean.

By 2000 BC Minoan society was controlled from palaces at Knossos, Phaistos, Mallia and Khania, probably the capitals of small kingdoms. A number of smaller palaces were probably subordinate centers. The palaces, which incorporated vast storehouses for grain, oil and other products, were centers for redistributing produce collected as taxes or tribute for rations to support administrators, craftsmen or traders. The Minoans had a hieroglyphic script by 2000, but this was superseded by a syllabic script three centuries later. Neither script has been deciphered so the ethnic identity of the Minoans is unknown, but they did not speak an Indo-European language and were therefore not Greeks.

Around 1700 most of the Minoan palaces were destroyed by fire, probably as a result of warfare between the palace states; they were subsequently rebuilt, but only Knossos regained its former splendor, taking control of the whole island and reducing the other palaces to tributary status. In 1626 the palaces were damaged by ash falls and earthquakes resulting from a volcanic eruption on the nearby island of Thera. The palaces were rebuilt and the Minoan civilization endured until it collapsed in about 1450 after conquest by the Mycenaeans.

The Mycenaeans, or Achaeans as they probably called themselves, were a Greek-speaking people who had moved to the Greek peninsula from the Balkans around 2000 BC. By around 1600 small kingdoms based on fortified towns were beginning to develop and a system of writing, based on the Cretan syllabic script, had been adopted. The earliest

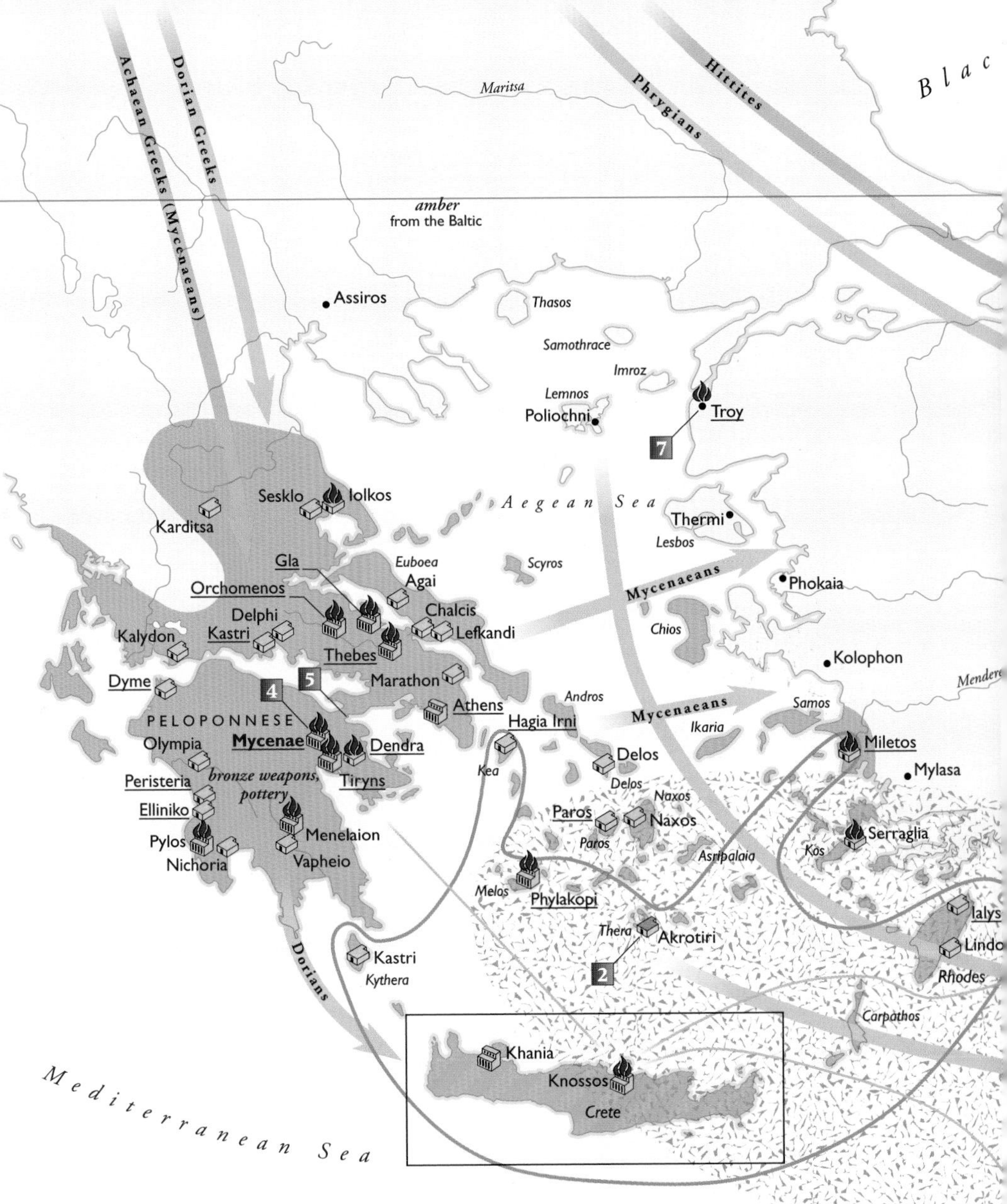

Achaean Greeks (Mycenaeans)
Dorian Greeks
Maritsa
Phrygians
Hittites
Blac
amber
from the Baltic
Assiros
Thasos
Samothrace
Imroz
Lemnos
Poliochni
Troy
7
Sesklo
Iolkos
Karditsa
Aegean Sea
Thermi
Lesbos
Gla
Euboea
Agai
Scyros
Orchomenos
Delphi
Kastri
Chalcis
Lefkandi
Mycenaeans
Phokaia
Kalydon
Thebes
Chios
Kolophon
Dyme
4
5
Marathon
Athens
Andros
Mendere
PELOPONNESE
Hagia Irni
Mycenaeans
Samos
Olympia
Mycenae
Dendra
Ikaria
Miletos
Kea
Delos
Delos
Mylasa
Peristeria
bronze weapons, pottery
Tiryns
Naxos
Elliniko
Paros
Naxos
Paros
Serraglia
Pylos
Menelaion
Astypalaia
Kos
Nichoria
Vapheio
Melos
Phylakopi
Ialys
Thera
Akrotiri
Lindo
Dorians
Kastri
Kythera
2
Rhodes
Carpathos
Khania
Knossos
Crete
Mediterranean Sea

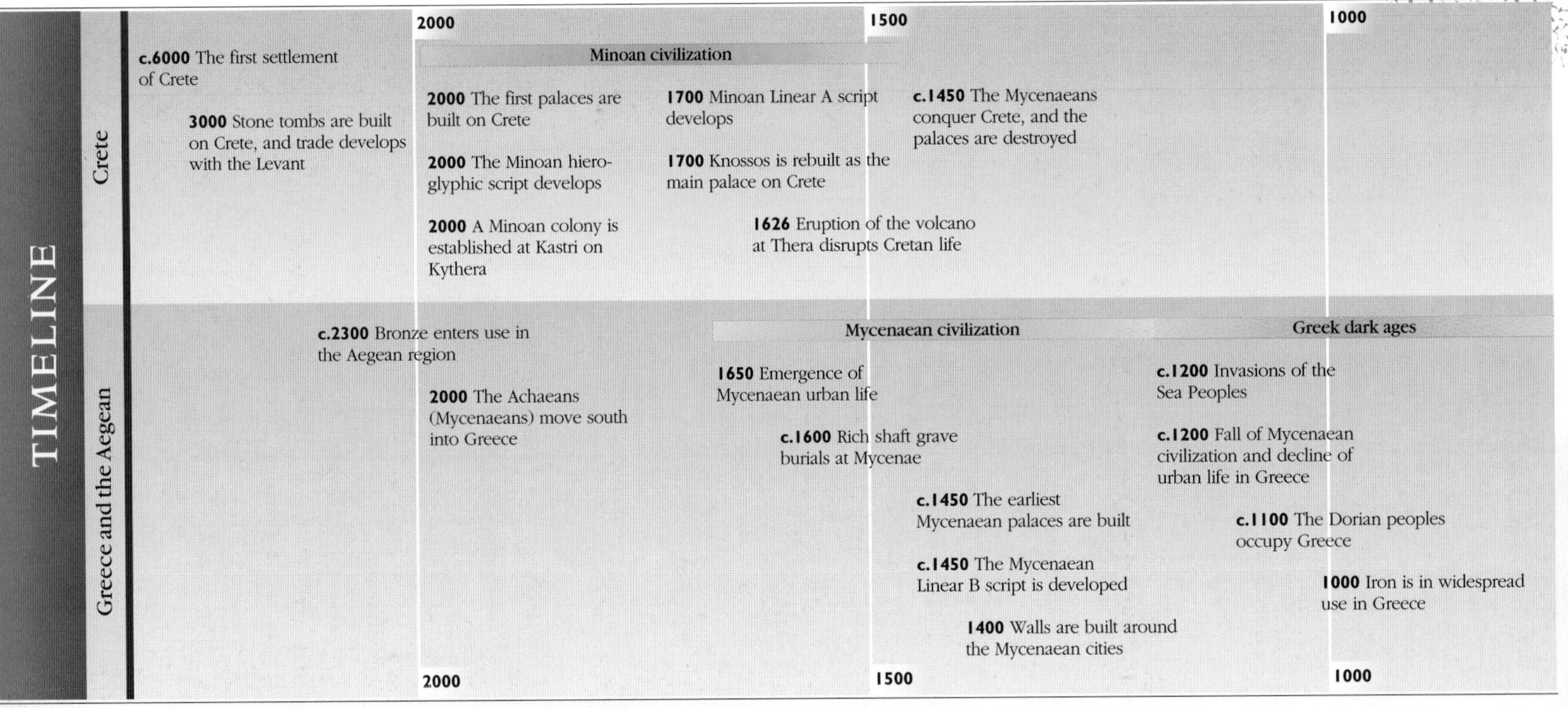

TIMELINE
Crete
Greece and the Aegean
2000
1500
1000
Minoan civilization
c.6000 The first settlement of Crete
3000 Stone tombs are built on Crete, and trade develops with the Levant
2000 The first palaces are built on Crete
2000 The Minoan hieroglyphic script develops
2000 A Minoan colony is established at Kastri on Kythera
1700 Minoan Linear A script develops
1700 Knossos is rebuilt as the main palace on Crete
1626 Eruption of the volcano at Thera disrupts Cretan life
c.1450 The Mycenaeans conquer Crete, and the palaces are destroyed
Mycenaean civilization
Greek dark ages
c.2300 Bronze enters use in the Aegean region
2000 The Achaeans (Mycenaeans) move south into Greece
1650 Emergence of Mycenaean urban life
c.1600 Rich shaft grave burials at Mycenae
c.1450 The earliest Mycenaean palaces are built
c.1450 The Mycenaean Linear B script is developed
1400 Walls are built around the Mycenaean cities
c.1200 Invasions of the Sea Peoples
c.1200 Fall of Mycenaean civilization and decline of urban life in Greece
c.1100 The Dorian peoples occupy Greece
1000 Iron is in widespread use in Greece
2000
1500
1000

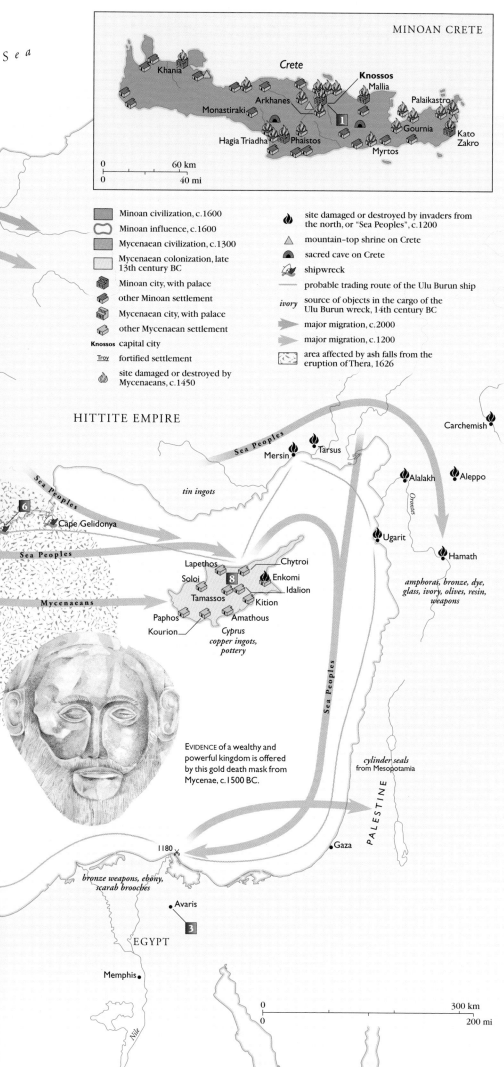

evidence of Mycenaean civilization is a series of richly furnished shaft graves at Mycenae, dating to between 1650 and 1550. The grave goods reveal a wealthy warrior society and include hoards of bronze weapons, gold, silver and electrum tableware, jewelry and gold deathmasks. Mycenaean warriors rode to battle in horse-drawn chariots, but fought on foot with spear, sword and dagger. The towns were well defended, especially after the 14th century, by strong walls, built with massive blocks of stone and bastioned gateways. From the 15th century, Mycenaean rulers were buried in vaulted *tholos* (beehive shaped) tombs in which rituals related to a cult of kingship could be performed.

Each Mycenaean stronghold was ruled over by a king with a warrior aristocracy. The kings controlled many craftsmen – the king of Pylos employed about four hundred bronzesmiths – and hundreds of mainly female slaves. The royal palaces were smaller than those on Crete. According to a survey preserved in Homer's *Iliad*, known as the Catalog of Ships, there were some twenty kingdoms theoretically acknowledging the leadership of Mycenae.

Around 1450 the Mycenaeans expanded in the Aegean, conquering Crete and founding Miletos on the Anatolian coast: they may also have raided Egypt and the Hittite empire and, perhaps, they sacked Troy. They traded throughout the eastern Mediterranean and as far west as Malta, Sicily and Italy.

The Mycenaean civilization came to a violent end around 1200. Most of the major centers were sacked, town life came to an end and writing fell out of use. The whole Aegean entered a dark age which lasted about four centuries. The attackers were probably the Sea Peoples who also brought chaos to Egypt and the Levant. Some Mycenaeans sought refuge on Cyprus and on the coast of Anatolia; others may have joined with the Sea Peoples – Mycenaean influence is evident in Palestine where some of them settled. A power vacuum developed in Greece into which another Greek-speaking people, the Dorians, migrated around 1100, overrunning the Peloponnese, Crete and Rhodes: of the old Mycenaean centers only Athens retained its independence.

1 Knossos, the greatest of the Cretan palaces, was first built around 2000 and was rebuilt several times after earthquake damage or war.

2 The Minoan city of Akrotiri was preserved by ashfalls after the volcanic eruption on Thera in 1626.

3 Avaris was an Egyptian city which contained a Minoan colony founded in about 1550.

4 Mycenae had rich tombs and massive defenses built between 1600 and 1200. According to Homer, its king Agamemnon led the Greeks in the Trojan War.

5 A defensive wall was built across the Isthmus of Corinth in the late 13th century to protect the Peloponnese from invasion from the north.

6 A 14th-century shipwreck found at Ulu Burun near Kas had a cargo from around the east Mediterranean.

7 Troy was sacked twice in the 13th century, and again in 1100.

8 Mycenaeans reached Cyprus in the 15th century but the main settlement was 300 years later.

MINOAN CRETE

Crete
Khania
Knossos
Mallia
Arkhanes
Monastiraki
Palaikastro
Gournia
Kato Zakro
Hagia Triadha
Phaistos
Myrtos
1
0 60 km
0 40 mi

- Minoan civilization, c.1600
- Minoan influence, c.1600
- Mycenaean civilization, c.1300
- Mycenaean colonization, late 13th century BC
- Minoan city, with palace
- other Minoan settlement
- Mycenaean city, with palace
- other Mycenaean settlement
- Knossos capital city
- Troy fortified settlement
- site damaged or destroyed by Mycenaeans, c.1450
- site damaged or destroyed by invaders from the north, or "Sea Peoples", c.1200
- mountain-top shrine on Crete
- sacred cave on Crete
- shipwreck
- probable trading route of the Ulu Burun ship
- *ivory* source of objects in the cargo of the Ulu Burun wreck, 14th century BC
- major migration, c.2000
- major migration, c.1200
- area affected by ash falls from the eruption of Thera, 1626

Sea
HITTITE EMPIRE
Sea Peoples
Mersin
Tarsus
Carchemish
Alalakh
Aleppo
tin ingots
6
Cape Gelidonya
Sea Peoples
Sea Peoples
Ugarit
Orontes
Hamath
Lapethos
Chytroi
Soloi
8
Enkomi
Idalion
Tamassos
Kition
Mycenaeans
Paphos
Amathous
Kourion
Cyprus
copper ingots, pottery
amphoras, bronze, dye, glass, ivory, olives, resin, weapons
Sea Peoples
cylinder seals from Mesopotamia
PALESTINE
Gaza
1180
bronze weapons, ebony, scarab brooches
Avaris
3
EGYPT
Memphis
Nile
0 300 km
0 200 mi

EVIDENCE of a wealthy and powerful kingdom is offered by this gold death mask from Mycenae, c.1500 BC.

See also 1.12 (Sea Peoples); 1.18 (Egypt); 1.24 (Greek city-states)

1.23 Phoenician and Greek expansion in the Mediterranean • 900 – 500 BC •

As the eastern Mediterranean recovered from the disruptions of the late second millennium, the Phoenicians and Greeks began to establish trade routes and colonies throughout the western Mediterranean and, in the case of the Greeks, the Black Sea.

The first to extend their trade routes into the western Mediterranean were the Phoenicians, a Levantine people culturally and linguistically closely related to the Canaanites. The Phoenician homeland had the best natural harbors on the coastline of the Levant, where small ports had grown up as early as the third millennium BC, trading cedar wood, purple dye and other commodities with Egypt. The leading Phoenician ports had developed into independent city-states by 1500 BC. In the earliest records the Phoenician cities were ruled by hereditary kings, but by the 6th century monarchy had been replaced by elected officials. The Phoenician cities never exercised control far inland and for the greater part of their history they were dominated by one or other of the region's great powers.

The earliest evidence of Phoenician expansion overseas is at Kition, originally a Mycenaean colony, on Cyprus about 1000 BC. Cyprus was an important source of copper and had had close trade links with Phoenicia for centuries before this. The main period of Phoenician expansion, however, extended from the late 9th century to the mid 7th century. The main concentration of Phoenician colonies were in Tunisia, Sicily and Sardinia, which gave them control over the main approaches to the western Mediterranean. By the 7th century Carthage, a Tyrian colony, had become the leading Phoenician city in the west. By the 8th century Phoenician trade routes extended through the Straits of Gibraltar and some way along the Atlantic coasts of Spain and Morocco. At first the Phoenicians maintained only seasonal trading posts in this area, but permanent colonies, such as Tingis and Gades, were established in the 7th century. Phoenician colonies technically remained subject to their parent cities, but they were forced to become independent when Phoenicia was conquered by the Babylonians in the 6th century.

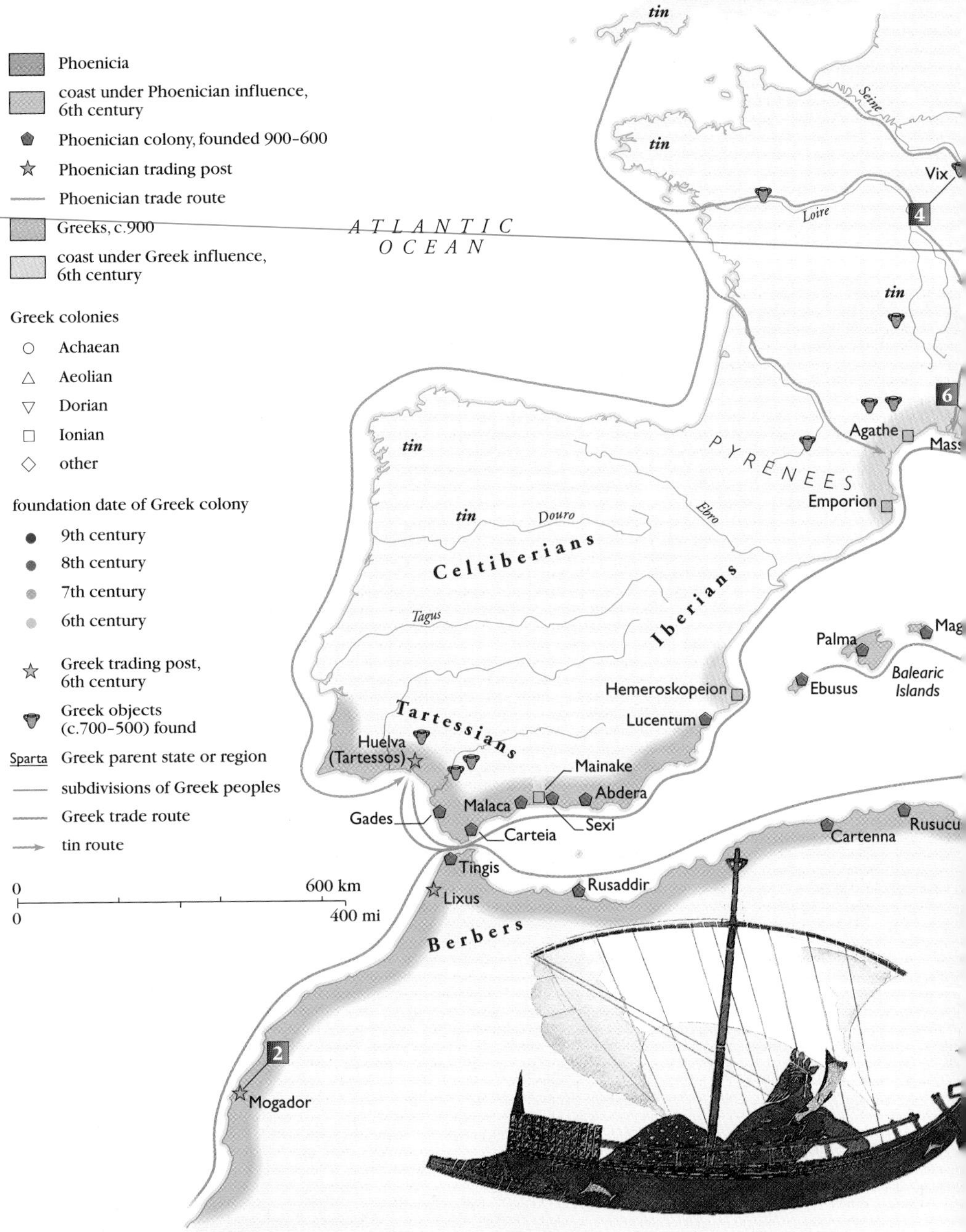

Phoenicia
coast under Phoenician influence, 6th century
Phoenician colony, founded 900–600
Phoenician trading post
Phoenician trade route
Greeks, c.900
coast under Greek influence, 6th century

Greek colonies
Achaean
Aeolian
Dorian
Ionian
other

foundation date of Greek colony
9th century
8th century
7th century
6th century

Greek trading post, 6th century
Greek objects (c.700–500) found
Sparta Greek parent state or region
subdivisions of Greek peoples
Greek trade route
tin route

0 600 km
0 400 mi

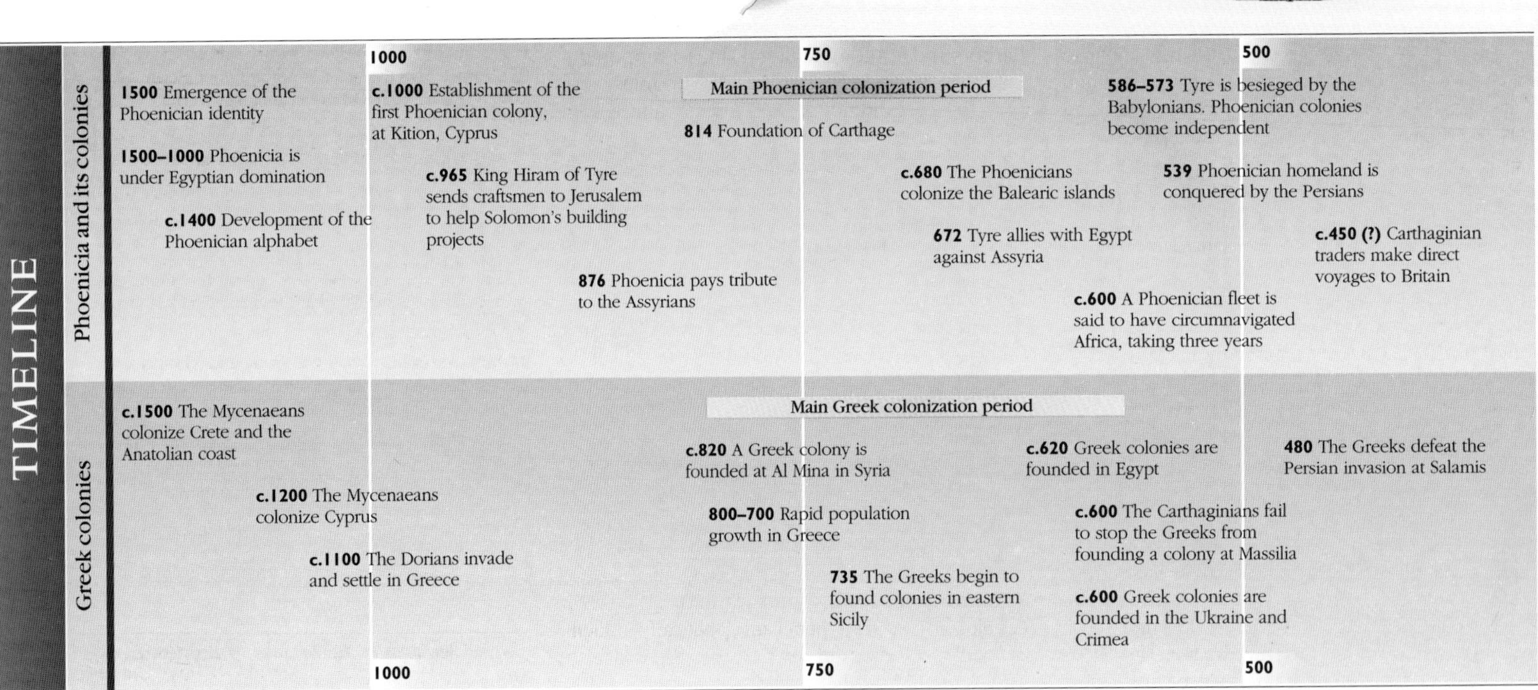
TIMELINE
Phoenicia and its colonies
1000
750
500
1500 Emergence of the Phoenician identity
1500–1000 Phoenicia is under Egyptian domination
c.1400 Development of the Phoenician alphabet
c.1000 Establishment of the first Phoenician colony, at Kition, Cyprus
c.965 King Hiram of Tyre sends craftsmen to Jerusalem to help Solomon's building projects
876 Phoenicia pays tribute to the Assyrians
Main Phoenician colonization period
814 Foundation of Carthage
c.680 The Phoenicians colonize the Balearic islands
672 Tyre allies with Egypt against Assyria
586–573 Tyre is besieged by the Babylonians. Phoenician colonies become independent
539 Phoenician homeland is conquered by the Persians
c.600 A Phoenician fleet is said to have circumnavigated Africa, taking three years
c.450 (?) Carthaginian traders make direct voyages to Britain
Greek colonies
c.1500 The Mycenaeans colonize Crete and the Anatolian coast
c.1200 The Mycenaeans colonize Cyprus
c.1100 The Dorians invade and settle in Greece
Main Greek colonization period
c.820 A Greek colony is founded at Al Mina in Syria
800–700 Rapid population growth in Greece
735 The Greeks begin to found colonies in eastern Sicily
c.620 Greek colonies are founded in Egypt
c.600 The Carthaginians fail to stop the Greeks from founding a colony at Massilia
c.600 Greek colonies are founded in the Ukraine and Crimea
480 The Greeks defeat the Persian invasion at Salamis
1000
750
500

GORGON's head handles and a frieze of soldiers and chariots embellish this head-height bronze *krater* (a vessel for mixing wine and water). Of 6th-century Greek manufacture, it was found at Vix, France

SHIPBUILDING and navigation were essential skills. This detail of a vase painting c.540 shows the god Dionysus at sea (having escaped capture by pirates).

For almost three centuries after the collapse of the Mycenaean civilization, Greece remained impoverished and isolated. Recovery began around 900 as the Greeks reestablished trade links with the Levant and Italy. By the 8th century prosperity had returned, urban life was restored and the Greek population was rising rapidly. The earliest Greek overseas colonies, such as Al Mina in Syria and Pithekoussai and Kymai in Italy, were motivated by trade. The earliest long-distance trade was in iron ore, slaves and luxury goods; in return the Greeks offered wine and acted as middlemen. Even before the end of the 8th century, colonies had also become a way for the Greek cities to resettle surplus population. Often colonists were chosen by lot. Most active as colonizers were the Ionian Greeks, descendants of the Mycenaeans, and the Dorians. The Greek colonies, unlike Phoenician colonies, were founded from the outset to be independent states in their own right, although relations with the parent states often remained close.

The Greeks initially looked west. The first major colonizing efforts in the 8th century were in southern Italy and Sicily, where there were many good harbors and fertile agricultural land to support the colonists. Relations with the native peoples were poor, but that did not prevent Greek culture from having a great impact in Italy, especially on the Etruscans in the north. The Italian colonies were initially highly successful – Syracuse, for example, was the most populous Greek city in the 5th century – but the constant hostility of the natives sapped their strength and by the 3rd century they were in decline. Further west in the Mediterranean, the Greeks faced the opposition of the Phoenicians but Massilia was founded around 600. The Celtic chiefs of Gaul prospered greatly from trade with the Greeks, as the superb quality of Greek artifacts found in burials, such as that at Vix, shows.

In the 7th and 6th centuries the effort of colonization shifted to the coasts of Thrace and the Black Sea. The Greek colonies here traded luxury goods with the steppe peoples for wheat to feed the cities of the Greek homeland. The same period also saw colonies founded in Cyrenaica and Egypt. The Greek colonies in Egypt became politically influential and through them the Greeks gained a deep knowledge of Egyptian art and architecture.

1 Carthage was the most important Phoenician colony, founded in 814. It became a powerful independent state in the 6th century.

2 Phoenician trading posts on the African coast, such as Mogador, were occupied for only part of the year.

3 The Scythians traded grain with the Greek Black Sea colonies in return for luxury goods

4 The burial mound at Vix of a 6th-century Celtic princess has yielded some of the finest Greek bronzework yet found.

5 Syracuse, founded by Corinth around 733, became the wealthiest and most powerful of the western Greek colonies.

6 Massilia, founded around 600 to exploit the tin trade, declined after 500 when the trade routes shifted to the Atlantic and the Alpine passes.

7 Greek mercenaries played a key role in Egyptian armies around 600.

See also 1.14 (Bible lands), 1.22 (Mycenaeans), 1.24 (Mainland Greece), 1.25 (Carthage)

1.24 The emergence of the Greek city-states • 1100 – 500 BC •

During the dark ages (1200–800 BC), the Greeks lived in tribal communities under chiefs or kings who combined the roles of warleader and chief priest but who had to consult a council of elders and the warrior aristocracy. Their subjects sometimes paid tribute to the kings, but there was no regular system of taxation. There were no palaces, and kings lived in houses distinguished from those of their subjects only by their greater size. Town life almost ceased and such long-distance trade as survived was controlled by the Phoenicians. War, hunting and lavish displays of hospitality were the hallmarks of dark-age Greek culture. One of the most important developments of the period was that iron replaced bronze.

By the 9th century power began to pass to the hereditary aristocracy, and by the end of the 7th century only Sparta, Argos and Thera still had monarchies. Little is known about the institutions of aristocratic government but it was under their rule that trade and city life revived in Greece and that Greek colonization overseas began. The *polis* (city-state) became the dominant form of political organization. The cities dominated the countryside and became the main centers of political power, commerce and cultural life. The revival of trade made it necessary to re-invent writing in the 8th century, as the Mycenaean script had been entirely forgotten. The Greeks adopted the Phoenician consonantal alphabet and by adding separate signs for vowels turned it into a far more flexible and simple writing system. As a result writing became a common accomplishment in Greece. This was to be a major factor in the brilliant flowering of Greek civilization in the 6th and 5th century.

In the 7th century aristocratic government became unpopular. New military tactics, involving large numbers of heavily armed infantry, deprived them of their status as a warrior elite. There was discontent also among the newly rich who, not having aristocratic birth, were excluded from political power. In many Greek city-states these discontents led, between 660 and 485, to revolutions under popular leaders known as "tyrants" (a term describing rulers who had gained power through their own efforts, rather than by virtue of birth). Most tyrannies endured only a few decades before they were overthrown and replaced with "oligarchies", in which the aristocracy was influential but had no monopoly on power. Other Greek city-states reformed their constitutions without revolutions and by the 6th century most were ruled by oligarchies: the remaining strongholds of aristocratic power were in the north of Greece, where there were few cities, and in Sicily.

The most far-reaching political upheavals took place in Athens. Faced with mounting internal problems, the Athenians sought to avoid revolution by

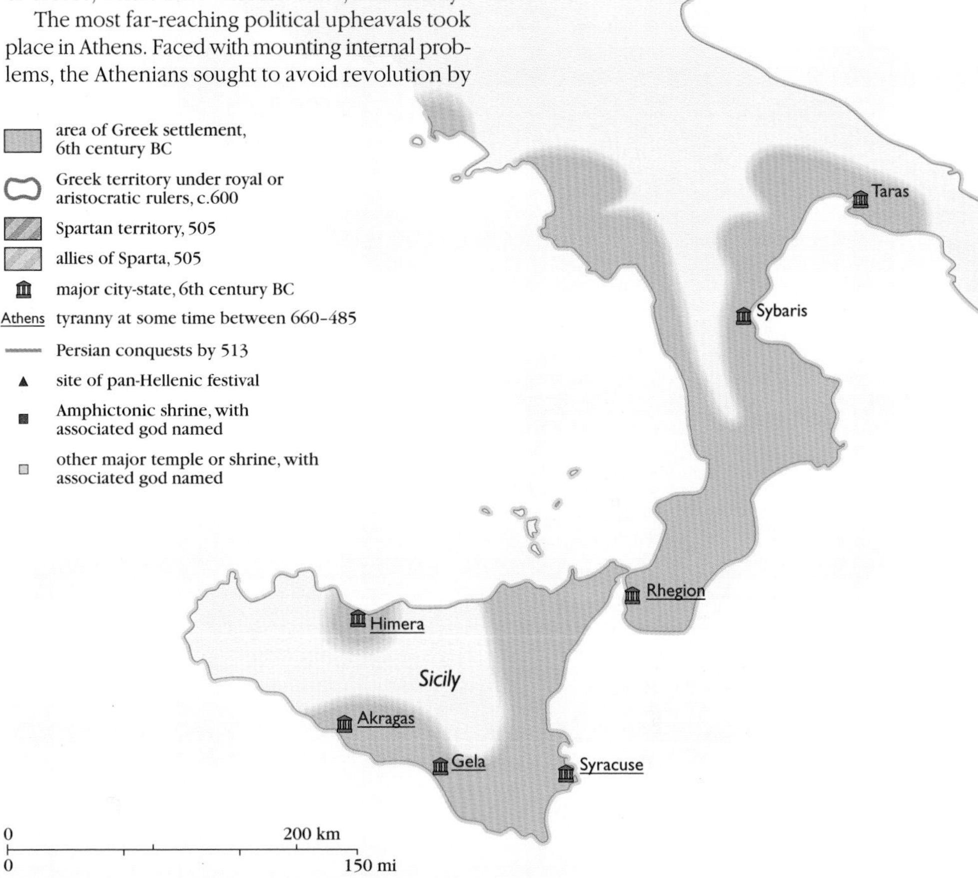

area of Greek settlement, 6th century BC
Greek territory under royal or aristocratic rulers, c.600
Spartan territory, 505
allies of Sparta, 505
major city-state, 6th century BC
Athens tyranny at some time between 660–485
Persian conquests by 513
site of pan-Hellenic festival
Amphictonic shrine, with associated god named
other major temple or shrine, with associated god named
Taras
Sybaris
Rhegion
Himera
Sicily
Akragas
Gela
Syracuse
0
200 km
0
150 mi

TIMELINE

Political change

- **c.900** Foundation of Sparta
- **900–800** The first city-states are established in Ionia and Aeolia.
- **c.800** Foundation of Corinth
- **c.800** Beginning of the main period of Greek expansion overseas
- **800–750** Sparta conquers Laconia
- **700–650** The "phalanx" infantry formation is developed
- **683** End of the monarchy in Athens
- **657–580** Corinth, the leading power in Greece, is ruled by a tyranny
- **c.640** The kingdom of Macedon is founded
- **594** Solon reforms the Athenian constitution
- **560–510** Rule of the tyrants in Athens
- **c.560** Sparta is the leading military power in Greece
- **546–540** The Persians conquer Ionia
- **509–507** A democratic constitution is implemented in Athens
- **480** The Greeks defeat the Persians at Salamis

Cultural change

- **800–700** The population begins to rise in Greece
- **776** The earliest known Olympic Games are held
- **c.750** Homer composes the *Iliad* and the *Odyssey*
- **c.750** The Greek alphabet is developed
- **c.650** Written law codes are created in Greece
- **c.650** A strong eastern influence is felt on Greek art
- **c.600** Coinage is adopted in the Greek mainland
- **c.580** A distinctive school of philosophy emerges in Ionia
- **550–500** Egyptian influences are felt on Greek art and architecture

800 700 600 500

1 A century of far-reaching political reforms transformed Athens from a backwater in 600 into a leading state in 500.

2 Regarded by the Greeks as a barbarian kingdom, Macedon had a mixed population of Illyrians, Thracians and Dorian Greeks.

3 Olympia was the wealthiest religious center in Greece; pan-Hellenic games were held in honor of Zeus every four years from 776 BC to AD 393.

4 The oracle of Apollo at Delphi was widely consulted by the Greek states on important political matters; it was famous for its ambiguous answers.

5 Corinth benefited from its strategic position on the isthmus between the Gulf of Corinth and the Aegean Sea to become a major trading power.

6 The Ionians were the most culturally sophisticated Greeks in the 7th and 6th centuries, taking advantage of close links with the Middle Eastern civilizations.

7 Argos was a bitter rival of Sparta for control of the Peloponnese from the 7th to the 5th century.

8 Coinage was introduced by Lydian kings in about 700; its use had spread to Greece by about 600.

BURIED under the ruins of the Acropolis when the Persians attacked Athens in 480, this marble *kore* (maiden) would once have been brightly painted.

appointing Solon to reform the constitution in 594. The result was a compromise that satisfied nobody and in 546 the tyrant Peisistratus seized power. Peisistratus was an effective and popular ruler who broke the aristocratic hold on power and did much to address the problems of the peasantry. Peisistratos was succeeded by his less able son Hippias who was overthrown by an aristocratic faction in 510. After three years of internal strife the aristocratic party was defeated. The reformer Kleisthenes "took the people into partnership" and introduced a democratic constitution which gave all 45,000 male citizens the right to attend the assembly and vote on all major decisions and appointments.

By actively involving its citizens in government, Athens had become a self-confident and assertive state by 500, but for most of the 6th century the most powerful state was Sparta, which had taken the lead in developing new infantry tactics in which armored spearmen fought in a close-packed phalanx, presenting an impenetrable hedge of spears to the enemy. Sparta formed a league of similar cities based on a hoplite franchise, through which it dominated the Peloponnese.

The first Greeks to fall under Persian power were the Ionians on the Anatolian coast. Since about 600 the Ionians had paid tribute to the kings of Lydia but relations were good: the Greeks adopted coinage as a result of Lydian influences and the Lydians themselves became increasingly Hellenized. Persian rule was not particularly oppressive but it was more unpopular than the loose control of the Lydians.

Despite their rivalries, Greeks had a strong sense of common identity by the 8th century, expressed through the name they gave themselves – Hellenes – and by religion. All Greeks worshiped the same gods and celebrated pan-Hellenic festivals, such as the Olympic Games, during which hostilities had to cease. The neutrality of shrines of pan-Hellenic importance was protected and supported by leagues (*amphictonies*) of neighboring states, such as the Amphictony of Delphi. A cultural heritage had also emerged, epitomized by the epic poems of Homer, which were composed in the 8th century.

See also 1.15 (Persia), 1.22 (Minoans and Mycenaeans), 1.25 (western Mediterranean)

1.25 Etruscans, Greeks and Carthaginians • 800 – 480 BC •

The first cities and states in the western Mediterranean developed in the early Iron Age. The first were the Etruscan city-states of northern Italy, which had emerged by 800 BC. Then in the 8th century many cities were founded on the coasts of southern Italy, France, Spain and north Africa by Phoenician and Greek colonists. The Greeks had a strong impact on the Etruscan civilization while the Phoenician colonies in Spain influenced the growth of cities and states among the native Tartessian, Turdetanian and Iberian peoples by 500 BC.

The origin of the Etruscans is uncertain. Their language was unrelated to any other European language, suggesting that the Etruscans may have migrated into Italy from the Middle East. There is no convincing evidence of this, however, and it is more likely that the Etruscans were an indigenous people. The forerunner of the Etruscan civilization was the Villanova culture – the first iron-using culture in Italy – which developed in Tuscany around 900 and later spread north into the Po valley. This culture itself seems to have developed out of local Urnfield cultures. In Tuscany the Villanova culture was replaced by the Etruscan civilization in the 8th century BC but it survived in the Po valley until the 6th century, when the area was overrun by the Etruscans.

Etruria was rich in iron and copper ores, had good agricultural land and a coastline with many natural harbors, which encouraged the Etruscans to become active seafarers and traders. Most early Etruscan cities were sited a few kilometers from the coast, close enough for convenience but not vulnerable to pirate raids. Each city was an independent state ruled by a king but the twelve most important cities were loosely united in the Etruscan league. From the 8th century the Etruscans faced competition from Greek and Phoenician colonies in the western Mediterranean. The foundation of the Greek colony at Massilia around 600 was a particularly serious development as it shut the Etruscans out of the important trans-Gallic tin routes. To some extent this was offset by Etruscan expansion into the Po valley in the 6th century, which brought them control of the transalpine and Adriatic trade routes and diverted some trade away from the Greek colonies. With Carthaginian help, the Etruscans succeeded in driving the Greeks out of Corsica in 535 but attacks on the Greeks at Kymai (Cumae) in southern Italy were repulsed in 524, 505 and 474. Despite these hostilities, Etruscan culture had become very Hellenized by the 6th century.

The other major group of peoples in Italy were the Italic speakers who had probably migrated into Italy from central Europe during Urnfield times. Though most of the Italic peoples were still organized into tribes in 500 BC, city-states had developed among the Latins as a result of Etruscan influence. The leading Latin city was Rome. The Romans expelled their Etruscan king in 509 and founded a republic but Rome was still little more than a market town.

Carthage was not the earliest Phoenician colony in north Africa but its fine harbor and strategic position had made it into the most important by the mid 7th century.

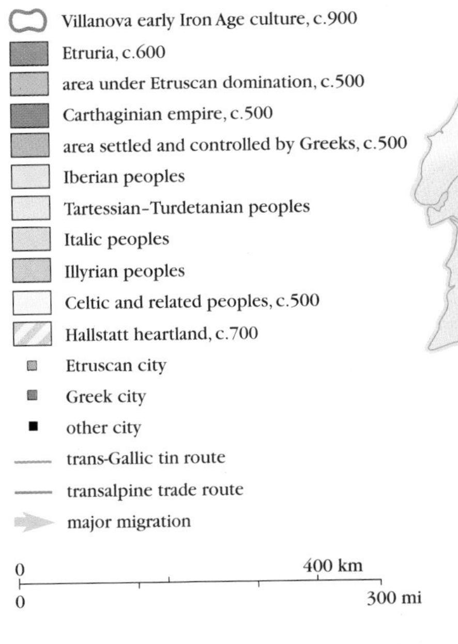

Villanova early Iron Age culture, c.900
Etruria, c.600
area under Etruscan domination, c.500
Carthaginian empire, c.500
area settled and controlled by Greeks, c.500
Iberian peoples
Tartessian–Turdetanian peoples
Italic peoples
Illyrian peoples
Celtic and related peoples, c.500
Hallstatt heartland, c.700
Etruscan city
Greek city
other city
trans-Gallic tin route
transalpine trade route
major migration
0
400 km
0
300 mi

ATLANTIC OCEAN

Elviña
Coaña
Rianxo
Cameixa
El Redal
Ebro
Cortes de Navarra
Douro
Azaila
Terroso
Soldeana
Celtiberians
Lusitanians
Iberi
Tagus
Saguntum
Guadiana
Pedra de Oiro
Hemeroskopei
KINGDOM OF TARTESSOS c.600
Lucentum
Elche
Tartessians
Guadalquivir
Porcuna
Niebla
El Carambolo
Turdetanians
Tartessos (Huelva)
Osuna
1
Mainake
Gades
Malaca
Sexi
Abdera
Carteia
Tingis
Lixus
Rusaddir
Berbers

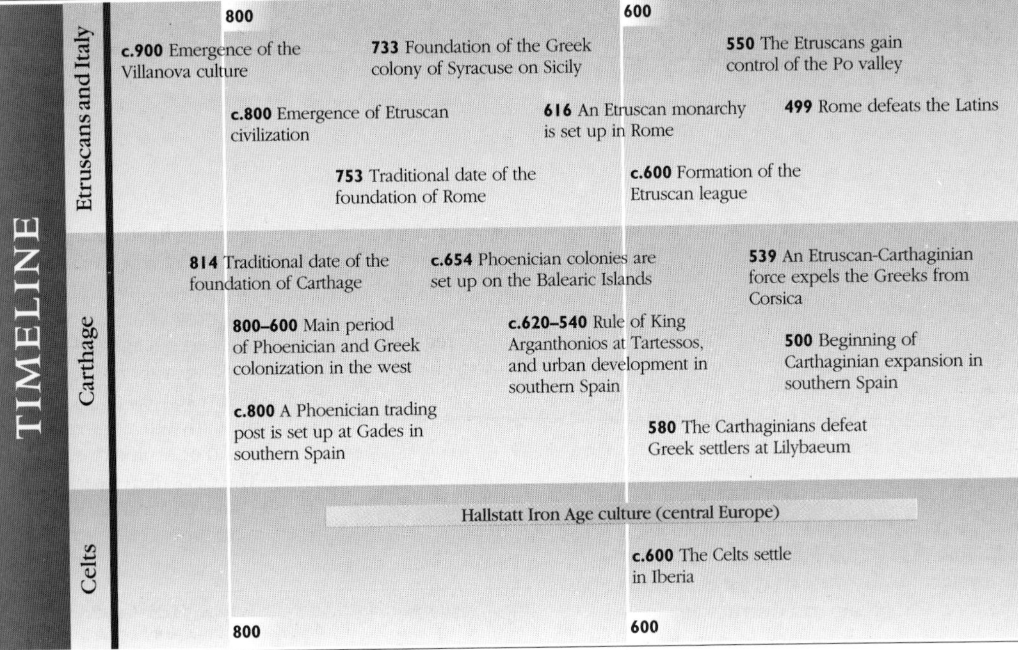

TIMELINE
Etruscans and Italy
800
600
c.900 Emergence of the Villanova culture
733 Foundation of the Greek colony of Syracuse on Sicily
550 The Etruscans gain control of the Po valley
c.800 Emergence of Etruscan civilization
616 An Etruscan monarchy is set up in Rome
499 Rome defeats the Latins
753 Traditional date of the foundation of Rome
c.600 Formation of the Etruscan league
Carthage
814 Traditional date of the foundation of Carthage
c.654 Phoenician colonies are set up on the Balearic Islands
539 An Etruscan-Carthaginian force expels the Greeks from Corsica
800–600 Main period of Phoenician and Greek colonization in the west
c.620–540 Rule of King Arganthonios at Tartessos, and urban development in southern Spain
500 Beginning of Carthaginian expansion in southern Spain
c.800 A Phoenician trading post is set up at Gades in southern Spain
580 The Carthaginians defeat Greek settlers at Lilybaeum
Celts
Hallstatt Iron Age culture (central Europe)
c.600 The Celts settle in Iberia
800
600

1 By 600 BC, Tartessos was the capital of a wealthy kingdom, and the region saw rapid urban growth under Phoenician and Carthaginian influence in the 6th century.

2 The Hallstatt Iron Age culture (c.750–450) is named for a rich cemetery at an ancient salt-mining center in the Austrian Alps.

3 The stone defenses of the 6th-century Celtic fort at Heuneburg show the influence of Greek architecture.

4 Until the end of the 6th century, the main importance of the small market town of Rome was its control of the main crossing point of the river Tiber.

5 The Lipari Islands were the base for Greek pirates in the 6th and 5th centuries.

6 A joint Carthaginian–Etruscan force defeated the Greeks off Corsica in 539, halting Greek colonization in the western Mediterranean.

7 Populonia was the main iron-working center of Italy from the 6th century; around 10,000 tonnes of iron ore were imported from Elba and smelted there annually.

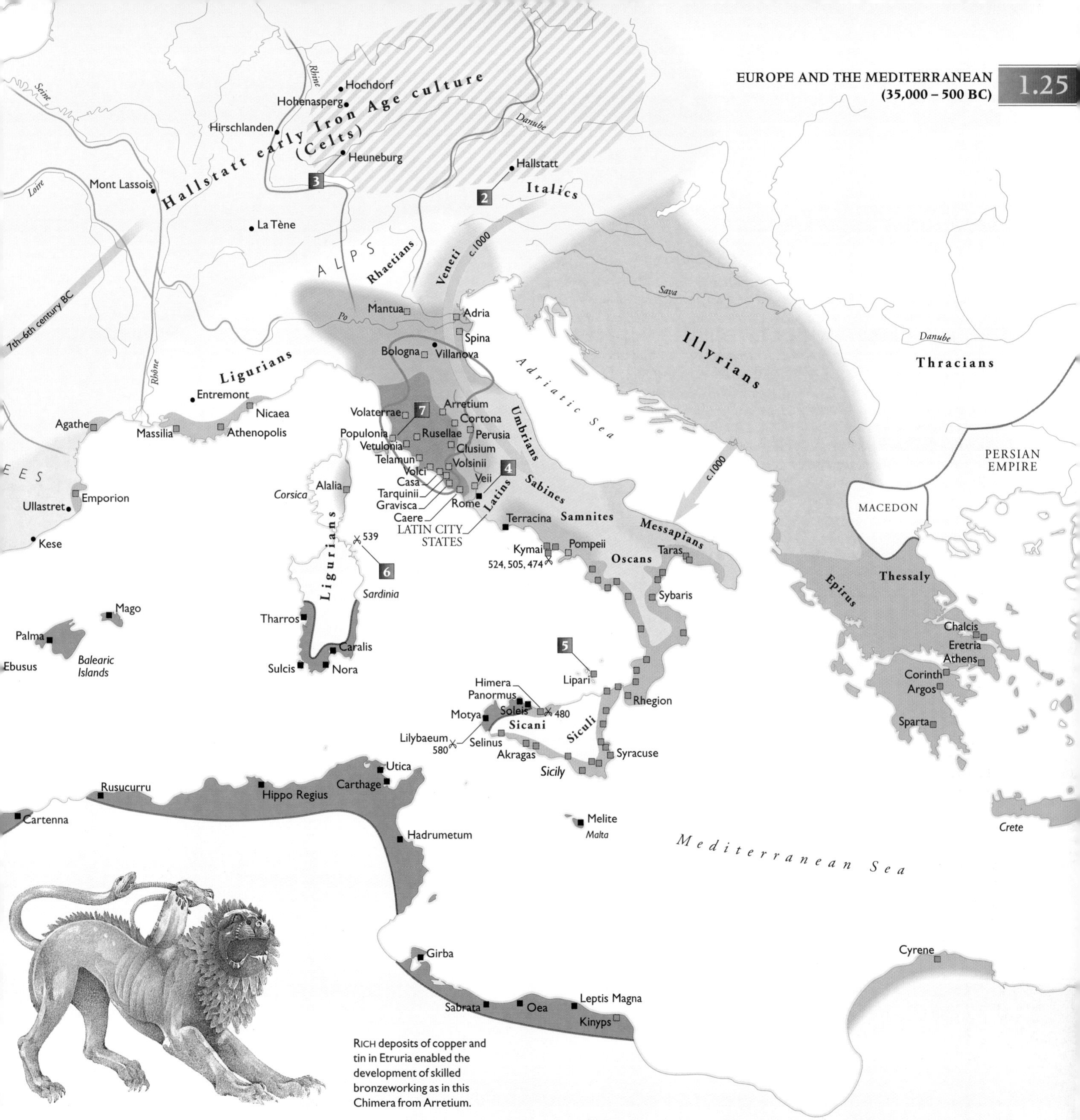

RICH deposits of copper and tin in Etruria enabled the development of skilled bronzeworking as in this Chimera from Arretium.

Although technically still subject to its parent city Tyre, Carthage had by this time begun its own independent colonization of the Balearic Islands. In 580 Carthage intervened in Sicily to protect Motya against the Greek city of Selinus and shortly after to support the Phoenician colonies in Sardinia against the natives. These actions established Carthage as the protector of the Phoenician colonies in the west, and by 500 it had become the capital of a loose-knit maritime empire which dominated the western Mediterranean trade routes. The Greeks, however, succeeded in gaining control of most of Sicily in 480.

The area most influenced by the Phoenicians and Carthaginians was southern Spain. Gades (Cadiz) was an important Phoenician trading post from at least the 8th century, if not earlier, and Huelva – almost certainly the ancient city of Tartessos – was a port with trading links with the Greeks, Phoenicians and Atlantic Europe by around 800. Excavations at Huelva have yielded huge quantities of imported pottery. Huelva's prosperity was based on exports of silver and other metals from southern Spain and of tin from Galicia, Brittany and Cornwall. By the 6th century a Tartessian kingdom had developed and fortified towns were being founded in the Guadalquivir valley. Phoenician techniques were incorporated into local metalworking and sculpture and a script based on the Phoenician alphabet was adopted. Urban development was also beginning in the Iberian area on the east coast of Spain by 500. Here too a Phoenician-based script was adopted.

The dominant influence in west and central Europe in the 7th and 6th centuries was the Hallstatt culture, which is generally identified with the Celts. The Hallstatt culture began to develop in the 12th century BC from the Urnfield cultures of the upper Danube region. Bronze-using in its earlier stages, the Hallstatt culture adopted iron working in about 750. In the early 7th century the Celts spread west across Germany and France and by the early 6th century they had crossed the Pyrenees and occupied over half of the Iberian peninsula. The Celts there were quickly assimilated with the native peoples to produce a distinctive Celtiberian culture.

See also 1.21 (Bronze Age Europe), 1.23 (Greek and Phoenician colonization)

1.26 The first civilizations of south Asia • 6000 – 500 BC •

The first civilization of south Asia emerged in the Indus river valley around 2600 BC. The Indus civilization covered the greatest geographical extent of the Bronze Age civilizations. In its origins it resembled the Mesopotamian civilization, arising on the arid flood plain of a great and unpredictable river where the need for large-scale irrigation and flood defense schemes led to the development of a well-organized hierarchical society.

The first farming communities in south Asia developed at sites such as Mehrgarh in the mountains of Baluchistan as early as 6000 BC and spread from there into the Indus valley in the 4th millennium. There was considerable interaction between the valley settlements and those in the highlands. Highland peoples took their flocks to winter in the valley and traded metals, semiprecious stones and timber for grain and other foodstuffs. The early farming communities of the Indus valley showed no signs of social ranking, but the transition to a hierarchical society occurred very rapidly in about 2600 BC. This may have been a result of the establishment of trading contacts with Mesopotamia. Towns grew up in the Indus valley as a result of this trade. The metals and other products of the highlands were gathered in the towns and sent on to Mesopotamia: a shipment of 5,900 kilograms of copper was recorded on one occasion. The growth of trade also led to the development of small towns, such as Nindowari, in the highlands.

Most of the cities and towns in the Indus valley were small but two, Mohenjo-Daro and Harappa (from which the Indus civilization gets its alternative name, "Harappan"), had populations of around 30,000–40,000, placing them among the largest Bronze Age cities anywhere. Both Mohenjo-Daro and Harappa, as well as several of the smaller cities such as Kalibangan, had impressive mud-brick city walls, a citadel with public buildings and granaries and streets laid out on a grid pattern. The civilization was literate but its pictographic script has not been deciphered. As a result, the identity of the Indus people is unknown: they may have been related to the modern Dravidian peoples of southern India.

By 1800 BC the Indus cities were in decline and a century later they had been abandoned. Writing fell

farming settlement, c.6000
spread of farming, c.4000–3000
Kulli complex, c.4000–3000
Banas culture, c.2200–1500
major settlement of Indus valley civilization, 2600–1700
minor settlement of Indus valley civilization, 2600–1700
Harappa possible capital
ancient river course
desert

0 400 km
0 300 mi

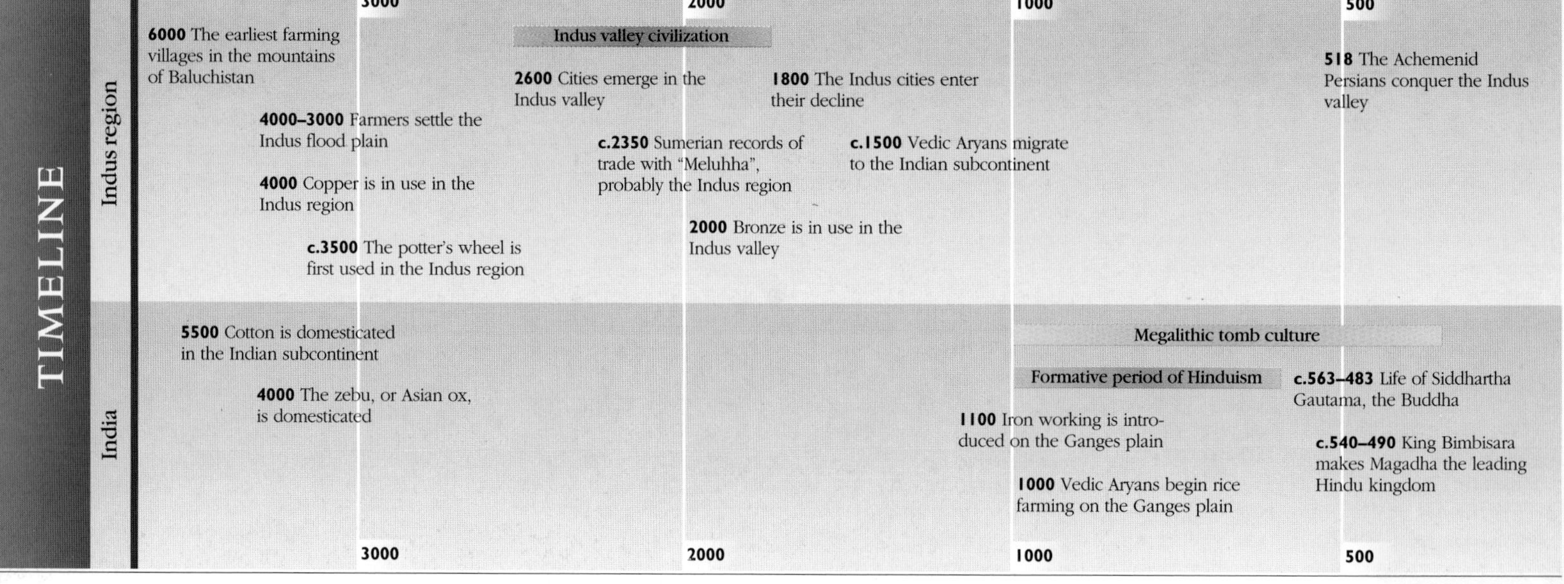

TIMELINE
Indus region
India
3000
2000
1000
500
6000 The earliest farming villages in the mountains of Baluchistan
4000–3000 Farmers settle the Indus flood plain
4000 Copper is in use in the Indus region
c.3500 The potter's wheel is first used in the Indus region
Indus valley civilization
2600 Cities emerge in the Indus valley
c.2350 Sumerian records of trade with "Meluhha", probably the Indus region
2000 Bronze is in use in the Indus valley
1800 The Indus cities enter their decline
c.1500 Vedic Aryans migrate to the Indian subcontinent
518 The Achemenid Persians conquer the Indus valley
5500 Cotton is domesticated in the Indian subcontinent
4000 The zebu, or Asian ox, is domesticated
Megalithic tomb culture
Formative period of Hinduism
1100 Iron working is introduced on the Ganges plain
1000 Vedic Aryans begin rice farming on the Ganges plain
c.563–483 Life of Siddhartha Gautama, the Buddha
c.540–490 King Bimbisara makes Magadha the leading Hindu kingdom
3000
2000
1000
500

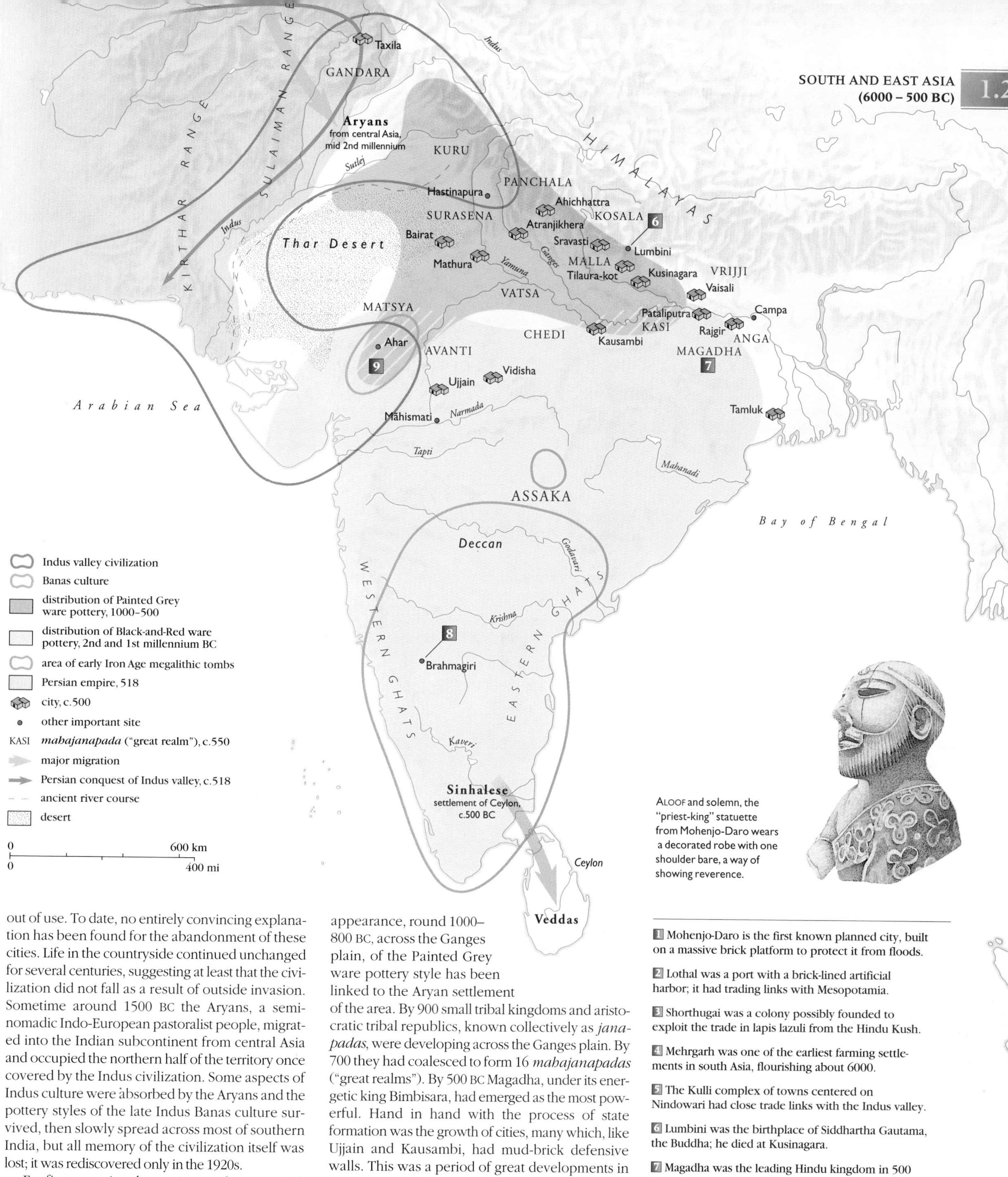
Taxila
GANDARA
SULAIMAN RANGE
KIRTHAR RANGE
Indus
Aryans
from central Asia,
mid 2nd millennium
KURU
Sutlej
HIMALAYAS
PANCHALA
Hastinapura
Ahichhattra
SURASENA
Atranjikhera
KOSALA
6
Thar Desert
Bairat
Sravasti
Lumbini
Mathura
Yamuna
Ganges
MALLA
Tilaura-kot
Kusinagara
VRIJJI
Vaisali
VATSA
MATSYA
Pataliputra
KASI
Campa
Rajgir
ANGA
CHEDI
Kausambi
Ahar
AVANTI
MAGADHA
9
7
Vidisha
Ujjain
Arabian Sea
Mahismati
Narmada
Tamluk
Tapti
Mahanadi
ASSAKA
Bay of Bengal
Deccan
Godavari
WESTERN GHATS
EASTERN GHATS
Krishna
8
Brahmagiri
Kaveri
Sinhalese
settlement of Ceylon,
c.500 BC
Ceylon
Veddas
Indus valley civilization
Banas culture
distribution of Painted Grey ware pottery, 1000–500
distribution of Black-and-Red ware pottery, 2nd and 1st millennium BC
area of early Iron Age megalithic tombs
Persian empire, 518
city, c.500
other important site
KASI *mahajanapada* ("great realm"), c.550
major migration
Persian conquest of Indus valley, c.518
ancient river course
desert
0 600 km
0 400 mi

ALOOF and solemn, the "priest-king" statuette from Mohenjo-Daro wears a decorated robe with one shoulder bare, a way of showing reverence.

out of use. To date, no entirely convincing explanation has been found for the abandonment of these cities. Life in the countryside continued unchanged for several centuries, suggesting at least that the civilization did not fall as a result of outside invasion. Sometime around 1500 BC the Aryans, a semi-nomadic Indo-European pastoralist people, migrated into the Indian subcontinent from central Asia and occupied the northern half of the territory once covered by the Indus civilization. Some aspects of Indus culture were absorbed by the Aryans and the pottery styles of the late Indus Banas culture survived, then slowly spread across most of southern India, but all memory of the civilization itself was lost; it was rediscovered only in the 1920s.

For five centuries, the semi-nomadic Aryans left little physical trace of their presence, but a mythic record of their migrations and wars with the indigenous peoples has been preserved in the *Vedic Hymns*. These, the holiest books of the Hindu religion, were transmitted orally for centuries until they were written down in the 6th century BC. Around 1100 BC the Aryans adopted iron working, possibly independently of outside influence, and soon afterward they moved east and began to settle down in villages on the Ganges plain as rice farmers. The appearance, round 1000–800 BC, across the Ganges plain, of the Painted Grey ware pottery style has been linked to the Aryan settlement of the area. By 900 small tribal kingdoms and aristocratic tribal republics, known collectively as *janapadas*, were developing across the Ganges plain. By 700 they had coalesced to form 16 *mahajanapadas* ("great realms"). By 500 BC Magadha, under its energetic king Bimbisara, had emerged as the most powerful. Hand in hand with the process of state formation was the growth of cities, many which, like Ujjain and Kausambi, had mud-brick defensive walls. This was a period of great developments in religion: it was the formative period of the Hindu religion and the late 6th century witnessed the lives and teachings of Mahavira, the founder of Jainism, and of Siddhartha Gautama, the Buddha.

By 500 BC the Gangetic civilization extended as far south as the River Godavari. South of this were iron-using, tribally organized farming peoples, many of whom buried their dead in megalithic cists (box-shaped tombs). Only towards the end of the 1st millennium did state formation and urban development start in this area.

1 Mohenjo-Daro is the first known planned city, built on a massive brick platform to protect it from floods.

2 Lothal was a port with a brick-lined artificial harbor; it had trading links with Mesopotamia.

3 Shorthugai was a colony possibly founded to exploit the trade in lapis lazuli from the Hindu Kush.

4 Mehrgarh was one of the earliest farming settlements in south Asia, flourishing about 6000.

5 The Kulli complex of towns centered on Nindowari had close trade links with the Indus valley.

6 Lumbini was the birthplace of Siddhartha Gautama, the Buddha; he died at Kusinagara.

7 Magadha was the leading Hindu kingdom in 500 BC, later forming the center of the Mauryan empire.

8 Brahmagiri is a major site of the south Indian Iron Age megalithic, with 300 tombs and stone circles.

9 Black-and-Red ware pottery appeared in the Banas region in late Indus times and spread across southern India after 1800 BC.

See also 1.10 (Mesopotamia), 1.15 (Persia), 2.22 (Mauryan India)

1.27 The first civilizations of east Asia • 6000 – 500 BC •

The first civilization of east Asia developed in the Yellow river valley in the 18th century BC from indigenous Neolithic cultures. Farming began as early as 5800 BC on the broad band of loess soils that stretches across the Yellow river basin. By 5000 millet farming villages of the Yangshao culture were spread across much of the region. At the same time rice farming communities were spreading among the wetlands of the Yangtze valley. Rice farming spread to the Yellow river valley in the late 4th millennium and the Longshan cultures emerged. In favorable areas, the Longshan cultures practiced intensive rice cultivation using irrigation. The population rose, copper came into use, regional trading networks developed and a warrior class emerged. There is evidence of warfare, such as rammed earth fortifications and massacres of prisoners. A system of divination based on the use of "oracle bones" was developed.

According to Chinese traditions, civilization was founded by the emperor Huang Di around 2698 BC while the first dynasty, the Xia, was founded by Yu the Great in about 2205. However, there is no evidence for states in China in the 3rd millennium BC.

The first historically and archeologically attested Chinese dynasty is the Shang. This was founded about 1766 BC by King Tang, around the time of the appearance of the Erlitou culture. Cities with monumental buildings began to develop craft specialization and advanced bronze-casting techniques were adopted. The appearance of rich burials points to the emergence of a powerful ruling elite. A pictographic script came into use: the modern Chinese script is its direct descendant. Shang cultural influence extended across most of northern China and as far south as the Yangtze river. Like many early states, the Shang kingdom combined directly run provinces and vassal states.

Around 1122 the Shang king Di-xin was defeated and overthrown by his vassal king Wu of Zhou. The dynasty established by Wu became the longest lived of Chinese history and the early centuries of its rule were looked back on as a golden age. To legitimize their rule after their usurpation of the Shang, the Zhou rulers introduced the theory of the "Mandate

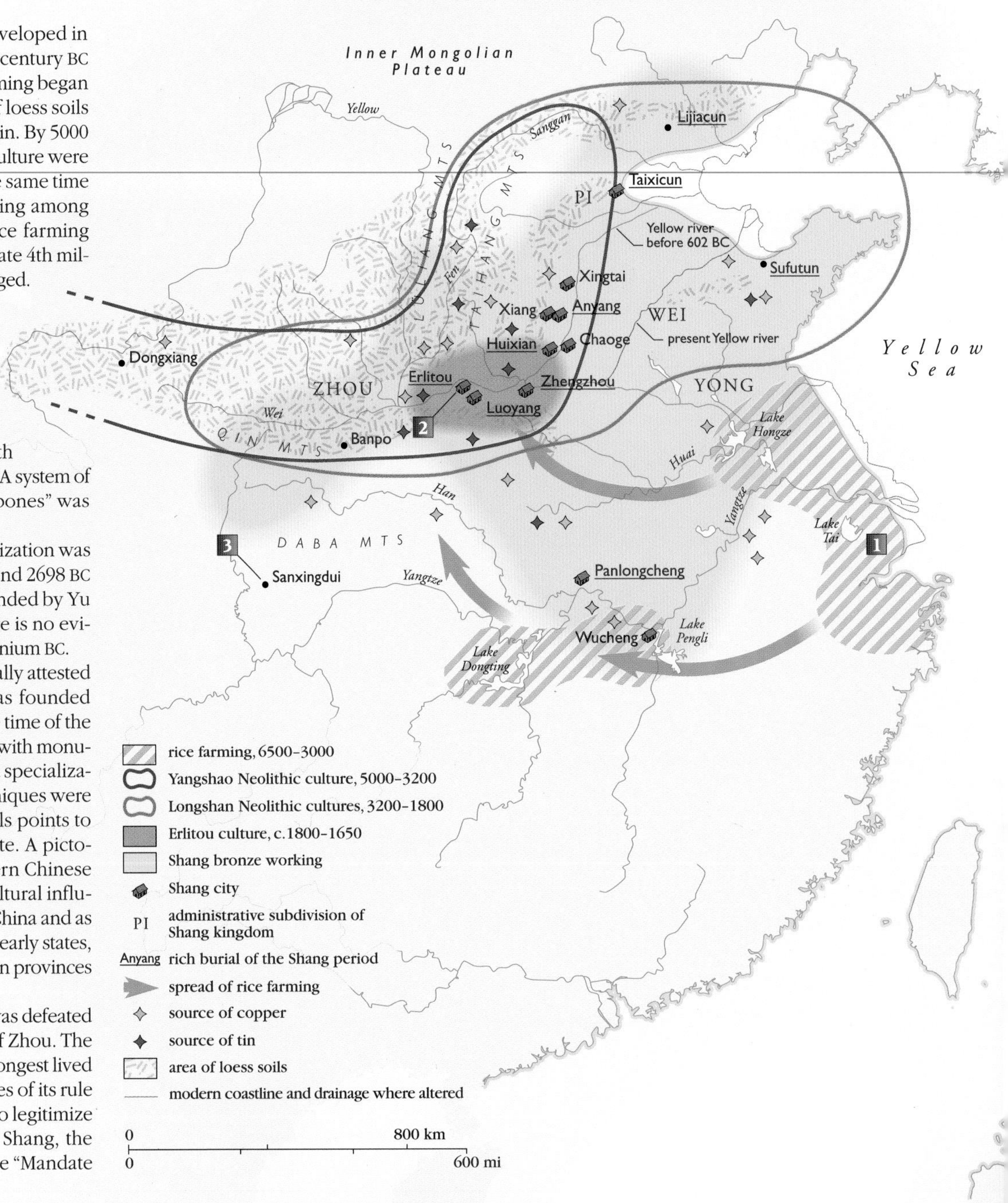

rice farming, 6500–3000
Yangshao Neolithic culture, 5000–3200
Longshan Neolithic cultures, 3200–1800
Erlitou culture, c.1800–1650
Shang bronze working
Shang city
PI administrative subdivision of Shang kingdom
Anyang rich burial of the Shang period
spread of rice farming
source of copper
source of tin
area of loess soils
modern coastline and drainage where altered

0 800 km
0 600 mi

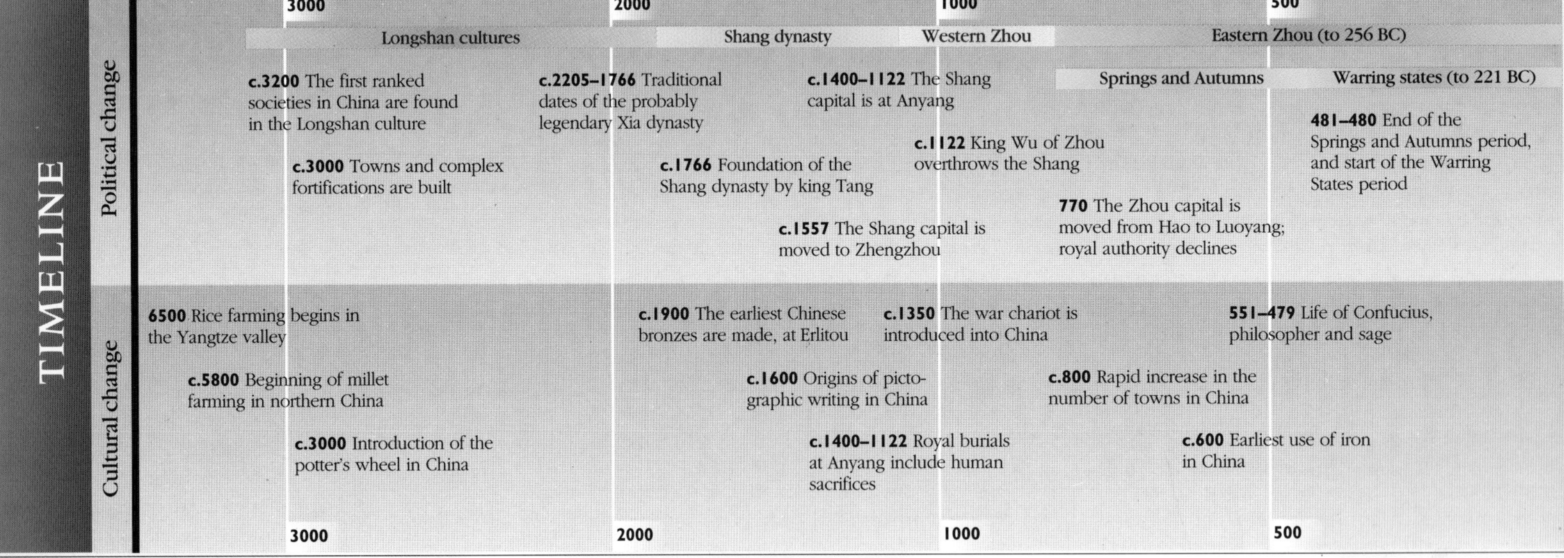

TIMELINE

3000 | 2000 | 1000 | 500

Longshan cultures | Shang dynasty | Western Zhou | Eastern Zhou (to 256 BC)

Springs and Autumns | Warring states (to 221 BC)

Political change

c.3200 The first ranked societies in China are found in the Longshan culture

c.3000 Towns and complex fortifications are built

c.2205–1766 Traditional dates of the probably legendary Xia dynasty

c.1766 Foundation of the Shang dynasty by king Tang

c.1557 The Shang capital is moved to Zhengzhou

c.1400–1122 The Shang capital is at Anyang

c.1122 King Wu of Zhou overthrows the Shang

770 The Zhou capital is moved from Hao to Luoyang; royal authority declines

481–480 End of the Springs and Autumns period, and start of the Warring States period

Cultural change

6500 Rice farming begins in the Yangtze valley

c.5800 Beginning of millet farming in northern China

c.3000 Introduction of the potter's wheel in China

c.1900 The earliest Chinese bronzes are made, at Erlitou

c.1600 Origins of pictographic writing in China

c.1400–1122 Royal burials at Anyang include human sacrifices

c.1350 The war chariot is introduced into China

c.800 Rapid increase in the number of towns in China

551–479 Life of Confucius, philosopher and sage

c.600 Earliest use of iron in China

3000 | 2000 | 1000 | 500

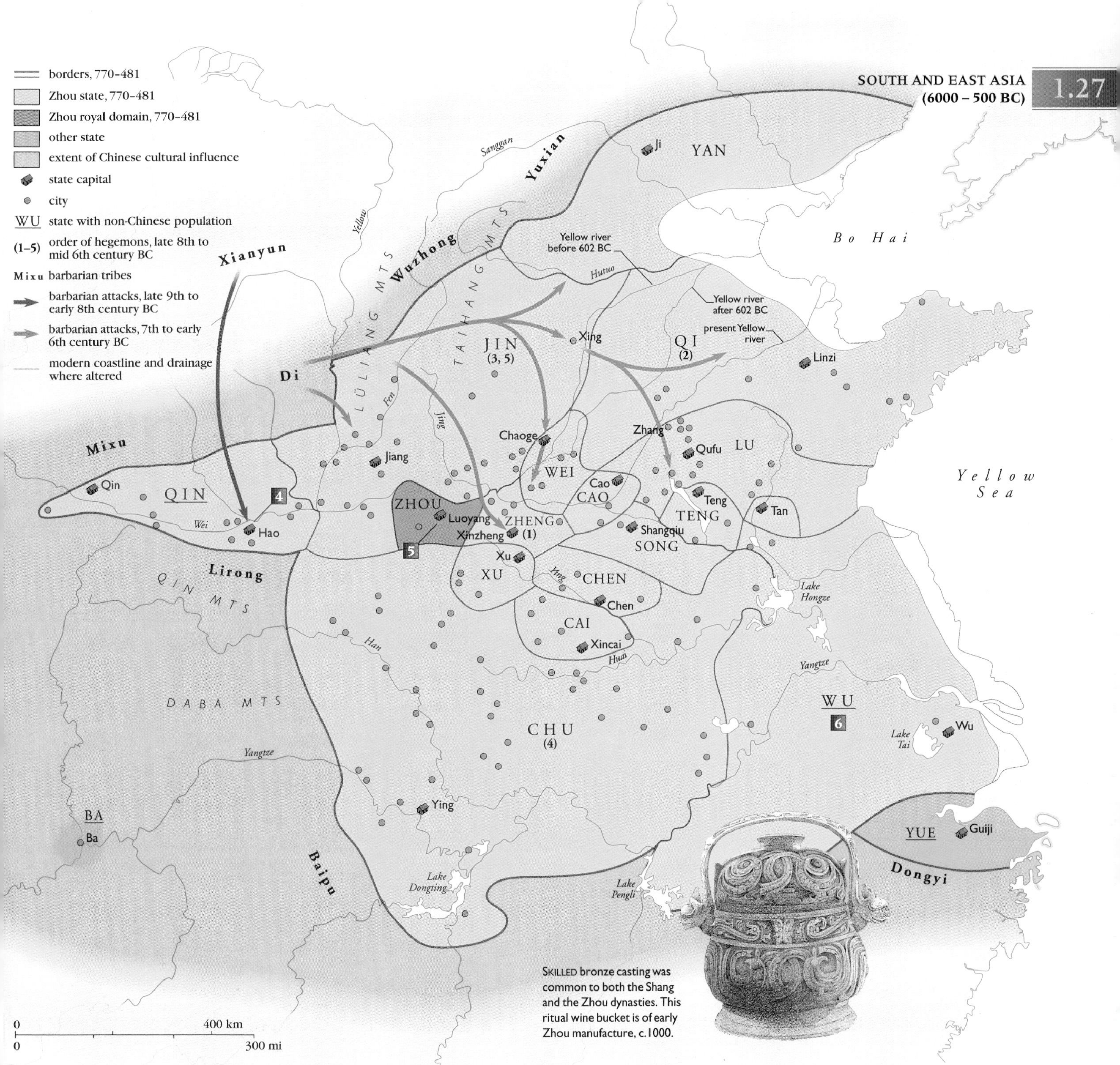

- borders, 770–481
- Zhou state, 770–481
- Zhou royal domain, 770–481
- other state
- extent of Chinese cultural influence
- state capital
- city
- WU state with non-Chinese population
- (1–5) order of hegemons, late 8th to mid 6th century BC
- Mixu barbarian tribes
- barbarian attacks, late 9th to early 8th century BC
- barbarian attacks, 7th to early 6th century BC
- modern coastline and drainage where altered

0 400 km
0 300 mi

SKILLED bronze casting was common to both the Shang and the Zhou dynasties. This ritual wine bucket is of early Zhou manufacture, c.1000.

of Heaven". The ruler was the "Son of Heaven" and "All under Heaven" was his lawful domain so long as he was just and moral. Should a ruler become unjust, Heaven would send him a warning and if he failed to reform, the Mandate would be given to another. Di-xin had been a sadist so Heaven had transferred the right to rule to the Zhou. This theory, which could be used both to condemn disobedience to the ruler and to justify successful usurpation, remained central to Chinese imperial ideology.

The Zhou kingdom was a decentralized feudal state, divided into fiefs governed by dukes chosen from among the king's relatives and trusted supporters. Only the royal domain was directly ruled by the king. In 770 barbarian attacks on Hao forced the Zhou to move their capital to Luoyang. This event was a turning-point in the history of the dynasty and marks the beginning of the period of disorder and fragmentation known as the Springs and Autumns period (after the title of the annals of the state of Lu).

Luoyang was more centrally situated than Hao but it removed the dynasty from its traditional heartland in the west; its authority began to decline. By this time the king controlled less land than most of his dukes who now became, in effect, the rulers of independent states, making almost constant war on one another. However, the dukes continued to recognize the sovereignty of the king and also recognized the duke of the leading state of the time as hegemon (with general primacy over all other states). The Springs and Autumns period turned into the Warring States period (480–221), which saw the decline of feudal relationships and the rise of a professional bureaucracy.

The Springs and Autumns period was a brutal age but it saw great creativity in literature and religious and philosophical thought. The end of the period saw Confucius found the ethical system, which remains fundamental to Chinese thought. Iron working was adopted around 600, probably in Wu, though iron tools and weapons did not replace bronze in everyday use until the 2nd century BC.

1 More than a hundred wet-rice farming villages (using flooded fields) were established in this region 6500–4000 BC.

2 Erlitou was the site of the first Chinese bronzes c.1900 BC; it was probably also the first Shang capital.

3 The city and ritual offering pits at Sanxingdui, discovered in the 1990s, are evidence of a bronze-using civilization contemporary with the Shang.

4 Hao, in the original Zhou heartland, was abandoned as the capital in 770 after barbarian attacks. The move initiated a decline in Zhou authority.

5 The Zhou royal domain was limited to a small area around Luoyang by the 7th century.

6 Wu, the dominant state in southern China in the late 6th century, was destroyed by Yue in 473 BC.

See also 1.03 (agriculture), 2.24 (Warring states and after)

The first civilizations of the Americas • 4000 – 500 BC •

The domestication of maize around 2700 made possible the development of permanent farming villages in Mesoamerica by 2300. Most early farmers practiced slash-and-burn agriculture, which cannot support dense populations. However, on fertile river flood-plains in the tropical forests of southeastern Mexico, reliable rainfall and year-round warmth made it possible to raise four crops of maize a year, which provided the economic base for the Olmec civilization.

By 1250 BC the Olmec lived in chiefdoms or small states ruled by a powerful hereditary elite. The most important sites were ceremonial centers with earth pyramid mounds and monumental stone sculptures of gods and chiefs. Associated with the ceremonial centers were settlements of two to three thousand people. The ritual centers were periodically destroyed and sculptures defaced or buried. Though possibly due to warfare between chiefdoms or states, it is more likely that this served a ritual purpose, marking the end of calendrical cycles, the death of a ruler or the accession of a new dynasty. Trade and gift exchange played an important part in the Olmec way of life. The Olmec lands have few natural resources and the raw materials for everyday tools, stone sculpture and status enhancing display objects had to be imported over long distances. Gift exchange played an important part in the diffusion of Olmec culture as the emerging elites of neighboring communities took up Olmec beliefs and artifacts to enhance their prestige. Late in their history, the Olmec developed a rudimentary hieroglyphic script which was used mainly for astronomical inscriptions. They used – and may have originated – both the Mesoamerican 260-day sacred year and the 52-year "long-count" calendar.

The Maya originated about 1200 BC in the Guatemalan highlands, developing from earlier Archaic cultures, and began to spread out into the lowlands of the Yucatán peninsula around 1000. By draining and canalizing swamps the Maya were able to

Pavón
El Opeño
Capacha
Valley of Mexico
Tlatilco
Cuicuilco
Tlapacoya
Gualupita
Chalcatzinco
Los Bocas
Balsas
Oxtotitlan
Tehuacán Valley
Juxtiahuaca
Monte Negro
San José Mogote
Las Limas
Oaxaca Valley
Dainzú
Monte Albán
El Trapiche
El Viejón
Gulf of Mexico
Tres Zapotes
Laguna de los Cerros
La Venta
San Lorenzo
Komchen
Dzibilchaltun
Yucatán Peninsula
Balancán
Nakbe
Cuello
Lamanai
Uaxactún
Tikal
Altar de Sacrificios
Padre Piedra
Pijijiapan
Xoc
Salinas la Blanca
Izapa
Abaj Takalik
Copán
Kaminaljuyú
Chalchuapa
PACIFIC OCEAN
1
2
3
4
Olmec, c.1250–400
Maya, c.1000
Maya, c.800
Zapotec, c.1400–400
Olmec ceremonial center
site with Olmec or Olmec influenced art
Olmec trade route
source of basalt
source of hematite
source of jade
source of obsidian
source of serpentine
northern limit of farming cultures, c.500 BC
0 600 km
0 400 mi

CARVED in rare blue jade, this tiny bust of a woman has the distinctive monumental quality which characterizes all Olmec sculpture.

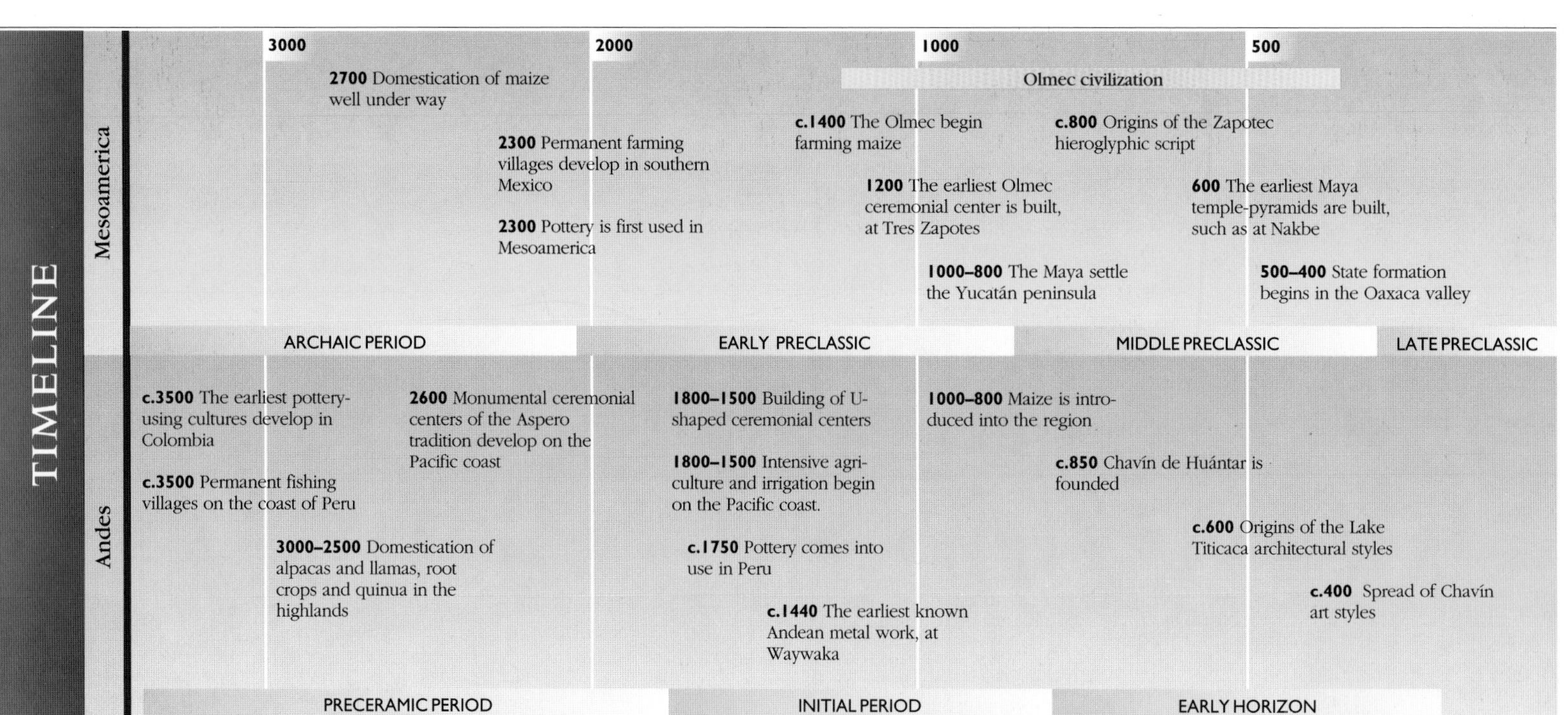
TIMELINE
Mesoamerica
3000
2000
1000
500
2700 Domestication of maize well under way
Olmec civilization
2300 Permanent farming villages develop in southern Mexico
2300 Pottery is first used in Mesoamerica
c.1400 The Olmec begin farming maize
c.800 Origins of the Zapotec hieroglyphic script
1200 The earliest Olmec ceremonial center is built, at Tres Zapotes
600 The earliest Maya temple-pyramids are built, such as at Nakbe
1000–800 The Maya settle the Yucatán peninsula
500–400 State formation begins in the Oaxaca valley
ARCHAIC PERIOD
EARLY PRECLASSIC
MIDDLE PRECLASSIC
LATE PRECLASSIC
Andes
c.3500 The earliest pottery-using cultures develop in Colombia
c.3500 Permanent fishing villages on the coast of Peru
2600 Monumental ceremonial centers of the Aspero tradition develop on the Pacific coast
3000–2500 Domestication of alpacas and llamas, root crops and quinua in the highlands
1800–1500 Building of U-shaped ceremonial centers
1800–1500 Intensive agriculture and irrigation begin on the Pacific coast.
c.1750 Pottery comes into use in Peru
c.1440 The earliest known Andean metal work, at Waywaka
1000–800 Maize is introduced into the region
c.850 Chavín de Huántar is founded
c.600 Origins of the Lake Titicaca architectural styles
c.400 Spread of Chavín art styles
PRECERAMIC PERIOD
INITIAL PERIOD
EARLY HORIZON

produce sufficient food to support a complex society and by 600 towns, such as Nakbe and Komchen, with monumental temple pyramids, were developing. Complex societies also developed among the Zapotec people of the Oaxaca valley by the 1st millennium BC. Here food production was increased by simple irrigation techniques and terracing. By 400 BC there were at least seven small states in the valley, the most important of which was centered on Monte Albán, and a system of hieroglyphic writing had been developed. In the Valley of Mexico highly productive agriculture using *chinampas* – raised fields built on reclaimed swamps – led to the development of trading networks, a market economy, craft specialization and large villages by around 200 BC.

The earliest complex societies in South America developed on the desert coast of Peru in settled fishing communities during the Preceramic period (3750–1800 BC). The marine resources of this area are unusually rich and these communities were able to free labor for the construction of temples and ceremonial centers under the direction of village leaders. One of the earliest such centers was built at Aspero around 2600: it consisted of six mounds nine meters high, topped with masonry ceremonial structures. Cotton, squash and gourds (used as floats for fishing nets) were cultivated but farming did not make a significant contribution to the diet. In the highlands, herding alpacas or llamas and cultivation of root crops such as potatoes, ullucu and oca or quinua, a cereal, gradually replaced hunting and gathering during the Preceramic; permanent villages with small ceremonial buildings also developed.

During the Initial Period (1800–800 BC) the area of cultivable land in the coastal lowlands was greatly extended through irrigation works, diverting water from the rivers which flowed from the Andes through the desert to the coast. Pottery was adopted. Huge U-shaped ceremonial centers, requiring the control of considerable resources of labor, food supplies and raw materials, were constructed: one at Garagay is estimated to have required 3.2 million work-days to complete. These sites were probably focal points for local chiefdoms but burial practices show few distinctions of wealth or rank. Interaction between the fishing communities on the coast and the farming communities in the desert river valleys and the mountains was considerable, with salt, seaweed and dried fish from the coast being exchanged for carbohydrate foods such as root crops and grain from the highlands and river valleys.

The Early Horizon (about 800–200 BC) saw the development of sophisticated architecture and complex sculptural styles at the highland ceremonial center of Chavín de Huántar. The Chavín style was the culmination of styles which had originated as early as 1200 in other Andean and coastal sites and by 400 its influence had spread over a wide area of coastal and highland Peru. Chavín had a population of two to three thousand at its peak in the 4th century but thereafter it declined, without developing into a full urban civilization. Complex societies, united by common beliefs, also developed in the Lake Titicaca basin during the Early Horizon. Particularly important is the ceremonial center at Chiripa, built 600–400 BC, in which can be seen the origins of the architectural styles of the 5th-century AD Tiahuanaco state. Maize became an important crop in the Andes during this period.

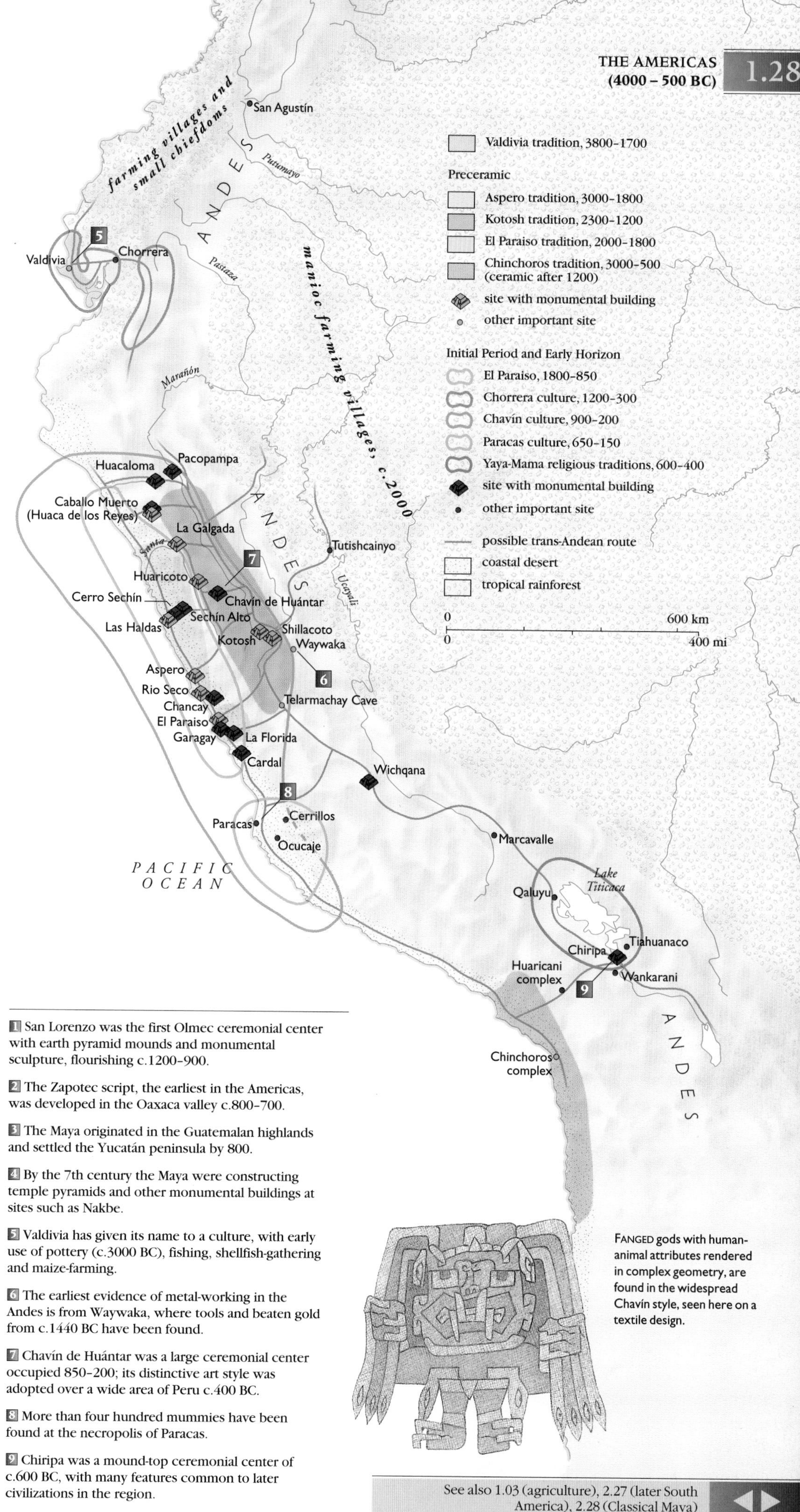

Valdivia tradition, 3800–1700
Preceramic
Aspero tradition, 3000–1800
Kotosh tradition, 2300–1200
El Paraiso tradition, 2000–1800
Chinchoros tradition, 3000–500 (ceramic after 1200)
site with monumental building
other important site
Initial Period and Early Horizon
El Paraiso, 1800–850
Chorrera culture, 1200–300
Chavín culture, 900–200
Paracas culture, 650–150
Yaya-Mama religious traditions, 600–400
site with monumental building
other important site
possible trans-Andean route
coastal desert
tropical rainforest
0 600 km
0 400 mi
farming villages and small chiefdoms
manioc farming villages, c.2000
ANDES
PACIFIC OCEAN
San Agustín
Putumayo
Pastaza
Marañón
Santa
Ucayali
Valdivia
Chorrera
Huacaloma
Pacopampa
Caballo Muerto (Huaca de los Reyes)
La Galgada
Huaricoto
Cerro Sechín
Chavín de Huántar
Sechín Alto
Las Haldas
Kotosh
Shillacoto
Waywaka
Tutishcainyo
Aspero
Rio Seco
Chancay
El Paraiso
Garagay
La Florida
Cardal
Telarmachay Cave
Wichqana
Paracas
Cerrillos
Ocucaje
Marcavalle
Lake Titicaca
Qaluyu
Chiripa
Tiahuanaco
Huaricani complex
Wankarani
Chinchoros complex
5
6
7
8
9

1 San Lorenzo was the first Olmec ceremonial center with earth pyramid mounds and monumental sculpture, flourishing c.1200–900.

2 The Zapotec script, the earliest in the Americas, was developed in the Oaxaca valley c.800–700.

3 The Maya originated in the Guatemalan highlands and settled the Yucatán peninsula by 800.

4 By the 7th century the Maya were constructing temple pyramids and other monumental buildings at sites such as Nakbe.

5 Valdivia has given its name to a culture, with early use of pottery (c.3000 BC), fishing, shellfish-gathering and maize-farming.

6 The earliest evidence of metal-working in the Andes is from Waywaka, where tools and beaten gold from c.1440 BC have been found.

7 Chavín de Huántar was a large ceremonial center occupied 850–200; its distinctive art style was adopted over a wide area of Peru c.400 BC.

8 More than four hundred mummies have been found at the necropolis of Paracas.

9 Chiripa was a mound-top ceremonial center of c.600 BC, with many features common to later civilizations in the region.

FANGED gods with human-animal attributes rendered in complex geometry, are found in the widespread Chavín style, seen here on a textile design.

See also 1.03 (agriculture), 2.27 (later South America), 2.28 (Classical Maya)

Part 2

THE CLASSICAL

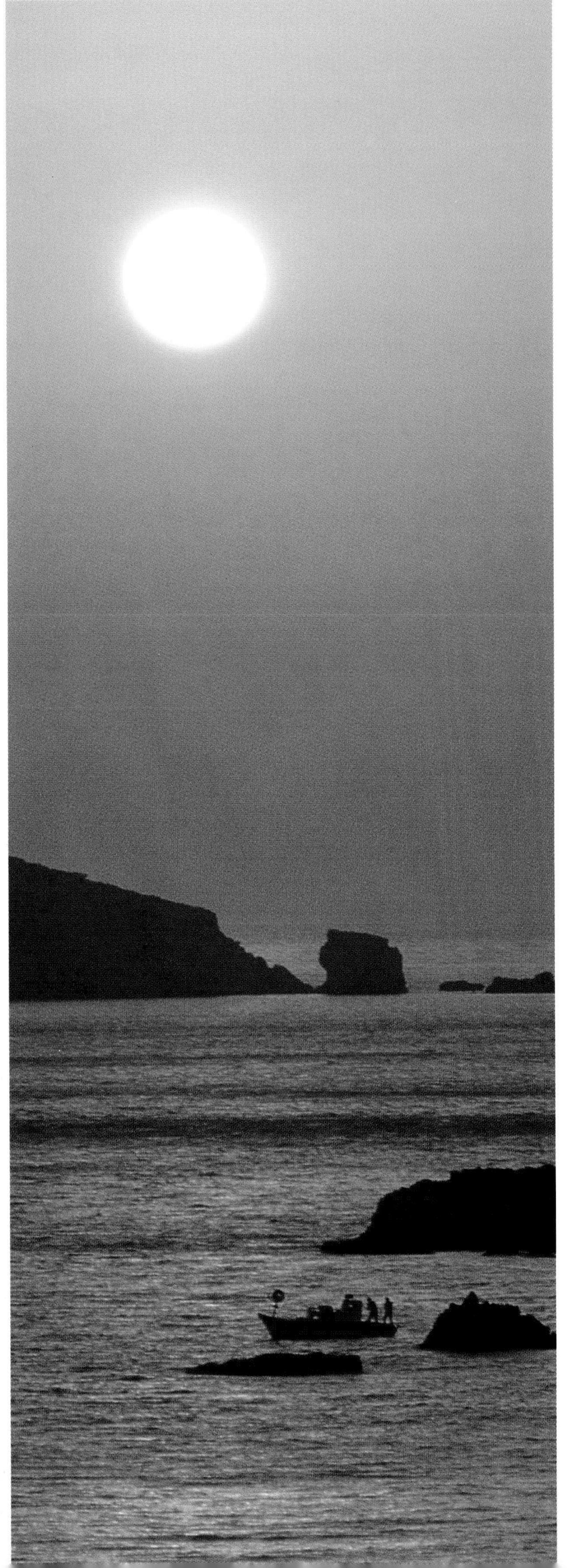

In the thirty generations between 500 BC and AD 600, the world was transformed. Across the globe, populations increased, sometimes startlingly so; states with complex systems of social and economic control emerged; food production intensified, allowing specialists such as artists, architects, poets and thinkers to develop their skills of adorning, exploring and explaining their world. By AD 600 empires had come and gone and all the major religions, with the exception of Islam, had taken root.

Amidst the vivid mass of detail, certain themes recur. In certain areas, favored by their access to natural resources and their position astride important communication routes, the pace of change accelerated and centers of social or economic innovation sprang up. Powerful individuals commanded their own territories, now known as chiefdoms. They survived by competing with and copying from one another: prestige goods were acquired and displayed in life and on death, for lesser beings and rivals to wonder at. The Scythian chieftain buried at Pazyryk in central Asia about 600 BC was provided in his grave with everything a paramount would wish for – a funerary vehicle, feasting and hunting gear and gold; but this collection of finery was as much an opportunity for his family to display the extent of their wealth and power to their rivals, as to offer the deceased a comfortable afterlife. Conspicuous consumption and ritual destruction of luxuries by burying them with chieftains meant that ever more prestige goods were needed. This gave momentum to trade and exchange and, from time to time, encouraged latent hostility to flare into outright physical aggression.

In some areas chiefdoms were transformed into states, often through a complex phase of warfare and rapid social reordering. Thus the Mycenaean chiefdoms of the late second millennium BC became the young city-states of Greece two

WORLD

500 BC – AD 600

centuries later. On the other side of the world in about 500 BC, in the Oaxaca valley of Mesoamerica, three competing chiefdoms came together to found a new political capital on the mountain-top of Monte Albán; it remained preeminent for more than a thousand years. The unification of rival polities under a single authority was a recurring pattern, seen on different scales and at different times throughout the world. In 408 BC, a century after the foundation of Monte Albán, three rival Greek cities on the island of Rhodes agreed to found the city of Rhodes. This kind of coalescence the Greeks well understood – they called it synoicism.

There was a dynamic, interdependent relationship between these innovating centers and the peripheries around them. A complex state system needed raw materials and human power to maintain it. A regular supply of rare metals, exotic stones and woods, furs and fabrics was essential to support the structure of the social hierarchy. Human power, too, whether in the form of slaves or a supply of food for a free workforce, was a prerequisite for supporting the labor-intensive adjuncts of a state, whether the bureaucracy and professional army of Qin China in the 3rd century BC, or the scholarly elite of Gupta India in the 4th century AD, who created some of the greatest works of law, medicine, astronomy, mathematics and philosophy in the Sanskrit language.

The demands of centralizing powers encouraged trade with the surrounding peripheries. African and Indian communities were drawn into the economic sphere of the Roman empire in the first four centuries AD, despite knowing little or nothing of the Roman state that gave them pottery, coins and trinkets in return for raw materials and slaves. Communities closer to the innovating centers were in a better position to learn from their neighbors and emulate their ways, thus becoming increasingly powerful.

There was a continual drift of creative power and energy from the center to the periphery, as the seeds of innovation took root in the fertile periphery while the core decayed. The early core of Europe developed in the Greek cities around the Aegean in the eighth to sixth centuries BC; later, in the fifth century, the focus for innovation was on the Greek mainland. Power then shifted to the central Mediterranean where, after the third century BC, Rome emerged preeminent. It maintained its leadership for some six centuries until power moved back to the peripheral Black Sea region, with the rise of Constantinople and the Byzantine empire. In Mesoamerica a similar pattern can be seen, with the spread of innovating power from the Oaxaca valley in the second half of the first millennium BC to the Valley of Mexico in the central highlands and then the Maya area of the Yucatán in the early first millennium AD. The pattern is still with us, as economic vitality and productivity shifts at the end of the 20th century from the north Atlantic toward the Pacific rim.

The cycle of growth and decay and the inexorable shift of centers of power were frequently accelerated by warfare and invasion. The Celtic tribes from eastern France and southern Germany who attacked the Greek and Roman world in the fourth and third centuries BC confronted energetic Mediterranean states well able to defend themselves; but the succession of attacks by Germanic peoples around AD 400 found the Roman empire in a state of decay. The "barbarian" Germans rapidly overran the old empire and set up a number of new kingdoms within its carcass.

The collapse of empires – a common theme in this period – is a subject of great fascination. Each case is different and the reasons are always many and interacting: natural catastrophy, population decline, economic over-extension, invasion, disease. In the purely prehistoric context of Mesoamerica,

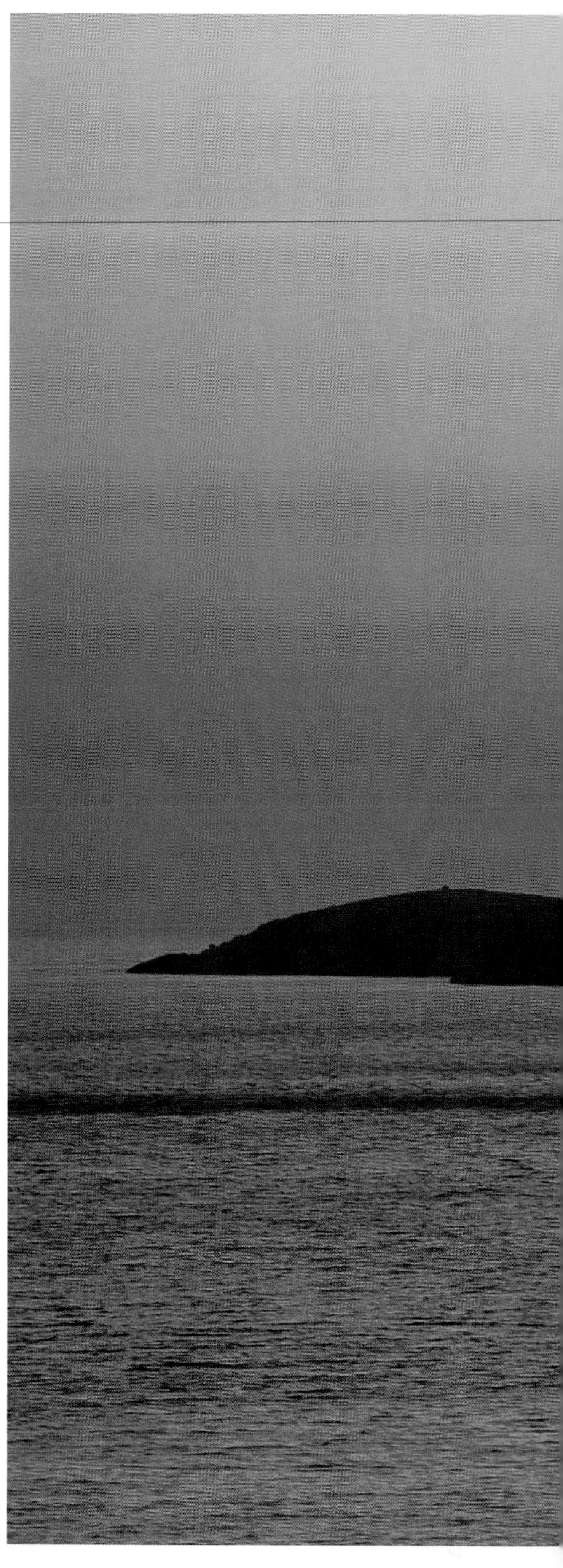

The Aegean islands and the surrounding mainland regions of Greece and Asia Minor were the scene of many key developments in civilization, state-building and economic life around 500 BC. The sea itself, vividly described in Homer's poetry, held a special place in the affections of the Greeks in classical times and beyond.

archeologists can only speculate about "ecological overshoot" and the destructive role of parasitic elites; whereas in China, detailed written records reveal the processes leading to the collapse of the Han empire in AD 220 – foreign wars, internal power struggles and peasant rebellions. In the end, the empire which had held China together for four centuries disintegrated into many rival factions of local warlords.

Yet it is possible to turn the notions of center and periphery inside out and to see the states and empires of Europe, India and China not as centers but as developments on the periphery of the huge, central landmass of Asia – an unending steppe land, home of horse-riding nomads who for century after century moved out to strike terror into the hearts of their sedentary, civilized neighbors. In Europe the first recorded invaders from the steppe were the Cimmerians in about 700 BC. Then followed the Scythians, the Sarmatians, the Alans and the Huns, the last contributing to the chaos at the end of the Roman era. Other groups moved through the Indus valley into the heart of the subcontinent, while the northern borders of China were constantly at risk after the eighth century BC – a threat which the Great Wall, with its garrison of half a million troops, was eventually built to avert. The history of Old World civilization was intimately bound up with the population pressures of the deepest Eurasian steppes.

During the millennium 500 BC–AD 600, many foundations of the modern world were created. Pyrotechnical skills developed; bronze and iron became widely available throughout the Old World and steel was developed in Han China. The powers of wind and water were harnessed; horse-riding was transformed by the development of the stirrup about 200 BC; and science, astronomy and mathematics made enormous strides in the Hellenistic world, India, China and to some extent in Mesoamerica. By AD 600 a plateau had been reached. There was to be little further advance until the fifteenth century when the arts of navigation and seamanship opened up the world and, in doing so, unleashed new dynamic forces ■

2.01 THE WORLD • 323 BC •

In 500 BC the world's most impressive state was the Achemenid empire of Persia, extending from Libya to the Indus. The empire's first setback occurred when Xerxes I invaded Greece (▷2.07). The quarrelsome Greek city-states united in the face of the common enemy and defeated the Persians at sea at Salamis and on land at Plataea. The Greeks went back to their quarrels and did little to follow up their victory: Persia lost its foothold in Europe but continued to dominate the Middle East for eighty years (▷2.11). Then, in 404, Egypt rebelled and Persian control was not restored until 343. In 380 Persia's Indian provinces were lost.

Late 5th-century Greece was dominated by rivalry between Sparta and Athens, culminating in the Peloponnesian war which engulfed most of the Greek world but settled nothing. Further indecisive wars between shifting alliances ensued. Meanwhile, the Balkan kingdom of Macedon rose unopposed under Philip II and in 338 all the Greek city-states were forcibly enrolled in the Macedonian-dominated Hellenic league. Philip planned to invade Persia but his assassination in 336 left it to his son Alexander to carry out his plans. In only six years he conquered almost all the Persian empire, opening the whole Middle East to Greek influence (▷ 2.09).

By the 4th century the old south Arabian kingdom of Saba had been joined by the new states of Qataban and Hadramaut, driven by a demand from the Mediterranean for the precious gums, frankincense and myrrh, which were produced in the region. By the same period Sabean influence was seen in Damot on the African Red Sea coast.

Through most of the 5th and 4th centuries the main power in the western Mediterranean was Carthage. Carthage was more interested in commerce than conquest and its empire grew little between 500 and 323. Most of central and western Europe was now dominated by Celtic peoples. Around 400, Celts crossed the Alps and invaded Italy, breaking the power of the Etruscans and settling the Po valley. Though still insignificant on the map, by 323 Rome was a major power in Italy, having conquered its Latin and Etruscan neighbors earlier in the century (▷ 2.12).

The strongest state in India in 500 was Magadha in the lower Ganges plain. From 364 it brought most of northern India under its control (▷2.22). Southern India was a mosaic of minor states and chiefdoms with little urban development. The Zhou kingdom of China, which had broken up into a dozen competing states in the 8th century, was still disunited, although many of the smaller states had been absorbed by the bigger players (▷2.24). The continual warfare

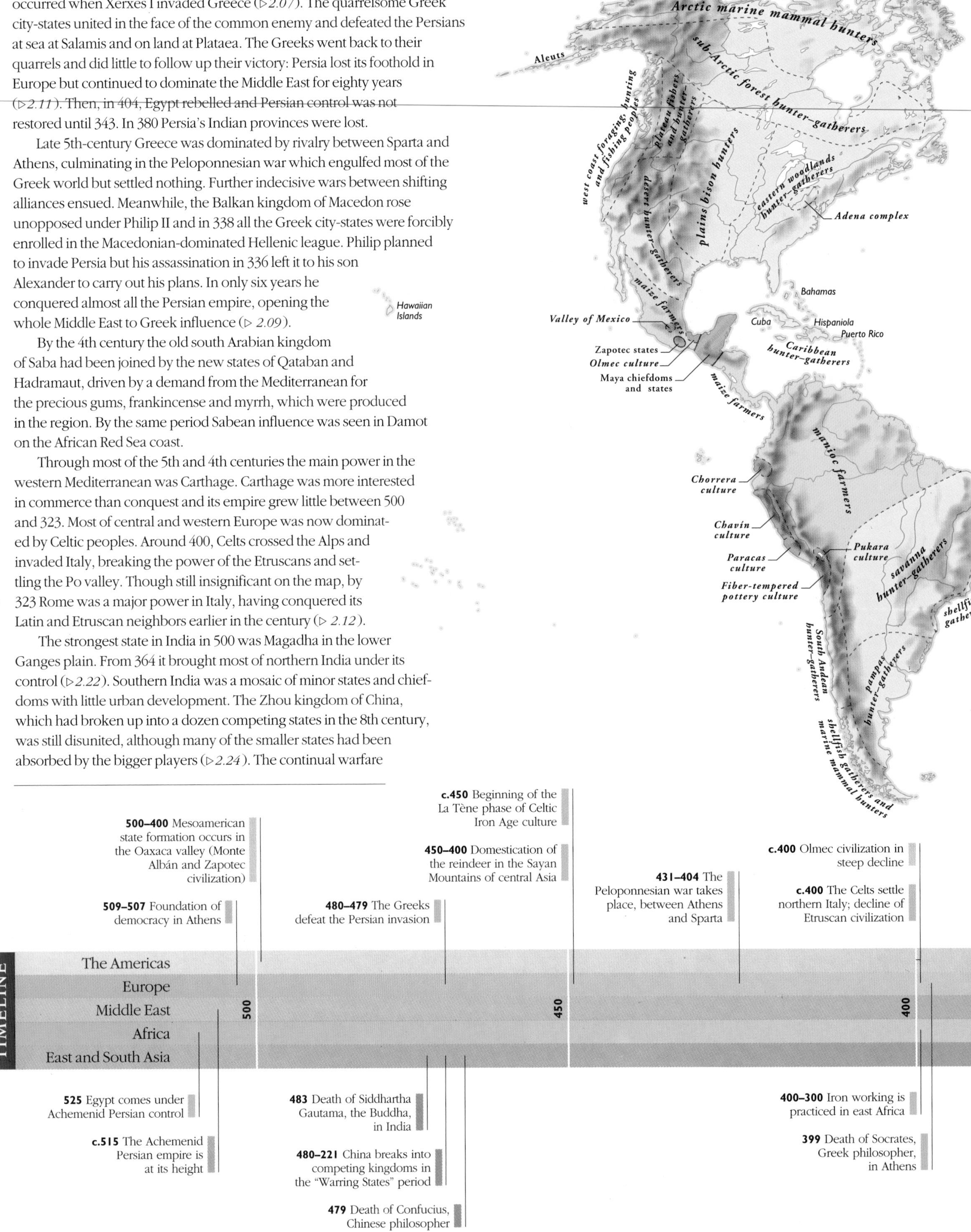

Arctic marine mammal hunters
sub-Arctic forest hunter-gatherers
Aleuts
west coast foraging, hunting and fishing peoples
plateau fishers and hunter-gatherers
desert hunter-gatherers
plains bison hunters
eastern woodlands hunter-gatherers
Adena complex
maize farmers
Hawaiian Islands
Bahamas
Valley of Mexico
Cuba
Hispaniola
Puerto Rico
Caribbean hunter-gatherers
Zapotec states
Olmec culture
Maya chiefdoms and states
maize farmers
manioc farmers
Chorrera culture
Chavín culture
Paracas culture
Pukara culture
savanna hunter-gatherers
Fiber-tempered pottery culture
shellfish gatherers
South Andean hunter-gatherers
pampas hunter-gatherers
shellfish gatherers and marine mammal hunters
500–400 Mesoamerican state formation occurs in the Oaxaca valley (Monte Albán and Zapotec civilization)
509–507 Foundation of democracy in Athens
c.450 Beginning of the La Tène phase of Celtic Iron Age culture
450–400 Domestication of the reindeer in the Sayan Mountains of central Asia
480–479 The Greeks defeat the Persian invasion
431–404 The Peloponnesian war takes place, between Athens and Sparta
c.400 Olmec civilization in steep decline
c.400 The Celts settle northern Italy; decline of Etruscan civilization
TIMELINE
The Americas
Europe
Middle East
Africa
East and South Asia
500
450
400
525 Egypt comes under Achemenid Persian control
c.515 The Achemenid Persian empire is at its height
483 Death of Siddhartha Gautama, the Buddha, in India
480–221 China breaks into competing kingdoms in the "Warring States" period
479 Death of Confucius, Chinese philosopher
400–300 Iron working is practiced in east Africa
399 Death of Socrates, Greek philosopher, in Athens

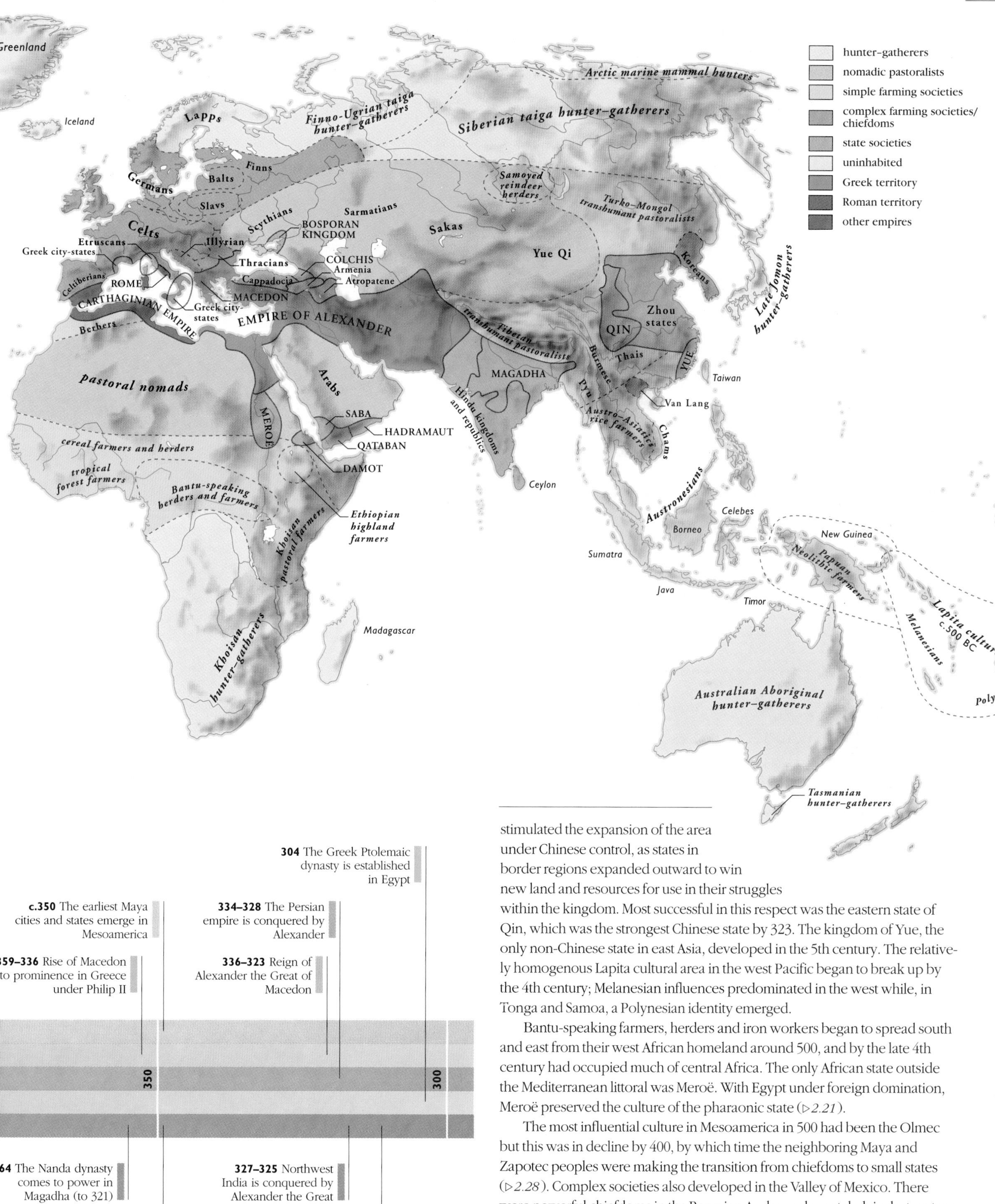
hunter-gatherers
nomadic pastoralists
simple farming societies
complex farming societies/ chiefdoms
state societies
uninhabited
Greek territory
Roman territory
other empires
Greenland
Iceland
Lapps
Finno-Ugrian taiga hunter-gatherers
Arctic marine mammal hunters
Siberian taiga hunter-gatherers
Finns
Germans
Balts
Slavs
Samoyed reindeer herders
Turko-Mongol transhumant pastoralists
Sarmatians
Scythians
BOSPORAN KINGDOM
Sakas
Celts
Etruscans
Greek city-states
Illyrian
Thracians
COLCHIS
Armenia
Atropatene
Yue Qi
Koreans
Late Jomon hunter-gatherers
Celtiberians
ROME
Cappadocia
MACEDON
Greek city-states
CARTHAGINIAN EMPIRE
EMPIRE OF ALEXANDER
Tibetan transhumant pastoralists
Zhou states
QIN
Berbers
Thais
YUE
Burmese
Taiwan
MAGADHA
Pastoral nomads
Arabs
MEROE
SABA
HADRAMAUT
QATABAN
DAMOT
Hindu kingdoms and republics
Pyu
Van Lang
Austro-Asiatic rice farmers
Chams
cereal farmers and herders
tropical forest farmers
Bantu-speaking herders and farmers
Ethiopian highland farmers
Ceylon
Austronesians
Celebes
Borneo
New Guinea
Papuan Neolithic farmers
Sumatra
Khoisan pastoral farmers
Java
Timor
Lapita culture c.500 BC
Melanesians
Madagascar
Khoisan hunter-gatherers
Australian Aboriginal hunter-gatherers
Polynesians
Tasmanian hunter-gatherers
304 The Greek Ptolemaic dynasty is established in Egypt
c.350 The earliest Maya cities and states emerge in Mesoamerica
334–328 The Persian empire is conquered by Alexander
359–336 Rise of Macedon to prominence in Greece under Philip II
336–323 Reign of Alexander the Great of Macedon
350
300
364 The Nanda dynasty comes to power in Magadha (to 321)
327–325 Northwest India is conquered by Alexander the Great
350–320 The Qin state rises to dominance in China
321 Chandragupta Maurya becomes king of Magadha and founds the Mauryan empire

stimulated the expansion of the area under Chinese control, as states in border regions expanded outward to win new land and resources for use in their struggles within the kingdom. Most successful in this respect was the eastern state of Qin, which was the strongest Chinese state by 323. The kingdom of Yue, the only non-Chinese state in east Asia, developed in the 5th century. The relatively homogenous Lapita cultural area in the west Pacific began to break up by the 4th century; Melanesian influences predominated in the west while, in Tonga and Samoa, a Polynesian identity emerged.

Bantu-speaking farmers, herders and iron workers began to spread south and east from their west African homeland around 500, and by the late 4th century had occupied much of central Africa. The only African state outside the Mediterranean littoral was Meroë. With Egypt under foreign domination, Meroë preserved the culture of the pharaonic state (▷2.21).

The most influential culture in Mesoamerica in 500 had been the Olmec but this was in decline by 400, by which time the neighboring Maya and Zapotec peoples were making the transition from chiefdoms to small states (▷2.28). Complex societies also developed in the Valley of Mexico. There were powerful chiefdoms in the Peruvian Andes and coastal plain, but no true states in South America. In North America hunting, gathering or fishing continued as the dominant way of life. Many groups augmented their food supply by cultivating wild plants but this activity was more gardening than farming ■

2.02 THE WORLD • 200 BC •

Alexander's empire did not survive his death in 323 – the immediate cause of its breakup being his failure to provide an heir – and within a few years his generals had become the rulers of independent kingdoms (▷*2.10*). Seleucos built a state which incorporated most of Anatolia, Mesopotamia, and Iran and extended into central Asia; despite successful rebellions by the Bactrian Greeks in 239 and the Parthians in 238, the Seleucid kingdom was still the largest of the successor states in 200. Ptolemy seized Egypt and founded a dynasty which was to last until 31 BC, ending only with Cleopatra's suicide after the battle of Actium. Macedon itself fell to Antipater, who reasserted Macedonian supremacy in Greece in the face of an Athenian-led rebellion. Macedon was still the leading power in Greece in 200.

The leading power in the western Mediterranean by 200 was Rome. The Romans had completed the conquest of peninsular Italy in 272, and in 264 were drawn into a war with Carthage over Sicily. This, the First Punic War, dragged on for over twenty years until the Romans had wrested control of Sicily, Sardinia and Corsica. Carthaginian expansion in Spain, arousing Roman hostility once again, led in 218 to the outbreak of the Second Punic War. The Carthaginian general Hannibal surprised the Romans by attacking Italy from the north, but counterattacks in Spain and north Africa brought Rome crushing victory, and Carthage was shorn of its empire (▷*2.12*).

Several centuries of stability on the Eurasian steppes came to an end in the 3rd century as the Sarmatians began to push westward against the Scythians. On the far eastern steppes the Turko-Mongol pastoralists made the transition to a horse-mounted fully nomadic way of life around 300, and by 200 they were united in the powerful Xiongnu confederation. Their use of the composite bow gave the Xiongnu a decided military advantage over their nomadic Iranian neighbors to the west and made them a formidable adversary for the newly united Chinese (▷*2.20*).

In 321 Chandragupta Maurya (321–c. 293) seized the throne of the kingdom of Magadha, overthrowing the Nanda dynasty. Chandragupta spent most of his reign building a strong central administration, but he defeated a Seleucid invasion, adding all of northwest India to his domains (▷*2.22*). His son Bindusara also conquered much of southern India. Under Ashoka the Mauryan empire reached its greatest extent. Appalled by his bloody conquest of the east coast kingdom of Kalinga in 261, Ashoka abjured further warfare and, becoming a Buddhist, tried to impose Buddhist standards of behavior on his people. Little is known

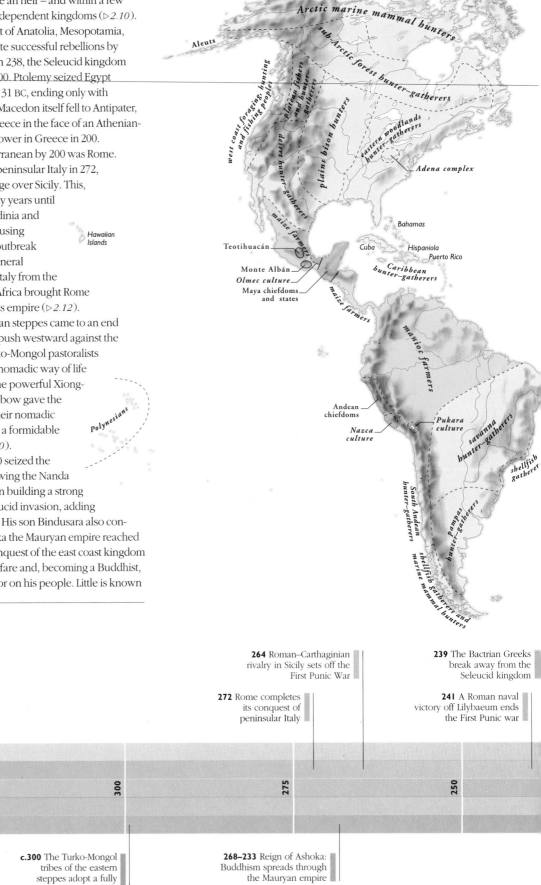

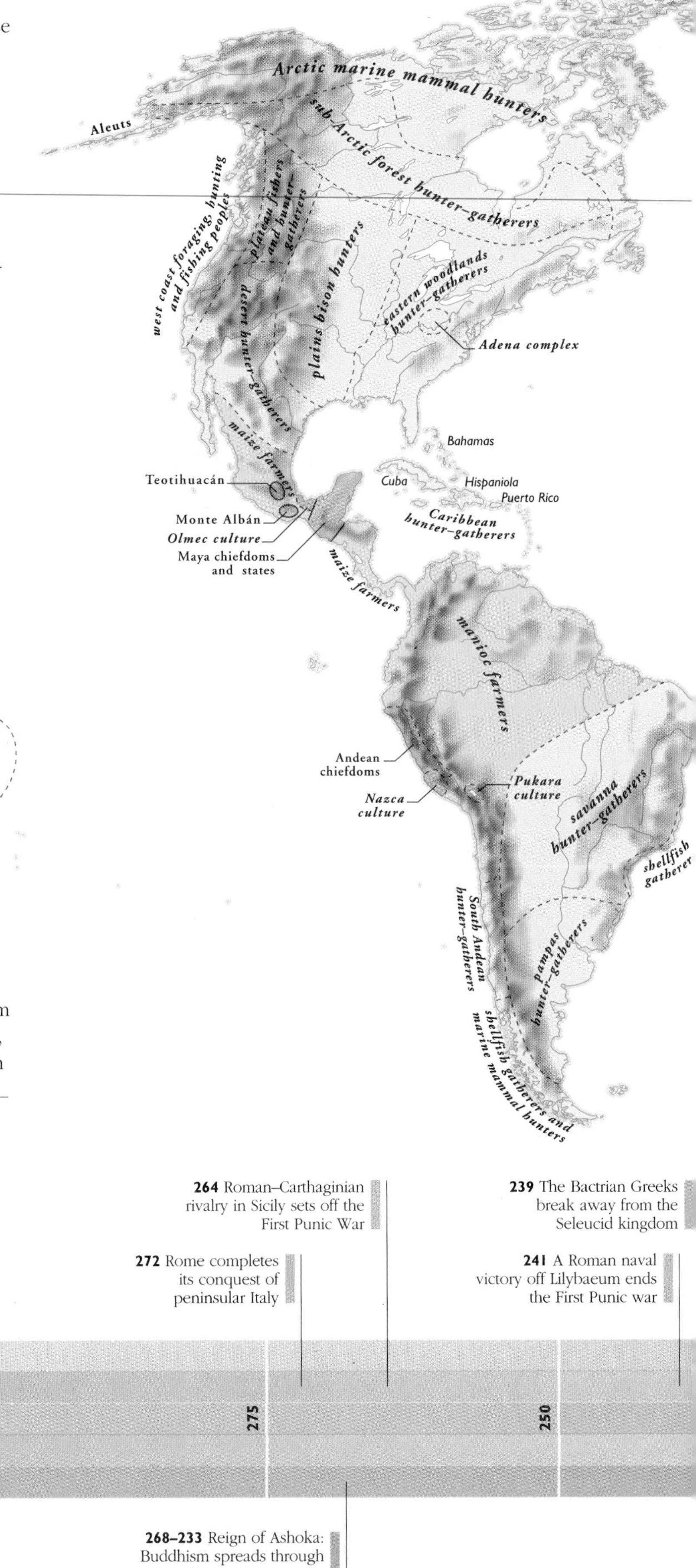
Hawaiian Islands
Polynesians
Aleuts
Arctic marine mammal hunters
sub-Arctic forest hunter-gatherers
west coast foraging, hunting and fishing peoples
plateau fishers and hunter-gatherers
desert hunter-gatherers
plains bison hunters
eastern woodlands hunter-gatherers
Adena complex
maize farmers
Teotihuacán
Monte Albán
Olmec culture
Maya chiefdoms and states
Bahamas
Cuba
Hispaniola
Puerto Rico
Caribbean hunter-gatherers
maize farmers
manioc farmers
Andean chiefdoms
Nazca culture
Pukara culture
savanna hunter-gatherers
shellfish gatherers
South Andean hunter-gatherers
pampas hunter-gatherers
shellfish gatherers and marine mammal hunters

TIMELINE

The Americas | Europe | Middle East | Africa | East and South Asia

325 | 300 | 275 | 250

323–280 Wars of the Diadochi: Alexander's generals split up his empire

323 Alexander the Great dies without naming a successor

321 Chandragupta Maurya, founder of the Mauryan empire, becomes king of Magadha

c.300 The Turko-Mongol tribes of the eastern steppes adopt a fully nomadic way of life

c.300 Beginning of rice farming in Japan

272 Rome completes its conquest of peninsular Italy

268–233 Reign of Ashoka: Buddhism spreads through the Mauryan empire

264 Roman–Carthaginian rivalry in Sicily sets off the First Punic War

241 A Roman naval victory off Lilybaeum ends the First Punic war

239 The Bactrian Greeks break away from the Seleucid kingdom

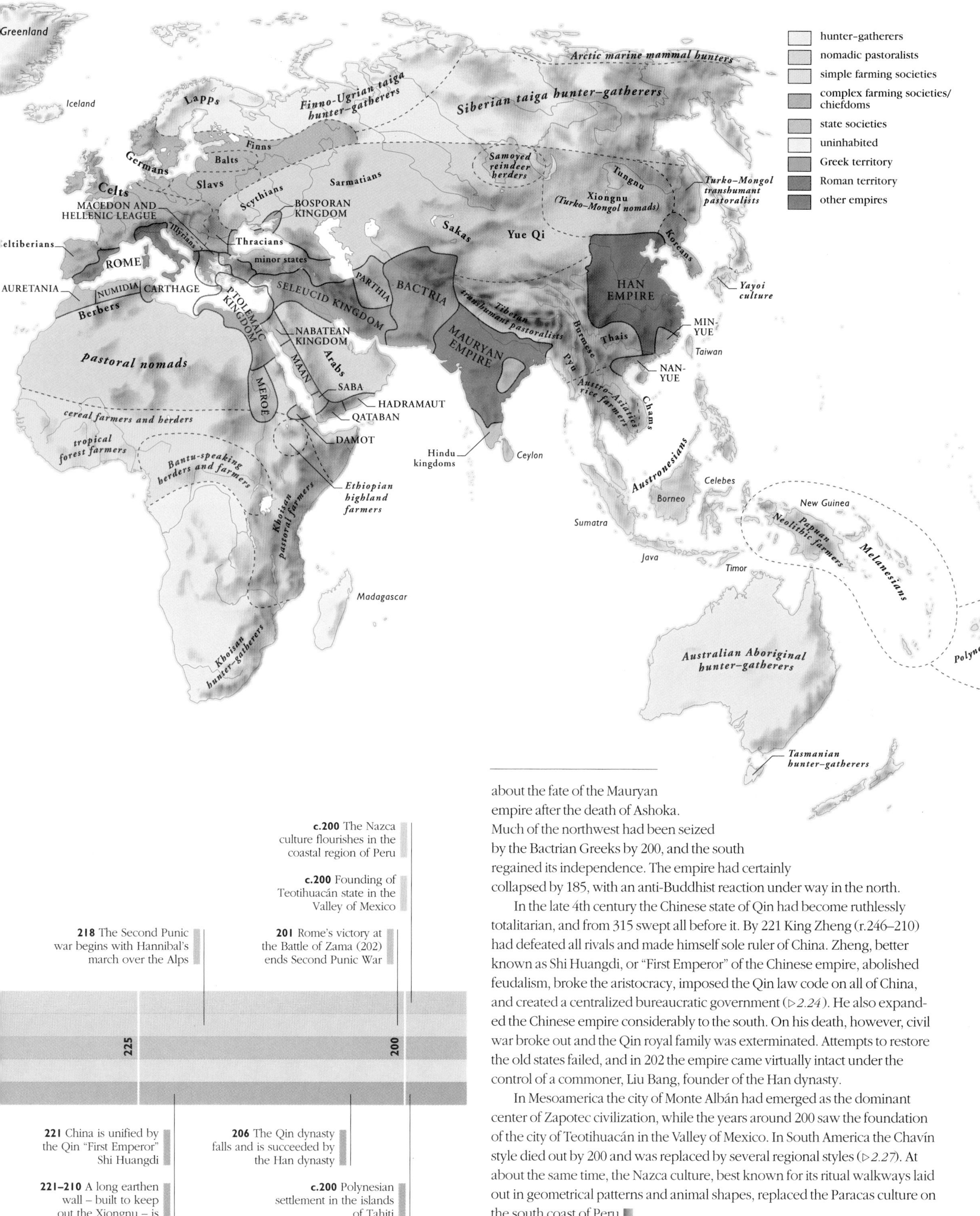
hunter-gatherers
nomadic pastoralists
simple farming societies
complex farming societies/ chiefdoms
state societies
uninhabited
Greek territory
Roman territory
other empires
Greenland
Iceland
Lapps
Finno-Ugrian taiga hunter-gatherers
Arctic marine mammal hunters
Siberian taiga hunter-gatherers
Finns
Balts
Germans
Slavs
Celts
Sarmatians
Scythians
Samoyed reindeer herders
Tungnu
Xiongnu (Turko-Mongol nomads)
Turko-Mongol transhumant pastoralists
MACEDON AND HELLENIC LEAGUE
BOSPORAN KINGDOM
eltiberians
Illyrians
Thracians
minor states
ROME
Sakas
Yue Qi
Koreans
Yayoi culture
AURETANIA
NUMIDIA
CARTHAGE
PTOLEMAIC KINGDOM
SELEUCID KINGDOM
PARTHIA
BACTRIA
Tibetan transhumant pastoralists
HAN EMPIRE
Berbers
NABATEAN KINGDOM
Arabs
MAURYAN EMPIRE
Burmese
Thais
MIN-YUE
Taiwan
pastoral nomads
MAAN
MEROE
Pyu
NAN-YUE
SABA
HADRAMAUT
QATABAN
Austro-Asiatic rice farmers
Chams
cereal farmers and herders
DAMOT
tropical forest farmers
Bantu-speaking herders and farmers
Hindu kingdoms
Ceylon
Austronesians
Celebes
Ethiopian highland farmers
Borneo
New Guinea
Sumatra
Papuan Neolithic farmers
Melanesians
Khoisan pastoral farmers
Java
Timor
Madagascar
Khoisan hunter-gatherers
Australian Aboriginal hunter-gatherers
Polynesians
Tasmanian hunter-gatherers
225
200

about the fate of the Mauryan empire after the death of Ashoka. Much of the northwest had been seized by the Bactrian Greeks by 200, and the south regained its independence. The empire had certainly collapsed by 185, with an anti-Buddhist reaction under way in the north.

In the late 4th century the Chinese state of Qin had become ruthlessly totalitarian, and from 315 swept all before it. By 221 King Zheng (r.246–210) had defeated all rivals and made himself sole ruler of China. Zheng, better known as Shi Huangdi, or "First Emperor" of the Chinese empire, abolished feudalism, broke the aristocracy, imposed the Qin law code on all of China, and created a centralized bureaucratic government (▷*2.24*). He also expanded the Chinese empire considerably to the south. On his death, however, civil war broke out and the Qin royal family was exterminated. Attempts to restore the old states failed, and in 202 the empire came virtually intact under the control of a commoner, Liu Bang, founder of the Han dynasty.

In Mesoamerica the city of Monte Albán had emerged as the dominant center of Zapotec civilization, while the years around 200 saw the foundation of the city of Teotihuacán in the Valley of Mexico. In South America the Chavín style died out by 200 and was replaced by several regional styles (▷*2.27*). At about the same time, the Nazca culture, best known for its ritual walkways laid out in geometrical patterns and animal shapes, replaced the Paracas culture on the south coast of Peru ■

c.200 The Nazca culture flourishes in the coastal region of Peru

c.200 Founding of Teotihuacán state in the Valley of Mexico

218 The Second Punic war begins with Hannibal's march over the Alps

201 Rome's victory at the Battle of Zama (202) ends Second Punic War

221 China is unified by the Qin "First Emperor" Shi Huangdi

221–210 A long earthen wall – built to keep out the Xiongnu – is completed in China

206 The Qin dynasty falls and is succeeded by the Han dynasty

c.200 Polynesian settlement in the islands of Tahiti

A decisive Roman victory at the battle of Cynoscephalae in 197 BC had broken the power of Macedon, who had supported Carthage in the Second Punic War. This victory opened the way for Roman domination of Greece. In 146 Rome brought the whole of Greece under direct control; and in the same year ruthlessly destroyed Carthage, though it had long ceased to be a threat (▷2.12). The Hellenistic kingdoms of the east were also powerless to prevent Roman expansion. By 64 BC most of Anatolia and the Levant were under Roman rule and Egypt had been made a protectorate. Direct rule was imposed on Egypt in 30 BC (▷2.13).

Rome's successes put its republican system of government – designed for a city-state, not a world empire – under increasing strain: and a succession of civil wars between 50 and 31 BC brought about the collapse of the Roman republic. The eventual victor, Octavian, created a new form of government – in effect, an absolute monarchy. King in all but name, he took the titles *princeps* (first citizen) and Augustus. His successors used the title *imperator* (commander or emperor).

In northern Europe, the Celts found themselves caught between the Romans, who were expanding northward, and the Germans, who were pushing south: by 1 BC the only remaining independent Celts were in the British Isles (▷2.18).

In Africa, the Sabean colonies had developed into the kingdom of Axum around 100 BC. At about the same time the dromedary camel was introduced to the northern Sahara, transforming the lives of the desert nomads much as horse riding had earlier changed the steppe pastoralist way of life, enabling them to range widely and raid settled peoples almost at will. By 1 BC pastoralism had spread among the Khoisan-speaking peoples as far south as the Transvaal region and Bantu-speaking peoples had begun to settle on the east African plateau (▷2.21).

Following his victory in the civil war in China (202), Liu Bang restored prosperity by introducing a series of agricultural and administrative reforms but, despite heroic efforts, failed to stop damaging raids by the nomadic Xiongnu who continued to be a serious threat to China until 38 BC. The Han period saw Chinese expansion in the south (▷2.24), where the non-Chinese kingdoms of Min-yue and Nan-yue were conquered, and in Korea. Small kingdoms had begun to develop in parts of Korea not under Chinese occupation by 50 BC.

The rise of the Xiongnu had a destabilizing effect on the Iranian nomads to the west (▷2.20). In 170 the Xiongnu inflicted a crushing defeat on the Yue Qi, who fled westward, unsettling the Sakas, before overrunning the Bactrian kingdom around 135. The Sakas headed south, first invading the Parthian

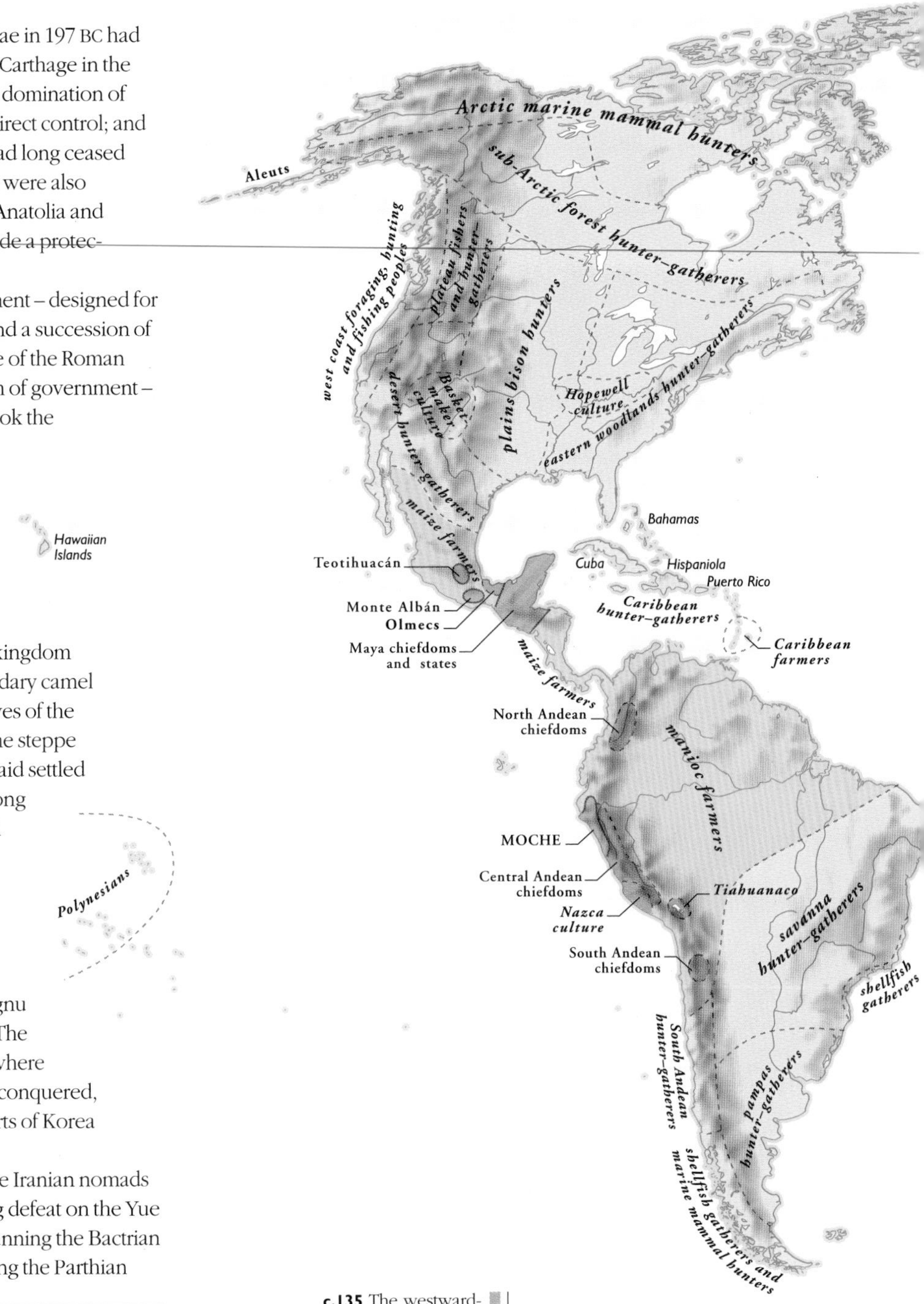

Arctic marine mammal hunters
sub-Arctic forest hunter-gatherers
Aleuts
west coast foraging, hunting and fishing peoples
plateau fishers and hunter-gatherers
plains bison hunters
Basket maker culture
desert hunter-gatherers
Hopewell culture
eastern woodlands hunter-gatherers
maize farmers
Hawaiian Islands
Bahamas
Teotihuacán
Cuba
Hispaniola
Puerto Rico
Monte Albán
Olmecs
Caribbean hunter-gatherers
Maya chiefdoms and states
Caribbean farmers
maize farmers
North Andean chiefdoms
manioc farmers
MOCHE
Central Andean chiefdoms
Tiahuanaco
Nazca culture
Polynesians
savanna hunter-gatherers
South Andean chiefdoms
shellfish gatherers
South Andean hunter-gatherers
pampas hunter-gatherers
shellfish gatherers and marine mammal hunters

c.135 The westward-driven Yue Qi overrun the Bactrian kingdom

170–141 The Parthians conquer the Seleucid kingdom

146 Roman control is extended throughout Greece

c.100 Foundation of the Moche state in the region of Peru

TIMELINE

The Americas
Europe
Middle East
Africa
East and South Asia

200 150 100

c.185 Fall of the Mauryan dynasty after Bactrians invade the Punjab

149–146 The Third Punic War: Rome levels the city of Carthage to the ground

101 China under the Han dynasty conquers Van Lang

170 The Hsiung-nu defeat the Yue Qi and dominate the eastern steppes

c.141 The Sakas invade the Parthian empire and northern India

c.100 The beginning of camel nomadism in the Sahara desert

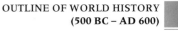

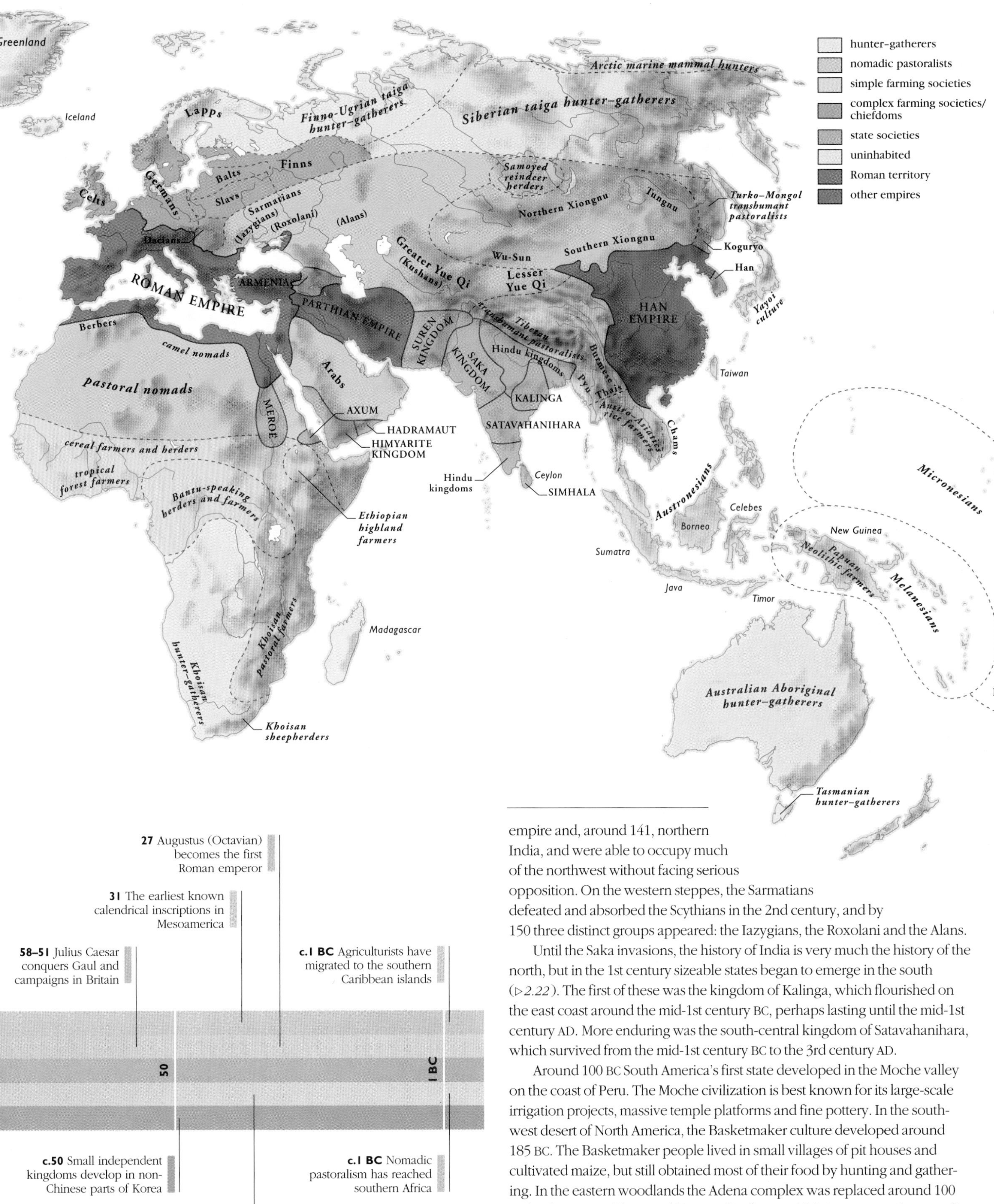
hunter-gatherers
nomadic pastoralists
simple farming societies
complex farming societies/ chiefdoms
state societies
uninhabited
Roman territory
other empires
Greenland
Iceland
Lapps
Finno-Ugrian taiga hunter-gatherers
Arctic marine mammal hunters
Siberian taiga hunter-gatherers
Celts
Germans
Balts
Finns
Slavs
Sarmatians (Iazygians) (Roxolani)
(Alans)
Samoyed reindeer herders
Northern Xiongnu
Tungnu
Turko-Mongol transhumant pastoralists
Dacians
Southern Xiongnu
Koguryo
Han
Greater Yue Qi (Kushans)
Wu-Sun
Lesser Yue Qi
ROMAN EMPIRE
ARMENIA
PARTHIAN EMPIRE
HAN EMPIRE
Yayoi culture
Berbers
camel nomads
SUREN KINGDOM
Tibetan transhumant pastoralists
Hindu kingdoms
SAKA KINGDOM
Burmese
Pyu
Thais
Taiwan
Arabs
pastoral nomads
MEROË
AXUM
HADRAMAUT
HIMYARITE KINGDOM
KALINGA
SATAVAHANIHARA
Austro-Asiatic rice farmers
Chams
cereal farmers and herders
tropical forest farmers
Bantu-speaking herders and farmers
Ethiopian highland farmers
Hindu kingdoms
Ceylon
SIMHALA
Austronesians
Borneo
Celebes
Micronesians
New Guinea
Papuan Neolithic farmers
Melanesians
Sumatra
Java
Timor
Madagascar
Khoisan pastoral farmers
Khoisan hunter-gatherers
Khoisan sheepherders
Australian Aboriginal hunter-gatherers
Polynesians
Tasmanian hunter-gatherers

empire and, around 141, northern India, and were able to occupy much of the northwest without facing serious opposition. On the western steppes, the Sarmatians defeated and absorbed the Scythians in the 2nd century, and by 150 three distinct groups appeared: the Iazygians, the Roxolani and the Alans.

Until the Saka invasions, the history of India is very much the history of the north, but in the 1st century sizeable states began to emerge in the south (▷2.22). The first of these was the kingdom of Kalinga, which flourished on the east coast around the mid-1st century BC, perhaps lasting until the mid-1st century AD. More enduring was the south-central kingdom of Satavahanihara, which survived from the mid-1st century BC to the 3rd century AD.

Around 100 BC South America's first state developed in the Moche valley on the coast of Peru. The Moche civilization is best known for its large-scale irrigation projects, massive temple platforms and fine pottery. In the southwest desert of North America, the Basketmaker culture developed around 185 BC. The Basketmaker people lived in small villages of pit houses and cultivated maize, but still obtained most of their food by hunting and gathering. In the eastern woodlands the Adena complex was replaced around 100 BC by the more widespread Hopewell culture, which incorporated many of its key characteristics such as construction of burial mounds. It was probably around 1 BC that farming peoples began to migrate from the South American mainland to the Caribbean islands ■

58–51 Julius Caesar conquers Gaul and campaigns in Britain

31 The earliest known calendrical inscriptions in Mesoamerica

27 Augustus (Octavian) becomes the first Roman emperor

c.1 BC Agriculturists have migrated to the southern Caribbean islands

50 | 1 BC

c.50 Small independent kingdoms develop in non-Chinese parts of Korea

30 Egypt becomes a Roman province after the death of Cleopatra

c.1 BC Nomadic pastoralism has reached southern Africa

The area of the – now Christian – Roman empire in AD 400, though slightly greater than in 1 BC, disguises Rome's true position. Although the emperor Diocletian (r.284–305) had given the empire a new lease of life by dividing it into eastern and western halves and completely reforming the administration and army, Rome was a state under siege. Pressure on the empire's borders was constant and the cost of maintaining defenses ruinous, especially in the poorer west. When the Huns, a Turkic-dominated nomad confederation from somewhere in central Asia, arrived in eastern Europe around 372, destabilizing the Germanic tribes, the empire was plunged back into crisis (▷2.15). To the east, the Sasanians, who had overthrown the Parthian empire in 226, were also posing a threat.

From around AD 50 the Kushan clan, which had become dominant among the Yue Qi, established an empire extending from the Aral Sea to the Indian Ocean and into northwest India. The empire had fallen by the late 4th century. Northern India continued to be divided into small states, until around 350, when Samudragupta (d.c.380) founded the Gupta empire (▷2.23), which by 410 had reached its greatest extent under Chandragupta II (r.380–414).

Farther east, the authority of the Han dynasty, which had reached the summit of its power in the 1st century, began to decline. In 189 the empire collapsed in chaos as army and court factions struggled to control an isolated and powerless emperor. The dynasty was overthrown in 220, when the empire split into three kingdoms (▷2.25). In 280 unity was briefly restored, but civil war again broke out, giving the Xiongnu the opportunity to conquer the north of the country. A second wave of nomads – the Turkic Toba tribes – arrived in 386 and won control of the north. The Toba Wei state itself was threatened by the Juan-juan, a Mongol-dominated nomad confederation which arose in the late 4th century and controlled the eastern steppes by 400.

Small states sprang up in southern Japan in the 2nd or 3rd centuries, though most of these had been incorporated into the Yamato kingdom of Honshu by 400. The first southeast Asian states – the trading kingdom of Funan and the Cham kingdom of Champa – had developed by the 2nd century. Madagascar had been discovered and settled by Austronesian peoples from Indonesia in the 1st century AD, a voyaging feat to be matched by the Polynesians, who by 400 had colonized Hawaii and Easter Island.

In Africa the kingdom of Meroë collapsed around 350 as a result of nomad

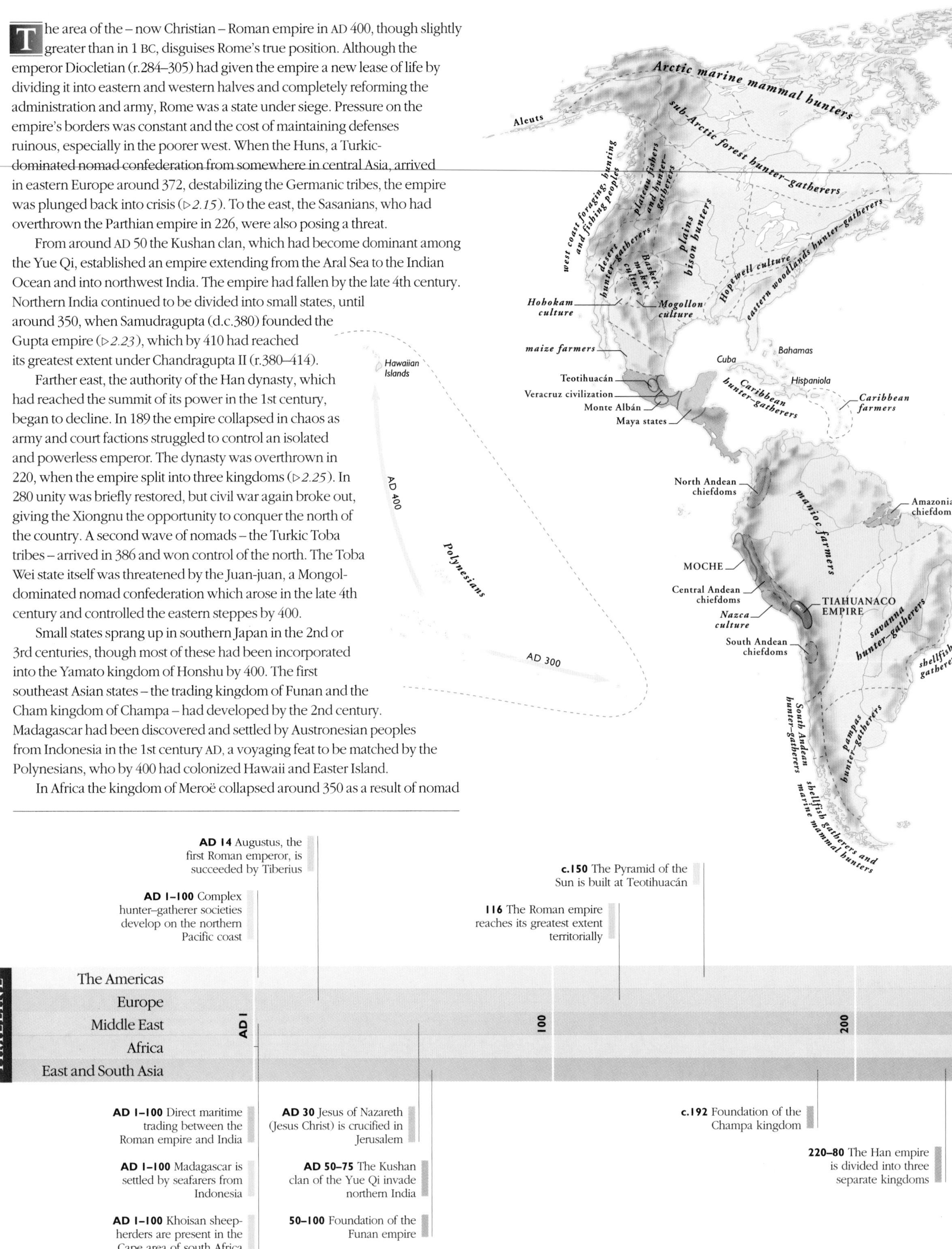
Arctic marine mammal bunters
sub-Arctic forest hunter-gatherers
Aleuts
west coast foraging, hunting and fishing peoples
plateau fishers and hunter-gatherers
plains bison hunters
desert hunter-gatherers
Basket maker culture
Hopewell culture
eastern woodlands hunter-gatherers
Hohokam culture
Mogollon culture
maize farmers
Hawaiian Islands
Bahamas
Cuba
Hispaniola
Teotihuacán
Veracruz civilization
Monte Albán
Maya states
Caribbean hunter-gatherers
Caribbean farmers
North Andean chiefdoms
manioc farmers
Amazonian chiefdoms
AD 400
Polynesians
MOCHE
Central Andean chiefdoms
Nazca culture
TIAHUANACO EMPIRE
savanna hunter-gatherers
South Andean chiefdoms
AD 300
shellfish gatherers
South Andean hunter-gatherers
pampas hunter-gatherers
shellfish gatherers and marine mammal hunters
AD 14 Augustus, the first Roman emperor, is succeeded by Tiberius
AD 1–100 Complex hunter–gatherer societies develop on the northern Pacific coast
c.150 The Pyramid of the Sun is built at Teotihuacán
116 The Roman empire reaches its greatest extent territorially
TIMELINE
The Americas
Europe
Middle East
Africa
East and South Asia
AD 1
100
200
AD 1–100 Direct maritime trading between the Roman empire and India
AD 30 Jesus of Nazareth (Jesus Christ) is crucified in Jerusalem
c.192 Foundation of the Champa kingdom
220–80 The Han empire is divided into three separate kingdoms
AD 1–100 Madagascar is settled by seafarers from Indonesia
AD 50–75 The Kushan clan of the Yue Qi invade northern India
AD 1–100 Khoisan sheep-herders are present in the Cape area of south Africa
50–100 Foundation of the Funan empire

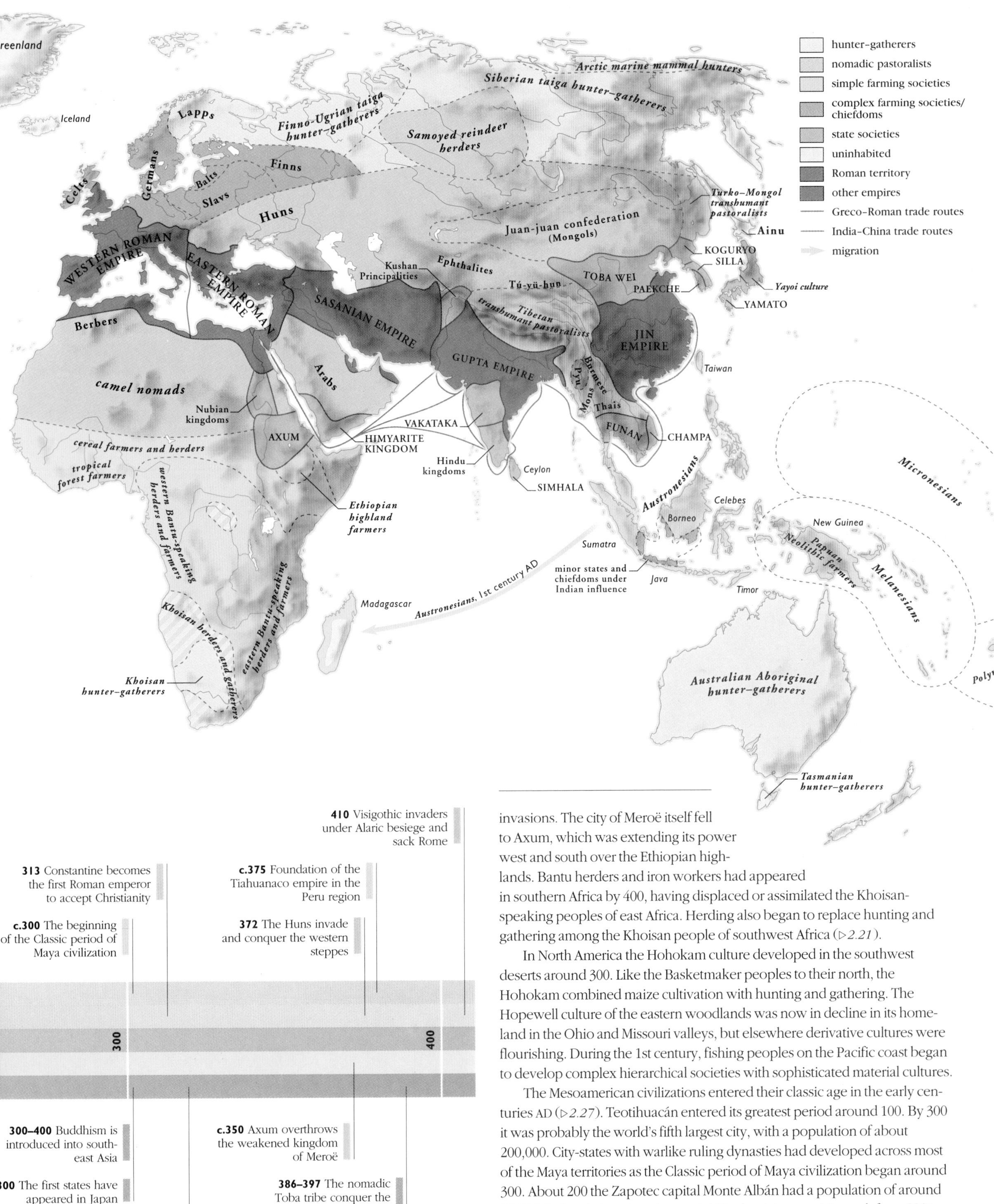
hunter-gatherers
nomadic pastoralists
simple farming societies
complex farming societies/ chiefdoms
state societies
uninhabited
Roman territory
other empires
Greco-Roman trade routes
India-China trade routes
migration
Greenland
Iceland
Lapps
Finno-Ugrian taiga hunter-gatherers
Samoyed reindeer herders
Arctic marine mammal hunters
Siberian taiga hunter-gatherers
Celts
Germans
Balts
Finns
Slavs
Huns
Juan-juan confederation (Mongols)
Turko-Mongol transhumant pastoralists
Ainu
KOGURYO
SILLA
PAEKCHE
Yayoi culture
YAMATO
WESTERN ROMAN EMPIRE
EASTERN ROMAN EMPIRE
Kushan Principalities
Ephthalites
Tú-yü-hun
TOBA WEI
Tibetan transhumant pastoralists
SASANIAN EMPIRE
JIN EMPIRE
Berbers
Arabs
GUPTA EMPIRE
Burmese
Pyu
Mons
Thais
Taiwan
camel nomads
Nubian kingdoms
AXUM
VAKATAKA
HIMYARITE KINGDOM
FUNAN
CHAMPA
cereal farmers and herders
tropical forest farmers
Hindu kingdoms
Ceylon
SIMHALA
Austronesians
Micronesians
western Bantu-speaking herders and farmers
Ethiopian highland farmers
Borneo
Celebes
New Guinea
Papuan Neolithic farmers
Sumatra
minor states and chiefdoms under Indian influence
Java
Timor
Melanesians
Austronesians, 1st century AD
Madagascar
Khoisan herders and gatherers
eastern Bantu-speaking herders and farmers
Khoisan hunter-gatherers
Australian Aboriginal hunter-gatherers
Polynesians
Tasmanian hunter-gatherers
300
400

410 Visigothic invaders under Alaric besiege and sack Rome

313 Constantine becomes the first Roman emperor to accept Christianity

c.375 Foundation of the Tiahuanaco empire in the Peru region

c.300 The beginning of the Classic period of Maya civilization

372 The Huns invade and conquer the western steppes

300–400 Buddhism is introduced into south-east Asia

c.350 Axum overthrows the weakened kingdom of Meroë

300 The first states have appeared in Japan

386–397 The nomadic Toba tribe conquer the Wei state in north China

320 Foundation of the Gupta kingdom in northern India

invasions. The city of Meroë itself fell to Axum, which was extending its power west and south over the Ethiopian highlands. Bantu herders and iron workers had appeared in southern Africa by 400, having displaced or assimilated the Khoisan-speaking peoples of east Africa. Herding also began to replace hunting and gathering among the Khoisan people of southwest Africa (▷*2.21*).

In North America the Hohokam culture developed in the southwest deserts around 300. Like the Basketmaker peoples to their north, the Hohokam combined maize cultivation with hunting and gathering. The Hopewell culture of the eastern woodlands was now in decline in its homeland in the Ohio and Missouri valleys, but elsewhere derivative cultures were flourishing. During the 1st century, fishing peoples on the Pacific coast began to develop complex hierarchical societies with sophisticated material cultures.

The Mesoamerican civilizations entered their classic age in the early centuries AD (▷*2.27*). Teotihuacán entered its greatest period around 100. By 300 it was probably the world's fifth largest city, with a population of about 200,000. City-states with warlike ruling dynasties had developed across most of the Maya territories as the Classic period of Maya civilization began around 300. About 200 the Zapotec capital Monte Albán had a population of around 30,000. In South America, the coastal Moche state was at its peak from 200 to 400, and the Tiahuanaco state, in the Lake Titicaca highlands, was beginning a period of imperial expansion (▷*2.28*) ■

2.05 THE WORLD • AD 600 •

The western half of the Roman empire, altogether poorer and less populated than the east, was also more exposed to Germanic barbarian attack. In 406 German tribes – Goths, Franks, Vandals and others – overran the Rhine frontier and by 476 the western Roman empire was almost entirely under their control. The wealthy eastern half of the Roman empire survived more or less unscathed and its emperor Justinian counter-attacked against the barbarians in the 530s, restoring Roman rule in Italy, north Africa and southern Spain (▷*2.17*). However, the empire was put back on the defensive after Justinian's death; much of Italy fell to the Lombards and most of southern Spain to the Visigoths by 600. The most successful of the Germanic invaders were the Franks, who had settled northern Gaul in the early 5th century. From 486 they were united by Clovis, who extended his kingdom into southern Gaul and east into Germany. By 600 the Frankish kingdom stretched from the Pyrenees almost to the Elbe. The end of Roman rule in Britain saw a revival of Celtic culture but in about 450 Angles and Saxons from north Germany began to settle the fertile east of Britain, driving the Celts to the hillier west.

Fear of the Huns drove the Germanic peoples to invade the Roman empire. The Huns extended their control as far west as the Rhine – further west than any steppe nomads in history – and raided both halves of the Roman empire under Attila (r. 433–453). However, after his death the Hun confederation broke up and returned to the steppes. Between 460 and 515 the Ephthalite (or "White") Huns destroyed the last Kushan principalities of central Asia, raided the Sasanian empire and conquered northwest India, only to be driven out in 528 (▷*2.20*). On the eastern steppes, the Mongol-dominated Juan-juan confederacy was broken by a rebellion of the Turks in 552. By 600 the Turks had destroyed the Ephthalites and dominated the steppes as far west as the Aral Sea. The Khazars, another Turkic people, were established on the Caspian steppes. A part of the Juan-juan, the Avars, fled from the Turks and arrived on the European steppes in about 562 where they mopped up the remnants of the Huns and raided the Balkans. North of the Caucasus the Alans – the sole remnant of the Iranian peoples who had once dominated the steppes – re-emerged from Hunnic dominance in the 450s.

In Africa, Christianity had spread to Nubia and Axum by the 6th century, strengthening cultural and political links with the eastern Roman empire (▷*2.21*). With Roman encouragement, the Axumites conquered southwest Arabia in 528 but were expelled by the Sasanians in 574, ending Christian influence in Arabia just four years after the birth of Muhammad at Mecca. In west Africa intensive dry-rice farming led to a rising population on the upper Niger and the foundation of large villages in the 3rd and 4th centuries. One of these, Jenne-jeno, became the center of a wideranging network of west

Arctic marine mammal hunters
Aleuts
sub-Arctic forest hunter-gatherers
west coast foraging, hunting and fishing peoples
plateau fishers and hunter-gatherers
desert hunter-gatherers
Basket maker culture
plains bison hunters
Hopewell culture
eastern woodlands hunter-gatherers
Hohokam culture
Mogollon culture
maize farmers
Hawaiian Islands
Bahamas
Cuba
Teotihuacán
Hispaniola
Veracruz civilization
Puerto Rico
Caribbean hunter-gatherers
Caribbean farmers
Monte Albán
Maya states
North Andean chiefdoms
Amazonian chiefdoms
manioc farmers
Polynesians
MOCHE
HUARI EMPIRE
farming (replacing hunter-gatherers)
TIAHUANACO EMPIRE
savanna hunter-gatherers
South Andean hunter-gatherers
pampas hunter-gatherers
shellfish gatherers and marine mammal hunters

c.500 Foundation of the Huari empire in the highlands of Peru

481–511 Reign of Clovis, undisputed Frankish king of Gaul from 486

476 Fall of the western Roman empire when the the emperor Romulus is deposed

410 The Visigoths, led by Alaric, sack Rome

c.450 The Angles and Saxons begin to settle eastern Britain

533–54 Roman emperor Justinian reconquers most of north Africa and Italy

TIMELINE

The Americas
Europe
Middle East
Africa
East and South Asia

400 450 500 550

c.400 Iron working reaches southern Africa

c.400 Jenne-jeno flourishes as the first town in west Africa

429 A wealthy Vandal kingdom is set up in north Africa

460–528 The Ephthalite Huns ("Hunas") invade northwest India

c.470 Decline of the Gupta empire in northern India

531–79 Sasanian Persia achieves its maximum extent under Chosroes I

c.540 Christianity is introduced into Nubia

c.550 The Turkish khanates are dominant throughout central Asia

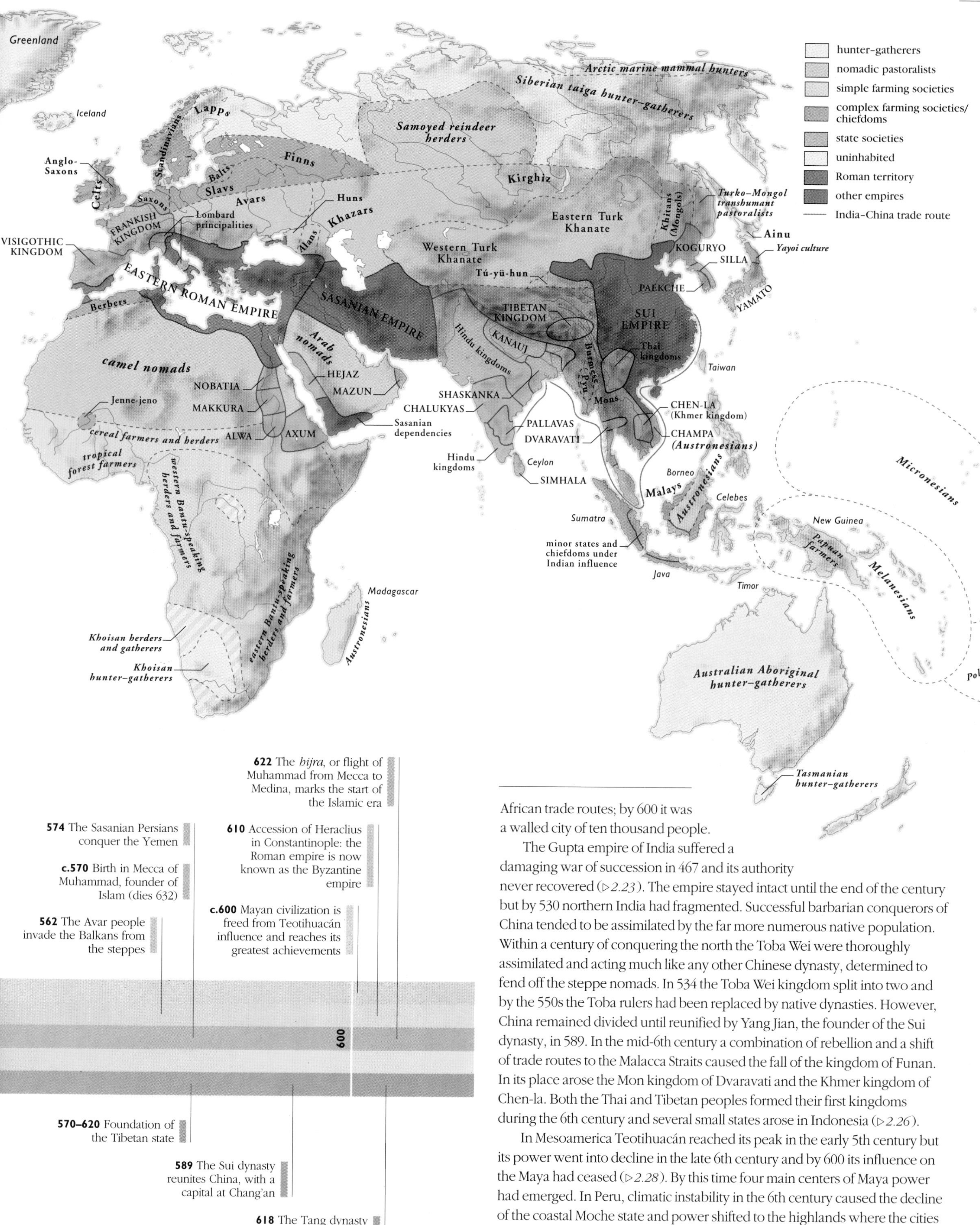
hunter-gatherers
nomadic pastoralists
simple farming societies
complex farming societies/ chiefdoms
state societies
uninhabited
Roman territory
other empires
India–China trade route
Greenland
Iceland
Lapps
Scandinavians
Anglo-Saxons
Celts
Saxons
Balts
Finns
Slavs
Avars
FRANKISH KINGDOM
Lombard principalities
Huns
Khazars
Alans
VISIGOTHIC KINGDOM
EASTERN ROMAN EMPIRE
Berbers
SASANIAN EMPIRE
Arab nomads
camel nomads
NOBATIA
MAKKURA
ALWA
AXUM
HEJAZ
MAZUN
Sasanian dependencies
Jenne-jeno
cereal farmers and herders
tropical forest farmers
western Bantu-speaking herders and farmers
eastern Bantu-speaking herders and farmers
Khoisan herders and gatherers
Khoisan hunter-gatherers
Madagascar
Austronesians
Arctic marine mammal hunters
Siberian taiga hunter-gatherers
Samoyed reindeer herders
Kirghiz
Eastern Turk Khanate
Western Turk Khanate
Khitans (Mongols)
Turko-Mongol transhumant pastoralists
Ainu
Yayoi culture
KOGURYO
SILLA
PAEKCHE
YAMATO
Tú-yü-hun
TIBETAN KINGDOM
KANAUJ
Hindu kingdoms
SUI EMPIRE
Thai kingdoms
Burmese
Pyu
Mons
Taiwan
SHASKANKA
CHALUKYAS
PALLAVAS
DVARAVATI
CHEN-LA (Khmer kingdom)
CHAMPA (Austronesians)
Hindu kingdoms
Ceylon
SIMHALA
Borneo
Malays
Austronesians
Celebes
Sumatra
minor states and chiefdoms under Indian influence
Java
Timor
New Guinea
Papuan farmers
Melanesians
Micronesians
Polynesians
Australian Aboriginal hunter-gatherers
Tasmanian hunter-gatherers
622 The hijra, or flight of Muhammad from Mecca to Medina, marks the start of the Islamic era
574 The Sasanian Persians conquer the Yemen
610 Accession of Heraclius in Constantinople: the Roman empire is now known as the Byzantine empire
c.570 Birth in Mecca of Muhammad, founder of Islam (dies 632)
c.600 Mayan civilization is freed from Teotihuacán influence and reaches its greatest achievements
562 The Avar people invade the Balkans from the steppes
600
570–620 Foundation of the Tibetan state
589 The Sui dynasty reunites China, with a capital at Chang'an
618 The Tang dynasty replaces the Sui in China

African trade routes; by 600 it was a walled city of ten thousand people.

The Gupta empire of India suffered a damaging war of succession in 467 and its authority never recovered (▷*2.23*). The empire stayed intact until the end of the century but by 530 northern India had fragmented. Successful barbarian conquerors of China tended to be assimilated by the far more numerous native population. Within a century of conquering the north the Toba Wei were thoroughly assimilated and acting much like any other Chinese dynasty, determined to fend off the steppe nomads. In 534 the Toba Wei kingdom split into two and by the 550s the Toba rulers had been replaced by native dynasties. However, China remained divided until reunified by Yang Jian, the founder of the Sui dynasty, in 589. In the mid-6th century a combination of rebellion and a shift of trade routes to the Malacca Straits caused the fall of the kingdom of Funan. In its place arose the Mon kingdom of Dvaravati and the Khmer kingdom of Chen-la. Both the Thai and Tibetan peoples formed their first kingdoms during the 6th century and several small states arose in Indonesia (▷*2.26*).

In Mesoamerica Teotihuacán reached its peak in the early 5th century but its power went into decline in the late 6th century and by 600 its influence on the Maya had ceased (▷*2.28*). By this time four main centers of Maya power had emerged. In Peru, climatic instability in the 6th century caused the decline of the coastal Moche state and power shifted to the highlands where the cities of Tiahuanaco and Huari had built considerable empires by 600 (▷*2.27*) ■

The years 1000 BC–AD 600 saw the emergence of every major world religion except Islam (a world religion is one that has endured and influenced diverse civilizations). Hinduism and Judaism had earlier roots but assumed their present form at this time; Christianity, Buddhism, Zoroastrianism, Daoism and Confucianism all arose 600 BC–AD 600.

Early Hinduism was based on the Vedas, hymns of the Aryans who invaded India around 1500 BC, but was also influenced by indigenous Dravidian traditions. Vedic Hinduism looked forward to a future existence in heaven; it was not until the 6th century BC that the belief in *karma* and rebirth, central to modern Hinduism, developed. The complex rituals of early Hinduism gave rise to a distinctive feature of Indian civilization, the caste system – the priestly Brahmins forming the highest caste. By 500 BC Hinduism dominated the Indian subcontinent, but discontent with Brahminical traditions grew on the Gangetic plain, where urbanization created a more materialistic society. New sects developed there, the most successful of them being Buddhism.

The founder of Buddhism was Siddhartha Gautama, known as the Buddha, or "Enlightened One." Many legends have become associated with the Buddha and little is known for certain of his life: even his original teachings are a matter of debate as the canon of Buddhist scripture was not written down until four centuries after his death. Buddhism remained a minor sect until the Mauryan emperor Ashoka converted in 260 BC. Under his patronage Buddhist missionaries spread the religion throughout India and to Ceylon and the Iranian nomads in central Asia. In northern India Buddhism supplanted Hinduism as the majority religion. It then spread from central Asia along the Silk Route, reaching China in the 1st century AD; Indian seafarers took it to southeast Asia in the 4th century. By the 3rd century AD Buddhism had divided into two schools: Theravada (Doctrine of the Elders), which adhered strictly to the established Buddhist canon, and Mahayana (Great Vehicle), a more liberal, eclectic tradition. Hinduism responded to the rise of Buddhism by becoming more flexible and tolerant, and by AD 400 it was beginning to recover in India. In the 5th century Hinduism spread to southeast Asia.

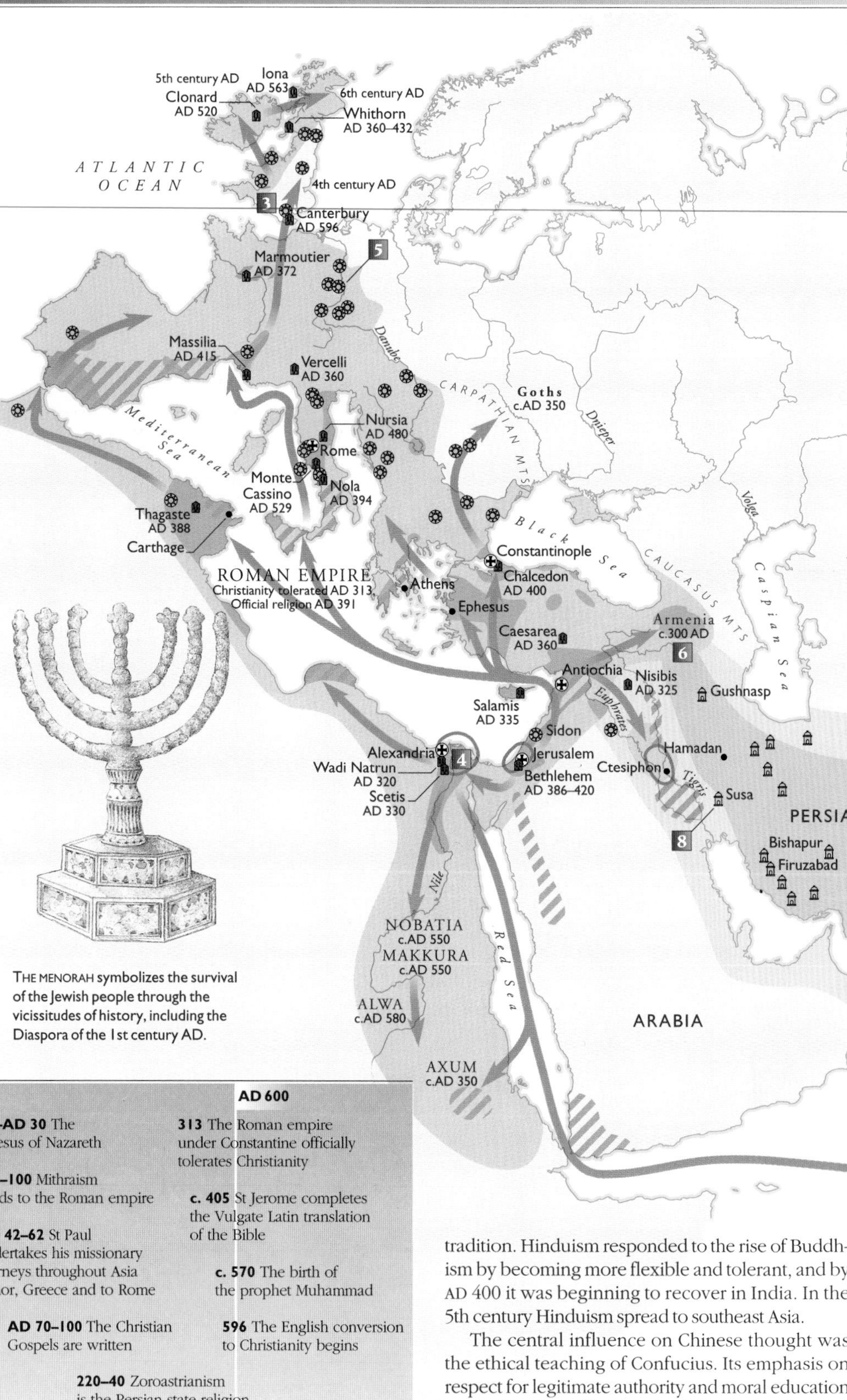

5th century AD
Clonard AD 520
Iona AD 563
6th century AD
Whithorn AD 360–432
ATLANTIC OCEAN
4th century AD
3
Canterbury AD 596
Marmoutier AD 372
5
Massilia AD 415
Vercelli AD 360
Danube
CARPATHIAN MTS
Goths c.AD 350
Dnieper
Mediterranean Sea
Nursia AD 480
Rome
Monte Cassino AD 529
Nola AD 394
Thagaste AD 388
Carthage
Black Sea
Constantinople
Chalcedon AD 400
CAUCASUS MTS
Volga
Caspian Sea
ROMAN EMPIRE
Christianity tolerated AD 313, Official religion AD 391
Athens
Ephesus
Caesarea AD 360
Armenia c.300 AD
6
Antiochia
Nisibis AD 325
Gushnasp
Euphrates
Salamis AD 335
Sidon
Jerusalem
Bethlehem AD 386–420
Alexandria
4
Wadi Natrun AD 320
Scetis AD 330
Hamadan
Ctesiphon
Tigris
Susa
PERSIA
8
Bishapur
Firuzabad
Nile
NOBATIA c.AD 550
MAKKURA c.AD 550
Red Sea
ALWA c.AD 580
AXUM c.AD 350
ARABIA

THE MENORAH symbolizes the survival of the Jewish people through the vicissitudes of history, including the Diaspora of the 1st century AD.

TIMELINE

Middle East and Europe

600 BC

c.630–553 The life of Zoroaster, founder of Zoroastrianism

587 The Jews are deported to Babylonia by Nebuchadnezzar. This marks the beginning of the Diaspora

AD 1

c.6 BC–AD 30 The life of Jesus of Nazareth

AD 1–100 Mithraism spreads to the Roman empire

AD 42–62 St Paul undertakes his missionary journeys throughout Asia Minor, Greece and to Rome

AD 70–100 The Christian Gospels are written

220–40 Zoroastrianism is the Persian state religion

AD 600

313 The Roman empire under Constantine officially tolerates Christianity

c. 405 St Jerome completes the Vulgate Latin translation of the Bible

c. 570 The birth of the prophet Muhammad

596 The English conversion to Christianity begins

South and east Asia

800–400 The *Upanishads* of Hinduism are composed

6th century The life of Lao Zi, the inspirer of Daoism

c.563–483 Life of Siddhartha Gautama, the Buddha

551–479 The life of the Chinese sage Confucius

600 BC

260 The Mauryan emperor Ashoka becomes a Buddhist and sends Buddhist missions to Ceylon and central Asia

c.240 BC The *Dao De Jing*, the basic text of Daoism, is composed

AD 1–100 Mahayana Buddhism develops

AD 1

253–333 The life of Ko Hung, founder of religious Daoism

259 Chinese Buddhists begin pilgrimages to India

300–500 The Hindu epics the *Ramayana* and the *Mahabharata* are written down in their final form

AD 600

The central influence on Chinese thought was the ethical teaching of Confucius. Its emphasis on respect for legitimate authority and moral education made this the official orthodoxy under the Han dynasty (206 BC–AD 220). In the disorder following the fall of the Han, Confucianism declined and Buddhism became a stronger influence in China. Buddhism was itself influenced by Chinese philosophies, particularly Daoism, a system inspired by the teachings of Lao Zi, a philosopher of the 6th century BC. The traditional Chinese practice of ancestor worship remained strong throughout these changes.

Although it was the religion of a minor and relatively unimportant people, the Hebrews, Judaism was the most influential religion of the Middle East. It was the first major monotheistic religion and its

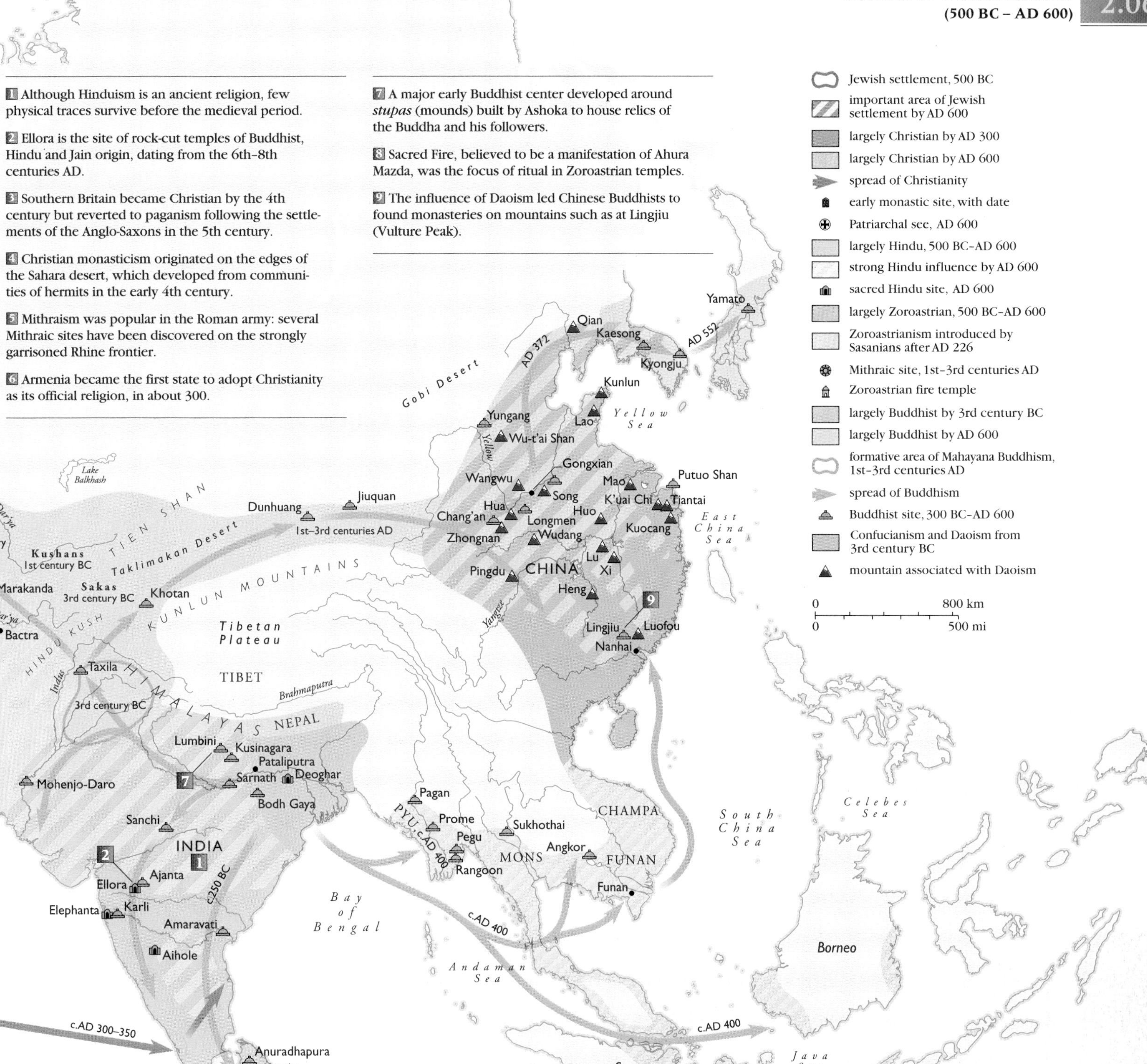
1 Although Hinduism is an ancient religion, few physical traces survive before the medieval period.
2 Ellora is the site of rock-cut temples of Buddhist, Hindu and Jain origin, dating from the 6th–8th centuries AD.
3 Southern Britain became Christian by the 4th century but reverted to paganism following the settlements of the Anglo-Saxons in the 5th century.
4 Christian monasticism originated on the edges of the Sahara desert, which developed from communities of hermits in the early 4th century.
5 Mithraism was popular in the Roman army: several Mithraic sites have been discovered on the strongly garrisoned Rhine frontier.
6 Armenia became the first state to adopt Christianity as its official religion, in about 300.
7 A major early Buddhist center developed around *stupas* (mounds) built by Ashoka to house relics of the Buddha and his followers.
8 Sacred Fire, believed to be a manifestation of Ahura Mazda, was the focus of ritual in Zoroastrian temples.
9 The influence of Daoism led Chinese Buddhists to found monasteries on mountains such as at Lingjiu (Vulture Peak).
Jewish settlement, 500 BC
important area of Jewish settlement by AD 600
largely Christian by AD 300
largely Christian by AD 600
spread of Christianity
early monastic site, with date
Patriarchal see, AD 600
largely Hindu, 500 BC–AD 600
strong Hindu influence by AD 600
sacred Hindu site, AD 600
largely Zoroastrian, 500 BC–AD 600
Zoroastrianism introduced by Sasanians after AD 226
Mithraic site, 1st–3rd centuries AD
Zoroastrian fire temple
largely Buddhist by 3rd century BC
largely Buddhist by AD 600
formative area of Mahayana Buddhism, 1st–3rd centuries AD
spread of Buddhism
Buddhist site, 300 BC–AD 600
Confucianism and Daoism from 3rd century BC
mountain associated with Daoism
0 800 km
0 500 mi
Yamato
AD 552
Qian
Kaesong
Kyongju
AD 372
Gobi Desert
Kunlun
Yellow Sea
Yungang
Lao
Wu-t'ai Shan
Yellow
Gongxian
Putuo Shan
Wangwu
Mao
Song
K'uai Chi
Tiantai
Hua
Huo
Chang'an
Longmen
East China Sea
Zhongnan
Wudang
Kuocang
Lu
Pingdu
CHINA
Xi
Heng
Yangtze
Lingjiu
Luofou
Nanhai
Lake Balkhash
TIEN SHAN
Dunhuang
Jiuquan
1st–3rd centuries AD
Taklimakan Desert
Kushans 1st century BC
Marakanda
Sakas 3rd century BC
Khotan
KUNLUN MOUNTAINS
Bactra
HINDU KUSH
Tibetan Plateau
Taxila
TIBET
Indus
3rd century BC
Brahmaputra
HIMALAYAS
NEPAL
Lumbini
Kusinagara
Pataliputra
Sarnath
Deoghar
Mohenjo-Daro
Bodh Gaya
Sanchi
INDIA
Ajanta
Ellora
c.250 BC
Elephanta
Karli
Amaravati
Aihole
Pagan
PYU c.AD 400
Prome
Pegu
Sukhothai
CHAMPA
Rangoon
MONS
Angkor
FUNAN
Funan
South China Sea
Celebes Sea
Bay of Bengal
c.AD 400
Andaman Sea
Borneo
c.AD 300–350
Anuradhapura
Kandy
Ceylon
c.AD 400
Sumatra
Srivijaya
Java Sea
Java
INDIAN OCEAN

teachings provided the basis of Christianity and Islam. Judaism was a national religion and did not actively seek converts among non-Jews; yet the Hebrews' turbulent history meant that it became very widespread in the Mediterranean and Middle East by AD 600. The Diaspora, or dispersal of the Jews, began in the 6th century BC when communities of exiles from Palestine were established in Egypt and Mesopotamia. The greatest dispersal of Jews occurred in the 1st and 2nd centuries AD, following rebellions in Palestine against Roman rule.

Christianity originated in the teachings of a Jew, Jesus of Nazareth, who rejected the current practice of Judaism. Christianity developed initially as a Jewish sect, but the influence of St Paul and others made the religion more attractive to non-Jews, and by AD 70 its separation from Judaism was complete. Because of their refusal to pay formal homage to the state gods, Christians often faced persecution by the Roman emperors. Despite this Christianity was well established, especially in the eastern empire, by 312 when the emperor Constantine converted, introducing formal toleration the following year. Christianity made rapid progress after this, and in 391 it became the Roman empire's official religion. Christians came to believe that God had created the Roman empire specifically for the purpose of spreading Christianity.

An early rival to Christianity in the Roman empire was Mithraism, a derivative of the Persian Zoroastrian religion. Zoroaster, the religion's founder, reformed the ancient Iranian religion, dividing the pantheon into good and evil deities. It developed into a dualist religion which taught that the chief god Ahura Mazda, aided by Mithra, was locked in combat to protect the world from his evil rival Ahriman. Zoroastrianism became the religion of the Achemenid rulers of Persia and flourished under the Parthians and Sasanians. Although in its pure form it won few converts outside Persia, its teaching on the nature of good and evil had an important influence on Hellenistic, Jewish, Christian and Islamic thought.

See also 1.26 (early India); 2.15 (the Christian empire); 3.05 (medieval world religions)

2.07 The Persian wars and 5th-century Greece • 499 – 435 BC •

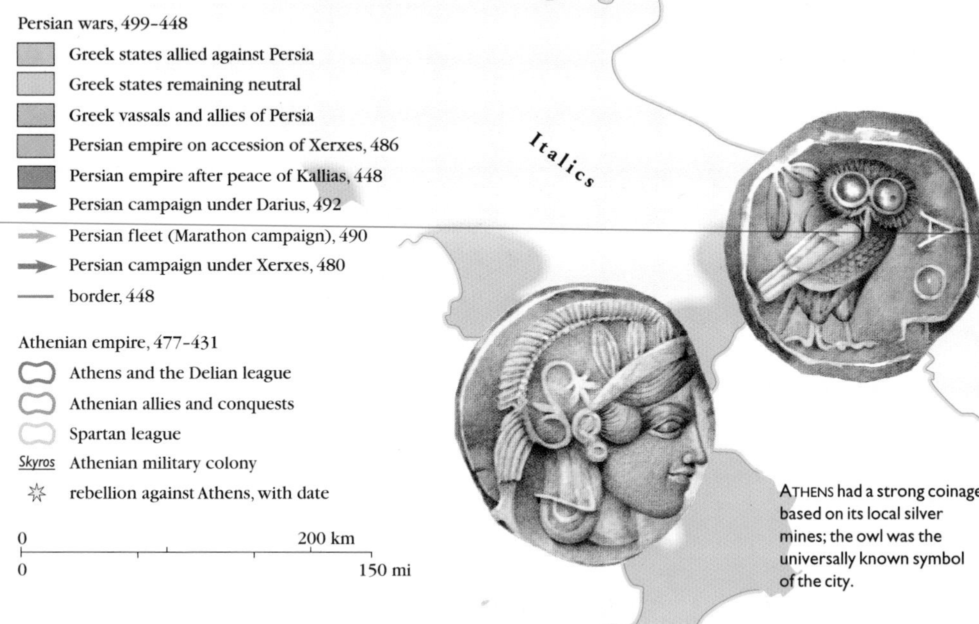
Persian wars, 499–448
Greek states allied against Persia
Greek states remaining neutral
Greek vassals and allies of Persia
Persian empire on accession of Xerxes, 486
Persian empire after peace of Kallias, 448
Persian campaign under Darius, 492
Persian fleet (Marathon campaign), 490
Persian campaign under Xerxes, 480
border, 448
Athenian empire, 477–431
Athens and the Delian league
Athenian allies and conquests
Spartan league
Skyros Athenian military colony
rebellion against Athens, with date
0 200 km
0 150 mi
Italics

ATHENS had a strong coinage based on its local silver mines; the owl was the universally known symbol of the city.

After Cyrus, founder of the Persian empire, conquered Lydia in 546 BC, his generals mopped up the relatively insignificant Greek cities of Ionia, but in 499 they rebelled again under the leadership of Aristagoras of Miletos and introduced democratic rule. The rebels received aid from Athens and this provoked the Persian king Darius (r.521–486) to plan a punitive invasion of Greece after the revolt had been crushed in 494.

Darius' first invasion, in 492, was defeated by the weather when the fleet supporting his army was destroyed in a storm rounding Mount Athos. After a second expedition was humiliatingly defeated by the Athenians at Marathon in 490, Darius decided that the conquest of the whole of Greece was needed to secure the Persian position in Ionia. He died before his preparations were complete and it was left to his son Xerxes to carry out his plans. Meanwhile the Greeks prepared for an invasion, with Themistocles persuading Athens – by far the largest and wealthiest *polis* or city-state – to invest in an urgent naval building program.

The history of this invasion was memorably recorded by the Ionian-born Herodotos, the first major Greek prose writer and historian, later in the 5th century. Xerxes' army, said to have been 200,000 strong, was one of the largest forces ever assembled in antiquity and was supported by a fleet of perhaps a thousand ships. Faced with this vast force, most of the northern Greek states opted for neutrality or (in a few cases) alliance with Persia. The southern Greek states, however, united under the leadership of Athens and Sparta and prepared to resist the Persians. The resulting struggle was less uneven than expected. The very size of the Persian army proved a serious handicap; it was difficult to supply and impossible to control effectively on a battlefield; the quality of its troops varied enormously and only around 10,000 were elite troops. In contrast the Greeks, though greatly outnumbered, were heavily armed, experienced, disciplined and highly motivated: they were citizens defending their states, homes and families.

The Greeks, led by Sparta, attempted to halt the Persian invasion at Thermopylae but were defeated after heroic resistance. The Persians went on to occupy Athens, although its population had been evacuated to Salamis. The Persian fleet, which was needed to outflank Spartan defenses on the Isthmus of Corinth, was now ambushed and destroyed by the Athenian navy at Salamis. Since it was clear that Greece could not now be conquered in a single campaign, Xerxes returned to Asia with half of the army: the remainder wintered in Greece only to be defeated decisively by a Spartan-led army at Plataea in the following year. The threat to Greece ended, the old rivalries of the Greek world resurfaced and Sparta and most of the other states withdrew from the war against Persia. Athens and its allies continued hostilities, destroying the last Persian garrisons in Europe, re-opening the Bosporus to Greek shipping by 475, and freeing the Ionian Greeks from Persian rule in 468. The Athenians also intervened unsuccessfully against the Persians in Egypt in 454 and captured Cyprus in 450. Hostilities came to a formal end in 448 when the Persians recognized Ionian independence.

To pursue its war aims, Athens created the anti-Persian Delian league of Aegean cities, with a common treasury on the island of Delos to which all members contributed. As its richest member and greatest naval power, Athens dominated the league and came increasingly to regard it as its empire. Some states, such as Aegina, were forcibly enrolled, and if a dissatisfied member tried to withhold contributions, the Athenian fleet was sent to enforce obedience. When the Athenians moved the treasury to Athens in 454 its domination became even more apparent. Despite this, many members remained loyal, being grateful to Athens for its role in the Persian wars and for introducing democracy. After the end of the war with Persia the league became as much a commercial as a military organization, although still serving Athenian interests. Athenian coinage, weights and measures were introduced throughout the league.

Under the leadership of the highly nationalistic Pericles, Athens also extended its power on the mainland and by 460 had achieved a dominant position in central Greece. Sparta – unusual in still having a monarchical constitution – had the strongest army in Greece and was unwilling to surrender its primacy to the increasingly arrogant Athenians. Throughout the 460s the Spartans were preoccupied with a *helot* (serf) revolt, but moves to increase the influence of Athens within the Peloponnese led to the outbreak of war between the two rivals in 457.

Athens was unable to sustain a war against Persia and Sparta at the same time, but the peace treaty with Persia in 448 in some ways weakened the Athenian position. Without the fear of a return to Persian rule, many members of the Delian league felt less closely bound to Athens. Sparta, which had no navy, concentrated its attack on the Athenian position on the mainland of central Greece while attempting to foment rebellion in the league. The Athenians successfully put down rebellions in

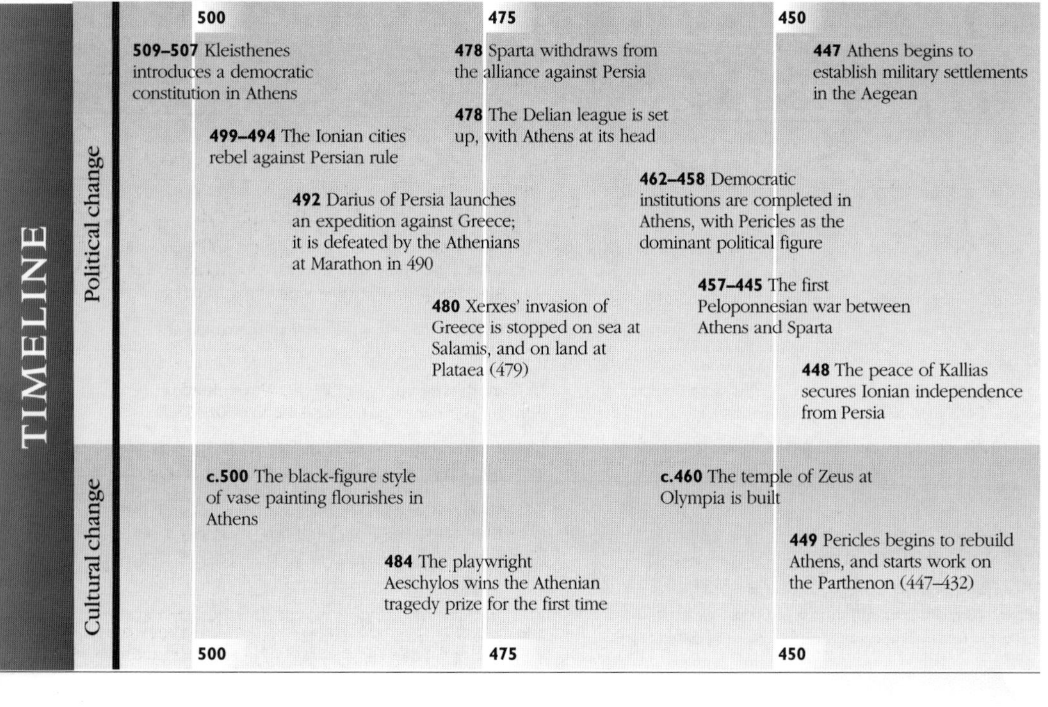
TIMELINE
Political change
500
475
450
509–507 Kleisthenes introduces a democratic constitution in Athens
499–494 The Ionian cities rebel against Persian rule
492 Darius of Persia launches an expedition against Greece; it is defeated by the Athenians at Marathon in 490
480 Xerxes' invasion of Greece is stopped on sea at Salamis, and on land at Plataea (479)
478 Sparta withdraws from the alliance against Persia
478 The Delian league is set up, with Athens at its head
462–458 Democratic institutions are completed in Athens, with Pericles as the dominant political figure
457–445 The first Peloponnesian war between Athens and Sparta
447 Athens begins to establish military settlements in the Aegean
448 The peace of Kallias secures Ionian independence from Persia
Cultural change
c.500 The black-figure style of vase painting flourishes in Athens
484 The playwright Aeschylos wins the Athenian tragedy prize for the first time
c.460 The temple of Zeus at Olympia is built
449 Pericles begins to rebuild Athens, and starts work on the Parthenon (447–432)
500
475
450

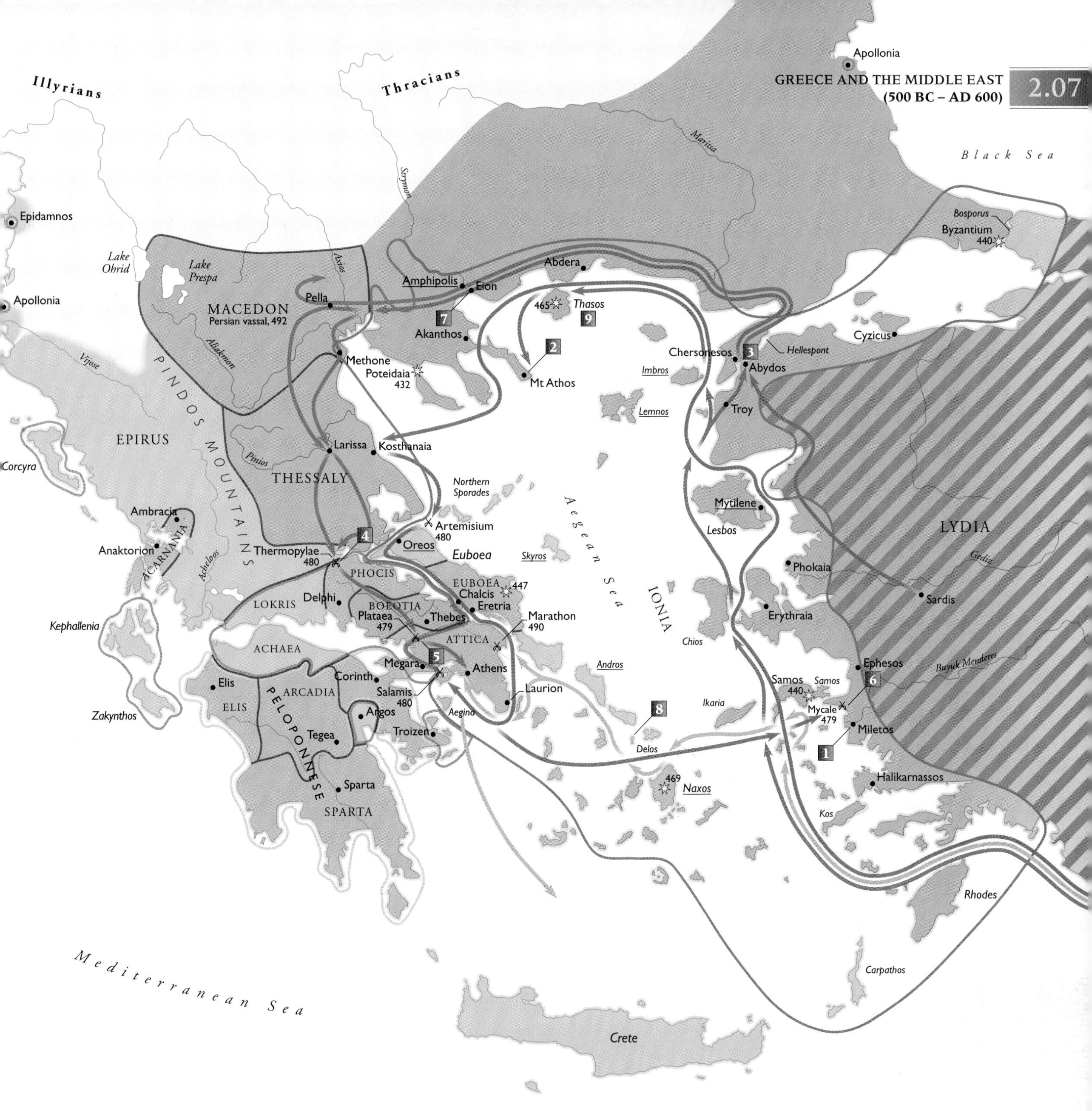

Euboea and Thasos, but by 445 they had lost control in central Greece and agreed to peace terms which recognized Spartan dominance in the Peloponnese.

Despite being almost constantly at war, Athens flourished economically in the 5th century as a result of its dominance of eastern Mediterranean and Black Sea trade and its own rich silver mines – worked by more than 20,000 slaves – at Laurion in Attica. Athenian democratic institutions continued to be developed and by 458 all citizens (excluding slaves, women and foreigners) were eligible to vote for and (except for the poorest) to serve in the highest offices of the government and the judiciary. The triumph in the war with Persia led to an exceptional outburst of cultural confidence in Greece as a whole, and especially in Athens, where vase-painting, sculpture and drama all reached new heights. The city, and notably its Acropolis, were rebuilt and the "classical" style of art and architecture matured. No other Greek city-state saw such a program of public building at this time.

1 The Greek cities of Ionia, led by Miletos, rebelled against Persian rule in 499 and sacked Sardis.

2 A Persian fleet was destroyed rounding Mt Athos in 492. To avoid the same thing happening in 480, the Persians dug a canal across the peninsula neck.

3 A bridge of boats was built across the Hellespont for Xerxes' expedition in 480.

4 At Thermopylae, the Greeks under Leonidas of Sparta were outflanked; most withdrew, but the Spartans' heroic stand inspired later Greek defense.

5 At the comprehensive Greek victory of Plataea, the Persian general Mardonios was killed and the leading Theban allies of the Persians were executed.

6 The last of the Persian fleet was destroyed at Mycale in 479.

7 Eion, the last important Persian stronghold in Europe, was captured by the Athenians in 475.

8 The common treasury of the Delian league was kept on Delos, but was removed to Athens in 454.

9 Delian league member Thasos rebelled in 465, but the Athenians invaded and tore down the city walls.

See also 1.15 (Achemenid Persia); 1.24 (archaic Greece); 2.08 (Peloponnesian war)

2.08 The Peloponnesian War and the rise of Macedon • 435 – 336 BC •

The first Peloponnesian War had been indecisive and a second, much larger, war broke out in 431. Although the war eventually broke the power of Athens, it did not leave Sparta, the victor, strong enough to achieve the undisputed dominance in Greece. The war confirmed that no Greek city-state could achieve permanent dominance.

In the 430s, Athens was entering its most exceptional age, with the Parthenon completed in 432, and with values embodied in Periclean rhetoric and the plays of Sophocles and Euripides. In 430 Socrates began his career as teacher and philosopher. The 4th century brought philosophers such as Plato and Aristotle (who was to be the tutor of Alexander of Macedon). And the Peloponnesian War found in Thucydides a great Athenian historian able to record the complex chain of events.

In 435 a minor war broke out between the Corcyreans and Corinth, an ally of Sparta. Anxious that Corinth would seek revenge, the victorious Corcyreans allied with Athens in 433 but this only led the Spartans to fear that the Athenians once again had expansionist ambitions. When Athens attacked the northern city of Poteidaia for defecting from the Delian league, the Spartans demanded that Athens free all members of the league.

Sparta's strength was its army, Athens' its navy: when war broke out between the two in 431, they pursued very different strategies. Sparta's hope was that Athens could be starved into surrender by ravaging its agricultural hinterland in Attica. However, the Athenians had planned for this contingency. Attica was abandoned – its population taken within the city walls – while the city's wealth and command of the sea was harnessed to supply Athens from overseas and to raid the Peloponnese. However this overcrowding led to a plague (430–426) in which a third of the city's population died. By 421 neither side had achieved a decisive advantage and a peace was negotiated but on terms which alienated Sparta's allies Corinth, Elis, Mantineia and Argos, which then allied with Athens in 419. War broke out again unofficially but after a Spartan victory at Mantineia in 418 this new alliance broke up. The war entered a decisive phase in 416 when the Athenians, to deprive their enemies of Sicilian food exports, agreed to send an expedition to besiege Syracuse. The expedition of the following year was a disaster from which Athens failed to recover. Sparta re-entered the war officially in 414 and sent help to Syracuse. The Athenians were catastrophically defeated in Sicily the following year, losing most of their 45,000-strong force. In the same year, Sparta garrisoned Dekeleia in Attica, forcing the closure of Athens' silver mines.

In 412 Persia, in return for a free hand in Ionia, paid for the construction of a Spartan fleet, tipping the balance of power decisively away from Athens.

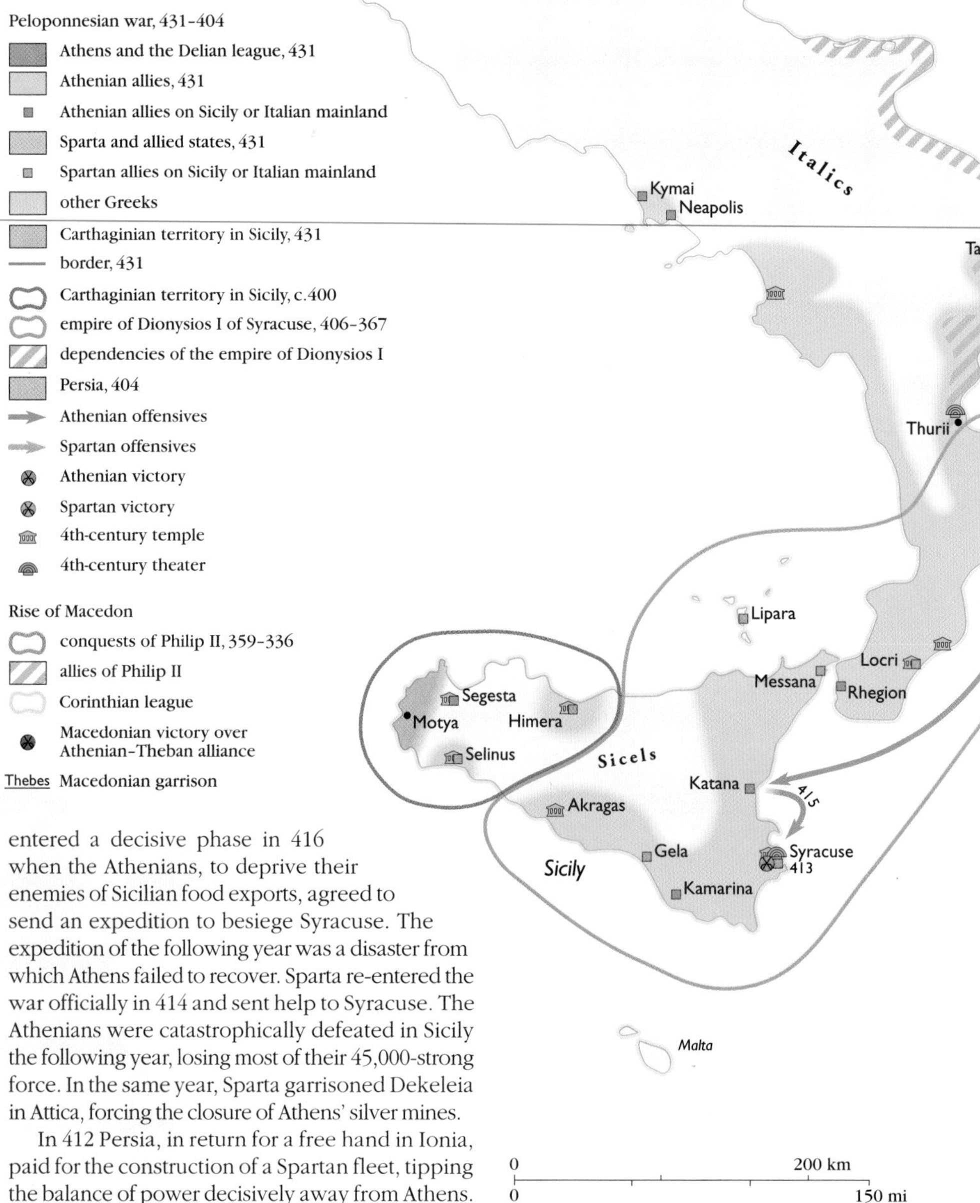

Peloponnesian war, 431-404
Athens and the Delian league, 431
Athenian allies, 431
Athenian allies on Sicily or Italian mainland
Sparta and allied states, 431
Spartan allies on Sicily or Italian mainland
other Greeks
Carthaginian territory in Sicily, 431
border, 431
Carthaginian territory in Sicily, c.400
empire of Dionysios I of Syracuse, 406-367
dependencies of the empire of Dionysios I
Persia, 404
Athenian offensives
Spartan offensives
Athenian victory
Spartan victory
4th-century temple
4th-century theater
Rise of Macedon
conquests of Philip II, 359-336
allies of Philip II
Corinthian league
Macedonian victory over Athenian-Theban alliance
Thebes Macedonian garrison
Kymai
Neapolis
Italics
Taras
Thurii
Lipara
Locri
Messana
Rhegion
Segesta
Motya
Himera
Selinus
Sicels
Katana
415
Akragas
Gela
Syracuse
413
Sicily
Kamarina
Malta
0
200 km
0
150 mi

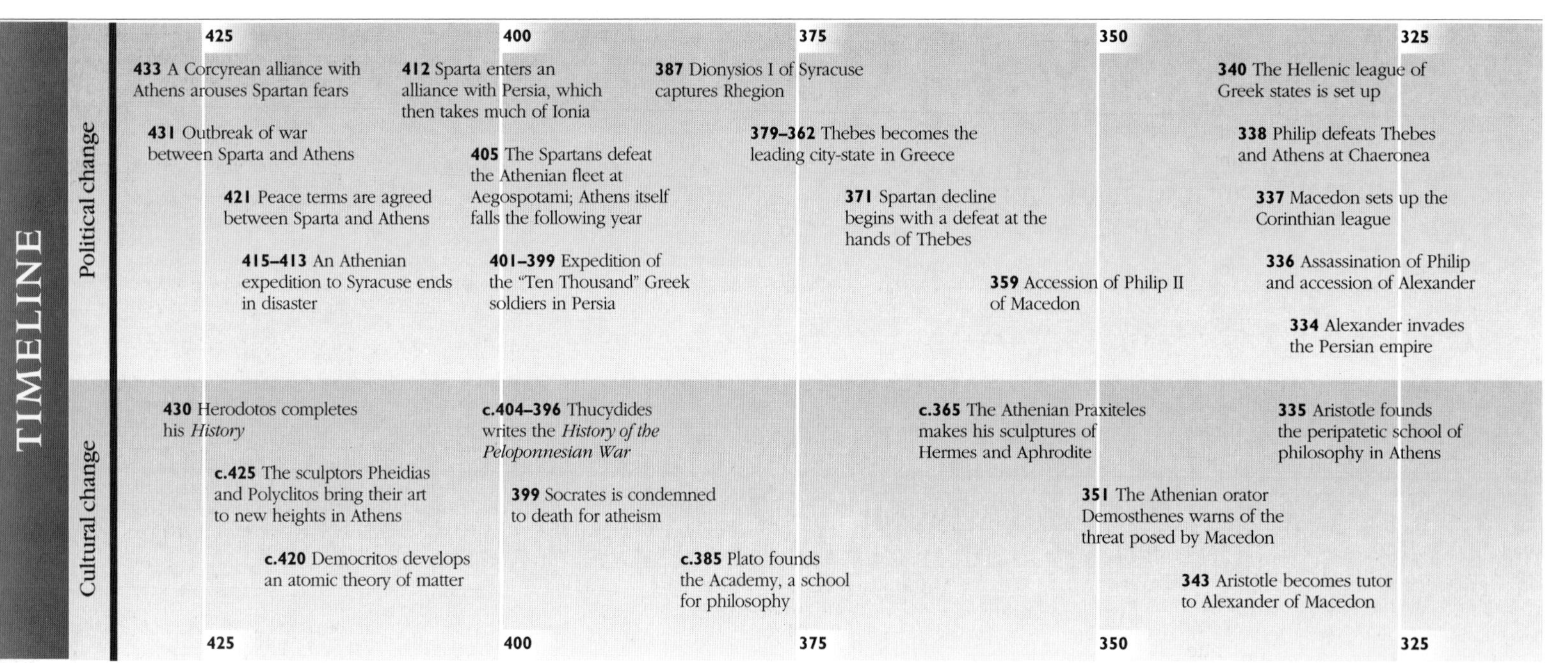

TIMELINE
Political change
Cultural change
425
400
375
350
325
433 A Corcyrean alliance with Athens arouses Spartan fears
431 Outbreak of war between Sparta and Athens
421 Peace terms are agreed between Sparta and Athens
415–413 An Athenian expedition to Syracuse ends in disaster
412 Sparta enters an alliance with Persia, which then takes much of Ionia
405 The Spartans defeat the Athenian fleet at Aegospotami; Athens itself falls the following year
401–399 Expedition of the "Ten Thousand" Greek soldiers in Persia
387 Dionysios I of Syracuse captures Rhegion
379–362 Thebes becomes the leading city-state in Greece
371 Spartan decline begins with a defeat at the hands of Thebes
359 Accession of Philip II of Macedon
340 The Hellenic league of Greek states is set up
338 Philip defeats Thebes and Athens at Chaeronea
337 Macedon sets up the Corinthian league
336 Assassination of Philip and accession of Alexander
334 Alexander invades the Persian empire
430 Herodotos completes his History
c.425 The sculptors Pheidias and Polyclitos bring their art to new heights in Athens
c.420 Democritos develops an atomic theory of matter
c.404–396 Thucydides writes the History of the Peloponnesian War
399 Socrates is condemned to death for atheism
c.385 Plato founds the Academy, a school for philosophy
c.365 The Athenian Praxiteles makes his sculptures of Hermes and Aphrodite
351 The Athenian orator Demosthenes warns of the threat posed by Macedon
343 Aristotle becomes tutor to Alexander of Macedon
335 Aristotle founds the peripatetic school of philosophy in Athens
425
400
375
350
325

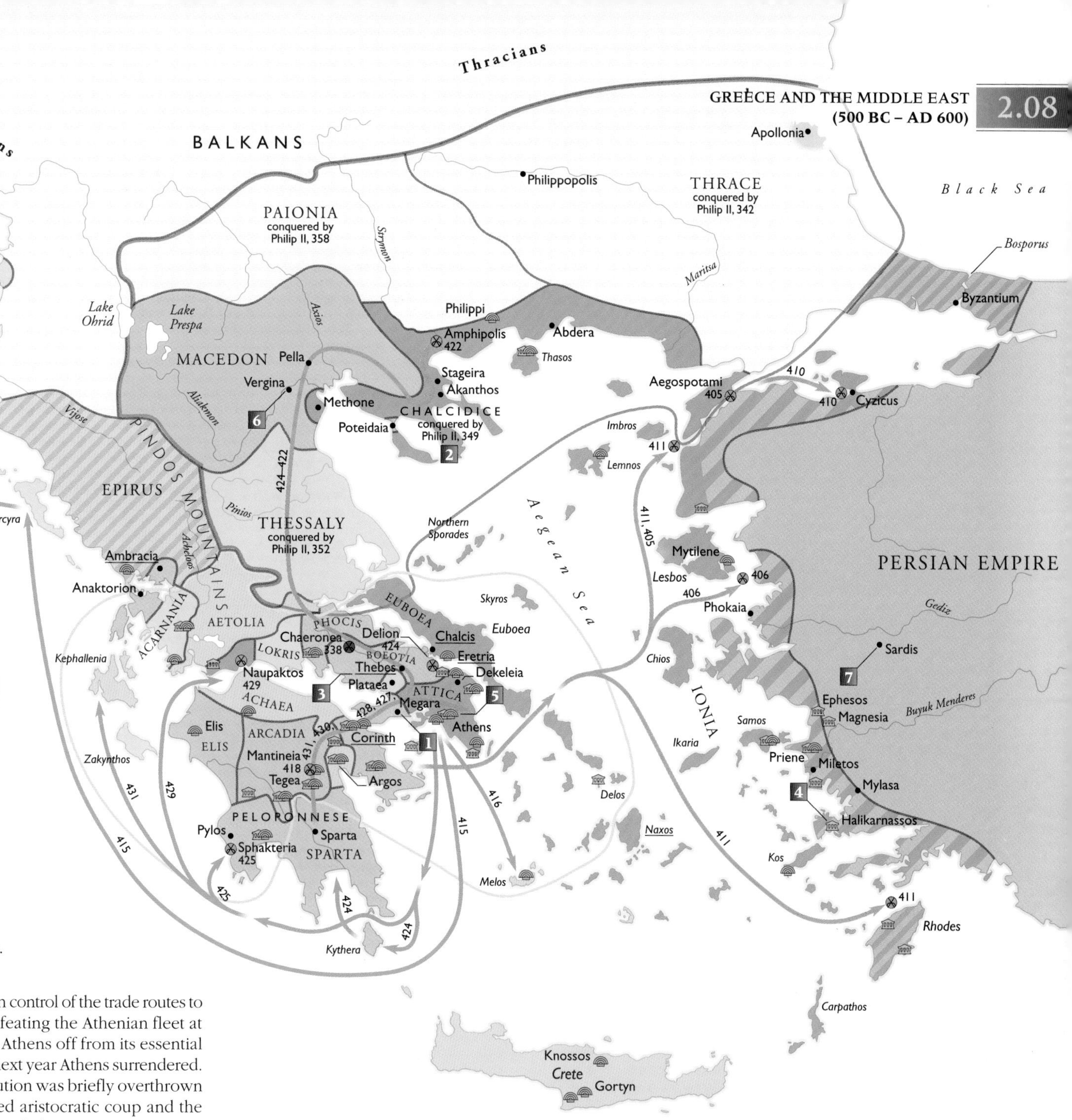

PHILIP of Macedon, an able and ruthless soldier, is seen here on an ivory carving found in his tomb at Vergina.

In 405 the Spartans won control of the trade routes to the Black Sea after defeating the Athenian fleet at Aegospotami, cutting Athens off from its essential imports of grain. The next year Athens surrendered. Its democratic constitution was briefly overthrown by a Spartan-supported aristocratic coup and the Delian league was disbanded.

Sparta was now the strongest Greek state but its victory had been paid for by Persian gold. When Sparta went to war against Persia in 400, the Persians simply switched their subsidies to Athens and the increasingly powerful Thebes, and Spartan ambitions faded. The Greek states continued to struggle fruitlessly for another fifty years until unity was imposed on them by Philip II (r.359–336) of Macedon.

Macedon had a mixed population of Greeks, Illyrians and Thracians but, even though the Athenians liked to regard it as a barbarian kingdom, it was a thoroughly hellenized state by Philip's accession. Macedon was now transformed from a backwater into a superpower. Philip ignored the convention of Greek warfare that restricted campaigning to specific times of the year and introduced siege engines to take cities quickly by storm rather than by long blockade. Philip's first conquest, Paionia in the Balkans, paid with its rich mineral resources for the expansion of the Macedonian army and thereafter his progress was inexorable. In 340 Athens made a last-ditch effort to halt Philip's expansion, forming the anti-Macedonian Hellenic league. Philip crushed this alliance at Chaeronea in 338, after which all the major Greek states, except Sparta, were forced to join the Macedonian-controlled Corinthian league.

Philip now announced a war of all Greece against Persia. The military weakness of Persia had been exposed in 401 when the rebel Persian governor of Sardis recruited an army of 10,000 Greek mercenaries to support his bid for the throne. The "Ten Thousand" marched into the heart of the Persian empire and, when their employer was killed in Babylonia, fought their way home again, demonstrating the military superiority of the Greeks. Philip's confidence was well placed but he was assassinated before his expedition was ready.

In the late 5th century the Greeks came close to being expelled from Sicily after Segesta called on the support of its ally Carthage during a boundary dispute with the aggressive Greek city of Selinus in 410. The Carthaginians went on to occupy the western half of Sicily by 405. The Greeks were united by Dionysios (r.406–367), tyrant of Syracuse, who recovered much of the territory lost to Carthage. Dionysios later extended his power to the Italian mainland where the Greek cities accepted him as their protector against the Italic peoples.

1 Megara was a neighbor and rival of Athens; when Athens blockaded it in the 430s, Sparta found an excuse for war.

2 Athens lost control of Chalcidice as a result of a campaign by the Spartan general Brasidas in 424–422.

3 The war-weariness of Sparta and Athens allowed Thebes to become dominant in Greece 379–362.

4 Halikarnassos was the site of the monument (Mausoleum) to Mausolos, a Lydian king who ruled from Mylasa and tried to build an empire in the 350s.

5 In Athens, Demosthenes spoke passionately about the Macedonian threat but failed to stem it.

6 The opulently furnished tomb of Philip II at Vergina was discovered in 1977. It contained his cremated body, his bronze armor and elegant grave goods.

7 Cyrus, governor of Sardis, recruited 10,000 Greek mercenaries to support his bid for the Persian throne in 401. Their progress was described by Xenophon.

See also 2.07 (5th-century Greece); 2.09 (Alexander); 2.12 (Sicily, Carthage and Rome)

2.09 The conquests of Alexander the Great • 336 – 300 BC •

In only eight years of tireless campaigning, Alexander of Macedon (r. 336–323) conquered the Persian empire and the Indus valley. Although his empire broke up on his death, Alexander's conquests determined that Hellenism would be the dominant cultural influence in the Middle East well into the Christian era.

Alexander was eighteen years old when his father, Philip II, was assassinated. He was bold, imaginative, well educated – Aristotle had been his tutor – and a promising soldier. In the first two years of his reign Alexander proved his abilities by securing Macedon's northern borders and subduing the rebellious Greeks. In 334, his home base now stable, Alexander launched his father's planned invasion of Persia, routing the army sent to stop him at the river Granicus. He then marched down the Anatolian coast, liberating and restoring the Greek cities of Ionia. Only Miletos and Halikarnassos, where the garrisons had been supplied by the Persian fleet, offered serious resistance. To prevent further naval interference, Alexander proceeded to conquer Phoenicia and Egypt, after first crushing a large Persian army, commanded personally by Darius III, at the river Issus in 333. With Persian naval power eliminated, Alexander marched into the heart of the Persian empire in 331, and at Gaugamela inflicted another humiliating defeat on Darius. Persian resistance crumbled, and Babylon and the Persian treasury at Susa were captured.

The following year, at the Persian Gates pass, Alexander destroyed the last sizeable Persian army and swept on to loot and burn the Persian capital, Persepolis. It took Alexander three more years of tough campaigning in Bactria and Sogdiana to complete his conquest of the Persian empire, before invading the Indus valley in 327. There, in 326, Alexander won his last major battle, over King Porus at the river Hydaspes. Alexander wanted to press on and invade the Ganges plain, but his soldiers, after marching 25,000 kilometers (15,000 miles), had had enough and they refused. Instead Alexander marched down the Indus to the sea and turned west, reaching Babylon in 324, where, the following year, aged only 32, he died, an overweight alcoholic. Shortly before his death his adoption of the styles of oriental kingship had lost him the loyalty of some of his original Macedonian followers.

The most important factor in Alexander's success was his military genius, but he was also aided by the centuries-long tradition of imperial rule in the Middle East, which had weakened local identities and loyalties. The provincial populations of the Persian empire were used to foreign rule and, as Alexander respected local customs and did not make unreasonable demands for tribute, a change from Persian to Macedonian rule was a matter of indifference to them. Alexander's empire broke

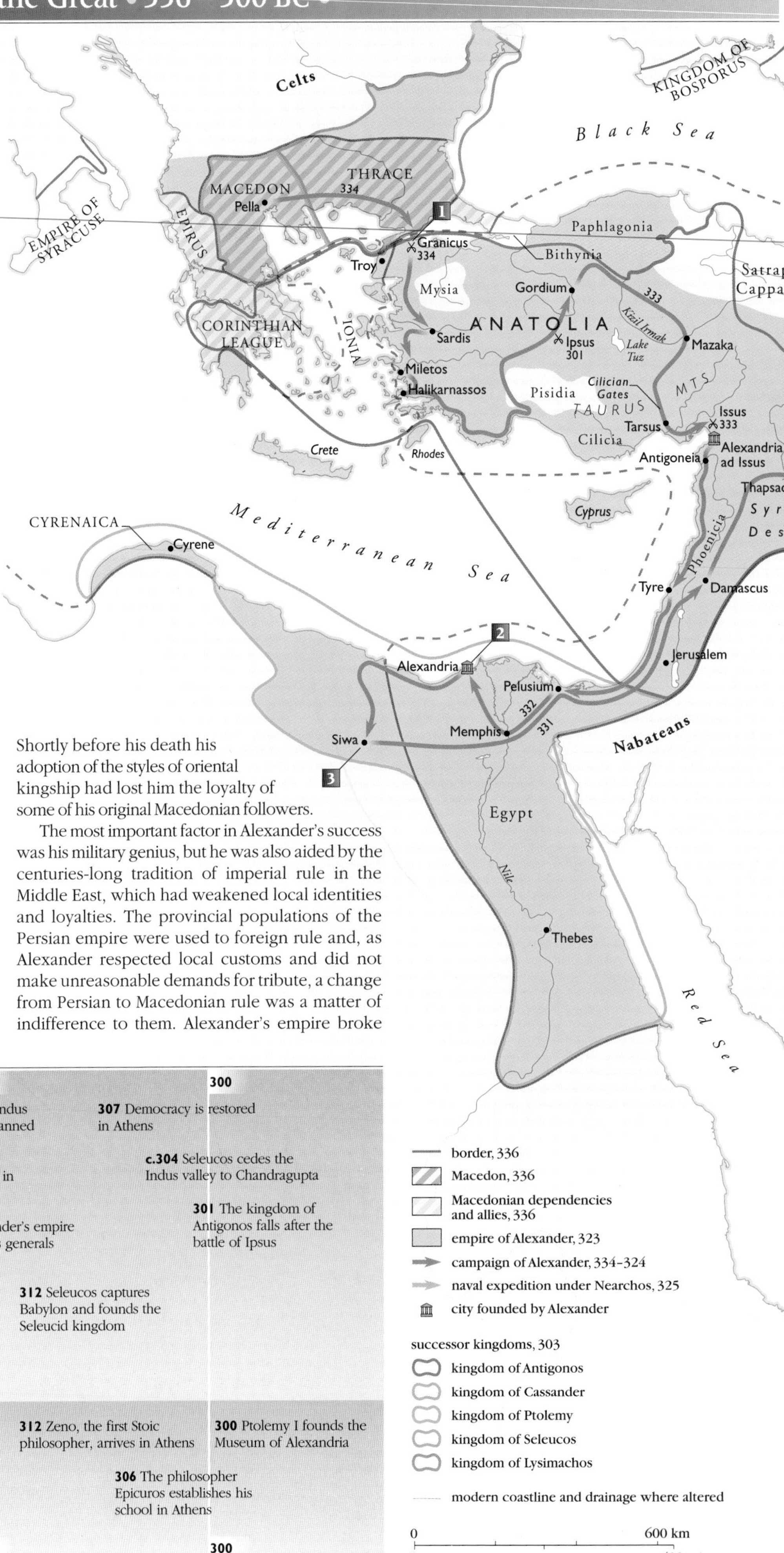

Scythians
Celts
KINGDOM OF BOSPORUS
Black Sea
THRACE
334
MACEDON
Pella
EPIRUS
EMPIRE OF SYRACUSE
1
Granicus
334
Troy
Paphlagonia
Bithynia
Mysia
Gordium
Satrapy
Cappad
333
Kizil Irmak
CORINTHIAN LEAGUE
IONIA
ANATOLIA
Sardis
Ipsus
301
Lake Tuz
Mazaka
Miletos
Halikarnassos
Pisidia
Cilician Gates
TAURUS MTS
Issus
333
Tarsus
Cilicia
Alexandria ad Issus
Antigoneia
Crete
Rhodes
Thapsacu
Syri
Dese
Cyprus
CYRENAICA
Cyrene
Mediterranean Sea
Phoenicia
Tyre
Damascus
2
Jerusalem
Alexandria
Pelusium
332
331
Memphis
Siwa
Nabateans
3
Egypt
Nile
Thebes
Red Sea
border, 336
Macedon, 336
Macedonian dependencies and allies, 336
empire of Alexander, 323
campaign of Alexander, 334–324
naval expedition under Nearchos, 325
city founded by Alexander
successor kingdoms, 303
kingdom of Antigonos
kingdom of Cassander
kingdom of Ptolemy
kingdom of Seleucos
kingdom of Lysimachos
modern coastline and drainage where altered
0
600 km
0
400 mi

TIMELINE

330 | 315 | 300

Political change

- **334** Alexander invades Anatolia, repulsing a Persian army at the Granicus river
- **333** Darius III is defeated at the Battle of Issus
- **332** Alexander conquers Egypt and founds the city of Alexandria
- **331** At Gaugamela, Alexander defeats Darius again, and goes on to sack Persepolis
- **329** Alexander conquers Bactria and Sogdiana
- **326** Alexander, in the Indus valley, abandons his planned conquest of India
- **323** Alexander dies in Babylon
- **321–316** Alexander's empire breaks up as his generals seize territory
- **312** Seleucos captures Babylon and founds the Seleucid kingdom
- **307** Democracy is restored in Athens
- **c.304** Seleucos cedes the Indus valley to Chandragupta
- **301** The kingdom of Antigonos falls after the battle of Ipsus

Cultural change

- **335** Aristotle founds his school of philosophy in Athens
- **c.325–300** Pytheas of Massilia circumnavigates Britain
- **312** Zeno, the first Stoic philosopher, arrives in Athens
- **306** The philosopher Epicuros establishes his school in Athens
- **300** Ptolemy I founds the Museum of Alexandria

330 | 315 | 300

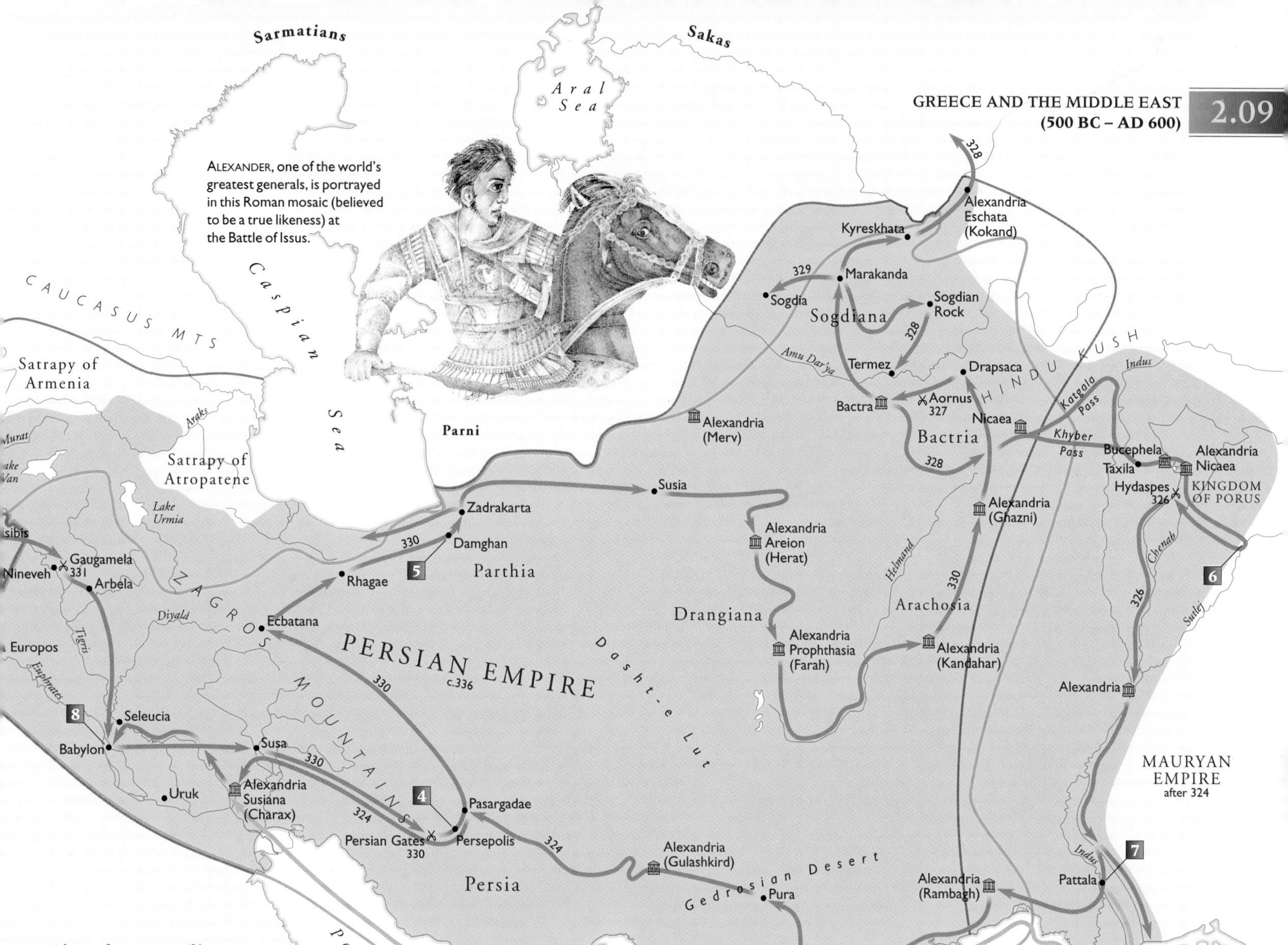

ALEXANDER, one of the world's greatest generals, is portrayed in this Roman mosaic (believed to be a true likeness) at the Battle of Issus.

Sarmatians
Sakas
Aral Sea
Caspian Sea
CAUCASUS MTS
Satrapy of Armenia
Satrapy of Atropatene
Lake Urmia
Parni
Parthia
PERSIAN EMPIRE c.336
ZAGROS MOUNTAINS
Dasht-e Lut
Drangiana
Arachosia
Bactria
Sogdiana
HINDU KUSH
KINGDOM OF PORUS
MAURYAN EMPIRE after 324
Persia
Gedrosian Desert
Persian Gulf
Gulf of Oman
Arabian Sea
Nineveh
Gaugamela 331
Arbela
Europos
Seleucia
Babylon
Uruk
Susa
Alexandria Susiana (Charax)
Ecbatana
Rhagae
Damghan
Zadrakarta
Susia
Alexandria Areion (Herat)
Alexandria Prophthasia (Farah)
Alexandria (Kandahar)
Alexandria (Ghazni)
Alexandria (Merv)
Pasargadae
Persepolis
Persian Gates 330
Alexandria (Gulashkird)
Pura
Alexandria (Rambagh)
Pattala
Alexandria
Bucephela
Taxila
Alexandria Nicaea
Hydaspes 326
Khyber Pass
Katgala Pass
Nicaea
Bactra
Aornus 327
Drapsaca
Termez
Sogdian Rock
Sogdia
Marakanda
Kyreskhata
Alexandria Eschata (Kokand)

up within a few years of his death, but this was for dynastic reasons; there were no popular rebellions against his successors. Alexander founded cities of Greek colonists (usually named after himself) throughout his empire, and his successors founded dozens more. These cities were scattered from the Mediterranean to central Asia, and became the agents for the vast expansion of Greek cultural influence over west Asia that was perhaps the most important consequence of Alexander's conquests.

Alexander left as his heirs a posthumous son and a mentally ill brother, neither of whom was capable of ruling in his own right. The regent Perdiccas maintained the central administration until his murder in 321, but under his successor, Antipater (d.319), the governor of Macedon, power in the provinces was seized by the generals and the empire fragmented in a series of conflicts known as the Wars of the Diadochi ("successors"). By 304 five successor kingdoms had arisen. Cassander, Antipater's son, ruled in Macedon; Lysimachos in Thrace; Antigonos had seized power in Anatolia; Seleucos in Mesopotamia and the east; and Ptolemy in Egypt. Of the five, only Antigonos aspired to recreate Alexander's empire, but this simply united the other Diadochi against him. When Antigonos was killed in battle against the combined armies of Seleucos, Lysimachos and Cassander at Ipsus in 301, his kingdom was divided up among the victors: Lysimachos taking Anatolia, Seleucus Syria and Cilicia, and Ptolemy, who had been campaigning separately, Palestine and Cyprus. Although the battle of Ipsus did not bring an end to the struggles of the Diadochi, it did set the seal on the break-up of Alexander's empire.

During the chaos that followed his death, Alexander's empire had also begun to fray at the edges. His conquests had been rapid and the rulers of the northern satrapies of Bithynia, Paphlagonia, Cappadocia, Armenia and Atropatene had been allowed to retain their provinces after making only token submission. Alexander's early death prevented these provinces being brought into full submission, and during the Diadochan wars they became fully independent kingdoms. The Indus valley was also lost by the Greeks after Alexander's death. Preoccupied with the war against Antigonos, Seleucos ceded the Indian provinces to the Mauryan empire in 304 in return for a herd of war elephants (which he used to good effect at Ipsus). In Greece, now only a small part of the Hellenistic world, the cities of the Corinthian league rebelled unsuccessfully against Macedonian control in 323 and then defected to Antigonos in 307. However, after the defeat of Antigonos at Ipsus, Macedonian control was restored.

1 Alexander won control of Anatolia after defeating an army sent to intercept him at the river Granicus.

2 Founded in 332, Alexandria was to become the largest and richest Greek city in the 3rd century.

3 The oracle of Amun at Siwa claimed Alexander to be son of the god and heir to the Egyptian throne.

4 The burning of the palace of Xerxes at Persepolis in 330 marked the end of the Panhellenic war of revenge but not of Alexander's personal desire for conquest.

5 Darius III was murdered at Damghan by his courtiers as he fled, seeking refuge in Bactria.

6 Only when Alexander's exhausted and homesick army refused to follow him into the Ganges valley did he at last relent and turn back.

7 Nearchos built a fleet of more than 100 ships at Pattala to explore and control the Gulf coast.

8 Alexander died in Babylon in 323, having caught a fever after several days of heavy drinking.

See also 1.15 (Achemenid Persia); 2.08 (rise of Macedon); 2.10 (Hellenistic world)

2.10 The Hellenistic world • 301 – 30 BC •

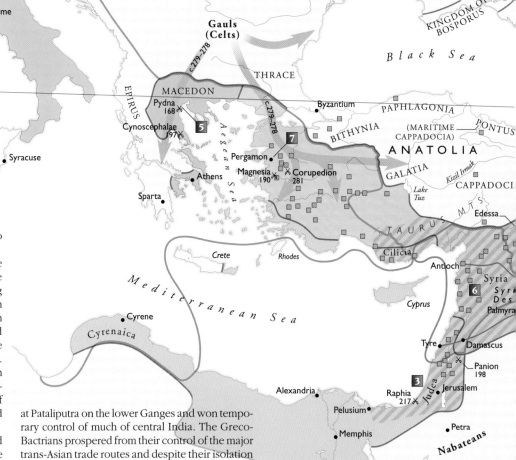

The struggles of the Diadochi continued for twenty years after the battle of Ipsus (301), during which time Lysimachos's Thracian kingdom was eliminated. Lysimachos himself was killed at the battle of Corupedion in 281, after which Seleucos took control of western Anatolia. Two years later Thrace was overrun by a Gaulish (Celtic) invasion. Some of these Gauls crossed into Anatolia, eventually establishing themselves in the region known subsequently as Galatia, from where they plundered the surrounding countryside for the next fifty years. The spate of Greek colonization of the east begun by Alexander continued until about 250. Dozens of new cities were founded and many established ones were hellenized: Greek became the common tongue from the Mediterranean to central Asia and the Indus valley.

Macedon gradually strengthened its hold on the Greek city-states during the 3rd century, but made an enemy of Rome by supporting Carthage during the Second Punic War (221–201). When Pergamon and Rhodes appealed to the Romans for protection against Macedon, Rome was happy to oblige, and at the battle of Cynoscephalae in 197 broke the kingdom's power and freed the Greek city-states. When Macedon attempted to reassert its position in Greece it was again defeated and annexation followed in 148. By this time the Romans had tired of the constant disputes of the Greek city-states and these were brought under direct Roman rule in 146.

The largest of the Hellenistic kingdoms at the end of the Diadochian wars was the Seleucid, but by the mid-3rd century it had begun a long slow decline. The first loss was the city of Pergamon in 262 BC. In 239 the Bactrian Greeks rebelled and founded an independent kingdom. The history of the Bactrian Greeks is little known, but they won back control of the Indus valley from the ailing Mauryan empire by the early 2nd century. In the 180s Greco-Bactrian rulers campaigned as far east as the Mauryan capital at Pataliputra on the lower Ganges and won temporary control of much of central India. The Greco-Bactrians prospered from their control of the major trans-Asian trade routes and despite their isolation remained in contact with the mainstream of Greek culture. However, Bactria was exposed to attacks by the steppe nomads and around 135 BC most of the kingdom was overrun. Some independent Greek principalities survived in the upper Indus valley but were extinguished by the end of the 1st century BC.

The Seleucid kingdom suffered a further territorial loss in 238 when Parthia became independent

TIMELINE

Political change

- **c.300** The Parni, Iranian nomads, settle in Parthia
- **279–278** Gaulish Celts overrun Thrace and invade Anatolia
- **239** Foundation of the Greco-Bactrian kingdom
- **238** Foundation of the Parthian kingdom
- **214-205** The First Macedonian War marks the beginning of Roman intervention in Greece
- **198** The Seleucids win control of Palestine at the battle of Panion
- **190** The Romans defeat Antiochus III at Magnesia
- **c.180** The peak of Greco-Bactrian power
- **171 and 168** Seleucid invasions of Egypt
- **166–160** The revolt of Judas Maccabeus in Judea
- **148–146** Macedon and Greece are annexed by Rome
- **141** The Parthians conquer Mesopotamia
- **c.135** The Kushans destroy the Bactrian kingdom
- **c.94** Taxila becomes the capital of the Saka kingdom
- **88-63** Mithridates of Pontus fights three wars to free the Greeks from Rome
- **83** The Seleucid kingdom finally collapses
- **30** Egypt becomes a Roman province

Cultural change

- **275** The Pharos lighthouse at Alexandria is completed
- **c.270** Aristarchos of Samos (c.320–c.250), first proposes a heliocentric universe
- **c.235** Eratosthenes (c.276–c.194) measures the Earth's circumference
- **c.140** The Venus de Milo sculpture is completed
- **c.120** The Greek ambassador Heliodoros erects a monument at Vidisha in central India
- **c.105** A college of technology is founded at Alexandria

200 100

- border, c.270
- Macedon, c.270
- Ptolemaic kingdom, c.270
- Roman empire, c.270
- Seleucid kingdom, c.270
- Greco-Bactrians, c.185
- Parthian empire, c.185
- Seleucid kingdom, c.185
- Parthian empire, c.90
- Roman empire, c.90
- Seleucid kingdom, c.90
- trans-Asia trade route
- migration, with date
- cities with Hellenistic foundations
- modern coastline and drainage where altered

0 600 km
0 400 mi

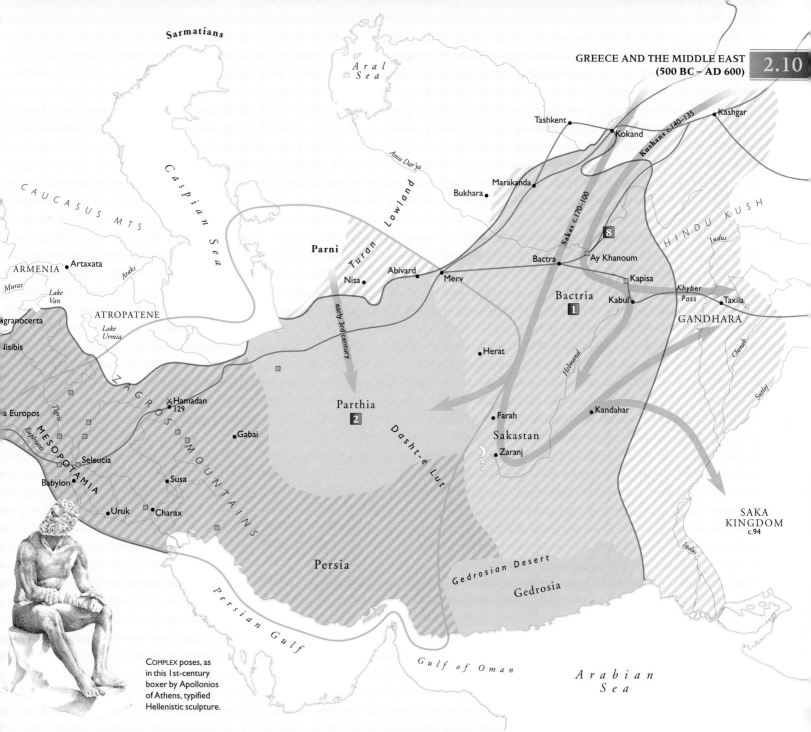

COMPLEX poses, as in this 1st-century boxer by Apollonios of Athens, typified Hellenistic sculpture.

under the Arsacid dynasty. The Arsacids were descendants of the ruling house of the Parni, Iranian nomads who had settled in Parthia earlier in the century. Under Antiochus III (223–187) the Seleucid kingdom conquered Armenia, Atropatene and Palestine and contained the expansion of Parthia and Bactria. Unfortunately, Antiochus's success alarmed the Romans, who declared war on him in 192 and two years later inflicted a crushing defeat on him at Magnesia. Armenia and Atropatene quickly regained their independence, while the Romans awarded western Anatolia to their ally Pergamon. Then in 166 Antiochus IV (r.174–163) faced a serious Jewish revolt. Around the middle of the century the Parthians conquered Persia and overran Mesopotamia, reducing the Seleucid kingdom to little more than Syria. However, the Parthians were prevented from completing the conquest of the Seleucid kingdom by the invasion of their eastern provinces by the Sakas in the 130s. The Sakas were contained by 90 BC and their main settlements, later known as Sakastan, came under the control of the Parthian Suren family, who founded a semi-independent kingdom that lasted over a century.

The most enduring of the Hellenistic kingdoms was the Ptolemaic kingdom of Egypt. Egypt had the strongest and most recent traditions of independence – it had successfully thrown off Persian rule from 404 to 341– and its population was resentful of the Greeks and Macedonians who now dominated the government and army. To placate the native Egyptians the Ptolemies adopted many of the trappings of the pharaohs and became patrons of the traditional religious cults. By the 2nd century some Egyptians had become hellenized; and some Egyptian cults, such as that of the goddess Isis, had found favor with the Greeks. Egyptians began to play an important role in the army. However, there was no real assimilation of the populations. Alexandria became the largest and richest Greek city in the world and even overshadowed Athens as a cultural center. The Ptolemaic kingdom was the major naval power of the eastern Mediterranean for most of the 3rd century but began to decline during a period of dynastic instability after the death of Ptolemy IV in 203. When, in 168, Antiochus IV conquered Egypt, only the intervention of the Romans secured the restoration of the Ptolemaic dynasty.

1 The Bactrian kingdom, independent from 239 and at its peak c.180, was destroyed by the Kushans c.135.

2 The Parthian kingdom, founded by Arsaces in 238, had conquered Persia and Mesopotamia by 141.

3 The Jewish Maccabean revolt against the Seleucids in 166–160 led to Judean independence in 142–141.

4 Ptolemaic Egypt, though ruled from the Greek city of Alexandria, saw its cultural traditions preserved.

5 The Romans broke the power of Macedon at Pydna in 168, and formally annexed the kingdom in 148.

6 The final remnant of the Seleucid kingdom was conquered in 83 BC by the Armenian king Tigranes I.

7 Under the Attalids, Pergamon was an important cultural center with a vast library, and spectacular architecture.

8 Hellenistic settlers spread Greek institutions across Asia. Gymnasia – centers of athletics and debating – have been discovered as far east as Ay Khanoum.

See also 2.09 (Alexander); 2.11 (Parthians and Sasanians); 2.13 (growth of the Roman empire)

2.11 Parthian and Sasanian Persia • 238 BC – AD 636 •

In the chaos that followed the death of Alexander the Great, the Parni, an Iranian nomadic people, migrated from the Caspian steppes into Parthia. There they adopted Parthian language and customs, and their dominant family, the Arsacids, became the local rulers as vassals of the Seleucid kingdom. Arsaces I (r.c.247–c.211) declared his independence in 238, founding the independent Parthian state. The Seleucids contained Parthian expansion until the reign of Mithradates I (170–138), who turned Parthia into a major power by conquering Iran and Mesopotamia. Further expansion was prevented by invasions from the east by the Sakas and the Kushans and by dynastic problems. By 90–80 BC the eastern border was stabilized and the Sakas were settled in a vassal kingdom under the Parthian Suren family. Around the beginning of the Christian era this kingdom extended its control into the Indus valley. After 66 BC the Parthians had an opportunity to expand into Atropatene and seize northern Mesopotamia, where they established a common frontier with the Romans on the Euphrates.

The Romans initially regarded the Parthians as barbarians but learned to respect them when a major Roman army was destroyed at Carrhae by their horse archers almost as soon as it crossed the frontier in 53 BC. Internal troubles in Parthia saved the Romans from paying an even heavier price for their unprovoked attack. The Romans itched to avenge the humiliation, and wars between the two powers were frequent. The Roman infantry never got the measure of the Parthian horse archers and they made little headway until the 2nd century AD when the emperor Trajan took Armenia and Mesopotamia in 115–17. However, Trajan's successor Hadrian gave them up on his accession in 117. The Parthians had previously lost the Suren sub-kingdom to the Kushans, around AD 50–75.

The early Parthian kings adopted the Hellenistic traditions and governmental institutions of the Seleucid kingdom and continued to use Greek as an official language and on coinage. By the 1st century BC, however, the Parthian kingdom had developed into a decentralized feudal state made up of directly ruled provinces, vassal sub-kingdoms under local dynasties, and the fiefs of semi-independent nobles. Hellenistic cultural influence, strong at first, had also begun to decline by this time in the face of a resurgence of Persian traditions.

The frequent wars with Rome sapped the strength of the Parthian dynasty and in AD 224–26 it was overthrown following the rebellion of Ardashir I (r.c.220–40), the sub-king of Persia, who founded the Sasanian dynasty (named for Ardashir's grandfather, Sasan). The Sasanians saw themselves as the successors of the Achemenids and pursued far more aggressive and expansionist policies than the Parthians. Shapur I (r. 240–72) attempted to take Syria from the Romans but despite some spectacular victories, including the capture of the emperor Valerian at Edessa in 260, the Romans held on grimly. Shapur gained some territory from the Armenians and enjoyed spectacular success in the

Suren kingdom, AD 1
Kushan empire, c.AD 50–240
Parthia, c.AD 114
Roman empire, AD 114
temporary Roman conquest, AD 114–17
Sasanian empire, c.AD 260
temporary Sasanian conquest, AD 607–28
important city of the Parthian period
rock relief of the Parthian period
important city of the Sasanian period
rock relief of the Sasanian period
Parthian or Sasanian victory
Parthian or Sasanian defeat
Sasanian defensive earthworks
border, c.AD 114
trans-Asian trade route
campaign of Heraclius, AD 622–27
major migration
modern coastline and drainage where altered

0 600 km
0 400 mi

Black Se
AD 623
Byzantium
(Constantinople after AD 330)
Aegean Sea
AD 622
ANATOLIA
Lake Tuz
Kizil I
TAURUS
Ginda
Crete
Rhodes
AD 622
Antioch
Cyprus
Mediterranean Sea
Damascu
Tyre
Palestine
Jerus
Alexandria
Petra
Egypt
Nile
Red Sea

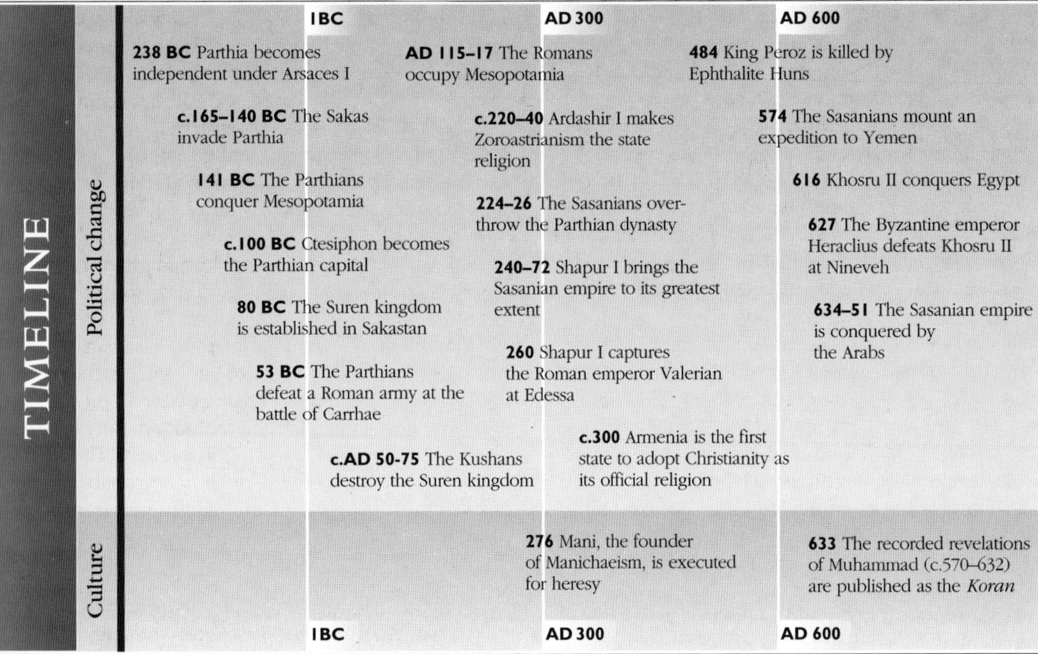

TIMELINE
Political change
Culture
1 BC
AD 300
AD 600
238 BC Parthia becomes independent under Arsaces I
c.165–140 BC The Sakas invade Parthia
141 BC The Parthians conquer Mesopotamia
c.100 BC Ctesiphon becomes the Parthian capital
80 BC The Suren kingdom is established in Sakastan
53 BC The Parthians defeat a Roman army at the battle of Carrhae
c.AD 50-75 The Kushans destroy the Suren kingdom
AD 115–17 The Romans occupy Mesopotamia
c.220–40 Ardashir I makes Zoroastrianism the state religion
224–26 The Sasanians overthrow the Parthian dynasty
240–72 Shapur I brings the Sasanian empire to its greatest extent
260 Shapur I captures the Roman emperor Valerian at Edessa
c.300 Armenia is the first state to adopt Christianity as its official religion
484 King Peroz is killed by Ephthalite Huns
574 The Sasanians mount an expedition to Yemen
616 Khosru II conquers Egypt
627 The Byzantine emperor Heraclius defeats Khosru II at Nineveh
634–51 The Sasanian empire is conquered by the Arabs
276 Mani, the founder of Manichaeism, is executed for heresy
633 The recorded revelations of Muhammad (c.570–632) are published as the *Koran*
1 BC
AD 300
AD 600

1 The capital of Arsaces I, founder of the Parthian state, was Abivard. The royal necropolis was at Nisa.

2 A former Parthian winter capital, Ctesiphon was the Sasanian capital from AD 226 until 637.

3 The Kushans were conquered by Shapur I (r.240–72) but briefly regained most of their territory during the minority of Shapur II (r.309–79).

4 At Naqsh-i Rustam a monumental relief carved on a cliff face commemorates the capture of the Roman emperor Valerian by Shapur I in AD 260.

5 "Alexander's Barrier" was actually a Sasanian earthwork built as a defense against steppe nomads.

6 The fire-temples complex at Gushnasp was the holiest site of the Sasanians' Zoroastrian state church.

7 The Sasanian state collapsed after defeats by the Arabs at Al Qadisiya (637) and Nehavend (642).

8 Dura Europos was a major Parthian border fortress city, captured by the Romans in AD 165 and abandoned after it was taken by the Sasanians in 256.

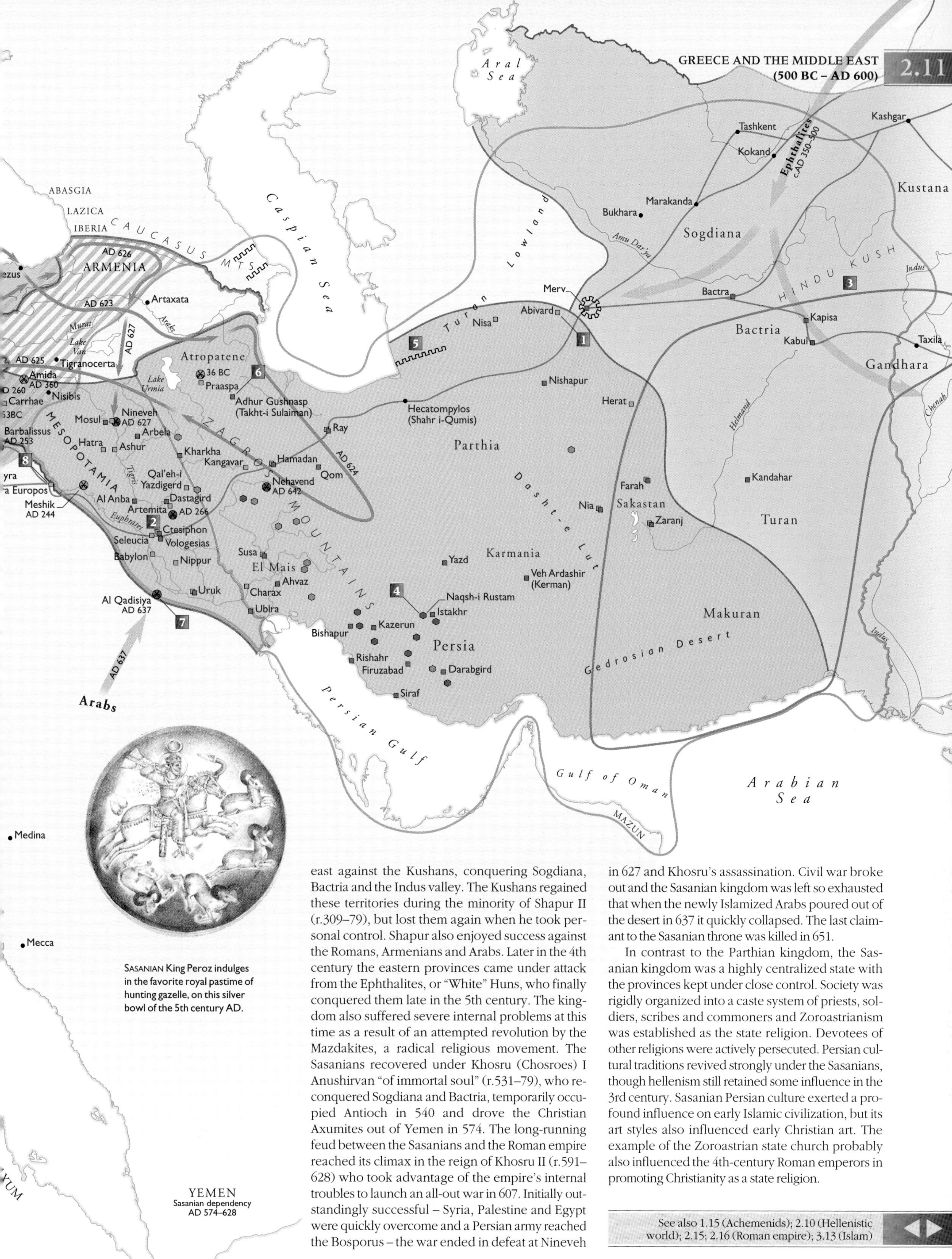
Aral Sea
Caspian Sea
Persian Gulf
Gulf of Oman
Arabian Sea
ABASGIA
LAZICA
IBERIA
CAUCASUS MTS
ARMENIA
AD 626
AD 623
AD 627
AD 625
Artaxata
Araks
Murat
Lake Van
Tigranocerta
Amida
AD 360
Nisibis
Carrhae
Barbalissus
AD 253
Meshik
AD 244
Atropatene
36 BC
Praaspa
Lake Urmia
Adhur Gushnasp
(Takht-i Sulaiman)
Mosul
Nineveh
AD 627
Arbela
Hatra
Ashur
MESOPOTAMIA
Tigris
Kharkha
Kangavar
Hamadan
Qal'eh-i Yazdigerd
Dastagird
Al Anba
Artemita
AD 266
Euphrates
Ctesiphon
Seleucia
Vologesias
Babylon
Nippur
Uruk
Al Qadisiya
AD 637
Arabs
AD 637
ZAGROS MOUNTAINS
Nehavend
AD 642
Qom
Ray
AD 624
Susa
El Mais
Ahvaz
Charax
Ublra
Bishapur
Kazerun
Rishahr
Firuzabad
Siraf
Darabgird
Persia
Naqsh-i Rustam
Istakhr
Yazd
Karmania
Veh Ardashir
(Kerman)
Hecatompylos
(Shahr i-Qumis)
Parthia
Dasht-e Lut
Nishapur
Nisa
Abivard
Turan
Lowland
Merv
Herat
Farah
Nia
Sakastan
Zaranj
Turan
Makuran
Gedrosian Desert
MAZUN
Bukhara
Amu Dar'ya
Marakanda
Sogdiana
Tashkent
Kokand
Ephthalites
c.AD 350–500
Kashgar
Kustana
HINDU KUSH
Bactra
Bactria
Kapisa
Kabul
Taxila
Gandhara
Indus
Helmand
Kandahar
Chenab
Medina
Mecca
YEMEN
Sasanian dependency
AD 574–628

SASANIAN King Peroz indulges in the favorite royal pastime of hunting gazelle, on this silver bowl of the 5th century AD.

east against the Kushans, conquering Sogdiana, Bactria and the Indus valley. The Kushans regained these territories during the minority of Shapur II (r.309–79), but lost them again when he took personal control. Shapur also enjoyed success against the Romans, Armenians and Arabs. Later in the 4th century the eastern provinces came under attack from the Ephthalites, or "White" Huns, who finally conquered them late in the 5th century. The kingdom also suffered severe internal problems at this time as a result of an attempted revolution by the Mazdakites, a radical religious movement. The Sasanians recovered under Khosru (Chosroes) I Anushirvan "of immortal soul" (r.531–79), who reconquered Sogdiana and Bactria, temporarily occupied Antioch in 540 and drove the Christian Axumites out of Yemen in 574. The long-running feud between the Sasanians and the Roman empire reached its climax in the reign of Khosru II (r.591–628) who took advantage of the empire's internal troubles to launch an all-out war in 607. Initially outstandingly successful – Syria, Palestine and Egypt were quickly overcome and a Persian army reached the Bosporus – the war ended in defeat at Nineveh in 627 and Khosru's assassination. Civil war broke out and the Sasanian kingdom was left so exhausted that when the newly Islamized Arabs poured out of the desert in 637 it quickly collapsed. The last claimant to the Sasanian throne was killed in 651.

In contrast to the Parthian kingdom, the Sasanian kingdom was a highly centralized state with the provinces kept under close control. Society was rigidly organized into a caste system of priests, soldiers, scribes and commoners and Zoroastrianism was established as the state religion. Devotees of other religions were actively persecuted. Persian cultural traditions revived strongly under the Sasanians, though hellenism still retained some influence in the 3rd century. Sasanian Persian culture exerted a profound influence on early Islamic civilization, but its art styles also influenced early Christian art. The example of the Zoroastrian state church probably also influenced the 4th-century Roman emperors in promoting Christianity as a state religion.

See also 1.15 (Achemenids); 2.10 (Hellenistic world); 2.15; 2.16 (Roman empire); 3.13 (Islam)

2.12 Early Rome and the Punic wars • 509 – 201 BC •

Founded probably around 800 BC, Rome had by about 600 BC fallen under the control of an Etruscan dynasty. Rome benefited from its strategic position on the lowest crossing point of the Tiber but remained a minor city. In 509 the monarchy was overthrown by an aristocratic coup and a republic was founded. The first century of its history was dominated by a struggle between the lower classes (the plebeians) and the leading families (the patricians). By the end of the 5th century the senate had codified the law and granted the plebeians their own representatives: the tribunes. In the 4th century the plebeians also won the right to run for the major offices of state – though voting in the popular assembly was structured to favor the richer classes. The extension of rights to the plebeians helped build a community of interest between the classes that sustained the republic through many crises.

Roman expansion began as a series of minor wars against its immediate neighbors. There was no imperial masterplan at this stage: these wars were intended primarily to make Rome more secure from attack. Around 400 BC, Gauls crossed the Alps and made extensive settlements in the Po valley, which became known as Cisalpine Gaul (Gaul "this side of the Alps") to distinguish it from the Gaulish homeland to the north. The Gauls raided widely, even sacking Rome in 390, but mainly they weakened the Etruscans. In 354 the Romans allied against the Gauls with the Samnites, a powerful tribal confederation, but the alliance did not last. The Romans and Samnites had competing interests in central Italy, which led to the inconclusive First Samnite War (343–341). Rome conquered the Latins (340–338), before renewing its conflict with the Samnites in the Second (327–304) and Third (298–290) Samnite wars. A Roman victory at Sentinum in 295 was followed by the collapse of Samnite power and by 290 Rome dominated central Italy. The Romans planted colonies of Roman citizens in subdued territories and awarded their allies half-citizenship rights which could, if loyalty was proved, eventually be increased to full Roman citizenship.

The Romans began to bring the Greek cities of southern Italy under their sway. The Greeks appealed for protection to King Pyrrhus of Epirus. In 280 Pyrrhus invaded Italy after a hard-fought battle at Heraclea. The king's losses were so great that he remarked after the battle that a few more victories like this and he would lose the war. This is what in fact happened: the Romans resisted doggedly and in 275 Pyrrhus withdrew. Three years later the Romans took Tarentum, completing their conquest of peninsular Italy. Rome was now a Mediterranean power.

In 264 Rome went to war with Carthage, the major naval power of the western Mediterranean, over a dispute about spheres of influence in Sicily. The Romans called the Carthaginians "Poeni" (Phoenicians) – and the wars with Carthage came to be known as the Punic wars. Rome had no tradition of naval warfare but learned quickly, and in 260 its newly built fleet won its first victory over the Carthaginians at Mylae. In 255 the Romans tried to bring the war to a quick conclusion by invading north Africa but were repulsed. The war dragged on until 241, when the Carthaginians were vanquished at sea off Lilybaeum. Sicily became a Roman province; and in 238 the Romans also occupied Corsica

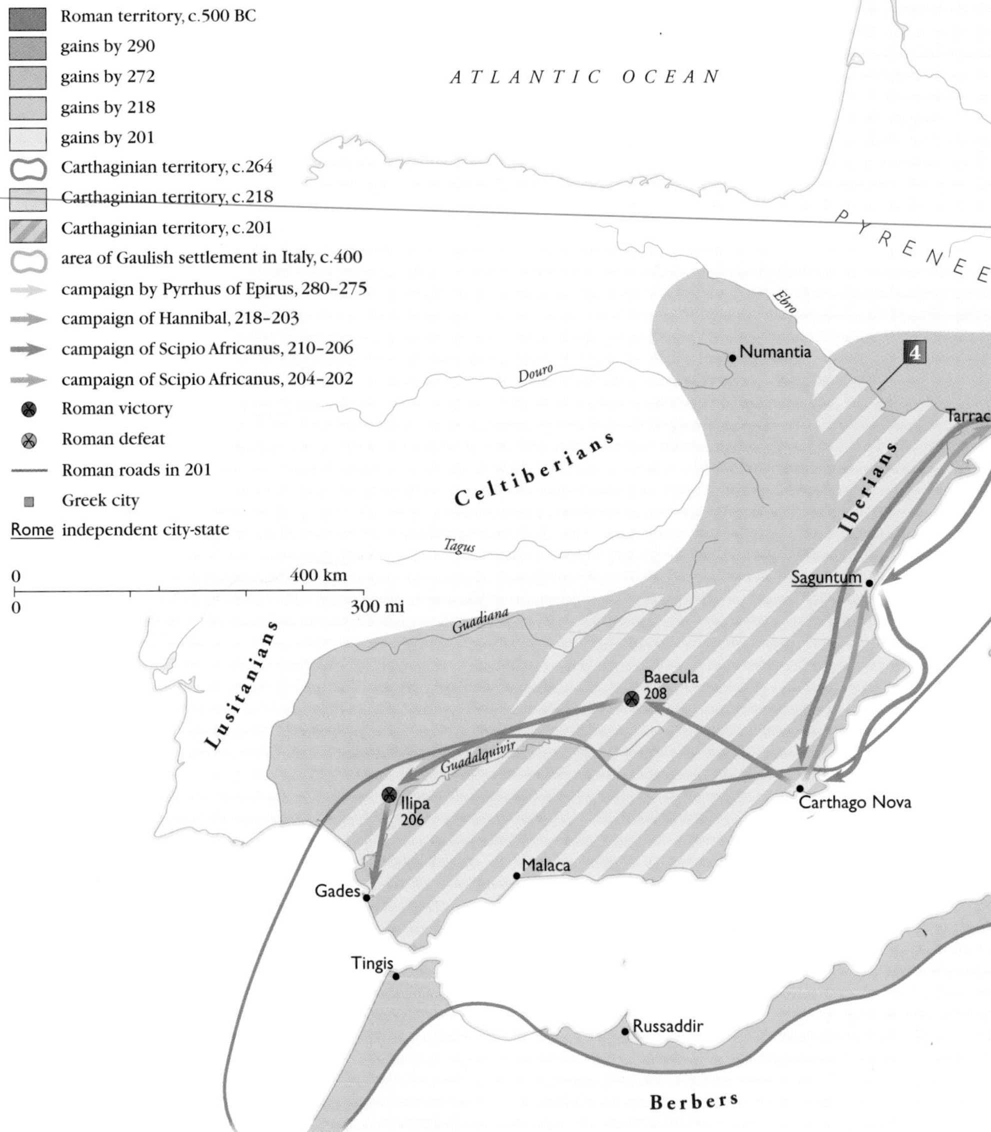

Roman territory, c.500 BC
gains by 290
gains by 272
gains by 218
gains by 201
Carthaginian territory, c.264
Carthaginian territory, c.218
Carthaginian territory, c.201
area of Gaulish settlement in Italy, c.400
campaign by Pyrrhus of Epirus, 280–275
campaign of Hannibal, 218–203
campaign of Scipio Africanus, 210–206
campaign of Scipio Africanus, 204–202
Roman victory
Roman defeat
Roman roads in 201
Greek city
Rome independent city-state
0 400 km
0 300 mi
ATLANTIC OCEAN
PYRENEES
Ebro
Numantia
4
Tarraco
Douro
Celtiberians
Iberians
Tagus
Saguntum
Guadiana
Lusitanians
Baecula 208
Guadalquivir
Ilipa 206
Carthago Nova
Malaca
Gades
Tingis
Russaddir
Berbers

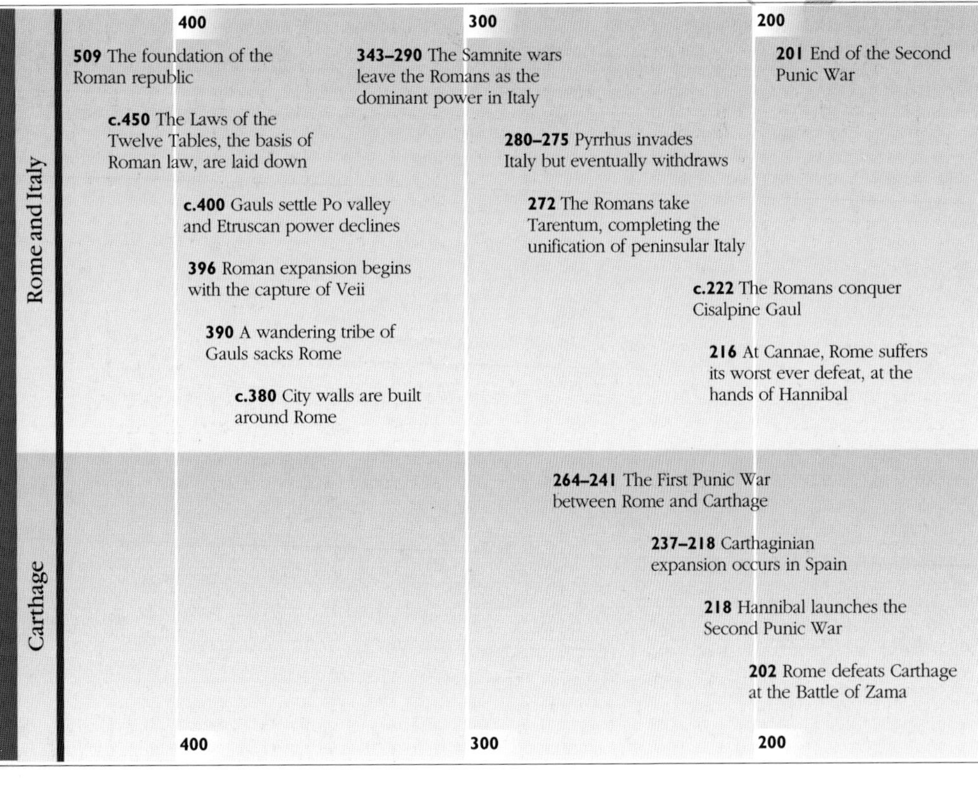

TIMELINE
Rome and Italy
Carthage
400
300
200
509 The foundation of the Roman republic
c.450 The Laws of the Twelve Tables, the basis of Roman law, are laid down
c.400 Gauls settle Po valley and Etruscan power declines
396 Roman expansion begins with the capture of Veii
390 A wandering tribe of Gauls sacks Rome
c.380 City walls are built around Rome
343–290 The Samnite wars leave the Romans as the dominant power in Italy
280–275 Pyrrhus invades Italy but eventually withdraws
272 The Romans take Tarentum, completing the unification of peninsular Italy
c.222 The Romans conquer Cisalpine Gaul
216 At Cannae, Rome suffers its worst ever defeat, at the hands of Hannibal
201 End of the Second Punic War
264–241 The First Punic War between Rome and Carthage
237–218 Carthaginian expansion occurs in Spain
218 Hannibal launches the Second Punic War
202 Rome defeats Carthage at the Battle of Zama
400
300
200

Gauls (Celts)
ALPS
Aquileia
Mediolanum
Ticinus River 218
CISALPINE GAUL
Po
Venetians
Rhône
GAUL
Trebia River 218
Genua
Ligurians
Arausio
Ariminum
Metaurus River 207
Ancona
Sentinum 295
Pisa
Massilia
Narbo
Lake Trasimenus 217
Umbrians
Castrum Novum
Etruscans
Saturnia
Cosa
Sabines
Veii
Rome
Corfinium
Ostia
Samnites
Latins
Cannae 216
Beneventum
Capua
Caudine Forks 321
Neapolis
Paestum
Brundisium
Tarentum
Messapians
Lucanians
Heraclea 280
Aleria
Corsica
Emporiae (Ampurias)
Sardinia
Carales
Balearic Islands
Croton
Bruttians
MAGNA GRAECIA
Mylae 260
Rhegium
Panormus
Messana
Drepanum 249
Lilybaeum 241
Sicily
Catana
Agrigentum 262
Syracusae
Ecnomus 256
Mediterranean Sea
Hippo Regius
Utica
Carthage
Bagradas 255
Zama 202
Cirta 203
Hadrumetum
Malta
NUMIDIA
Kingdom of Syphax
Kingdom of Massinissa
Leptis Magna
Sava
Danube
Illyrians
Adriatic Sea
Epidamnus
MACEDON
Apollonia
EPIRUS
Ambracia

ELEPHANTS carried soldiers to battle, but were used to scare the enemy rather than as cavalry. This Roman plate shows one carrying a fort.

and Sardinia. In the 230s Carthage began to recoup its losses by expansion in Spain; and in the 220s Rome conquered Cisalpine Gaul. In 226 Rome and Carthage agreed on respective spheres of influence, but when Hannibal, Carthage's foremost general, attacked Saguntum, a city within Carthage's sphere but friendly to Rome, the Second Punic War broke out. Roman naval power compelled Hannibal to invade Italy by marching overland and crossing the Alps. In Italy Hannibal found ready allies in the newly conquered Gauls in the north and the Greek cities in the south – and also in the kingdom of Macedon, which viewed with concern the expansion of Roman power into Greece in the 220s. Hannibal was a brilliant general but lacked the strength to take Rome itself and so win the war. The Romans, after a catastrophic defeat at Cannae, did their best to avoid facing Hannibal in open battle, trying simply to contain him in southern Italy. The main Roman counterattack was aimed at Carthage's Spanish possessions. The decisive campaign began in 210 under Scipio Africanus, and by 206 the Carthaginians had been driven out of Spain. Then in 204 Scipio launched an invasion of north Africa and persuaded the Numidian king Massinissa to side with Rome. Hannibal was recalled from Italy to face Scipio, and in 202 the two generals met in battle at Zama. The result was a crushing defeat for Hannibal and Carthage surrendered on harsh terms. Rome annexed Spain and the Balearic Islands, and the Numidians were given most of Carthage's north African territory. Carthage itself was reduced to a heartland in modern Tunisia: it had to disband its fleet and agree not to go to war without Rome's permission. Although in Spain the Romans faced rebellions – which for seventy years frustrated their attempts to gain control of their new possessions – Rome now dominated the western Mediterranean.

1 The capture of nearby Veii, an Etruscan city, in 396, was the first step in the Roman conquest of Italy.

2 Rome disputed control of Italy with the Samnites, a confederation of the Caraceni, Caudini, Hirpini and Pentri tribes, in a series of wars, from 343 to 290.

3 In the growing rivalry between Rome and Carthage, Sicily was the flashpoint that led in 264 to the outbreak of the First Punic War.

4 In 226 the Ebro was the agreed border between Roman and Carthaginian spheres of influence.

5 A Roman campaign against Illyria was mounted in 229–228 to suppress pirates infesting the Adriatic Sea.

6 Hannibal's crossing of the Alps took 15 days: only a handful of his original 38 elephants survived.

7 Hannibal's base for operations in southern Italy was at Tarentum until the Romans retook the city in 209.

8 Numidia's Berber kingdoms, longtime suppliers of cavalry to Carthage, sided with Rome at Zama in 202.

See also 1.25 (Carthage and the Etruscans);
2.13 (growth of the Roman empire)

2.13 The growth of the Roman empire • 201 BC – AD 117 •

Soon after the Second Punic War, Rome was drawn into further wars to protect its position in Italy, Spain and Greece. Cisalpine Gaul was reconquered by 191. The need to protect the new Spanish provinces from native attack drew Rome into a piecemeal conquest of the whole peninsula. Rome also launched a punitive campaign in 200 against Macedon, which had allied itself with Carthage in the Second Punic War. In 197, after the battle of Cynoscephalae, Macedon was forced to liberate the Greek city-states. At this time Rome took no territory for itself. However, the weight of constant disputes among the Greek cities and the Hellenistic kingdoms had become so onerous by 146 that the Romans imposed direct rule on Greece: opposition was ruthlessly suppressed. Also in 146 a Roman army, which had been besieging Carthage for three years, finally razed the city to the ground, its territory becoming the Roman province of Africa. Expansion into the Middle East began in 133, when the last king of Pergamon bequeathed his kingdom to Rome, and Pergamon became the province of Asia. Southern Gaul was conquered and became the province of Gallia Narbonensis in 121.

As the empire grew, the booty of successful campaigns – treasure and slaves – flooded back to Rome. The largest class of the early republic had been peasant freeholders, but they could not compete with the new slave-run estates of the rich and were forced off the land to swell the ranks of the urban poor. Demands for constitutional reform led to bitter class conflict in Rome, as defenders of aristocratic privilege resorted to acts of violence, such as the murder of the reformist tribune Tiberius Gracchus in 133. Gaius Marius then reformed the Roman army, opening recruitment for the first time to landless citizens. These soldiers looked to their commanders to reward their service with grants of land to settle on when discharged. This had a dramatic effect on Roman politics as successful generals could usually count on their armies to support their political ambitions. Success in war was now the surest route to political power: it was the main motive for Pompey's campaigns in Anatolia and Syria (67–64 BC), Julius Caesar's conquest of Gaul (58–51 BC) and Crassus's ill-fated attack on Parthia, which ended in his death at Carrhae, in 53 BC. The generals' need to reward their veterans led to the foundation of colonies throughout the empire in the late republic: these became important agents of Romanization.

The competition for power between generals led to civil war in 49 BC and ultimately to the fall of the republic. The victor was Caesar, who defeated his opponent Pompey at Ilerda in Spain (49 BC) and Pharsalus in Greece (48 BC). By 44 BC Caesar had crushed all military opposition, but a month after he declared himself dictator for life he was murdered by republican conspirators. Instability and civil war continued until Caesar's nephew Octavian, later known as Augustus, defeated Mark Antony and Cleopatra at Actium in 31 BC. In 27 BC Augustus introduced a new constitutional settlement, which he claimed "restored the republic" but in reality

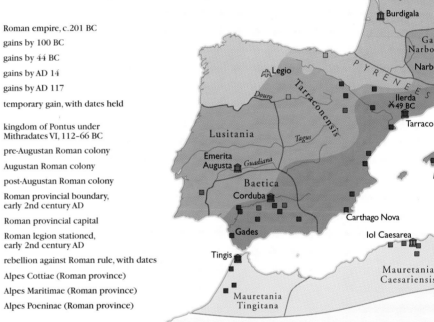

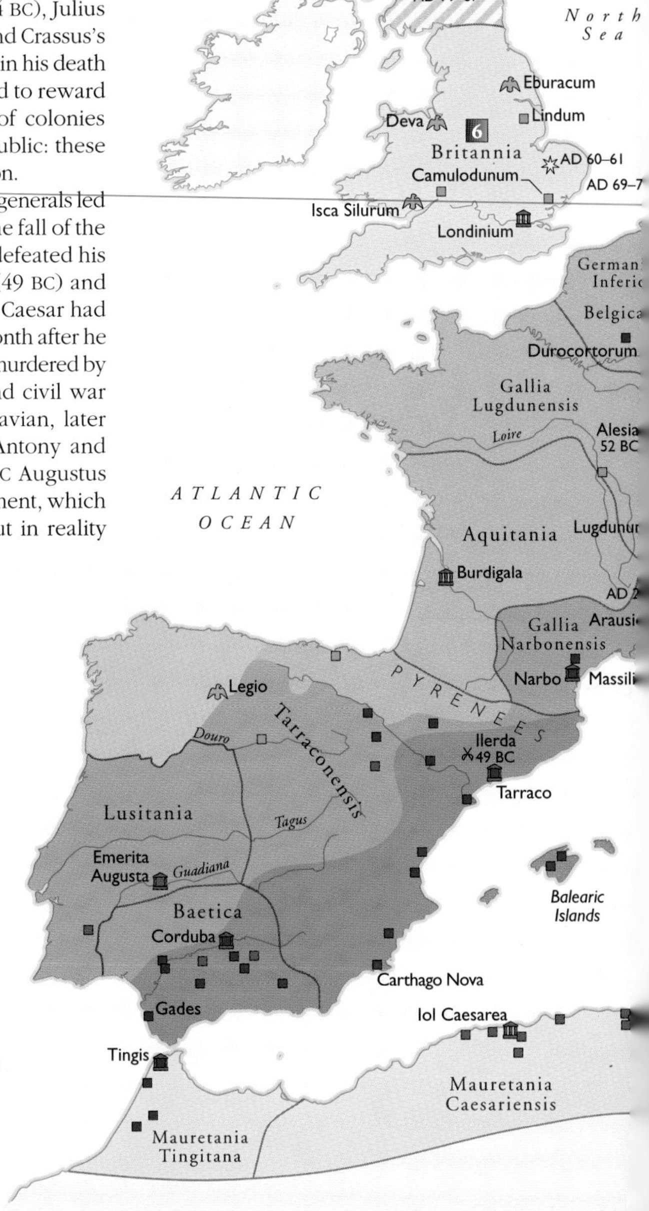

Roman empire, c.201 BC
gains by 100 BC
gains by 44 BC
gains by AD 14
gains by AD 117
temporary gain, with dates held
kingdom of Pontus under Mithradates VI, 112–66 BC
pre-Augustan Roman colony
Augustan Roman colony
post-Augustan Roman colony
Roman provincial boundary, early 2nd century AD
Roman provincial capital
Roman legion stationed, early 2nd century AD
rebellion against Roman rule, with dates
AC Alpes Cottiae (Roman province)
AM Alpes Maritimae (Roman province)
AP Alpes Poeninae (Roman province)
AD 79–87
North Sea
Eburacum
Deva
Lindum
6
Britannia
AD 60–61
Camulodunum
AD 69–7
Isca Silurum
Londinium
German
Inferi
Belgica
Durocortorum
Gallia Lugdunensis
Loire
Alesia 52 BC
ATLANTIC OCEAN
Aquitania
Lugdunu
Burdigala
Gallia Narbonensis
Arausi
Narbo
Massili
PYRENEES
Legio
Douro
Tarraconensis
Ilerda 49 BC
Tarraco
Lusitania
Tagus
Emerita Augusta
Guadiana
Baetica
Corduba
Balearic Islands
Carthago Nova
Gades
Iol Caesarea
Tingis
Mauretania Caesariensis
Mauretania Tingitana

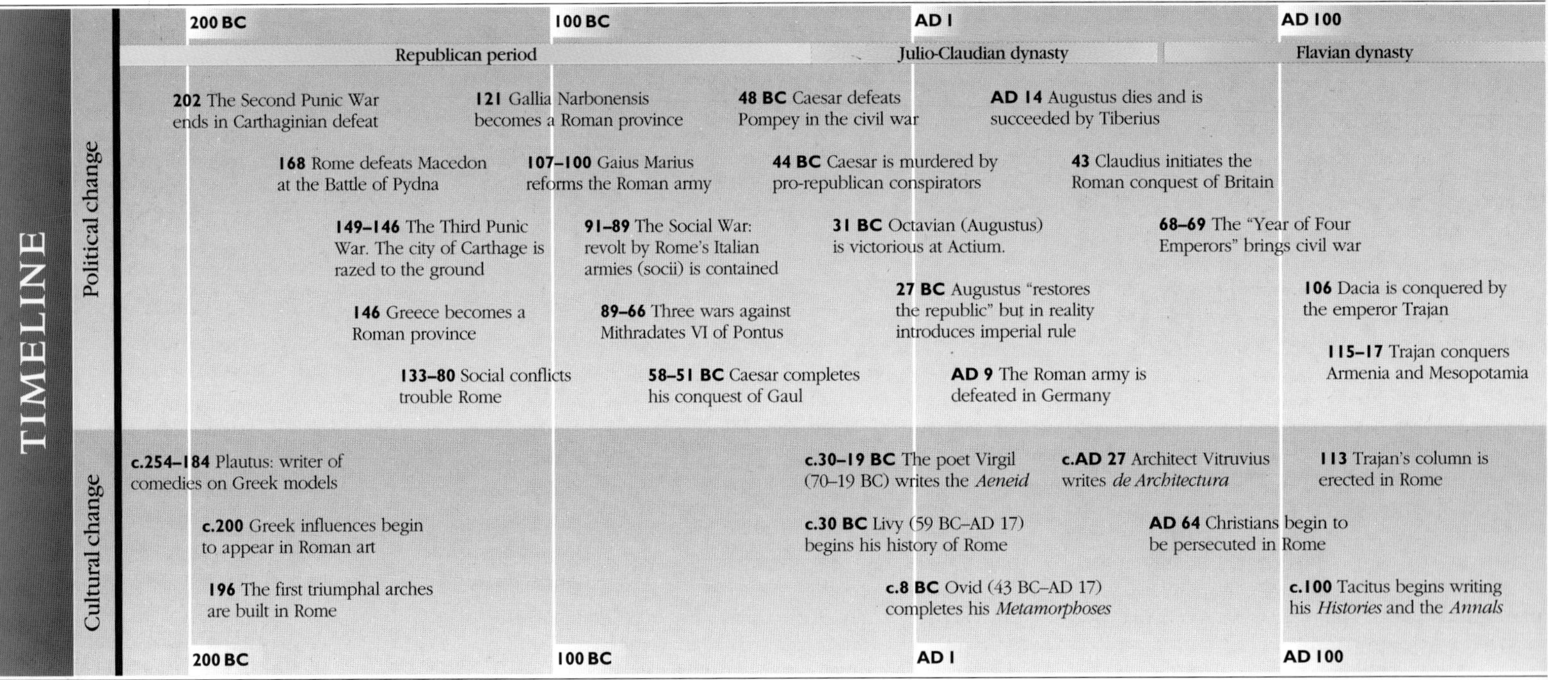

TIMELINE
Political change
Cultural change
200 BC
100 BC
AD 1
AD 100
Republican period
Julio-Claudian dynasty
Flavian dynasty
202 The Second Punic War ends in Carthaginian defeat
168 Rome defeats Macedon at the Battle of Pydna
149–146 The Third Punic War. The city of Carthage is razed to the ground
146 Greece becomes a Roman province
133–80 Social conflicts trouble Rome
121 Gallia Narbonensis becomes a Roman province
107–100 Gaius Marius reforms the Roman army
91–89 The Social War: revolt by Rome's Italian armies (socii) is contained
89–66 Three wars against Mithradates VI of Pontus
58–51 BC Caesar completes his conquest of Gaul
48 BC Caesar defeats Pompey in the civil war
44 BC Caesar is murdered by pro-republican conspirators
31 BC Octavian (Augustus) is victorious at Actium.
27 BC Augustus "restores the republic" but in reality introduces imperial rule
AD 9 The Roman army is defeated in Germany
AD 14 Augustus dies and is succeeded by Tiberius
43 Claudius initiates the Roman conquest of Britain
68–69 The "Year of Four Emperors" brings civil war
106 Dacia is conquered by the emperor Trajan
115–17 Trajan conquers Armenia and Mesopotamia
c.254–184 Plautus: writer of comedies on Greek models
c.200 Greek influences begin to appear in Roman art
196 The first triumphal arches are built in Rome
c.30–19 BC The poet Virgil (70–19 BC) writes the Aeneid
c.30 BC Livy (59 BC–AD 17) begins his history of Rome
c.8 BC Ovid (43 BC–AD 17) completes his Metamorphoses
c.AD 27 Architect Vitruvius writes de Architectura
AD 64 Christians begin to be persecuted in Rome
113 Trajan's column is erected in Rome
c.100 Tacitus begins writing his Histories and the Annals
200 BC
100 BC
AD 1
AD 100

GAULS were respected opponents of the Romans in the west and in Anatolia; this statue of a dying Gaul was made in Pergamon, 2nd century BC.

introduced a monarchical type of government. He took the title *princeps* (first citizen), leaving it to his successors to call themselves *imperator* (emperor).

Expansion continued under the emperors. In Augustus' reign Egypt and Galatia were annexed, the last native resistance was extinguished in Spain, the Alpine tribes were conquered, and the empire's northern frontier was pushed to the Danube. Augustus also tried to conquer Germany but gave up the attempt after a humiliating defeat at the battle of the Teutoburgerwald in AD 9. This defeat convinced Augustus that the empire had reached its natural limits and he advised his successors not to seek any more territories. Despite this advice, the empire continued to expand for another century after the death of Augustus. Much of the expansion was simply a tidying-up operation. The annexation of Lycia (AD 43) and the client kingdom of Mauretania (AD 44) gave Rome control of the entire Mediterranean coastline. In AD 43, Claudius, a weak emperor who needed a triumph to strengthen his position, began the conquest of Britain but only the southern two-thirds of the island were actually brought under Roman rule. The last emperor to pursue an all-out expansionist policy was Trajan. Between 101 and 106 Trajan conquered the Dacian kingdom, which posed a threat to the security of the Danube frontier. His ambition was to conquer the Parthian empire, and he brought Armenia and Mesopotamia under Roman rule. However, his successor Hadrian (r.117–38), judging these eastern conquests to be undefendable, withdrew from all of them except Edessa. Later in the 2nd century the border was pushed northward in Britain, and northern Mesopotamia was wrested from the Parthians, but from this time on the empire was mainly on the defensive.

1 Willed to the empire by the king of Pergamon, Asia became Rome's first Anatolian province in 133 BC.

2 Rebellions – the "Social War" – forced Rome to concede equal political rights to non-Roman Italians.

3 Mithradates VI of Pontus fought Rome in three wars from 89 until his final defeat in 66 BC.

4 Augustus' victory at Actium in 31 BC ended the civil war and brought Egypt under Roman rule.

5 Carthage, refounded as a Roman colony, became the center of Roman administration in Africa in 29 BC.

6 The Roman conquest of Britain began in AD 43, nearly a century after Caesar's raids in 55 and 54 BC.

See also 2.06 (religion); 2.10 (Hellenistic kingdoms); 2.11 (Persia); 2.14 (later Roman empire)

.14 Economy and society of the Roman empire • 27 BC – AD 305 •

The Roman empire created a vast free-trade area with a single currency where commerce could flourish without the threat of piracy or war. Good roads, bridges and harbors further aided trade. The empire's prosperity began to falter only in the 3rd century when the high cost of defending the empire caused emperors progressively to debase coinage, setting off runaway inflation.

The vast majority of the population of the Roman empire were peasant farmers or slaves whose needs were adequately met by local producers, but there was also considerable long-distance trade in both luxury goods and basic commodities such as metals, pottery and foodstuffs. The lifestyles of the small wealthy class were geared to conspicuous consumption, and luxury products such as silk, spices, aromatic resins, pigments and ivory were imported from as far afield as China, the East Indies and equatorial Africa to satisfy their tastes. Moralistic Romans worried that these expensive imports were a drain on the wealth of the empire; but finds of Roman metal and glassware, as well as coinage, from India and southeast and central Asia suggest that there was also a healthy demand for Roman exports. Luxury goods apart, the empire was essentially self-sufficient in everyday necessities and what was lacking in one region could easily be supplied by another. Most trade was generated by the needs of the empire's growing urban populations. Rome itself had to import 400,000 tons of grain annually, most of which came from Egypt, Africa and Sicily. The army also generated trade. Over 100,000 tons of grain were needed for rations each year; while the tents for one legion alone required the hides of 54,000 calves. The needs of the army stimulated agriculture and metalworking in the border areas, where most troops were stationed, but also called for much to be brought from elsewhere.

The empire's system of roads was built primarily to provide the army with fast all-weather routes, but they also promoted local trade. However, land transport was expensive because the volumes that could be transported were small. Long-distance cargoes therefore went by water, both by sea and along navigable rivers. Sea-going merchant ships capable of carrying up to 350 tons made it cheaper for the city of Rome to import grain from across the Mediterranean than to cart it into the city from the surrounding countryside. For the same reason the Romans preferred to run frontiers along navigable rivers providing access to border garrisons – and fleets were maintained on the Rhine and the Danube for this purpose.

Although trade was essential to its survival, the empire's commercial classes remained small and enjoyed neither the wealth nor the status of the landowning aristocracy. Goods such as pottery were mass-produced in factories, but most production in the empire was small-scale and under-capitalized, the rich preferring to invest in land. It is in any case doubtful, in view of the poverty of most of the empire's population, whether the markets existed to support a greater degree of industrial production. This is probably one of the factors behind the surprising lack of technological innovation in the empire. Although the Romans were excellent engineers, they did not extensively exploit their understanding of the principles of water and wind power. The ready availability of cheap slave labor may also have deterred investment in expensive machinery.

The wealth and population of the empire were not evenly spread: the eastern half was wealthier, more densely urbanized and had a higher population than the western half which, outside Italy, was relatively underdeveloped. In most of the west, as in Gaul and Britain, urbanization was still in its early stages at the time of the Roman conquest, and the promotion of town life became part of the program of Romanization. The Romans founded dozens of new towns, each complete with baths, theaters, amphitheaters and other trappings of Roman civilization. But most of the west was too poor and underpopulated to support this level of urbanization and towns remained primarily administrative or military centers. This contrast between east and west was to have an important bearing on the fate of the empire in the 5th century.

The Roman empire united many different ethnic groups into a single state, but over time, helped by the progressive extension of citizenship, local

1 The main port for Rome was Puteoli until Claudius improved the harbor at Ostia, though this remained unsafe until Trajan rebuilt it in the early 2nd century.

2 Rome, with about a million inhabitants, was the largest city in the empire. Some 200,000 people relied on state handouts of grain for survival.

3 Egypt was the main granary of the Roman empire: the fertile Nile flood plain was the most productive agricultural area in the empire.

4 Carnuntum was the main center for trading Baltic amber with the German tribes.

5 Northwest Spain was one of the most important mining regions in the Roman empire.

6 Palmyra was a desert city which became an important trading destination for trans-Asian caravans.

7 The Rhineland was an important center of glass manufacturing: much was exported across the Rhine.

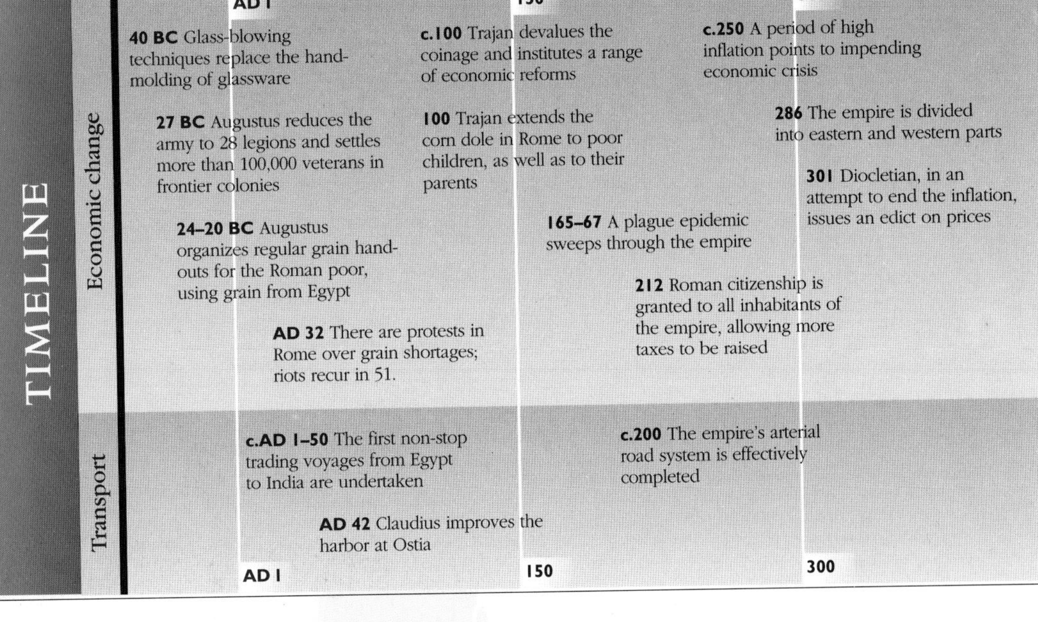

TIMELINE
Economic change
Transport
AD 1
150
300
40 BC Glass-blowing techniques replace the hand-molding of glassware
27 BC Augustus reduces the army to 28 legions and settles more than 100,000 veterans in frontier colonies
24–20 BC Augustus organizes regular grain hand-outs for the Roman poor, using grain from Egypt
AD 32 There are protests in Rome over grain shortages; riots recur in 51.
c.100 Trajan devalues the coinage and institutes a range of economic reforms
100 Trajan extends the corn dole in Rome to poor children, as well as to their parents
165–67 A plague epidemic sweeps through the empire
c.250 A period of high inflation points to impending economic crisis
286 The empire is divided into eastern and western parts
301 Diocletian, in an attempt to end the inflation, issues an edict on prices
212 Roman citizenship is granted to all inhabitants of the empire, allowing more taxes to be raised
c.AD 1–50 The first non-stop trading voyages from Egypt to India are undertaken
AD 42 Claudius improves the harbor at Ostia
c.200 The empire's arterial road system is effectively completed
AD 1
150
300

Roman empire, c.AD 117
main concentration of cities
city with population over 100,000
city with population over 30,000
main road
sea and river route
caravan route
division between Greek and Latin languages
CELTIC local language surviving within Roman empire
furs source of goods from outside Roman empire
goods traded within Roman empire
copper
gold
iron
lead
silver
tin
grain
olive oil
wine
slaves
brass and bronze
glass
pottery
timber
marble
textiles
purple dye
0 600 km
0 400 mi
Vänern
furs
Vättern
Lake Peipus
Baltic Sea
amber
amber
Vistula
animal hides, slaves
Elbe
Oder
Dnieper
animal hides, honey, grain
Colonia Agrippina
Augusta Treverorum
Castra Regina
Rhine
Danube
Carnuntum
CARPATHIAN MTS
Olbia
Panticapaeum
flax, wine, iron
ALPS
Aquileia
Sarmizegethusa
Po
Sava
Genua
Ravenna
Singidunum
Danube
Tomi
Black Sea
Ancona
Salonae
Naissus
Sinope
Trapezus
THRACIAN
ILLYRIAN
Ostia
Rome
Byzantium
Nicomedia
Dyrrhachium
Ancyra
Megalopolis
Sardinia
Puteoli
Brundisium
Thessalonica
ANATOLIA
Amida
wild animals from Asia
Carthage to Ostia - 3–5 days
Pergamon
Smyrna
Ephesus
Edessa
Athens
Corinth
Aphrodisias
Tarsus
Antiochia
silk from China
Sicily
Syracusae
Rhodus
Rhodes
Dura Europus
Carthage
Cyprus
Palmyra
Crete
Paphus
Ctesiphon
Malta
Gaza to Byzantium - 10–12 days
ARAMAIC/SYRIAC
Mediterranean Sea
Caesarea to Rome - 20 days
Tyrus
Damascus
Alexandria to Puteoli - 15–20 days
Caesarea
Bostra
Jerusalem
Gaza
Cyrene
Leptis Magna
Alexandria
Petra
NABATAEAN
Clysma
slaves and wild animals from tropical Africa
LIBYAN
Memphis
DEMOTIC/COPTIC
Myos Hormus
Thebes
Berenice
Syene
perfume, spices and muslin from India
aromatic resins from Arabia
slaves, ivory, ebony and wild animals from tropical Africa

identities were weakened, and by the 4th century the vast majority of the empire's citizens considered themselves Roman. In the west local languages were gradually replaced by Latin. Distinct local dialects of Latin developed in Italy, Iberia, Dacia and Gaul, eventually developing into the Romance languages – Italian, Spanish, Portuguese, Romanian and French. Celtic languages survived in Britain, Basque in the Pyrenees and Libyan in much of North Africa. Latin made little headway in the east. Here it was Greek which gradually replaced local languages, such as Phrygian, in Anatolia. However, Greek did not take over as completely as Latin did in the west and there remained large communities of Demotic (late ancient Egyptian) and Aramaic speakers.

MERCHANT ships were slow and heavy but were capable of ocean-going voyages: this illustration comes from Trajan's Column in Rome (AD 113).

See also 2.06 (religion and culture); 2.11 (Persia); 2.13 (Diocletian's reforms);

2.15 Crisis and recovery of the Roman empire • AD 117 – 376 •

After Hadrian withdrew from Trajan's eastern conquests in 117, the borders of the Roman empire remained stable for almost 150 years. The only significant change was in the east, where successful campaigning by Septimius Severus between 195 and 198 wrested northern Mesopotamia from the Parthians. The 2nd century was a time of unrivaled peace and prosperity for the empire but this was not to last. The wealth of the empire was attractive to the Germanic tribes along the Rhine and Danube frontiers, and these began to unite in powerful confederations and raid Roman territory. In 167 Marcomannic raiders crossed into Italy, and though the emperor, Marcus Aurelius, successfully secured the borders, pressure on the northern frontier was thereafter continuous. Another problem was the imperial succession: there was no accepted way of deposing an incompetent or tyrannical emperor, nor of selecting a new emperor if a dynasty died out or was overthrown. When the incompetent, tyrannical Nero was overthrown in AD 68 the frontier armies promoted their own candidates for the succession, who then fought it out in a civil war. The same happened after the murder of the mad Commodus.

Pressure on the northern frontiers became critical in the 3rd century, and a new threat appeared in 226 when the Parthians were overthrown by the aggressive Persian Sasanian dynasty. In these conditions, the emperor had to be above all a good soldier. While rival candidates for power, promoted by different legions, fought each other for control of the empire, the borders were left undefended and open to invasion. For example, when Valerian (r. 253–60) withdrew troops from the Rhine to fight a usurper, the Franks immediately invaded Gaul. The efforts of emperors to buy the loyalty of their troops led them to debase the coinage to raise money, but this added runaway inflation to the empire's woes. Urban life now declined, especially in the west, where many towns shrank to a fortified administrative core. Civil war and invasion were incessant between 235 and 284: of the twenty-six emperors who ruled in this period all but one died by violence.

Not all the usurpers aimed at control of the whole empire. After Valerian was captured by the Persians at Edessa in 260, defense of the east devolved on Odenathus, ruler of the desert city of Palmyra. He defeated the Persians but then built an independent kingdom for himself. Under his wife and successor Queen Zenobia, it came to include Egypt, Syria and much of Anatolia. In the west the usurper Postumus founded an independent Gallic empire, winning over the people of Gaul, Britain and Spain; he promised to concentrate on defending the frontiers and not to march on Rome.

The Roman empire began to revive in the reign of Aurelian, with the reconquest of Palmyra (272) and the Gallic empire (274), though Dacia was permanently abandoned to the Germans. Political and economic stability were restored by Diocletian (r. 284–305), who reformed the whole structure of the empire. Diocletian greatly expanded the army and reformed the tax system to pay for it. Price regulation was introduced to curb inflation, though it drove goods off the markets. To restore respect to the imperial office, elaborate court ritual was introduced and the idea of the emperor as "first citizen" was abandoned: he was now "lord and god." Civilian and military authority were separated: provinces

Roman empire, c.235
Roman territory lost permanently, 163–378
kingdom of Palmyra, 260–72
Gallic empire, 260–74
strong Christian communities by 300
Goths major Germanic peoples, 3rd century
Picts other barbarians, 3rd century
attacks on Roman empire, with dates
city sacked
Roman victory
Roman defeat
battle between Roman forces
frontier wall or rampart
Italia Diocletianic diocese
borders of Diocletianic dioceses

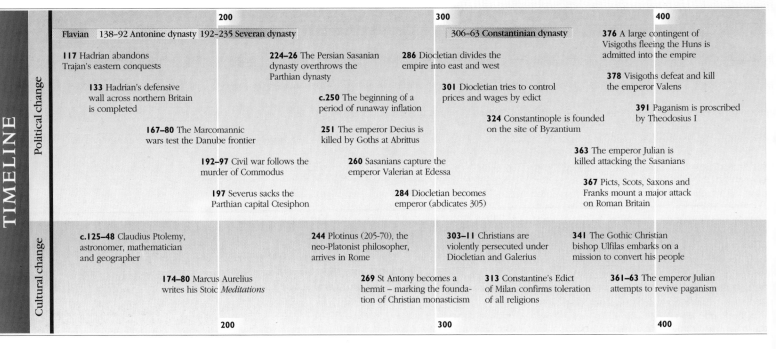

TIMELINE

Political change

Flavian | 138–92 Antonine dynasty | 192–235 Severan dynasty | 306–63 Constantinian dynasty

117 Hadrian abandons Trajan's eastern conquests

133 Hadrian's defensive wall across northern Britain is completed

167–80 The Marcomannic wars test the Danube frontier

192–97 Civil war follows the murder of Commodus

197 Severus sacks the Parthian capital Ctesiphon

224–26 The Persian Sasanian dynasty overthrows the Parthian dynasty

c.250 The beginning of a period of runaway inflation

251 The emperor Decius is killed by Goths at Abrittus

260 Sasanians capture the emperor Valerian at Edessa

284 Diocletian becomes emperor (abdicates 305)

286 Diocletian divides the empire into east and west

301 Diocletian tries to control prices and wages by edict

324 Constantinople is founded on the site of Byzantium

363 The emperor Julian is killed attacking the Sasanians

367 Picts, Scots, Saxons and Franks mount a major attack on Roman Britain

376 A large contingent of Visigoths fleeing the Huns is admitted into the empire

378 Visigoths defeat and kill the emperor Valens

391 Paganism is proscribed by Theodosius I

Cultural change

c.125–48 Claudius Ptolemy, astronomer, mathematician and geographer

174–80 Marcus Aurelius writes his Stoic *Meditations*

244 Plotinus (205-70), the neo-Platonist philosopher, arrives in Rome

269 St Antony becomes a hermit – marking the foundation of Christian monasticism

303–11 Christians are violently persecuted under Diocletian and Galerius

313 Constantine's Edict of Milan confirms toleration of all religions

341 The Gothic Christian bishop Ulfilas embarks on a mission to convert his people

361–63 The emperor Julian attempts to revive paganism

200 | 300 | 400

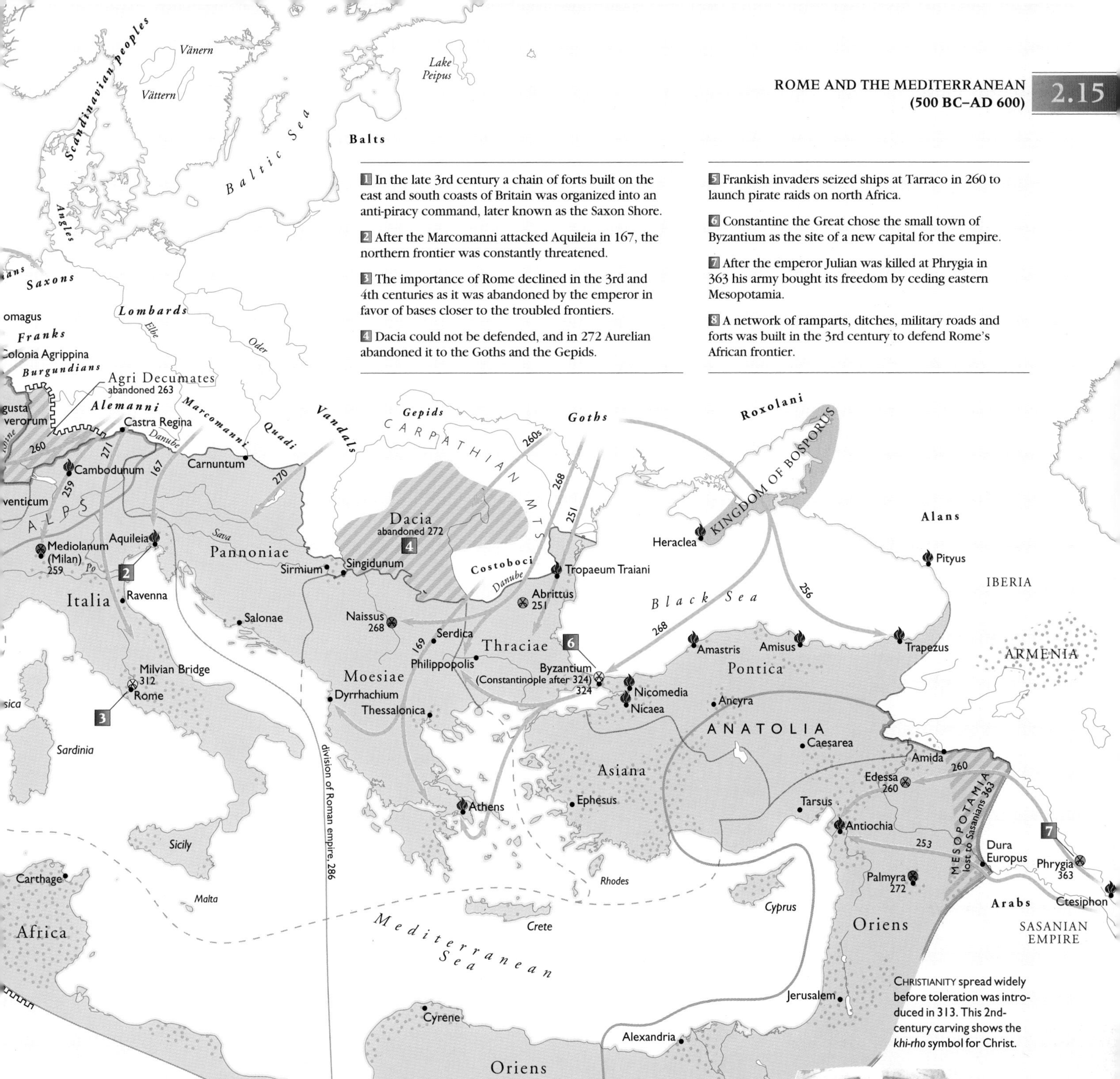

1 In the late 3rd century a chain of forts built on the east and south coasts of Britain was organized into an anti-piracy command, later known as the Saxon Shore.

2 After the Marcomanni attacked Aquileia in 167, the northern frontier was constantly threatened.

3 The importance of Rome declined in the 3rd and 4th centuries as it was abandoned by the emperor in favor of bases closer to the troubled frontiers.

4 Dacia could not be defended, and in 272 Aurelian abandoned it to the Goths and the Gepids.

5 Frankish invaders seized ships at Tarraco in 260 to launch pirate raids on north Africa.

6 Constantine the Great chose the small town of Byzantium as the site of a new capital for the empire.

7 After the emperor Julian was killed at Phrygia in 363 his army bought its freedom by ceding eastern Mesopotamia.

8 A network of ramparts, ditches, military roads and forts was built in the 3rd century to defend Rome's African frontier.

were subdivided and organized in dioceses under "vicars" who were directly responsible to the emperor. Diocletian realized that the problems of defending the empire were too great for one ruler and in 286 he appointed Maximian as co-emperor to rule the west while he concentrated on the east.

In the 4th century the empire underwent a cultural transformation as traditional paganism was supplanted by Christianity. The pagan Roman empire was a tolerant state and was prepared to accept any religion that did not involve human sacrifice, so long as its devotees were prepared to pay lip-service to the state gods. Christians were not prepared to do this and had faced frequent persecutions as a result, one of the worst being ordered by Diocletian. Despite this,Christianity had spread steadily through the urban lower and middle classes, and by 300 it was well established throughout the empire. In 312 the emperor Constantine (r. 306–37) became convinced that the Christian God had helped him win a victory over a rival at the Milvian Bridge, and in 313 he granted Christian toleration. Constantine subsequently presided over church councils, founded churches and was baptized on his deathbed. There is no reason to doubt the sincerity of his conversion, but he may also have seen Christianity as a unifying force for the embattled empire. Constantine's successors continued to promote Christianity and, despite a short-lived pagan revival under Julian (r.361–63), the new religion began to exert a strong influence on all aspects of Roman life, from personal morality to art and literature. Christianity finally became the empire's official religion in 391, when Theodosius I abolished pagan worship.

CHRISTIANITY spread widely before toleration was introduced in 313. This 2nd-century carving shows the *khi-rho* symbol for Christ.

See also 2.11 (Sasanians): 2.14 (earlier Roman empire); 2.16 (fall of the empire); 2.19 (Germans)

2.16 The fall of the western Roman empire • AD 376 – 480 •

The fragile stability of the 4th-century empire was maintained at great cost to its citizens. Taxation was kept at a high level to pay for the large armies needed to defend the frontiers against increasingly well organized Germanic barbarians; yet the economy, particularly in the west, was in decline. The rich used their political influence to avoid paying taxes, so the tax burden fell heavily upon the poorer classes. Even in Egypt's fertile Nile valley, peasant farmers could not afford to pay their taxes and abandoned their fields. The empire's population contracted and manpower shortages began to affect the armies. The western army relied increasingly on barbarian mercenaries to fill its ranks.

In the 370s pressures on the empire's northern frontier increased dramatically. The Huns, a Turkic nomad people, migrated to the eastern European steppes from central Asia and, around 372, crushed the Ostrogoths. The defeat of this the most powerful Germanic tribe caused panic among the rest. In 376 the Visigoths, seeking sanctuary from the Huns, requested permission to settle in the Roman empire. The eastern emperor, Valens, who saw the Visigoths as a valuable source of recruits for the army, settled them on vacant lands in Thrace. There, however, they were treated badly by the corrupt officials in charge of their settlement; and in 378 they rebelled, defeating and killing Valens in battle at Adrianople. Under a new agreement in 382 the emperor Theodosius gave the Visigoths the status of federates (allies); but they rebelled again in 395 under their ambitious new leader, Alaric. He had previously commanded Gothic troops in the Roman army, but now ravaged Greece and Dalmatia before invading Italy in 401. Stilicho, a Roman general of Germanic origin, drove the Visigoths back into Dalmatia; but the situation deteriorated in 406 when a coalition of Vandals, Suevi and Alans invaded Gaul before crossing the Pyrenees into Spain in 409. They were followed into Gaul by Franks, Burgundians and Alemanni. In 410 Alaric rebelled yet again, and when his demands were refused the Visigoths sacked Rome. Though no longer the administrative capital of the empire, Rome remained a potent symbol of its history and power, and the attack was deeply shocking. Alaric died soon afterward, and his successors were more inclined to cooperate with the Romans. In 418 the Visigoths, as allies of the Romans, attacked the Suevi, Alans and Vandals in Spain, before being settled on rich lands in Aquitaine as federates under nominal Roman suzerainty.

Although the Huns were indirectly responsible for the empire's woes, they initially maintained good

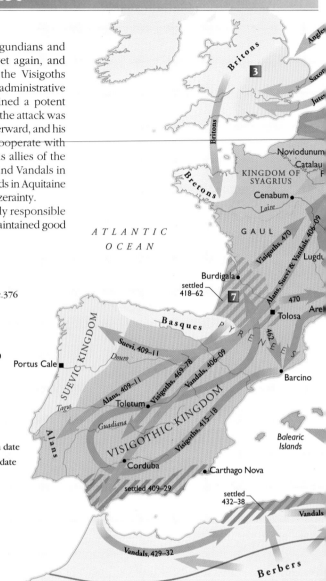

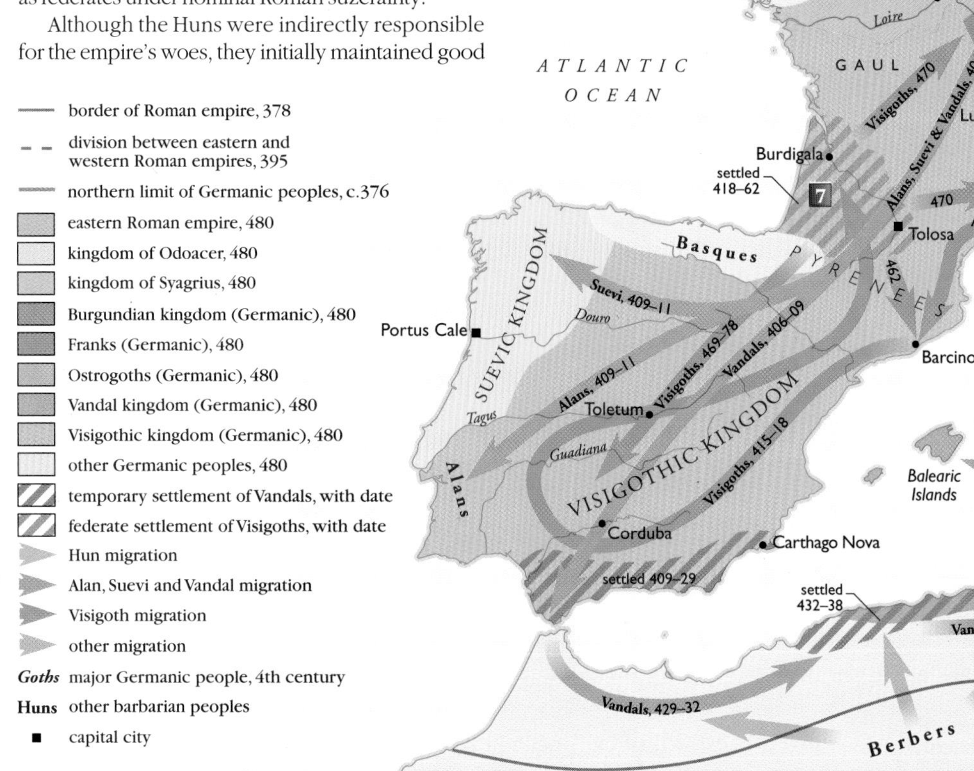

Picts
Angles
Saxons
Jutes
Britons
3
Britons
Bretons
Noviodunum
Catalau
KINGDOM OF SYAGRIUS
Cenabum
Loire
GAUL
ATLANTIC OCEAN
Visigoths, 470
Alans, Suevi & Vandals, 406–09
Lugdu
Burdigala
settled 418–62
7
470
Tolosa
Arel
Basques
PYRENEES
462
SUEVIC KINGDOM
Suevi, 409–11
Douro
Portus Cale
Barcino
Visigoths, 469–78
Vandals, 406–09
Alans, 409–11
Toletum
Tagus
Guadiana
VISIGOTHIC KINGDOM
Visigoths, 415–18
Alans
Corduba
Balearic Islands
Carthago Nova
settled 409–29
settled 432–38
Vandals
Vandals, 429–32
Berbers
border of Roman empire, 378
division between eastern and western Roman empires, 395
northern limit of Germanic peoples, c.376
eastern Roman empire, 480
kingdom of Odoacer, 480
kingdom of Syagrius, 480
Burgundian kingdom (Germanic), 480
Franks (Germanic), 480
Ostrogoths (Germanic), 480
Vandal kingdom (Germanic), 480
Visigothic kingdom (Germanic), 480
other Germanic peoples, 480
temporary settlement of Vandals, with date
federate settlement of Visigoths, with date
Hun migration
Alan, Suevi and Vandal migration
Visigoth migration
other migration
Goths major Germanic people, 4th century
Huns other barbarian peoples
capital city

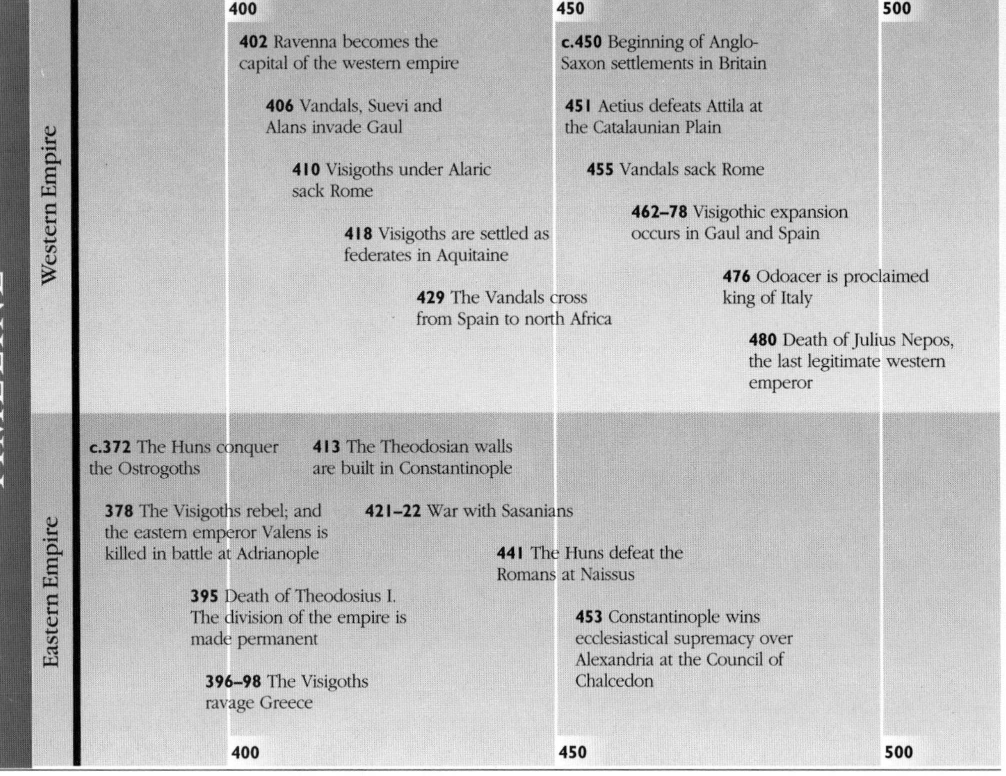

TIMELINE
Western Empire
400
450
500
402 Ravenna becomes the capital of the western empire
406 Vandals, Suevi and Alans invade Gaul
410 Visigoths under Alaric sack Rome
418 Visigoths are settled as federates in Aquitaine
429 The Vandals cross from Spain to north Africa
c.450 Beginning of Anglo-Saxon settlements in Britain
451 Aetius defeats Attila at the Catalaunian Plain
455 Vandals sack Rome
462–78 Visigothic expansion occurs in Gaul and Spain
476 Odoacer is proclaimed king of Italy
480 Death of Julius Nepos, the last legitimate western emperor
Eastern Empire
c.372 The Huns conquer the Ostrogoths
378 The Visigoths rebel; and the eastern emperor Valens is killed in battle at Adrianople
395 Death of Theodosius I. The division of the empire is made permanent
396–98 The Visigoths ravage Greece
413 The Theodosian walls are built in Constantinople
421–22 War with Sasanians
441 The Huns defeat the Romans at Naissus
453 Constantinople wins ecclesiastical supremacy over Alexandria at the Council of Chalcedon
400
450
500

1 The arrival of the Huns in eastern Europe around 370 completely destabilized the Germanic tribes, causing many to seek refuge in the Roman empire.

2 In 402 the capital of the western empire was moved from Rome to Ravenna, allowing more rapid communication with the northern frontier and Constantinople.

3 Most of Britain's garrison was withdrawn in 407 by the usurper Constantine to fight in a civil war. In 410 Honorius told the Britons to see to their own defenses.

4 Rome was sacked twice in the 5th century: in 410 by the Visigoths; and in 455 by the Vandals.

5 Saxons, Angles and Jutes from north Germany and Denmark began to settle in eastern Britain c.450.

6 The position and strong fortifications of Constantinople saved Anatolia from barbarian invaders in the 5th century.

7 In the 460s Visigoths, settled by the Romans in Aquitaine in 418, expanded into Gaul and Spain.

8 In 476 Italy came under the rule of Odoacer, a barbarian general, who deposed the "last" western emperor: the puppet usurper Romulus Augustulus, who was still a boy.

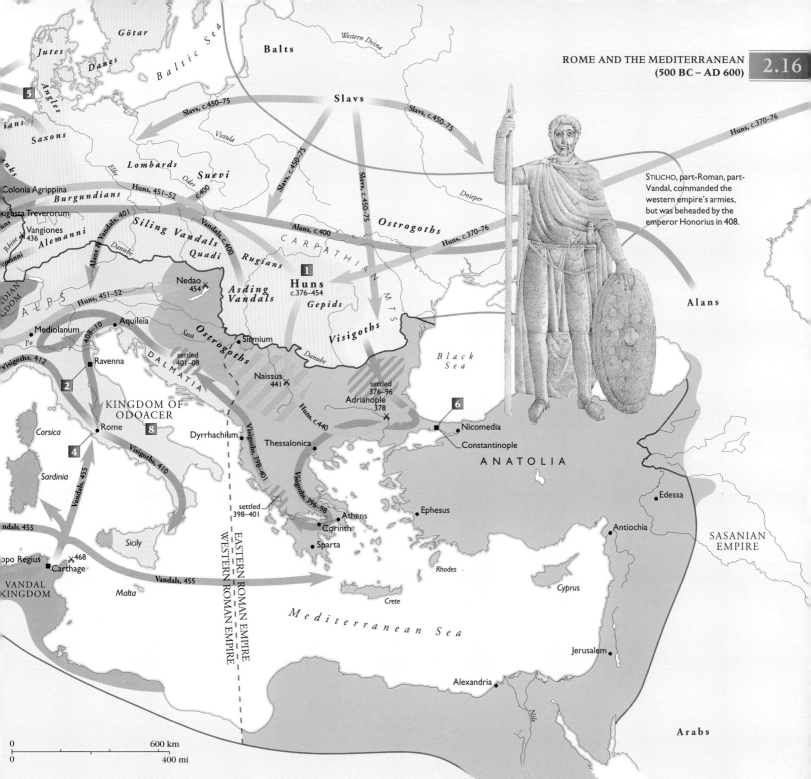

STILICHO, part-Roman, part-Vandal, commanded the western empire's armies, but was beheaded by the emperor Honorius in 408.

relations with Rome. The Roman general Aetius used Hun mercenaries widely in the 430s to impose federate status on the Burgundians and other barbarian settlers in Gaul, but in 441 Attila turned on the empire, ravaging the Balkans and pushing his western border to the Rhine. In 451 Attila invaded Gaul but was defeated by a coalition of Romans, Visigoths, Burgundians and Franks under Aetius at the Catalaunian Plain. After Attila's death in 453 the Huns' German subjects rebelled, breaking their power at the battle of Nedao in 454. The collapse of the Huns in fact worked against Rome: fear of them had kept Rome's Germanic allies reasonably loyal, now they had less cause to be cooperative.

In 429 the Vandals had crossed from Spain to Africa and in 439 captured Carthage and set up a completely independent kingdom. This was the most serious blow the barbarians had so far struck against the empire, as north Africa was Italy's main source of grain. The Vandals turned to piracy, and in 455 went on to sack Rome itself. The assassination in this year of Aetius, the west's most able general, and of Valentinian III, last of the Theodosian dynasty, were further blows. The western empire now began to crumble and by the 470s was reduced to little more than Italy. The last legitimate western emperor, Julius Nepos, was driven out of Italy in 475 by a palace coup which placed a boy usurper, Romulus Augustulus, on the throne. The following year Odoacer, a barbarian general, deposed Augustulus and was proclaimed king by his soldiers. Odoacer recognized the suzerainty of the eastern emperor Zeno and offered to rule Italy as imperial viceroy. The deposing of Augustulus in 476 is widely accepted as marking the end of the western Roman empire, but Julius Nepos continued to rule a rump empire in Dalmatia from 475 until his death in 480. Dalmatia then became part of Odoacer's kingdom.

The main cause of the fall of the western Roman empire was its exposure to barbarian attack – far greater than in the east, which had only a short northern frontier. This problem was exacerbated by the division of the empire in the 4th century, which deprived the poorer, less populated and more vulnerable west of the resources of the richer east. Eastern emperors did assist their western colleagues, but their main priority was ensuring that the east did not go the same way as the west. The west was also politically less stable than the east. From the time of Honorius onward western emperors were dominated by overbearing generals. After the death of Valentinian III in 455, the western emperors became the puppets of barbarian generals: when they outlived their usefulness or tried to act independently, they were murdered. The high cost of defending the empire undermined positive loyalty to it. There was little popular resistance to the barbarians and, as they were inefficient tax collectors, most people probably felt themselves better off without the empire.

See also 2.11 (Sasanians); 2.17 (rise of Byzantium); 2.19 (Germans and Slavs); 2.20 (steppe peoples)

2.17 Justinian and the origins of the Byzantine empire • AD 480 – 629 •

For twelve years after Odoacer's takeover of Italy, Zeno, the eastern emperor, did nothing. Then in 488 he commissioned Theodoric, king of the Ostrogoths, to overthrow Odoacer and rule Italy until he, the emperor, was able to claim sovereignty in person. By 493 Odoacer was dead and Theodoric was master of Italy. Under Theodoric, who wished to preserve Roman civilization, Italy enjoyed peace and prosperity, but there was no assimilation between Roman and Goth. The main barrier was religion. The Goths had converted to Christianity in the 4th century but were followers of the teachings of Arius, who denied the divinity of Christ – which their Roman subjects regarded as heretical. The Burgundians, Visigoths and Vandals were also Arians and assimilation was equally limited in those kingdoms. Arianism also prevented good relations between the barbarian kingdoms and the eastern emperor, who regarded himself as the guardian of orthodox Christianity. The only barbarians to escape the taint of heresy were the Franks, who converted directly from paganism to orthodox Christianity around 500. This earned them the friendship and support of the eastern emperors and the loyalty and cooperation of their Gallo-Roman subjects. Because of this the Frankish kingdom became the strongest power in western Europe by 600.

Although it was frequently at war with Sasanian Persia, the eastern empire prospered after the fall of the west. The emperor Anastasius (r. 491–518) even managed to cut taxes and still leave his successor, Justin (r. 518–27), with a full treasury. Justin was succeeded by his nephew Justinian (r. 527–65), the last great Roman emperor. Justinian had a very clear idea of the responsibilities of a Roman emperor, chief of which was maintaining the territorial integrity of the empire. To Justinian it was a disgrace that the western provinces of the empire were occupied by barbarians and he launched a concerted effort to recover them. In 533 he sent a force under Belisarius which, against expectations, destroyed the Vandal kingdom in north Africa. The Vandal campaign had been made possible by the cooperation of the pro-Roman Ostrogothic queen Amalasuntha,

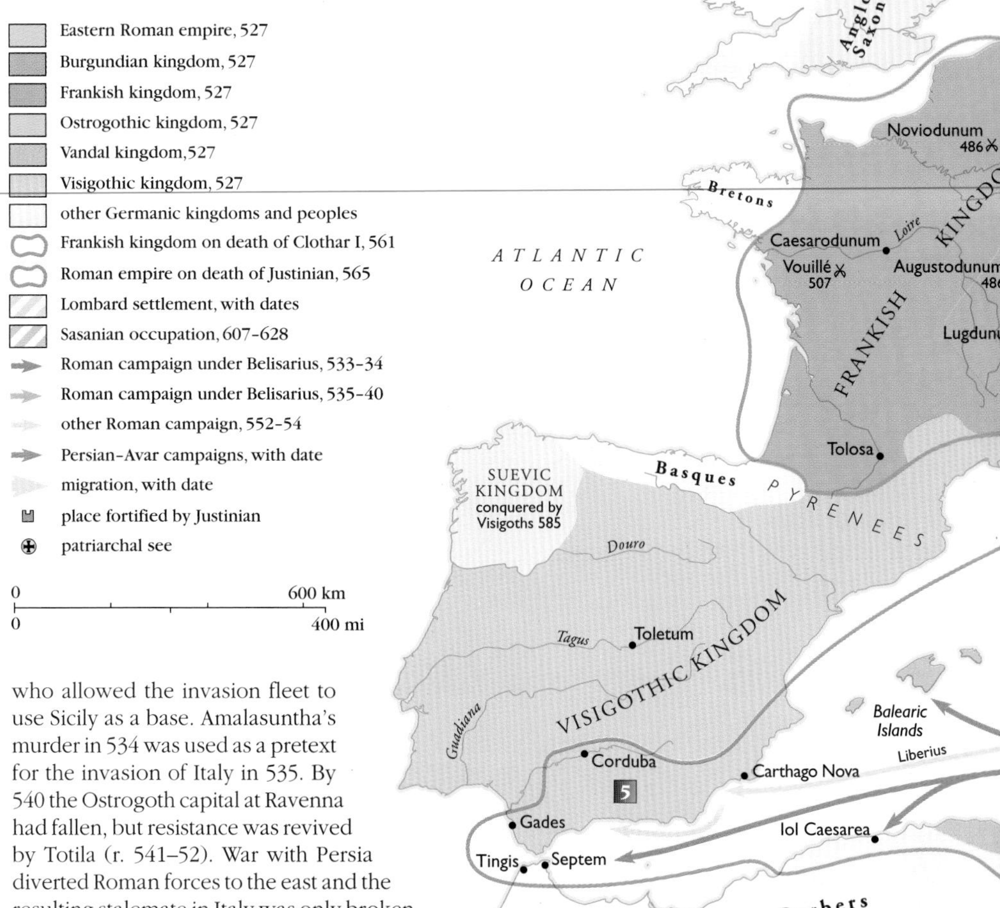

Eastern Roman empire, 527
Burgundian kingdom, 527
Frankish kingdom, 527
Ostrogothic kingdom, 527
Vandal kingdom, 527
Visigothic kingdom, 527
other Germanic kingdoms and peoples
Frankish kingdom on death of Clothar I, 561
Roman empire on death of Justinian, 565
Lombard settlement, with dates
Sasanian occupation, 607–628
Roman campaign under Belisarius, 533–34
Roman campaign under Belisarius, 535–40
other Roman campaign, 552–54
Persian–Avar campaigns, with date
migration, with date
place fortified by Justinian
patriarchal see
0 600 km
0 400 mi
Scots
North Sea
Anglo-Saxons
Noviodunum 486
Bretons
ATLANTIC OCEAN
Caesarodunum
Loire
Vouillé 507
Augustodunum 486
FRANKISH KINGDOM
Lugdunum
Tolosa
SUEVIC KINGDOM conquered by Visigoths 585
Basques
PYRENEES
Douro
Tagus
Toletum
VISIGOTHIC KINGDOM
Guadiana
Balearic Islands
Corduba
Carthago Nova
Liberius
5
Gades
Iol Caesarea
Tingis
Septem
Berbers

who allowed the invasion fleet to use Sicily as a base. Amalasuntha's murder in 534 was used as a pretext for the invasion of Italy in 535. By 540 the Ostrogoth capital at Ravenna had fallen, but resistance was revived by Totila (r. 541–52). War with Persia diverted Roman forces to the east and the resulting stalemate in Italy was only broken in 552 when a new Roman army under Narses arrived from Constantinople. By 554 all of Italy south of the Po was in Roman hands, but north of the river Ostrogothic resistance continued until 562. The last of Justinian's conquests was southern Spain, seized opportunistically during a Visigothic civil war in 554.

Justinian's reconquests restored Roman control of the Mediterranean but put the empire under serious economic strain. The concentration of forces in the west left the Balkans exposed to Slavic raiding and settlement, and the Persians made serious incursions in the east. Italy was devastated by years of war and much of the province was soon lost again following an invasion by the Lombards in 572. However, north Africa and Sicily proved to be valuable additions to the empire's resources.

In about 560 a new wave of nomads, the Avars, arrived in eastern Europe. The Romans paid them to wipe out the remnants of the Huns, but in 580 a dispute over possession of Singidunum (modern

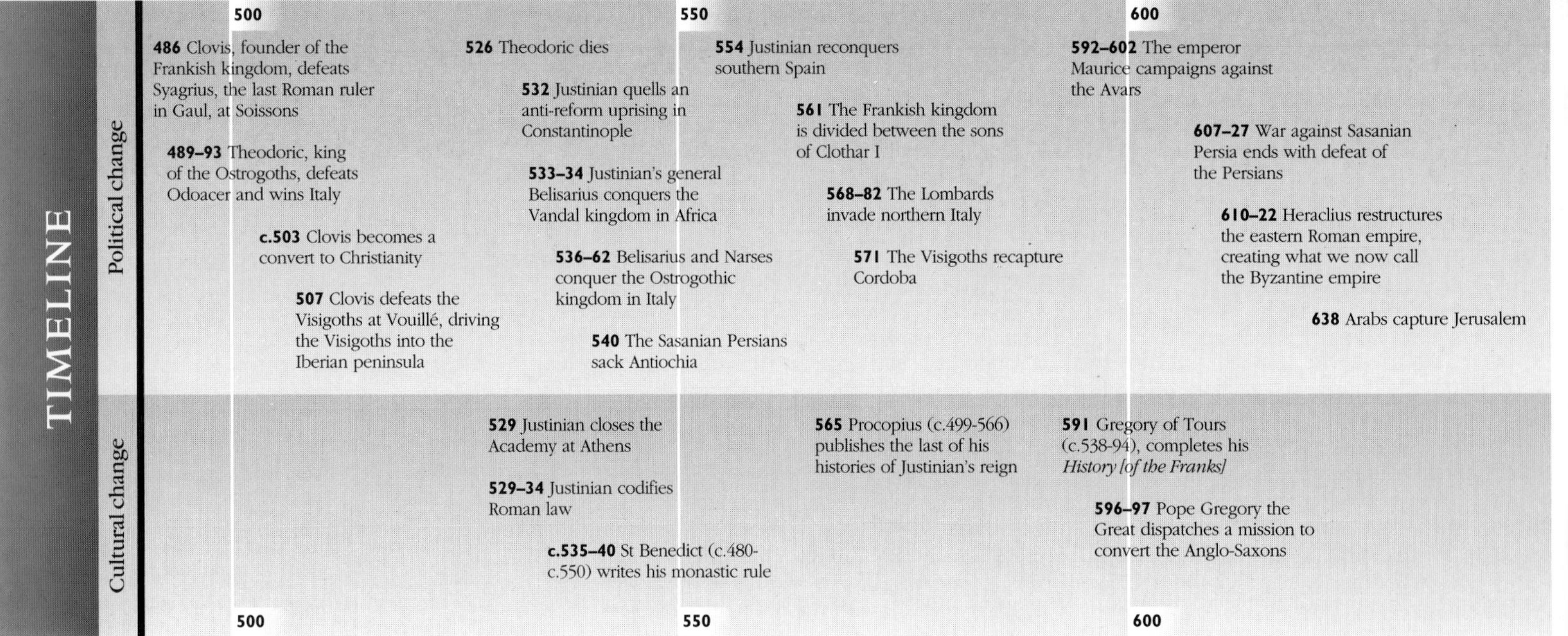

TIMELINE
Political change
500
550
600
486 Clovis, founder of the Frankish kingdom, defeats Syagrius, the last Roman ruler in Gaul, at Soissons
489–93 Theodoric, king of the Ostrogoths, defeats Odoacer and wins Italy
c.503 Clovis becomes a convert to Christianity
507 Clovis defeats the Visigoths at Vouillé, driving the Visigoths into the Iberian peninsula
526 Theodoric dies
532 Justinian quells an anti-reform uprising in Constantinople
533–34 Justinian's general Belisarius conquers the Vandal kingdom in Africa
536–62 Belisarius and Narses conquer the Ostrogothic kingdom in Italy
540 The Sasanian Persians sack Antiochia
554 Justinian reconquers southern Spain
561 The Frankish kingdom is divided between the sons of Clothar I
568–82 The Lombards invade northern Italy
571 The Visigoths recapture Cordoba
592–602 The emperor Maurice campaigns against the Avars
607–27 War against Sasanian Persia ends with defeat of the Persians
610–22 Heraclius restructures the eastern Roman empire, creating what we now call the Byzantine empire
638 Arabs capture Jerusalem
Cultural change
529 Justinian closes the Academy at Athens
529–34 Justinian codifies Roman law
c.535–40 St Benedict (c.480-c.550) writes his monastic rule
565 Procopius (c.499-566) publishes the last of his histories of Justinian's reign
591 Gregory of Tours (c.538-94), completes his *History [of the Franks]*
596–97 Pope Gregory the Great dispatches a mission to convert the Anglo-Saxons
500
550
600

JUSTINIAN was portrayed in this mosaic at Ravenna, supported by religious and military forces.

Belgrade) led to war. For ten years the Avars raided the Balkans until the emperor, Maurice, launched a series of effective counterattacks in 592. Maurice was close to breaking Avar power, when his army mutinied in 602: he was deposed and murdered by his successor, Phocas, an incompetent despot. The administrative structure of the empire now began to fall apart. Slavs and Avars overran the Balkans and the Persians took the fortresses of Roman Mesopotamia one by one. The chaotic state of the empire prompted the governor of Africa to equip his son Heraclius with an army in 610 and send him to Constantinople to overthrow Phocas.

The reign of Heraclius was a turning point. The structure of the empire of Diocletian, Constantine and Justinian could not be revived. Heraclius spent the first years of his reign rebuilding the administrative and military structure of the empire. Greek, which had always been the majority language in the eastern empire, replaced Latin in official documents. Heraclius worked closely with the patriarch of Constantinople, who willingly used the wealth and authority of the church to support the state. While Heraclius was reforming the empire, the war with Persia continued to go badly and by 616 Syria, Palestine and Egypt had been lost. In 622 Heraclius launched a bold campaign directly into the heart of the Sasanian empire and five years later destroyed the Persian army at Nineveh, bringing the war to an end. Heraclius had saved the empire, but his reforms are considered to mark the end of the eastern Roman empire and the beginning of the medieval Greek Byzantine empire (named for the old Greek name for Constantinople).

1 Rome regained importance in the 6th century as the chief center of Christianity in western Europe.

2 The Ostrogothic queen Amalasuntha allowed Justinian's general Belisarius to use Sicily as a base for his attack on the Vandals in 533.

3 Ravenna, the Ostrogothic capital, was taken by Belisarius in 540; resistance continued for many years.

4 The Avars, a Mongol people, migrated to Europe after being defeated by the Turks in central Asia (552).

5 Civil war in the Visigothic kingdom gave Justinian the opportunity to reconquer southern Spain in 554.

6 Originally Roman allies against the Ostrogoths, the Lombards invaded and settled Italy 568–82.

7 Justinian's concentration on the west left the Balkans exposed to frequent Slav raids and settlement.

8 A joint Persian–Avar attack on Constantinople in 626 failed when the Byzantine fleet prevented the two attacking armies from uniting.

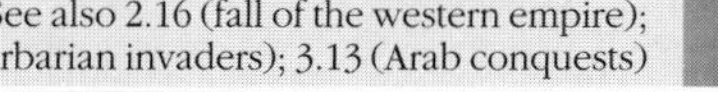
See also 2.16 (fall of the western empire); 2.20 (barbarian invaders); 3.13 (Arab conquests)

The name Celts was used by Greek writers from the 5th century BC onward to describe a group of peoples of central and western Europe. Roman writers called the same peoples Gauls. The origins of the Celts are uncertain but are probably to be found in the northern Alps in the Bronze Age Urnfield (from mid-2nd millennium BC) and the late Bronze–early Iron Age Hallstatt cultures (1200–450 BC). There were at least two waves of Celtic migration out of central Europe. The first, from around 1000, took the Urnfield culture across western Europe into northern Spain by the 7th century; and a second, beginning in the 8th century, had by 500 BC spread the Hallstatt culture across France, Spain, Portugal, Germany, the Low Countries, and southern Britain.

A new phase of Celtic history began around 450 BC with the development in Germany and France of the La Tène culture. This was distinguished by a vigorous art style based on geometrical patterns and stylized animal images. It developed from Hallstatt art but also showed the influence of Etruscan and Scythian styles. The La Tène culture spread quickly across central and western Europe and reached the British Isles by about 400 BC, passed on partly by trade contacts and partly by smallscale migrations of continental Celts, such as the Parisii, who settled in Yorkshire. The La Tène culture did not spread to Spain, where the earlier Celtic settlers and the native population had become assimilated, forming a distinctive Celtiberian culture.

Around 400 BC there were major migrations of Celtic peoples into Italy and the lower Danube region. In Italy the Celts raided widely, sacked Rome, permanently weakened the Etruscans, and settled densely in the Po valley. The Celts on the lower Danube began to migrate into the Balkans in the 3rd century BC. A major raid on Delphi was repulsed, but the Hellenistic kingdom of Thrace was destroyed by their attacks. Three tribes crossed the Dardanelles and settled in central Anatolia, from where they raided the surrounding kingdoms.

The early 3rd century marked the high tide of Celtic expansion. The Romans began the conquest of the Celts of the Po valley at the battle of Telamon in 225 and captured the last center of resistance in Italy at Bononia (modern Bologna) in 192. The Thracians restored their kingdom around 220; and the Anatolian Celts were pacified by Pergamon in 230. In the 230s the Carthaginians began the conquest of the Celtiberians, and this was continued by the Romans after they had expelled the Carthaginians from Spain in 206. The Roman victory at Numantia in 133 brought them control of most of Spain, but Celtiberian resistance continued in the northwest until 19 BC. By the first century AD the continental Celts were caught firmly in a vise between the northward expansion of the Roman empire and the southward and westward expansion of the Germanic tribes and the Dacians. Between 58

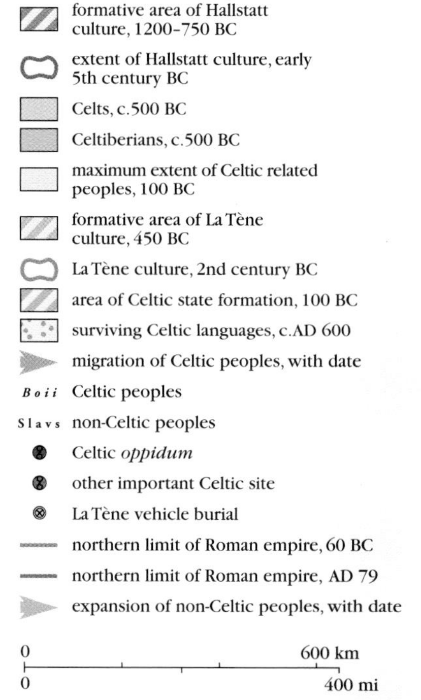
formative area of Hallstatt culture, 1200–750 BC
extent of Hallstatt culture, early 5th century BC
Celts, c.500 BC
Celtiberians, c.500 BC
maximum extent of Celtic related peoples, 100 BC
formative area of La Tène culture, 450 BC
La Tène culture, 2nd century BC
area of Celtic state formation, 100 BC
surviving Celtic languages, c.AD 600
migration of Celtic peoples, with date
Boii Celtic peoples
Slavs non-Celtic peoples
Celtic oppidum
other important Celtic site
La Tène vehicle burial
northern limit of Roman empire, 60 BC
northern limit of Roman empire, AD 79
expansion of non-Celtic peoples, with date
0 600 km
0 400 mi

Mons Graupius
AD 83
Caledonii
c.AD 525
Votadini
Scots
Navan
(Emain Macha)
Brigantes
IERNE
Tara
Peni
Drumanagh
Arras
Parisii
Desi
ALBION
9
AD 61
Iceni
8
Silures
Hengistbury Head
Atrebates
Calleva
Dumnonii
c.100 BC
c.50 BC
c.AD 450
Pari
Veneti
Carnutes
7
56 BC
Loire
ATLANTIC OCEAN
Pictones
GAU
Bituri
Bibract
6
Arve
Aquitani
Brigantium
Gallaeci
PYRENEES
Numantia
Douro
133 BC
5
Celtiberians
Iberians
Tagus
Lusitanii
Guadiana
Tartessians
Gades
Bale
Isla

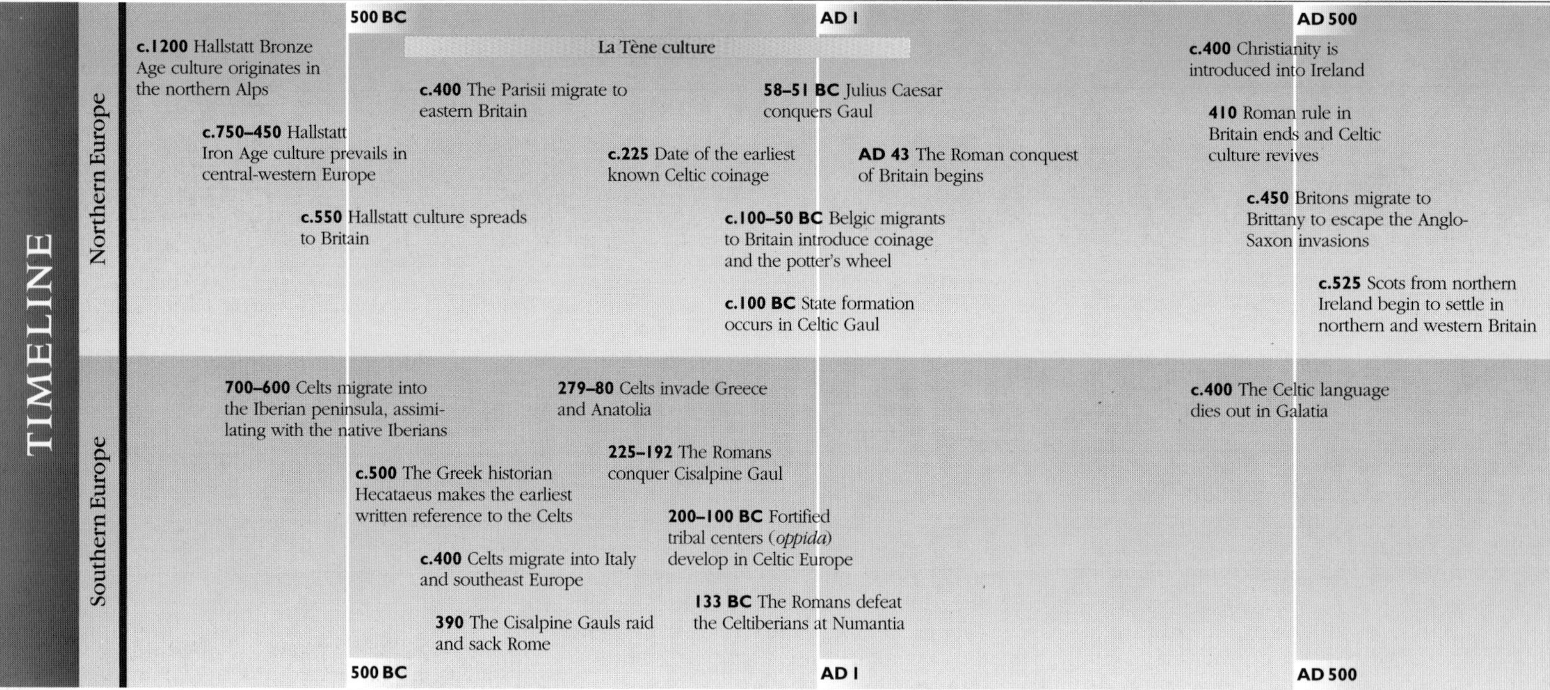
TIMELINE
Northern Europe
Southern Europe
500 BC
AD 1
AD 500
La Tène culture
c.1200 Hallstatt Bronze Age culture originates in the northern Alps
c.750–450 Hallstatt Iron Age culture prevails in central-western Europe
c.550 Hallstatt culture spreads to Britain
c.400 The Parisii migrate to eastern Britain
c.225 Date of the earliest known Celtic coinage
58–51 BC Julius Caesar conquers Gaul
AD 43 The Roman conquest of Britain begins
c.100–50 BC Belgic migrants to Britain introduce coinage and the potter's wheel
c.100 BC State formation occurs in Celtic Gaul
c.400 Christianity is introduced into Ireland
410 Roman rule in Britain ends and Celtic culture revives
c.450 Britons migrate to Brittany to escape the Anglo-Saxon invasions
c.525 Scots from northern Ireland begin to settle in northern and western Britain
700–600 Celts migrate into the Iberian peninsula, assimilating with the native Iberians
c.500 The Greek historian Hecataeus makes the earliest written reference to the Celts
c.400 Celts migrate into Italy and southeast Europe
390 The Cisalpine Gauls raid and sack Rome
279–80 Celts invade Greece and Anatolia
225–192 The Romans conquer Cisalpine Gaul
200–100 BC Fortified tribal centers (oppida) develop in Celtic Europe
133 BC The Romans defeat the Celtiberians at Numantia
c.400 The Celtic language dies out in Galatia
500 BC
AD 1
AD 500

Vänern
Vättern
Gundestrup
North Sea
5th century AD
Anglo-Saxons
Elbe
Germans
Vistula
500–1 BC
500–1 BC
500–1 BC
500–1 BC
Oder
Rhine
Volcae
Boii
Danube
Manching
Hallstatt
Helvetii
La Tène
ALPS
Scordisci
PANNONIA
c.400 BC
Dardani
Sava
Scythians
CARPATHIAN MTS
c.60 BC
Dacians
c.60 BC
Danube
Insubres
CISALPINE GAUL
Po
Telamon
225 BC
Bononia
192 BC
Boii
Senones
c.400 BC
Etruscans
Illyrians
Corsica
390 BC
Rome
1
Italics
Sardinia
Black Sea
4
Thracians
279 BC
279–275 BC
Tectosages
GALATIA
Tolistobogii
Trocmi
Pergamon
230 BC
2
3
Delphi
Greeks
Sicily
Rhodes
Cyprus
Malta
Crete
Mediterranean Sea

HORSES, chariots and armor were important elements in the Celtic love of display. This bronze head comes from Yorkshire, Britain.

1 The Celts (Gauls) sacked Rome in 390 BC, after defeating a Roman army at the river Allia.

2 An invasive Celtic migration as far south as Delphi was turned back by Greek resistance in 279 BC .

3 Celtic raids in Anatolia ceased after the victory of Attalus I of Pergamon around 230 BC.

4 Survivors of the Celtic attack on Delphi in 279 founded a kingdom in Thrace that lasted until 213 BC.

5 The main Celtiberian resistance to Roman rule was broken when, after a 20-year siege, Numantia fell in 133 BC.

6 Trade contacts with the Roman empire led to the formation of tribal states in southern Gaul in the 1st century BC.

7 Julius Caesar's victory over Vercingetorix at Alesia in 52 BC, the climax of an eight-year campaign (58–51 BC), secured Roman control of Gaul.

8 The Iceni, led by their queen, Boudicca, rebelled unsuccessfully against Roman rule in AD 60.

9 Celtic culture and art revived in Britain after the end of Roman rule in AD 410.

and 51 BC Julius Caesar conquered the Celts of Gaul. Under Augustus the tribes of the Alps and Pannonia were brought under Roman rule. By AD 1 the only independent Celts on mainland Europe were enclaves in German territory north of the Danube.

Celtic society was hierarchical and competitive and by the 2nd century BC was in the early stages of state formation. Fortified centers, or *oppida*, spread across Europe: some, such as Manching on the Danube, were large towns by the 1st century BC. Coinage and, in some areas, writing came into use. In southern Gaul small tribal states in direct contact with the Roman empire had developed by 60 BC. The Roman conquest prevented the Celts from developing a full urban civilization of their own.

The Celtic resistance to Rome failed for two main reasons. The Celts were politically disunited and the Romans easily exploited rivalries between states or tribes to their own advantage. Also, Celtic warriors saw war as an opportunity to seek personal glory and this put them at a disadvantage to the drilled and disciplined legions. After the Roman conquest the La Tène culture died out on the continent and Celtic language was gradually replaced by Latin; but Celtic religion continued to be practiced. *Oppida* were superseded by planned Romanized towns.

Apart from two punitive raids by Caesar in 55–54 BC, it was AD 43 before the Romans began to subjugate the Celts in Britain. By this time contacts with the Romans across the Channel had already led to considerable Romanization of the southern British tribes and to the development of *oppida* and small tribal states. The Romans could never conquer all of Britain: the closest they came was in AD 83 when they defeated the Caledonians at "Mons Graupius". Harsh weather, mountainous terrain and long lines of communication meant that the highland tribes of Scotland stayed independent, as did the Celts in Ireland, where pagan Celtic culture survived into the early Middle Ages. La Tène art died out in southern Britain in the 2nd century AD, but Celtic art traditions continued in the far north and Ireland, while Celtic languages survived throughout the British Isles. After the end of Roman rule in Britain in 410, Celtic art revived but was strongly influenced by late Roman and Anglo-Saxon art. The introduction of Christianity to Ireland in the 5th century inspired the development of a Celtic monastic civilization which, through missionary activity, had begun to exert a strong influence in Britain and the continent by 600.

See also 1.25 (Hallstatt); 2.13 (growth of the Roman empire); 2.19 (Germans); 3.06 (Dark Ages)

.19 The Germans and the Slavs • 750 BC – AD 600 •

The Germans originated in southern Scandinavia and the north German plain in the first half of the 1st millennium BC, probably descended from peoples long settled there. The first contact between the Germans and the Mediterranean civilizations occurred around 350 BC, when the Greek navigator Pytheas of Massilia explored the North Sea coasts. However, his account of his voyage was not widely believed and Mediterranean writers first became aware of the Germans as a group distinct from the Celts only at the end of the 2nd century BC. At this time the Germans' society and way of life resembled that of the Celts, but showed no evidence of power centralization or urban development.

In the second half of the 1st millennium BC the Germans expanded out of north Germany, mainly at the expense of the Celtic peoples to their south and west. These movements were for the most part gradual, but around 120 the Cimbri and the Teutones, two peoples from Jutland, began a twenty-year migration that took them across west-central Europe. When the tribes attacked the Taurisci in 113, their Roman allies sent an army to protect them. The Cimbri and Teutones crushed this army at Noreia but then headed northwest into Gaul. In 109 the tribes invaded southern Gaul and inflicted a succession of defeats on Roman armies, culminating in their victory at Arausio (Orange) in 105. At this point the tribes split up, the Cimbri invading Spain and the Teutones going to northern Gaul. The Roman dictator Marius used the respite to reorganize the legions, and when the Teutones returned to southern Gaul in 102, he defeated them at Aquae Sextiae (Aix-en-Provence). In 101 Marius defeated the Cimbri – who had finally invaded Italy – at Vercellae. Fear of future Germanic invasions was a major motive for Roman expansion northward in the 1st century BC.

Julius Caesar conquered the tribes on the west bank of the Rhine in 56 BC, but these were to be the only Germans permanently under Roman rule. By AD 6 the Germanic tribes as far east as the Elbe were pacified, but a rebellion under Arminius destroyed the Roman army of occupation in AD 9. After AD 12

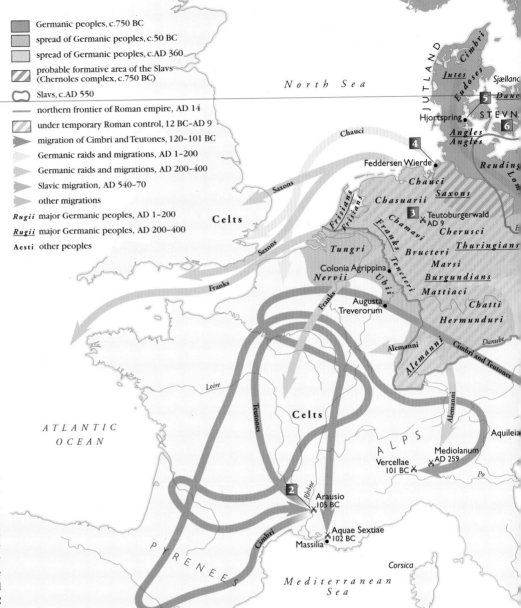

Germanic peoples, c.750 BC
spread of Germanic peoples, c.50 BC
spread of Germanic peoples, c.AD 360
probable formative area of the Slavs (Chernoles complex, c.750 BC)
Slavs, c.AD 550
northern frontier of Roman empire, AD 14
under temporary Roman control, 12 BC–AD 9
migration of Cimbri and Teutones, 120–101 BC
Germanic raids and migrations, AD 1–200
Germanic raids and migrations, AD 200–400
Slavic migration, AD 540–70
other migrations
Rugii major Germanic peoples, AD 1–200
Rugii major Germanic peoples, AD 200–400
Aesti other peoples

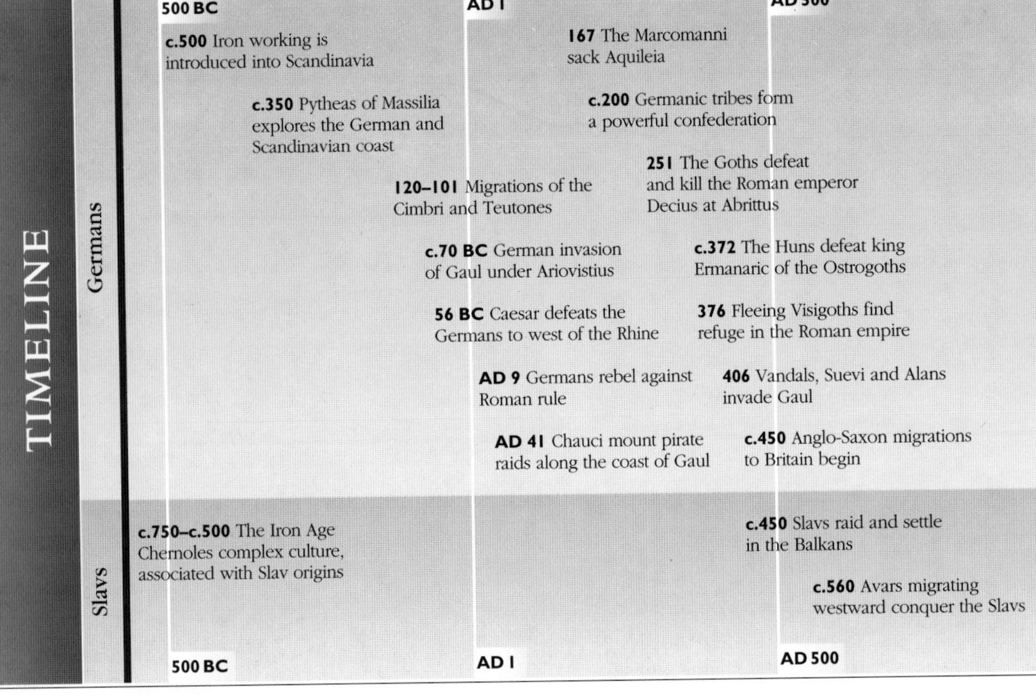

TIMELINE
Germans
Slavs
500 BC
AD 1
AD 500
c.500 Iron working is introduced into Scandinavia
c.350 Pytheas of Massilia explores the German and Scandinavian coast
120–101 Migrations of the Cimbri and Teutones
c.70 BC German invasion of Gaul under Ariovistius
56 BC Caesar defeats the Germans to west of the Rhine
AD 9 Germans rebel against Roman rule
AD 41 Chauci mount pirate raids along the coast of Gaul
167 The Marcomanni sack Aquileia
c.200 Germanic tribes form a powerful confederation
251 The Goths defeat and kill the Roman emperor Decius at Abrittus
c.372 The Huns defeat king Ermanaric of the Ostrogoths
376 Fleeing Visigoths find refuge in the Roman empire
406 Vandals, Suevi and Alans invade Gaul
c.450 Anglo-Saxon migrations to Britain begin
c.750–c.500 The Iron Age Chernoles complex culture, associated with Slav origins
c.450 Slavs raid and settle in the Balkans
c.560 Avars migrating westward conquer the Slavs
500 BC
AD 1
AD 500

1 The Balts were farming peoples whose cultural identity emerged as early as 1800 BC.

2 Two Roman armies were destroyed by the Cimbri and Teutones at Arausio in 105 BC.

3 In AD 9 Rome lost three legions at the battle of the Teutoburgerwald against Germans under Arminius.

4 A Germanic farming village of fifty houses occupied from the 1st century BC to the 5th century AD was found at Feddersen Wierde.

5 Votive offerings were a feature of Germanic religion: one of the richest finds, at Hjortspring, included a ship and many weapons sunk in a bog.

6 A 3rd-century kingdom centered in Stevns controlled the flow of Roman trade in the southern Baltic.

7 The Goths, Burgundians and other Germans believed they had migrated from Scandinavia – called "the womb of peoples" – in the 6th century AD.

8 Some historians think that the "Scythian farmers" were Slavs living under Scythian domination.

9 In the 540s–60s, while the armies of the eastern Roman emperor Justinian (r.527–65) campaigned in Italy, the Slavs raided and settled in the Balkans.

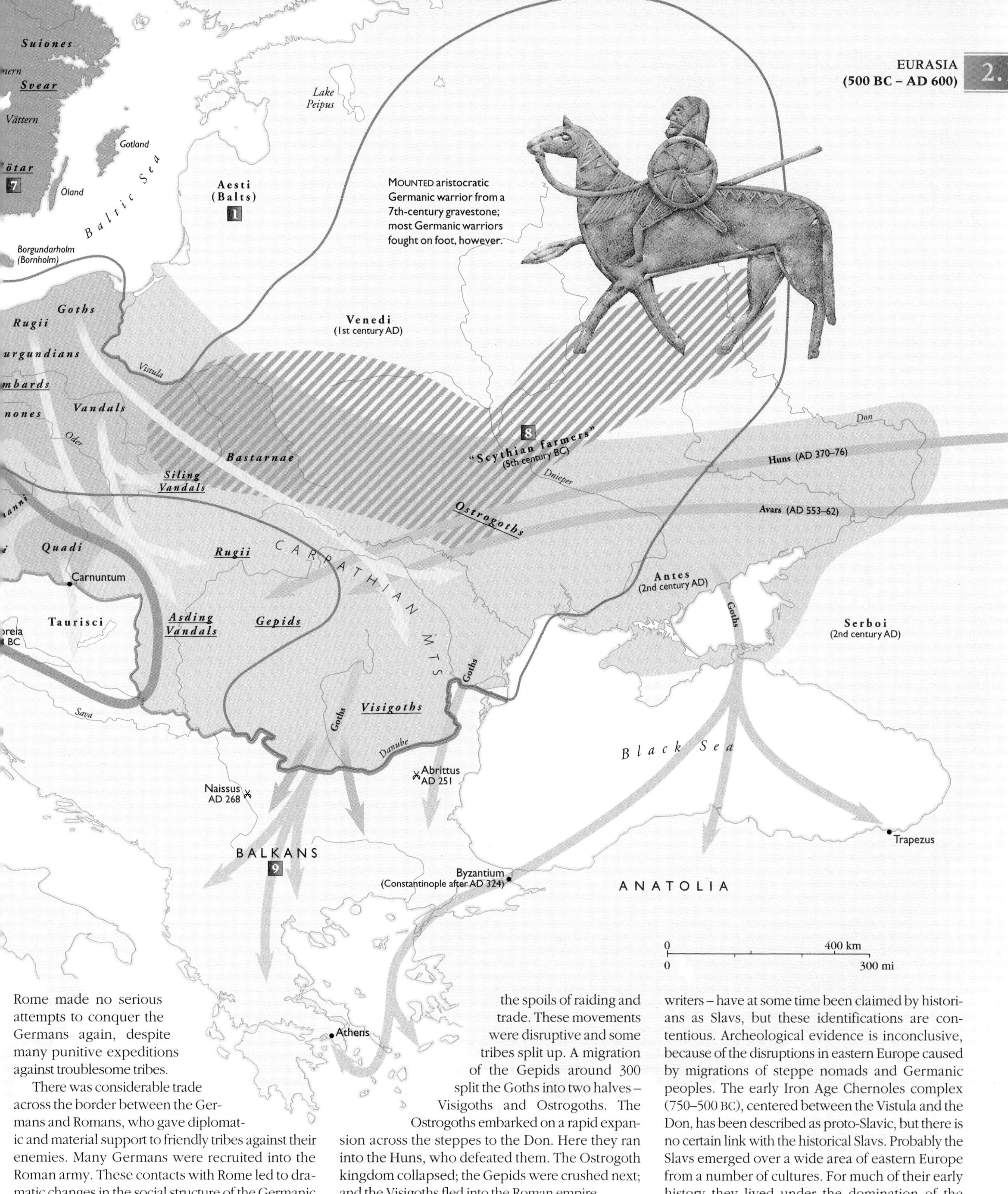
Suiones
Svear
Vättern
Gotland
Öland
Baltic Sea
Borgundarholm
(Bornholm)
Aesti
(Balts)
1
7
Lake
Peipus
Goths
Rugii
Vandals
Vistula
Oder
Venedi
(1st century AD)
Bastarnae
Siling
Vandals
"Scythian farmers"
(5th century BC)
8
Dnieper
Don
Huns (AD 370–76)
Avars (AD 553–62)
Ostrogoths
Quadi
Carnuntum
Rugii
CARPATHIAN MTS
Tauri sci
Asding
Vandals
Gepids
Antes
(2nd century AD)
Serboi
(2nd century AD)
Goths
Visigoths
Sava
Danube
Black Sea
Abrittus
AD 251
Naissus
AD 268
BALKANS
9
Byzantium
(Constantinople after AD 324)
ANATOLIA
Trapezus
Athens
400 km
300 mi

MOUNTED aristocratic Germanic warrior from a 7th-century gravestone; most Germanic warriors fought on foot, however.

Rome made no serious attempts to conquer the Germans again, despite many punitive expeditions against troublesome tribes.

There was considerable trade across the border between the Germans and Romans, who gave diplomatic and material support to friendly tribes against their enemies. Many Germans were recruited into the Roman army. These contacts with Rome led to dramatic changes in the social structure of the Germanic tribes in the late 2nd–early 3rd centuries. Small tribes merged to form powerful confederations: thus, on the Rhine, the Chasuarii, Chamavi, Bructeri, Tencteri and other tribes emerged as the Frankish confederacy in the early 3rd century. These confederations were dangerous enemies and the empire suffered from Germanic invasions in the 3rd century. Many tribes, like the Burgundians, moved closer to the borders of the Roman empire, hoping to share in the spoils of raiding and trade. These movements were disruptive and some tribes split up. A migration of the Gepids around 300 split the Goths into two halves – Visigoths and Ostrogoths. The Ostrogoths embarked on a rapid expansion across the steppes to the Don. Here they ran into the Huns, who defeated them. The Ostrogoth kingdom collapsed; the Gepids were crushed next; and the Visigoths fled into the Roman empire.

The earliest records of the Slavs date from the mid-6th century AD when they began to raid and settle in the Balkans. They were tribal farming peoples, ruled by warrior chiefs. By this time Slavs occupied much of eastern Europe, so peoples speaking Slavonic languages must have existed long before this. However, their origins are obscure. The Venedi, Antes, Serboi and the Scythian farmers – all eastern European peoples mentioned by classical writers – have at some time been claimed by historians as Slavs, but these identifications are contentious. Archeological evidence is inconclusive, because of the disruptions in eastern Europe caused by migrations of steppe nomads and Germanic peoples. The early Iron Age Chernoles complex (750–500 BC), centered between the Vistula and the Don, has been described as proto-Slavic, but there is no certain link with the historical Slavs. Probably the Slavs emerged over a wide area of eastern Europe from a number of cultures. For much of their early history they lived under the domination of the Scythians, Sarmatians, Ostrogoths and Huns, and they were conquered in the late 6th century by the Avars. When Avar power declined in the 7th century, the Slavs emerged to play an important role in the formation of early medieval Europe.

See also 1.21 (Bronze Age Europe); 2.15 (Roman empire); 2.18 (Celts); 2.20 (steppe peoples)

2.20 The steppe nomads • 900 BC – AD 600 •

The steppes are a vast area of grassland stretching from eastern Europe across central Asia to Manchuria, which were colonized in the 5th millennium BC by farmers from western Eurasia. The harsh climate was not well suited to arable farming, so the steppe farmers relied primarily on their herds of cattle, horses, sheep and goats. Around 3500 BC wheeled vehicles came into use. This new mobility allowed the farmers to develop a transhumant lifestyle (moving their flocks and herds between summer and winter pastures), significantly increasing the grazing resources available to them. In the second half of the 2nd millennium BC bits and bridles were introduced, which made horseback riding possible. This allowed the steppe peoples to manage large herds over vast ranges, and led to the adoption of a fully nomadic way of life around 900.

The earliest nomads were Iranian-speakers who occupied the steppes as far east as the Ordos desert in China by the 8th century. The Cimmerians on the Russian steppes in the early 1st millennium were the first known nomad power. About 700 they were eclipsed by the Scythians, another Iranian people from central Asia or Siberia. Pursued across the Caucasus by the Scythians, a group of Cimmerians migrated to Anatolia, destroying the Phrygian kingdom on the way. This was the first instance of conflicts on the steppes setting off migrations that had destructive effects on remote urban civilizations – a frequent cycle over the next two millennia.

The Scythians were ruled by powerful chiefs, who were buried in underground chambers with offerings of weapons, jewelry, horses, wagons and human sacrifices, and covered with a *kurgan*, or barrow. An important group of burials at Pazyryk in the Altay mountains, revealed that the Scythians

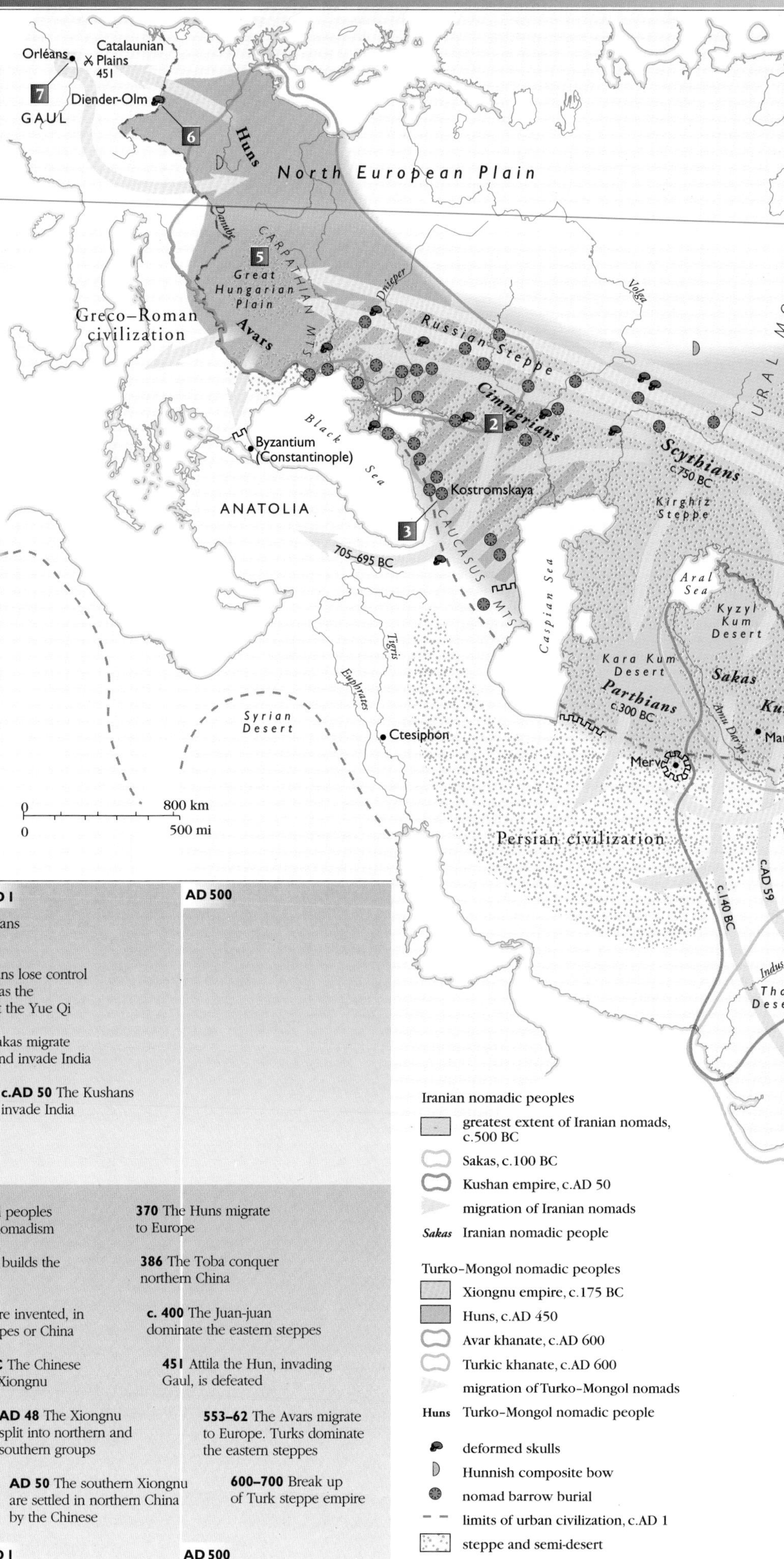

Orléans
Catalaunian Plains 451
7
GAUL
Diender-Olm
6
Huns
North European Plain
Danube
CARPATHIAN MTS
5
Great Hungarian Plain
Greco–Roman civilization
Avars
Dnieper
Volga
Russian Steppe
Cimmerians
2
Scythians c.750 BC
URAL MOUNTA
Black Sea
Byzantium (Constantinople)
Kostromskaya
3
ANATOLIA
705–695 BC
CAUCASUS MTS
Kirghiz Steppe
Aral Sea
Caspian Sea
Kyzyl Kum Desert
Kara Kum Desert
Sakas
Parthians c.300 BC
Kusha
Maracan
Tigris
Euphrates
Syrian Desert
Ctesiphon
Merv
Amu Darya
Persian civilization
c.AD 59
c.140 BC
Indus
Thar Desert
0 800 km
0 500 mi
Iranian nomadic peoples
greatest extent of Iranian nomads, c.500 BC
Sakas, c.100 BC
Kushan empire, c.AD 50
migration of Iranian nomads
Sakas Iranian nomadic people
Turko-Mongol nomadic peoples
Xiongnu empire, c.175 BC
Huns, c.AD 450
Avar khanate, c.AD 600
Turkic khanate, c.AD 600
migration of Turko-Mongol nomads
Huns Turko-Mongol nomadic people
deformed skulls
Hunnish composite bow
nomad barrow burial
limits of urban civilization, c.AD 1
steppe and semi-desert
defensive barrier

TIMELINE

500 BC | AD 1 | AD 500

Iranian nomads

c.900 The Iranian steppe peoples adopt horse-mounted nomadism

c.900–700 The Cimmerians dominate the western steppes

705–695 The Cimmerians invade Anatolia

c.700–300 The Scythians now dominate the steppes

500–300 BC Rich Scythian burials at Pazyryk

c.300 BC The Sarmatians conquer the Scythians

175–170 Iranians lose control of the steppes as the Xiongnu defeat the Yue Qi

c.140 The Sakas migrate southward and invade India

c.AD 50 The Kushans invade India

Turko-Mongol nomads

c.300 Turko-Mongol peoples adopt horse-based nomadism

209–174 Motun builds the Xiongnu empire

c.200 Stirrups are invented, in the eastern steppes or China

128–36 BC The Chinese pacify the Xiongnu

AD 48 The Xiongnu split into northern and southern groups

AD 50 The southern Xiongnu are settled in northern China by the Chinese

370 The Huns migrate to Europe

386 The Toba conquer northern China

c. 400 The Juan-juan dominate the eastern steppes

451 Attila the Hun, invading Gaul, is defeated

553–62 The Avars migrate to Europe. Turks dominate the eastern steppes

600–700 Break up of Turk steppe empire

500 BC | AD 1 | AD 500

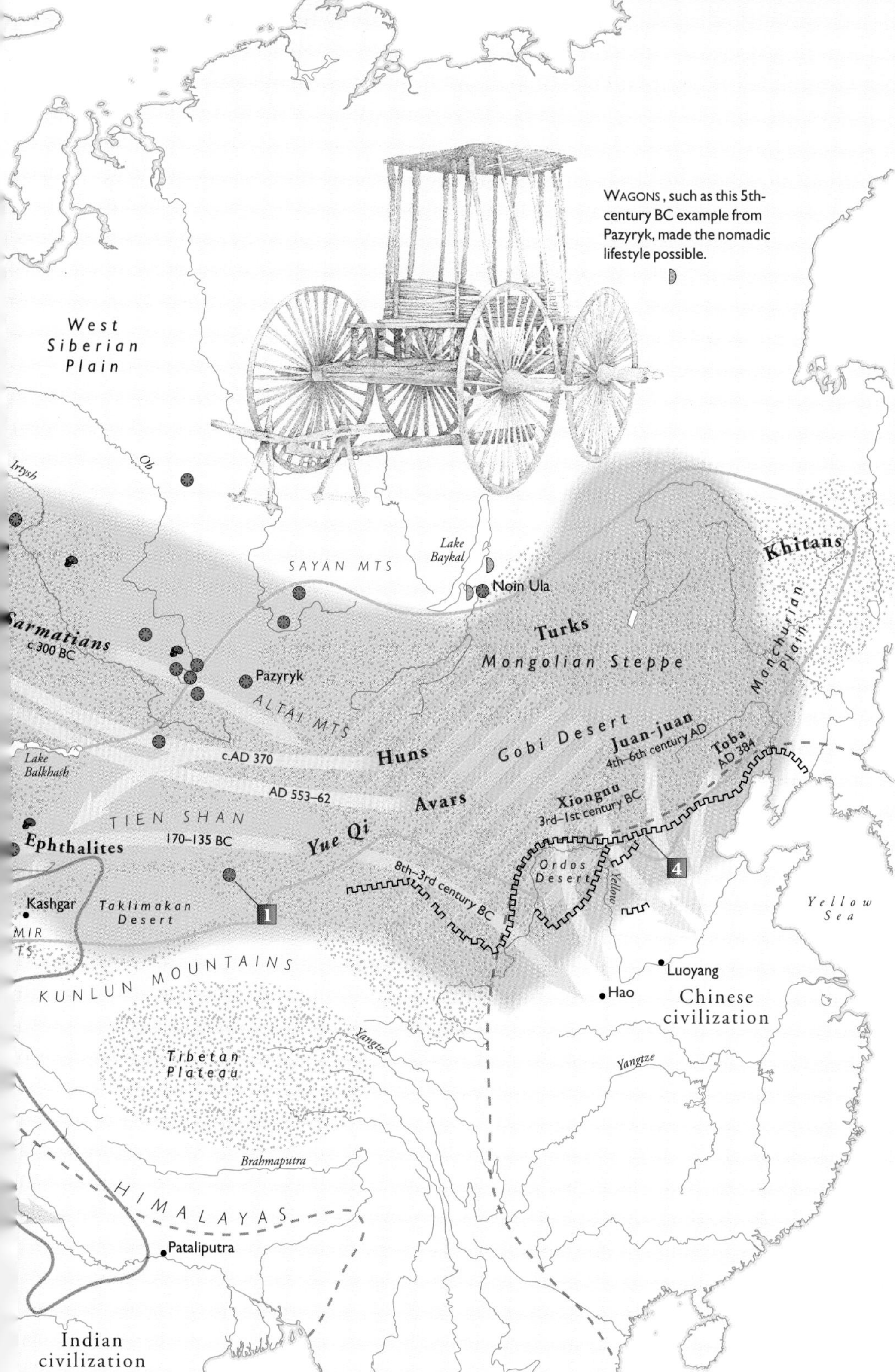
West
Siberian
Plain
Irtysh
Ob
Lake
Baykal
SAYAN MTS
Noin Ula
Khitans
Sarmatians
c.300 BC
Pazyryk
Turks
Mongolian Steppe
ALTAI MTS
Manchurian
Plain
Gobi Desert
Juan-juan
4th–6th century AD
Toba
AD 384
Lake
Balkhash
c.AD 370
Huns
AD 553–62
Avars
Xiongnu
3rd–1st century BC
TIEN SHAN
Ephthalites
170–135 BC
Yue Qi
Ordos
Desert
Yellow
4
8th–3rd century BC
Kashgar
Taklimakan
Desert
1
Yellow
Sea
KUNLUN MOUNTAINS
Luoyang
Hao
Chinese
civilization
Yangtze
Tibetan
Plateau
Yangtze
Brahmaputra
HIMALAYAS
Pataliputra
Indian
civilization

WAGONS, such as this 5th-century BC example from Pazyryk, made the nomadic lifestyle possible.

1 Burials in the Tarim basin indicate that European-type peoples were settled in the eastern steppes around 2000 BC.

2 The Cimmerians, the first steppe peoples to adopt a fully nomadic way of life, dominated the steppes c.900–700 BC.

3 Site of the barrow burial of a Scythian chieftain of the 7th or 6th century BC which included offerings of weapons and sacrificed servants and horses.

4 Chinese rulers began to build great defensive walls to deter nomad raiders, in the 4th century BC.

5 The Hungarian plain, the most westerly area of steppe capable of supporting large herds of horses, became the center of the Hun and Avar empires.

6 Hunnish burials are notable for their distinctively deformed skulls caused by binding children's heads.

7 Orleans, besieged by the Huns in AD 451, was the farthest west that steppe nomads ventured.

decorated their bodies with elaborate tattoos. The Scythians produced a vigorous art style based on stylized animals, and imported Greek metalwork and other goods. Scythian power waned in the 3rd century and their place on the western steppes was taken by the Sarmatians. The defeated Scythians were probably not exterminated, but absorbed by the Sarmatians.

The practice of assimilating defeated rivals explains both the rapid rise of steppe peoples and their rapid extinctions. The numbers of a successful tribe were swelled by assimilated enemies and by other tribes who joined voluntarily to share in the prestige and plunder of the victors. By the same means an apparently numerous and powerful people could suddenly vanish. Although very destructive, nomad armies rarely made lasting conquests outside the steppe zone. Only on the steppes was there sufficient grazing for the huge numbers of horses that nomad armies needed. Where nomads did make lasting conquests outside the steppe zone, as in India and China, they abandoned their lifestyle and became assimilated into the culture of the more numerous settled population.

The Turko-Mongol peoples of the eastern steppes made the transition from transhumant pastoralism to full horse-mounted nomadism around 300 BC. In the short composite bow (made of glued strips of horn and wood) the Turko-Mongol nomads had a weapon ideally suited to fast moving cavalry warfare, and they soon proved a formidable threat to Iranian nomads and urban civilizations alike. The first nomad power of the eastern steppes was the Xiongnu, a Turkic dominated confederation. Under Motun (r.209–174 BC) they raided the Han empire of China, exacting huge amounts in tribute. In 170 the Xiongnu defeated the Iranian Yue Qi nomads and drove them to the west, in turn forcing the Sakas to move south around 140 through the Parthian empire into India, where they founded a kingdom which lasted until about AD 400. The dominant Yue Qi clan, the Kushans, built an empire which by AD 50 extended from the Aral Sea to the Indian Ocean and controlled the Asian trade routes.

Between 128 and 36 BC the Chinese fought a series of campaigns that succeeded in reducing the Xiongnu to tributary status. In AD 48 the Xiongnu split into two groups; and they finally disappeared from history around AD 400. In the late 4th century the Huns, a Turkic people, migrated west from central Asia to the steppes of east Europe, destabilizing the Germanic tribes and causing them to invade the Roman empire in search of safer lands to settle. The Huns reached the height of their power under Attila (r.434–53), but their empire collapsed after his death. Another Hunnish people, the Ephthalite ("White") Huns, invaded Persia and India in the late 5th century, preventing the Sasanians from exploiting the problems of the Roman empire and destroying the declining Gupta empire.

For several centuries after the collapse of Xiongnu power, no one people achieved dominance on the eastern steppes. At times of internal weakness China was raided, and in 386 the north was conquered by the Toba nomads, who held power there for over 150 years. Around 400 the Juan-juan, a Mongol-dominated confederation, built an empire which covered much the same area as the earlier Xiongnu empire. The Juan-juan were themselves overthrown in 553 by their Turkish subjects, who went on to create an empire that stretched from Manchuria to the Aral Sea by 600. Part of the Juan-juan confederation, the Avars, fled west and in 562 arrived in eastern Europe where, in alliance with the Sasanians, they almost destroyed the eastern Roman empire. To save the empire reforms had to be introduced – changes so far-reaching that historians consider them the beginning of the Byzantine empire.

See also 1.06 (the world 500 BC); 2.19 (Germans); 2.23 (Kushans and Guptas); 2.24 (China)

2.21 Early states of Africa • 500 BC – AD 600 •

The earliest African state formed in Egypt's Nile valley, where a centralized kingdom had emerged by 3000 BC. By this time desertification had turned the Sahara into a major barrier to travel and the only easy land route between Egypt and tropical Africa lay along the narrow valley of the middle Nile through Nubia. By 2500 several chiefdoms had emerged in Nubia. These were consolidated by 1700 into a large state, known to the Egyptians as Kush, whose capital was at Kerma. Nubia was rich in natural resources, especially gold, and was subjected to Egyptian plundering expeditions. It may, therefore, have been the impetus to organize an effective defense against the Egyptians that provided the impetus for state formation in this area. Kush was conquered by the Egyptians about 1500 at the start of Egypt's imperialistic New Kingdom period. When Egyptian power declined at the end of the New Kingdom (1070 BC), Kush regained its independence. In 770 the kings of Kush conquered southern Egypt and in 712 Shabaka (r.712–698) brought the whole kingdom under Nubian rule. Assyrian attacks on Egypt drove the Nubians from northern Egypt, and by 657 they had lost control of the whole country. The Egyptians expelled the Assyrians in 653 and launched campaigns into Nubia, forcing the Nubians to move their capital south to Meroë around 590. The kingdom of Meroë, as Kush is subsequently known, remained a major power that was taken seriously by the Persians, Greco-Macedonians and Romans who in turn ruled Egypt after 525 BC. In the 4th century Meroë suffered attacks from desert nomads; it collapsed about 350, after the capital was taken by the Axumites. Three small states, Nobatia, Makkura and Alwa, arose as successors to Meroë but Makkura conquered Nobatia in the 8th century.

Nubia was strongly influenced by Egyptian religion, kingship and culture. Until about 200 BC, when an indigenous Meroitic script was developed, Egyptian scripts and language were used for inscriptions, and the use of pyramids for royal burials continued into the Christian era, long after the practice had ceased in Egypt. Christianity was introduced to Nubia in the 6th century and remained strong until the region was put under pressure by the Arabs in the 13th century.

The second state to develop in tropical Africa, Axum emerged in northern Ethiopia in the 1st century AD. Urban development had begun at sites such as Yeha in the 5th century BC and the cultural development of the area was strongly influenced by the Sabeans of Arabia, whose alphabet, architecture and religion were adopted. In the 1st century AD the port of Adulis was exporting ivory, rhinoceros horn, tortoise-shell, obsidian and aromatic resins to the Roman empire via Red Sea trade routes. The city of Axum itself included complexes of monumental buildings and palaces. Among the most remarkable monuments at Axum are monoliths carved to resemble multistory buildings: the tallest still standing is 69 feet (21 meters) high. The kingdom of Axum reached a peak in the reign of King Ezana around 350. About this time also, Ezana converted to Christianity, the first African ruler to do so. In 522 the Axumites invaded and conquered the Yemen and held it until driven out by the Sasanians in 574. In the 8th century, attacks by the Arabs accelerated the decline of Axum, and by the 10th century power had shifted to the Ethiopian highlands.

Another area of Africa in which state formation occurred was the Maghrib, where the Berber kingdoms of Numantia and Mauretania emerged around 200 BC in the power vacuum left by the defeat of Carthage in the Second Punic War (226–201 BC). However, these states were soon swallowed up by the expanding empire of Rome. The most significant development in north Africa was the introduction of the camel to the Sahara around 100 BC. Camels were ideal for desert warfare, and settled communities on the fringes of the desert soon suffered badly from nomad raids. Camels also had the endurance for long desert crossings – horses, mules and bullocks had previously been the main beasts of burden in the Sahara. Now cross-desert trade began to expand, and by AD 500 camel caravans forged strong trade links between the Mediterranean and west Africa (maritime links were never established, because of adverse winds south of Cape Bojador).

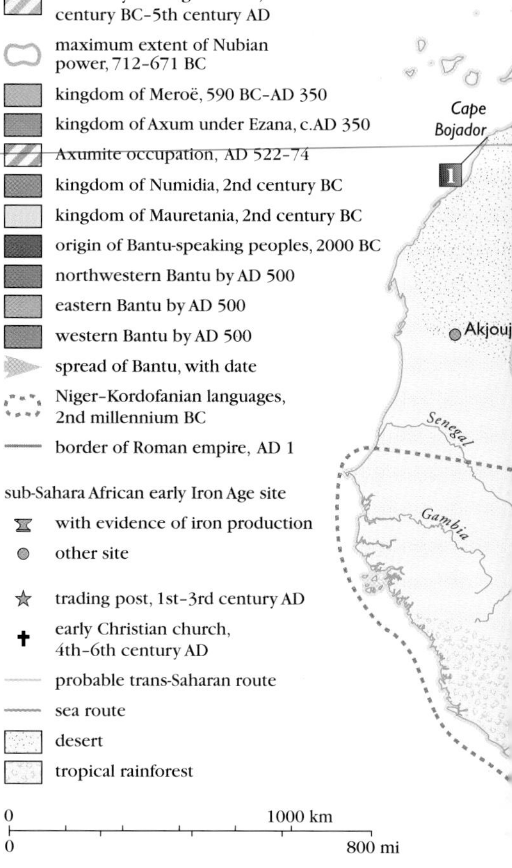

Nok early Iron Age culture, 6th century BC–5th century AD
maximum extent of Nubian power, 712–671 BC
kingdom of Meroë, 590 BC–AD 350
kingdom of Axum under Ezana, c.AD 350
Axumite occupation, AD 522–74
kingdom of Numidia, 2nd century BC
kingdom of Mauretania, 2nd century BC
origin of Bantu-speaking peoples, 2000 BC
northwestern Bantu by AD 500
eastern Bantu by AD 500
western Bantu by AD 500
spread of Bantu, with date
Niger–Kordofanian languages, 2nd millennium BC
border of Roman empire, AD 1
sub-Sahara African early Iron Age site
with evidence of iron production
other site
trading post, 1st–3rd century AD
early Christian church, 4th–6th century AD
probable trans-Saharan route
sea route
desert
tropical rainforest
0
1000 km
0
800 mi
Cape Bojador
1
Akjouj
Senegal
Gambia

TIMELINE
Northern Africa
600 BC
AD 1
AD 600
712–671 Egypt is under Nubian rule
c.200 Berber kingdoms emerge in north Africa
c.350 Fall of the kingdom of Meroë
590 Meroë becomes the capital of Nubia
146 The Romans destroy the city of Carthage
c.350 King Ezana of Axum converts to Christianity
525–523 Egypt is conquered by Persia
c.100 BC The camel is introduced into the Sahara
522–74 The kingdom of Axum rules in the Yemen
c.500 Sabeans settle in Ethiopia, later contributing to rise of the kingdom of Axum
AD 1–100 The kingdom of Axum emerges
c.540 The Nubians are converted to Christianity
Southern Africa
700–600 Iron working is first known in the central Sahara region
c.200 Date of the earliest occupation at Jenne-jeno
c.400 City walls are built at Jenne-jeno
c.480 Taruga, Nigeria, flourishes as an iron working center
c.AD 1 Khoisans in southern Africa are herding sheep
400–500 Iron working reaches southern Africa
AD 1–100 Madagascar is settled by Austronesians from southeast Asia
500–600 Cattle and iron working are widespread in southern Africa
400–300 Iron working is established in the east African highlands
100–300 Greco-Roman merchants sail to east Africa for ivory
600 BC
AD 1
AD 600

The earliest Iron Age culture of west Africa, the Nok culture of Nigeria (c. 500 BC– AD 400), is noted for its sophisticated terracotta sculptures, which are often seen as being ancestral to the art styles of the medieval Ibo and Yoruba peoples. By AD 600 many areas of west Africa had dense farming populations, and one city, Jenne-jeno, had developed as a regional trading center. Many large burial mounds in this region point to the emergence of powerful elites and the beginnings of state formation.

The major development in Africa south of the Equator was the expansion of the Bantu-speaking peoples, mixed farming and, later, iron working. The Bantu languages belong to the Niger-Kordofanian group, confined to tropical west Africa in the second millennium BC. The original homeland of the Bantu was in southern Nigeria and Cameroon, but around 2000 BC Bantu-speakers began to spread into central and east Africa, and by AD 500 they had reached southern Africa. Bantu languages were spread partly by migrations of iron-using farmers, but also by the assimilation to Bantu culture of the Khoisan-speaking Stone Age herders and hunter–gatherers of eastern and southern Africa.

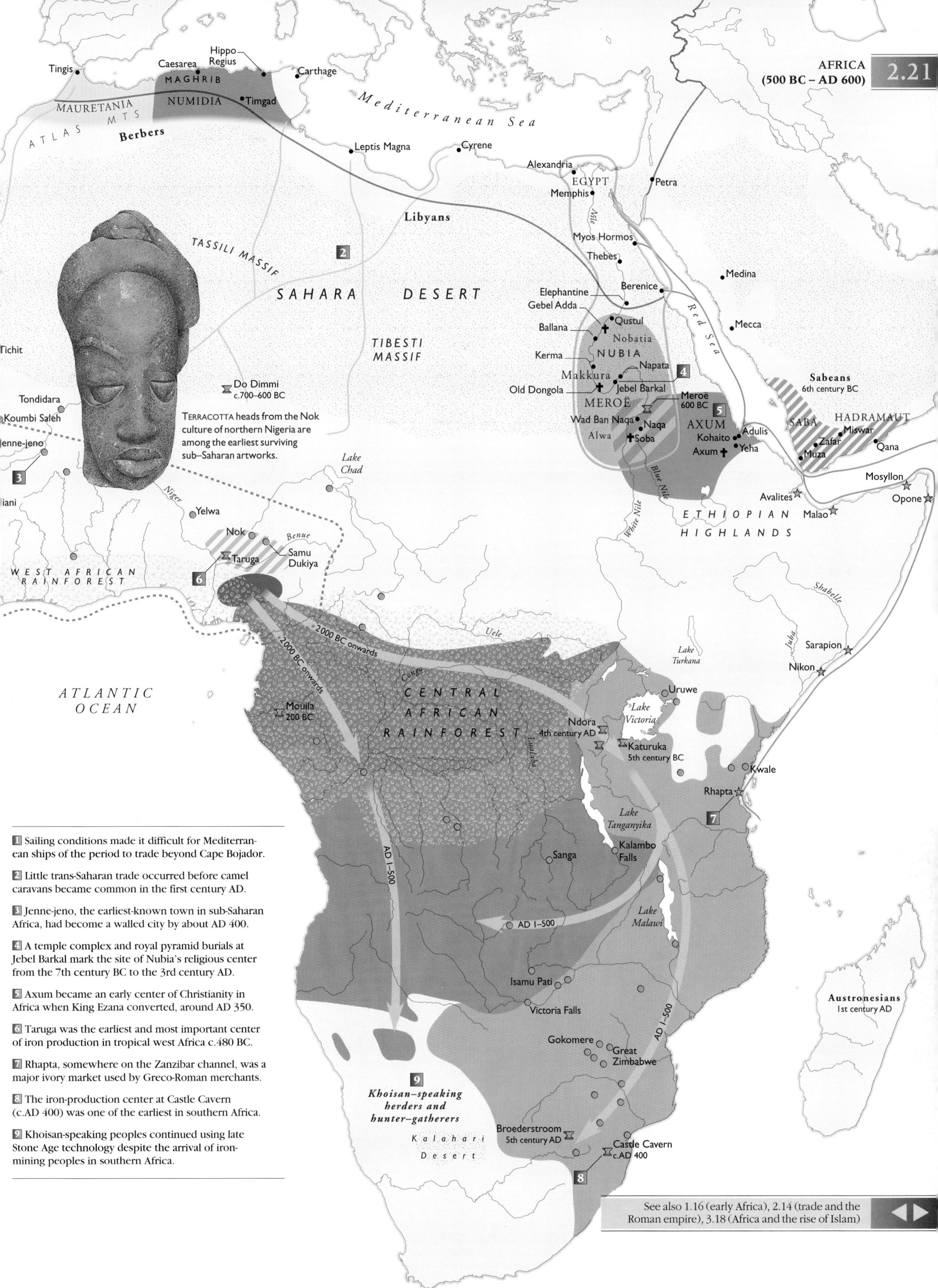
AFRICA
(500 BC – AD 600)
2.21
Tingis
Caesarea
Hippo Regius
Carthage
MAGHRIB
NUMIDIA
Timgad
MAURETANIA
ATLAS MTS
Berbers
Mediterranean Sea
Leptis Magna
Cyrene
Alexandria
EGYPT
Memphis
Petra
Nile
Libyans
Myos Hormos
Thebes
Medina
TASSILI MASSIF
SAHARA DESERT
Elephantine
Gebel Adda
Berenice
Red Sea
Ballana
Qustul
Mecca
Nobatia
NUBIA
Kerma
TIBESTI MASSIF
Tichit
Napata
Makkura
Old Dongola
Jebel Barkal
MEROË
Meroë 600 BC
Sabeans 6th century BC
Do Dimmi c.700–600 BC
Tondidara
Koumbi Saleh
Wad Ban Naqa
Naqa
Alwa
Soba
AXUM
Kohaito
Adulis
Axum
Yeha
SABA
HADRAMAUT
Miswar
Zafar
Muza
Qana
Jenne-jeno
TERRACOTTA heads from the Nok culture of northern Nigeria are among the earliest surviving sub-Saharan artworks.
Lake Chad
Blue Nile
Mosyllon
Avalites
Opone
Malao
Niger
Yelwa
White Nile
ETHIOPIAN HIGHLANDS
Nok
Benue
Taruga
Samu Dukiya
WEST AFRICAN RAINFOREST
Shabelle
Uele
2000 BC onwards
2000 BC onwards
Lake Turkana
Juba
Sarapion
Nikon
Congo
ATLANTIC OCEAN
CENTRAL AFRICAN RAINFOREST
Uruwe
Mouila 200 BC
Lake Victoria
Ndora 4th century AD
Katuruka 5th century BC
Lualaba
Kwale
Rhapta
Lake Tanganyika
AD 1–500
Kalambo Falls
Sanga
Lake Malawi
AD 1–500
Isamu Pati
Victoria Falls
Austronesians 1st century AD
AD 1–500
Gokomere
Great Zimbabwe
Khoisan-speaking herders and hunter-gatherers
Kalahari Desert
Broederstroom 5th century AD
Castle Cavern c.AD 400

1 Sailing conditions made it difficult for Mediterranean ships of the period to trade beyond Cape Bojador.

2 Little trans-Saharan trade occurred before camel caravans became common in the first century AD.

3 Jenne-jeno, the earliest-known town in sub-Saharan Africa, had become a walled city by about AD 400.

4 A temple complex and royal pyramid burials at Jebel Barkal mark the site of Nubia's religious center from the 7th century BC to the 3rd century AD.

5 Axum became an early center of Christianity in Africa when King Ezana converted, around AD 350.

6 Taruga was the earliest and most important center of iron production in tropical west Africa c.480 BC.

7 Rhapta, somewhere on the Zanzibar channel, was a major ivory market used by Greco-Roman merchants.

8 The iron-production center at Castle Cavern (c.AD 400) was one of the earliest in southern Africa.

9 Khoisan-speaking peoples continued using late Stone Age technology despite the arrival of iron-mining peoples in southern Africa.

See also 1.16 (early Africa), 2.14 (trade and the Roman empire), 3.18 (Africa and the rise of Islam)

In 500 BC northern India was divided into several Hindu kingdoms, the most powerful being Magadha, ruled by king Bimbisara. Southern India was still dominated by tribal peoples under Hindu influence. In 364 Magadha came under the control of the expansionist Nanda dynasty, which by about 340 dominated northern India. The Nandas' reputation for oppressive taxation, however, led to their overthrow in a coup by Chandragupta Maurya (r. 321–c.293). Chandragupta's origins are obscure but he appears to have been a military commander in the northwest border provinces at the time of Alexander the Great's invasion of the Indus valley: he fought against Greek outposts in the area and may have met Alexander.

By 311 Chandragupta had extended his kingdom to the Indus, bringing him into conflict with Seleucos, who had seized power after Alexander's death. In 305 Chandragupta defeated Seleucos and was ceded control of the whole Indus valley in return for a gift of 500 war elephants. Chandragupta maintained a large standing army and imposed a harsh penal code on his people. He also created an effective central bureaucracy, which controlled economic activity and carried out road building, irrigation and other public works. In about 293 he abdicated in favor of his son Bindusara (r.c. 293–268) and became a Jain monk, dying around 286. Bindusara continued the expansionist program of his father and extended the Mauryan empire far into southern India. In 268 he was succeeded by his son Ashoka, one of India's most remarkable rulers. Reportedly overcome with remorse after a bloody conquest of the east-coast district of Kalinga in 261, Ashoka converted to Buddhism in about 260.

Buddhism had its origins in the teachings of Siddhartha Gautama, the Buddha, (c.563–483), in the heartland of late 6th-century Magadha. It was just one among many sects influenced by, but reacting against, India's traditions of Brahmanic Hinduism, until the missionary work started by Ashoka in 258 began its transformation from minor sect to major world religion. Ashoka adopted the Buddhist principles of right conduct and non-violence, assured neighboring states of his goodwill, ameliorated his grandfather's penal code and sought to rule as far as possible by moral authority alone. To spread Buddhist values he had edicts on morality and the way of compassion carved on rock-faces and pillars throughout his empire. Over thirty of these survive, forming the most important source of information about Ashoka's reign. Ashoka intervened in doctrinal matters and it was his initiative that led to the defining of the Buddhist canon at the Third Buddhist council at Pataliputra around 240. Ashoka also promoted Buddhism abroad, sending missions to Indonesia, southern India, Ceylon, the Greek states of western Asia and the nomads of central Asia.

Although Ashoka's empire was the largest state to exist in India before the coming of the Mughal empire in the 17th century AD, it did not long survive

A CARVING of about AD 100 from Sanchi, exemplifying a common Hindu theme of a dancing woman with a flowering tree.

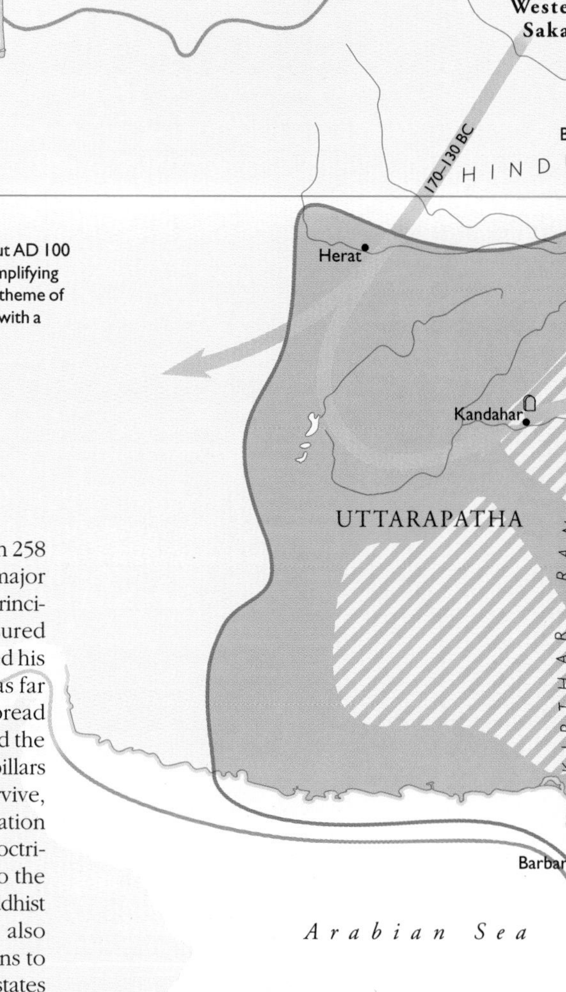
Marakanda
170–130 BC
Herat
Kandahar
UTTARAPATHA
Arabian Sea

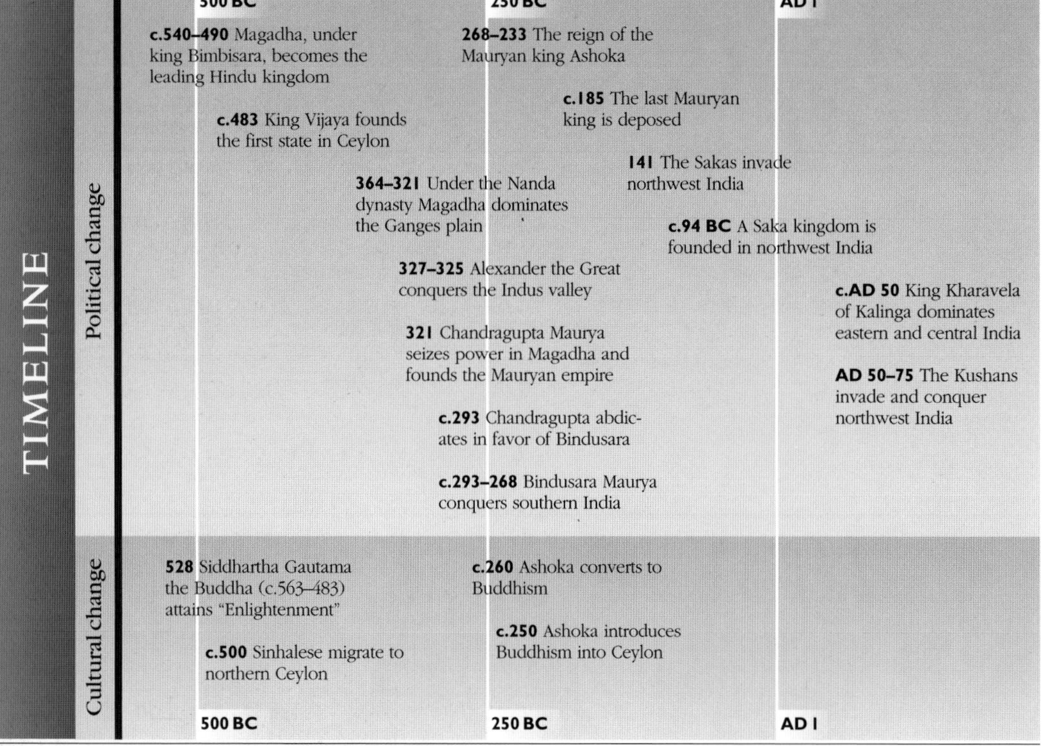
TIMELINE
Political change
500 BC
250 BC
AD 1
c.540–490 Magadha, under king Bimbisara, becomes the leading Hindu kingdom
c.483 King Vijaya founds the first state in Ceylon
364–321 Under the Nanda dynasty Magadha dominates the Ganges plain
327–325 Alexander the Great conquers the Indus valley
321 Chandragupta Maurya seizes power in Magadha and founds the Mauryan empire
c.293 Chandragupta abdicates in favor of Bindusara
c.293–268 Bindusara Maurya conquers southern India
268–233 The reign of the Mauryan king Ashoka
c.185 The last Mauryan king is deposed
141 The Sakas invade northwest India
c.94 BC A Saka kingdom is founded in northwest India
c.AD 50 King Kharavela of Kalinga dominates eastern and central India
AD 50–75 The Kushans invade and conquer northwest India
Cultural change
528 Siddhartha Gautama the Buddha (c.563–483) attains "Enlightenment"
c.500 Sinhalese migrate to northern Ceylon
c.260 Ashoka converts to Buddhism
c.250 Ashoka introduces Buddhism into Ceylon
500 BC
250 BC
AD 1

- empire of Alexander the Great, c.325 BC
- kingdom of Magadha under Nanda dynasty, c.324 BC

Mauryan empire

- territory gained by Chandragupta Maurya, 320–305 BC
- territory gained by Bindusara, c.293–268 BC
- territory gained by Ashoka, 268–260 BC
- maximum extent of empire under Ashoka, c.260 BC
- weak or nominal Mauryan control
- provincial capital
- VANGA province under Ashoka
- Ashokan rock edict
- Ashokan pillar edict
- heartland of Satavahanihara kingdom late 1st century BC
- maximum extent of Saka rule, 1st century BC
- Western Sakas, 2nd century AD
- formative area of Buddhism
- Buddhist monument, before 187 BC
- Buddhist monument, 187 BC–AD 50
- migration of peoples
- ancient river course
- modern coastline where altered

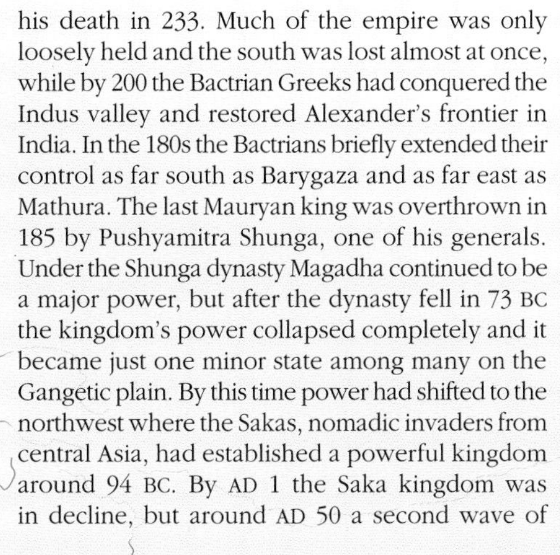

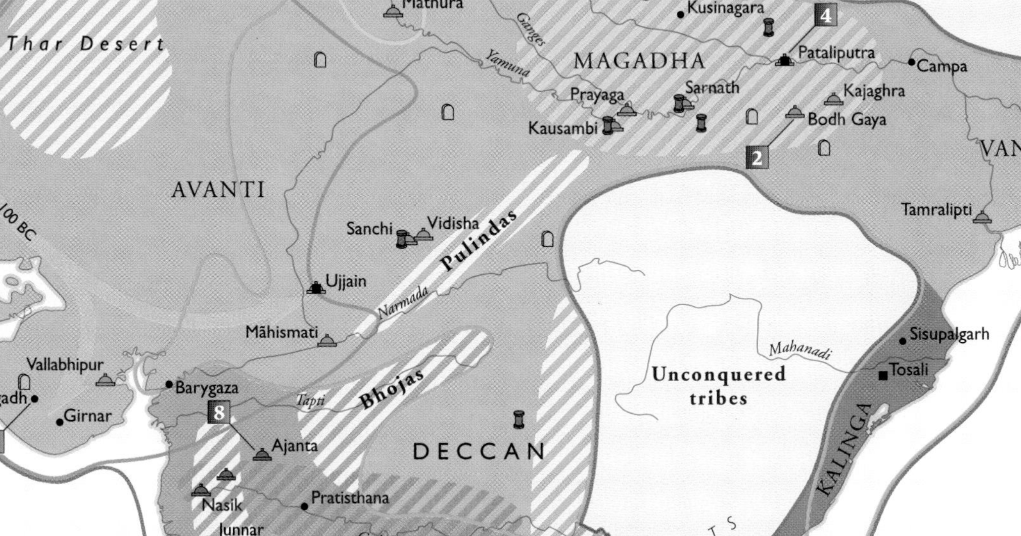
Sakas
Northern Sakas
Khotan
(Buddhism introduced in 3rd century BC)
Sakas
KUNLUN MTS
HIMALAYAS
Indus
141 BC
Taxila
Chenab
Sutlej
Thar Desert
Mathura
Sravasti
Lumbini
Kusinagara
Ganges
Yamuna
MAGADHA
Pataliputra
Campa
Prayaga
Sarnath
Kajaghra
Kausambi
Bodh Gaya
VANGA
AVANTI
110–100 BC
Sanchi
Vidisha
Pulindas
Tamralipti
Ujjain
Narmada
Māhismati
Vallabhipur
Junagadh
Girnar
Barygaza
Tapti
Bhojas
Ajanta
DECCAN
Unconquered tribes
Mahanadi
Sisupalgarh
Tosali
KALINGA
Bay of Bengal
Pratisthana
Nasik
Junnar
Godavari
Rathikas
EASTERN GHATS
Dantapura
DAKSHINAPATHA
Amaravati
WESTERN GHATS
Krishna
Suvarnagiri
Satiyaputras
Kaveri
Cholas
Keralaputras
Pandyas
Sinhalese
Ceylon
Anuradhapura
VIJAYANA
Veddas
Mahagoma
0 400 km
0 300 mi

his death in 233. Much of the empire was only loosely held and the south was lost almost at once, while by 200 the Bactrian Greeks had conquered the Indus valley and restored Alexander's frontier in India. In the 180s the Bactrians briefly extended their control as far south as Barygaza and as far east as Mathura. The last Mauryan king was overthrown in 185 by Pushyamitra Shunga, one of his generals. Under the Shunga dynasty Magadha continued to be a major power, but after the dynasty fell in 73 BC the kingdom's power collapsed completely and it became just one minor state among many on the Gangetic plain. By this time power had shifted to the northwest where the Sakas, nomadic invaders from central Asia, had established a powerful kingdom around 94 BC. By AD 1 the Saka kingdom was in decline, but around AD 50 a second wave of nomads, the Kushans, invaded and founded another major kingdom in the northwest.

The advent of the Mauryan empire accelerated state formation in southern India – trade contacts, colonies of northerners and Buddhist missions ending the area's relative isolation. The first considerable state in the region, Kalinga, dominated eastern India and extended its power into the Gangetic plain in the middle of the 1st century BC under King Kharavela. Soon after Kharavela's death, however, it sank back into obscurity. More stable was the state of Satavahanihara, centered around Pratisthana, which also rose to prominence in the 1st century BC and remained the dominant power in the south until the 3rd century AD. Ceylon was colonized by Sinhalese from southern India around 500 BC and the native Veddas were pushed into the interior. Traditionally the first state in Ceylon was founded around 483, by King Vijaya in the north of the island. Ashoka's missionaries took Buddhism to Ceylon, where the religion set down particularly deep roots.

1 The trading city of Taxila, occupied successively by Persians, Greeks, Mauryans, Sakas and Kushans, became a melting pot of different cultures.

2 Bodh Gaya, where Buddha gained "Enlightenment" c.528 BC, was and remains a sacred site of Buddhism.

3 Anuradhapura was founded in 437 BC as the capital of a Sinhalese kingdom of northern Ceylon.

4 Pataliputra was capital of Magadha and the Mauryan empire and one of the largest cities in the ancient world, defended by a timber wall with 500 towers.

5 A dam, reservoir and irrigation project of the Mauryan period at Junagadh was one of the first such large projects to be built under government direction.

6 Southern India was (most probably) conquered by Chandragupta's son Bindusara (r. c.293–268 BC).

7 Amaravati was the main Buddhist center in southern India from the 3rd century BC to the 14th AD.

8 A complex of rock-cut Buddhist temples and monasteries with fine wall paintings was built at Ajanta from the 2nd century BC to the 5th AD.

9 Trade in pearls, diamonds and gold led to state formation in southern India by the 1st century BC.

See also 1.26 (early India); 2.09 (Alexander's empires); 2.20 steppe peoples; 2.23 (Guptas)

2.23 Kushan and Gupta India • AD 50 – 570 •

Around AD 50 the Kushans made northwest India part of an empire stretching from the Ganges to the Aral Sea. They were a clan of the Yue Qi nomads who had overrun the Greek kingdom of Bactria around 135 BC. The Kushan state was set up in Bactria around AD 25 by Kujala Kadphises, who invaded India and conquered Gandhara and the Northern Sakas around AD 50. Kujala's successor, Vima Kadphises (r.c.75–100), conquered the Indus valley and much of the Gangetic plain. The empire reached its peak under Kanishka (r.c.100–130). He was a devout Buddhist and a patron of the arts, supporting both the Indo-Hellenistic school of Gandhara and the Hindu school of Mathura. Under Kanishka's successors, the Kushan empire maintained its borders until the 3rd century, when most of the empire's western provinces were conquered by the Sasanian King Shapur I. Although the Kushans briefly regained their independence in the 4th century, the united Kushan empire was not restored.

The Kushan empire was never highly centralized and the king ruled through a host of dependent subkings or *yaghbus*. Kushan rulers used an eclectic range of titles, including *maharaja* (great king), *rajatiraja* (king of kings), the Greek title *basileus* (king) and *kaisara* (from the Latin *caesar*). They also instituted a cult of ruler worship and used the title *devaputra* (son of God). Kushan culture was equally eclectic, mixing Hellenistic, Indian and central Asian styles. Kushan rulers were tolerant in matters of religion. Most of the early rulers were Buddhists and the later ones Hindus, but all showed respect for a wide range of Persian, Greek and even Roman deities. The empire was always wealthy, prospering by its control of all the major trans-Asian overland trade routes. High-quality gold coinage was made by melting down gold Roman coins flooding into the empire to pay for luxury goods such as Chinese silk.

The Kushans did not have a monopoly on east–west trade. By the 1st century AD, Mediterranean seafarers had discovered how to exploit the monsoon winds to sail across the Indian Ocean, bringing increased trade between the Roman empire and southern India. The region's most valuable exports were spices, which the Romans paid for in gold. South Indian rulers did not issue their own coinage and Roman coins circulated freely. The most powerful south Indian state at this period was Satavahanihara; but the influx of wealth led to the formation of several small tribal kingdoms and cities in the region.

The decline of Kushan power made possible the rise of the Gupta kingdom in the 4th century. Minor princes in the Varanasi area in the later 3rd century, the Guptas may have been feudatories of Magadha. The dynasty began with the reign of Chandragupta I (r.320–35), who made an advantageous marriage alliance with the Licchavis. This brought him control of Magadha, the fertile and densely populated heartland of the former Mauryan empire. Chandragupta was succeeded by his son Samudragupta (r.335–80), whose long reign saw the kingdom expand across northern India, reducing the Kushans to tributary status. Samudragupta also fought a major campaign in the southeast, reducing many rulers to tributaries. He formed strong alliances with the Sakas and the Vakatakas (in power in Satavahanihara), but his son and successor, Chandragupta II (r.380–414), turned on the Western Sakas, conquered their kingdom and imposed direct rule. The empire ruled by Chandragupta II was almost as large as the Mauryan empire, but was very loose-knit. Gupta inscriptions approximately cover the area in which the dynasty exercised direct rule – the rest of the empire was ruled by tributary kings and barely-subdued tribes.

The Guptas were patrons of the arts and sciences and the period was one of great creativity. They were devout Hindus and some of the main features of Hinduism, such as image-worship, appeared under their rule. The Hindu epics of the *Ramayana* and the *Mahabharata* reached their final form at this time. Sanskrit poetry and drama flourished, causing the Gupta period to be regarded as the classical age of Indian literature. Advances were made in astronomy and mathematics, including the invention of the decimal system of numerals, later adopted by the Arabs and, through them, by the Europeans.

After the death of Chandragupta II, the empire ceased expanding but remained powerful, and under Skandagupta (r.c.455–67) defeated a major Hunnish invasion. However, a war of succession followed Skandagupta's death and the empire went into decline as tributary kings and nominally conquered tribes reasserted their independence. The final blow came from an invasion of the Hunas (Ephthalite Huns) in 505–11, who founded a kingdom in northwest India, destroying the last remnants of the Kushans. In 528 a coalition of Indian princes defeated the Hunas, but the Guptas played only a minor role in this campaign. Gupta rulers continued in Magadha until around 720, but only as mere princes. Except for a brief period under Harsha (r.606–47) of Kanauj, who united the states on the Gangetic plain, no supraregional state reappeared in India until the 13th century.

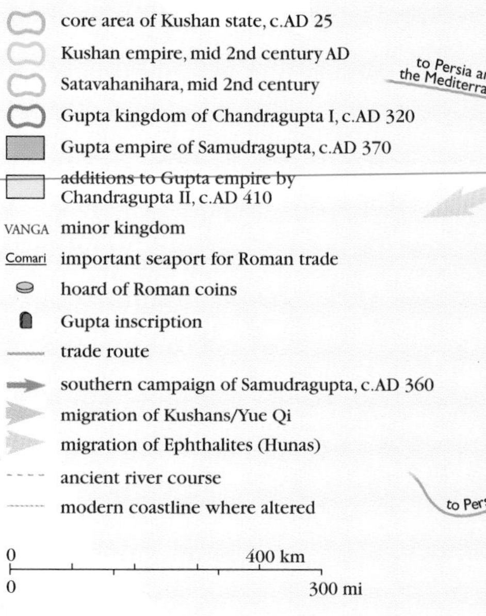

core area of Kushan state, c.AD 25
Kushan empire, mid 2nd century AD
Satavahanihara, mid 2nd century
Gupta kingdom of Chandragupta I, c.AD 320
Gupta empire of Samudragupta, c.AD 370
additions to Gupta empire by Chandragupta II, c.AD 410
VANGA minor kingdom
Comari important seaport for Roman trade
hoard of Roman coins
Gupta inscription
trade route
southern campaign of Samudragupta, c.AD 360
migration of Kushans/Yue Qi
migration of Ephthalites (Hunas)
ancient river course
modern coastline where altered
0
400 km
0
300 mi
to Persia and the Mediterranean
to Persia

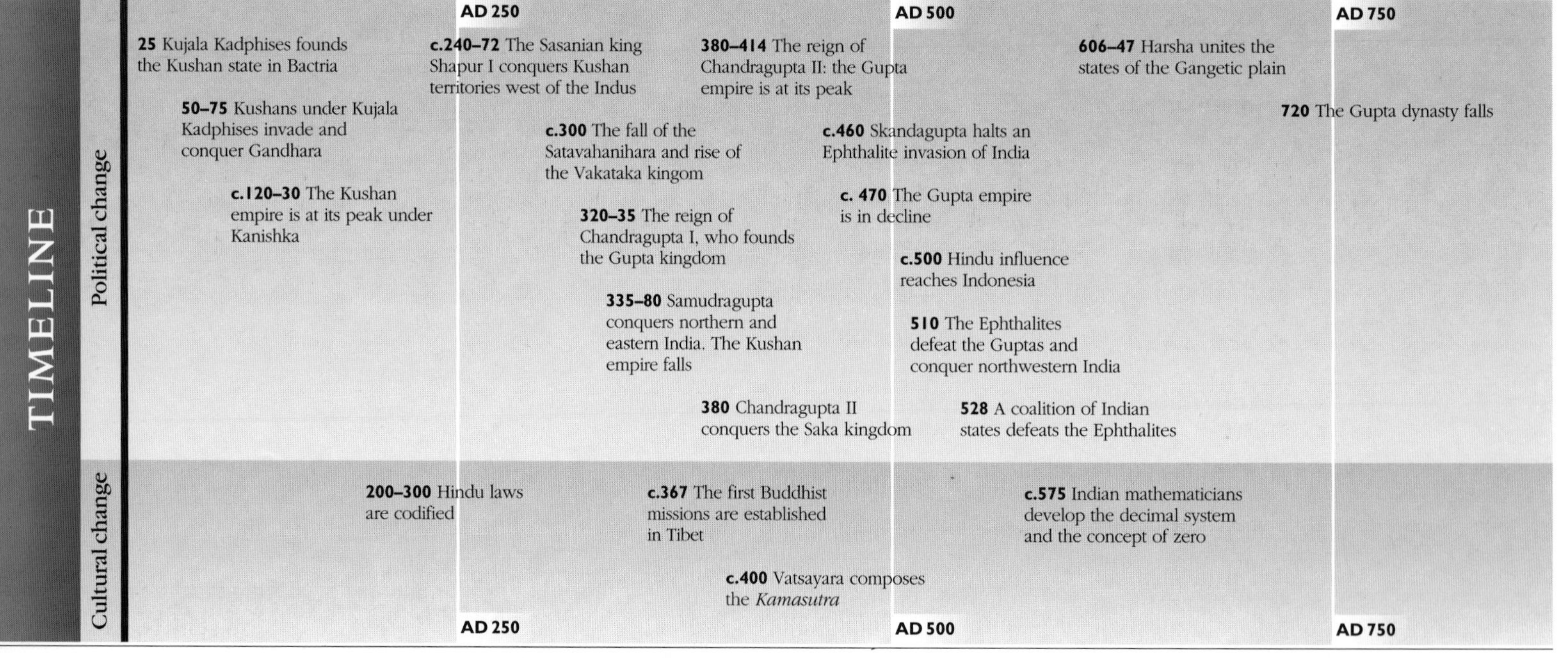

TIMELINE
Political change
Cultural change
AD 250
AD 500
AD 750
25 Kujala Kadphises founds the Kushan state in Bactria
50–75 Kushans under Kujala Kadphises invade and conquer Gandhara
c.120–30 The Kushan empire is at its peak under Kanishka
c.240–72 The Sasanian king Shapur I conquers Kushan territories west of the Indus
c.300 The fall of the Satavahanihara and rise of the Vakataka kingom
320–35 The reign of Chandragupta I, who founds the Gupta kingdom
335–80 Samudragupta conquers northern and eastern India. The Kushan empire falls
380–414 The reign of Chandragupta II: the Gupta empire is at its peak
380 Chandragupta II conquers the Saka kingdom
c.460 Skandagupta halts an Ephthalite invasion of India
c. 470 The Gupta empire is in decline
c.500 Hindu influence reaches Indonesia
510 The Ephthalites defeat the Guptas and conquer northwestern India
528 A coalition of Indian states defeats the Ephthalites
606–47 Harsha unites the states of the Gangetic plain
720 The Gupta dynasty falls
200–300 Hindu laws are codified
c.367 The first Buddhist missions are established in Tibet
c.400 Vatsayara composes the Kamasutra
c.575 Indian mathematicians develop the decimal system and the concept of zero
AD 250
AD 500
AD 750

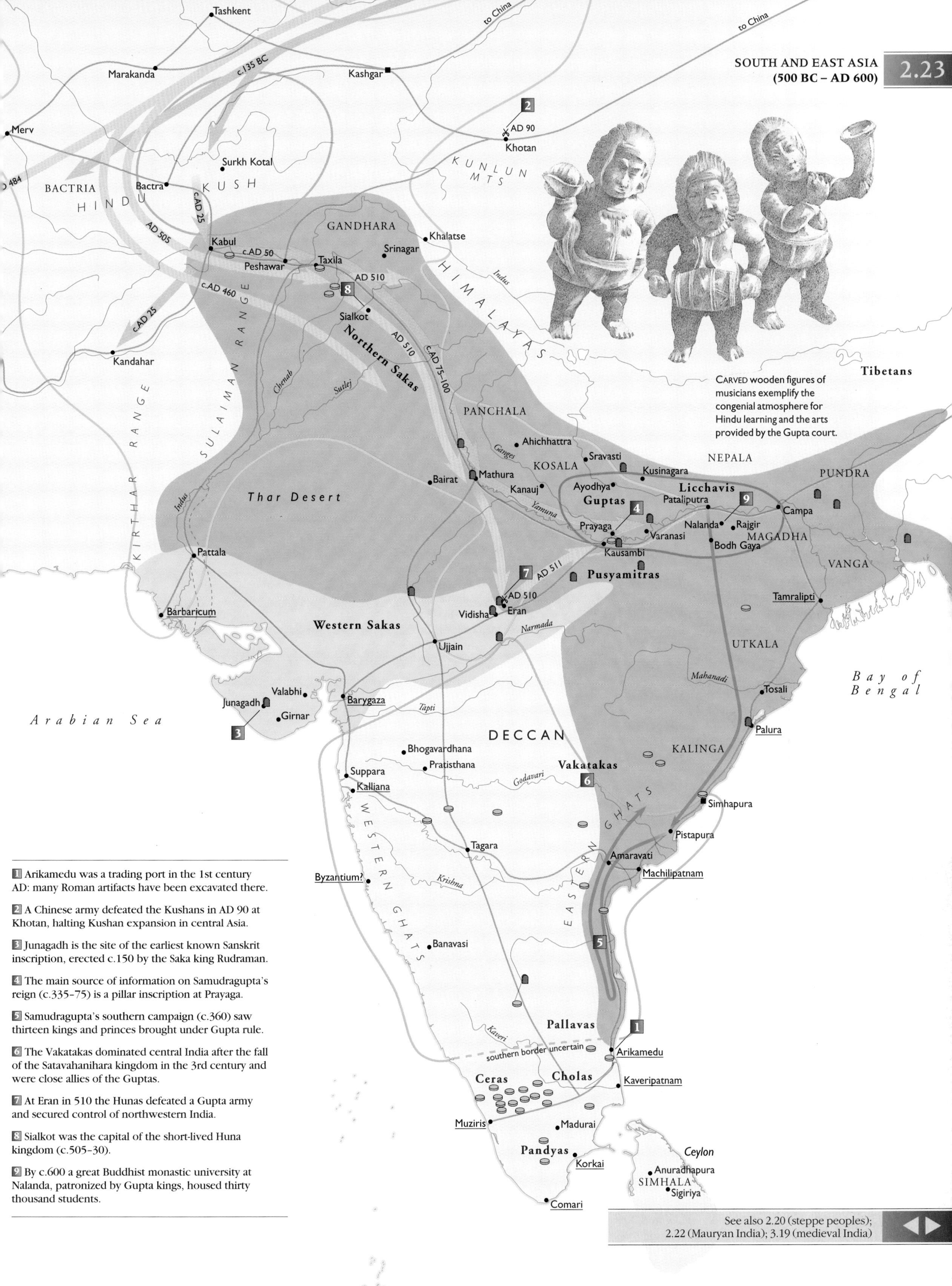
Tashkent
Marakanda
Kashgar
to China
to China
c.135 BC
Merv
AD 90
Khotan
KUNLUN MTS
Surkh Kotal
BACTRIA
Bactra
HINDU KUSH
c.AD 25
AD 505
GANDHARA
Khalatse
Kabul
c.AD 50
Peshawar
Taxila
Srinagar
AD 510
c.AD 460
Sialkot
c.AD 25
Kandahar
HIMALAYAS
Indus
SULAIMAN RANGE
Northern Sakas
AD 510
c.AD 75–100
Chenab
Sutlej
Tibetans
PANCHALA
Ahichhattra
Ganges
Sravasti
KOSALA
Kusinagara
NEPALA
PUNDRA
Bairat
Mathura
Kanauj
Ayodhya
Licchavis
Guptas
Pataliputra
Campa
Thar Desert
KIRTHAR RANGE
Yamuna
Prayaga
Varanasi
Nalanda
Rajgir
MAGADHA
Bodh Gaya
Kausambi
Pattala
AD 511
Pusyamitras
VANGA
AD 510
Eran
Vidisha
Tamralipti
Barbaricum
Western Sakas
Narmada
Ujjain
UTKALA
Mahanadi
Bay of Bengal
Valabhi
Junagadh
Girnar
Barygaza
Tapti
Tosali
Arabian Sea
Palura
DECCAN
KALINGA
Bhogavardhana
Pratisthana
Vakatakas
Suppara
Kalliana
Godavari
Simhapura
WESTERN GHATS
EASTERN GHATS
Pistapura
Tagara
Amaravati
Machilipatnam
Byzantium?
Krishna
Banavasi
Pallavas
Kaveri
southern border uncertain
Arikamedu
Ceras
Cholas
Kaveripatnam
Muziris
Madurai
Pandyas
Ceylon
Korkai
Anuradhapura
SIMHALA
Sigiriya
Comari
1
2
3
4
5
6
7
8
9

CARVED wooden figures of musicians exemplify the congenial atmosphere for Hindu learning and the arts provided by the Gupta court.

1 Arikamedu was a trading port in the 1st century AD: many Roman artifacts have been excavated there.

2 A Chinese army defeated the Kushans in AD 90 at Khotan, halting Kushan expansion in central Asia.

3 Junagadh is the site of the earliest known Sanskrit inscription, erected c.150 by the Saka king Rudraman.

4 The main source of information on Samudragupta's reign (c.335–75) is a pillar inscription at Prayaga.

5 Samudragupta's southern campaign (c.360) saw thirteen kings and princes brought under Gupta rule.

6 The Vakatakas dominated central India after the fall of the Satavahanihara kingdom in the 3rd century and were close allies of the Guptas.

7 At Eran in 510 the Hunas defeated a Gupta army and secured control of northwestern India.

8 Sialkot was the capital of the short-lived Huna kingdom (c.505–30).

9 By c.600 a great Buddhist monastic university at Nalanda, patronized by Gupta kings, housed thirty thousand students.

See also 2.20 (steppe peoples); 2.22 (Mauryan India); 3.19 (medieval India)

China from warring states to the first empires • 480 BC – AD 220 •

Zhou China (1122–256 BC) was a decentralized feudal state: the king exercised direct authority only over his own domain, while the provinces were held as fiefs by dukes who ruled in his name. Gradually the dukes became, in effect, the rulers of independent states; the Zhou king reigned from his capital at Luoyang but did not rule. The Warring States period (480–221 BC) saw the stronger states eliminate the weaker and absorb their territory: by 300 eleven states were left, and by 256, when the last Zhou king was deposed, there were seven. By 221 one state – Qin – was supreme.

Qin's rise to dominance began under Xiao (r.361–338). Shang Yang, Xiao's prime minister, ended the power of the feudal aristocracy and enacted a series of reforms that turned Qin into a centralized state based on a settled and productive peasantry and a strong army. Qin's frontier position gave it opportunities for expansion at the expense of the tribal peoples to the west, while its mountainous borders protected it from the aggression of other states. By 315 it was the strongest of the surviving states. The Qin dukes had already abandoned the pretence of subservience to the Zhou by adopting the title of king. In the 3rd century Qin waged almost constant warfare against the other Chinese states, which failed to combine against it and were picked off one at a time. The unification of China was completed in a series of lightning campaigns by Zheng (r.246–210) between 230 and 221, after which he adopted the title Shi Huangdi, the "First Emperor".

Shi Huangdi is regarded as the founder of the Chinese empire and the pattern of centralized totalitarian government he established has endured to the present day. Qin laws and institutions were extended to the whole of China. The aristocracies of the defeated states were deported, the remnants of feudalism were abolished and a non-hereditary central and local bureaucracy was created. The empire was divided into 36 districts or commanderies, governed by civilian and military officials responsible directly to the autocratic emperor. Coinage, weights and measures, scripts and even the axle sizes of wagons were standardized. In an attempt to ensure that Chinese history began with him, Shi Huangdi ordered the destruction of all works of history, along with all "subversive" works of literature: scholars who protested were executed. Military campaigns extended the empire in the south while armies of conscripted laborers linked the frontier walls, which had been built by the Warring States against nomad invasions, into a continuous defensive system.

The cost of Shi Huangdi's reforms ruined the economy and his despotic rule caused such discontent that, after his death in 210, a civil war broke out. In 206 rebels massacred the entire Qin royal family. However, there was no restoration of the old states and the empire passed intact under the rule of Liu Bang, a commoner who had become a Qin official, and who became the first ruler of the Han dynasty. Gaozu (to use his more common posthumous title) ameliorated the severe Qin laws, reduced taxes and introduced reforms to restore prosperity. He rewarded some generals and bureaucrats with small fiefs but these were strictly controlled and the centralized state of Shi Huangdi was preserved.

The Former Han period (206 BC–AD 9) saw major territorial gains in central Asia and the south but northern China suffered severely from raids by the Xiongnu nomads until they were pacified in a long series of Han campaigns between 128 and 36 BC.

A TERRACOTTA army, six thousand men and horses strong, was buried with Shi Huangdi at Xianyang.

Turfan
105 BC
6
Dunhuang
108 BC
Cherchen
Gansu Corridor
8
Changye
QILIAN MTS
Wu-su
Lake Qinghai
Tibetans

- Jin, c.500 BC
- Warring States border, c.300 BC
- Qin state, c.350 BC
- Qin gains by 300 BC
- Qin gains, 300–250 BC
- Qin gains, 230–221 BC
- Qin gains by 206 BC
- empire of the former Han dynasty, c.AD 6
- Han protectorates, c.59 BC–AD 23, AD 73–127
- territorial gains of Later Han dynasty
- independent kingdom of Nan-yue, 206–113 BC
- Warring States capital
- capital of Zhou empire
- capital of Qin dynasty
- capital of former Han dynasty and Later Han dynasty
- Qin fort
- frontier wall
- Chinese campaign
- Xiongnu campaign
- modern coastline and drainage where altered

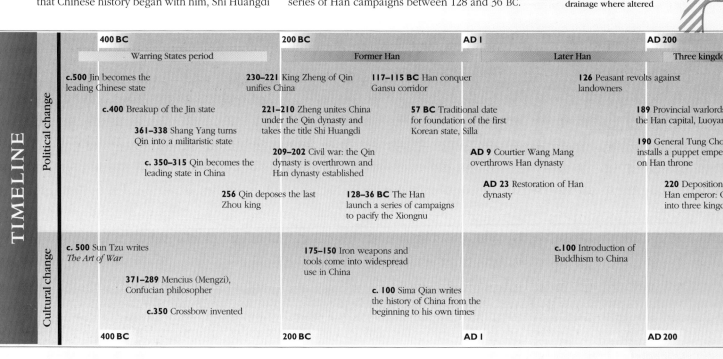

TIMELINE

400 BC | 200 BC | AD 1 | AD 200

Warring States period | Former Han | Later Han | Three kingdoms period

Political change

c.500 Jin becomes the leading Chinese state

c.400 Breakup of the Jin state

361–338 Shang Yang turns Qin into a militaristic state

c. 350–315 Qin becomes the leading state in China

256 Qin deposes the last Zhou king

230–221 King Zheng of Qin unifies China

221–210 Zheng unites China under the Qin dynasty and takes the title Shi Huangdi

209–202 Civil war: the Qin dynasty is overthrown and Han dynasty established

117–115 BC Han conquer Gansu corridor

128–36 BC The Han launch a series of campaigns to pacify the Xiongnu

57 BC Traditional date for foundation of the first Korean state, Silla

AD 9 Courtier Wang Mang overthrows Han dynasty

AD 23 Restoration of Han dynasty

126 Peasant revolts against landowners

189 Provincial warlords seize the Han capital, Luoyang

190 General Tung Cho installs a puppet emperor on Han throne

220 Deposition of last Han emperor: China splits into three kingdoms

Cultural change

c. 500 Sun Tzu writes *The Art of War*

371–289 Mencius (Mengzi), Confucian philosopher

c.350 Crossbow invented

175–150 Iron weapons and tools come into widespread use in China

c. 100 Sima Qian writes the history of China from the beginning to his own times

c.100 Introduction of Buddhism to China

400 BC | 200 BC | AD 1 | AD 200

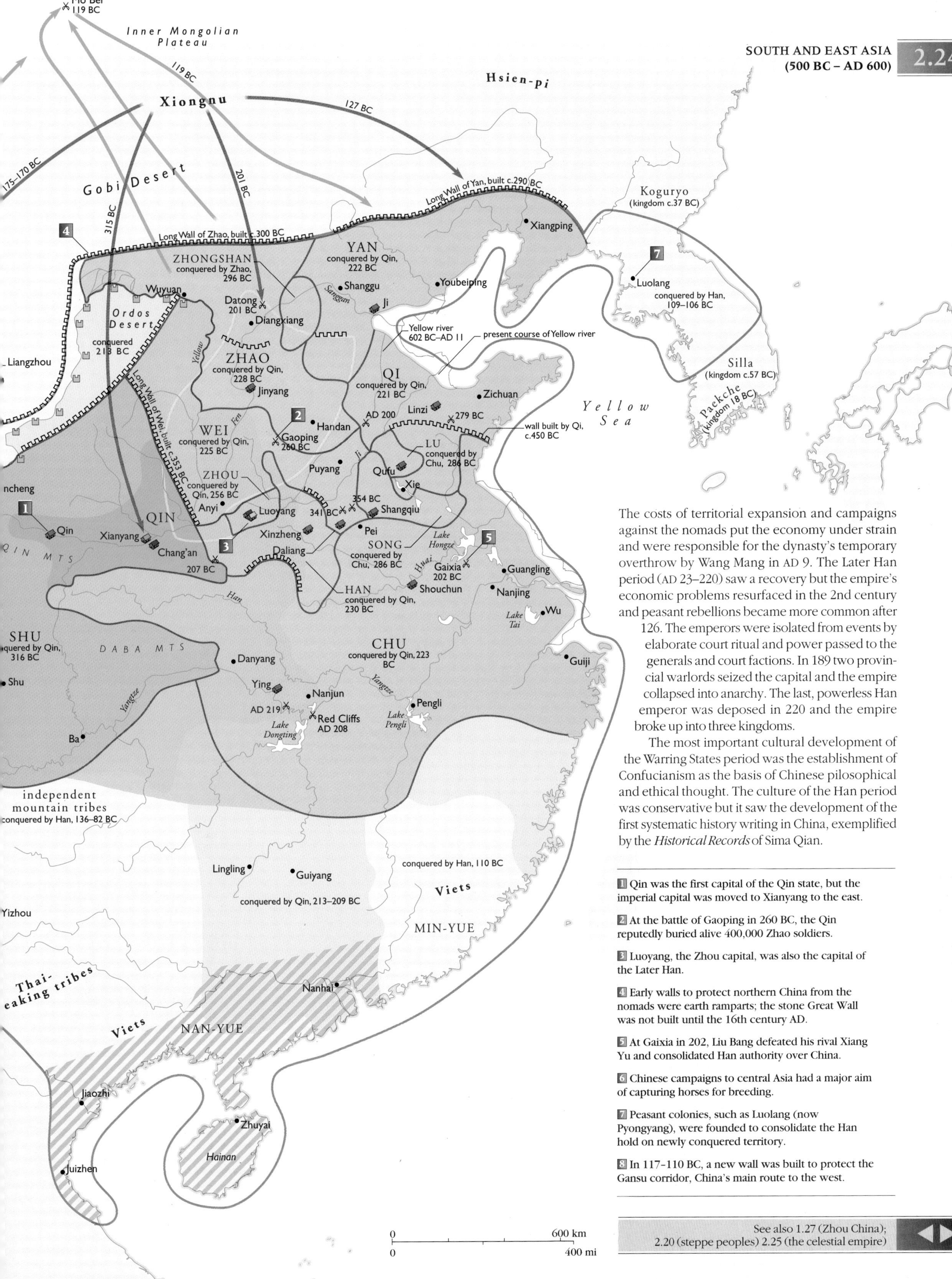
Mo Bei 119 BC
Inner Mongolian Plateau
Hsien-pi
Xiongnu
119 BC
127 BC
175–170 BC
Gobi Desert
201 BC
315 BC
Long Wall of Yan, built c.290 BC
Long Wall of Zhao, built c.300 BC
Koguryo (kingdom c.37 BC)
Xiangping
YAN conquered by Qin, 222 BC
ZHONGSHAN conquered by Zhao, 296 BC
Luolang conquered by Han, 109–106 BC
Wuyuan
Datong 201 BC
Diangxiang
Shanggu
Ji
Youbeiping
Sanggan
Ordos Desert
conquered 213 BC
Liangzhou
Yellow river 602 BC–AD 11
present course of Yellow river
ZHAO conquered by Qin, 228 BC
Jinyang
QI conquered by Qin, 221 BC
Silla (kingdom c.57 BC)
Paekche (kingdom 18 BC)
Zichuan
Yellow Sea
Long Wall of Wei, built c.353 BC
Linzi
279 BC
wall built by Qi, c.450 BC
WEI conquered by Qin, 225 BC
Fen
Handan
AD 200
Gaoping 260 BC
LU conquered by Chu, 286 BC
ZHOU conquered by Qin, 256 BC
Puyang
Qufu
Xie
ncheng
Anyi
Luoyang
341 BC
354 BC
Shangqiu
QIN
Qin
Xianyang
Chang'an
QIN MTS
207 BC
Xinzheng
Pei
SONG conquered by Chu, 286 BC
Daliang
Lake Hongze
Huai
Gaixia 202 BC
Guangling
Nanjing
HAN conquered by Qin, 230 BC
Shouchun
Lake Tai
Wu
Han
SHU conquered by Qin, 316 BC
DABA MTS
CHU conquered by Qin, 223 BC
Danyang
Guiji
Shu
Ying
Nanjun
Yangtze
Pengli
AD 219
Red Cliffs AD 208
Lake Dongting
Lake Pengli
Ba
independent mountain tribes conquered by Han, 136–82 BC
Lingling
Guiyang
conquered by Han, 110 BC
Viets
conquered by Qin, 213–209 BC
Yizhou
MIN-YUE
Thai-speaking tribes
Nanhai
Viets
NAN-YUE
Jiaozhi
Zhuyai
Hainan
Juizhen
0 600 km
0 400 mi

The costs of territorial expansion and campaigns against the nomads put the economy under strain and were responsible for the dynasty's temporary overthrow by Wang Mang in AD 9. The Later Han period (AD 23–220) saw a recovery but the empire's economic problems resurfaced in the 2nd century and peasant rebellions became more common after 126. The emperors were isolated from events by elaborate court ritual and power passed to the generals and court factions. In 189 two provincial warlords seized the capital and the empire collapsed into anarchy. The last, powerless Han emperor was deposed in 220 and the empire broke up into three kingdoms.

The most important cultural development of the Warring States period was the establishment of Confucianism as the basis of Chinese pilosophical and ethical thought. The culture of the Han period was conservative but it saw the development of the first systematic history writing in China, exemplified by the *Historical Records* of Sima Qian.

1 Qin was the first capital of the Qin state, but the imperial capital was moved to Xianyang to the east.

2 At the battle of Gaoping in 260 BC, the Qin reputedly buried alive 400,000 Zhao soldiers.

3 Luoyang, the Zhou capital, was also the capital of the Later Han.

4 Early walls to protect northern China from the nomads were earth ramparts; the stone Great Wall was not built until the 16th century AD.

5 At Gaixia in 202, Liu Bang defeated his rival Xiang Yu and consolidated Han authority over China.

6 Chinese campaigns to central Asia had a major aim of capturing horses for breeding.

7 Peasant colonies, such as Luolang (now Pyongyang), were founded to consolidate the Han hold on newly conquered territory.

8 In 117–110 BC, a new wall was built to protect the Gansu corridor, China's main route to the west.

See also 1.27 (Zhou China); 2.20 (steppe peoples) 2.25 (the celestial empire)

.25 China disunited and the rise of Japan • AD 220 – 600 •

China's "period of disunion" between the fall of the Han dynasty in 220 and the reunification of the empire under the Sui in 589 saw constant warfare and nomad invasion. It was also critically important in Chinese cultural and economic history.

None of the warlords whose rivalries had brought down the Han could command universal allegiance, and the empire split into three kingdoms. The strongest – and the most populous – was the northern state of Wei, which included the wealthy Yellow river valley. The weakest and least populated kingdom was Shu, which relied on its mountainous frontiers for protection. Wu was the largest by area but its population was only slightly more than that of Shu. Each kingdom considered itself the legitimate successor to the Han, and wars between them were frequent and devastating: many towns were ruined and the total population of China fell sharply.

The first kingdom to fall was Shu. In 263 the Wei general, Sima Yen, sent an army through hundreds of kilometers of trackless mountain country to descend unexpectedly on Chengdu, the Shu capital. Shu capitulated but many of its nobles and troops fled west, eventually finding a refuge in Persia. Two years later Sima Yen seized power in Wei and, as Wudi (r.265–89), became the first emperor of the Jin dynasty. Wudi's main interest was his harem but he found time to conquer Wu in 280, briefly reuniting China. Shortly after Wudi's death, civil wars broke out between his sons, reaching their peak in the "rebellion of the eight princes" (291–306). To support their struggles the princes recruited troops from among the steppe peoples, but this made the weakness of the empire only too obvious to the nomads, who turned on their employers: northern China fragmented into a mosaic of Chinese and nomad states. Southern China stayed under the stable but oppressive rule of the Jin dynasty until 420, after which several short-lived dynasties ruled until 589.

The destruction afflicting northern China caused large numbers of landowners and peasants to flee

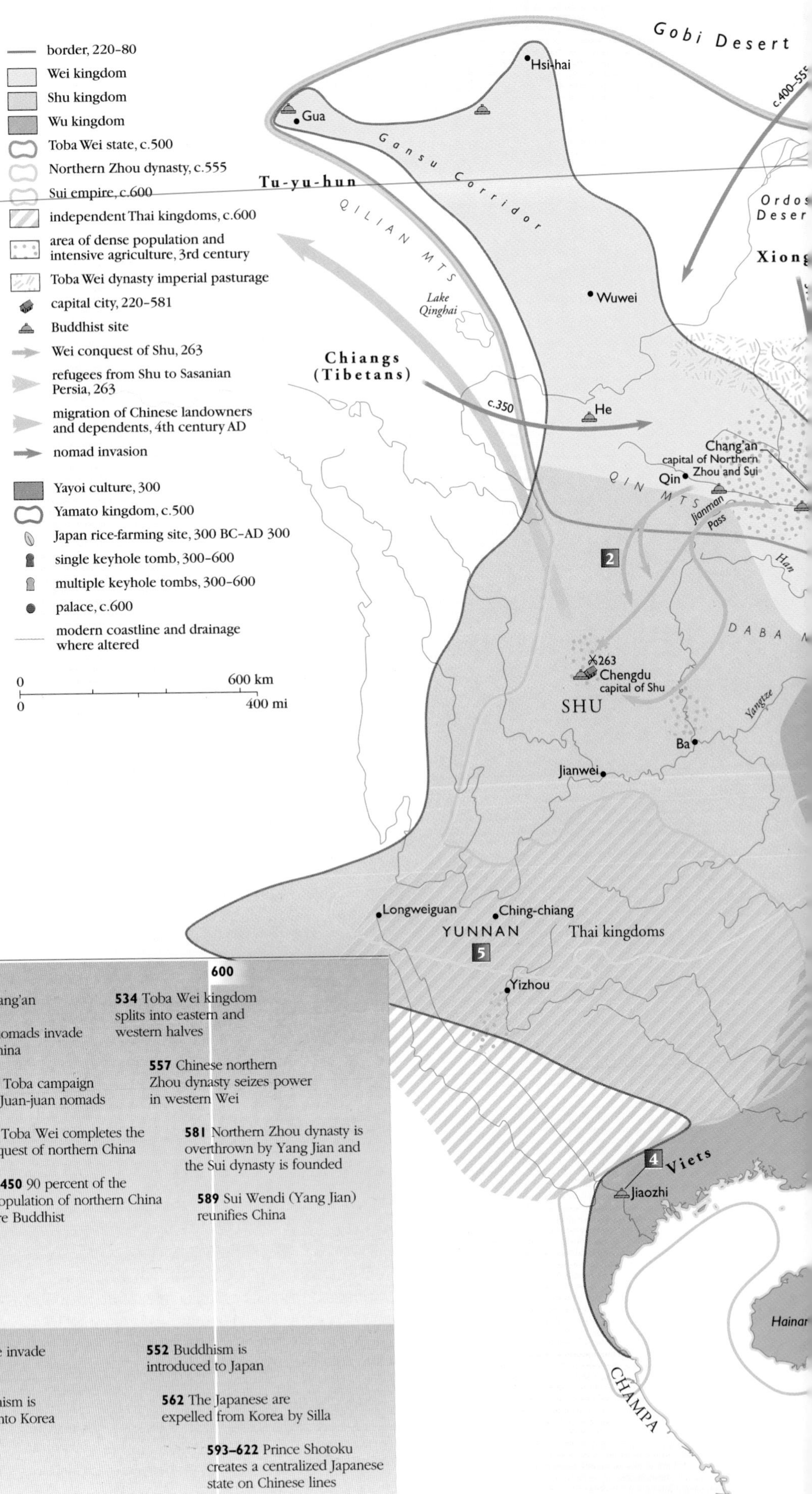

border, 220–80
Wei kingdom
Shu kingdom
Wu kingdom
Toba Wei state, c.500
Northern Zhou dynasty, c.555
Sui empire, c.600
independent Thai kingdoms, c.600
area of dense population and intensive agriculture, 3rd century
Toba Wei dynasty imperial pasturage
capital city, 220–581
Buddhist site
Wei conquest of Shu, 263
refugees from Shu to Sasanian Persia, 263
migration of Chinese landowners and dependents, 4th century AD
nomad invasion
Yayoi culture, 300
Yamato kingdom, c.500
Japan rice-farming site, 300 BC–AD 300
single keyhole tomb, 300–600
multiple keyhole tombs, 300–600
palace, c.600
modern coastline and drainage where altered
0
600 km
0
400 mi
Gobi Desert
Hsi-hai
Gua
Gansu Corridor
Tu-yu-hun
QILIAN MTS
Ordos Desert
Xiong
Lake Qinghai
Wuwei
Chiangs (Tibetans)
c.350
He
Chang'an capital of Northern Zhou and Sui
Qin
QIN MTS
Jianman Pass
Han
DABA
263
Chengdu capital of Shu
SHU
Yangtze
Ba
Jianwei
Longweiguan
Ching-chiang
YUNNAN
Thai kingdoms
Yizhou
Viets
Jiaozhi
Hainan
CHAMPA

TIMELINE

300 — 600

China

200–300 Growth of Buddhist influence in China

220 Deposition of last Han emperor

263 Kingdom of Wei conquers Shu

265 Jin dynasty comes to power in Wei

280 China is reunified as the kingdom of Jin conquers Wu

291–306 Northern China fragments

311 Xiongnu sack Luoyang

316 Xiongnu sack Chang'an

386 Toba nomads invade northern China

407–49 Toba campaign against Juan-juan nomads

439 Toba Wei completes the conquest of northern China

c.450 90 percent of the population of northern China are Buddhist

534 Toba Wei kingdom splits into eastern and western halves

557 Chinese northern Zhou dynasty seizes power in western Wei

581 Northern Zhou dynasty is overthrown by Yang Jian and the Sui dynasty is founded

589 Sui Wendi (Yang Jian) reunifies China

Neighboring states

239 Embassy from Queen Himiko of Wa (Japan) to China

259 Chinese Buddhists begin to make pilgrimages to India

c. 300 State formation begins in Japan

366 The Japanese invade Korea

c.372 Buddhism is introduced into Korea

552 Buddhism is introduced to Japan

562 The Japanese are expelled from Korea by Silla

593–622 Prince Shotoku creates a centralized Japanese state on Chinese lines

300 — 600

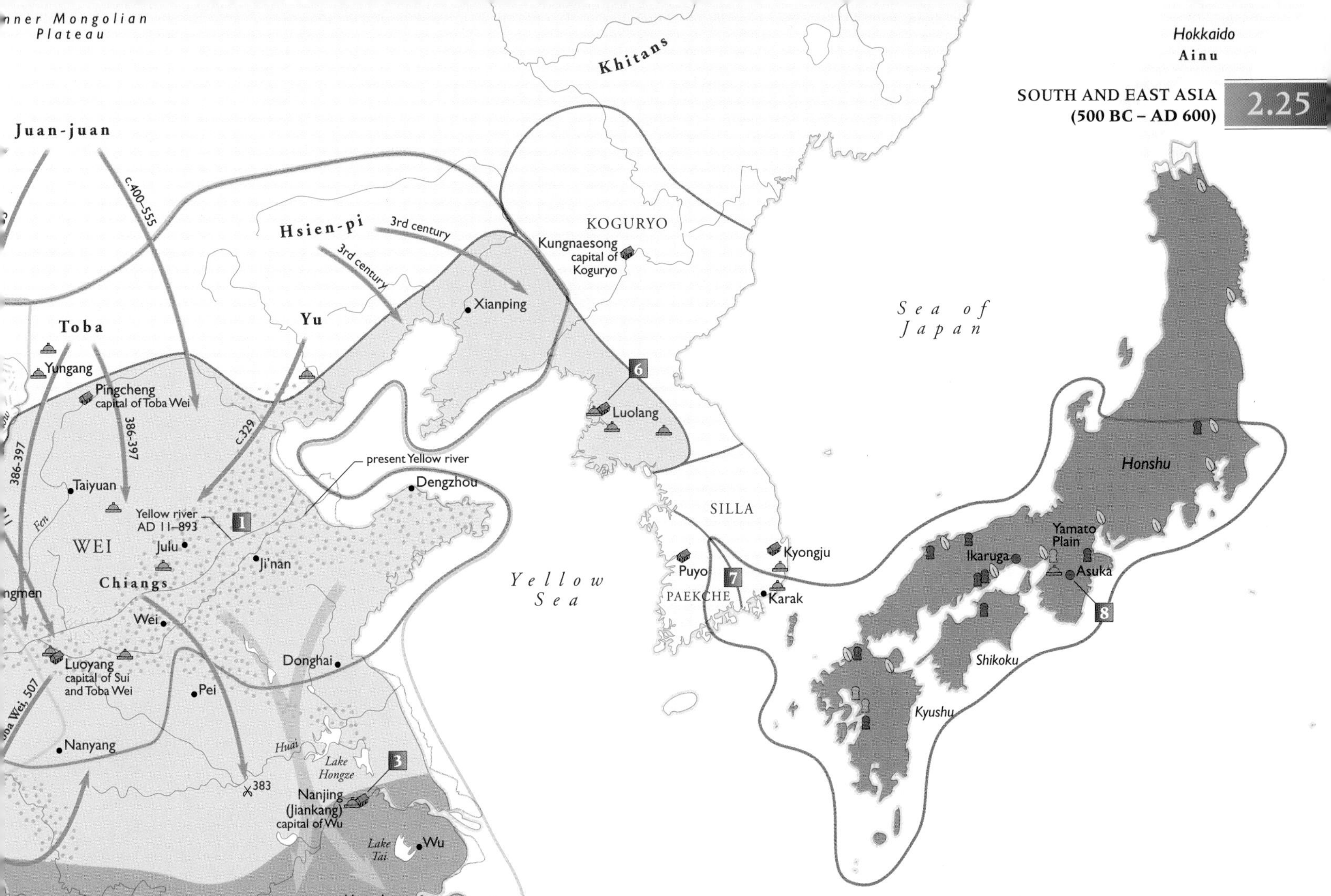

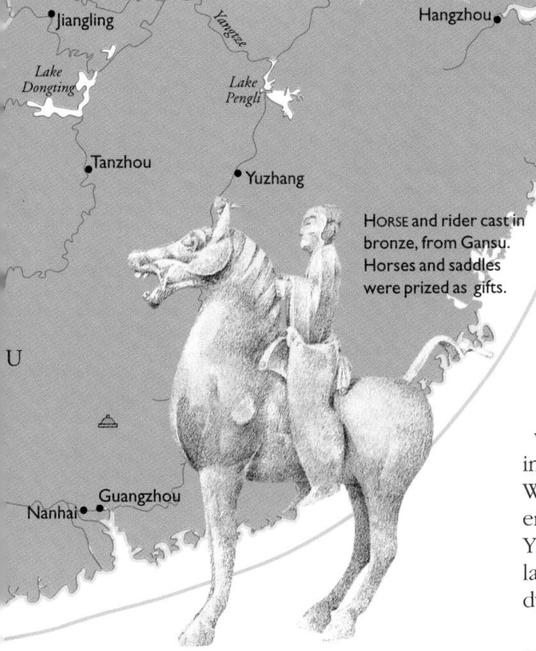

HORSE and rider cast in bronze, from Gansu. Horses and saddles were prized as gifts.

south and settle on the fertile but sparsely populated Yangtze plain. This sparked a period of economic and population growth in southern China which, within a few centuries, saw it overtake the north as the most populous and prosperous part of China.

The position in the north began to stabilize after the Toba, a Turkic nomad confederation, invaded the north in 386–97 and re-established the Wei state. The Toba were a small minority among the Chinese population and they had little administrative expertise. However, they gained the cooperation of the northern landowners who saw the restoration of strong government as a way to protect their interests against a discontented peasantry. The Toba knew that their power depended on military strength, and large areas of the state were reserved as pasture for cavalry horses. The Toba were quickly assimilated into Chinese culture and behaved much like any other Chinese dynasty, defending the northern frontier effectively against the powerful Juan-juan nomad confederacy and launching many campaigns to extend their authority over all of China. The Toba Wei state split into eastern and western halves after a civil war in 534. The Chinese Northern Zhou dynasty seized power in western Wei in 557. The Northern Zhou expanded into southwest China and in 577 conquered eastern Wei, reuniting the north. Four years later the Northern Zhou were overthrown by one of their generals, Yang Jian, who founded the Sui dynasty. In 589 he launched a campaign against the southern Chen dynasty and reunified China under his rule.

The major cultural development of this period of disunion was the rise of Buddhism. Buddhism was introduced into China in the 1st century AD but it only became popular after the fall of the Han: its emphasis on personal salvation and otherworldliness being attractive to a deeply troubled society. Buddhism introduced Indian art, architecture, philosophy and science and was the strongest outside influence on China before the 19th century AD.

While China was undergoing disunion, the first states appeared in Japan. Complex societies began to develop in Japan in the Yayoi culture (300 BC–AD300) which saw rice farming become established in Kyushu, Honshu and Shikoku. Early in the Yamato period (AD 300–710) large tombs appeared (called "keyhole tombs" for their shape) with rich furnishings, pointing to the existence of powerful chiefdoms and small states. By the end of the 4th century the rulers of the Yamato plain in Honshu had created an extended kingdom. The Chinese script was adopted and in about 552 Buddhism was introduced from Korea. At the end of the 6th century, Prince Shotoku transformed the Yamato kingdom by strengthening the authority of the court over the provincial nobles and building an administration based on the Chinese model. He also promoted Chinese esthetic values, and introduced Chinese craftworkers and the Chinese calendar.

1 The fertile, densely populated river region made Wei the most powerful kingdom in the 3rd century.

2 The Wei conquest of Shu involved forced marches through difficult terrain.

3 Nanjing (Jiankang) was capital of southern Chinese dynasties 220–280 and 317–589 and was a major cultural center.

4 The Viets, an Austroasiatic people, carried out an unsuccessful rebellion against Chinese rule in 541–47.

5 Thai-speaking peoples of Yunnan founded several independent kingdoms by 600, benefitting from Chinese weakness.

6 Luolang became the capital of Koguryo after its capture in 313.

7 The southern Korean peninsula was conquered by the Japanese 366–562.

8 Asuka, capital of the late Yamato kingdom, was a complex of palaces, tombs and temples, c.550–650.

See also 2.06 (spread of Buddhism); 2.24 (the first emperor); 3.20 (Tang China)

2.26 The Pacific and southeast Asia • 2000 BC – AD 600 •

In AD 600 the Austronesian language group spanned the Indian and Pacific oceans. Austronesian-speaking peoples had originated in Taiwan around 3000 BC. The introduction of rice farming from China a millennium earlier led to population growth, followed by expansion into the Philippines, Indonesia and Malaysia, where Austronesians had become the dominant peoples by about 2000 BC. In the early first millennium BC Austronesians settled the coast of modern Vietnam and in the 1st century AD Austronesians from the Indonesian archipelago sailed west to colonize the uninhabited island of Madagascar.

Australia, New Guinea and the Solomon Islands had been settled many millennia earlier by Australoid peoples. Around 2000 BC Austronesians began moving into the coastal regions of New Guinea (they did not penetrate the highlands) and the islands. The Lapita culture (named for a site in New Caledonia), characterized by tools of shell and by distinctive pottery, developed here around 1600. By 1000 the Lapita culture had spread eastward to New Caledonia, Fiji, Samoa and Tonga. This migration probably followed the inventions of the sail-powered canoe with outrigger and the twin-hulled voyaging canoe.

The Australian Aborigines remained (except in the far north) isolated from the rest of the world, and the hunter–gatherer way of life established at least 40,000 years ago survived, adapting to environmental changes, until European contact in the 18th century AD. Differing styles of art have been found widely dispersed across the continent.

In the middle of the first millennium BC the Lapita culture-area began to divide. In the west the culture was absorbed into the diverse cultural traditions of the long-established Australoid peoples, ancestors of the modern Melanesians. In the Fiji–Samoa–Tonga triangle the Lapita developed into the ancestral Polynesian culture. The early Polynesians lived

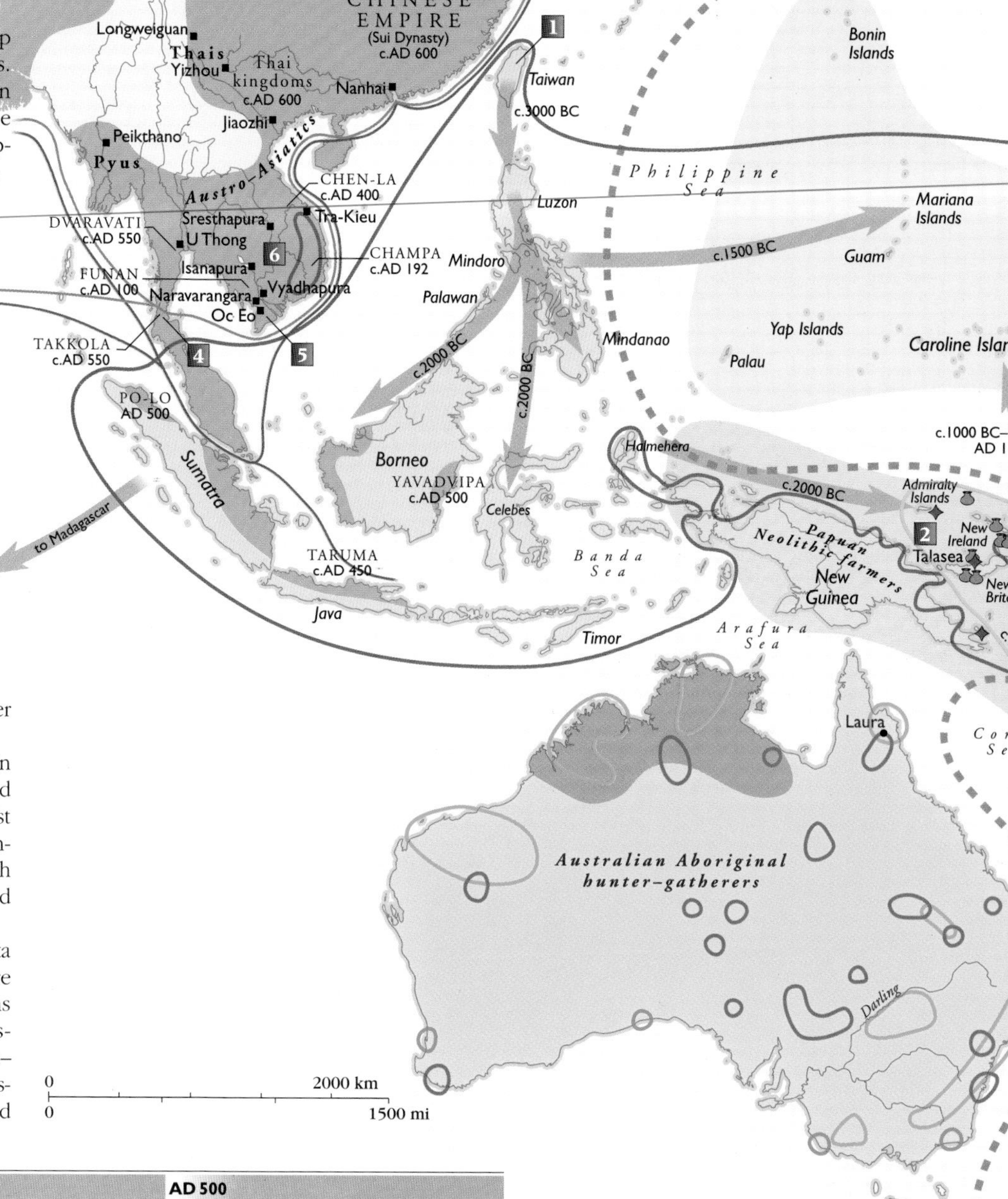
CHINESE EMPIRE
(Sui Dynasty)
c.AD 600
Longweiguan
Thais
Yizhou
Thai kingdoms
c.AD 600
Nanhai
Jiaozhi
Peikthano
Pyus
Austro-Asiatics
CHEN-LA
c.AD 400
Tra-Kieu
DVARAVATI
c.AD 550
Sresthapura
U Thong
Isanapura
CHAMPA
c.AD 192
FUNAN
c.AD 100
Naravarangara
Vyadhapura
Oc Eo
TAKKOLA
c.AD 550
PO-LO
AD 500
Sumatra
to Madagascar
TARUMA
c.AD 450
Java
Borneo
YAVADVIPA
c.AD 500
Celebes
Banda Sea
Timor
Arafura Sea
Taiwan
c.3000 BC
Luzon
Mindoro
Palawan
Mindanao
c.2000 BC
Philippine Sea
c.1500 BC
Mariana Islands
Guam
Bonin Islands
Yap Islands
Palau
Caroline Islands
c.1000 BC–AD 1
Halmehera
c.2000 BC
Admiralty Islands
New Ireland
Talasea
New Britain
Papuan Neolithic farmers
New Guinea
Laura
Australian Aboriginal hunter–gatherers
Darling
Tasmania
Tasmanian hunter–gatherers
0 2000 km
0 1500 mi
1
2
4
5
6

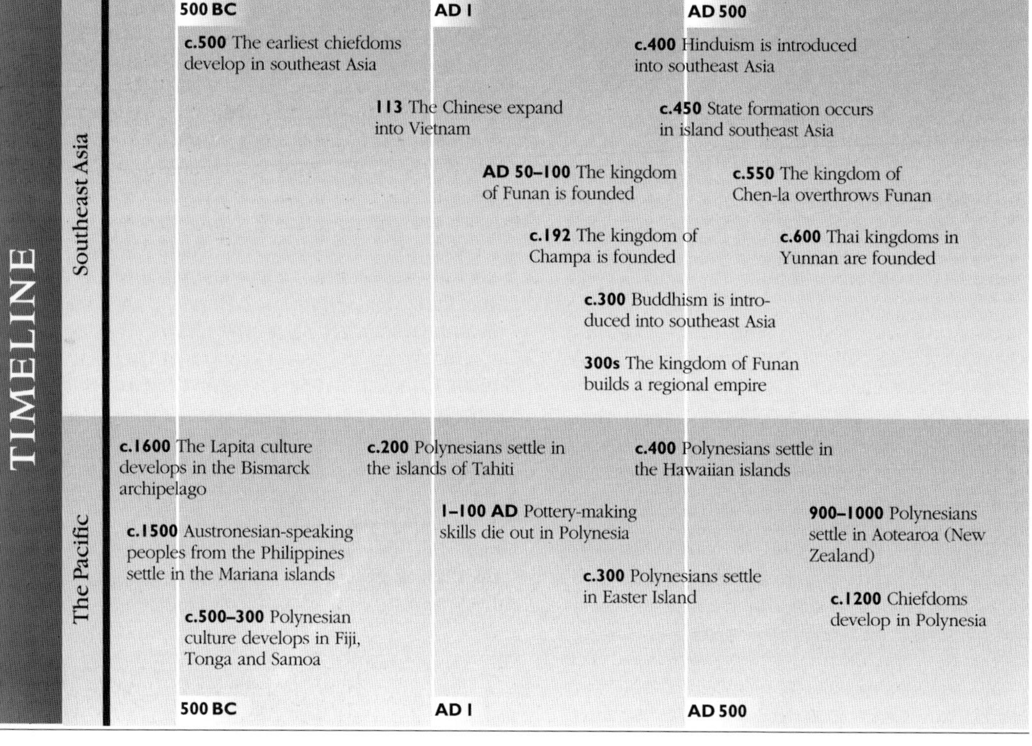

TIMELINE

	500 BC	AD 1	AD 500
Southeast Asia	**c.500** The earliest chiefdoms develop in southeast Asia	**113** The Chinese expand into Vietnam; **AD 50–100** The kingdom of Funan is founded; **c.192** The kingdom of Champa is founded; **c.300** Buddhism is introduced into southeast Asia; **300s** The kingdom of Funan builds a regional empire	**c.400** Hinduism is introduced into southeast Asia; **c.450** State formation occurs in island southeast Asia; **c.550** The kingdom of Chen-la overthrows Funan; **c.600** Thai kingdoms in Yunnan are founded
The Pacific	**c.1600** The Lapita culture develops in the Bismarck archipelago; **c.1500** Austronesian-speaking peoples from the Philippines settle in the Mariana islands; **c.500–300** Polynesian culture develops in Fiji, Tonga and Samoa	**c.200** Polynesians settle in the islands of Tahiti; **1–100 AD** Pottery-making skills die out in Polynesia; **c.300** Polynesians settle in Easter Island	**c.400** Polynesians settle in the Hawaiian islands; **900–1000** Polynesians settle in Aotearoa (New Zealand); **c.1200** Chiefdoms develop in Polynesia

1 Austronesian languages originated in Taiwan before 3000 BC and began to spread through the southeast Asian islands before 2000 BC.

2 The Lapita culture originated in the Bismarck archipelago (New Britain and New Ireland) c.1600 BC and by 1000 had spread to New Caledonia, Fiji and Tonga.

3 Polynesian culture developed in the Fiji-Samoa-Tonga triangle c.500–300 BC, but was later displaced in Fiji by waves of Melanesian settlers.

4 Important trade routes crossed the Kra isthmus in the early centuries AD, stimulating the growth of several small short-lived kingdoms.

5 Oc Eo was a major trading port in the 2nd and 3rd centuries AD, declining in the 4th century when trade routes shifted to the Malacca straits.

6 By AD 400 the kingdom of Funan dominated most of the territory of modern Cambodia and Thailand.

7 Powerful chiefdoms, megalithic monuments and a system of pictographic writing developed on Easter island in the 17th century AD.

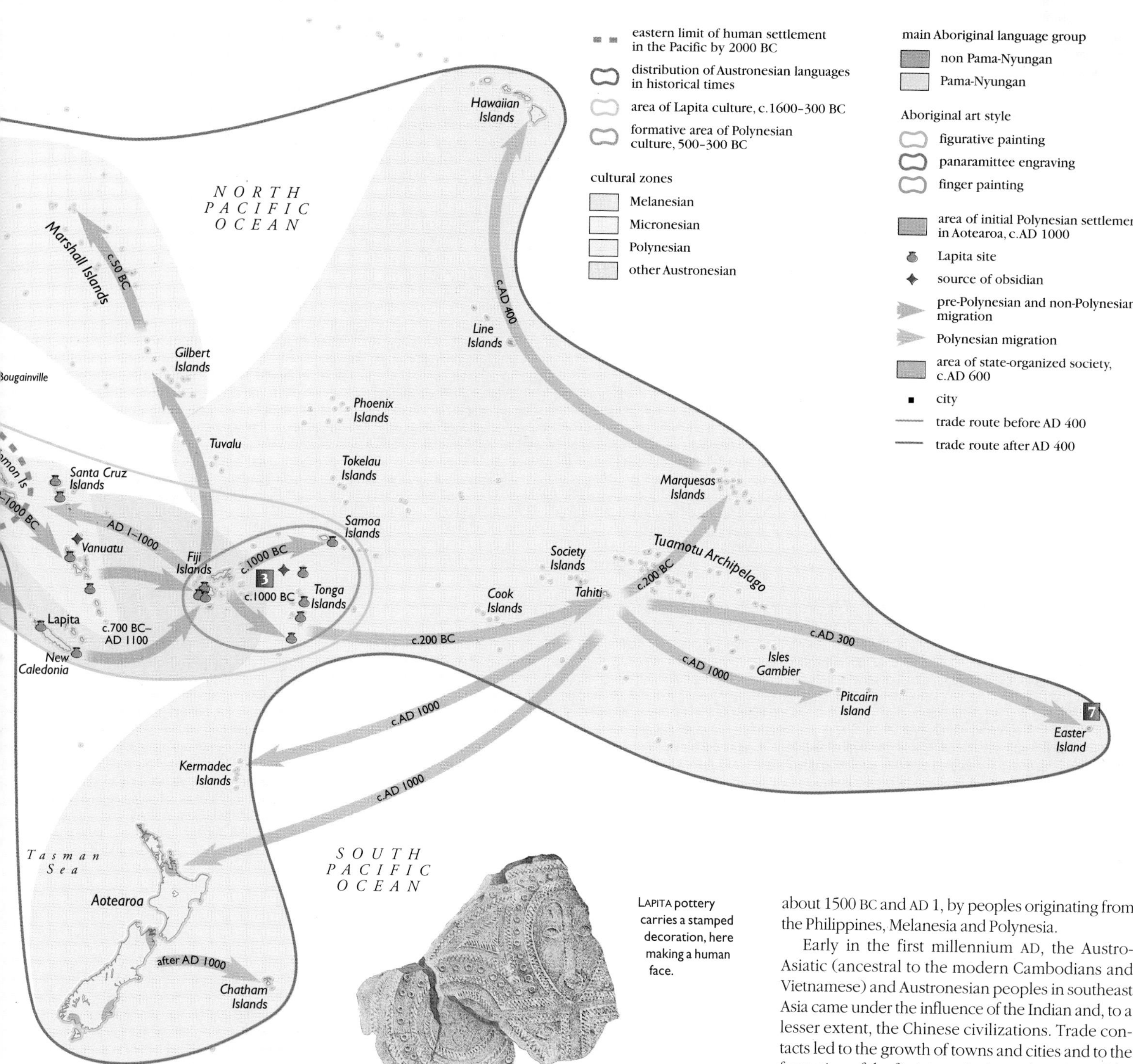
eastern limit of human settlement in the Pacific by 2000 BC
distribution of Austronesian languages in historical times
area of Lapita culture, c.1600–300 BC
formative area of Polynesian culture, 500–300 BC
cultural zones
Melanesian
Micronesian
Polynesian
other Austronesian
main Aboriginal language group
non Pama-Nyungan
Pama-Nyungan
Aboriginal art style
figurative painting
panaramittee engraving
finger painting
area of initial Polynesian settlement in Aotearoa, c.AD 1000
Lapita site
source of obsidian
pre-Polynesian and non-Polynesian migration
Polynesian migration
area of state-organized society, c.AD 600
city
trade route before AD 400
trade route after AD 400
NORTH PACIFIC OCEAN
Hawaiian Islands
Marshall Islands
c.50 BC
c.AD 400
Line Islands
Gilbert Islands
Bougainville
Phoenix Islands
Tuvalu
Santa Cruz Islands
Tokelau Islands
Marquesas Islands
AD 1–1000
Samoa Islands
Vanuatu
Fiji Islands
c.1000 BC
3
Tonga Islands
c.1000 BC
Society Islands
Tuamotu Archipelago
c.200 BC
Tahiti
Cook Islands
Lapita
c.700 BC– AD 1100
c.200 BC
c.AD 300
New Caledonia
c.AD 1000
Isles Gambier
Pitcairn Island
7
Easter Island
c.AD 1000
Kermadec Islands
c.AD 1000
Tasman Sea
SOUTH PACIFIC OCEAN
Aotearoa
after AD 1000
Chatham Islands

LAPITA pottery carries a stamped decoration, here making a human face.

by a mixture of farming, fishing and gathering tree-products such as coconuts; their crops and domestic animals – taro, yams, breadfruit, pigs, dogs and chickens – had been brought by their ancestors from southeast Asia.

The Polynesians migrated farther east to Tahiti, the Tuamotu archipelago and the Marquesas Islands by about 200 BC. Polynesian settlement of the Pacific was the result of planned voyages of discovery. Polynesian seafarers accumulated extensive practical knowledge of the stars, weather, ocean wildlife, sea conditions and currents, and this enabled them to navigate accurately across vast distances of open ocean. Easter Island was settled around AD 300 and the Hawaiian islands a hundred years later. The final pulse of Polynesian expansion took place around AD 1000 with the settlement of Aotearoa (New Zealand). Few of the Polynesians' traditional crops would grow in Aotearoa's temperate climate, so the Maoris cultivated native plants and hunted sea mammals and flightless birds. There was also migration westward in the first millennium AD to the Solomon Islands, but the Polynesians here were cut off from the main Polynesian regions by a Melanesian migration from Vanuatu to Fiji around 1100. Some Polynesians probably made contact with the Americas, as the Maoris and eastern Polynesians cultivated the sweet potato, a native of South America. The Polynesians formed simple tribal societies in the colonization period, but by 1200 chiefdoms appeared throughout the region.

The third Pacific culture-area, Micronesia, has a much more confused history but scattered islands of this region seem to have been settled between about 1500 BC and AD 1, by peoples originating from the Philippines, Melanesia and Polynesia.

Early in the first millennium AD, the Austro-Asiatic (ancestral to the modern Cambodians and Vietnamese) and Austronesian peoples in southeast Asia came under the influence of the Indian and, to a lesser extent, the Chinese civilizations. Trade contacts led to the growth of towns and cities and to the formation of the first states in the region. One of the earliest states to emerge was Funan, centered on the lower Mekong, which by AD 100 became an intermediary in trade between China and India. In the 4th century Funan became an imperial power and for a time dominated mainland southeast Asia. Another important kingdom was Champa in southern Vietnam. In the 4th and 5th centuries Champa took advantage of Chinese divisions to launch cross-border raids, but its kings were forced to pay tribute to China after 586. State formation began later in island southeast Asia, but by 600 many small Buddhist- and Hindu-influenced states had arisen in Sumatra, Java and Borneo. An important factor here was a shifting of trade routes away from Funan, south to the Malacca straits in the 4th century.

See also 1.02 (earliest populations); 3.01 (Polynesian migrations); 3.25 (southeast Asia)

The foundations of Mesoamerican civilization were laid in the Middle Preclassic period (900–300 BC) by the Olmec peoples of the Gulf coast and the Zapotecs of the Oaxaca valley. The influence of the Olmec civilization had declined by the start of the Late Preclassic (300–1 BC), but the Zapotec remained influential, particularly with regard to its hieroglyphic script. However, by the end of the period the Zapotec civilization was overshadowed by Teotihuacán and the Maya.

Teotihuacán first appeared around 200 BC as one of many large, prosperous farming communities in the fertile and well watered Valley of Mexico. The growth of Teotihuacán began at the beginning of the Classic period (AD 1–650), when a monumental ceremonial center, palaces and a large urban settlement were built on a carefully planned grid pattern. At its peak around AD 500, Teotihuacán covered twenty square kilometers (eight square miles) – a greater area than ancient Rome, although with a rather smaller population (between one and two hundred thousand). Considerable areas of the city were devoted to craft workshops, including those of obsidian workers, potters, stonemasons, plasterers and bricklayers. The city also contained quarters for foreign residents, such as Zapotec merchants. Trade was important to Teotihuacán, and it is likely that the caste of armed merchants, known in Aztec times as *pochteca*, had their origins there.

In its heyday Teotihuacán was the most important cultural, religious and economic center in Mesoamerica. The art, architecture, religions and costume of the Olmec, Maya and Zapotecs all show the influence of Classic Teotihuacán. Although the Teotihuacán civilization was probably literate, no inscriptions or other written records have survived. For unknown reasons – possibly soil erosion caused by overcultivation and deforestation – Teotihuacán began to decline around AD 600. Soon after 700 the city was sacked and burned, probably by forces from the nearby city of Cholula. The site continued to be occupied on a small scale, but by the time of the Aztecs – the cultural heirs of Teotihuacán – its origins had been forgotten.

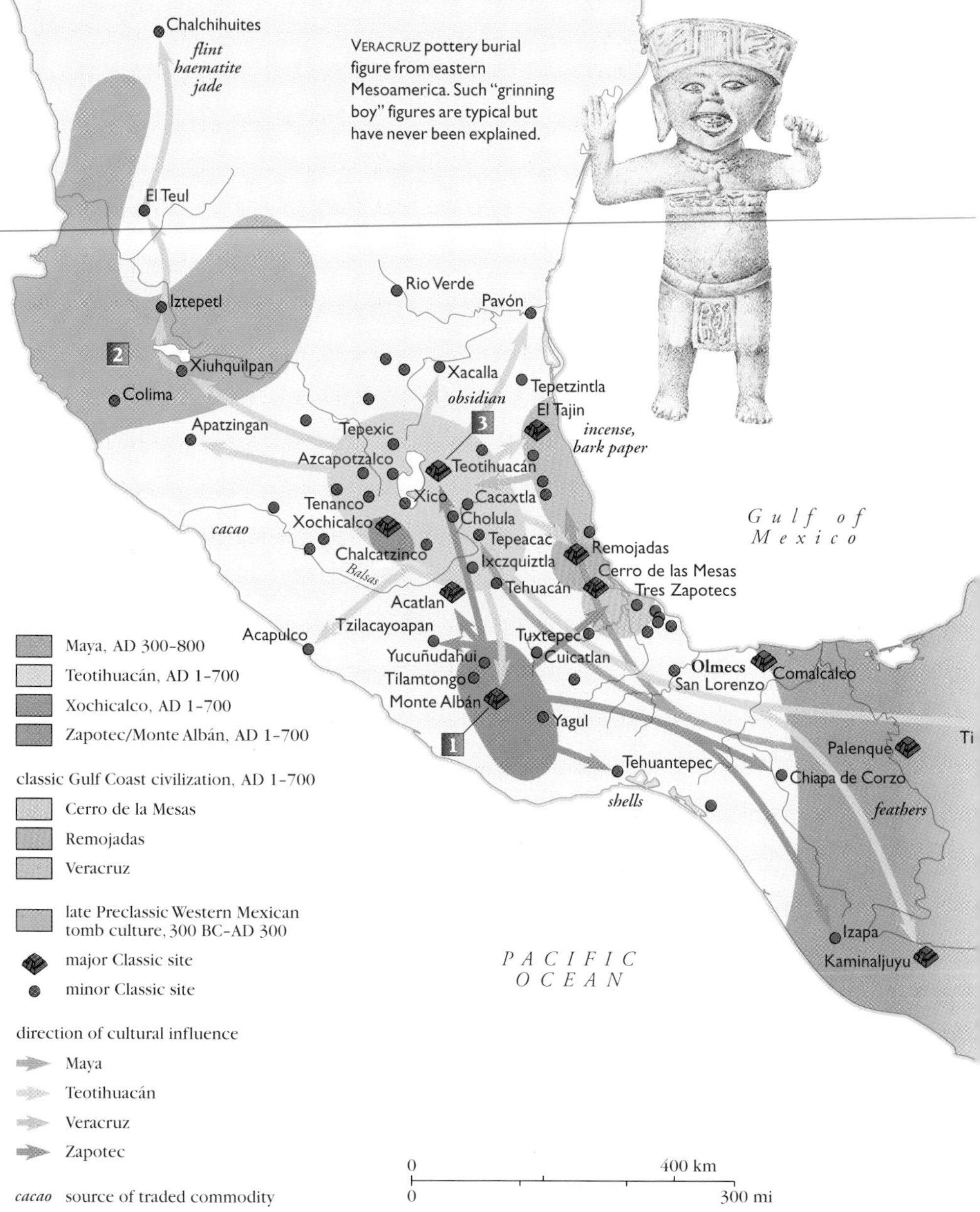
Chalchihuites
flint
haematite
jade
El Teul
Iztepetl
Xiuhquilpan
Colima
Apatzingan
Rio Verde
Pavón
Xacalla
obsidian
Tepetzintla
El Tajín
incense, bark paper
Tepexic
Azcapotzalco
Teotihuacán
Tenanco
Xico
Cacaxtla
Cholula
Xochicalco
cacao
Chalcatzinco
Balsas
Tepeacac
Ixczquiztla
Remojadas
Cerro de las Mesas
Tres Zapotecs
Tehuacán
Acatlan
Tzilacayoapan
Acapulco
Tuxtepec
Cuicatlan
Yucuñudahui
Tilamtongo
Monte Albán
Yagul
Olmecs
San Lorenzo
Comalcalco
Tehuantepec
shells
Palenque
Chiapa de Corzo
feathers
Izapa
Kaminaljuyu
Gulf of Mexico
PACIFIC OCEAN
1
2
3
Maya, AD 300–800
Teotihuacán, AD 1–700
Xochicalco, AD 1–700
Zapotec/Monte Albán, AD 1–700
classic Gulf Coast civilization, AD 1–700
Cerro de la Mesas
Remojadas
Veracruz
late Preclassic Western Mexican tomb culture, 300 BC–AD 300
major Classic site
minor Classic site
direction of cultural influence
Maya
Teotihuacán
Veracruz
Zapotec
cacao source of traded commodity
0 400 km
0 300 mi

VERACRUZ pottery burial figure from eastern Mesoamerica. Such "grinning boy" figures are typical but have never been explained.

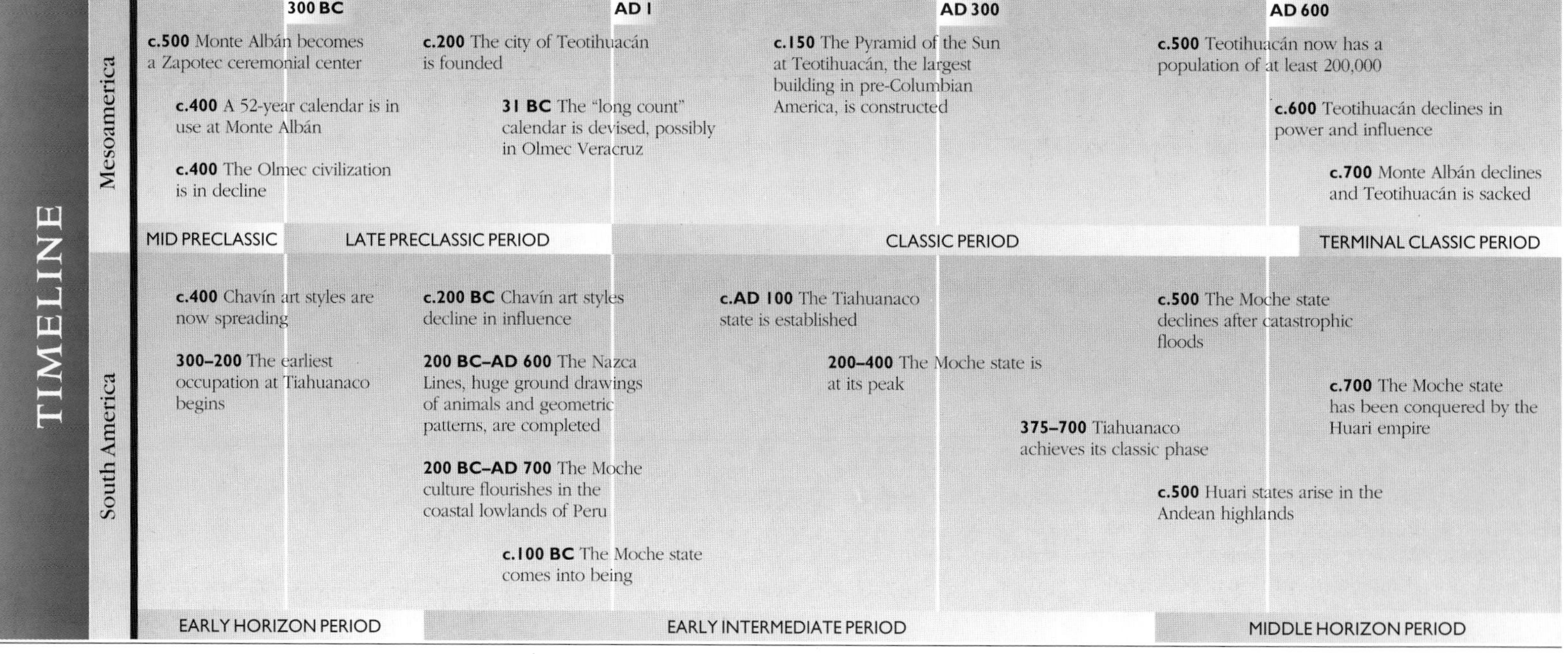

TIMELINE

300 BC | AD 1 | AD 300 | AD 600

Mesoamerica

c.500 Monte Albán becomes a Zapotec ceremonial center

c.400 A 52-year calendar is in use at Monte Albán

c.400 The Olmec civilization is in decline

c.200 The city of Teotihuacán is founded

31 BC The "long count" calendar is devised, possibly in Olmec Veracruz

c.150 The Pyramid of the Sun at Teotihuacán, the largest building in pre-Columbian America, is constructed

c.500 Teotihuacán now has a population of at least 200,000

c.600 Teotihuacán declines in power and influence

c.700 Monte Albán declines and Teotihuacán is sacked

MID PRECLASSIC | LATE PRECLASSIC PERIOD | CLASSIC PERIOD | TERMINAL CLASSIC PERIOD

South America

c.400 Chavín art styles are now spreading

300–200 The earliest occupation at Tiahuanaco begins

c.200 BC Chavín art styles decline in influence

200 BC–AD 600 The Nazca Lines, huge ground drawings of animals and geometric patterns, are completed

200 BC–AD 700 The Moche culture flourishes in the coastal lowlands of Peru

c.100 BC The Moche state comes into being

c.AD 100 The Tiahuanaco state is established

200–400 The Moche state is at its peak

375–700 Tiahuanaco achieves its classic phase

c.500 The Moche state declines after catastrophic floods

c.500 Huari states arise in the Andean highlands

c.700 The Moche state has been conquered by the Huari empire

EARLY HORIZON PERIOD | EARLY INTERMEDIATE PERIOD | MIDDLE HORIZON PERIOD

Intensive irrigation-based agriculture and powerful chiefdoms, sophisticated artistic and architectural traditions all developed in many areas of the central Andes during the Initial period (1800–800 BC) and Early Horizon period (800–200 BC). The dominant cultural influence over a wide area of highland and coastal Peru by about 400 BC was the Chavín art style; its declined about 200 BC and it was succeeded by a variety of local styles.

The decline of Chavín influence marks the start of the Early Intermediate period (200 BC–AD 500), which saw the first states and empires in South America. Warfare was more prevalent and large fortifications were built through the region. The earliest state formed around the coastal site of Moche in about 100 BC. Moche was a vast ceremonial center, including two huge adobe (mud brick) platforms: the pyramids of the Sun and the Moon. Between the two is a cemetery which has yielded richly furnished royal burials. Moche craftsmen were among the most skilled in the New World, producing fine polychrome ceramics, textiles and metalwork in gold, silver and copper. Some pottery was mass-produced using molds. Moche craftsmen were full-time specialists, some of whom worked in teams under the direction of supervisors, while laborers were drafted for work on major public projects as necessary. The Moche economy was based on fishing and agriculture, growing maize, potatoes, cotton, peppers and peanuts in irrigated fields. By AD 200 the Moche culture was spread by conquest to all the neighboring coastal valleys, where provincial capitals and fortresses were built. Moche itself was abandoned around AD 500, after massive flooding, and the capital was moved north to Pampa Grande, where it remained until the Moche state was absorbed by the Huari empire between 600 and 700. At the same time that Moche became an imperial state, other small states were emerging among the coastal Nazca people and among the highland Huarpa and Recuay peoples and, farther south, at Tiahuanaco in the lake Titicaca basin.

The site of Tiahuanaco was first occupied about 300 BC, but its growth as a major power began in the period AD 100–375, when major building and agricultural improvement projects began. At the heart of Tiahuanaco was a precinct of temples, platforms, tombs and palaces around which was a large residential area, housing between twenty and forty thousand people. The outstanding feature of Tiahuanaco architecture is its meticulously finished drystone walls and monolithic sculptures. In its Classic period (AD 375–700) Tiahuanaco built an empire which dominated the southern Andes and extended to the Pacific coast and the edge of the Amazonian rainforest. Expansion to the north was blocked by the rise of the aggressive Huari empire in the 6th century. The motive for the expansion of Tiahuanaco, and all the successive highland empires up to the Inca in the 15th century, was the desire to achieve control over supplies of lowland and coastal products. Both Tiahuanaco and Huari were abandoned around 1000, possibly because of prolonged drought conditions.

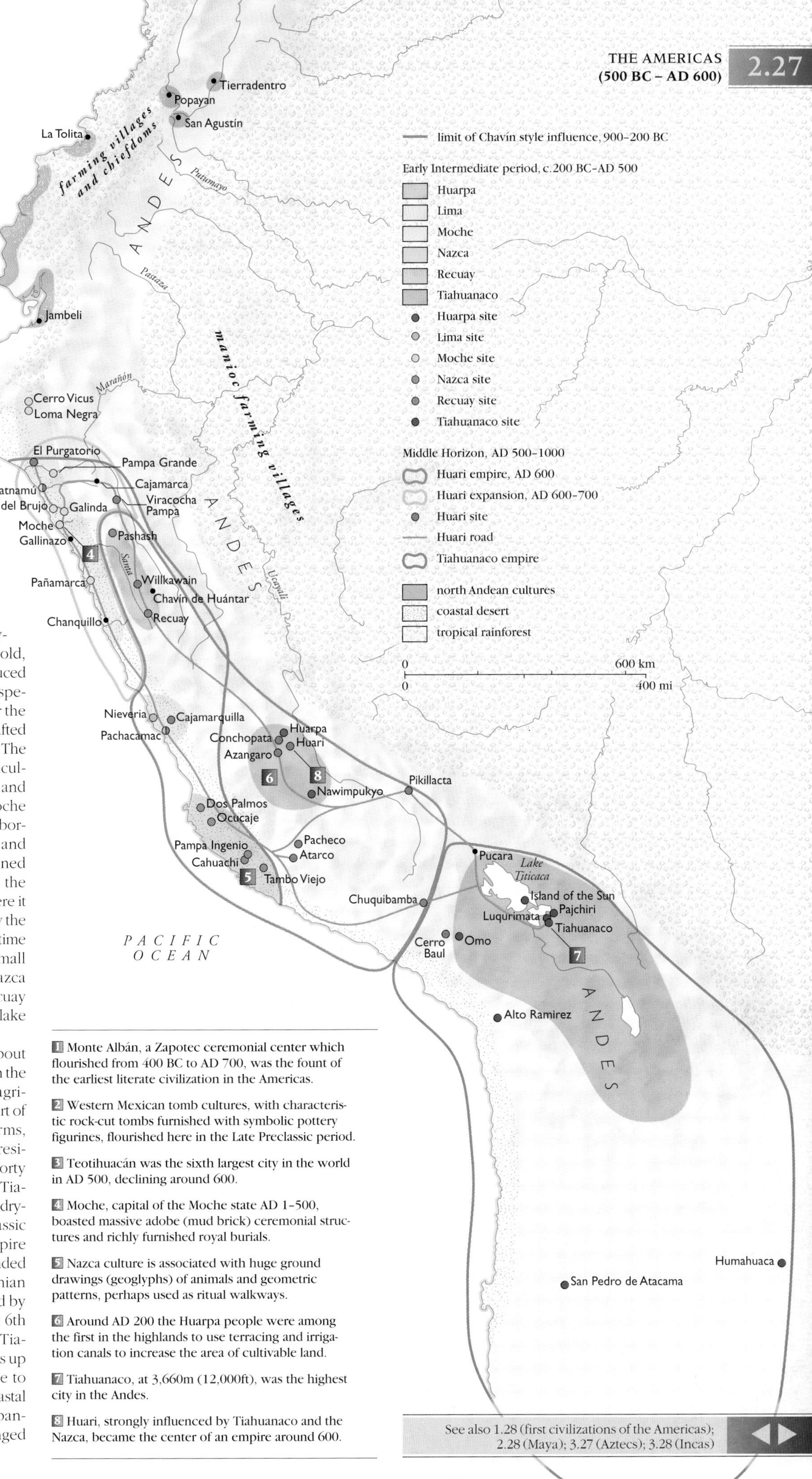
limit of Chavín style influence, 900–200 BC
Early Intermediate period, c.200 BC–AD 500
Huarpa
Lima
Moche
Nazca
Recuay
Tiahuanaco
Huarpa site
Lima site
Moche site
Nazca site
Recuay site
Tiahuanaco site
Middle Horizon, AD 500–1000
Huari empire, AD 600
Huari expansion, AD 600–700
Huari site
Huari road
Tiahuanaco empire
north Andean cultures
coastal desert
tropical rainforest
0 600 km
0 400 mi
Tierradentro
Popayan
San Agustín
La Tolita
farming villages and chiefdoms
Putumayo
ANDES
Pastaza
Jambeli
manioc farming villages
Marañón
Cerro Vicus
Loma Negra
El Purgatorio
Pampa Grande
Cajamarca
Pacatnamú
Huaca del Brujo
Galinda
Viracocha Pampa
Moche
Gallinazo
Pashash
Santa
Pañamarca
Willkawain
Chavín de Huántar
Recuay
Chanquillo
Ucayali
Nievería
Cajamarquilla
Pachacamac
Huarpa
Conchopata
Huari
Azangaro
Nawimpukyo
Pikillacta
Dos Palmos
Ocucaje
Pacheco
Atarco
Pampa Ingenio
Cahuachi
Tambo Viejo
Pucara
Lake Titicaca
Island of the Sun
Chuquibamba
Luqurimata
Pajchiri
Tiahuanaco
Cerro Baul
Omo
PACIFIC OCEAN
Alto Ramirez
Humahuaca
San Pedro de Atacama
Aguada
Hualfin

1 Monte Albán, a Zapotec ceremonial center which flourished from 400 BC to AD 700, was the fount of the earliest literate civilization in the Americas.

2 Western Mexican tomb cultures, with characteristic rock-cut tombs furnished with symbolic pottery figurines, flourished here in the Late Preclassic period.

3 Teotihuacán was the sixth largest city in the world in AD 500, declining around 600.

4 Moche, capital of the Moche state AD 1–500, boasted massive adobe (mud brick) ceremonial structures and richly furnished royal burials.

5 Nazca culture is associated with huge ground drawings (geoglyphs) of animals and geometric patterns, perhaps used as ritual walkways.

6 Around AD 200 the Huarpa people were among the first in the highlands to use terracing and irrigation canals to increase the area of cultivable land.

7 Tiahuanaco, at 3,660m (12,000ft), was the highest city in the Andes.

8 Huari, strongly influenced by Tiahuanaco and the Nazca, became the center of an empire around 600.

See also 1.28 (first civilizations of the Americas); 2.28 (Maya); 3.27 (Aztecs); 3.28 (Incas)

2.28 The ancient Maya • 300 BC – AD 800 •

- late Preclassic site with monumental sculpture, 300 BC–AD 300
- other late Preclassic site, 300 BC–AD 300
- area of Classic Maya civilization, AD 300–800
- Puuc style
- Chenes style
- Rio Bec style
- Cotzumalhuapan style
- major Classic site
- minor Classic site
- pre-eminent regional center
- influence of Tikal, 5th century AD
- Tikal dynastic histories deciphered
- city-state border, AD 790
- trade route
- *cacao* source of traded commodity

area with intensive agriculture

- raised fields
- stone-faced terraces

0 200 km
0 150 mi

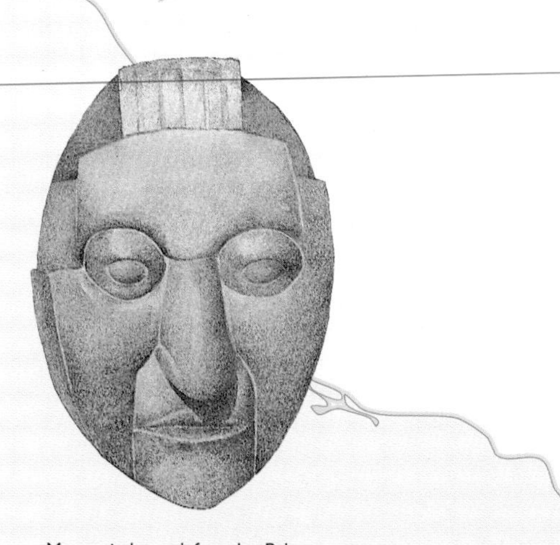

MOSAIC jade mask found at Palenque, possibly a representation of Pacal, ruler of Palenque in the 7th century.

The most sophisticated of the pre-Columbian civilizations of the Americas was the Maya of Guatemala, Petén and Yucatán. By draining and canalizing the swamplands, agricultural production rose in the Middle Preclassic period (700–300 BC), making it possible to support large populations. Chiefdoms and small states appeared and the first towns and monumental structures were built. During the Late Preclassic (300 BC–AD 300) powerful city-states emerged, writing came into use, advanced mathematical and astronomical studies were pursued, and a calendrical system was adopted. The new states were competitive and warlike and many cities were fortified. Underlying these developments may have been such factors as population pressure, agricultural intensification, long-distance trade and increased warfare. The main influences on the development of Mayan civilization were the Olmecs and the Zapotecs, from whom the Maya received, among other things, the 52-year "long count" calendar, writing and the sacred ball game.

The most important Maya center of the Late Preclassic period was the city of El Mirador, occupied 150 BC–AD 150. It had large temple pyramids, a fortified palace area, marketplaces and a population approaching 80,000. Causeways known as *sacbes* linked El Mirador with its subordinate villages. Although there is some evidence of writing at El Mirador, the best evidence for its use by the Preclassic Maya comes from the southern highland area, where many *stelae* (stone monuments) were erected at sites like Kaminaljuyú, in the 1st and 2nd centuries AD, to commemorate royal ancestors. The earliest known inscription, found at El Baul, carries a "long-count" date equivalent to AD 36. The Maya did not invent writing themselves, but their hieroglyphic script was the only pre-Columbian script that could fully express the spoken language. The Mayan script included both ideographic and phonetic elements. About 800 glyphs are known. The southern Maya declined in the 3rd century AD and the tradition of erecting commemorative *stelae* died out. The cause was probably a volcanic eruption that blew apart Mount Ilopango, covering thousands of square kilometers with ash and ruining agriculture for years.

Commemorative *stelae* with hieroglyphic inscriptions began to be erected by the Maya in the central lowland rainforest area around AD 300, a development that marks the beginning of the Classic period (AD 300–800). The earliest show clear stylistic links with the highland Maya. Until about AD 400 *stelae* were only erected at Tikal, Uaxactún and a few nearby centers, but thereafter the practice spread throughout the central area. Palenque, Yaxchilán, Copán and Calakmul all developed into major regional powers, but the dominant city-state for much of the Classic period was Tikal, with a population of 75,000–100,000. At its peak under King Stormy Sky (r.411–57), Tikal dominated most of the central area and maintained cultural and trade links with Teotihuacán, the greatest power in Mesoamerica. Tikal went into decline after its defeat by Caracol in 562; and although it recovered under Ah Cacau (r.682–723) it did not regain its preeminence.

Warfare was common among the Classic Maya city-states, although the aim was more often to exact tribute and take prisoners than to annex territory permanently. The normal fate of prisoners was ritual torture and mutilation, after which they were sacrificed to the gods. Human sacrifices were needed to dedicate new temples, to accompany the dead and to mark important events such as the completion of calendrical cycles. Mayan rulers were expected to take part in painful bloodletting rites as a means of communicating with ancestral spirits. Marriage alliances were the usual means of forging friendly relations between states.

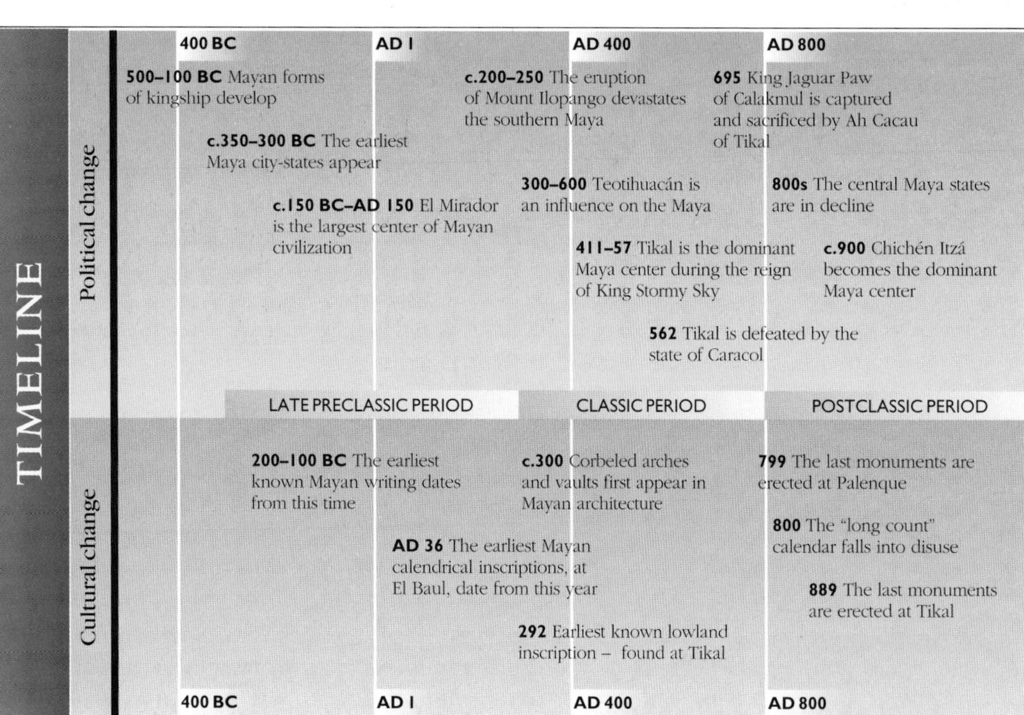

TIMELINE
Political change
400 BC
AD 1
AD 400
AD 800
500–100 BC Mayan forms of kingship develop
c.200–250 The eruption of Mount Ilopango devastates the southern Maya
695 King Jaguar Paw of Calakmul is captured and sacrificed by Ah Cacau of Tikal
c.350–300 BC The earliest Maya city-states appear
300–600 Teotihuacán is an influence on the Maya
800s The central Maya states are in decline
c.150 BC–AD 150 El Mirador is the largest center of Mayan civilization
411–57 Tikal is the dominant Maya center during the reign of King Stormy Sky
c.900 Chichén Itzá becomes the dominant Maya center
562 Tikal is defeated by the state of Caracol
LATE PRECLASSIC PERIOD
CLASSIC PERIOD
POSTCLASSIC PERIOD
Cultural change
200–100 BC The earliest known Mayan writing dates from this time
c.300 Corbeled arches and vaults first appear in Mayan architecture
799 The last monuments are erected at Palenque
800 The "long count" calendar falls into disuse
AD 36 The earliest Mayan calendrical inscriptions, at El Baul, date from this year
889 The last monuments are erected at Tikal
292 Earliest known lowland inscription – found at Tikal
400 BC
AD 1
AD 400
AD 800

1 El Mirador was the largest Maya center in the Late Preclassic period, before being abandoned c.AD 150.

2 Lake Ilopango now fills the crater left by the catastrophic eruption of Mount Ilopango c.AD 200-250, which caused the decline of the southern Maya .

3 Tikal was the largest Maya city. It reached its peak under King Stormy Sky (r.AD 411–57) and dominated the central Maya until conquered by Caracol in 562.

4 Classic Maya ceremonial centers were often aligned on astronomical events. The earliest such center, at Uaxactún, was aligned on the midwinter, equinoctial and midsummer sunrises.

5 Copán, a major Maya center during the Classic period, was supplanted by Quirigua in 738.

6 The raised causeway, or *sacbe*, linking Cobá with Yaxuná runs for some 100 kilometers (62 miles).

7 Murals at Bonampak celebrating a victory of King Chan Muan c.790 provide vivid evidence of the warlike character of Maya civilization.

8 Power and population moved to the north in the Early Postclassic period (AD 900–1200), when Chichén Itzá became the dominant Maya center.

The civilization of the Classic Maya was not uniform: several regional decorative styles are known, and there was considerable variation in architectural styles. The Maya were highly skilled craftsmen, producing monumental stone sculpture, jade carving, pottery, paintings and obsidian tools of the highest quality. A few gold and copper objects have been found at Mayan sites, but metals were little used before Postclassic times.

The Classic period came to an end around the beginning of the 9th century, when the city-states of the central lowlands began to collapse. The population declined dramatically, new building ceased, and the tradition of erecting commemorative *stelae* was abandoned. The last monuments were erected at Palenque in 799, at Yaxchilan in 808, at Quirigua 810, at Copán in 822 and Tikal in 889. By 950 all the major central Mayan cities lay in ruins. The "long count" calendar fell out of use.

The collapse is thought to be an indirect consequence of the fall of Teotihuacán around 750. Mayan rulers competed, through warfare and by commissioning more and more ambitious building projects, to fill the power vacuum created by the fall of Teotihuacán. Pressures on the peasantry to supply food and labor increased to such a point that the agricultural economy collapsed; malnutrition, population decline and political collapse followed. Classic Mayan civilization did not die out, but continued to flourish in the semiarid north of the Yucatán peninsula until around 1000, when the area was invaded by the Toltecs, from central Mexico.

See also 1.28 (first civilizations of Mesoamerica); 2.27 (Teotihuacán); 3.27 (Toltecs and late Maya)

Part 3

THE MEDIEVAL

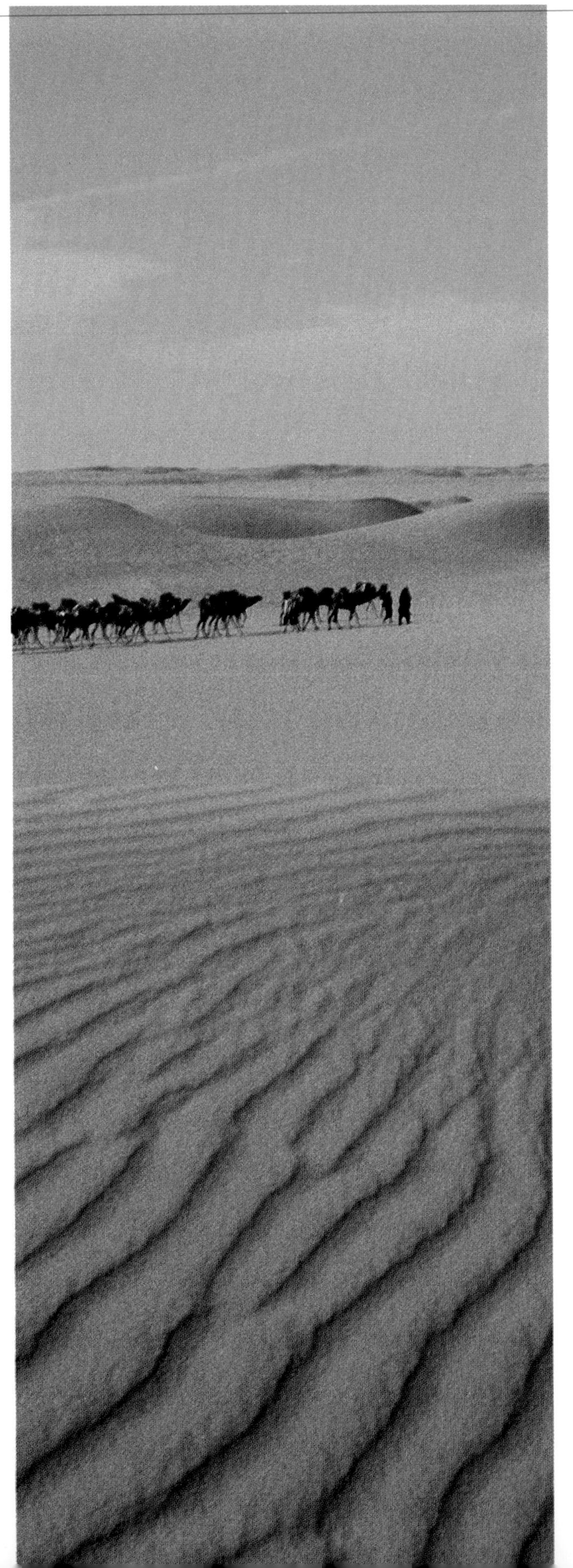

The centuries between 600 and 1492 saw the entire life cycle of several important civilizations. Shortly after 600 the Islamic community was founded in Medina under the leadership of prophet Muhammad. For many centuries Islam and other civilizations farther east were the most dynamic cultures in the world. The year 1492, however, saw the discovery of the Antilles by Christopher Columbus, the prelude to the conquest and settlement of the New World by Europeans. Six years later the Portuguese explorer Vasco da Gama sailed around Africa to the Indian port of Calicut. The foundation of western hegemony was thus laid at the end of the fifteenth century. Two great phases of world expansion, that of Arab people and Islamic civilization, and that of European descendants of Germanic tribes, characterize this period.

Just as the "barbarian" invasions from the 5th century AD led to the eclipse of the classical civilization of western Europe, so the Muslim Arab expansion displaced the political domination of ancient Persian empires in the Middle East and the surviving Roman empire in the eastern Mediterranean. The intensity of the spiritual and material success of Islam is still unexplained, but there is no doubt about its significance. The unification of large parts of the Mediterranean, the Middle East, and the Indian Ocean by the Umayyad and Abbasid caliphates was a great cultural, technological, and economic operation, as well as a political achievement. The spread and usage of Arabic as a language of the *Koran* and of intercultural communication, education, and administration played an important role. The Bedouins of the Arabian peninsula, the Berber converts of north Africa, Arab conquerors in Andalusia, the Copts of Egypt, the Nabateans of Mesopotamia, and the converted Iranians all shared the Koranic prayers recited in Arabic and a common body of family and civil law.

WORLD

AD 600 – 1492

Islam revitalized old urban centers and founded new ones. Both Medina and Mecca attracted a huge concourse of pilgrims each year, while Damascus became the first Islamic capital under the Umayyads, the predominantly Byzantine city being greatly enlarged by successive caliphs. Under the Abbasids, the capital shifted to Baghdad, the first planned capital city to be built by Muslims. This in turn was followed by Samarra. The great urban centers of the Islamic world included Basra, Alexandria, Cairo, Tunis, and Córdoba. Arab writers drew often attention to the splendors of these cities as well as to the forces of their relative decline.

Contemporaries knew that the urban gravitation of Islamic expansion required an economic surplus and food resources. This was achieved by bringing new land under cultivation and reviving existing regions of agricultural production. Arab engineers and farmers proved skillful in constructing irrigation projects. Long, subterranean conduits brought water from the mountains to arid valleys and desert plains and made intensive cultivation of crops possible. The water-lifting machinery known as the Persian wheel also increased efficiency. New plants such as hard wheat, sugar cane, citrus fruits, vegetables, and legumes were imported from India and southeast Asia and disseminated throughout the oasis agriculture of north Africa and in the arid areas of southern Spain. The Islamic green revolution was a notable feat and sustained the new settlements in garrison towns.

Similar developments took place in China and southeast Asia. The Chinese perfected ways of containing and controlling the great rivers of northern China to develop the rice-growing areas of Szechuan and the Yangtze valley. Subsequent demographic expansion, combined with the instability of climate, created an endemic problem of feeding the world's most advanced political empire. The emperors of the Song dynasty were acutely aware that this problem was a product of the previous agricultural success, which had created densely populated cities and rural areas. Relief was provided by the state distribution of food in times of scarcity, and by encouraging the cultivation of a new strain of rice that ripened in sixty days as against the three to six months taken by traditional varieties.

Chinese civilization and administration was a matter of wonder to the rest of the world. China developed a class of professional bureaucratic administrators who were given formal instructions in writing and who had to report to the imperial court through written memoranda. Science, mathematics, and engineering kept pace with the development in the state system. China invented papermaking and the moving-type printing press; its alchemists discovered gunpowder and engineers may also have learned to convert the circular motion generated by a water-driven turbine into the longitudinal motion of a piston capable of pushing and pulling the bellows of a blast-furnace.

China's capacity for industrial production was evident in the quality of its porcelain and silk textiles. The Indian subcontinent had a similar lead in the production of cotton textiles. These products sustained a long-distance trade from the South China Sea to the eastern Mediterranean. Luxury goods were not the only articles of international trade in the Indian Ocean or medieval Europe. Marine risk was minimized by mixing low-value bulk commodities with high-value luxury goods, although caravan traders could most profitably cross the Gobi Desert with valuable porcelain, silk, and foodstuffs. Such an extended system of exchange required emporia where merchants of different nationalities could meet.
A whole network of trading cities grew up in response to these needs. Ports such as Hangzhou were linked to Malacca in the

THE CAMEL CARAVAN made possible the political and cultural unity of north Africa, the Middle East and central Asia, as the Arabs built an empire and spread Islam. It also made possible the overland trade routes that stretched from the heart of China to the Mediterranean world. Europe was peripheral for much of this period.

tip of Malay peninsula. This in turn was connected to the seaports of India, the Persian Gulf and the Red Sea. The city-states on the coast of east Africa completed the final side of this commercial rectangle.

The Mongol conquests of central Asia in the thirteenth century disrupted this trade and thus dealt a severe blow to the ancient civilizations of the Indian Ocean, preparing the way for a resurgent Europe, where Arab intellectual knowledge had slowly penetrated through the intermediary of Jewish scholars and scientists living and working in Spain.

Europe's main contribution to world history to this point was its fighting technique. The adoption of the horse stirrup made it possible gradually to increase the armament of the mounted warrior using a heavy lance. A new breed of powerful horses capable appeared and the mounted knights had such spectacular success in battle during the Crusades that European cavalry tactics were copied by the new class of Middle Eastern warriors. European success in the New World and the Indian Ocean later owed a great deal also to the invention of square-rigged ships armed with artillery capable of not only attacking other vessels at sea but also bombarding towns and cities. The reinforced hull made it possible to pierce gunports and add a gun-deck without encroaching on the vessel's cargo capacity. The result was a floating fortress that was also a floating warehouse.

European expansion and new oceanic discoveries were embedded in a larger process of scientific and intellectual advances. The new navigational methods – the use of compass, marine charts, scientific mapmaking and astronomical navigation – were linked to the invention of the fighting ships which provided the logistical support for the global expansion of the west. As a result, when, in the 15th century, Europeans sought new routes to the east that would avoid the hostile Ottoman lands, the technology was at hand to enable them to dominate these new waters. The consequences were to be dramatically evident in the three centuries after 1500 ■

3.01 THE WORLD • AD 800 •

The years between AD 600 and 800 saw the final breakup of the world of classical antiquity and the dramatic rise of an Arab Islamic civilization. Islam has its origins in the teachings of Muhammad (c.570–632). Islam united the Arabs and created a theocratic state. Despite civil war after the prophet's death, the caliph or "successor" Umar turned Arab energies outward in campaigns of conquest and conversion (▷ *3.13*).

Circumstances were favorable to Arab expansion. From 602 to 627 the Persian Sasanian empire and the surviving eastern half of the Roman empire were locked in total war. The Romans emerged triumphant but the reforms introduced by the emperor Heraclius created an essentially new, Greek, state, known as the Byzantine empire. Neither Persia nor Byzantium was thus in a fit state to withstand the sudden invasions of Arab armies, which began with the capture of Damascus in 635. By 642 the Arabs had captured Syria, Palestine and Egypt from the Byzantines and completely destroyed the Sasanian empire. A second wave of conquests began after the Umayyad dynasty came to power in 661. In 698 Byzantine Carthage fell and in 711 the Arabs crossed the Straits of Gibraltar and conquered the Visigothic kingdom of Spain; in the east Arab armies reached the Indus and Samarkand. Failure to take Constantinople in 717 and defeat by the Franks at Poitiers in 732 marked the end of the Arab victories. The unity of the Arab world ended in 749–50 when the Umayyads were overthrown and slaughtered by the Abbasids, except for one who escaped to Spain and founded an independent state. By 800 the Abbasids had also lost control of Morocco and Tunisia (▷ *3.14*).

In 600 the Frankish kingdom was the leading state in western Europe but dynastic instability led to a decline in the late 7th century (▷ *3.06*). Frankish power recovered under the Carolingian dynasty, named for Charlemagne who controlled most of Christian western Europe and expanded into the pagan lands of eastern Europe. He was crowned Roman emperor by the pope in Rome on Christmas Day, 800. In the British Isles, the Anglo-Saxons confined the Celts to the hilly west. The Scandinavians were beginning state formation, a by-product of which was the onset of Viking raids on western Europe.

China, divided for almost four centuries, was reunited by the Sui dynasty in 589 (▷ *3.20*). The Sui's ambitions overstretched the empire's resources and they were overthrown by the Tang dynasty in 618. China flourished under the early Tang emperors and campaigns in central Asia extended

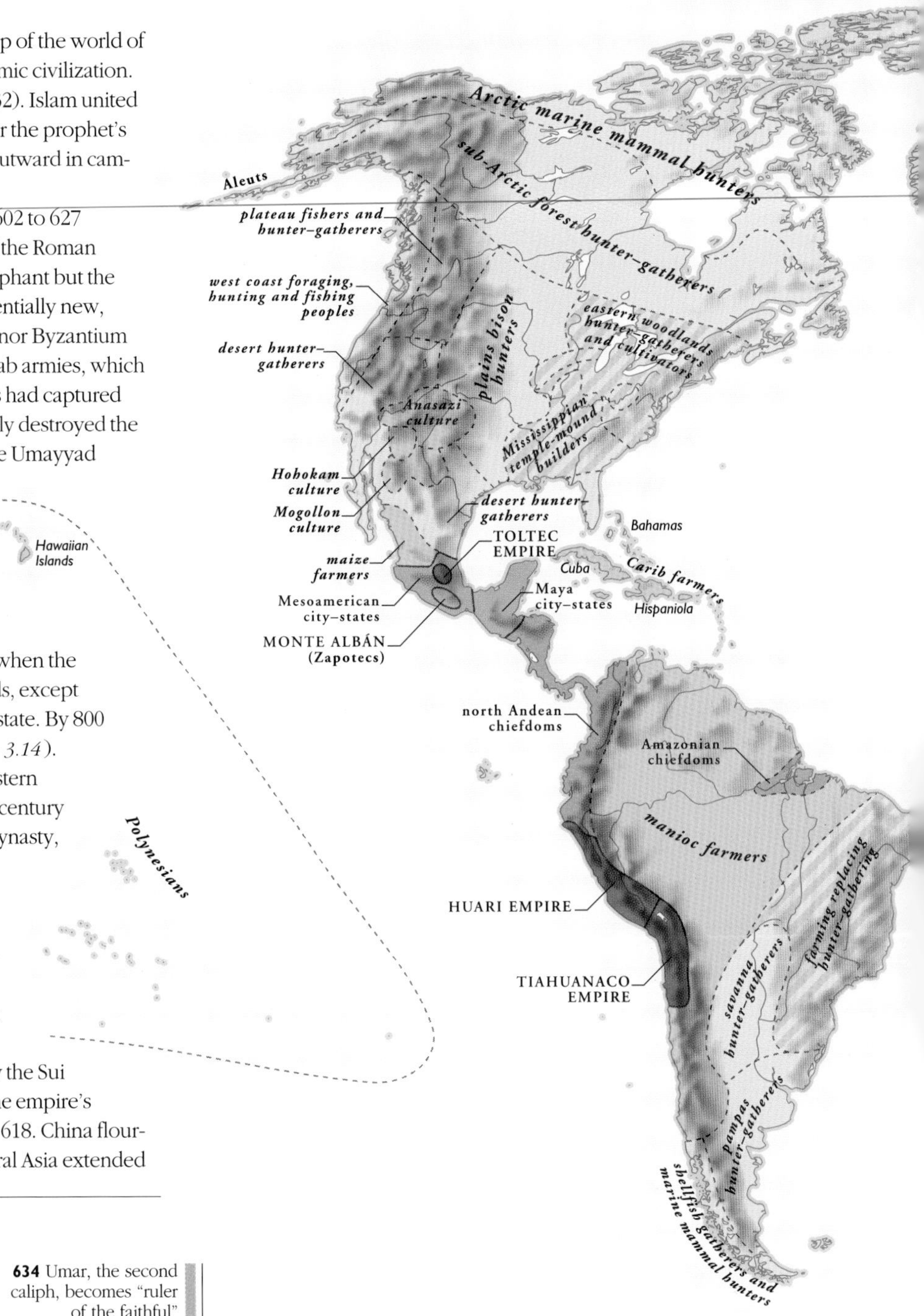

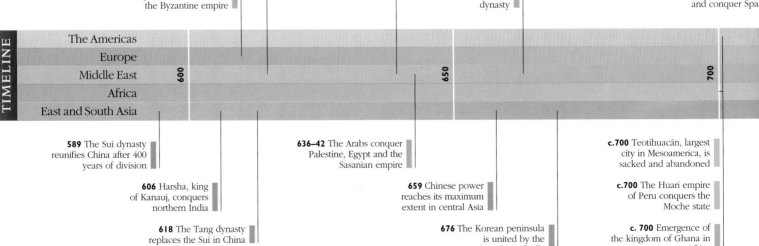

622 Muhammad flees from Mecca to Medina (*hijra*); beginning of the Islamic calendar

634 Umar, the second caliph, becomes "ruler of the faithful"

610 Accession of Heraclius; Eastern Roman empire is now known as the Byzantine empire

661 Caliph Muawiya founds the Umayyad dynasty

711 The Arabs invad and conquer Spai

TIMELINE

The Americas

Europe

Middle East

Africa

East and South Asia

600

650

700

589 The Sui dynasty reunifies China after 400 years of division

636–42 The Arabs conquer Palestine, Egypt and the Sasanian empire

c.700 Teotihuacán, largest city in Mesoamerica, is sacked and abandoned

606 Harsha, king of Kanauj, conquers northern India

659 Chinese power reaches its maximum extent in central Asia

c.700 The Huari empire of Peru conquers the Moche state

618 The Tang dynasty replaces the Sui in China

676 The Korean peninsula is united by the kingdom of Silla

c. 700 Emergence of the kingdom of Ghana in west Africa

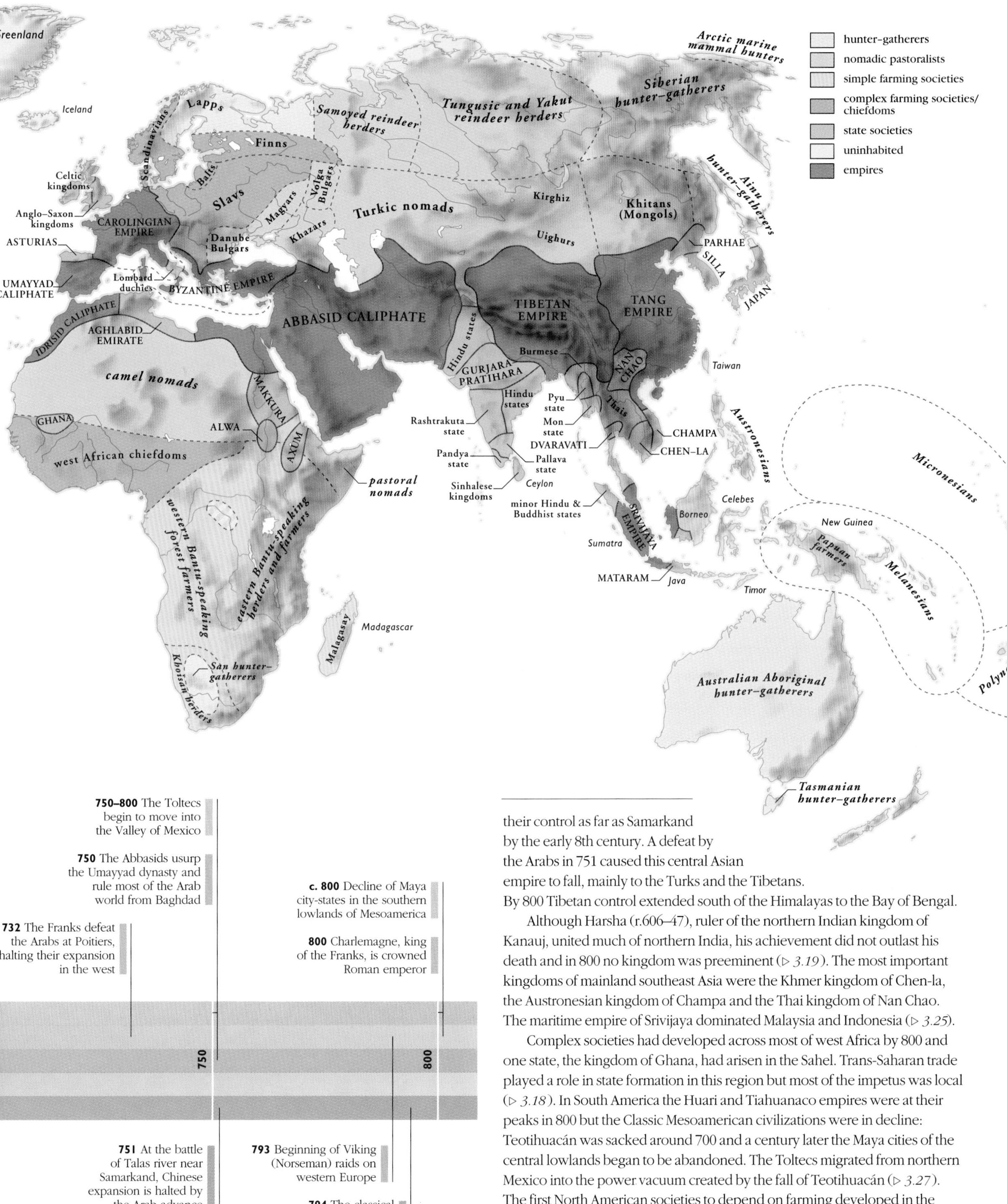

Greenland
Iceland
Lapps
Scandinavians
Finns
Balts
Celtic kingdoms
Anglo-Saxon kingdoms
CAROLINGIAN EMPIRE
ASTURIAS
UMAYYAD CALIPHATE
Slavs
Magyars
Volga Bulgars
Danube Bulgars
Khazars
Lombard duchies
BYZANTINE EMPIRE
IDRISID CALIPHATE
AGHLABID EMIRATE
ABBASID CALIPHATE
Samoyed reindeer herders
Tungusic and Yakut reindeer herders
Siberian hunter-gatherers
Arctic marine mammal hunters
Turkic nomads
Kirghiz
Uighurs
Khitans (Mongols)
Ainu hunter-gatherers
PARHAE
SILLA
JAPAN
TIBETAN EMPIRE
TANG EMPIRE
Hindu states
GURJARA PRATIHARA
Burmese
NAN CHAO
Taiwan
Hindu states
Pyu state
Mon state
Rashtrakuta state
DVARAVATI
Thais
CHAMPA
CHEN-LA
Pandya state
Pallava state
Sinhalese kingdoms
Ceylon
minor Hindu & Buddhist states
SRIVIJAYA EMPIRE
Sumatra
Borneo
Celebes
Austronesians
Micronesians
New Guinea
Papuan farmers
Melanesians
Polynesians
MATARAM
Java
Timor
camel nomads
GHANA
ALWA
MAKKURA
AXUM
west African chiefdoms
pastoral nomads
western Bantu-speaking forest farmers
eastern Bantu-speaking herders and farmers
Malagasy
Madagascar
San hunter-gatherers
Khoisan herders
Australian Aboriginal hunter-gatherers
Tasmanian hunter-gatherers
hunter-gatherers
nomadic pastoralists
simple farming societies
complex farming societies/ chiefdoms
state societies
uninhabited
empires

750–800 The Toltecs begin to move into the Valley of Mexico

750 The Abbasids usurp the Umayyad dynasty and rule most of the Arab world from Baghdad

732 The Franks defeat the Arabs at Poitiers, halting their expansion in the west

c. 800 Decline of Maya city-states in the southern lowlands of Mesoamerica

800 Charlemagne, king of the Franks, is crowned Roman emperor

750

800

751 At the battle of Talas river near Samarkand, Chinese expansion is halted by the Arab advance

793 Beginning of Viking (Norseman) raids on western Europe

794 The classical Heian period in Japan is established by emperor Kammu, who moves his capital to Kyoto

their control as far as Samarkand by the early 8th century. A defeat by the Arabs in 751 caused this central Asian empire to fall, mainly to the Turks and the Tibetans. By 800 Tibetan control extended south of the Himalayas to the Bay of Bengal.

Although Harsha (r.606–47), ruler of the northern Indian kingdom of Kanauj, united much of northern India, his achievement did not outlast his death and in 800 no kingdom was preeminent (▷ *3.19*). The most important kingdoms of mainland southeast Asia were the Khmer kingdom of Chen-la, the Austronesian kingdom of Champa and the Thai kingdom of Nan Chao. The maritime empire of Srivijaya dominated Malaysia and Indonesia (▷ *3.25*).

Complex societies had developed across most of west Africa by 800 and one state, the kingdom of Ghana, had arisen in the Sahel. Trans-Saharan trade played a role in state formation in this region but most of the impetus was local (▷ *3.18*). In South America the Huari and Tiahuanaco empires were at their peaks in 800 but the Classic Mesoamerican civilizations were in decline: Teotihuacán was sacked around 700 and a century later the Maya cities of the central lowlands began to be abandoned. The Toltecs migrated from northern Mexico into the power vacuum created by the fall of Teotihuacán (▷ *3.27*). The first North American societies to depend on farming developed in the southwestern deserts in the 7th–8th centuries. In the eastern woodlands maize was a widespread crop by 800. The Hopewell cultures were replaced by the more complex Mississippian temple-mound building cultures (▷ *3.26*) ■

3.02 THE WORLD • AD 1000 •

In the 9th century Christian Europe was under attack from Viking raiders from Scandinavia, Muslim pirates from Spain and north Africa, and steppe nomads, the Magyars and Bulgars (▷ *3.07*). The cultural and economic revival fostered by the Carolingian empire collapsed under the impact of the attacks and the empire itself broke up between 843 and 889. However, by 1000 European civilization was expanding and many of the states of medieval Europe had begun to emerge as stable political units: France was a decentralized, weak feudal kingdom but the German kings built a strong state based on their control of the church. In 962 the German king Otto I adopted the title Roman emperor, founding the Holy Roman empire. He ended the Magyar threat in 955, after which the Magyars founded the Christian kingdom of Hungary. Viking attacks on the British Isles were a catalyst in the formation of the kingdoms of England and Scotland and by 1000 stable kingdoms had developed in Scandinavia itself. Swedish Vikings founded the first Russian state about 862 but by 1000 this had lost its Scandinavian character and was a Slavic state under Byzantine influence.

The Arab world continued to fragment and by 1000 the Abbasid caliphs were no more than spiritual figureheads (▷ *3.14*). Persia passed under the control of native dynasties; Egypt, Syria and Palestine became independent under the Tulunid emirs in 868; most of Arabia was lost around 900; and the Christian Armenians recovered their independence in 886. Abbasid power revived in the early 10th century and control over Egypt and southern Iran was recovered, but it collapsed for good when the Persian Buwayhids seized Baghdad in 945: they ruled in the name of the caliph who was retained only for his spiritual authority. Between 967 and 973 the Tunisian Fatimid dynasty conquered Egypt, Palestine and Syria and were the most powerful Muslim rulers in 1000. Despite the disunity, the Muslim world continued to expand in the 9th and 10th centuries, the most important gain being the conversion of the Ghuzz Turks.

Despite the collapse of the Tibetan empire around 850, the Tang Chinese empire continued to decline in the 9th century (▷ *3.20*). The government's fiscal problems led to persecutions and expropriation of property belonging to Buddhists, Nestorian Christians and Manichaeans. Landlords began to reverse the earlier Tang land reforms, leading to a peasant uprising in 874–84 which broke the authority of the dynasty. Power devolved to provincial warlords and the empire split into several states. In 916 the far north was conquered by the nomad Khitans (a Mongol people), who founded the

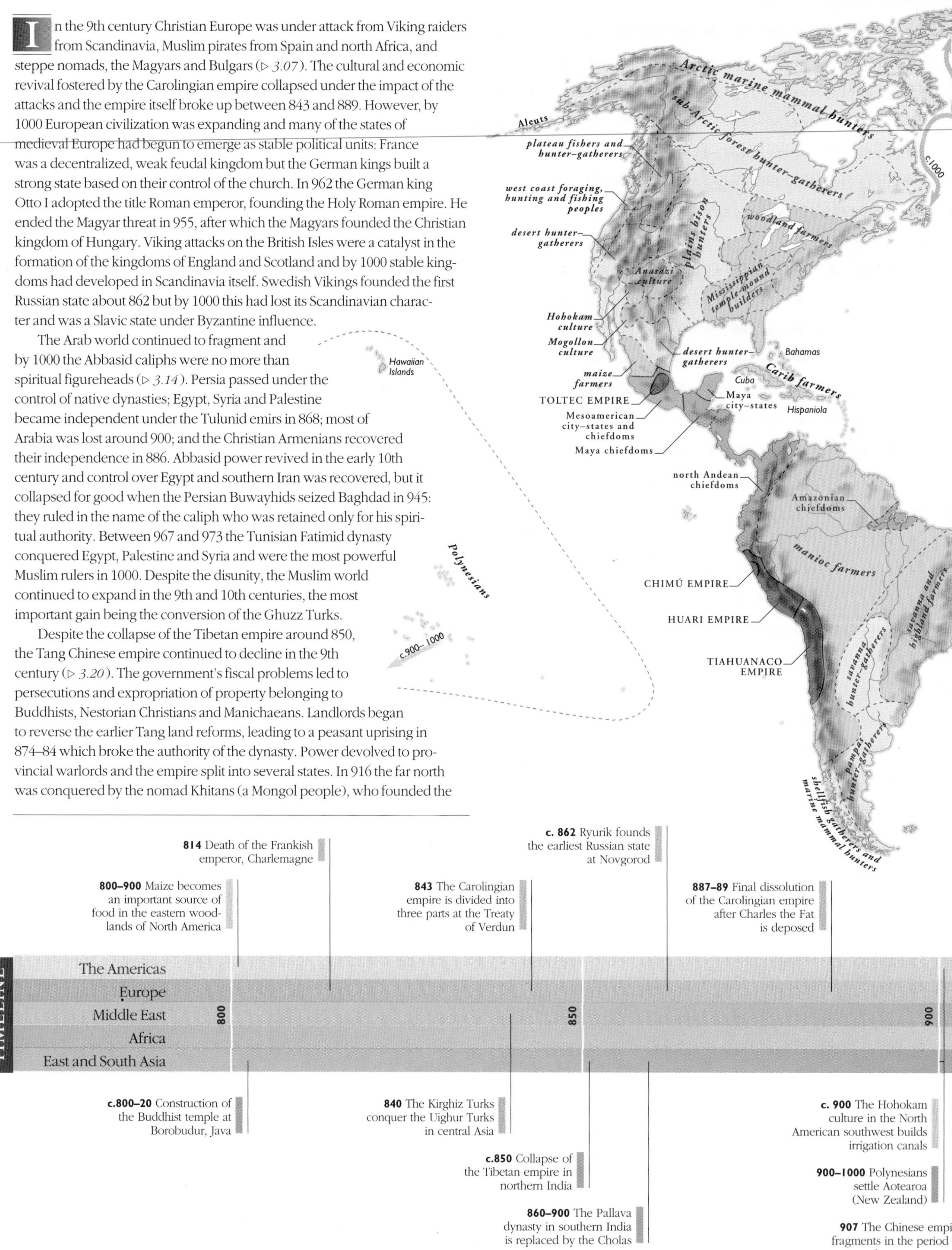

Arctic marine mammal hunters
sub-Arctic forest hunter-gatherers
Aleuts
plateau fishers and hunter-gatherers
west coast foraging, hunting and fishing peoples
desert hunter-gatherers
plains bison hunters
woodland farmers
Anasazi culture
Mississippian temple-mound builders
Hohokam culture
Mogollon culture
desert hunter-gatherers
Bahamas
maize farmers
Cuba
Carib farmers
TOLTEC EMPIRE
Maya city-states
Hispaniola
Mesoamerican city-states and chiefdoms
Maya chiefdoms
Hawaiian Islands
c.1000
Polynesians
c.900–1000
north Andean chiefdoms
Amazonian chiefdoms
manioc farmers
CHIMÚ EMPIRE
HUARI EMPIRE
TIAHUANACO EMPIRE
savanna and highland farmers
savanna hunter-gatherers
pampas hunter-gatherers
shellfish gatherers and marine mammal hunters

TIMELINE

The Americas | Europe | Middle East | Africa | East and South Asia

800 · 850 · 900

800–900 Maize becomes an important source of food in the eastern woodlands of North America

814 Death of the Frankish emperor, Charlemagne

c.800–20 Construction of the Buddhist temple at Borobudur, Java

840 The Kirghiz Turks conquer the Uighur Turks in central Asia

843 The Carolingian empire is divided into three parts at the Treaty of Verdun

c.850 Collapse of the Tibetan empire in northern India

860–900 The Pallava dynasty in southern India is replaced by the Cholas

c. 862 Ryurik founds the earliest Russian state at Novgorod

887–89 Final dissolution of the Carolingian empire after Charles the Fat is deposed

c. 900 The Hohokam culture in the North American southwest builds irrigation canals

900–1000 Polynesians settle Aotearoa (New Zealand)

907 The Chinese empire fragments in the period of the Five Dynasties

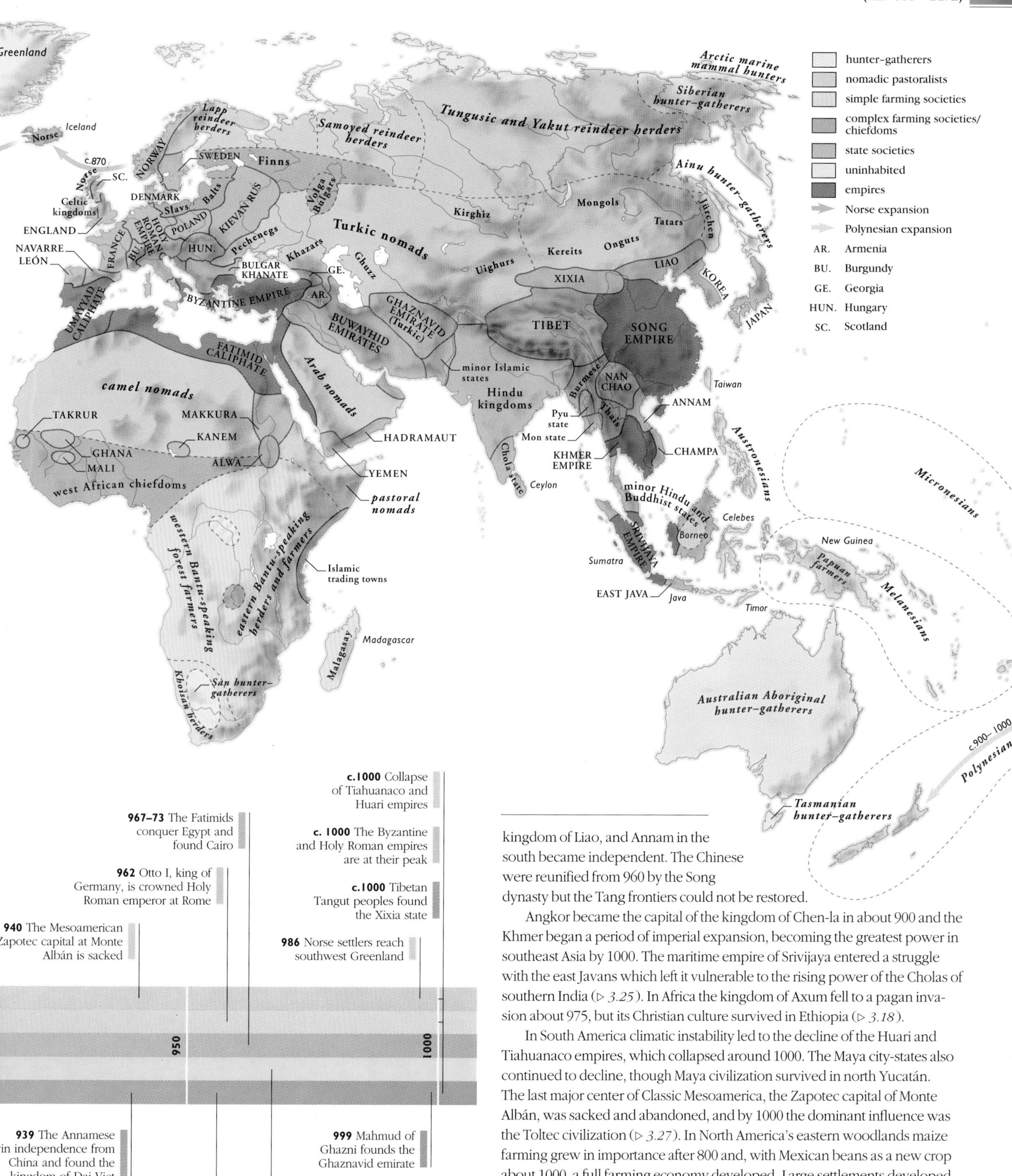
hunter-gatherers
nomadic pastoralists
simple farming societies
complex farming societies/ chiefdoms
state societies
uninhabited
empires
Norse expansion
Polynesian expansion
AR. Armenia
BU. Burgundy
GE. Georgia
HUN. Hungary
SC. Scotland
Greenland
Iceland
Norse
c.870
SC.
Celtic kingdoms
ENGLAND
NAVARRE
LEÓN
FRANCE
DENMARK
NORWAY
SWEDEN
Lapp reindeer herders
Finns
Balts
Slavs
POLAND
HOLY ROMAN EMPIRE
HUN.
KIEVAN RUS
Pechenegs
Khazars
Volga Bulgars
BULGAR KHANATE
GE.
AR.
BYZANTINE EMPIRE
UMAYYAD CALIPHATE
FATIMID CALIPHATE
Samoyed reindeer herders
Tungusic and Yakut reindeer herders
Arctic marine mammal hunters
Siberian hunter-gatherers
Ainu hunter-gatherers
Turkic nomads
Ghuzz
Kirghiz
Mongols
Tatars
Jurchen
Kereits
Onguts
Uighurs
XIXIA
LIAO
KOREA
JAPAN
GHAZNAVID EMIRATE (Turkic)
BUWAYHID EMIRATES
TIBET
SONG EMPIRE
minor Islamic states
Hindu kingdoms
Burmese
NAN CHAO
Thais
Pyu state
Mon state
KHMER EMPIRE
ANNAM
CHAMPA
Taiwan
Chola state
Ceylon
Arab nomads
HADRAMAUT
YEMEN
camel nomads
TAKRUR
MAKKURA
KANEM
GHANA
MALI
ALWA
west African chiefdoms
pastoral nomads
western Bantu-speaking forest farmers
eastern Bantu-speaking herders and farmers
Islamic trading towns
Malagasy
Madagascar
San hunter-gatherers
Khoisan herders
minor Hindu and Buddhist states
SRIVIJAYA EMPIRE
Sumatra
Borneo
Celebes
EAST JAVA
Java
Timor
Austronesians
Micronesians
New Guinea
Papuan farmers
Melanesians
Australian Aboriginal hunter-gatherers
Tasmanian hunter-gatherers
c.900–1000
Polynesians

c. 940 The Mesoamerican Zapotec capital at Monte Albán is sacked

962 Otto I, king of Germany, is crowned Holy Roman emperor at Rome

967–73 The Fatimids conquer Egypt and found Cairo

c.1000 Collapse of Tiahuanaco and Huari empires

c. 1000 The Byzantine and Holy Roman empires are at their peak

c.1000 Tibetan Tangut peoples found the Xixia state

986 Norse settlers reach southwest Greenland

950

1000

939 The Annamese win independence from China and found the kingdom of Dai Viet

960 The Chinese empire is restored by the Song dynasty

c.975 The Christian kingdom of Axum falls to pagan invaders

999 Mahmud of Ghazni founds the Ghaznavid emirate

kingdom of Liao, and Annam in the south became independent. The Chinese were reunified from 960 by the Song dynasty but the Tang frontiers could not be restored.

Angkor became the capital of the kingdom of Chen-la in about 900 and the Khmer began a period of imperial expansion, becoming the greatest power in southeast Asia by 1000. The maritime empire of Srivijaya entered a struggle with the east Javans which left it vulnerable to the rising power of the Cholas of southern India (▷ *3.25*). In Africa the kingdom of Axum fell to a pagan invasion about 975, but its Christian culture survived in Ethiopia (▷ *3.18*).

In South America climatic instability led to the decline of the Huari and Tiahuanaco empires, which collapsed around 1000. The Maya city-states also continued to decline, though Maya civilization survived in north Yucatán. The last major center of Classic Mesoamerica, the Zapotec capital of Monte Albán, was sacked and abandoned, and by 1000 the dominant influence was the Toltec civilization (▷ *3.27*). In North America's eastern woodlands maize farming grew in importance after 800 and, with Mexican beans as a new crop about 1000, a full farming economy developed. Large settlements developed by 1000 in the southwestern deserts and the Mississippi area (▷ *3.26*).

Two large uninhabited landmasses were colonized at this time. Scandinavians, mainly from Norway, began to settle in Iceland about 870, and by 1000 had also settled southwest Greenland and reached the American mainland. At the same time Polynesians reached Aotearoa (New Zealand) ■

3.03 THE WORLD • AD 1279 •

Western Europe's confidence grew in the 11th and 12th centuries, as shown in its Gothic cathedrals and in crusades against the Muslims in the Holy Land and the pagan Slavs in eastern Europe (▷ *3.17*). Spain's Christian kingdoms expanded until by 1279 the Muslims were confined to Granada. The Holy Roman empire looked impressive, but disputes with the papacy undermined its authority. By the mid-13th century the empire was becoming a confederation of semi-independent states. In contrast, England and France had become strong centralized kingdoms (▷ *3.08*).

Although Islam lost ground in Europe it continued to expand elsewhere. The Ghaznavid emirate conquered northwest India and in 1206 a Muslim sultanate was founded at Delhi: by 1279 it was the largest state in India since the fall of the Gupta empire (▷ *3.19*). Islam was spread by merchants to west Africa in the 11th century, and by the 13th century, Timbuktu, the capital of the kingdom of Mali, was a center of Muslim culture. Trade with the Muslim world was a factor in the emergence of the first powerful chiefdom of southern Africa at Great Zimbabwe around 1200 (▷ *3.18*)

The dominant Muslim power in the 11th century was the Seljuks (▷ *3.16*). Originally a clan of Ghuzz Turk mercenaries who rebelled against their employer, the Ghaznavid emir, in 1037, the Seljuks overran Persia, the Abbasid caliphate, Syria and the Holy Land, and in 1071 won control of Anatolia. Although the First Crusade, which captured Jerusalem in 1099, allowed the Byzantines to reclaim some lost territory, the empire never fully recovered. By this time Seljuk political unity had broken down, and hostility between them and the Fatimids of Egypt meant that Muslim counterattacks against the Crusaders were ineffective. The Crusaders were put on the defensive after the Seljuk Zangid sultanate of Aleppo overthrew the Fatimids 1169–71 and seized Egypt, but the Zangids were themselves overthrown five years later by Saladin, who retook Jerusalem in 1187. The Crusader states were finally destroyed in 1291 by the Mamlukes who had seized power in Egypt in 1250.

The nomadic Mongol peoples had been gradually expanding westward since the breakup of the Turkish steppe empire in the 8th century. Though superb cavalry fighters they did not threaten the settled civilizations of Eurasia until they were

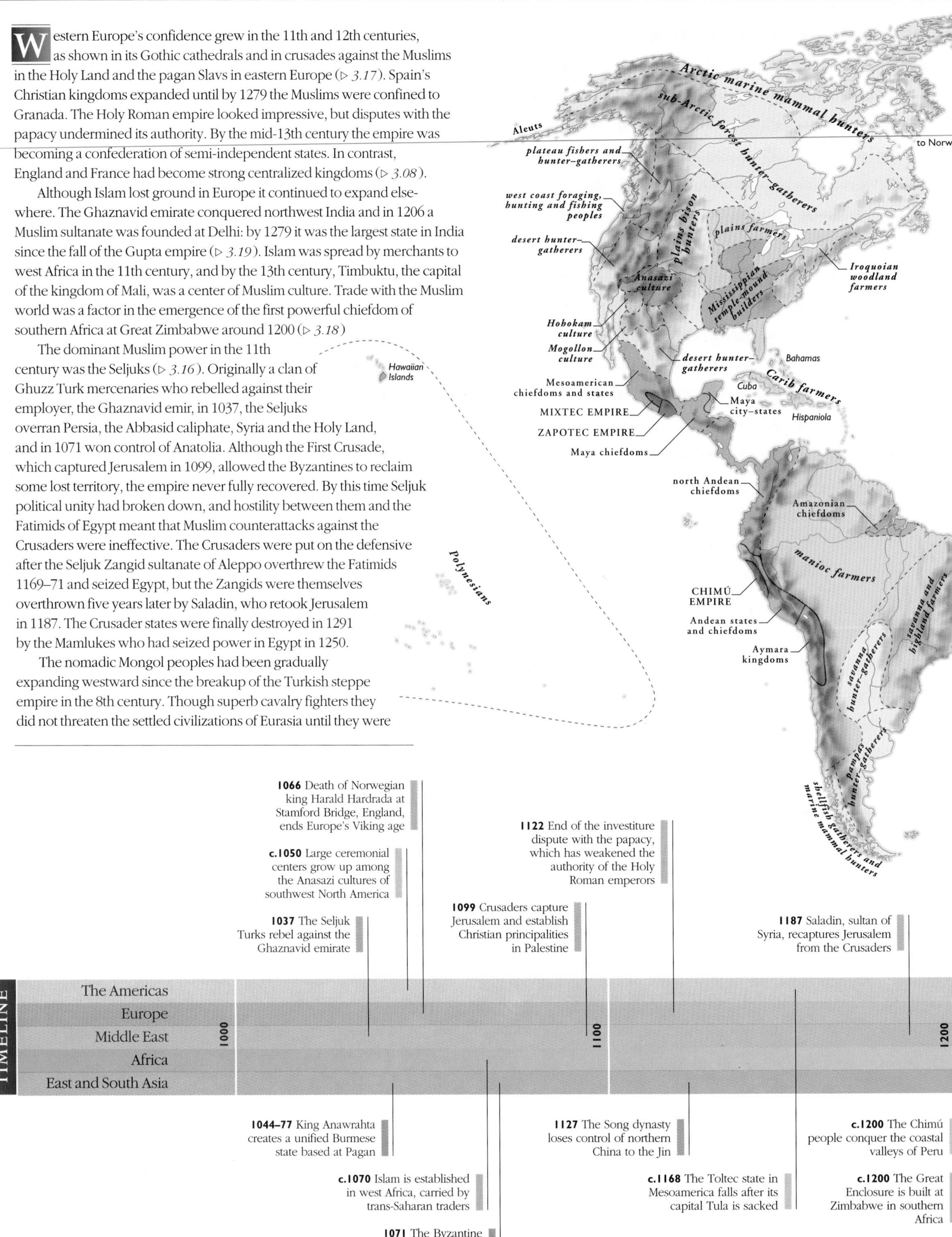

Arctic marine mammal hunters
sub-Arctic forest hunter-gatherers
Aleuts
to Norway
plateau fishers and hunter-gatherers
west coast foraging, hunting and fishing peoples
desert hunter-gatherers
plains bison hunters
plains farmers
Iroquoian woodland farmers
Anasazi culture
Mississippian temple-mound builders
Hobokam culture
Mogollon culture
desert hunter-gatherers
Bahamas
Hawaiian Islands
Mesoamerican chiefdoms and states
Cuba
Carib farmers
MIXTEC EMPIRE
Maya city-states
Hispaniola
ZAPOTEC EMPIRE
Maya chiefdoms
north Andean chiefdoms
Amazonian chiefdoms
Polynesians
manioc farmers
CHIMÚ EMPIRE
savanna and highland farmers
Andean states and chiefdoms
Aymara kingdoms
savanna hunter-gatherers
pampas hunter-gatherers
shellfish gatherers and marine mammal hunters
TIMELINE
The Americas
Europe
Middle East
Africa
East and South Asia
1000
1100
1200

1066 Death of Norwegian king Harald Hardrada at Stamford Bridge, England, ends Europe's Viking age

c.1050 Large ceremonial centers grow up among the Anasazi cultures of southwest North America

1037 The Seljuk Turks rebel against the Ghaznavid emirate

1122 End of the investiture dispute with the papacy, which has weakened the authority of the Holy Roman emperors

1099 Crusaders capture Jerusalem and establish Christian principalities in Palestine

1187 Saladin, sultan of Syria, recaptures Jerusalem from the Crusaders

1044–77 King Anawrahta creates a unified Burmese state based at Pagan

c.1070 Islam is established in west Africa, carried by trans-Saharan traders

1071 The Byzantine empire is defeated by the Seljuk Turks at Manzikert

1127 The Song dynasty loses control of northern China to the Jin

c.1168 The Toltec state in Mesoamerica falls after its capital Tula is sacked

c.1200 The Chimú people conquer the coastal valleys of Peru

c.1200 The Great Enclosure is built at Zimbabwe in southern Africa

c.1200 The first chiefdoms develop in Polynesia

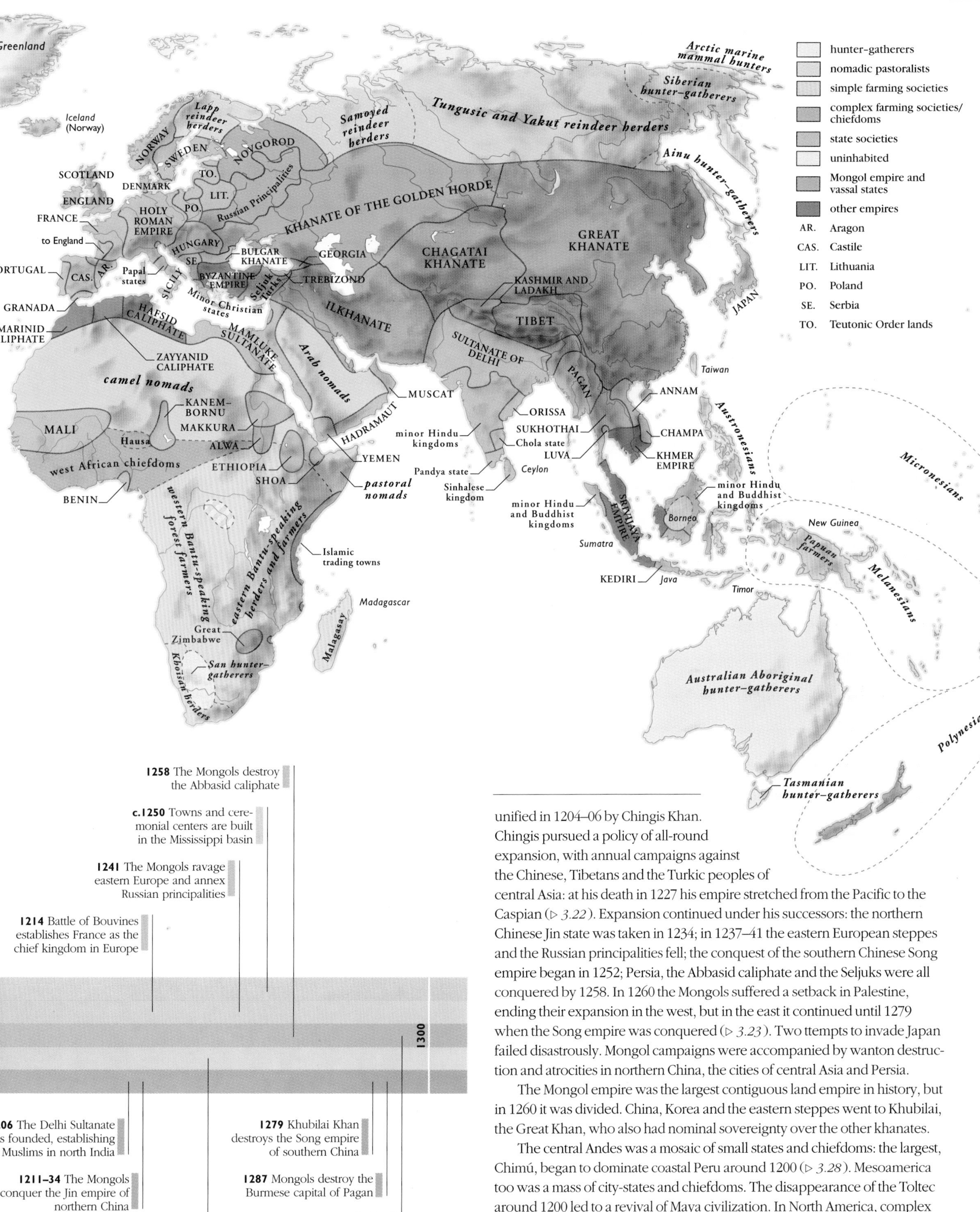
hunter-gatherers
nomadic pastoralists
simple farming societies
complex farming societies/ chiefdoms
state societies
uninhabited
Mongol empire and vassal states
other empires
AR. Aragon
CAS. Castile
LIT. Lithuania
PO. Poland
SE. Serbia
TO. Teutonic Order lands
Greenland
Iceland (Norway)
Arctic marine mammal hunters
Siberian hunter-gatherers
Tungusic and Yakut reindeer herders
Samoyed reindeer herders
Lapp reindeer herders
NORWAY
SWEDEN
NOVGOROD
Russian Principalities
SCOTLAND
DENMARK
ENGLAND
FRANCE
to England
HOLY ROMAN EMPIRE
HUNGARY
BULGAR KHANATE
GEORGIA
TREBIZOND
BYZANTINE EMPIRE
Seljuk Turks
Papal states
SICILY
Minor Christian states
PORTUGAL
GRANADA
MARINID CALIPHATE
HAFSID CALIPHATE
ZAYYANID CALIPHATE
KHANATE OF THE GOLDEN HORDE
CHAGATAI KHANATE
GREAT KHANATE
Ainu hunter-gatherers
JAPAN
KASHMIR AND LADAKH
TIBET
ILKHANATE
SULTANATE OF DELHI
MAMLUKE SULTANATE
Arab nomads
camel nomads
KANEM-BORNU
MAKKURA
ALWA
MALI
Hausa
west African chiefdoms
ETHIOPIA
SHOA
BENIN
MUSCAT
HADRAMAUT
YEMEN
pastoral nomads
minor Hindu kingdoms
ORISSA
SUKHOTHAI
Chola state
LUVA
Pandya state
Sinhalese kingdom
Ceylon
PAGAN
ANNAM
CHAMPA
KHMER EMPIRE
Taiwan
Austronesians
Micronesians
minor Hindu and Buddhist kingdoms
Borneo
SRIVIJAYA EMPIRE
Sumatra
KEDIRI
Java
New Guinea
Papuan farmers
Melanesians
Timor
western Bantu-speaking forest farmers
eastern Bantu-speaking herders and farmers
Islamic trading towns
Madagascar
Malagasy
Great Zimbabwe
San hunter-gatherers
Khoisan herders
Australian Aboriginal hunter-gatherers
Polynesians
Tasmanian hunter-gatherers
1300

1258 The Mongols destroy the Abbasid caliphate

c.1250 Towns and ceremonial centers are built in the Mississippi basin

1241 The Mongols ravage eastern Europe and annex Russian principalities

1214 Battle of Bouvines establishes France as the chief kingdom in Europe

206 The Delhi Sultanate is founded, establishing Muslims in north India

1211–34 The Mongols conquer the Jin empire of northern China

c.1235 Rise of kingdom of Mali under Sun Diata Keita

1279 Khubilai Khan destroys the Song empire of southern China

1287 Mongols destroy the Burmese capital of Pagan

1291 Acre, the last Crusader stronghold, falls to the Mamlukes

unified in 1204–06 by Chingis Khan. Chingis pursued a policy of all-round expansion, with annual campaigns against the Chinese, Tibetans and the Turkic peoples of central Asia: at his death in 1227 his empire stretched from the Pacific to the Caspian (▷ *3.22*). Expansion continued under his successors: the northern Chinese Jin state was taken in 1234; in 1237–41 the eastern European steppes and the Russian principalities fell; the conquest of the southern Chinese Song empire began in 1252; Persia, the Abbasid caliphate and the Seljuks were all conquered by 1258. In 1260 the Mongols suffered a setback in Palestine, ending their expansion in the west, but in the east it continued until 1279 when the Song empire was conquered (▷ *3.23*). Two ttempts to invade Japan failed disastrously. Mongol campaigns were accompanied by wanton destruction and atrocities in northern China, the cities of central Asia and Persia.

The Mongol empire was the largest contiguous land empire in history, but in 1260 it was divided. China, Korea and the eastern steppes went to Khubilai, the Great Khan, who also had nominal sovereignty over the other khanates.

The central Andes was a mosaic of small states and chiefdoms: the largest, Chimú, began to dominate coastal Peru around 1200 (▷ *3.28*). Mesoamerica too was a mass of city-states and chiefdoms. The disappearance of the Toltec around 1200 led to a revival of Maya civilization. In North America, complex societies arose in the Anasazi culture of the southwest in the 11th century. Towns developed around ceremonial sites in the Mississippi area (▷ *3.26*) ■

3.04 THE WORLD • AD 1492 •

At the end of the 13th century Islam began to spread through Malaya and the islands of southeast Asia, gradually supplanting Hinduism and Buddhism. At the same time, the Mongols tried to expand into southeast Asia, but with little success. Their vast empire broke up in the 14th century. In China they were overthrown by the native Ming dynasty in 1368, following peasant rebellions and internal power struggles. The Ming ruled in the tradition of the Tang dynasty and reasserted Chinese power in southeast Asia. One of their first acts was to forbid Chinese from traveling abroad. This isolated China, ruined Chinese trade and led to a fateful neglect of maritime matters just as the Europeans were about to begin their own oceanic exploration. By the time the interdict was lifted in 1567, the initiative had passed irretrievably to the Europeans.

The Mongols remained a power on the eastern steppes and the khanates of the Chagatai and the Golden Horde survived at the end of the 15th century, but their mainly Turkic subjects had already reasserted their independence. In the Middle East the Mongols converted to Islam and were assimilated by their Persian and Turkic subjects. Fragmentation followed and by 1350 the Ilkhanate had dissolved into a number of Turkish, Persian and nominally Mongol states. One of these, the Ottoman Turk sultanate, had by 1400 conquered most of Anatolia and the Balkans and reduced the Byzantine empire to its capital Constantinople (▷ *3.16*). Attempts to build a united Christian front to counter this new Muslim threat to Europe foundered amid international rivalries. The Ottomans, however, were defeated in 1402 by Timur the Lame (r.1361–1405), ruler of Samarkand, who claimed Chingis Khan as his ancestor and saw himself as restorer of the Mongol empire, though he was culturally more Turk than Mongol. In a devastating reign of terror, Timur rebuilt the Ilkhanate, broke the power of the Delhi sultanate and was only prevented from invading China by his death. The empire he had built broke up shortly after.

Ottoman power revived after Timur's death and the advance into Europe began again. In 1453 Constantinople fell after an epic siege and the Byzantine empire finally died. In 1475 the Ottomans crossed the Danube and pushed west. Although Byzantium had fallen, much of its heritage survived in the

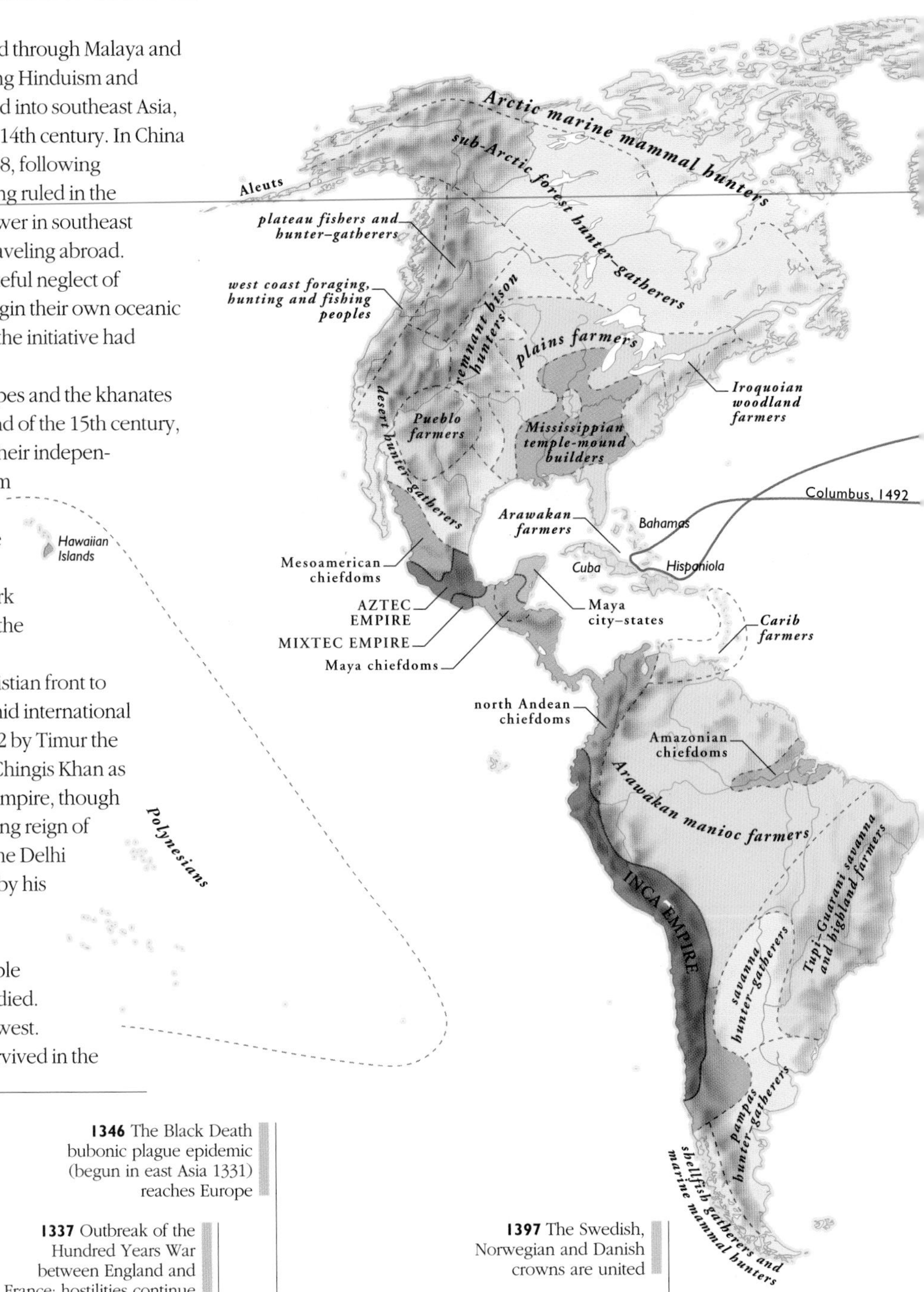

Arctic marine mammal hunters
sub-Arctic forest hunter-gatherers
Aleuts
plateau fishers and hunter-gatherers
west coast foraging, hunting and fishing peoples
remnant bison hunters
plains farmers
Iroquoian woodland farmers
desert hunter-gatherers
Pueblo farmers
Mississippian temple-mound builders
Columbus, 1492
Hawaiian Islands
Arawakan farmers
Bahamas
Mesoamerican chiefdoms
Cuba
Hispaniola
AZTEC EMPIRE
MIXTEC EMPIRE
Maya chiefdoms
Maya city-states
Carib farmers
north Andean chiefdoms
Amazonian chiefdoms
Arawakan manioc farmers
Polynesians
INCA EMPIRE
savanna hunter-gatherers
Tupi-Guarani savanna and highland farmers
pampas hunter-gatherers
shellfish gatherers and marine mammal hunters

c.1300 Decline of the Anasazi and other farmers of southwestern deserts

c.1300 The Renaissance begins in Italy as Classical forms in art, architecture and literature are revived

1293 Osman I, a Turkish chief in Anatolia, founds the Ottoman dynasty

1346 The Black Death bubonic plague epidemic (begun in east Asia 1331) reaches Europe

1337 Outbreak of the Hundred Years War between England and France: hostilities continue sporadically until 1453

c.1325 Arrival of the Aztecs in Mexico

1397 The Swedish, Norwegian and Danish crowns are united

1378 The "Great Schism" in the Catholic church begins, with popes in both Rome and Avignon

1428 The Aztec empire is founded by Itzcóatl (r.1428–40)

TIMELINE

The Americas
Europe
Middle East
Africa
East and South Asia

1300

1400

1290 Merchants introduce Islam into Indonesia and Malaysia

1317 Christian Makkura is overthrown by Muslim Arab nomads

c.1330 The sultanate of Delhi reaches its maximum extent under Muhammad ibn Tughluk

1361–1405 From his capital at Samarkand Timur the Lame leads a resurgence of Mongol power in the Middle East

1368 The establishment of the Ming dynasty ends Mongol rule in China

1370 The kingdom of Vijayanagara dominates southern India

1415 The Portuguese take Ceuta in Morocco, their first African possession

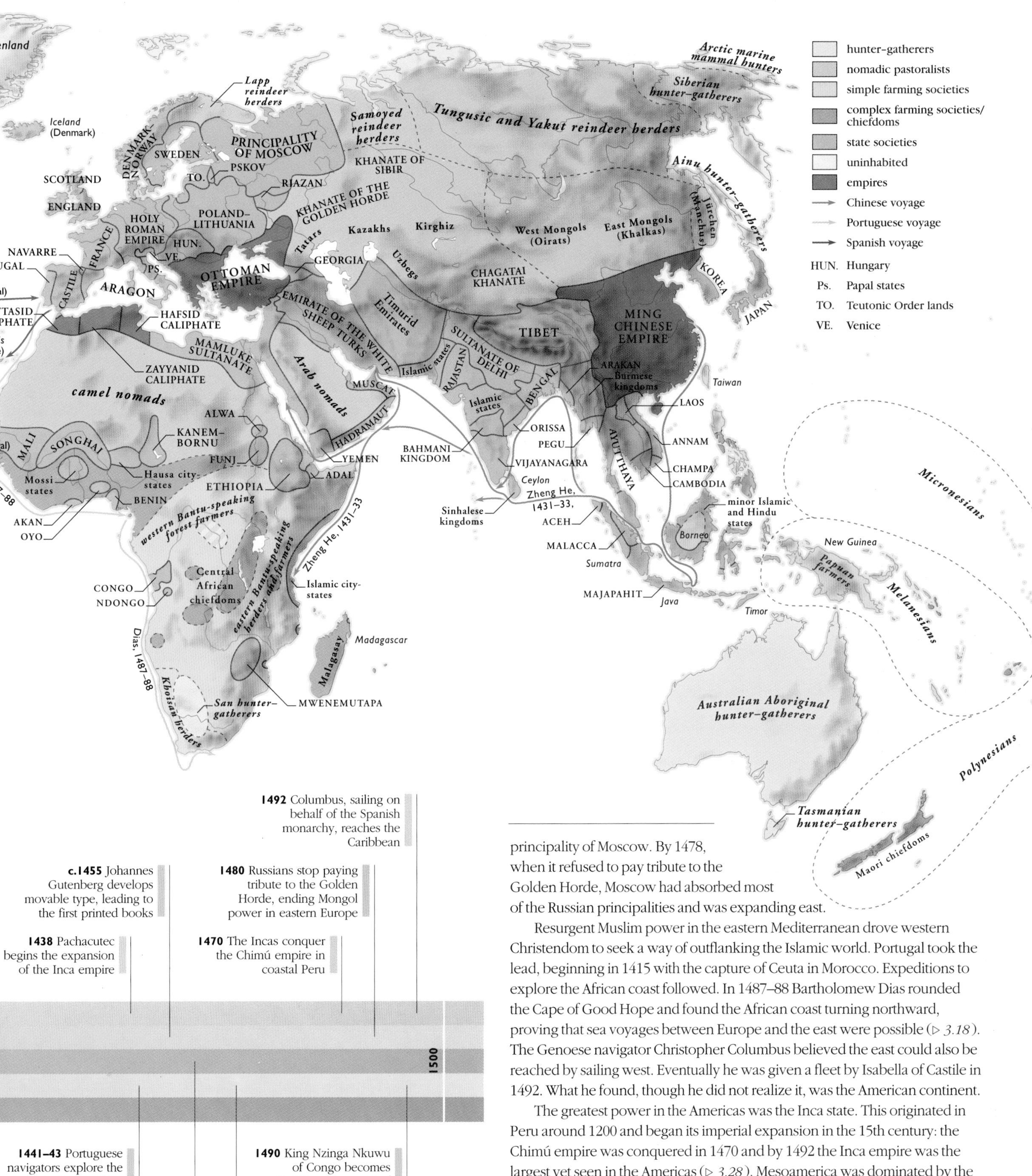
hunter-gatherers
nomadic pastoralists
simple farming societies
complex farming societies/ chiefdoms
state societies
uninhabited
empires
Chinese voyage
Portuguese voyage
Spanish voyage
HUN. Hungary
Ps. Papal states
TO. Teutonic Order lands
VE. Venice
Iceland (Denmark)
Lapp reindeer herders
Samoyed reindeer herders
Tungusic and Yakut reindeer herders
Arctic marine mammal hunters
Siberian hunter-gatherers
Ainu hunter-gatherers
SCOTLAND
ENGLAND
DENMARK-NORWAY
SWEDEN
PRINCIPALITY OF MOSCOW
PSKOV
TO.
RIAZAN
KHANATE OF SIBIR
KHANATE OF THE GOLDEN HORDE
POLAND-LITHUANIA
HOLY ROMAN EMPIRE
HUN.
VE.
PS.
FRANCE
NAVARRE
CASTILE
ARAGON
OTTOMAN EMPIRE
GEORGIA
Tatars
Kazakhs
Kirghiz
Uzbegs
West Mongols (Oirats)
East Mongols (Khalkas)
Jürchen (Manchus)
KOREA
JAPAN
CHAGATAI KHANATE
Timurid Emirates
EMIRATE OF THE WHITE SHEEP TURKS
TIBET
MING CHINESE EMPIRE
HAFSID CALIPHATE
ZAYYANID CALIPHATE
MAMLUKE SULTANATE
Arab nomads
MUSCAT
HADRAMAUT
YEMEN
ADAL
Islamic states
RAJASTAN
SULTANATE OF DELHI
BENGAL
Islamic states
BAHMANI KINGDOM
ORISSA
PEGU
VIJAYANAGARA
ARAKAN
Burmese kingdoms
LAOS
ANNAM
CHAMPA
CAMBODIA
AYUTTHAYA
Taiwan
Ceylon
Zheng He, 1431–33,
Sinhalese kingdoms
ACEH
MALACCA
Sumatra
MAJAPAHIT
Java
Borneo
minor Islamic and Hindu states
New Guinea
Papuan farmers
Timor
Micronesians
Melanesians
Polynesians
Australian Aboriginal hunter-gatherers
Tasmanian hunter-gatherers
Maori chiefdoms
camel nomads
ALWA
KANEM-BORNU
FUNJ
MALI
SONGHAI
Mossi states
Hausa city-states
BENIN
ETHIOPIA
AKAN
OYO
western Bantu-speaking forest farmers
Central African chiefdoms
eastern Bantu-speaking herders and farmers
Zheng He, 1431–33
Islamic city-states
CONGO
NDONGO
Dias, 1487–88
Madagascar
Malagasay
MWENEMUTAPA
San hunter-gatherers
Khoisan herders
1500

1438 Pachacutec begins the expansion of the Inca empire

1441–43 Portuguese navigators explore the coast of west Africa

c.1455 Johannes Gutenberg develops movable type, leading to the first printed books

1453 The Ottoman Turks take Constantinople and end the Byzantine empire

1464 Songhai eclipses Mali as the chief power in west Africa

1470 The Incas conquer the Chimú empire in coastal Peru

1480 Russians stop paying tribute to the Golden Horde, ending Mongol power in eastern Europe

1490 King Nzinga Nkuwu of Congo becomes Christian as a result of Portuguese influence

1492 Columbus, sailing on behalf of the Spanish monarchy, reaches the Caribbean

principality of Moscow. By 1478, when it refused to pay tribute to the Golden Horde, Moscow had absorbed most of the Russian principalities and was expanding east.

Resurgent Muslim power in the eastern Mediterranean drove western Christendom to seek a way of outflanking the Islamic world. Portugal took the lead, beginning in 1415 with the capture of Ceuta in Morocco. Expeditions to explore the African coast followed. In 1487–88 Bartholomew Dias rounded the Cape of Good Hope and found the African coast turning northward, proving that sea voyages between Europe and the east were possible (▷ *3.18*). The Genoese navigator Christopher Columbus believed the east could also be reached by sailing west. Eventually he was given a fleet by Isabella of Castile in 1492. What he found, though he did not realize it, was the American continent.

The greatest power in the Americas was the Inca state. This originated in Peru around 1200 and began its imperial expansion in the 15th century: the Chimú empire was conquered in 1470 and by 1492 the Inca empire was the largest yet seen in the Americas (▷ *3.28*). Mesoamerica was dominated by the Aztecs (▷ *3.27*), who settled the valley of Mexico about 1325 and became an imperial power under Itzcóatl (r.1428–40). The complex cultures of the south-western deserts of North America collapsed at the end of the 13th century after prolonged droughts. The towns of the Mississippian cultures were in decline by 1492 and the region's center had lost its population. Buffalo-hunting on the Great Plains was dying out as farming spread along river valleys (▷ *3.26*) ■

3.05 The spread of the world religions • AD 600 – 1500 •

The birth of Islam, the most recent of the world religions, dominated the era known to Europeans as the Middle Ages, and it deeply affected all the established world religions.

Islam originated in the teachings of the prophet Muhammad. From 610 Muhammad received a series of revelations which are recorded in the sacred book of Islam, the *Koran*. Islam drew much from Judaism and, to a lesser extent, Christianity; the *Koran* asserts that Muhammad is the last of a line of prophets that included Adam, Abraham, Noah, Moses and Jesus.

By the time of Muhammad's death in 632 Arabs had generally acknowledged him as their religious and political leader and had accepted Islam. Muhammad had no male heir and the decades following his deathwere marked by prolonged disputes over the succession, which erupted into civil war during the caliphate of Muhammad's son-in-law Ali (r.656–61). When Ali was murdered in 661, his supporters recognized his son Husain as successor (caliph) in preference to Muawiya, founder of the Umayyad dynasty. Husain's death in battle at Karbala in 680 led to his martyrdom, and the development among his supporters of the Shiite tradition of Islam.

Shiism has continued to be distinguished from the majority Sunni tradition by its stress on martyrdom and its radically different theories of religious leadership. In the 9th century doctrinal disputes resulted in the secession from Shiism of the Ismaili sect. Until the 13th century, the Ismailis (who are also known as the Assassins) habitually murdered their enemies. Moreover, the spread of both the Sunni and Shiite Islamic traditions was promoted by the growth, from the 8th century onward, of the mystical movement known as Sufism, which laid a heavy emphasis on piety and zeal.

The rise of Islam halved the area under Christian domination between 600 and 750. Islam tolerated Christians but the social and financial advantages of conversion were great and Christianity soon declined in the areas conquered by the Arabs. However, freedom from Orthodox persecution enabled some minority Christian sects, such as the Nestorians, to spread widely in Asia. Although it regained some ground through missionary work and military conquest – most notably the Crusades that temporarily restored Christian

ATLANTIC OCEAN
Glasgow
Nidaros (Trondheim)
SCANDINAVIA Christianity, c.950–1100
Uppsala
York
Lincoln
Salisbury
London
Canterbury
Roskilde
Santiago de Compostela
Rouen
Paris
Chartres
Amiens
Saxons Christianity, 785
Cologne
Reims
Bourges
León
Burgos
Danzig
LITHUANIA Christianity, 1386
Novgorod
SPAIN Christianity, 750–1492
Toledo
Seville
Córdoba
Strasbourg
Freiburg
Ulm
Prague
Regensburg
Poles Christianity, c.1000
Russians Christianity, 989
Moscow
Milan
Vienna
Fez
Tlemcen
Magyars (Hungarians) Christianity, c.1000
Kiev
Dnieper
Rome
KHAZAR KHANATE Jewish ruling dynasty, c.800–1242
Bulgars Christianity, 890
Constantinople
Mt Athos
Black Sea
BYZANTINE EMPIRE Islam, 1071–1453
GEORGIA
Konya
Mediterranean Sea
TEKRUR Islam, c.1030
GHANA Islam, 1076
Niger
Timbuktu
MALI Islam, c.1250
AIR Islam, c.1350
Barda
Nisibis
Masyaf
Tigris
Euphrates
Arbela
Kirkuk
Bethlehem
Damascus
Jerusalem
Baghdad
Tanta
Cairo
Karbala
Seleucia
Umm Abida
Kaskar
Basra
Rev-Ardashir
Shiraz
Nile
Medina
Humaithira
Mecca
MAKKURA Islam, 1317
ALWA
Red Sea
Axum
Lalibela
Debre Libanos
ETHIOPIA
Harer
Socotra
Somalis Islam, c.1100
CONGO Christianity, 1490
Kilwa

TIMELINE

700 | 1000 | 1300

South and east Asia

600–700 Beginning of the Bakhti revival of Hinduism in India

600–800 Spread of Chan and Pure Land Buddhism in China

c.700 Persian Zoroastrians settle in India: origin of Parsis

762 Uighur nomads adopt Manichaeanism as religion

791 Buddhism becomes the state religion in Tibet

843 Manichaeanism in China is destroyed by persecution

845 Buddhists face persecution in China

900–1000 Pilgrimages are established as an important expression of Hindu devotion

1191 Zen (Chan) Buddhism is introduced to Japan

1200–1300 Buddhism dies out in northern India

Middle East

622 Muhammad's flight (*hijra*) from Mecca to Medina

700–800 Growth of the Sufi mystical movement in Islam

c.970 Turks convert to Islam

c.1070 Islam spreads to sub-Saharan Africa

1258 Mongols destroy the Abbasid caliphate of Baghdad

Europe

726–843 Iconoclast controversy: destruction of religious images in Byzantine empire

965 Harald Bluetooth of Denmark is baptized: the first Christian king of Scandinavia

1054 Roman–Orthodox schism becomes permanent

1095–99 The First Crusade is called; Jerusalem is taken

1209–29 Crusades are launched against Cathar (Manichaean) heretics

1232 The Church sets up the Inquisition to fight heresy

1378–1417 Great Schism damages papal authority

700 | 1000 | 1300

SHIVA, one of the major deities of Hinduism, is seen in his form as Nataraja (Lord of Dance).

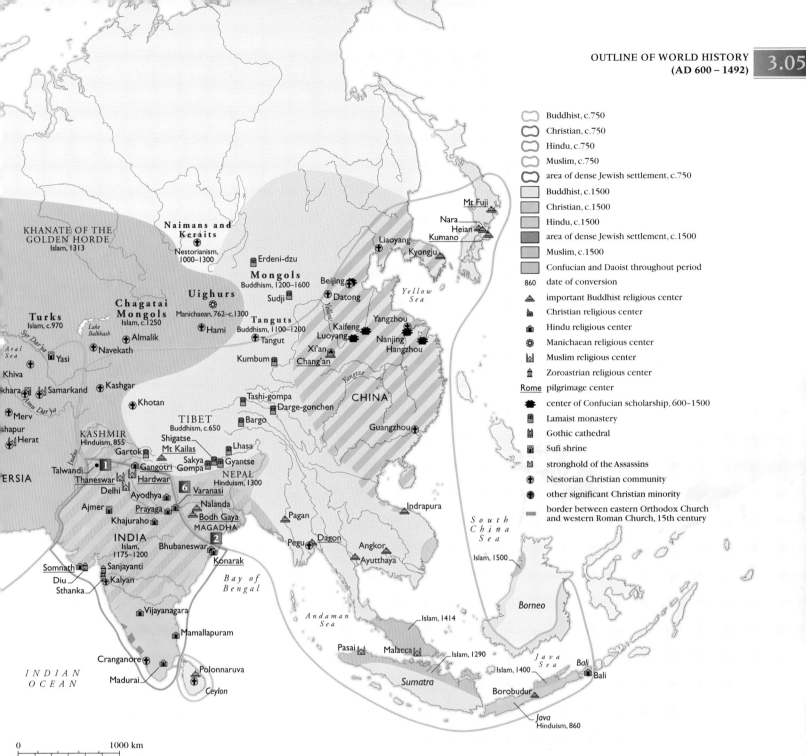

- Buddhist, c.750
- Christian, c.750
- Hindu, c.750
- Muslim, c.750
- area of dense Jewish settlement, c.750
- Buddhist, c.1500
- Christian, c.1500
- Hindu, c.1500
- area of dense Jewish settlement, c.1500
- Muslim, c.1500
- Confucian and Daoist throughout period
- 860 date of conversion
- important Buddhist religious center
- Christian religious center
- Hindu religious center
- Manichaean religious center
- Muslim religious center
- Zoroastrian religious center
- Rome pilgrimage center
- center of Confucian scholarship, 600–1500
- Lamaist monastery
- Gothic cathedral
- Sufi shrine
- stronghold of the Assassins
- Nestorian Christian community
- other significant Christian minority
- border between eastern Orthodox Church and western Roman Church, 15th century

0 1000 km
0 600 mi

control to the Holy Land – Christianity was again in retreat by the 15th century, as the Muslim Ottoman Turks overran the Byzantine empire and moved into the Balkans.

The Arab conquests destroyed Zoroastrianism in its Persian homeland but small communities of emigrants established themselves on India's west coast where the religion still survives among the Parsis.

The Bakhti (devotional) revival movement in the 7th century caused Hinduism to reassert itself against Buddhism, which had been dominant in the preceding centuries. The 8th-century philosopher Shankara gave impetus to the recovery by assimilating popular aspects of Buddhist devotion into Hinduism. An important aspect of the Bakhti revival was the great increase in the popularity of pilgrimages to sacred sites such as Varanasi on the River Ganges. A number of Hindus, especially from the lower castes, converted to Islam following the Muslim conquest around 1200, yet Hinduism remained India's principal religion.

Indian Buddhism, however, was destroyed by the Muslim conquest, continuing to flourish only in Ceylon. Buddhism also declined in southeast Asia following the introduction there of Islam in the 13th century. Chinese Buddhism reached the peak of its influence in the 7th and 8th centuries as a result of patronage by the Tang court. The period saw the spread of the meditative school of Chan (known in Japan as Zen) Buddhism and the populist Pure Land school which promised its adherents rebirth in paradise. Some 40,000 Buddhist temples and monasteries, all with tax-exempt estates, sprang up; they proved a severe drain on state income by 800. A brief imperial persecution in 845 closed many of these monasteries and forced 250,000 monks back into secular life. Buddhism recovered but never regained its former prestige.

The most important new converts to Buddhism in this period were the Tibetans. Here elements of Tibetan shamanism were assimilated to Buddhism to form a distinctive tradition known as Lamaism.

1 Talwandi was the birthplace in 1469 of Guru Nanak, founder of the Sikh religion.

2 Buddhism declined in its original heartland of Magadha after 600 and had been supplanted by Hinduism and Islam by the 13th century.

3 Jerusalem, site of Jesus' crucifixion, was believed by medieval Christians to be the center of the world.

4 Jews were tolerated in Muslim Spain but faced expulsion or forcible conversion after the Christian reconquest.

5 Constantinople, the greatest Christian city of the East, became a leading center of Islamic culture after its conquest by the Ottoman Turks in 1453.

6 Varanasi is Hinduism's most holy site: pilgrimages to bathe in the Ganges had become popular by 1050.

See also 3.09 (religion in medieval Europe); 3.17 (the Crusades); 3.19 (medieval India)

3.06 The rise of the Carolingian empire • 600 – 814 •

Of the Germanic kingdoms set up within the territory of the western Roman empire in the 5th century, only the Frankish and the Visigothic still survived in 600. The Visigothic kings preserved the late Roman administrative structure but, in contrast to the Franks who were able to win the cooperation and loyalty of their subjects, they remained distant from their Hispano-Roman subjects. This was a fatal weakness. Faced with an invasion of Muslim Arabs and Berbers from North Africa in 711, the Visigoths received no support and the kingdom abruptly collapsed. The invaders took only two years to overrun most of the Iberian peninsula, bringing it within the Umayyad caliphate. Only in the mountains of the far north was there substantial resistance. Here the small Christian kingdom of Asturias developed, based at Oviedo. By 800 it had won back a sizable part of the northwest peninsula from the Arabs.

Since the mid 5th century the Merovingian dynasty had ruled the Frankish kingdom. They followed the Germanic custom of dividing the kingdom between all male heirs, leading to a complex sequence of subdivisions as generation succeeded generation. The succession was rarely a simple matter, and civil wars and assassinations were frequent. In the mid 7th century real authority passed into the hands of court officials known as the mayors of the palace. Frankish power declined and some peripheral areas of the kingdom were lost: most were recovered early in the 8th century but Aquitaine, which broke away in 670, was not taken back until 768. The most successful of the mayors was Pepin II of Herstal (mayor 679–714), who was effective ruler of the entire kingdom by 687. Founder of the Carolingian dynasty, he began an expansion of Frankish power which continued under his son Charles Martel (mayor 714–41). In 732 he turned back an Arab invasion at Poitiers, ending Muslim expansion in the west.

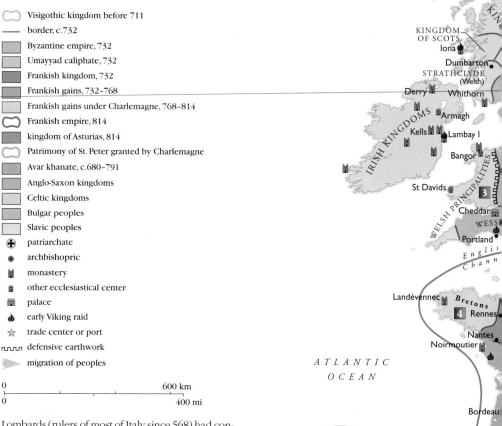

Charles' successor Pepin III (r.741–68) formed an alliance with the papacy in 751. The year before, the Lombards (rulers of most of Italy since 568) had conquered the Byzantine exarchate of Ravenna and were threatening Rome itself. In return for military aid, the pope authorized Pepin to depose the last Merovingian king and assume the kingship of the Franks himself. Pepin died in 768, and the kingdom was divided between his two sons, Charlemagne and Carloman. On the latter's death in 771 Charlemagne was sole ruler; he doubled the size of the Frankish realm in thirty years of campaigning. He was also an energetic legislator and administrator and was devoutly religious, even intervening in matters of doctrine. He promoted missionary activity among the pagan Saxons in the northeast and, anxious to improve the quality of the clergy, encouraged the revival of classical learning known as the Carolingian renaissance. Charlemagne made considerable donations of land to the papacy and, influenced by Byzantine ideas of rulership, had himself crowned emperor by the pope on Christmas Day 800, an act he probably saw as restoring the Roman empire in the west. In line with Frankish custom, Charlemagne made provisions for his empire to be divided between his three sons after his death but was survived by only one, Louis the Pious.

In the British Isles, the Anglo-Saxons had overrun most of the fertile lowland zone by 600 and were

Visigothic kingdom before 711
border, c.732
Byzantine empire, 732
Umayyad caliphate, 732
Frankish kingdom, 732
Frankish gains, 732–768
Frankish gains under Charlemagne, 768–814
Frankish empire, 814
kingdom of Asturias, 814
Patrimony of St. Peter granted by Charlemagne
Avar khanate, c.680–791
Anglo-Saxon kingdoms
Celtic kingdoms
Bulgar peoples
Slavic peoples
patriarchate
archbishopric
monastery
other ecclesiastical center
palace
early Viking raid
trade center or port
defensive earthwork
migration of peoples

0 600 km
0 400 mi

KINGDOM OF SCOTS
Iona
Dumbarton
STRATHCLYDE (Welsh)
Derry
Whithorn
IRISH KINGDOMS
Armagh
Kells
Lambay I
Bangor
WELSH PRINCIPALITIES
St Davids
3
Cheddar
WESS
Portland
English Chann
Landévennec
Bretons
4
Rennes
Nantes
Noirmoutier
ATLANTIC OCEAN
Bordeau
Basques
2
Oviedo
Covadonga 718
KINGDOM OF ASTURIAS
Roncesvalles 778
Galicia
Douro
Segoyuela 713
Zaragoza
UMAYYAD CALIPHATE
Tagus
Toledo
Lisbon
Guadiana
7
Alicante
Córdoba
Seville
Ecija 711
Jerez de la Frontera 711
Algeciras

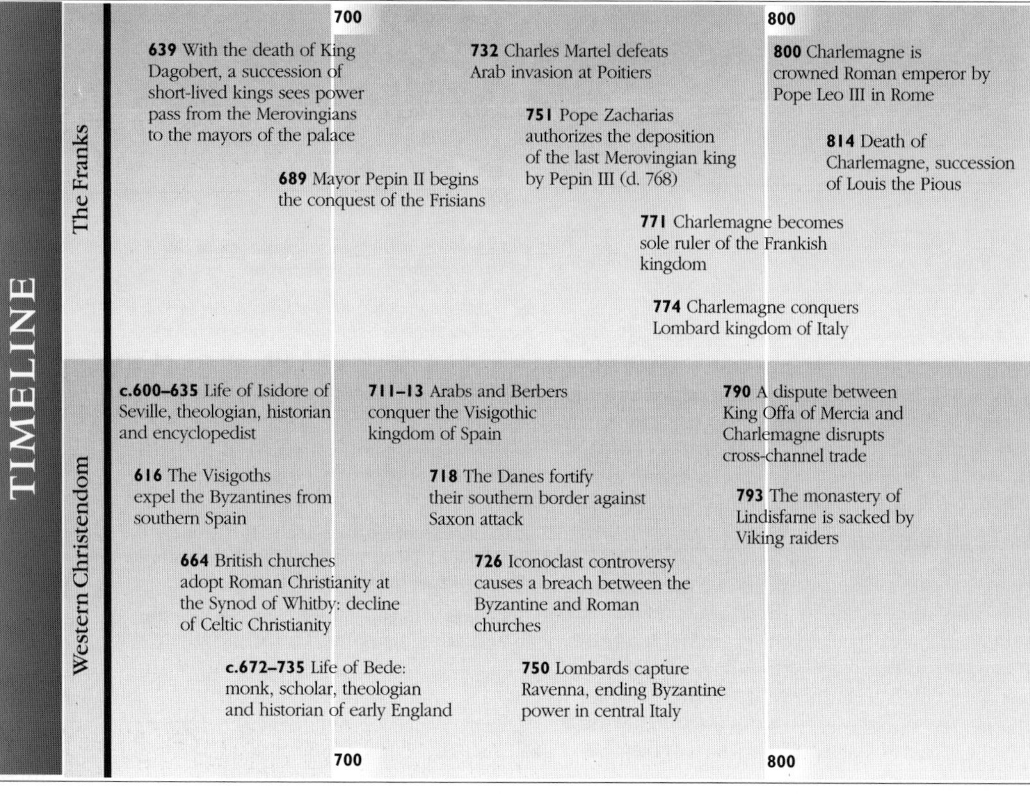

TIMELINE
The Franks
700
800
639 With the death of King Dagobert, a succession of short-lived kings sees power pass from the Merovingians to the mayors of the palace
689 Mayor Pepin II begins the conquest of the Frisians
732 Charles Martel defeats Arab invasion at Poitiers
751 Pope Zacharias authorizes the deposition of the last Merovingian king by Pepin III (d. 768)
771 Charlemagne becomes sole ruler of the Frankish kingdom
774 Charlemagne conquers Lombard kingdom of Italy
800 Charlemagne is crowned Roman emperor by Pope Leo III in Rome
814 Death of Charlemagne, succession of Louis the Pious
Western Christendom
c.600–635 Life of Isidore of Seville, theologian, historian and encyclopedist
616 The Visigoths expel the Byzantines from southern Spain
664 British churches adopt Roman Christianity at the Synod of Whitby: decline of Celtic Christianity
c.672–735 Life of Bede: monk, scholar, theologian and historian of early England
711–13 Arabs and Berbers conquer the Visigothic kingdom of Spain
718 The Danes fortify their southern border against Saxon attack
726 Iconoclast controversy causes a breach between the Byzantine and Roman churches
750 Lombards capture Ravenna, ending Byzantine power in central Italy
790 A dispute between King Offa of Mercia and Charlemagne disrupts cross-channel trade
793 The monastery of Lindisfarne is sacked by Viking raiders
700
800

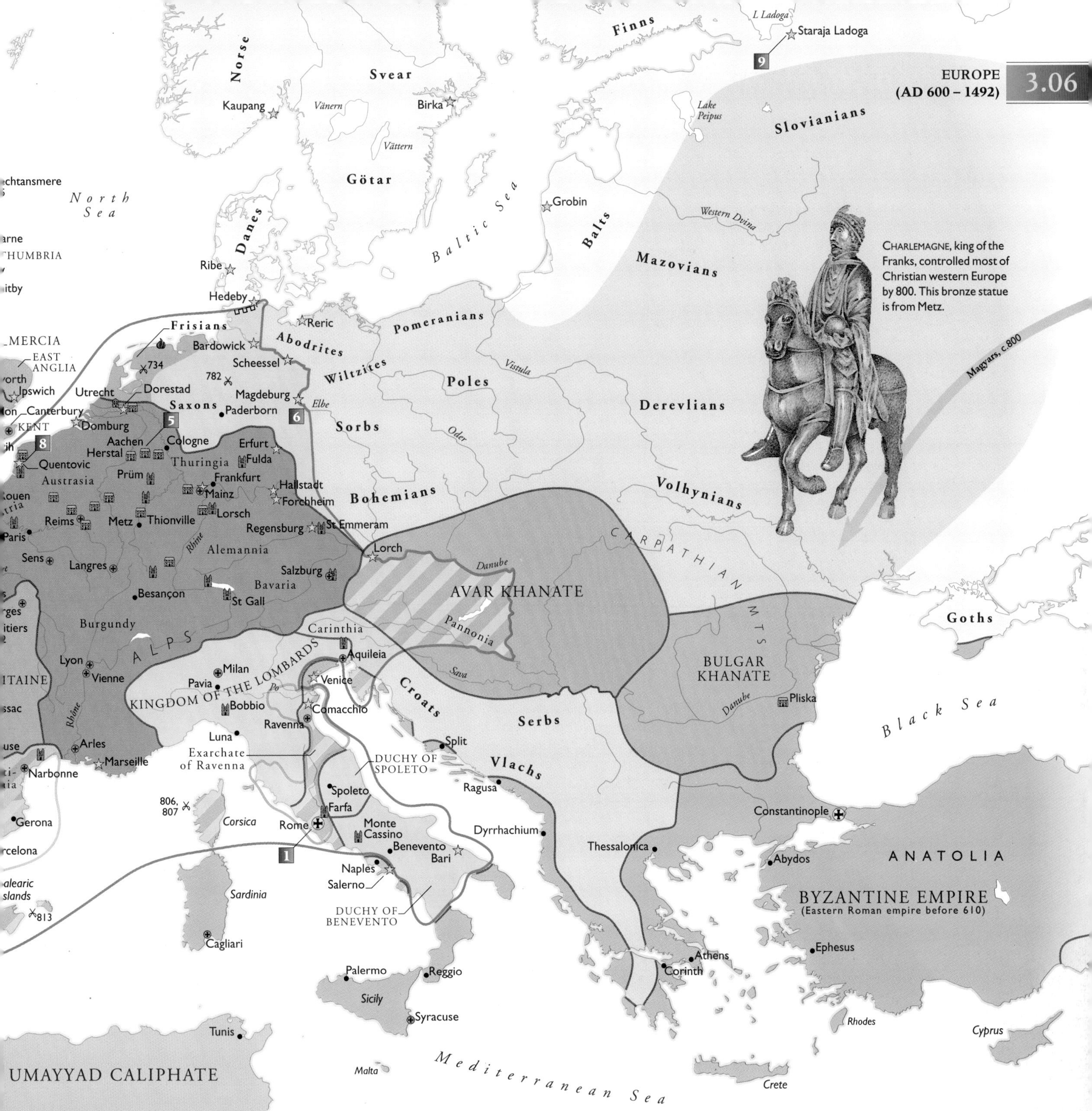

CHARLEMAGNE, king of the Franks, controlled most of Christian western Europe by 800. This bronze statue is from Metz.

beginning to form regional kingdoms, the most powerful being Northumbria. The Anglo-Saxon migrations into southern Britain had cut off British Christianity from contact with the Roman church. The Celtic church developed a distinctive identity and in Ireland fostered the creation of a monastic civilization that was to have significant influence on cultural and religious life in Europe. Irish and Roman missionaries both won converts among the Anglo-Saxons in the 7th century, and it was only with difficulty that the Celtic church was persuaded to rejoin the Roman church in 664. Northumbrian power declined after defeat by the Picts in 685, and in the 8th century the Mercian kingdom rose to dominance under Aethelbald (r.716–57) and Offa (r.757–96).

Frankish overrule brought a modest revival of trade and towns to western Europe, most marked around the southern North Sea and the Baltic where ports and seasonal trading places developed by 800. Though threatened by the Viking raids that broke out in the 790s, it was the start of the process that shifted the focus of economic life from the Mediterranean to the North Sea and Atlantic coasts.

1 Rome found a new role as the seat of the papacy and the spiritual capital of western Christendom.

2 The Asturian victory at Covadonga is regarded as the beginning of the Christian reconquest of Spain.

3 King Offa of Mercia built a 240km (185 mile) earth and timber rampart on his frontier with the Welsh.

4 The Bretons fiercely resisted Frankish expansion: subdued by Charlemagne in 799, they revolted in 812.

5 Charlemagne built an impressive palace, administrative and ecclesiastical complex at Aachen in the 790s.

6 Charlemagne set up a chain of customs posts to regulate trade with the Slavs in 806.

7 Córdoba, the capital of Muslim Spain, was the largest city in western Europe by the 9th century.

8 Trading centers such as Hamwih and Quentovic were evidence of the growing commercial importance of northern Europe.

9 Scandinavian merchants were established at the Finnic settlement of Staraja Ladoga by 750.

See also 3. 07 (Viking age), 3.13 (Arab conquests); 3.15 (Byzantine empire)

The Vikings – pagan raiders from Denmark and Norway – burst upon western Europe at the end of the 8th century as a bolt from the blue. The targets for their attacks were defenseless coastal monasteries which offered rich plunder. Their first known raid was against the monastery at Lindisfarne, the center of Northumbrian Christianity, in 793. Six years later they raided the Frankish coast, prompting Charlemagne to set up coastal defenses. But the full weight of Viking raids came in the 830s, when they arrived each year in ever greater numbers and began to sail up navigable rivers like the Rhine to sack inland ports such as Dorestad. Viking activity entered a new phase in 865 when the Danish "Great Army" invaded England with permanent settlement rather than plunder in mind. Much of eastern and northern England was overrun and settled (the area known as the Danelaw, with its capital at York) but the Wessex king Alfred (r.871–99) resisted the Danish advance. By 954 Alfred's successors had conquered the Scandinavian settlements and in the process created a united English kingdom. Traders and farmers as well as pirates, the Vikings also established colonies in Normandy, the Shetland and Orkney Islands, Ireland, the Faroe Islands and Iceland. A final migration across the Atlantic about 1000 led to the colonization of Greenland and the first European exploration in the Americas. In eastern Europe, Swedish venturers known as Rus pioneered trade routes along the rivers of Russia to the Black and Caspian Seas, giving their name to the Russian state which developed at Novgorod around 862.

The Viking raids and settlements were prompted by developments within Scandinavia itself. By the late 8th century power was becoming centralized, creating an intensely competitive society. For many, pirate raids overseas became a means to acquire wealth, a reputation and an armed following to support their ambitions at home. Others, denied the chance to rule at home, sought to conquer lands for themselves and their followers abroad. Trade and land hunger, caused by a rising population, were other important factors in the Viking phenomenon.

During the 10th century Denmark and Norway emerged as stable territorial states, a process completed in Sweden by the 12th century. The same period saw the start of the Scandinavians' conversion to Christianity. Denmark's hegemony briefly included England and Norway under Cnut (r.1016–35). In the east the Slavs assimilated the Rus ruling class and by 1000 Kievan Rus was a powerful Slavic state, strongly influenced by the Byzantines who introduced Orthodox Christianity. In Normandy the Vikings adopted French culture and language by 1000, but remained effectively independent of the French monarchy, which had passed from the Carolingian line with the accession of Hugh Capet in 987.

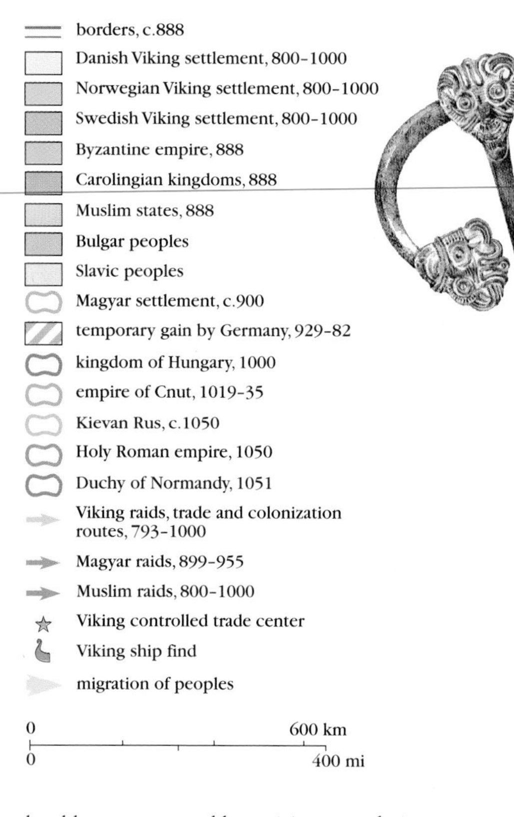
borders, c.888
Danish Viking settlement, 800–1000
Norwegian Viking settlement, 800–1000
Swedish Viking settlement, 800–1000
Byzantine empire, 888
Carolingian kingdoms, 888
Muslim states, 888
Bulgar peoples
Slavic peoples
Magyar settlement, c.900
temporary gain by Germany, 929–82
kingdom of Hungary, 1000
empire of Cnut, 1019–35
Kievan Rus, c.1050
Holy Roman empire, 1050
Duchy of Normandy, 1051
Viking raids, trade and colonization routes, 793–1000
Magyar raids, 899–955
Muslim raids, 800–1000
Viking controlled trade center
Viking ship find
migration of peoples
0 600 km
0 400 mi

BRONZEWORKING was highly developed among the Vikings, as in this decorated brooch from Denmark.

Iceland
c.870 Norse settlement
c.986 to Greenland
Faroe Islands
c.825 Norse settlement
Orkney Islands
Hebrides
KINGDOM OF SCOTS
Iona
Scone
KINGDOM OF STRATHCLYDE (Welsh)
Lindisfarne
IRISH KINGDOMS
2
KINGDOM OF YORK
Dublin
Limerick
Waterford
Wexford
KINGDOM OF WESSEX
WELSH PRINCIPALITIES
Edington
878
London
Winchester
914–39 occupied but not settled by Vikings
BRITTANY
3
Nantes
Loire
ATLANTIC OCEAN
Bordeaux
NAVARRE
Oviedo
Santiago de Compostela
León
Toulouse
KINGDOM OF ASTURIAS AND LEÓN
Douro
Zaragoza
Barcelona
951
997
981
Tagus
Toledo
Lisbon
Mérida
Guadiana
UMAYYAD EMIRATE
Alicante
Córdoba
Seville
IDRISID CALIPHATE

TIMELINE

The Viking world

900 | 1000

830s Viking raids on English and Frankish coast increase

845 The Franks buy off raiders by paying Danegeld

859–62 Viking raiders in the Mediterranean

878 Alfred, king of Wessex, defeats the Danes at Edington

882 Oleg makes Kiev capital of the Rus state

911 Charles the Simple allows Viking settlement in Normandy

954 Fall of Viking kingdom of York

965 Harald Bluetooth of Denmark is baptised first Christian king in Scandinavia

986 Erik the Red founds Norse settlements in Greenland

c.1000 Norse Greenlanders found shortlived settlement in Newfoundland

1014 Danes under Svein Forkbeard conquer England

1016–35 Cnut reigns in England, Denmark and Norway

Western Christendom

840 Death of Louis the Pious

843 Treaty of Verdun divides Carolingian empire into three

846 Muslim pirates sack the Vatican

889 Final breakup of the Carolingian empire

898–99 Magyars invade Italy and sack Pavia

910 Cluny abbey is founded in Burgundy, initiating period of monastic reform

911 End of Carolingian rule in Germany and accession of Henry the Fowler, founder of Saxon dynasty

962 Otto I crowned Roman emperor in Rome: Holy Roman empire founded

1002 Umayyad caliphate collapses into petty states

1027 Arrival of Norman mercenaries in southern Italy

1043 Edward the Confessor is crowned king of England

900 | 1000

The Viking invasions occurred at a time when the Carolingian empire was weakened by internal squabbles. The emperor Louis the Pious (r.814–40) was not willing, as Charlemagne had been, to contemplate the equal division of the empire between his sons. Louis' younger sons and many of the Franks regarded the settlement as unjust and in 827 civil war broke out. The succession was not resolved until the Treaty of Verdun (843) which saw the empire divided into three parts. By this time royal authority was weakened and defenses against the Vikings had collapsed. Charles the Fat briefly reunited the Carolingian empire from 885–87, but it broke up finally in 889 into five kingdoms: West Francia (France), East Francia (Germany), Italy, Burgundy and Provence.

The Vikings were not the only threat facing western Christendom. Muslim pirates from Spain and Tunisia raided the Mediterranean coast and preyed on travelers over the Alpine passes. In the east a nomadic people, the Magyars, crossed the Carpathians around 900 to settle in the Danube plain in the old Roman province of Pannonia, from where they raided Italy, Germany and France. By 1000, however, the Muslim and Magyar threats had ended and Viking activity was limited mainly to the British Isles. Leading the recovery was Germany. With the ending of Carolingian rule there in 911, power passed into the hands of the Saxon kings. Under Otto I (r.936–73) the Magyars were defeated at the battle of Lechfeld (955) and were converted to Christianity. Expansion against the Slavs continued, and Otto annexed the kingdom of Italy in 951–61. Crowned Roman emperor in 962, he founded what became known as the Holy Roman empire. By the 11th century the German emperors had emerged as the clear leaders of western Christendom.

1 The monastery of Luxeuil was sacked successively by Viking raiders, Muslim pirates and Magyars between 886 and 924.

2 The Viking raids damaged Ireland's monastic culture, but also founded its first towns at Dublin, Wexford, Waterford and Limerick in the 9th century.

3 Paris first rose to prominence as a result of its determined resistance to a Viking siege in 885–86.

4 Conversion of the Poles to Christianity began in 966: the first Polish archbishopric, at Gniezno, was founded in 1000.

5 German protectorates from 935, Burgundy and Provence were united in a single kingdom in 948 and absorbed into the Holy Roman empire in 1033.

6 Rus traders traveled down the river Volga to Bulgar to trade slaves and furs with Arab merchants.

7 Strategically placed, Gotland was an important center of Baltic trade: over 40,000 Arab, 38,000 Frankish and 28,000 Anglo-Saxon silver coins have been found there.

See also 3.05 (world religions); 3.06 (Carolingians); 3.26 (North America)

3.08 Feudal Europe • 1050 – 1300 •

Feudalism was a contractual system by which a lord granted a fief (or estate) to a vassal, usually a knight or nobleman, in return for sworn homage and military service. The Carolingian kings used the system to bind the nobility in loyalty to the crown, but under a weak ruler it could undermine royal authority and decentralize power. By the late 11th century feudalism had been introduced to England and Sicily by the Normans and was highly developed in Spain. It was present, though less dominant, in Scotland, Scandinavia, northern Italy and eastern Europe. By 1200 the military importance of feudalism was in decline, as kings could raise money to hire professional soldiers, and vassals could make a cash payment in lieu of military service. Fiefs had become heritable and were treated by vassals as family estates.

HAROLD II, last Anglo-Saxon king of England (r.1066), is shown here being crowned in the Bayeux Tapestry (c.1080).

Decentralization was most extreme in France, where the royal lands (the demesne) were confined in the 11th century to the area around Paris and Orléans, while powerful vassals like the dukes of Normandy and the counts of Anjou and Aquitaine were semi-independent rulers of vast fiefs. When William of Normandy became king of England by conquest in 1066, he became more powerful than his feudal lord, the French king. In the 1150s Henry Plantagenet of Anjou accumulated, through inheritance and marriage, fiefs covering half of France, dwarfing the royal demesne. In 1154 he inherited the English throne to become, as Henry II, the most powerful ruler in Europe. Yet he tried to avoid open warfare with the French king, feeling he should not set a bad example to his own vassals. Philip Augustus (r.1180–1223) revived the French monarchy and recovered all the Angevin fiefs except Gascony. In 1214 he repulsed a German invasion at Bouvines, making France the strongest power in Europe.

The German kings and emperors avoided the problems of the French monarchy by granting land as fiefs to the church. Literate priests and abbots were well equipped to administer its fiefs, and celibate churchmen could not found dynasties, so the lands returned into the gift of the king. As long as the king retained control over ecclesiastical appointments, this system offered a counterweight to the territorial nobility. But when emperor Henry III died in 1056, leaving his son Henry IV (r.1056–1106) in the control of a weak regency, the papacy asserted itself. The ensuing Investiture Contest (1075–1122), a dispute over who had the right to nominate to vacant sees, gave the popes greatly enhanced authority. A sign of their new prestige was the summoning of the First Crusade in 1095, which led to the capture of Jerusalem in 1099.

The Hohenstaufen emperor Frederick Barbarossa (r. 1152–90) found his authority challenged in Germany by powerful territorial princes, such as Henry the Lion of the Welf family. He tried to compensate by tightening imperial control in Italy but was defeated by the Lombard league of cities in 1176. His successors did little better. Though the Hohenstaufens won control of the Norman kingdom of Sicily in 1194, they failed to assert their authority over the German princes, and the Holy Roman empire disintegrated into a loose federation of states. The emperor Frederick II (r.1210–50) attempted to consolidate his

Faroe Islands
Earldom of Orkney
Orkney Islands
Hebrides
SCOTLAND
Perth
Edinburgh
North Sea
Kingdom of Man
IRISH KINGDOMS & CHIEFDOMS
Dublin
York
Stamford Bridge 1066
ENGLAND
Norwich
Oxford
London
Canterb
Hastings 1066
WELSH PRINCIPALITIES
Brug
Bouvine 121
Rouen
Bayeux
Normandy
Paris
Brittany
Maine
Orléan
Loire
Tours
Anjou
ATLANTIC OCEAN
FRANCE
Clermont
Aquitaine
Bordeaux
Gascony
County of Toulouse
Toulouse
Mar
LEÓN
León
NAVARRE
Douro
ARAGON
CASTILE
Barcelona
Coimbra
PORTUGAL
Tagus
Toledo
Lisbon
Guadiana
Valencia
Las Navas de Tolosa 1212
EMIRATE OF MALLO
1
Córdoba
ALMOHAD CALIPHATE until 1230
Granada

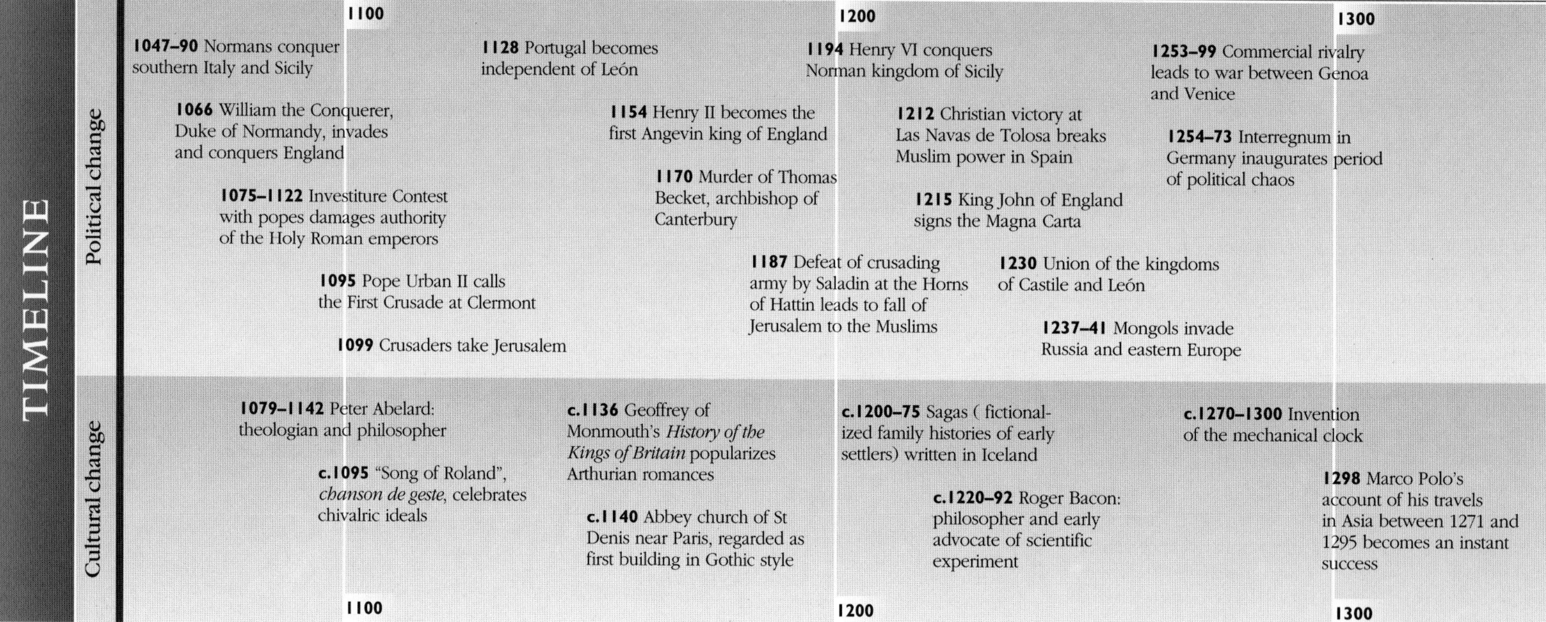

TIMELINE

Political change

1047–90 Normans conquer southern Italy and Sicily

1066 William the Conquerer, Duke of Normandy, invades and conquers England

1075–1122 Investiture Contest with popes damages authority of the Holy Roman emperors

1095 Pope Urban II calls the First Crusade at Clermont

1099 Crusaders take Jerusalem

1100

1128 Portugal becomes independent of León

1154 Henry II becomes the first Angevin king of England

1170 Murder of Thomas Becket, archbishop of Canterbury

1187 Defeat of crusading army by Saladin at the Horns of Hattin leads to fall of Jerusalem to the Muslims

1194 Henry VI conquers Norman kingdom of Sicily

1200

1212 Christian victory at Las Navas de Tolosa breaks Muslim power in Spain

1215 King John of England signs the Magna Carta

1230 Union of the kingdoms of Castile and León

1237–41 Mongols invade Russia and eastern Europe

1253–99 Commercial rivalry leads to war between Genoa and Venice

1254–73 Interregnum in Germany inaugurates period of political chaos

1300

Cultural change

1079–1142 Peter Abelard: theologian and philosopher

c.1095 "Song of Roland", *chanson de geste*, celebrates chivalric ideals

1100

c.1136 Geoffrey of Monmouth's *History of the Kings of Britain* popularizes Arthurian romances

c.1140 Abbey church of St Denis near Paris, regarded as first building in Gothic style

c.1200–75 Sagas (fictionalized family histories of early settlers) written in Iceland

1200

c.1220–92 Roger Bacon: philosopher and early advocate of scientific experiment

c.1270–1300 Invention of the mechanical clock

1298 Marco Polo's account of his travels in Asia between 1271 and 1295 becomes an instant success

1300

Trondheim
Finns
Lake Onega
NORWAY
Bergen
Christiania
SWEDEN
Uppsala
Vänern
Vättern
Visby
Åbo
River Neva 1240
Lake Ladoga
Ladoga
Beloozero
REPUBLIC OF NOVGOROD
Novgorod
Revel
Estonians
Lake Peipus 1242
Lake Peipus
Pskov
Livs
Riga
Western Dvina
PRINCIPALITY OF VLADIMIR
Volga
Bulgar
Volga Bulgars
Vladimir
Murom
Moscow
Ryazan
PRINCIPALITY OF SMOLENSK
Smolensk
PRINCIPALITY OF MUROM–RYAZAN
PRINCIPALITY OF CHERNIGOV
Lithuanians
Polotsk
PRINCIPALITY OF POLOTSK
Minsk
Baltic Sea
Århus
DENMARK
Roskilde
Lund
Königsberg
Schleswig
Danzig
Wends
Prus
Holstein
Hamburg
Stettin
Bremen
Saxony
Magdeburg
Brandenburg
Vistula
PRINCIPALITY OF TUROV–PINSK
Pinsk
Chernigov
Don
Cumans (Turkic)
POLAND
Elbe
Thuringia
Breslau
Oder
PRINCIPALITY OF VOLHYNIA
PRINCIPALITY OF KIEV
Kiev
PRINCIPALITY OF PEREYASLAV
Pereyaslav
PRINCIPALITY OF NOVGOROD–SEVERSK
Cologne
GERMANY
Frankfurt
Mainz
Franconia
Krakow
Prague
BOHEMIA
Dnieper
Galich
PRINCIPALITY OF GALICIA
Nuremberg
Rhine
Danube
Bavaria
Swabia
Vienna
Austria
Salzburg
Styria
Gran
Pest
Cumans (Turkic)
to Kiev
Alans
Carinthia
HUNGARY
Legnano 1176
Milan
Aquileia
Venice
Sava
Belgrade
VENICE
KINGDOM OF ITALY
Bologna
Genoa
Zara
Pisa
Florence
PISA
Danube
Black Sea
Ragusa
BYZANTINE EMPIRE
GEORGIA
Corsica
Rome
PAPAL STATES
Constantinople
Dyrrachium
Thessalonica
Benevento 1266
Bari
Sardinia
Naples
KINGDOM OF SICILY
Palermo
Sicily
Tunis
ALMOHAD CALIPHATE until 1230
Malta
Mediterranean Sea
Crete
0 600 km
0 400 mi
Duchy of Normandy, 1066
Norman gains in England and southern Italy by 1154
Holy Roman empire, c.1175
Hohenstaufen demesne
Welf demesne
Church land
other
borders, c.1175
effective Angevin (Anjou) control, c.1175
nominal Angevin control, c.1175
French royal demesne, c.1175
Angevin fiefs in France after 1214
Byzantine empire, 1175
Norwegian territory, 1175
Swedish territory, 1175
Holy Roman empire, 1175
expansion of German settlement, 12th–13th centuries
Lombard league city, 1167
German city founded in 13th century
ARAGON fief of the Papacy during the pontificate of Innocent III, 1198–1216
German and Danish crusades against the pagan Slavs and Balts, 12th–13th centuries
Swedish expansion, 12th–13th centuries
western limit of Mongol conquests, 1240
Spanish states, 1300
Aragon
Castile
emirate of Granada
Portugal
controlled by the Teutonic Knights, c.1300
Russian states
pagan area

position in Italy but, faced with the hostility of the papacy and the Lombard cities, his reign ended in failure and the dynasty was overthrown in 1266. Despite the political fragmentation of the empire, the 13th century saw German influence expand to the east through the establishment of peasant settlements and new towns, and the activities of traders and the crusading order of the Teutonic Knights in the Baltic.

The Slavic state of Kievan Rus broke up into several principalities in 1132, most of which were overrun by the Mongols in 1237–41. Alexander Nevsky (r.1236–63), ruler of Novgorod, submitted voluntarily to the Mongol invasion, and was therefore able to concentrate his resources on resisting incursions by Swedish forces and the Teutonic Knights. In 1252, he added the principality of Vladimir to his possessions.

1 Lisbon was captured from the Muslims by a fleet from northern Europe *en route* to the Second Crusade in the Holy Land in 1147.

2 Alexander Nevsky's victory at the river Neva in 1240 halted further Swedish expansion eastward.

3 Austria was founded as a duchy by Frederick Barbarossa in 1156 to counter Welf power in Bavaria.

4 The wealthy cities of Lombardy formed defensive leagues in 1167 and 1226 to resist imperial attempts to restrict their freedoms.

5 A major concern of the Papacy was to prevent a political union between the Holy Roman empire and the kingdom of Sicily.

6 Sicily passed to the Normans (1091); to emperor Henry IV (1194); to the Angevin dynasty (1266); to the Aragonese (1282); to independence (1295).

See also 3.09 (religion in medieval Europe); 3.17 (Crusades); 3.22 (Mongol empire)

3.09 Religion in medieval Europe • 800 – 1300 •

The church's split into the opposing camps of eastern Orthodoxy and western Catholicism dated from late Roman times. Five sees – Jerusalem, Alexandria, Antioch, Constantinople and Rome – were recognized as having patriarchal status. As the direct heirs of St Peter, the popes (the name given to the Roman patriarchs) claimed, but failed to establish, primacy over the rest. In the 7th century Antioch, Jerusalem and Alexandria came under Muslim rule and declined in importance, but the popes continued to press their claims against the patriarch of Constantinople. Animosity hardened as the two churches competed for influence among the Magyars and Slavs: the conversion of Hungary and Poland was brought about by Catholic missionaries; Serbia, Bulgaria and Russia by Orthodox. Schisms between the two branches of the church were frequent, and in 1054 the breach became permanent when the pope excommunicated the patriarch for refusing to accept his authority. Although the Byzantine emperor appealed to the west for help in expelling the Turks from Asia Minor after the battle of Manzikert, relations between the Greeks and the Latin Crusaders were always strained, even before the sack of Constantinople in 1204.

Standards in the western church had declined in the 9th century: the papacy itself was corrupt and under the control of the Roman nobility, and clerical morals were lax. A reform movement spreading out from monastic centers such as Gorze in Germany and Cluny in Burgundy during the 10th century gradually widened the demand for church reform. In 1046 emperor Henry III (r.1039–56) deposed three rival popes at the synod of Sutri and appointed his own reformist candidate. But a strengthened and reformed papacy soon determined to assert its independence of imperial control. Reform in Rome was led by the German churchman Hildebrand who, as Pope Gregory VII (r.1073–85), banned laymen from investing bishops and claimed papal primacy in secular affairs. Papal authority increased through the 12th century, reaching its zenith under Innocent III (r.1198–1216), an able lawyer and administrator.

In the hands of such men the church became a wealthy and worldly institution. By the 12th century abbeys such as Cluny had moved away from their ideals of poverty, prompting a new call for monastic reform. The Cistercian order, with an austere rule of labor, prayer and study, spread throughout Europe under the charismatic leadership of St Bernard of Clairvaux. The dissatisfaction of many lay people with the laxity of the church fed the growth of anti-clerical movements, such as the Waldensians. Others embraced the antimaterialistic Cathar heresy, which held that the universe is ruled by two powers, one good, one evil. To combat such heresies the papacy authorized new preaching orders of friars and launched the Albigensian Crusade against the Cathars of southwest France.

border, c.1200
Muslim dominated lands
Catholic Christendom
Orthodox Christendom
Georgian rite
Greek rite
Slavonic rite
main concentration of Jews
pagan
heretics
Bogomils (Manichaeans)
Cathars
Waldensians
maximum extent of Crusader control, c.1144
patriarchal see
metropolitan see
archbishopric
Benedictine or Cluniac monastery
Cistercian monastery
Orthodox monastery
other monastery
university founded before 1300, with date
monastic school
cathedral school
Rome pilgrimage destination
pilgrim route
Faroe Islands to Norway
Shetland Islands to Norway
Orkney Islands to Norway
Kingdom of Man to Norway
SCOTLAND
North Sea
Iona
Dunfermline
Melrose
Lindisfarne
Furness
Mount Grace
Armagh
Rievaulx
Tuam
Mellifont
Fountains
York
IRELAND
Dublin
Cashel
ENGLAND
WALES
Cambridge 1209
Peterborough
Oxford c.1190
Bury St Edmunds
Tintern
St Albans
Glastonbury
London
Lewes
Canterbury
Boulogne
Fécamp
Rouen
Mont-St-Michel
Bec
Paris c.1170
St Denis
Savigny
Chartres
Clairvaux
Angers 1229
Fleury
Sens
Tours
Fontevrault
Bourges
Citeaux
Poitiers
Cluny
ATLANTIC OCEAN
FRANCE
Bordeaux
Grand Chartreuse
Moissac
Albi
Auch
Toulouse 1229
Narbonne
Santiago de Compostela
LEÓN
NAVARRE
Sahagún
Las Huelgas
Moruela
ARAGON
Braga
Palencia 1208
Lérida 1300
Poblet
Douro
Salamanca 1243
Huerta
Coimbra 1290
CASTILE
Santa Creus
PORTUGAL
Alcobaça
Tagus
Toledo
Lisbon 1290
Guadiana
Balearic Islands
ALMOHAD CALIPHATE
Seville 1254

TIMELINE

Catholic church

927–941 Cluny (founded 910) becomes center of monastic reform movement under Odo

c.1000–1100 The cult of the Virgin Mary becomes an important element in popular Catholic religion

1046 The synod of Sutri places the papacy at the head of the reform movement

1054 Pope excommunicates patriarch of Constantinople, precipating final split between churches

1095 Pope Urban II's call for a crusade to free the holy places of Jerusalem sparks off wave of Jewish massacres in the Rhineland

1115 Cistercians found their third house at Clairvaux with St Bernard as abbot (until 1153)

1123 First Lateran Council (general council of the Catholic church) condemns simony and clerical marriage

c.1173 Peter Valdes, a merchant, founds the heretical Waldensian movement

1209 Franciscan order of. friars founded by St Francis of Assisi receives papal approval

1209–29 Albigensian crusades against Cathars in southwest France

1232 Inquisition established to investigate and prosecute heretics

1267–73 St Thomas Aquinas (c.1224–74) writes the *Summa Theologiae*

Orthodox

988 The baptism of Vladimir of Kiev leads to the conversion of Russia to Orthodox Christianity

1071 Defeat of Greek army by Seljuk Turks at Manzikert leads to loss of Byzantine influence in Asia Minor

1110 Basil, leader of the heretical Bogomil sect with strong support in the Balkans, is burnt in Constantinople

1204 Army of the Fourth Crusade sacks Constantinople and expels Greek emperor (until 1261)

1000 1100 1200

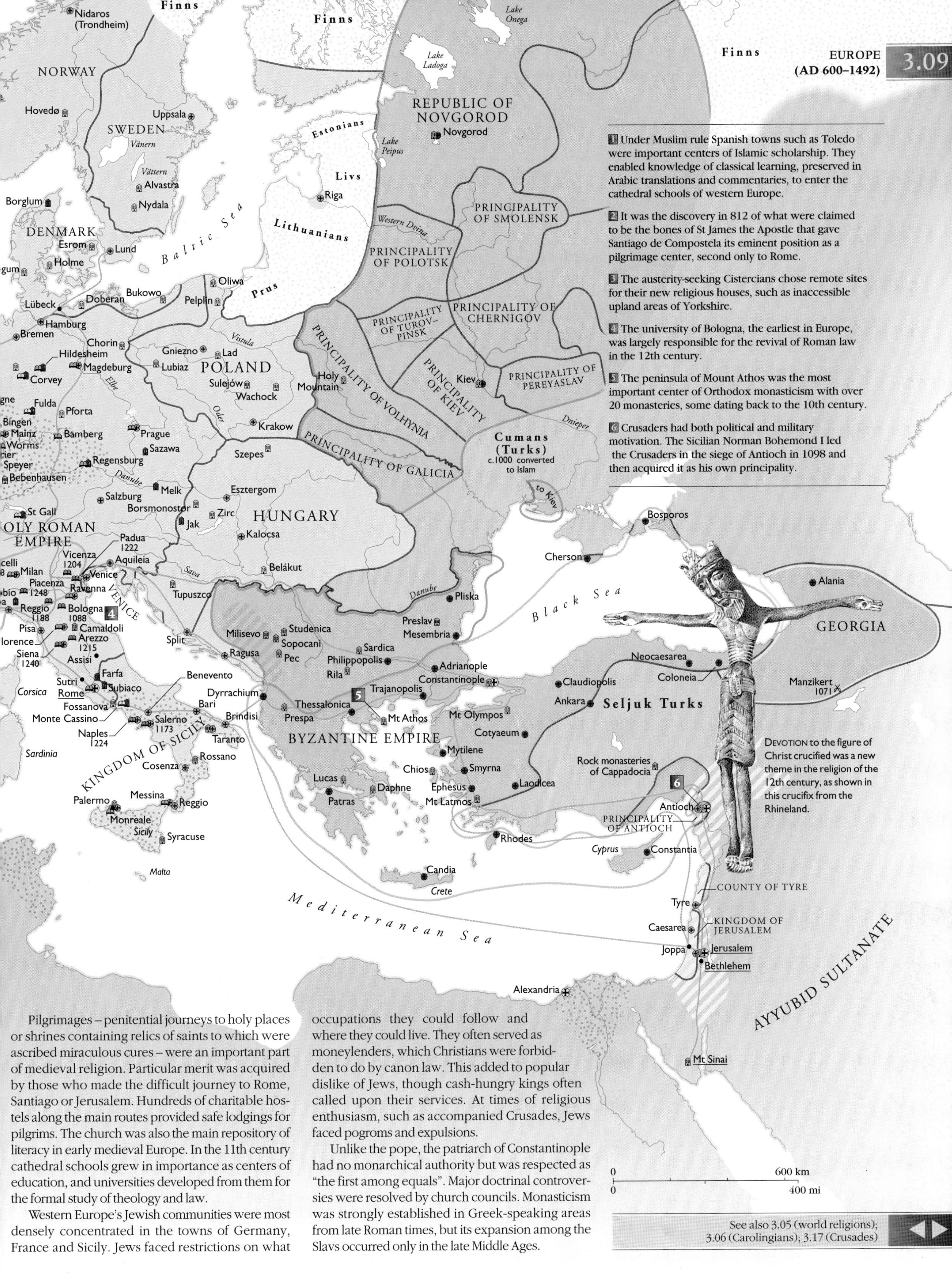
Finns
Nidaros (Trondheim)
NORWAY
Hovedø
Uppsala
SWEDEN
Vänern
Vättern
Alvastra
Nydala
Borglum
DENMARK
Esrom
Lund
Holme
Baltic Sea
Lübeck
Doberan
Bukowo
Oliwa
Pelplin
Prus
Hamburg
Bremen
Chorin
Hildesheim
Magdeburg
Corvey
Gniezno
Lad
Lubiaz
POLAND
Sulejów
Wachock
Vistula
Oder
Elbe
Fulda
Pforta
Bingen
Mainz
Worms
Speyer
Bamberg
Prague
Sazawa
Regensburg
Bebenhausen
Krakow
Szepes
Danube
Salzburg
Melk
Esztergom
Borsmonostor
Zirc
HUNGARY
Jak
Kalocsa
St Gall
OLY ROMAN EMPIRE
Padua 1222
Vicenza 1204
Aquileia
Venice
Milan
Piacenza 1248
Ravenna
Reggio 1188
Bologna 1088
VENICE
Pisa
Camaldoli
Arezzo 1215
Siena 1240
Assisi
Farfa
Sutri
Rome
Subiaco
Corsica
Fossanova
Monte Cassino
Benevento
Salerno 1173
Naples 1224
Sardinia
Bari
Brindisi
Taranto
Rossano
Cosenza
KINGDOM OF SICILY
Messina
Reggio
Palermo
Monreale
Sicily
Syracuse
Malta
Sava
Belákut
Tupuszco
Split
Ragusa
Milisevo
Studenica
Sopocani
Pec
Sardica
Philippopolis
Rila
Dyrrachium
Thessalonica
Prespa
Trajanopolis
Mt Athos
Adrianople
Constantinople
Preslav
Mesembria
Pliska
Danube
BYZANTINE EMPIRE
Lucas
Patras
Daphne
Chios
Mytilene
Smyrna
Ephesus
Mt Latmos
Mt Olympos
Cotyaeum
Rhodes
Candia
Crete
Mediterranean Sea
Lake Onega
Lake Ladoga
Finns
REPUBLIC OF NOVGOROD
Novgorod
Estonians
Lake Peipus
Livs
Riga
Lithuanians
Western Dvina
PRINCIPALITY OF SMOLENSK
PRINCIPALITY OF POLOTSK
PRINCIPALITY OF TUROV-PINSK
PRINCIPALITY OF CHERNIGOV
PRINCIPALITY OF VOLHYNIA
Holy Mountain
PRINCIPALITY OF KIEV
Kiev
PRINCIPALITY OF PEREYASLAV
Dnieper
PRINCIPALITY OF GALICIA
Cumans (Turks)
c.1000 converted to Islam
to Kiev
Bosporos
Cherson
Black Sea
Alania
GEORGIA
Neocaesarea
Coloneia
Claudiopolis
Ankara
Seljuk Turks
Manzikert 1071
Rock monasteries of Cappadocia
Laodicea
Antioch
PRINCIPALITY OF ANTIOCH
Cyprus
Constantia
COUNTY OF TYRE
Tyre
Caesarea
KINGDOM OF JERUSALEM
Joppa
Jerusalem
Bethlehem
Alexandria
AYYUBID SULTANATE
Mt Sinai
0 600 km
0 400 mi

DEVOTION to the figure of Christ crucified was a new theme in the religion of the 12th century, as shown in this crucifix from the Rhineland.

1 Under Muslim rule Spanish towns such as Toledo were important centers of Islamic scholarship. They enabled knowledge of classical learning, preserved in Arabic translations and commentaries, to enter the cathedral schools of western Europe.

2 It was the discovery in 812 of what were claimed to be the bones of St James the Apostle that gave Santiago de Compostela its eminent position as a pilgrimage center, second only to Rome.

3 The austerity-seeking Cistercians chose remote sites for their new religious houses, such as inaccessible upland areas of Yorkshire.

4 The university of Bologna, the earliest in Europe, was largely responsible for the revival of Roman law in the 12th century.

5 The peninsula of Mount Athos was the most important center of Orthodox monasticism with over 20 monasteries, some dating back to the 10th century.

6 Crusaders had both political and military motivation. The Sicilian Norman Bohemond I led the Crusaders in the siege of Antioch in 1098 and then acquired it as his own principality.

Pilgrimages – penitential journeys to holy places or shrines containing relics of saints to which were ascribed miraculous cures – were an important part of medieval religion. Particular merit was acquired by those who made the difficult journey to Rome, Santiago or Jerusalem. Hundreds of charitable hostels along the main routes provided safe lodgings for pilgrims. The church was also the main repository of literacy in early medieval Europe. In the 11th century cathedral schools grew in importance as centers of education, and universities developed from them for the formal study of theology and law.

Western Europe's Jewish communities were most densely concentrated in the towns of Germany, France and Sicily. Jews faced restrictions on what occupations they could follow and where they could live. They often served as moneylenders, which Christians were forbidden to do by canon law. This added to popular dislike of Jews, though cash-hungry kings often called upon their services. At times of religious enthusiasm, such as accompanied Crusades, Jews faced pogroms and expulsions.

Unlike the pope, the patriarch of Constantinople had no monarchical authority but was respected as "the first among equals". Major doctrinal controversies were resolved by church councils. Monasticism was strongly established in Greek-speaking areas from late Roman times, but its expansion among the Slavs occurred only in the late Middle Ages.

See also 3.05 (world religions); 3.06 (Carolingians); 3.17 (Crusades)

3.10 War, revolt and plague in 14th-century Europe • 1300–1400 •

The authority of the papacy – already in decline in the face of royal attempts to build centralized nation-states – faced a further setback in 1303 when it fell under the domination of the French monarchy. In 1309 it took up residence at Avignon. It returned to Rome in 1377, but a disputed papal election led to the Great Schism in 1378, with rival popes sitting at Rome and Avignon. The schism stayed unresolved until 1417 as neither pope would submit to the judgment of a church council. It divided Europe and exacerbated existing political differences. France supported the Avignon papacy, for example, so England – then involved in the Hundred Years War (1337–1453) with France – gave its allegiance to the Roman papacy while Scotland, antagonistic to England, joined the French party.

The Hundred Years War had been sparked off by French attempts to recover English lands in France. After English victories at Crécy (1346) and Poitiers (1356), the French ceded Aquitaine and Gascony at the treaty of Bretigny (1360). But fighting broke out again and when a 28-year truce was agreed in 1396 the English held less land in France than they had in 1337. In 1363, the French monarchy stored up future trouble by granting the duchy of Burgundy out of the royal desmesne to Philip the Bold, the younger son of John II. Through marriage to the heiress of the Count of Flanders (1369), Philip later added the imperial county of Burgundy (the Franche-Comté) and the wool towns of Flanders to his possessions.

War was endemic throughout the Holy Roman empire.The powerful city-states of northern Italy, where imperial control was now purely nominal, engaged armies of mercenaries to fight one another. The German princes were occupied in dynastic struggles to gain primacy and thus win control of imperial elections. The Wittelsbachs gained the upper hand from the Habsburgs in 1325, only to lose it to the Luxembourgs (1346–1438). From 1377–89 the princes formed a united front to reduce the independence of the cities of south Germany and the Rhineland. In 1388, after a century of rebellion, the Swiss confederation of eight cantons secured their independence from the dukes of Habsburg. In eastern Europe in 1354, the Ottoman Turks took

Faroe Islands to Norway
Shetland Islands to Norway
Orkney Islands to Norway
borders, c.1360–61
Muslim states
Orthodox states
English possessions
Genoese possessions
Venetian possessions
Holy Roman empire
Habsburg lands
Luxembourg lands
Wittelsbach lands
other
Great Schism, 1378
supporting Avignon papacy
supporting Roman papacy
supporting Roman papacy, but with shifting allegiances on a local level
antisemitic rioting and massacres
urban revolt
rural revolt
lands acquired for Burgundy by Philip the Bold, c.1396
spread of Black Death, with date
area relatively lightly affected by the Plague
Lollard heretic movement, c.1400
0 600 km
0 400 mi
Hebrides
SCOTLAND
Bannockburn 1314
Edinburgh
North Sea
ENGLAND
York
Ireland
Dublin
Chester
Wexford
Norwich
East Anglia
Oxford
Bristol
London
Southampton
Friesland
Holland
mid 1349
Utre
Antwerp
Bruges
Ypres
Flanders
Crécy 1346
Cherbourg
Amiens
Laon
Rouen
Reims
Paris
Luxembourg
Brittany
Orléans
Nantes
Loire
Franche-Comté
FRANCE
Burgun
Poitiers 1356
Aquitaine
Lyon
Vienne
Bordeaux
Gascony
Avignon
Toulouse
Arles
Marseill
NAVARRE
Burgos
CASTILE
Douro
ARAGON
ANDORRA
Barcelona
Segovia
PORTUGAL
Aljubarrota 1385
Tagus
Toledo
Lisbon
Guadiana
Valencia
Balearic Islands to Aragon
Córdoba
Seville
EMIRATE OF GRANADA
Granada
MOORISH EMIRATES
ATLANTIC OCEAN
late 1349
mid 1349
late 1348
mid 1348
late 1348
mid 1348
1347

TIMELINE

Political change

1325	1350	1375
1302 Territorial expansion of Muscovy begins	**1326** Cannon first used in Europe by Florentine army	**1378–1417** The Great Schism leads to rival popes at Rome and Avignon
1309–77 The papacy is resident at Avignon	**1331–35** Serbian empire of Stephen Dushan dominates the Balkans	**1380** Muscovites inflict major defeat on Golden Horde at Kulikovo
1310 John of Luxembourg becomes king of Bohemia	**1346–7** Louis IV of Wittelsbach loses imperial title to Charles of Luxembourg	**1389** Serbian defeat at Kosovo makes them vassals of Ottomans
1314–25 War between Wittelsbachs and Habsburgs ends in victory for Louis IV of Wittelsbach	**1347–51** The Black Death devastates Europe	**1397** Union of Calmar unites Scandinavia under the Danish crown
1323 Wars between Scotland and England ends; confirmed by treaty of Edinburgh (1328)	**1356** Charles IV issues the Golden Bull ending papal role in imperial elections	

Cultural change

1325	1350	1375
1305 Frescoes of the Arena Chapel, Padua painted by Giotto	**1348–53** Boccaccio writes the *Decameron*	**1386–1400** Geoffrey Chaucer writes the *Canterbury Tales*
c.1314–21 Dante writes the *Divine Comedy*	**1351** Petrarch, Italian poet, moves from Rome to Provence and begins his *Rime*	

1 A Genoese attempt to destroy the power of its trading rival Venice was defeated at Chioggia in 1380.

2 Bohemia, acquired in 1310, served as the Luxembourgs' power base in Germany. Under their rule Prague became a major European cultural center.

3 The success of English archers over French armored cavalry at Crécy in 1346 showed the increasing importance of infantry in late medieval warfare.

4 Moscow owed its independence to Prince Daniel (r.1263–1304) who began its territorial expansion.

5 The Lithuanians, Europe's last pagans, resisted the attempt of the Teutonic Knights to convert them by force, but voluntarily adopted Christianity in 1386.

6 Defeat at Bannockburn in 1314 forced the English to recognize Scottish independence in 1328, but both kingdoms continued to raid each other's territory.

7 A Castilian invasion of Portugal was defeated in 1385, securing its future as an independent state.

BLACK DEATH victims – shown in this French wall-painting – were buried immediately, often in unconsecrated ground.

Gallipoli on the European shore of the Dardanelles; by the end of the century they had overrun most of the Balkans. Political conflicts and the paralysis of the papacy ensured that there was no purposeful response to the Ottoman threat apart from the unsuccessful Crusade of Nicopolis, led by John the Fearless of Burgundy to support Hungary in 1396.

But the event that dominated the 14th century was the Black Death, a combined epidemic of bubonic and pneumonic plague that broke out on the east Asian steppes in the 1330s and spread along the Silk Road to reach the Genoese port of Kaffa in the Crimea in late 1346. From here it was carried (by the parasitic fleas that infested ships' rats) to Venice, Genoa and Marseille, all ports with strong links to the east, and then spread amazingly quickly along the main trade routes of Europe. One factor explaining the Black Death's rapid inroads may lie in the series of crop failures earlier in the century which caused extensive famines in areas where overpopulation was rife. The effects of malnutrition probably weakened resistence to the disease. The impact of the Black Death was catastrophic: even in the most lightly affected areas, ten to fifteen percent of the population died, and in the worst affected areas (Tuscany, East Anglia and Norway) mortality may have been fifty percent or more. Overall, around a third of Europe's population died between 1346 and 1351. The plague remained endemic in Europe for 250 years and many cities had still not regained their pre-plague population levels by the 16th century.

Outbreaks of the plague were often accompanied by religious hysteria, and blame fell on Jews and foreigners who were subjected to attacks. Depopulation caused prices and rents to fall and wages to rise, loosening the traditional bonds of service. Social disruption increased and urban and rural uprisings such as the Jacquerie wars in northern France (1358) and the English peasants' revolt of 1381 were frequent. Mob violence was mainly directed at landlords, tax officials and rich urban oligarchies, and there was often an element of anticlericalism, found also in the rise of heretical movements such as the Lollards in England. In eastern Europe, in contrast, a largely free peasantry had serfdom imposed upon them by lords who were anxious not to lose tenants.

See also 3.09 (religion in medieval Europe); 3.23 (break-up of the Mongol empire)

3.11 The economy of medieval Europe • 1000 – 1500 •

Over 90 percent of the population of medieval Europe were peasant farmers. The manorial system – by which a lord divided up an estate (the manor) between individual peasants who farmed it – was widespread, though there were regional variations. The lord was expected to protect his peasants in times of war, provide relief in times of famine and administer justice, in return for payments of produce, labor and money. Many peasants were unfree serfs or villeins, tied for life to the land on which they worked and passing their servile status onto their descendants, but they were not slaves and had certain established rights. By the end of the Middle Ages serfs had been replaced by tenant farmers and wage laborers in the British Isles, Italy and Iberia, but serfdom survived into the 18th century in some parts of western Europe and in Russia until 1861.

A number of agricultural improvements took place in the early Middle Ages. Most important was the widespread adoption around the year 700 of a three-field system of crop rotation, in which one field was used for cereals, one for vegetables such as beans and the third left fallow, to preserve soil fertility. The introduction of the wheeled plow, and later of the padded shoulder collar that enabled horses – 50 percent more efficient than oxen – to be used for plowing, allowed the heavy soils of northern Europe to be worked more efficiently. In these ways productivity was boosted far beyond the levels achieved in Roman times and peasant prosperity increased steadily. Most surplus agricultural produce was sold at local markets but wool, hides, wine, dairy products, salt, fish and grain were traded in large quantities over long distances. Moving goods by land was slow and expensive, so most bulk trade went by sea or river boat. Various industrial activities such as mining, ore smelting, logging, charcoal burning, quarrying and salt extraction were also important in the countryside. Both agriculture and rural industry benefited from technological improvements that

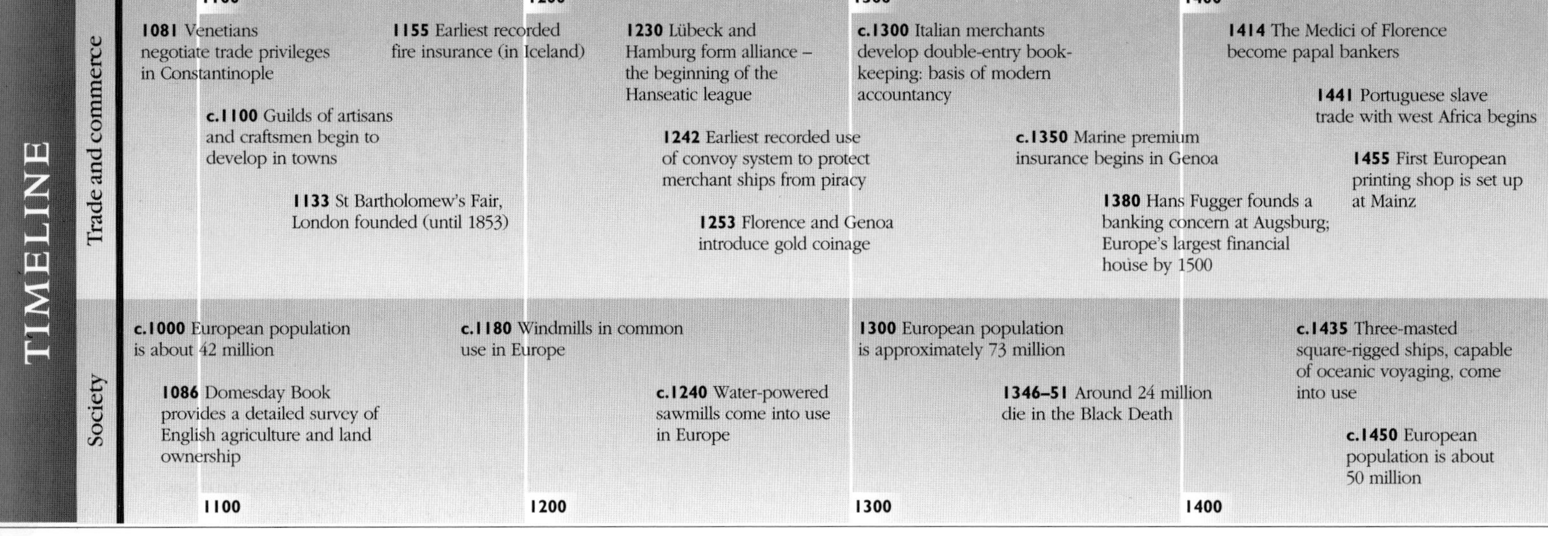

TIMELINE

1100 | 1200 | 1300 | 1400

Trade and commerce

1081 Venetians negotiate trade privileges in Constantinople

c.1100 Guilds of artisans and craftsmen begin to develop in towns

1133 St Bartholomew's Fair, London founded (until 1853)

1155 Earliest recorded fire insurance (in Iceland)

1230 Lübeck and Hamburg form alliance – the beginning of the Hanseatic league

1242 Earliest recorded use of convoy system to protect merchant ships from piracy

1253 Florence and Genoa introduce gold coinage

c.1300 Italian merchants develop double-entry bookkeeping: basis of modern accountancy

c.1350 Marine premium insurance begins in Genoa

1380 Hans Fugger founds a banking concern at Augsburg; Europe's largest financial house by 1500

1414 The Medici of Florence become papal bankers

1441 Portuguese slave trade with west Africa begins

1455 First European printing shop is set up at Mainz

Society

c.1000 European population is about 42 million

1086 Domesday Book provides a detailed survey of English agriculture and land ownership

c.1180 Windmills in common use in Europe

c.1240 Water-powered sawmills come into use in Europe

1300 European population is approximately 73 million

1346–51 Around 24 million die in the Black Death

c.1435 Three-masted square-rigged ships, capable of oceanic voyaging, come into use

c.1450 European population is about 50 million

1100 | 1200 | 1300 | 1400

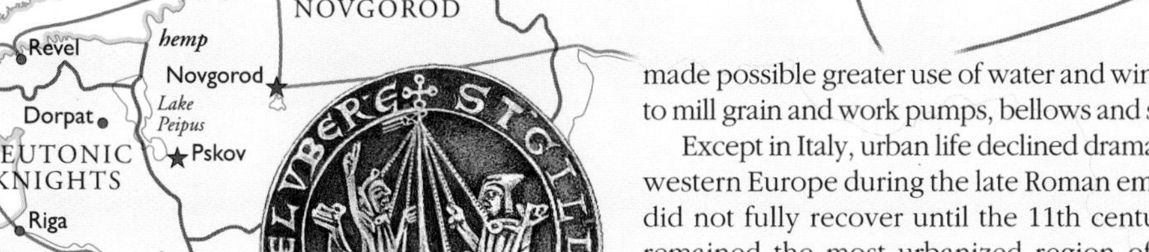

LÜBECK was a center of the Hanseatic trade in the Baltic, using sturdy ships called cogs, as shown on this seal of 1258.

made possible greater use of water and wind power to mill grain and work pumps, bellows and sawmills.

Except in Italy, urban life declined dramatically in western Europe during the late Roman empire and did not fully recover until the 11th century. Italy remained the most urbanized region of Europe throughout the Middle Ages. Compared with contemporary towns in the Arab world and China, medieval European towns were small and, outside northern Italy and Flanders, rarely had populations above 10,000. They were unhygienic places and, as deaths exceeded births, they relied on immigration from the countryside to maintain their populations. Townspeople were free of servile obligations but citizenship, and with it a right to participate in local government, was normally restricted to property owners. The trade and craft activities of towns were regulated by associations of merchants or craftsmen known as guilds. These prescribed standards of quality and training and provided members with welfare benefits, but their principal function was protectionist, to exclude outside competition. Manufactured goods produced in towns were generally intended for the local market but production of high-quality goods for export was important in some areas, such as Flanders where there was a flourishing woolen textile industry. Seasonal trade fairs were important commercial events, attracting merchants from a far wider area than the weekly town markets; some, for example the Champagne fairs, developed into major centers of international business.

One of the most powerful trade associations of the Middle Ages was the Hanseatic league, membership of which extended to 37 north German and Baltic towns at its peak in the 14th century. The league negotiated trading privileges for its members, prepared navigational charts, suppressed piracy and even waged war. It maintained offices called *kontors* in London, Bergen, Bruges and Novgorod where its merchants lived and traded permanently, as well as subsidiary depots in many other cities. The league's power declined at the end of the Middle Ages, when it was faced with greater competition from England and the Netherlands. In the Mediterranean, maritime trade was dominated by Venice and Genoa. Both took advantage of the Crusades to build up trade links with Asia, the source of luxury products such as silks, spices and gems, and maintained a bitter rivalry between themselves.

By the 13th century merchants were assuming the role of capitalists to finance craft production, so that productivity increased but craftsmen lost their independence. International banking houses such as the Medici and the Fuggers emerged, and the principles of modern insurance and accountancy were established.

population density per sq km, early 14th century
- over 30
- 21–30
- 11–20
- 10 or under
- city with population over 10,000, c.1300
- branch of Fugger bank
- branch of Medici bank
- Kiev — city with important trade fair
- major Hanseatic league member
- other Hanseatic league member
- Hanseatic *kontor* (foreign depot)
- Genoese trading center
- Venetian trading center
- grain exporting area
- wine exporting area
- woollen cloth producing area
- *furs* — main trade commodity

- borders, c.1325
- Hanseatic trade route
- Genoese trade route
- Venetian trade route
- Gascon wine trade route
- other trade route

0 – 600 km
0 – 400 mi

1 Flanders was a leading center of Europe's growing textile industry; its prosperity was enshrined in grand town halls, as at Ghent.

2 England's prosperity resulted from it being Europe's main source of wool for cloth-making.

3 The Arabs introduced papermaking to Europe at Valencia in the 12th century.

4 The church's prohibition on eating meat on fast days maintained demand for salted fish from the Baltic and North Seas.

5 The fairs of Champagne flourished as centers of north–south trade in the 12th and 13th centuries.

6 The importance of the Black Sea as a trading area increased after the 13th-century Mongol invasions improved access to the east for European traders.

See also 3.10 (war, revolt and plague); 4.12 (European economy 1500–1800)

3.12 Renaissance Europe • 1400 – 1492 •

The Renaissance, the great cultural movement of 15th-century Europe, had its origins in the revival of interest in classical philosophy, science and literature that first emerged during the 12th century, but its immediate roots lay in 14th-century Italy in the work of artists such as Giotto and humanist scholars such as Petrarch. By the early 15th century, men like Masaccio and Donatello in Florence were evolving new styles of painting and sculpture, while Brunelleschi was leading the revival of classical forms of architecture. In the course of the century Italy's city-states came to be ruled by dynastic princes. Italian Renaissance rulers – whether the powerful Medici family in Florence or the heads of ducal courts such as Mantua or Urbino – dispensed patronage as an arm of government, to secure prestige and influence. In Venice, a large urban aristocracy was keen to publicize its wealth and status. The technology of printing, developed in Germany in the mid-1450s, aided the spread of the new arts and learning outside Italy. By the early 16th century they were beginning to find their place in the courts of Europe's "new monarchs", who were emerging from periods of dynastic rivalry and civil war with strong centralized governments.

In the early 15th century France was divided by the rivalry between the Burgundian and Armagnac families, who disputed control of mad king Charles VI (r.1380–1422). Henry V of England (r.1413–22), anxious to secure the legitimacy of the Lancastrian dynasty established by his father Henry IV in 1399, seized the opportunity to reopen the Hundred Years War. His major victory at Agincourt (1415) and conquest of northern France led to his recognition as Charles VI's heir in 1420. After Henry's death and the revival of French morale under the leadership of Joan of Arc, English fortunes declined. By 1453 they had lost all their French possessions except Calais. Defeat provoked dynastic wars in England (the Wars of the Roses) until Henry VII (r.1485–1509), founder of the Tudor dynasty, restored stable government.

The dukes of Burgundy profited from France's troubles to enhance their own position by forming an alliance with the English which lasted until 1435. Under Philip the Good (r.1419–67) they acquired further territory in the Netherlands. His successor Charles the Bold wanted to establish an independent kingdom and tried to build a corridor of lands to link his southern and northern possessions, but died in battle against the Swiss at Nancy in 1477. When his heiress Mary married Maximilian of Habsburg, the Burgundian lands descended to the Habsburgs, who had ruled the Holy Roman empire since 1438, having already united their lands with those of Luxembourg. Louis XI (r.1461– 83) seized and retained the lands of the duchy of Burgundy in France. Franche-Comté was ceded to France on the betrothal of the *dauphin* (later Charles VIII) to Mary's daughter in 1482, but reverted to the Habsburgs when the engagement was revoked.

borders, 1429-33
Burgundian territory, 1429
English territory, 1429
nominally English territory, 1429
Aragonese territory, 1430
Byzantine empire, 1430
Genoese territory, 1430
Habsburg territory, 1430
Hungarian territory, 1430
Muscovy, 1430
Ottoman empire, 1430
Poland-Lithuania, 1430
Venetian territory, 1430
Polish acquisition, 1466
Habsburg acquisition, 1477
temporary Hungarian gain under Matthias Corvinus, 1477–90
maximum extent of Burgundian kingdom under Charles the Bold, 1477
kingdom of Aragon & Castile, 1492
kingdom of France, 1492
Muscovy, 1492
Ottoman empire, 1492
Portuguese base
printing center, with date
Milan early Renaissance cultural center
Tatar campaign
Hussite movement, 1415-36
0 600 km
0 400 mi

SHETLAND
1469 to Scotland
ORKNEY
1468 to Scotland
Lordship of the Isles
SCOTLAND
1460–88 recovered by Scotland
Edinburgh
ENGLAND
Irish
Irish Pale
Dublin
Towton 1461
York
Chester
Shrewsbury 1403
Bosworth 1485
Wales
Oxford 1478
Bristol
London 1476
Southampton
Calais
Agincourt 1415
PICARDY
Rouen
Formigny 1450
Normandy
BRITTANY
Orleans 1429
Nantes
Tours
Bourges
ATLANTIC OCEAN
Bordeaux
Castillon 1453
Gascony
León
Burgos 1490
NAVARRE
ANDORRA
Douro
Barcelona 1475
ARAGON
PORTUGAL
Madrid
Tagus
CASTILE
1479 union of crowns with Aragon
Valencia 1475
Lisbon 1489
GRANADA 1485–92 to Castile
Guadiana
Seville 1492
Granada
Almeria
Cartagena
Cádiz
Málaga
Tangier 1471
Ceuta 1415
Asilah 1471

TIMELINE

Political change

1425 · 1450 · 1475

1405–06 Florence captures Pisa, giving it an outlet to the sea

1417 The Council of Constance ends the Great Schism of the papacy

1419 John the Fearless, Duke of Burgundy, murdered during peace conference with Armagnacs

1429 Joan of Arc relieves the siege of Orléans: turning point of Hundred Years War

1434 Cosimo de' Medici becomes the ruler of Florence (d.1464)

1438 Albert II of Austria, a Habsburg, is elected Holy Roman emperor: the office remains with the Habsburgs until it is abolished in 1806

1453 Ottoman Turks capture Constantinople, bringing the Byzantine empire to an end

1455–85 The Wars of the Roses in England

1463–79 Venice loses Euboea and the Greek islands to the Ottomans

1469 Ferdinand of Aragon marries Isabella of Castile

1478 Foundation of the Spanish Inquisition

1492 Fall of Granada. Columbus' first voyage to the New World

1494 Beginning of the Italian Wars between France and the Habsburgs

1497–98 Vasco da Gama sails to India

Cultural change

1411–66 fl. Donatello, Florentine sculptor

1420–36 Brunelleschi builds dome on Florence cathedral

1422–40 fl. Jan van Eyck, Netherlandish painter

1435 Rogier van der Weyden's *Descent from the Cross* (wooden altarpiece) painted

1455 First commercially printed book, the *Gutenberg Bible*, is published at Mainz

1456–57 Botticelli, Florentine painter, completes *Primavera*

1476 William Caxton sets up the first printing press in London

1495–97 Leonardo da Vinci paints *The Last Supper* in Milan

1425 · 1450 · 1475

GERMAN and Italian armorers brought plate armor to its highest development in the 15th century. This finely-crafted plumed helmet was made for Ferdinand of Aragon.

In the Iberian peninsula a century or more of rivalry between Castile and Aragon (which added the kingdom of Naples to its extensive Mediterranean empire in 1442), came to an end in 1469 with the marriage of Ferdinand of Aragon to Isabella of Castile. Under their joint leadership Granada, the last Muslim state in Spain, was conquered in 1485–92. Portugal, prevented from expanding in the peninsula by Castile, turned its attention to North Africa, beginning with the capture of Ceuta in 1415. In the 1430s Portuguese navigators began to explore the African coast and in 1487 entered the Indian Ocean. Even more significant was the voyage of Columbus, commissioned by Isabella of Castile, which led to the discovery of the New World in 1492.

Eastern Europe saw the creation of a strong but short-lived kingdom: Poland–Lithuania, under Casimir IV (r.1447–92) the largest state in Europe. Hungary, which resisted Ottoman expansion in the Balkans, dominated central Europe under Matthias Corvinus (r.1477–90). By the end of the century Muscovy had absorbed most of the other Russian principalities. With the fall of the Byzantine empire in 1453, it was left as the only significant Orthodox state: Ivan III married a Byzantine princess in 1472, adopting the title of *czar*(caesar).

1 The Union of Calmar, proclaimed in 1397, was unpopular in Sweden, where it led to several revolts before its final collapse in 1523.

2 The defeat by Poland–Lithuania of the Teutonic Knights at Tannenberg saw the start of their decline.

3 The burning for heresy of the Bohemian religious reformer Jan Hus at Constance in 1415 sparked a 20-year revolutionary uprising by his followers.

4 In 1480 Ivan III of Muscovy ceased paying tribute to buy off the Golden Horde, by now a shadow of its former strength.

5 In 1492, after their victory over the Muslims, Ferdinand and Isabella expelled from Spain around 150,000 Jews who refused to convert to Christianity.

6 England's preoccupation with war in France in the 15th century allowed much of Ireland to achieve effective independence.

7 The patronage of the wealthy Medici family made Florence the leading cultural center of the age, as well as a center for banking and trade, and the dominant political entity of central Italy.

See also 3.11 (economy of medieval Europe); 3.23 (decline of the Mongol empire)

3.13 The great Arab conquests • 632 – 750 •

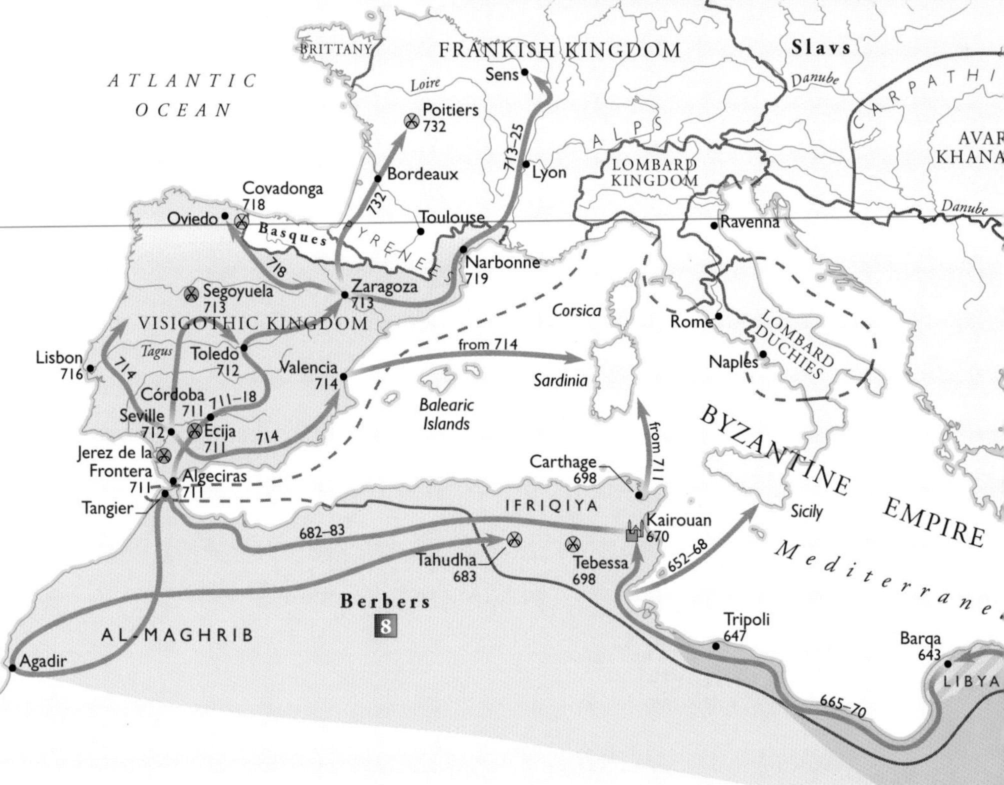

BRITTANY
FRANKISH KINGDOM
Slavs
Danube
CARPATHI
AVAR KHANA
ATLANTIC OCEAN
Loire
Sens
Poitiers 732
713–25
ALPS
Lyon
LOMBARD KINGDOM
Bordeaux
732
Covadonga 718
Oviedo
Basques
PYRENEES
Toulouse
Ravenna
Danube
Narbonne 719
718
Segoyuela 713
Zaragoza 713
VISIGOTHIC KINGDOM
Corsica
Rome
LOMBARD DUCHIES
from 714
Lisbon 716
Tagus
Toledo 712
Valencia 714
Sardinia
Naples
714
Córdoba 711–18
Seville 712
Ecija 711
714
Balearic Islands
BYZANTINE EMPIRE
Jerez de la Frontera 711
Algeciras 711
Carthage 698
from 711
Tangier
IFRIQIYA
Kairouan 670
Sicily
682–83
Tahudha 683
Tebessa 698
652–68
Mediterranean
Berbers
8
Tripoli 647
Barqa 643
AL-MAGHRIB
Agadir
LIBYA
665–70

The great empires of the Mediterranean and the Middle East had for centuries been accustomed to raids by Arab border tribes. Though troublesome, these raids were prevented from becoming a serious threat by the political disunity of the Arabs. However, this situation changed dramatically in the early 7th century as a result of the rise of Islam.

The faith of Islam (meaning "submission to the will of God") was founded by Muhammad (c.570–632), a member of the Meccan Quraysh tribe. From about 610, Muhammad began to experience the revelations that formed the basis of the *Koran*. Muhammad's espousal of monotheism met with opposition from the Quraysh, so to escape persecution the prophet and his followers fled in 622 to Medina, a commercial rival of Mecca. This event, the *hijra* (flight), marks the beginning of the Muslim era and is the first year of the Islamic calendar. Muhammad used Medina as a base to fight the Quraysh and in 630 he returned to Mecca in triumph. However, Muhammad continued to live at Medina, which became the capital of a theocratic Islamic state. In the last two years of his life, Muhammad used diplomacy and force to spread Islam to other Arab tribes.

Muhammad was succeeded by his father-in-law Abu Bakr, the first *caliph* (successor). After putting down an anti-Islamic rebellion, Abu Bakr completed the political and religious unification of the Arabs. Under the next two caliphs, Umar and Uthman, the Arabs began an explosive expansion which saw the Byzantine empire lose the rich and populous provinces of Syria, Palestine, Egypt and Libya, and the complete destruction of the Persian Sasanian empire. On Uthman's death civil war broke out between supporters of the caliph Ali, Muhammad's son-in-law, and Muawiya, a member of Uthman's Umayyad family. After Ali's murder in 661, Muawiya became caliph, founding the Umayyad dynasty. Ali's son Husain tried to win the caliphate on Muawiya's death but was killed in battle with the Umayyads at Karbala in 680. Consequently, Islam split into its two main branches: the Sunnites (from *sunna*, "tradition of Muhammad"), who formed a majority, and the Shiites (from *shi'atu Ali*, "party of Ali").

Arab expansion continued under the early Umayyads and by 715 the Islamic caliphate, extending from the Indus and central Asia to the Pyrenees, was the largest state the world had yet seen. Yet their attempts to complete the conquest of the Byzantine empire and the west failed, with two unsuccessful sieges of Constantinople in 677 and 717 and defeat by the Franks at Poitiers in 732.

The caliphs were both religious and political leaders. Whereas the early caliphs had been elected, the Umayyads introduced hereditary succession, claiming divine appointment and demanding total obedience. By adapting Byzantine bureaucracy, they created an administrative system capable of ruling a world empire. As this empire could not be ruled effectively from the remote Arabian city of Medina, Muawiya moved the capital to Damascus in 661. The Umayyad period saw the beginning of the successful Arabization of the conquered populations through conversion to Islam, the adoption of Arabic as a common language, and by intermarriage. The Arabs in turn were influenced by the Persian and Byzantine civilizations that they had conquered. One of the most important cultural developments of

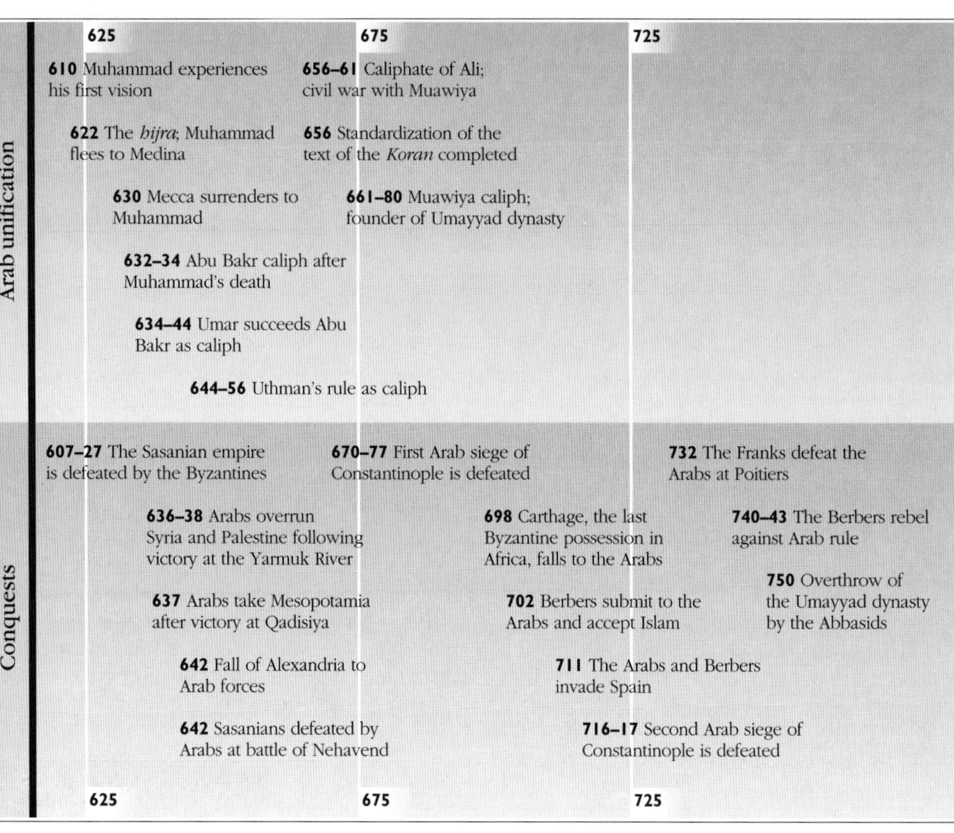

TIMELINE
625
675
725
Arab unification
610 Muhammad experiences his first vision
622 The *hijra*; Muhammad flees to Medina
630 Mecca surrenders to Muhammad
632–34 Abu Bakr caliph after Muhammad's death
634–44 Umar succeeds Abu Bakr as caliph
644–56 Uthman's rule as caliph
656–61 Caliphate of Ali; civil war with Muawiya
656 Standardization of the text of the *Koran* completed
661–80 Muawiya caliph; founder of Umayyad dynasty
Conquests
607–27 The Sasanian empire is defeated by the Byzantines
636–38 Arabs overrun Syria and Palestine following victory at the Yarmuk River
637 Arabs take Mesopotamia after victory at Qadisiya
642 Fall of Alexandria to Arab forces
642 Sasanians defeated by Arabs at battle of Nehavend
670–77 First Arab siege of Constantinople is defeated
698 Carthage, the last Byzantine possession in Africa, falls to the Arabs
702 Berbers submit to the Arabs and accept Islam
711 The Arabs and Berbers invade Spain
716–17 Second Arab siege of Constantinople is defeated
732 The Franks defeat the Arabs at Poitiers
740–43 The Berbers rebel against Arab rule
750 Overthrow of the Umayyad dynasty by the Abbasids
625
675
725

1 Mecca was an important trading city and the main cult center for the pre-Islamic Arabs' pagan religion.

2 Arab military settlements, such as Al-Fustat (Cairo), were sited close to the edge of the desert, where the Arabs could take refuge in the event of rebellions.

3 The Taurus mountains proved an effective barrier against further Arab conquests in Anatolia.

4 The last Sasanian king, Yezdegird III, was murdered near Merv in 652, so ending Persian resistance.

5 Karbala became a major pilgrimage site for Shiite Muslims after Husain, Muhammad's grandson, was killed there by the Umayyads.

6 With the transfer of the Arab capital to Damascus in 661, Arabia gradually declined in significance.

7 The two attempts by the Arabs to take the heavily fortified city of Constantinople were costly failures.

8 Berber resistance to the Arabs was fierce; they were only subdued and converted to Islam in 702.

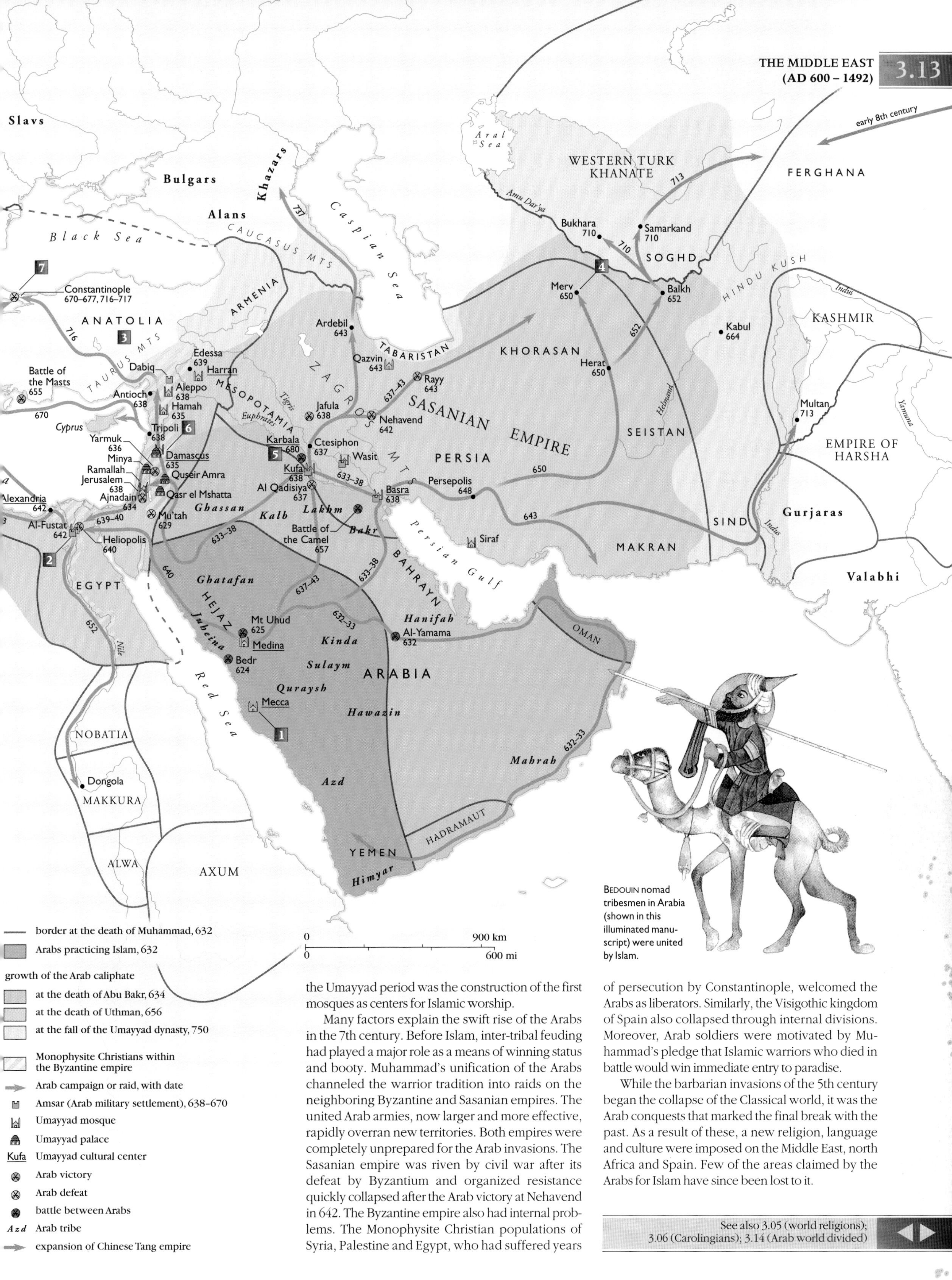

Slavs
Bulgars
Khazars
Alans
Black Sea
CAUCASUS MTS
Caspian Sea
Aral Sea
WESTERN TURK KHANATE
FERGHANA
early 8th century
Amu Dar'ya
Bukhara 710
Samarkand 710
713
710
SOGHD
HINDU KUSH
Merv 650
Balkh 652
Kabul 664
KASHMIR
Indus
Constantinople 670–677, 716–717
ANATOLIA
TAURUS MTS
716
737
ARMENIA
Ardebil 643
TABARISTAN
Qazvin 643
KHORASAN
Herat 650
652
Edessa 639
Harran
Dabiq
Battle of the Masts 655
Antioch 638
Aleppo 638
Hamah 635
MESOPOTAMIA
ZAGROS MTS
Tigris
Euphrates
Jafula 638
Rayy 643
637–43
Nehavend 642
SASANIAN EMPIRE
Helmand
SEISTAN
Multan 713
Yamuna
670
Cyprus
Tripoli 638
Yarmuk 636
Minya
Damascus 635
Ramallah
Quseir Amra
Jerusalem 638
Ajnadain 634
Qasr el Mshatta
Karbala 680
Ctesiphon 637
Wasit
Kufa 638
Al Qadisiya 637
633–38
PERSIA
Basra 638
Persepolis 648
650
EMPIRE OF HARSHA
Alexandria 642
Al-Fustat 642
Heliopolis 640
639–40
Mu'tah 629
Ghassan
Kalb
Lakhm
Bakr
Battle of the Camel 657
643
Siraf
MAKRAN
SIND
Gurjaras
Persian Gulf
BAHRAYN
633–38
637–43
640
EGYPT
Ghatafan
HEJAZ
Valabhi
Juheina
Mt Uhud 625
Medina
632–33
Hanifah
Al-Yamama 632
OMAN
652
Nile
Kinda
Bedr 624
Sulaym
ARABIA
Red Sea
Quraysh
Mecca
Hawazin
NOBATIA
Mahrah
632–33
Dongola
MAKKURA
Azd
HADRAMAUT
YEMEN
ALWA
AXUM
Himyar
0 900 km
0 600 mi
border at the death of Muhammad, 632
Arabs practicing Islam, 632
growth of the Arab caliphate
at the death of Abu Bakr, 634
at the death of Uthman, 656
at the fall of the Umayyad dynasty, 750
Monophysite Christians within the Byzantine empire
Arab campaign or raid, with date
Amsar (Arab military settlement), 638–670
Umayyad mosque
Umayyad palace
Kufa Umayyad cultural center
Arab victory
Arab defeat
battle between Arabs
Azd Arab tribe
expansion of Chinese Tang empire

BEDOUIN nomad tribesmen in Arabia (shown in this illuminated manuscript) were united by Islam.

the Umayyad period was the construction of the first mosques as centers for Islamic worship.

Many factors explain the swift rise of the Arabs in the 7th century. Before Islam, inter-tribal feuding had played a major role as a means of winning status and booty. Muhammad's unification of the Arabs channeled the warrior tradition into raids on the neighboring Byzantine and Sasanian empires. The united Arab armies, now larger and more effective, rapidly overran new territories. Both empires were completely unprepared for the Arab invasions. The Sasanian empire was riven by civil war after its defeat by Byzantium and organized resistance quickly collapsed after the Arab victory at Nehavend in 642. The Byzantine empire also had internal problems. The Monophysite Christian populations of Syria, Palestine and Egypt, who had suffered years of persecution by Constantinople, welcomed the Arabs as liberators. Similarly, the Visigothic kingdom of Spain also collapsed through internal divisions. Moreover, Arab soldiers were motivated by Muhammad's pledge that Islamic warriors who died in battle would win immediate entry to paradise.

While the barbarian invasions of the 5th century began the collapse of the Classical world, it was the Arab conquests that marked the final break with the past. As a result of these, a new religion, language and culture were imposed on the Middle East, north Africa and Spain. Few of the areas claimed by the Arabs for Islam have since been lost to it.

See also 3.05 (world religions); 3.06 (Carolingians); 3.14 (Arab world divided)

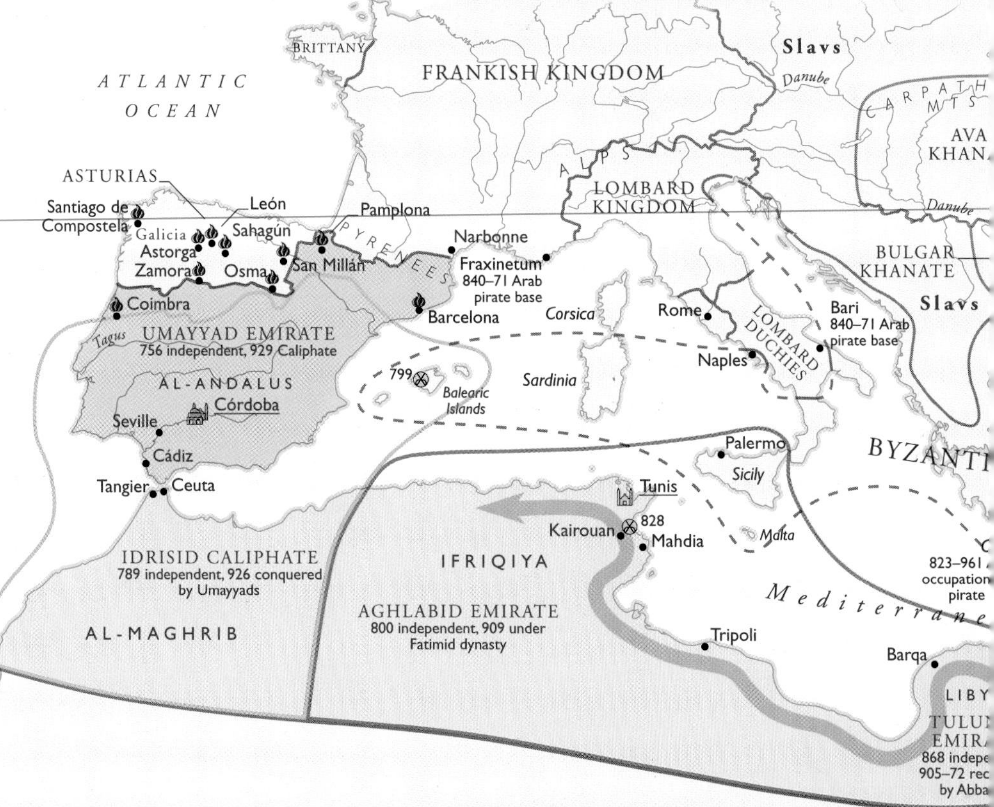

ATLANTIC OCEAN
BRITTANY
FRANKISH KINGDOM
Slavs
Danube
CARPATHIAN MTS
AVAR KHAN.
ALPS
LOMBARD KINGDOM
ASTURIAS
Santiago de Compostela
León
Pamplona
Galicia
Sahagún
Astorga
Zamora
Osma
San Millán
PYRENEES
Narbonne
Fraxinetum 840–71 Arab pirate base
BULGAR KHANATE
Slavs
Coimbra
Barcelona
Corsica
Rome
LOMBARD DUCHIES
Bari 840–71 Arab pirate base
Tagus
UMAYYAD EMIRATE 756 independent, 929 Caliphate
Naples
799
Balearic Islands
Sardinia
AL-ANDALUS
Córdoba
Seville
Cádiz
Palermo
BYZANTI
Tangier
Ceuta
Tunis
Sicily
828
Kairouan
Mahdia
Malta
IDRISID CALIPHATE 789 independent, 926 conquered by Umayyads
IFRIQIYA
823–961 occupation pirate
Mediterrane
AGHLABID EMIRATE 800 independent, 909 under Fatimid dynasty
AL-MAGHRIB
Tripoli
Barqa
LIBY
TULU EMIR 868 indepe 905–72 rec by Abba

The authority of the Umayyad caliphs was gradually undermined in the 8th century by the Shiite-Sunnite conflict, the re-emergence of tribal feuding among the Arabs and by discontent among new converts to Islam in the conquered lands who were resentful of the tax and political privileges enjoyed by the Arabs. Rebellion broke out in the province of Khorasan in 747 and in 749 Abu al-Abbas of the Sunni Abbasid family was proclaimed caliph by the rebels. Following the Abbasid victory at the Battle of the Zab in 750, there was a general massacre of the Umayyad family. One of the few to survive, Abd al-Rahman (r.756–88), escaped to Spain and seized power in Córdoba in 756. His founding of an independent emirate began the political fragmentation of the Arab world. Abd al-Rahman faced internal opposition to his rule for several years, which allowed the Christians of Asturias to regain Galicia and give their kingdom a firm territorial base: the Franks were also able to recapture Narbonne. The Abbasid caliphate suffered further losses in 789 when the Idrisid emirs of the Maghrib rejected its political and spiritual authority and founded a Shiite caliphate. In 800 the Aghlabid emirs of Ifriqiya (Tunisia) also became independent.

Despite these losses the accession of the Abbasids ushered in a "golden age" of Islamic civilization. The caliphate's vast wealth, acquired partly from the exploitation of rich silver mines in the Hindu Kush Mountains, funded lavish building projects and patronage of the arts and sciences. Baghdad, founded as a new capital to replace Damascus in 763, had within forty years become probably the world's largest city and its greatest cultural center. The assimilation of Persian literary forms and Greek science and philosophy to Islamic and Arab tradition initiated a period of great achievements in many intellectual fields. Medieval Europe would owe most of its knowledge of astronomy, geography, medicine, mathematics and even Greek philosophy to Arab scholars. Religious and racial pluralism also characterized Abbasid rule: strict observance of Islam did not preclude tolerance of the faith of people of other religions, while Arabs were no longer accorded a privileged status.

The Abbasids reached their zenith under Harun al-Rashid but civil war broke out between his sons soon after his death. The caliph's authority began to decline in favour of the provincial emirs. In 868 Egypt and Palestine became independent under the Tulunids, while the eastern provinces seceded under the native Persian Saffarid and Samanid dynasties. The Abbasids lost Arabia after the rebellion of the Shiite Qarmatian sect in 899. The Christians of Armenia had also regained their independence in 886. The Abbasids recovered briefly around 900, retaking Palestine and Egypt in 905, and aided by the Sunnite Samanid emirate's annexation of the troublesome Shiite Saffarid emirate. However, in 914 the Fatimids, who had come to power in Ifriqiya in 909, began the conquest of Egypt; by 1000 they were the dominant Islamic power. In about 913 the Buwayhids, a tribal confederation from Daylam, conquered Persia. Their capture of Baghdad in 945 ended Abbasid territorial power. Though the caliphate was kept as a spiritual office, the Sunnite caliph was merely a figurehead, behind whom the Shiite Buwayhids held real power.

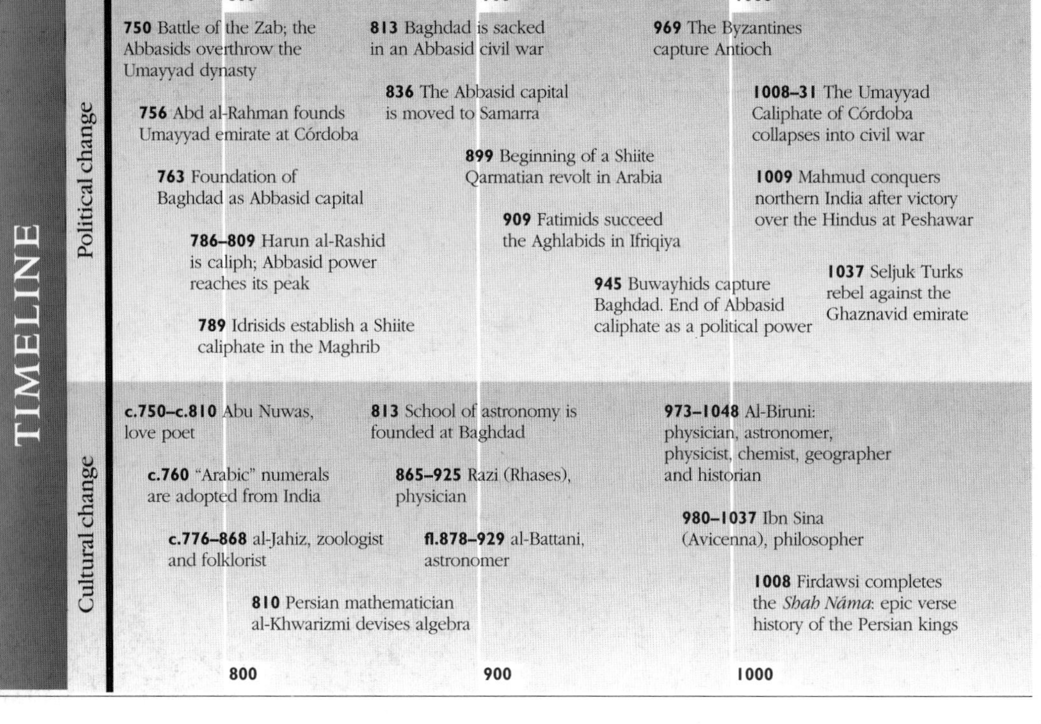

TIMELINE
800
900
1000
Political change
750 Battle of the Zab; the Abbasids overthrow the Umayyad dynasty
756 Abd al-Rahman founds Umayyad emirate at Córdoba
763 Foundation of Baghdad as Abbasid capital
786–809 Harun al-Rashid is caliph; Abbasid power reaches its peak
789 Idrisids establish a Shiite caliphate in the Maghrib
813 Baghdad is sacked in an Abbasid civil war
836 The Abbasid capital is moved to Samarra
899 Beginning of a Shiite Qarmatian revolt in Arabia
909 Fatimids succeed the Aghlabids in Ifriqiya
945 Buwayhids capture Baghdad. End of Abbasid caliphate as a political power
969 The Byzantines capture Antioch
1008–31 The Umayyad Caliphate of Córdoba collapses into civil war
1009 Mahmud conquers northern India after victory over the Hindus at Peshawar
1037 Seljuk Turks rebel against the Ghaznavid emirate
Cultural change
c.750–c.810 Abu Nuwas, love poet
c.760 "Arabic" numerals are adopted from India
c.776–868 al-Jahiz, zoologist and folklorist
810 Persian mathematician al-Khwarizmi devises algebra
813 School of astronomy is founded at Baghdad
865–925 Razi (Rhases), physician
fl.878–929 al-Battani, astronomer
973–1048 Al-Biruni: physician, astronomer, physicist, chemist, geographer and historian
980–1037 Ibn Sina (Avicenna), philosopher
1008 Firdawsi completes the *Shah Nāma*: epic verse history of the Persian kings
800
900
1000

- border, 763
- Abbasid caliphate, 763
- Abbasid caliphate, 900
- Umayyad emirate, 763
- Umayyad caliphate, c.990
- Buwayhid emirates, c.990
- Fatimid caliphate, c.990
- empire of Mahmud of Ghazni at greatest extent, c.1030
- eastern border of Byzantine empire, 1022–71
- city founded by the Abbasids
- Abbasid mosque
- Abbasid palace
- Umayyad mosque
- Umayyad palace
- Rayy Muslim cultural center
- town sacked by Almanzor, 985–1002
- Arab victory
- Arab defeat
- battle between Muslim states
- victory for Mahmud of Ghazni
- Qarmatian raid, 899–930
- migration of Arab nomads, 7th to 11th centuries
- expansion of Turkish peoples

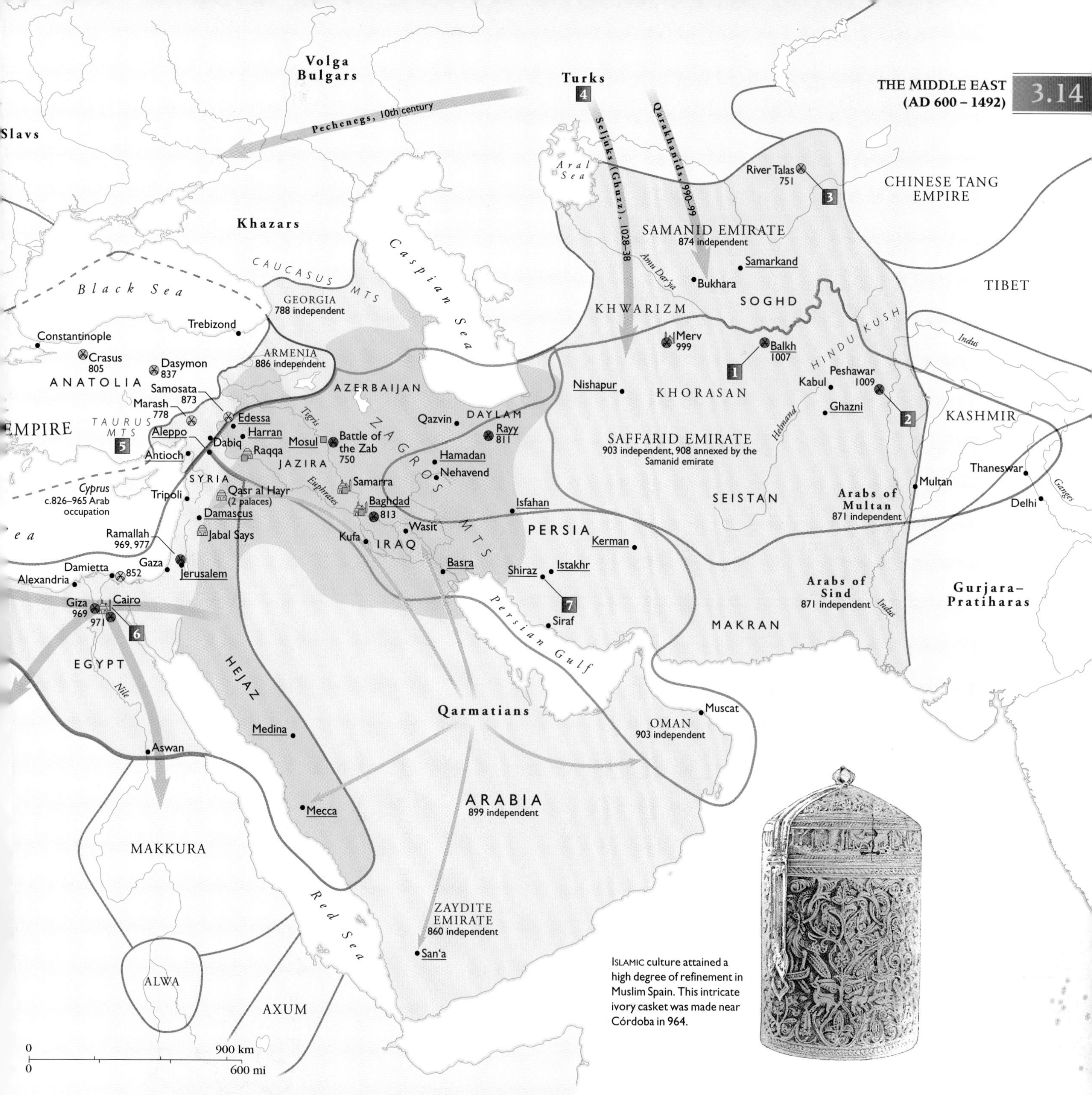
Volga Bulgars
Turks
4
Slavs
Pechenegs, 10th century
Seljuks (Ghuzz), 1028–38
Qarakhanids, 990–99
Aral Sea
River Talas 751
3
CHINESE TANG EMPIRE
Khazars
SAMANID EMIRATE 874 independent
Samarkand
Bukhara
TIBET
Black Sea
CAUCASUS MTS
GEORGIA 788 independent
Caspian Sea
Amu Dar'ya
KHWARIZM
SOGHD
HINDU KUSH
Trebizond
Constantinople
Crasus 805
Dasymon 837
ARMENIA 886 independent
Merv 999
Balkh 1007
1
Indus
ANATOLIA
Samosata 873
Marash 778
AZERBAIJAN
Nishapur
KHORASAN
Kabul
Peshawar 1009
Ghazni
2
KASHMIR
EMPIRE
TAURUS MTS
5
Aleppo
Edessa
Harran
Dabiq
Raqqa
Tigris
Mosul
Battle of the Zab 750
ZAGROS MTS
Qazvin
DAYLAM
Rayy 811
Hamadan
Nehavend
SAFFARID EMIRATE 903 independent, 908 annexed by the Samanid emirate
Helmand
Antioch
JAZIRA
SYRIA
Euphrates
Samarra
Thaneswar
Multan
Ganges
Cyprus c.826–965 Arab occupation
Tripoli
Qasr al Hayr (2 palaces)
Damascus
Baghdad 813
Isfahan
SEISTAN
Arabs of Multan 871 independent
Delhi
Jabal Says
Ramallah 969, 977
Kufa
IRAQ
Wasit
PERSIA
Kerman
Gaza
Damietta 852
Jerusalem
Basra
Shiraz
Istakhr
Arabs of Sind 871 independent
Gurjara–Pratiharas
Alexandria
Giza 969
Cairo 971
6
7
Siraf
Persian Gulf
MAKRAN
EGYPT
HEJAZ
Nile
Qarmatians
Muscat
OMAN 903 independent
Medina
Aswan
ARABIA 899 independent
Mecca
MAKKURA
Red Sea
ZAYDITE EMIRATE 860 independent
San'a
ALWA
AXUM
0 900 km
0 600 mi

ISLAMIC culture attained a high degree of refinement in Muslim Spain. This intricate ivory casket was made near Córdoba in 964.

The rise of the Buwayhids was accompanied by the decline of the Samanid emirate. Its northern provinces were lost to the Qarakhanid Turks in the 990s while the rest was seized by a rebel Turkish mercenary, Mahmud of Ghazni, who defeated the Samanids near Merv. Thereafter, Mahmud expanded into the Buwayhid emirates and northern India. A militant Muslim, Mahmud conducted holy wars against the Hindu kingdoms, deliberately destroying Hindu temples. The Ghaznavid emirate was the first of the Turkish empires of the Middle East, yet it declined rapidly following an invasion by the Ghuzz Turks led by members of the Seljuk clan in 1037.

After its initial setbacks, the Umayyad emirate in Spain consolidated its position, and in 929 Abd al-Rahman III (r.912–61) declared himself caliph. Conquest of the Maghrib in 973 and the great successes of his general Almanzor (al-Mansur) against the Christians of the north seemed to justify his confidence. However, in 1008 civil war broke out: the caliphate collapsed and Muslim power in Spain never fully recovered. Despite mainly hostile relations, Muslim Spain was, with Sicily, the most important route for the transmission of Arab culture to Christian Europe.

1 The Qarakhanid Turks overran Soghd in 990–95, but further expansion was halted by their defeat by Mahmud of Ghazni at Balkh in 1007.

2 Mahmud of Ghazni's victory over a coalition of Hindu princes at Peshawar in 1009 made him the dominant power in northwest India.

3 The Arab victory at the River Talas led to the collapse of China's central Asian empire.

4 The Turks, who converted to Islam c.970, were an important source of mercenaries for the armies of the Abbasid caliphate and its successor states: many Turks achieved positions of power and influence.

5 The long Arab–Byzantine struggle for control of the Taurus Mountains was won by the Byzantines in the 960s, after which they occupied northern Syria.

6 Cairo (Al-Qahirah) was founded in 969 as the capital of the Fatimid dynasty, and began to supplant Alexandria as Egypt's most important city.

7 The Shiite Buwayhids established their capital at Shiraz c.913 after conquering Persia. They captured Baghdad in 945.

See also 3.06 (Carolingians); 3.13 (the rise of Islam); 3.19 (medieval India)

3.15 The Byzantine empire • 610 – 1204 •

The Byzantine empire is the term modern historians use to describe the continuation of the eastern Roman empire after the accession of Heraclius (r.610–41). When Heraclius came to the throne, the empire was facing defeat by the neighboring Persian Sasanian empire. To save it Heraclius reformed the army and administration to create what was effectively a new state. Greek, which had always been the majority language of the eastern Roman empire, replaced Latin as the official language of government. Because of this, medieval western Europeans saw the Byzantine empire as a Hellenistic state; however, the Byzantines continued to think of themselves as Romans, until the final fall of their empire to the Ottoman Turks in 1453.

Heraclius' reforms saw Byzantium emerge victorious from its war with Persia in 627. However, the exhausted empire was unprepared for the attacks by the Arabs, newly united by Islam, that began in 633. Syria, Palestine, Egypt and North Africa were lost by 698 but Arab attempts to take Constantinople in 670–77 and 716–17 failed. Other powers also benefited from Byzantine weakness: the Lombards captured Genoa in 640 and the Bulgars overran much of the Balkans in 679. The empire continued to lose ground in the 8th and early 9th centuries: the Lombards conquered the exarchate of Ravenna in 751 and the Arabs began the conquest of Sicily in 827.

The shrinkage of the empire was eventually reversed by the emperors of the Macedonian dynasty (867–1059), who restored the frontiers in the north and the east close to where they had been in late Roman times. Though the Macedonians were fine soldiers, they were also helped by the political fragmentation of the Arab world in the 9th century and the weakening of the Bulgars by Magyar and Rus attacks in the 10th. Under Basil II (r.976–1025; the "Bulgar-slayer"), the Byzantine empire reigned supreme in Europe and the Middle East, yet within 20 years of his death it was again losing ground. By 1071 the Normans had largely driven the Byzantines out of Italy. In the same year a crushing defeat by the Seljuk Turks at Manzikert was followed by the loss of Anatolia, the empire's main source of army recruits.

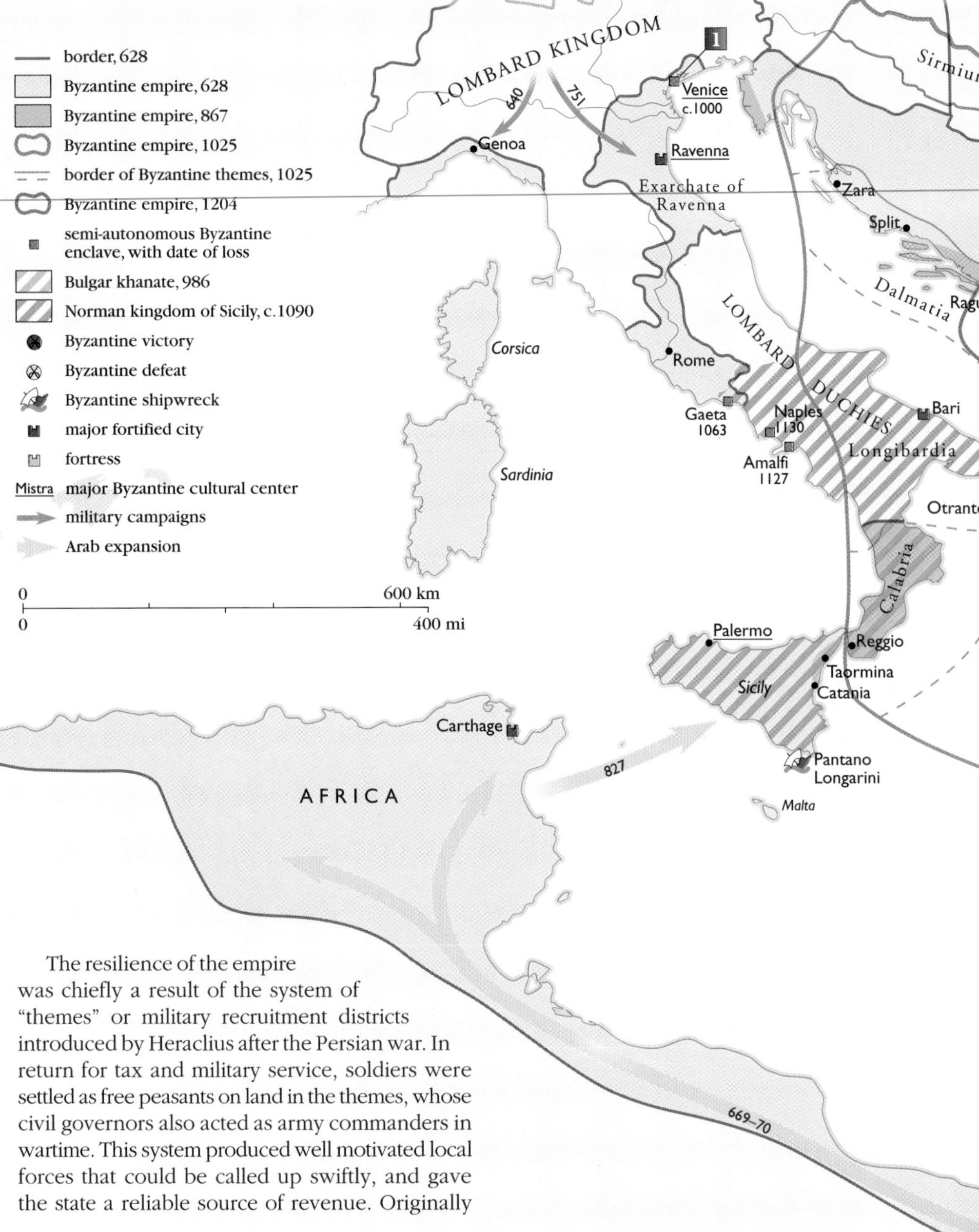

border, 628
Byzantine empire, 628
Byzantine empire, 867
Byzantine empire, 1025
border of Byzantine themes, 1025
Byzantine empire, 1204
semi-autonomous Byzantine enclave, with date of loss
Bulgar khanate, 986
Norman kingdom of Sicily, c.1090
Byzantine victory
Byzantine defeat
Byzantine shipwreck
major fortified city
fortress
Mistra major Byzantine cultural center
military campaigns
Arab expansion
0 600 km
0 400 mi
1
LOMBARD KINGDOM
640
751
Venice c.1000
Genoa
Ravenna
Exarchate of Ravenna
Sirmium
Zara
Split
Dalmatia
Ragusa
LOMBARD DUCHIES
Corsica
Rome
Gaeta 1063
Naples 1130
Amalfi 1127
Bari
Longibardia
Sardinia
Otranto
Calabria
Palermo
Reggio
Taormina
Catania
Sicily
Carthage
AFRICA
827
Pantano Longarini
Malta
669–70

The resilience of the empire was chiefly a result of the system of "themes" or military recruitment districts introduced by Heraclius after the Persian war. In return for tax and military service, soldiers were settled as free peasants on land in the themes, whose civil governors also acted as army commanders in wartime. This system produced well motivated local forces that could be called up swiftly, and gave the state a reliable source of revenue. Originally

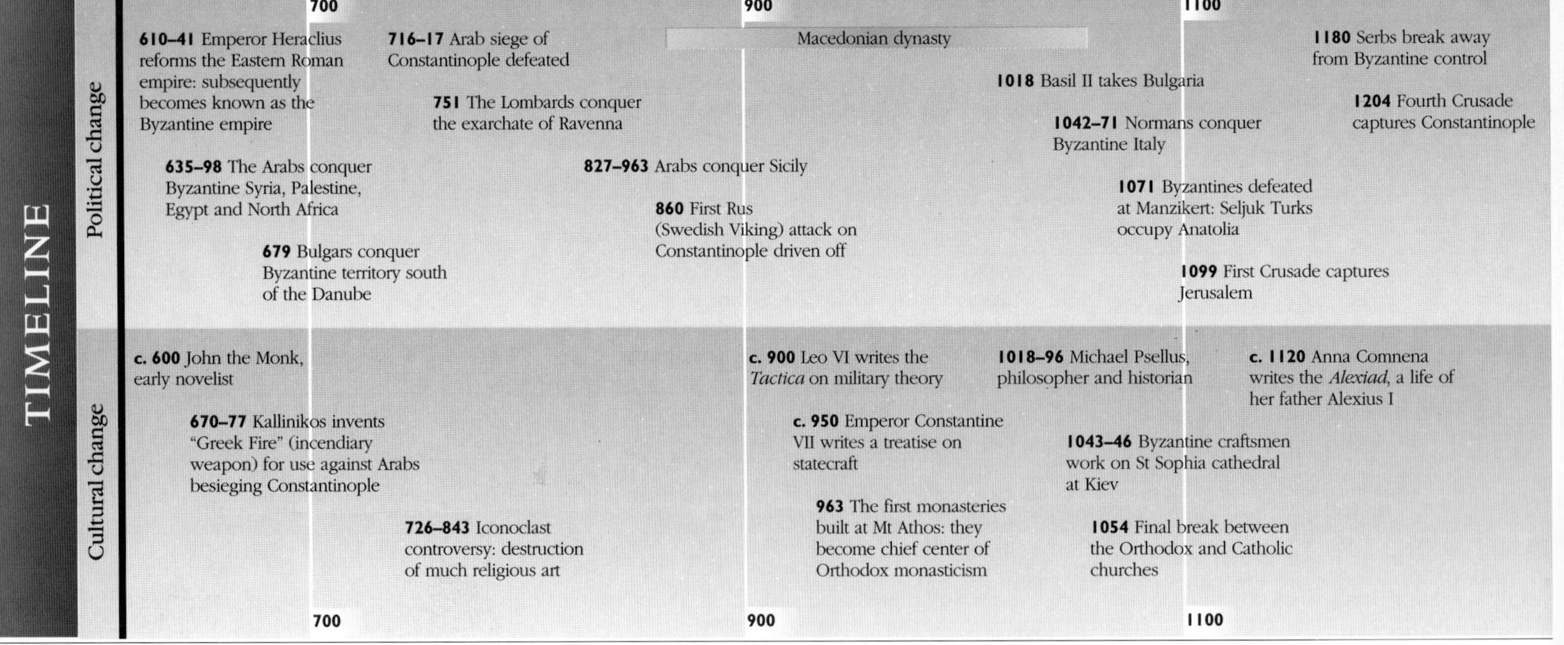

TIMELINE
Political change
700
900
1100
610–41 Emperor Heraclius reforms the Eastern Roman empire: subsequently becomes known as the Byzantine empire
716–17 Arab siege of Constantinople defeated
Macedonian dynasty
1180 Serbs break away from Byzantine control
1018 Basil II takes Bulgaria
751 The Lombards conquer the exarchate of Ravenna
1204 Fourth Crusade captures Constantinople
1042–71 Normans conquer Byzantine Italy
635–98 The Arabs conquer Byzantine Syria, Palestine, Egypt and North Africa
827–963 Arabs conquer Sicily
1071 Byzantines defeated at Manzikert: Seljuk Turks occupy Anatolia
860 First Rus (Swedish Viking) attack on Constantinople driven off
679 Bulgars conquer Byzantine territory south of the Danube
1099 First Crusade captures Jerusalem
Cultural change
c. 600 John the Monk, early novelist
c. 900 Leo VI writes the *Tactica* on military theory
1018–96 Michael Psellus, philosopher and historian
c. 1120 Anna Comnena writes the *Alexiad*, a life of her father Alexius I
670–77 Kallinikos invents "Greek Fire" (incendiary weapon) for use against Arabs besieging Constantinople
c. 950 Emperor Constantine VII writes a treatise on statecraft
1043–46 Byzantine craftsmen work on St Sophia cathedral at Kiev
963 The first monasteries built at Mt Athos: they become chief center of Orthodox monasticism
726–843 Iconoclast controversy: destruction of much religious art
1054 Final break between the Orthodox and Catholic churches
700
900
1100

AVAR
KHANATE
Dnieper
Dniester
Bulgars, 679
Rus (Vikings), 860, 907, 941
Bosporus
Cherson
Cherson
Sirmium
Belgrade
Dorostalon
971
4
Danube
Pliska
Nicopolis
Preslav
Nish
Paristrion
Mesembria
817
Black Sea
Sinope
Constantinople
670–77, 716–17
1204
Amastris
Philippopolis
Adrianople
Arcadiopolis
970
6
Bulgaria
Balathista
1014
Strymon
Macedonia
Thrace
Paphlagonia
Armeniakon
Trebizond
Chaldia
Ani
Theodosiopolis
ARMENIA
2
Thessalonica
Philippi
Nicomedia
Optimaton
Bucellarion
Gangra
Amasia
Seljuk Turks, 1071–80
Colonea
Colonea
Theodosiopolis
Vaspurakan
Manzikert
1071
Nicaea
Ancyra
Sebastea
Iberia
Mt Athos
Abydos
Dorylaeum
Charsianon
Sebastea
Mesopotamia
Aghtamar
Larisa
Opsikion
Amorion
ANATOLIA
Taron
Pelagos
Mytilene
Caesarea
Melitene
Melitene
Nicopolis
Hellas
Chios
Myriocephalum
1176
Arabissos
Smyrna
Sardes
Anatolikon
Cappadocia
Lycandos
Aegean
Naupactus
Thebes
Thracesion
Iconium
Tyana
Loulon
Samosata
873
Samos
Ephesus
Laodicea
Edessa
Corinth
Athens
Cilicia
Tarsus
Teleuch
Poleis
Parephratidiai
SASANIAN EMPIRE
642 conquered by Arabs
Peloponnesus
5
Yassi Ada
Cibyrrhaeoton
Attalia
Seleucia
Seleucia
Aleppo
Mistra
Antioch
Euphrates
Serçe
Liman
Rhodes
Myra
Antiochia
SYRIA
Rhodes
Crete
Cyprus
7
637–43
Gortyn
Crete
Cyprus
633–40
633–40
Damascus
Mediterranean Sea
Tyre
Yarmuk River
635
3
Caesarea
633–40
Jerusalem
PALESTINE
LIBYA
Alexandria
642–43
Heliopolis
640
640
Nile
EGYPT
Arabs

EMPRESS ZOE (r.1028–50), is shown here in the mosaic artform that was Byzantium's finest cultural achievement.

1 Byzantine influence endured in Venice long after the city's independence. St Mark's Cathedral (begun 1063) is a fine example of Byzantine architecture.

2 Christian Armenia joined the empire voluntarily in 1020, seeking protection from its Muslim neighbors.

3 The Byzantine defeat on the Yarmuk River led to the Arab occupation of Palestine and Syria.

4 The Bulgarian capital at Pliska was built around a fortified palace; at its height (c.800) the city covered a larger area than Constantinople.

5 Wreck of a 7th-century Byzantine merchant ship carrying wine; long-distance trade flourished in the Byzantine empire in the early Middle Ages.

6 After their defeat of the Bulgars at Balathista (1014), the Byzantines pushed their frontier to the Danube.

7 Cyprus changed hands several times: Arab 649–746, Byzantine 746–c.826, Arab c.826–965, Byzantine 965–1191 when it was captured by Richard I of England during the Third Crusade.

numbering 13, the themes had grown to over 40 by the 11th century. After Basil II's death, the system was deliberately neglected by weak rulers who feared the army's strength, and the empire was unprepared to face the Seljuk invasions.

The loss of Anatolia was a fatal blow for the empire. Though the western districts were regained by Alexius I Comnenus (r.1081–1118) following the success of the First Crusade, the themes had been obliterated and the area depopulated. The landed aristocracy reduced the surviving free peasantry to servile status, leading to the total collapse of the theme system. Thus the empire was left dependent on expensive mercenaries at a time when its income base was being undermined. The state was further impoverished in the 12th century as Venice and Genoa gradually took control of Byzantine trade. Byzantium's residual prestige and its proverbially devious diplomacy maintained the semblance of a great power until the Seljuks inflicted another crushing defeat, at Myriocephalum, in 1176.

The Seljuks did not follow up their victory, however, and it was the Fourth Crusade's capture and plunder of Constantinople that delivered the fatal blow in 1204. Although the Byzantines retook their capital in 1261, the restored empire was a shadow of its former self: prone to civil war, its survival depended on its enemies' weaknesses and misfortunes.

For most of the Middle Ages Byzantium was Christendom's most sophisticated state, producing outstanding sacred art, literature and architecture. Yet its frequent schisms with the western (Roman) church engendered mutual suspicion and hostility. As a result, Byzantium's cultural influence was strongest in areas where Orthodox Christianity prevailed: the Balkans, Georgia and, especially, Russia, which came to see itself as the legitimate successor to the Byzantine state after 1453.

See also 2.17 (the empire of Justinian); 3.16 (the rise of the Turks; 3.17 (the Crusades)

3.16 The medieval Turkish empires • 1038 – 1492 •

Turkish power in the Middle East grew rapidly after the Seljuk invasion of the Ghaznavid emirate in 1037. Three years later, under Toghril Beg (r.1038–63), they had occupied the emirate's western provinces. In 1054–55 the Seljuks, heeding an appeal for help by the Abbasid caliph of Baghdad, drove the Buwayhids from the city. As Sunni Muslims, the Seljuks accorded the caliph greater respect than had the Shiite Buwayhids, but they were no less firm in ruling the city. Under Toghril Beg's successor, Alp Arslan (r.1063–72), the Seljuks overran Syria and routed the Byzantines at Manzikert. Alp Arslan was killed in 1072 repelling a Qarakhanid Turk invasion at Berzem but in the reign of his successor Malik Shah (r.1072–92), Byzantine Anatolia was occupied and the Fatimids expelled from Palestine.

Malik Shah's death sparked civil war and the Seljuk sultanate began to fragment. By 1095 the sultanate of Rum and the Danishmend emirate in Anatolia had seceded and by 1100 there were dozens of independent Seljuk states. The main beneficiaries were the Byzantine empire and the First Crusade, which between them deprived the Seljuks of western Anatolia and northern Syria, and the Fatimids, who retook Palestine in 1098, only to lose it again almost at once to the Crusaders.

Turkish power in the west began to recover under Zangi, the *atabeg* (governor) of Mosul (r.1127–46), who united northern Syria and recaptured Edessa from the Crusaders in 1144. Zangi's son Nur al-Din (r.1146–74) conquered the rest of Muslim Syria and destroyed the Shiite Fatimid caliphate of Egypt. After his death, Saladin, Kurdish governor of Egypt, rebelled against the Zangids and by 1177 controlled the emirate. The Ayyubid dynasty founded by Saladin held power until 1250 when the Mamlukes, a caste of mainly Turkish slave soldiers, seized power. This military elite continued to rule Egypt and Syria until 1517, surviving as a class until 1811. The Seljuks of Rum also recovered their power and defeated the Byzantines at Myriocephalum in 1176.

In the east Turkish power continued to wane in the 12th century and in 1156 the Abbasid caliphate enjoyed a revival. Although its political authority extended only to Iraq, its spiritual authority enabled it to arbitrate in disputes between the Seljuk states. Then in the early 13th century the eastern Seljuk states were absorbed by a new Turkish power, the shahdom of Khwarizm. However, its growth was abruptly halted by the Mongol invasion of 1219. At a stroke, Chingis Khan broke the shahdom's power.

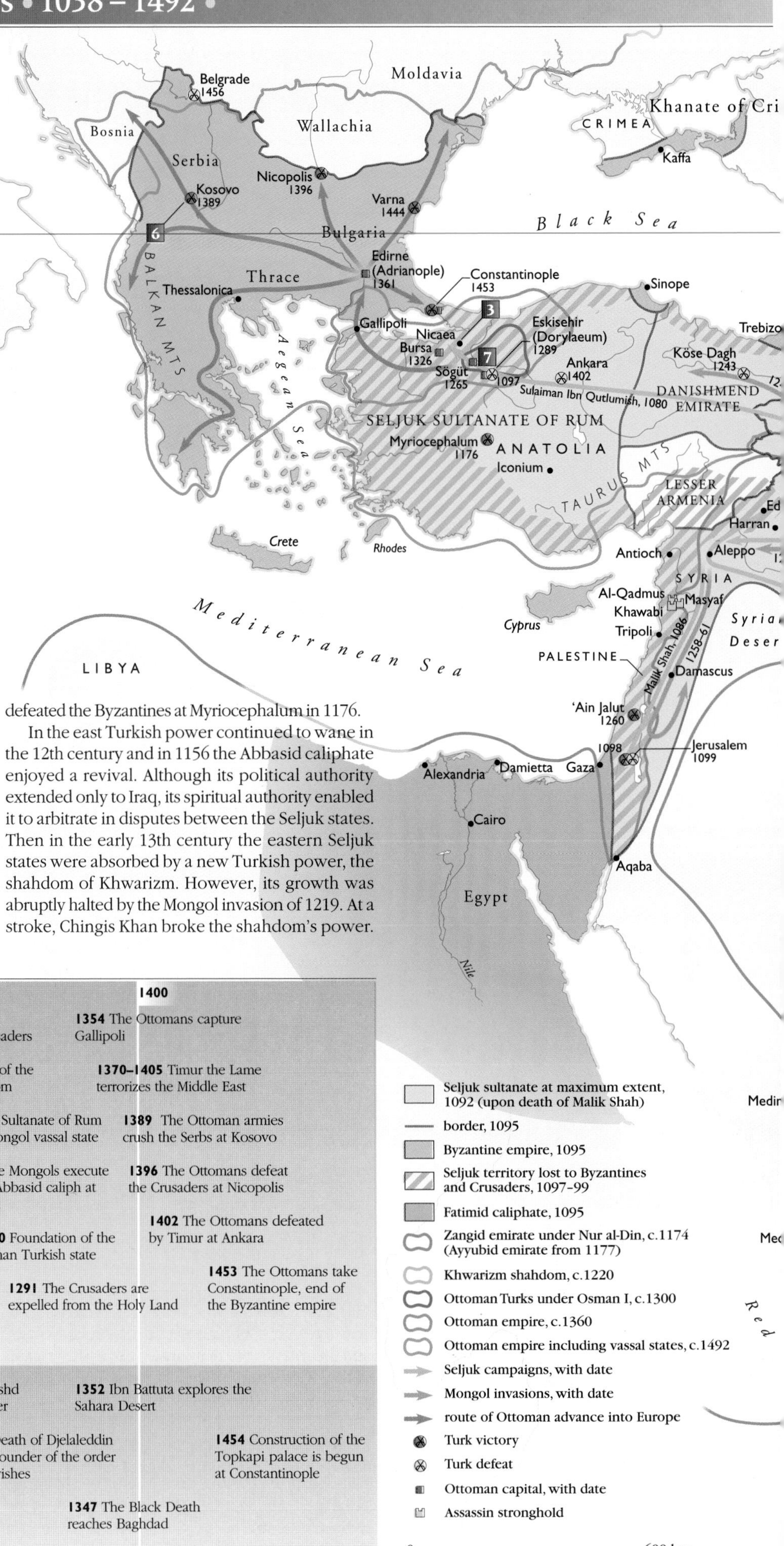

Belgrade 1456
Moldavia
Khanate of Cri
CRIMEA
Kaffa
Bosnia
Wallachia
Serbia
Kosovo 1389
Nicopolis 1396
Varna 1444
Black Sea
6
Bulgaria
BALKAN MTS
Edirne (Adrianople) 1361
Constantinople 1453
Sinope
Thrace
Thessalonica
3
Gallipoli
Nicaea
Bursa 1326
Eskisehir (Dorylaeum) 1289
Trebizo
Aegean Sea
Söğüt 1265
7
1097
Ankara 1402
Köse Dagh 1243
Sulaiman Ibn Qutlumish, 1080
DANISHMEND EMIRATE
SELJUK SULTANATE OF RUM
Myriocephalum 1176
ANATOLIA
Iconium
TAURUS MTS
LESSER ARMENIA
Harran
Crete
Rhodes
Antioch
Aleppo
SYRIA
Al-Qadmus
Masyaf
Khawabi
Mediterranean Sea
Cyprus
Tripoli
Syrian Desert
PALESTINE
Malik Shah, 1086
1258–61
LIBYA
Damascus
'Ain Jalut 1260
1098
Jerusalem 1099
Alexandria
Damietta
Gaza
Cairo
Aqaba
Egypt
Nile
Red
Seljuk sultanate at maximum extent, 1092 (upon death of Malik Shah)
border, 1095
Byzantine empire, 1095
Seljuk territory lost to Byzantines and Crusaders, 1097–99
Fatimid caliphate, 1095
Zangid emirate under Nur al-Din, c.1174 (Ayyubid emirate from 1177)
Khwarizm shahdom, c.1220
Ottoman Turks under Osman I, c.1300
Ottoman empire, c.1360
Ottoman empire including vassal states, c.1492
Seljuk campaigns, with date
Mongol invasions, with date
route of Ottoman advance into Europe
Turk victory
Turk defeat
Ottoman capital, with date
Assassin stronghold
0 600 km
0 400 mi

TIMELINE

1100 | 1250 | 1400

Political change

1038–40 The Seljuks conquer Khorasan

1055 Seljiks capture Baghdad

1071 The Seljuks defeat Byzantines at Manzikert

1092 Death of Malik Shah; Seljuk sultanate disintegrates

1099 The First Crusade captures Jerusalem

1127–46 Zangi, emir of Mosul, unites Turkish emirates of Syria

1169–71 Saladin conquers Egypt for the Zangid emirate

1187 Saladin recaptures Jerusalem from the Crusaders

1210 Foundation of the Khwarizm shahdom

1243 Seljuk Sultanate of Rum becomes Mongol vassal state

1258 The Mongols execute the last Abbasid caliph at Baghdad

c.1280 Foundation of the Ottoman Turkish state

1291 The Crusaders are expelled from the Holy Land

1354 The Ottomans capture Gallipoli

1370–1405 Timur the Lame terrorizes the Middle East

1389 The Ottoman armies crush the Serbs at Kosovo

1396 The Ottomans defeat the Crusaders at Nicopolis

1402 The Ottomans defeated by Timur at Ankara

1453 The Ottomans take Constantinople, end of the Byzantine empire

Cultural change

1027–1123 Omar Khayyam: Persian scientist and poet

1065–67 Nizamayeh academy (Baghdad) is founded

c. 1080 Construction of the Friday Mosque in Isfahan

1198 Death of Ibn Rushd (Averröes): philosopher

1273 Death of Djelaleddin Rumi, founder of the order of Dervishes

1352 Ibn Battuta explores the Sahara Desert

1347 The Black Death reaches Baghdad

1454 Construction of the Topkapi palace is begun at Constantinople

1100 | 1250 | 1400

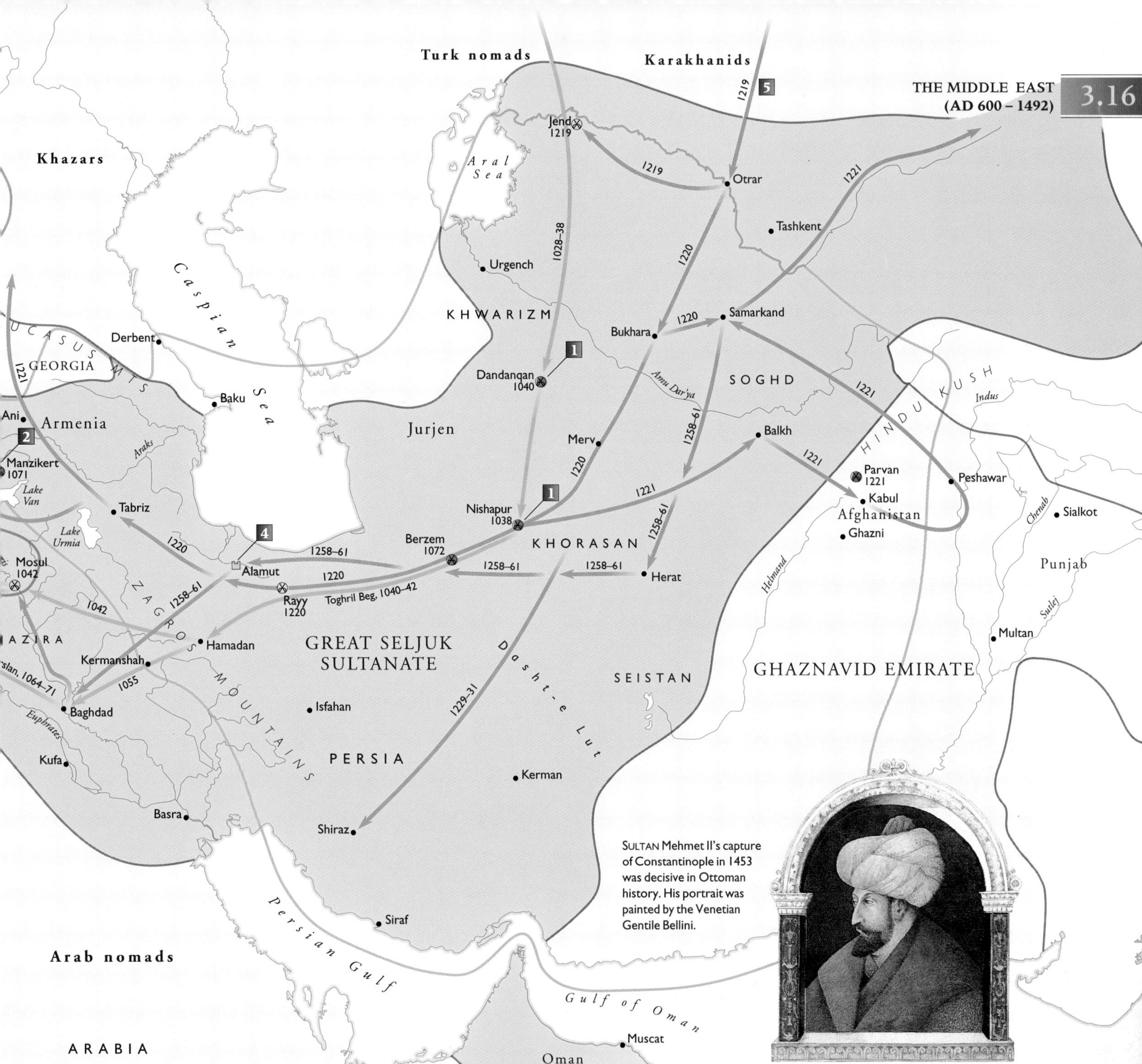
Turk nomads
Karakhanids
Khazars
Aral Sea
Jend 1219
1219
Otrar
Tashkent
1221
1220
1028–38
Urgench
Caspian Sea
KHWARIZM
Bukhara
Samarkand
Derbent
CAUCASUS MTS
GEORGIA
Dandanqan 1040
SOGHD
Amu Dar'ya
Baku
Ani
Armenia
Araks
Manzikert 1071
Lake Van
Jurjen
Merv
1258–61
Balkh
HINDU KUSH
Indus
Parvan 1221
Kabul
Afghanistan
Ghazni
Peshawar
Chenab
Sialkot
Punjab
Tabriz
Lake Urmia
Nishapur 1038
Berzem 1072
KHORASAN
Alamut
Herat
Mosul 1042
Rayy 1220
Toghril Beg, 1040–42
ZAGROS MOUNTAINS
Hamadan
Kermanshah
1055
1042
Baghdad
Euphrates
GREAT SELJUK SULTANATE
Dasht-e Lut
SEISTAN
Helmand
GHAZNAVID EMIRATE
Multan
Sutlej
Isfahan
1229–31
PERSIA
Kerman
Kufa
Basra
Shiraz
Siraf
Persian Gulf
Gulf of Oman
Muscat
Oman
Arab nomads
ARABIA

SULTAN Mehmet II's capture of Constantinople in 1453 was decisive in Ottoman history. His portrait was painted by the Venetian Gentile Bellini.

1 The Ghaznavids lost their western territories to the Seljuks after defeats at Nishapur and Dandanqan.

2 Sultan Alp Arslan's victory over the Byzantines at Manzikert began the Seljuk conquest of Anatolia.

3 Nicaea became the capital of the Seljuk sultanate of Rum ("Rome", from *Romaivi*, as the Byzantine Greeks called themselves) in 1080; when it fell to the Crusaders in 1097, the capital was moved to Iconium.

4 Alamut was the main stronghold of the Shiite Ismaili Nizari sect (the Assassins).

5 The Mongol invaders of the 13th century occupied or imposed vassalage on all the Middle East except Palestine, Egypt, Syria and Arabia.

6 Their defeat by the Ottomans at Kosovo is deeply ingrained on the Serbian national consciousness; for many, it justified the "ethnic cleansing" of Muslims in the Bosnian civil war of 1992–95.

7 The Ottoman state is named after Osman I (r.1280–1324), a Turkish chieftain who ruled Sögüt.

The Seljuks of Rum were reduced to vassals in 1243, the Abbasid caliphate was destroyed, this time for good, in 1258 and in 1260 the Mongols drove the Mamlukes out of Syria. Though the Mamlukes recovered much of this territory after their victory over the Mongols at 'Ain Jalut later that year, the Mongols remained the dominant power in the Middle East until Timur the Lame's death in 1405.

Following the Mongol conquests, the Seljuk sultanate of Rum broke up. The Byzantine empire was now too weak to benefit, while the Serbs, Bulgars and the Latins were busy arguing over the remains of the dying empire. The Ottoman state began its growth under the minor Anatolian chief Osman I, and by the death of Orhan (r.1324–60) the Ottomans occupied most of northwest Anatolia and had begun to expand into Europe, capturing Gallipoli in 1354. In 1361 Murad I (r.1360–89) captured Adrianople and, renaming it Edirne, transferred the capital there. Timur the Lame's invasion in 1402, and his victory at Ankara, led to the temporary collapse of the sultanate but the Ottomans rallied quickly, expanding again by 1430. Constantinople, and with it the Byzantine empire, fell in 1453. Although further expansion into central Europe was checked by the Hungarians at Belgrade in 1456, the Ottoman sultanate was still a rising power in 1492.

A major factor in Ottoman success was the weakness of the neighboring Christian and Turkish states. The divisions in Europe caused by the Hundred Years' War and the Great Schism precluded a concerted Christian resistance, while the Seljuks were weakened by the Mongols, who subsequently withdrew from Anatolia. Religious zeal was another vital element. Osman I had been a *ghazi*, an Islamic warrior, and commitment to spreading the faith through holy war motivated the Ottoman armies. This was especially true of its elite Janissary corps which was composed of the children of Christians, who were raised as devout Muslims.

See also 3.14 (the rise of the Turks); 3.17 (the Crusades); 4.15 (the peak of the Ottoman empire)

3.17 The Crusades • 1096 – 1291 •

The Crusades were holy wars fought to defend the Catholic church and the Christian people against those who were regarded as external and internal enemies of Christendom. Although the main crusading effort was directed against the Muslims in the Holy Land, Crusades were also conducted against the pagan Slavs of the Baltic, Muslim Spain, the Ottoman Turks in the Balkans and heretics, such as the Cathars, within western Christendom itself. Though considered peripheral at the time, it was these campaigns, particularly those in Spain and the Baltic, that were ultimately the most successful. The movement did not die out completely until the 18th century; however, the main period of crusading activity lasted from 1096 to 1291, which saw eight major campaigns and dozens of smaller expeditions.

The Crusaders saw their role as part of the pilgrimage tradition. Pilgrimages to holy places were undertaken as penance and to acquire spiritual merit. The ultimate pilgrimage was to Jerusalem, and when the Turks began to harass pilgrims in the 11th century an armed pilgrimage to restore Christian control was thought fully justified. This appealed both to the piety and the adventurous spirit of the feudal knightly class, who saw themselves as protectors of Christendom. As an inducement the papacy offered Crusaders spiritual and legal privileges, most important of which was remission of the penances due for sin. This was popularly interpreted as a guarantee of immediate entry to heaven if the Crusader were to die on the expedition.

The First Crusade was called by Pope Urban II at the Council of Clermont in 1095 in response to an appeal from the Byzantine emperor Alexius I Comnenus for military help against the Seljuk Turks. The first army to set out, a motley band of poorly armed pilgrims, was wiped out near Nicomedia. However, the main army, mostly French and Norman knights, fought its way across Anatolia to Antioch and on to Jerusalem, which was taken in 1099. The First Crusade was the most successful, thanks in part to divisions in the Muslim world. Four Crusader states were set up in Syria and Palestine: the Kingdom of Jerusalem, the County of Tripoli, the Principality of Antioch and the County of Edessa.

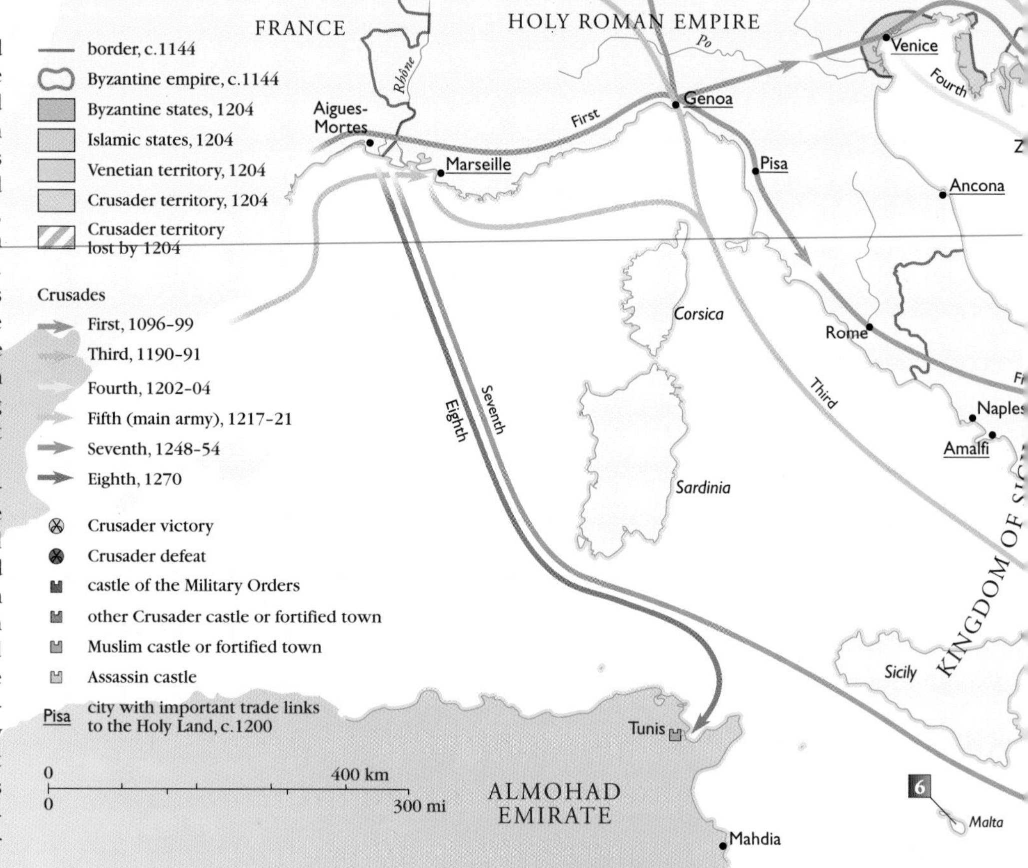

border, c.1144
Byzantine empire, c.1144
Byzantine states, 1204
Islamic states, 1204
Venetian territory, 1204
Crusader territory, 1204
Crusader territory lost by 1204
Crusades
First, 1096–99
Third, 1190–91
Fourth, 1202–04
Fifth (main army), 1217–21
Seventh, 1248–54
Eighth, 1270
Crusader victory
Crusader defeat
castle of the Military Orders
other Crusader castle or fortified town
Muslim castle or fortified town
Assassin castle
Pisa
city with important trade links to the Holy Land, c.1200
0
400 km
0
300 mi
FRANCE
HOLY ROMAN EMPIRE
Po
Rhône
Venice
Fourth
Genoa
First
Aigues-Mortes
Marseille
Pisa
Ancona
Corsica
Rome
Third
Naples
Amalfi
Seventh
Eighth
Sardinia
Sicily
Tunis
ALMOHAD EMIRATE
Mahdia
6
Malta

Muslim unity began to be restored by Zangi, governor of Mosul, who retook Edessa in 1144; this loss prompted the Second Crusade (1147–49), which was badly mauled crossing Anatolia and achieved nothing. The loss of Jerusalem after Saladin's victory at Hattin in 1187 led to the calling of the Third Crusade under Richard I (Lionheart) of England and Philip II Augustus of France. Although this failed to recover Jerusalem, by retaking the coast of Palestine it ensured the survival of the Crusader states.

In the 13th century, Crusaders showed an increasingly sophisticated strategic approach to defense of the Holy Land. It was realized that Christian control of the region could never be secure so long as Egypt remained the center of Muslim power. The Fourth Crusade (1202–04) was the first called with the intention of attacking Egypt but it never reached its destination. Assembled in Venice, the Crusaders were unable to pay for their transit to Egypt, and so agreed to help the Venetians capture the Hungarian city of Zara. Thereafter, the Crusade was diverted to Constantinople in support of a claimant for the Byzantine throne who promised support for the expedition. When this was not forthcoming, the Crusaders sacked Constantinople and made it the center of a Latin Empire. The Fifth Crusade (1217–21) took Damietta at the mouth of the Nile but was defeated by river flooding as it

TIMELINE

Eastern Mediterranean

1095 Pope Urban II calls the First Crusade at Clermont

1098 Crusaders take Edessa and Antioch

1099 Crusaders capture Jerusalem. Defeat of Egyptian relief army at Ascalon

1113 Founding of Order of the Hospital of St John in Jerusalem (Hospitallers)

1118 Founding of the Order of the Knights Templar

1144 Zangi, governor of Mosul takes Edessa

1149 The Second Crusade ends in failure

1187 Saladin defeats Christians at Hattin and recaptures Jerusalem

1190–92 Third Crusade under Richard I: Cyprus captured

1200

1204 The Fourth Crusade takes Constantinople; founding of the Latin Empire

1217–21 The Fifth Crusade attacks Egypt

1228–29 The Sixth Crusade secures Jerusalem

1248–54 Louis IX leads the Seventh Crusade in Egypt

1261 Byzantines recapture Constantinople: fall of the Latin Empire

1270 Louis IX (St Louis) dies besieging Tunis on the Eighth Crusade

1291 Mamlukes capture Acre: fall of Kingdom of Jerusalem

1300

1302 Fall of Ruad. Crusaders are expelled from Holy Land

1310 The Hospitallers are established on Rhodes

1312 The Order of the Knights Templar is dissolved

1396 The Ottomans defeat Burgundian–Hungarian Crusade at Nicopolis

1400

1456 Crusaders defend Belgrade against the Ottomans

Other Crusades

1096 Urban II offers privileges to Crusaders fighting the Spanish Muslims

1147 Crusades against the pagan Wends (Slavs) in the Baltic. Crusaders take Lisbon

1200

1208 Pope Innocent III calls a Crusade against the Cathar heretics in southern France

1227 The Teutonic Knights begin crusading against the pagan Prussians

1300

1309 The Teutonic Knights launch a permanent Crusade against the pagan Lithuanians

1400

1420 A Crusade is proclaimed against the Hussite heretics in Bohemia

1492 The fall of Granada completes the Christian reconquest of Spain

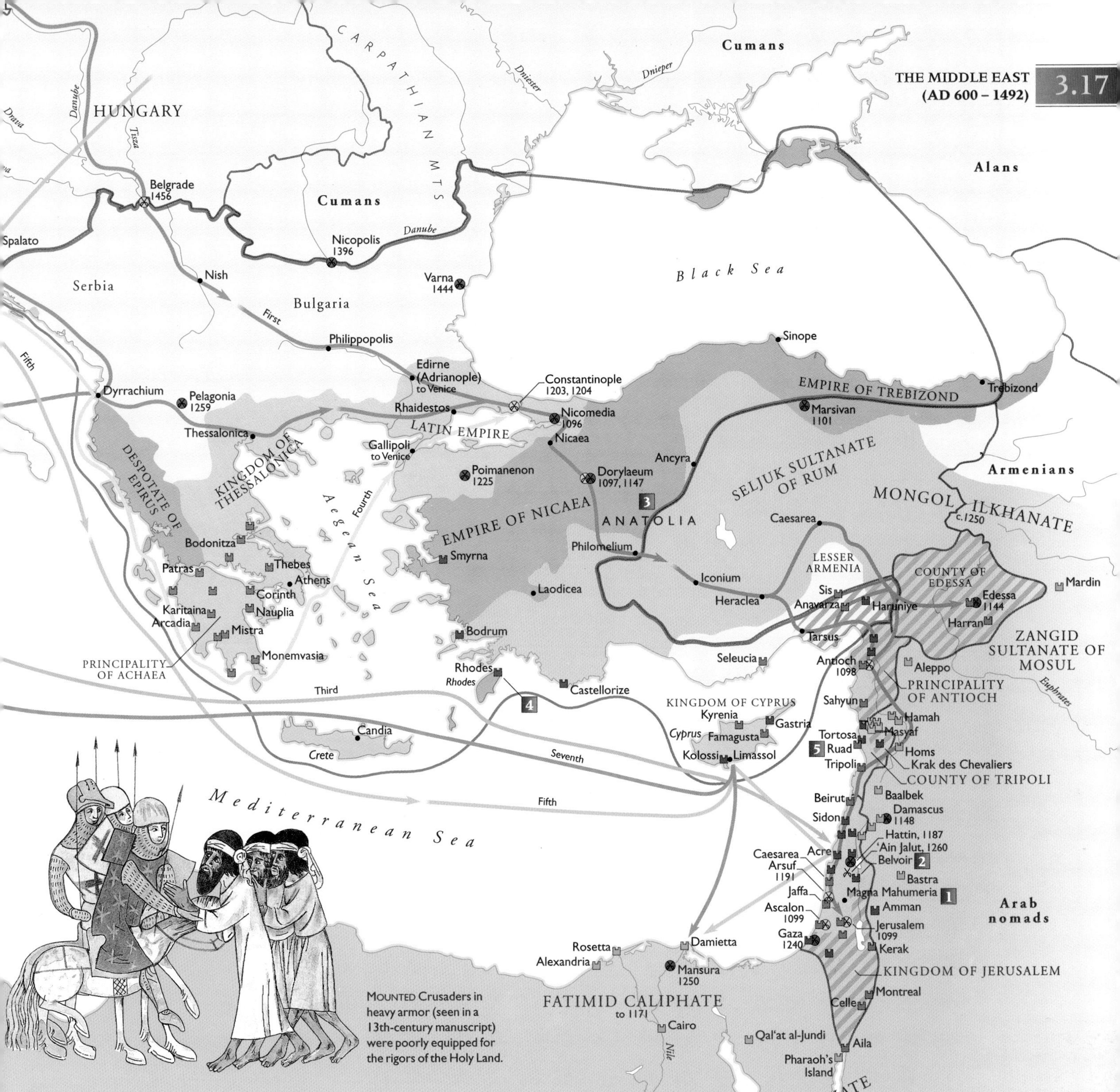

MOUNTED Crusaders in heavy armor (seen in a 13th-century manuscript) were poorly equipped for the rigors of the Holy Land.

1 Magna Mahumeria was a farming settlement of volunteers from France, Spain and Italy, occupied 1120–87 with a population of c.700. Settlers received land on easy terms in return for military service.

2 The concentric castle was the most important innovation of Crusader military architecture. The earliest, begun in 1168, is at Belvoir.

3 Food and water shortages and Turkish attacks made Anatolia highly dangerous for Crusaders. After the Second Crusade failed, most went to Palestine by sea.

4 Occupied by the Hospitallers in 1310, Rhodes became an major Crusader base for campaigns against the Turks until its capture by the Ottomans in 1522.

5 The fortress island of Ruad was the last Christian stronghold in the Holy Land to fall to the Muslims, being taken by the Mamlukes in 1302.

6 Malta, the last bastion of the Crusading movement, was home to the Hospitallers from 1530 to 1798, when they were expelled by Napoleon.

advanced on Cairo. The Holy Roman emperor Frederick II gained Jerusalem through diplomacy on the Sixth Crusade (1228–29) but did not win enough territory to ensure its defense once the truce broke down, and the city was lost again in 1244. The Seventh Crusade (1248–54) under Louis IX of France was an exact repeat of the Fifth. The Eighth Crusade (1270), also led by Louis IX and directed against Tunis with the intention of using it as a base for further attacks on Egypt, was also a costly failure. Far more significant than the Crusades in ensuring the survival of the Crusader states in the 13th century were the Mongol attacks on the Muslim world. After decisively defeating the Mongols at ʻAin Jalut in 1260 the Mamlukes turned their full attention to the Crusader states, which finally fell in 1291.

Throughout their existence the Crusader states suffered from a critical shortage of manpower. Attempts to attract settlers foundered on the extreme inhospitability of the region. Instead, castle building became highly sophisticated; these castles were often garrisoned by military monastic orders, such as the Knights Templars and the Knights Hospitallers, founded to help defend the Holy Land.

The Crusades had considerable effects on the Islamic world, where they briefly revived the concept of the *jihad* (holy war). Nevertheless, Arab historians of the time gave them only scanty attention, and saw the Mongols as a far more potent threat to Islamic civilization.

See also 3.05 (the world religions); 3.09 (medieval Christianity); 3.16 (the medieval Turkish empires)

In sub-Saharan Africa, the period 600–1500 witnessed the rise of chiefdoms, cities, states and empires so that by 1500 most Africans lived in complex societies of some sort. While the causes of state formation were primarily internal, Islam, introduced by Arab merchants, also exerted a strong influence on west and east Africa from the 10th century onward. From the mid-15th century Catholicism was introduced to west and central Africa by the Portuguese. Except possibly in the far southwest, iron was in everyday use in sub-Saharan Africa by the 11th century and in west Africa metalworkers made artifacts of high technical and artistic quality.

Too little is known at present to determine the exact causes of state formation in sub-Saharan Africa. In the west African part of the Sahel (the southern fringe of the Sahara), state formation had begun by 600 and the earliest known state, the kingdom of Ghana, had emerged by 700. Population growth and the development of regional trade routes in the early first millennium AD led to the growth of many large settlements along rivers and at waterholes even before AD 600. It is unclear whether state formation was a response to urbanization or a cause of it, but the west African states grew out of amalgamations of smaller units – chiefdoms with populations of between two and ten thousand people, which dominated areas no more that 30–50 kilometers (20–30 miles) across and were often centered on a single large settlement. These units did not lose their identities in the early states but remained the focus for local loyalties.

The first west African state about which any substantial information exists is the empire of Mali. Arising in the 13th century, Mali centered on fertile farmlands on the inland delta of the upper Niger and controlled access to rich goldfields. Its government and army, which included a strong cavalry element, were strongly influenced by the Muslim states of north Africa. Trans-Saharan trade by camel caravan played an important part in the economy of Mali. Cities such as Koumbi Saleh and Timbuktu at the southern termini of the caravan routes grew rapidly to be centers where African slaves, ivory and gold were exchanged for salt, cloth, glass, ceramics, horses and other luxuries from the north. By 1500 Songhai, another cavalry state, had supplanted Mali as the chief west African power. By 1300 small states such as Benin were developing in the west African forest. State formation here is presumed to have had internal causes: contact with the Sahelian states and, later, the Portuguese was too fleeting to be decisive.

Trade was vital to the growth of city-states on the east African coast. These cities were founded before the arrival of Islam by local Bantu-speaking peoples, perhaps to exploit trade links with the Mediterranean, Middle East and India that had existed since Classical times. Islam was brought by Arab merchants in about AD 1000, yet despite strong cultural influence (such as literacy and stone architecture), no large scale immigration occurred.

States had also begun to emerge in southern Africa by 1500. From about AD 1000, many small chiefdoms had developed between the Zambezi and Limpopo rivers. As cattle formed the basis of the region's wealth, competition over grazing rights possibly led to state formation, and by the 13th century Great Zimbabwe was predominant. Its imposing stone architecture was unequalled in sub-Saharan Africa at the time. Yet as power shifted north to the emerging state of Mwenemutapa in about 1450, Great Zimbabwe declined.

The oldest states in sub-Saharan Africa in 600 were the Christian states in Nubia and Ethiopia. Makkura, the strongest Nubian state, conquered its neighbor Nobatia in the 8th century but finally succumbed to Arab pressure in the 14th century. Another, Alwa, survived until 1505 when it was conquered by an alliance of Arabs and the southern Funj people. By 600 the Ethiopian kingdom of Axum was in decline and the city of Axum itself was abandoned. The last traces of the state survived until 975 when they were destroyed by pagan invaders from the southeast, and through them Christianity survived in the highlands. By the 12th century a successor state, the kingdom of Ethiopia, had emerged around Lalibela. Under the Solomonid dynasty (1270–1777), Ethiopia expanded, bringing most of the Ethiopian highlands under its control by the 15th century and often exacting tribute from its Muslim neighbors.

1 Cruciform churches of solid rock, such as that at Lalibela (c.1300), are the most important monuments of the medieval Ethiopian kingdom.

2 In c.1400, Great Zimbabwe had a population of between 5,000 and 18,000: its Great Enclosure was the largest stone building in sub-Saharan Africa.

3 Cemetery of Mecca-oriented burials with rich grave goods from Persia, Egypt and China indicates settlement by Muslim traders by the 10th–13th centuries.

4 Under the Songhais in the 15th century, Timbuktu became the main center of Islamic culture in west Africa and of trade in salt, gold, ivory and slaves.

5 A fortress was built in 1482 by the Portuguese to protect their trade in gold from Spanish interference: the coast became known as Elmina, "the mine".

6 To mark where they had been, Portuguese explorers built stone columns ("mariners' milestones") with their country's arms and the date of arrival.

SCULPTURES of chieftains and kings were made in bronze and terracotta at Ife, west Africa, from the 12th century.

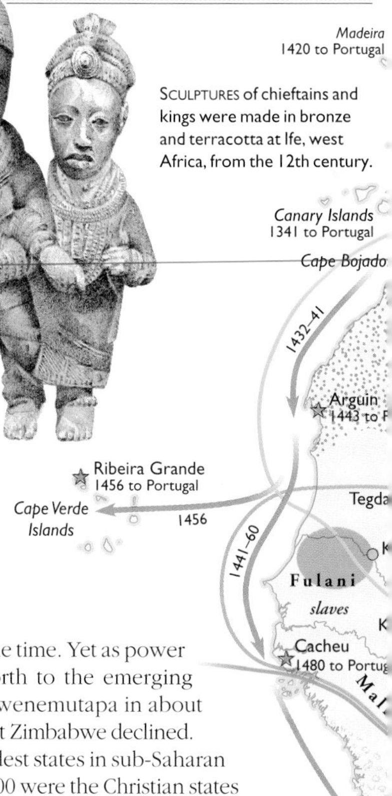

Madeira
1420 to Portugal
Canary Islands
1341 to Portugal
Cape Bojado
1432–41
Arguin
1443 to P
Ribeira Grande
1456 to Portugal
Cape Verde
Islands
1456
Tegda
1441–60
Fulani
slaves
Cacheu
1480 to Portug

TIMELINE

	600–900	900–1200	1200–1500
West	**c.700** Foundation of the kingdom of Ghana **738** The Arabs raid west Africa for slaves **c.750** Trans-Saharan trade begins to increase	**c.1000** Islam becomes established in west Africa **1056–94** Yahya ibn Masa creates the Sanhaja Berber Almoravid emirate **c.1076** Ghana is invaded by the Almoravids	**c.1250** The empire of Malinke becomes the predominant state of west Africa **c.1250** Founding of kingdom of Benin **c.1260–77** Mansa Uli, king of Mali, makes the pilgrimage to Mecca (*hajj*) **c.1400** The lost-wax bronze casting technique introduced to west Africa **1432** Portuguese navigators begin the exploration of the west African coast **1464** Sanni Ali makes Songhai the leading power in west Africa
East and south	**c.800** Trading towns are founded on the east African coast, including Kilwa Kisiwani	**c.1000** Islamic influence begins at Kilwa	**c.1200** Construction of the Great Enclosure at Zimbabwe **c.1200** The first coinage in east Africa is issued at Kilwa **c.1450** Great Zimbabwe is superseded by Mwenemutapa **1490** Portuguese convert King Nzinga Nkuwu of Congo to Christianity
Northeast	**652** The first Islamic Arab invasion of Makkura	**c.975** Pagan invaders destroy kingdom of Axum	**1270** Solomonid dynasty comes to power in Ethiopia **1317** Muslim Arab nomads destroy kingdom of Makkura **1415** Ethiopians kill the Muslim ruler of Saylac

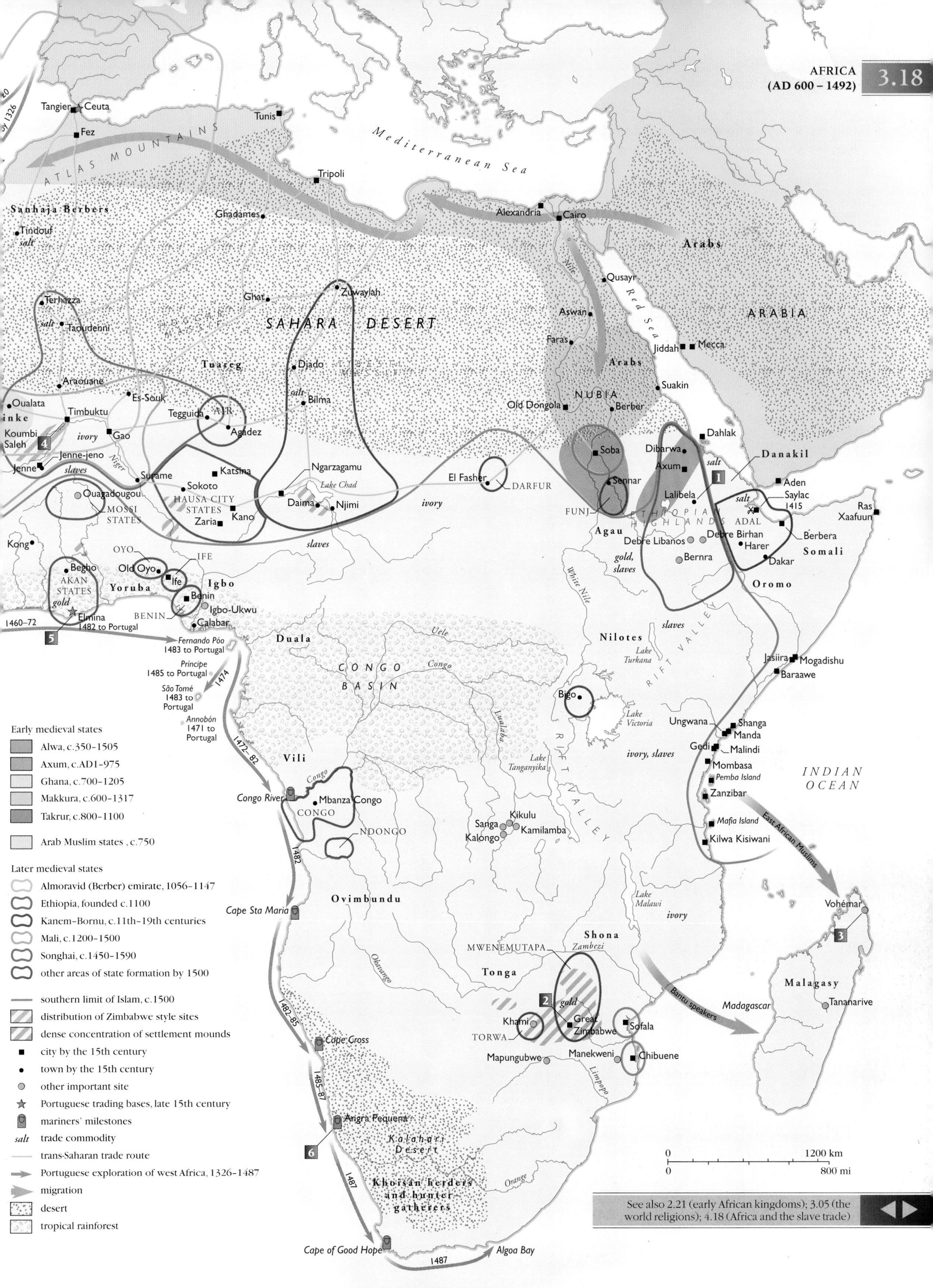
AFRICA
(AD 600 – 1492)
3.18
Mediterranean Sea
ATLAS MOUNTAINS
SAHARA DESERT
HOGGAR MASSIF
TIBESTI MASSIF
ARABIA
Red Sea
Arabs
Sanhaja Berbers
Tuareg
Tangier
Ceuta
Fez
Tunis
Tripoli
Ghadames
Alexandria
Cairo
Qusayr
Aswan
Faras
Jiddah
Mecca
Suakin
Old Dongola
Berber
NUBIA
Soba
Sennar
FUNJ
Dibarwa
Axum
Dahlak
Lalibela
Danakil
Aden
Saylac
1415
Ras Xaafuun
Berbera
ADAL
Harer
Dakar
Debre Libanos
Debre Birhan
Bernra
ETHIOPIAN HIGHLANDS
Agau
gold, slaves
Somali
Oromo
Tindouf
salt
Terhazza
Taoudenni
Araouane
Oualata
Es-Souk
Timbuktu
Koumbi Saleh
ivory
Gao
Tegguida
AÏR
Agadez
Ghat
Zuwaylah
Djado
Bilma
Jenne-jeno
Jenne
slaves
Niger
Surame
Katsina
Sokoto
HAUSA CITY STATES
Kano
Zaria
Ngarzagamu
Lake Chad
Daima
Njimi
El Fasher
DARFUR
Ouagadougou
MOSSI STATES
Kong
OYO
Old Oyo
Ife
IFE
Yoruba
Igbo
Benin
Igbo-Ukwu
BENIN
Calabar
Begho
AKAN STATES
gold
Elmina
1482 to Portugal
1460–72
Fernando Póo
1483 to Portugal
Príncipe
1485 to Portugal
1474
São Tomé
1483 to Portugal
Annobón
1471 to Portugal
1472–82
Duala
CONGO BASIN
Uele
Congo
Lualaba
White Nile
Nilotes
Lake Turkana
RIFT VALLEY
Bigo
Lake Victoria
Lake Tanganyika
ivory, slaves
Jasiira
Mogadishu
Baraawe
Ungwana
Shanga
Manda
Gedi
Malindi
Mombasa
Pemba Island
Zanzibar
Mafia Island
Kilwa Kisiwani
INDIAN OCEAN
East African Muslims
Vili
Congo River
Mbanza Congo
CONGO
NDONGO
1482
Sanga
Kikulu
Kamilamba
Kalongo
Cape Sta Maria
Ovimbundu
Okavango
Lake Malawi
ivory
Shona
MWENEMUTAPA
Zambezi
Tonga
gold
Khami
Great Zimbabwe
TORWA
Sofala
Mapungubwe
Manekweni
Chibuene
Limpopo
Bantu speakers
Vohémar
Malagasy
Madagascar
Tananarive
1482–85
Cape Cross
1485–87
Angra Pequena
Kalahari Desert
1487
Orange
Khoisan herders and hunter-gatherers
Cape of Good Hope
Algoa Bay
0 1200 km
0 800 mi
Early medieval states
Alwa, c.350–1505
Axum, c.AD1–975
Ghana, c.700–1205
Makkura, c.600–1317
Takrur, c.800–1100
Arab Muslim states , c.750
Later medieval states
Almoravid (Berber) emirate, 1056–1147
Ethiopia, founded c.1100
Kanem-Bornu, c.11th–19th centuries
Mali, c.1200–1500
Songhai, c.1450–1590
other areas of state formation by 1500
southern limit of Islam, c.1500
distribution of Zimbabwe style sites
dense concentration of settlement mounds
city by the 15th century
town by the 15th century
other important site
Portuguese trading bases, late 15th century
mariners' milestones
salt trade commodity
trans-Saharan trade route
Portuguese exploration of west Africa, 1326–1487
migration
desert
tropical rainforest

See also 2.21 (early African kingdoms); 3.05 (the world religions); 4.18 (Africa and the slave trade)

At the beginning of the 7th century the most powerful Indian kingdom was Kanauj, which dominated the Gangetic plain. Shortly after his ascending the throne of the minor kingdom of Thaneswar, Harsha also became king of Kanauj and began a career of conquest that united most of northern India under his rule. However, Harsha's attempt to conquer the Deccan was defeated in 633 by the Chalukyas, the dominant power of central India. Harsha's empire fell apart after he was murdered in 647; no other northern ruler would again attempt to conquer the south until the 13th century.

For the 600 years after the fall of Harsha's empire, the history of India is dominated by the rise and fall of regional kingdoms and short-lived dynasties. Regional wars were frequent; however, because the main kingdoms were roughly comparable in wealth, population, military strength and tactics, a balance of power existed that precluded the formation of supraregional states. The period saw a strong revival of Hinduism and a commensurate decline of Buddhism throughout India with the exception of Ceylon. Hinduism also began to replace Buddhism in much of southeast Asia, largely through the influence of the Tamil kingdom of the Cholas, a major mercantile and naval power.

The entire period from 700 to 1500 was dominated by the spread of Islam as a cultural and political force. Introduced into India by the Arabs, who conquered Sind and Multan in the early 8th century, Islam's advance under the Arabs was halted by the Gurjara-Pratiharas, a military Rajput dynasty that had become the main power in the north after the fall of Harsha's empire. However, in 1000 the militant Muslim ruler Mahmud of Ghazni (r.999–1030) launched the first of his 17 invasions of India. Mahmud broke the power of the Gurjara-Pratiharas and the Chandellas but only incorporated the Punjab into his empire, as his main concern was with plunder, and with despoiling Hindu temples. After Mahmud's death the Ghaznavid emirate declined and for 150 years there was no further Islamic advance in India. In 1151 the Ghaznavids were overthrown by the governor of Ghur. From 1175 onwards, Muhammad of Ghur (r.1173–1206) made a concerted effort to conquer northern India. Following his victory over a confederation of Rajput rulers at the second battle of Tarain in 1192, Hindu resistance began to crumble. By 1200 he was master of the Indus and Gangetic plains and had laid the foundations for 600 years of Muslim dominance in India. Muhammad's victory was the result of both Muslim strength and Hindu weakness. The Muslim army was a professional force of disciplined and highly mobile horse archers. Many Muslim soldiers were slaves, trained for battle from childhood, but a military career was open to all – unlike in the Hindu states – and rapid advancement was possible for anyone who showed ability, enslaved or free. Also, the Muslims were invading a country rich in plunder, and were further motivated by religious fervor.

On the death of Muhammad in 1206 the Turkish slave-general Qutb-ud-Din broke away from the Ghurid empire, founding an independent sultanate at Delhi. Qutb-ud-Din faced widespread Hindu rebellions and his successor Iltutmish (r.1211–36) consolidated the Muslim conquest of northern India. Qutb-ud-Din's dynasty was overthrown in 1290 by the Khalji dynasty (1290–1320). Under the second Khalji ruler Ala-ud-Din, the sultanate's control was extended south of the Narmada river in the Deccan. The sultanate reached its greatest territorial extent under Muhammad ibn Tughluk (d.1351). Determined to make the whole of the Deccan an integral part of the Delhi sultanate, he transferred his center of government to the massive hilltop fortress of Daulatabad in central India but by moving away from Delhi he lost control of the north while failing to consolidate his hold on the south. Muhammad was forced to return to Delhi to restore order, leaving the Deccan in the charge of a governor, Hasan Gungu, who revolted in 1347 to establish the independent Bahmani sultanate. At the same time the Hindu kingdom of Vijayanagara started to establish

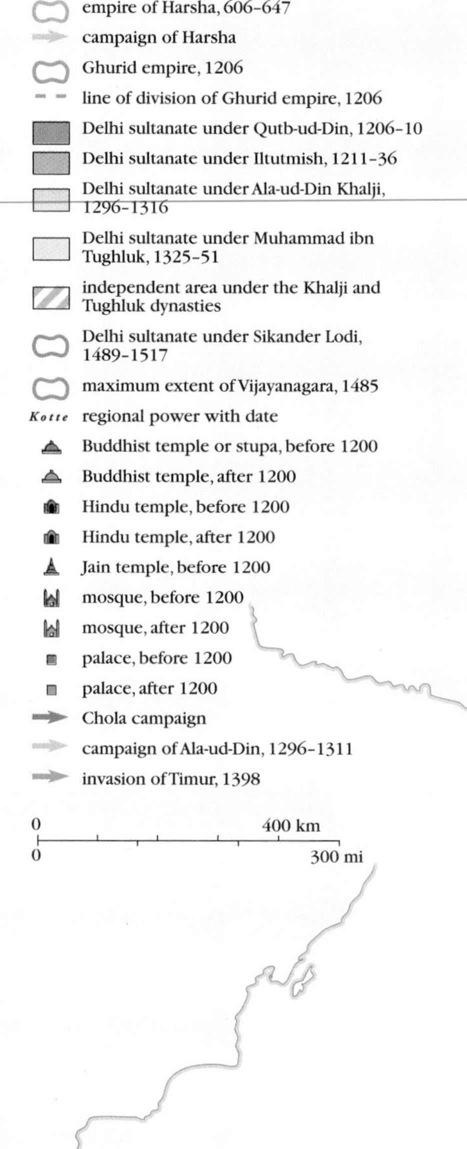
empire of Harsha, 606–647
campaign of Harsha
Ghurid empire, 1206
line of division of Ghurid empire, 1206
Delhi sultanate under Qutb-ud-Din, 1206–10
Delhi sultanate under Iltutmish, 1211–36
Delhi sultanate under Ala-ud-Din Khalji, 1296–1316
Delhi sultanate under Muhammad ibn Tughluk, 1325–51
independent area under the Khalji and Tughluk dynasties
Delhi sultanate under Sikander Lodi, 1489–1517
maximum extent of Vijayanagara, 1485
Kotte regional power with date
Buddhist temple or stupa, before 1200
Buddhist temple, after 1200
Hindu temple, before 1200
Hindu temple, after 1200
Jain temple, before 1200
mosque, before 1200
mosque, after 1200
palace, before 1200
palace, after 1200
Chola campaign
campaign of Ala-ud-Din, 1296–1311
invasion of Timur, 1398
0
400 km
0
300 mi

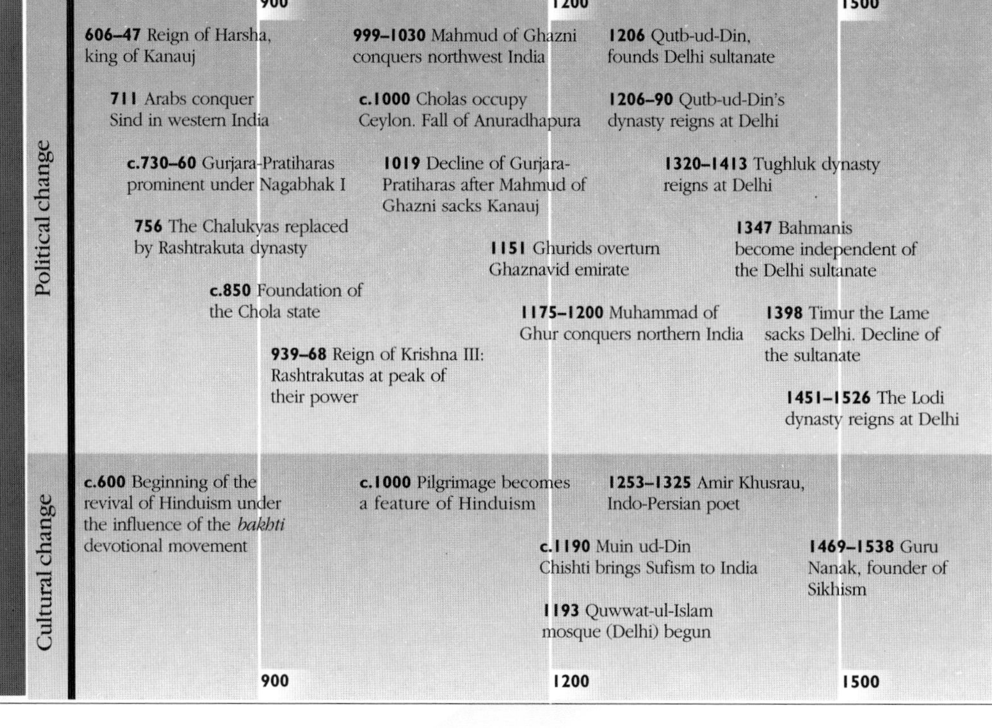
TIMELINE
900
1200
1500
Political change
606–47 Reign of Harsha, king of Kanauj
711 Arabs conquer Sind in western India
c.730–60 Gurjara-Pratiharas prominent under Nagabhak I
756 The Chalukyas replaced by Rashtrakuta dynasty
c.850 Foundation of the Chola state
939–68 Reign of Krishna III: Rashtrakutas at peak of their power
999–1030 Mahmud of Ghazni conquers northwest India
c.1000 Cholas occupy Ceylon. Fall of Anuradhapura
1019 Decline of Gurjara-Pratiharas after Mahmud of Ghazni sacks Kanauj
1151 Ghurids overturn Ghaznavid emirate
1175–1200 Muhammad of Ghur conquers northern India
1206 Qutb-ud-Din, founds Delhi sultanate
1206–90 Qutb-ud-Din's dynasty reigns at Delhi
1320–1413 Tughluk dynasty reigns at Delhi
1347 Bahmanis become independent of the Delhi sultanate
1398 Timur the Lame sacks Delhi. Decline of the sultanate
1451–1526 The Lodi dynasty reigns at Delhi
Cultural change
c.600 Beginning of the revival of Hinduism under the influence of the bakhti devotional movement
c.1000 Pilgrimage becomes a feature of Hinduism
c.1190 Muin ud-Din Chishti brings Sufism to India
1193 Quwwat-ul-Islam mosque (Delhi) begun
1253–1325 Amir Khusrau, Indo-Persian poet
1469–1538 Guru Nanak, founder of Sikhism
900
1200
1500

1 Harsha's attempt to capture the Deccan in 633 was decisively repulsed by the Chalukyas.

2 The complex of over 20 Hindu and Jain temples of the 9th–11th centuries at Khajuraho is virtually the sole relic of the powerful Chandella kingdom.

3 Delhi was a minor fortress town until Qutb-ud-Din, its first sultan, adopted it as his capital.

4 The Cholas were the dominant south Indian power in the 10th and 11th centuries, with a major naval and trading empire. The kingdom survived until 1279.

5 Two battles fought at Tarain 1191 and 1192 between the Rajputs and Muhammad of Ghur were followed by the Muslim conquest of northern India.

6 Buddhism, long in decline in India, was finally extinguished when the Ghurids destroyed the university at Nalanda in 1199.

7 The ruins of Vijayanagara ("city of victory"), capital of the largest Hindu state from the 14th century onward, cover some 25 sq km (9 sq miles).

8 Daulatabad, a massive hilltop fortress and walled city, was chosen by Muhammad Tughluk as a new capital in the Deccan in 1339.

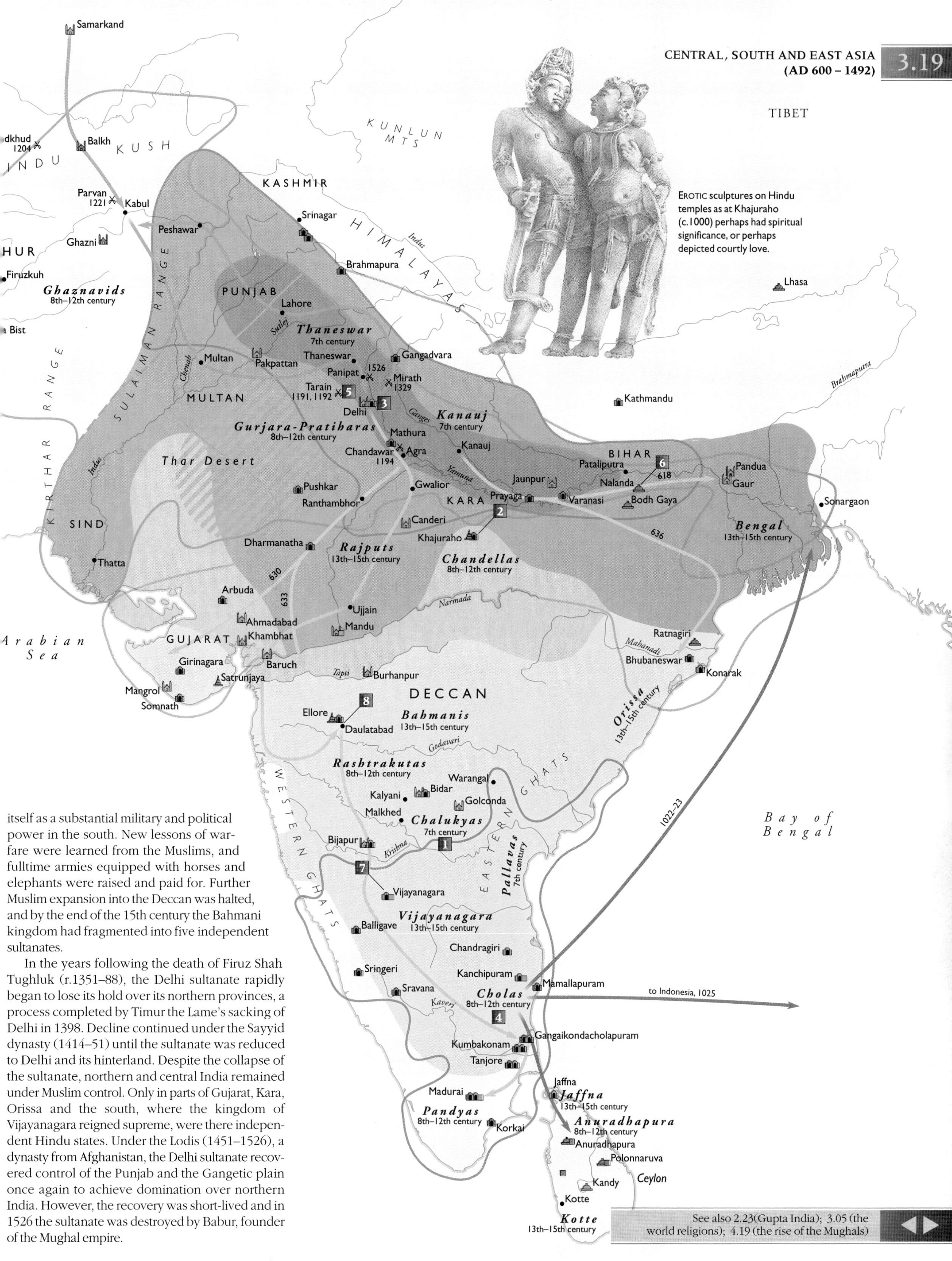
Samarkand
TIBET
KUNLUN MTS
dkhud 1204
Balkh
HINDU KUSH
KASHMIR
Parvan 1221
Kabul
Srinagar
HIMALAYAS
Indus
Peshawar
Ghazni
HUR
Brahmapura
Firuzkuh
Ghaznavids
8th–12th century
PUNJAB
Lahore
Lhasa
Bist
SULAIMAN RANGE
Sutlej
Thaneswar
7th century
Multan
Pakpattan
Thaneswar
Gangadvara
Chenab
Panipat
1526
Mirath
1329
Brahmaputra
Tarain
1191, 1192
5
MULTAN
Delhi
3
Kathmandu
KIRTHAR RANGE
Ganges
Kanauj
7th century
Gurjara-Pratiharas
8th–12th century
Mathura
Indus
Chandawar
1194
Agra
Kanauj
Thar Desert
BIHAR
6
Pataliputra
618
Pandua
Yamuna
Jaunpur
Nalanda
Gaur
Gwalior
Pushkar
Prayaga
Varanasi
Bodh Gaya
Sonargaon
Ranthambhor
KARA
2
SIND
Canderi
Bengal
13th–15th century
636
Khajuraho
Dharmanatha
Rajputs
13th–15th century
Chandellas
8th–12th century
Thatta
630
Arbuda
633
Narmada
Ujjain
Ahmadabad
Mandu
Arabian Sea
GUJARAT
Khambhat
Ratnagiri
Mahanadi
Bhubaneswar
Girinagara
Baruch
Konarak
Tapti
Burhanpur
Satrunjaya
Mangrol
Somnath
DECCAN
8
Orissa
13th–15th century
Ellore
Bahmanis
Daulatabad
13th–15th century
Godavari
Rashtrakutas
8th–12th century
EASTERN GHATS
WESTERN GHATS
Warangal
Bidar
Kalyani
Golconda
Malkhed
Chalukyas
7th century
1022–23
Bay of Bengal
Bijapur
Krishna
1
Pallavas
7th century
7
Vijayanagara
Vijayanagara
13th–15th century
Balligave
Chandragiri
Sringeri
Kanchipuram
Mamallapuram
Sravana
Cholas
8th–12th century
to Indonesia, 1025
Kaveri
4
Gangaikondacholapuram
Kumbakonam
Tanjore
Jaffna
Madurai
Jaffna
13th–15th century
Pandyas
8th–12th century
Korkai
Anuradhapura
8th–12th century
Anuradhapura
Polonnaruva
Ceylon
Kandy
Kotte
Kotte
13th–15th century

EROTIC sculptures on Hindu temples as at Khajuraho (c.1000) perhaps had spiritual significance, or perhaps depicted courtly love.

itself as a substantial military and political power in the south. New lessons of warfare were learned from the Muslims, and fulltime armies equipped with horses and elephants were raised and paid for. Further Muslim expansion into the Deccan was halted, and by the end of the 15th century the Bahmani kingdom had fragmented into five independent sultanates.

In the years following the death of Firuz Shah Tughluk (r.1351–88), the Delhi sultanate rapidly began to lose its hold over its northern provinces, a process completed by Timur the Lame's sacking of Delhi in 1398. Decline continued under the Sayyid dynasty (1414–51) until the sultanate was reduced to Delhi and its hinterland. Despite the collapse of the sultanate, northern and central India remained under Muslim control. Only in parts of Gujarat, Kara, Orissa and the south, where the kingdom of Vijayanagara reigned supreme, were there independent Hindu states. Under the Lodis (1451–1526), a dynasty from Afghanistan, the Delhi sultanate recovered control of the Punjab and the Gangetic plain once again to achieve domination over northern India. However, the recovery was short-lived and in 1526 the sultanate was destroyed by Babur, founder of the Mughal empire.

See also 2.23(Gupta India); 3.05 (the world religions); 4.19 (the rise of the Mughals)

3.20 Sui and Tang China • 589 – 907 •

The centralized Chinese empire created by Shi Huangdi survived until AD 220, when it split into three rival states. Unity was restored in 589 by Yang Jian, who as emperor Wen (r.589–604) became the founder of the Sui dynasty. Wen, a tyrannical but able ruler, re-established a strong centralized bureaucracy and increased the prosperity of the peasantry through a land redistribution scheme. Granaries were built and the canal system expanded. As a result of Wen's reforms, the economy grew rapidly and the state amassed large reserves of cash and commodities. These were squandered by Wen's successor Yang (r.604–17) on building projects and opulent court life. Moreover, a disastrous war against the Korean kingdom of Koguryo caused the peasants of the northeast to rebel. The empire was saved only by the coup of Li Yuan, military governor of Taiyuan, who captured the Sui capital at Luoyang in 617 and became, after Yang's murder in 618, the first emperor of the Tang dynasty (as Gaozu, r.618– 26). Gaozong was then deposed by his son Taizong (r.626–49), one of Chinese history's ablest rulers.

Taizong based his government loosely on the Han model but without the feudal elements. At its head was the emperor, whose authority (in theory if not always in practice) was absolute. The central administration consisted of three bodies, the Imperial Chancellery, the Imperial Secretariat and the Department for State Affairs. This latter department supervised the six ministries – officials, finances, religious rites, the army, justice and public works – while a Board of Censors oversaw the actions of officials. The empire was divided into 15 administrative regions or "circuits", under an inspecting commissioner. The examination system became more important for selecting bureaucratic staff, yet the cost of education precluded all but the rich landowning classes from pursuing a career in administration.

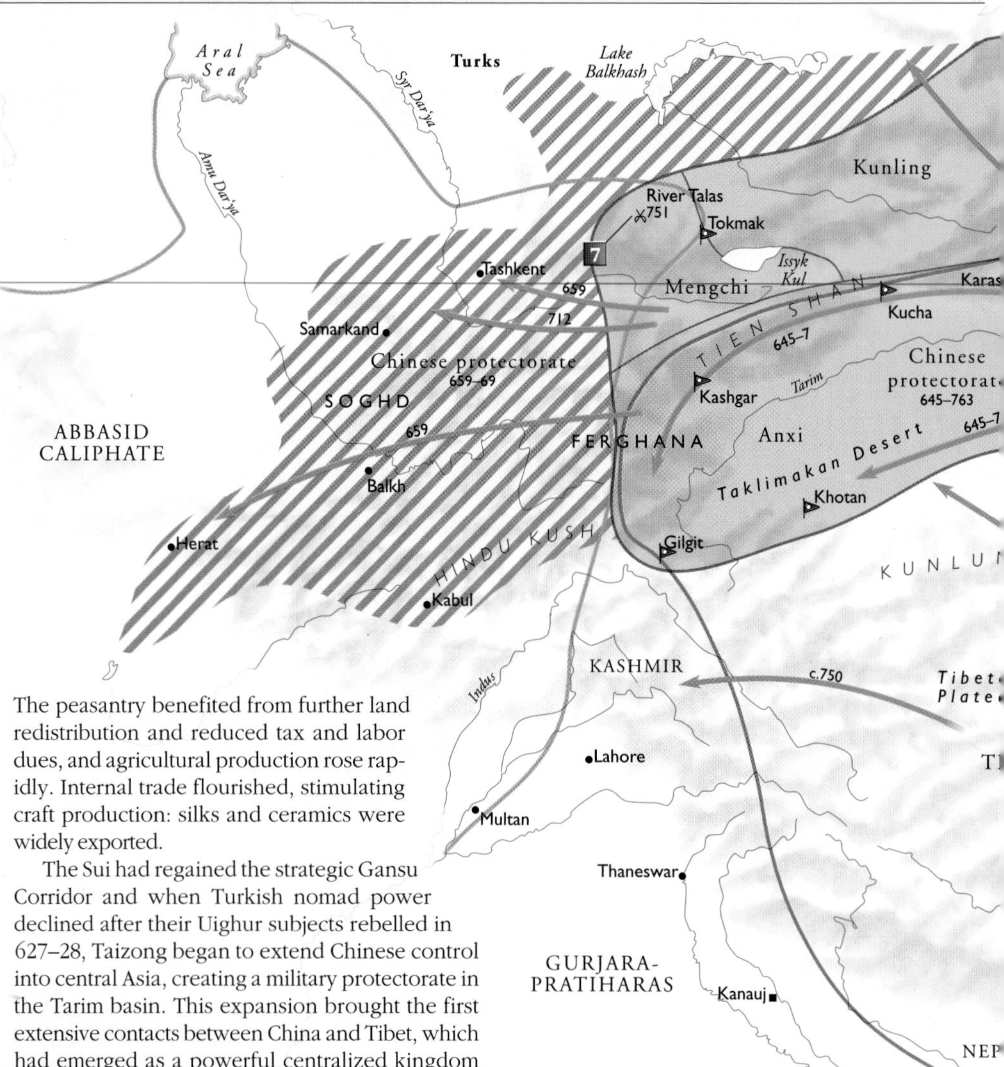

Aral Sea
Turks
Lake Balkhash
Syr Dar'ya
Amu Dar'ya
Kunling
River Talas
751
Tokmak
7
Tashkent
Issyk Kul
659
Mengchi
Karas
712
TIEN SHAN
Kucha
Samarkand
645–7
Chinese protectorate
659–69
Kashgar
Tarim
Chinese protectorate
645–763
SOGHD
659
ABBASID CALIPHATE
FERGHANA
Anxi
645–7
Taklimakan Desert
Balkh
Khotan
Herat
HINDU KUSH
Gilgit
KUNLUN
Kabul
KASHMIR
c.750
Tibet Plate
Indus
Lahore
Multan
Thaneswar
GURJARA-PRATIHARAS
Kanauj
NEP

The peasantry benefited from further land redistribution and reduced tax and labor dues, and agricultural production rose rapidly. Internal trade flourished, stimulating craft production: silks and ceramics were widely exported.

The Sui had regained the strategic Gansu Corridor and when Turkish nomad power declined after their Uighur subjects rebelled in 627–28, Taizong began to extend Chinese control into central Asia, creating a military protectorate in the Tarim basin. This expansion brought the first extensive contacts between China and Tibet, which had emerged as a powerful centralized kingdom under Sron-btsan-sgampo (r.605–49). Gaozong

TIMELINE

700 · 800 · 900

Political change

589 Yang Jian unites China and founds Sui dynasty

c. 600 Emergence of Tibet and Nan Chao states

611–14 A Sui attempt to conquer Koguryo defeated with heavy loss

618 Li Yuan becomes the first emperor of the Tang dynasty

640–59 The Chinese expand into central Asia

676 Silla becomes the leading Korean kingdom

751 Arab victory over the Tang at the River Talas

755–63 Rebellion of An Lushan leads to breakdown of central administration

780 Collapse of the kingdom of Silla

791 Chinese lose control of Gansu corridor after defeat of Chinese–Uighur army by Tibetans at Tingzhou

874–84 Major peasant rebellions: decline of the Tang dynasty

907–60 The Five Dynasties and Ten Kingdoms

907 Final collapse of the Tang dynasty

936 Foundation of the kingdom of Koryo (Korea)

939 Annam becomes independent of China

960–79 Song Taizu and Song taizong reunite China

Cultural change

606–09 The Grand Canal from Beijing to Yue is built

635 Nestorian Christian missionaries reach China

c. 700–800 Earliest text produced by block printing

c. 701–761 Life of the poet Li Po

713–68 Life of the poet Du Fu

780 Lu Yu's *The Classic of Tea* describes tea use

c.825 Chamber lock in use on Chinese canals

845 Persecution of non-Chinese religions including Buddhism and Christianity

c.850 Possible earliest use of gunpowder

700 · 800 · 900

- border, 750
- "circuits" of Tang empire, 742
- civil administration
- military government
- temporary expansion, 7th century
- Abbasid caliphate, c.751
- maximum extent of Tibetan kingdom, c.800
- capital
- seat of circuit-inspecting commissioner, 742
- seat of government-general, 800
- Chinese garrison
- non-Chinese capital
- outbreak of An Lushan's rebellion, 755
- other rebellion against the Tang
- concentration of pottery kilns
- Sui campaign
- Tang campaign
- Tibetan expansion
- frontier wall
- major migration
- major canal
- modern coastline and drainage where altered

0 – 800 km
0 – 500 mi

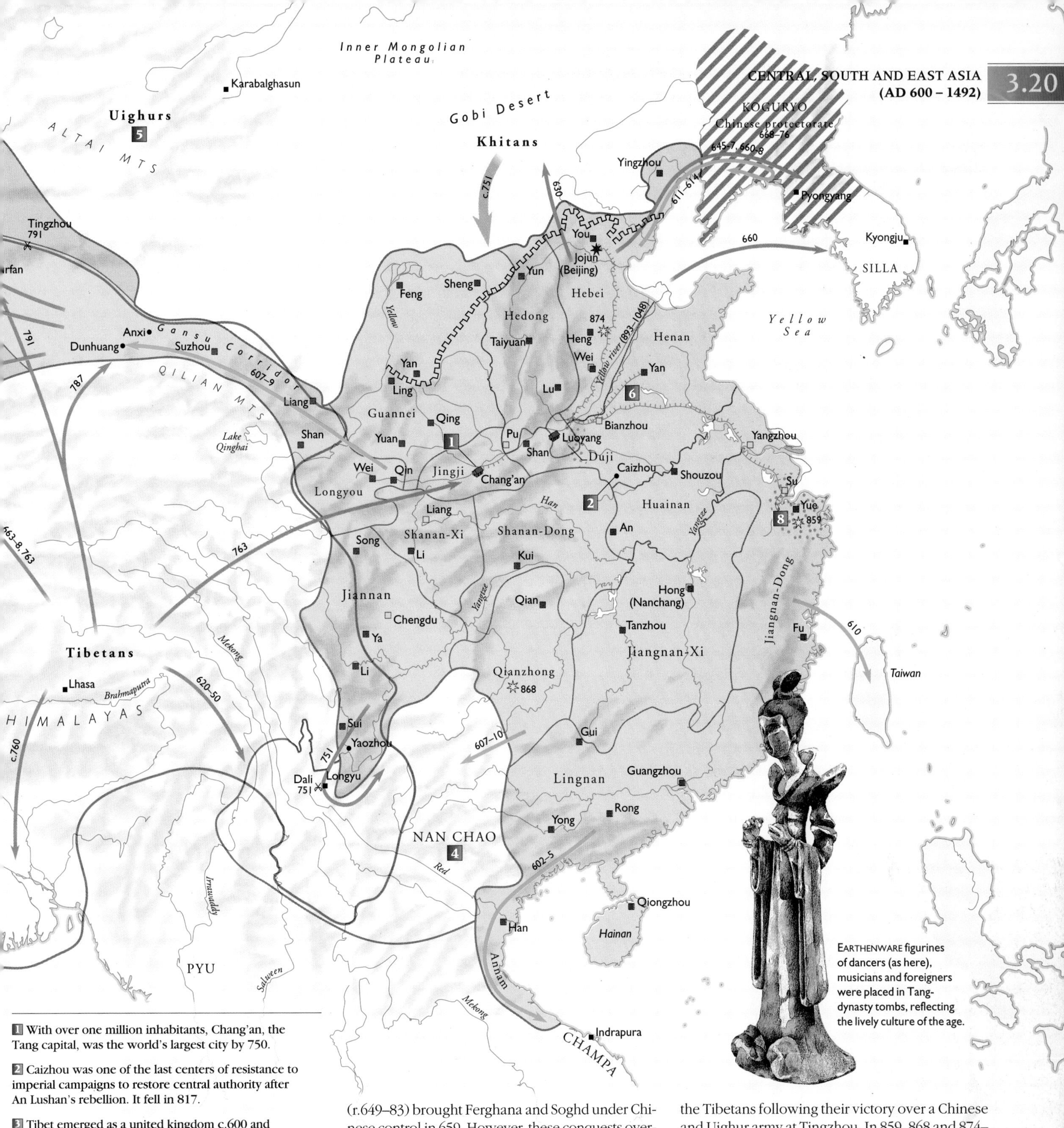

Inner Mongolian Plateau
Karabalghasun
Uighurs
5
ALTAI MTS
Gobi Desert
Khitans
c.751
630
KOGURYO
Chinese protectorate
668–76
645–7, 660–8
Yingzhou
611–614
Pyongyang
660
Kyongju
SILLA
Tingzhou
791
rfan
You
Jojun
(Beijing)
Yun
Hebei
Feng
Sheng
Yellow
Hedong
874
Taiyuan
Heng
Henan
Wei
Yellow river (893–1048)
Yan
Yellow Sea
791
Anxi
Gansu Corridor
Dunhuang
Suzhou
607–9
787
QILIAN MTS
Yan
Ling
Lu
6
Liang
Guannei
Qing
Bianzhou
Lake Qinghai
Shan
Yuan
1
Pu
Luoyang
Yangzhou
Shan
Duji
Wei
Qin
Jingji
Chang'an
Caizhou
Shouzou
Longyou
Su
Liang
Han
2
Huainan
Yue
8
859
An
Song
Shanan-Xi
Shanan-Dong
Yangtze
Li
663–8, 763
763
Kui
Jiangnan-Dong
Hong
(Nanchang)
Jiannan
Qian
Chengdu
Yangtze
Tanzhou
610
Ya
Fu
Mekong
Jiangnan-Xi
Tibetans
Li
Qianzhong
Taiwan
868
Lhasa
Brahmaputra
620–50
HIMALAYAS
Sui
Gui
Yaozhou
607–10
c.760
751
Dali
751
Longyu
Guangzhou
Lingnan
Rong
Yong
NAN CHAO
4
Red
602–5
Irrawaddy
Qiongzhou
Han
Hainan
PYU
Salween
Annam
Mekong
Indrapura
CHAMPA

EARTHENWARE figurines of dancers (as here), musicians and foreigners were placed in Tang-dynasty tombs, reflecting the lively culture of the age.

1 With over one million inhabitants, Chang'an, the Tang capital, was the world's largest city by 750.

2 Caizhou was one of the last centers of resistance to imperial campaigns to restore central authority after An Lushan's rebellion. It fell in 817.

3 Tibet emerged as a united kingdom c.600 and reached its greatest extent c.800.

4 Nan Chao, a Thai kingdom in modern Yunnan province, emerged c.600.

5 The Uighurs were a Turkic nomad tribe allied with the Chinese against the Turks and Tibetans.

6 The canal system linked the grain-producing Yangtze valley with the political center of the empire and the northern frontier zone.

7 The decisive battle at the River Talas, which led to the fall of China's central Asian empire, followed an appeal to the Arabs from the ruler of Tashkent for protection against the Chinese.

8 The first true porcelain was made in eastern China during the Tang period.

(r.649–83) brought Ferghana and Soghd under Chinese control in 659. However, these conquests overextended the empire and they were lost by 665. In the east, the Chinese subdued Koguryo in 668 but the Korean kingdom of Silla expelled them in 676.

The Chinese position in central Asia was dealt further blows in 751, with defeats by the Arabs at the River Talas and by the Thai kingdom of Nan Chao at Dali. The Mongol Khitan nomads emerged as a threat in the north in the 8th century. At home, landlord–peasant conflict increased, and the emperors from Gaozong onward proved ineffectual. A rebellion of the general An Lushan in 755 threatened the Tang; it was suppressed in 763 but central authority did not recover and power devolved to around forty semi-independent military governments-general. In 791 the empire lost control of the Gansu Corridor to the Tibetans following their victory over a Chinese and Uighur army at Tingzhou. In 859, 868 and 874–84 peasant rebellions broke out. The emperor's authority was damaged beyond repair and power was again seized by provincial warlords. The Tang struggled on until 907, finally collapsing in a period of disunity known as the Five Dynasties and Ten Kingdoms (907–960).

The Tang period is regarded as the golden age of Chinese poetry. The dynasty also presided over major achievements in historiography and painting, and restored Confucianism as the state ideology after it had declined during the Period of Disunion.

See also 2.24 (early imperial China); 3.05 (the world religions); 3.21 (the Song dynasty)

3.21 Song China • 907 – 1279 •

The disunity of the Five Dynasties and Ten Kingdoms period began to come to an end when Song Taizu (r.960–76) overthrew the last of the Five Dynasties, which had ruled the Yellow River valley since 907, in a military coup. Taizu skillfully consolidated his hold on power by bringing the military under effective civilian political control and in 963 he began a series of diplomatic and military campaigns to reunify China. This process was completed by his equally able brother Song Taizong (r.976–97), so creating the third Chinese empire. In accomplishing this, the Song benefited from the idea of China as an indivisible state, which had become established under the Tang. Only in Taiyuan, which had the support of the nomadic Khitans, and Houshu did the Song meet determined resistance, while Wuyue was secured through diplomacy alone. However, the Song were not able to restore the borders of the Tang empire and its authority was confined to areas of ethnic Chinese settlement. Unlike the Tang, the Song empire was surrounded by well-organized states that effectively blocked Chinese expansion.

The most powerful of these states was the Khitan Liao kingdom. The Khitans were a Turko-Mongol nomadic people, who had won control of the northern Chinese plains in 916 and went on to dominate the eastern steppes. Taizong attempted to drive the Khitans back to the steppes in 979 but was badly defeated near Beijing. A Khitan attack on the Song capital Kaifeng in 1004 was bought off for a heavy annual tribute of silver, silk and tea and thereafter relations between Song and Liao were peaceful. The Khitans adopted Chinese administrative practices to govern their kingdom and by the end of the 11th century they had become thoroughly assimilated. In 1114 the Jürchen people of Manchuria broke off payments of tribute to the Khitans and three years later launched an invasion of Liao, which collapsed in 1124. The Song initially supported the Jürchen attack on Liao but when the Jürchen created their own state under the Jin dynasty they found themselves faced with an even more formidable enemy.

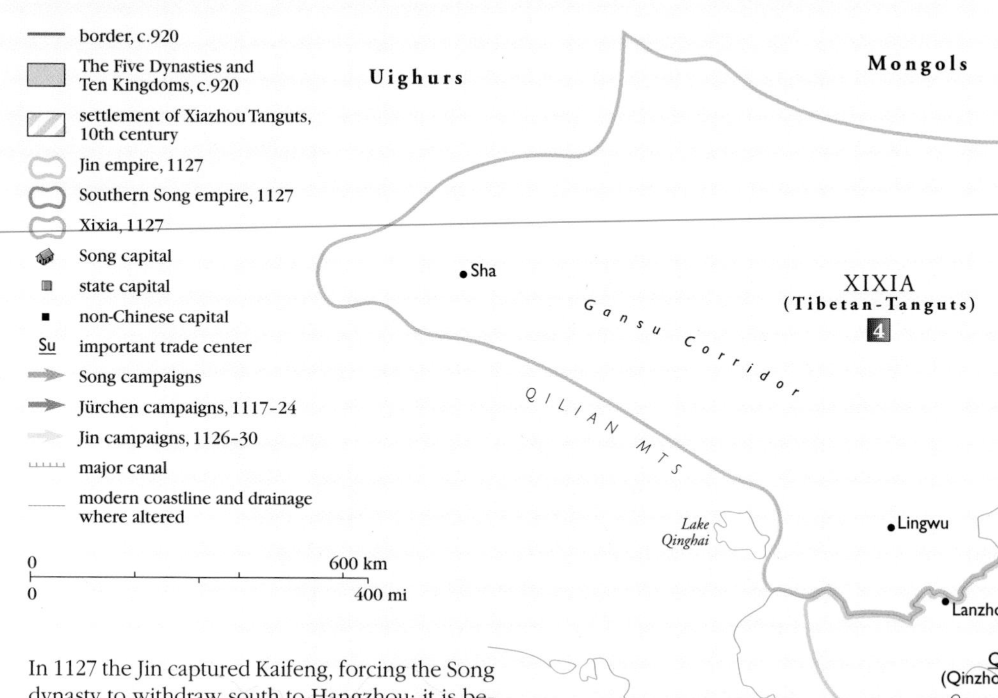
border, c.920
The Five Dynasties and Ten Kingdoms, c.920
settlement of Xiazhou Tanguts, 10th century
Jin empire, 1127
Southern Song empire, 1127
Xixia, 1127
Song capital
state capital
non-Chinese capital
Su important trade center
Song campaigns
Jürchen campaigns, 1117–24
Jin campaigns, 1126–30
major canal
modern coastline and drainage where altered
0
600 km
0
400 mi
Uighurs
Mongols
Sha
XIXIA
(Tibetan-Tanguts)
4
Gansu Corridor
QILIAN MTS
Lake Qinghai
Lingwu
Lanzhou
Qin
(Qinzhou)

In 1127 the Jin captured Kaifeng, forcing the Song dynasty to withdraw south to Hangzhou: it is because of this move that the Song is divided into Northern (pre-1127) and Southern (post-1127) periods. However, attempts by the Jin to consolidate their success with the conquest of China failed. Because of population shifts over the preceding centuries, the loss of the north did not cripple the Song. The south now had the majority of China's population and wealth so the Song remained strong enough to keep the Jin at bay. The Song made no attempt, though, to reconquer the north from the Jin.

Less powerful than Liao but a more serious obstacle to Chinese expansion was the kingdom of Xixia, which dominated the Gansu corridor, shutting the Song out of central Asia. Xixia was founded in the late 10th century by the Xiazhou clan of the nomadic Tangut people. With a mixed Tangut, Tibetan and Chinese population, it never became as sinicized as Liao. In the south the Thai kingdom of Nan Chao and the Viet kingdom of Annam blocked expansion.

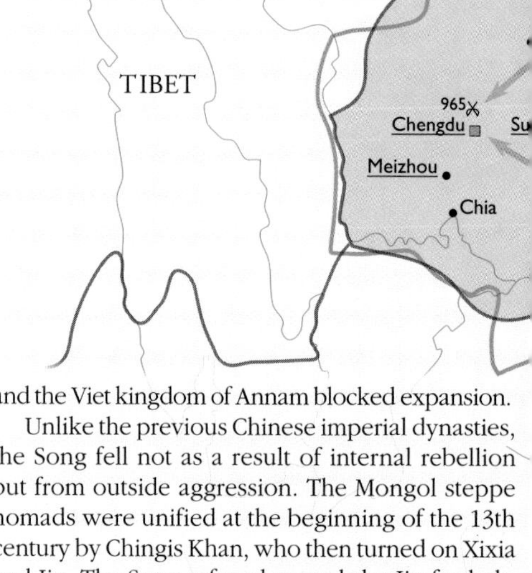
TIBET
965
Chengdu
Meizhou
Chia

Unlike the previous Chinese imperial dynasties, the Song fell not as a result of internal rebellion but from outside aggression. The Mongol steppe nomads were unified at the beginning of the 13th century by Chingis Khan, who then turned on Xixia and Jin. The Song refused appeals by Jin for help and, repeating their earlier disastrous policy towards the Jürchen, even supplied the Mongols with much-needed troops who were skilled in siege warfare. When the Song tried to profit from the fall of Jin in 1234 by seizing Kaifeng and Luoyang, they simply caused the Mongols to turn on them. Song resistance to the Mongols was determined but swiftly collapsed after the capture of Hangzhou in 1276. The last Song emperor was drowned three years later following a naval battle off the island of Yaishan.

Although theirs was the smallest of the Chinese empires, the Song are regarded as one of the most capable and humane dynasties in Chinese history. The Song period was one of remarkable economic prosperity, technological innovation and rapid population growth, especially in the south, which experienced an influx of refugees from the Jin in the 12th century. Agricultural productivity was greatly increased by the introduction of Vietnamese strains

TIMELINE

1000 · 1100 · 1200

Northern Song period | Southern Song period

Political change

960 Song Taizu is declared emperor in the Five Dynasties state

963 Song Taizu begins the reunification of China

979 Song Taizong completes the reunification of China

1068–86 Minister Wang Anshi introduces unsuccessful land reform program

1117–24 Jürchen destroy Liao state and establish Jin empire

1127 Jin take Kaifeng. Song capital is moved to Hangzhou

1226 Xixia is destroyed by the Mongols

1234 Jin empire conquered by the Mongols. First Mongol attack on Southern Song

1279 Mongols conquer Southern Song empire

Cultural change

969 Gunpowder rockets are first used in warfare

c.1000 Rise of Song school of landscape painting

c.1000 Movable type printing is invented

c.1086 Scientist Shen Gua writes the *Dreampool Jottings*

1090 Water-driven mechanical clock built for Song court

1130–1200 Zhu Xi, neo-Confucian philosopher

1130 Paddle-wheel-driven ships are in use

1150 Chinese navigators use the magnetic compass

1259 Song forces use bamboo-tube firearms

c.1200 Chinese ships built with watertight bulkheads

c.1200 Waterpowered textile machinery is in use

1000 · 1100 · 1200

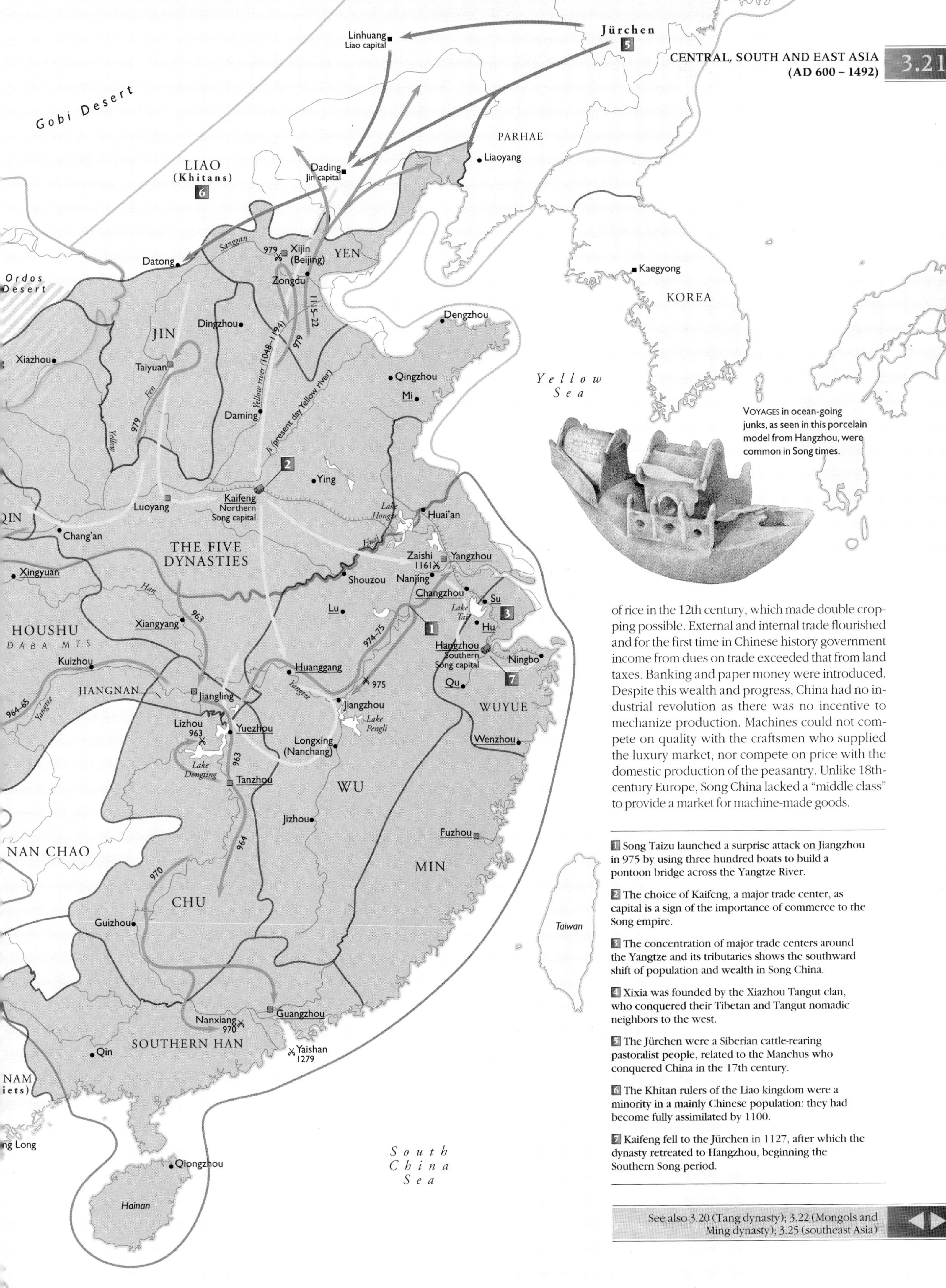
Jürchen
5
Linhuang
Liao capital
Gobi Desert
PARHAE
Liaoyang
LIAO
(Khitans)
6
Dading
Jin capital
Sanggan
979
Xijin
(Beijing)
YEN
Datong
Ordos
Desert
Zongdu
1115–22
979
Yellow river (1048–1194)
Dingzhou
JIN
Taiyuan
Xiazhou
Fen
979
Yellow
Daming
Ji (present day Yellow river)
Kaegyong
KOREA
Dengzhou
Qingzhou
Mi
Yellow
Sea
2
Ying
Kaifeng
Northern
Song capital
Luoyang
QIN
Chang'an
THE FIVE
DYNASTIES
Lake
Hongze
Huai'an
Huai
Zaishi
1161
Yangzhou
Xingyuan
Shouzou
Nanjing
Changzhou
Han
Su
Lake
Tai
3
Hu
Lu
HOUSHU
DABA MTS
963
Xiangyang
974–75
1
Hangzhou
Southern
Song capital
Ningbo
7
Kuizhou
Huanggang
975
Qu
JIANGNAN
Jiangling
Yangtze
Jiangzhou
Lake
Pengli
WUYUE
964–65
Yangtze
Lizhou
963
Yuezhou
Longxing
(Nanchang)
Wenzhou
Lake
Dongting
963
Tanzhou
WU
Jizhou
Fuzhou
NAN CHAO
964
970
MIN
CHU
Taiwan
Guizhou
Guangzhou
Nanxiang
970
SOUTHERN HAN
Yaishan
1279
Qin
NAM
iets)
ng Long
Qiongzhou
South
China
Sea
Hainan

VOYAGES in ocean-going junks, as seen in this porcelain model from Hangzhou, were common in Song times.

of rice in the 12th century, which made double cropping possible. External and internal trade flourished and for the first time in Chinese history government income from dues on trade exceeded that from land taxes. Banking and paper money were introduced. Despite this wealth and progress, China had no industrial revolution as there was no incentive to mechanize production. Machines could not compete on quality with the craftsmen who supplied the luxury market, nor compete on price with the domestic production of the peasantry. Unlike 18th-century Europe, Song China lacked a "middle class" to provide a market for machine-made goods.

1 Song Taizu launched a surprise attack on Jiangzhou in 975 by using three hundred boats to build a pontoon bridge across the Yangtze River.

2 The choice of Kaifeng, a major trade center, as capital is a sign of the importance of commerce to the Song empire.

3 The concentration of major trade centers around the Yangtze and its tributaries shows the southward shift of population and wealth in Song China.

4 Xixia was founded by the Xiazhou Tangut clan, who conquered their Tibetan and Tangut nomadic neighbors to the west.

5 The Jürchen were a Siberian cattle-rearing pastoralist people, related to the Manchus who conquered China in the 17th century.

6 The Khitan rulers of the Liao kingdom were a minority in a mainly Chinese population: they had become fully assimilated by 1100.

7 Kaifeng fell to the Jürchen in 1127, after which the dynasty retreated to Hangzhou, beginning the Southern Song period.

See also 3.20 (Tang dynasty); 3.22 (Mongols and Ming dynasty); 3.25 (southeast Asia)

3.22 The creation of the Mongol empire • 1204 – 1260 •

The dramatic expansion of the Mongols that began under Temujin was the most important event in world history in the 13th century. The son of a minor Mongol chief, Temujin's brilliant leadership in inter-tribal warfare enabled him to unify the Mongol peoples in a ruthless two-year campaign.

To mark his success he was proclaimed Chingis ("universal") Khan in 1206. During his unification campaign, he created what has often been called the finest cavalry army that the world has ever seen. If the army was not to break up, and his khandom with it, he had to find work for it to do and wealth with which to reward it. He therefore adopted a policy of all-round aggression and by his death in 1227 he had conquered an empire that included most of central Asia and northern China.

His successors, his son Ogedai and grandsons Küyük and Möngke, continued his expansionist policy and by 1259 they had carried the Mongol conquests into Europe and the Middle East. In China only the southern Song empire stood out against the Mongols, though it too would fall within 20 years. However, Mongol unity was fragile and already the achievement of Chingis Khan had started to unravel.

The Mongol conquests formed the largest land empire in history. The achievement is all the more remarkable in that the Mongols had few governmental institutions and did not even possess basic metalworking skills. They were fortunate in being able to exploit existing disunity among their enemies: China was divided into three hostile kingdoms; the powerful Turkish empires of Kara-Khitai and Khwarizm were mutually hostile and had dynastic problems; and Russia, like most of Europe, was a mosaic of quarrelsome states which cooperated only reluctantly and ineffectually against the common enemy.

The key factor in the Mongol success, however, was the magnificent army that Chingis created. Unlike the armies of their opponents, where birth usually determined rank, promotion in the Mongol army was by merit only. The discipline and mobility of the Mongol army enabled it to execute complex battlefield maneuvers, giving it decisive advantages over any opponent. A frequent tactic was the feigned retreat, used to lure rash pursuers into ambushes on unfavorable ground where they could be destroyed. The Mongols had an excellent long-range weapon in the composite bow, which enabled them to inflict casualties while keeping out of danger themselves. The Mongols also committed horrific atrocities, systematically creating terror to sap their enemies' will to resist. This persuaded many Turks, Uighurs, Kipchaks and Chinese to defect to the Mongols rather than risk defeat.

The Mongol military machine had its limitations. Except in China, the boundaries of the Mongol empire were very close to those of the Eurasian

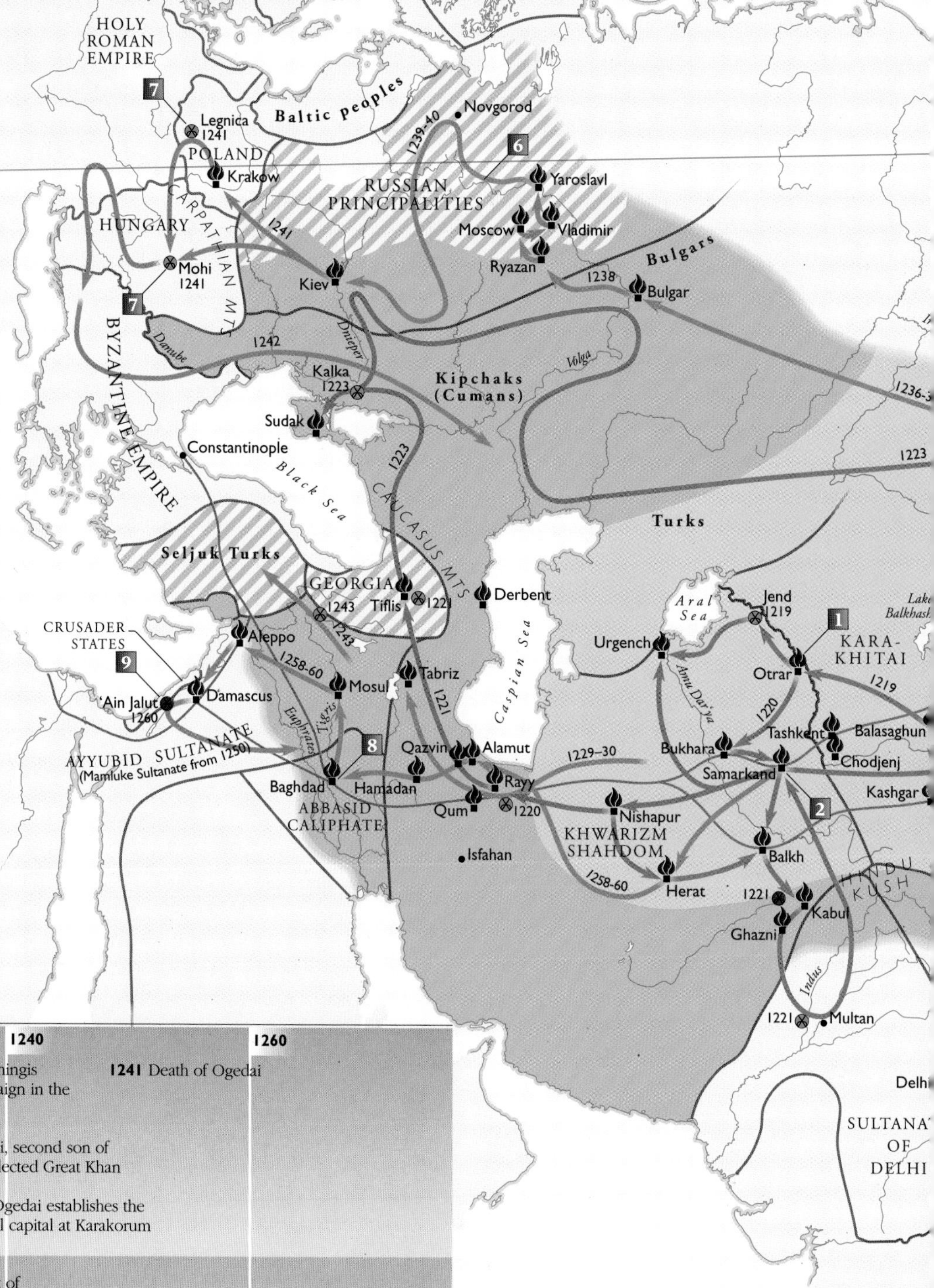

HOLY ROMAN EMPIRE
Baltic peoples
Novgorod
Legnica 1241
POLAND
Krakow
RUSSIAN PRINCIPALITIES
Yaroslavl
Moscow
Vladimir
Ryazan
Bulgars
Bulgar
HUNGARY
CARPATHIAN MTS
Mohi 1241
Kiev
1241
1239–40
1238
1242
Danube
Dnieper
Volga
BYZANTINE EMPIRE
Kalka 1223
Kipchaks (Cumans)
Sudak
Constantinople
Black Sea
CAUCASUS MTS
1223
1236–
Turks
Seljuk Turks
GEORGIA
Tiflis
1221
1243
Derbent
Aral Sea
Jend 1219
KARA-KHITAI
Otrar
1219
CRUSADER STATES
Aleppo
1258–60
Mosul
Tabriz
Urgench
Amu Darya
Caspian Sea
'Ain Jalut 1260
Damascus
Euphrates
Tigris
AYYUBID SULTANATE
(Mamluke Sultanate from 1250)
Qazvin
Alamut
1229–30
Bukhara
Tashkent
Balasaghun
Chodjenj
Samarkand
Kashgar
1220
Baghdad
Hamadan
ABBASID CALIPHATE
Rayy
Qum
1220
Nishapur
KHWARIZM SHAHDOM
Balkh
Isfahan
1258–60
Herat
1221
Kabul
HINDU KUSH
Ghazni
Indus
1221
Multan
Delhi
SULTANATE OF DELHI

TIMELINE

	1220	1240	1260
The Mongol world	**c1167** Birth of Temujin (Chingis Khan) **1204–06** Temujin unites the Mongol tribes and is proclaimed Chingis Khan	**1227** Death of Chingis Khan on a campaign in the Jin empire **1229** Ogedai, second son of Chingis, is elected Great Khan **1235** Ogedai establishes the Mongol capital at Karakorum	**1241** Death of Ogedai
Eastern conquests	**1209** The Mongols attack Xixia and Uighurs **1211** The first Mongol attacks on China (Jin empire) **1215** The Mongols capture Dadu (Beijing) **1218** Kara-Khitai empire is conquered by the Mongols	**1226** The conquest of Xixia is complete **1234** The Jin capital Kaifeng falls to the Mongols	**1252** The conquest of the Song empire (southern China) begins
The West	**1219–21** Chingis Khan invades Khwarizm shahdom **1220–23** Chingis Khan sends a force to Russia	**1237–41** The Mongols invade Russia and eastern Europe	**1258** Baghdad falls to the Mongols, and the last Abbasid caliph is executed **1260** The Mongols are defeated by the Mamlukes at 'Ain Jalut

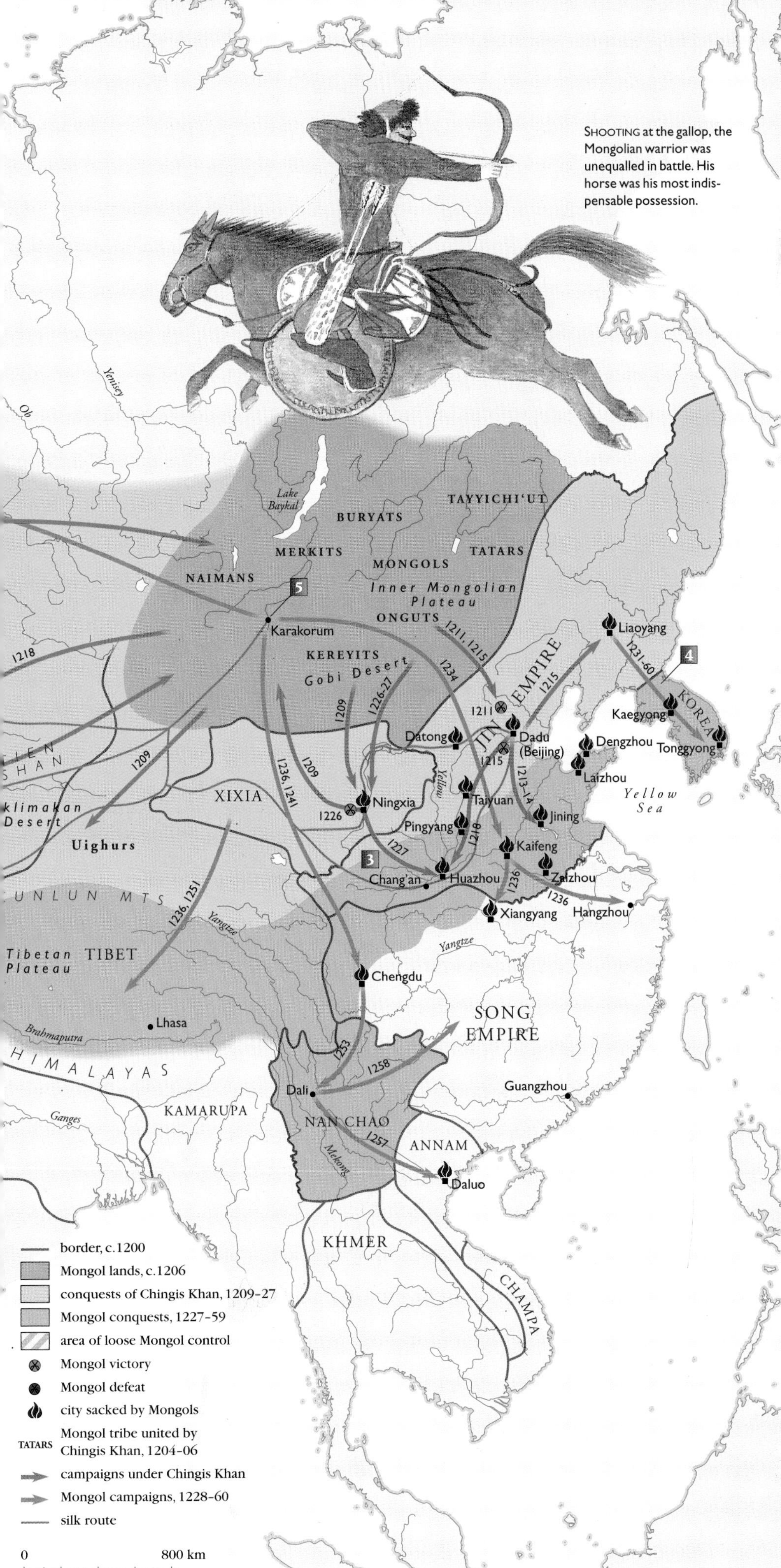
Yenisey
Ob
Lake Baykal
BURYATS
TAYYICHI'UT
MERKITS
TATARS
MONGOLS
NAIMANS
Inner Mongolian Plateau
ONGUTS
Karakorum
KEREYITS
Gobi Desert
1218
1209
1226-27
1234
1211, 1215
1215
1211
JIN EMPIRE
Liaoyang
1231-60
Kaegyong
KOREA
Tonggyong
Datong
Dadu (Beijing)
Dengzhou
1215
1213-14
Laizhou
Yellow Sea
TIEN SHAN
XIXIA
1236, 1241
Ningxia
1226
Yellow
Taiyuan
Jining
Taklimakan Desert
Uighurs
Pingyang
1218
1227
Kaifeng
Chang'an
Huazhou
Zhizhou
1236
1236
Xiangyang
Hangzhou
KUNLUN MTS
1236, 1251
Yangtze
Tibetan Plateau
TIBET
Chengdu
Lhasa
SONG EMPIRE
Brahmaputra
HIMALAYAS
1253
1258
Dali
Guangzhou
Ganges
KAMARUPA
NAN CHAO
1257
Mekong
ANNAM
Daluo
KHMER
CHAMPA
border, c.1200
Mongol lands, c.1206
conquests of Chingis Khan, 1209–27
Mongol conquests, 1227–59
area of loose Mongol control
Mongol victory
Mongol defeat
city sacked by Mongols
TATARS Mongol tribe united by Chingis Khan, 1204–06
campaigns under Chingis Khan
Mongol campaigns, 1228–60
silk route
0 800 km
0 500 mi

SHOOTING at the gallop, the Mongolian warrior was unequalled in battle. His horse was his most indispensable possession.

steppes and grasslands which alone could provide the necessary grazing for the vast herds of horses that accompanied every Mongol army. The defeat suffered by the Mongols at the hands of the Mamlukes at 'Ain Jalut in 1260 was to some extent the result of poor grazing in the Syrian desert. This, rather than the strength of local resistance, was probably also the reason why the Mongols never returned to Europe after their invasion of 1241–42. The army also needed plenty of room for maneuver, so it was less effective in forested, mountainous or intensively farmed areas than in open country. This helps to explain, for example, the relative slowness of the conquest of China.

The period of the Mongols' expansion had few beneficial results: they destroyed far more than they built. The most sophisticated civilizations of the time – the Muslim and the Chinese – suffered the worst. The Abbasid caliphate of Baghdad, spiritual, cultural and (for much of the time) political leader of the Muslim world since the 8th century, was overthrown. The ancient cities of central Asia were devastated and never recovered their former prosperity. Depopulation and the neglect of irrigation channels meant that most of Iraq and west Persia was reduced to desert for centuries. Northern China suffered depopulation and the Mongol conquest isolated Russia from the mainstream of European development for almost two centuries. The impact of the Mongols on the rest of Christendom was fleeting, and by disrupting the Muslim world they granted a brief stay of execution to the Crusader states and allowed a shortlived revival of the crumbling Byzantine empire. Eventually, Christendom benefited from the Mongol conquests in Asia, as Muslim control of the silk route ended and the way was opened for westerners such as Marco Polo to travel to east Asia for the first time.

1 The governor of Otrar provoked Chingis Khan's invasion of the Khwarizm shahdom by executing merchants and envoys from the Mongols in 1218.

2 Chingis Khan divided his army at Samarkand, despatching a smaller force to pursue the Khwarizm Shah and then cross the Caucasus to gather intelligence in Europe.

3 Chingis Khan died here in 1227 on campaign against the Jin empire.

4 Fighting in unfavorable mountainous terrain, it took the Mongols 30 years to force the Koreans to submit. Thereafter the Koreans became close allies.

5 Karakorum, favorite campsite of Chingis, became the capital of the Mongol empire in 1235.

6 Using frozen rivers as highways, the Mongols launched the only successful winter invasion in Russian history in 1238–39. The Russians paid tribute to the Mongols for two centuries.

7 The combined armies of eastern Europe were routed at Legnica and Mohi in 1241. The Mongols withdrew on news of Ogedai Khan's death.

8 The fall of Baghdad was followed by the massacre of 200,000 captives (20 percent of the population).

9 The first major defeat of the Mongols was at the hands of the Mamlukes at 'Ain Jalut in 1260.

See also 2.20 (steppe peoples); 3.08 (Europe); 3.16 (Muslim world); 3.23 (later Mongols)

The break-up of the Mongol empire • 1260 – 1502 •

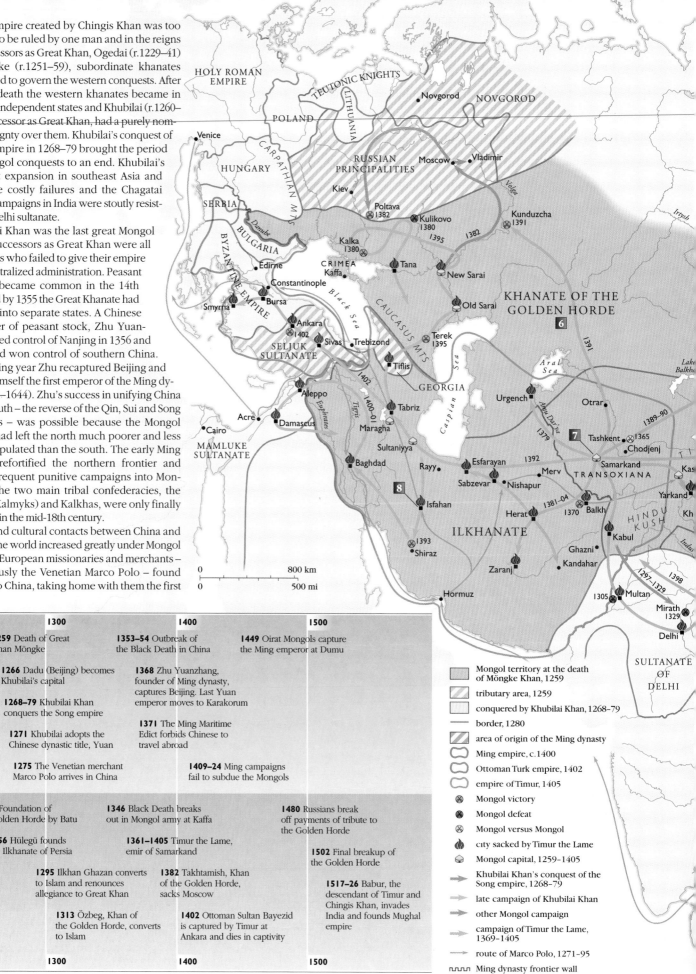

The empire created by Chingis Khan was too vast to be ruled by one man and in the reigns of his successors as Great Khan, Ogedai (r.1229–41) and Möngke (r.1251–59), subordinate khanates were created to govern the western conquests. After Möngke's death the western khanates became in effect fully independent states and Khubilai (r.1260–94), his successor as Great Khan, had a purely nominal sovereignty over them. Khubilai's conquest of the Song empire in 1268–79 brought the period of the Mongol conquests to an end. Khubilai's attempts at expansion in southeast Asia and Japan were costly failures and the Chagatai khanate's campaigns in India were stoutly resisted by the Delhi sultanate.

Khubilai Khan was the last great Mongol ruler: his successors as Great Khan were all mediocrities who failed to give their empire a stable centralized administration. Peasant rebellions became common in the 14th century and by 1355 the Great Khanate had broken up into separate states. A Chinese rebel leader of peasant stock, Zhu Yuanzhang, seized control of Nanjing in 1356 and by 1367 had won control of southern China. The following year Zhu recaptured Beijing and declared himself the first emperor of the Ming dynasty (1368–1644). Zhu's success in unifying China from the south – the reverse of the Qin, Sui and Song unifications – was possible because the Mongol invasions had left the north much poorer and less densely populated than the south. The early Ming emperors refortified the northern frontier and launched frequent punitive campaigns into Mongolia but the two main tribal confederacies, the Oirats (or Kalmyks) and Kalkhas, were only finally subjugated in the mid-18th century.

Trade and cultural contacts between China and the rest of the world increased greatly under Mongol rule. Many European missionaries and merchants – most famously the Venetian Marco Polo – found their way to China, taking home with them the first

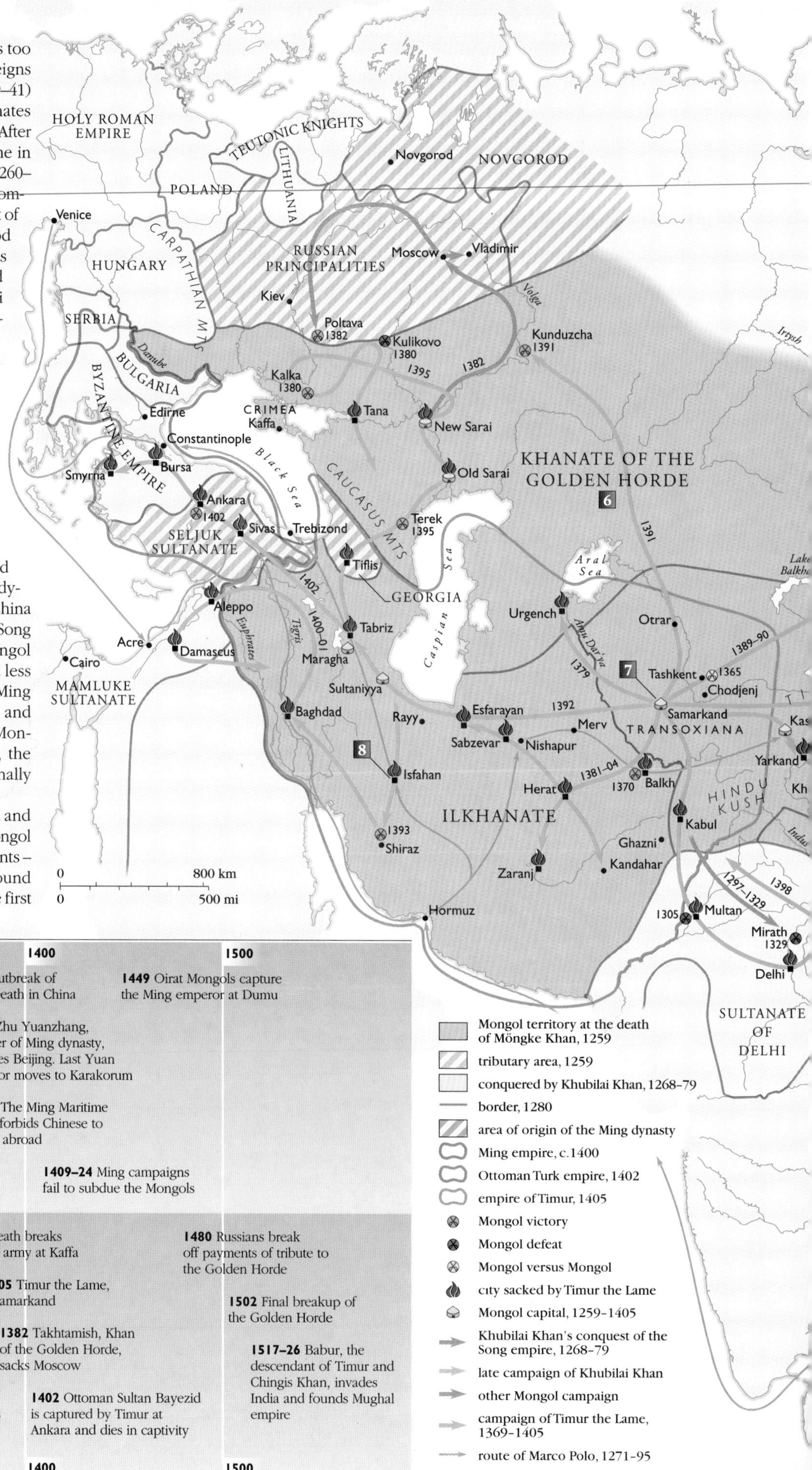
HOLY ROMAN EMPIRE
TEUTONIC KNIGHTS
LITHUANIA
Novgorod
NOVGOROD
POLAND
Venice
CARPATHIAN MTS
HUNGARY
RUSSIAN PRINCIPALITIES
Moscow
Vladimir
Volga
Kiev
SERBIA
Danube
BULGARIA
Poltava 1382
Kulikovo 1380
1395
1382
Kunduzcha 1391
Irtysh
Kalka 1380
BYZANTINE EMPIRE
Edirne
CRIMEA
Kaffa
Tana
New Sarai
Constantinople
Black Sea
Bursa
Smyrna
CAUCASUS MTS
Old Sarai
KHANATE OF THE GOLDEN HORDE
6
Ankara 1402
SELJUK SULTANATE
Sivas
Trebizond
Terek 1395
1391
Tiflis
Aral Sea
Lake Balkhash
GEORGIA
Caspian Sea
1402
Aleppo
Euphrates
Tigris
1400–01
Tabriz
Urgench
Otrar
Amu Dar'ya
1389–90
Acre
Damascus
Maragha
Cairo
1379
7
Tashkent 1365
Chodjenj
MAMLUKE SULTANATE
Sultaniyya
Samarkand
1392
Baghdad
Rayy
Esfarayan
Merv
TRANSOXIANA
Kas
Sabzevar
Nishapur
8
Yarkand
Isfahan
1381–04
Balkh
1370
Herat
HINDU KUSH
Kh
ILKHANATE
Kabul
1393
Shiraz
Indus
Ghazni
0 800 km
0 500 mi
Zaranj
Kandahar
1398
1297–1329
Hormuz
1305
Multan
Mirath 1329
Delhi
SULTANATE OF DELHI
Mongol territory at the death of Möngke Khan, 1259
tributary area, 1259
conquered by Khubilai Khan, 1268–79
border, 1280
area of origin of the Ming dynasty
Ming empire, c.1400
Ottoman Turk empire, 1402
empire of Timur, 1405
Mongol victory
Mongol defeat
Mongol versus Mongol
city sacked by Timur the Lame
Mongol capital, 1259–1405
Khubilai Khan's conquest of the Song empire, 1268–79
late campaign of Khubilai Khan
other Mongol campaign
campaign of Timur the Lame, 1369–1405
route of Marco Polo, 1271–95
Ming dynasty frontier wall

TIMELINE

East Asia

1259 Death of Great Khan Möngke

1266 Dadu (Beijing) becomes Khubilai's capital

1268–79 Khubilai Khan conquers the Song empire

1271 Khubilai adopts the Chinese dynastic title, Yuan

1275 The Venetian merchant Marco Polo arrives in China

1353–54 Outbreak of the Black Death in China

1368 Zhu Yuanzhang, founder of Ming dynasty, captures Beijing. Last Yuan emperor moves to Karakorum

1371 The Ming Maritime Edict forbids Chinese to travel abroad

1409–24 Ming campaigns fail to subdue the Mongols

1449 Oirat Mongols capture the Ming emperor at Dumu

Europe and west Asia

1241 Foundation of the Golden Horde by Batu

1256 Hülegü founds the Ilkhanate of Persia

1295 Ilkhan Ghazan converts to Islam and renounces allegiance to Great Khan

1313 Özbeg, Khan of the Golden Horde, converts to Islam

1346 Black Death breaks out in Mongol army at Kaffa

1361–1405 Timur the Lame, emir of Samarkand

1382 Takhtamish, Khan of the Golden Horde, sacks Moscow

1402 Ottoman Sultan Bayezid is captured by Timur at Ankara and dies in captivity

1480 Russians break off payments of tribute to the Golden Horde

1502 Final breakup of the Golden Horde

1517–26 Babur, the descendant of Timur and Chingis Khan, invades India and founds Mughal empire

1300 1400 1500

detailed accounts of Chinese civilization. Although the Christian and Islamic worlds benefited from these cultural contacts, China itself did not. Most trade was controlled by foreigners and currency drained out of China. The painful experience of Mongol rule seemed to the Chinese to vindicate their ancient xenophobia and sense of cultural superiority. Thus, when Mongol rule ended, they unwisely renounced all foreign influences just as China was losing its economic and technological lead.

The Ilkhanate of Persia, founded in 1256, was the shortest-lived of the Mongol khanates, lasting only until 1335 despite a series of able rulers. By 1300 most Mongols had converted to Islam, while their lavish patronage of scholarship and the arts had helped repair the damage inflicted by their conquests. On the death of the last khan, the Ilkhanate split into several Mongol, Turkish and Persian states.

The steppe khanates of the Golden Horde and the Chagatai, where the Mongols could pursue their traditional way of life, survived the longest. The population of the Golden Horde was mainly Turkish: their adoption of Turkish as the official language in about 1280 and of Islam in the early 14th century alienated them from their Christian Russian tributaries. The Chagatai khanate was divided into an eastern area, characterized by paganism and nomadism, and a western, dominated by the great Muslim cities of the Silk Route. Antagonism between them was exploited by the last Mongol conqueror, Timur the Lame (r.1361–1405). Though a nomad who claimed descent from Chingis Khan, Timur was a Muslim and culturally and linguistically Turkish. Timur was appointed emir of Samarkand in 1361, and established a power base in Transoxiana by organizing defenses against nomad raiders from Mughulistan. In 1370 he captured Balkh, murdered its ruler and massacred its populace. Timur spent the rest of his life in almost constant campaigning, yet the empire he built died with him. His campaigns were marked by appalling savagery and widespread plundering, and he made no attempt to impose institutional unity on the lands he gained. Samarkand thrived on war booty, but Timur's legacy was otherwise entirely negative. A militant Muslim, he left the Islamic world in ruins; moreover, though claiming to restore Chingis Khan's empire, he weakened the Golden Horde and the Chagatai khanate. These states did, however, survive Timur's attacks. The Chagatai khanate was reduced to the lands around Kashgar; it was ultimately annexed by the Manchus in the late 17th century. The Golden Horde split up in 1438, finally disappearing from history in 1502. The khanate of the Crimean Tatars, virtually the last vestige of the Mongol empire, was annexed by Russia in 1783.

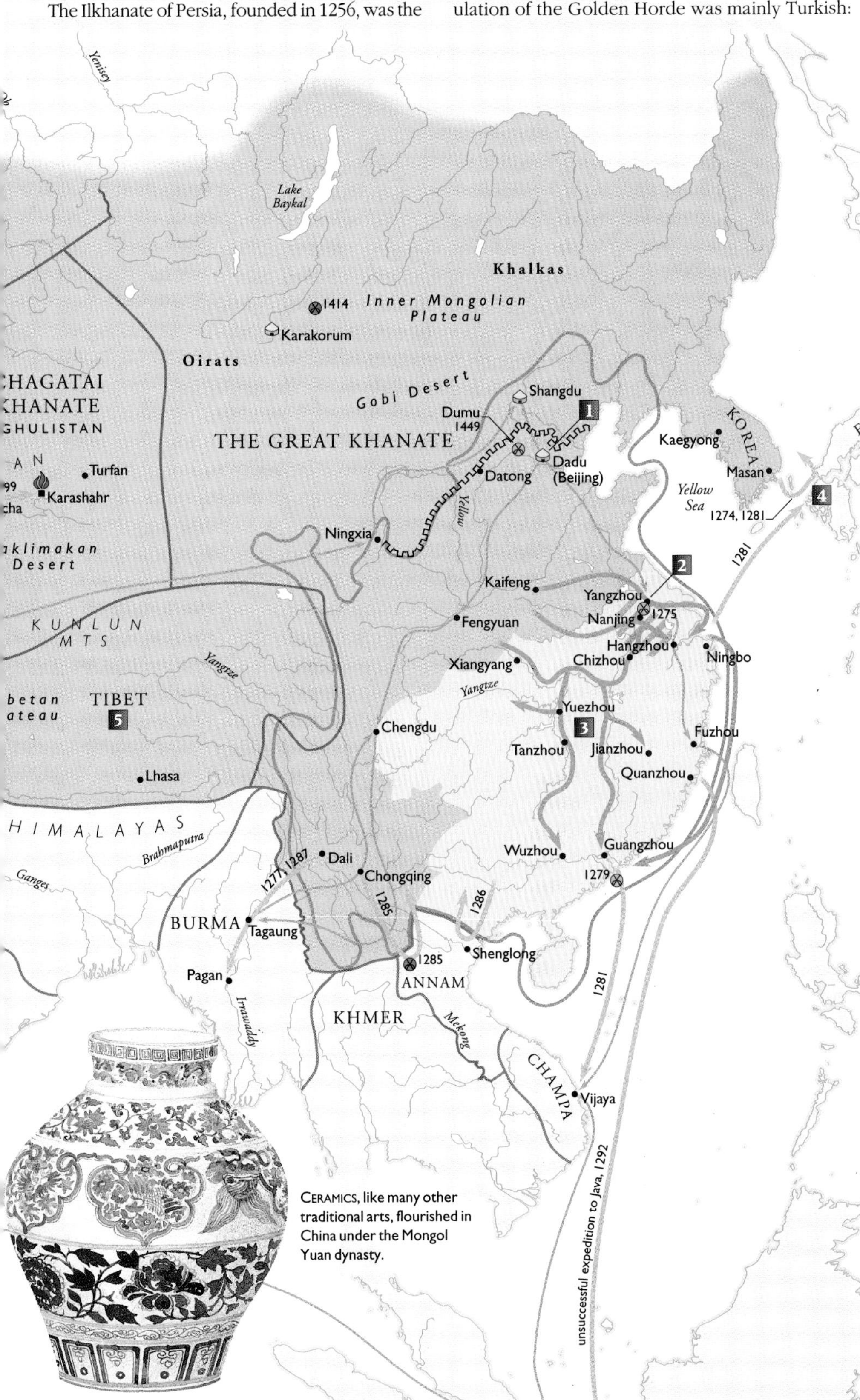
Yenisey
Lake Baykal
Khalkas
1414
Inner Mongolian Plateau
Karakorum
Oirats
CHAGATAI
KHANATE
GHULISTAN
Gobi Desert
Shangdu
Dumu 1449
1
THE GREAT KHANATE
Dadu (Beijing)
Datong
Turfan
Karashahr
Kaegyong
KOREA
Masan
EMPIRE OF JAPAN
Yellow Sea
1274, 1281
4
Ningxia
Yellow
1281
2
Kaifeng
Yangzhou
1275
Nanjing
Fengyuan
KUNLUN MTS
Hangzhou
Ningbo
Chizhou
Xiangyang
Yangtze
TIBET
5
Yuezhou
3
Chengdu
Fuzhou
Tanzhou
Jianzhou
Quanzhou
Lhasa
HIMALAYAS
Brahmaputra
Wuzhou
Guangzhou
1277, 1287
Dali
Chongqing
1279
Ganges
1285
1286
BURMA
Tagaung
1285
Shenglong
Pagan
ANNAM
1281
Irrawaddy
KHMER
Mekong
CHAMPA
Vijaya
unsuccessful expedition to Java, 1292

CERAMICS, like many other traditional arts, flourished in China under the Mongol Yuan dynasty.

1 Dadu (Beijing) became the capital of the Great Khanate in 1266: Shangdu in the cooler north was the summer capital.

2 Marco Polo claimed to have been appointed governor of Yangzhou for three years by Khubilai, though he was probably only a minor trade official.

3 Khubilai Khan wanted to capture the Song empire intact, and so avoided the pillaging and massacres that had characterized earlier Mongol campaigns.

4 The myth of Mongol invincibility was shattered by the failure of Khubilai Khan's attempted invasions of Japan in 1274 and 1281. The invasion fleets were scattered by a typhoon, from which the Japanese term *kamikaze* ("divine wind") is derived.

5 After Khubilai Khan's death in 1294, Tibet regained its independence: the Mongols retained nominal superiority until 1368.

6 The Golden Horde is thought to be named for the color of the first Khan's tent.

7 Enslaved craftsmen from throughout the Middle East labored to build some of the Islamic world's finest surviving mosques, mausoleums and public buildings at Timur's capital Samarkand.

8 Isfahan was the scene of one of Timur the Lame's worst atrocities: 70,000 people were slaughtered so that he could build towers with their skulls.

See also 3.22 (rise of the Mongols); 3.24 (medieval Japan); 4.17 (central Asia and the Safavids)

3.24 Medieval Japan and Korea • 600 – 1500 •

The early states of Japan and Korea were strongly influenced by Chinese civilization. By 600 Chinese administrative practices and political ideologies were being introduced by Japanese and Korean rulers as they attempted to build centralized states. These endeavors had been largely successful in Korea by the 15th century but in Japan initial success was followed by progressive decentralization of authority and, in the 15th century, the growth of feudalism. The elite culture of Korea was heavily influenced by that of China in this period; there were similar forces in Japan but also a much greater retention of distinctively Japanese ideas and practices.

In Japan, the attempt to build a centralized state on Chinese lines began late in the Yamato period (AD 300–710). Prince Shotoku (r.593–622) introduced a constitution in 604 asserting the power of the emperor over the nobility. The Taika reforms that followed in 646 brought all land into imperial ownership and instituted a tax system. In 702 the Taiho laws – new civil and penal codes – were introduced. Buddhism was promoted as a way of increasing imperial authority. Finally in 710 a permanent administrative capital, modeled on Chang'an, was established at Nara. Yet the achievement of the Yamato period reformers was superficial and the centralized state was never able to consolidate its authority.

Nara became an important religious center and the Buddhist clergy soon began to exert strong political influence over the emperors. To escape this interference, emperor Kammu moved the court to a new capital at Heian (modern Kyoto) in 794. Here the emperors came under the sway of the aristocratic Fujiwara family, who skillfully strengthened their political influence by marrying into the imperial family. Buddhist monasteries and great families such as the Fujiwara were able to amass extensive landholdings at imperial expense by obtaining *shoen* (private tax-free estates) as rewards for good service.

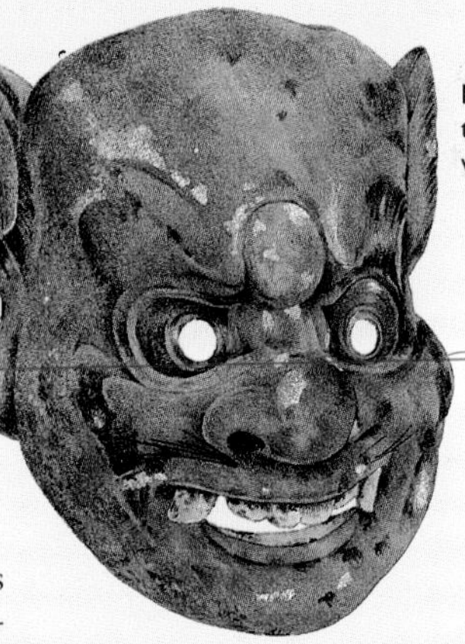

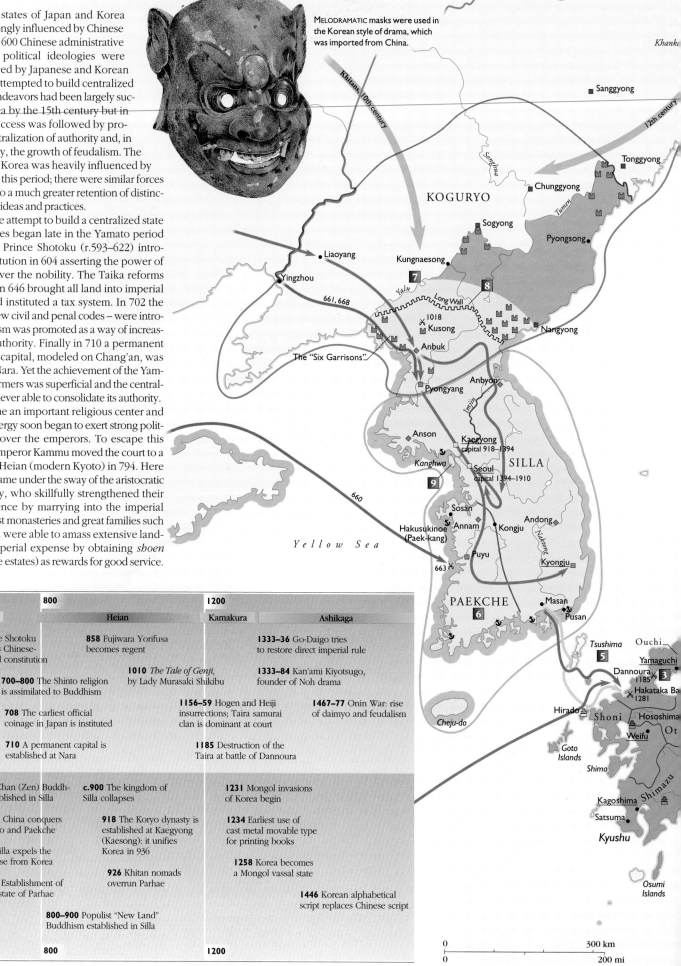

MELODRAMATIC masks were used in the Korean style of drama, which was imported from China.

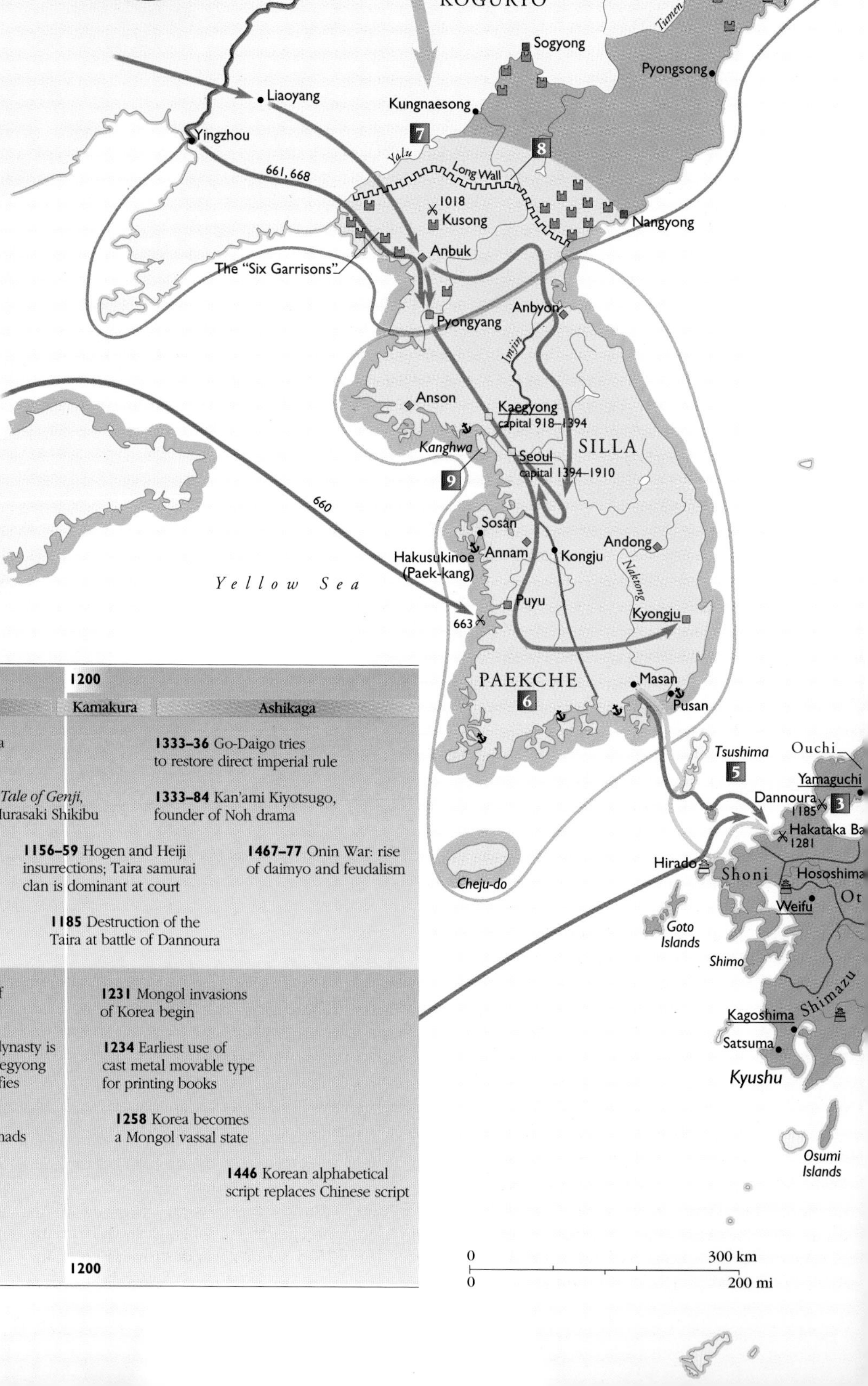

TIMELINE

Periods (Japan): Yamato; Heian (from 800); Kamakura (from 1200); Ashikaga

Japan

- **604** Prince Shotoku introduces Chinese-influenced constitution
- **700–800** The Shinto religion is assimilated to Buddhism
- **708** The earliest official coinage in Japan is instituted
- **710** A permanent capital is established at Nara
- **858** Fujiwara Yorifusa becomes regent
- **1010** *The Tale of Genji*, by Lady Murasaki Shikibu
- **1156–59** Hogen and Heiji insurrections; Taira samurai clan is dominant at court
- **1185** Destruction of the Taira at battle of Dannoura
- **1333–36** Go-Daigo tries to restore direct imperial rule
- **1333–84** Kan'ami Kiyotsugu, founder of Noh drama
- **1467–77** Onin War: rise of daimyo and feudalism

Korea

- **600–700** Chan (Zen) Buddhism is established in Silla
- **660–68** China conquers Koguryo and Paekche
- **676** Silla expels the Chinese from Korea
- **694** Establishment of the state of Parhae
- **800–900** Populist "New Land" Buddhism established in Silla
- **c.900** The kingdom of Silla collapses
- **918** The Koryo dynasty is established at Kaegyong (Kaesong): it unifies Korea in 936
- **926** Khitan nomads overrun Parhae
- **1231** Mongol invasions of Korea begin
- **1234** Earliest use of cast metal movable type for printing books
- **1258** Korea becomes a Mongol vassal state
- **1446** Korean alphabetical script replaces Chinese script

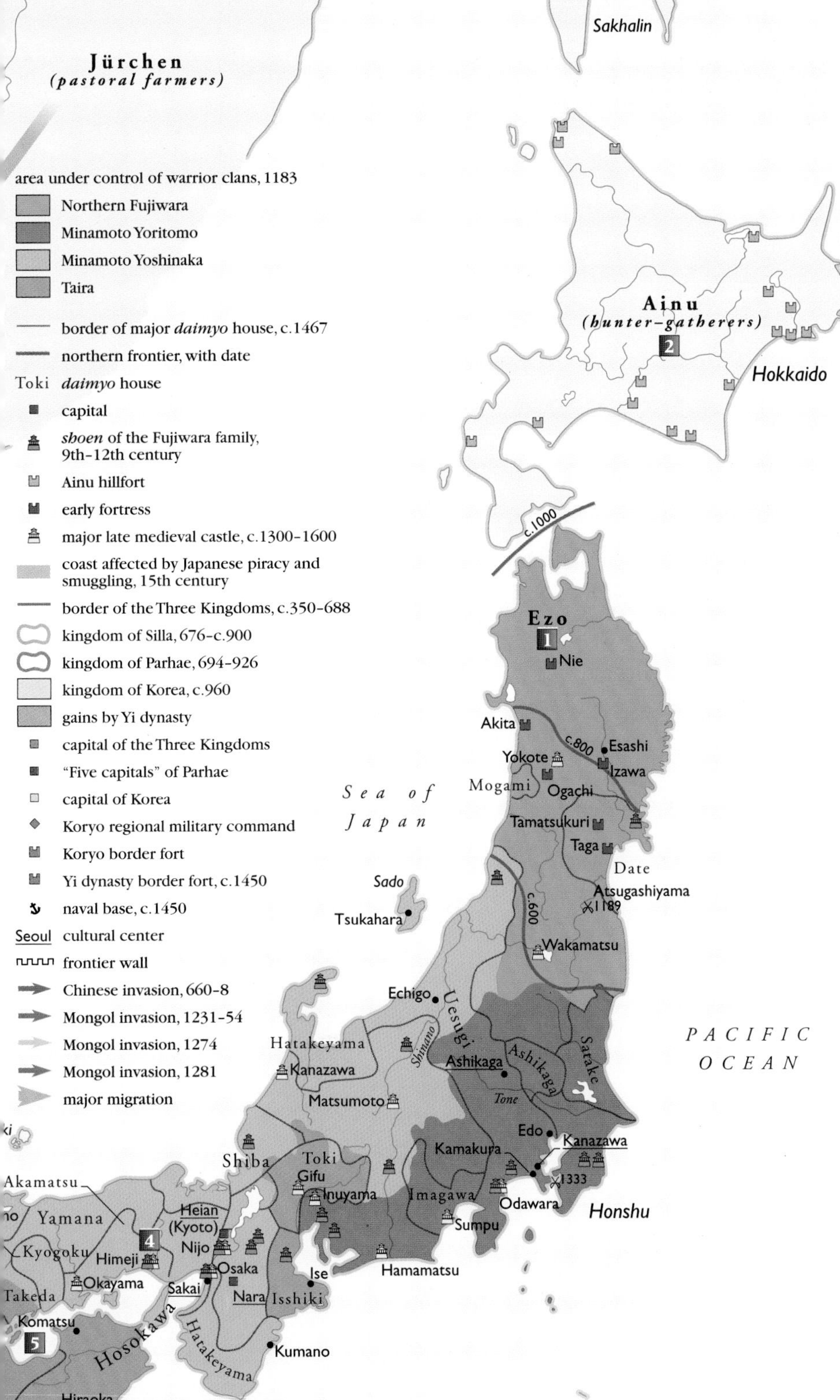
Jürchen
(pastoral farmers)
area under control of warrior clans, 1183
Northern Fujiwara
Minamoto Yoritomo
Minamoto Yoshinaka
Taira
border of major daimyo house, c.1467
northern frontier, with date
Toki daimyo house
capital
shoen of the Fujiwara family, 9th-12th century
Ainu hillfort
early fortress
major late medieval castle, c.1300-1600
coast affected by Japanese piracy and smuggling, 15th century
border of the Three Kingdoms, c.350-688
kingdom of Silla, 676-c.900
kingdom of Parhae, 694-926
kingdom of Korea, c.960
gains by Yi dynasty
capital of the Three Kingdoms
"Five capitals" of Parhae
capital of Korea
Koryo regional military command
Koryo border fort
Yi dynasty border fort, c.1450
naval base, c.1450
Seoul cultural center
frontier wall
Chinese invasion, 660-8
Mongol invasion, 1231-54
Mongol invasion, 1274
Mongol invasion, 1281
major migration
Sakhalin
Ainu
(hunter-gatherers)
Hokkaido
c.1000
Ezo
Nie
Akita
c.800
Esashi
Yokote
Izawa
Mogami
Ogachi
Tamatsukuri
Taga
Date
Atsugashiyama
1189
c.900
Wakamatsu
Sea of Japan
Sado
Tsukahara
Echigo
Uesugi
Shinano
Satake
Ashikaga
Hatakeyama
Kanazawa
Matsumoto
Tone
PACIFIC OCEAN
Edo
Kanazawa
Kamakura
1333
Shiba
Toki
Gifu
Inuyama
Imagawa
Odawara
Honshu
Akamatsu
Yamana
Heian (Kyoto)
Nijo
Kyogoku
Himeji
Sumpu
Osaka
Okayama
Sakai
Nara
Isshiki
Ise
Hamamatsu
Takeda
Komatsu
Hosokawa
Hatakeyama
Kumano
Hiraoka
Shikoku

1 The Ezo people of Honshu, related to the Ainu, fiercely resisted Japanese expansion but were conquered by the 12th century.

2 The Ainu were an aboriginal hunter-gatherer people, linguistically and physically unrelated to any other east Asian peoples, who were only brought under Japanese rule in the 17th century.

3 The destruction of the Taira at the battle of Dannoura was made the subject of the *Tale of the Heike*, the major literary work of 13th-century Japan.

4 One of the best preserved Japanese medieval castles is White Heron Castle at Himeji (14th century).

5 Fishing villages in the Inland Sea and on Tsushima became bases for smugglers and pirates, breaking tight Korean and Chinese restrictions on trade.

6 The kingdom of Paekche fell after its Japanese allies were defeated by Silla in a naval battle in 663.

7 The Koryo dynasty extended its control to the Yalu River c.960, since when it has remained Korea's northwestern border.

8 The Long Wall was built in 1033–44 to defend Korea against Khitan and Jürchen invasions.

9 During the Mongol invasions, the Korean royal court moved to the greater safety of Kanghwa Island.

The exquisitely refined culture of Heian court life contrasted with growing disorder in the provinces. In the absence of a centralized military system, monasteries and aristocratic houses formed private armies and a class of rural warriors – the *samurai* – developed. Sporadic warfare increased, and with it arose the culture of the warrior.

In the 12th century samurai clans became involved in court politics and Fujiwara influence declined. Following the Gempei war (1180–85) between the Taira and Minamoto clans, Minamoto Yoritomo founded the Kamakura shogunate, beginning a period of military government that would last until 1868. The Kamakura shogunate was overthrown in 1333 and replaced five years later by the Ashikaga shogunate. The shoguns ruled in alliance with the *shugo* (military constables), who gradually became powerful regional rulers, undermining the authority of the shoguns. When a dispute over the shogunal succession escalated into a fullscale civil war between 1467–77, the shugo lost control of their regional power bases. Control of the provinces fell to new feudal warlords, or *daimyo*. The daimyo feuded almost constantly among themselves, deploying armies of samurai vassals who held small estates in return for military service. The castles of the daimyo became the main centers of government and of warrior culture. Castles attracted craftsmen and merchants and many became a focus for urban development. Though the Ashikaga shogunate survived until 1573, the civil war destroyed its remaining authority and by 1500 Japan had fragmented into almost 400 effectively independent states. The emperors continued to reign in Heian (Kyoto) but they were powerless and impoverished figureheads.

In Korea three kingdoms – Koguryo, Silla and Paekche – had emerged by 600. In 660 the expansionist Chinese Tang dynasty invaded the peninsula and in alliance with Silla conquered Paekche and Koguryo. On finding that it was not to share in the spoils, Silla drove the Chinese from the peninsula in 676. Silla occupied Paekche and southern Koguryo: northern Koguryo remained in chaos until a successor state, Parhae, emerged in 694. Both Korean states developed as centralized kingdoms on the Tang model. In 780 a struggle between the monarchy and the aristocracy broke out in Silla and in the 9th century the kingdom broke up. A new kingdom was created in 918–36 by Wang Kon (r.918–45), founder of the Koryo dynasty from which Korea gets its name. Parhae was extinguished about the same time by the Khitan nomads. Despite Khitan opposition, Korea had established a heavily fortified frontier on the Yalu River by the early 11th century.

A coup in 1170 deprived the monarchy of real power, leaving Korea leaderless until the military Choe family seized power in 1196. The Choe led resistance to the Mongols but unrest grew more widespread as the wars dragged on: the dynasty was overthrown in 1258 and Korea became a Mongol vassal state. The end of Mongol rule in 1356 brought a return to political instability and the Koryo dynasty was eventually overthrown with Chinese help by the general Yi Songgye (r.1392–98), founder of the Yi dynasty (1392–1910). Under the Yi, Confucianism replaced Buddhism as Korea's main ethical code and was made the basis of the bureaucratic and educational systems. The Yi resumed expansion to the northeast and by the 15th century the country's modern borders had been established.

See also 3.05 (the world religions); 3.23 (Mongol invasion); 4.23 (later Japan)

3.25 The kingdoms of southeast Asia • 600 – 1500 •

Several small and unstable states arose in mainland and island southeast Asia during the first half of the first millennium AD. Yet by 1000 many stable kingdoms and large empires had emerged. Local rulers, influenced by India, consolidated their power by adopting Buddhist and Hindu concepts of sacred kingship: most southeast Asian states before 1500 were royal theocracies. Indeed, Indian cultural influences remained strong throughout the period; China, however, despite close trade and diplomatic links with some southeast Asian states, only exerted influence on states directly bordering on it.

The most powerful mainland state for much of this period was the Khmer empire of Cambodia. The Khmers had been united in the state of Chen-la around AD 400: this peaked under Jayavarman I in about 700 but soon declined. In 802 Jayavarman II (r.802–50), a minor king in the Angkor district, proclaimed himself *devaraja* ("god-king"), reuniting the Khmer peoples. By the reign of Indravarman I (r.877–89) the Khmer ruled the Mon and Thai peoples to the north and west. Yasovarman I (r.889–910) founded a new capital at Angkor, the Khmer empire's most impressive monument. The empire was at its height under Suryavarman I (r.1010–50) and Suryavarman II (r.1113–50). Under pressure from the expanding Thai peoples and the pull of maritime commerce, the Khmer capital moved to the safer location of Caturmukha (near Phnom Penh) in 1431 and abandoned Angkor in 1440. By 1500 the Khmer had become a minor regional power.

The earliest Thai state, the warlike Nan Chao, emerged in about 600; it was finally conquered by the Mongols in 1253. From about 1000 Thai peoples began moving south into Mon and Khmer territories. Around 1250, a Thai dynasty established a powerful kingdom at Sukhothai and a century later another Thai kingdom was founded at Ayutthaya. Ayutthaya conquered Sukhothai in about 1378 and became the dominant power of the Gulf of Thailand by the 15th century after driving the Khmers from Angkor.

About 600, Buddhist states began to form among the Mon and Pyu peoples of the Irrawaddy valley.

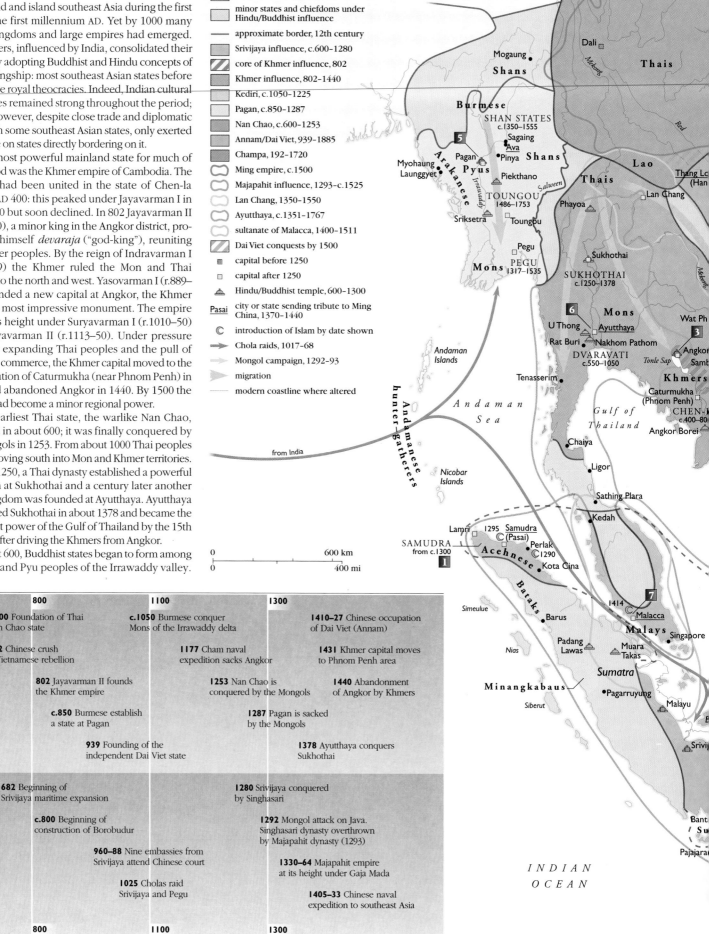

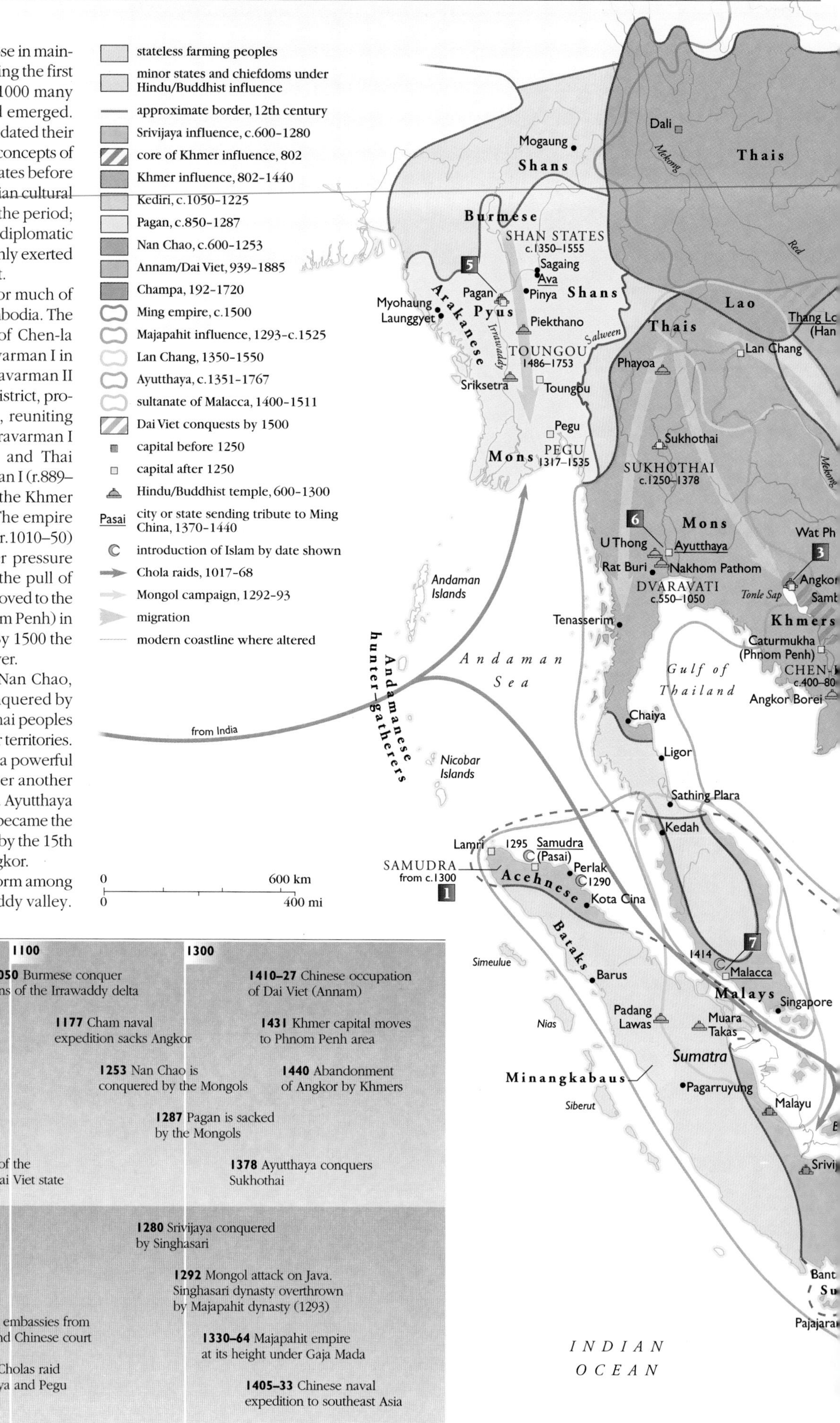

stateless farming peoples
minor states and chiefdoms under Hindu/Buddhist influence
approximate border, 12th century
Srivijaya influence, c.600–1280
core of Khmer influence, 802
Khmer influence, 802–1440
Kediri, c.1050–1225
Pagan, c.850–1287
Nan Chao, c.600–1253
Annam/Dai Viet, 939–1885
Champa, 192–1720
Ming empire, c.1500
Majapahit influence, 1293–c.1525
Lan Chang, 1350–1550
Ayutthaya, c.1351–1767
sultanate of Malacca, 1400–1511
Dai Viet conquests by 1500
capital before 1250
capital after 1250
Hindu/Buddhist temple, 600–1300
Pasai city or state sending tribute to Ming China, 1370–1440
introduction of Islam by date shown
Chola raids, 1017–68
Mongol campaign, 1292–93
migration
modern coastline where altered
0 600 km
0 400 mi
Dali
Mogaung
Shans
Thais
Burmese
SHAN STATES c.1350–1555
Sagaing
Ava
Pinya
Shans
Pagan
Pyus
Myohaung
Launggyet
Arakanese
Irrawaddy
Piekthano
Salween
TOUNGOU 1486–1753
Toungou
Sriksetra
Lao
Thais
Thang Lo (Han
Lan Chang
Phayoa
Pegu
PEGU 1317–1535
Mons
Sukhothai
SUKHOTHAI c.1250–1378
Mekong
Red
Mons
U Thong
Ayutthaya
Rat Buri
Nakhom Pathom
DVARAVATI c.550–1050
Wat Ph
Angkor
Tonle Sap
Khmers
Caturmukha (Phnom Penh)
CHEN-
c.400–80
Angkor Borei
Andaman Islands
Andamanese hunter–gatherers
Tenasserim
Andaman Sea
Gulf of Thailand
from India
Chaiya
Ligor
Nicobar Islands
Sathing Plara
Kedah
Lamri
1295 Samudra (Pasai)
SAMUDRA from c.1300
Perlak 1290
Acehnese
Kota Cina
Bataks
Simeulue
Barus
1414
Malacca
Malays
Singapore
Padang Lawas
Muara Takas
Nias
Sumatra
Minangkabaus
Pagarruyung
Siberut
Malayu
Srivij
Bant
Su
Pajajara
INDIAN OCEAN

TIMELINE

Mainland southeast Asia

- **c.600** Foundation of Thai Nan Chao state
- **602** Chinese crush a Vietnamese rebellion
- **802** Jayavarman II founds the Khmer empire
- **c.850** Burmese establish a state at Pagan
- **939** Founding of the independent Dai Viet state
- **c.1050** Burmese conquer Mons of the Irrawaddy delta
- **1177** Cham naval expedition sacks Angkor
- **1253** Nan Chao is conquered by the Mongols
- **1287** Pagan is sacked by the Mongols
- **1378** Ayutthaya conquers Sukhothai
- **1410–27** Chinese occupation of Dai Viet (Annam)
- **1431** Khmer capital moves to Phnom Penh area
- **1440** Abandonment of Angkor by Khmers

Island Southeast Asia

- **682** Beginning of Srivijaya maritime expansion
- **c.800** Beginning of construction of Borobudur
- **960–88** Nine embassies from Srivijaya attend Chinese court
- **1025** Cholas raid Srivijaya and Pegu
- **1280** Srivijaya conquered by Singhasari
- **1292** Mongol attack on Java. Singhasari dynasty overthrown by Majapahit dynasty (1293)
- **1330–64** Majapahit empire at its height under Gaja Mada
- **1405–33** Chinese naval expedition to southeast Asia

800 | 1100 | 1300

The Pyu states were destroyed by Nan Chao about 835; shortly after the Burmese moved into the valley and built a state around Pagan. By the mid-11th century Pagan subdued the Mons, the coastal Arakanese and the Thai-speaking Shan hill peoples, building the first unified state in the Irrawaddy basin. Pagan was eventually destroyed by the Mongols. The Shan, Mon and Arakanese were reconquered by the Burmese Toungou dynasty (16th century).

Vietnam had been the site of complex societies from early times and occupied by the Chinese since the 3rd century BC. Only in 939, after centuries of rebellion, did the Vietnamese found an independent state, known to them as Dai Viet and to the Chinese as Annam. This was the sole state of southeast Asia in which Chinese cultural influences predominated. Once China had abandoned hopes of reconquest in 1427, relations between the two states improved.

The first large state to dominate the sea passages was Srivijaya, in Sumatra. Srivijaya began its imperial expansion in 682 and reached its peak in 800. Raids by the Cholas of south India in the 11th century eroded its power but its demise was hastened in the first quarter of the 13th century by the imperial expansion of the east Javan Singhasari dynasty. This was in turn succeeded by a new dynasty at Majapahit in 1293. For the next century Majapahit dominated maritime Indonesia but was in decline by 1400. Like the earlier maritime empires, Majapahit was not centralized: only central and east Java was under its direct control, while provincial rulers retained power locally. Payment of tribute was enforced by the threat of punitive naval action.

Islam, which was brought to island southeast Asia by Indian Muslim merchants at the end of the 13th century, undermined theocratic kingship, founded coastal states and defeated the remnants of Hindu–Buddhist Majapahit by 1527. When the Europeans arrived in the 16th century, they found island southeast Asia divided into dozens of petty states.

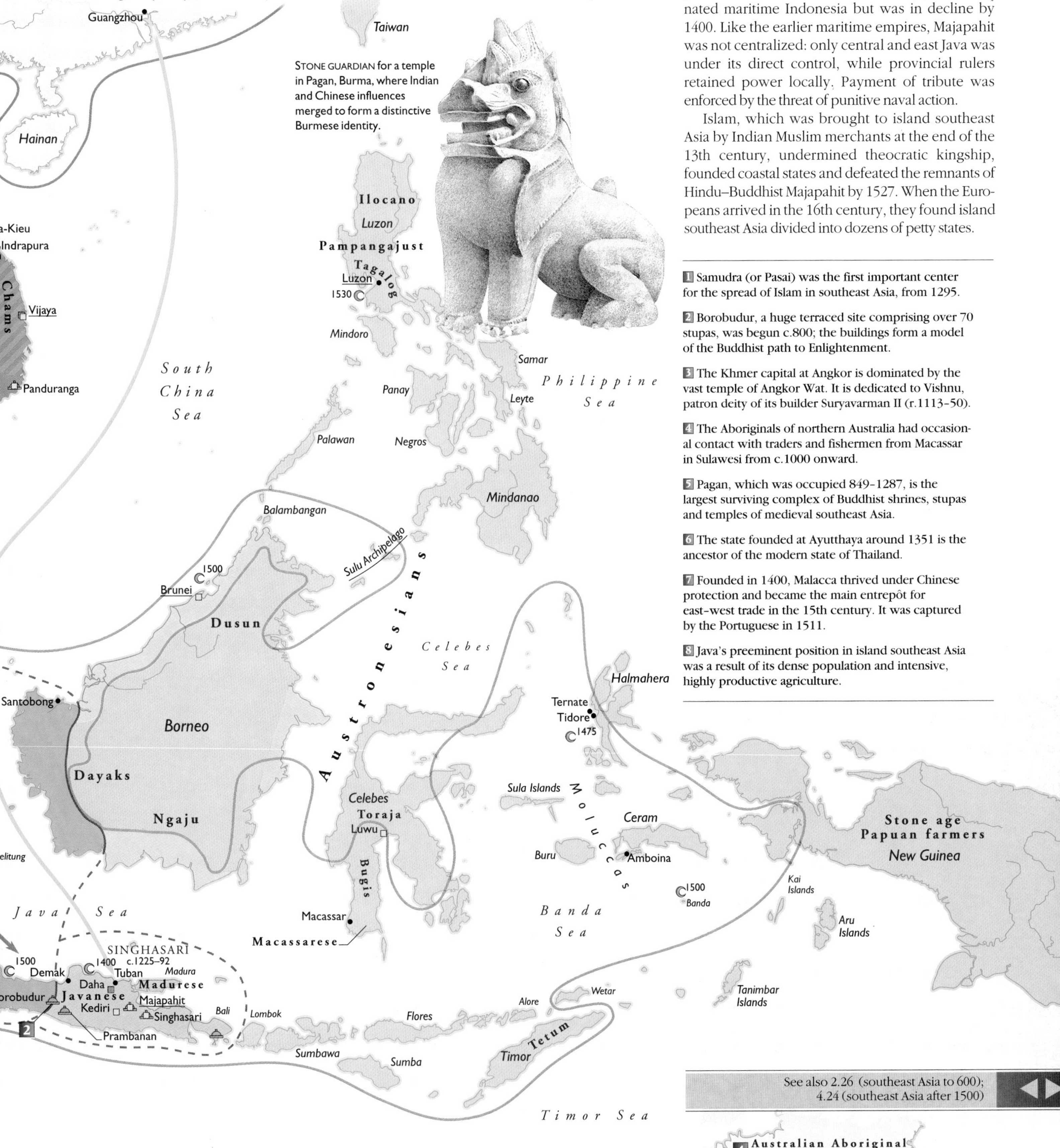
Guangzhou
Taiwan
Hainan
a-Kieu
Indrapura
Chams
Vijaya
Panduranga
South China Sea
Ilocano
Luzon
Pampangajust
Tagalog
Luzon
1530
Mindoro
Samar
Philippine Sea
Panay
Leyte
Palawan
Negros
Mindanao
Balambangan
Sulu Archipelago
1500
Brunei
Dusun
Austronesians
Celebes Sea
Halmahera
Santobong
Borneo
Ternate
Tidore
1475
Dayaks
Ngaju
Celebes
Toraja
Luwu
Sula Islands
Moluccas
Ceram
Buru
Amboina
Stone age Papuan farmers
New Guinea
Belitung
Bugis
1500
Banda
Kai Islands
Java Sea
Macassar
Banda Sea
Aru Islands
Macassarese
SINGHASARI c.1225–92
1500
1400
Demak
Tuban
Madura
Daha
Madurese
Borobudur
Javanese
Majapahit
Kediri
Singhasari
Bali
Lombok
Prambanan
Flores
Alore
Wetar
Tanimbar Islands
Tetum
Timor
Sumbawa
Sumba
Timor Sea
Australian Aboriginal hunter–gatherers

STONE GUARDIAN for a temple in Pagan, Burma, where Indian and Chinese influences merged to form a distinctive Burmese identity.

1 Samudra (or Pasai) was the first important center for the spread of Islam in southeast Asia, from 1295.

2 Borobudur, a huge terraced site comprising over 70 stupas, was begun c.800; the buildings form a model of the Buddhist path to Enlightenment.

3 The Khmer capital at Angkor is dominated by the vast temple of Angkor Wat. It is dedicated to Vishnu, patron deity of its builder Suryavarman II (r.1113–50).

4 The Aboriginals of northern Australia had occasional contact with traders and fishermen from Macassar in Sulawesi from c.1000 onward.

5 Pagan, which was occupied 849–1287, is the largest surviving complex of Buddhist shrines, stupas and temples of medieval southeast Asia.

6 The state founded at Ayutthaya around 1351 is the ancestor of the modern state of Thailand.

7 Founded in 1400, Malacca thrived under Chinese protection and became the main entrepôt for east-west trade in the 15th century. It was captured by the Portuguese in 1511.

8 Java's preeminent position in island southeast Asia was a result of its dense population and intensive, highly productive agriculture.

See also 2.26 (southeast Asia to 600); 4.24 (southeast Asia after 1500)

Native cultures of North America • 600 – 1500 •

The initial settlement of North America began around 12,000 years ago as bands of Paleoindians, the ancestors of modern Native Americans, spread south from Alaska. At first, Paleoindian culture was relatively homogeneous but adaptation to particular environments led to the emergence of well defined regional cultures by the end of the first millennium BC. From early times hunter–gatherers in many areas of North America had cultivated favored food plants on a small scale. Some native plant species, such as sunflowers, had been domesticated by the end of the first millennium BC and maize and beans had been introduced from Mexico. As wild food sources remained abundant, true farming communities were slow to develop.

The first mainly agricultural North American societies developed in the southwest deserts in about AD 300. Maize, beans, squash and cotton were first cultivated close to permanent water sources but by about 900 elaborate irrigation systems were in use. By the 9th century three main cultural traditions had developed – the Hohokam, Mogollon and Anasazi – together with two subsidiary cultures, the Patayan and the Fremont. In some areas (such as Chaco Canyon) these cultures developed considerable social complexity. Their most distinctive remains are the multi-roomed dwellings known as pueblos, and their fine pottery. Droughts caused their decline from around 1300.

True farming began to emerge in the eastern woodlands once hardier strains of maize and beans appeared after 700. The resulting growth in food production stimulated the rise of North America's first towns, in the Mississippi basin, by the 12th century. These centered around large earthwork temple mounds. The Mississippian cultures shared a common religion known as the Southern Cult, and were hierarchical; their rulers were buried in mound-top mortuaries with rich grave goods and even human sacrifices. Large Mississippian towns, such as Cahokia, were the centers of powerful chiefdoms. By the 15th century, Mississippian culture was declining and its heartland was depopulated (the so-called "vacant quarter"). By about 1000 permanent farming villages were established throughout the eastern woodlands. Warfare spread and by the time of European contact defensive tribal confederacies, such as the Iroquois league, were forming.

Elsewhere in North America hunting, fishing and gathering remained the dominant way of life. On the Pacific coast, ocean resources were so abundant that relatively dense populations and permanent village settlements emerged, with a level of social and cultural complexity far beyond that normally achieved by hunter–gatherer peoples. The Great Plains and the sub-Arctic forests were sparsely populated, though the advent of the bow and arrow in the first millennium AD made big-game hunting more efficient. At the time of European contact buffalo hunting was gradually giving way to farming, but the introduction of the horse (native American horses died out around 10,000 years ago), led many settled Plains peoples to abandon farming for nomadism.

The Paleoindians did not for the most part settle in Arctic North America. The region was uninhabited until about 2500–1900 BC when the ancestors of the modern Inuit peoples arrived in Alaska from Siberia. Early Inuit cultures became increasingly well adapted to the Arctic environment, culminating in the Thule tradition which survived to the modern age. This originated during the Old Bering Sea Stage (200 BC–AD 800) among specialized marine mammal hunters on St Lawrence and other Bering Sea islands, from where it spread along Alaska's west coast and north to Point Barrow. From there Thule Inuit migrated east, displacing or assimilating the earlier Dorset Inuit until they reached Greenland in the 13th century. Here they made contact with Norse settlers, with whom they traded and fought. The Norse were not well adapted to life in the Arctic and by about 1500 their settlements had died out and been occupied by the Thule.

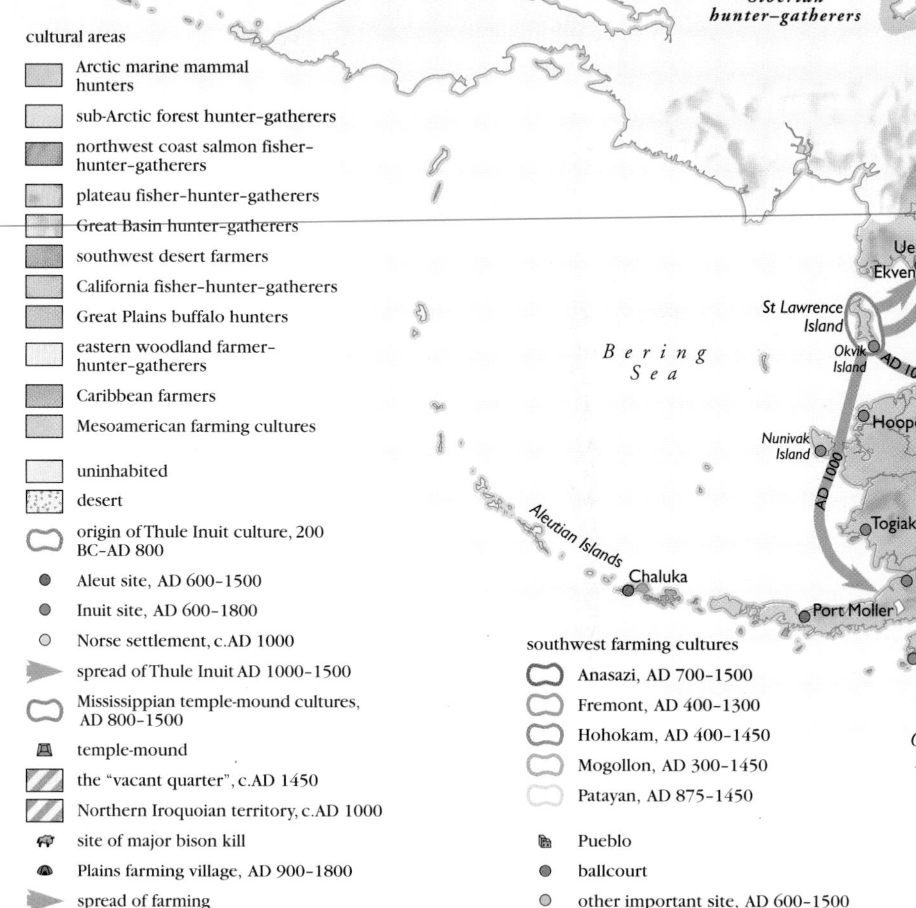

cultural areas
Arctic marine mammal hunters
sub-Arctic forest hunter-gatherers
northwest coast salmon fisher-hunter-gatherers
plateau fisher-hunter-gatherers
Great Basin hunter-gatherers
southwest desert farmers
California fisher-hunter-gatherers
Great Plains buffalo hunters
eastern woodland farmer-hunter-gatherers
Caribbean farmers
Mesoamerican farming cultures
uninhabited
desert
origin of Thule Inuit culture, 200 BC-AD 800
Aleut site, AD 600-1500
Inuit site, AD 600-1800
Norse settlement, c.AD 1000
spread of Thule Inuit AD 1000-1500
Mississippian temple-mound cultures, AD 800-1500
temple-mound
the "vacant quarter", c.AD 1450
Northern Iroquoian territory, c.AD 1000
site of major bison kill
Plains farming village, AD 900-1800
spread of farming
southwest farming cultures
Anasazi, AD 700-1500
Fremont, AD 400-1300
Hohokam, AD 400-1450
Mogollon, AD 300-1450
Patayan, AD 875-1450
Pueblo
ballcourt
other important site, AD 600-1500
Siberian hunter–gatherers
Siberian Inuit
Bering Sea
St Lawrence Island
Okvik Island
Nunivak Island
Aleutian Islands
Chaluka
Port Moller
Kodiak Island
Gulf of Alaska
Uelen
Ekven
Kungitavik
Hooper Bay
Togiak
Naknek
AD 1000

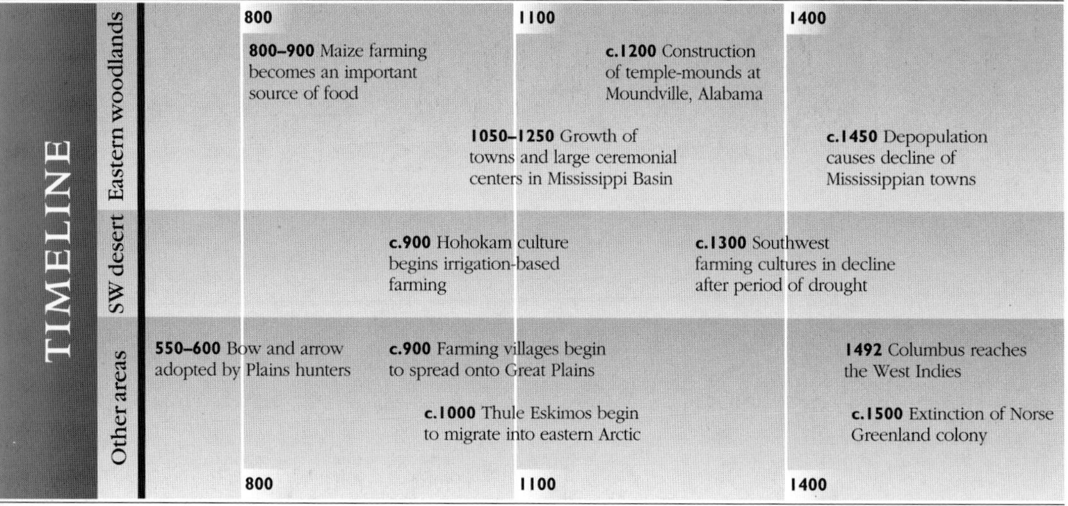

TIMELINE
Eastern woodlands
SW desert
Other areas
800
1100
1400
800–900 Maize farming becomes an important source of food
c.1200 Construction of temple-mounds at Moundville, Alabama
1050–1250 Growth of towns and large ceremonial centers in Mississippi Basin
c.1450 Depopulation causes decline of Mississippian towns
c.900 Hohokam culture begins irrigation-based farming
c.1300 Southwest farming cultures in decline after period of drought
550–600 Bow and arrow adopted by Plains hunters
c.900 Farming villages begin to spread onto Great Plains
1492 Columbus reaches the West Indies
c.1000 Thule Eskimos begin to migrate into eastern Arctic
c.1500 Extinction of Norse Greenland colony
800
1100
1400

1 Here a cliff was used as a "jump" over which buffalo were stampeded to their deaths, from c.5400 BC to European contact.

2 A small Norse settlement occupied for about twenty years c.AD 1000 is the only sure evidence that Europeans reached the Americas before Columbus.

3 Ritual ball courts at Snaketown and Casa Grande indicate that the Hohokam culture was influenced by Mesoamerican civilizations.

4 From 900–1300, Chaco Canyon was the hub of a network of 125 planned villages linked by 400 kilometers (250 miles) of roads.

5 Iron ship rivets, textiles and chain mail found at sites at Flagler Bay show contact between the Thule Inuit and the Norse Greenlanders.

6 Sub-Arctic hunters typically sited their camps at river crossings used by herds of caribou (reindeer).

Greenland
AD 1200–1500
Ellesmere Island
Inuarfissuaq
Flagler Bay
Thule
Illummersuit
Inussuk
Sermermiut
AD 1200–1500
Utqiagvik
Birnick
Point Barrow
Bathurst Island
Craig Harbour
Melville Island
de Blicquy
Devon Island
Maxwell Bay
Resolute
Nunguvik
Western Settlement
Illutalik
Kangeq
Eastern Settlement
Middle Settlement
Beaufort Sea
AD 1000–1200
AD 1000–1200
Mittimatalik
Banks Island
Prince of Wales Island
Strathcona Sound
Baffin Island
Kuujja
Victoria Island
Memorana
Jackson
Pingitkalik
Klo-kut
Bell
Pembroke
Clark
Maleruakik
AD 1000–1200
Crystal II
Labrador Sea
Lady Franklin Point
Naujan
Southampton Island
Chimi
Great Bear Lake
Mackenzie
Silumiut
Igluligardjuk
L'Anse aux Meadows
Frank Channel
Hudson Bay
Yukon
Great Slave Lake
Newfoundland
Indian Point
Charlot River
Mingan
Lake Athabasca
Reindeer Lake
Peace
Athabasca
ROCKY MOUNTAINS
COAST MOUNTAINS
Dodge Island
Queen Charlotte Islands
Tailrace Bay
Lake Winnipeg
Metabetchouan
Saskatchewan
Fraser
Godard Point
Nesikep
Old Women's Buffalo jump
Avonlea
Lake Superior
St Lawrence
Vancouver Island
Head-Smashed-In
Columbia
Lake Ontario
Maxon-Derby
Ozette
Hoko River
Missouri
Big Hidatsa
Lake Huron
Nodwell
Sackett
Lake Michigan
Molander
Netarts Sand Spit
Wakemap Mound
Vore
Mississippi
Great Plains
Lake Erie
ATLANTIC OCEAN
Arzberger
APPALACHIAN MTS
Big Goose Creek
Oneota
Snake
Glenrock
Proctorville
Gunther Island
Platte
Fort Ancient
Hogup Cave
Old Fort
Ohio
Clay Mound
Wardell
Cahokia
Angel
SIERRA NEVADA
Medicine Creek
Town Creek
Middle Mississippian
Kings Mound
San Francisco Bay
Hiwassee Island
Colorado
Arkansas
Alkali Ridge
Shiloh
Etowah
Mesa Verde
Pueblo Bonito
Knapp Mounds
Salmon Ruin
Pecos Pueblo
Lamar
Canyon de Chelly
Chaco Canyon
Caddoan
Moundville
South Appalachian Mississippian
Santa Barbara
Topoc Maze
Montezuma Castle
Winterville
Lake Jackson
Mogollon
Plaquemine Mississippian
Emerald Mound
Pueblo Grande
Snaketown
Garnsey
Casa Grande
Mimbres Valley
Coles Creek
Safety Harbor
Casas Grandes
PACIFIC OCEAN
Rio Grande
Gulf of Mexico
La Candelaria
Cuba
0 1200 km
0 800 mi

GEOMETRICAL design on pottery was typical of the Mimbres Valley in the south-west's Mogollon culture.

See also 4.25 (Spanish empire); 4.26 (European exploration of North America)

3.27 Toltecs and Aztecs • 800 – 1520 •

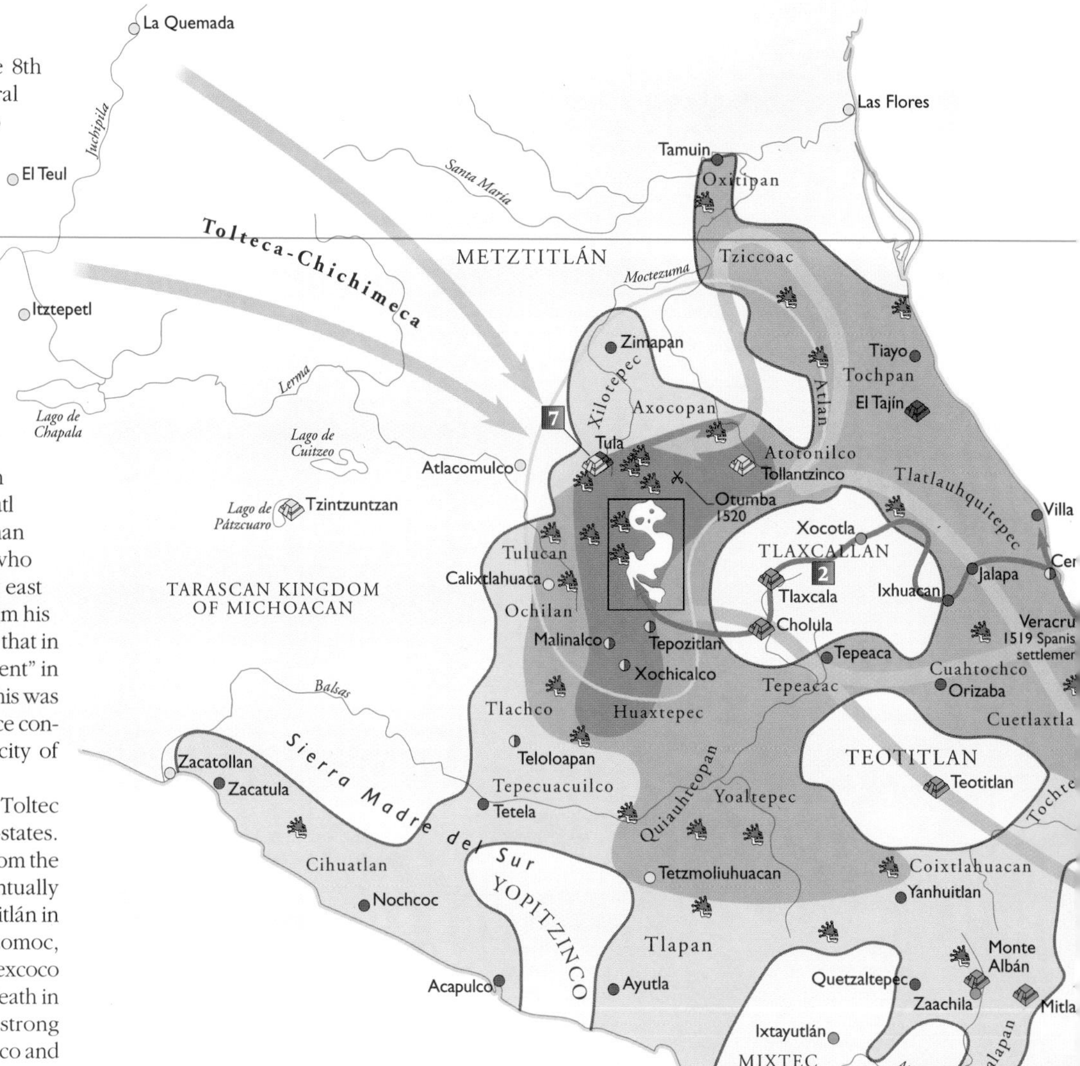

The destruction of Teotihuacán in the 8th century left a power vacuum in central Mexico, which allowed new peoples to migrate to the region. The Chichimeca and the Nonoalca settled to the north of the Valley of Mexico, where they merged to form the Toltec nation. By around 900 a Toltec state was established around Tula, from where they expanded over the Valley of Mexico. Little is known of the history of the Toltecs, but their legends feature prominently in the traditions of the Aztecs, who claimed descent from them. The most important legend concerns the Toltec ruler Topiltzin-Quetzalcóatl, a real person born in 935 or 947, who soon came to be identified with the god Quetzalcóatl ("feathered serpent"). His opposition to human sacrifice offended the god Tezcatlipoca, who overthrew him: Topiltzin-Quetzalcóatl fled east overseas, vowing to return one day to reclaim his kingdom. Intriguingly, Mayan records show that in 987 a man called Kukulcán ("feathered serpent" in Mayan) conquered Yucatán. Whether or not this was the Toltec Quetzalcóatl, archeological evidence confirms that in about 1000 the main Mayan city of Chichén Itzá was occupied by Toltecs.

Tula was sacked in about 1168 and the Toltec empire was supplanted by many rival city-states. Around 1200 the Aztecs, a farming people from the west, moved into the Valley of Mexico, eventually founding a permanent settlement at Tenochtitlán in 1325. First serving as mercenaries for Tezozomoc, ruler of Azcapotzalco, the Aztecs allied with Texcoco to destroy Azcapotzalco after Tezozomoc's death in 1426. Two years later Itzcóatl established a strong Aztec monarchy. In 1434 Tenochtitlán, Texcoco and Tlacopan formed the Triple Alliance, imposing tributary status on the other states of the Valley of Mexico. Expansion continued under Itzcóatl's successors; by 1500 the alliance ruled over some 10 million people. The empire peaked under Moctezuma II (r.1502–20) but was abruptly ended by Hernán Cortés' invasion of 1519–21. Though Cortés had great advantages in weaponry and armor, these were not decisive against overwhelming Aztec superiority of numbers. Moctezuma vacillated, believing Cortés to be the returning Quetzalcóatl, whom the legends described as fair-skinned and bearded. The Mesoamerican custom of taking prisoners for sacrifice also hampered the Aztecs against the conquistadors, who fought to kill. Moreover, Cortés found willing allies in the Tlaxcallans, the Aztecs' main source of sacrificial victims. Finally, diseases brought by the Spanish, such as smallpox, decimated the Aztecs.

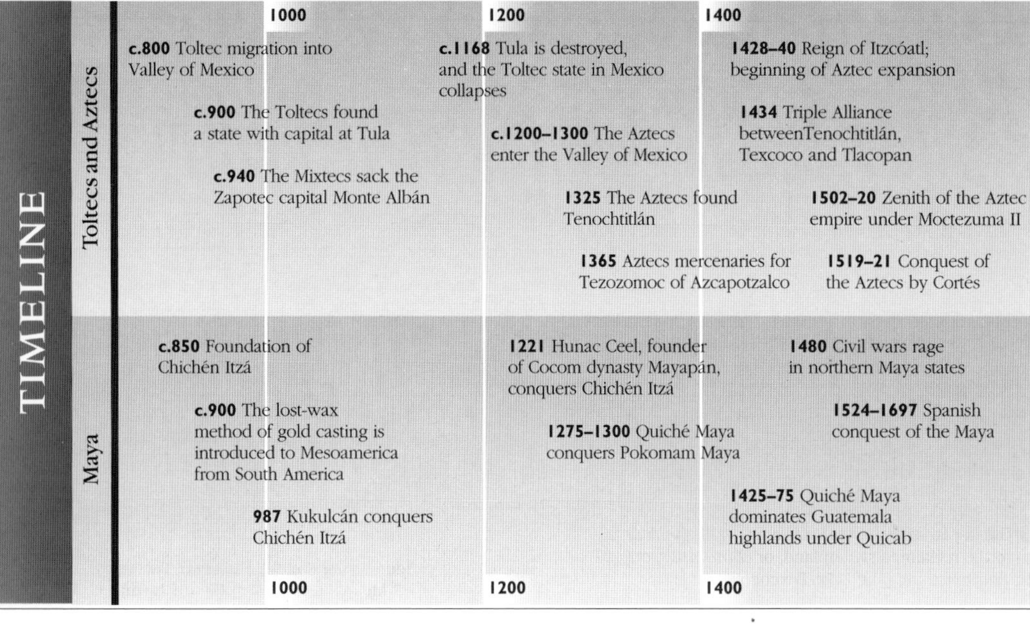

TIMELINE

Toltecs and Aztecs

c.800 Toltec migration into Valley of Mexico

c.900 The Toltecs found a state with capital at Tula

c.940 The Mixtecs sack the Zapotec capital Monte Albán

c.1168 Tula is destroyed, and the Toltec state in Mexico collapses

c.1200–1300 The Aztecs enter the Valley of Mexico

1325 The Aztecs found Tenochtitlán

1365 Aztecs mercenaries for Tezozomoc of Azcapotzalco

1428–40 Reign of Itzcóatl; beginning of Aztec expansion

1434 Triple Alliance betweenTenochtitlán, Texcoco and Tlacopan

1502–20 Zenith of the Aztec empire under Moctezuma II

1519–21 Conquest of the Aztecs by Cortés

Maya

c.850 Foundation of Chichén Itzá

c.900 The lost-wax method of gold casting is introduced to Mesoamerica from South America

987 Kukulcán conquers Chichén Itzá

1221 Hunac Ceel, founder of Cocom dynasty Mayapán, conquers Chichén Itzá

1275–1300 Quiché Maya conquers Pokomam Maya

1480 Civil wars rage in northern Maya states

1524–1697 Spanish conquest of the Maya

1425–75 Quiché Maya dominates Guatemala highlands under Quicab

1000 1200 1400

At the time of the conquest, Aztec society was a class-based hierarchy. Relatives of the king formed the aristocracy, while the commoners (the largest class) comprised members of 20 clans. Each clan had its own quarter of the city with its own schools, temples and communal farms. The lowest class were conquered peoples, who served the aristocracy as farmers and laborers. There were also slaves, usually war captives, and a merchant class, the *pochteca*.

After the Classic Maya cities of the Petén lowlands were abandoned in about 800, Mayan civilization continued in northern Yucatán. Around 850–900 the Putún or Itza Maya settled at Chichén Itzá, which quickly became the dominant Maya center. Around 1000 Yucatán was conquered by the Toltecs, whose rule ended in 1221 with the fall of Chichén Itzá to Hunac Ceel, ruler of Mayapán. The Cocom dynasty he founded dominated Yucatán for over 200 years. When the Spanish landed on Yucatán in 1517 the northern Maya were divided into 16 rival states. This made them harder to subdue than the Aztecs, as there were no key institutions. Thus, Tayasal, the last independent Maya state, did not fall until 1697.

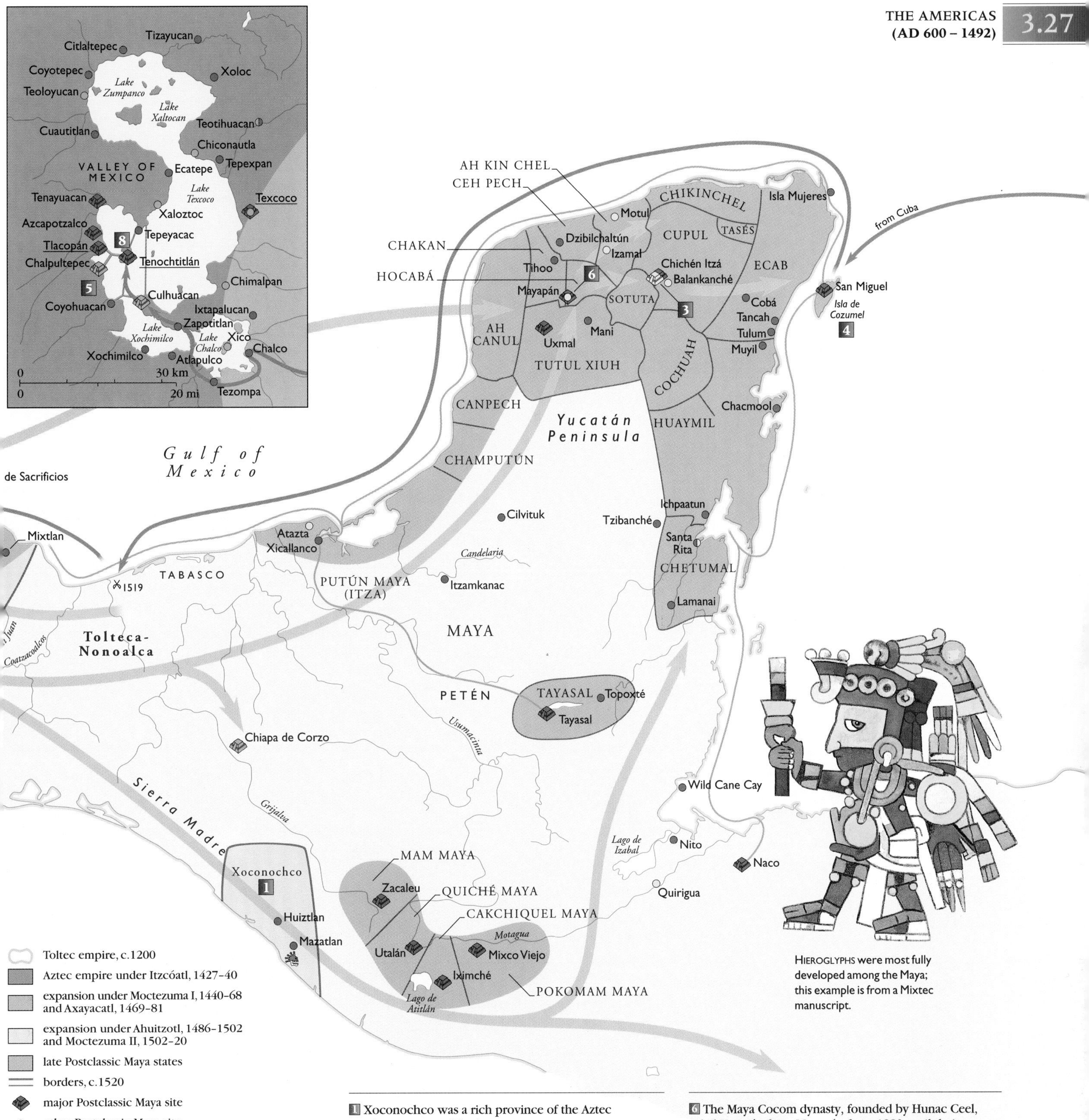

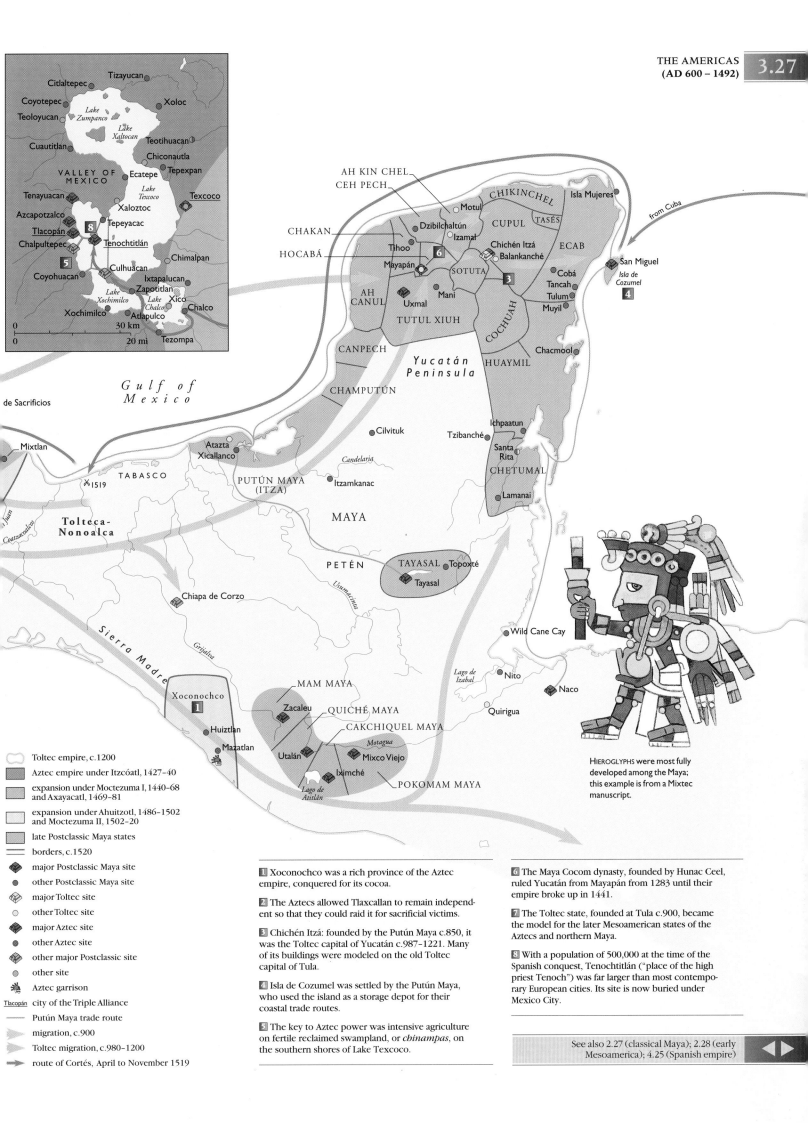

- Toltec empire, c.1200
- Aztec empire under Itzcóatl, 1427–40
- expansion under Moctezuma I, 1440–68 and Axayacatl, 1469–81
- expansion under Ahuitzotl, 1486–1502 and Moctezuma II, 1502–20
- late Postclassic Maya states
- borders, c.1520
- major Postclassic Maya site
- other Postclassic Maya site
- major Toltec site
- other Toltec site
- major Aztec site
- other Aztec site
- other major Postclassic site
- other site
- Aztec garrison
- Tlacopán city of the Triple Alliance
- Putún Maya trade route
- migration, c.900
- Toltec migration, c.980–1200
- route of Cortés, April to November 1519

HIEROGLYPHS were most fully developed among the Maya; this example is from a Mixtec manuscript.

1 Xoconochco was a rich province of the Aztec empire, conquered for its cocoa.

2 The Aztecs allowed Tlaxcallan to remain independent so that they could raid it for sacrificial victims.

3 Chichén Itzá: founded by the Putún Maya c.850, it was the Toltec capital of Yucatán c.987–1221. Many of its buildings were modeled on the old Toltec capital of Tula.

4 Isla de Cozumel was settled by the Putún Maya, who used the island as a storage depot for their coastal trade routes.

5 The key to Aztec power was intensive agriculture on fertile reclaimed swampland, or *chinampas*, on the southern shores of Lake Texcoco.

6 The Maya Cocom dynasty, founded by Hunac Ceel, ruled Yucatán from Mayapán from 1283 until their empire broke up in 1441.

7 The Toltec state, founded at Tula c.900, became the model for the later Mesoamerican states of the Aztecs and northern Maya.

8 With a population of 500,000 at the time of the Spanish conquest, Tenochtitlán ("place of the high priest Tenoch") was far larger than most contemporary European cities. Its site is now buried under Mexico City.

See also 2.27 (classical Maya); 2.28 (early Mesoamerica); 4.25 (Spanish empire)

The collapse of the highland Tiahuanaco and Huari empires in about 1000 ushered in a long period of political fragmentation in the Andean civilizations. Both in the highlands and on the coast many local states emerged, most of which, like the Sicán state of Lambayeque, controlled no more than a single valley. Around 1200 the Chimú state, centered on Chan Chan in the Moche valley, began a period of gradual imperial expansion until in the 15th century it controlled over a thousand kilometers (620 miles) of the Peruvian coast. Around the same time that the Chimú began to expand, a semi-legendary figure, Manco Capac, founded the Inca state at Cuzco in the Killke cultural area of the highlands. For most of its history the Inca state controlled little more than the valley around Cuzco but in the 15th century it became the greatest of all the empires of the pre-Columbian Americas: it was also destined to be the last.

At its peak in around 1500 the Inca empire encompassed much of modern Peru and Bolivia, together with sizable portions of Chile, Argentina and Equador, and ruled over some 12 million people. The Incas' remarkable territorial expansion took place almost entirely during the reigns of Pachacutec (r.1438–71) and his equally able son Tupac Yupanqui (r.1471–93). The Incas overcame the Chimú, their only serious rivals as an imperial power, with little difficulty, capturing their capital Chan Chan in 1470. By the end of Tupac's reign the Inca empire was reaching the practicable limits of its expansion. The Amazonian rainforest to the east and the southern Andes had sparse, mobile populations that would have proved difficult to control and had environments that were unsuited to the settled intensive agriculture that might make their conquest and colonization worthwhile.

Some new territorial gains were made in the north under Huayna Capac (r. 1493–1525) but on his death a bloody civil war broke out between his sons Atahuallpa and Huáscar. Atahuallpa finally triumphed in 1532 but he had no opportunity to restore the weakened empire. In the same year the Spanish conquistador Francisco Pizarro invaded and captured Atahuallpa in a daring assault on Cajamarca. In 1533 the Spanish executed Atahuallpa and installed a puppet ruler at Cuzco: however, when he rebelled in 1536, they assumed direct rule. Inca resistance continued from inaccessible mountain strongholds but was finally crushed in 1572.

There are many reasons for the Incas' spectacular rise and equally rapid decline. They were fortunate in having able generals as rulers. Inca nobles were brought up in the arts of war and a standing army was maintained, so the empire was able to react quickly to any threat. Uniquely among Andean states, the Incas built a network of strategic roads estimated to have been more than 20,000 kilometers (12,500 miles) long – second only in size to the Roman empire's among pre-industrial civilizations – which allowed troops to move quickly to quell trouble on the borders or in the provinces. Conquests were consolidated by a policy of deporting rebellious populations to the heart of the empire where they could be supervised, while their lands were resettled by loyal Inca subjects.

Probably the main factor in Inca success, however, was their complex administrative system – maintained without any system of writing, and with record-keeping done using an elaborate system of knotted strings known as *quipu* – which allowed them to marshal the empire's human resources with great efficiency. Inca society was highly centralized and rigidly hierarchical. At its head was the semidivine emperor. Below the emperor, and directly answerable to him, were the prefects of the

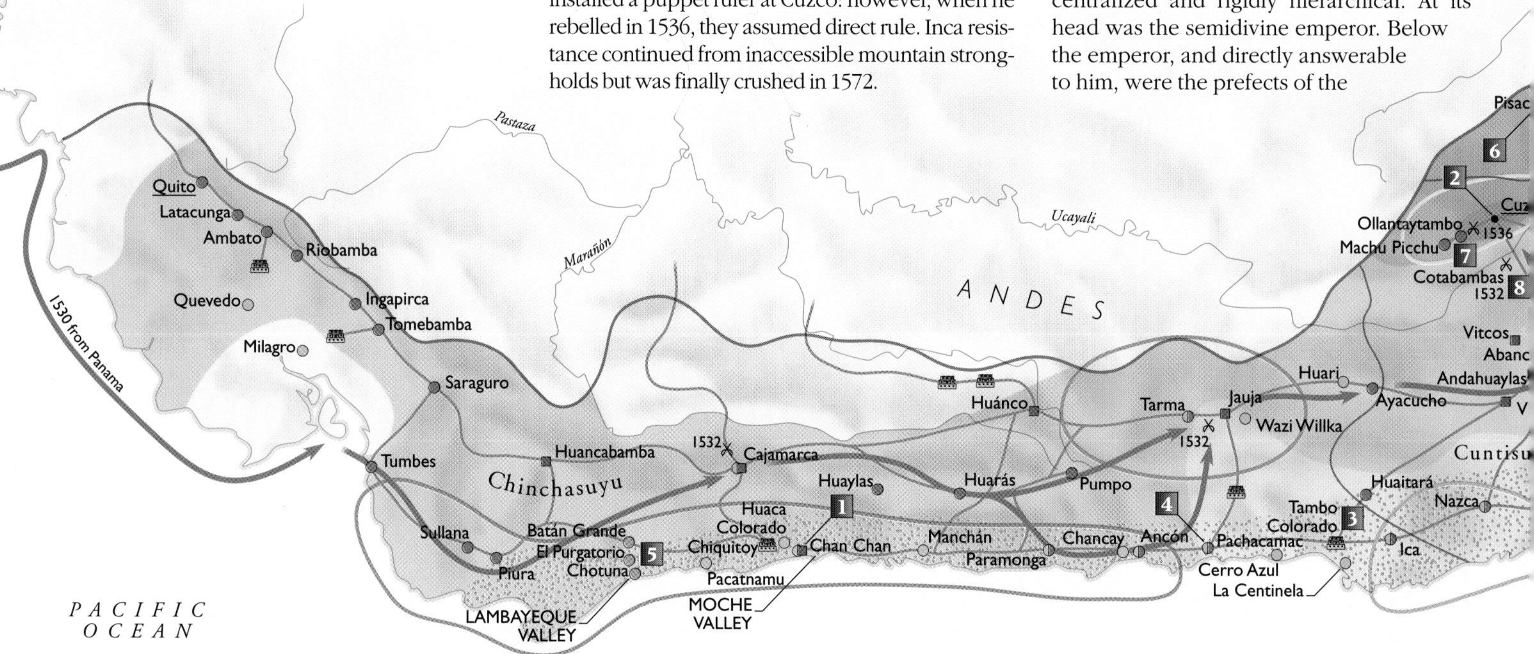
Pisac
6
2
Ollantaytambo
1536
Machu Picchu
7
Cotabambas
1532
8
Vitcos
Andahuaylas
Ayacucho
Huari
Pastaza
Marañón
Ucayali
ANDES
Quito
Latacunga
Ambato
Riobamba
Quevedo
Ingapirca
Tomebamba
Milagro
1530 from Panama
Saraguro
Tumbes
Huancabamba
1532
Cajamarca
Chinchasuyu
Huánco
Tarma
Jauja
Wazi Willka
1532
Huaylas
Huarás
Pumpo
Huaitará
Nazca
Tambo Colorado
3
4
1
5
Huaca Colorado
Sullana
Batán Grande
El Purgatorio
Piura
Chotuna
Chiquitoy
Chan Chan
Manchán
Paramonga
Chancay
Ancón
Pachacamac
Ica
Pacatnamu
Cerro Azul
La Centinela
MOCHE VALLEY
LAMBAYEQUE VALLEY
PACIFIC OCEAN

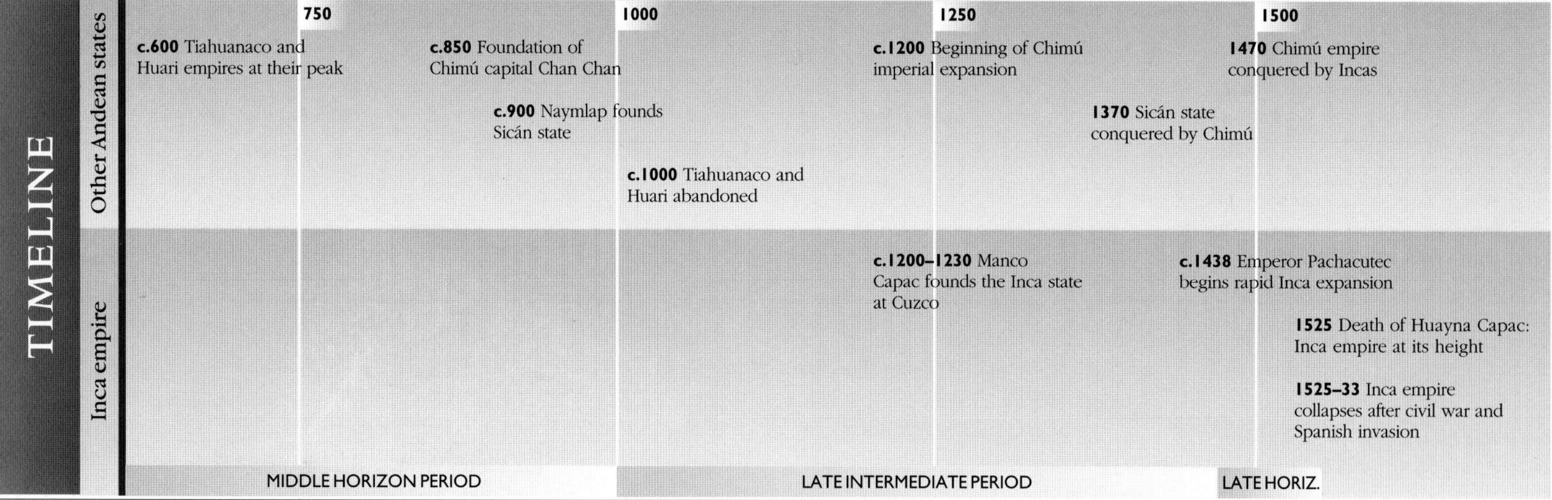
TIMELINE
Other Andean states
Inca empire
750
1000
1250
1500
c.600 Tiahuanaco and Huari empires at their peak
c.850 Foundation of Chimú capital Chan Chan
c.900 Naymlap founds Sicán state
c.1000 Tiahuanaco and Huari abandoned
c.1200 Beginning of Chimú imperial expansion
1370 Sicán state conquered by Chimú
1470 Chimú empire conquered by Incas
c.1200–1230 Manco Capac founds the Inca state at Cuzco
c.1438 Emperor Pachacutec begins rapid Inca expansion
1525 Death of Huayna Capac: Inca empire at its height
1525–33 Inca empire collapses after civil war and Spanish invasion
MIDDLE HORIZON PERIOD
LATE INTERMEDIATE PERIOD
LATE HORIZ.

Four Quarters and below them provincial governors, followed by district officers, local chiefs and, at the bottom, foremen each responsible for supervising ten families. Farmland was divided into thirds, for the support of the state, the gods and the people respectively. All Inca men and women contributed taxation in the form of labor on those parts of the land allocated to the state and the gods. Able-bodied men also paid tax through a labor draft known as *mit'a*. This could last for months and range from military service to work on major construction projects, such as roads and fortresses, or agricultural improvements, such as terracing steep hillsides. This system enabled the empire to raise and supply large armies and keep them in the field for long campaigns.

Although Pizarro was fortunate in having his invasion coincide with the end of a long and destructive civil war, the centralized hierarchy of the Inca empire was also partly responsible for its swift demise. No major decision could be taken without the emperor, whch meant that the empire was paralyzed once Atahuallpa had been captured. Diseases also contributed to the Incas' defeat; as in Mesoamerica, the indigenous population had no resistance to epidemics brought by the Spanish. Indeed, the civil war that first weakened the Inca empire was indirectly caused by a disease introduced from Europe: Huayna Capac died of a smallpox epidemic that spread south from the Spanish base at Panama.

1 Chan Chan was the capital of the Chimú empire from c.850–1470: at the heart of the city were ten walled palace-mausoleum compounds.

2 The Inca capital Cuzco was regarded as the center of the universe, from which radiated the "Four Quarters" of the world. In the Quechua language of the Incas (still widely spoken in the Andes), *cuzco* means "navel".

3 *Tambos*, roadside hostels and storehouses, were sited at intervals of one day's journey on all the empire's roads; one of the largest and best preserved is Tambo Colorado.

4 The oracle of the god Pachacamac, dating to around AD 200, was a major pilgrimage center and rival to the Incas' state solar cult.

5 The Lambayeque valley was the center of the wealthy Sicán state from c.900 until its conquest by the Chimú in c.1370.

6 The Inca increased the area of farmland by terracing mountainsides: many, as at Pisac, are still farmed today.

7 Machu Picchu, the most famous Inca site, was a remote mountain-top religious center and frontier outpost.

8 The victory of Atahuallpa's forces over his rival Huáscar at Cotabambas ended the Inca civil war.

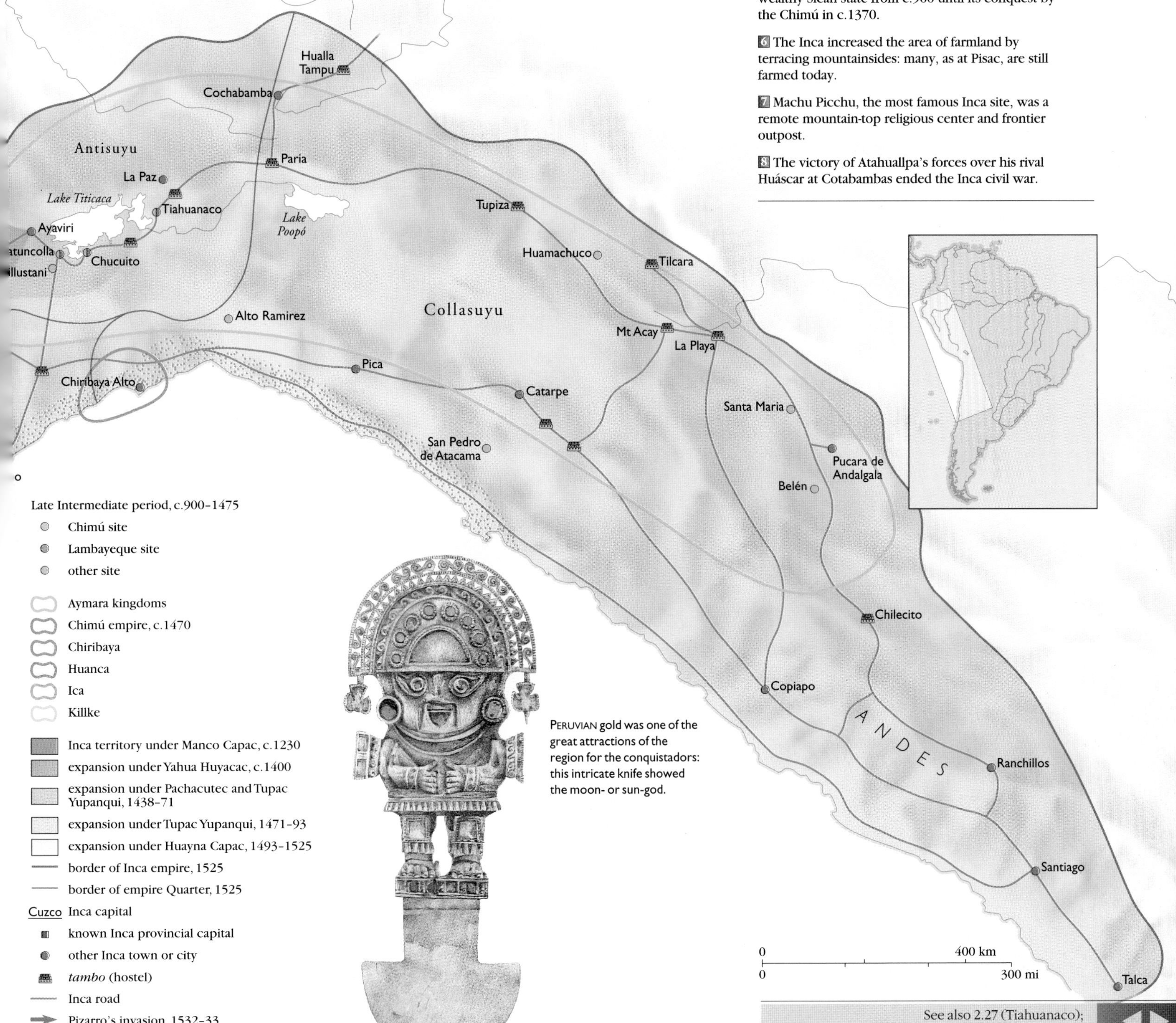
Hualla Tampu
Cochabamba
Antisuyu
Paria
La Paz
Lake Titicaca
Tiahuanaco
Lake Poopó
Tupiza
Ayaviri
Chucuito
Huamachuco
Tilcara
Alto Ramirez
Collasuyu
Mt Acay
La Playa
Pica
Chiribaya Alto
Catarpe
Santa Maria
San Pedro de Atacama
Pucara de Andalgala
Belén
Chilecito
Copiapo
ANDES
Ranchillos
Santiago
Talca
0 400 km
0 300 mi
Late Intermediate period, c.900–1475
Chimú site
Lambayeque site
other site
Aymara kingdoms
Chimú empire, c.1470
Chiribaya
Huanca
Ica
Killke
Inca territory under Manco Capac, c.1230
expansion under Yahua Huyacac, c.1400
expansion under Pachacutec and Tupac Yupanqui, 1438–71
expansion under Tupac Yupanqui, 1471–93
expansion under Huayna Capac, 1493–1525
border of Inca empire, 1525
border of empire Quarter, 1525
Cuzco Inca capital
known Inca provincial capital
other Inca town or city
tambo (hostel)
Inca road
Pizarro's invasion, 1532–33
coastal desert

PERUVIAN gold was one of the great attractions of the region for the conquistadors: this intricate knife showed the moon- or sun-god.

See also 2.27 (Tiahuanaco); 4.25 (Spanish empire)

Part 4

FROM COLUMBUS

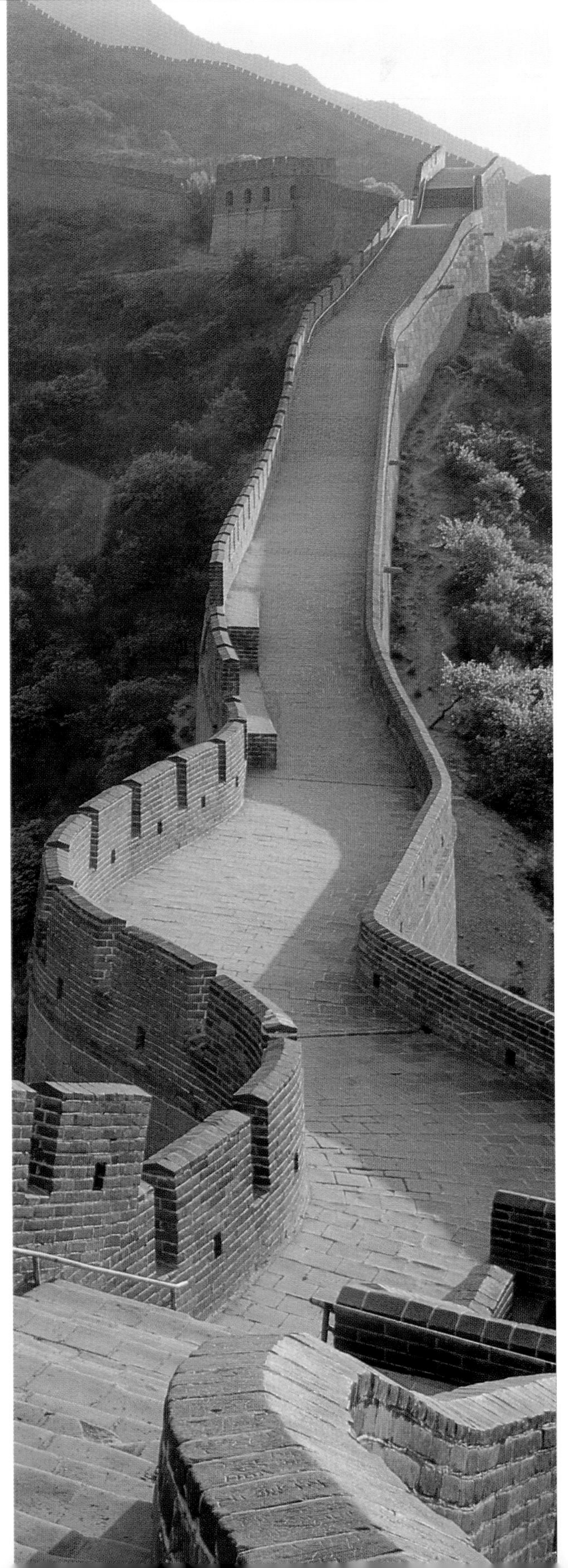

The three centuries after 1492 saw the different parts of the world interact with one another as never before, and at the same time witnessed the rise of European power. The period (often called the "early modern period") began with the European "discovery" of the New World by Christopher Columbus, and ended, ironically, with the throwing off by Britain's North American colonies of European rule – an act that presaged further vast changes, intellectual and technological as well as political and economic, in the Old World of Eurasia and the indigenous empires of Asia and Africa as well as in the New World itself. The rise of Europe and the shrinking of the world were linked. First Spain and Portugal, and later England, France and the Dutch all conquered and settled important portions of North and South America. It was through the projection of Portuguese naval power from the 1490s that European military strength began to make its impact in the Indian Ocean; again, the other powers, notably the Dutch and British, but also the French and Spanish, soon followed in their wake.

The result was a shift in global power. For much of the preceding millennium, Europe had been fairly inconsequential on the world stage. Indeed, in the fifteenth century Europeans had been unable to prevent the advance of the Ottoman Turks into the Balkans, a process that led to the fall of Constantinople, last bastion of the old Roman empire, to Mehmet II in 1453. At that time, no European king could match Mehmet's power. And at the same date, Chinese ships dominated Asian waters; indeed in the first half of the century the Chinese sent fleets into the Indian Ocean that were far larger than any contemporary European fleet.

Over the next 150 years, the impact of Europe on the rest of the world grew enormously. By 1600, the Turks had, it is true, advanced further in Europe and the Mediterranean, capturing

TO AMERICAN INDEPENDENCE

1492 – 1783

Belgrade, defeating Hungary and conquering Cyprus; but their invasion of southern Italy was repelled and they were held at Vienna, Corfu and Malta. From the early 1570s a rough division of the Mediterranean into Ottoman and Christian spheres of influence was established. Further afield, however, the shift was far more dramatic. Spain made dramatic gains in the New World in the early decades of the sixteenth century, overthrowing the powerful empires of the Aztecs of Mexico and the Incas of Peru. The supply of precious metals from these two regions sustained the European economy throughout the century. When Spanish forces began to take control of the Philippines in the 1570s, King Philip II of Spain – for whom the islands were renamed – became the world's first ruler with an empire on which the sun never set. Portuguese warships in the Indian Ocean had destroyed the leading Indian fleets of Calicut and Gujarat – and also those of Egypt and Turkey; Portugal also laid claim to the coast of Brazil.

The tide of transoceanic European maritime activity and territorial expansion was maintained throughout the following two centuries. In the seventeenth century the English and French set up their own colonies – initially little more than fragile footholds but eventually growing to lay claim to much of the eastern seaboard – in North America, while the Dutch, defeated in North America by the English, took over some of the spice-producing regions of the East Indies, regions that brought with them a fantastically profitable trade. Meanwhile, the Russians expanded eastward across Siberia to the Pacific, as a result of which even China acquired a land-frontier with a European state.

In the first three quarters of the eighteenth century, European power expanded in the New World, with the Portuguese pressing deep into the interior of Brazil, the Spaniards pushing north from Mexico into California and the English and French competing for supremacy in the Great Lakes region. In India, the British took over Bengal and became the leading power on the southeast coast. The only serious defeat that Europeans were to experience occurred in North America, where the Thirteen Colonies fought their way into independence from Britain. Yet, even this defeat was at the hands of people of European descent, armed with European weapons and fighting with the assistance of a European state, France.

It would be misleading to imply that the Europeans were everywhere victorious. Their territorial expansion in Africa was still very limited, even though the demands of the European slave trade to the New World carried political and demographic ramifications deep in the interior of the continent. In east Asia the most expansive state in the eighteenth century was still China. At the same time, the Russians found it difficult to make lasting headway against the Persians while, despite major defeats, the Turks displayed great resilience against Austria.

However, the world was increasingly one where the crucial links between distant parts were controlled or created by Europeans. This helped to ensure that a "world economy" developed: that distant regions traded with one another under European auspices, so that the British shipped tea from India to North America or the Dutch moved Chinese porcelain to Europe. This trade was to the profit of the European maritime powers that controlled it, and maritime rivalry was the source of several conflicts between Britain, France and the Netherlands in the seventeenth and eighteenth centuries. Eventual British dominance in this trade helped make London the world's financial center in the eighteenth century and ensured that Britain was well-placed for the rapid economic growth that would lead to the Industrial Revolution by the year 1800.

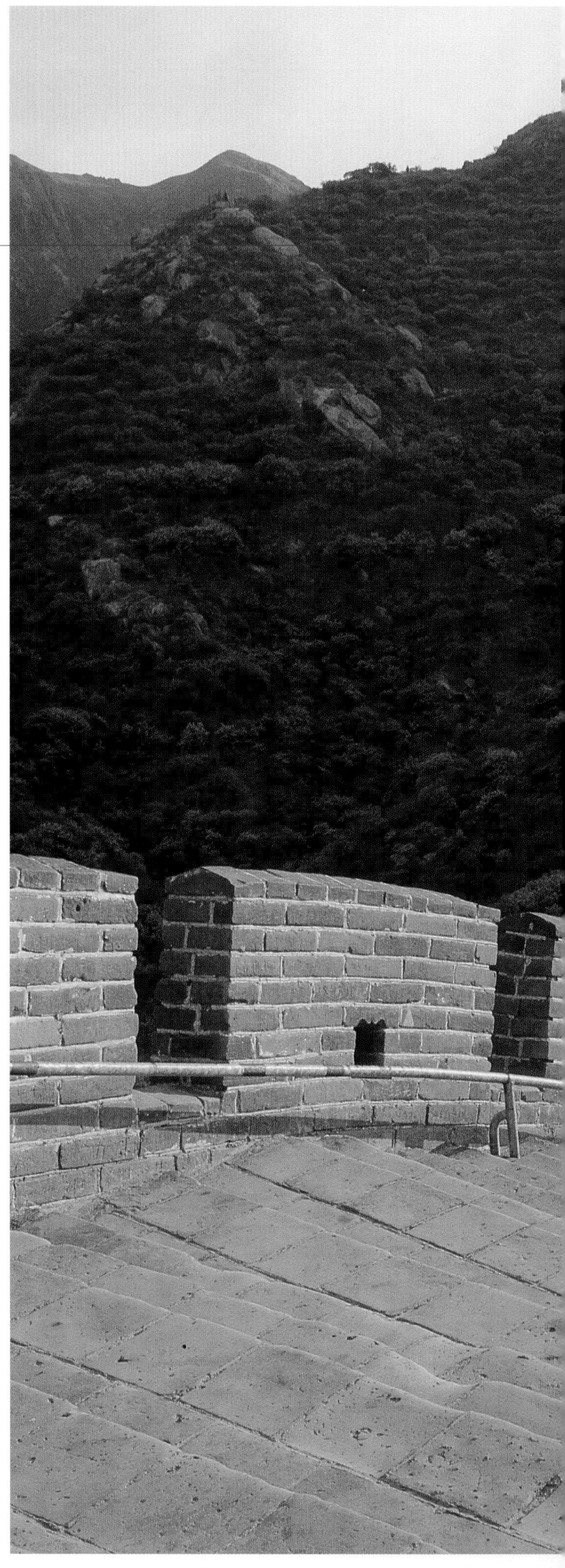

THE GREAT WALL OF CHINA achieved its final form in the 17th century but had been built up over two thousand years to prserve the civilization of China from nomadsfrom the north. Despite the vast effort of building and manning the wall, the real threat to Manchu China would come in future from European ships, and not from nomads on horseback.

European maritime control also had demographic consequences across the globe. It made possible a major migration of Europeans and another – involuntary – of African slaves to the New World, and permanently altered the demography of the latter continent. The European population expanded in the sixteenth century, and, after a period of protracted stagnation, from the 1740s. This growth provided the people both to settle Pennsylvania and to move the frontier of settled agriculture south across the Russian steppes.

The theme of European expansion might sometimes appear exaggerated. Much of the world had never seen a European. European maps of central Asia or of inland Africa were either blanks or full of errors. To talk of European power would have seemed curious in Tibet, conquered by China in 1720, in Mombasa, whence the Omani Arabs expelled the Portuguese in 1698, or on the west coast of Africa where the kingdom of Dahomey dominated European coastal trading posts from the 1720s.

Yet, however limited their political or military impact in some areas, Europeans were to be found off the coast of Asia, not Asians off that of Europe. It was Europeans who charted the oceans, who explored their dark side of the world – the Pacific – and thus acquired the knowledge that helped them to profit from their strength. The world was increasingly renamed by the Europeans, its spaces organized in and by their maps. European products became sought-after, and European selfconfidence enhanced. Many consequences of European ambition were unattractive, most obviously the slave trade, though even this reflected the crucial European ability to plan and execute long-range economic exchanges. Today we can consider the rise of Europe without applauding its consequences. Yet it is difficult to challenge its importance. This was the era when Europeans remolded the world, creating new political, economic, demographic, religious and cultural spaces and forging links between different regions that still affect the world in which we live ■

4.01 THE WORLD • AD 1530 •

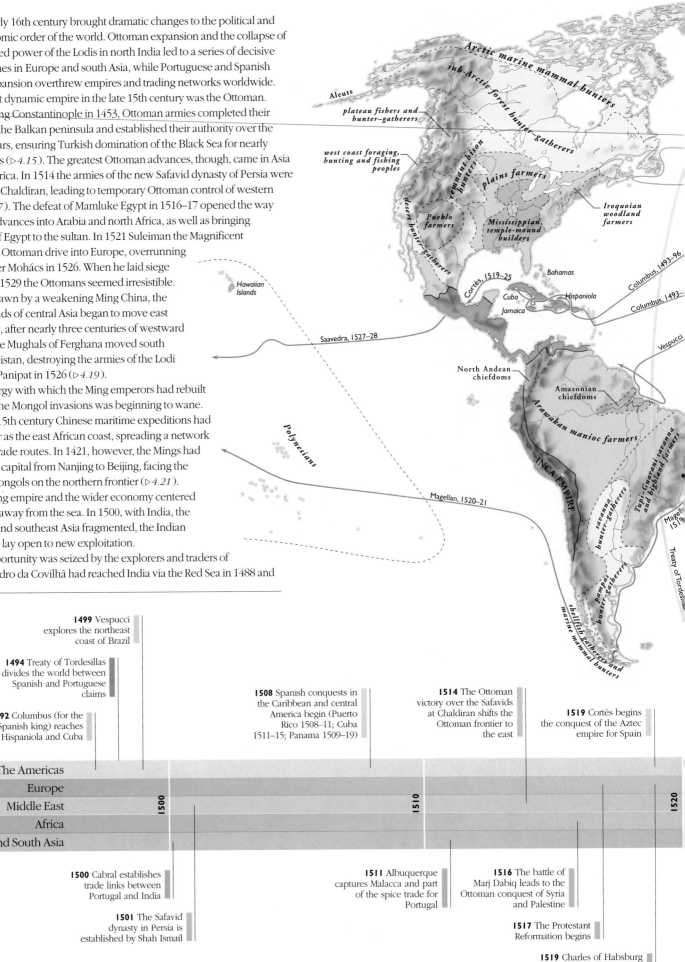

The early 16th century brought dramatic changes to the political and economic order of the world. Ottoman expansion and the collapse of the established power of the Lodis in north India led to a series of decisive military clashes in Europe and south Asia, while Portuguese and Spanish maritime expansion overthrew empires and trading networks worldwide.

The most dynamic empire in the late 15th century was the Ottoman. After capturing Constantinople in 1453, Ottoman armies completed their conquest of the Balkan peninsula and established their authority over the Crimean Tatars, ensuring Turkish domination of the Black Sea for nearly two centuries (▷*4.15*). The greatest Ottoman advances, though, came in Asia and north Africa. In 1514 the armies of the new Safavid dynasty of Persia were destroyed at Chaldiran, leading to temporary Ottoman control of western Persia (▷*4.17*). The defeat of Mamluke Egypt in 1516–17 opened the way for further advances into Arabia and north Africa, as well as bringing the wealth of Egypt to the sultan. In 1521 Suleiman the Magnificent resumed the Ottoman drive into Europe, overrunning Hungary after Mohács in 1526. When he laid siege to Vienna in 1529 the Ottomans seemed irresistible.

Partly drawn by a weakening Ming China, the Turkic nomads of central Asia began to move east around 1500, after nearly three centuries of westward pressure. The Mughals of Ferghana moved south from Afghanistan, destroying the armies of the Lodi sultanate at Panipat in 1526 (▷*4.19*).

The energy with which the Ming emperors had rebuilt China after the Mongol invasions was beginning to wane. In the early 15th century Chinese maritime expeditions had ranged as far as the east African coast, spreading a network of Chinese trade routes. In 1421, however, the Mings had moved their capital from Nanjing to Beijing, facing the resurgent Mongols on the northern frontier (▷*4.21*). Both the Ming empire and the wider economy centered on it turned away from the sea. In 1500, with India, the East Indies and southeast Asia fragmented, the Indian Ocean trade lay open to new exploitation.

The opportunity was seized by the explorers and traders of Portugal. Pedro da Covilhã had reached India via the Red Sea in 1488 and

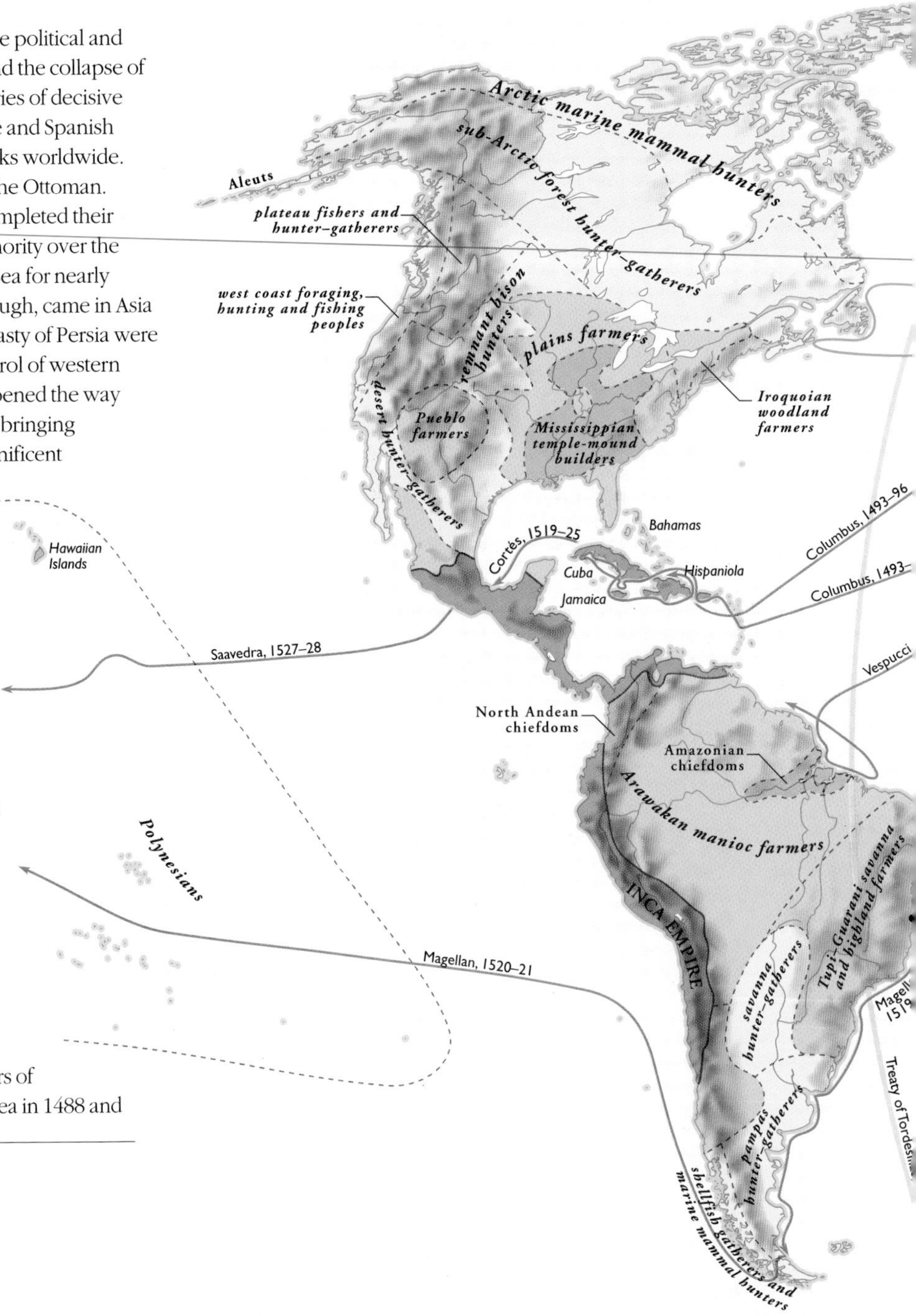

Arctic marine mammal hunters
sub-Arctic forest hunter-gatherers
Aleuts
plateau fishers and hunter-gatherers
west coast foraging, hunting and fishing peoples
remnant bison hunters
plains farmers
Iroquoian woodland farmers
desert hunter-gatherers
Pueblo farmers
Mississippian temple-mound builders
Hawaiian Islands
Bahamas
Cortés, 1519–25
Cuba
Hispaniola
Jamaica
Columbus, 1493–96
Columbus, 1493–
Saavedra, 1527–28
Vespucci
North Andean chiefdoms
Amazonian chiefdoms
Arawakan manioc farmers
Polynesians
INCA EMPIRE
Tupi-Guarani savanna and highland farmers
savanna hunter-gatherers
Magellan, 1520–21
Treaty of Tordesillas
pampas hunter-gatherers
shellfish gatherers and marine mammal hunters

TIMELINE

Rows: The Americas | Europe | Middle East | Africa | East and South Asia — 1500 | 1510 | 1520

1492 Columbus (for the Spanish king) reaches Hispaniola and Cuba

1494 Treaty of Tordesillas divides the world between Spanish and Portuguese claims

1499 Vespucci explores the northeast coast of Brazil

1500 Cabral establishes trade links between Portugal and India

1501 The Safavid dynasty in Persia is established by Shah Ismail

1508 Spanish conquests in the Caribbean and central America begin (Puerto Rico 1508–11; Cuba 1511–15; Panama 1509–19)

1511 Albuquerque captures Malacca and part of the spice trade for Portugal

1514 The Ottoman victory over the Safavids at Chaldiran shifts the Ottoman frontier to the east

1516 The battle of Marj Dabiq leads to the Ottoman conquest of Syria and Palestine

1517 The Protestant Reformation begins

1519 Cortés begins the conquest of the Aztec empire for Spain

1519 Charles of Habsburg is elected Charles V, Holy Roman emperor

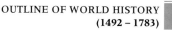

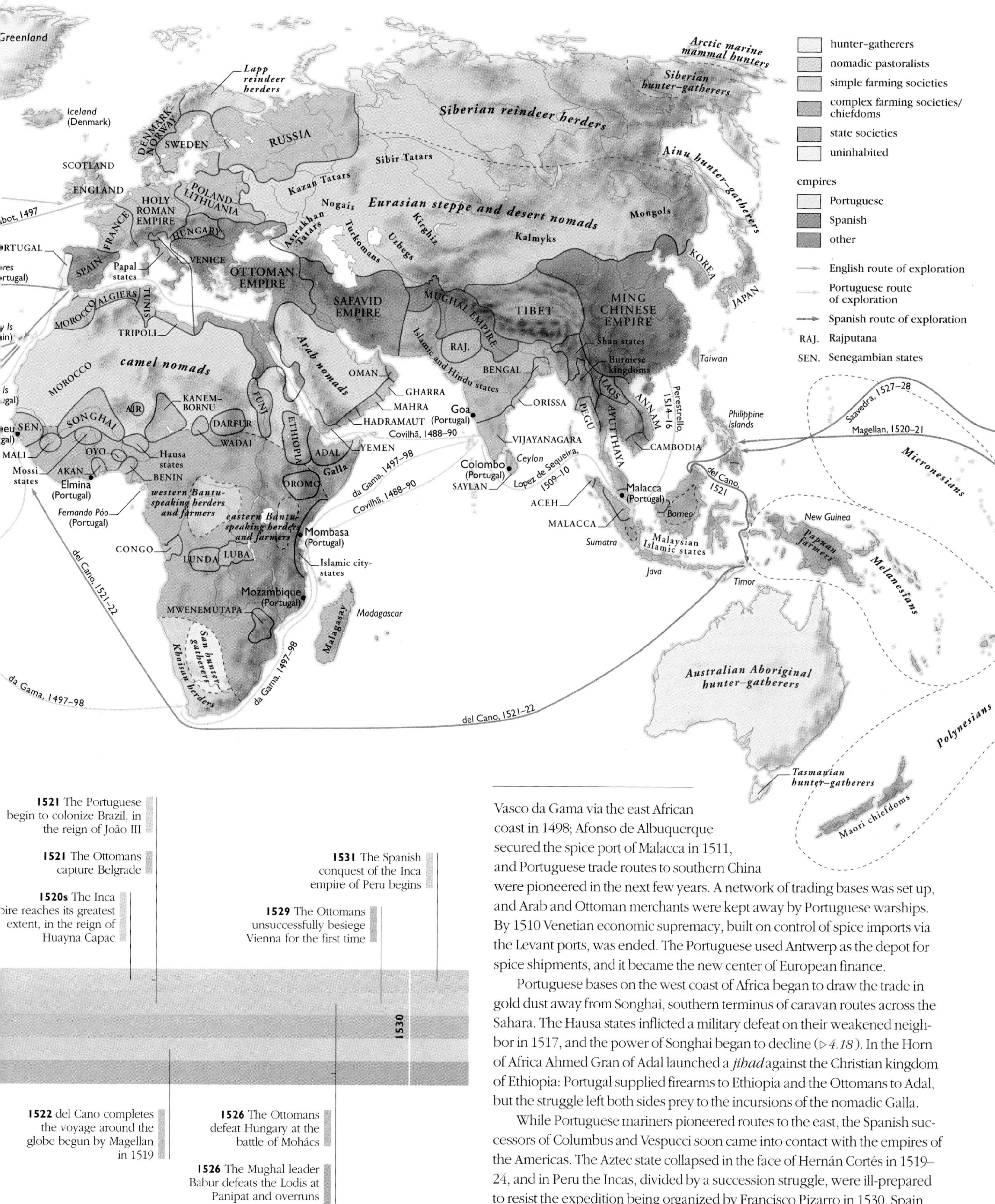
hunter-gatherers
nomadic pastoralists
simple farming societies
complex farming societies/ chiefdoms
state societies
uninhabited
empires
Portuguese
Spanish
other
English route of exploration
Portuguese route of exploration
Spanish route of exploration
RAJ. Rajputana
SEN. Senegambian states
Greenland
Iceland (Denmark)
Lapp reindeer herders
Arctic marine mammal hunters
Siberian hunter-gatherers
Siberian reindeer herders
Ainu hunter-gatherers
DENMARK-NORWAY
SWEDEN
RUSSIA
SCOTLAND
ENGLAND
Sibir Tatars
Kazan Tatars
POLAND-LITHUANIA
HOLY ROMAN EMPIRE
Nogais
Eurasian steppe and desert nomads
Mongols
Astrakhan Tatars
Turkomans
Kirghiz
Uzbegs
Kalmyks
FRANCE
HUNGARY
VENICE
SPAIN
Papal states
OTTOMAN EMPIRE
SAFAVID EMPIRE
MUGHAL EMPIRE
TIBET
MING CHINESE EMPIRE
KOREA
JAPAN
ALGIERS
TUNIS
MOROCCO
TRIPOLI
Arab nomads
Islamic and Hindu states
RAJ.
Shan states
Burmese kingdoms
Taiwan
camel nomads
OMAN
BENGAL
GHARRA
MAHRA
HADRAMAUT
Goa (Portugal)
ORISSA
PEGU
LAOS
ANNAM
Perestrello, 1514–16
Philippine Islands
Saavedra, 1527–28
Magellan, 1520–21
Micronesians
KANEM-BORNU
AIR
SONGHAI
DARFUR
WADAI
FUNJ
ETHIOPIA
Covilhã, 1488–90
YEMEN
VIJAYANAGARA
AYUTTHAYA
CAMBODIA
SEN.
MALI
Mossi states
OYO
Hausa states
AKAN
Elmina (Portugal)
BENIN
ADAL
Galla
OROMO
da Gama, 1497–98
Colombo (Portugal)
SAYLAN
Ceylon
Lopez de Sequeira, 1509–10
ACEH
Malacca (Portugal)
del Cano, 1521
Borneo
New Guinea
Papuan farmers
Fernando Póo (Portugal)
western Bantu-speaking herders and farmers
eastern Bantu-speaking herders and farmers
Mombasa (Portugal)
MALACCA
Sumatra
Malaysian Islamic states
Java
Melanesians
CONGO
LUNDA
LUBA
Islamic city-states
Timor
del Cano, 1521–22
Mozambique (Portugal)
MWENEMUTAPA
Madagascar
Malagasay
San hunter-gatherers
Khoisan herders
Australian Aboriginal hunter-gatherers
da Gama, 1497–98
del Cano, 1521–22
Polynesians
Tasmanian hunter-gatherers
Maori chiefdoms
1530

1521 The Portuguese begin to colonize Brazil, in the reign of João III

1521 The Ottomans capture Belgrade

1520s The Inca empire reaches its greatest extent, in the reign of Huayna Capac

1531 The Spanish conquest of the Inca empire of Peru begins

1529 The Ottomans unsuccessfully besiege Vienna for the first time

1522 del Cano completes the voyage around the globe begun by Magellan in 1519

1526 The Ottomans defeat Hungary at the battle of Mohács

1526 The Mughal leader Babur defeats the Lodis at Panipat and overruns northern India

Vasco da Gama via the east African coast in 1498; Afonso de Albuquerque secured the spice port of Malacca in 1511, and Portuguese trade routes to southern China were pioneered in the next few years. A network of trading bases was set up, and Arab and Ottoman merchants were kept away by Portuguese warships. By 1510 Venetian economic supremacy, built on control of spice imports via the Levant ports, was ended. The Portuguese used Antwerp as the depot for spice shipments, and it became the new center of European finance.

Portuguese bases on the west coast of Africa began to draw the trade in gold dust away from Songhai, southern terminus of caravan routes across the Sahara. The Hausa states inflicted a military defeat on their weakened neighbor in 1517, and the power of Songhai began to decline (▷*4.18*). In the Horn of Africa Ahmed Gran of Adal launched a *jihad* against the Christian kingdom of Ethiopia: Portugal supplied firearms to Ethiopia and the Ottomans to Adal, but the struggle left both sides prey to the incursions of the nomadic Galla.

While Portuguese mariners pioneered routes to the east, the Spanish successors of Columbus and Vespucci soon came into contact with the empires of the Americas. The Aztec state collapsed in the face of Hernán Cortés in 1519–24, and in Peru the Incas, divided by a succession struggle, were ill-prepared to resist the expedition being organized by Francisco Pizarro in 1530. Spain was on the verge of a huge territorial expansion, and about to tap a source of silver that would drive the world's economy for over a century (▷*4.25*) ■

4.02 THE WORLD • AD 1600 •

By 1600, Europe and Asia had enjoyed a century of population growth. European prosperity was matched by a rise in living conditions in Asia, India and the Middle East. African populations and material conditions stayed stable, but in the Americas the Europeans brought demographic catastrophe.

Spanish and Portuguese penetration of the Americas was slow after the collapse of the Inca empire: beyond the highly-organized Inca and Aztec states, populations were sparse, distances huge and political structures lacking, and the conquistadors had little incentive to explore. Instead they exploited their conquests (▷*4.25*). In 1545 production began at the rich mines of Potosí; silver was shipped to Seville and spread through Europe, as the Genoese backers of Spain's voyages multiplied its value by sophisticated credit mechanisms. Spanish silver was also used by Europe's merchants to buy into other trading networks around the world. Antwerp's reign as financial capital of Europe had ended by 1576 when it was sacked by Spanish mutineers: from 1557 Genoa called the tune in Europe's economy (▷*4.12*).

Spanish political and military power reached its peak in the 1580s when Philip II seized the crown of Portugal. For sixty years the two crowns were united, although Portuguese overseas possessions were still administered from Lisbon. As the Netherlands began a campaign of conquest against the Portuguese trading bases worldwide, Portuguese power in Asia declined.

European politics spilled over into the Spanish empire. Dutch and English pirates raided the Spanish–American cities and attempted to seize bullion fleets. French Huguenot (Protestant) colonists reached Florida and the mouth of the Amazon: they were driven from the former by Spanish forces, but the Portuguese could not dislodge them from the latter for over a century. French explorers such as Jacques Cartier penetrated North America via the St Lawrence river, while the Spaniard Francisco Coronado pioneered routes north from Mexico (▷*4.26*).

In Africa, the Ottomans steadily reduced the Spanish footholds in North Africa, while Morocco's stunning defeat of a major Portuguese expedition at Alcazarquivir in 1578 led directly to the union of Portugal with Spain. The Moroccans then mounted an even more spectacular expedition across the Sahara in 1590–91 to overthrow the weakened Songhai empire at Tondibi. In sub-Saharan Africa, the Muslim empire of Kanem-Bornu emerged as the most

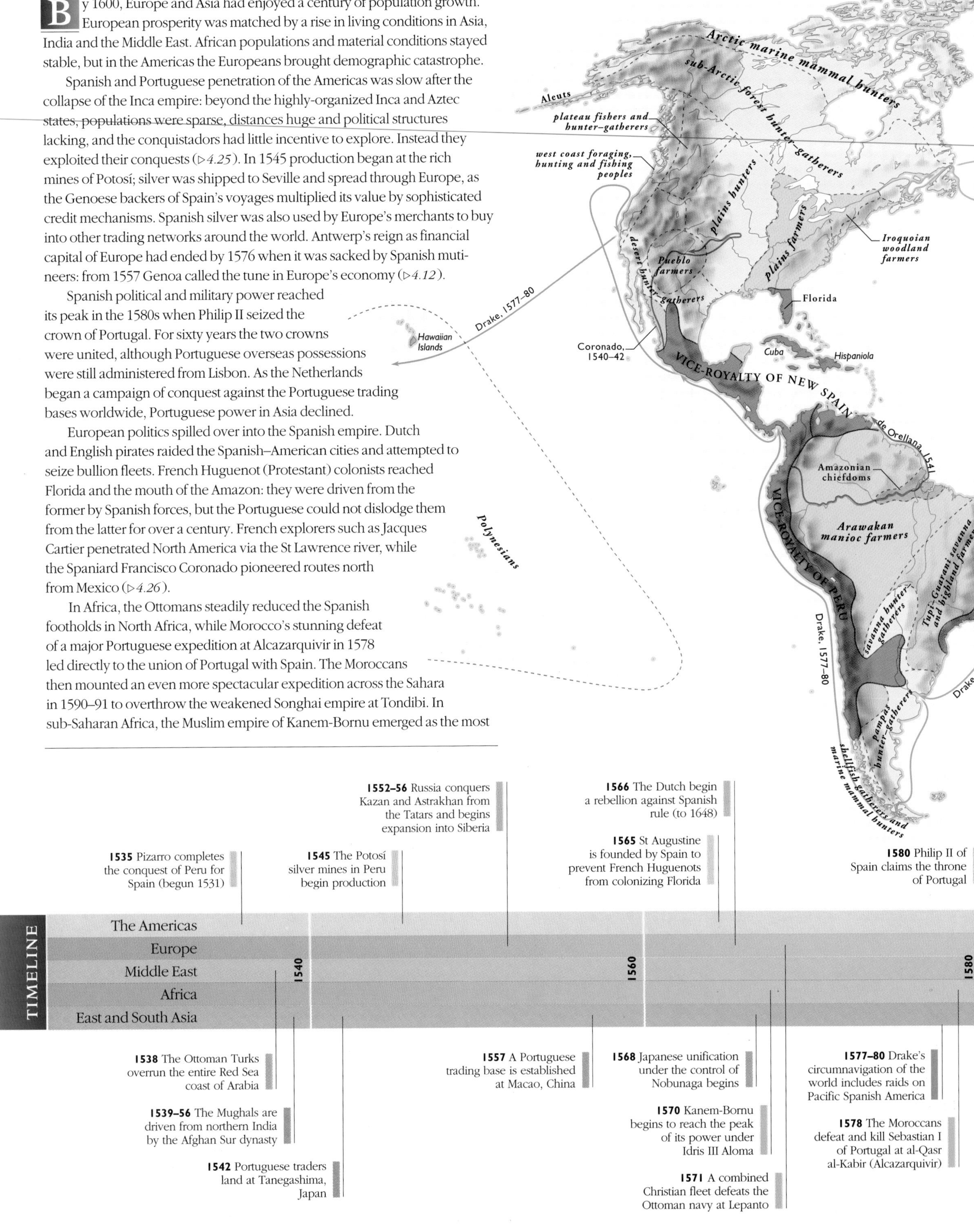

Arctic marine mammal hunters
sub-Arctic forest hunter-gatherers
Aleuts
plateau fishers and hunter-gatherers
west coast foraging, hunting and fishing peoples
plains hunters
plains farmers
Iroquoian woodland farmers
desert hunter-gatherers
Pueblo farmers
Florida
Drake, 1577–80
Hawaiian Islands
Coronado, 1540–42
Cuba
Hispaniola
VICE-ROYALTY OF NEW SPAIN
de Orellana, 1541
Amazonian chiefdoms
Arawakan manioc farmers
VICE-ROYALTY OF PERU
Tupi-Guarani savanna and highland farmers
savanna hunter-gatherers
Polynesians
pampas hunter-gatherers
shellfish gatherers and marine mammal hunters

TIMELINE

The Americas / Europe / Middle East / Africa / East and South Asia

1540 · 1560 · 1580

1535 Pizarro completes the conquest of Peru for Spain (begun 1531)

1538 The Ottoman Turks overrun the entire Red Sea coast of Arabia

1539–56 The Mughals are driven from northern India by the Afghan Sur dynasty

1542 Portuguese traders land at Tanegashima, Japan

1545 The Potosí silver mines in Peru begin production

1552–56 Russia conquers Kazan and Astrakhan from the Tatars and begins expansion into Siberia

1557 A Portuguese trading base is established at Macao, China

1565 St Augustine is founded by Spain to prevent French Huguenots from colonizing Florida

1566 The Dutch begin a rebellion against Spanish rule (to 1648)

1568 Japanese unification under the control of Nobunaga begins

1570 Kanem-Bornu begins to reach the peak of its power under Idris III Aloma

1571 A combined Christian fleet defeats the Ottoman navy at Lepanto

1577–80 Drake's circumnavigation of the world includes raids on Pacific Spanish America

1578 The Moroccans defeat and kill Sebastian I of Portugal at al-Qasr al-Kabir (Alcazarquivir)

1580 Philip II of Spain claims the throne of Portugal

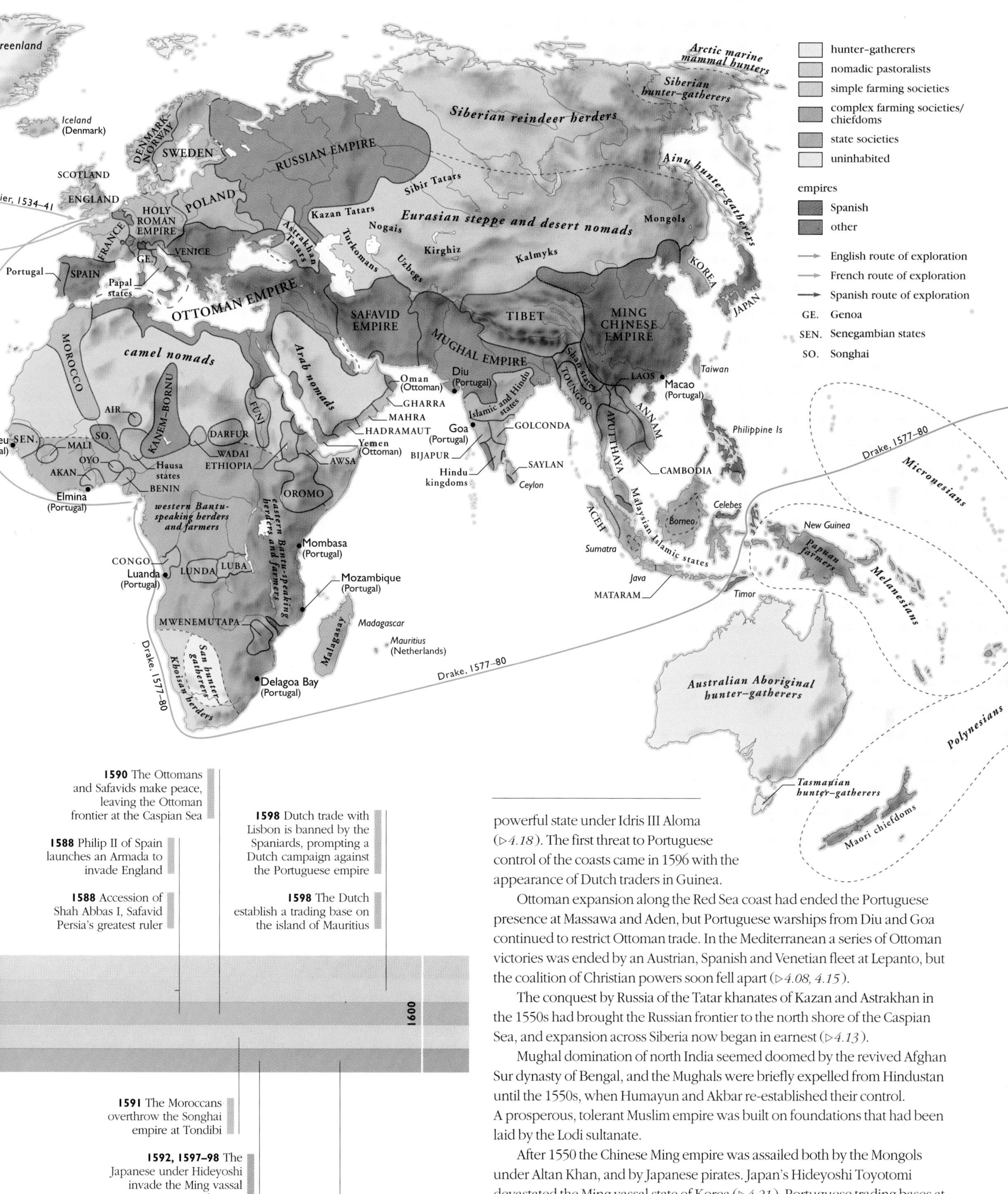
hunter-gatherers
nomadic pastoralists
simple farming societies
complex farming societies/ chiefdoms
state societies
uninhabited
empires
Spanish
other
English route of exploration
French route of exploration
Spanish route of exploration
GE. Genoa
SEN. Senegambian states
SO. Songhai
Greenland
Iceland (Denmark)
SCOTLAND
ENGLAND
DENMARK-NORWAY
SWEDEN
RUSSIAN EMPIRE
POLAND
HOLY ROMAN EMPIRE
FRANCE
GE.
VENICE
Portugal
SPAIN
Papal states
OTTOMAN EMPIRE
Astrakhan Tatars
Kazan Tatars
Sibir Tatars
Nogais
Turkomans
Uzbegs
Kirghiz
Kalmyks
Eurasian steppe and desert nomads
Mongols
Siberian reindeer herders
Arctic marine mammal hunters
Siberian hunter-gatherers
Ainu hunter-gatherers
KOREA
JAPAN
SAFAVID EMPIRE
TIBET
MING CHINESE EMPIRE
MUGHAL EMPIRE
Shan states
TOUNGOO
LAOS
ANNAM
AYUTTHAYA
CAMBODIA
Taiwan
Macao (Portugal)
Philippine Is
Oman (Ottoman)
Diu (Portugal)
Islamic and Hindu states
GHARRA
MAHRA
HADRAMAUT
Yemen (Ottoman)
Goa (Portugal)
GOLCONDA
BIJAPUR
Hindu kingdoms
SAYLAN
Ceylon
Arab nomads
MOROCCO
camel nomads
AIR
KANEM-BORNU
FUNJ
DARFUR
WADAI
ETHIOPIA
AWSA
SEN.
MALI
SO.
OYO
AKAN
Hausa states
BENIN
Elmina (Portugal)
OROMO
western Bantu-speaking herders and farmers
eastern Bantu-speaking herders and farmers
Mombasa (Portugal)
CONGO
Luanda (Portugal)
LUNDA
LUBA
Mozambique (Portugal)
Madagascar
Malagasy
Mauritius (Netherlands)
MWENEMUTAPA
San hunter-gatherers
Khoisan herders
Delagoa Bay (Portugal)
Drake, 1577–80
ACEH
Malaysian Islamic states
Sumatra
Borneo
Celebes
Java
MATARAM
Timor
New Guinea
Papuan farmers
Melanesians
Micronesians
Polynesians
Australian Aboriginal hunter-gatherers
Tasmanian hunter-gatherers
Maori chiefdoms

1590 The Ottomans and Safavids make peace, leaving the Ottoman frontier at the Caspian Sea

1588 Philip II of Spain launches an Armada to invade England

1588 Accession of Shah Abbas I, Safavid Persia's greatest ruler

1598 Dutch trade with Lisbon is banned by the Spaniards, prompting a Dutch campaign against the Portuguese empire

1598 The Dutch establish a trading base on the island of Mauritius

1600

1591 The Moroccans overthrow the Songhai empire at Tondibi

1592, 1597–98 The Japanese under Hideyoshi invade the Ming vassal state of Korea

1596 The first Dutch trading expedition reaches the East Indies

powerful state under Idris III Aloma (▷*4.18*). The first threat to Portuguese control of the coasts came in 1596 with the appearance of Dutch traders in Guinea.

Ottoman expansion along the Red Sea coast had ended the Portuguese presence at Massawa and Aden, but Portuguese warships from Diu and Goa continued to restrict Ottoman trade. In the Mediterranean a series of Ottoman victories was ended by an Austrian, Spanish and Venetian fleet at Lepanto, but the coalition of Christian powers soon fell apart (▷*4.08, 4.15*).

The conquest by Russia of the Tatar khanates of Kazan and Astrakhan in the 1550s had brought the Russian frontier to the north shore of the Caspian Sea, and expansion across Siberia now began in earnest (▷*4.13*).

Mughal domination of north India seemed doomed by the revived Afghan Sur dynasty of Bengal, and the Mughals were briefly expelled from Hindustan until the 1550s, when Humayun and Akbar re-established their control. A prosperous, tolerant Muslim empire was built on foundations that had been laid by the Lodi sultanate.

After 1550 the Chinese Ming empire was assailed both by the Mongols under Altan Khan, and by Japanese pirates. Japan's Hideyoshi Toyotomi devastated the Ming vassal state of Korea (▷*4.21*). Portuguese trading bases at Macao and in Japan brought the European and Asian economies into direct contact, but, with traditional suspicion of outsiders, both China and Japan acted to keep the European traders under close control (▷*4.23*) ■

4.03 THE WORLD • AD 1650 •

The first half of the 17th century saw a downturn in material conditions in Eurasia so widespread that many historians consider a global climatic change to be the only sufficient explanation. The population growth of the 16th century was sharply reversed amid widespread famine, plague and warfare. Even Europe's exploration of the wider world came to a halt, with the exception of Tasman's voyage to Australia and New Zealand.

All the great empires were shaken, but the greatest casualty of the "crisis of the 17th century" was Ming China, in 1600 still the most powerful in the world (▷ *4.21*). Mongol and Japanese attacks at the end of the 16th century added to taxation and economic pressures, and from the 1620s peasant revolts and military rebellions threatened the dynasty. In 1644 it was swept away by a nomad people from the north, the Manchus, and by 1650 northern and central China were under Manchu control (▷ *4.22*).

Although Shah Jahan extended Mughal territory in mid-century, religious intolerance and political instability grew rapidly in his reign (▷ *4.20*). Safavid Persia had enjoyed a period of prosperity under Shah Abbas I, but after 1629 the Ottomans retook Mesopotamia and the Safavid empire began to decline rapidly (▷ *4.17*). The Ottoman empire itself was shaken by a series of revolts during the reign of Murad IV, and made little progress in wars with Austria and Venice (▷ *4.16*).

Russia fell into renewed chaos during the early 17th century, with civil strife and military intervention by Poland and Sweden. Russian merchants spread through Siberia, creating an empire tyrannized by its own vast size, but the Russian sphere of influence remained open to exploitation by traders from both Europe and Asia (▷ *4.13*).

In Europe, the tensions of the Protestant Reformation had already brought widespread bloodshed to France, Germany and the Netherlands, and several other regions. The outbreak of the Thirty Years War in 1618, however, devastated much of Europe. Contemporaries were horrified at the scale of destruction. The predominance of Spain was ended, and the Holy Roman empire was torn apart (▷ *4.10*). There were few winners on the Protestant side either: the German Protestant states were ruined, and their backers Denmark and Sweden were exhausted by their military efforts.

The only states to emerge strengthened from the war were France (by its victories over its rivals, the Habsburgs) and the United Provinces

Arctic marine mammal hunters
sub-Arctic forest hunter-gatherers
plateau fishers and hunter-gatherers
west coast foraging, hunting and fishing peoples
desert hunter-gatherers
plains hunters
Iroquoian woodland farmers
Acadia
New France
Massachusetts Bay
New Amsterdam
Virginia
plains farmers
Pueblo farmers
Florida
Bahamas
Hawaiian Islands
Cuba
Belize
Hispaniola
Puerto Rico
Jamaica
VICE-ROYALTY OF NEW SPAIN
Essequibo
Surinam
Cayenne
Amazonian chiefdoms
Dutch 1642/54
Polynesians
Arawakan manioc farmers
Tupi-Guarani savanna and highland farmers
VICE-ROYALTY OF PERU
Portuguese
savanna hunter-gatherers
pampas hunter-gatherers
shellfish gatherers and marine mammal hunters

TIMELINE

The Americas
Europe
Middle East
Africa
East and South Asia

1600

1600 The English East India Company is established; the Dutch East India Company is set up two years later

1602–18 Ottomans lose Azerbaijan, Georgia and, temporarily, Baghdad and Mosul in a war with Persia

1603 Foundation of the Tokugawa shogunate in Japan, with its capital at Edo (Tokyo)

1604–13 The "Time of Troubles" brings political chaos to Russia

1608 French settlers found the colony at Quebec

1609 The Netherlands agree a 12-year truce in their rebellion against Spain

1610

1611 The accession of Gustavus II Adolphus begins Sweden's great power period

1615 The Manchus unite under Nurhachi and begin the conquest of the ailing Ming empire

1618 Outbreak of the Thirty Years War, which engulfs much of Europe and severely weakens Spanish power

1619 The Dutch build a trading post and headquarters of the Dutch East India Company at Batavia

1620

1620 English colonists (the "Pilgrims") arrive at Cape Cod, Massachusetts

1622 English merchants and Persian troops take Hormuz from the Portuguese

1623 The Dutch destroy the English base at Amboina and end English trade in the East Indies, Ayutthaya and Japan

1625 The first French settlements in the Caribbean are founded

1626 The Dutch found the colony of New Amsterdam (New York)

1629 The accession of Shah Safi marks the beginning of Safavid decline

1630

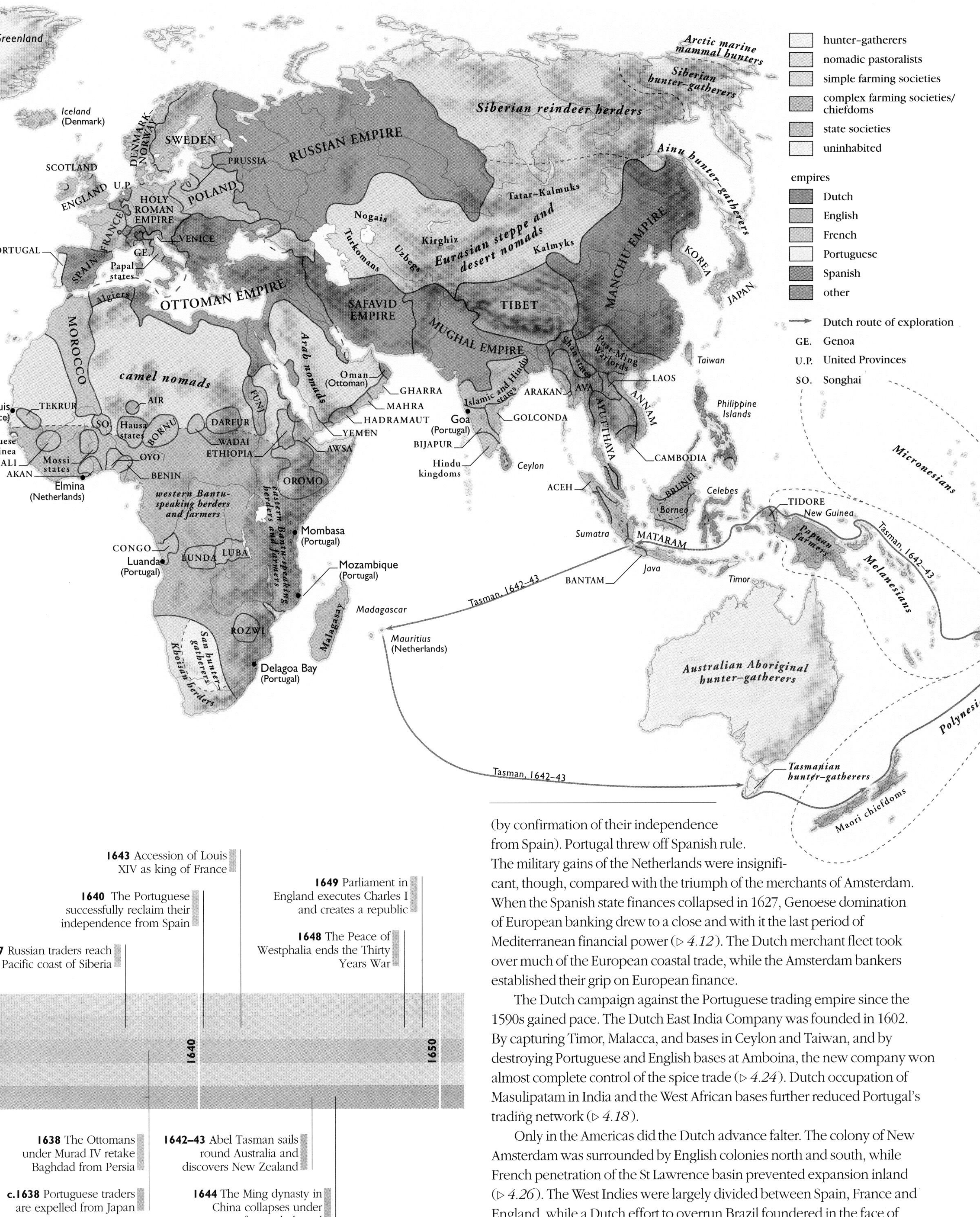
Greenland
Iceland (Denmark)
SCOTLAND
ENGLAND
U.P.
DENMARK-NORWAY
SWEDEN
PRUSSIA
POLAND
RUSSIAN EMPIRE
HOLY ROMAN EMPIRE
FRANCE
PORTUGAL
SPAIN
GE.
VENICE
Papal states
Algiers
OTTOMAN EMPIRE
MOROCCO
camel nomads
TEKRUR
SO.
AIR
Hausa states
BORNU
DARFUR
WADAI
FUNJ
ETHIOPIA
Mossi states
OYO
BENIN
AKAN
Elmina (Netherlands)
OROMO
western Bantu-speaking herders and farmers
eastern Bantu-speaking herders and farmers
CONGO
Luanda (Portugal)
LUNDA
LUBA
Mombasa (Portugal)
Mozambique (Portugal)
ROZWI
San hunter-gatherers
Khoisan herders
Delagoa Bay (Portugal)
Malagasy
Madagascar
Mauritius (Netherlands)
Arab nomads
Oman (Ottoman)
GHARRA
MAHRA
HADRAMAUT
YEMEN
AWSA
Nogais
Turkomans
Uzbegs
Kirghiz
Eurasian steppe and desert nomads
Kalmyks
Tatar-Kalmuks
SAFAVID EMPIRE
MUGHAL EMPIRE
TIBET
Islamic and Hindu states
Goa (Portugal)
BIJAPUR
GOLCONDA
Hindu kingdoms
Ceylon
ARAKAN
AVA
Shan states
Post-Ming Warlords
LAOS
ANNAM
AYUTTHAYA
CAMBODIA
ACEH
Sumatra
MATARAM
BANTAM
Java
BRUNEI
Borneo
Celebes
Timor
TIDORE
New Guinea
Papuan farmers
Melanesians
Micronesians
Polynesians
Philippine Islands
Taiwan
MANCHU EMPIRE
KOREA
JAPAN
Ainu hunter-gatherers
Siberian reindeer herders
Siberian hunter-gatherers
Arctic marine mammal hunters
Australian Aboriginal hunter-gatherers
Tasmanian hunter-gatherers
Maori chiefdoms
Tasman, 1642–43
hunter-gatherers
nomadic pastoralists
simple farming societies
complex farming societies/ chiefdoms
state societies
uninhabited
empires
Dutch
English
French
Portuguese
Spanish
other
Dutch route of exploration
GE. Genoa
U.P. United Provinces
SO. Songhai
1640
1650

1643 Accession of Louis XIV as king of France

1640 The Portuguese successfully reclaim their independence from Spain

7 Russian traders reach Pacific coast of Siberia

1649 Parliament in England executes Charles I and creates a republic

1648 The Peace of Westphalia ends the Thirty Years War

1638 The Ottomans under Murad IV retake Baghdad from Persia

c.1638 Portuguese traders are expelled from Japan

1642–43 Abel Tasman sails round Australia and discovers New Zealand

1644 The Ming dynasty in China collapses under pressure from rebels and the Qing (Manchus)

(by confirmation of their independence from Spain). Portugal threw off Spanish rule. The military gains of the Netherlands were insignificant, though, compared with the triumph of the merchants of Amsterdam. When the Spanish state finances collapsed in 1627, Genoese domination of European banking drew to a close and with it the last period of Mediterranean financial power (▷ *4.12*). The Dutch merchant fleet took over much of the European coastal trade, while the Amsterdam bankers established their grip on European finance.

The Dutch campaign against the Portuguese trading empire since the 1590s gained pace. The Dutch East India Company was founded in 1602. By capturing Timor, Malacca, and bases in Ceylon and Taiwan, and by destroying Portuguese and English bases at Amboina, the new company won almost complete control of the spice trade (▷ *4.24*). Dutch occupation of Masulipatam in India and the West African bases further reduced Portugal's trading network (▷ *4.18*).

Only in the Americas did the Dutch advance falter. The colony of New Amsterdam was surrounded by English colonies north and south, while French penetration of the St Lawrence basin prevented expansion inland (▷ *4.26*). The West Indies were largely divided between Spain, France and England, while a Dutch effort to overrun Brazil foundered in the face of guerrilla warfare by the Portuguese (▷ *4.25*) ■

The global demographic crisis became less severe after about 1670. The bubonic plague which had appeared in India in 1616 and Turkey in 1661 spread as far as London by 1665, then declined – one of the last great plagues in Eurasian history. A great famine of 1709 also proved to be Europe's last. In Asia, the population of China reached 100 million by 1650, and began to expand at a rate that would take it to nearly 300 million by 1800.

Dutch domination of European worldwide trade survived three damaging wars with England. France under Louis XIV, though, was Europe's greatest power, its population in 1700 as large as that of the Spanish and Austrian Habsburg lands combined (▷ *4.11*). But Louis XIV failed to break the hold of the Amsterdam bankers on French trade, revealing the enduring financial power of the last great European city-state.

Dutch might was built on control of trade within Europe, but trade with the rest of the world also grew. As silver production in Spanish America fluctuated and Asia's demand for silver was partially assuaged, the Dutch took over the Asian coastal trade. Bills of exchange from Amsterdam underpinned credit transactions worldwide.

The rise of France pursuing a consistently anti-Habsburg policy upset the balance between Austria and Turkey in the Balkans. After a near-disastrous campaign against Crete (1645–69), Ottoman reforms led to a new, though unsuccessful, siege of Vienna (1683). This, however, was followed by a Russian and Austrian onslaught on Ottoman territory, while in Africa the corsair rulers of Algiers confirmed their independence (▷ *4.16*). After taking Azov from the Turks in 1696, Peter the Great of Russia embarked on war with Sweden: his victory at Poltava marked the end of Sweden's dominance of northern Europe and Russia's rise to the status of great power (▷ *4.09, 4.13*).

The campaigns of Aurangzeb against the Hindu Marathas extended Mughal frontiers into the Deccan, but his empire began to fall apart on his death in 1707. By 1715 the Marathas were the most powerful of the successor states within the empire's nominal borders. The foundation of British trading bases at Bombay and Calcutta, and French at Pondicherry, however, established both Britain and France as future players in Indian affairs (▷ *4.20*).

Manchu control over southern China was finallyconfirmed. The Ming warlord Zheng Cheng-gong had driven the Dutch from Taiwan in 1661–62,

Arctic marine mammal hunters
sub-Arctic forest hunter-gatherers
plateau fishers and hunter-gatherers
Rupert's Land
New France
Newfou
west coast foraging, hunting and fishing peoples
Iroquoian woodland farmers
plains hunters
Nova Scotia
desert hunter-gatherers
Pueblo farmers
plains farmers
British American colonies
Louisiana
South Carolina
Florida
Bahamas
Hawaiian Islands
Cuba
Saint-Domingue
Belize
Hispaniola
Jamaica
VICE-ROYALTY OF NEW SPAIN
Mosquito Coast
Guyana
Cayenne
Arawakan manioc farmers
Polynesians
VICE-ROYALTY OF PERU
Tupi-Guarani savanna and highland farmers
VICE-ROYALTY OF BRAZIL
savanna hunter-gatherers
pampas hunter-gatherers
shellfish gatherers and marine mammal hunters

TIMELINE

The Americas
Europe
Middle East
Africa
East and South Asia

1650 · 1670 · 1690

1636 The Mughals begin to expand into the Deccan

1643 Louis XIV succeeds to the French throne (to 1715)

1652 Cape Town is founded by Dutch settlers

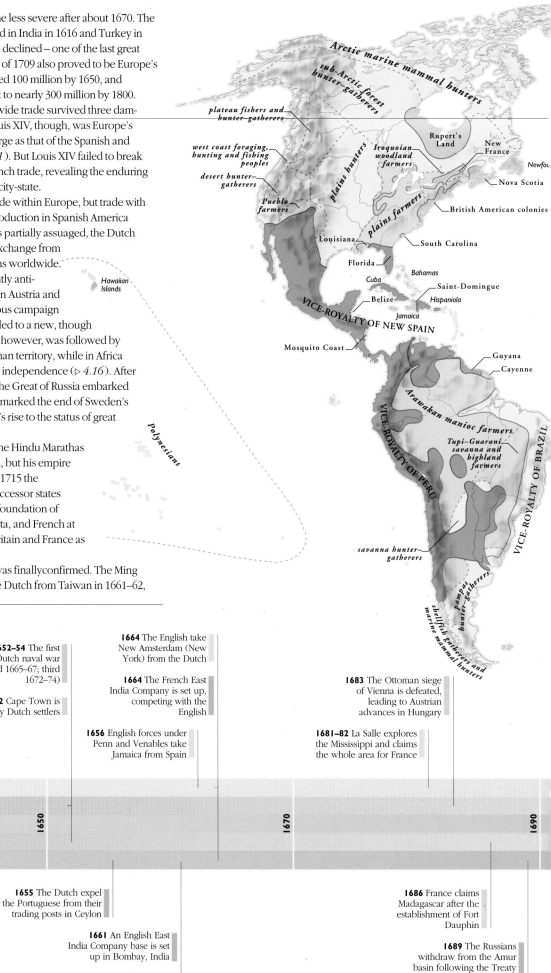

1652–54 The first Anglo–Dutch naval war (second 1665–67; third 1672–74)

1655 The Dutch expel the Portuguese from their trading posts in Ceylon

1656 English forces under Penn and Venables take Jamaica from Spain

1661 An English East India Company base is set up in Bombay, India

1661–62 Jeng Cheng-gong takes Taiwan

1664 The English take New Amsterdam (New York) from the Dutch

1664 The French East India Company is set up, competing with the English

1681–82 La Salle explores the Mississippi and claims the whole area for France

1683 The Ottoman siege of Vienna is defeated, leading to Austrian advances in Hungary

1686 France claims Madagascar after the establishment of Fort Dauphin

1689 The Russians withdraw from the Amur basin following the Treaty of Nerchinsk with China

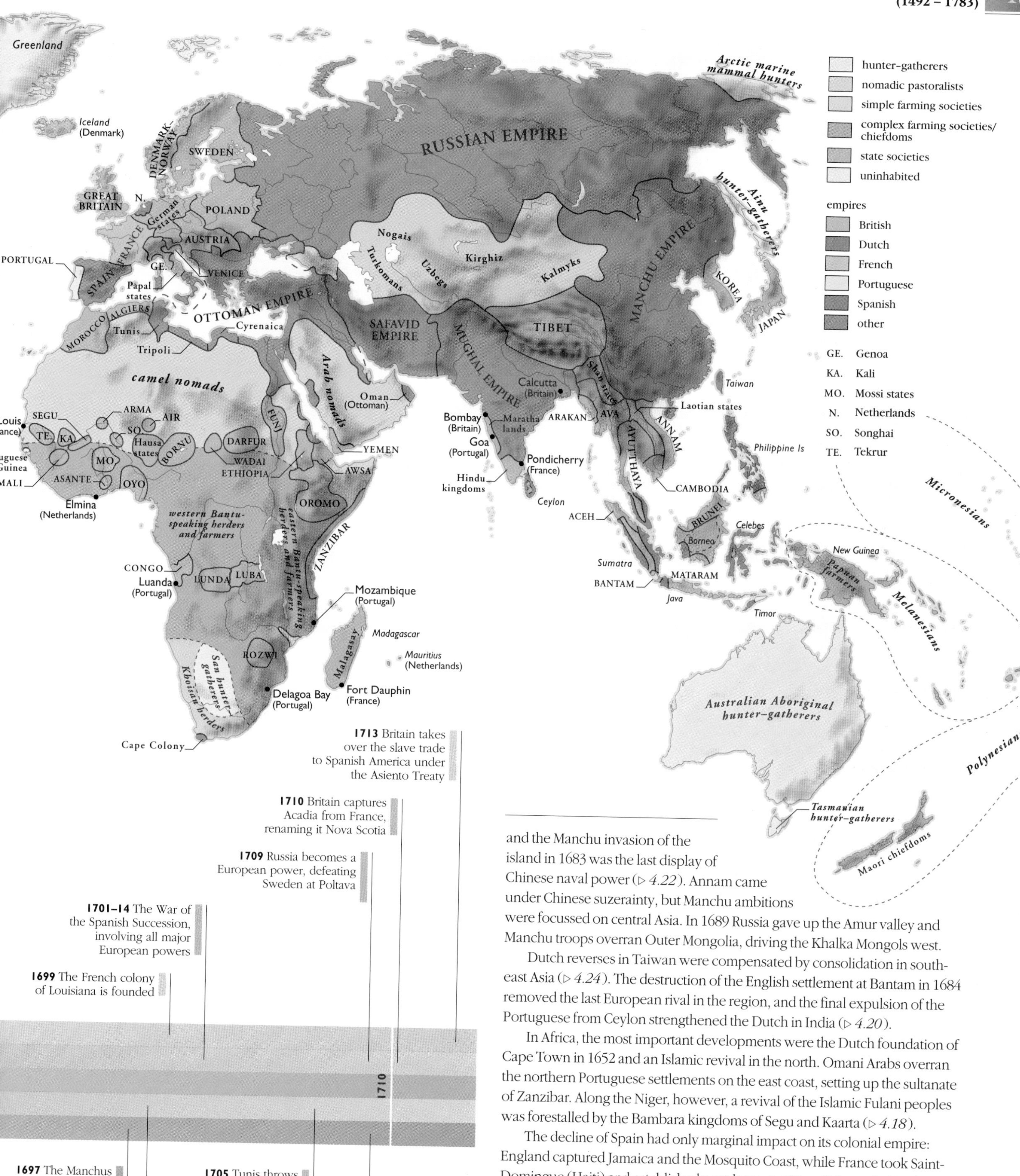
hunter-gatherers
nomadic pastoralists
simple farming societies
complex farming societies/ chiefdoms
state societies
uninhabited
empires
British
Dutch
French
Portuguese
Spanish
other
GE. Genoa
KA. Kali
MO. Mossi states
N. Netherlands
SO. Songhai
TE. Tekrur
Greenland
Iceland (Denmark)
DENMARK-NORWAY
SWEDEN
RUSSIAN EMPIRE
Arctic marine mammal hunters
GREAT BRITAIN
N.
German states
POLAND
PORTUGAL
SPAIN
FRANCE
AUSTRIA
GE.
VENICE
Papal states
ALGIERS
MOROCCO
Tunis
Tripoli
OTTOMAN EMPIRE
Cyrenaica
Nogais
Turkomans
Uzbegs
Kirghiz
Kalmyks
MANCHU EMPIRE
KOREA
JAPAN
Ainu hunter-gatherers
SAFAVID EMPIRE
TIBET
MUGHAL EMPIRE
Arab nomads
Oman (Ottoman)
camel nomads
Calcutta (Britain)
Shan states
Taiwan
Laotian states
Bombay (Britain)
Maratha lands
Goa (Portugal)
ARAKAN
AVA
ANNAM
AYUTTHAYA
Philippine Is
Pondicherry (France)
Hindu kingdoms
Ceylon
CAMBODIA
ACEH
BRUNEI
Borneo
Celebes
Sumatra
BANTAM
MATARAM
Java
Timor
New Guinea
Papuan farmers
Micronesians
Melanesians
Polynesians
Australian Aboriginal hunter-gatherers
Tasmanian hunter-gatherers
Maori chiefdoms
SEGU
ARMA
AIR
SO.
TE.
KA.
Hausa states
BORNU
DARFUR
FUNJ
YEMEN
MO.
WADAI
ETHIOPIA
AWSA
ASANTE
OYO
MALI
Elmina (Netherlands)
OROMO
western Bantu-speaking herders and farmers
eastern Bantu-speaking herders and farmers
ZANZIBAR
CONGO
Luanda (Portugal)
LUNDA
LUBA
Mozambique (Portugal)
Madagascar
Malagasy
Mauritius (Netherlands)
ROZWI
San hunter-gatherers
Khoisan herders
Delagoa Bay (Portugal)
Fort Dauphin (France)
Cape Colony
1710

1713 Britain takes over the slave trade to Spanish America under the Asiento Treaty

1710 Britain captures Acadia from France, renaming it Nova Scotia

1709 Russia becomes a European power, defeating Sweden at Poltava

1701–14 The War of the Spanish Succession, involving all major European powers

1699 The French colony of Louisiana is founded

1697 The Manchus verrun Outer Mongolia (Khalka)

1705 Tunis throws off Ottoman rule

1698 The Omanis drive the Portuguese from Mombasa and set up the Zanzibar sultanate

1709 The Afghans rebel against Safavid rule and assert their independence

and the Manchu invasion of the island in 1683 was the last display of Chinese naval power (▷ 4.22). Annam came under Chinese suzerainty, but Manchu ambitions were focussed on central Asia. In 1689 Russia gave up the Amur valley and Manchu troops overran Outer Mongolia, driving the Khalka Mongols west.

Dutch reverses in Taiwan were compensated by consolidation in south-east Asia (▷ 4.24). The destruction of the English settlement at Bantam in 1684 removed the last European rival in the region, and the final expulsion of the Portuguese from Ceylon strengthened the Dutch in India (▷ 4.20).

In Africa, the most important developments were the Dutch foundation of Cape Town in 1652 and an Islamic revival in the north. Omani Arabs overran the northern Portuguese settlements on the east coast, setting up the sultanate of Zanzibar. Along the Niger, however, a revival of the Islamic Fulani peoples was forestalled by the Bambara kingdoms of Segu and Kaarta (▷ 4.18).

The decline of Spain had only marginal impact on its colonial empire: England captured Jamaica and the Mosquito Coast, while France took Saint-Domingue (Haiti) and established a settlement at New Orleans. In North America, Frenchman Robert La Salle explored the Mississippi, while English control of the eastern seaboard was confirmed by the capture of Dutch New Amsterdam (New York) (▷ 4.26). The English colonies grew rapidly in population, the English built a presence beyond the French-controlled St Lawrence, and took control of French Acadia, renaming it Nova Scotia in 1710 ■

4.05 World trade • 1492 – 1783 •

Trade between the Mediterranean and the east was of very ancient origin. The "Silk Route" linked the Middle East with China from classical times (▷ *3.22*): ancient Rome, like 16th-century Europe, imported goods from China and paid for them in gold and silver. India developed a money-based economy before the Christian era despite a lack of local precious metals, by attracting gold through the sale of cheap cotton textiles (▷ *2.23*). Credit facilities for merchants, which made long-distance trade possible, developed at an early date in both China and India, and achieved roughly their modern form in Europe by 1200.

The period 1500–1800, however, brought three new developments in world trade, all of them originating in Europe. First was the establishment of regular routes around Africa from Europe to India and China. These routes, and the permanent bases along them, meant that European traders no longer had to rely on the overland caravan routes and Islamic middlemen.

The second development resulted from the Spanish conquests in the Americas. By the second half of the 16th century, as the gold mines of southern Germany and Hungary were nearing exhaustion, vast shipments of silver from Peru and Mexico began to arrive at Seville. Much of the Spanish–American silver found its way into the general European economy, where it made possible a huge increase in the credit available to European merchants, and helped avert financial collapse during the grim 17th century (▷ *4.12*).

American silver bought European access to the other world markets. Until 1750, only in shipbuilding did European technology enjoy the superiority over its world rivals that was to characterize the 19th century, and European manufactured goods had little allure for Indian or Chinese merchants. Europeans could only obtain the goods they desired – southeast Asian spices, Indian cottons or Chinese silks and porcelain – by paying in gold or silver. The huge quantities of American silver flowing into Europe after about 1550 therefore flowed out again to the east almost as quickly – some via the Ottoman empire (the old trade routes never completely closed), some (after the opening of Siberia) via Russia, and some by sea. Meanwhile large quantities of American silver were reaching the Asian economies from the Americas, via the Philippines. In the hands of the Dutch, and then their British successors, Spanish–American silver became the means of establishing a permanent

furs
Québec
fish
timber
furs, grain, meat
Boston
New York
dyes, rice, tobacco
Charleston
New Orleans
cotton
to Manila
£5.0 milli
£4.5
Hawaiian Islands
silver
Veracruz
Acapulco
Cuba
Havana
Bahamas
sugar
Hispaniola
coffee, cotton, sugar
Jamaica
sugar
Guadeloupe
cacao, dyes
Panama
cacao, dyes
New Amsterdam
Cayenne
sugar
"Middle Passa
silver
sugar, tobacc
Callao
Bahia
coffee, sugar
sugar
Arica
Potosí
silver
Rio de Janeiro
coffee, diamonds, gold, silver
hides
Buenos Aires
Falkland Islands

TIMELINE

The Americas
Europe
Middle East
Africa
Asia and Australasia

1550
1650

1498 Vasco da Gama reaches Calicut, initiating European maritime trade links with India

1503 The Spanish office of American trade is set up at Seville

1521 Lisbon and Oporto are licensed as monopoly ports for trade with Brazil

1545 The Potosí silver mine in Peru enters production for Spain

c.1550 The first slave-worked sugar plantations are established in Brazil

1557 A permanent Portuguese trading base is established at Macao

1575 The slaving town of Luanda is founded in Portuguese Angola to supply slaves for Brazil

1600 The English East India Company is set up (its first base is founded at Bantam in 1602)

1602 The Dutch East India Company is founded in Amsterdam

1619 The Dutch East India Company headquarters is set up at Batavia on Java

1625 British settlement begins in the West Indies: by 1640 plantation-grown sugar is the principal crop

1641 The Dutch capture Malacca to win control of the East Indies trade

1661–62 The Dutch lose Formosa (Taiwan) to the Chinese

1664 The Frenc East India Compan (*Compagnie des Inde* is founde

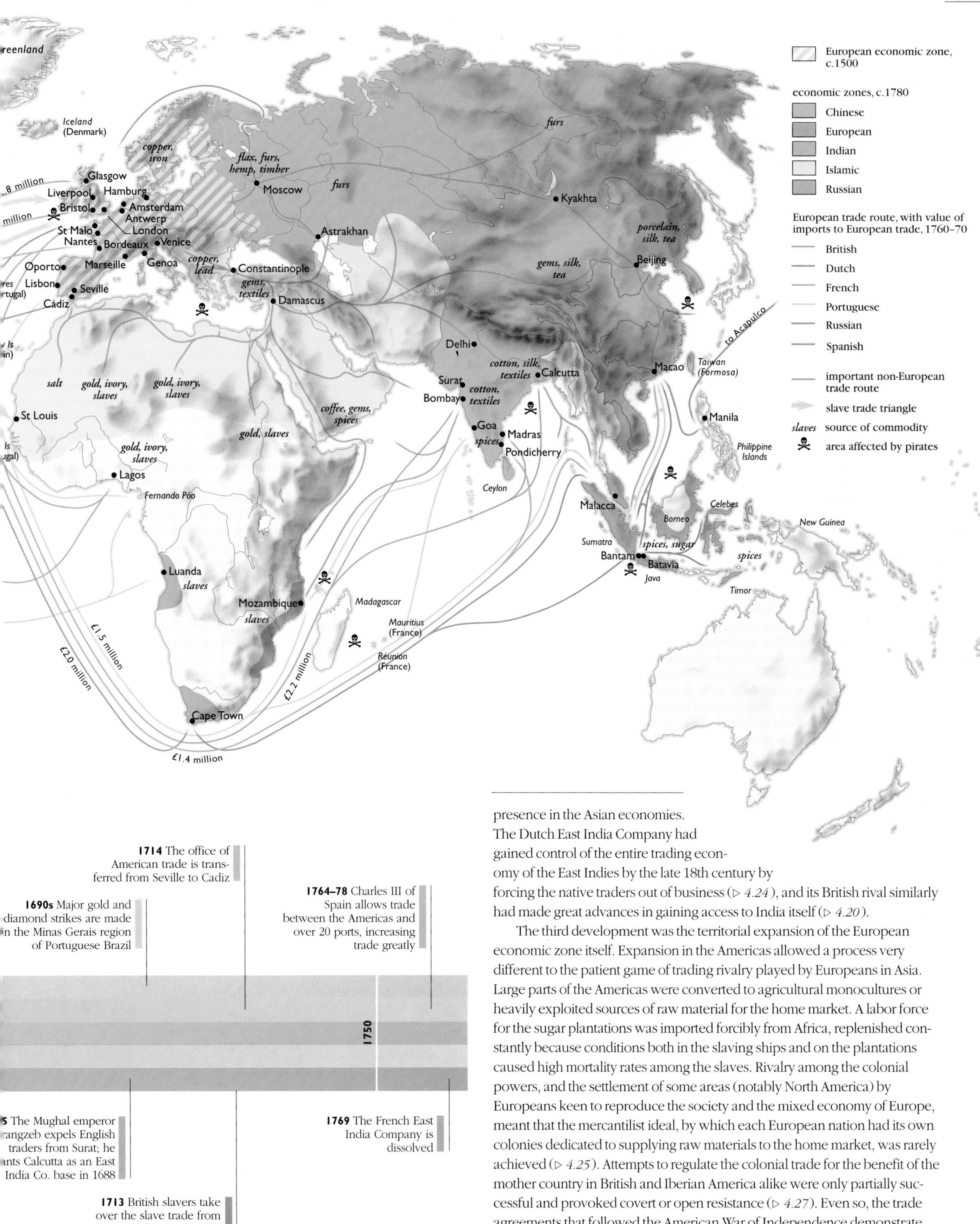
European economic zone, c.1500
economic zones, c.1780
Chinese
European
Indian
Islamic
Russian
European trade route, with value of imports to European trade, 1760–70
British
Dutch
French
Portuguese
Russian
Spanish
important non-European trade route
slave trade triangle
slaves source of commodity
area affected by pirates
reenland
Iceland (Denmark)
copper, iron
flax, furs, hemp, timber
furs
furs
Glasgow
Liverpool
Hamburg
Bristol
Amsterdam
Antwerp
London
St Malo
Nantes
Bordeaux
Venice
Genoa
Marseille
copper, lead
Oporto
Lisbon
Seville
Cádiz
Moscow
Astrakhan
Constantinople
gems, textiles
Damascus
Kyakhta
porcelain, silk, tea
gems, silk, tea
Beijing
to Acapulco
Delhi
cotton, silk, textiles
Calcutta
Surat
cotton, textiles
Bombay
Macao
Taiwan (Formosa)
Manila
Philippine Islands
Goa
spices
Madras
Pondicherry
Ceylon
salt
gold, ivory, slaves
gold, ivory, slaves
coffee, gems, spices
gold, slaves
St Louis
gold, ivory, slaves
Lagos
Fernando Póo
Malacca
Borneo
Celebes
New Guinea
Sumatra
spices, sugar
spices
Bantam
Batavia
Java
Timor
Luanda
slaves
Mozambique
slaves
Madagascar
Mauritius (France)
Réunion (France)
Cape Town
£1.5 million
£2.0 million
£2.2 million
£1.4 million
.8 million
million
1750

1714 The office of American trade is transferred from Seville to Cadiz

1690s Major gold and diamond strikes are made in the Minas Gerais region of Portuguese Brazil

1764–78 Charles III of Spain allows trade between the Americas and over 20 ports, increasing trade greatly

5 The Mughal emperor rangzeb expels English traders from Surat; he nts Calcutta as an East India Co. base in 1688

1769 The French East India Company is dissolved

1713 British slavers take over the slave trade from West Africa to Spanish America for 30 years under the Asiento agreement

presence in the Asian economies. The Dutch East India Company had gained control of the entire trading economy of the East Indies by the late 18th century by forcing the native traders out of business (▷ *4.24*), and its British rival similarly had made great advances in gaining access to India itself (▷ *4.20*).

The third development was the territorial expansion of the European economic zone itself. Expansion in the Americas allowed a process very different to the patient game of trading rivalry played by Europeans in Asia. Large parts of the Americas were converted to agricultural monocultures or heavily exploited sources of raw material for the home market. A labor force for the sugar plantations was imported forcibly from Africa, replenished constantly because conditions both in the slaving ships and on the plantations caused high mortality rates among the slaves. Rivalry among the colonial powers, and the settlement of some areas (notably North America) by Europeans keen to reproduce the society and the mixed economy of Europe, meant that the mercantilist ideal, by which each European nation had its own colonies dedicated to supplying raw materials to the home market, was rarely achieved (▷ *4.25*). Attempts to regulate the colonial trade for the benefit of the mother country in British and Iberian America alike were only partially successful and provoked covert or open resistance (▷ *4.27*). Even so, the trade agreements that followed the American War of Independence demonstrate how intimately these colonial economies remained tied to Europe ■

4.06 THE WORLD • AD 1783 •

After more than a century of worldwide famine, plague, warfare and hardship, recovery took place in the course of the 18th century. In China, the population rose from 120 million in 1680 to nearly 300 million by 1790. In Europe perhaps 100 million in 1650 had become 187 million by 1800. Even in the Americas, 13 million inhabitants in 1650 had doubled by 1800. Only in Africa did the overall population of 100 million stay unchanged, though here several million were forcibly moved under the slave trade.

It is often said that medical and sanitation advances gave humankind the means to escape the tyranny of plague and high infant mortality. Such advances were indeed made in parts of Europe, but nowhere else. A more general cause may have been climatic, a gradual rise in the temperature of the planet leading to improved harvests and greater resistance to disease.

Politically, the 18th century brought the struggle between the most dynamic nation-states of western Europe, France and Great Britain, to the world stage. British gains in the Americas were extended during the War of the Austrian Succession (1740–48), but French successes in India and in Europe meant that the Treaty of Aix-la-Chapelle (1748) simply restored the pre-war status quo (▷ *4.14*). In the Seven Years War (1756–63), however, British naval superiority was decisive. James Wolfe's victory at Quebec in 1759 delivered New France to Britain, and all French possessions in the West Indies except Saint-Domingue were taken in 1762. In the same year, British forces captured Havana, heart of the Spanish– American empire, and twelve months later Florida was ceded. In India, the English East India Company, struggling to reverse the French gains of 1748, won a decisive victory at Plassey (1759) over France's ally Siraj ud-Daulah of Bengal (▷ *4.20*). By 1763, France held only Pondicherry in India, and had lost all footholds in America east of the Mississippi.

Britain's attempts to tighten fiscal control over colonial America and its concern at illicit trade between its American subjects and French, Dutch and Spanish colonies led to war with its largest colonial possession. France, supporting the colonials, sent troops and a fleet to threaten British North America and the economically valuable West Indies. By 1783 Britain had secured the West Indies but lost America (▷ *4.28*).

New powers emerged elsewhere in the world in the 18th century. In Europe, the Prussia of Frederick the Great mounted

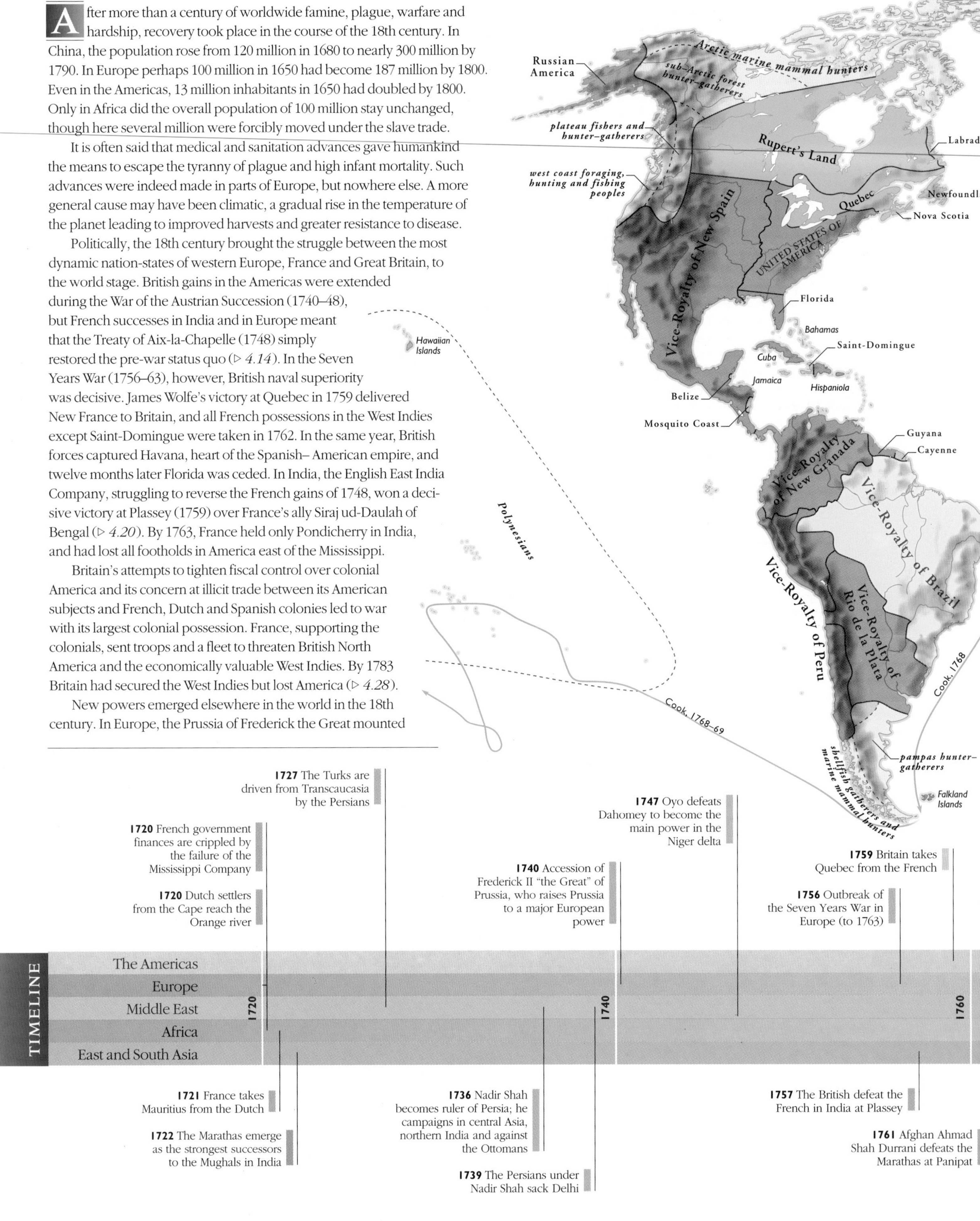

Russian America
Arctic marine mammal hunters
sub-Arctic forest hunter-gatherers
plateau fishers and hunter-gatherers
west coast foraging, hunting and fishing peoples
Rupert's Land
Quebec
Nova Scotia
Vice-Royalty of New Spain
UNITED STATES OF AMERICA
Florida
Bahamas
Saint-Domingue
Cuba
Jamaica
Hispaniola
Belize
Mosquito Coast
Hawaiian Islands
Guyana
Cayenne
Vice-Royalty of New Granada
Vice-Royalty of Brazil
Polynesians
Vice-Royalty of Peru
Vice-Royalty of Rio de la Plata
Cook, 1768
Cook, 1768–69
pampas hunter-gatherers
shellfish gatherers and marine mammal hunters
Falkland Islands

TIMELINE

The Americas · Europe · Middle East · Africa · East and South Asia

1720

1720 French government finances are crippled by the failure of the Mississippi Company

1720 Dutch settlers from the Cape reach the Orange river

1721 France takes Mauritius from the Dutch

1722 The Marathas emerge as the strongest successors to the Mughals in India

1727 The Turks are driven from Transcaucasia by the Persians

1736 Nadir Shah becomes ruler of Persia; he campaigns in central Asia, northern India and against the Ottomans

1739 The Persians under Nadir Shah sack Delhi

1740

1740 Accession of Frederick II "the Great" of Prussia, who raises Prussia to a major European power

1747 Oyo defeats Dahomey to become the main power in the Niger delta

1756 Outbreak of the Seven Years War in Europe (to 1763)

1757 The British defeat the French in India at Plassey

1759 Britain takes Quebec from the French

1760

1761 Afghan Ahmad Shah Durrani defeats the Marathas at Panipat

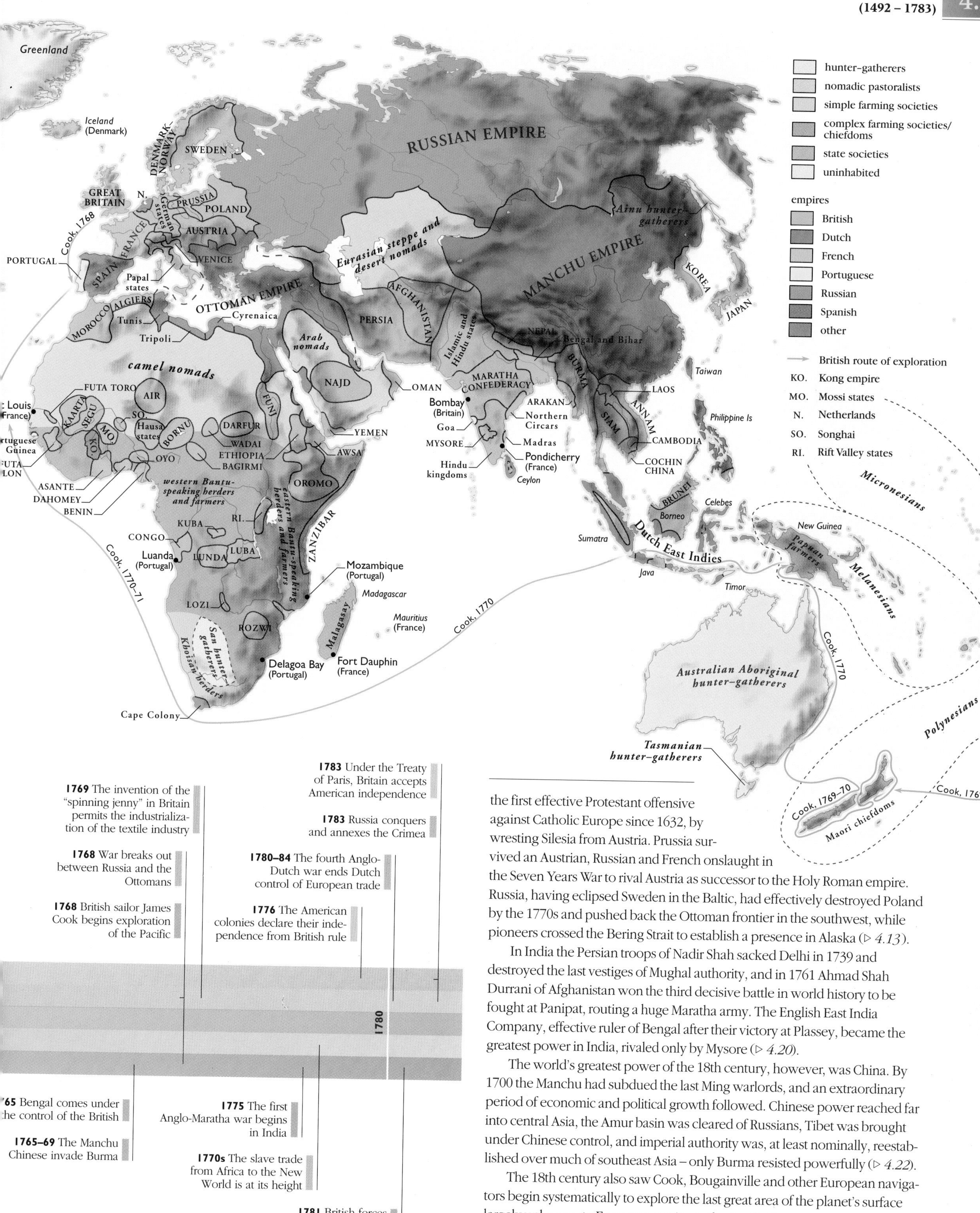
hunter-gatherers
nomadic pastoralists
simple farming societies
complex farming societies/chiefdoms
state societies
uninhabited
empires
British
Dutch
French
Portuguese
Russian
Spanish
other
British route of exploration
KO. Kong empire
MO. Mossi states
N. Netherlands
SO. Songhai
RI. Rift Valley states
Greenland
Iceland (Denmark)
DENMARK-NORWAY
SWEDEN
GREAT BRITAIN
N.
German states
PRUSSIA
POLAND
AUSTRIA
FRANCE
VENICE
PORTUGAL
SPAIN
Papal states
Cook, 1768
RUSSIAN EMPIRE
Eurasian steppe and desert nomads
Ainu hunter-gatherers
MANCHU EMPIRE
KOREA
JAPAN
OTTOMAN EMPIRE
ALGIERS
MOROCCO
Tunis
Tripoli
Cyrenaica
AFGHANISTAN
PERSIA
Islamic and Hindu states
NEPAL
Bengal and Bihar
Arab nomads
NAJD
OMAN
YEMEN
MARATHA CONFEDERACY
Bombay (Britain)
Goa
MYSORE
Hindu kingdoms
ARAKAN
Northern Circars
Madras
Pondicherry (France)
Ceylon
BURMA
LAOS
ANNAM
SIAM
CAMBODIA
COCHIN CHINA
Taiwan
Philippine Is
BRUNEI
Borneo
Celebes
Sumatra
Java
Dutch East Indies
Timor
New Guinea
Papuan farmers
Micronesians
Melanesians
Polynesians
camel nomads
FUTA TORO
AIR
Louis (France)
KAARTA
SEGU
SO.
MO.
KO.
Hausa states
BORNU
DARFUR
FUNJ
WADAI
ETHIOPIA
BAGIRMI
AWSA
OYO
Portuguese Guinea
FUTA JALON
ASANTE
DAHOMEY
BENIN
western Bantu-speaking herders and farmers
OROMO
eastern Bantu-speaking herders and farmers
KUBA
RI.
CONGO
Luanda (Portugal)
LUNDA
LUBA
ZANZIBAR
Mozambique (Portugal)
Madagascar
Mauritius (France)
Malagasy
LOZI
ROZWI
San hunter-gatherers
Khoisan herders
Delagoa Bay (Portugal)
Fort Dauphin (France)
Cape Colony
Cook, 1770–71
Cook, 1770
Australian Aboriginal hunter-gatherers
Tasmanian hunter-gatherers
Cook, 1769–70
Cook, 1769
Maori chiefdoms
1780

1783 Under the Treaty of Paris, Britain accepts American independence

1783 Russia conquers and annexes the Crimea

1780–84 The fourth Anglo-Dutch war ends Dutch control of European trade

1776 The American colonies declare their independence from British rule

1769 The invention of the "spinning jenny" in Britain permits the industrialization of the textile industry

1768 War breaks out between Russia and the Ottomans

1768 British sailor James Cook begins exploration of the Pacific

'65 Bengal comes under the control of the British

1765–69 The Manchu Chinese invade Burma

1775 The first Anglo-Maratha war begins in India

1770s The slave trade from Africa to the New World is at its height

1781 British forces take Dutch settlements in west Sumatra

the first effective Protestant offensive against Catholic Europe since 1632, by wresting Silesia from Austria. Prussia survived an Austrian, Russian and French onslaught in the Seven Years War to rival Austria as successor to the Holy Roman empire. Russia, having eclipsed Sweden in the Baltic, had effectively destroyed Poland by the 1770s and pushed back the Ottoman frontier in the southwest, while pioneers crossed the Bering Strait to establish a presence in Alaska (▷ *4.13*).

In India the Persian troops of Nadir Shah sacked Delhi in 1739 and destroyed the last vestiges of Mughal authority, and in 1761 Ahmad Shah Durrani of Afghanistan won the third decisive battle in world history to be fought at Panipat, routing a huge Maratha army. The English East India Company, effective ruler of Bengal after their victory at Plassey, became the greatest power in India, rivaled only by Mysore (▷ *4.20*).

The world's greatest power of the 18th century, however, was China. By 1700 the Manchu had subdued the last Ming warlords, and an extraordinary period of economic and political growth followed. Chinese power reached far into central Asia, the Amur basin was cleared of Russians, Tibet was brought under Chinese control, and imperial authority was, at least nominally, reestablished over much of southeast Asia – only Burma resisted powerfully (▷ *4.22*).

The 18th century also saw Cook, Bougainville and other European navigators begin systematically to explore the last great area of the planet's surface largely unknown to European mariners, the Pacific ■

4.07 Reformation Europe • 1492 – 1560 •

As the 15th century neared its close, the monarchies of western Europe consolidated their positions and brought civil wars within their territories to an end. Louis XI of France (r.1461–81) overcame his Burgundian rivals, Henry Tudor brought England's long Wars of the Roses to an end in 1485, and Ferdinand of Aragon and Isabella of Castile oversaw the unification of their kingdoms and the final conquest of Moorish Granada in 1492. As feudal relationships continued to break down, the near-independence of the great nobles in times of weak kings was gradually curtailed by the rise of administrators and financiers. Europe's monarchs became distributors of patronage in a world where finance was beginning to count for more than fealty.

The territorial kingdoms of 16th-century Europe were very different to the monolithic states of today. Material conditions, slow communications and the stubborn survival of local customs, economies and even laws limited royal power. The nation-state was still a novelty.

The old notion of a secular empire transcending the state endured. Charles VIII of France invaded Italy in 1494 in pursuit of such an aim, prompting a long struggle in which French, Spanish and German armies rampaged through the peninsula, almost destroying the achievements of the Italian Renaissance. In 1519, Charles of Habsburg, grandson both of Ferdinand of Aragon and Emperor Maximilian I, became Emperor Charles V: the empire itself was weak and fragmented, but Charles now held the Austrian Habsburg lands in Spain, the Netherlands, Franche-Comté and much of Italy, as well as Spain's new overseas possessions, creating a power bloc that dominated Europe until the late 17th century.

Alarmingly, though, the defeat of Louis II of Hungary by the Ottomans at Mohács in 1526 raised the specter that the empire that would unify Europe might not even be a Christian one. In both central Europe and the Mediterranean (where Barbarossa's victory at Prevesa in 1538 ensured Ottoman and Barbary corsair domination), Charles V shouldered the responsibility for halting the Ottoman advance.

Against this background of imperial commitments the greatest event of the 16th century, the Reformation, was played out. What began as a challenge by a monk, Martin Luther, to corrupt practices in the church became an expression of German nationalism, and then of local interests asserted against the emperor. The Peasants' Wars, uprisings partly fueled by religious unrest, were vigorously put down by the German nobility, who then began to adopt the reformed faith themselves, often for political reasons. Charles won a crushing victory at Mühlberg over the Protestant nobles, but otherwise did little to halt the spread of reform.

The papacy faced Luther's challenge hamstrung

major faith, 1550
- Anglican
- Catholic
- Calvinist
- Lutheran
- Muslim
- Orthodox
- mixed

- state with significant Catholic minority, 1550
- state with significant Protestant minority, 1550
- borders, 1560
- territory controlled by Christian military orders, 1500
- Austrian Habsburg land
- Spanish Habsburg land
- Ottoman empire, 1492
- European territory lost to Ottomans by 1560
- Christian defeat by Ottomans
- major Ottoman siege
- Ottoman advance against Christian Europe
- popular uprising, with date
- major printing center, 15th–16th centuries
- Spanish *presidio* fort

Italian wars
- French victory
- Spanish Habsburg victory
- Venetian victory
- invasion route of Charles VIII of France, 1494

0 600 km
0 400 mi

ATLANTIC OCEAN

Ireland
Irish Pale
Dublin
1549, Western Rebellion
Britta 1491 to F
La Roc
Bor
La Coruña
Santander
Pamplona
Nav 1512
Burgos
1521–22, Comunero revolt
Douro
SPAIN
Ara 1479
Madrid
PORTUGAL
Tagus
Castile 1479 to Spain
Lisbon
Valenci
Córdoba
Seville
Granada
Granada 1492 to Spain
Cart
Tangier
Asilah
Ceuta
Melilla 1497 to Spain
Oran 1509 to Spain

LUTHER was caricatured as the Devil's plaything in this typically grotesque woodcut of 1525.

TIMELINE

Habsburg lands

1500 | 1530 | 1560

1492 The conquest of Granada completes Spain's *reconquista*; Castile and Aragon are united by the marriage of Ferdinand and Isabella

1509 Spain takes Oran, beginning a campaign to take key bases in North Africa

1517 Martin Luther writes his 95 Theses against abuse in the Catholic Church

1519 Charles of Habsburg, king of Spain since 1516, is elected Holy Roman emperor

1521 Protestant Reformation begins as Luther is outlawed

1524–25 The Peasants' War breaks out across Germany

1527 Imperial troops sack Rome

1529 Vienna is besieged unsuccessfully by the Turks

1530 German Protestants publish 28 articles of faith to avoid a split with the Church

1534 Anabaptists seize control of Münster, prophesying the end of the world

1547 Charles V defeats the Schmalkaldic league of Protestant princes at Mühlberg

1555 The Peace of Augsburg allows each prince in the Holy Roman empire to select the faith of his subjects

1556 Charles V abdicates; he is succeeded by Philip II in Spain, and by Ferdinand I as emperor

Other lands

1494–95 Charles VIII of France invades Italy, initiating a series of wars with Spain

1503 Pope Alexander VI, a Borgia, dies; Julius II becomes pope

1515 Francis I of France defeats Swiss at Marignano to control northern Italy

1525 Francis I is captured by the Spaniards at Pavia; he is held for a year

1534 Henry VIII asserts his claim to be the supreme head of the Church in England

1541 Calvin introduces a puritan Protestant society to Geneva

1558 The Protestant Elizabeth I succeeds her Catholic sister Mary to the English throne

1559 The treaty of Cateau-Cambrésis ends Italian wars

1500 | 1530 | 1560

by a decline in the need for a unified church (literacy, once the church's preserve, had become more widely diffused in the previous two centuries) and by the widespread perception that the pope was merely a cynical participant in the complex web of Italian politics. The authority of the church was challenged even by rulers with no particular religious motive: first by Ferdinand of Aragon, who threatened in 1508 to withdraw his kingdoms from obedience to the pope; in 1527 by Gustavus Vasa's seizure of church lands in Sweden; and by Henry VIII of England who repudiated papal authority in 1532.

The Reformation was driven by a shift in religious sensibilities, as the spread of printing gave the new demands for a more personal spirituality an unprecedented mobility and resilience. Even as political compromise between the faiths was agreed in 1555 within the empire (the Peace of Augsburg) and between France and Spain in Italy in 1559 (the treaty of Cateau-Cambrésis), the Catholic response to church reform was taking shape: the Council of Trent formulated a statement of Catholic doctrine and the Jesuit Order was adopted by the papacy as the spearhead of a new pastoral effort.

1 A defeat at the hands of the English at Flodden ensured Scotland did not interfere in English affairs for most of the Tudor period.

2 Martin Luther, an Augustinian monk, nailed his *95 Theses* to the Wittenberg cathedral door in 1517, challenging church abuses and initiating the Reformation.

3 The château of Chambord, built by Francis I from 1519, is a classic of French Renaissance architecture.

4 The Christian stronghold of Rhodes fell to the Ottomans in 1522, after vigorous defense by the Knights of St John.

5 The unexpected defeat and capture of Francis I of France by Spanish forces at Pavia in 1525 was the climax of the Italian wars.

6 The brutal sack of Rome in 1527 by Spanish and German mercenaries in the service of Charles V shocked the whole of Europe.

7 In three sessions from 1545, the Council of Trent decrees laid the basis of modern Catholicism in doctrines directly opposing Protestantism.

See also 3.12 (Renaissance Europe); 4.08 (Counter-Reformation Europe); 4.15 (Ottoman empire)

4.08 Counter-Reformation Europe • 1560 – 1600 •

The peace agreements of the 1550s were greeted with palpable relief in a Europe which, despite sustained economic growth since 1510, had known anything but peace. Yet the relief was short-lived. Religious conflict, averted in Germany, broke out with unexpected savagery in France and the Netherlands, while the Baltic lands of the former Teutonic Knights became a battleground for Polish, Danish, Swedish and Russian armies. At the same time, Europe's climate entered a two-century-long mini-ice age. Rivers froze in the long, cold winters, while the cool, wet summers all but wiped out the recent advances in agriculture. Population growth ended. Worse would follow in the early 17th century: the period 1550–1650 was known to contemporaries as the "Iron Century".

The Reformation entered a new phase in the 1560s with the spread of Calvinism, more radical and uncompromising than Lutheranism. Scotland adopted the new faith in 1560, and its growth in the Netherlands underlay the Dutch revolt against Spanish rule in 1566. By 1600 Nassau, the Palatinate and Ansbach in the empire had adopted Calvinism, and large Calvinist minorities existed in Bohemia, Moravia and Transylvania. Above all, Calvinism unified and motivated the Huguenot (Protestant) minority in France. By 1600 almost 40 percent of the European population had renounced the Catholic faith. In Germany, although Calvinism was excluded from the tolerance extended by the Peace of Augsburg, the principle enshrined in the Peace that the prince was to determine the religion of his subjects (*cuius regio, eius religio*) allowed it to take root.

In France the Huguenot congregations included many of the most important figures in the royal administration as well as many citizens in the towns of the south, and much of the nobility including Henry of Navarre. A formidable political and military force, the Huguenots took up arms in 1562 and remained a threat to the French crown for the rest of the century, despite a string of military defeats and the slaughter of 30,000 men and women in the 1572 Massacre of St Bartholomew. Henry of Navarre renounced his faith to become Henry IV, first Bourbon king of France, and offered the Huguenots toleration, but the threat to the monarchy remained.

The Church's response to the Reformation was twofold. A pastoral and doctrinal offensive saw the spread of colleges of the formidable Jesuit Order, the revival of the medieval Inquisition, the establishment of an Index of Prohibited Books and a clearer restatement of the nature of Catholic faith than ever before. Politically, the Church found a champion in Philip II of Spain willing and able to take military action against its enemies.

border of territory under Dutch control, 1577
border of territory under Dutch control, 1588
predominantly Anglican, 1598
predominantly Calvinist/Huguenot, 1598
predominantly Catholic, 1598
recovered for Catholicism by 1600
predominantly Lutheran, 1598
with Calvinist/Catholic/Lutheran faiths, 1598
borders, 1600
Austrian Habsburg land
Spanish Habsburg land
Ottoman empire, 1560
Ottoman gains by 1600
Spanish Habsburg victory
European defeat by Ottomans
major Ottoman siege
Huguenot refuge
major Jesuit center or seminary
major center of St Bartholomew massacre, 1572
major revolt or unrest
Spanish *presidio* fort
Spanish military communication route by 1600
campaign route
Vigo Spanish port raided by Drake
Irish rebel march
0 600 km
0 400 mi
ATLANTIC OCEAN
O'Neill's rebellion, 1593–1603
O'Donnell's rebellion, 1594–1601
Ireland
Irish Pale
Dublin
Fitzmaurice's rebellion, 1579
Kinsale 1601
Southam
Plymouth
Spanish Armada, 1588
Drake, Norris 1589
La Coruña
Santiago de Compostela
Santander
Bilbao
Pamplona
Nav
Drake, Norris 1589
Vigo
Valladolid
Douro
Salamanca
The Escorial
Madrid
Portugal
Tagus
Alcántara 1580
Toledo
Lisbon
Drake, Norris 1589
SPAIN
Valenci
Córdoba
Seville
Cartagena
Morisco revolt, 1569–71
Howard, Essex 1596
Cádiz
to West Indies
Tangier
Ceuta
Mostagane
Melilla
Alcazarquivir 1578

TIMELINE

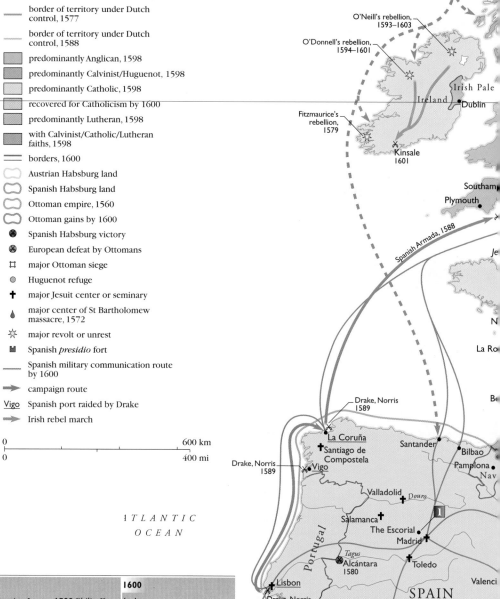

Spain and the Papacy

1560 – 1580 – 1600

- **1556** Accession of Philip II to the Spanish throne (to 1598)
- **1561** Madrid is established as the Spanish capital
- **1568–70** A revolt of the Moriscos in southern Spain is put down
- **1571** A Christian fleet defeats the Ottomans at Lepanto
- **1578** Portugal's Sebastian I is killed at Alcazarquivir
- **1580** Spain defeats Portugal at Alcántara; Philip II takes the Portuguese throne
- **1581** Spain makes peace with the Ottomans
- **1585-90** Reforming pontificate of Pope Sixtus V
- **1588** Philip II sends the Armada to invade England
- **1598** Death of Philip II, accession of Philip III

Western Europe

French wars of religion

- **1563** The proclamation of the 39 Articles initiates the Anglican church in England
- **1566** The Dutch revolt against Spanish rule begins; Alva invades the Netherlands
- **1572** Protestant leaders across France die in the Massacre of St Bartholomew
- **1576** Pacification of Ghent unites Protestant and Catholic Netherlands against Spain
- **1578–88** Spanish troops under Parma reconquer most of the southern Netherlands
- **1579** The northern provinces of the Netherlands formally unite in the Union of Utrecht
- **1587** The Catholic Mary Queen of Scots is executed by Elizabeth of England
- **1589** The once-Protestant Henry IV becomes French king, initiating Bourbon rule
- **1593–1603** O'Neill's revolt threatens English control of Ireland
- **1598** The Edict of Nantes grants a degree of religious toleration, ending French wars of religion

1560 – 1580 – 1600

1 Philip II built the Escorial, his palace, in 1563–84. Its severe architecture symbolized his approach to the task of leading Counter-Reformation Europe.

2 The fall of Tunis to an Ottoman fleet three years after Lepanto ended Spanish hopes of maintaining a significant military presence in north Africa.

3 Unpaid and starving Spanish troops sacked Antwerp in November 1576. The Pacification of Ghent, a statement of opposition to the Spanish troops by all the provinces, was a result of the sack.

4 A Dutch-English victory at Zutphen interrupted the Spanish general Parma's reconquest of the rebellious provinces of the Netherlands.

5 The success of Henry of Navarre (Henry IV) in occupying staunchly Catholic Paris after the battle of Ivry brought the French Wars of Religion to an end.

6 Protestants were expelled from Bavaria and Austria; imperialist attempts to repeat the process in Bohemia and Moravia in the early 17th century were to prompt the Thirty Years War.

7 English ships under Howard and Essex raided Cadiz in 1596 but failed in the plan of intercepting a bullion fleet from the Americas.

The challenges facing Philip were many, and his administration was strained to the limit despite vast quantities of American silver that flowed through Spain. Faced with the Ottoman threat, he abandoned the effort to hold Tunis as Venice opted for rivalry with Spain in preference to the agreed counterattack on the Turks (spectacularly but briefly successful at Lepanto in 1571). Philip put down the revolt of the Moriscos (converted Moors) of southern Spain and acquired the crown of Portugal. He also struggled to meet the most serious threat to Habsburg authority, the Dutch revolt.

The dukes of Alva and Parma failed to bring the Dutch to heel, though they recaptured most of the southern Netherlands. From 1571 Dutch corsairs (the "Sea Beggars") cut the Spanish sea route to the Netherlands, and in 1585 the hard-pressed Hollanders received military support from Protestant England, led by the earl of Leicester.

England had seen the final triumph of Protestantism only in 1563, after Mary Tudor's brief and bloody reimposition of Catholicism (1553–58). Queen Elizabeth's position was secured in 1587 by the execution of her Catholic cousin and focus for discontent, Mary Queen of Scots. Philip reacted to English support for the Dutch by sending the great naval expedition known as the Armada, to spearhead a fullscale invasion in 1588. It failed, largely through violent weather and poor planning. Victory over the Armada is often seen as the beginning of English naval power and the end of that of Spain; but the Spanish fleet was rebuilt within two years, Francis Drake led a "counter-Armada" in 1589 which met with an equal lack of success, and English attempts to intercept Spanish bullion fleets over the next decade were beaten off with ease. Spain landed troops in Ireland in 1601 to support the rebellion of Hugh O'Neill, earl of Tyrone. The threat of Spanish military intervention in England as in France, remained real until the end of the century.

See also 4.01 (European empires);
4.07 (Reformation Europe); 4.15 (Ottoman empire)

4.09 Sweden's bid for Baltic dominance • 1561 – 1721 •

Late medieval trade in the Baltic region was dominated by the Hanseatic league; its politics by the league and by the united kingdoms of Denmark–Norway and Sweden. The Hanseatic trading network, centered on Lübeck, reached from London to Novgorod and provided a counterweight to the Venetian trading network in southern Europe. Control of the river ports that handled Baltic products – grain, copper, furs and the "naval stores" (timber, flax, hemp, pitch and tar) which made possible Europe's overseas expansion – was central to the region's politics.

In the early 16th century the hold of the Teutonic Knights on the eastern Baltic began to weaken, and English and Dutch merchants began to rival those of the league. In 1520 the Swedes under Gustavus Vasa rebelled against Christian II of Denmark, and were supported by Lübeck. The victorious Swedes then joined a concerted effort by Lübeck's rivals to break the Hanseatic hold on Baltic trade.

Sweden was an unlikely inheritor of the leading role in the region. Domination of both sides of the Sound gave Denmark a natural stranglehold on Baltic trade with the outside world. Sweden's internal communications were poor, the merchant fleet was made up almost entirely of small-tonnage vessels, its main ports were icebound in winter and its population smaller than that of any of its rivals. Moreover, the eastern Baltic, the "natural" area for Swedish expansion, was equally natural for Poland and Russia, and the Danes had a stepping stone to the region in the island of Gotland, acquired from the Knights in 1407.

Swedish expansion at first proceeded by opportunistic steps, made possible by a precociously efficient royal administration and a strictly-enforced system of military service that made maximum use of the limited manpower. An early spur to Swedish expansion was the English establishment of a trade route to Russia via Archangel, bypassing the Baltic altogether. Thereafter, Swedish territorial gains were aimed at control of the Baltic river ports through which grain and naval stores flowed to western Europe and beyond: the conquest of Livonia, for example, brought customs revenues equal to 25 percent of Swedish state income.

Throughout the period, however, the Dutch hold on Baltic trade increased steadily, sometimes in partnership with Sweden and sometimes in opposition. The highly advanced Swedish metallurgical industry around Falun, for example, was entirely financed from Amsterdam – but a Dutch fleet helped destroy Swedish naval power off Öland in 1676.

The Livonian War (1557–82) saw Russia's first attempt to acquire a Baltic coastline defeated: Sweden gained the whole of Estonia. Polish–Swedish rivalry became open warfare after the deposition in 1598 of Sigismund III, Vasa ruler of both kingdoms, from the Swedish throne. Poles and Swedes backed opposing factions in Russia during the "Time of Troubles" (1604-13); the Swedes acquired Karelia from the hard-pressed czar in return for aid, and then extended their hold into eastern Karelia and Ingria by the treaty of Stolbovo (1617) in return for recognition of Michael Romanov and the return of occupied lands around Novgorod. An indecisive struggle around Calmar and Älvsborg marked Sweden's first war with Denmark.

Under Gustavus Adolphus (r.1611–32) the scope of Swedish involvement in Europe expanded. A campaign against Poland secured Livonia and ensured that, when Gustavus intervened in the Thirty Years War in 1630, the Swedish army was formidably experienced as well as tactically superior to the imperialist forces it faced. While the mastermind behind Swedish intervention was Cardinal Richelieu of France, Gustavus's success took the Swedes to the center stage of European politics. A crisis came when Gustavus was killed at Lützen (1632) and his army defeated at Nördlingen (1634), but Swedish fortunes were restored in the grim final years of the war by Axel Oxenstierna and Lennart Torstensson,

former Teutonic Order and associated Church lands
Swedish empire, 1561
Swedish gains to 1660
maximum extent of Swedish territory in the Holy Roman empire, 1632-35
Denmark-Norway, 1644
Denmark-Norway gain, 1660
Brandenburg-Prussia, 1660
Poland-Lithuania, 1660
Russia, 1689
Brandenburg-Prussia gains, 1719
Russian gains by 1721
borders, 1660
major Swedish victory
major Swedish defeat
major center of Baltic trade
major Swedish shipbuilding center
important Baroque architecture
flax source of traded commodity
Swedish campaign under Lewenhaupt, 1708
Swedish campaign under Charles XII, 1708-1709
trade route
sea frozen in winter

0 400 km
0 300 mi

North Sea
Principality of Bremen 1648–1715 to Sweden
Amsterdam
Netherl
London
tea, textiles, tobacco, sugar, wine
Kleve
Meuse

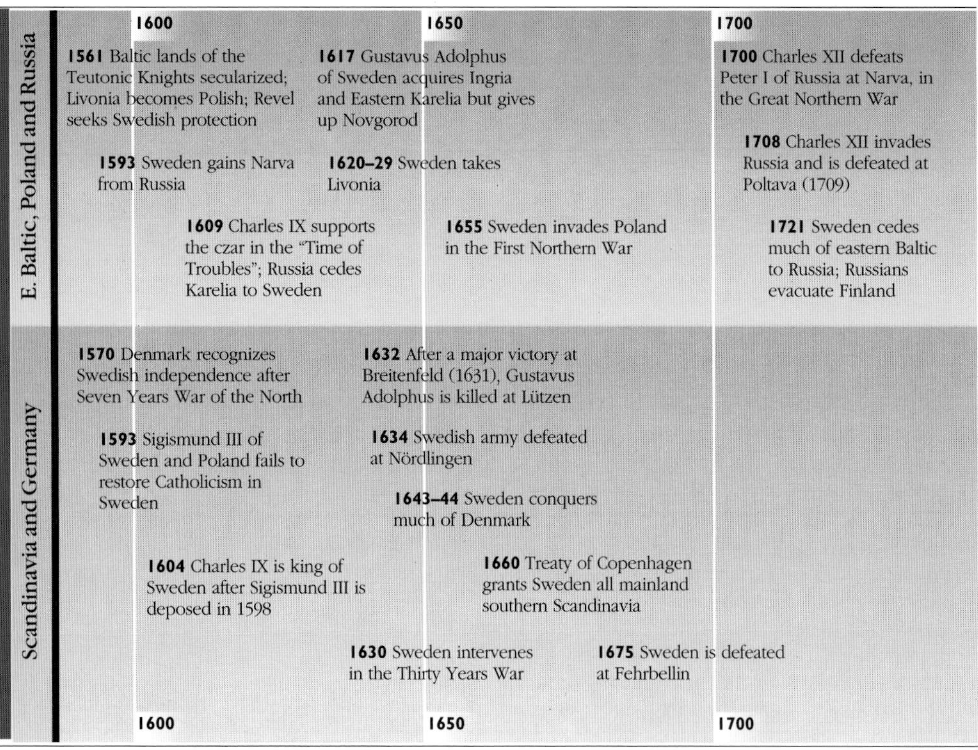
TIMELINE
1600
1650
1700
E. Baltic, Poland and Russia
1561 Baltic lands of the Teutonic Knights secularized; Livonia becomes Polish; Revel seeks Swedish protection
1617 Gustavus Adolphus of Sweden acquires Ingria and Eastern Karelia but gives up Novgorod
1700 Charles XII defeats Peter I of Russia at Narva, in the Great Northern War
1593 Sweden gains Narva from Russia
1620–29 Sweden takes Livonia
1708 Charles XII invades Russia and is defeated at Poltava (1709)
1609 Charles IX supports the czar in the "Time of Troubles"; Russia cedes Karelia to Sweden
1655 Sweden invades Poland in the First Northern War
1721 Sweden cedes much of eastern Baltic to Russia; Russians evacuate Finland
Scandinavia and Germany
1570 Denmark recognizes Swedish independence after Seven Years War of the North
1632 After a major victory at Breitenfeld (1631), Gustavus Adolphus is killed at Lützen
1593 Sigismund III of Sweden and Poland fails to restore Catholicism in Sweden
1634 Swedish army defeated at Nördlingen
1643–44 Sweden conquers much of Denmark
1604 Charles IX is king of Sweden after Sigismund III is deposed in 1598
1660 Treaty of Copenhagen grants Sweden all mainland southern Scandinavia
1630 Sweden intervenes in the Thirty Years War
1675 Sweden is defeated at Fehrbellin
1600
1650
1700

1 English trade to Archangel was pioneered by Hugh Willoughby and Richard Chancellor in 1553 and Anthony Jenkinson in 1557–58; Swedish expansion northward was partly an attempt to control this trade.

2 The flagship *Kronen* was destroyed in 1676 by an explosion during Sweden's defeat by a Dutch-Danish fleet in Louis XIV's second war with the Netherlands.

3 Falun was the center of a metallurgical industry; its copper and iron exports underpinned Sweden through the 17th century.

4 The provinces of Dalecarlia and Uppland were the heart of Sweden; during the Great Northern War they lost nearly a third of their adult male population.

5 Göteborg was Sweden's only direct trading outlet to the North Sea. Protected by Fort Älfsborg, it was besieged repeatedly by Denmark.

6 Swedish territorial expansion south and east of the Baltic was aimed at control of the great river ports.

7 Finland was overrun by Russia after Poltava, and Sweden's naval presence in the eastern Baltic ended.

LAPLAND
Norwegian Sea
Västerbotten 1560–1661 to Sweden
Luleå
Archangel
1560–95 to Sweden
1658–1660 to Sweden 1660 to Denmark-Norway
Trondheim
Jamtland 1645 to Sweden
Ångermanland
Umeå
Gulf of Bothnia
Österbotten
Vasa
Storkyra 1714
Finland
Karelia 1617 to Sweden 1721 to Russia
Lake Onega
Härjedalen
Medelpad
Dalecarlia
Falun
Gävle
Nystad
timber
Nyland
Vyborg
Lake Ladoga
Bergen
Christiania
copper, iron, timber
Dal
Uppland
Åland Is
Åbo
Helsingfors (Helsinki)
St Petersburg
Stolbovo
DENMARK-NORWAY
SWEDEN
Västerås
Uppsala
Stockholm
1720
1714
Estonia 1561 to Sweden 1721 to Russia
Narva 1700
RUSSIA
Drottningholm
Dagö
Revel
1610 to Sweden 1617 to Russia
Ingria 1583, 1617 to Sweden 1595, 1721 to Russia
Vänern
Södermanland
1582 to Sweden 1721 to Russia
1718
Jerwen 1582 to Sweden 1721 to Russia
flax, hemp, hides
Novgorod
Älvsborg
Bohuslän
Linköping
Westgotland
Vättern
Ösel 1645 to Sweden 1721 to Russia
1582 to Sweden 1721 to Russia
Lake Peipus
Göteborg
Jönköping
Ostgotland
Visby
Gotland 1645 to Sweden
Livonia 1629 to Sweden 1721 to Russia
Pskov
Ålborg
Halland
Småland
Windau
Tver
Volga
Calmar
Öland
Baltic Sea
Courland
Riga
Kircholm 1605
Moscow
JUTLAND
Helsingborg 1710
1658 to Sweden
Blekinge
Brömesbro
Libau
Mitau
Kokenhausen 1601
flax, furs, grain, hemp, timber
Fredericia
Copenhagen 1658
Skane
The Sound
Western Dvina
Klushino 1610
Odense
ZEELAND
1658 to Sweden 1660 to Denmark-Norway
Ermeland 1629 to Sweden 1635 to Brandenburg-Prussia
Memel
Samogitia
Polotsk
Vitebsk
Schleswig
West Pomerania 1648 to Sweden
Bornholm
Smolensk
Königsberg
Vilna
Lübeck
Wismar
Stralsund
Kolberg
East Pomerania
Danzig
Elbing
Andrusovo
Hamburg
Mecklenberg
Stuhm 1629
Prussia Polish suzerainty until 1657/60
flax, grain, hemp, timber.
Holowczyn 1708
Minsk
Mogilev
Stettin
Grodno
Brandenburg
Verden
Lesnaya 1708
Fehrbellin 1675
Berlin
Minden
Pultusk 1656
POLAND
Starodub
Magdeburg
Poznan
Vistula
Bug
Gomel
Ravensberg
Mark
grain
1656
Warsaw
Pinsk
Pripet
Gorki
Breitenfeld 1631
Elbe
Podolesia
Saxony
Dresden
Desna
Lublin
Breslau
Oder
Lützen 1632
Volhynia
Kiev
Ukraine
Klissow 1702
Prague
Krakow
HOLY ROMAN EMPIRE
Jankau 1645
Lemberg (Lvov)
Poltava 1709
Dnieper
Nördlingen 1634
Zaporogian Cossacks
Ochakov
1 2 3 4 5 6 7

engineer of the crushing victory over the imperial forces at Jankau (1645) and a punitive invasion of Denmark in 1643–44. Swedish gains by 1648 included West Pomerania, the ports of Stettin and Wismar, and the former bishoprics of Bremen and Verden.

The First Northern War (1655–60) saw Swedish military success in Poland in alliance with Brandenburg, but fear of further Swedish expansion galvanized a coalition of Russia, Denmark and the empire to resist, and Brandenburg quickly changed sides.

Swedish gains were limited to the former Danish possessions on the Swedish side of the Sound. In 1675 a new campaign against Brandenburg in support of France ended in a humiliating defeat at Fehrbellin. The last phase of Swedish greatness came under Charles XII (r.1697– 1718), whose reign was devoted largely to the Great Northern War against an alliance of Russia, Denmark, and Poland under Augustus II (also Elector of Saxony). Charles soon defeated the Danes and in 1700 destroyed a Russian army five times the size of his own at Narva. Victories against Poland and Saxony followed, and in 1708 Charles marched east. Russian scorched-earth tactics drew him south in pursuit of an alliance with the Ukrainian Cossacks. Finally, at Poltava in 1709, the exhausted Swedes were routed by a superior Russian force, in a battle that marked the end of Sweden's imperial dream and Russia's emergence as a great power. By 1721 all Swedish possessions southeast of the Baltic were in Russian hands.

Dutch domination of the former Hanseatic trade network was almost total by 1600, and Sweden's economic base was almost entirely in Dutch control.

GUSTAVUS ADOLPHUS built up the military and political strength of Sweden and intervened in the Thirty Years War in the early 1630s.

See also 3.11 (economy of medieval Europe); 4.10 (Thirty Years War); 4.13 (the rise of Russia)

4.10 Europe in the age of the Thirty Years War • 1600 – 1648 •

The "crisis of the 17th century" brought social upheaval, religious violence and economic hardship from Portugal to Russia. Monarchs tried to increase their power at the expense of the nobility, local corporations and the peripheral regions.

Religious tensions abounded, heightened by the uncompromising stances of both Calvinism and Counter-Reformation Catholicism. Religion was, however, seldom the overriding factor in conflict. In England and France it gave an edge to political and social struggles, while in the shifting alliances of the Thirty Years War, religious affiliation was often little more than a kind of badge for armies recruited indiscriminately from all faiths, or for princes prepared to change religion to further a political advantage.

After the assassination of Henry IV in 1610, France underwent a period of weak government until Cardinal Richelieu became chief minister in 1624. Plots against him by the brother of Louis XIII led to a renewal of hostilities between the administration and the nobility. The Huguenots demanded concessions and rose in revolt again. Richelieu laid siege to their chief stronghold, La Rochelle; the defenders were starved into submission. Thereafter Richelieu concentrated on dismembering the Habsburg empire. Offensives against the strategic route to Flanders were narrowly defeated by Spanish and imperialist forces, but in the1640s Richelieu and his successor Mazarin brought the scheme to fruition, with military success in Flanders, the Rhineland, Italy and the Pyrenees, and French-sponsored revolts in Portugal, Catalonia, Sicily and Naples. Spain's empire appeared doomed, but unrest in France proved the cost of these efforts.

Contemporaries recognized the war that broke out in 1618 as one which subsumed all Europe's other conflicts. The Thirty Years War consisted of several stages. First, the Bohemian–Palatinate war (1618–23) in which a Bohemian Protestant and Transylvanian threat to Habsburg Vienna was defeated and the Calvinist Lower Palatinate was conquered by imperial and Spanish troops. Second, the Danish war (1625–29) in which an intervention on behalf of the German Protestants by Denmark was shattered at Lutter, and the Edict of Restitution strengthened the position of the Catholics in Germany. Third, the Swedish war (1630–35) in which Sweden briefly carried the war to the the heart of Catholic southern Germany. Fourth, the French– Swedish war (1635-48), in which the French defeated successive Spanish invasions and undertook counter-offensives against all the Spanish possessions, Sweden defeated the imperialists and various armies spread unprecedented devastation over much of Germany before a peace was agreed.

Spain's role as Catholic champion of Europe was the greatest casualty of the war. The years of relative peace in the early 17th century were wasted and the reform program initiated after 1621 by the chief minister Olivares could not be sustained, as the cost of financing a war effort across the continent escalated while silver revenues dwindled. With the revolts of Catalonia and Portugal in 1640, Spain was forced to divert resources to deal with domestic difficulties.

James VI and I of Scotland and England planted Ulster with Protestant settlers, but avoided commitment to the Protestant cause on Europe's mainland. Constitutional and religious opposition to his son Charles I led to war in Scotland (1639–40), to a massacre of the Ulster Protestants, and then to civil war in England. The victory of his Parliamentary enemies did not end unrest; the king was executed in 1649 (though few sought such a radical solution) and a Commonwealth established under Oliver Cromwell.

The Dutch alone gained from Europe's long, grim war. By weathering years of Spanish assaults they preserved their trading empire and won their independence; they now set about commercial expansion. By 1650 Amsterdam's financiers dominated the entire European economy.

Austrian Habsburg territory, 1618
Spanish Habsburg territory, 1618
Habsburg allies, 1618
France, 1618
German Protestant states
United Provinces, 1609
Sweden, 1618
other state hostile to Habsburgs
borders, 1648
French offensive
Protestant offensive
Spanish offensive
Swedish offensive
Habsburg and imperialist victory
Habsburg and imperialist defeat
major siege
town sacked
major revolt or unrest
major Dutch fortifications built 1605-06
Spanish blockade of Dutch trade, 1624-27
major Habsburg strategic route
major Dutch trade route
Spanish naval patrol
British settlement in Ireland, 1613
"Plantations" of James I, 1613-25
Eastern Association of pro-Parliamentary counties, 1643
royalist victory
royalist defeat

Ireland
Limerick
Tralee
Cork
ATLANT
OCEAN
to the Atlantic and East Indies
to Spanish Netherlands
La Coruña
Santa
Valladolid
Oporto
SPAIN
PORTUGAL
Portuguese revolt, 1640
Tagus
1640
Lisbon
Córdoba
Seville
to the Americas
Tangier
Ceuta
Mel
0 400 km
0 300 mi

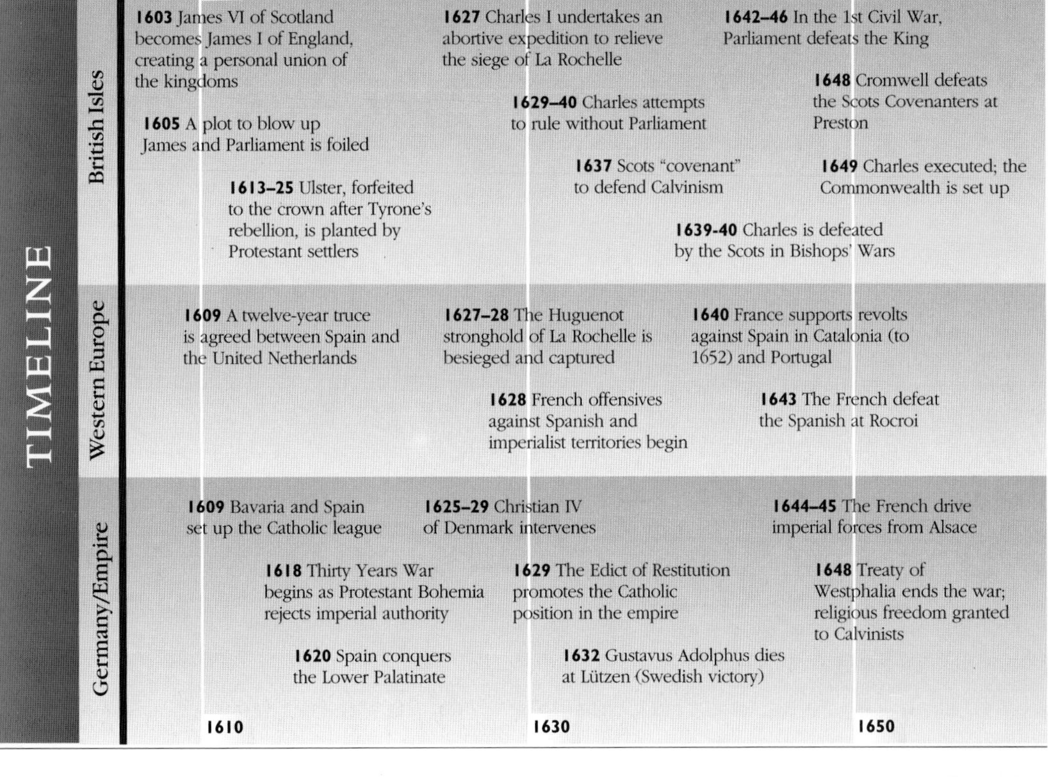

TIMELINE

British Isles

1603 James VI of Scotland becomes James I of England, creating a personal union of the kingdoms

1605 A plot to blow up James and Parliament is foiled

1613–25 Ulster, forfeited to the crown after Tyrone's rebellion, is planted by Protestant settlers

1627 Charles I undertakes an abortive expedition to relieve the siege of La Rochelle

1629–40 Charles attempts to rule without Parliament

1637 Scots "covenant" to defend Calvinism

1639-40 Charles is defeated by the Scots in Bishops' Wars

1642–46 In the 1st Civil War, Parliament defeats the King

1648 Cromwell defeats the Scots Covenanters at Preston

1649 Charles executed; the Commonwealth is set up

Western Europe

1609 A twelve-year truce is agreed between Spain and the United Netherlands

1627–28 The Huguenot stronghold of La Rochelle is besieged and captured

1628 French offensives against Spanish and imperialist territories begin

1640 France supports revolts against Spain in Catalonia (to 1652) and Portugal

1643 The French defeat the Spanish at Rocroi

Germany/Empire

1609 Bavaria and Spain set up the Catholic league

1618 Thirty Years War begins as Protestant Bohemia rejects imperial authority

1620 Spain conquers the Lower Palatinate

1625–29 Christian IV of Denmark intervenes

1629 The Edict of Restitution promotes the Catholic position in the empire

1632 Gustavus Adolphus dies at Lützen (Swedish victory)

1644–45 The French drive imperial forces from Alsace

1648 Treaty of Westphalia ends the war; religious freedom granted to Calvinists

1610 1630 1650

Stockholm
SWEDEN
Vänern
Vättern
DENMARK–NORWAY
Auldcarn
1645
to Greenland, Newfoundland and Shetlands fisheries
Scotland
Tippermuir
1644
Solemn League and Covenant, 1639–40
North Sea
to Baltic ports
Edinburgh
Philiphaugh
1645
Bishops' Wars, 1639–40
Massacre of Protestants, 1641
Newburn
1640
Copenhagen
Christian IV, 1625
Gustavus Adolphus, 1631–32
Baltic Sea
England
Marston Moor
1644
York
Preston
1648
Hull
1643
Mansfeld, 1626
West Pomerania
Stralsund
1628
Kolberg
East Pomerania
Königsberg
Danzig
Royal Prussia
PRUSSIA
Lübeck
Wismar
Mecklenberg
Friedrichstadt
Bremen
Nantwich
1644
Nottingham
Naseby
1645
Worcester
1651
Edgehill
1642
Fenland revolt, 1630–38
Gloucester
1642, 1644
Levellers, 1647
Oxford
1642–6
Putney Debates, 1647
Bristol
Roundway Down
1643
Newbury
1643
London
Downs
1639
Turnham Green
1643
Lostwithiel
1644
Dunkirk
Dunkirkers
FLANDERS
UNITED PROVINCES
Amsterdam
Breda
Kleve
Antwerp
Brussels
Spanish Netherlands
1642–46
Magdeburg
1631
Ravensberg
Westphalia
Lutter
1626
Brandenburg
Landsberg
Frankfurt
Wallenstein, 1627–28
Vistula
Anhalt
Saxony
Mark
Hesse
HOLY ROMAN EMPIRE
Lützen
1632
Breitenfeld
1631
POLAND
Oder
Silesia
White Mountain
1620
Prague
Bohemia
Bayreuth
Krakow
Jankau
1645
Moravia
Corbie
1636
Rouen
Rocroi
1643
Spinola, 1621
Frankfurt
Heidelberg
Ansbach
'Nu-pieds', 1639–40
Paris
Lower Palatinate
ALSACE
Rhine
Württemberg
Nördlingen
1634
Regensburg
Bethlen Gabor, 1619
George Rakóczy, 1645
1634
1634, 1637–48
Austria
Danube
Vienna
Orléans
Breisach
Ferla, 1633
Munich
Bavaria
Gran
Buda
Nantes
Loire
Franche-Comté
SWISS CONFEDERATION
Tyrol
Salzburg
Styria
IMPERIAL HUNGARY
TRANSYLVANIA
Bourges
Charolais
Carinthia
La Rochelle
1627–28
Huguenots, 1621–28
FRANCE
1629
VALTELLINE
HUNGARY
Geneva
Lyon
SAVOY
MILAN
1637–48
Carniola
Peasant 'Croquants', 1636–37, 1643–45
Milan
Mantua
Venice
Turin
Po
Bordeaux
VENICE
PARMA
MODENA
Ravenna
Guyenne revolt, 1641, 1645
Languedoc revolt, 1641, 1643–45
Rhône
Genoa
PAPAL STATES
OTTOMAN EMPIRE
Guetaria
1638
Toulouse
Avignon
GENOA
Bilbao
1638
1640–52
Provence revolt, 1639, 1643–45
Florence
Marseille
1646
TUSCANY
Pamplona
Perpignan
Roussillon
1642 to France
Piombino
Porto Longone
Ragusa
Montenegro
ANDORRA
PIOMBINO
Orbetello
Lérida
1647
Catalan revolt, 1640
Corsica
to Genoa
Rome
Barcelona
Montjuich
1641
1647
Naples
NAPLES
BENEVENTO
Valencia
Palma
Balearic Islands
Sardinia
SARDINIA
Cagliari
Palermo
1647
Messina
SICILY
Sicily
Mediterranean Sea
MALTA

1 The offensive of Albrecht von Wallenstein in 1627–28 against the Baltic ports was intended to destroy Dutch trade; instead it prompted Sweden's entry into the war in Germany.

2 Dunkirk was a key Spanish naval base and a threat to both Dutch and English trade until captured by French troops in 1646. Spain retook it in 1652.

3 France actively supported the Neapolitan insurrection of 1647 to break Spain's hold on Italy.

4 The Habsburgs were threatened in 1629–32 by the Swedish advance and French attacks on Mantua and the Valtelline; they revived by 1634.

5 The sack of Magdeburg by the imperialist Count Tilly in 1631 encouraged savage reprisals between Swedes and imperialists for the rest of the war.

6 The Catalan revolt of 1640 was supported by France, and the subsequent French invasion led to a long, inconclusive war.

See also 4.08 (Counter-Reformation Europe); 4.11 (age of Louis XIV)

4.11 Europe in the age of Louis XIV • 1648 – 1715 •

The Thirty Years War concluded the conflicts that had threatened Europe since the Reformation and brought a revulsion against religious and social extremism. Only in Britain, where Cromwell's regime faced mounting discontent until it collapsed in 1660, did the radical opponents of the existing social order achieve power. Instead there was a general extension of royal control over the affairs of the state, and the doctrine of the absolute power of the monarch emerged. The long struggle between kings and territorial magnates was at last resolved, nowhere more so than in France, Europe's most populous and most influential state: local administration was put in the hands of officials while aristocrats were required to dance attendance on the king at his court, and representative institutions were stripped of the power to criticize the government.

The seven decades after 1648 saw Louis XIV systematically pursue his ambition of supplanting Habsburg Spain as Europe's dominant power. The Netherlands, formerly banker and mainstay of the anti-Habsburg cause, allied itself with Spain against the growing threat of France and England. Under Cromwell and the later Stuart kings, England took a pro-France, anti-Spain stance, leading it into a series of damaging naval wars with the Netherlands. The dramatic accession of the Dutchman William of Orange to the English throne in 1688–89 reversed this pattern and Anglo-French enmity again became a feature of European history. Austria, once the junior partner in Habsburg Europe, emerged as a power while Spanish might waned. Sweden, France's partner against the Habsburgs in the 1630s and 40s, suffered a defeat at Fehrbellin while supporting Louis XIV against the Netherlands, and thereafter shrank from direct involvement in western Europe. In Italy, Savoy eclipsed Habsburg Milan, while the Spanish possessions in the south survived the French-supported revolts of the 1640s and passed to Austrian control after 1713 as Spain's European territories were shared out between the new Bourbon king of Spain, Philip V, and the Austrian Habsburgs.

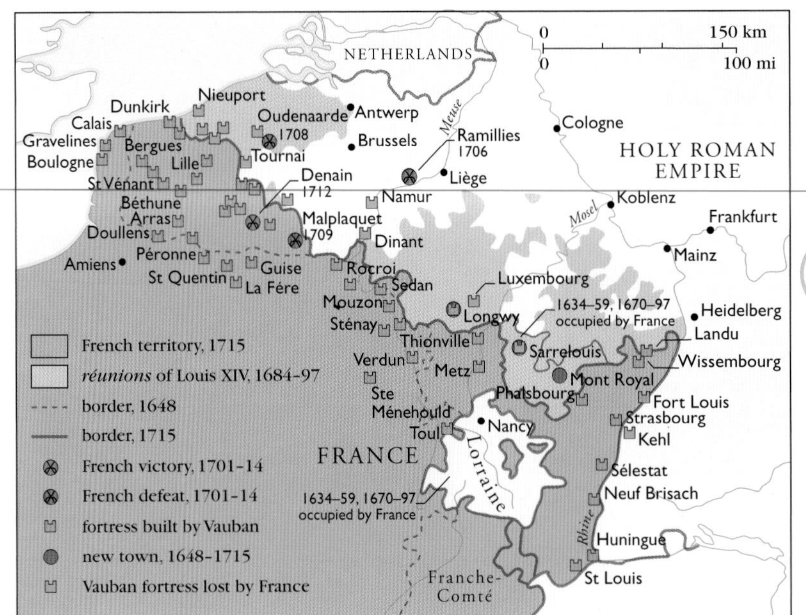
0 150 km
0 100 mi
NETHERLANDS
Dunkirk
Nieuport
Calais
Gravelines
Boulogne
Bergues
Lille
Oudenaarde 1708
Tournai
Antwerp
Brussels
Ramillies 1706
Liège
Meuse
Cologne
HOLY ROMAN EMPIRE
St Venant
Béthune
Arras
Doullens
Denain 1712
Namur
Malplaquet 1709
Dinant
Koblenz
Mosel
Frankfurt
Mainz
Amiens
Péronne
St Quentin
Guise
La Fère
Rocroi
Sedan
Mouzon
Sténay
Luxembourg
Longwy
1634–59, 1670–97 occupied by France
Heidelberg
Landu
Thionville
Sarrelouis
Wissembourg
Verdun
Metz
Mont Royal
Phalsbourg
Fort Louis
Strasbourg
Kehl
Ste Ménehould
Toul
Nancy
FRANCE
Lorraine
Sélestat
Neuf Brisach
Rhine
Huningue
St Louis
Franche-Comté
1634–59, 1670–97 occupied by France
French territory, 1715
réunions of Louis XIV, 1684–97
border, 1648
border, 1715
French victory, 1701–14
French defeat, 1701–14
fortress built by Vauban
new town, 1648–1715
Vauban fortress lost by France

Louis' military aggressiveness raised a coalition of hostile powers against him. He achieved much in modernizing the French state but failed to control and centralize the economy, ultimately ensuring social upheaval and economic collapse for his successors. Furthermore his revocation of the Edict of Nantes led to the flight of 200,000 Huguenots and ended any hope of again enlisting the Protestant German states against the Habsburgs.

Louis relied for most of his reign on a small group of competent ministers: Colbert (responsible for economic and financial policy, and building up the armed forces), Louvois (minister of war), Vauban (an engineer whose fortresses secured the northern and eastern frontiers for the first time since the Roman era), and a group of exceptional generals (Turenne, Condé, Luxembourg and Villars). France fought four major wars in his reign, making substantial territorial gains and dominating Europe's seas for thirty years. The widespread imitation of Louis' palace at Versailles throughout Europe in the 18th century is a testament to the influence of France in his reign.

In Britain, the accession of William of Orange had other effects than the realignment of foreign policy. In 1714 the equally Protestant George I, Elector of Hanover, came to the British throne, keeping the Catholics from power and involving

ATLANTIC
OCEAN

La Coruña
Santander
Oporto
Douro
Castile
Villaviciosa
Madrid (La Granja)
Tagus
PORTUGAL
Lisbon (Queluz)
1657–59, 1663, 1665
Elvas 1659
Vila Viçosa 1665
SPAIN
Talavera
7
Almanza 1707
Lagos
1693
Seville
Málaga
1704
Cádiz 1656
Gibraltar 1713 to Britain
3
Tangier
Melilla

TIMELINE

1650 | 1675 | 1700

France and Spain

1643 Louis accedes to the French throne aged five; Mazarin runs the government

1648 The Fronde, a noble and parliamentary revolt, causes widespread disorder

1661 Louis XIV's personal rule begins

1667–68 French War of Devolution against the Spanish Netherlands

1672 Louis attacks the Netherlands (except Holland), and occupies most by 1678

1681 France annexes Strasbourg

1685 Revocation of the Edict of Nantes ends Huguenot toleration in France

1688–97 War of the League of Augsburg: Sweden, Spain, the Palatinate, Bavaria and Saxony oppose France

1701 Outbreak of the War of the Spanish Succession after death of Charles II of Spain

1710 Madrid is briefly occupied by the anti-Bourbon alliance

1713 The Treaty of Utrecht divides Spanish territories between Philip V of Bourbon and the Austrian Habsburgs

Rest of Europe

1649 Execution of Charles I of England and establishment of the Commonwealth

1651 England's Navigation Act leads to the 1st Anglo-Dutch war (1652–54); 2nd war 1665–67; 3rd war 1672–74)

1660 Restoration of the English monarchy under Charles II

1665 Great Plague in London, followed by the Great Fire in 1666

1675 The Swedes, allies of Louis, are defeated by Brandenburg at Fehrbellin

1683 The Ottoman siege of Vienna is defeated

1688 In England's Glorious Revolution, Stuart King James II is replaced by William III of Orange and Queen Mary

1688 Death of Frederick William, "Great Elector" of Brandenburg since 1640

1699 Treaty of Karlowitz cedes most of Hungary to Austria

1707 Act of Union unites Scotland and England as Great Britain

1714 The Elector of Hanover becomes King George I of Britain

1650 | 1675 | 1700

- British territory, 1648
- French territory, 1648
- Austrian Habsburg territory, 1648
- Spanish Habsburg territory, 1648
- Russian territory, 1648
- Savoy-Piedmont territory, 1648
- Ottoman territory, 1648
- Venetian territory, 1648
- British territorial gains by 1715
- French territorial gains by 1715
- Austrian Habsburg territorial gains by 1715
- Spanish Bourbon territory, 1715
- Savoy-Piedmont territorial gains by 1720
- Venetian territorial gains by 1715
- borders, 1715
- French and Bourbon victory
- French and Bourbon defeat
- Ottoman victory
- Ottoman siege
- town sacked
- revolt
- fortress built by Vauban
- French naval base
- palace modeled on Versailles built in 18th century
- French strategic offensive, 1648–97
- Spanish Habsburg invasion of Portugal, 1657–68
- Ottoman campaign
- relief of Vienna, 1683
- Marlborough's campaign, 1704
- major Habsburg strategic route
- state generally in alliance with Louis XVI
- state generally opposed to Louis XVI
- campaign of Oliver Cromwell, 1649–51
- area granted to veterans of Cromwell's army, 1651
- advance of William of Orange, 1688

0 400 km
0 300 mi

Britain deeply in European politics for the remainder of the century. The deposed Stuart royal family became a focus for political discontent for several decades, with the threat of a counter-coup first manifested in the Earl of Mar's revolt in 1715.

After a series of reforms under Kara Mustafa, the Ottomans advanced a huge army against Vienna in 1683, but the city was relieved by a German and Polish army. Austrian Habsburg forces swiftly reconquered Hungary before Turkish resistance stiffened.

The War of the Spanish Succession (1701–14), fought on the death of the last Habsburg king of Spain, exemplified the changes that had taken place since 1648. Once Europe's predominant power, Spain was now little more than a battleground for French, Austrian, British and Portuguese armies, while Britain, Holland and the Austrian Habsburgs lined up against the house of Bourbon who claimed the throne with Louis' backing. The Bourbons ultimately succeeded despite several major French defeats, confirming the power-base Louis had built.

1 Cromwell's alliance with France against Spain allowed England to capture Dunkirk (1658); Charles II kept the alliance but sold the port to Louis (1662).

2 The Duchy of Hanover and Great Britain were temporarily united in 1714, when dynastic links allowed George of Hanover to succeed Queen Anne.

3 In 1656 English admiral Robert Blake captured a Spanish bullion fleet off Cadiz, a feat achieved before only by Dutchman Piet Hein in the Caribbean (1628).

4 The Netherlands were saved from occupation at the hands of Louis, Turenne and Condé (1672) by William of Orange, who flooded much of the country.

5 In 1704 an anti-Bourbon army led by Marlborough and Eugene of Savoy succeeded in knocking France's ally Bavaria out of the War of the Spanish Succession.

6 Louis XIV's naval base at Toulon played a major role in French naval campaigns against the Habsburgs.

7 The War of the Spanish Succession was most bitter in Spain itself; pro-Bourbon Castile prevailed against pro-Habsburg Catalonia.

See also 4.09 (Sweden and the Baltic); 4.10 (Thirty Years War); 4.14 (the *ancien régime*)

European economic development • 1492 – 1783 •

Europe's economy in 1783 still rested on a base of semi-subsistence agriculture, poor transport, local economies based partly on barter, lack of development capital and the slow adoption of technological advances. Important developments in agriculture, industry and commerce had taken place since the 16th century, most importantly in Britain and France, but their social impact was still slight.

The population growth of the 16th century had brought pressure on resources, resulting in rising prices and falling wages. Population stagnation in the 17th allowed a slight rise in living standards; but renewed population growth in the later 18th century was not matched by an equivalent increase in production and so brought hardship again. This contributed to the revolutionary explosion at the end of the century. Overall, however, Europe's population doubled between 1500 and 1800. The cities grew most: London and Paris exceeded 250,000 inhabitants by 1700.

It was in the cities that a higher level of economic activity took place. Sophisticated banking and credit systems emerged, providing finance not only for long-distance trade but also for monarchs and governments. Although neither standards of living nor technology were markedly superior in Europe to those in Asia or the Middle East, this new merchant capitalism made possible Europe's transformation into the economic powerhouse of the world.

The economic area dependent on European capitalism underwent an extraordinary expansion after 1492, reaching across the Atlantic to incorporate the Americas and spreading a galaxy of trading bases across south and east Asia. Its center of gravity, having see-sawed between Flanders and northern Italy, finally settled in the north, at Amsterdam in the 17th century and London in the late 18th. A succession of financially dominant cities took European capitalism progressively closer to world domination, in a contest between the nimble city-states of the past and the nation-states of the future; Britain's precocious national economy centered on London finally proved too powerful for its predecessors.

In the late 15th century, the dominant financial powers were still Venice and the Hanseatic league, each controlling a network of trade routes. Flemish and English incursions into Hanseatic areas, and the arrival of Portuguese ships with East Indies spices at Antwerp (bypassing the Venetian spice route through the Levant), resulted in the collapse of their partnership. From 1501 to 1568 European capitalism was dominated by the bankers of Antwerp. The distribution of the American silver flooding into Seville was handled from Flanders, while Dutch and Flemish ships dominated the Baltic grain trade to southern Europe – and reduced the Mediterranean to a peripheral area. In 1557 the pendulum swung back to the south. The first Spanish state bankruptcy damaged the Antwerp banking system, and the Genoese seized their chance. For the next seventy years Europe's finances were managed from Genoa, while the Netherlands subsided into religious war.

Whereas Antwerp and Genoa competed for dominance during the economic upswing of the 16th century, as the downturn gathered pace in the 1620s and silver remittances from Spanish America reduced, Amsterdam emerged as Europe's capitalist powerhouse. Maritime expertise combined with a stable, subtle and flexible credit system led to Dutch control of much European and Asian trade.

The foremost nation-states, Britain and France, made strenuous efforts to compete. The advantages of a stable banking system and an established system of national debt – and the benefit of huge investments after 1688 from the Dutch themselves – finally told in Britain's favor.

population density per sq km, c.1620
over 40
20–40
under 20
city with static population of over 40,000
city with significant population growth, 1500–1800
port for European external trade, 18th century
Genoa city dominating the European financial system at date shown
pioneering development in steam power
important development in iron manufacture and use
important development in the mechanization of the textile industry
commercial center for linen industry
area of coastal or marsh reclamation
textile area in the 18th century
grain exporting area in the 16th century
grain importing area in the 16th century
coalfield exploited by the late 18th century
advanced agricultural techniques practiced by the late 18th century
area of iron working in the 18th century
major metallurgical area in the 18th century
copper
lead and zinc
silver
tin
migration
major canal built by 1770

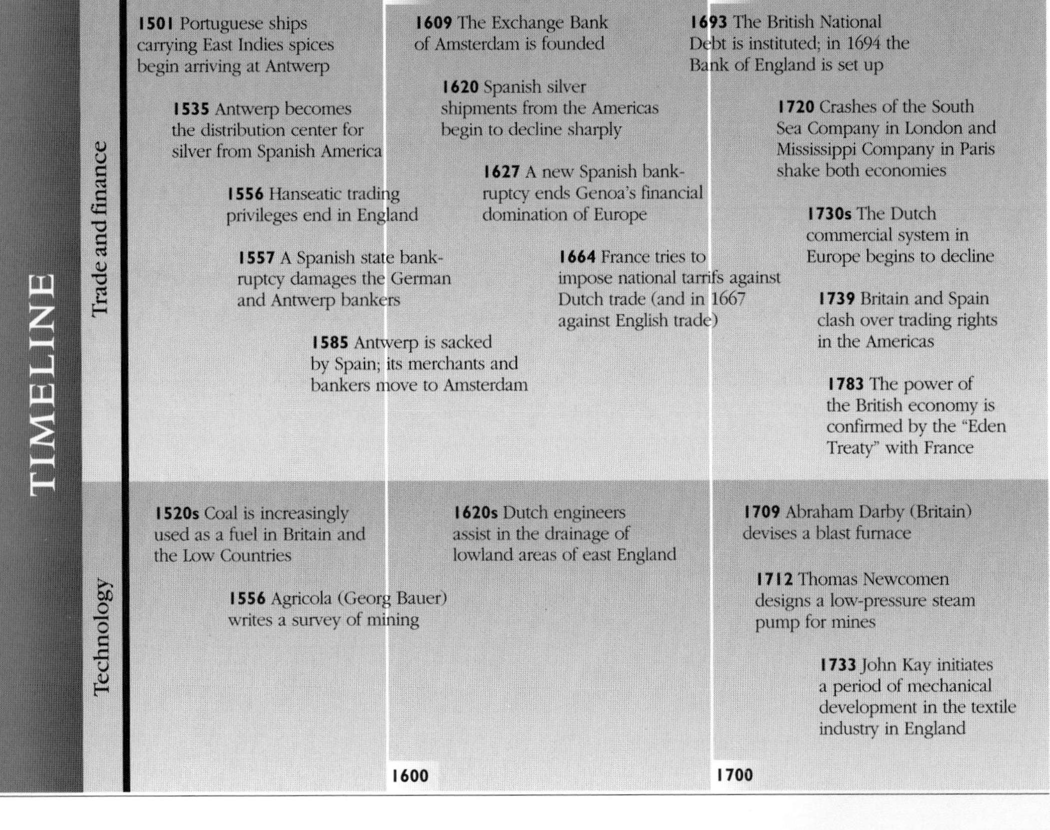
TIMELINE
Trade and finance
1600
1700
1501 Portuguese ships carrying East Indies spices begin arriving at Antwerp
1535 Antwerp becomes the distribution center for silver from Spanish America
1556 Hanseatic trading privileges end in England
1557 A Spanish state bankruptcy damages the German and Antwerp bankers
1585 Antwerp is sacked by Spain; its merchants and bankers move to Amsterdam
1609 The Exchange Bank of Amsterdam is founded
1620 Spanish silver shipments from the Americas begin to decline sharply
1627 A new Spanish bankruptcy ends Genoa's financial domination of Europe
1664 France tries to impose national tarrifs against Dutch trade (and in 1667 against English trade)
1693 The British National Debt is instituted; in 1694 the Bank of England is set up
1720 Crashes of the South Sea Company in London and Mississippi Company in Paris shake both economies
1730s The Dutch commercial system in Europe begins to decline
1739 Britain and Spain clash over trading rights in the Americas
1783 The power of the British economy is confirmed by the "Eden Treaty" with France
Technology
1520s Coal is increasingly used as a fuel in Britain and the Low Countries
1556 Agricola (Georg Bauer) writes a survey of mining
1620s Dutch engineers assist in the drainage of lowland areas of east England
1709 Abraham Darby (Britain) devises a blast furnace
1712 Thomas Newcomen designs a low-pressure steam pump for mines
1733 John Kay initiates a period of mechanical development in the textile industry in England
1600
1700

The counterpart to this struggle for the heights of European capitalism was the beginning of a transformation of the European economy itself. New agricultural techniques (notably the enclosure by private landlords of common land, improved crop rotation and animal husbandry techniques, and the drainage of marginal lands) in the 18th century spread across Britain and the Netherlands. At the same time, transportation was revolutionized by the construction of canal networks, and energy use by the exploitation of coalfields once bulk transport on the canals became possible. Thomas Newcomen's steam

Stockholm
Vänern
Vättern
Swedes
Baltic Sea
North Sea
4
Falkirk
Carron Iron Works, 1762
Glasgow
Watt, 1765
Edinburgh
Belfast
Newry–Lough Neagh canal, 1742
Newcastle
Bolton
Crompton, 1779
Bury
Kay, 1738
Dublin
Liverpool
Manchester
Hull
Bridgewater and Grand Trunk canal,
Cromford
Arkwright, 1771
Ironbridge
Darby, 1779
King's Lynn
Dudley
Newcomen, 1712
Birmingham
Norwich
Bristol
Southampton
London
from 1763
Savery, 1698
Copenhagen
Königsberg
Vilna
Danzig
Lübeck
Hamburg
Stettin
Bremen
Elbe
Elbe–Oder canal, 1745
Amsterdam
1627–1783
Deventer
Minden
Berlin
Vistula
Poles
Warsaw
Rotterdam
Bielefeld
Middelburg
Antwerp
1501–68
Elderfeld
Leipzig
Oder
Bruges
Ghent
Brussels
Cologne
7
Breslau
Lille
Jemappe
1729
Liège
Cambrai
Valenciennes
Frankfurt
Prague
Krakow
Lemberg
La Havre
Amiens
Rouen
Péronne
St Quentin
5
Huguenots
Nuremberg
Serbs
St Malo
Passy
May/Meeres, 1726
Paris
Strasbourg
Rhine
Augsburg
Danube
Orléans
Troyes
Vienna
Nantes
Loire
Canal d'Orléans, 1692
Ravensburg
Salzburg
Buda
Swiss
St Gallen
Poitiers
Geneva
Lyon
Vaucanson, 1742
Brescia
Verona
Milan
Trieste
Venice
1378–1510
Turin
Po
Cremona
Bordeaux
Genoa
1557–1627
Bologna
Toulouse
Montpellier
Nice
Pisa
Florence
Livorno
Ancona
Aigues-Mortes
Marseille
Piombino
Sofia
Ebro
Zaragoza
Corsica
Rome
Barcelona
Albanians
Naples
Thessalonica
Moriscoes
Palma
Balearic Islands
Sardinia
Valencia
Cagliari
Crotone
Athens
Mediterranean Sea
2
Palermo
Messina
Sicily
1
0 400 km
0 300 mi

SELECTIVE breeding contributed to the agricultural revolution of the 18th century. This British illustration shows a prize pig.

engine, which was developed in 1712 in England as a means of pumping water from mines (and soon imitated in Europe), was turned into a source of mechanical power by the Scottish inventor James Watt and his partner Matthew Boulton in 1776. Metallurgy was revolutionized by Abraham Darby and others. Above all, the mechanization of the textile industry initiated by John Kay, Samuel Crompton and Richard Arkwright led directly to the first modern-style factories – and the beginnings of the transformation of work itself in what became known as the Industrial Revolution.

1 Portugal broke Venetian control of the spice trade in the early 1500s, but Venice was a center of trade, finance and manufacturing until the late 18th century.

2 English and Dutch merchant ships entered the Mediterranean in the 1570s to break the dominance of Venice and Genoa.

3 After the golden years of the empire, Spain's economy stagnated, with low investment, little technological innovation and entrenched local interests.

4 The North Sea and Atlantic fishing and whaling fleets contributed greatly to Dutch prosperity.

5 Steam pumps in a mine at Jemappe and the Paris water works at Passy were among the first to be used.

6 Agricultural advances transformed Ireland from a subsistence economy into an efficient supplier of butter and meat for Britain in the 18th century.

7 Urbanization, transport and metallurgical advances gave 18th-century Germany a dynamic economy.

See also 3.11 (medieval economy); 4.05 (world trading networks); 5.10 (Industrial Revolution)

4.13 The expansion of Russia • 1492 – 1783 •

By the late 15th century the Grand Principality of Muscovy was deeply isolated. The fall of Constantinople left the Russian church the only significant Orthodox alternative to Catholicism, and their long struggle against the Tatars had convinced the Russians that the west had survived the last great nomad onslaught only at Muscovy's expense. Despite a Hanseatic presence in Novgorod, Russian trade was mainly with the south and east – Persia, the Black Sea, the Ottoman lands and central Asia.

Ivan III of Muscovy ended the independence of its rival Novgorod in 1478. Two years later Muscovy finally threw off the Tatar yoke. As the 16th century opened, Ivan was pressing the Polish–Lithuanian border around Smolensk and the Dnieper. His kingdom suffered from the weaknesses that were to afflict Russia until modern times: huge distances and a sparse population, oppressive social control intended to ensure that landlords could retain their labor force, and the temptation of open frontier regions to which dissatisfied peasants could migrate.

Ivan IV ("the Terrible") oversaw the Russian conquest of the Tatar khanates of Kazan and Astrakhan from 1552, opening trade routes down the Volga to the Caspian and through the southern Urals toward central Asia. To the west, however, Ivan's plans went disastrously wrong after 1558. Ivan struck toward the Baltic: in the resulting Livonian War, Sweden, Denmark and Poland all intervened against Russia. Lacking the resources for a professional army and unable to rely on the semi-independent *boyars*(high nobility), in 1565 Ivan took the drastic step of converting the former Novgorod lands to a personal fief, dispossessing the *boyars* and redistributing their estates to a service nobility entirely dependent on the czar. All remaining free peasant communities were destroyed. In the resulting civil war a Crimean Tatar army sacked Moscow. By 1595 Russian control over Pskov and eastern Ukraine was secure, but further progress to the north or west was impossible.

Incursions by other European powers continued during the "Time of Troubles" (1604–13): Poland and Sweden intervened in the civil war that devastated much of western Russia. Meanwhile, Russian traders pursued furs across northern Asia, brushing aside the tiny native communities and establishing a series of trading fairs in southern Siberia. Official trade was highly regulated, but huge quantities of furs and other goods were traded illicitly to central Asia and China. Russian pioneers reached the Pacific coast by 1637, but were forced out of the Amur basin in 1689. By 1800 they had established a string of fur-trading posts and forts in Russian America (Alaska).

The first of several huge rebellions shook southern Russia in 1670, but with no independent nobility to support them and little tradition of local autonomy, all were overcome, while a rebellion of the Don and Dnieper Cossacks against Poland allowed Russia to extend its frontiers south to the Ottoman client state of the Crimea and as far west as Kiev.

The defining moment in Russian history came at the end of the century. Peter I "the Great" rejected traditional Russian antagonism to the West and traveled to Europe in 1697–98 in pursuit of ideas, technology and assistance in modernizing his empire. By 1721 the power of Russia's deadliest northern rival, Sweden, had been broken, the trading ports of the eastern Baltic were in Russian hands, and Peter's new capital, St Petersburg, had risen from the Neva marshes to attract French culture and English and Dutch trade eastward. Large state-run iron and copper industries grew up in the Urals in the 18th century, along with a vast armory at Tula and shipyards elsewhere. The economy remained vulnerable to exploitation by European, Armenian, Indian, Ottoman and Chinese merchants, but Russia never became an economic colony of these interests.

When Russian suzerainty over the Zaporogian Cossacks was accepted, the czars came into direct confrontation with the Ottoman empire. Through the 18th century Russian armies gradually drove the Ottomans from the Crimea and southern Ukraine, opening the Black Sea to Russian trade. The czar's new status as a major player in European politics also involved Russia in new wars: its participation in the Seven Years War almost destroyed Prussia, while Russia, Austria and Prussia partitioned Poland in 1772. By 1783, though still a world apart with a unique culture and its extra-European economy, Russia was now a key element in European history.

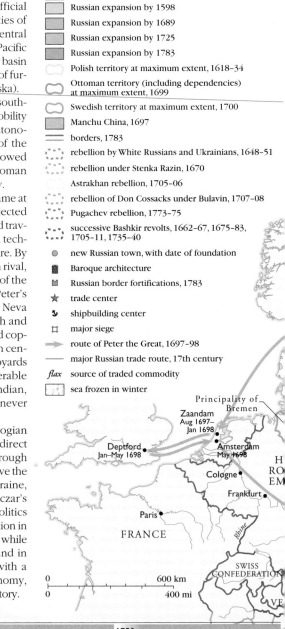

Russia, 1505
Russian expansion by 1598
Russian expansion by 1689
Russian expansion by 1725
Russian expansion by 1783
Polish territory at maximum extent, 1618–34
Ottoman territory (including dependencies) at maximum extent, 1699
Swedish territory at maximum extent, 1700
Manchu China, 1697
borders, 1783
rebellion by White Russians and Ukrainians, 1648–51
rebellion under Stenka Razin, 1670
Astrakhan rebellion, 1705–06
rebellion of Don Cossacks under Bulavin, 1707–08
Pugachev rebellion, 1773–75
successive Bashkir revolts, 1662–67, 1675–83, 1705–11, 1735–40
new Russian town, with date of foundation
Baroque architecture
Russian border fortifications, 1783
trade center
shipbuilding center
major siege
route of Peter the Great, 1697–98
major Russian trade route, 17th century
flax source of traded commodity
sea frozen in winter

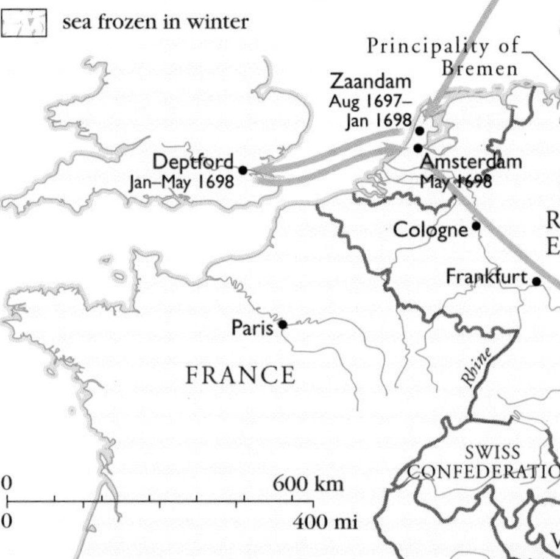

Principality of Bremen
Zaandam
Aug 1697–
Jan 1698
Amsterdam
May 1698
Deptford
Jan–May 1698
Cologne
Frankfurt
Paris
FRANCE
Rhine
SWISS CONFEDERATION
0
600 km
0
400 mi

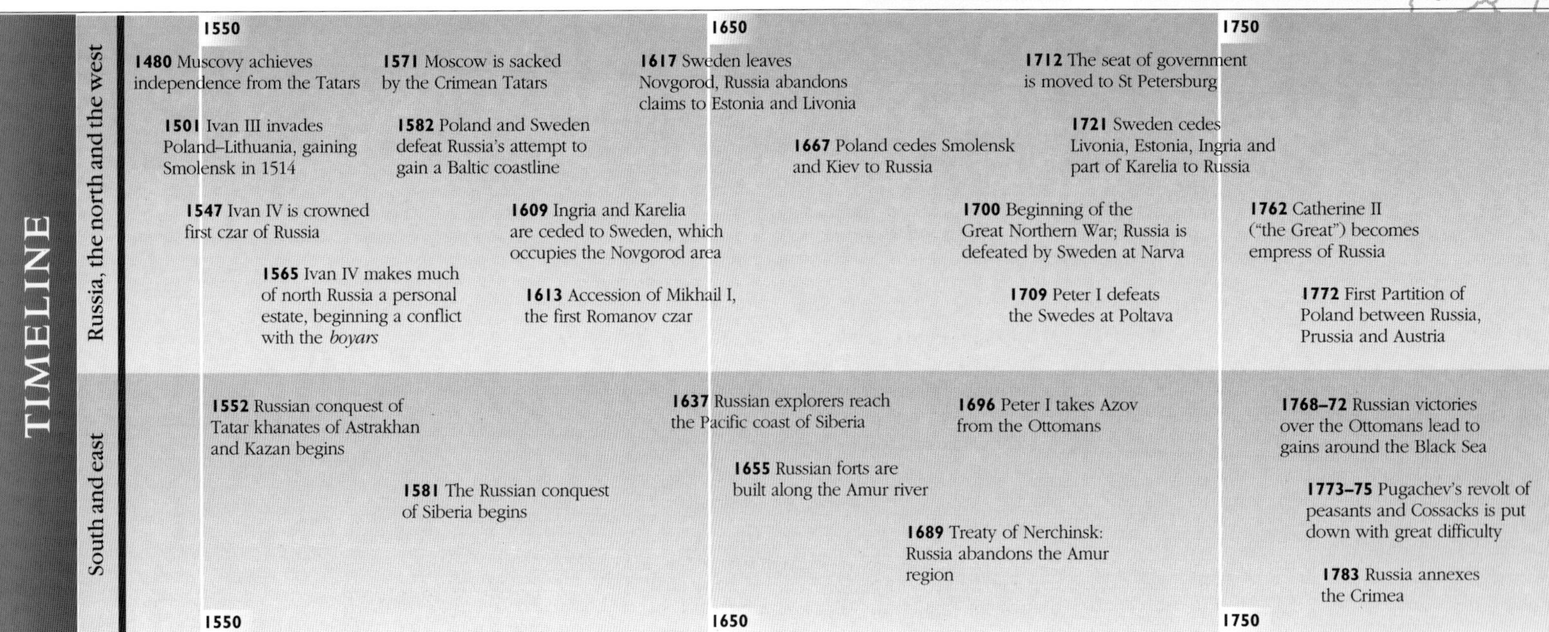

TIMELINE
Russia, the north and the west
1550
1650
1750
1480 Muscovy achieves independence from the Tatars
1501 Ivan III invades Poland–Lithuania, gaining Smolensk in 1514
1547 Ivan IV is crowned first czar of Russia
1565 Ivan IV makes much of north Russia a personal estate, beginning a conflict with the *boyars*
1571 Moscow is sacked by the Crimean Tatars
1582 Poland and Sweden defeat Russia's attempt to gain a Baltic coastline
1609 Ingria and Karelia are ceded to Sweden, which occupies the Novgorod area
1613 Accession of Mikhail I, the first Romanov czar
1617 Sweden leaves Novgorod, Russia abandons claims to Estonia and Livonia
1667 Poland cedes Smolensk and Kiev to Russia
1700 Beginning of the Great Northern War; Russia is defeated by Sweden at Narva
1709 Peter I defeats the Swedes at Poltava
1712 The seat of government is moved to St Petersburg
1721 Sweden cedes Livonia, Estonia, Ingria and part of Karelia to Russia
1762 Catherine II ("the Great") becomes empress of Russia
1772 First Partition of Poland between Russia, Prussia and Austria
South and east
1552 Russian conquest of Tatar khanates of Astrakhan and Kazan begins
1581 The Russian conquest of Siberia begins
1637 Russian explorers reach the Pacific coast of Siberia
1655 Russian forts are built along the Amur river
1689 Treaty of Nerchinsk: Russia abandons the Amur region
1696 Peter I takes Azov from the Ottomans
1768–72 Russian victories over the Ottomans lead to gains around the Black Sea
1773–75 Pugachev's revolt of peasants and Cossacks is put down with great difficulty
1783 Russia annexes the Crimea
1550
1650
1750

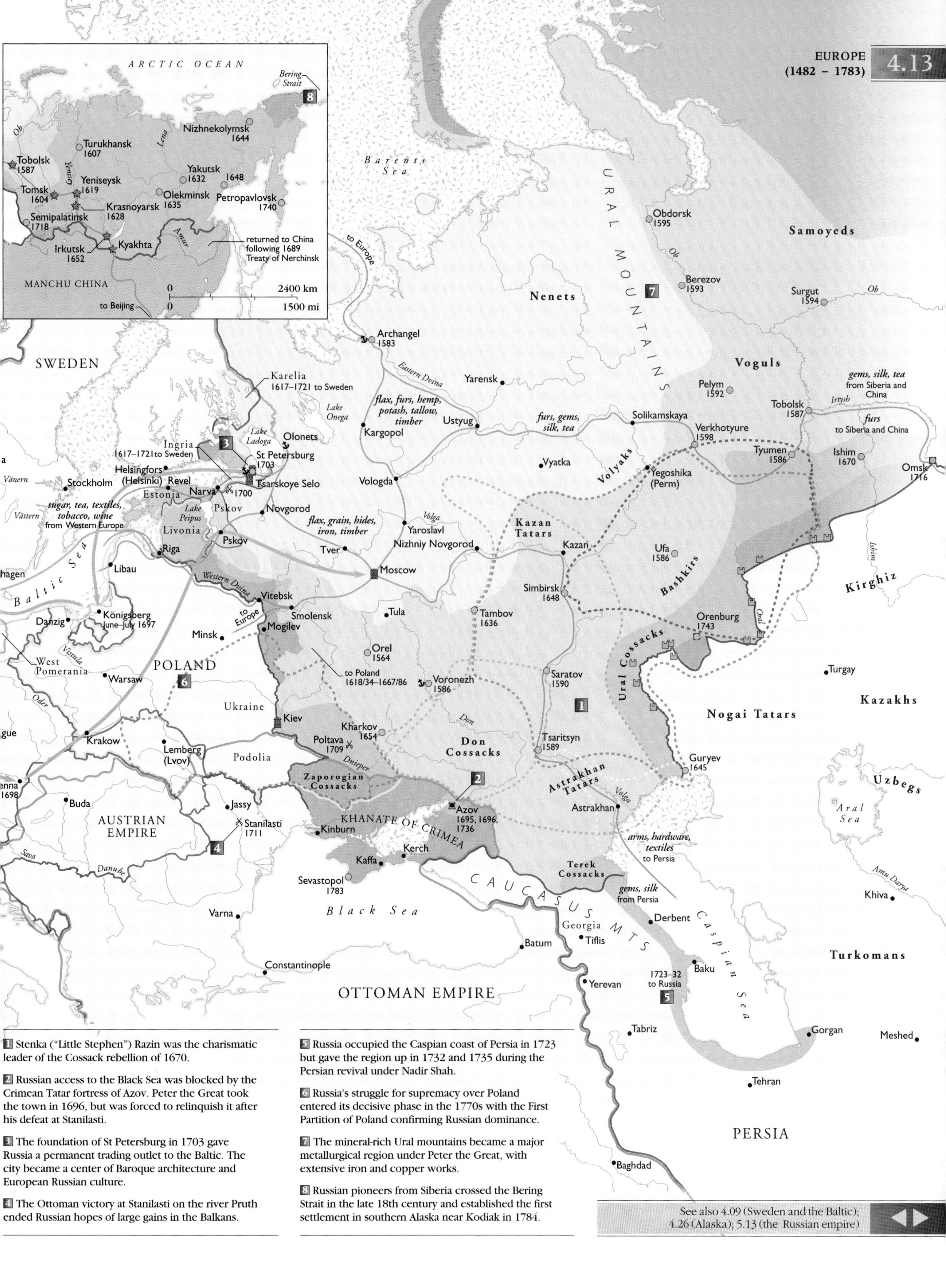
ARCTIC OCEAN
Bering Strait
8
Ob
Lena
Nizhnekolymsk 1644
Turukhansk 1607
Tobolsk 1587
Yenisey
Yakutsk 1632
1648
Yeniseysk 1619
Tomsk 1604
Olekminsk 1635
Petropavlovsk 1740
Krasnoyarsk 1628
Semipalatinsk 1718
Amur
Irkutsk 1652
Kyakhta
returned to China following 1689 Treaty of Nerchinsk
MANCHU CHINA
0 2400 km
0 1500 mi
to Beijing
Barents Sea
URAL MOUNTAINS
Obdorsk 1595
Samoyeds
Ob
Berezov 1593
to Europe
Nenets
7
Surgut 1594
Archangel 1583
SWEDEN
Eastern Dvina
Voguls
Yarensk
Karelia 1617–1721 to Sweden
flax, furs, hemp, potash, tallow, timber
Lake Onega
Pelym 1592
gems, silk, tea from Siberia and China
Ustyug
furs, gems, silk, tea
Solikamskaya
Tobolsk 1587
Irtysh
Kargopol
Verkhotyure 1598
furs to Siberia and China
Lake Ladoga
Olonets
Ingria 1617–1721 to Sweden
3
St Petersburg 1703
Tyumen 1586
Ishim 1670
Omsk 1716
Vyatka
Volyaks
Yegoshika (Perm)
Helsingfors (Helsinki)
Revel
Vänern
Stockholm
Tsarskoye Selo
Vologda
Estonia
Narva 1700
sugar, tea, textiles, tobacco, wine from Western Europe
Vättern
Lake Peipus
Pskov
Novgorod
flax, grain, hides, iron, timber
Volga
Yaroslavl
Kazan Tatars
Livonia
Pskov
Nizhniy Novgorod
Kazan
Ufa 1586
Riga
Tver
Baltic Sea
Libau
Moscow
Bashkirs
Ishim
Kirghiz
Western Dvina
Simbirsk 1648
Vitebsk
Königsberg June–July 1697
Danzig
to Europe
Smolensk
Tula
Tambov 1636
Orenburg 1743
Minsk
Mogilev
Ural
Vistula
Orel 1564
Ural Cossacks
West Pomerania
POLAND
Warsaw
6
to Poland 1618/34–1667/86
Voronezh 1586
Saratov 1590
Turgay
Oder
Ukraine
1
Kazakhs
Kiev
Nogai Tatars
Don
Kharkov 1654
Krakow
Poltava 1709
Lemberg (Lvov)
Don Cossacks
Tsaritsyn 1589
Podolia
Dnieper
Guryev 1645
Zaporogian Cossacks
2
Astrakhan Tatars
Uzbegs
Volga
Buda
Jassy
Azov 1695, 1696, 1736
Astrakhan
Aral Sea
AUSTRIAN EMPIRE
Stanilasti 1711
KHANATE OF CRIMEA
Kinburn
4
arms, hardware, textiles to Persia
Sava
Danube
Kerch
Kaffa
Terek Cossacks
Amu Darya
Sevastopol 1783
CAUCASUS MTS
gems, silk from Persia
Khiva
Black Sea
Varna
Derbent
Caspian Sea
Georgia
Tiflis
Batum
Turkomans
Baku
Constantinople
Yerevan
1723–32 to Russia
OTTOMAN EMPIRE
5
Tabriz
Gorgan
Meshed
Tehran
PERSIA
Baghdad

1 Stenka ("Little Stephen") Razin was the charismatic leader of the Cossack rebellion of 1670.

2 Russian access to the Black Sea was blocked by the Crimean Tatar fortress of Azov. Peter the Great took the town in 1696, but was forced to relinquish it after his defeat at Stanilasti.

3 The foundation of St Petersburg in 1703 gave Russia a permanent trading outlet to the Baltic. The city became a center of Baroque architecture and European Russian culture.

4 The Ottoman victory at Stanilasti on the river Pruth ended Russian hopes of large gains in the Balkans.

5 Russia occupied the Caspian coast of Persia in 1723 but gave the region up in 1732 and 1735 during the Persian revival under Nadir Shah.

6 Russia's struggle for supremacy over Poland entered its decisive phase in the 1770s with the First Partition of Poland confirming Russian dominance.

7 The mineral-rich Ural mountains became a major metallurgical region under Peter the Great, with extensive iron and copper works.

8 Russian pioneers from Siberia crossed the Bering Strait in the late 18th century and established the first settlement in southern Alaska near Kodiak in 1784.

See also 4.09 (Sweden and the Baltic); 4.26 (Alaska); 5.13 (the Russian empire)

In 1713 the Treaty of Utrecht partitioned the former Spanish Habsburg territories between the Bourbons and Austrian Habsburgs, and confirmed that no single empire controlled the affairs of Europe. A new concept emerged of the balance of power; it proved its worth when France, Britain, Austria and the Netherlands formed an unlikely alliance to stop Philip V of Spain from undoing the territorial provisions of Utrecht in Italy. Yet the Europe of the *ancien régime* was still a network of dynastic states, with little effective representation in government by financial or mercantile groups (except in Britain and the Netherlands).

Western Europe now began a period of economic growth, overseen by Robert Walpole in Britain and Cardinal Fleury in France. The religious wars of the 17th century had turned many people toward natural philosophy (science), which seemed to offer a surer route to peace and harmony. The spread of academies of science and observatories was one manifestation of the Enlightenment, as were new movements in art, architecture and music. Equally important were new attitudes to society itself. Influential thinkers such as Voltaire questioned their assumptions about social order and sought a new, rational basis for human affairs. This mainly aristocratic intelligentsia tried to persuade dynastic rulers to remodel society, introducing new ideas to many regions, including the ending of judicial torture and the abolition – despite opposition – of serfdom.

Rising population and economic growth brought prosperity for some but hardship for many. Where serfdom survived, rising prices, falling wages and poor agricultural techniques increased social tensions. Even in Britain, the Netherlands, Scandinavia and parts of France, Spain and Prussia, where agricultural yields improved, the beneficiaries were merchants, financiers and industrialists rather than the majority employed in agricultural production.

Relative peace in central and northeastern Europe allowed the rulers of Austria and Russia to concentrate on domestic reform and the struggle to roll back the Ottomans. The Habsburgs rebuilt their authority in the Holy Roman empire and extended their sway in Hungary. Russia pushed south, and its Baltic fleet sailed round Europe in 1770 to destroy the Ottoman fleet at Chesmé.

From mid-century a new series of dynastic wars overtook Europe, exacerbated by a worldwide conflict between the Netherlands, France and Britain. In the case of Poland (1733–35), a proxy war between France, Spain, Savoy and Austria was largely fought in Italy, resulting in a kind of musical chairs with the Habsburg territories: Poland itself was left entirely dominated by Austria and Russia, its decline finally confirmed by the First Partition in 1772. The Holy Roman empire was effectively swept away in 1740, with the opening of a 130-year struggle for dominance between Austria and Prussia, newly promoted to the rank of great power through the policies and reforms of Frederick William I. His son, Frederick the Great, wrested Silesia from the Habsburgs after the extinction of their male line. Louis XV, allied to Prussia, suffered a defeat at British–Hanoverian hands at Dettingen, but overran the Austrian Netherlands after defeating a British army at Fontenoy. Frederick tightened his hold on Silesia, and Britain (which had to deal in 1745 with a rebellion in Scotland on behalf of the Stuarts) feared the loss of its naval dominance in Europe to France.

Maria Theresa of Austria sought revenge in the Seven Years War, allied with France and Russia against Prussia and Britain. Despite a string of defensive victories, Frederick of Prussia was saved only by the accession of his admirer, Peter III, to the

Austrian Habsburg territory, 1715
Brandenburg-Prussia, 1715
France, 1715
Great Britain & Hanover (in personal union from 1714)
Ottoman empire, 1715
Russia, 1715
Savoy-Piedmont, 1715
Spanish Bourbon lands, 1715
Austrian Habsburg gains by 1783
Brandenburg-Prussia gains by 1783
French gains by 1783
Hanover gains by 1783
Ottoman gains by 1783
Russian gains by 1783
Savoy-Piedmont gains by 1783
gains by cadet branch of Spanish Bourbon family, 1735
borders, 1783
nominal border of Holy Roman empire, 1783
SPAIN state in which Enlightenment ideas were influential in state reform
Spanish siege
scientific society
observatory
route of Jacobite forces under Charles Edward Stuart, 1745–46

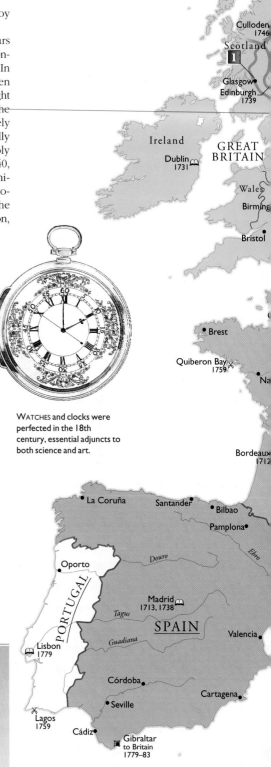

WATCHES and clocks were perfected in the 18th century, essential adjuncts to both science and art.

Culloden 1746
Scotland
1
Glasgow
Edinburgh 1739
Ireland
Dublin 1731
GREAT BRITAIN
Wales
Birming
Bristol
Brest
Quiberon Bay 1759
Na
Bordeaux 1712
La Coruña
Santander
Bilbao
Pamplona
Ebro
Douro
Oporto
PORTUGAL
Madrid 1713, 1738
Tagus
SPAIN
Valencia
Guadiana
Lisbon 1779
Córdoba
Cartagena
Seville
Lagos 1759
Cádiz
Gibraltar to Britain 1779–83

TIMELINE

Military and diplomatic

1717 Philip V of Spain tries to supplant Austrian rule in the former Spanish lands in Italy, but is defeated in 1720

1733 Following the War of the Polish Succession (to 1735) Austria and Russia dominate Poland

1740 Prussia takes Austrian Silesia, beginning War of the Austrian Succession (to 1748)

1756 France supports Austria against Prussia in the Seven Years War

1763 Treaties of Paris and Hubertusberg end the Seven Years War

1772 First Partition of Poland by Russia, Austria and Prussia

1776 Thirteen of Britain's North American colonies declare their independence

Internal affairs

1720 France and Britain endure financial crises

1721 Robert Walpole is the first British prime minister (to 1742), ushering in a period of stability and growth

1740 Frederick II "the Great" of Prussia introduces religious and economic reform and consolidates royal authority

1751–57 Chief minister Pombal introduces Enlightenment reforms to Portugal

1762 Catherine the Great tries to establish an enlightened despotism in Russia

1774 Accession of Louis XVI, last pre-revolutionary king of France

1778 French participation in the war of American independence leads to a financial crisis

1725 1750 1775

Russian throne and the withdrawal of Russia from the alliance against him. An Anglo-Brunswick victory at Minden saved Hanover from French invasion; British naval supremacy was restored by victories over the French at Lagos and Quiberon Bay; Britain also overran French North America.

Louis XVI had a chance for revenge when Britain's American colonies rebelled, but French participation in the American victory caused a financial crisis which ultimately cost Louis his head. By contrast Britain's strength was underlined in the last Anglo-Dutch War (climaxing at the battle of Dogger Bank in 1782), the final nail in the coffin of Amsterdam's economic hegemony.

1 Adam Smith's *Wealth of Nations*, written in Glasgow in 1776, represents the first detailed development of modern economic theories.

2 The Pantheon, begun in 1775 in Paris by Jacques-Germain Soufflot, was an outstanding example of the Neoclassical architecture of the later 18th century.

3 Voltaire (François-Marie Arouet), a central figure of the Enlightenment, was given refuge in the 1750s at Frederick's Sans Souci palace.

4 Johann Sebastian Bach was director of church music in Leipzig, 1723–50. A deeply religious Lutheran, he also wrote outstanding music for the Catholic church.

5 A century of invasions had devastated the grain lands of Poland by the 1750s; demographic and economic collapse led to the partition of Poland.

6 Joseph II abolished serfdom throughout the Austrian empire in 1781, but noble opposition meant that many peasants were not truly free until 1848.

7 In 1778 and 1785, Austrian attempts to annex Bavaria by granting the Austrian Netherlands and a royal crown to the Elector were blocked by Prussia.

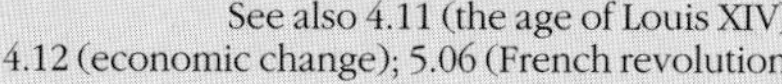
See also 4.11 (the age of Louis XIV); 4.12 (economic change); 5.06 (French revolution)

4.15 The rise of the Ottoman empire • 1492 – 1640 •

The rise of the Ottoman Turkish state from a regional power in Asia Minor in the mid-15th century to the greatest empire in Europe and the Middle East by the mid-16th was a dramatic one. In less than a century, the house of Osman had destroyed Byzantium and become unquestioned leaders of the Islamic world, wealthy patrons of a confident culture and rulers of an empire stretching from the Atlas Mountains to the Caspian Sea.

The key moment in this transformation is often considered to be the capture of Constantinople by Mehmet II in 1453, but the second decade of the 16th century perhaps has a better claim. Between 1516 and 1520 the armies of Selim I (r.1512–20) drove the Safavid Persians out of Kurdistan, destroyed the empire of the Mamlukes on the battlefields of Marj Dabiq and al-Raydaniyya, and secured from the *sharif* of Mecca recognition of their sultan as caliph, or leader of the Islamic faithful.

The conquest of Syria and Egypt from the Mamlukes made the Ottoman territories an integral part of a vast network of overland caravan routes from Morocco to the gates of Beijing. At one end of this network were the spices, drugs, silks and (later) porcelain of the east; at the other the traders in gold dust, slaves, gems and other products of the African interior, and the shipments of textiles, glass, hardware, timber and currency from Europe.

Christian Europe responded ambivalently to the Ottomans. Venice was anxious to retain as great a share as possible of trade with the Levant – even, ultimately, at the expense of Venetian territory – while Francis I of France openly allied himself with

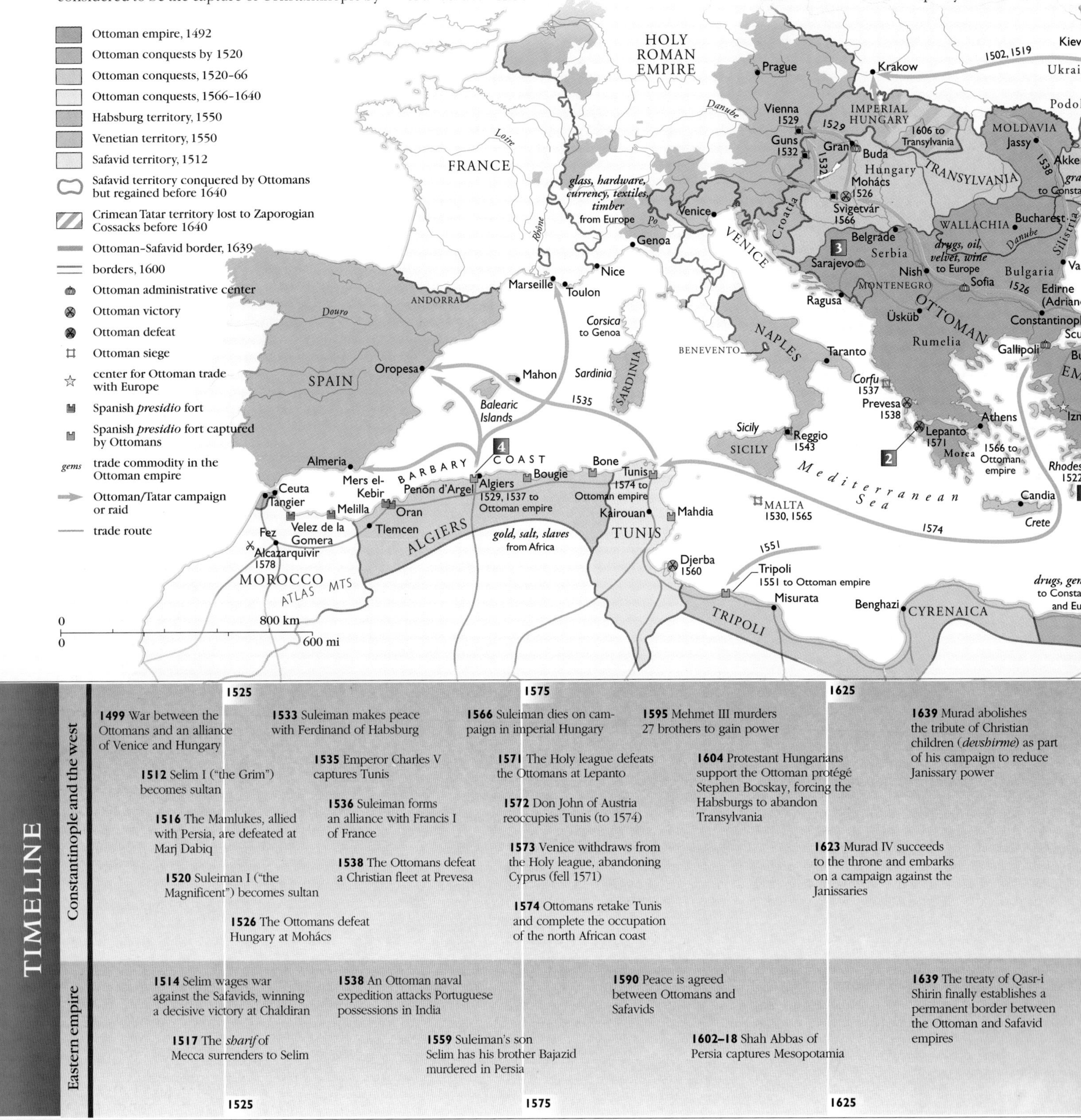

Ottoman empire, 1492
Ottoman conquests by 1520
Ottoman conquests, 1520–66
Ottoman conquests, 1566–1640
Habsburg territory, 1550
Venetian territory, 1550
Safavid territory, 1512
Safavid territory conquered by Ottomans but regained before 1640
Crimean Tatar territory lost to Zaporogian Cossacks before 1640
Ottoman–Safavid border, 1639
borders, 1600
Ottoman administrative center
Ottoman victory
Ottoman defeat
Ottoman siege
center for Ottoman trade with Europe
Spanish *presidio* fort
Spanish *presidio* fort captured by Ottomans
gems trade commodity in the Ottoman empire
Ottoman/Tatar campaign or raid
trade route
HOLY ROMAN EMPIRE
FRANCE
SPAIN
ANDORRA
Douro
Loire
Rhône
Danube
Po
Prague
Krakow
Kiev
Ukrai
Podol
1502, 1519
Vienna 1529
Guns 1532
1529
1532
IMPERIAL HUNGARY
1606 to Transylvania
Gran
Buda
Hungary
Mohács 1526
TRANSYLVANIA
MOLDAVIA
Jassy
1538
Akker
grai to Constar
Svigetvár 1566
Croatia
WALLACHIA
Bucharest
Silistria
Belgrade
Serbia
drugs, oil, velvet, wine to Europe
Sarajevo
Nish
Bulgaria
Var
Sofia
1526
Edirne (Adrianc
MONTENEGRO
Ragusa
Üsküb
OTTOMAN
Constantinopl
Rumelia
Scu
Gallipoli
Bu
EM
glass, hardware, currency, textiles, timber from Europe
Venice
VENICE
Genoa
Nice
Marseille
Toulon
Corsica to Genoa
Sardinia
SARDINIA
BENEVENTO
NAPLES
Taranto
Corfu 1537
Prevesa 1538
Athens
Izm
Lepanto 1571
Morea
1566 to Ottoman empire
Rhodes 1522
Candia
Crete
Oropesa
Mahon
Balearic Islands
1535
Sicily
SICILY
Reggio 1543
Mediterranean Sea
MALTA 1530, 1565
1574
Almeria
Ceuta
Tangier
Mers el-Kebir
BARBARY COAST
Penõn d'Argel
Algiers 1529, 1537 to Ottoman empire
Bougie
Bone
Tunis 1574 to Ottoman empire
Kairouan
Mahdia
TUNIS
Melilla
Oran
Tlemcen
Velez de la Gomera
Fez
Alcazarquivir 1578
ALGIERS
gold, salt, slaves from Africa
MOROCCO
ATLAS MTS
Djerba 1560
1551
Tripoli 1551 to Ottoman empire
Misurata
TRIPOLI
Benghazi
CYRENAICA
drugs, gem to Constar and Eur
0 800 km
0 600 mi

TIMELINE

Constantinople and the west

1525 · 1575 · 1625

1499 War between the Ottomans and an alliance of Venice and Hungary

1512 Selim I ("the Grim") becomes sultan

1516 The Mamlukes, allied with Persia, are defeated at Marj Dabiq

1520 Suleiman I ("the Magnificent") becomes sultan

1526 The Ottomans defeat Hungary at Mohács

1533 Suleiman makes peace with Ferdinand of Habsburg

1535 Emperor Charles V captures Tunis

1536 Suleiman forms an alliance with Francis I of France

1538 The Ottomans defeat a Christian fleet at Prevesa

1566 Suleiman dies on campaign in imperial Hungary

1571 The Holy league defeats the Ottomans at Lepanto

1572 Don John of Austria reoccupies Tunis (to 1574)

1573 Venice withdraws from the Holy league, abandoning Cyprus (fell 1571)

1574 Ottomans retake Tunis and complete the occupation of the north African coast

1595 Mehmet III murders 27 brothers to gain power

1604 Protestant Hungarians support the Ottoman protégé Stephen Bocskay, forcing the Habsburgs to abandon Transylvania

1623 Murad IV succeeds to the throne and embarks on a campaign against the Janissaries

1639 Murad abolishes the tribute of Christian children (*devshirme*) as part of his campaign to reduce Janissary power

Eastern empire

1514 Selim wages war against the Safavids, winning a decisive victory at Chaldiran

1517 The *sharif* of Mecca surrenders to Selim

1538 An Ottoman naval expedition attacks Portuguese possessions in India

1559 Suleiman's son Selim has his brother Bajazid murdered in Persia

1590 Peace is agreed between Ottomans and Safavids

1602–18 Shah Abbas of Persia captures Mesopotamia

1639 The treaty of Qasr-i Shirin finally establishes a permanent border between the Ottoman and Safavid empires

1525 · 1575 · 1625

1 Rhodes was captured by the Ottomans in 1522, when help from Europe failed to arrive for the defending Knights of St John (Hospitallers).

2 At the Battle of Lepanto, Ali Pasha's Ottoman fleet was defeated by a Don John of Austria. Casualties included writer Miguel de Cervantes, who lost an arm.

3 The Ottomans were initially welcomed by many of the inhabitants of the Balkans; in Bosnia, descendants of the Bogomil heretics voluntarily converted to Islam.

4 After the Spanish fort of Peñon d'Argel was taken by the Ottoman admiral Khaireddin in 1529, Algiers became a major base for Barbary corsairs.

5 The deployment of artillery – which their opponents lacked – was decisive in the Ottoman victories of Chaldiran and at al-Raydaniyya.

6 An expedition to Muscat in 1551 secured Ottoman control of Oman and raided Portuguese bases in India, but the Ottomans failed to expel the Portuguese from the Indian Ocean or to dominate the region's trade.

Suleiman the Magnificent (r.1520–66) against the Habsburgs. Reformation and Counter-Reformation helped to weaken the crusading spirit that had once united Europe against Islam. Suleiman reduced Hungary to vassal status after his victory at Mohács in 1526, then conquered a swathe of European territory from Croatia to the Black Sea; his siege of Vienna in 1529 was broken more by the winter weather and the length of Ottoman supply lines than by Habsburg action. Ultimately, though, it was the Ottoman commitment to a savage and apparently endless religious war with Safavid Persia that saved Habsburg central Europe.

The Ottoman–Christian frontier on the Danube achieved a kind of equilibrium after the death of Suleiman. In the Mediterranean, Ottoman conquest of the north African coast was facilitated by the naval victory at Prevesa, but Charles V's (initially successful) offensive at Tunis (1535) and the Christian victory at Lepanto (1571) restored the *status quo*: a rough division of the sea along a line through Italy, Sicily and Tunisia. The Ottoman fleet was quickly rebuilt, but there was no new naval confrontation.

The wars between Ottomans and Christians never entirely halted trade between Europe and the Levant. European merchant ships continued to arrive at Iskanderun or Tripoli in Syria, or at Alexandria, and to unload cargoes of European goods and quantities of Spanish–American gold and silver destined for Asia. These cargoes were carried through the Ottoman and Safavid empires in caravans forbidden to Europeans, meticulously organized, secure, regular and often faster than the European sea routes. The same system of caravans brought Asian goods back for export to Europe from Mediterranean ports. Until the mid-17th century, this trade flourished, enriching the Ottoman empire and ensuring that European technology remained available to the sultan.

The most costly of the Ottoman–Safavid wars broke out in 1602; the reorganized and re-equipped armies of the Persians reversed almost all the Ottoman gains of the previous century before a peace was agreed. Constantinople was devastated by plagues and economic crises. The empire was further weakened by instability, which derived both from the lack of a clear custom of succession (the "law of fratricide" often settled the matter) and from the growing independence and political influence of the Janissaries. These were originally an elite military and administrative caste recruited from the *devshirme* system, by which children of Balkan Christians were surrendered as tribute to Constantinople. This caste increasingly played the role of the empire's kingmakers. From the mid-16th century, too, the caravan routes' profitability began to wane under pressure from alternative European and Russian routes to the East. By the death of Murad IV (r.1623–40), the Ottoman empire was starting to fall behind its European rivals in military technology, in wealth and even in political unity.

SULEIMAN I was renowned as a lawgiver, soldierand art patron. The Venetian artist Titian painted his portrait.

See also 3.16 (rise of the Ottomans); 4.07 and 4.08 (16th-century Europe); 4.16 (Ottoman decline)

4.16 The decline of the Ottoman empire • 1640 – 1783 •

The decline of the Ottoman empire was a slow process, interrupted by periods of revival or stability. The signs of decay became more acute in the 17th and 18th centuries, in protracted conflicts with Venice, the Holy league and Russia. Economic and social difficulties also increased steadily. Nevertheless, in 1783 the empire still extended from the Balkans through Greece, Asia Minor, the Levant and Egypt to the holy places of Islam.

An unsuccessful Ottoman attempt in 1645 to occupy Crete, the last Venetian possession in the eastern Mediterranean, was perhaps the first sign of the empire's failing power. The fleet, mothballed during the Thirty Years War and the Ottoman struggle with the Safavid empire under Shah Abbas, had been allowed to rot. A Venetian fleet blockaded the Dardanelles and threatened Constantinople itself in 1648. Sultan Ibrahim (r. 1640–48) was deposed by the Janissaries during the resulting political crisis.

The deposition of Ibrahim heralded a period of reform and revival under the Köprülüs, an Albanian dynasty that was to occupy the office of grand vizier to the sultans until the early 18th century. Mehmet Köprülü eventually brought the Cretan war to a successful conclusion, stabilized the Danube front against Austria and annexed Podolia, bringing the Ottomans into direct confrontation with Russia for the first time. In 1683, however, his successor Kara Mustafa mounted the empire's last challenge to Christian Europe, culminating in a new siege of Vienna. A concerted German and Polish response, masterminded by

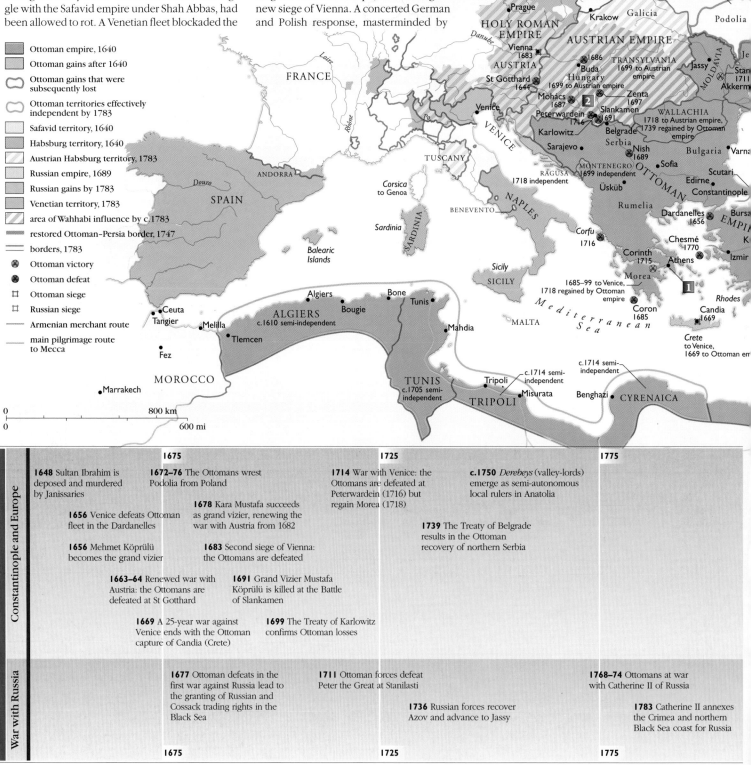

Ottoman empire, 1640
Ottoman gains after 1640
Ottoman gains that were subsequently lost
Ottoman territories effectively independent by 1783
Safavid territory, 1640
Habsburg territory, 1640
Austrian Habsburg territory, 1783
Russian empire, 1689
Russian gains by 1783
Venetian territory, 1783
area of Wahhabi influence by c.1783
restored Ottoman–Persia border, 1747
borders, 1783
Ottoman victory
Ottoman defeat
Ottoman siege
Russian siege
Armenian merchant route
main pilgrimage route to Mecca
Narva
RUSSI
Novgoro
ESTONIA
Libau
Western Dvina
Vitebsk
Smolensk
Vistula
PRUSSIA
POLAND
Warsaw
1672 to Ottoman empire, 1699 to Poland
Podolia
Prague
Krakow
Galicia
HOLY ROMAN EMPIRE
Danube
AUSTRIAN EMPIRE
Vienna 1683
AUSTRIA
1686 Buda
Hungary
1699 to Austrian empire
TRANSYLVANIA 1699 to Austrian empire
Jassy
MOLDAVIA
Stan 1711
Akkerm
St Gotthard 1644
Mohács 1687
Zenta 1697
Slankamen 1691
Peterwardein 1716
Venice
WALLACHIA 1718 to Austrian empire, 1739 regained by Ottoman empire
Karlowitz
Belgrade
Serbia
Sarajevo
Nish 1689
Bulgaria
Varna
FRANCE
Loire
Rhône
Po
VENICE
TUSCANY
RAGUSA 1718 independent
MONTENEGRO 1699 independent
Sofia
Scutari
Edirne
Constantinople
Üsküb
OTTOMAN
Rumelia
ANDORRA
Douro
SPAIN
Corsica to Genoa
Sardinia
SARDINIA
NAPLES
BENEVENTO
Dardanelles 1656
Bursa
EMPI
Corfu 1716
Chesmé 1770
Izmir
Balearic Islands
Corinth 1715
Athens
Sicily
SICILY
Morea
1685–99 to Venice, 1718 regained by Ottoman empire
Rhodes
Algiers
Bone
Tunis
Bougie
Ceuta
Tangier
ALGIERS c.1610 semi-independent
Melilla
Tlemcen
Mahdia
Mediterranean Sea
MALTA
Coron 1685
Candia 1669
Crete to Venice, 1669 to Ottoman em
Fez
MOROCCO
Marrakech
TUNIS c.1705 semi-independent
Tripoli
c.1714 semi-independent
TRIPOLI
Misurata
Benghazi
CYRENAICA
0 800 km
0 600 mi

TIMELINE

Constantinople and Europe

1648 Sultan Ibrahim is deposed and murdered by Janissaries

1656 Venice defeats Ottoman fleet in the Dardanelles

1656 Mehmet Köprülü becomes the grand vizier

1663–64 Renewed war with Austria: the Ottomans are defeated at St Gotthard

1669 A 25-year war against Venice ends with the Ottoman capture of Candia (Crete)

1672–76 The Ottomans wrest Podolia from Poland

1678 Kara Mustafa succeeds as grand vizier, renewing the war with Austria from 1682

1683 Second siege of Vienna: the Ottomans are defeated

1691 Grand Vizier Mustafa Köprülü is killed at the Battle of Slankamen

1699 The Treaty of Karlowitz confirms Ottoman losses

1714 War with Venice: the Ottomans are defeated at Peterwardein (1716) but regain Morea (1718)

1739 The Treaty of Belgrade results in the Ottoman recovery of northern Serbia

c.1750 *Derebeys* (valley-lords) emerge as semi-autonomous local rulers in Anatolia

War with Russia

1677 Ottoman defeats in the first war against Russia lead to the granting of Russian and Cossack trading rights in the Black Sea

1711 Ottoman forces defeat Peter the Great at Stanilasti

1736 Russian forces recover Azov and advance to Jassy

1768–74 Ottomans at war with Catherine II of Russia

1783 Catherine II annexes the Crimea and northern Black Sea coast for Russia

1675 1725 1775

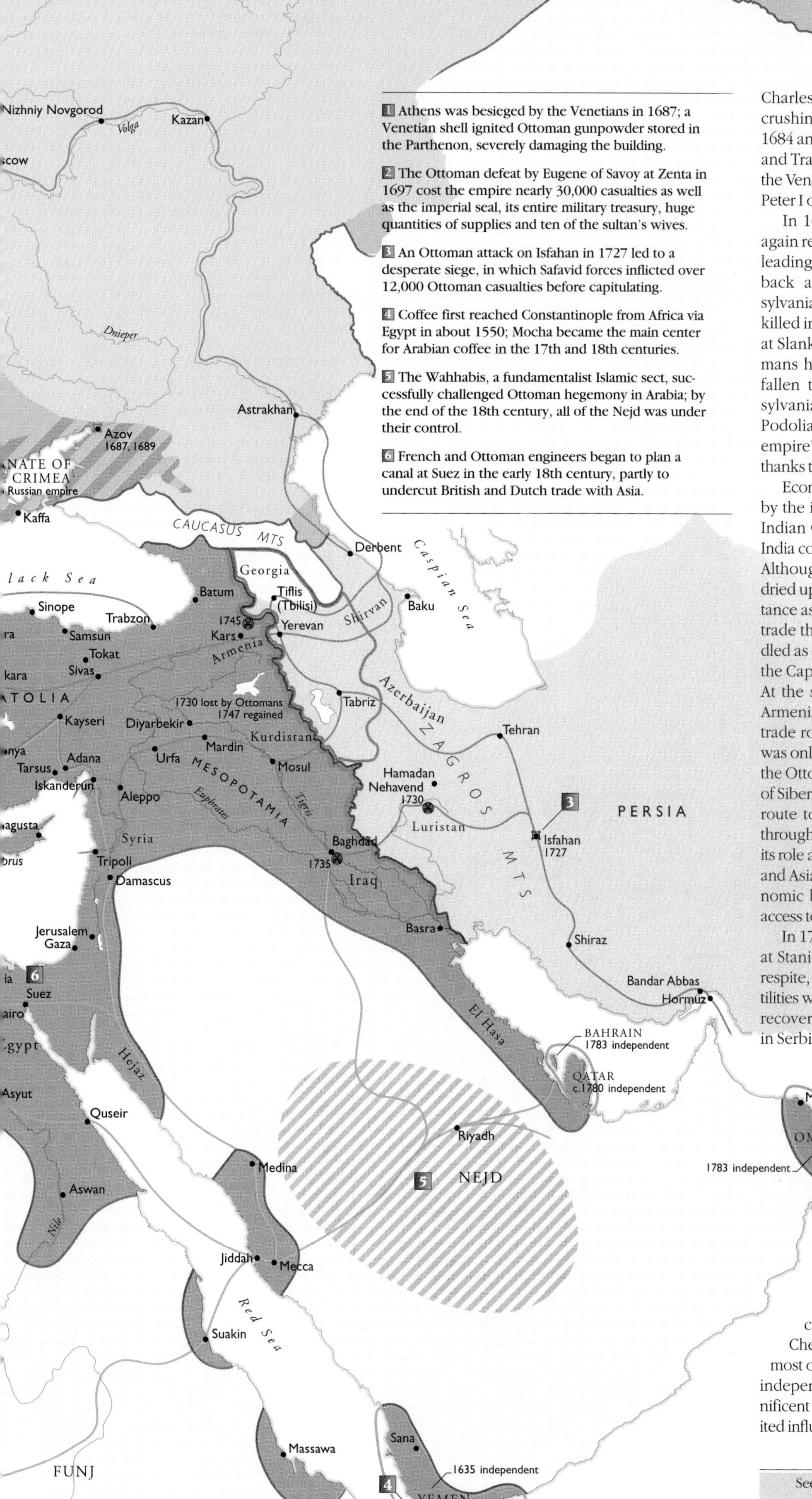
Nizhniy Novgorod
Volga
Kazan
Astrakhan
Azov 1687, 1689
Kaffa
CAUCASUS MTS
Derbent
Caspian Sea
Georgia
Batum
Tiflis (Tbilisi)
Baku
Sinope
Trabzon
1745
Yerevan
Shirvan
Samsun
Kars
Armenia
Tokat
Sivas
1730 lost by Ottomans 1747 regained
Tabriz
Azerbaijan
Kayseri
Diyarbekir
Kurdistan
Tehran
Mardin
Adana
Tarsus
Urfa
MESOPOTAMIA
Mosul
Iskanderun
Aleppo
Euphrates
Tigris
Hamadan
Nehavend
1730
ZAGROS MTS
Syria
Luristan
Baghdad
Isfahan 1727
PERSIA
Tripoli
Damascus
1735
Iraq
Jerusalem
Gaza
Basra
Shiraz
Suez
Bandar Abbas
Hormuz
El Hasa
BAHRAIN 1783 independent
Hejaz
QATAR c.1780 independent
Muscat
Asyut
Quseir
Riyadh
OMAN
1783 independent
Medina
NEJD
Aswan
Nile
Jiddah
Mecca
Red Sea
Suakin
Massawa
Sana
1635 independent
FUNJ
YEMEN
Mocha
Aden
ETHIOPIA

1 Athens was besieged by the Venetians in 1687; a Venetian shell ignited Ottoman gunpowder stored in the Parthenon, severely damaging the building.

2 The Ottoman defeat by Eugene of Savoy at Zenta in 1697 cost the empire nearly 30,000 casualties as well as the imperial seal, its entire military treasury, huge quantities of supplies and ten of the sultan's wives.

3 An Ottoman attack on Isfahan in 1727 led to a desperate siege, in which Safavid forces inflicted over 12,000 Ottoman casualties before capitulating.

4 Coffee first reached Constantinople from Africa via Egypt in about 1550; Mocha became the main center for Arabian coffee in the 17th and 18th centuries.

5 The Wahhabis, a fundamentalist Islamic sect, successfully challenged Ottoman hegemony in Arabia; by the end of the 18th century, all of the Nejd was under their control.

6 French and Ottoman engineers began to plan a canal at Suez in the early 18th century, partly to undercut British and Dutch trade with Asia.

Charles of Lorraine and John Sobieski, inflicted a crushing defeat on the Ottoman forces. Between 1684 and 1690, Austrian armies broke into Hungary and Transylvania (Belgrade was captured in 1688), the Venetians overran Morea (the Peloponnese) and Peter I of Russia threatened Azov.

In 1690 a new grand vizier, Mustafa Köprülü, again restored the empire's fortunes in the Balkans, leading a counteroffensive that drove the Austrians back across the Danube and recovered Transylvania. The following year, however, Mustafa was killed in a major Ottoman defeat by Louis of Baden at Slankamen. By the end of the century the Ottomans had again been routed at Zenta, Azov had fallen to the Russians, and Hungary and Transylvania had been ceded to the Habsburgs (and Podolia to Poland) by the Treaty of Karlowitz. The empire's European territories were preserved only thanks to a renewed Austrian war with France.

Economically, the empire's decline was hastened by the increasingly aggressive monopolization of Indian Ocean trade by the British and Dutch East India companies from the mid-17th century onward. Although Ottoman commerce with the east never dried up entirely (and Mocha rose steadily in importance as an international center of the coffee trade), trade through the Red Sea and Persian Gulf dwindled as ever more Asian goods were carried around the Cape of Good Hope to Amsterdam or London. At the same time, the enterprise of the empire's Armenian and Jewish merchants in pioneering new trade routes up the Volga to Moscow and beyond was only matched by their inventiveness in evading the Ottoman tax system. Moreover, the opening up of Siberia gave Russian and European traders a land route to China that bypassed the caravan routes through Ottoman and Safavid territories. The loss of its role as trade intermediary between Europe, Africa and Asia reduced much Ottoman territory to an economic backwater. It also deprived the empire of access to the latest European military technology.

In 1711 an Ottoman victory over Peter the Great at Stanilasti brought recovery of Azov and a brief respite, but the period 1714–18 saw a revival of hostilities with Venice and Austria, in which the empire's recovery of Morea was offset by Austrian advances in Serbia (Belgrade was lost in 1717). The collapse of Safavid power allowed an agreement with Russia to partition western Persia, but the counteroffensives of Nadir Shah after 1730 cost the empire its Mesopotamian and Transcaucasian provinces. Although combined Austrian and Russian attacks after 1736 were initially withstood, the Ottomans soon felt the full weight of Russian expansion. A series of defeats after 1768 led to the final loss of the Crimea, while a Russian fleet commanded by British officers crushed the empire's painfully rebuilt navy at Chesmé in 1770. By the end of the 18th century most outlying Ottoman territories were effectively independent and the empire of Suleiman the Magnificent had become a mid-ranking power, with limited influence outside the Middle East.

See also 4.15 (expansion of the Ottoman empire); 5.14 (collapse of Ottoman power)

4.17 Central Asia and the Safavids • 1500 – 1800 •

Between 1500 and 1800 Asia saw the rise and retrenchment of Safavid Persia, the expansion of Russia across Siberia and the emergence of powerful new states in Afghanistan and Manchu China. This was the period of the last nomad migrations in Eurasian history. In the 16th and early 17th centuries the nomad peoples once drawn westward by the weakness of Europe flowed back to the east and southeast, sweeping away the settled regimes in India and Ming China. In the late 17th and 18th centuries they were driven west once more by a resurgent China and penned into the harsh lands bordered by Persia, Afghanistan, Russian Siberia and the Manchu empire.

In the 13th and 14th centuries, nomadic Turkic and Mongol peoples had spread throughout Eurasia, from Beijing to the Black Sea. By 1500, most had been converted to Islam and a number of Muslim khanates had emerged, in particular around the oasis-cities of the Silk Route. From Kazan and the Crimea to the Oirat Mongol lands north of the Great Wall, these descendants of Chingis Khan were still hated and feared by their settled neighbors for their capacity to expand explosively whenever their own pastures became exhausted or economic circumstances worsened.

In the early 15th century, the Ming Chinese had expelled the Mongols from their eastern steppe and desert homeland north of the Great Wall. The Ming had then gradually retired behind the Wall. Pressured by the rise of new empires in the west and Russian encroachment into the northern khanates of Kazan and Astrakhan, the nomads of central Asia moved east to fill this power vacuum from 1500.

As part of this eastward movement, the formidable Uzbegs expanded into Ferghana, homeland of the Turkic Mughals. Under Babur (r. 1501–30, a direct descendant of Chingis Khan and Timur), the Mughals established a base at Kabul, then crossed into northern India. Babur's subjugation of the Delhi sultanate led to the founding of the powerful Mughal empire, which endured until the late 18th century.

Safavid Persia grew rapidly under Shah Ismail (r.1501–24), expanding from Azerbaijan to occupy the area between the Caspian Sea and the Persian Gulf, and capturing Khorasan from the Uzbegs. This growth was abruptly halted by defeat at the hands of the Ottomans at Chaldiran in 1514. Seven decades of internecine struggle and desperate defense against repeated invasions by the Uzbegs and Ottomans ensued. Abbas the Great (r.1588–1629), however,

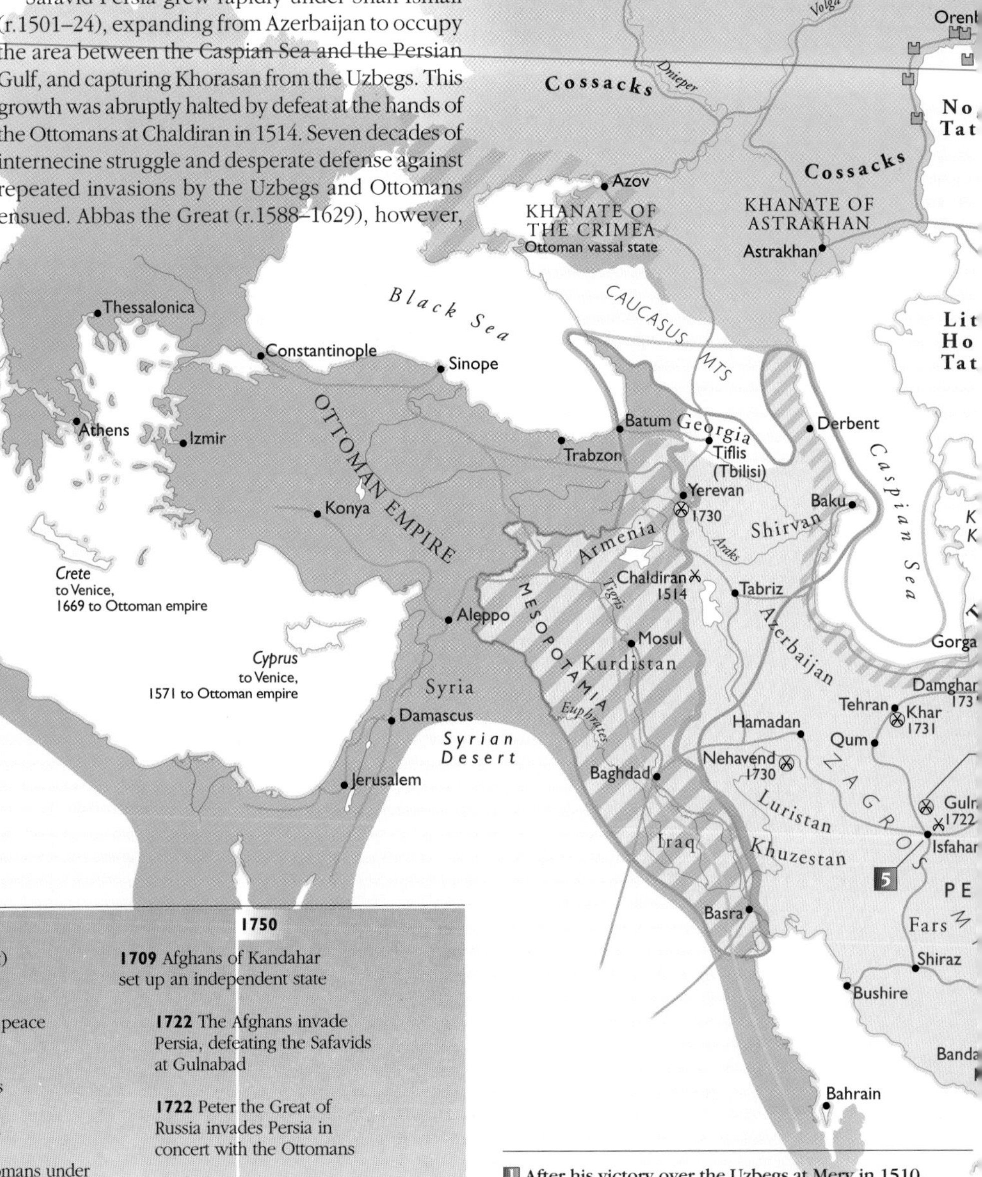

Moscow
Nizhniy Novgorod
Kazan
KHANATE OF KAZAN
Volga
Orenb
Dnieper
Cossacks
Cossacks
Azov
KHANATE OF THE CRIMEA
Ottoman vassal state
KHANATE OF ASTRAKHAN
Astrakhan
Black Sea
CAUCASUS MTS
Thessalonica
Constantinople
Sinope
OTTOMAN EMPIRE
Athens
Izmir
Konya
Crete
to Venice, 1669 to Ottoman empire
Cyprus
to Venice, 1571 to Ottoman empire
Trabzon
Batum
Georgia
Tiflis (Tbilisi)
Yerevan
1730
Derbent
Baku
Shirvan
Caspian Sea
Armenia
Araks
Chaldiran
1514
Tabriz
Aleppo
MESOPOTAMIA
Tigris
Mosul
Kurdistan
Azerbaijan
Syria
Damascus
Syrian Desert
Jerusalem
Euphrates
Hamadan
Tehran
Khar
1731
Damghar
Qum
Nehavend
1730
ZAGROS
Baghdad
Luristan
Gulnabad
1722
Isfahan
Iraq
Khuzestan
5
Basra
Fars
Shiraz
Bushire
Banda
Bahrain
Gorga

1 After his victory over the Uzbegs at Merv in 1510, Shah Ismail had the skull of Mohammed Shaibani, the Uzbeg leader, made into a drinking cup.

2 Hormuz was occupied by Portuguese traders from 1507 to 1622, when it was captured by the English East India Company and Persian forces.

3 The powerful Uzbeg khanate of Bukhara repeatedly threatened Safavid rule in Khorasan, and the Mughals in northwest India.

4 Kyakhta was the main center for Russian trade with China – chiefly furs and European silver for tea, and silk – which grew rapidly from the 17th century.

5 Abbas the Great designated Isfahan the Persian capital from 1587; public works included the Chahan Bagh avenue and the Maidan marketplace.

6 Kandahar and the surrounding area changed hands repeatedly between the Safavids and Mughals for most of the 17th century.

7 The westward movement of the Oirat Mongols led to a long confrontation between Oirats and Kazakhs in the lands west of Lake Balkhash.

TIMELINE

1550 | 1650 | 1750

Persia and Afghanistan

1500 "White Sheep" Turkoman rulers of Persia are overthrown by the Safavid leader Ismail

1510 Ismail drives the Uzbegs out of Khorasan

1514 Safavid forces are defeated by the Ottomans at Chaldiran

1588 Abbas I (the Great) becomes shah

1590 Abbas concludes peace with the Ottomans

1603–23 Abbas takes Baghdad, Mosul and most of Mesopotamia

1630 The Ottomans under Murad IV regain most areas lost to Abbas

1709 Afghans of Kandahar set up an independent state

1722 The Afghans invade Persia, defeating the Safavids at Gulnabad

1722 Peter the Great of Russia invades Persia in concert with the Ottomans

1726 The Safavids retake Isfahan from the Afghans

1736–47 Reign of Nadir Shah in Persia

Central Asia

1519 Babur invades India; he sets up Mughal power (1526)

1540 The Uzbegs re-take Balkh from the Safavids

1552–56 Russia subdues the khanates of Kazan and Astrakhan

1582 Russian Cossack mercenaries overrun the Sibir khanate

1600 The Janid dynasty succeeds the Shaibanis as rulers of the Uzbeg khanates

1678 The khanate of Kashgar is overthrown by Kokand with Oirat assistance

1696 The Oirat Mongols are defeated at Ulan Bator by a Manchu punitive expedition

1717 Oirat Mongols descend into Tibet and sack Lhasa

1759 The Manchus destroy the Oirats

1759 The khanate of Kokand acknowledges Manchu suzerainty

1550 | 1650 | 1750

RUSSIAN EMPIRE
Tobolsk
Tyumen
KHANATE OF SIBIR
Omsk
Tomsk
Ob
Irtysh
Yenisey
Lake Baykal
Buriats
Irkutsk
SAYAN MOUNTAINS
Kyakhta
Ulan Bator
1696
Oirat Mongols
Mongolian Steppe
Semipalatinsk
Kabdo
ALTAI MOUNTAINS
Gobi Desert
1755
Middle Horde Tatars
Golden Horde Tatars
Tarbagatai
Kazakhs
Kalmyk Tatars
Lake Balkhash
DZUNGARIA
Hami
Khalka Tatars
Urumqi
Turfan
Ganzhou
Suzhou
1755-59
Lanzhou
Gansu
Great Wall
Yellow
Ili
KHANATE OF TURFAN
TIEN SHAN
Aksu
Yasi
Kizil Kum
TRANSOXIANA
Tashkent
KHANATE OF KASHGAR
Taklimakan Desert
Uzbegs
Kokand
Kashgar
Samarkand
KHANATE OF KOKAND
Yarkand
Bukhara
Amu Dar'ya
Badakshan
FERGHANA
Khotan
KHANATE OF BUKHARA
KUNLUN MOUNTAINS
1510
Merv
HINDU KUSH
Kashmir
Balkh
Khorasan
Meshed
LADAKH
KARAKORUM
Indus
Tibetan Plateau
Kabul
Peshawar
Afghanistan
TIBET
1642 occupied by Kalmyk Tatars
Herat
Seistan
Punjab
Lahore
Brahmaputra
Helmand
Kandahar
1738
Karnal
1739
SIKKIM
Kathmandu
Multan
Baluchistan
MUGHAL EMPIRE
Delhi
Thar Desert
Sind
Makran
Thatta
Arabian Sea
Safavid empire under Shah Ismail, 1512
empire of Nadir Shah, 1740–47
area disputed between Uzbegs and Safavids
Ottoman conquest after 1512 and subsequently disputed until 1639
Ottoman empire, c.1566
Russia, 1505
occupied by Russia, 1722–32
Russian territorial gains by 1783
Ming empire, c.1600
territorial gains by Manchus, 1783
Mughal empire, 1707
stabilized Ottoman–Persian frontier, 1639–1724 and after 1747
major victory of Nadir Shah, with date
cultural center of the central Asian khanates, with Islamic madrasas (centers of learning)
Russian border fortification, 1783
Russian campaign against the Oirat Mongols, 1720
Manchu campaign against the Kalmyk Tatars, with date
Oirat Mongol migration, 17th and 18th centuries
major trade route
defensive barrier
0 800 km
0 600 mi

NADIR Shah was one of Persia's greatest leaders; in this painting he is seen destroying Delhi in 1739.

brought a cultural renaissance and a renewed period of expansion. Persia regained most of the lands lost to the Ottomans, took and held Kandahar against the Mughals and finally prevailed over the Uzbegs in Khorasan. The Uzbegs now turned east, tightening their hold on Ferghana and establishing the new khanate of Kokand. The Safavid empire, despite a succession of mediocre rulers after Abbas, survived until 1722, when it was overrun by the Afghans.

In the east, the Chagatai khanate of Kashgar had annexed Kashmir and Ladakh before being overrun from Kokand, while Manzur Khan of Turfan had launched raids into Gansu. At the end of the 16th century came the last great nomad conquest. The Manchus, a mixed people of largely Mongol stock, crossed the Great Wall to overthrow the greatest settled state on earth, Ming China, in 1644. As in Mughal India, the invaders soon created a dynamic new state out of the ruins of the old.

In 1696 the Manchus destroyed the Oirat Mongol capital Ulan Bator, causing a westward migration that became a flood in the 18th century. Harried by Manchu campaigns, the Oirats and Kalmyk Tatars destroyed the khanates of Dzungaria and pressed on to the lands around the Aral Sea. The Uzbeg khanates, impoverished by the decline of overland trade, faced a Persia revitalized by Nadir Shah (r.1736–47). Khiva, Afghanistan and Balkh were lost; only Bukhara withstood the Persian onslaught.

Northward expansion of the Mongol peoples was held in check by the line of border forts that the Russians had established in Siberia during their relentless advance eastward. Initial conflict between Russia and Manchu China was eventually resolved in a trade agreement that signaled the final demise of the Silk Route.

Even the collapse of Persia after the death of Nadir Shah could not restore nomad fortunes. A strong Afghan state emerged to dominate the lands south of Bukhara, while China extended its hegemony to the shores of Lake Balkhash by the end of the 18th century. In the space of three centuries, the once-fearsome nomads of central Asia had been confined to a cultural and economic backwater.

See also 3.23 (central Asia and the Mongols); 4.13 (Russia); 4.19 (Mughal India); 4.21 (Ming China)

4.18 Sub-Saharan Africa • 1500 – 1800 •

The arrival of Europeans in sub-Saharan Africa caused dislocations in old patterns of trade and cultural exchange that were unresolved by 1800. Nonetheless, outside influence was nowhere so extensive or systematic that it overwhelmed indigenous culture: several important African states emerged in this period.

The geographical barriers of the oceans and the Sahara, and Africa's abundance of natural resources, had inhibited the growth of an African seafaring or long-distance trading culture. Even coastal trade was minimal until it was developed by the Portuguese and the Dutch. Nevertheless the empires of the Sahel (the southern fringe of the Sahara), notably Songhai, traded gold, ivory and slaves in exchange for salt, glass and other luxuries. Other states flourished and traded with one another along the great river routes, especially those of west Africa.

Portuguese navigators first appeared off west Africa in the mid-15th century; the coastal bases they established drew trade away from the upper Niger. Following a long struggle with the Hausa people to the east, the Songhai empire was overthrown in 1591 by a Moroccan mercenary army at the battle of Tondibi, and a Moroccan *pashalik* (governorship) was established on the Niger. Neither Morocco nor the new African states on the upper Niger – the short-lived Manding empire and the Bambara kingdoms of Segu and Kaarta – could match the power of Songhai at its height.

The early 16th century saw the emergence of other states to the south of the Sahara, including the Mossi around Ouagadougou and, later, the Oyo states of the Niger delta. Asante and Dahomey emerged in the 17th century, first in the interior and later dominating the coast. By the late 18th century both of these were centralized, bureaucratic kingdoms. South of the Equator was the culturally dynamic Congo kingdom, where rivalry with Ndongo allowed the Portuguese to establish a colony in Angola after 1575, which was to become a major base for the transatlantic slave trade. Nevertheless, Ndongo's Queen Njinga (r.1624–63) prevented any further European expansion here. Further inland, the powerful Lunda empire arose in the mid-18th century, and pressed westward.

1 The Funj were pagan nomadic cattle-herders who overran the Islamic state of Nubia in the early 16th century, but then converted to Islam themselves.

2 The Portuguese force sent to support Christian Ethiopia against Ahmad Gran was commanded by Cristoforo da Gama, son of the explorer Vasco.

3 The Songhai empire rose to prominence under Sonni Ali (r.1464–92); its trading towns, notably Timbuktu, were celebrated centers of Islamic culture.

4 The Dutch traded on the Guinea coast in 1595 as part of a campaign against Portuguese trading bases; by 1637 the Portuguese had gone.

5 The Gold Coast-Benin area was the hub of the west African slave trade; in the 18th century 35,000 slaves a year were transported from here.

6 By 1783 the Dutch colony in the Cape region was the largest concentration of Europeans in Africa.

European influence in the states of the southern edge of the Sahara was minimal, and here Islam made its greatest progress. From 1570, Idris Aloma of Kanem-Bornu created the most purely Islamic state in Africa, and built up its power by importing firearms from the Ottomans. Its conversion of the pagan Wadai and Bagirmi states to the east was one of the few genuine territorial advances of Islam during this period. An Islamic revival, though, took place in Senegambia in the late 18th century.

In east Africa, a direct conflict arose between Islam and Christianity, mainly because of the survival of the ancient Christian kingdom of Ethiopia. The conversion of the Funj to Islam was accompanied by a rebellion of Adal, an alliance of Islamic states, against Ethiopian rule in 1527. Ahmed Gran, an Adali *imam*, ravaged Ethiopia for thirteen years before being killed by a Portuguese–Ethiopian force. On the east African coast, Portugal established a string of bases from Delagoa Bay to Socotra to dominate Indian Ocean trade. These were largely successful until the end of the 17th century, when the sultanate of Oman, semi-independent of the Ottoman empire, capitalized on a fierce conflict between the Portuguese and the Dutch by occupying most of the northern bases. Omani and Indian trade across the Indian Ocean revived as a result.

The most dramatic impact of the Europeans on Africa was the transatlantic slave trade, which began early in the 16th century. A trade in slaves within Africa had been known long before; but the demand for labor in the plantations in the Americas and the willingness of many African states to deal with Europeans led to a true explosion of the trade in the 17th century. States such as Dahomey used the provision of slaves as part of their own political processes – waging war in their traditional manner to obtain slaves, or enslaving and selling parts of their own populations. The human cost of transporting some ten million people to the Americas is incalculable.

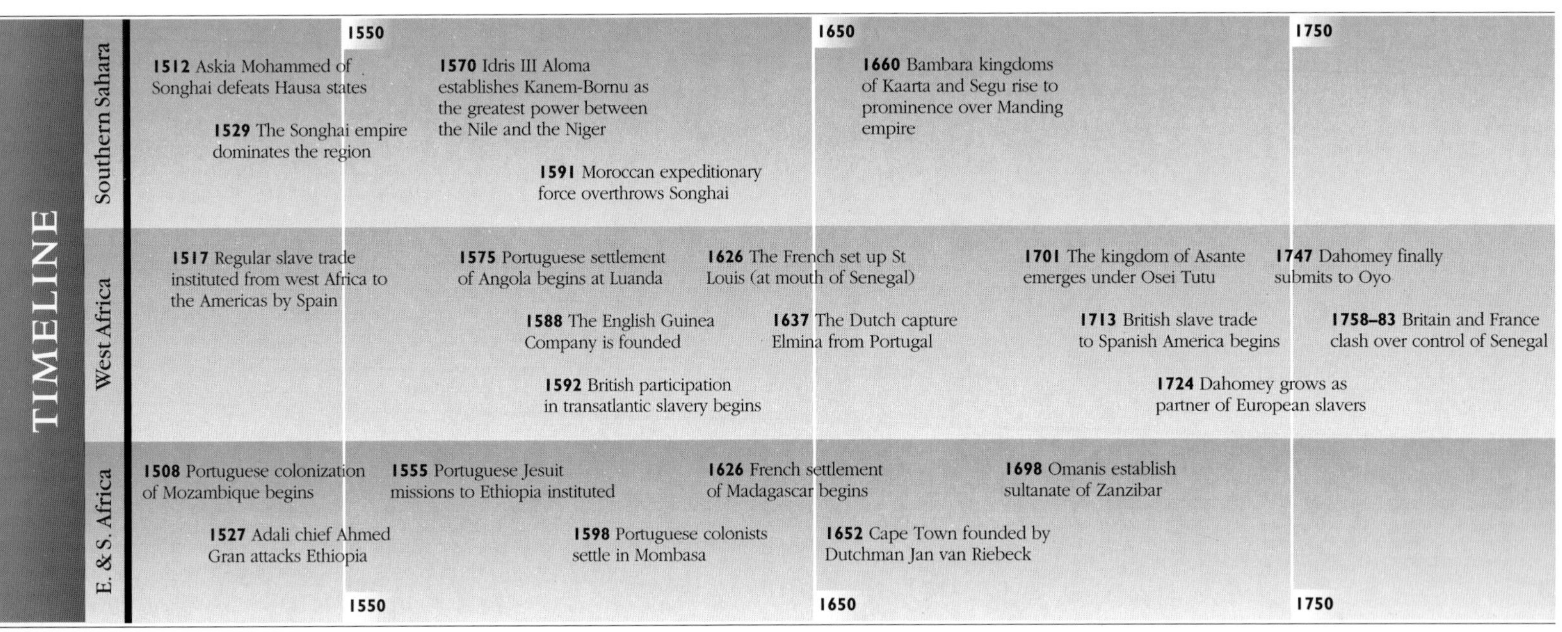
TIMELINE
1550
1650
1750
Southern Sahara
1512 Askia Mohammed of Songhai defeats Hausa states
1529 The Songhai empire dominates the region
1570 Idris III Aloma establishes Kanem-Bornu as the greatest power between the Nile and the Niger
1591 Moroccan expeditionary force overthrows Songhai
1660 Bambara kingdoms of Kaarta and Segu rise to prominence over Manding empire
West Africa
1517 Regular slave trade instituted from west Africa to the Americas by Spain
1575 Portuguese settlement of Angola begins at Luanda
1588 The English Guinea Company is founded
1592 British participation in transatlantic slavery begins
1626 The French set up St Louis (at mouth of Senegal)
1637 The Dutch capture Elmina from Portugal
1701 The kingdom of Asante emerges under Osei Tutu
1713 British slave trade to Spanish America begins
1724 Dahomey grows as partner of European slavers
1747 Dahomey finally submits to Oyo
1758–83 Britain and France clash over control of Senegal
E. & S. Africa
1508 Portuguese colonization of Mozambique begins
1527 Adali chief Ahmed Gran attacks Ethiopia
1555 Portuguese Jesuit missions to Ethiopia instituted
1598 Portuguese colonists settle in Mombasa
1626 French settlement of Madagascar begins
1652 Cape Town founded by Dutchman Jan van Riebeck
1698 Omanis establish sultanate of Zanzibar
1550
1650
1750

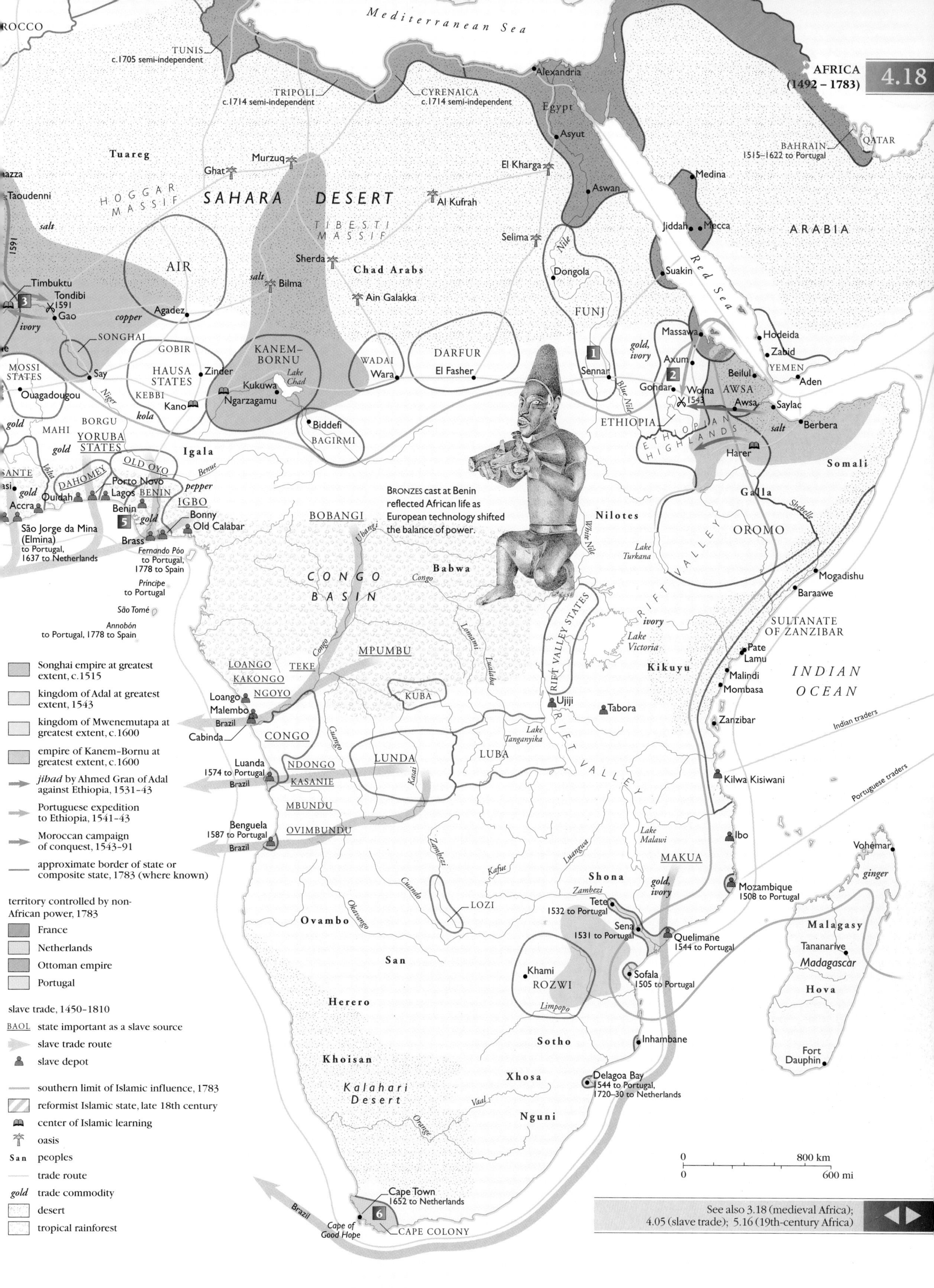

AFRICA (1492 – 1783)
4.18
Mediterranean Sea
ROCCO
TUNIS c.1705 semi-independent
TRIPOLI c.1714 semi-independent
CYRENAICA c.1714 semi-independent
Alexandria
Egypt
Asyut
El Kharga
Aswan
BAHRAIN 1515–1622 to Portugal
QATAR
Medina
Jiddah
Mecca
ARABIA
Red Sea
Suakin
Tuareg
Murzuq
Ghat
Taoudenni
HOGGAR MASSIF
SAHARA DESERT
TIBESTI MASSIF
Al Kufrah
Selima
Nile
Dongola
salt
1591
AIR
Sherda
Chad Arabs
Bilma
Timbuktu
Tondibi 1591
Gao
copper
ivory
Agadez
Ain Galakka
FUNJ
SONGHAI
GOBIR
KANEM-BORNU
WADAI
DARFUR
Massawa
Hodeida
Zabid
YEMEN
Aden
gold, ivory
Axum
Sennar
Wara
El Fasher
MOSSI STATES
Say
HAUSA STATES
Zinder
Lake Chad
Kukuwa
Ngarzagamu
Gondar
Woina 1543
AWSA
Beilul
Awsa
Saylac
Berbera
Ouagadougou
KEBBI
Kano
kola
Niger
Blue Nile
ETHIOPIA
ETHIOPIAN HIGHLANDS
salt
gold
MAHI
BORGU
Biddefi
BAGIRMI
YORUBA STATES
Igala
OLD OYO
Harer
Somali
ANTE
DAHOMEY
Porto Novo
Lagos
BENIN
Benue
pepper
gold
Ouidah
Accra
Benin
IGBO
Bonny
Old Calabar
Brass
São Jorge da Mina (Elmina) to Portugal, 1637 to Netherlands
Fernando Póo to Portugal, 1778 to Spain
Príncipe to Portugal
São Tomé
Annobón to Portugal, 1778 to Spain
BOBANGI
Ubangi
Nilotes
White Nile
Galla
Shebelle
OROMO
Lake Turkana
RIFT VALLEY
CONGO BASIN
Congo
Babwa
Mogadishu
Baraawe
RIFT VALLEY STATES
ivory
Lake Victoria
SULTANATE OF ZANZIBAR
MPUMBU
Lomami
Lualaba
Kikuyu
Pate
Lamu
Malindi
Mombasa
INDIAN OCEAN
LOANGO
TEKE
KAKONGO
NGOYO
KUBA
Loango
Malembo
Brazil
Cabinda
CONGO
Cuango
Ujiji
Tabora
Zanzibar
Indian traders
LUNDA
LUBA
Lake Tanganyika
Luanda 1574 to Portugal
Brazil
NDONGO
KASANIE
Kasai
Kilwa Kisiwani
Portuguese traders
MBUNDU
Benguela 1587 to Portugal
Brazil
OVIMBUNDU
Zambezi
Lake Malawi
Luangwa
Ibo
Vohémar
MAKUA
Kafue
Shona
gold, ivory
Mozambique 1508 to Portugal
ginger
Cuando
Okavango
LOZI
Zambezi
Tete 1532 to Portugal
Sena 1531 to Portugal
Quelimane 1544 to Portugal
Ovambo
Malagasy
Tananarive
Madagascar
San
Khami
ROZWI
Sofala 1505 to Portugal
Hova
Herero
Limpopo
Sotho
Inhambane
Fort Dauphin
Khoisan
Xhosa
Delagoa Bay 1544 to Portugal, 1720–30 to Netherlands
Kalahari Desert
Vaal
Orange
Nguni
Cape Town 1652 to Netherlands
Brazil
Cape of Good Hope
CAPE COLONY
0 800 km
0 600 mi
Songhai empire at greatest extent, c.1515
kingdom of Adal at greatest extent, 1543
kingdom of Mwenemutapa at greatest extent, c.1600
empire of Kanem-Bornu at greatest extent, c.1600
jihad by Ahmed Gran of Adal against Ethiopia, 1531–43
Portuguese expedition to Ethiopia, 1541–43
Moroccan campaign of conquest, 1543–91
approximate border of state or composite state, 1783 (where known)
territory controlled by non-African power, 1783
France
Netherlands
Ottoman empire
Portugal
slave trade, 1450–1810
BAOL state important as a slave source
slave trade route
slave depot
southern limit of Islamic influence, 1783
reformist Islamic state, late 18th century
center of Islamic learning
oasis
San peoples
trade route
gold trade commodity
desert
tropical rainforest

BRONZES cast at Benin reflected African life as European technology shifted the balance of power.

See also 3.18 (medieval Africa); 4.05 (slave trade); 5.16 (19th-century Africa)

4.19 The rise of Mughal India • 1500 – 1707 •

The eastward migration of Mongols and Tatars in the late 15th and early 16th centuries meant that the Mughals, a people descended from Timur's Mongols, were driven out of the principality they had established in Ferghana. Under their leader Babur (r.1501–30), the Mughals conquered an area around Kabul in 1504, and made the first of several exploratory invasions of India in 1519, culminating in a fullscale attempt in 1526. The Indian subcontinent at the time was a patchwork of warring Muslim and Hindu states, among which the Rajput lands southwest of Delhi, the ancient Hindu kingdom of Vijayanagara in the south and the Afghan Lodi sultanate of Delhi were the most powerful. Babur's force of 12,000 men, supported by artillery, overcame the army of Ibrahim Shah Lodi at Panipat in 1526. Mughal conquest thereafter was swift; by Babur's death, all the former Lodi lands had been subdued, while his son Humayun (r.1530–40; 1555–56) invaded Gujarat in 1535, taking the fortress of Champanir. In the 1540s, however, a rebellion of the Afghan Sur dynasty of south Bihar against their new masters almost spelt the end of the Mughal dynasty. The Surs captured the Gangetic plain and Delhi, and forced Humayun to take refuge in Persia. Only in 1555 did Humayun succeed in reoccupying Delhi, but his reconquest was cut short by his death.

Babur's grandson Akbar (r.1556–1605) not only managed to regain all the lands lost to the Surs, but created one of the world's most powerful states. In 1572 the conquest of Gujarat brought access to the sea, while control of Bengal in 1576 secured India's richest region for the Mughals. By 1605 their advance into the Deccan had begun with the subjugation of Khandesh and Berar, with the loyalty of the Rajputs assured by military force and dynastic intermarriage. Akbar's reign brought administrative efficiency and social reform. The empire was divided into provinces (*subahs*) which were administered by professional civil servants who were appointed on merit. Moreover, though himself a devout Muslim, the sophisticated Akbar promoted religious toleration throughout his empire.

Other external powers also arrived in India after 1500. The Portuguese acquired trading bases at Goa, Daman and Diu in the early 16th century. Conflict ensued; the Portuguese defeated a combined Indian and Mamluke Egyptian fleet off Diu in 1509, and repulsed an Ottoman-Gujarati attack on the same base in1538. In general, though, the Indians found mercantile benefits in cooperating with Europeans. By 1500 Indian banking and credit facilities supported a commercial network that covered most of Asia and east Africa, and extended as far as Moscow. Since Roman times Europeans had exchanged silver or gold for Indian silks, cottons, spices and dyes, and European access to the silver mines of Latin America made possible a huge increase in this trade. Trading links with European companies became more and more important in the Mughal economy.

Mughal agriculture was highly efficient (cereal yields were higher than those of Europe until the 19th century), and cash crops (indigo, cotton, sugar, opium, pepper and later tobacco) were developed within a centrally controlled internal market. Indian industry, based on cheap labor and proven, low-level technology, included both the world's largest textile industry (whose products were exported worldwide) and an iron industry producing high-quality steel and cannon the equal of any in Europe. The Mughals kept a standing army of about one million men who were equipped with weapons that, until the 18th century, rivaled European arms. Yet the vast Mughal empire was already fragmenting by the death of the last great emperor, Aurangzeb (r.1658–1707). Religious intolerance had grown under Akbar's successors Jahangir, Shah Jahan and Aurangzeb himself, leading to increasingly frequent revolts even as the empire reached its greatest territorial extent with the conquest of Ahmadnagar (1636), Bijapur (1686) and Golconda (1687). As bases of the Dutch and English East India companies spread in the later 17th century, largely displacing the Portuguese, the Hindu Marathas of the Western Ghats were already asserting their independence of the Mughal empire.

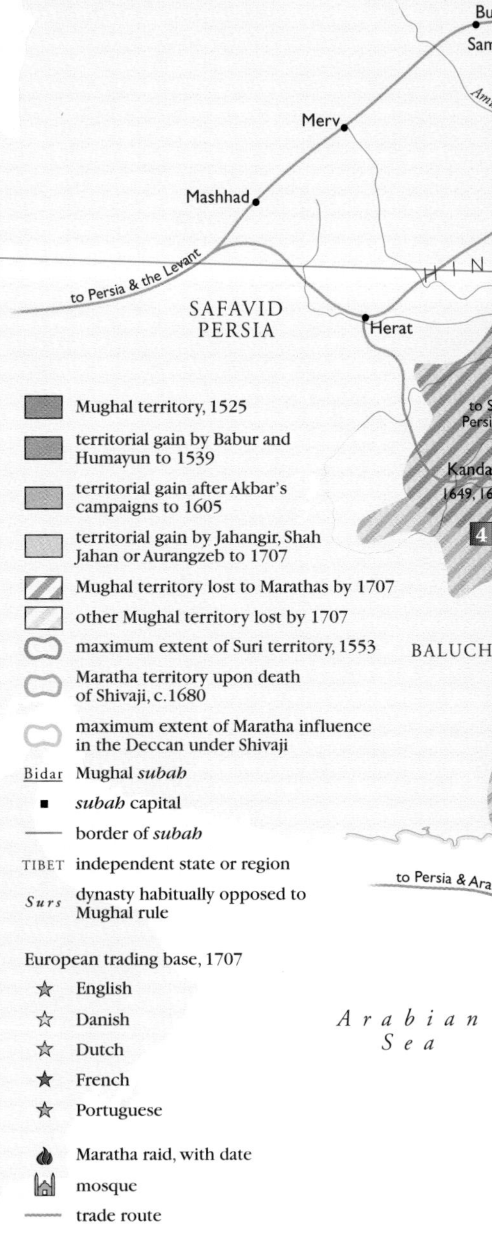

Buk
Sama
Amu
Merv
Mashhad
to Persia & the Levant
HIND
SAFAVID PERSIA
Herat
to Saf Persia
Kandaha
1649, 1652
4
BALUCHIS
to Persia & Arabia
Arabian Sea
Mughal territory, 1525
territorial gain by Babur and Humayun to 1539
territorial gain after Akbar's campaigns to 1605
territorial gain by Jahangir, Shah Jahan or Aurangzeb to 1707
Mughal territory lost to Marathas by 1707
other Mughal territory lost by 1707
maximum extent of Suri territory, 1553
Maratha territory upon death of Shivaji, c.1680
maximum extent of Maratha influence in the Deccan under Shivaji
Bidar Mughal subah
subah capital
border of subah
TIBET independent state or region
Surs dynasty habitually opposed to Mughal rule
European trading base, 1707
English
Danish
Dutch
French
Portuguese
Maratha raid, with date
mosque
trade route

TIMELINE

1525 · 1600 · 1675

Mughal empire

1504 The Mughals under Babur are expelled from Ferghana by the Uzbegs

1526 Babur defeats Shah Ibrahim Lodi of the sultanate of Delhi at Panipat

1535 Humayun invades Gujarat

1539 Suri Afghans of Bihar under Sher Shah rebel and reconquer much Mughal territory

1556 Mughals under Akbar rout the Suri army at Panipat

1568–69 Akbar captures the Rajput fortresses of Chittaurgarh and Rathambhor

1571 Construction of new capital Fatehpur Sikri begins

1572 Conquest of Gujarat gives the Mughals a seaport

1576 The Mughal conquest of Bengal is completed

1598 The Mughal capital is moved to Agra

1632 Shah Jahan begins the Mughal conquest of Deccan

1659–70 The Hindu Maratha leader Shivaji defeats Bijapur and sacks Surat

1669–78 Religious persecution prompts rebellions by the Jats and Sikhs

1679–1709 War between the Mughals and Hindu Rajputs

1707 Death of Aurangzeb marks the start of the disintegration of the Mughal empire

Europeans in India

1498 A Portuguese expedition under Vasco da Gama reaches the Malabar Coast

1509 The Portuguese under Francisco de Almeida defeat Egyptian–Indian fleet at Diu

1538 The Portuguese defeat an attack on Diu by Ottoman and Gujarati forces

1608 The English East India Company receives its first trading concessions in India

1612 The English East India Company defeats a Portuguese fleet at Surat

1661 The English East India Company gains a base at Bombay

1664 The French East India Company is founded

1685 The English are expelled from Surat by Aurangzeb

1525 · 1600 · 1675

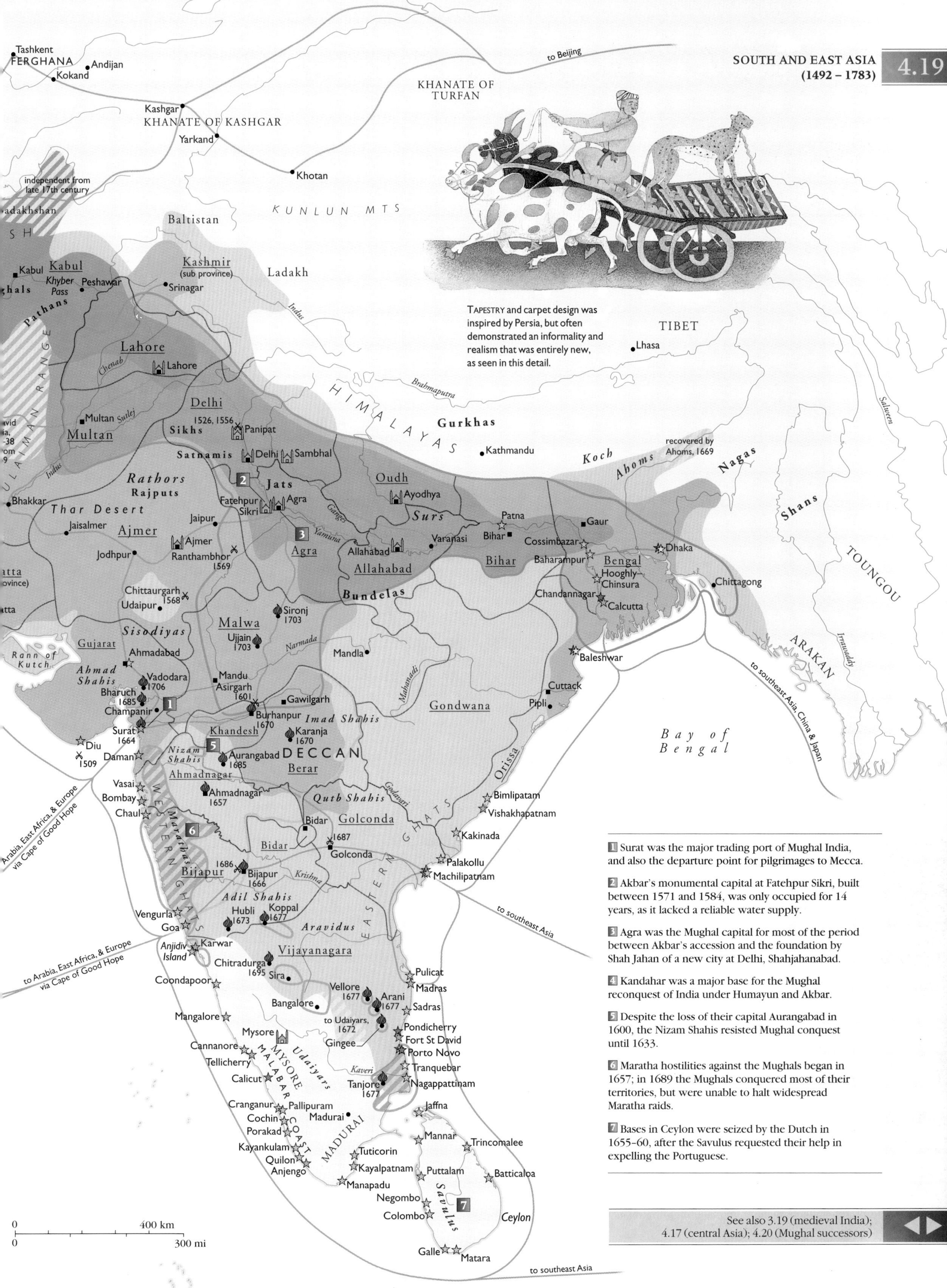
Tashkent
FERGHANA
Andijan
Kokand
to Beijing
KHANATE OF TURFAN
Kashgar
KHANATE OF KASHGAR
Yarkand
Khotan
independent from late 17th century
KUNLUN MTS
Baltistan
Kabul
Kabul
Khyber Pass
Peshawar
Kashmir
(sub province)
Srinagar
Ladakh
Pathans
Indus
Lahore
Chenab
Lahore
TIBET
Lhasa
Brahmaputra
HIMALAYAS
Salween
Delhi
Multan
Sutlej
Multan
1526, 1556
Panipat
Sikhs
Satnamis
Delhi
Sambhal
Gurkhas
Kathmandu
recovered by Ahoms, 1669
Koch
Ahoms
Nagas
Rathors
Rajputs
Jats
Fatehpur Sikri
Agra
Oudh
Ayodhya
Bhakkar
Thar Desert
Jaisalmer
Ajmer
Jaipur
Ajmer
Ranthambhor
1569
Jodhpur
Agra
Yamuna
Ganges
Surs
Patna
Bihar
Gaur
Varanasi
Allahabad
Allahabad
Bihar
Cossimbazar
Baharampur
Bengal
Hooghly
Chinsura
Dhaka
Shans
TOUNGOU
Chittagong
Chandannagar
Calcutta
Bundelas
Chittaurgarh
1568
Udaipur
Sironj
1703
Malwa
Ujjain
1703
Narmada
Sisodiyas
Gujarat
Rann of Kutch
Ahmadabad
Ahmad Shahis
Vadodara
1706
Bharuch
1685
Champanir
Mandu
Asirgarh
1601
Mandla
Mahanadi
Gawilgarh
Burhanpur
1670
Imad Shahis
Gondwana
Baleshwar
Cuttack
Pipli
ARAKAN
Irrawaddy
to southeast Asia, China & Japan
Surat
1664
Diu
1509
Daman
Khandesh
Karanja
1670
Nizam Shahis
Aurangabad
1685
DECCAN
Berar
Bay of Bengal
Orissa
Ahmadnagar
Ahmadnagar
1657
Vasai
Bombay
Chaul
WESTERN GHATS
Godavari
Qutb Shahis
Bimlipatam
Vishakhapatnam
Marathas
Bidar
Golconda
1687
Golconda
Bidar
Kakinada
EASTERN GHATS
Arabia, East Africa, & Europe via Cape of Good Hope
1686
Bijapur
Bijapur
1666
Krishna
Palakollu
Machilipatnam
Adil Shahis
Vengurla
Goa
Hubli
1673
Koppal
1677
Aravidus
to southeast Asia
Anjidiv Island
Karwar
Chitradurga
1695
Vijayanagara
Sira
to Arabia, East Africa, & Europe via Cape of Good Hope
Pulicat
Madras
Coondapoor
Vellore
1677
Arani
1677
Sadras
Bangalore
Mangalore
to Udaiyars, 1672
Mysore
Pondicherry
Fort St David
Porto Novo
Gingee
Cannanore
Tellicherry
MYSORE
Udaiyars
MALABAR
Calicut
Kaveri
Tranquebar
Tanjore
1677
Nagappattinam
Cranganur
Pallipuram
Cochin
Porakad
Madurai
COAST
MADURAI
Jaffna
Mannar
Trincomalee
Kayankulam
Quilon
Anjengo
Tuticorin
Kayalpatnam
Puttalam
Batticaloa
Manapadu
Negombo
Savulus
Colombo
Ceylon
Galle
Matara
to southeast Asia
0 400 km
0 300 mi

TAPESTRY and carpet design was inspired by Persia, but often demonstrated an informality and realism that was entirely new, as seen in this detail.

1 Surat was the major trading port of Mughal India, and also the departure point for pilgrimages to Mecca.

2 Akbar's monumental capital at Fatehpur Sikri, built between 1571 and 1584, was only occupied for 14 years, as it lacked a reliable water supply.

3 Agra was the Mughal capital for most of the period between Akbar's accession and the foundation by Shah Jahan of a new city at Delhi, Shahjahanabad.

4 Kandahar was a major base for the Mughal reconquest of India under Humayun and Akbar.

5 Despite the loss of their capital Aurangabad in 1600, the Nizam Shahis resisted Mughal conquest until 1633.

6 Maratha hostilities against the Mughals began in 1657; in 1689 the Mughals conquered most of their territories, but were unable to halt widespread Maratha raids.

7 Bases in Ceylon were seized by the Dutch in 1655–60, after the Savulus requested their help in expelling the Portuguese.

See also 3.19 (medieval India); 4.17 (central Asia); 4.20 (Mughal successors)

4.20 The successors to Mughal India • 1707 – 1783 •

The beginning of the decline of Mughal power in India is variously dated at 1707 (death of Aurangzeb), 1739 (sack of Delhi by the Persians), 1757 (victory of Robert Clive at Plassey) or even 1761 (defeat of the Marathas, apparent successors to the Mughals, by the Afghans at Panipat). What is beyond question is that by the last quarter of the 18th century India had suffered a long period of devastating wars and foreign intervention, and the major powers in the subcontinent were the Maratha Confederacy, Mysore and the British East India Company. The Mughal empire survived in name only.

The empire's disintegration may be traced to the latter part of the reign of Aurangzeb (r.1658–1707). The cultural and religious pluralism fostered by Akbar began to disappear, partly because of religious intolerance promoted by Aurangzeb himself. The empire had reached its natural frontiers in Assam, Nepal and the far south of India; with no fresh lands to dispense, the emperor could not keep the loyalty of the class of public officials, or *mansabdars*, without high taxation. The crucial link between wealth and public service began to break down as more *mansabdars* became directly involved in trade and sought ways of making their wealth hereditary rather than reverting to the emperor at their death. Provincial governors and viceroys (*subadars* and *nawabs*) became increasingly independent throughout India in the 18th century.

The greatest threat to the Mughal empire came from the Marathas, a Hindu people from the Western Ghats. Under Sivaji (r.1647–80), the Marathas resisted all attempts at Mughal conquest and began to raid extensively across central India, sacking Surat, the empire's main port, in 1664. The covert support of many Hindu merchants enabled the Marathas to acquire superior weaponry, which, combined with great mobility, made them formidable opponents.

Mughal military problems multiplied in the course of the 18th century. In 1739 the Persian leader Nadir Shah (r.1736–47) defeated a Mughal army at Karnal and sacked Delhi. In 1740 the Marathas launched an invasion of the Carnatic; their defeat of the *nawab* at Damalcherry prompted intervention by the semi-independent Nizam of Hyderabad. By 1744, both French and English East India Companies had been drawn into the conflict. The French occupied Madras, the principal British base in the Carnatic, in 1746.

Further hostilities in 1749 saw the deposition of the Nizam's appointed *nawab* of Arcot by the French and their protégé, Chanda Sahib. The Nizam himself was killed, and his successor appointed the French administrator Joseph Dupleix governor of all of Mughal south India in return for a military alliance. The British Company allied itself with Mysore and the Marathas, and Robert Clive won a spectacular victory over Chanda Sahib and the French at Arcot. While Maratha forces overran the west of the Nizam's territories, Clive forced the French to surrender at Trichinopoly in 1752.

In 1756 British interests were again threatened by an independent Mughal *nawab*, this time in Bengal. Siraj ud-Daulah (r.1756–57) captured the Company's base at Calcutta. Clive responded by securing the loyalty of the Bengali army commander Mir Jafar Khan, and using the Company's naval supremacy to transport troops to Bengal from the Carnatic. The

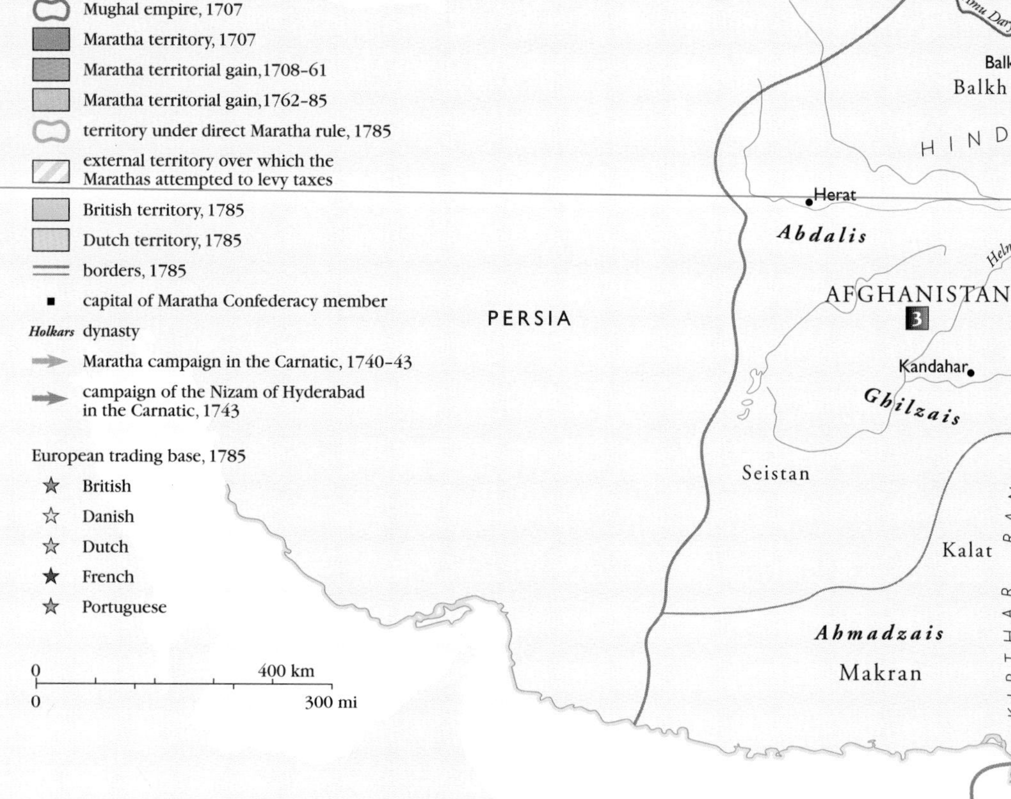

Mughal empire, 1707
Maratha territory, 1707
Maratha territorial gain, 1708–61
Maratha territorial gain, 1762–85
territory under direct Maratha rule, 1785
external territory over which the Marathas attempted to levy taxes
British territory, 1785
Dutch territory, 1785
borders, 1785
capital of Maratha Confederacy member
Holkars dynasty
Maratha campaign in the Carnatic, 1740–43
campaign of the Nizam of Hyderabad in the Carnatic, 1743
European trading base, 1785
British
Danish
Dutch
French
Portuguese
0
400 km
0
300 mi
PERSIA
KHANATE BUKHA
Amu Darya
Balkh
Balkh
HIND
Herat
Abdalis
AFGHANISTAN
3
Kandahar
Ghilzais
Seistan
Kalat
Ahmadzais
Makran
KIRTHAR RANGE

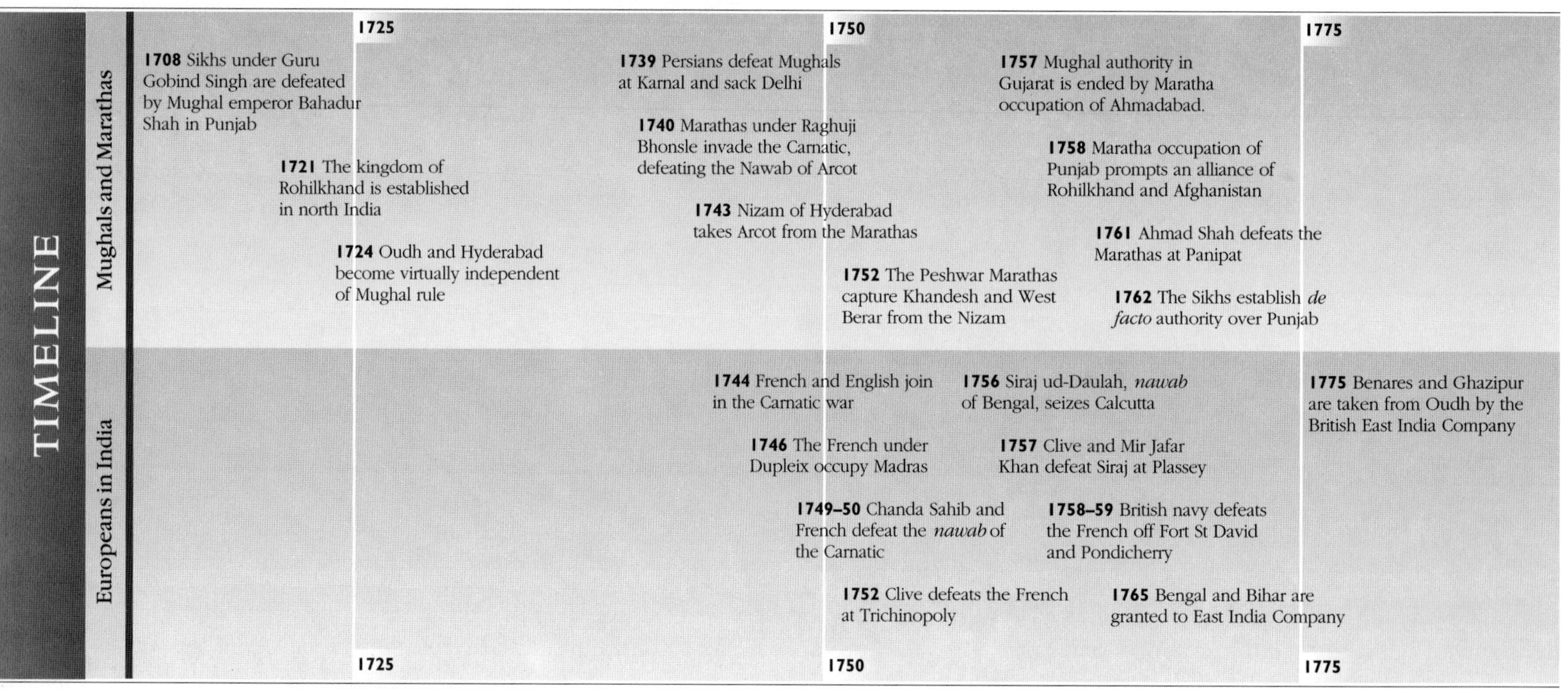

TIMELINE
Mughals and Marathas
1725
1750
1775
1708 Sikhs under Guru Gobind Singh are defeated by Mughal emperor Bahadur Shah in Punjab
1721 The kingdom of Rohilkhand is established in north India
1724 Oudh and Hyderabad become virtually independent of Mughal rule
1739 Persians defeat Mughals at Karnal and sack Delhi
1740 Marathas under Raghuji Bhonsle invade the Carnatic, defeating the Nawab of Arcot
1743 Nizam of Hyderabad takes Arcot from the Marathas
1752 The Peshwar Marathas capture Khandesh and West Berar from the Nizam
1757 Mughal authority in Gujarat is ended by Maratha occupation of Ahmadabad.
1758 Maratha occupation of Punjab prompts an alliance of Rohilkhand and Afghanistan
1761 Ahmad Shah defeats the Marathas at Panipat
1762 The Sikhs establish de facto authority over Punjab
Europeans in India
1744 French and English join in the Carnatic war
1746 The French under Dupleix occupy Madras
1749–50 Chanda Sahib and French defeat the nawab of the Carnatic
1752 Clive defeats the French at Trichinopoly
1756 Siraj ud-Daulah, nawab of Bengal, seizes Calcutta
1757 Clive and Mir Jafar Khan defeat Siraj at Plassey
1758–59 British navy defeats the French off Fort St David and Pondicherry
1765 Bengal and Bihar are granted to East India Company
1775 Benares and Ghazipur are taken from Oudh by the British East India Company
1725
1750
1775

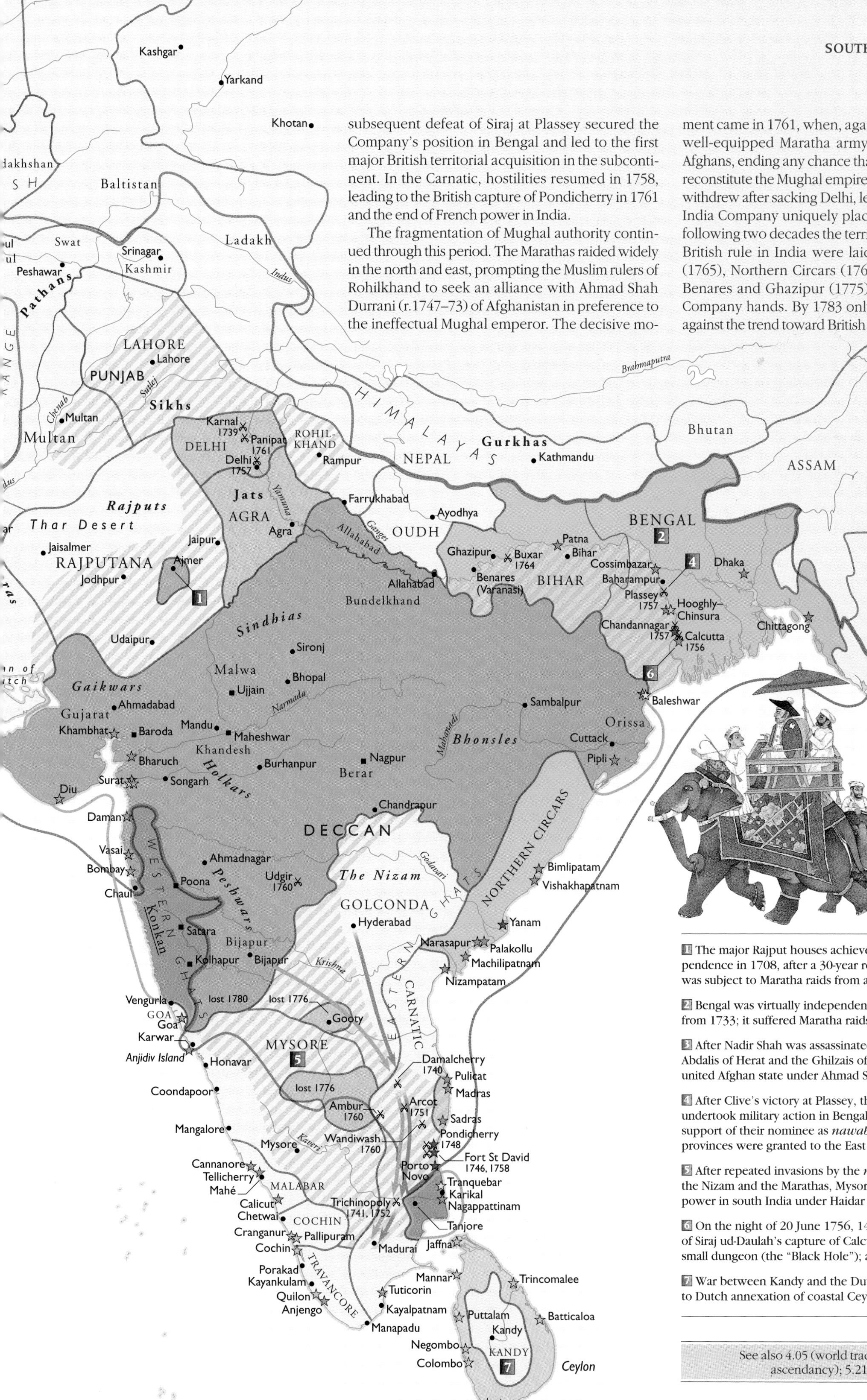
Kashgar
Yarkand
Khotan
Badakhshan
Baltistan
Swat
Srinagar
Kashmir
Ladakh
Indus
Peshawar
Pathans
LAHORE
Lahore
PUNJAB
Sutlej
Chenab
Sikhs
Multan
Multan
Brahmaputra
HIMALAYAS
Karnal 1739
Panipat 1761
DELHI
Delhi 1757
ROHILKHAND
Rampur
Gurkhas
NEPAL
Kathmandu
Bhutan
ASSAM
Nagas
Shans
Jats
AGRA
Yamuna
Agra
Rajputs
Thar Desert
Jaipur
Jaisalmer
RAJPUTANA
Ajmer
Jodhpur
Farrukhabad
Ayodhya
OUDH
Ganges
Allahabad
Allahabad
Bundelkhand
BENGAL
2
Patna
Bihar
Ghazipur
Buxar 1764
Benares (Varanasi)
BIHAR
Cossimbazar
4
Dhaka
Baharampur
Plassey 1757
Hooghly–Chinsura
Chandannagar 1757
Calcutta 1756
BURMA
Chittagong
Chins
ARAKAN
Irrawaddy
1
Udaipur
Sindhias
Sironj
Malwa
Bhopal
Ujjain
Narmada
Gaikwars
Ahmadabad
Gujarat
Khambhat
Baroda
Mandu
Maheshwar
Khandesh
Bharuch
Surat
Songarh
Burhanpur
Holkars
Nagpur
Berar
Mahanadi
Bhonsles
Sambalpur
6
Baleshwar
Orissa
Cuttack
Pipli
Diu
Daman
Chandrapur
DECCAN
NORTHERN CIRCARS
Vasai
Bombay
Chaul
WESTERN GHATS
Ahmadnagar
Poona
Peshwars
Udgir 1760
The Nizam
Godavari
GOLCONDA
Hyderabad
Bimlipatam
Vishakhapatnam
Yanam
Konkan
Satara
Bijapur
Kolhapur
Bijapur
Krishna
Narasapur
Palakollu
Machilipatnam
Nizampatam
EASTERN GHATS
CARNATIC
Vengurla
GOA
Goa
lost 1780
lost 1776
Gooty
Karwar
Anjidiv Island
MYSORE
5
Honavar
Coondapoor
Damalcherry 1740
Pulicat
Madras
lost 1776
Ambur 1760
Arcot 1751
Sadras
Mangalore
Wandiwash 1760
Pondicherry 1748
Mysore
Kaveri
Fort St David 1746, 1758
Cannanore
Tellicherry
Mahé
MALABAR
Porto Novo
Tranquebar
Karikal
Nagappattinam
Calicut
Chetwai
COCHIN
Trichinopoly 1741, 1752
Tanjore
Cranganur
Pallipuram
Cochin
Madurai
Jaffna
TRAVANCORE
Porakad
Kayankulam
Quilon
Anjengo
Mannar
Tuticorin
Trincomalee
Kayalpatnam
Manapadu
Puttalam
Batticaloa
Kandy
Negombo
Colombo
KANDY
7
Ceylon
Galle
Matara

subsequent defeat of Siraj at Plassey secured the Company's position in Bengal and led to the first major British territorial acquisition in the subcontinent. In the Carnatic, hostilities resumed in 1758, leading to the British capture of Pondicherry in 1761 and the end of French power in India.

The fragmentation of Mughal authority continued through this period. The Marathas raided widely in the north and east, prompting the Muslim rulers of Rohilkhand to seek an alliance with Ahmad Shah Durrani (r.1747–73) of Afghanistan in preference to the ineffectual Mughal emperor. The decisive moment came in 1761, when, again at Panipat, a large, well-equipped Maratha army was routed by the Afghans, ending any chance that the Marathas might reconstitute the Mughal empire. Ahmad Shah's army withdrew after sacking Delhi, leaving the British East India Company uniquely placed to benefit. In the following two decades the territorial foundations of British rule in India were laid: Bengal and Bihar (1765), Northern Circars (1768), and the cities of Benares and Ghazipur (1775) passed into British Company hands. By 1783 only Mysore stood firm against the trend toward British predominance.

BRITISH expansion in India was accompanied by the adoption of some native symbols of authority.

1 The major Rajput houses achieved *de facto* independence in 1708, after a 30-year rebellion; Ajmer was subject to Maratha raids from about 1740.

2 Bengal was virtually independent of the Mughals from 1733; it suffered Maratha raids 1742–51.

3 After Nadir Shah was assassinated in 1747, the Abdalis of Herat and the Ghilzais of Kandahar set up a united Afghan state under Ahmad Shah Durrani.

4 After Clive's victory at Plassey, the British undertook military action in Bengal and Bihar in support of their nominee as *nawab*; in 1765 both provinces were granted to the East India Company.

5 After repeated invasions by the *nawab* of Arcot, the Nizam and the Marathas, Mysore became a major power in south India under Haidar Ali (r.1761–82).

6 On the night of 20 June 1756, 145 British survivors of Siraj ud-Daulah's capture of Calcutta were shut in a small dungeon (the "Black Hole"); all but 23 died.

7 War between Kandy and the Dutch in 1761–63 led to Dutch annexation of coastal Ceylon after 1766.

See also 4.05 (world trade); 4.19 (the Mughal ascendancy); 5.21 (19th-century India)

4.21 Ming China • 1368 – 1644 •

By the beginning of the 16th century the great Ming imperial dynasty of China, which had been established by Zhu Yuanzhang in 1368, was on the decline. Ming reconquest of the country from the Mongols had been followed by the long process of rebuilding the economy and by a period of aggressive foreign policy. Yet repeated invasions of Mongolia in the early 15th century came to an end in 1449 with the capture of the Mongol emperor, and the adoption of a new defensive strategy that included major reconstruction of the Great Wall. In the same period extensive maritime expeditions of admiral Zheng He had spread Ming military and economic power as far as the east coast of Africa, but these also ended with the admiral's death in 1433. A significant indication of Ming China's changing priorities was the transfer of the capital from Nanjing to Beijing in 1421: the focus thus shifted from the heart of the maritime trading region of China to the Mongol border, and with it vanished any prospect of Chinese maritime contact with Renaissance Europe.

Ming economic policy was at best unsympathetic to external trade, favoring instead a regulated and self-sufficient domestic economy. Relative peace and stability after 1449 brought a steady population increase (from 60 million in the aftermath of the Mongol conquest to almost 130 million by 1580), and a huge manufacturing and trading economy emerged, stimulated by such initiatives as the reconstruction of the transport system centered on the Grand Canal. Long-distance trade prospered, despite government attempts at regulation and despite the monopolies operated by regional merchant oligarchies. Cotton fields in northern China, planted under the Mongols, supplied a booming textile industry. Along with other commodities (such as silk and tea), cotton goods were exported to Japan in exchange for metals and spices, and to southeast Asia (and thence to Europe) in exchange for silver from the Americas.

The first direct foreign involvement in Ming external commerce came with the establishment of a permanent Portuguese trading base at Macao in 1557 and a Dutch fortified settlement on Taiwan (Formosa) in 1622. Relations between the European merchants and Ming authorities were frequently uncomfortable.

One consequence of the Ming efforts to control export and import was the growth of the *Wako* in the mid-16th century. These pirate-trader bands were mainly based in southern Japan, from where they descended on the Chinese coast in strength from the 1520s onward, until the spread of Japanese central authority deprived them of most of their bases. Raids by the *Wako* coincided with a renewed military threat in Mongolia posed by the migration of central Asian nomads back to the east. Mongol forces under Altan Khan (r.1543–83) invaded northern China twice in mid-century and were only repelled at great cost.

In 1592, the Ming vassal state of Korea was attacked by a newly unified Japan under Hideyoshi

DZUNGARIA
Kalmyk Tatars
Gobi Desert
Turfan
Hami
Anxi
Ordos Desert
Suzhou
Ganzhou
Ningxia
Yulin
QILIAN MTS
Liangzhou
Lake Qinghai
Xining
Lanzhou
Shaanxi
QIN MTS
Chang'
Fengxian
Guangyuan
DABA
Chamdo
Mekong
Jinsha
Yalong
Chengdu
Sichuan
Chongqing
Luzhou
Naga Hills
Guizhou
Zhaotong
Guiyang
Dali
Menghua
2
Yunnan
Yunnan
Guang
Mekong
YUENAN (ANNAM)
Jichangmen (Cua Hoi)
borders, c.1590
Ming territory, c.1590
Ming tributary or buffer state, c.1590
area subject to attack by Japanese Wako pirates in the 15th and 16th centuries
area occupied by Wako pirates after 1550
Wako pirate base area
popular uprisings, 1636–41
kingdom of Zhang Xianzhong, 1641–44
kingdom of Li Zucheng, 1641–45
Chinese trade route under the Ming empire
Portuguese trade route
Spanish "Manila Galleon" trade route
Chinese trading base
Dutch trading base
Portuguese trading base
Spanish trading base
silk major export from China
silver major import to China
Ming national capital, with date
Ming provincial capital
Great Wall
Willow Palisade
canal of the Ming period
modern coastline and drainage where altered
migration of Mongol and Tatar nomads, 16th century
0 800 km
0 600 mi

TIMELINE

Ming and Manchu dynasties

- **1520–21** The first direct Chinese-European trade contact is made with a Portuguese expedition
- **1522** The Portuguese are expelled from China for piracy by the new Ming emperor Jia Qing
- **1556** The worst earthquake in Chinese history kills over 850,000 in Shanxi province
- **1577** Altan Khan accepts the authority of reformed Tibetan Buddhism over the Mongols
- **1582** The Ming imperial government in Beijing begins to decline into corruption
- **1615** Nurhachi becomes leader of Jürchen (Manchu) peoples of eastern Manchuria
- **1621** Nurhachi establishes the Manchu capital at Liaoyang
- **1636** The Manchus proclaim themselves the Qing dynasty of China at Mukden
- **1641** Rival post-Ming regimes emerge in China under Li Zucheng and Zhang Xianzhong

Invasions and revolts

- **1523** Ming repel major attack by *wako* pirates from Japan
- **1542** The Mongols under Altan Khan invade China
- **1550** A second Mongol invasion is defeated by Ming
- **1552–55** The *Wako* again attack China, besieging Nanjing
- **1592–93** The Japanese invasion of Korea is repulsed
- **1597–98** A second Japanese invasion of Korea is defeated
- **1627** Peasant rebellions begin in central and northern China
- **1627–37** A Manchu coup deposes the Ming regime in Korea
- **1644** The Manchus wrest control of Beijing from Li Zuchang

1550 1600 1650

Jürchen
(Manchus)
Mongols
Kaiyuan
Shenyang
(Mukden)
Liaoyang
7
Haizhou
Liaodong
3
Rehe
Kalgan
Beijing
1421 onwards
Shanhaiguan
Datong
Jinzhou
Sea of Japan
Wonsan
Pyongyang
Seoul
CHAOXIAN
(KOREA)
Ulsan
Pusan
RIBEN
(JAPAN)
Osaka
Zhili
Da Yunhe
(Grand Canal)
present course of Yellow river
Dengzhou
Pingdu
Ji'nan
Shanxi
Shandong
Yellow
Sea
6
Nagasaki
copper, silver,
spices
Kaifeng
Yellow river
1324–1853
Henan
Lake
Hongze
Huai
Huai'an
Nanjing
1368–1403
4
Nanzhili
cotton textiles,
silk, wine
Hangzhou
Mingzhou
(Ningbo)
Wuchang
Yangtze
Jingzhou
Jujiang
Lake
Pengli
Zhejiang
East
China
Sea
Lake
Dongting
Nanchang
Wenzhou
Haobaijiang
(Naha)
Tanzhou
Jiangxi
Hengzhou
5
Fuzhou
Fujian
Jilong
Tingzhou
Ganzhou
Zhangzhou
Xiamen
(Amoy)
Taiwan
(Formosa)
Tainan
Fort Zeelandia
Guangdong
Xi
Guangzhou
(Canton)
cotton textiles,
ironware, silk, tea
Macao
cotton textiles,
porcelain, silk
1
Qiongzhou
to the Indonesian
archipelago
South
China
Sea
Dajiang
(Port San Vicente)
to Champa and Siam
from Goa
silver
from Europe
Pengjiashilan
(Pangasinan)
Philippine
Islands
Lusong
(Manila)
silver
from Central
America
to Central America
from
Central America

PORCELAIN, invented under the Tang, reached its peak in Ming China, with refined shape and materials and formal or floral motifs.

Toyotomi, with an army of some 200,000 troops equipped with firearms copied from Portuguese prototypes. The Ming responded by deploying an army said to have numbered one million men, and a substantial naval force. The Japanese were driven back to the south coast of Korea after heavy fighting; a second invasion in 1597–98 met with the same fate.

The cost to China of these incursions was huge. Plagues and crop failures had already caused devastation in much of the north of the country at the end of the 16th century (the population falling below 100 million once more), and growing corruption in the imperial bureaucracy fueled popular resentment. Harsh rises in taxation (the burden of which fell on agriculture under the Ming rather than on trade) and requisitions for the war effort provoked a wave of violent unrest that escalated into open insurrection in cities throughout China and widespread peasant revolts after 1627. Ming authority now crumbled: Liaodong and territories north of the Wall were annexed by a new rival power, the Manchus, who also engineered a successful coup against the Ming-allied rulers of Korea. After 1641 rebel regimes sprang up in north and west China proper, led by Li Zucheng and Zhang Xianzhong. The last Ming emperor, Chongzhen (r.1627–44), committed suicide as Li's forces entered Beijing in 1644.

The Manchus under Dorgun (r.1628–50) had laid claim to the leadership of China in 1636, and were well placed to exploit this period of unrest. Responding to a request for aid by the beleaguered Ming, they drove Li Zucheng from Beijing in 1644 with the help of the frontier general Wu Sangui, and then proceeded to install their own Qing dynasty.

1 Chinese maritime trade over an area from Ceylon to Timor to Osaka continued throughout the Ming period; many ports had large Chinese communities.

2 An efficient courier service was established by the Ming to all parts of the empire. Communication from Beijing to Yunnan nevertheless took six to seven weeks each way.

3 The early Ming period saw major reconstruction along the Great Wall as the renewed threat from nomad migration increased; by the 1630s most areas beyond the Wall were already under Manchu control.

4 Despite official Ming antipathy to long-distance trade, the cities of the Yangtze delta became major manufacturing centers for cotton textiles. Raw cotton was shipped from the north via the Grand Canal and from the west via the Yangtze itself.

5 Ming trade was dominated by groups of merchants who operated on a national scale; much of the export trade was in the hands of Fujian maritime traders.

6 As well as Japanese, the *Wako* included unofficial traders and freebooters, plus many renegade Chinese and Portuguese. As many Chinese traders had a vested interest in their activities, the effectiveness of Ming countermeasures was limited.

7 Han Chinese settlement in Liaodong was protected under the Ming by a continuous wooden palisade with gate towers, known as the Willow Palisade. In 1621 the Manchus won control of the whole enclave.

See also 3.23 (rise of the Ming);
4.23 (Tokugawa Japan)

4.22 The rise of Manchu China • 1644 – 1783 •

The Manchus originated as one of the Jürchen tribes – themselves part of a larger group of Tungusic (Siberian) peoples – from the area to the north of the Korean peninsula adjoining the Han Chinese enclave of Liaodong. They began to emerge as a political force under the leadership of Nurhachi (r.1586–1626). Nurhachi imposed a Mongol-style military administration on his people in 1615, and took the title Jin Khan the following year to indicate continuity with the Jürchen Jin (or Ruzhen) dynasty that had ruled northern China in the 12th century.

In the 1620s and 1630s the peoples united by Nurhachi profited from Ming weakness to establish their control over the Mongol lands just north of the Wall, the Liaodong basin and the Ming vassal state of Korea. Although Nurhachi died in battle, his son Dorgun (r.1628–50) gained control of Beijing in 1644 and acted as regent to his nephew who was installed as the first Manchu (Qing) emperor of China, under the name Shunzhi, in the same year. Over the next 15 years, Ming resistance was suppressed, with the far southwestern province of Yunnan the last to fall.

The Manchus adopted a more subtle approach to administrative reform than that of China's previous conquerors, the Mongols. Manchu officials were given senior posts in existing Ming institutions, and military garrisons were set up in the major provincial cities, but new structures were not imposed wholesale. The Manchus were initially quick to require cultural changes (such as their characteristic shaven head and pigtail), but their numerical inferiority to the Han Chinese meant that, by the 18th century, their culture had become fully assimilated. Their most significant contribution was to inject an unprecedented dynamism and efficiency into Chinese political and military life.

Resistance to Manchu rule was rekindled in 1674. An attempt by the Beijing government to assert its authority over the southern province of Guangdong, which had been allowed considerable autonomy since its subjugation, prompted a popular revolt led by Wu Sangui, governor of Yunnan and Guizhou. Wu, supported by Shang Zhixin of Guangdong and Geng Jingzhong of Fujian (the "Three Feudatories"), was only defeated after five years of campaigning. At the same time, the government was confronted with a rebellion by the Ming-loyalist warlord Zheng Jing, whose father Zheng Cheng-gong (Koxinga) had expelled the Dutch from Taiwan in 1662.

After this, only the uprising of non-Han tribal peoples in Yunnan in 1726–29 disrupted more than

Manchu homeland, early 17th century

Manchu territorial expansion

- to 1644, with date of acquisition
- 1644–97, with date of acquisition
- 1697–1783, with date of acquisition
- vassal state acquired before 1644, with date
- vassal state acquired or confirmed after 1697, with date
- area affected by Wu Sangui's rebellion, 1674–81
- area held by Ming loyalists, 1662–83
- rebellion of non-Han people against Manchu rule
- Manchu national capital
- Manchu provincial capital
- trade route of the Manchu empire
- area of extensive coastal trade
- silk — major export from Manchu China
- *rice* — major import to Manchu China
- migration of Kalmyk Tatars, mid-17th century
- migration of Oirat Mongols, late 17th to early 18th centuries
- internal migration of Han Chinese, 18th century
- borders, c.late 18th century
- Great Wall
- Willow Palisade
- Grand Canal
- modern coastline and drainage where altered

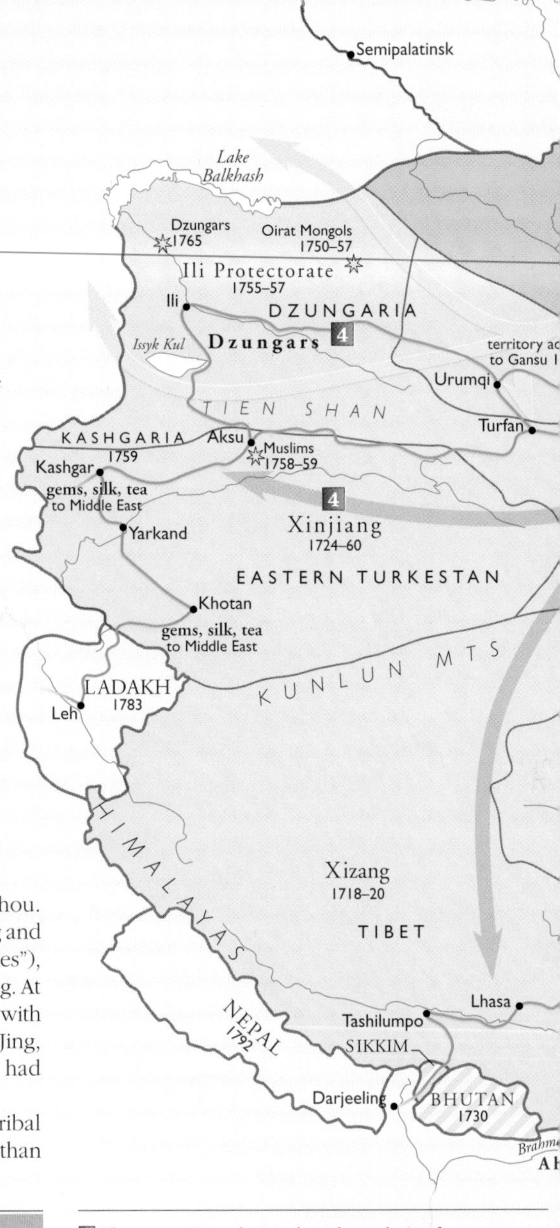

Semipalatinsk
Lake Balkhash
Dzungars 1765
Oirat Mongols 1750–57
Ili Protectorate 1755–57
Ili
DZUNGARIA
Issyk Kul
Dzungars
4
territory ac to Gansu 1
Urumqi
Turfan
TIEN SHAN
KASHGARIA 1759
Aksu
Muslims 1758–59
Kashgar
gems, silk, tea to Middle East
4
Yarkand
Xinjiang 1724–60
EASTERN TURKESTAN
Khotan
gems, silk, tea to Middle East
KUNLUN MTS
LADAKH 1783
Leh
HIMALAYAS
Xizang 1718–20
TIBET
Lhasa
Tashilumpo
NEPAL 1792
SIKKIM
Darjeeling
BHUTAN 1730

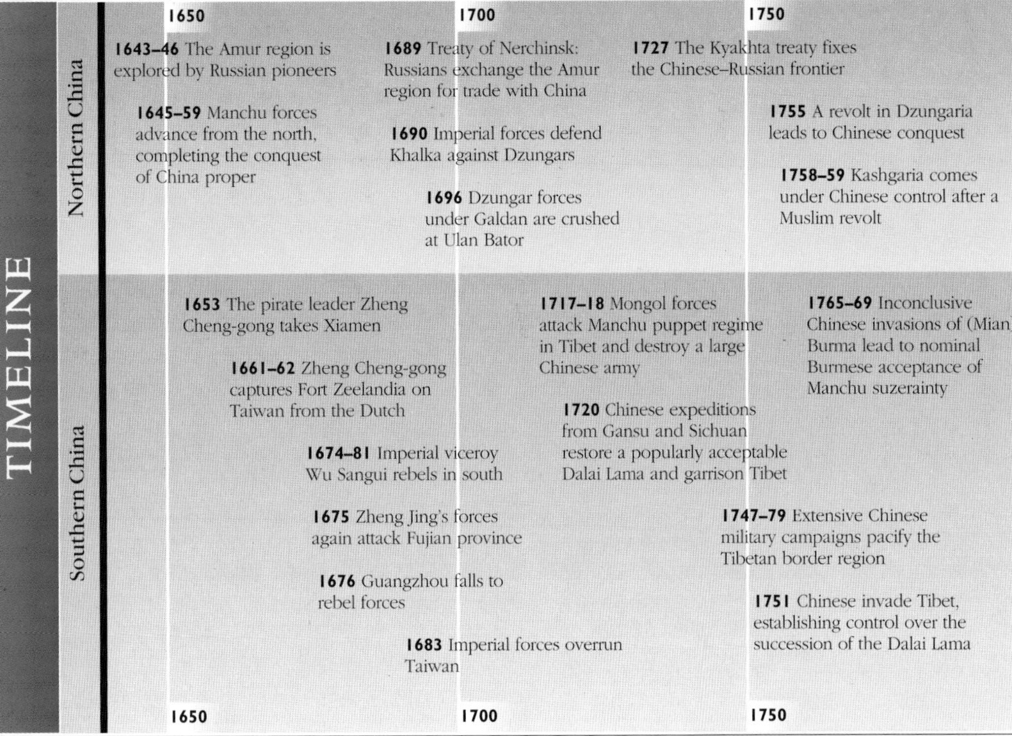

TIMELINE
Northern China
1650
1700
1750
1643–46 The Amur region is explored by Russian pioneers
1645–59 Manchu forces advance from the north, completing the conquest of China proper
1689 Treaty of Nerchinsk: Russians exchange the Amur region for trade with China
1690 Imperial forces defend Khalka against Dzungars
1696 Dzungar forces under Galdan are crushed at Ulan Bator
1727 The Kyakhta treaty fixes the Chinese–Russian frontier
1755 A revolt in Dzungaria leads to Chinese conquest
1758–59 Kashgaria comes under Chinese control after a Muslim revolt
Southern China
1653 The pirate leader Zheng Cheng-gong takes Xiamen
1661–62 Zheng Cheng-gong captures Fort Zeelandia on Taiwan from the Dutch
1674–81 Imperial viceroy Wu Sangui rebels in south
1675 Zheng Jing's forces again attack Fujian province
1676 Guangzhou falls to rebel forces
1683 Imperial forces overrun Taiwan
1717–18 Mongol forces attack Manchu puppet regime in Tibet and destroy a large Chinese army
1720 Chinese expeditions from Gansu and Sichuan restore a popularly acceptable Dalai Lama and garrison Tibet
1765–69 Inconclusive Chinese invasions of (Mian) Burma lead to nominal Burmese acceptance of Manchu suzerainty
1747–79 Extensive Chinese military campaigns pacify the Tibetan border region
1751 Chinese invade Tibet, establishing control over the succession of the Dalai Lama
1650
1700
1750

1 The name "Manchu" is thought to derive from Manjusri, a Buddhist *bodhisattva* recognized in Mongolia from 1579; the term was not used until 1652.

2 The Willow Palisade around the Liaodong region was retained after the Manchu conquest of China as a barrier to Han Chinese settlement in Manchuria.

3 The province of Gansu was created in 1715; the large area of former Mongol territory added to the province in 1759 was directly administered by the imperial bureaucracy in Beijing.

4 The Ili (Dzungaria) and Xinjiang regions remained under military control throughout the Manchu period.

5 Manchu administrative reforms resulted in the creation of the new provinces of Anhui (1662) and Hunan (1664), as well as Gansu.

6 The Russian fort built at Albazin in 1651 was ceded to China in return for trade concessions that created a large market for Russian furs in Beijing.

7 The vast population growth of China in the 18th century stimulated internal migration to outlying areas; Sichuan and Yunnan provinces experienced extensive Han Chinese immigration.

8 The Manchu conquest of 1683 brought imperial Chinese control to Taiwan for the first time, but the inhospitable eastern side of the island was barely settled by Han Chinese until the late 19th century.

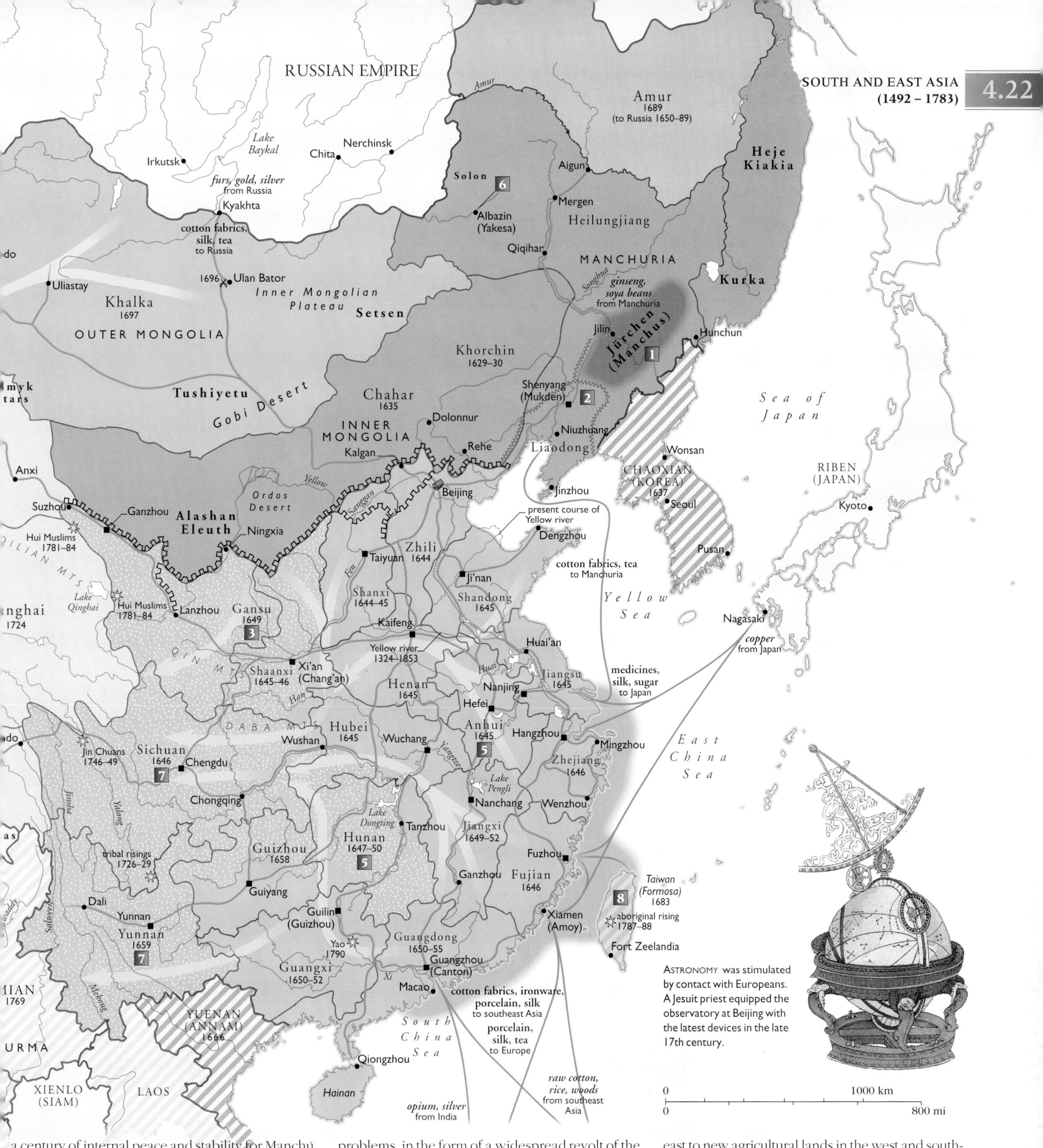

ASTRONOMY was stimulated by contact with Europeans. A Jesuit priest equipped the observatory at Beijing with the latest devices in the late 17th century.

a century of internal peace and stability for Manchu China. An aggressive campaign of territorial expansion, however, resulted in the creation of the greatest Eurasian land empire since the Mongols. Russian incursions into the Amur region were ended by the Treaty of Nerchinsk in 1689. The Manchus then embarked on a sustained campaign to end the Mongol menace. Military expeditions of great ferocity finally subdued the formidable Dzungars (West Mongols), and by 1783 Manchu colonial administration had been extended to Tibet and – nominally at least – its vassal states (Bhutan, Sikkim and Ladakh) and the former Turkic khanates of eastern Turkestan. (This extension of Chinese authority brought its own problems, in the form of a widespread revolt of the Muslim Hui people in 1781–84.) Burma and Laos were reduced to nominal vassal status, and Manchu troops were poised to invade Nepal and Annam.

Following the conflicts and plagues that had afflicted the region during the 17th century, peace and prosperity caused a demographic explosion within the Manchu empire. The Chinese population swelled from 100 million in 1650 to 300 million in 1800. This expansion created growing tensions. A ban imposed by the Manchus on the settlement of Han Chinese north of the Wall led to largescale internal migrations in the late 17th and 18th centuries from the overpopulated Yangtze basin and south-east to new agricultural lands in the west and south-west. The authorities maintained Chinese external trade but were able to restrict foreign merchants to Guangzhou in the south and Kyakhta in the north. The export of Chinese luxury goods for silver continued to ensure a strong monetary economy. At the end of the 18th century, however, Manchu China's decline was about to begin, with growing government corruption, social unrest and the start of the European opium trade to China.

See also 4.21 (Ming China); 4.24 (European empires); 5.19 (19th-century China)

4.23 Japan and the Tokugawa shogunate • 1500 – 1800 •

The last century of the Ashikaga shogunate (1338–1573) in Japan was dominated by the political fragmentation arising from the Onin war of 1467–77. Following this protracted civil conflict, real power devolved to small, feudal units subject to the changing allegiances of local lords (*daimyo*), while the authority of the emperor and his military commander, the *shogun*, was only nominal. Instability was heightened by ever more frequent popular uprisings, often fomented by the powerful Buddhist monasteries. Both this tradition of religious militancy and the independent merchant guilds provided an alternative focus for popular loyalty.

The lack of political stability did not, however, prevent the steady growth of Japanese trade and industry throughout the later 15th and early 16th centuries, although the proliferation of local customs boundaries did preclude a truly national economy. Japan also remained culturally vibrant, with many great *daimyo* patronizing such diverse art forms as *noh* drama, poetry, the tea ceremony and painting. At the same time, traveling balladeers, preachers and dancers helped create a popular culture that transcended Japan's political fragmentation.

In 1568, the first of a series of leaders powerful enough to attempt the political unification of Japan emerged. Nobunaga, lord of the Oda clan, captured the imperial capital Kyoto in that year, and embarked on the destruction of the Buddhist temples and slaughter of the monks. Warfare in Japan had been transformed by the introduction of firearms by the Portuguese in 1542: muskets were copied in large numbers, and sophisticated new tactics developed to utilize this firepower. Even more significant was the construction by Nobunaga of an entirely new type of castle at Azuchi. In contrast to earlier mountain strongholds, Azuchi was built to dominate the rice fields and communications of the plain, and was an administrative center as well as a fortress. Its importance was such that the age of national

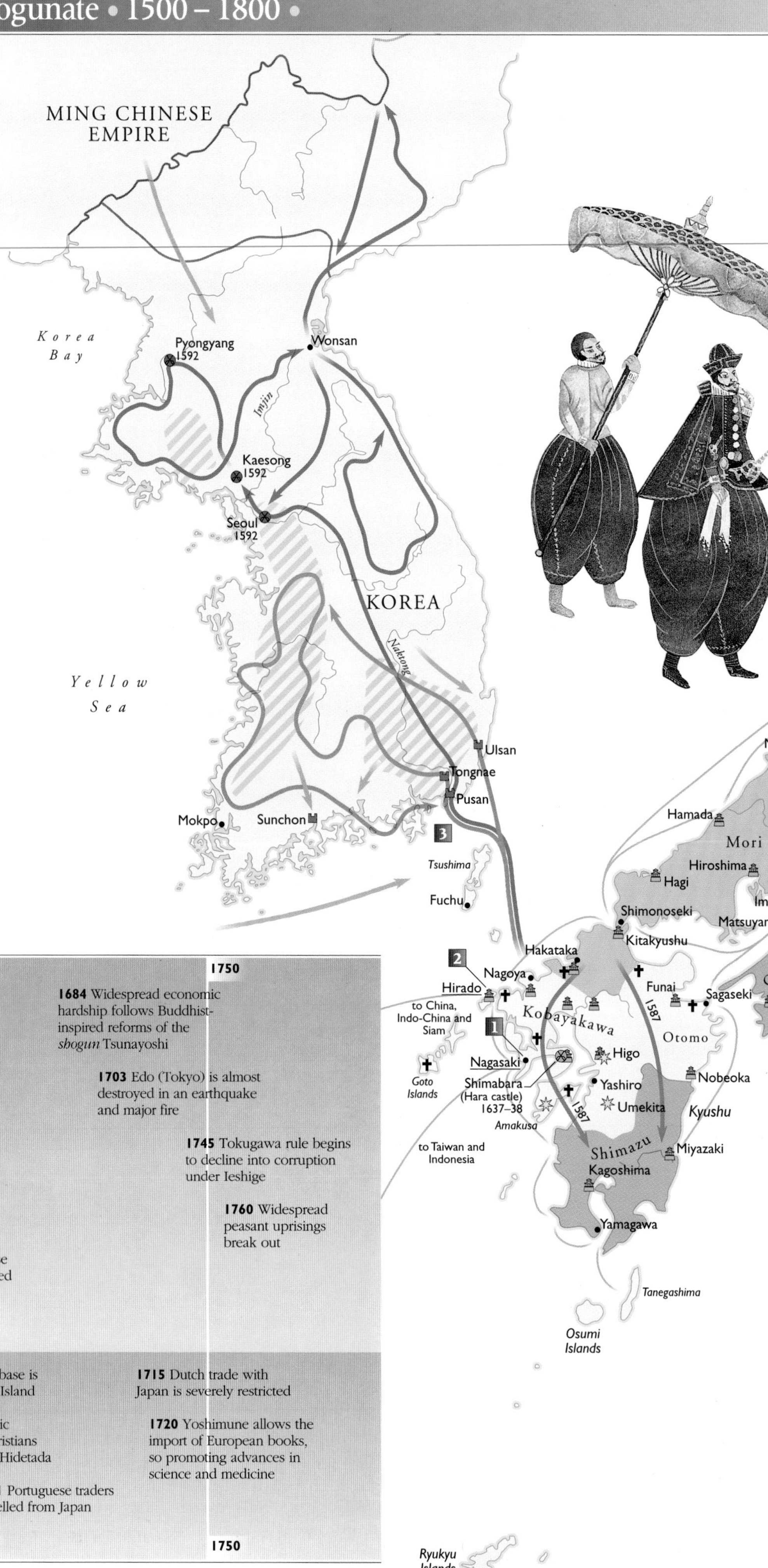

MING CHINESE EMPIRE
Korea Bay
Pyongyang 1592
Wonsan
Imjin
Kaesong 1592
Seoul 1592
KOREA
Naktong
Yellow Sea
Ulsan
Tongnae
Pusan
Mokpo
Sunchon
3
Tsushima
Fuchu
Hamada
Mori
Hiroshima
Hagi
Shimonoseki
Matsuyama
Kitakyushu
Hakataka
2
Nagoya
Hirado
to China, Indo-China and Siam
Kobayakawa
1
Funai
Sagaseki
1587
Otomo
Nagasaki
Higo
Goto Islands
Shimabara (Hara castle) 1637–38
Yashiro
Nobeoka
Umekita
Kyushu
Amakusa
1587
to Taiwan and Indonesia
Shimazu
Miyazaki
Kagoshima
Yamagawa
Tanegashima
Osumi Islands
Ryukyu Islands

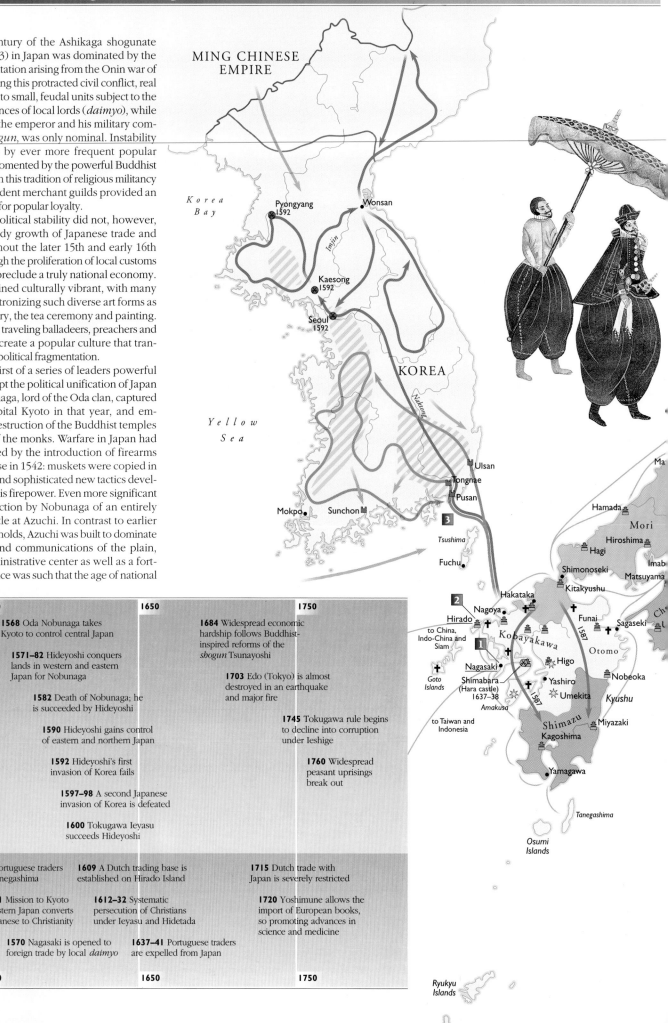

TIMELINE

Unification of Japan

1550 | 1650 | 1750

1568 Oda Nobunaga takes Kyoto to control central Japan

1571–82 Hideyoshi conquers lands in western and eastern Japan for Nobunaga

1582 Death of Nobunaga; he is succeeded by Hideyoshi

1590 Hideyoshi gains control of eastern and northern Japan

1592 Hideyoshi's first invasion of Korea fails

1597–98 A second Japanese invasion of Korea is defeated

1600 Tokugawa Ieyasu succeeds Hideyoshi

1684 Widespread economic hardship follows Buddhist-inspired reforms of the *shogun* Tsunayoshi

1703 Edo (Tokyo) is almost destroyed in an earthquake and major fire

1745 Tokugawa rule begins to decline into corruption under Ieshige

1760 Widespread peasant uprisings break out

Foreign influences

1542 First Portuguese traders arrive on Tanegashima

1548–51 Mission to Kyoto and western Japan converts first Japanese to Christianity

1570 Nagasaki is opened to foreign trade by local *daimyo*

1609 A Dutch trading base is established on Hirado Island

1612–32 Systematic persecution of Christians under Ieyasu and Hidetada

1637–41 Portuguese traders are expelled from Japan

1715 Dutch trade with Japan is severely restricted

1720 Yoshimune allows the import of European books, so promoting advances in science and medicine

1550 | 1650 | 1750

Hokkaido
Hakodate
Miyuma
Hirosaki
Hachinohe
Noshiro
Morioka
Miyako
Akita
Senpoku
Sea of Japan
Honjo
Oshu Kaido
Ichinoseki
Shinjo
Shonai
Ozaki
Tsuruoka
Sendai
Yamagata
Sado
Niigata
Shibata
Yonezawa
Tsukahara
Fukushima
eastward coastal route
Aizu
Wajima
Nagaoka
Iwaki
Shirakawa
Takata
JAPAN
Uesugi
Nikko
Utsunomiya
Toyama
Zenkoji
Kanazawa
Sasa
Takeda
Takasaki
Nikko Kaido
westward coastal route
Maeda
Nakasendo
7
5
Hojo
Choshi
Honshu
Fukui
Koshu Kaido
Edo
Shibata
Odawara
1590
Iida
Obama
Sekigahara
1600
Tottori
4
Fukuchiyama
Akechi
Nagoya
Numazu
Tokaido
6
Kyoto
Azuchi
Tokugawa
Himeji
Momoyama
Yoshida
Shimoda
Osaka
1614–15
Kobe
Sakai
PACIFIC OCEAN
Ise
Toba
Osaka–Edo route
Takamatsu
1584–85
Tokushima
Tanabe
Shingu
Shikoku
Oshima

EUROPEAN traders (seen in this Japanese painting) and missionaries were initially welcomed, but repression increased in the 1630s.

1 Nagasaki was an unimportant fishing village until it was developed as Japan's main port for foreign trade by the local lord Omura in 1570.

2 The Dutch East India Company base on Hirado Island was moved to Deshima Island, near Nagasaki, in 1641. The Dutch officials had to undergo various symbolic indignities to retain their trading privileges.

3 Hideyoshi's invasion of Korea was commanded by Kato Kiyomasa and Konishi Yukinaga. Konishi took Pusan in 1592, but the Ming navy almost destroyed the Japanese fleet, leaving the army cut off.

4 Azuchi castle, on the shores of Lake Biwa, was begun by Oda Nobunaga in 1576. This pioneering castle was widely imitated by other *daimyo* over the next few decades.

5 Edo (Tokyo) became the administrative and military base of Tokugawa Ieyasu in 1590. In the 1600s it became a rival to the ancient capital, Kyoto.

6 Osaka castle, stronghold of Hideyoshi's son Hideyori, became a center for opposition to the rule of Ieyasu, until Ieyasu's forces sacked it in 1614–15.

7 The Five Highways (*gokaido*) formed an efficient transport network converging on the *shogun*'s court; *daimyo* traveling to the court had their travel papers checked at control points on the highways.

- Oda land, 1560
- area conquered by Nobunaga and Hideyoshi by 1582
- main *daimyo* house opposed to Hideyoshi, 1582
- Mori *daimyo* house, 16th–17th centuries
- campaigns of Hideyoshi, 1584–90
- Hideyoshi's first invasion of Korea, 1592
- Hideyoshi's second invasion of Korea, 1597–98
- Korean and Ming Chinese counteroffensives
- main areas of Korean resistance to Hideyoshi
- Japanese base in Korea retained after 1593
- Hideyoshi victory
- castle town
- Japanese peasant revolt against Hideyoshi's land survey
- victory of Tokugawa Ieyasu or his successors
- area with significant number of Christian converts
- Hirado trading port used by Europeans
- "Five Highways" of Tokugawa Japan
- coastal shipping route

0 200 km
0 150 mi

unification is known in Japan as the Azuchi–Momoyama period, after Nobunaga's castle and its counterpart built by his lieutenant Hideyoshi.

Hideyoshi, who acquired the surname Toyotomi ("the Wealthy"), was a military genius of humble origins. Under his leadership, Oda forces overran the lands of their rivals in central Japan, the Akechi, Shibata and Mori, and then expanded eastward into Takeda and Uesugi territory. After Nobunaga's death in 1582, Hideyoshi became ruler of most of central Japan in alliance with Tokugawa Ieyasu, his most dangerous rival. Campaigns against rival daimyo on the islands of Shikoku and Kyushu followed, and in 1590 Hideyoshi's capture of the Hojo clan's castle at Odawara also gave him control of eastern Japan.

Hideyoshi's conquests were accompanied by political changes designed to prevent further unrest. He disarmed the peasantry and insisted that the *samurai* (warrior-class) live in castle towns, which ensured that potentially rebellious farming communities could no longer rely on local samurai support. Taxation was reformed in an unpopular land survey, which initially caused widespread unrest. Trade was brought under government control, and steps were taken to suppress Christianity, which had spread from the Portuguese base at Nagasaki (founded 1572) but which now seemed alien and subversive.

Ieyasu succeeded Hideyoshi after two Japanese invasions of Korea in the 1590s were beaten back by the Koreans with the help of Ming China. He continued the policies of his predecessor, as did subsequent *shoguns* of the Tokugawa dynasty which he founded in 1603. Christianity, persecuted under Hidetada (r.1605–23), was eradicated by the massacre of 37,000 Japanese Christians at Hara castle (1638). Social and economic stability were maintained by strict segregation of farming and trade, a ban on private investment and official discouragement of any contact between different parts of the country that did not use the closely controlled Five Highways. Portuguese ships were banned from Japan in 1639, export restricted to Dutch and Chinese bases at Nagasaki, and Japanese citizens were forbidden to travel abroad (while those long resident in ports throughout Asia were forbidden to return). The construction of large ships was banned in 1638 to prevent the Japanese from traveling abroad.

Despite these repressive measures, the early Edo period (1603–1867) was remarkable for its economic prosperity and agricultural productivity (led by growing demand from the booming cities), and for its technological advancement. The population grew rapidly in the 17th and early 18th centuries to nearly 30 million, and a vigorous merchant class had its heyday in the late 17th century. However, economic and social ills did begin to accumulate. By the mid-18th century many peasants had left the land, many samurai had fallen into debt, and unrest was again becoming common. Lifting both of social strictures and of the ban on European books under the enlightened shogun Yoshimune (r.1716–45) brought some relief, but famine, natural disasters and government corruption provoked frequent peasant uprisings after 1760. The late 18th century saw the growth of an opposition movement around the emperor to the rule of the Tokugawa shoguns and a new Japanese awareness of the threat from expanding European influence in Asia.

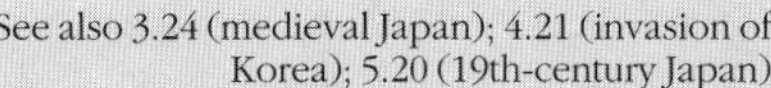
See also 3.24 (medieval Japan); 4.21 (invasion of Korea); 5.20 (19th-century Japan)

4.24 Southeast Asia • 1500 – 1800 •

European influence grew in the islands of southeast Asia between 1500 and 1800, yet the vitality of the states and peoples of the mainland restricted foreign incursions to a minimum. The trading economies of the island-states of the Indonesian archipelago rivaled those of the European powers until the mid-18th century, while Islam also played a part in keeping the Europeans at bay.

On the mainland, the Burmese, Arakanese, Thai, Khmer, Vietnamese and Laotian peoples all established or consolidated existing states between 1500 and 1800, while the Shans and Mons failed to do so. The first attempt to create a unified Burmese–Mon kingdom was made by Tabin Shweti (r.1535–50) of Toungou in the 1540s. Toungou expanded north to incorporate the ancient Burmese capital of Pagan, and south to overrun the Mon kingdom of Pegu by 1546. Laotians from Lan Chang extended their control westward over the Thai state of Chiangmai in 1548. In the same year, Toungou unsuccessfully invaded the Thai kingdom of Ayutthaya – initiating a long Burmese–Thai enmity that was to influence much of the subsequent history of southeast Asia. It then annexed Ava (weakened by two decades of warfare against the Shans) and wrested Chiangmai from the Laotians in 1556. This Burmese empire survived until 1600, when a new Burmese state, based on Ava, emerged to dominate much the same area.

The Vietnamese state of Annam (formerly Dai Viet) steadily expanded southward at the expense of the Hindu kingdom of Champa, finally capturing its capital Vijaya in 1471 and driving a remnant court to the south. But once Vietnamese began to populate the multiethnic and maritime central coast they proved hard for Hanoi to control. The kingdom split around 1600: ancient Dai Viet of the Red River delta became known to Europeans as Tongking, and the southern state with its capital near modern Hue as Cochin-China. The Tay-son rebellion of 1773–92 destroyed first the south and then the north, effectively reuniting the kingdom.

Cochin-China continued a policy of expansion, at the expense first of the remnant Champa and then Cambodia. The Saigon area was under its control by 1690 and the remains of the Cambodia kingdom was under Vietnamese or Siamese suzerainty for most of the 18th century. The Lao state of Lansang also broke up in the 17th century into the three principalities of Luang Prabang, Vientiane and Champassak, each

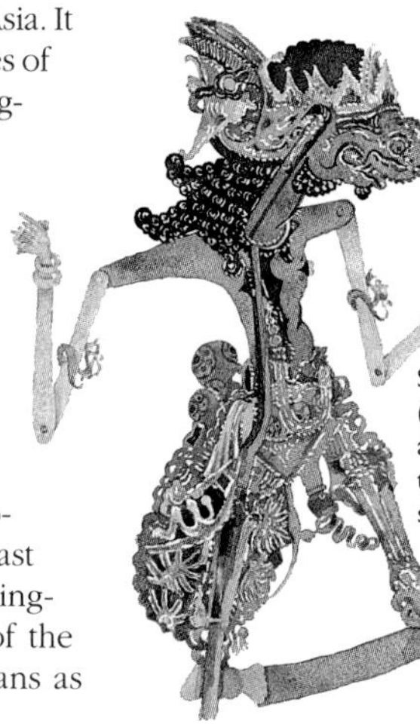

SHADOW-PUPPETRY (*wayang*), a Javanese artform, flourished in the 18th century, and spread to Europe.

TIMELINE

Mainland southeast Asia

- **1519–20** Portuguese establish trading bases at Mataban and Syriam
- **1533** Dai Viet kingdom fragments into petty states
- **1539** Tabin Shweti of Toungou begins to unify Burma
- **1555** Toungou conquers Ava and destroys Chiangmai (1556)
- **1602** The Dutch establish a trading base at Patani
- **1610** The Burmese kingdom of Ava conquers Toungou
- **1611** Final absorption of Champa by Cochin-China
- **1688** A rebellion in Ayutthaya overthrows King Narai in reaction to French pressure
- **1740** The Mon kingdom of Pegu rebels against Burmese rule, taking Ava in 1752
- **1753** Alaungpaya re-establishes a united Burma and expels foreign interests
- **1766** The Manchus launch the first of four invasion attempts of Burma
- **1767** The Burmese destroy Ayutthaya

Maritime southeast Asia

- **1511** Portuguese under Albuquerque capture Malacca
- **1520** Rise of the Muslim states of Aceh and Bantam
- **1571** Spanish found Manila as capital of the Philippines
- **1596** The first Dutch fleet arrives at Bantam
- **1602** Dutch East Indies Company is founded, headquarters at Batavia from 1619
- **1624–62** The Dutch occupy Taiwan
- **1631–60** Sultanate of Macassar reaches its greatest influence
- **1667** The Dutch conquer the sultanate of Macassar
- **1684** The Dutch East India Company occupies the sultanate of Bantam
- **1685** The English set up a base for pepper at Benkulen
- **1762–64** A British fleet occupies Manila
- **1773–75** The British East India Company occupies a base at Balambangan
- **1781** British conquer all Dutch territories in West Sumatra; later exchanged for trading concessions

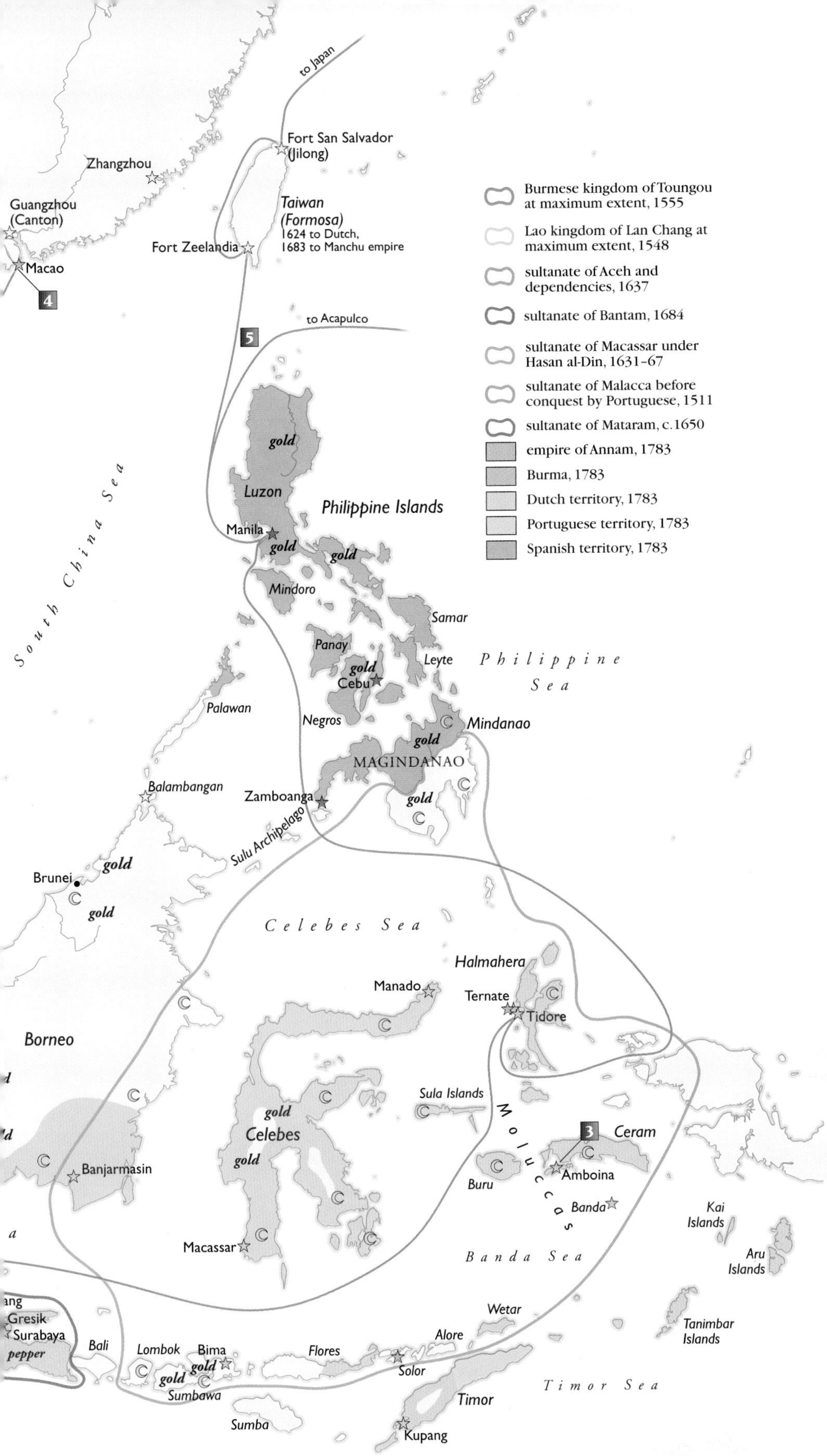

Burmese kingdom of Toungou at maximum extent, 1555
Lao kingdom of Lan Chang at maximum extent, 1548
sultanate of Aceh and dependencies, 1637
sultanate of Bantam, 1684
sultanate of Macassar under Hasan al-Din, 1631–67
sultanate of Malacca before conquest by Portuguese, 1511
sultanate of Mataram, c.1650
empire of Annam, 1783
Burma, 1783
Dutch territory, 1783
Portuguese territory, 1783
Spanish territory, 1783

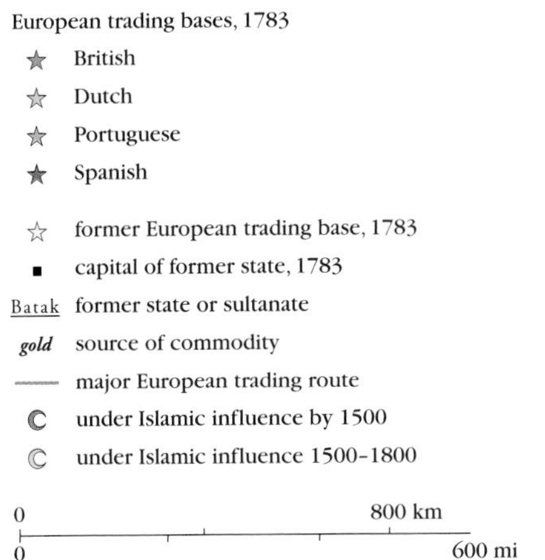
European trading bases, 1783
British
Dutch
Portuguese
Spanish
former European trading base, 1783
capital of former state, 1783
Batak former state or sultanate
gold source of commodity
major European trading route
under Islamic influence by 1500
under Islamic influence 1500–1800
0 800 km
0 600 mi

having to pay tribute to Siam, Tongking or Cochin-China at different periods.

After initially finding European guns and trade wealth very useful for their wars of expansion, the major mainland states all began to fear their power. In 1688 an anti-foreigner revolution overthrew the Siamese monarchy, and both Siam and the Vietnamese states thereafter reoriented their trade to the less threatening Chinese.

Magellan had visited the Philippine Islands in 1521 (he was killed there), but Spanish settlement began, around Manila, only in 1571, under Miguel Lopez de Legazpi. Manila became the center for Spanish trade with Asia and for Christianizing northern and central Philippines by 1650, but the Islamic states of Sulu and Magindanao resisted their control in the southern islands.

In the Indonesian archipelago the sultanate of Malacca focussed much of the trade between the Indian Ocean, China and southeast Asia until 1511, when the Portuguese conquered the city and built a fort which they held until the Dutch took it in 1641. Muslim traders dispersed, strengthening the new Islamic powers of the 16th and 17th centuries, notably Aceh, Bantam and Mataram. Aceh and Bantam controlled trade in Sumatran and west Javan pepper, which dominated the world supply by 1600. Further east the Portuguese built forts in Ternate and Amboina to control the supply of cloves and in Solor and Kupang for sandalwood, but never got the better of a still lively Islamic trading network. By 1605 the rising power of Macassar adopted Islam and became the main trade center of east Indonesia.

The Dutch East India Company (VOC) was more formidable. It took control of Amboina in 1606, Jakarta (renamed Batavia) in 1619, the nutmeg-producing Banda Islands in 1621 and monopolized clove production in the Moluccas by the 1650s. VOC was the greatest commercial power of maritime Asia by 1650, though it controlled negligible territory. In the 18th century VOC shifted its interest to the internal affairs of Java, including production of coffee and sugar, but its trade monopolies collapsed after 1770 in the face of stronger British, French, American and Chinese trade.

1 Under the unifying influence of Islam and trade, the diverse Indonesian peoples began to adopt Malay as a language for trade in the 15th and 16th centuries.

2 Under Sultan Agung (r.1613-46) Mataram dominated all of Java except the Dutch enclave of Batavia; in the later 17th century the Dutch gradually acquired control of most of the island.

3 The Dutch sacked the English trading base at Amboina in 1623, ending direct English involvement in the spice trade.

4 After the loss of Malacca to the Dutch in 1641, the Portuguese merchants of Macao became the main suppliers of Chinese silk to the Spanish for the "Manila Galleon" trade.

5 The "Manila Galleon" trade route brought silver from Acapulco and returned with Chinese silk; it remained a closed, Spanish route until the British occupation of Manila in 1762–64.

6 Ayutthaya was destroyed by a Burmese invasion in 1767. A new Siamese kingdom was established at Thon Buri (Bangkok) in 1782.

7 Britain conquered the Dutch settlements in west Sumatra in 1781, but returned them in 1783 in return for trading rights throughout the Dutch East Indies.

See also 3.25 (southeast Asia before the Europeans); 5.22 (19th-century southeast Asia)

4.25 The Spanish–American empire • 1492 – 1783 •

Spanish conquest in the New World profoundly affected both the region itself and Europe. Spain's empire was the largest in world history to date other than that of the Mongols. It destroyed ancient cultures and decimated native populations who proved disastrously vulnerable to diseases introduced from the Old World. Meanwhile, the mining of huge silver deposits financed Spanish Habsburg ambitions and underpinned the whole of European trade. Nor was the traffic in disease all one-way: syphilis, caught by Spanish sailors in the Caribbean, became a feared killer in Europe from the early 16th century.

Spain's incursion in the Americas began with royal sponsorship of the voyages of the Italian navigator-merchants Christopher Columbus and Amerigo Vespucci at the end of the 15th century. In particular, Columbus' discovery of the West Indies for Spain soon led to permanent settlements. Colonization of the Caribbean islands began on Santo Domingo (Hispaniola) and provided a foretaste of Spanish rule on the mainland; administrative, legal, and religious structures were rapidly put in place, while the aboriginal Arawak and Carib peoples fell victim to maltreatment and disease.

The Spanish empire was territorial from the outset, concerned with the government, economic exploitation and religious conversion of its native subjects; it was perhaps less careless of the welfare of its subject peoples than were some other colonial empires. Paradoxically, its rapid growth depended on existing political structures and communications networks. Hernán Cortés and Francisco Pizarro encountered, in the Aztec and Inca empires respectively, centralized, populous and formidable states, yet internal divisions helped them swiftly to destroy any resistance. Beyond their boundaries, the population was sparse and the environment hostile and virtually impenetrable to Europeans. These hinterlands were still only partially conquered by 1800.

The prosperity of the empire was built above all on Mexican and Peruvian gold and silver. These precious metals had been extracted on a modest scale by the Aztecs and Incas for use in ceremonial artifacts, but were now mined and shipped in huge quantities by the Spanish. This enterprise required regular commercial fleets with permanent naval escorts, linking Seville and Veracruz on the east coast of Mexico, and Peru and the west coast of the Central American isthmus. The maintenance and protection of these fleets was one of the great maritime and commercial achievements of the age.

Challenges by Spain's European rivals to the Spanish–American empire itself were frequent but largely unsuccessful; indeed, Spanish America proved more resilient than Spain's European territories to challenges from the other powers. From the 1570s, major ports were subjected to numerous assaults. The English capture of Jamaica in 1655 was an important strategic loss, but the empire remained largely secure until the Seven Years War (1756–63). In 1762, the British occupied Havana; Spain only regained control by ceding Florida. However, the demise of France as a colonial power in America allowed Spain to acquire Louisiana while, in the American War of Independence, it regained Florida and checked British expansion on the Mississippi.

Spain was not the only significant colonial power in South America. In 1494, Spain and Portugal

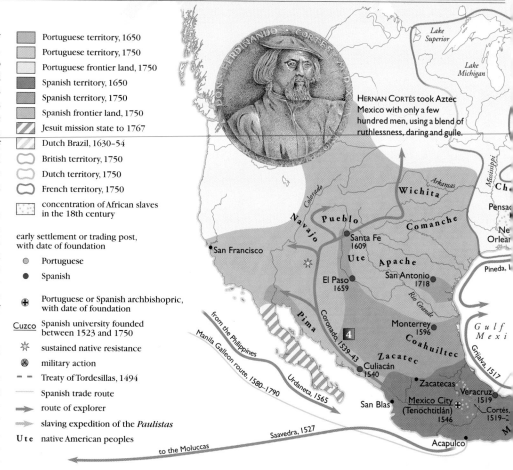

Portuguese territory, 1650
Portuguese territory, 1750
Portuguese frontier land, 1750
Spanish territory, 1650
Spanish territory, 1750
Spanish frontier land, 1750
Jesuit mission state to 1767
Dutch Brazil, 1630–54
British territory, 1750
Dutch territory, 1750
French territory, 1750
concentration of African slaves in the 18th century

early settlement or trading post, with date of foundation
Portuguese
Spanish
Portuguese or Spanish archbishopric, with date of foundation
Cuzco Spanish university founded between 1523 and 1750
sustained native resistance
military action
Treaty of Tordesillas, 1494
Spanish trade route
route of explorer
slaving expedition of the *Paulistas*
Ute native American peoples

HERNAN CORTÉS took Aztec Mexico with only a few hundred men, using a blend of ruthlessness, daring and guile.

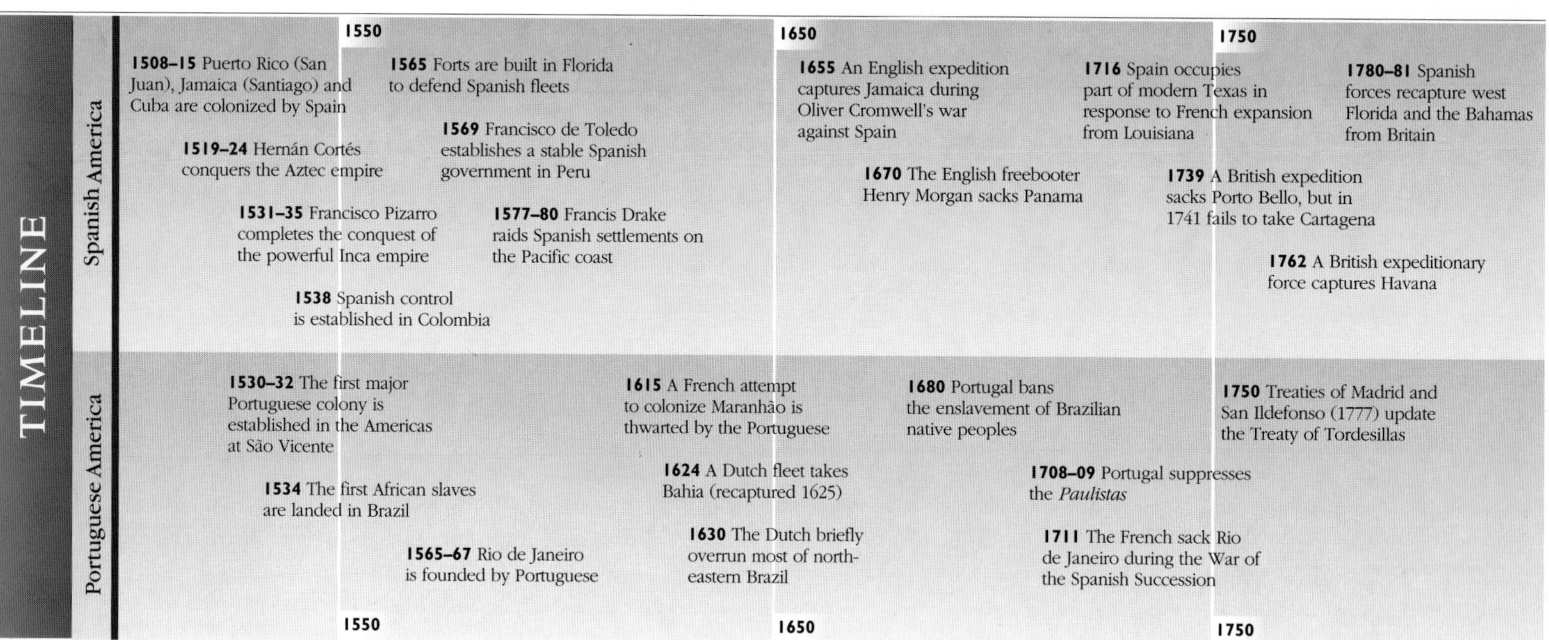
TIMELINE
Spanish America
1550
1650
1750
1508–15 Puerto Rico (San Juan), Jamaica (Santiago) and Cuba are colonized by Spain
1519–24 Hernán Cortés conquers the Aztec empire
1531–35 Francisco Pizarro completes the conquest of the powerful Inca empire
1538 Spanish control is established in Colombia
1565 Forts are built in Florida to defend Spanish fleets
1569 Francisco de Toledo establishes a stable Spanish government in Peru
1577–80 Francis Drake raids Spanish settlements on the Pacific coast
1655 An English expedition captures Jamaica during Oliver Cromwell's war against Spain
1670 The English freebooter Henry Morgan sacks Panama
1716 Spain occupies part of modern Texas in response to French expansion from Louisiana
1739 A British expedition sacks Porto Bello, but in 1741 fails to take Cartagena
1762 A British expeditionary force captures Havana
1780–81 Spanish forces recapture west Florida and the Bahamas from Britain
Portuguese America
1530–32 The first major Portuguese colony is established in the Americas at São Vicente
1534 The first African slaves are landed in Brazil
1565–67 Rio de Janeiro is founded by Portuguese
1615 A French attempt to colonize Maranhão is thwarted by the Portuguese
1624 A Dutch fleet takes Bahia (recaptured 1625)
1630 The Dutch briefly overrun most of north-eastern Brazil
1680 Portugal bans the enslavement of Brazilian native peoples
1708–09 Portugal suppresses the *Paulistas*
1711 The French sack Rio de Janeiro during the War of the Spanish Succession
1750 Treaties of Madrid and San Ildefonso (1777) update the Treaty of Tordesillas
1550
1650
1750

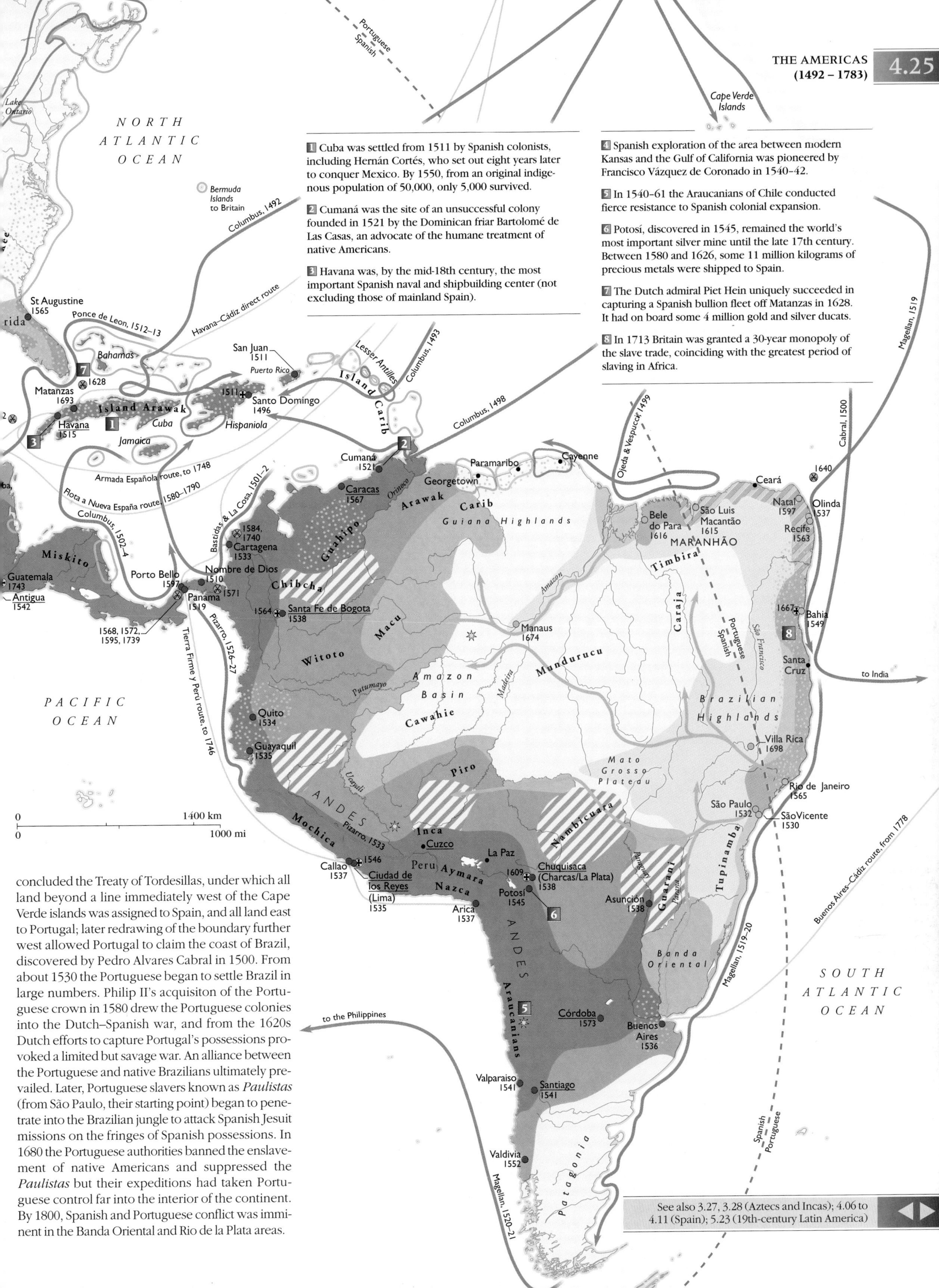
NORTH ATLANTIC OCEAN
Lake Ontario
Bermuda Islands to Britain
Columbus, 1492
Havana–Cádiz direct route
Ponce de Leon, 1512–13
St Augustine 1565
Bahamas
San Juan 1511
Puerto Rico
Lesser Antilles
Columbus, 1493
Island Carib
Matanzas 1693
1628
Island Arawak
Havana 1515
Cuba
Jamaica
1511 Santo Domingo 1496
Hispaniola
Columbus, 1498
Cumaná 1521
Armada Española route, to 1748
Flota a Nueva España route, 1580–1790
Columbus, 1502–4
Bastidas & La Cosa, 1501–2
Caracas 1567
Orinoco
Arawak
Georgetown
Paramaribo
Cayenne
Carib
Guiana Highlands
Guahipo
1584, 1740
Cartagena 1533
Nombre de Dios 1510
Miskito
Guatemala 1743
Antigua 1542
Porto Bello 1597
Panama 1519
1571
Chibcha
1564 Santa Fe de Bogota 1538
1568, 1572, 1595, 1739
Pizarro, 1526–27
Tierra Firme y Perú route, to 1746
Macu
Witoto
Amazon
Manaus 1674
Amazon Basin
Putumayo
Madeira
Mundurucu
Cawahie
PACIFIC OCEAN
Quito 1534
Guayaquil 1535
Piro
Ucayali
ANDES
Mochica
Pizarro, 1533
Inca
Cuzco
Callao 1537
1546
Ciudad de los Reyes (Lima) 1535
Peru
Aymara
Nazca
La Paz
1609
Chuquisaca (Charcas/La Plata) 1538
Potosí 1545
Arica 1537
Nambicuara
Paraguay
Guarani
Paraná
Asunción 1538
Tupinamba
Mato Grosso Plateau
Brazilian Highlands
Villa Rica 1698
Rio de Janeiro 1565
São Paulo 1532
São Vicente 1530
Caraja
Timbira
Bele do Para 1616
São Luis Macantão 1615
MARANHÃO
Ceará
Natal 1597
Olinda 1537
Recife 1563
1640
1667
Bahia 1549
Santa Cruz
São Francisco
Portuguese Spanish
Ojeda & Vespucci 1499
Cabral, 1500
Magellan, 1519
to India
Cape Verde Islands
Banda Oriental
Magellan, 1519–20
Buenos Aires–Cádiz route, from 1778
SOUTH ATLANTIC OCEAN
Araucanians
Córdoba 1573
Buenos Aires 1536
to the Philippines
Valparaiso 1541
Santiago 1541
Valdivia 1552
Patagonia
Magellan, 1520–21
Spanish Portuguese
0 1400 km
0 1000 mi

1 Cuba was settled from 1511 by Spanish colonists, including Hernán Cortés, who set out eight years later to conquer Mexico. By 1550, from an original indigenous population of 50,000, only 5,000 survived.

2 Cumaná was the site of an unsuccessful colony founded in 1521 by the Dominican friar Bartolomé de Las Casas, an advocate of the humane treatment of native Americans.

3 Havana was, by the mid-18th century, the most important Spanish naval and shipbuilding center (not excluding those of mainland Spain).

4 Spanish exploration of the area between modern Kansas and the Gulf of California was pioneered by Francisco Vázquez de Coronado in 1540–42.

5 In 1540–61 the Araucanians of Chile conducted fierce resistance to Spanish colonial expansion.

6 Potosí, discovered in 1545, remained the world's most important silver mine until the late 17th century. Between 1580 and 1626, some 11 million kilograms of precious metals were shipped to Spain.

7 The Dutch admiral Piet Hein uniquely succeeded in capturing a Spanish bullion fleet off Matanzas in 1628. It had on board some 4 million gold and silver ducats.

8 In 1713 Britain was granted a 30-year monopoly of the slave trade, coinciding with the greatest period of slaving in Africa.

concluded the Treaty of Tordesillas, under which all land beyond a line immediately west of the Cape Verde islands was assigned to Spain, and all land east to Portugal; later redrawing of the boundary further west allowed Portugal to claim the coast of Brazil, discovered by Pedro Alvares Cabral in 1500. From about 1530 the Portuguese began to settle Brazil in large numbers. Philip II's acquisiton of the Portuguese crown in 1580 drew the Portuguese colonies into the Dutch–Spanish war, and from the 1620s Dutch efforts to capture Portugal's possessions provoked a limited but savage war. An alliance between the Portuguese and native Brazilians ultimately prevailed. Later, Portuguese slavers known as *Paulistas* (from São Paulo, their starting point) began to penetrate into the Brazilian jungle to attack Spanish Jesuit missions on the fringes of Spanish possessions. In 1680 the Portuguese authorities banned the enslavement of native Americans and suppressed the *Paulistas* but their expeditions had taken Portuguese control far into the interior of the continent. By 1800, Spanish and Portuguese conflict was imminent in the Banda Oriental and Rio de la Plata areas.

See also 3.27, 3.28 (Aztecs and Incas); 4.06 to 4.11 (Spain); 5.23 (19th-century Latin America)

4.26 European exploration of North America • 1500 – 1783 •

The exploration of North America was unlike other achievements of the age of European expansion. Even though many of the cultures and civilizations encountered in other continents had had little recent contact with Europeans, they were not all wholly alien. Moreover, many had dynamic economies willing to supply in bulk products that Europe lacked. Even in Mexico and Peru, whose cultures were entirely new to Europeans, strong centralized states, a relatively dense population and an available fund of gold and silver were familiar elements. Only the Caribbean islands and the vast, empty interior of South America provided a foretaste of what confronted the first explorers of North America. From the first landing of John Cabot in 1497 until the 18th century, North America remained enigmatic; its true scale was not appreciated for a long time, nor did it offer any immediate returns on the investments of explorers and their backers.

Explorers were driven by a number of pervasive myths, and dogged by a sense of disappointment once their lack of substance was revealed. The earliest chanced upon North America while seeking a route to China; Columbus died convinced that he had found an island off the Asian mainland. After Giovanni da Verrazano had explored the length of the Atlantic seaboard and the first colonial ventures had encountered a densely wooded interior and native peoples hostile to exploration inland, the search began for a route around the continent. A possible northern passage remained an English obsession: Hudson, Davis and Baffin endured hardships in the Canadian north to find a northwest sea passage to China. Even James Cook, mapping the Alaskan coast in 1778–79, felt compelled to explore major inlets in search of the elusive seaway.

French exploration of the St Lawrence river was stimulated by the idea of a sea passage through the heart of the continent. Cartier, Champlain, the Jesuit fathers, the de la Vérendryes and generations of fur trappers progressed down the St Lawrence and through the Great Lakes, fueling the myth of a route westward to the Pacific. This myth finally evaporated in the endless expanse of the Great Plains beyond Lake Manitoba. The supreme French achievement, La Salle's descent of the Mississippi in 1682, did reveal a north–south passage, yet his disappointment at finding the Gulf of Mexico, rather than the Pacific, at the mouth of the river was profound.

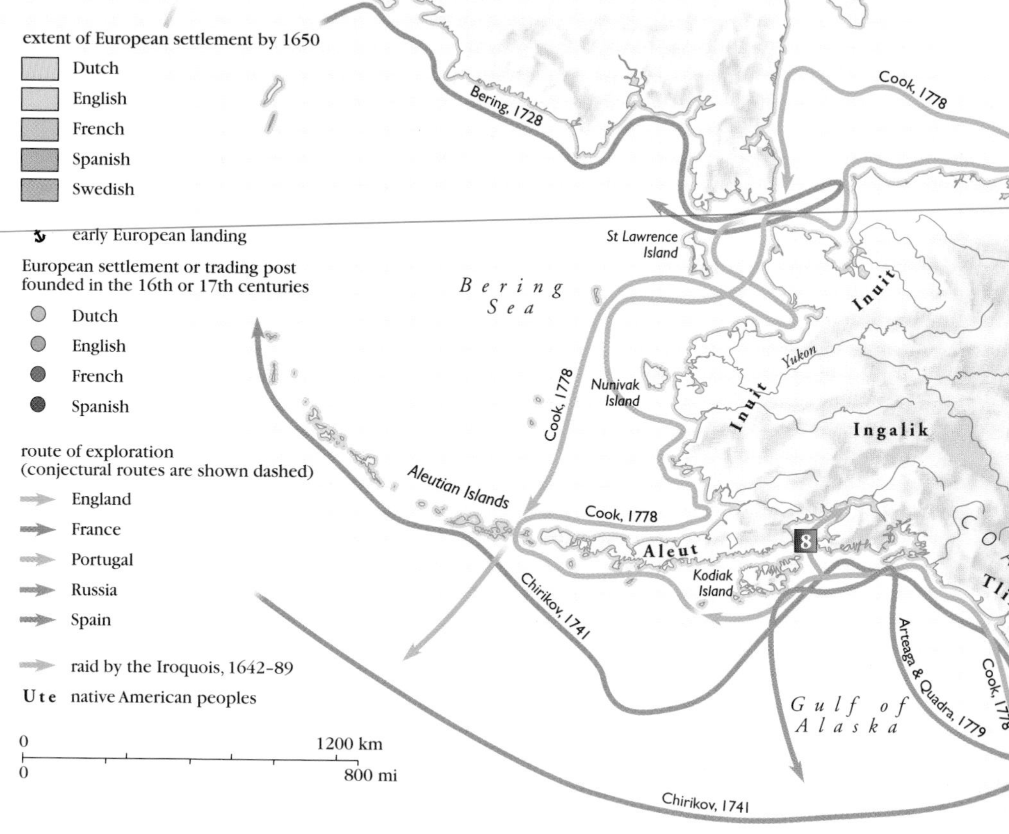

extent of European settlement by 1650
Dutch
English
French
Spanish
Swedish
early European landing
European settlement or trading post founded in the 16th or 17th centuries
Dutch
English
French
Spanish
route of exploration (conjectural routes are shown dashed)
England
France
Portugal
Russia
Spain
raid by the Iroquois, 1642–89
Ute native American peoples
0 1200 km
0 800 mi
Bering, 1728
Cook, 1778
St Lawrence Island
Bering Sea
Inuit
Nunivak Island
Yukon
Cook, 1778
Inuit
Ingalik
Aleutian Islands
Cook, 1778
Aleut
8
Kodiak Island
Chirikov, 1741
Arteaga & Quadra, 1779
Cook, 1778
Gulf of Alaska
Chirikov, 1741
Queen Cha

Initial Spanish exploration of North America from Mexico and the Caribbean under leaders such as de Soto and Coronado was mounted in a spirit of conquest, gold-lust and missionary zeal. Large military expeditions were equipped to build forts, establish missions and despoil the cities that reputedly lay to the north. After epic journeys, survivors of these expeditions returned exhausted and empty-handed. By the early 17th century, Spanish New Mexico was little more than a string of outposts in the *pueblo* villages around Santa Fé, surrounded by desert. Florida, which the Spaniards initially believed to be an island, was explored (and defended) for strategic reasons to protect the bullion fleet route to Europe. Similarly, the Spaniards began to venture up the Californian coast in the 17th century in response to a British and Russian threat.

By the 1650s the Caribbean and, to a lesser extent, the Atlantic seaboard had attracted settlers in number, but it was in the north that the true wealth of the American continent – rich farmland – began to be exploited. From the outset, the Dutch New Netherland colony encouraged settlement by farmers, while the English colonies quickly developed a European-style agricultural economy. The native peoples welcomed settlers for the trade they brought, but they prevented expansion inland; the Appalachian mountains also remained a formidable barrier. It was 180 years after Cabot's landing before English traders and explorers penetrated the basin of the Ohio, after European diseases and the erosion of native cultures had weakened resistance. In the years following the British conquest of French America, the trickle of pioneers across the Appalachians and into the fertile lands of Kentucky and Tennessee became a flood, marking a new era of truly profitable exploration.

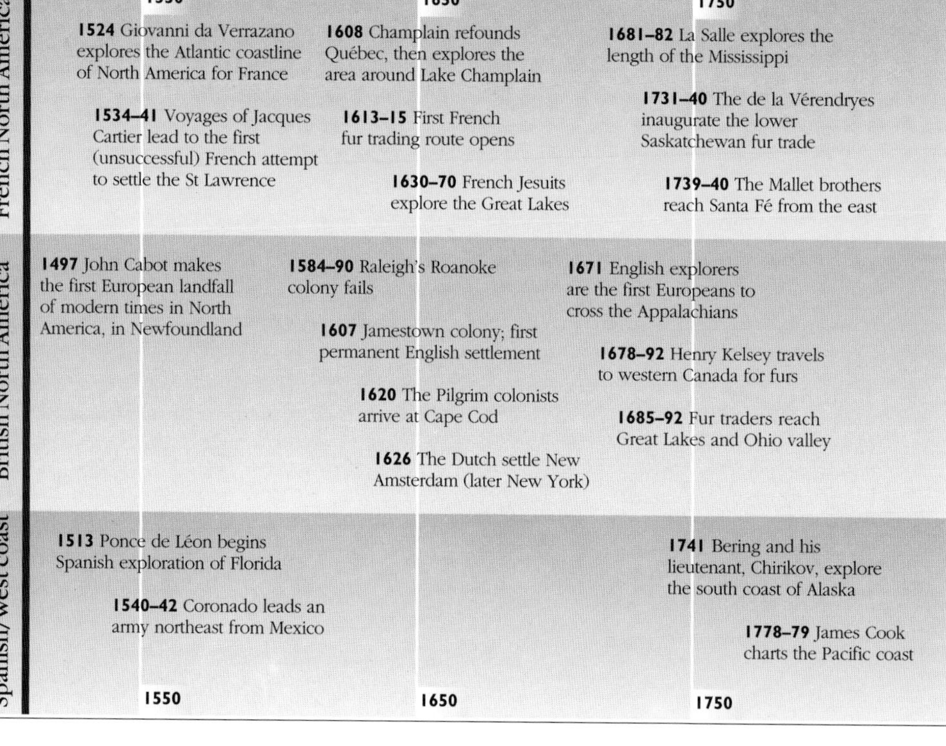

TIMELINE
French North America
1550
1650
1750
1524 Giovanni da Verrazano explores the Atlantic coastline of North America for France
1534–41 Voyages of Jacques Cartier lead to the first (unsuccessful) French attempt to settle the St Lawrence
1608 Champlain refounds Québec, then explores the area around Lake Champlain
1613–15 First French fur trading route opens
1630–70 French Jesuits explore the Great Lakes
1681–82 La Salle explores the length of the Mississippi
1731–40 The de la Vérendryes inaugurate the lower Saskatchewan fur trade
1739–40 The Mallet brothers reach Santa Fé from the east
British North America
1497 John Cabot makes the first European landfall of modern times in North America, in Newfoundland
1584–90 Raleigh's Roanoke colony fails
1607 Jamestown colony; first permanent English settlement
1620 The Pilgrim colonists arrive at Cape Cod
1626 The Dutch settle New Amsterdam (later New York)
1671 English explorers are the first Europeans to cross the Appalachians
1678–92 Henry Kelsey travels to western Canada for furs
1685–92 Fur traders reach Great Lakes and Ohio valley
Spanish/West coast
1513 Ponce de Léon begins Spanish exploration of Florida
1540–42 Coronado leads an army northeast from Mexico
1741 Bering and his lieutenant, Chirikov, explore the south coast of Alaska
1778–79 James Cook charts the Pacific coast
1550
1650
1750

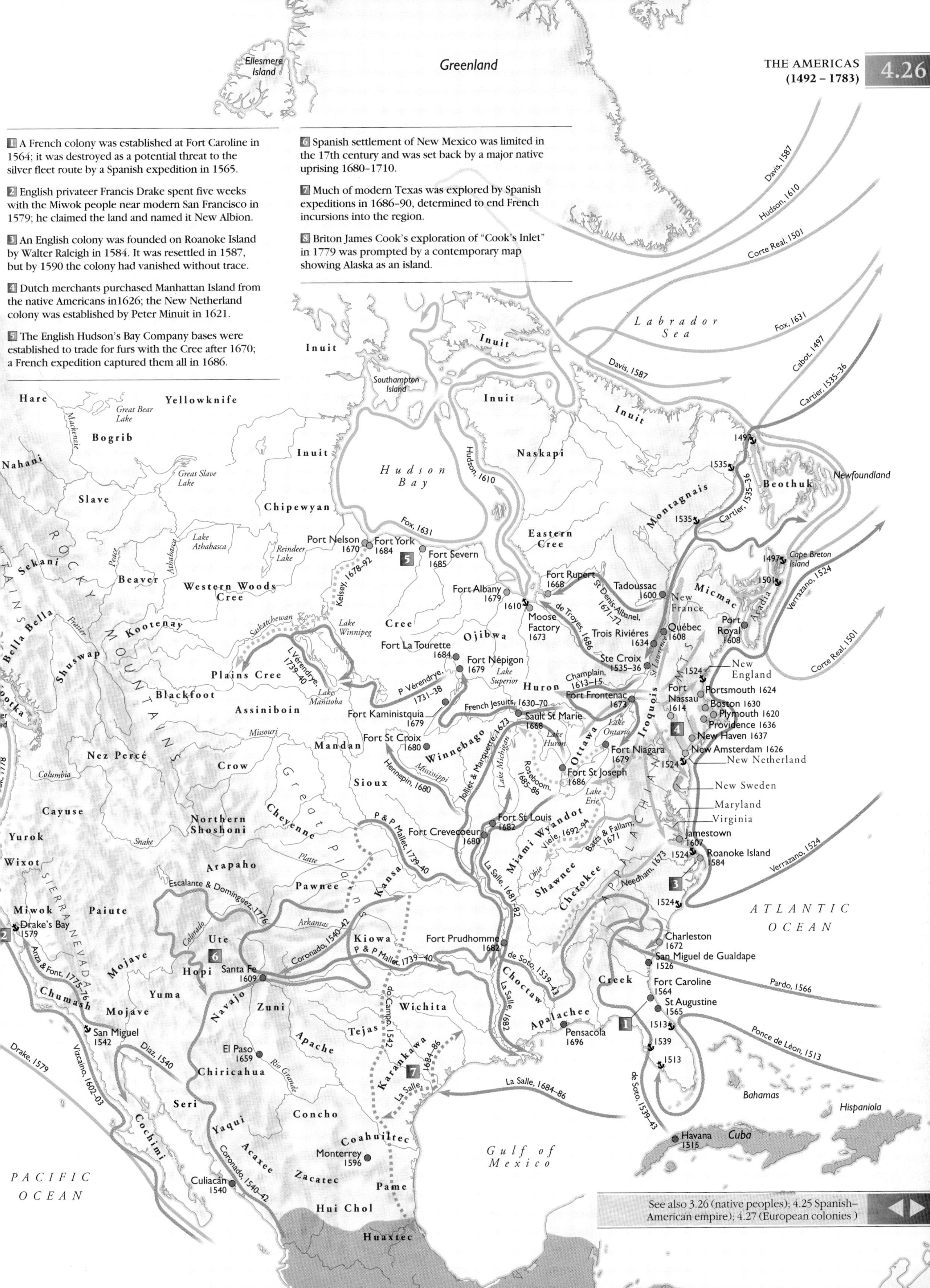
Ellesmere Island
Greenland
Labrador Sea
Davis, 1587
Hudson, 1610
Corte Real, 1501
Fox, 1631
Cabot, 1497
Cartier, 1535–36
Inuit
Southampton Island
Hudson Bay
Naskapi
Montagnais
Beothuk
Newfoundland
Eastern Cree
Cape Breton Island
Micmac
Acadia
Verrazano, 1524
Hare
Yellowknife
Great Bear Lake
Mackenzie
Bogrib
Nahani
Great Slave Lake
Slave
Chipewyan
Port Nelson 1670
Fort York 1684
Fort Severn 1685
Kelsey, 1678–92
Lake Athabasca
Reindeer Lake
Peace
Athabasca
Sekani
Beaver
Western Woods Cree
ROCKY MOUNTAINS
Bella Bella
Fraser
Kootenay
Shuswap
Saskatchewan
Lake Winnipeg
L Vérendrye, 1739–40
Lake Manitoba
Plains Cree
Blackfoot
Assiniboin
Cree
Fort Albany 1679
Fort Rupert 1668
Moose Factory 1673
de Troyes, 1686
St Denis-Albanel, 1671–72
Tadoussac 1600
New France
Québec 1608
Trois Rivières 1634
Ste Croix 1535–36
Port Royal 1608
Ojibwa
Fort La Tourette 1684
Fort Népigon 1679
Lake Superior
P Vérendrye, 1731–38
Fort Kaministquia 1679
French Jesuits, 1630–70
Sault St Marie 1668
Huron
Champlain, 1613–15
Fort Frontenac 1673
Lake Ontario
Iroquois
St Lawrence
New England
Portsmouth 1624
Fort Nassau 1614
Boston 1630
Plymouth 1620
Providence 1636
New Haven 1637
New Amsterdam 1626
New Netherland
New Sweden
Maryland
Virginia
Jamestown 1607
Roanoke Island 1584
Missouri
Mandan
Fort St Croix 1680
Winnebago
Jolliet & Marquette, 1673
Lake Michigan
Lake Huron
Ottawa
Fort Niagara 1679
Fort St Joseph 1686
Roseboom, 1685–86
Lake Erie
Nez Percé
Crow
Columbia
Mississippi
Hennepin, 1680
Sioux
Great Plains
Cayuse
Northern Shoshoni
Cheyenne
P & P Mallet, 1739–40
Fort Crevecoeur 1680
Fort St Louis 1682
Miami
Wyandot
Viele, 1692–94
Batts & Fallam, 1671
APPALACHIAN MTS
Yurok
Snake
Wixot
Platte
Arapaho
Escalante & Domínguez, 1776
Pawnee
Kansa
La Salle, 1681–82
Ohio
Shawnee
Cherokee
Needham, 1673
SIERRA NEVADA
Miwok
Drake's Bay 1579
Paiute
Colorado
Ute
Arkansas
Coronado, 1540–42
Kiowa
P & P Mallet, 1739–40
Fort Prudhomme 1682
de Soto, 1539–43
ATLANTIC OCEAN
Charleston 1672
San Miguel de Gualdape 1526
Anza & Font, 1775–76
Mojave
Hopi
Santa Fe 1609
Yuma
Choctaw
La Salle, 1682
Creek
Fort Caroline 1564
St Augustine 1565
Pardo, 1566
Chumash
Mojave
Navajo
Zuni
Wichita
do Campo, 1542
Apalachee
Pensacola 1696
San Miguel 1542
Díaz, 1540
El Paso 1659
Rio Grande
Apache
Tejas
Karankawa
1684–86
Ponce de León, 1513
Drake, 1579
Vizcaino, 1602–03
Chiricahua
La Salle
La Salle, 1684–86
de Soto, 1539–43
Bahamas
Hispaniola
Seri
Concho
Havana 1515
Cuba
Cochimi
Yaqui
Coronado, 1540–42
Acaxee
Coahuiltec
Monterrey 1596
Gulf of Mexico
PACIFIC OCEAN
Culiacán 1540
Zacatec
Pame
Hui Chol
Huaxtec

1 A French colony was established at Fort Caroline in 1564; it was destroyed as a potential threat to the silver fleet route by a Spanish expedition in 1565.

2 English privateer Francis Drake spent five weeks with the Miwok people near modern San Francisco in 1579; he claimed the land and named it New Albion.

3 An English colony was founded on Roanoke Island by Walter Raleigh in 1584. It was resettled in 1587, but by 1590 the colony had vanished without trace.

4 Dutch merchants purchased Manhattan Island from the native Americans in1626; the New Netherland colony was established by Peter Minuit in 1621.

5 The English Hudson's Bay Company bases were established to trade for furs with the Cree after 1670; a French expedition captured them all in 1686.

6 Spanish settlement of New Mexico was limited in the 17th century and was set back by a major native uprising 1680–1710.

7 Much of modern Texas was explored by Spanish expeditions in 1686–90, determined to end French incursions into the region.

8 Briton James Cook's exploration of "Cook's Inlet" in 1779 was prompted by a contemporary map showing Alaska as an island.

See also 3.26 (native peoples); 4.25 Spanish–American empire); 4.27 (European colonies)

4.27 Colonial North America • 1650 – 1763 •

From the 1650s most major European wars were also fought out in North America. First the smaller colonies were eliminated. After the Netherlands turned against France, the Dutch in 1655 took New Sweden (Delaware) from Louis XIV's European ally. Likewise, the New Netherland colony (in the Hudson River region) was overrun by English forces during the Anglo-Dutch naval wars (1664).

The main rivalry was between the French and the British. Early exploration had created distinct areas of influence on the St Lawrence and the eastern seaboard respectively. As these grew to include claims in the Mississippi basin, Georgia and the Appalachian foothills, some native peoples were drawn into the hostility between the colonists. Sporadic fighting erupted into the conflict known as King William's War (an extension of the War of the League of Augsburg in Europe), when a French expedition sacked English trading forts on Hudson Bay (1686), and French and Huron raids ravaged New England, despite England's alliance with the Iroquois.

Britain seized the opportunity of Queen Anne's War (the War of the Spanish Succession) to overrun the French territory of Acadia in 1710. Renamed Nova Scotia, the peninsula was confirmed as a British possession (together with Newfoundland) by the Treaty of Utrecht in 1713, while the Ile St Jean and Ile Royale remained French. However, the area remained the scene of regular skirmishes for fifty years. In King George's War – the War of the Austrian Succession – the French naval base at Louisbourg on Ile Royale was sacked (1745), a French naval expedition to reconquer Acadia was destroyed by a storm (1746), and an unsuccessful British and Iroquois attack on New France led to widespread French and Huron raids (1746–48). Hostilities continued after the war in the Ohio basin, where the French tried to halt British expansion westward by destroying the advanced post at Pickawillany.

The decisive phase of Anglo-French conflict came with the French and Indian War (1755–63), the American counterpart of the Seven Years War. The European population of New France and Louisiana was only one-tenth that of the British colonies, and despite strategically sited forts and alliances with the indigenous peoples, the French could no longer offset this imbalance. Though France had achieved naval parity after 1748, the Royal Navy was able to blockade both trade and military reinforcements from France. Initially Britain suffered defeat at Fort Duquesne, failed to take Crown Point (1755), and endured successful French counterattacks (1756) and defeat at Ticonderoga (1758). Thereafter, the war swung in Britain's favor. James Wolfe's victory over the Marquis de Montcalm on the Plains of Abraham near Québec in 1759 secured British supremacy. By 1760 the whole of New France was in British hands. At the same time, British naval forces captured all French possessions in the West Indies except Saint-Domingue. When France coerced Spain to enter the war, the British occupied Florida and Havana. In the Treaty of Paris (1763) Britain's control of the whole of North America east of the Mississippi was confirmed. French territories beyond the Mississippi passed to Spain, which also regained Havana in exchange for Florida.

Contact with Europeans initially brought some benefits to indigenous peoples. In the southwest, the Plains peoples reverted to buffalo-hunting after acquiring Spanish horses, while, in the mid-17th century, the Huron people of the Great Lakes were saved by their military alliance with France from destruction by the Iroquois. However, native Americans experienced a steady loss of their traditional lands. King Philip's War of 1675–76 ended native resistance to European encroachment in the northeast; the Tuscarora and Yamassee peoples were driven out of the Carolinas in 1711 and 1715 respectively; and from 1730 to 1755 the Shawnee and Delaware fled west down the Ohio. Only in the west, where French traders encountered the Sioux nation of the Plains, was European impact minimal.

extent of European settlement in 1713
- British
- French
- Spanish
- French territory acquired by Britain, 1713

European territorial claims, 1750
- British
- French
- Spanish
- British territory after 1763
- Spanish territory after 1763

settlement or trading post founded in the 18th century
- British
- French
- Spanish

French and Indian War, 1755-63
- British capture of fort or settlement
- French capture of fort or settlement
- British victory
- French victory
- Spanish victory
- raid by French and native allies on British settlements
- British campaign
- Spanish campaign
- Iroquois campaign, 1642-67
- migration of Delaware and Shawnee, 1730-55
- colonial road
- trade route of the native peoples
- Ute native American peoples

0 600 km
0 400 mi

Lake Athabasca
Western Woods Cree
Saskatchewan
Plains
Gros Ventre
Crow

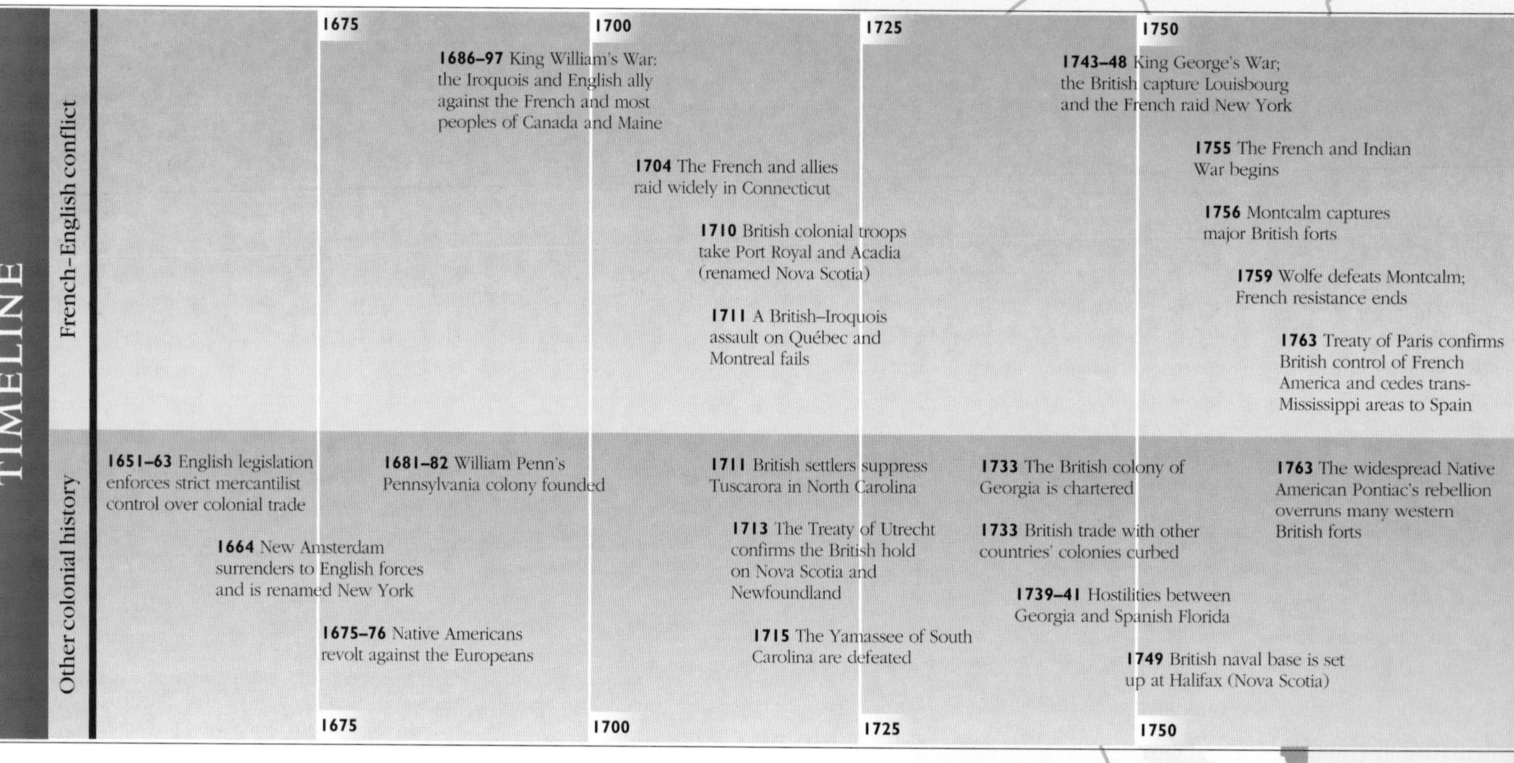

TIMELINE
French-English conflict
Other colonial history
1675
1700
1725
1750
1686–97 King William's War: the Iroquois and English ally against the French and most peoples of Canada and Maine
1704 The French and allies raid widely in Connecticut
1710 British colonial troops take Port Royal and Acadia (renamed Nova Scotia)
1711 A British–Iroquois assault on Québec and Montreal fails
1743–48 King George's War; the British capture Louisbourg and the French raid New York
1755 The French and Indian War begins
1756 Montcalm captures major British forts
1759 Wolfe defeats Montcalm; French resistance ends
1763 Treaty of Paris confirms British control of French America and cedes trans-Mississippi areas to Spain
1651–63 English legislation enforces strict mercantilist control over colonial trade
1664 New Amsterdam surrenders to English forces and is renamed New York
1681–82 William Penn's Pennsylvania colony founded
1675–76 Native Americans revolt against the Europeans
1711 British settlers suppress Tuscarora in North Carolina
1713 The Treaty of Utrecht confirms the British hold on Nova Scotia and Newfoundland
1715 The Yamassee of South Carolina are defeated
1733 The British colony of Georgia is chartered
1733 British trade with other countries' colonies curbed
1739–41 Hostilities between Georgia and Spanish Florida
1749 British naval base is set up at Halifax (Nova Scotia)
1763 The widespread Native American Pontiac's rebellion overruns many western British forts
1675
1700
1725
1750

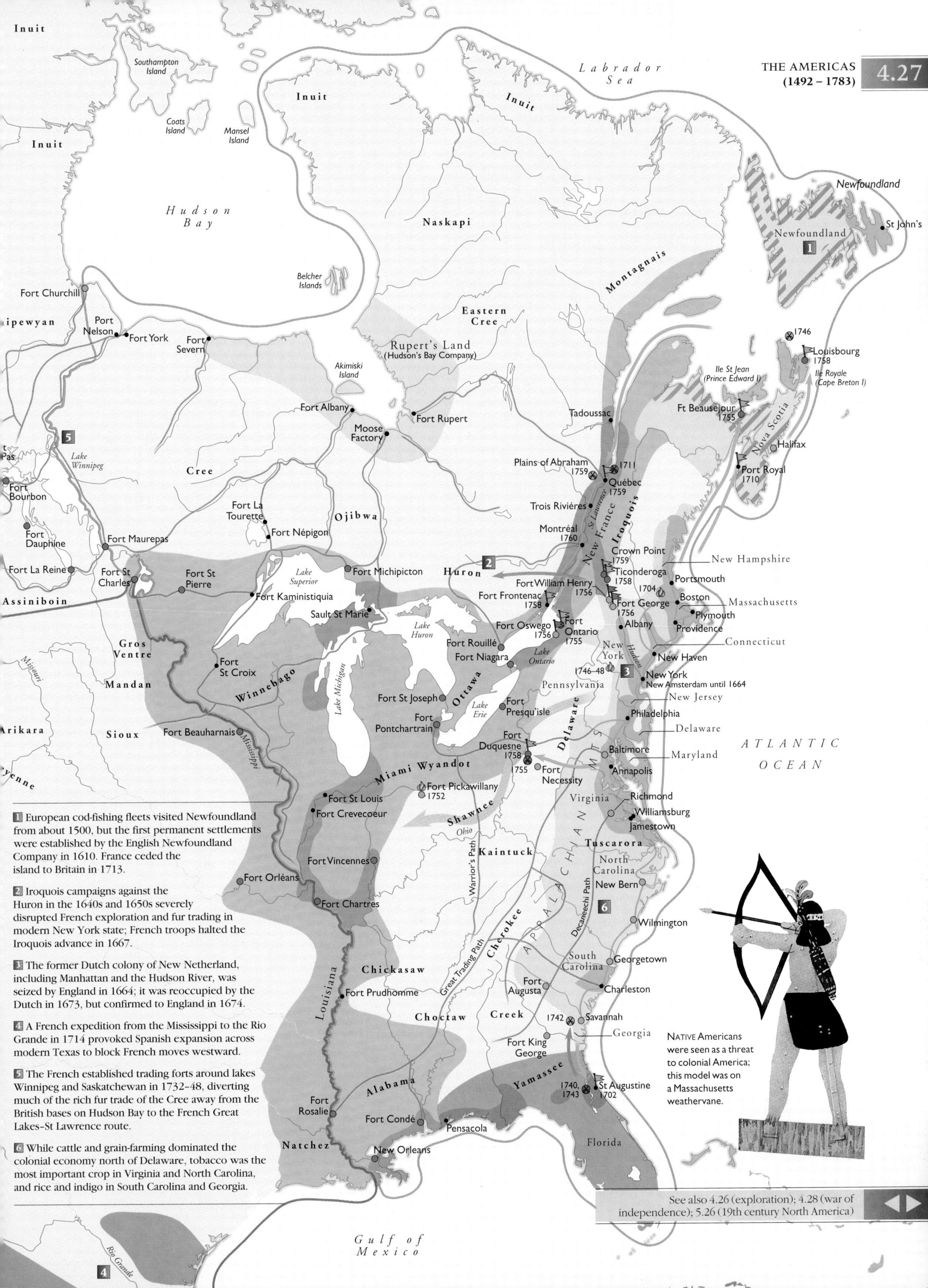
Inuit
Southampton Island
Coats Island
Mansel Island
Hudson Bay
Labrador Sea
Inuit
Naskapi
Newfoundland
St John's
Belcher Islands
Montagnais
Fort Churchill
Port Nelson
Fort York
Fort Severn
Eastern Cree
Rupert's Land (Hudson's Bay Company)
Akimiski Island
1746
Louisbourg 1758
Ile St Jean (Prince Edward I)
Ile Royale (Cape Breton I)
Fort Albany
Fort Rupert
Moose Factory
Tadoussac
Ft Beausejour 1755
Nova Scotia
Halifax
Lake Winnipeg
Cree
Plains of Abraham 1759
1711
Québec 1759
Port Royal 1710
Fort Bourbon
Fort La Tourette
Ojibwa
Fort Népigon
Trois Riviéres
St Lawrence
New France
Iroquois
Fort Dauphine
Fort Maurepas
Montréal 1760
Crown Point 1759
New Hampshire
Fort La Reine
Fort St Charles
Fort St Pierre
Lake Superior
Fort Michipicton
Huron
Ticonderoga 1758
Portsmouth
Fort William Henry 1756
1704
Boston
Massachusetts
Assiniboin
Fort Kaministiquia
Fort Frontenac 1758
Fort George 1756
Plymouth
Sault St Marie
Lake Huron
Fort Oswego 1756
Fort Ontario 1755
Albany
Providence
Gros Ventre
Fort Rouillé
Lake Ontario
New York
Hudson
Connecticut
Fort Niagara
New Haven
Missouri
Fort St Croix
1746–48
New York
New Amsterdam until 1664
Mandan
Winnebago
Ottawa
Pennsylvania
Lake Michigan
Fort St Joseph
New Jersey
Lake Erie
Fort Presqu'isle
Delaware
Philadelphia
Arikara
Sioux
Fort Beauharnais
Mississippi
Fort Pontchartrain
Delaware
Fort Duquesne 1758
Baltimore
Maryland
ATLANTIC OCEAN
1755
Fort Necessity
Annapolis
Miami Wyandot
Fort Pickawillany 1752
Fort St Louis
Fort Crevecoeur
Virginia
Richmond
Williamsburg
Jamestown
Shawnee
Ohio
Tuscarora
Kaintuck
Warrior's Path
North Carolina
Fort Vincennes
Fort Orléans
New Bern
Decaneechi Path
Fort Chartres
Wilmington
Cherokee
APPALACHIAN MTS
Great Trading Path
South Carolina
Georgetown
Chickasaw
Fort Augusta
Charleston
Louisiana
Fort Prudhomme
Choctaw
Creek
1742
Savannah
Georgia
Fort King George
Yamassee
Alabama
1740, 1743
St Augustine 1702
Fort Rosalie
Fort Condé
Pensacola
Natchez
New Orleans
Florida
Gulf of Mexico
Rio Grande

1 European cod-fishing fleets visited Newfoundland from about 1500, but the first permanent settlements were established by the English Newfoundland Company in 1610. France ceded the island to Britain in 1713.

2 Iroquois campaigns against the Huron in the 1640s and 1650s severely disrupted French exploration and fur trading in modern New York state; French troops halted the Iroquois advance in 1667.

3 The former Dutch colony of New Netherland, including Manhattan and the Hudson River, was seized by England in 1664; it was reoccupied by the Dutch in 1673, but confirmed to England in 1674.

4 A French expedition from the Mississippi to the Rio Grande in 1714 provoked Spanish expansion across modern Texas to block French moves westward.

5 The French established trading forts around lakes Winnipeg and Saskatchewan in 1732–48, diverting much of the rich fur trade of the Cree away from the British bases on Hudson Bay to the French Great Lakes–St Lawrence route.

6 While cattle and grain-farming dominated the colonial economy north of Delaware, tobacco was the most important crop in Virginia and North Carolina, and rice and indigo in South Carolina and Georgia.

NATIVE Americans were seen as a threat to colonial America; this model was on a Massachusetts weathervane.

See also 4.26 (exploration); 4.28 (war of independence); 5.26 (19th century North America)

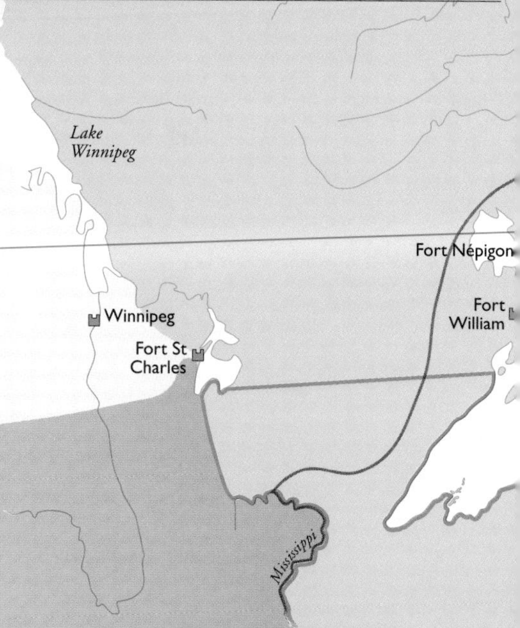

The 18th century witnessed a great increase in the colonial population of North America, particularly with the end of the struggle for supremacy between Britain and France in 1763. In just five years between 1769 and 1774, 152 ships from Irish ports alone brought over 44,000 new colonists. By 1774 Europeans in North America numbered two million – over a quarter of Britain's population. This growth altered the nature of the colonies and the allegiances of their inhabitants. In Pennsylvania, a flood of German and Irish Protestant immigrants in the 1720s outnumbered the original English Quakers. German soldiers sent to the colonies by the Hanoverian dynasty ruling Britain further swelled the non-British populace; Scots and Irish settlers, many with Jacobite (anti-Hanoverian) sympathies, also arrived. After 1775 loyalist support was concentrated in those longer-established colonies whose inhabitants could claim English ancestry. Even so, Virginia and the Carolinas, which attracted few non-British immigrants and were developing a distinctive plantation economy based on mass importation of slaves, showed little enthusiasm for the loyalist cause.

The influx of new immigrants, together with a rising birthrate in the colonies, are evidence of a booming economy. Agriculture was by far the most important activity, but it was commerce (particularly that of New England) that caused Britain most concern. Mercantilist theory maintained that colonial possessions should be developed to supply goods or raw materials unavailable in the home country, that these commodities should be paid for in manufactured goods for the colonists, and that the colonies should be discouraged from engaging in any other form of external trade. From the mid-17th century onward, these theories were imposed on the British colonies through a range of legislation, including the 1651 and 1673 Trade and Navigation Acts and the 1663 Staple Act. Yet the introduction of European-style agriculture into North America compromised the first of these conditions, while application of the second caused a currency shortage that rendered useless any attempts to restrict independent colonial trade. By the 18th century, the economy relied on smuggling: that is, trade other than with Britain. Merchants traded in fish, whale oil, horses, beef and timber to the Spanish, Dutch and French Caribbean in exchange for sugar, molasses, rum and silver coin. By the 1750s, they had begun to export dried fish, grain and flour to Europe in their own vessels, competing with British shippers and often bypassing British ports. In response, customs administration was tightened and a succession of laws passed in Britain from 1763 sought to curb this trade, including the 1764 Sugar Act. Along with the imposition of direct taxation in the Stamp Act of 1763, these caused great resentment in America.

At the same time, the costs that had been incurred in the war to gain control of the French colonies proved a severe drain on Britain's finances. In 1763–65 prime minister George Grenville forced the colonies to bear a greater share of this cost by imposing a series of taxes and other obligations. One that caused particular resentment was the Quartering Act of 1765, providing for the quartering of soldiers in colonial public buildings; it was seen as irrelevant once the French threat had dissipated.

Finally, the British attempted to forestall further hostilities over land with the indigenous peoples by setting limits to colonial expansion. The 1763 Proclamation Line defined a theoretical western boundary to the growth of the colonies. This aroused opposition (and was largely disregarded) in America, where the open frontier had already become an essential element in economic growth and the absorption of new immigrants. The 1774 Quebec Act, which provided for the government of former French colonies and extended Quebec's boundaries to the Ohio and Mississippi, was widely seen as a further attempt to restrict colonial freedom.

These issues combined to produce escalating tension and finally open war between colonists and British troops in 1775. Despite early reverses, the British commanders Sir William Howe and his brother Admiral Lord Howe had regained the initiative by the second year of the war, by capitalizing on the strategic mobility that their naval supremacy afforded. Subsequent campaigns confirmed the difficulty of holding large territories against an increasingly hostile population, but the intervention of France ultimately proved decisive. The victory of a French fleet over the Royal Navy off the Chesapeake Capes forced the surrender of a besieged British army at Yorktown. Although Britain saved the the economically vital West Indies by defeating a French invasion fleet in the eastern Caribbean in 1782, the American colonies were lost irretrievably. The Treaty of Paris of 1783 confirmed the independence of the new United States of America.

Lake Winnipeg

Fort Népigon

Fort William

Winnipeg

Fort St Charles

Mississippi

TIMELINE

Military campaigns

1770 | 1780

1770 The Boston Massacre; Bostonians are killed in fracas with British soldiers

1773 Boston Tea Party; protest against British tea-dumping in America

1775 Fighting erupts near Boston between British and colonial forces; Americans take Montréal but fail to capture Québec

1776 Declaration of Independence; British vacate Boston; Howe captures New York

1777 British advances on the Hudson are halted; Howe occupies Philadelphia

1778 France gives Americans military support; British forces secure Savannah

1779 Spain declares war on Britain and retakes Florida

1780 Charleston falls; Netherlands declares war on Britain

1781 British surrender after the siege at Yorktown

1782 British defeat French at The Saintes in West Indies

1783 The Treaty of Paris confirms US independence

Legislation

1763 Direct taxation is imposed on America

1765 The Stamp Act imposes the first direct taxation on the Brritish colonies

1766 The Declaratory Act affirms Britain's right to legislate in the colonies

1774 Massachusetts Government Act removes many rights; Quebec Act ends the growth of several colonies

1774 The First Continental Congress meets in Philadelphia

1776 Congress adopts the Declaration of Independence

1777 Congress adopts the Articles of Confederation, setting up the United States of America

1770 | 1780

1 The seizure of the vessel *Liberty* for smuggling at Boston in 1768 provoked a riot, followed by the refusal of the citizens to billet British troops.

2 The First Continental Congress met at Philadelphia on 5 September 1774; in 1776, the Second Congress proclaimed the Declaration of Independence.

3 Bunker Hill, the first engagement of the American revolution, was a British victory. However, as colonial forces inflicted heavy casualties on the British at little cost to themselves, the battle raised American morale.

4 Colonial forces besieged Québec in 1775-76, but withdrew when their commander was killed.

5 New York remained a loyalist stronghold after its capture by Sir William Howe in 1776, replacing Boston as the main British base in North America.

6 George Washington's Continental Army wintered in great hardship at Valley Forge in 1776-77, after its retreat across New Jersey from New York.

7 After British commander Samuel Hood's failure to prevent the French capture of St Kitts in 1782, George Rodney defeated de Grasse off The Saintes islands.

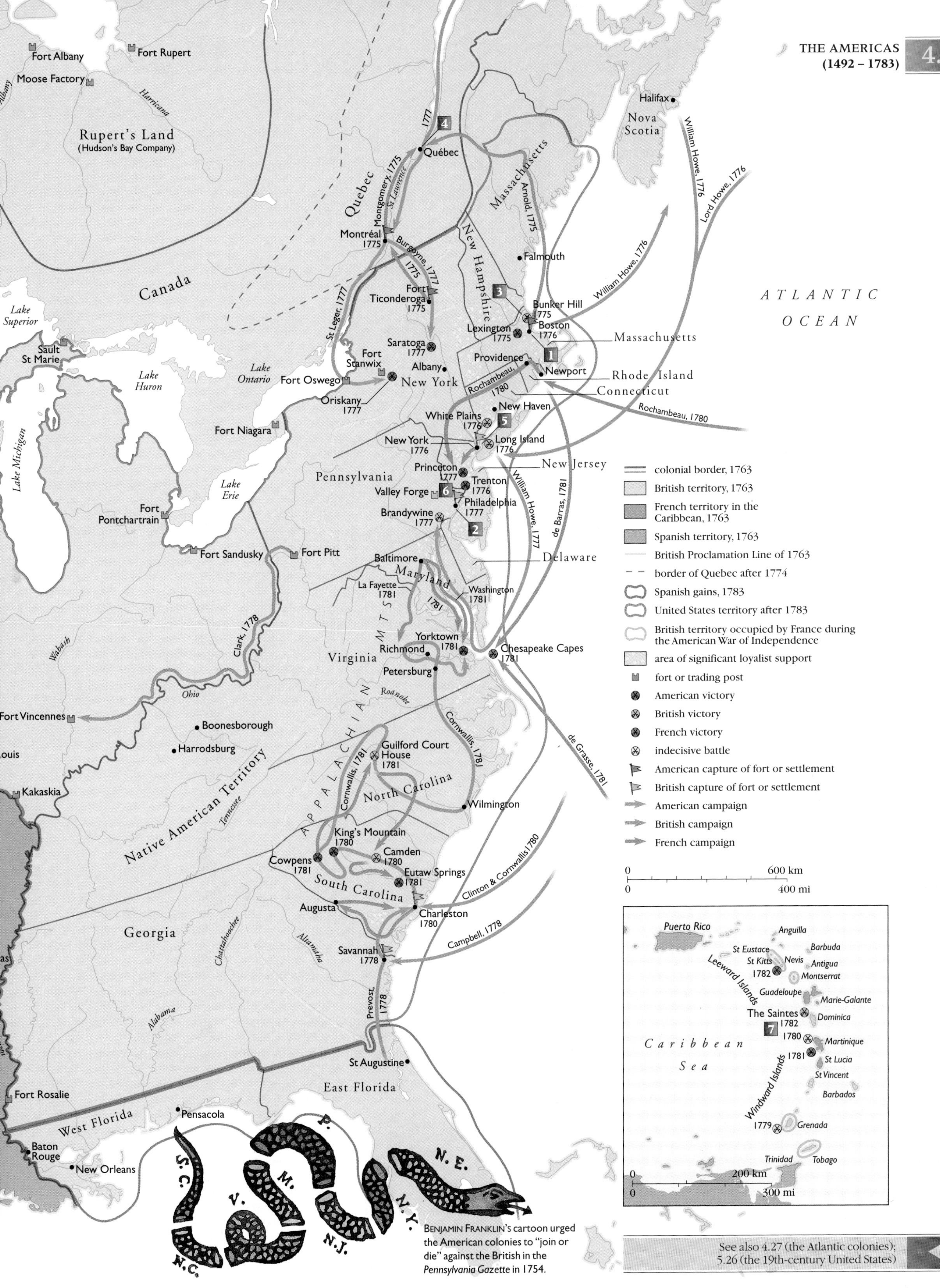

Fort Albany
Fort Rupert
Moose Factory
Albany
Harricana
Rupert's Land
(Hudson's Bay Company)
Canada
Lake Superior
Sault St Marie
Lake Huron
Lake Michigan
Lake Ontario
Lake Erie
Fort Niagara
Fort Oswego
Fort Pontchartrain
Fort Sandusky
Fort Pitt
Quebec
Québec
1777
Montgomery, 1775
St Lawrence
Montréal 1775
Burgoyne, 1777
1775
St Leger, 1777
Fort Ticonderoga 1775
Saratoga 1777
Fort Stanwix
Oriskany 1777
Albany
New York
Massachusetts
Arnold, 1775
New Hampshire
Falmouth
Bunker Hill 1775
Boston 1776
Lexington 1775
Massachusetts
Providence
Newport
Rhode Island
Connecticut
Rochambeau, 1780
New Haven
White Plains 1776
New York 1776
Long Island 1776
New Jersey
Princeton 1777
Trenton 1776
Valley Forge
Philadelphia 1777
Brandywine 1777
Pennsylvania
William Howe, 1777
de Barras, 1781
Delaware
Baltimore
Maryland
La Fayette 1781
Washington 1781
1781
Yorktown 1781
Richmond
Chesapeake Capes 1781
Virginia
Petersburg
Roanoke
APPALACHIAN MTS
Halifax
Nova Scotia
William Howe, 1776
Lord Howe, 1776
William Howe, 1776
ATLANTIC OCEAN
Clark, 1778
Wabash
Ohio
Fort Vincennes
Boonesborough
Harrodsburg
Kakaskia
Native American Territory
Tennessee
Cornwallis, 1781
de Grasse, 1781
Guilford Court House 1781
Cornwallis, 1781
North Carolina
Wilmington
King's Mountain 1780
Camden 1780
Cowpens 1781
Eutaw Springs 1781
South Carolina
Clinton & Cornwallis 1780
Augusta
Charleston 1780
Georgia
Chattahoochee
Altamaha
Savannah 1778
Campbell, 1778
Prevost, 1778
Alabama
St Augustine
East Florida
West Florida
Fort Rosalie
Pensacola
Baton Rouge
New Orleans
S.C.
N.C.
V.
M.
P.
N.J.
N.Y.
N.E.
colonial border, 1763
British territory, 1763
French territory in the Caribbean, 1763
Spanish territory, 1763
British Proclamation Line of 1763
border of Quebec after 1774
Spanish gains, 1783
United States territory after 1783
British territory occupied by France during the American War of Independence
area of significant loyalist support
fort or trading post
American victory
British victory
French victory
indecisive battle
American capture of fort or settlement
British capture of fort or settlement
American campaign
British campaign
French campaign
0 600 km
0 400 mi
Puerto Rico
Anguilla
St Eustace
Barbuda
St Kitts
Nevis
Antigua
1782
Montserrat
Leeward Islands
Guadeloupe
Marie-Galante
The Saintes
1782
Dominica
1780
Martinique
Caribbean Sea
1781
St Lucia
Windward Islands
St Vincent
Barbados
1779
Grenada
Trinidad
Tobago
0 200 km
0 300 mi

BENJAMIN FRANKLIN's cartoon urged the American colonies to "join or die" against the British in the *Pennsylvania Gazette* in 1754.

See also 4.27 (the Atlantic colonies); 5.26 (the 19th-century United States)

Part 5

THE NINETEENTH WORLD

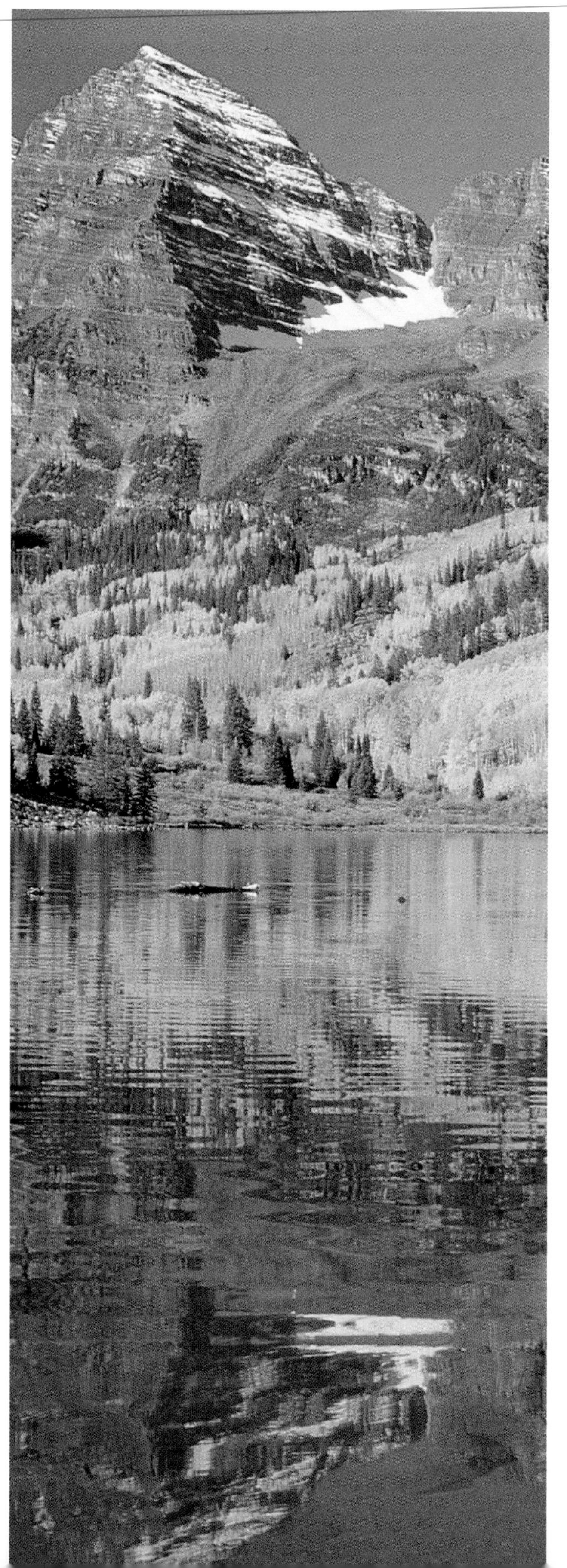

In 1783 Britain disconsolately accepted that its Thirteen Colonies in North America had won their independence. Yet, in the century and a quarter after the emergence of the United States, European powers rose to dominate most of the world. Their armies spread their authority, their navies charted the seas and their merchants welded the world together through a network of trade and investment. It was still organized primarily for the benefit of the European economy and to the profit of European exchequers, and this new age of European empires was by no means free from rivalries between the colonial powers, or between the parent countries and their colonies; yet now for the first time it brought a genuinely global economy.

The only part of the world effectively to resist the encroachment of the European powers in the nineteenth century was North America, but there the United States itself was a state ruled by people of European descent, its economy closely linked to and partly financed by Europe, and its culture was shaped by European influences. The railroads that effectively made the United States by linking the Atlantic and Pacific coasts owed much to British investment and technology. By the beginning of the twentieth century, the United States had challenged and overtaken much of Europe's economic and technological lead, and was poised to become the most powerful state in the world. By 1914, however, this was still not clear and Europe, its peoples, its industries and its empires remained the dominant force for change.

The impact of Europe on the United States was sustained by migration. Migration from Europe also totally altered the politics, economy and ethnic composition of Australasia and Canada, and greatly affected other regions including Algeria, South Africa and South America. It was the product both of European political power and of the growth in European

CENTURY 1783 – 1914

population, both absolutely and as a proportion of the world's peoples. Even in an age of rapid industrialization, Europe alone could never have sustained this rate of growth. Between 1815 and 1901, the United States took over eight million immigrants from the British Isles alone, and many more from Germany, Scandinavia and eastern and southern Europe.

Europeans were not the only people who moved, but those non-whites who journeyed long distances in pursuit of work – Chinese, Japanese, Indians, Malays as well as Africans – did so only with the consent of the European or North American states. Unlike the Europeans who were generally welcomed, despite their poverty, to assist in populating the newly acquired lands and building a new society, the non-Europeans were often contract laborers or worse, whose sojourn might only be temporary or against whom racial barriers were imposed. There was hostility, for example, to the arrival of Chinese in both Queensland and California.

The age of migrations reflected the potency of the new technologies of the age. Thanks to the steamship, the oceans shrank; long voyages became faster, safer, cheaper, more comfortable. Barbed wire, invented in the United States in 1873, made possible the fencing in of the prairies and thus the establishment of vast new ranches on what had been virgin land. Refrigerated shipholds allowed fresh meat grown on these ranches to be shipped to the cities of Europe and North America without spoilage, from temperate climates on the other side of the globe. Long-distance railroads, too, brought foodstuffs and other raw materials quickly and efficiently to the urban centers.As a result, Europe became the hub of a truly global agrarian system. North American grain, Argentine beef and Australasian wool and mutton were all crucial; without such imports, Europe could not have fed itself.

Trade was not restricted to raw materials. Heavy industry, light engineering, chemicals and textile manufacture now not only drove Europe's economy but also provided products for the rest of the world. In addition, Europe exported quantities of investment capital that acted as the engine of this global economy, financing the creation of the infrastructure for the new trade on every continent. The British empire, which encompassed more than a fifth of the Earth's landmass (its political and financial influence pervaded much of the rest in the later nineteenth century) was dominant in this flow of capital, though it was increasingly challenged by the United States, its powerful cultural and political offspring. As a result English became the international language of business, the language of profit across most of the globe.

The spread of European control and influence was not always peaceful. There was violent resistance, most common and widespread in Africa and China. Yet there was frequently also emulation, an attempt to borrow European techniques and practices. This was most apparent in Japan, which consciously embarked on an effective process of westernization from the 1870s. Similar choices were made in Egypt, Persia and Siam, all states more or less independent of direct European political control for much of the century but which saw the benefits of adopting western ways.

The formal European empires too ensured that their colonies were educated in European ways of government, law and culture as much as in technology and commerce. The value of this cultural imperialism, which was often conducted with little thought for the indigenous civilizations that were being usurped, was barely questioned by the Europeans. The *pax Britannica* was maintained across the globe by a combination of British gunboats and diplomats, but the introduction of British education, religion and the political institutions of Westminster were considered to bring undeniable benefits

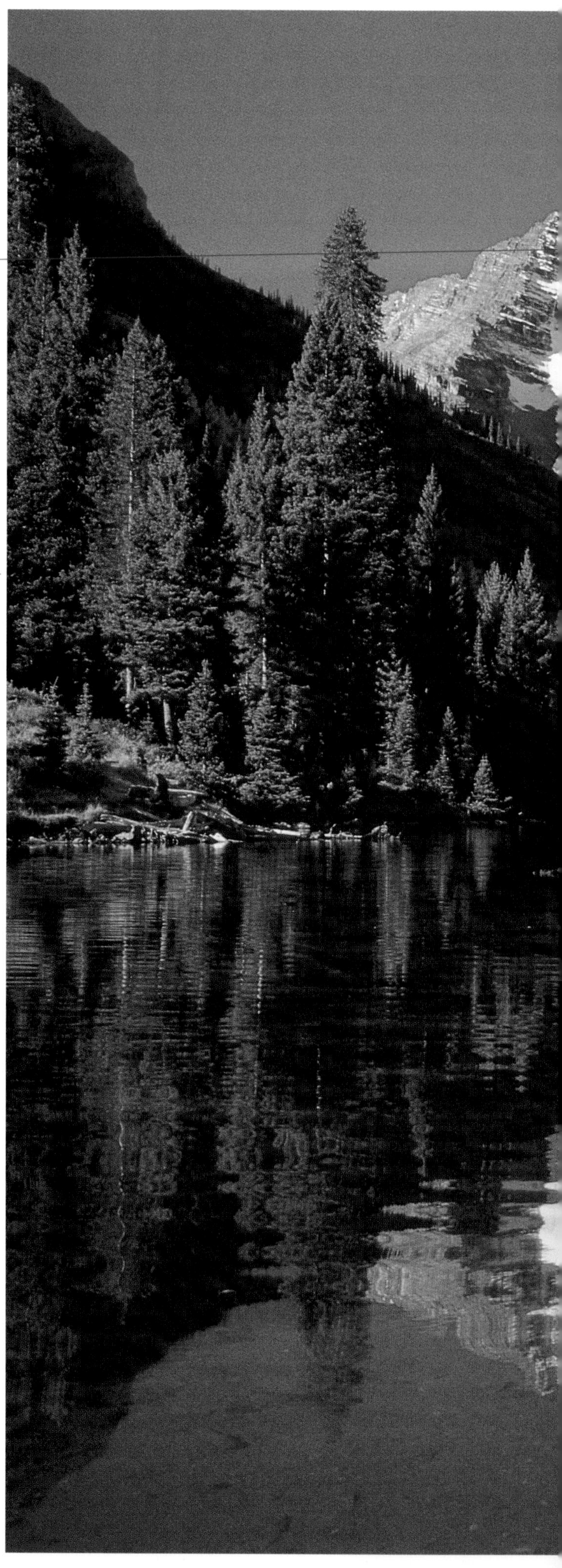

THE FRONTIER LANDS of North and South America, as well as Australia and Africa, provided space for westerners to expand their civilization, often at the expense of the indigenous peoples. The mountains of Colorado in the United States are shown here, where conflict between the two continued to the late 1870s.

to the "poor benighted heathen" of the rest of the world. Although some advantages undoubtedly accrued, the forcible imposition of European civilization with minimal adaptation to local conditions built up resentments that would grow throughout the first half of the twentieth century and result in often violent independence movements after 1945.

The nineteenth century was an age in which humanity increasingly sought to use advances in knowledge to mold the environment. Science – western science, conducted mainly in Germany, France, Britain and the United States – made great advances, and its power to change the world became undeniable. Scientific breeding and a thorough knowledge of the needs of plants and animals affected species and transformed economies: Malaya for example was changed utterly in the 1890s when the British introduced the rubber tree from South America, which could be grown on industrial-scale plantations in that country. Science seemed to hold the key to the future, to the creation and use of goods, new sources of power (electricity, high-performance steam engines, turbines and internal-combustion engines) and new materials (alloys, chemical dyes, fertilizers, explosives, among others). Equally revolutionary for the future were new forms of communication: telegraph, telephone and radio all shrank distance even more than had railroad and steamships: in 1901 Guglielmo Marconi transmitted radio signals across the Atlantic. Two years later the Wright brothers made the world's first heavier-than-air flight, giving the industrial countries, at least, access to an entirely new medium that would have profound implications, both civil and military.

Every such innovation contributed to a sense of change that was a solvent of former certainties, and in 1914, when the European powers began a conflict that engulfed their entire continent, the assumptions that had supported the previous century were exploded. To survive, the powers had to draw on the resources of their former colonies in ways that changed the relationships between them for ever ■

5.01 THE WORLD • AD 1812 •

The early 19th century saw Europe continue to open new markets and exploit new sources of raw materials worldwide. Another aspect of European expansion – colonialism – led many countries to expend considerable resources on the conquest and administration of new territories. Europeanization would influence every other culture in the world in some measure. Some, as in India, were long established and highly sophisticated; others, as in Africa, were at critical stages in their evolution. Many native cultures in North America, Australia and New Zealand would face the threat of displacement or extermination.

Both the United States of America and imperial Russia expanded their continental empires. The United States purchased Louisiana from France in 1803 and expeditions pioneered routes to the Pacific in 1805–12 (▷ *5.26*). Russia and Britain also promoted their North American interests, in Alaska and Vancouver respectively. American commerce grew after the revolution, first with China and then with Europe. Disruption to this trade, by Barbary pirates and the British blockade of Napoleonic Europe, met with a military response; American forces attacked Tripolitania in 1804 and British positions around Lakes Erie and Ontario in 1812 (▷ *5.25*).

The Ottomans still claimed suzerainty over Egypt, Tripolitania, Tunis and Algiers though all were now virtually independent (▷ *5.14*). European penetration of Africa was mainly confined to the voracious demands of the slave trade. Portuguese traders at the mouth of the Congo and the Zambezi made great profits from slavery. British involvement in the trade was also intensive until its abolition in 1807, by which time opponents of slavery had founded the state of Sierra Leone as a home for freed slaves (▷ *5.15*).

Africa was in a state of turmoil that was to worsen in the course of the 19th century. In west Africa, the Asante and Fulani empires were dominant; the Omani were rebuilding their trading empire on the east coast; and central African states were jostling for power. Further south, the Lozi and Kazembe empires controlled east–west trade along the Zambezi. Madagascar, gradually being absorbed by Merina, supplied slaves (as did Angola) to Brazil and the United States. Dutch settlers at the Cape were joined by the English (1795), who established a naval base at Simonstown in 1806. Before long they would

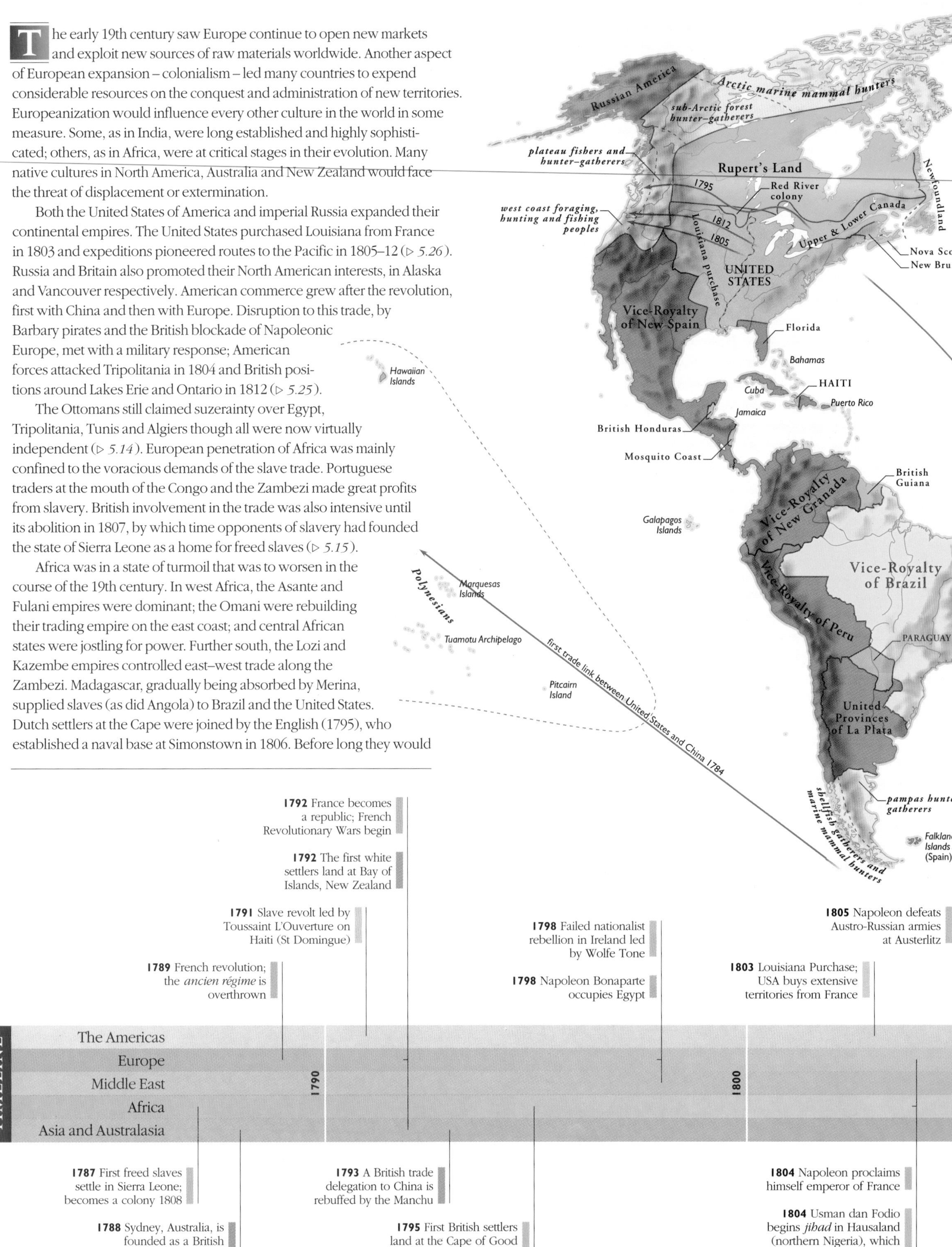

Russian America
Arctic marine mammal hunters
sub-Arctic forest hunter-gatherers
plateau fishers and hunter-gatherers
Rupert's Land
1795
Red River colony
Newfoundland
west coast foraging, hunting and fishing peoples
1812
1805
Louisiana Purchase
Upper & Lower Canada
Nova Scoti
New Bruns
UNITED STATES
Vice-Royalty of New Spain
Florida
Bahamas
Hawaiian Islands
Cuba
HAITI
Puerto Rico
Jamaica
British Honduras
Mosquito Coast
British Guiana
Vice-Royalty of New Granada
Galapagos Islands
Vice-Royalty of Brazil
Polynesians
Marquesas Islands
Vice-Royalty of Peru
Tuamotu Archipelago
PARAGUAY
first trade link between United States and China 1784
Pitcairn Island
United Provinces of La Plata
pampas hunter-gatherers
shellfish gatherers and marine mammal hunters
Falkland Islands (Spain)
1792 France becomes a republic; French Revolutionary Wars begin
1792 The first white settlers land at Bay of Islands, New Zealand
1791 Slave revolt led by Toussaint L'Ouverture on Haiti (St Domingue)
1789 French revolution; the ancien régime is overthrown
1798 Failed nationalist rebellion in Ireland led by Wolfe Tone
1798 Napoleon Bonaparte occupies Egypt
1805 Napoleon defeats Austro-Russian armies at Austerlitz
1803 Louisiana Purchase; USA buys extensive territories from France
TIMELINE
The Americas
Europe
Middle East
Africa
Asia and Australasia
1790
1800
1787 First freed slaves settle in Sierra Leone; becomes a colony 1808
1788 Sydney, Australia, is founded as a British convict settlement
1793 A British trade delegation to China is rebuffed by the Manchu
1795 First British settlers land at the Cape of Good Hope; Cape Colony under British control from 1806
1804 Napoleon proclaims himself emperor of France
1804 Usman dan Fodio begins jihad in Hausaland (northern Nigeria), which results in large Islamic state

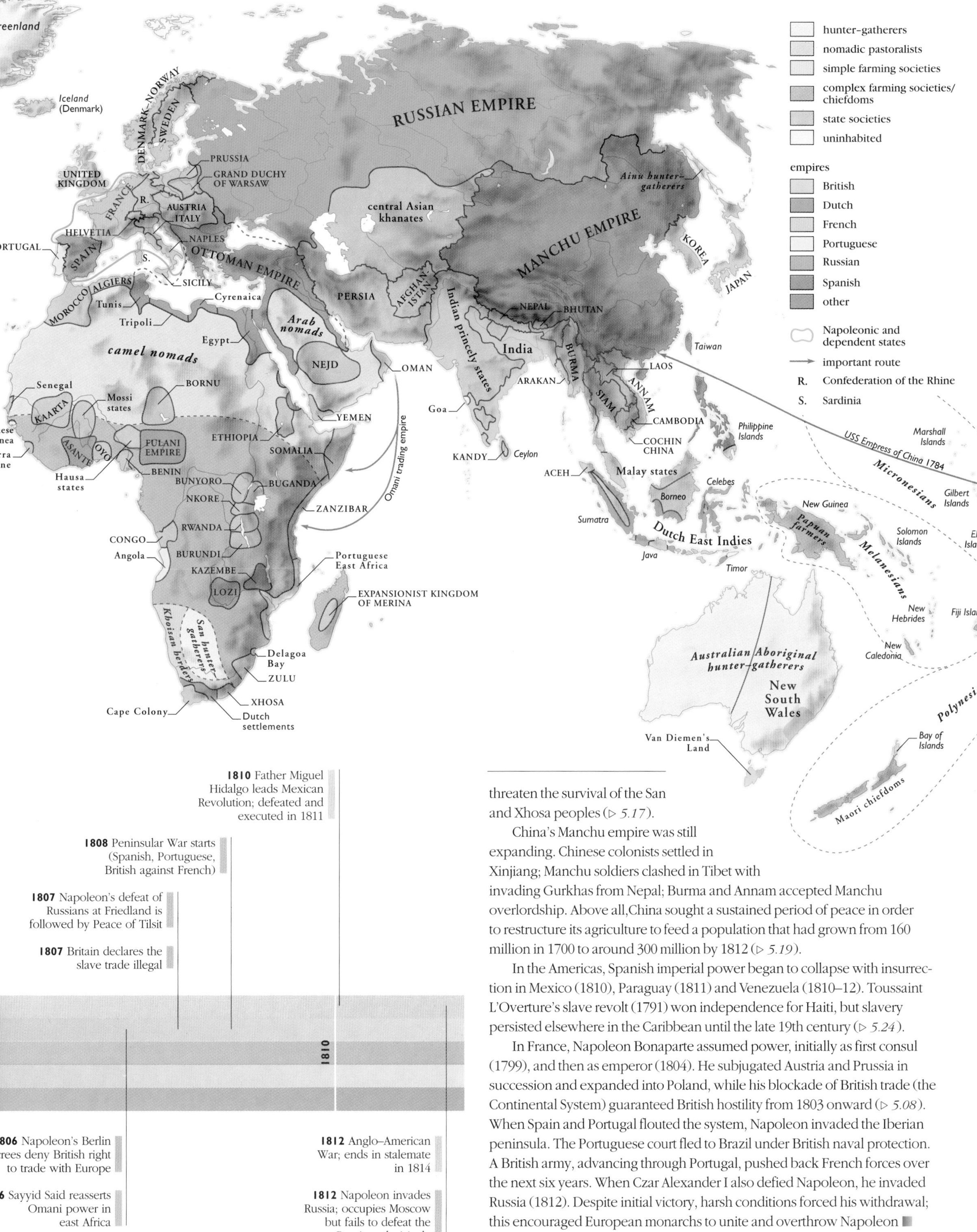
hunter-gatherers
nomadic pastoralists
simple farming societies
complex farming societies/ chiefdoms
state societies
uninhabited
empires
British
Dutch
French
Portuguese
Russian
Spanish
other
Napoleonic and dependent states
important route
R. Confederation of the Rhine
S. Sardinia
Greenland
Iceland (Denmark)
DENMARK-NORWAY
SWEDEN
RUSSIAN EMPIRE
PRUSSIA
GRAND DUCHY OF WARSAW
UNITED KINGDOM
FRANCE
AUSTRIA
ITALY
HELVETIA
NAPLES
PORTUGAL
SPAIN
SICILY
OTTOMAN EMPIRE
central Asian khanates
Ainu hunter-gatherers
MANCHU EMPIRE
KOREA
JAPAN
MOROCCO
ALGIERS
Tunis
Tripoli
Cyrenaica
Egypt
Arab nomads
PERSIA
AFGHANISTAN
Indian princely states
NEPAL
BHUTAN
India
Taiwan
camel nomads
NEJD
OMAN
BURMA
LAOS
ANNAM
SIAM
ARAKAN
Senegal
Mossi states
BORNU
KAARTA
ASANTE
OYO
FULANI EMPIRE
Hausa states
BENIN
ETHIOPIA
YEMEN
SOMALIA
Goa
Omani trading empire
KANDY
Ceylon
CAMBODIA
COCHIN CHINA
Philippine Islands
USS Empress of China 1784
Marshall Islands
Micronesians
Gilbert Islands
ACEH
Malay states
Celebes
Borneo
Sumatra
New Guinea
Papuan farmers
Dutch East Indies
Java
Timor
Solomon Islands
Ellice Islands
Melanesians
BUNYORO
BUGANDA
NKORE
ZANZIBAR
RWANDA
CONGO
Angola
BURUNDI
KAZEMBE
LOZI
Portuguese East Africa
EXPANSIONIST KINGDOM OF MERINA
Khoisan herders
San hunter-gatherers
Delagoa Bay
ZULU
XHOSA
Cape Colony
Dutch settlements
New Hebrides
Fiji Islands
New Caledonia
Australian Aboriginal hunter-gatherers
New South Wales
Polynesians
Van Diemen's Land
Bay of Islands
Maori chiefdoms
1810 Father Miguel Hidalgo leads Mexican Revolution; defeated and executed in 1811
1808 Peninsular War starts (Spanish, Portuguese, British against French)
1807 Napoleon's defeat of Russians at Friedland is followed by Peace of Tilsit
1807 Britain declares the slave trade illegal
1810
806 Napoleon's Berlin rees deny British right to trade with Europe
6 Sayyid Said reasserts Omani power in east Africa
1812 Anglo–American War; ends in stalemate in 1814
1812 Napoleon invades Russia; occupies Moscow but fails to defeat the Russians decisively

threaten the survival of the San and Xhosa peoples (▷ *5.17*).

China's Manchu empire was still expanding. Chinese colonists settled in Xinjiang; Manchu soldiers clashed in Tibet with invading Gurkhas from Nepal; Burma and Annam accepted Manchu overlordship. Above all,China sought a sustained period of peace in order to restructure its agriculture to feed a population that had grown from 160 million in 1700 to around 300 million by 1812 (▷ *5.19*).

In the Americas, Spanish imperial power began to collapse with insurrection in Mexico (1810), Paraguay (1811) and Venezuela (1810–12). Toussaint L'Overture's slave revolt (1791) won independence for Haiti, but slavery persisted elsewhere in the Caribbean until the late 19th century (▷ *5.24*).

In France, Napoleon Bonaparte assumed power, initially as first consul (1799), and then as emperor (1804). He subjugated Austria and Prussia in succession and expanded into Poland, while his blockade of British trade (the Continental System) guaranteed British hostility from 1803 onward (▷ *5.08*). When Spain and Portugal flouted the system, Napoleon invaded the Iberian peninsula. The Portuguese court fled to Brazil under British naval protection. A British army, advancing through Portugal, pushed back French forces over the next six years. When Czar Alexander I also defied Napoleon, he invaded Russia (1812). Despite initial victory, harsh conditions forced his withdrawal; this encouraged European monarchs to unite and overthrow Napoleon ■

The Congress of Vienna (1814–15) dismembered Napoleon's empire and transformed the map of Europe (▷ *5.08*). The German Confederation was formed, an alliance of states dominated by Austria and Prussia. Wholly new nations also arose: Greece wrested sovereignty from the Ottoman empire from 1821–28; Belgium rebelled against Dutch rule (1830) and won international recognition of its independence in 1839. Yet the restoration of autocratic monarchies by the Congress in the name of stability bred resentment, which erupted in a series of revolutions that swept the continent in 1848 (▷ *5.09*). Only Britain and Russia stayed unaffected; elsewhere, liberals and nationalists exploited economic hardship to foment revolts demanding representative forms of government. Internal divisions caused the revolutions to fail and conservative forces soon regained power.

In contrast, revolutions succeeded in toppling the Spanish and Portuguese empires in Central and South America. Brazil proclaimed an independent empire after King João VI returned to Portugal in 1822. The collapse of Spain during the Napoleonic Wars led to a succession of uprisings against Spanish rule in the Americas: eleven independent states were formed by 1826 (▷ *5.23*). The disparate nature of the region's cultures and the diversity of the revolutionaries' aspirations prevented the development of the envisaged Hispano–American state; Simón Bolívar's Gran Colombia (comprising modern Venezuela, Colombia, and Ecuador) fragmented in 1830, only eleven years after its formation.

Spain's fall benefited the United States, which gained the territories of East and West Florida in 1819–22. US foreign policy was outlined in the Monroe Doctrine of 1823, which stipulated separate spheres of interest for Europe and the Americas to forestall any renewal of European ambition in the region. The transcontinental expansion of the United States also accelerated during this period, with the annexation of Oregon in 1844, and Texas in 1845 (▷ *5.26*). War with Mexico (1846–48) led to the United States gaining California, where gold deposits were discovered soon after.

In Russia, Czar Alexander I and his successor Nicholas I maintained an implacable opposition to reform at home and abroad; an insurrection in Poland against Russian rule was suppressed (1830–31), while Russian troops were also sent to help Austria quell a Hungarian nationalist uprising in 1848–49. Russian forces

Russian America
Arctic marine mammal hunters
sub-Arctic forest hunter-gatherers
west coast foraging, hunting and fishing peoples
plateau fishers and hunter-gatherers
Rupert's Land
Newfoundland
Canada
Nova Scoti
New Bruns
UNITED STATES
MEXICO
Hawaiian Islands
Bahamas
HAITI
Cuba
Puerto Rico
Jamaica
DOMINICAN REPUBLIC
British Honduras
GUATEMALA
EL SALVADOR
HONDURAS
NICARAGUA
COSTA RICA
British Guiana
Dutch Guiana
French Guia
VENEZUELA
COLOMBIA
Galapagos Islands
ECUADOR
BRAZIL
PERU
Marquesas Islands (France)
Tuamotu Archipelago (France)
BOLIVIA
PARAGUAY
Pitcairn Island (Britain)
CHILE
ARGENTINA
URUGUAY
pampas hunter-gatherers
shellfish gatherers and marine mammal hunters
Falkland Islands (Britain)

TIMELINE

The Americas | Europe | Middle East | Africa | Asia and Australasia

1820 | 1830

1815 Defeat of Napoleon by British and Prussian forces at Waterloo

1816–20 Argentina declares its independence from Spain; war of liberation lasts for four years

1816 Shaka, king of the Zulu, begins to expand the Zulu empire

1816 Britain begins to recruit Gurkha soldiers from Nepal

1818 Border between Canada and United States is defined as 49th Parallel

1820 British settlers begin to arrive at the Cape in large numbers

1822 Brazil declares independence from Portugal

1823 Monroe Doctrine warns against further European expansion in the Americas

1824–26 British fight two unsuccessful wars against the Asante of west Africa

1828 Greeks win War of Independence (Ottomans recognize Greece 1832)

1830–31 Polish revolt against Russian rule

1833 Falkland Islands are occupied by Britain

1833 The Ottoman empire recognizes the independence of Egypt

1837 Natal Republic is founded by Afrikaners

1839 Belgian indepe dence is international guarantee

1839–42 Britain fights the First Afghan War to stop the southern spread of Russian influence

1839–42 First Opiu War is fought betwee Britain and Chi

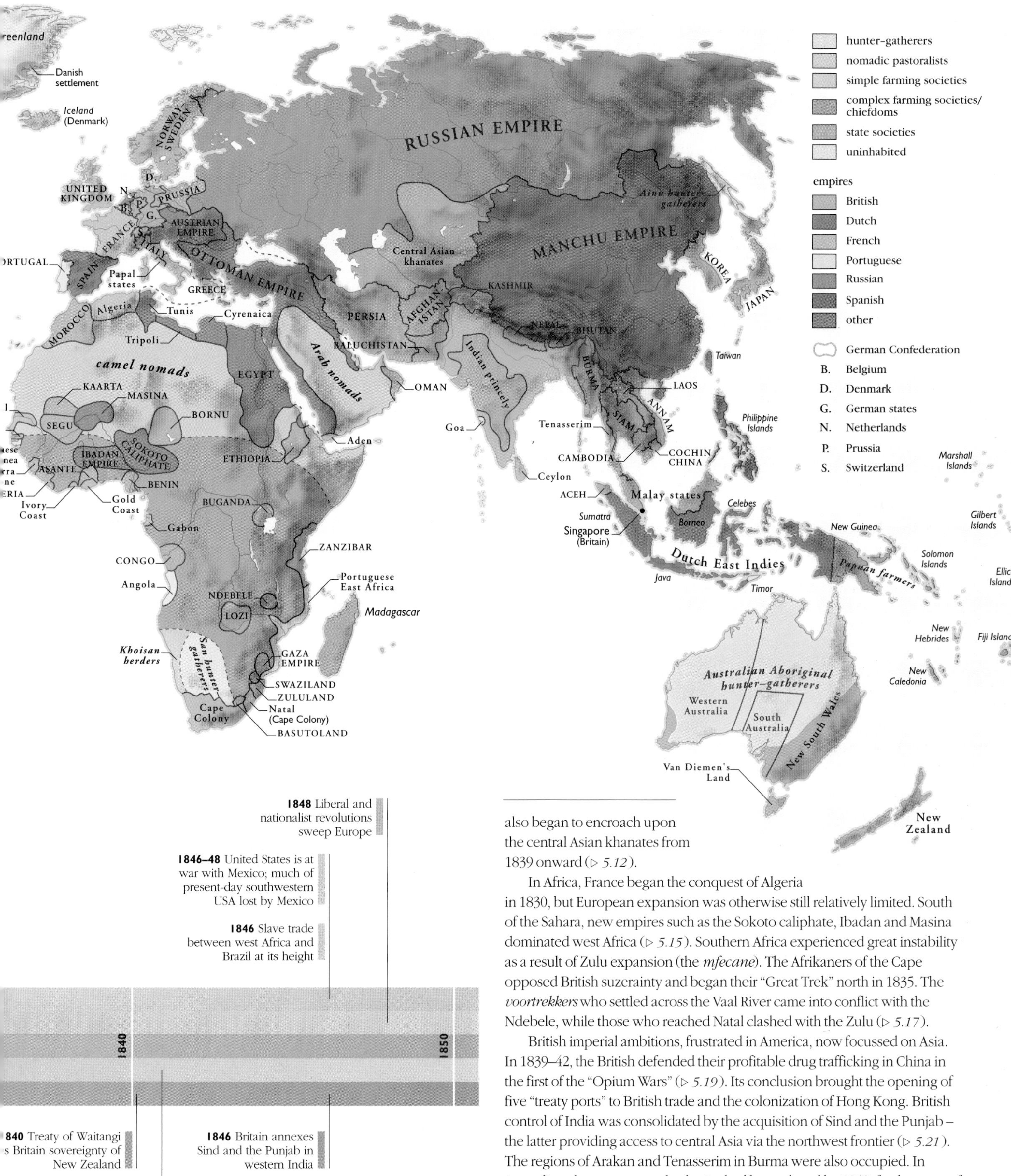
hunter-gatherers
nomadic pastoralists
simple farming societies
complex farming societies/ chiefdoms
state societies
uninhabited
empires
British
Dutch
French
Portuguese
Russian
Spanish
other
German Confederation
B. Belgium
D. Denmark
G. German states
N. Netherlands
P. Prussia
S. Switzerland
Danish settlement
Iceland (Denmark)
NORWAY SWEDEN
RUSSIAN EMPIRE
UNITED KINGDOM
N.
B.
P.
D.
G.
S.
PRUSSIA
AUSTRIAN EMPIRE
FRANCE
SPAIN
ITALY
Papal states
GREECE
OTTOMAN EMPIRE
Central Asian khanates
Ainu hunter-gatherers
MANCHU EMPIRE
KOREA
JAPAN
KASHMIR
AFGHANISTAN
PERSIA
BALUCHISTAN
NEPAL
BHUTAN
Taiwan
MOROCCO
Algeria
Tunis
Cyrenaica
Tripoli
camel nomads
Arab nomads
Indian princely
OMAN
EGYPT
KAARTA
MASINA
SEGU
BORNU
SOKOTO CALIPHATE
IBADAN EMPIRE
ASANTE
BENIN
Gold Coast
Ivory Coast
ETHIOPIA
Aden
Goa
Ceylon
BURMA
LAOS
ANNAM
SIAM
Tenasserim
CAMBODIA
COCHIN CHINA
Philippine Islands
Marshall Islands
ACEH
Malay states
Sumatra
Singapore (Britain)
Celebes
Borneo
New Guinea
Gilbert Islands
Dutch East Indies
Java
Timor
Papuan farmers
Solomon Islands
Ellice Islands
BUGANDA
Gabon
CONGO
Angola
ZANZIBAR
Portuguese East Africa
NDEBELE
LOZI
Madagascar
Khoisan herders
San hunter-gatherers
GAZA EMPIRE
SWAZILAND
ZULULAND
Natal (Cape Colony)
BASUTOLAND
Cape Colony
New Hebrides
Fiji Islands
New Caledonia
Australian Aboriginal hunter-gatherers
Western Australia
South Australia
New South Wales
Van Diemen's Land
New Zealand
1848 Liberal and nationalist revolutions sweep Europe
1846–48 United States is at war with Mexico; much of present-day southwestern USA lost by Mexico
1846 Slave trade between west Africa and Brazil at its height
1840
1850
1840 Treaty of Waitangi gives Britain sovereignty of New Zealand
1846 Britain annexes Sind and the Punjab in western India
1841 Ibadan empire expands in West Africa

also began to encroach upon the central Asian khanates from 1839 onward (▷ *5.12*).

In Africa, France began the conquest of Algeria in 1830, but European expansion was otherwise still relatively limited. South of the Sahara, new empires such as the Sokoto caliphate, Ibadan and Masina dominated west Africa (▷ *5.15*). Southern Africa experienced great instability as a result of Zulu expansion (the *mfecane*). The Afrikaners of the Cape opposed British suzerainty and began their "Great Trek" north in 1835. The *voortrekkers* who settled across the Vaal River came into conflict with the Ndebele, while those who reached Natal clashed with the Zulu (▷ *5.17*).

British imperial ambitions, frustrated in America, now focussed on Asia. In 1839–42, the British defended their profitable drug trafficking in China in the first of the "Opium Wars" (▷ *5.19*). Its conclusion brought the opening of five "treaty ports" to British trade and the colonization of Hong Kong. British control of India was consolidated by the acquisition of Sind and the Punjab – the latter providing access to central Asia via the northwest frontier (▷ *5.21*). The regions of Arakan and Tenasserim in Burma were also occupied. In Australia, where most penal colonies had been closed by 1848, fresh waves of migrants populated new settlements, such as Adelaide and Perth (▷ *5.18*). Conflict with the Maori in New Zealand resulted in 1840 in a treaty according to which the Maori recognized Queen Victoria as their sovereign; however, the treaty left many questions of land ownership and sale unresolved ■

Growing urbanization and industrialization, and a dramatic increase in population, were evident throughout the world by 1880. European cities developed rapidly, as ever more people were drawn away from rural life by factory work (▷ *5.10*). Technological advances, especially in communications, impelled industrial development and promoted colonial expansion; by the 1850s, the British had installed the first railroads and telegraph systems in India. Politically, while some ancient entities such as the Tokugawa shogunate in Japan did not survive the advent of the modern age, others – the Chinese Manchu dynasty, the Ottoman empire and czarist Russia – lingered into the 20th century, though torn by internal dissent.

Dynamic new nation-states arose as the 19th century progressed, changing the balance of power in Europe. In Italy, nationalist groupings in the north and south combined to bring about the unification of the country (▷ *5.09*). The struggle for domination in the German Confederation between Austria and Prussia resulted in conflict in 1866, from which Prussia emerged victorious (▷ *5.11*). Another crushing Prussian military victory in 1870–71 against France destroyed the empire of Napoleon III and led to Prussia forming the nucleus of the German "second empire".

Warfare was in the process of being radically altered by mechanization. The American Civil War (1861–65) was the first conflict to utilize the greatly enhanced mobility and firepower afforded respectively by railroads and the mass production of munitions (▷ *5.27*). Contested between the North and the South over the question of slavery and the extent of federal jurisdiction, the war exacted a huge toll in human lives. The North's far superior manpower and industrial capacity eventually allowed it to prevail. Despite the damage caused by the war, however, the United States was fast becoming the dominant power in the Western Hemisphere. Expansion continued with the purchase of the Gadsden Strip from Mexico (1853) and Alaska from Russia (1867). The inauguration of a transcontinental electric telegraph was swiftly followed by the linking of the Union Pacific and the Central Pacific railroads to form a coast-to-coast route in 1869 (▷ *5.26, 5.28*). In the 1870s and 1880s, the construction of another railroad across the North American continent played a vital role in unifying Canada, joining the new western territory of British Columbia to the eastern provinces that had declared the Dominion of Canada in 1867 (▷ *5.25*).

Central and South America were beset by armed conflict. France undertook an imperial adventure in Mexico in 1863–67, which ended disastrously.

Alaska
CANADA
Newfoundland
UNITED STATES
MEXICO
Hawaiian Islands (United States)
Bahamas
HAITI
Cuba
Puerto Rico
British Honduras
Jamaica
DOMINICAN REPUBLIC
GUATEMALA
EL SALVADOR
HONDURAS
NICARAGUA
COSTA RICA
British Guiana
Dutch Guiana
French Guia
VENEZUELA
COLOMBIA
Galapagos Islands (Ecuador)
ECUADOR
BRAZIL
Marquesas Islands (France)
PERU
Tuamotu Archipelago (France)
BOLIVIA
PARAGUAY
ARGENTINA
CHILE
PARAG
URUGUA
pampas hunter-gatherers
shellfish gatherers and marine mammal hunters
Falkland Islands (Britain)

TIMELINE

The Americas / Europe / Middle East / Africa / Asia and Australasia

1850

1860

1851–53 Gold rush in Australia

1852 French second empire: Louis Napoleon emperor (Napoleon III)

1853 US Commodore Matthew Perry opens up Japan to western trade

1854–56 Crimean War; Britain and France oppose Russian expansion into Ottoman territories

1857–58 Indian Mutiny; Muslims and Hindus rebel against British rule

1858 Piedmontese premier Camillo Cavour and Napoleon III plan Italian unification

1860 Abraham Lincoln elected US president on anti-slavery ticket

1861 Czar Alexander II undertakes reform by emancipating Russian serfs

1861–65 American Civil War; northern states fight to preserve Union against secessionist South

1863 Asante people of west Africa defeat British in Third Asante War

1866 Austro-Prussian War; Prussia defeats Austria

1867 Russia sells Alaska to the United States

1868 Japanese Tokugawa shogunate ends; Meiji dynasty restored

1869 Suez Canal, built by the French, opens

1870 Unification of Ita as Rome becomes pa of the kingdo

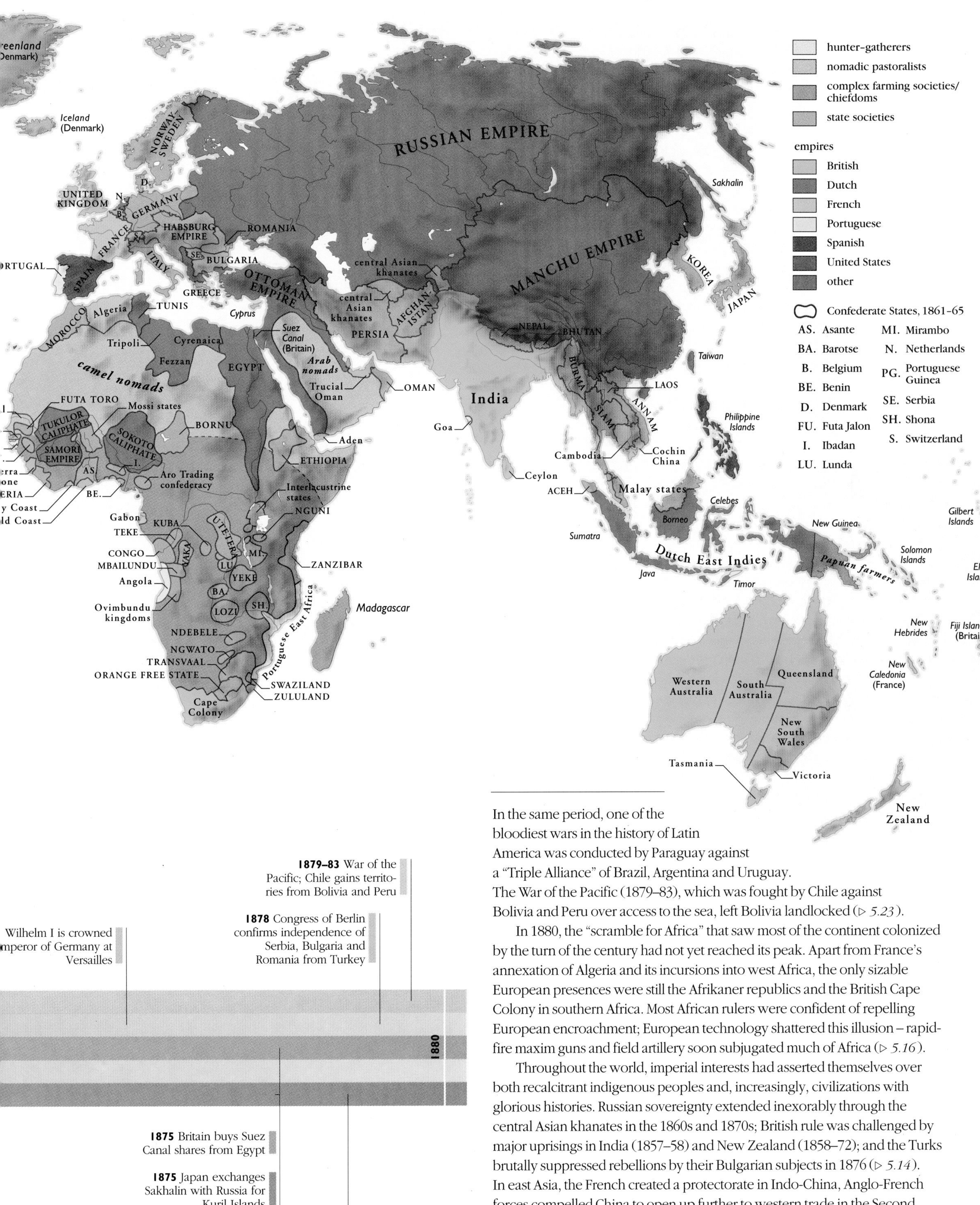
hunter-gatherers
nomadic pastoralists
complex farming societies/ chiefdoms
state societies
empires
British
Dutch
French
Portuguese
Spanish
United States
other
Confederate States, 1861-65
AS. Asante
BA. Barotse
B. Belgium
BE. Benin
D. Denmark
FU. Futa Jalon
I. Ibadan
LU. Lunda
MI. Mirambo
N. Netherlands
PG. Portuguese Guinea
SE. Serbia
SH. Shona
S. Switzerland
Iceland (Denmark)
NORWAY SWEDEN
RUSSIAN EMPIRE
UNITED KINGDOM
GERMANY
HABSBURG EMPIRE
ROMANIA
FRANCE
SPAIN
ITALY
BULGARIA
GREECE
OTTOMAN EMPIRE
central Asian khanates
AFGHANISTAN
PERSIA
MANCHU EMPIRE
KOREA
JAPAN
Sakhalin
Algeria
TUNIS
MOROCCO
Tripoli
Cyrenaica
Fezzan
Cyprus
Suez Canal (Britain)
Arab nomads
EGYPT
Trucial Oman
OMAN
camel nomads
FUTA TORO
Mossi states
TUKULOR CALIPHATE
SAMORI EMPIRE
SOKOTO CALIPHATE
BORNU
Aden
ETHIOPIA
Aro Trading confederacy
Interlacustrine states
NGUNI
Gabon
KUBA
TEKE
CONGO
MBAILUNDU
Angola
Ovimbundu kingdoms
UTETERA
YEKE
LOZI
ZANZIBAR
East Africa
Madagascar
NDEBELE
NGWATO
TRANSVAAL
ORANGE FREE STATE
Portuguese East Africa
SWAZILAND
ZULULAND
Cape Colony
NEPAL
BHUTAN
India
Goa
Ceylon
BURMA
SIAM
LAOS
ANNAM
Cambodia
Cochin China
Taiwan
Philippine Islands
ACEH
Malay states
Borneo
Celebes
Sumatra
Java
Dutch East Indies
Timor
New Guinea
Papuan farmers
Solomon Islands
Gilbert Islands
Ellice Islands
New Hebrides
Fiji Islands (Britain)
New Caledonia (France)
Western Australia
South Australia
Queensland
New South Wales
Victoria
Tasmania
New Zealand

1879–83 War of the Pacific; Chile gains territories from Bolivia and Peru

1878 Congress of Berlin confirms independence of Serbia, Bulgaria and Romania from Turkey

Wilhelm I is crowned emperor of Germany at Versailles

1880

1875 Britain buys Suez Canal shares from Egypt

1875 Japan exchanges Sakhalin with Russia for Kuril Islands

1876 Queen Victoria is proclaimed empress of India

In the same period, one of the bloodiest wars in the history of Latin America was conducted by Paraguay against a "Triple Alliance" of Brazil, Argentina and Uruguay. The War of the Pacific (1879–83), which was fought by Chile against Bolivia and Peru over access to the sea, left Bolivia landlocked (▷ *5.23*).

In 1880, the "scramble for Africa" that saw most of the continent colonized by the turn of the century had not yet reached its peak. Apart from France's annexation of Algeria and its incursions into west Africa, the only sizable European presences were still the Afrikaner republics and the British Cape Colony in southern Africa. Most African rulers were confident of repelling European encroachment; European technology shattered this illusion – rapid-fire maxim guns and field artillery soon subjugated much of Africa (▷ *5.16*).

Throughout the world, imperial interests had asserted themselves over both recalcitrant indigenous peoples and, increasingly, civilizations with glorious histories. Russian sovereignty extended inexorably through the central Asian khanates in the 1860s and 1870s; British rule was challenged by major uprisings in India (1857–58) and New Zealand (1858–72); and the Turks brutally suppressed rebellions by their Bulgarian subjects in 1876 (▷ *5.14*). In east Asia, the French created a protectorate in Indo-China, Anglo-French forces compelled China to open up further to western trade in the Second Opium War (1856–60), while a United States naval expedition in 1853 ended Japan's long diplomatic and commercial isolation (▷ *5.20*) ■

5.04 THE WORLD • AD 1914 •

By 1914 the dominion of European peoples had spread throughout the world – the imperial system was at its peak, and expeditions had explored both polar regions. Colonization was most extensive in Africa; the "scramble for Africa" that had begun among European powers after 1870 was formalized at the Berlin Conference of 1884–85, which divided virtually all of the continent between rival claimants (▷ *5.16*). Africans resisted the despoliation of their homelands, but usually to no avail; the Ethiopians successfully repulsed Italian invaders in 1896, but other peoples fought in vain against European troops equipped with superior weapons. Colonial forces also clashed; France and Britain disputed control of the upper Nile, and Germany's vigorous late pursuit of an African empire presaged the conflict to come in Europe. The Second Anglo-Boer War (1899–1902) was the culmination of decades of tension between settlers of Dutch and British origin in southern Africa; the British gained supremacy in a bitter struggle, but their failure to attract mass settlement left the Afrikaners dominant in the new Union of South Africa (▷ *5.17*).

The United States emerged as an imperial power, while the empires of Russia and Britain continued to grow. The British empire reached the height of its power, with important colonial possessions in every continent. The transoceanic remnants of Spain's empire – Cuba, Puerto Rico, Guam and the Philippines – fell to the United States in the Spanish–American War of 1898. In Central America, US technology succeeded in cutting the Panama Canal, which opened for navigation in 1914 (▷ *5.24*). The extension of the railroad network throughout the United States by the end of the 19th century was instrumental in opening up new territories; and, as the 20th century dawned, American engineers pioneered important new forms of transport. The first powered heavier-than-air flight was made in 1903, and mass automobile ownership was a fact by 1914.

Russia's expansion to the east brought it into conflict with Japan (▷ *5.12*). The industrializing and ambitious Japan routed Russian forces in 1904–05 and annexed Korea in 1910. Russia's humiliation sparked the first of a series of revolutions that led to the fall of the imperial regime in 1917.

Britain's prime interest was to protect its trade through the Suez Canal, including the new resource of oil which Britain received from the Persian Gulf. To this end, bases were developed in the Mediterranean. Egypt was also occupied in 1882. Further east, British

Alaska
CANADA
Newfoundland
UNITED STATES
MEXICO
Hawaiian Islands (United States)
Bahamas
HAITI
Puerto Rico (United States)
DOMINICAN REPUBLIC
CUBA
Jamaica
British Honduras
GUATEMALA
EL SALVADOR
HONDURAS
NICARAGUA
COSTA RICA
PANAMA
VENEZUELA
COLOMBIA
British Guiana
Dutch Guiana
French Guia
Galapagos Islands (Ecuador)
ECUADOR
BRAZIL
PERU
BOLIVIA
PARAGUAY
Marquesas Islands (France)
Tuamotu Archipelago (France)
Easter Island (Chile)
CHILE
ARGENTINA
URUGUA
Falkland Islands (Britain)

TIMELINE

The Americas | Europe | Middle East | Africa | Asia and Australasia

1882 Triple Alliance formed between Germany, Austria-Hungary, and Italy

1884–85 Berlin Conference divides up Africa between European powers

1885 Completion of Canadian Pacific Railway links east and west Canada

1885

1886 Discovery of gold in Transvaal initiates intensive mining activity throughout southern Africa

1888 Wilhelm II becomes German emperor (*Kaiser*)

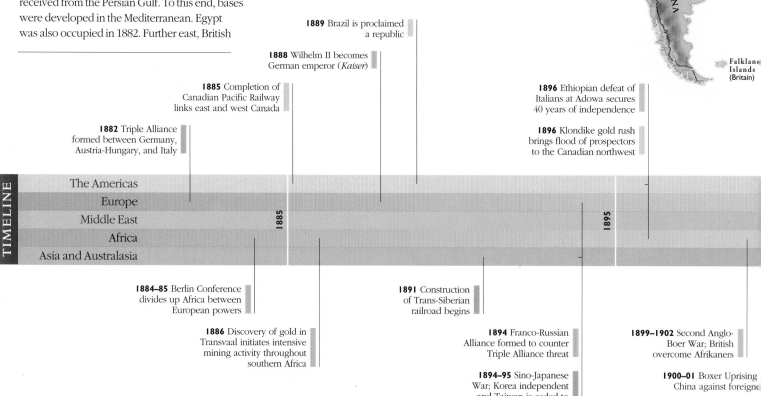

1889 Brazil is proclaimed a republic

1891 Construction of Trans-Siberian railroad begins

1894 Franco-Russian Alliance formed to counter Triple Alliance threat

1894–95 Sino-Japanese War; Korea independent and Taiwan is ceded to Japan on Chinese defeat

1895

1896 Ethiopian defeat of Italians at Adowa secures 40 years of independence

1896 Klondike gold rush brings flood of prospectors to the Canadian northwest

1899–1902 Second Anglo-Boer War; British overcome Afrikaners

1900–01 Boxer Uprising China against foreigne

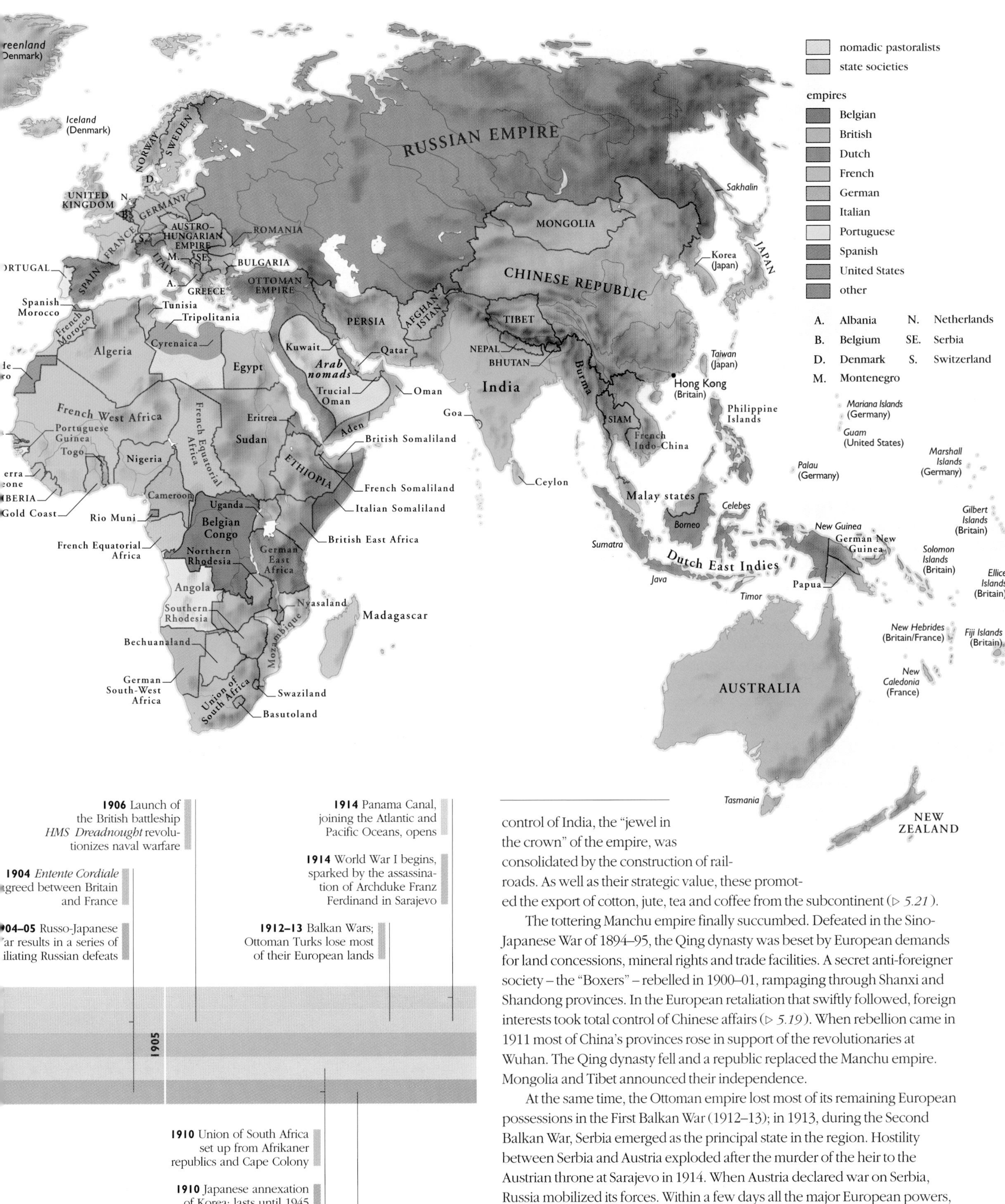
nomadic pastoralists
state societies
empires
Belgian
British
Dutch
French
German
Italian
Portuguese
Spanish
United States
other
A. Albania
B. Belgium
D. Denmark
M. Montenegro
N. Netherlands
SE. Serbia
S. Switzerland
reenland
Denmark)
Iceland
(Denmark)
NORWAY
SWEDEN
UNITED KINGDOM
GERMANY
FRANCE
SPAIN
ITALY
AUSTRO-HUNGARIAN EMPIRE
ROMANIA
BULGARIA
GREECE
OTTOMAN EMPIRE
RUSSIAN EMPIRE
MONGOLIA
CHINESE REPUBLIC
TIBET
PERSIA
AFGHANISTAN
NEPAL
BHUTAN
India
Burma
SIAM
French Indo-China
Sakhalin
Korea
(Japan)
JAPAN
Taiwan
(Japan)
Hong Kong
(Britain)
Philippine Islands
Mariana Islands
(Germany)
Guam
(United States)
Palau
(Germany)
Marshall Islands
(Germany)
Gilbert Islands
(Britain)
Malay states
Borneo
Celebes
Sumatra
Java
Dutch East Indies
Timor
New Guinea
German New Guinea
Papua
Solomon Islands
(Britain)
Ellice Islands
(Britain)
New Hebrides
(Britain/France)
Fiji Islands
(Britain)
New Caledonia
(France)
AUSTRALIA
Tasmania
NEW ZEALAND
Ceylon
Goa
Kuwait
Qatar
Arab nomads
Trucial Oman
Oman
Aden
)RTUGAL
Spanish Morocco
French Morocco
Tunisia
Tripolitania
Cyrenaica
Algeria
Egypt
French West Africa
Portuguese Guinea
Togo
Nigeria
French Equatorial Africa
Eritrea
Sudan
ETHIOPIA
British Somaliland
French Somaliland
Italian Somaliland
British East Africa
Cameroon
Uganda
Belgian Congo
Rio Muni
French Equatorial Africa
Northern Rhodesia
German East Africa
Angola
Nyasaland
Madagascar
Southern Rhodesia
Mozambique
Bechuanaland
German South-West Africa
Union of South Africa
Swaziland
Basutoland
BERIA
Gold Coast
1905

1906 Launch of the British battleship *HMS Dreadnought* revolutionizes naval warfare

1904 *Entente Cordiale* agreed between Britain and France

1904–05 Russo-Japanese War results in a series of humiliating Russian defeats

1914 Panama Canal, joining the Atlantic and Pacific Oceans, opens

1914 World War I begins, sparked by the assassination of Archduke Franz Ferdinand in Sarajevo

1912–13 Balkan Wars; Ottoman Turks lose most of their European lands

1910 Union of South Africa set up from Afrikaner republics and Cape Colony

1910 Japanese annexation of Korea; lasts until 1945

1911 Chinese Revolution overthrows Qing dynasty; republic established 1912

control of India, the "jewel in the crown" of the empire, was consolidated by the construction of railroads. As well as their strategic value, these promoted the export of cotton, jute, tea and coffee from the subcontinent (▷ *5.21*).

The tottering Manchu empire finally succumbed. Defeated in the Sino-Japanese War of 1894–95, the Qing dynasty was beset by European demands for land concessions, mineral rights and trade facilities. A secret anti-foreigner society – the "Boxers" – rebelled in 1900–01, rampaging through Shanxi and Shandong provinces. In the European retaliation that swiftly followed, foreign interests took total control of Chinese affairs (▷ *5.19*). When rebellion came in 1911 most of China's provinces rose in support of the revolutionaries at Wuhan. The Qing dynasty fell and a republic replaced the Manchu empire. Mongolia and Tibet announced their independence.

At the same time, the Ottoman empire lost most of its remaining European possessions in the First Balkan War (1912–13); in 1913, during the Second Balkan War, Serbia emerged as the principal state in the region. Hostility between Serbia and Austria exploded after the murder of the heir to the Austrian throne at Sarajevo in 1914. When Austria declared war on Serbia, Russia mobilized its forces. Within a few days all the major European powers, which had coalesced into two military blocs, were embroiled in World War I. This devastating global conflict was to bring the collapse of the Russian, German and Austro-Hungarian empires ■

5.05 World population and migration • 1830 – 1914 •

The world's population grew from around 950 million in 1830 to around 1,600 million in 1914. This increase was the result of many factors: improved food production and diet; a greater awareness of hygiene and the start of public health programs; and new labor opportunities in industrialized regions that allowed people to escape rural hardship. Yet in spite of these improvements, millions still lived in abject poverty; the biggest migrations ever recorded began in the 19th century. The reasons were diverse and complex. Europe experienced increased cycles of emigration after each economic depression, as emigrants tried to escape unemployment, poverty and poor housing. Substantial numbers from Russia and Ireland also fled from persecution or starvation. In all, over 40 million people left Europe between 1830 and 1914, yet during the same period the population of the continent increased by some 76 percent.

Migrants looked above all to the Americas as lands of unlimited opportunities. While the first of them to venture west did so aboard any cargo vessels that would take them, by mid-century passenger lines with purpose-built steamships were running regular services that offered cheap transatlantic passages in reasonable accommodation.

Up to 1895, immigrants to the United States and Canada tended to come from Scandinavia, Germany, Britain and Ireland (▷ *5.10*). Among those who endured the greatest hardship were the Irish, a trend dramatized by famine when the potato crop failed in 1845–47. Many prospective immigrants suffered from cholera and typhoid, and did not survive the passage. After 1895 most immigrants were of central and southern European origin. As a result of the huge influx (especially between 1900 and 1914), some regions of the United States were chiefly composed of either first- or second-generation European immigrants by 1914 (▷ *5.26*).

European imperial acquisitions also attracted their own immigration, with Italians moving to Libya, and French to north Africa (▷ *5.16*). The territories gained by Germany in inhospitable equatorial zones proved less inviting to emigrants from the home country. Many British people, especially Scots and Welsh, willingly emigrated to Canada, South Africa, Australia and New Zealand in order to find work (▷ *5.17, 5.18, 5.25*).

The Chinese emigrated in great numbers in this period; as early as 1850 Australian employers began shipping in Chinese "coolies" to undertake the

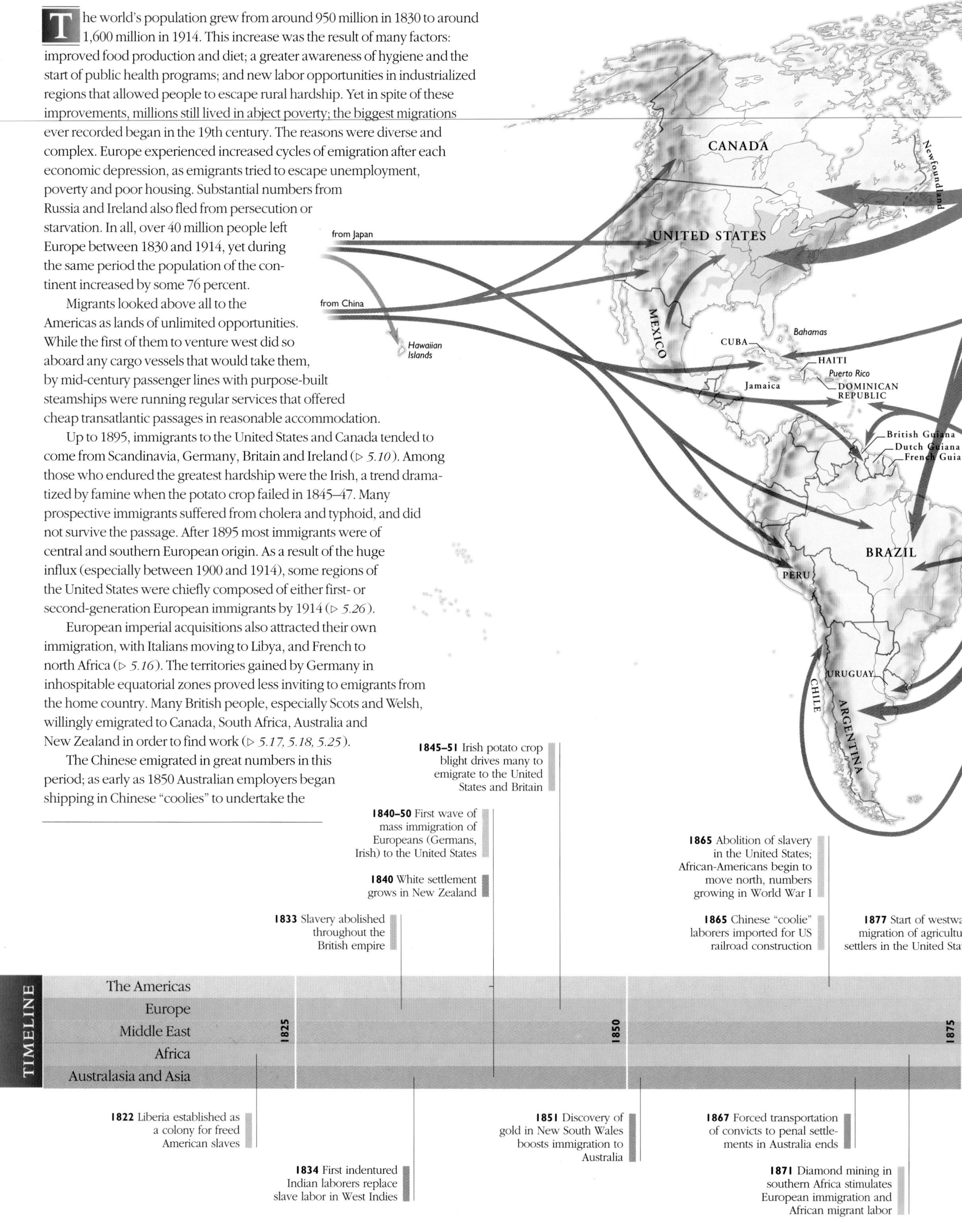

from Japan
from China
Hawaiian Islands
CANADA
Newfoundland
UNITED STATES
MEXICO
CUBA
Bahamas
HAITI
Puerto Rico
Jamaica
DOMINICAN REPUBLIC
British Guiana
Dutch Guiana
French Guia
BRAZIL
PERU
URUGUAY
CHILE
ARGENTINA
TIMELINE
The Americas
Europe
Middle East
Africa
Australasia and Asia
1825
1850
1875
1822 Liberia established as a colony for freed American slaves
1833 Slavery abolished throughout the British empire
1834 First indentured Indian laborers replace slave labor in West Indies
1840 White settlement grows in New Zealand
1840–50 First wave of mass immigration of Europeans (Germans, Irish) to the United States
1845–51 Irish potato crop blight drives many to emigrate to the United States and Britain
1851 Discovery of gold in New South Wales boosts immigration to Australia
1865 Abolition of slavery in the United States; African-Americans begin to move north, numbers growing in World War I
1865 Chinese "coolie" laborers imported for US railroad construction
1867 Forced transportation of convicts to penal settlements in Australia ends
1871 Diamond mining in southern Africa stimulates European immigration and African migrant labor
1877 Start of westwa migration of agricultu settlers in the United Stat

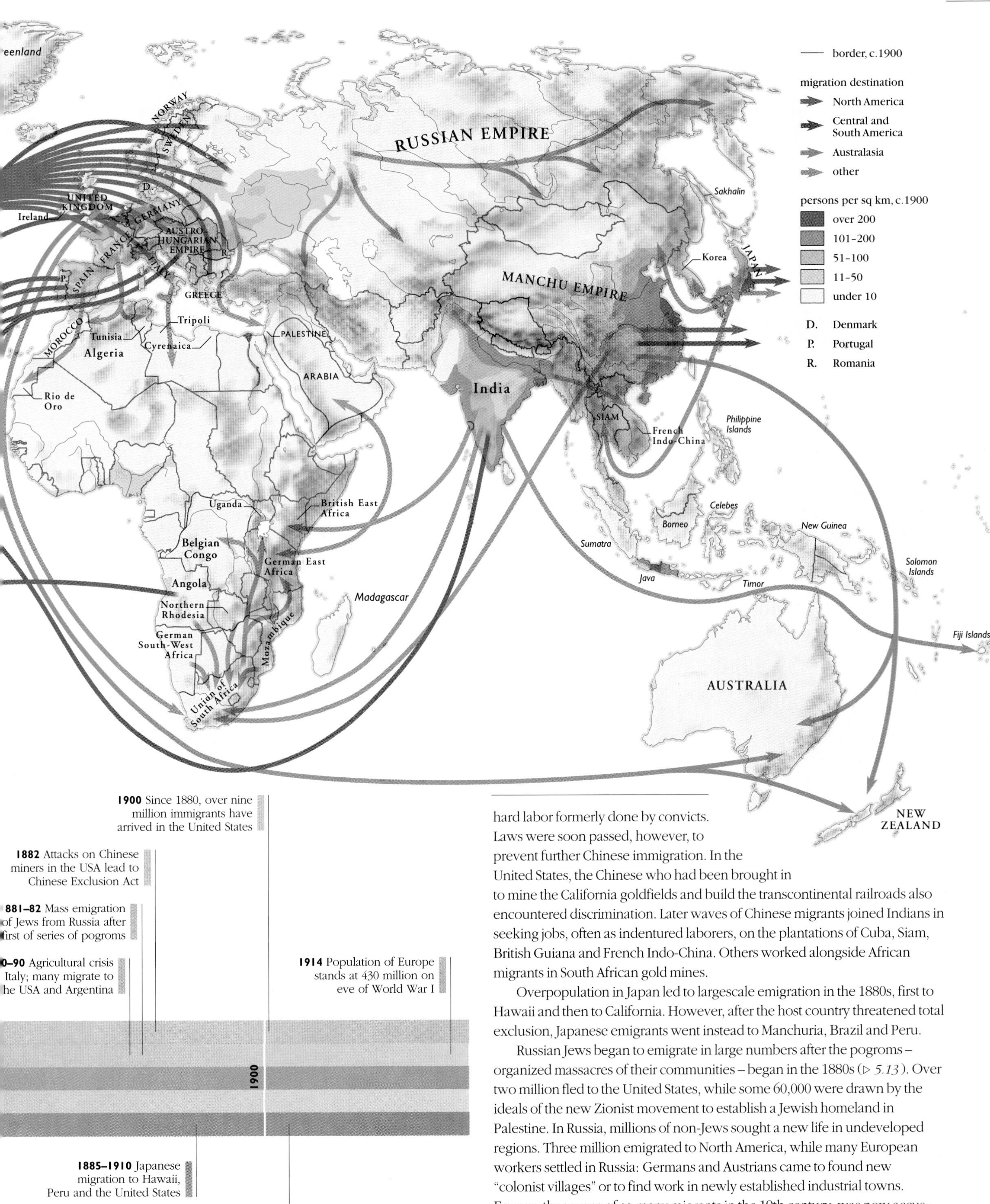

border, c.1900
migration destination
North America
Central and South America
Australasia
other
persons per sq km, c.1900
over 200
101–200
51–100
11–50
under 10
D. Denmark
P. Portugal
R. Romania
eenland
NORWAY
SWEDEN
RUSSIAN EMPIRE
UNITED KINGDOM
Ireland
D.
GERMANY
AUSTRO-HUNGARIAN EMPIRE
R.
FRANCE
SPAIN
P.
ITALY
GREECE
MOROCCO
Tunisia
Algeria
Tripoli
Cyrenaica
PALESTINE
ARABIA
Rio de Oro
Sakhalin
Korea
JAPAN
MANCHU EMPIRE
India
SIAM
French Indo-China
Philippine Islands
Uganda
British East Africa
Belgian Congo
German East Africa
Angola
Northern Rhodesia
German South-West Africa
Mozambique
Union of South Africa
Madagascar
Celebes
Borneo
Sumatra
Java
Timor
New Guinea
Solomon Islands
Fiji Islands
AUSTRALIA
NEW ZEALAND
1900

1900 Since 1880, over nine million immigrants have arrived in the United States

1882 Attacks on Chinese miners in the USA lead to Chinese Exclusion Act

881–82 Mass emigration of Jews from Russia after first of series of pogroms

0–90 Agricultural crisis Italy; many migrate to he USA and Argentina

1914 Population of Europe stands at 430 million on eve of World War I

1885–1910 Japanese migration to Hawaii, Peru and the United States

1902 Start of the "White Australia" policy; non-European immigrants excluded for over 60 years

hard labor formerly done by convicts. Laws were soon passed, however, to prevent further Chinese immigration. In the United States, the Chinese who had been brought in to mine the California goldfields and build the transcontinental railroads also encountered discrimination. Later waves of Chinese migrants joined Indians in seeking jobs, often as indentured laborers, on the plantations of Cuba, Siam, British Guiana and French Indo-China. Others worked alongside African migrants in South African gold mines.

Overpopulation in Japan led to largescale emigration in the 1880s, first to Hawaii and then to California. However, after the host country threatened total exclusion, Japanese emigrants went instead to Manchuria, Brazil and Peru.

Russian Jews began to emigrate in large numbers after the pogroms – organized massacres of their communities – began in the 1880s (▷ *5.13*). Over two million fled to the United States, while some 60,000 were drawn by the ideals of the new Zionist movement to establish a Jewish homeland in Palestine. In Russia, millions of non-Jews sought a new life in undeveloped regions. Three million emigrated to North America, while many European workers settled in Russia: Germans and Austrians came to found new "colonist villages" or to find work in newly established industrial towns. Europe, the source of so many migrants in the 19th century, was now accustomed to workers, capital and expertise constantly crossing national frontiers, a situation that would end abruptly with the outbreak of war in 1914 ■

5.06 World trade • 1830 – 1914 •

Between 1830 and 1914 world trade was dominated by the industrialized nations of Europe and the United States. These countries traded manufactured goods and foodstuffs with each other and, increasingly, with the traditional societies of Latin America, Asia and Africa.

The growth in production in the industrialized nations was accompanied by a rise in foreign trade, which had risen from 10 percent of all earnings in 1830 to 33 percent in 1914. This was based in large part on the systematic exploitation of traditional societies and their raw materials; the trade passing through the major ports constructed in China, Latin America and Africa hardly benefited the economies of the host countries. As a result, rural economies were often destroyed – as in Africa, India and the Dutch East Indies – and replaced by westernized agricultural patterns that dictated the nature of the crops grown, and the manner in which they were marketed. Accompanied by colonial warfare, this exploitation was the ultimate expression of imperialism between 1830 and 1914.

The infrastructure of global trade was financed by the industrialized nations. For example, the economic development of Africa required railroads to carry exports to the coast (▷ *5.16*). Rail links were vital, as the continent's great rivers were often ill suited to the mass transportation of freight, especially in sub-Saharan Africa. Similarly, investment by the industrialized nations built harbors, provided ships and established coaling stations worldwide. To handle the new commerce, port facilities were transformed in the industrialized countries themselves as well as in the colonies. Existing harbors, for example those in New York and Barcelona, were enlarged, while entirely new ports were built at Trieste in Italy and Le Havre in France.

Ship design also underwent radical change, with the advent of steam propulsion in 1833, iron hulls in 1837 and steel hulls in 1856. Sailing-ships reached their peak in the fast, elegant "clippers" that competed to transport commodities such as tea from China in record time. Yet by mid-century, purpose-built steamships with efficient engines were beginning to provide stiff competition for sailing vessels. Sail was dealt a further blow when the new canals cut at Suez, Kiel and Panama spared the need for long and often treacherous voyages around land-masses (▷ *5.14, 5.23*). Between 1850 and 1914 the world's merchant fleet expanded from 9 million net tonnes to over 35 million tonnes in 1914.

Increased global trade required changes in the way the world's economy

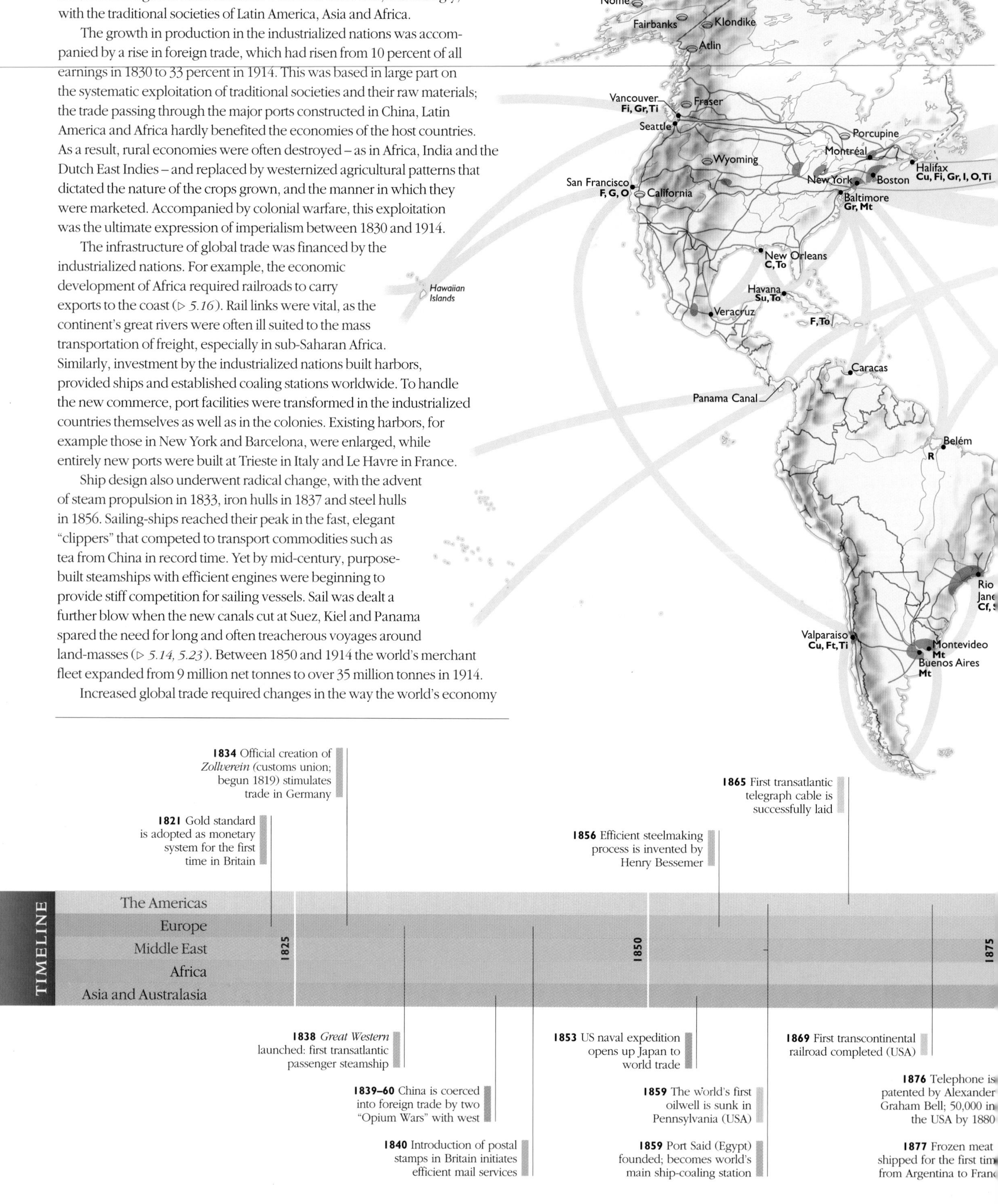

Nome
Fairbanks
Klondike
Atlin
Vancouver
Fi, Gr, Ti
Fraser
Seattle
Porcupine
Montréal
Wyoming
Halifax
Cu, Fi, Gr, I, O, Ti
San Francisco
F, G, O
California
New York
Boston
Baltimore
Gr, Mt
New Orleans
C, To
Hawaiian Islands
Havana
Su, To
Veracruz
F, To
Caracas
Panama Canal
Belém
R
Valparaiso
Cu, Ft, Ti
Montevideo
Mt
Buenos Aires
Mt

TIMELINE

The Americas | Europe | Middle East | Africa | Asia and Australasia

1825 | 1850 | 1875

1821 Gold standard is adopted as monetary system for the first time in Britain

1834 Official creation of *Zollverein* (customs union; begun 1819) stimulates trade in Germany

1838 *Great Western* launched: first transatlantic passenger steamship

1839–60 China is coerced into foreign trade by two "Opium Wars" with west

1840 Introduction of postal stamps in Britain initiates efficient mail services

1853 US naval expedition opens up Japan to world trade

1856 Efficient steelmaking process is invented by Henry Bessemer

1859 The world's first oilwell is sunk in Pennsylvania (USA)

1859 Port Said (Egypt) founded; becomes world's main ship-coaling station

1865 First transatlantic telegraph cable is successfully laid

1869 First transcontinental railroad completed (USA)

1876 Telephone is patented by Alexander Graham Bell; 50,000 in the USA by 1880

1877 Frozen meat shipped for the first tim from Argentina to Fran

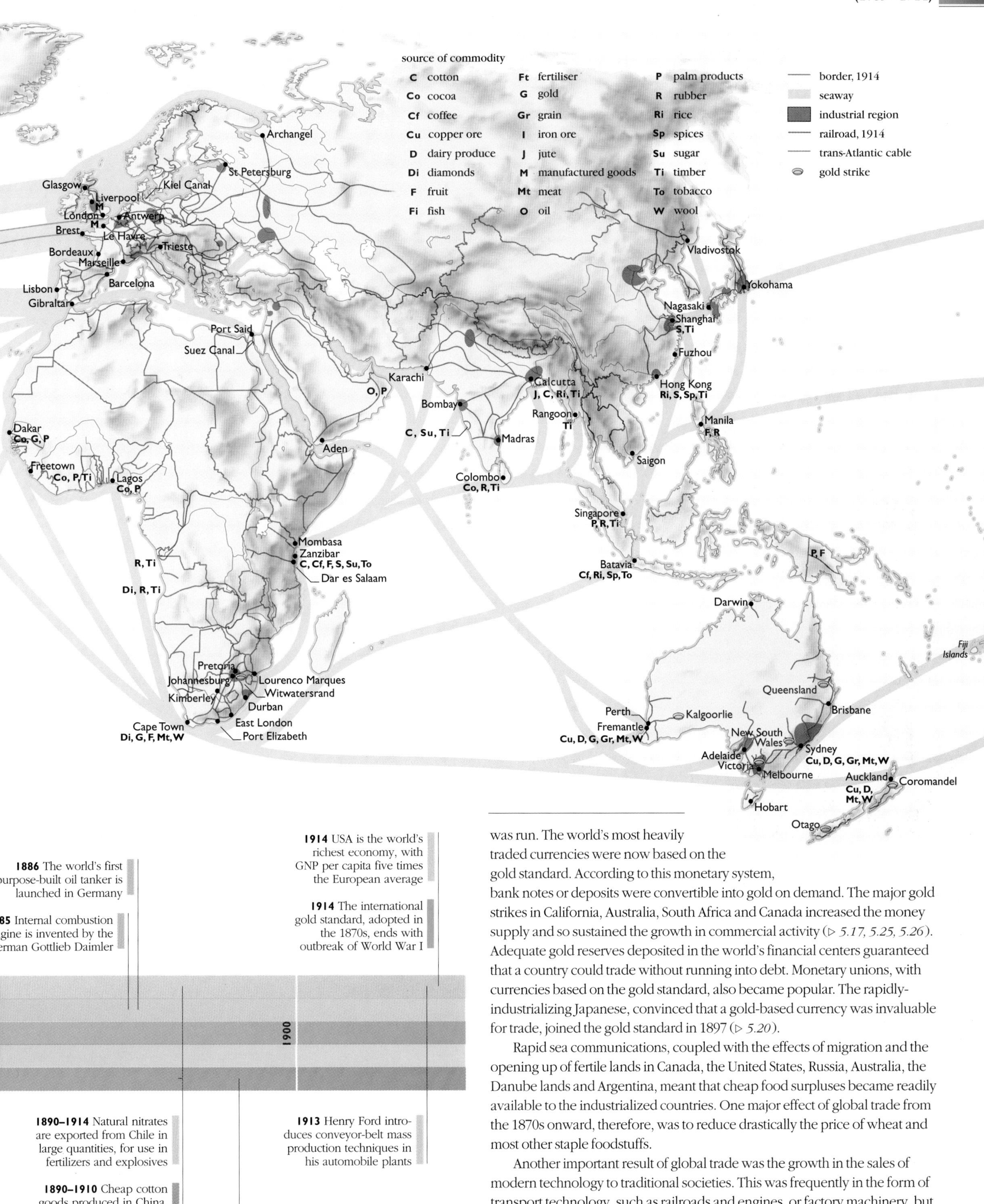
source of commodity
C cotton
Co cocoa
Cf coffee
Cu copper ore
D dairy produce
Di diamonds
F fruit
Fi fish
Ft fertiliser
G gold
Gr grain
I iron ore
J jute
M manufactured goods
Mt meat
O oil
P palm products
R rubber
Ri rice
Sp spices
Su sugar
Ti timber
To tobacco
W wool
border, 1914
seaway
industrial region
railroad, 1914
trans-Atlantic cable
gold strike
Archangel
St Petersburg
Kiel Canal
Glasgow
Liverpool
M
London
M
Antwerp
Brest
Le Havre
Trieste
Bordeaux
Marseille
Barcelona
Lisbon
Gibraltar
Port Said
Suez Canal
Karachi
O, P
Bombay
C, Su, Ti
Madras
Calcutta
J, C, Ri, Ti
Rangoon
Ti
Colombo
Co, R, Ti
Aden
Vladivostok
Yokohama
Nagasaki
Shanghai
S, Ti
Fuzhou
Hong Kong
Ri, S, Sp, Ti
Manila
F, R
Saigon
Singapore
P, R, Ti
Batavia
Cf, Ri, Sp, To
P, F
Darwin
Fiji Islands
Dakar
Co, G, P
Freetown
Co, P, Ti
Lagos
Co, P
Mombasa
Zanzibar
C, Cf, F, S, Su, To
Dar es Salaam
R, Ti
Di, R, Ti
Pretoria
Johannesburg
Kimberley
Lourenco Marques
Witwatersrand
Durban
East London
Port Elizabeth
Cape Town
Di, G, F, Mt, W
Queensland
Brisbane
Kalgoorlie
Perth
Fremantle
Cu, D, G, Gr, Mt, W
New South Wales
Sydney
Cu, D, G, Gr, Mt, W
Adelaide
Victoria
Melbourne
Auckland
Coromandel
Cu, D, Mt, W
Hobart
Otago

was run. The world's most heavily traded currencies were now based on the gold standard. According to this monetary system, bank notes or deposits were convertible into gold on demand. The major gold strikes in California, Australia, South Africa and Canada increased the money supply and so sustained the growth in commercial activity (▷ *5.17, 5.25, 5.26*). Adequate gold reserves deposited in the world's financial centers guaranteed that a country could trade without running into debt. Monetary unions, with currencies based on the gold standard, also became popular. The rapidly-industrializing Japanese, convinced that a gold-based currency was invaluable for trade, joined the gold standard in 1897 (▷ *5.20*).

Rapid sea communications, coupled with the effects of migration and the opening up of fertile lands in Canada, the United States, Russia, Australia, the Danube lands and Argentina, meant that cheap food surpluses became readily available to the industrialized countries. One major effect of global trade from the 1870s onward, therefore, was to reduce drastically the price of wheat and most other staple foodstuffs.

Another important result of global trade was the growth in the sales of modern technology to traditional societies. This was frequently in the form of transport technology, such as railroads and engines, or factory machinery, but also increasingly came to comprise advanced military hardware. The balance of power in regional conflicts was radically altered by this development ■

1886 The world's first purpose-built oil tanker is launched in Germany

1885 Internal combustion engine is invented by the German Gottlieb Daimler

1914 USA is the world's richest economy, with GNP per capita five times the European average

1914 The international gold standard, adopted in the 1870s, ends with outbreak of World War I

1900

1890–1914 Natural nitrates are exported from Chile in large quantities, for use in fertilizers and explosives

1890–1910 Cheap cotton goods produced in China, India and Japan undercut European cotton industry

1895 Malayan rubber plantations begin production

1913 Henry Ford introduces conveyor-belt mass production techniques in his automobile plants

5.07 Europe in the age of revolution • 1783 – 1800 •

Enlightenment thinkers of the mid-18th century often emphasized people's right to self-determination through a system of representative government. In this they expressed a hostility to the repressive forces – clerics, aristocrats and absolute monarchs – that still reigned supreme throughout Europe in the 18th century. Fueled by poverty, inflation and food shortages, and inspired by the successful revolution of American colonists against the British, this discontent was soon to erupt.

Uprisings occurred in 1784, when the Patriot party in the Dutch Netherlands tried to democratize government, and in 1787, when citizens of the neighboring territory of the Austrian Netherlands (Belgium) attempted to establish an independent republic. Neither insurrection achieved its goals.

A more widely based protest began against the *ancien régime* (autocratic royal government) in France when Louis XVI tried to raise taxes to avert state bankruptcy. He summoned the Estates-General – a periodic assembly of deputies from the three "Estates" (clergy, nobility, and commoners) – to approve his plans. However, Louis was faced with a political crisis when the Third Estate (made up of the rising middle class) withdrew to found a National Assembly and institute reform. Parisians feared an attack on the Assembly by Louis' forces and, on 14 July 1789, stormed the Bastille fortress, symbol of Bourbon tyranny. The rebellion spread rapidly .

In August 1789 the Assembly abolished the feudal system and issued its *Declaration of the Rights of Man*, which proclaimed freedom of conscience, property and speech, and established the principle that sovereign power resided in the nation rather than the king. After failing to escape from the country in 1791, Louis was compelled to approve a constitution that divested him of most of his power. By this stage, aristocrats who had managed to flee France had persuaded Prussia and the Habsburg empire (Austria) to intervene on Louis' behalf. Opposition to revolutionary France soon crystallized into the First Coalition of European powers. The ensuing Revolutionary Wars (1792–1802) saw the French repulse an initial invasion and then go on the attack. The king and queen and many of their aristocratic supporters were executed, counter-revolutionary risings were suppressed, internecine struggles broke out among the revolutionaries (the "Terror"), and the French tried to export revolution to their hostile neighbors the Netherlands, Spain and Britain (where they fomented rebellion in Ireland).

The First Coalition was broken by a series of French victories in 1794–95, culminating in a successful invasion of the Netherlands (ruled by France as the Batavian Republic until 1806). Prussia and Spain sued for peace, leaving Britain and the Habsburg empire isolated. Britain, though, maintained naval supremacy with victories over France, and latterly its Dutch and Spanish allies, from 1794–97. In 1798 a Second Coalition was formed.

Napoleon Bonaparte now began to emerge as the greatest of the French commanders through his brilliant campaigns in Italy and Austria. By late 1797, he had forced Austria to cede the Austrian Netherlands to France in exchange for Venice, in a peace treaty that also created French satellite states in northern Italy. As a prelude to his planned invasion

- borders, 1783
- border of Holy Roman empire, 1783
- Austrian Habsburg territory, 1783
- France, 1783
- Brandenburg-Prussia, 1783
- Great Britain & Hanover, 1783
- Ottoman empire, 1783
- Spanish Bourbon territory, 1783
- Russian empire, 1783
- Russian gains by 1795
- Brandenburg-Prussian gains by 1795
- Austrian Habsburg gains by 1797
- French gains by 1800
- Roman Republic – state established by Revolutionary France
- extent of the "Great Fear" within France, 1789
- French counter-revolution, 1793
- French campaign, 1796–98
- Russian campaign, 1798–1800
- town bombarded by Russian Black Sea fleet
- Naval mutiny in Great Britain
- major revolt, riot or disorder

THE SANS-CULOTTE, "man without breeches", symbolized the radical republicans of France in 1790.

TIMELINE

Revolts

1784–87 Revolts occur in Dutch and Austrian Netherlands

1788 Louis XVI of France summons the Estates-General

1789 French Revolution begins; the Bastille is stormed

1793 Execution of Louis XVI; a royalist rebellion begins in the Vendée

1794 Tadeusz Kosciuszko leads a national rebellion in Poland

1797 Mutinies in the British Royal Navy at Spithead and the Nore

1798 United Irishmen rebel in a vain effort to win independence from Britain

Revolutionary wars

1792 The Prussians are checked at Valmy; Austrians are defeated at Jemappes

1793 France blocks Anglo-Hanoverians at Hondschoote; defeats Austrians at Wattignies

1794 Britain beats France at the Battle of the First of June

1798 The French defeat the Mamlukes at the Battle of the Pyramids but are defeated by British at Battle of the Nile

1799 Bonaparte returns to France and seizes power

1800 Bonaparte defeats the Austrians at Marengo

Alliances & treaties

1783 Britain recognizes the independence of the United States in the Treaty of Paris

1792 Austria and Prussia ally against France: start of the French revolutionary wars

1793 Second Partition of Poland; Spain, Holland, Britain and the empire join First Coalition against France

1795 Third Partition of Poland

1797 Treaty of Campo Formio follows the French defeat of Austria

1798 Second Coalition against France

RUSSIAN EMPIRE
SWEDEN
DENMARK–NORWAY
North Sea
Baltic Sea
Christiania
Stockholm
Helsinki
Svenskund 1789, 1790
St Petersburg
Revel
Lake Peipus
Vänern
Vättern
Göteborg
Gotland to Sweden
Riga
Western Dvina
Samogitia
Copenhagen
Königsberg
East Prussia
New East Prussia from 1795
Minsk
Lithuania
Black Russia
Swedish Pomerania
Danzig
Ermland
West Prussia
PRUSSIA
Pomerania
Mazovia
Stettin
Netze
1795–1806 Batavian Republic
Camperdown 1797
Amsterdam
Nore
Hamburg
Bremen
Hanover
Brandenburg
Berlin
Elbe
Oder
Warsaw
POLAND
1794
Podlesia
Great Poland South Prussia from 1793
Little Poland West Galicia from 1795
NETHERLANDS
1784
1787
Brussels
Neerwinden 1793
Liège 1789
Fleurus 1794
Saxony
Dresden
Silesia
Volhynia
Red Russia
Vistula
Frankfurt
Nuremberg
Prague
Bohemia
Austrian Silesia
Moravia
Galicia and Lodomeria
Wissembourg 1793
Valmy 1792
Paris 1789
Versailles 1789
Saarwerden
Salm
Bavaria
Munich
Hohenlinden 1800
Austria
Danube
Vienna
HABSBURG EMPIRE
Bukovina
Montbeliard 1792–93
Rauracian Republic
Zürich 1799
Salzburg
Leoben
Styria
Buda
Hungary 1790
Transylvania
Jassy
Moldavia
Bessarabia
SWISS CONFEDERATION 1798–1803 Helvetic Republic
Tyrol
Carinthia
Carniola
Croatia
Slavonia
Banat
Wallachia
Sebastopol
Black Sea
Russian Black Sea fleet, 1798–1800
Geneva
Lyon
SARDINIA-PIEDMONT
Marengo 1800
Milan
Turin
Castiglione 1796
Rivoli 1797
Campo Formio
Mantua
Arcole 1796
Venice
1797–1802 Cisalpine Republic
VENICE
Mondovi 1796
Genoa
GENOA 1797–1805 Ligurian Republic
Avignon
Marseille
Nice
Toulon
Trouillas 1793
Vernet 1793
TUSCANY
PAPAL STATES
Fano
Bosnia
Serbia
Bulgaria
Varna
Herzegovina
MONTENEGRO
RAGUSA
Üsküb
Edirne
Constantinople
Rumelia
Albania
1798–99 Roman Republic
Corsica 1794–96 to Britain
Ajaccio
Civitavecchia
Rome
Naples
1798–99 Parthenopean Republic
Russian Black Sea fleet, 1798–1800
SARDINIA–PIEDMONT
Sardinia
1793
Minorca 1798 to Britain
Balearic Islands
KINGDOM OF NAPLES AND SICILY
Palermo
Messina
Sicily, 1799 independent of Naples
Ionian Islands Venetian, 1797 to France, 1799 to Russia
Janina
Morea
Athens
ANATOLIA
OTTOMAN EMPIRE
Rhodes
Cyprus
Crete
Cythera Venetian, 1797 to France, 1799 to Russia
Bonaparte, 1798
Tunis
Algiers
ALGIERS
Tunis
Malta Knights of St John, 1798 to France, 1800 to Britain
Mediterranean Sea
Tripoli
Cyrene
Aboukir Bay (Battle of the Nile) 1798
Alexandria
Acre
Mount Tabor 1798
Jaffa
Palestine
Cairo
Battle of the Pyramids 1798
Nile
Egypt
0 600 km
0 400 mi

1 In July and August 1789, a series of panics known as the "Great Fear" swept the French countryside, caused by rumors of brigands in the pay of aristocrats.

2 The Jacobin Maximilien Robespierre came to power in Paris in July 1793, initiating the revolutionary "Terror" and executing over a thousand people in the following twelve months.

3 The main counter-revolutionary revolt took place in the Vendée region of western France in 1793, and was brutally suppressed.

4 The Polish uprising against Russian rule in 1794 was led by Tadeusz Kosciuszko. Defeated and exiled, he refused to support subsequent attempts by France and Russia to grant Poland nominal independence.

5 Despite victories over France and its allies, harsh conditions in Britain's Royal Navy caused low morale, which led to two serious mutinies in 1797.

6 The French were persuaded by Wolfe Tone to support Irish risings against British rule. The rising of 1798 failed, and Tone committed suicide in prison.

of Britain, Bonaparte threatened Britain's trade route to India by attacking Egypt in 1798. Though victorious against Egypt's Mamluke rulers, his fleet was defeated by the British admiral Nelson at the Battle of the Nile. In response to reverses in Italy and on the Rhine, Bonaparte returned to France, overthrew the committee that had ruled France since 1795 (the "Directory") and installed himself as military dictator.

French military fortunes proceeded to rise; Napoleon's generals blocked an Anglo-Russian expedition to the Batavian Republic and defeated the Russians at Zürich, while he himself masterminded the defeat of the Austrians at Marengo (1800). Yet though his forces were all-powerful on land, his lack of naval superiority meant that he could not prevent raids from the Russian Black Sea fleet in 1798–1800, or – more importantly – deliver a decisive blow against the Second Coalition.

In eastern Europe, Poland embarked on a course of constitutional reform modeled on Enlightenment ideas in the 1790s. Russia under Catherine II, which had annexed part of the country in 1772, responded by invading in 1792. Further regions were annexed by Russia and Prussia in the Second Partition (1793). A rebellion against the foreign overlords ended with the capitulation of Warsaw in 1794, and the Third Partition (1795) saw the disappearance of Poland as a sovereign country for over 120 years.

See also 4.14 (*ancien regime* Europe); 5.08 (Napoleonic Europe)

French victories in 1800 virtually secured the defeat of Austria, but British naval power still frustrated Napoleon Bonaparte. His army in Egypt was forced out by the British in 1801, while the Danish fleet he hoped would keep Britain from the Baltic was destroyed at Copenhagen in the same year. A respite from war was confirmed by the Treaty of Amiens in 1802, enabling Britain to implement the Act of Union which incorporated Ireland into the United Kingdom, improving the islands' security.

War broke out again, however, in the spring of 1803. Napoleon revived his plan to invade Britain, which now stood alone against France, but he was unable to put it into action because of the undiminished strength of the Royal Navy. Britain's comprehensive naval victory at Trafalgar (1805), and the formation of the Third Coalition later that year, focussed Napoleon's attention back on the armies of Austria, overwhelming them at Ulm and Austerlitz. In 1806, Napoleon proclaimed the dissolution of the Holy Roman empire, united all the German states (apart from Austria and Prussia) into the Confederation of the Rhine, and then moved north to smash the Prussians at Jena–Auerstädt.

As in his earlier campaigns, Napoleon's generalship was unsurpassed and his army irresistible: the Treaty of Tilsit that followed his defeat of a Russian army at Friedland in 1807 broke the Third Coalition and placed Napoleon at the height of his power. He now turned to blockading all legitimate trade with Britain. The so-called "Continental System," established in Napoleon's Berlin and Milan decrees (1806, 1807), was designed to force the British to buy overpriced smuggled goods, thus depleting their gold reserves. Britain retaliated by prohibiting all French trade between one port and another.

Between 1804 (when he declared himself emperor) and 1814, Napoleon imposed his administrative and political ideas upon a conquered Europe while countering British attempts to probe the weak points in the continental blockade. In all his vassal states, he introduced the *Code Napoléon*, the French civil code that enshrined the revolutionary principles of equality and liberty, and provided the protection of private property.

A new phase of the Napoleonic wars opened in 1808, when a French army marched across the Iberian peninsula to force Portugal to adopt the Continental System. This sparked a uprising in Spain against the French, while the British under the command of Wellington established a base in Portugal. In a war of shifting fortunes, a number of hard-fought battles drained the reserves of both sides. At the same time, Napoleon was obliged to conduct another campaign against the Austrians, finally overcoming them at Wagram (1809) to reassert his position as master of Europe. Although this victory allowed Napoleon to concentrate his forces on Spain and temporarily reverse his setbacks suffered there, his decision to attack Russia in 1812 – again to enforce the Continental System – radically altered the situation. The campaign was a huge drain on men and supplies; after hunger, winter and Russian resistance forced a withdrawal from Moscow in late 1812, Napoleon's enemies seized the opportunity to create a Fourth Coalition. For the first time since 1795, a united Europe front opposed France.

Even the retreat from Russia did not break Napoleon's power; in 1813, his forces were still able to resist the new coalition at Lützen, Bautzen and Dresden but suffered heavy casualties in doing so. The loss of troops in Russia, combined with the huge international force ranged against him, finally proved decisive. At Leipzig – in the "Battle of the Nations"– Napoleon suffered his first major defeat and was forced to quit Germany. At the same time, Wellington managed to push north to Toulouse and conclude the Peninsular War. Allied armies pressed home their attack from Germany, and threatened Paris in 1814. Napoleon now abdicated and was sent

borders, 1812
French empire, 1812
state dependent on France, 1812
French ally, 1812
Ottoman empire, 1812
Russian empire, 1812
United Kingdom of Great Britain and Ireland, 1812
Confederation of the Rhine
France, 1815
Spanish guerrilla activity
French victory
French defeat
Austrian campaign
British campaign
French campaign
Napoleon's escape from Elba, and the Waterloo campaign, 1815
Prussian campaign
Russian campaign
Glasgow
Belfast
UNITED KINGDOM
Dublin
Ireland
Manchester
Wales
Brest
Nantes
ATLANTIC OCEAN
La Coruña 1809
Bayonne
Vitoria 1813
Burgos 1808
Valladolid
Zaragoza 1809
Oporto
Salamanca 1812
SPAIN
PORTUGAL
Ciudad Rodrigo
Madrid 1808
Talavera 1809
Ocana 1809
Valencia 1808
Torres Vedras
Lisbon
Badajoz 1812
La Albuera 1811
Córdoba
Bailen 1808
Seville
Granada
Cádiz
Málaga
Trafalgar 1805
Gibraltar to Britain
Ceuta to Spain
Tangier
Melilla to Spain
Oran
MOROCCO

into exile on the Mediterranean island of Elba.

While the victorious allies were redrawing the map of Europe at the Congress of Vienna, Napoleon escaped from exile and re-entered France in a final attempt to rebuild his empire. In his so-called "Hundred Days", he reformed his armies and challenged the combined British, Dutch and Prussian forces at Waterloo. The ensuing battle was closely contested, but ended in final defeat for Napoleon. He abdicated for a second time and was exiled to St Helena in the south Atlantic, where he died. Europe was finally at peace after twenty-three years of war.

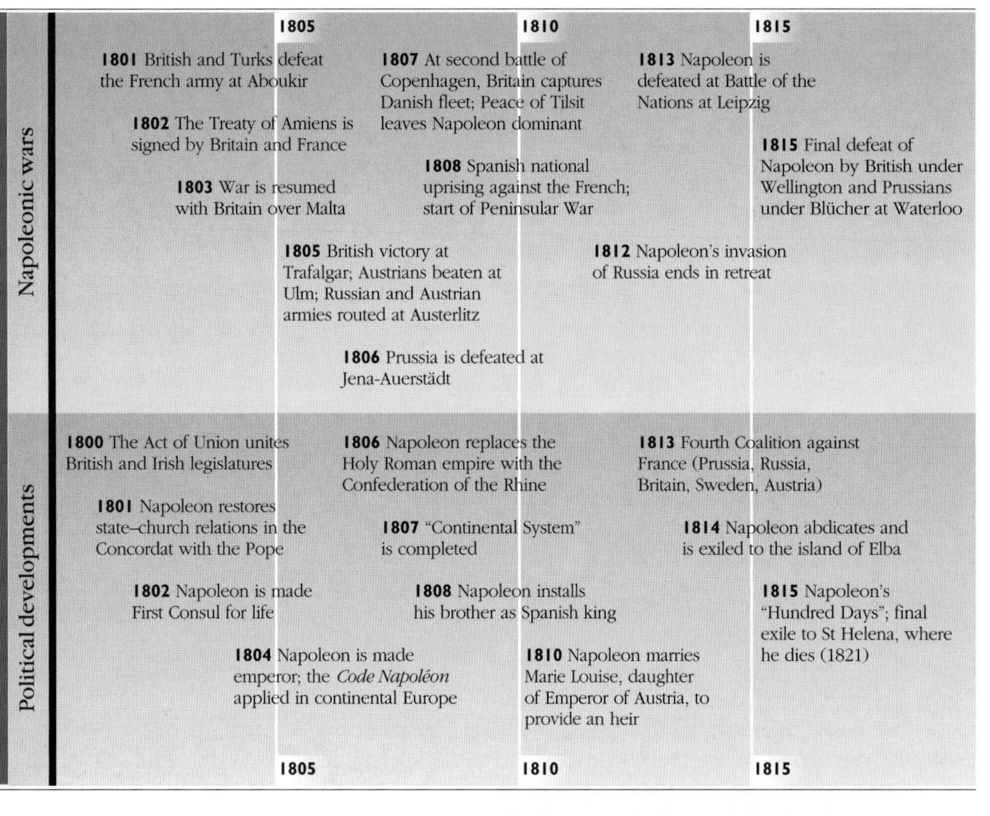
TIMELINE
1805
1810
1815
Napoleonic wars
1801 British and Turks defeat the French army at Aboukir
1802 The Treaty of Amiens is signed by Britain and France
1803 War is resumed with Britain over Malta
1805 British victory at Trafalgar; Austrians beaten at Ulm; Russian and Austrian armies routed at Austerlitz
1806 Prussia is defeated at Jena-Auerstädt
1807 At second battle of Copenhagen, Britain captures Danish fleet; Peace of Tilsit leaves Napoleon dominant
1808 Spanish national uprising against the French; start of Peninsular War
1812 Napoleon's invasion of Russia ends in retreat
1813 Napoleon is defeated at Battle of the Nations at Leipzig
1815 Final defeat of Napoleon by British under Wellington and Prussians under Blücher at Waterloo
Political developments
1800 The Act of Union unites British and Irish legislatures
1801 Napoleon restores state–church relations in the Concordat with the Pope
1802 Napoleon is made First Consul for life
1804 Napoleon is made emperor; the Code Napoléon applied in continental Europe
1806 Napoleon replaces the Holy Roman empire with the Confederation of the Rhine
1807 "Continental System" is completed
1808 Napoleon installs his brother as Spanish king
1810 Napoleon marries Marie Louise, daughter of Emperor of Austria, to provide an heir
1813 Fourth Coalition against France (Prussia, Russia, Britain, Sweden, Austria)
1814 Napoleon abdicates and is exiled to the island of Elba
1815 Napoleon's "Hundred Days"; final exile to St Helena, where he dies (1821)
1805
1810
1815

Christiania
SWEDEN
1815 union with Norway
Stockholm
Vänern
Vättern
Göteborg
Gotland
DENMARK–NORWAY
united until 1814
allied to France until 1814
1801–07
North Sea
Baltic Sea
Helsinki
St Petersburg
Revel
Lake Peipus
Riga
Copenhagen
1801, 1807
1807–11
Swedish Pomerania
1815 to Prussia
Heligoland
1807–14 to Britain
MECKLENBURG-SCHWERIN
1807
Hamburg
Bremen
Pomerania
PRUSSIA
1807–13 allied to France
Stettin
Danzig
Eylau
1807
Königsberg
Friedland
1807
East Prussia
Tilsit
Kovno
Vilna
Minsk
Berezina
1812
Krasnoi
1812
Vitebsk
Smolensk
1812
Western Dvina
Borodino
1812
Moscow
1812
Maloyaroslavets
1812
RUSSIAN EMPIRE
Amsterdam
Holland
Brandenburg
Berlin
GRAND DUCHY OF WARSAW
1815 to Russia
Warsaw
Kiev
Kharkov
WESTPHALIA
Elbe
Oder
HESSE
SAXONY
Jena-Auerstädt
1806
Lützen
1813
Leipzig
1813
Bautzen
1813
Dresden
1813
Silesia
Vistula
Dnieper
Waterloo
1815
Brussels
Ligny
1815
BERG
Amiens
Laon
1814
Frankfurt
Hanau
1813
WÜRZBURG
Prague
Bohemia
Moravia
Austrian Silesia
Austerlitz
1805
Galicia and Lodomeria
Château Thierry
1814
Reims
1814
Paris
1814
Mannheim
Champaubert
1814
La Fère Champenoise
1814
Montereau
1814
WÜRTTEMBERG
Ulm
1805
Ratisbon
1809
BAVARIA
Munich
Ebersberg
1809
Austria
Danube
Wagram
1809
Aspern
1809
Vienna
AUSTRIAN EMPIRE
1809–13 allied to France
Bukovina
Dniester
Bessarabia
1812 to Russian empire
Jassy
Moldavia
Ochakov
Orléans
BADEN
Rhine
Basel
Salzburg
Buda
Zürich
Styria
Hungary
Transylvania
Berne
HELVETIA
Carinthia
FRANCE
Geneva
Lyon
Milan
Venice
Slavonia
Banat
1806–12 under Russian occupation
Wallachia
Bucharest
Sebastopol
Grenoble
Turin
Illyrian Provinces
Sava
Belgrade
1811
Genoa
ITALY
Bosnia
Serbia
Bulgaria
Varna
Black Sea
Russian maritime operations, 1800–07
Avignon
LUCCA
Florence
Tuscany
Herzegovina
MONTENEGRO
Cannes
Marseille
PIOMBINO
Papal States
Corsica
Elba
Üsküb
Edirne
Constantinople
Rumelia
Catalonia
1812–13 to France
Ajaccio
Rome
NAPLES
Albania
Barcelona
1808
Sardinia
Naples
BENEVENTO
ANATOLIA
Janina
OTTOMAN EMPIRE
Corfu
to Russia,
1807 to France,
1815 to Britain
Balearic Islands
Athens
Morea
Palermo
Messina
SICILY
Ionian Islands
to Russia,
1807 to France,
1809 to Britain
1800–07
Rhodes
Cythera
to Russia,
1807 to France,
1809 to Britain
Crete
Tunis
Malta
to Britain
Mediterranean Sea
ALGIERS
Tunis
Cyrene
Cyrenaica
Aboukir
1799, 1801
Alexandria
EGYPT
0 600 km
0 400 mi

THE LÉGION D'HONNEUR, an award for all ranks for notable service to France, was created by Napoleon in 1802.

1 By the Treaty of Amiens (March 1802), Britain and France both agreed to return most conquests made since 1793. Peace, though, lasted barely a year.

2 The Battle of Trafalgar, in which the French lost over half of their ships, ended Napoleon's plans to invade Britain. British commander Lord Nelson died of injuries sustained in the action.

3 Borodino was a costly victory for Napoleon, who lost a quarter of his men. Only 30,000 troops of an original French force of 600,000 survived the Russian campaign.

4 Napoleon planned to invade England from Boulogne in 1804, and assembled a fleet of 2,000 ships; he failed, however, to control the Channel.

5 Naval bombardment forced Denmark to surrender its fleet to Britain in 1807, further weakening French opposition to British sea power.

6 Napoleonic armies lived off the land in invaded countries, a strategy that brought disaster in the severe Russian winter of 1812-13. In contrast, British success in the Peninsular War was based on sustaining strong defensive positions with supplies from home.

See also 5.07 (revolutionary Europe); 5.08 (mid-19th-century Europe); 5.10 (Industrial Revolution)

5.09 The growth of nationalism in Europe • 1815 – 1871 •

The decades after 1815 saw the emergence of nationalism in the aftermath of Napoleon's imperial rule. Liberals and democrats demanded nation-states embracing a common racial and linguistic identity and embodying constitutionally guaranteed rights for their citizens. Only a few nation-states were actually created in the early 19th century: Belgium, the Netherlands, Switzerland and Greece. More often, the monarchies restored after the fall of Napoleon (Prussia, Austria and Russia) stifled the nascent democracies. The strongest states to emerge – Italy and the German second empire – did so not through popular nationalist uprisings, but by coalescing around dynamic existing monarchies (Sardinia–Piedmont and Prussia respectively).

The Congress of Vienna (1814–15), convened at Napoleon's defeat, was intended to create a balance of power. Under the leadership of the conservative Austrian foreign minister Clemens Metternich, the Congress restored hereditary monarchies, created new enlarged kingdoms by unifying Norway with Sweden and Belgium with Holland, and established the "concert of Europe": congresses to deal with threats to political stability. A few concessions were made to nationalism: the Turkish sultan granted a measure of self-government to Serbia (1817) and to Moldavia and Wallachia (1829). However, when revolutions broke out in Naples, Spain and Portugal, the congresses at Troppau, Laibach and Verona authorized intervention; France sent troops to help conservatives suppress a liberal regime in Spain in 1823.

The Greek revolt against Ottoman rule broke out in 1821. The Greeks won control of the Peloponnese (Morea) by early 1822 when they declared Greece a sovereign state, but Turkish forces, bolstered by Egyptian troops, reinvaded in 1825. The conservative nature of the Greek rebellion, combined with strategic machinations against the crumbling Ottoman empire, led the European powers to approve

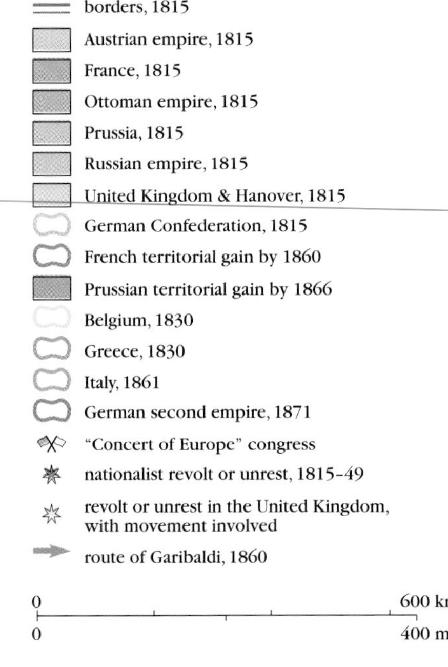

borders, 1815
Austrian empire, 1815
France, 1815
Ottoman empire, 1815
Prussia, 1815
Russian empire, 1815
United Kingdom & Hanover, 1815
German Confederation, 1815
French territorial gain by 1860
Prussian territorial gain by 1866
Belgium, 1830
Greece, 1830
Italy, 1861
German second empire, 1871
"Concert of Europe" congress
nationalist revolt or unrest, 1815–49
revolt or unrest in the United Kingdom, with movement involved
route of Garibaldi, 1860
0
600 km
0
400 mi

an autonomous Greek state. A British, French and Russian naval force destroyed the Turkish–Egyptian fleet at Navarino, and the Ottomans conceded Greek independence in 1832.

Revolutions in Modena, Parma, the Papal States, Poland and some areas of Germany broke out in 1830–31 but were all suppressed. The reactionary regime of Bourbon Charles X in France was ended by the July Revolution of 1830, though this lead not to a new republic but to the accession of the "citizen-king" Louis-Philippe. In the same year, Belgium began its struggle for independence from the Dutch.

The Congress of Vienna had replaced Napoleon's German state with an alliance of 39 states

Sco
Edinb
Glasgow
UNITED
KINGDO
Ireland
Dublin
Manch
1867 F
Liverpo
Tipperary
1848
Wale
Birmi
Newport
1839 Chartists
Bristo
Brest
Nante
ATLANTIC
OCEAN
Borde
La Coruña
1820
Oviedo
1820
Pamplona
1820
Burgos
Ebro
Oporto
1820, 1830
Valladolid
Douro
Zaragoza
1820
Salamanca
SPAIN
PORTUGAL
Madrid
Tagus
Lisbon
1820
Guadiana
Valencia
1820
Córdoba
Seville
2
Granada
Cádiz
1820
Málaga
Gibraltar
to Britain
Tangier
Ceuta
to Spain
Melilla
to Spain
Oran
MOROCCO

headed by Austria and Prussia, known as the German Confederation. Prussia gradually gained ascendancy, partly by forming the *Zollverein* free trade zone from 1819–44, isolating protectionist Austria.

The most serious challenge to Metternich came in 1848, the "Year of Revolutions". The catalyst was the fall of Louis-Philippe's regime to republicans in February. Unrest spread to Hungary, Croatia, and the Czech lands, where liberal governments were installed and democratic constitutions drafted. Metternich was forced to resign and flee abroad. Republics were proclaimed throughout Italy and a

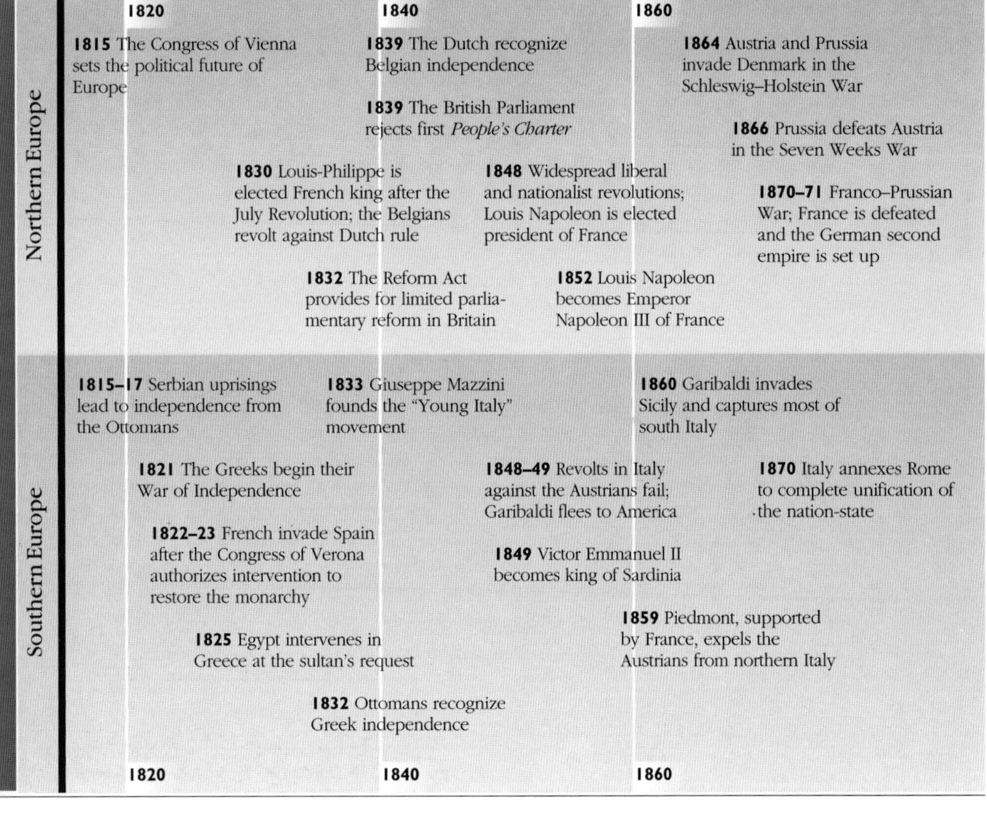

TIMELINE
1820
1840
1860
Northern Europe
1815 The Congress of Vienna sets the political future of Europe
1839 The Dutch recognize Belgian independence
1864 Austria and Prussia invade Denmark in the Schleswig–Holstein War
1839 The British Parliament rejects first *People's Charter*
1866 Prussia defeats Austria in the Seven Weeks War
1830 Louis-Philippe is elected French king after the July Revolution; the Belgians revolt against Dutch rule
1848 Widespread liberal and nationalist revolutions; Louis Napoleon is elected president of France
1870–71 Franco–Prussian War; France is defeated and the German second empire is set up
1832 The Reform Act provides for limited parliamentary reform in Britain
1852 Louis Napoleon becomes Emperor Napoleon III of France
Southern Europe
1815–17 Serbian uprisings lead to independence from the Ottomans
1833 Giuseppe Mazzini founds the "Young Italy" movement
1860 Garibaldi invades Sicily and captures most of south Italy
1821 The Greeks begin their War of Independence
1848–49 Revolts in Italy against the Austrians fail; Garibaldi flees to America
1870 Italy annexes Rome to complete unification of the nation-state
1822–23 French invade Spain after the Congress of Verona authorizes intervention to restore the monarchy
1849 Victor Emmanuel II becomes king of Sardinia
1859 Piedmont, supported by France, expels the Austrians from northern Italy
1825 Egypt intervenes in Greece at the sultan's request
1832 Ottomans recognize Greek independence
1820
1840
1860

1 The reunification of the northern and southern Netherlands in 1815 under the Protestant Dutch monarchy caused resentment in Catholic Belgium.

2 Ferdinand VII, king of Spain (r.1808–33) brutally suppressed liberal opposition after his return from exile in 1814. In 1820, the army he had assembled to reassert his rule in Latin America rose against him.

3 An early challenge to the rule of Louis-Philippe occurred in Lyon in 1831, when 600 protestors were killed in rioting.

4 A Roman republic was established by radicals (including Garibaldi) in 1848–49, but was ended when French troops restored Pope Pius IX to power

5 The head of the Bonaparte dynasty, Louis Napoleon, was elected French president in 1848. He became emperor Napoleon III after a coup (1851), but was exiled after defeat by Prussia in 1871.

LORD BYRON, the British Romantic poet, was inspired by the cause of Greek independence and died at Missolonghi in 1824.

parliamentary assembly met in Frankfurt with the aim of uniting Germany. Yet internal divisions prevailed, and by late 1849 the Habsburgs regained control in Austria, Italy and Hungary (the latter with Russian help); the German assembly collapsed under pressure from Prussia, which consolidated its power by means of swift victories over Denmark, Austria and France.

In Italy, revolutionary movements from 1820 onward, such as the Carbonari, had failed to expel the Austrians or unite the country. In mid-century an unlikely champion arose of the unification movement (*Risorgimento* or "resurrection"): the rich industrial state of Sardinia–Piedmont. The Piedmontese king Victor Emmanuel II and his prime minister Camillo di Cavour instituted liberal domestic reforms and secured the help of Napoleon III's France to drive the Austrians from northern Italy in 1859. The liberal constitutional monarchy sought by Piedmont was threatened when the revolutionary Giuseppe Garibaldi and his "redshirts" took Sicily and overran much of the southern mainland. Yet Garibaldi passed his conquests to Victor Emmanuel II, who effectively became king of a united Italy.

Britain was less affected by nationalist agitation, though the Chartists – supporters of a "People's Charter" – sought universal manhood suffrage after limited parliamentary reform was conceded in 1832. Irish nationalism was given urgency by the famine of 1845–47, and the Irish Republican Brotherhood (Fenians), precursor of the movement that won Irish independence in 1921, was set up in 1858.

See also 5.08 (Napoleonic Europe); 5.11 (the rise of Germany); 5.10 (Industrial Revolution)

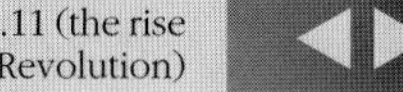

5.10 The industrial revolution in Europe • 1783 – 1914 •

From the last quarter of the 18th century to the outbreak of World War I, Europe was transformed from a series of traditional agrarian communities into a collection of modern industrial nations. Radical changes in the methods by which goods were produced – the widespread adoption of capitalism, mechanization and the factory system – gave rise to a period of unparalleled economic growth, though interrrupted by cyclical depressions. There was also a rapid increase in population and an influx of people from the countryside into the towns and cities that sprang up around the new workplaces.

The Industrial Revolution, as this transformation came to be known, had its origins in Britain. Its effects were first seen in the cotton and woollen industries in the north of the country. Mechanical innovations improved the speed and efficiency of weaving, and required new factories powered first by waterwheels and later by steam engines. These factories brought together the various operations involved in textile manufacture. Britain was ideally placed to pioneer and develop mass production, possessing abundant natural resources to power the new machinery, favorable terrain on which to construct extensive transport networks (canals in the late 18th and early 19th centuries, and rail from the 1830s onward), and a ready market for manufactured goods. By 1815, Britain's industrialists had already made it the "workshop of the world", with coal mining, textile production and pig-iron smelting exceeding the output of the rest of Europe combined. Industrialization had spread to mainland Europe at the end of the 18th century (for example, in the Belgian armaments industry or cotton weaving in Saxony and northern France), but Britain's embargo on the emigration of skilled artisans and the export of machinery during the Napoleonic period prevented a wider adoption of the new methods of production.

Beginning in the 1820s in Belgium, however, coal mining and the textile and metal industries took root in continental Europe. As in Britain, the new rail network played a prime role in promoting economic expansion; rail transport allowed rapid distribution of goods and its consumption

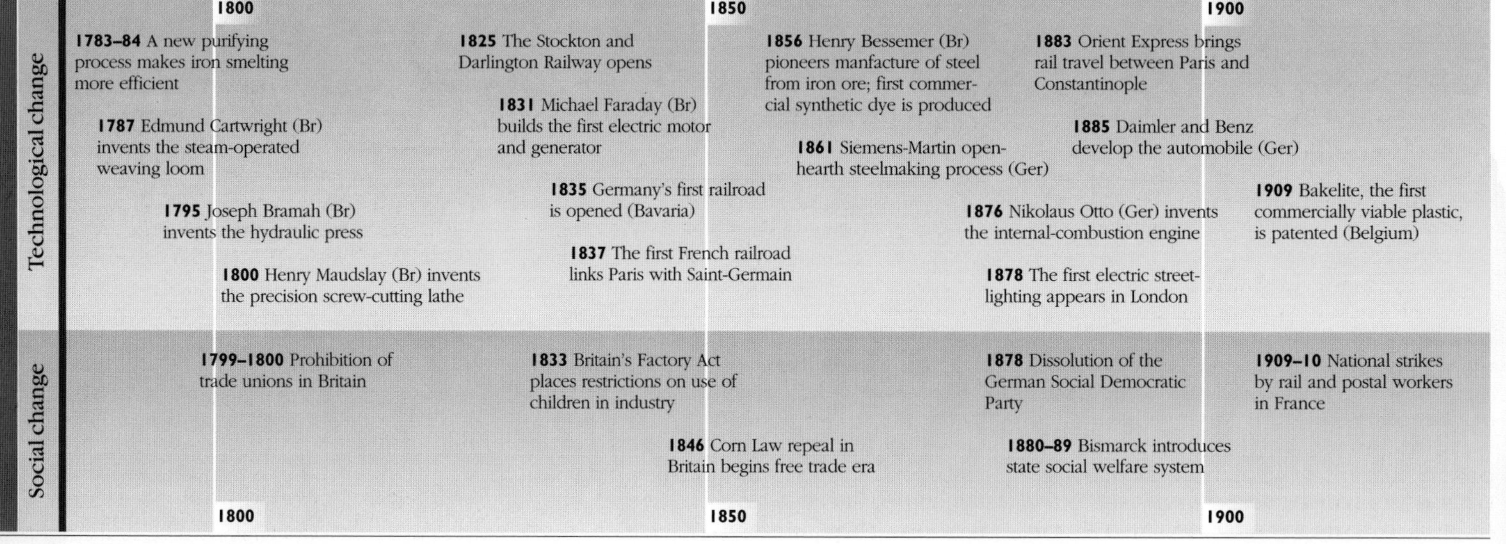

TIMELINE
Technological change
1800
1850
1900
1783–84 A new purifying process makes iron smelting more efficient
1787 Edmund Cartwright (Br) invents the steam-operated weaving loom
1795 Joseph Bramah (Br) invents the hydraulic press
1800 Henry Maudslay (Br) invents the precision screw-cutting lathe
1825 The Stockton and Darlington Railway opens
1831 Michael Faraday (Br) builds the first electric motor and generator
1835 Germany's first railroad is opened (Bavaria)
1837 The first French railroad links Paris with Saint-Germain
1856 Henry Bessemer (Br) pioneers manfacture of steel from iron ore; first commercial synthetic dye is produced
1861 Siemens-Martin open-hearth steelmaking process (Ger)
1876 Nikolaus Otto (Ger) invents the internal-combustion engine
1878 The first electric street-lighting appears in London
1883 Orient Express brings rail travel between Paris and Constantinople
1885 Daimler and Benz develop the automobile (Ger)
1909 Bakelite, the first commercially viable plastic, is patented (Belgium)
Social change
1799–1800 Prohibition of trade unions in Britain
1833 Britain's Factory Act places restrictions on use of children in industry
1846 Corn Law repeal in Britain begins free trade era
1878 Dissolution of the German Social Democratic Party
1880–89 Bismarck introduces state social welfare system
1909–10 National strikes by rail and postal workers in France
1800
1850
1900

Lake Onega
Lake Ladoga
Vyborg
Helsinki
St Petersburg
Narva
Revel
Lake Peipus
Riga
bau
Memel
Western Dvina
nigsberg
Vilna
Minsk
RUSSIAN EMPIRE
171m
Warsaw
Kiev
Dnieper
Vistula
akow
Lvov
(Lemberg)
Dniester
STRO-
NGARIAN
MPIRE
51m
pest
Odessa
Szeged
4
Ploisti
ROMANIA
7.1m
Bucharest
Danube
Belgrade
Black Sea
Varna
SERBIA
3.2m
Sofia
BULGARIA
4.3m
MONTENEGRO
0.6m
Edirne
Constantinople
ALBANIA
Thessalonica
Ankara
ANATOLIA
OTTOMAN EMPIRE
GREECE
Izmir
Konya
Athens
Damascus
Acre
Jerusalem
border, 1914
heavy industrial or mining area
major textile manufacturing area
other large coal deposit
other large iron ore deposit
urban population, 1914
under 100,000
100,000–500,000
500,000–1,000,000
over 1,000,000
oilfield, 1914
port
center of socialism
Berlin
research and development center for the chemical industry
19m
national population (million) where known, 1914
railroad constructed by 1870
railroad constructed 1870–1914
0
600 km
0
400 mi

CHILD-LABOR was common in the mines of early 19th-century Britain, but was banned in 1842.

of materials stimulated further growth. By 1890 nearly all the main rail routes across Europe had been completed.

Private investment lay behind the success of many major industrial ventures, such as some early railroads, but spectacular bankruptcies showed the need for a new method of funding capital projects. Especially in continental Europe, joint-stock limited liability companies, supported by development banks, were founded to provide credit. Free trade (the abolition of import tariffs protecting local producers from competition) was another crucial factor in industrial expansion. Britain lifted its high import duties on corn in 1846; agreements with France, the Prussian *Zollverein* and Belgium in the 1860s further encouraged the reduction of tariffs. By 1870 most European countries had expanded foreign trade and industrial production by lowering or abolishing their tariffs – though the position gradually reversed after the Franco-Prussian War (1870–71).

The social effects of the Industrial Revolution were as radical as its technological and financial consequences. The years of growth between 1840–70 also witnessed periodic financial crises and bouts of widespread unemployment. Harvests were critical, causing wild fluctuations in the price of food. Later, the import of cheap foodstuffs from Canada, the United States and Russia undercut agriculture in the industrializing states. New production methods threatened traditional skills, sometimes leading to machine-wrecking by disgruntled workers. As mechanization spread, working conditions became more hazardous. Employers exploited the large pool of child and female labor to depress wages. Living conditions deteriorated in the vastly expanding new cities, where sanitation failed to keep pace with population growth. Cholera and typhus epidemics were common. A second bout of industrialization after 1870, based on steel and the new power source of electricity, did little to alleviate these problems.

To challenge the effects of capital, both the industrial working classes and the rural peasantry (serfdom did not end in Russia until 1861) organized themselves into trade unions. These efforts met opposition from the state as well as the capitalists. Ideas for alternative ways of structuring society arose during this period. Socialist parties were formed to argue for a more equal distribution of wealth, becoming particularly strong in Germany and France. Karl Marx and Friedrich Engels published their *Communist Manifesto* in 1848, arguing for a class-based revolution in highly industrialized states such as Britain. Anarchists advocated the violent abolition of the state, while syndicalists sought worker-control of industry through general strikes. To forestall social upheaval, some governments enacted legislation to alleviate the worst effects of industrialization. Compulsory free state education was widely instituted; labor in factories and mines was gradually regulated; working hours were cut and wages rose (as did inflation); improved housing also became slowly available. The first decade of the 20th century was marked by widespread unrest, but the old problem of unemployment would be briefly answered by the demands of World War I.

For many people, the solution to poverty was to emigrate. Nearly half a million Poles moved west to find jobs in the industrialized Ruhr, and Italian farmers took harvest work in Germany, France and Austria. Yet far more people left Europe, emigrating in their millions to Australia and New Zealand, but above all to the Americas.

1 The world's first railroad to use steam locomotive traction was opened for coal traffic in 1825 between Stockton and Darlington in northeast England.

2 The new country of Belgium, flat and densely populated, was the first continental European state to complete its rail network, in the 1840s.

3 A major early corporate investment bank was Crédit Mobilier, founded in Paris in 1852; ill-advised speculation led to the bank's collapse in 1867.

4 In 1856, one of the world's first oil refineries opened in Ploisti. Foreign investment brought rapid expansion of the Romanian oilfields from 1895.

5 The major iron-ore deposits in Lorraine were a serious loss to France's nascent steelmaking industry after the area was annexed by Germany in 1871.

6 The German Social Democratic Party was the strongest prewar socialist party, despite laws banning it. The party claimed 1.5 million members in 1890.

7 Barcelona and Bilbao were the two main industrial centers of 19th-century Spain; Barcelona's powerful anarcho-syndicalist movement was set up in 1910.

8 A Luddite (machine-wrecker) revolt (1811–12) ended when its leaders were hanged in York 1813.

See also 4.12 (18th-century European economy); 5.05 (migration); 5.06 (world trade)

5.11 The unification of Germany • 1848 – 1871 •

In the north German states, the upheavals of 1848–49 largely took the form of political meetings and petitioning. A parliament was convened in Frankfurt by liberal forces to draft a national constitution, but it failed to reach consensus on the most suitable type of future government, and the assembly dissolved in disarray. One major rift was between the advocates of a "small Germany" (*Kleindeutschland*), excluding Austria, under Prussian leadership, and of a "big Germany" (*Grossdeutschland*) that included the huge Habsburg empire. For its part, Austria was anxious to protect its long predominance in central Europe. Thus, having restored internal order by 1850, Austria encouraged disunity among the small German principalities. In the meantime, Prussian influence temporarily declined.

In 1861Wilhelm I of the Hohenzollern dynasty ascended the Prussian throne. A conservative militarist, Wilhelm had been instrumental in putting down an insurrection in Baden in 1849. On gaining power, he was immediately faced with demands for a constitutional monarchy by liberals in the Prussian *Diet* (parliament), who opposed his plans to expand the army and introduce three-year military conscription. Wilhelm sought a strong minister-president to impose his will on the parliament, and chose Otto Karl von Bismarck (1815–98), an anti-liberal and member of the rightwing *Junker* party. Bismarck's success on the king's behalf began a partnership that was to last until the king's death in 1888, and that became the prime mover of German unification.

Bismarck's policy of strengthening Prussia by asserting its preeminence in the German-speaking world was first seen when Prussian troops (in concert with Austrian forces) were sent to end Danish occupation of the northern duchies of Holstein (1863) and Schleswig (1864). Prussian military expertise prevailed; in the peace settlement, Prussia received Schleswig and Austria gained Holstein.

Tensions between Austria and Prussia over Schleswig–Holstein were soon to erupt. In preparation for conflict, Bismarck had forged a secret alliance, promising Venetia in Italy in return for support against Austria. In a lightning campaign against Austria and its allies in the German Confederation (the Seven Weeks War), the Prussian forces occupied Holstein, moved south by rail and overcame the Hanoverian army at Langensalza, and then invaded Austria. Although the Austrians were successful against Italy, they were overwhelmed by Prussia at the battle of Königgrätz (Sadowa), and sued for peace in the Treaty of Prague. Prussia's swift victory sent shock waves of alarm through Europe.

At a stroke, Bismarck had recast the map of Europe. Prussia gained Holstein, and Italy received Venetia. His new German Confederation of states north of the River Main united all of north Germany except Saxony under the Hohenzollerns; while the south German states were equally dependent upon Berlin through the *Zollverein* (customs union) and a web of mutual defense treaties. Austrian influence in German affairs was irrevocably ended, not by the revolutionary tactics favored in 1848 but through diplomacy and skillful deployment of the new Prussian army.

France was now faced with a new and powerful neighbor in the form of Prussia. Nevertheless, the French emperor Napoleon III (r.1852–70) had a general sympathy for the cause of strong national identity, which led him to intervene in a nationalist rising in Mexico (1863–67) and in Italy. The same impulse led him initially to support Prussian ambitions in northern Germany. Growing fears among his ministers of Prussian dominance of Europe seemed to be vindicated when the vacant Spanish throne was offered to a member of the Hohenzollern dynasty. Although acceptance of the crown was withdrawn, the French felt that national pride demanded an assurance from Wilhelm I that the candidature would never be renewed. Bismarck, who now saw an opportunity to unite the southern German states with Prussia in opposing a common French enemy, manipulated the conciliatory royal reply (the so-called "Ems Telegram") to make it appear a diplomatic insult. An enraged French court duly declared war on Prussia. Prussian commanders once again used the mobility of deployment by rail to surprise the enemy; within two weeks, 500,000 troops had invaded France from the Rhineland, pinning down a large French force in the fortress of Metz, and then routing an army sent to relieve it at the Battle of Sedan. Napoleon III was captured and Prussian forces advanced through France to besiege Paris, which eventually fell in January 1871. The Prussians finally conducted successful campaigns against French armies in the provinces.

As Prussia's heavy siege artillery bombarded Paris, at Versailles Wilhelm I was proclaimed *Kaiser*, emperor of a united Germany. The new German "second empire" was a federation of twenty-five states plus the *Reichsland* of Alsace–Lorraine, ceded by a defeated France. Crucially, because German unification had been effected by the centralizing dominance of Prussia, the new Germany was a unitary state, with none of the multinationalism that had so weakened its erstwhile rival, Austria.

Meanwhile Paris, which had suffered greatly in the siege, underwent a violent conflict when a municipal council or "commune" was set up in March 1871 with a radical program of decentralization. National troops retook the city in May, at the cost of many thousands dead and imprisoned.

borders, 1848
Denmark, 1848
Italy, 1861
Austrian empire, 1866
France, 1866
Prussia, 1866
other German states, 1866
United Kingdom, 1866
German Confederation, 1866
southern border of North German Confederation, 1867
German empire, 1871
Austro-Prussian campaign, 1864
Prussian advance, with date
modern coastline where altered
0
300 km
0
200 mi
UNITED KINGDOM
London
Dunkirk
BELG
Boulogne
Dieppe
Amiens
1871
1870
St Q
1871
1870
Le Havre
Rouen
6
Champigny
Paris
1870
1870
FRANCE
Seine
Artenay
1870
Troy
Le Mans
1871
Patay
1870
1870
Colmiers
1870
Orléans
Beaugency
1870
Loire
Tours

TIMELINE

Political developments

1848 Franz-Josef becomes emperor of Austria; Louis Napoleon president of France

1849 The German National Assembly is dissolved

1852 The accession of Emperor Napoleon III begins the French second empire

1853 Hanover and Oldenburg join the *Zollverein*

1861 Wilhelm I succeeds to the Prussian throne

1862 Conservative Otto von Bismarck is appointed Prussian minister-president and foreign minister

1866–67 Prussia unilaterally ends the German Confederation and forms the North German Confederation

1870 The "Ems Telegram" arouses French national hostility towards Prussia

1871 Wilhelm I of Prussia is proclaimed emperor of Germany at Versailles

Military developments

1848 Austrian troops crush a Czech revolt in Prague and suppress revolution in Vienna

1857 Helmuth von Moltke is appointed chief of Prussian General Staff

1859 Austrians defeated by France and Sardinia-Piedmont

1863–64 A Prussian–Austrian invasion of Schleswig-Holstein expels the Danes

1866 Seven Weeks War: Austria, defeated by Prussia, loses Holstein and Venetia

1870 Franco-Prussian War begins; emperor Napoleon III surrenders at Sedan; end of the second empire; siege of Paris

1871 The German military occupation of Alsace-Lorraine begins

1850 · 1860 · 1870

Göteborg
SWEDEN
Gotland
Öland
Baltic Sea
North Sea
DENMARK
Copenhagen
Malmö
Fyn
Sjælland
Bornholm
Lolland
Falster
Dybböl
Als
Schleswig
1863 autonomous,
1865 to Prussia
Heligoland
to Britain
Kiel
Holstein
1865 to Austria,
1866 to Prussia
Lübeck
1865 to Prussia
Hamburg
Lauenberg
MECKLENBURG-SCWERIN
Pomerania
Stettin
Danzig
Königsberg
Prussia
RUSSIAN EMPIRE
Vistula
OLDENBURG
Bremen
HANOVER
1866 to Prussia
PRUSSIA
Berlin
Poznan
Warsaw
Amsterdam
ETHERLANDS
Hanover
SCHAUMBURG-LIPPE
BRUNSWICK
Brandenburg
Oder
Posen
Poland
ANHALT
LIPPE-DETMOLD
Westphalia
HESSE-KASSEL
1866 to Prussia
Elbe
Rhine
WALDECK
Saxony
Breslau
Langensalza
1866
Leipzig
Dresden
SAXONY
Silesia
Cologne
NASSAU
1866 to Prussia
THURINGIAN STATES
HESSE-DARMSTADT
Ems
LUXEMBOURG
Frankfurt
Main
Prague
Königgrätz
1866
Austrian Styria
Bohemia
Würzburg
Nuremberg
Moravia
Saarbrücken
LICHTENBERG
Metz
Spicheren
1870
Wissembourg
1870
Wörth
1870
BAVARIA
Stuttgart
Danube
AUSTRIAN EMPIRE
Strasbourg
WÜRTTEMBERG
ALSACE-LORRAINE
to German empire
BADEN
HOHENZOLLERN
1849 to Prussia
Munich
Upper Austria
Vienna
Lower Austria
Pressburg
Villersexel
1870
Salzburg
Buda
Pest
Hungary
Zürich
Lake Constance
Gastein
Lake Balaton
Besançon
LIECHTENSTEIN
Styria
Berne
Tyrol
Carinthia
SWITZERLAND
Lake Geneva
Küstenland
Carniola
Sava
Venetia
1866 to Italy
Savoy
1860 to France
Milan
Lombardy
1859 to Sardinia
then Italy
Custozza
1848, 1866
Venice
Trieste
Adige
Po
Croatia
Turin
Italian capital
1860–65
SARDINIA
1860 to Italy
Parma
1860 to Italy
Modena
1860 to Italy
Genoa
Bologna
1848 to France
SAN MARINO
Dalmatia
Florence
Italian capital
1865–70
MONACO
1861 independent
Adriatic Sea
Siena
PAPAL STATES
1860 to Italy
TUSCANY
1860 to Italy
Lissa
1866
Tiber
Patrimony of St Peter
1870 to Italy
Corsica
Rome
Italian capital
from 1870
KINGDOM OF THE TWO SICILIES
1860 to Italy
Mediterranean Sea
BENEVENTO
1870 to Italy
Sardinia
Naples

BISMARCK was known as the Iron Chancellor, apparently able to bend all Europe to his vision of German strength.

1 The middle-class Frankfurt National Assembly offered the German crown to Frederick William IV of Prussia in 1849. He declined, claiming that only the German princes were entitled to make such an offer.

2 In the Battle of Königgrätz (Sadowa), Prussian breech-loading needle guns had the advantage over Austrian slow muzzle-loading rifles.

3 The Battle of Lissa was fought between ironclad steamships but the Austrian navy triumphed over an Italian force using the ancient technique of ramming.

4 Austria's defeat in 1866 caused internal tensions to resurface in the Habsburg empire; the solution was the compromise (*Ausgleich*) of 1867, which created the Dual Monarchy of Austria–Hungary.

5 Alsace and Lorraine, which had large German-speaking populations, were annexed by Germany in 1871 to weaken France and to satisfy historic claims to the region.

6 Conditions in Paris during the Prussian siege of 1870–71 became so desperate that its inhabitants were compelled to eat the animals in the city's zoo.

See also 5.10 (the rise of nationalism); 5.13 (late 19th-century Europe)

The Russian empire, though ostensibly mighty, had structural weaknesses: above all, its sheer size made it difficult to govern and prevented ready exploitation of its abundant resources. As a result, corruption was rife and the country remained economically underdeveloped. Territorially, Russia continued to expand throughout the 18th and 19th centuries. Catherine the Great's energetic foreign policy added much of Poland and extended Russia's empire in the south. Czar Alexander I (r.1801–25) suffered Napoleon's invasion of 1812 but secured thereby a share of the spoils after the defeat of France. The Congress of Vienna ceded the remainder of Poland to Russia, thus augmenting its recent acquisitions in Finland and Bessarabia.

Territorial expansion left Russian rulers with a permanent fear of rebellion by conquered peoples. During the 1828–29 war with the Turks, Nicholas I (r.1825–55) was able to field barely 180,000 troops, as half a million frontline soldiers were committed to maintaining security in the Baltic provinces and the Caucasus. In 1830, a rising in Poland against Russian rule was only suppressed with difficulty. Internal dissent at autocratic rule began to grow; the "Decembrist" revolt of progressive army officers early in Nicholas I's reign was ruthlessly put down.

The principal aim of Nicholas' foreign policy was dominance over the Ottomans to ensure that Russia's grain exports had free passage across the Black Sea and through the Dardanelles to the Mediterranean. Russia endeavored to absorb Turkey's Balkan possessions and to encourage fellow Slavs to rebel against Ottoman rule in Europe. This policy brought Russia into conflict with the western powers. Britain saw its trade with India threatened by Russian expansion into the eastern Mediterranean, while France was concerned in its role as protector of the Catholic church within Turkish territories. Nicholas' decision to occupy the Ottoman provinces of Moldavia and Wallachia in 1853 provoked Britain and France to invade the Crimea (1854). Once again, mustering sufficient manpower to resist the invaders proved a severe problem.

Russia's defeat in the Crimean War, its withdrawal from Moldavia and Wallachia and the requirement that it "neutralize" the Black Sea compelled Alexander II (r.1855–81) to review his power base. Russian autocracy had always depended on the conscription of serfs, yet such a force was no match for the modern armies of France and Britain. The nobility, whose wealth was grounded in serfdom, was reluctant to innovate or invest in modern industrial plant. To forestall revolution from below, Alexander reformed from above, emancipating the serfs and moving Russia toward a capitalist economy. Even so, millions of former serfs had to pay redemption fees for the lands they tilled. Massive discontent remained, held in check only by conscripts and the secret police; the czar was assassinated in 1881.

Alexander II had begun to tap the vast resources of Siberia, had extended the empire in central Asia and had secured a warm-water port in east Asia. The territory of Alaska was sold to the United States to concentrate development efforts on eastern Siberia and Vladivostok. Alexander's armies gradually sub-

SWEDEN
GERMAN EMPIRE
Danube
Congress Poland 1815 to Russian empire
Finland 1809 to Russian empire
Libau
Revel
Tannenberg 1914
Riga
St Petersburg
Vienna
Warsaw
AUSTRO-HUNGARIAN EMPIRE
Vilna
MONTENEGRO
Minsk
Vitebsk
Archangel
1809–15 to Russian empire
Tarnopol
ALBANIA
Bessarabia 1812 to Russian empire
SERBIA
ROMANIA
BULGARIA
GREECE
Moscow
Yaroslavl
Kotlas
Tula
Ivanovo Voznesensk
Kishinev
Kiev
Odessa
Nikolayev
Kursk
Nizhniy Novgorod
Mediterranean Sea
Constantinople
Yekaterinoslav
Kharkov
Tambov
Volga
Sevastopol
CRIMEA
Berdyans'k
Lugansk
Kazan
Simbirsk
Taganrog
Novocherkassk
Saratov
Perm
Sinope
Rostov
Samara
Black Sea
OTTOMAN EMPIRE
Yekaterinodar
Tsaritsyn
1864 to Russian empire
Tobolsk
Poti
CAUCASUS MTS
Orenburg
URAL
Batumi
Astrakhan
1878 to Russian empire
Tiflis
1859 to Russian empire
Kars
Georgia 1801 to Russian empire
Euphrates
Tigris
Tabriz
Baku
Aral'sk
Aral Sea
Kazalinsk
Caspian Sea
Krasnovodsk
Kazakh Khanates from 1822–54 gained by Russian empire
1873 to Russian empire
Amu Dar'ya
Tehran
Khiva
1873 to Russian empire
Ashkhabad
Lake Balkhash
Merv
Bukhara
Tashkent
Samarkand
PERSIA
Kushka
1868 to Russian empire
AFGHANISTAN
WAKHAN
HINDU KUSH
Kabul
Indus
TIBET
1
2
3
4
5
0 800 km
0 600 mi

TIMELINE

1800 | 1850 | 1900

Domestic developments

1796 Death of Catherine II; brief reign of her son Paul I ends in assassination

1801 Alexander I ascends the throne; kingdom of Georgia voluntarily unites with Russia

1812 Napoleon invades Russia and occupies Moscow, but is forced to withdraw

1825 Accession of Czar Nicholas I; Decembrist revolt of army officers fails

1855 Alexander II becomes czar and institutes reform

1861 Russian serfs are emancipated by the "Czar Liberator" Alexander

1881 Assassination of Alexander II in St Petersburg; Alexander III becomes czar and reasserts autocratic rule

1891 Trans-Siberian Railroad is begun; completed in 1916

1894 Nicholas II, the last czar, ascends the throne

1905 Major uprisings sweep the country and lead to limited constitutional reform

1911 Pyotr Stolypin, reforming prime minister under the first *dumas*, is assassinated

Foreign policy

1810–50 Russia extends its dominion in central Asia

1815 Congress Poland is united with Russian empire, but retains its government

1830–31 Insurrection in Poland is brutally suppressed

1849 Russian troops are sent to crush Hungarian liberals

1854–56 Crimean War; British and French halt Russian Black Sea expansion

1860–70 Russian expansion into Turkestan

1867 Alaska is sold to the United States for US$7.2 million

1877–78 Last of a series of Russo-Turkish wars; creation of the vassal state of Bulgaria

1904–05 Russo-Japanese War; Russian forces are humiliated

1914 Russia mobilizes its army against Germany; on the outbreak of war it suffers a major defeat at the Battle of Tannenberg

1800 | 1850 | 1900

ARCTIC OCEAN
CANADA
Russian America
1867 to United States and renamed Alaska
Gulf of Alaska
Wrangel Island
1867 to Russian empire
Bering Sea
Aleutian Islands
PACIFIC OCEAN
Kureika
Turukhansk
RUSSIAN EMPIRE
Narym
Yenisey
Viluisk
Yakutsk
Tomsk
Krasnoyarsk
Lena
Verkholensk
Shushenskoye
Lake Baykal
Barguzin
Irkutsk
Chita
Kara
Kyakhta
Sea of Okhotsk
Nikolayevsk
1853 to Russian empire
Amur
1858 to Russian empire
Sakhalin
1875 to Russian empire, 1905 to Japan
Kuril Islands
Northern islands to Japan 1875
Khabarovsk
Ussuri
1860 to Russian empire
MONGOLIA
1900–14 under Russian influence
Manchuria
1900–05 Russian occupation
Harbin
Gobi Desert
Vladivostok
Mukden (Shenyang)
Yellow
Beijing
Port Arthur (Lushun)
Sea of Japan
JAPAN
KOREA
Seoul
Lanzhou
Edo (Tokyo)
Tsushima Strait 1905
Yellow Sea
MANCHU EMPIRE
Yangtze
Chongqing
Russian empire, 1802
Russian territorial gains, 1809-55
Russian territorial gains, 1855-1914
Russian sphere of influence, 1907
Austro-Hungarian empire, 1853
Ottoman empire, 1853
"Big Bulgaria", 1878
territory under Japanese control by 1910
Manchu empire, 1912
British India, 1914
British sphere of influence, 1907
border, 1914
Russian urban population, 1914
under 100,000
100,000-500,000
over 500,000
area of heavy grain export
area of heavy industry, 1914
coal mining, 1914
gold mining, 1914
iron ore mining, 1914
oilfield, 1914
port
Tula mutiny or strike, 1905
czarist prison/labor camp
railroad by 1917
trade route
Russian campaign, 1853
Anglo-French campaign, 1854
Jewish Pale of Settlement, subject to pogroms, 1881-1907

1 Catherine II annexed the Crimea in 1783 and ordered the construction of a huge naval facility at Sevastopol; this base was besieged by Anglo-French forces in 1854-56.

2 Congress Poland, so-called because it was awarded to Russia by the Congress of Vienna in 1815, lost its constitution after the 1830 revolt, and was entirely absorbed by Russia after another rebellion in 1863.

3 A strip of mountainous country known as Wakhan was appended to Afghanistan in 1905 to separate conflicting Russian and British interests in the region.

4 The revolution of 1905 spread to the armed forces; sailors of the battleship *Potemkin* seized control of the ship in Odessa and sought asylum in Romania.

5 Count Sergei Witte, Minister of Finance 1892-1903, was the driving force behind the Russian rail network and industrial expansion.

6 The loop of the Trans-Siberian railroad around Lake Baykal was completed in 1915, and the eastern Siberian link in 1916.

7 Thousands of political dissidents were sent to Siberian labor camps by the czarist regime, including the Bolsheviks Lenin (Shushenskoye), Stalin (Kureika), and Trotsky (Verkholensk).

dued the khanates in Bukhara, Khiva and Tashkent south of Lake Balkhash and the Aral Sea. However, a new war against Turkey and the creation of a client state in Bulgaria so alarmed the other great powers that Alexander let the Berlin Congress of 1878 put a brake on his Balkan ambitions.

Under his successor, Alexander III (r. 1881–94), Russia was poised to exploit trade routes in east Asia. The Trans-Siberian Railroad was begun, giving greater access to the mineral wealth of Siberia and central Asia and helping Russian entrepreneurs to penetrate Manchuria and Korea. This expansion brought Russia into collision with Britain and Japan. When antagonism eruped over the Russian occupation of Port Arthur, Japan humiliated the forces of czar Nicholas II (r.1894–1917) in 1904–05. Russia lost south Sakhalin, the lease of Port Arthur and control of the railroads in southern Manchuria.

Discontent grew in European Russia with news of the defeats in the east. In January 1905, a peaceful demonstration in St Petersburg was fired upon by troops. The authorities eventually acceded to liberal demands and allowed an elected national assembly (*duma*) with limited powers. In its foreign relations, Russia agreed "spheres of influence" in Persia with Britain in 1907. However, Russian interest revived in seeking access to the Mediterranean through the Balkans. Pan-Slavic Russian involvement with militant Serb groups opposing Austrian domination fueled the Balkan crisis of 1914 that sparked World War I. Within three years, Russia was beaten and the empire of the Russian czars had collapsed.

See also 4.13 (18th-century Russia); 5.20 (Russo-Japanese war); 6.15 (Russian revolution)

The European alliance system • 1871 – 1914 •

Bismarck, who initiated the complex web of alliances that developed after the Franco–Prussian War, now had as his ultimate objective the preservation of peace on the continent. He aimed to prevent France from launching a war of revenge by isolating it from any potential ally.

Bismarck's first step was to form the league of Three Emperors (*Dreikaiserbund*) between Germany, Austria–Hungary and Russia in 1873. In doing so, he had to reconcile a number of conflicting interests. Since the Crimean War, Russia had tried to reassert its position in Europe by championing the cause of Slav freedom from Austrian and Turkish rule. This brought Austria and Russia into conflict, as both empires cherished ambitions to secure the Balkan lands of the moribund Ottoman empire. The loose alliance that Bismarck forged was designed to stabilize southeast Europe, as its signatories agreed to act in concert against subversive movements in the region. In 1878, however, the Congress of Berlin forced Russia to renounce some of the excessive Balkan gains it had wrested from Turkey in 1877–78.

The chief beneficiary of the Berlin Congress was Austria, which negotiated a secret, defensive Dual Alliance with Germany (who, in World War I, were known as the Central powers). This relationship was to be the main focus of Bismarck's subsequent diplomacy; he publicly renewed the *Dreikaiserbund* in 1881 and distracted France by encouraging its colonial ambitions in north Africa, but secretly created a Triple Alliance between Germany, Austria and Italy.

When the *Dreikaiserbund* expired in 1887, Bismarck replaced it with a bilateral Reinsurance Treaty, which recognized the Balkans as a Russian sphere of influence and confirmed that Russia and Germany would stay neutral unless Germany attacked France, or Russia attacked Austria. This represented the pinnacle of Bismarck's diplomacy, which sought to secure German predominance in central Europe and avoid dangerous adventurism.

In 1890, a sea-change occurred in the politics of European alliances, when growing antagonism between the headstrong new emperor Wilhelm II and Bismarck brought the latter's resignation. The Reinsurance Treaty was allowed to lapse without renewal and the Russian harvest failed the same year. France offered aid to Russia, so laying the groundwork for a military alliance. This was duly signed in 1894, with the critical provision that if a Triple Alliance country mobilized its armies then Russia and France would do likewise. Mobilization of any armed forces was thus likely to lead to war.

- border proposed by the Treaty of San Stefano, 1878
- borders, 1912
- Allied powers, Aug 1914
- Central powers, Aug 1914

Schlieffen plan, 1905
- German army position
- route of German attack

- fortress of the Central powers
- fortress of the Allied powers
- Belgian fortress
- major naval base
- major armaments center
- league of Three Emperors, 1873–87
- Triple Alliance, 1882–1915
- *Entente Cordiale*, 1904
- Triple Entente, 1907
- key railroad line for transferring German troops to Russian front
- anticipated Russian attack
- Slavic language in central Europe

EUROPEAN royalty in the early 20th century had close family ties; Britain's King George V (shown here with Queen Mary) was cousin to Wilhelm II.

TIMELINE

1890 · 1910

Alliances and ententes

- **1873** Bismarck negotiates the League of the Three Emperors (*Dreikaiserbund*)
- **1879** Dual Alliance: Germany and Austria-Hungary
- **1882** Italy joins the Dual Alliance, thus creating the Triple Alliance
- **1887** German Reinsurance Treaty with Russia
- **1890** Bismarck resigns over differences with Kaiser Wilhelm II
- **1894** Franco-Russian military alliance is announced after France aids Russian famine
- **1902** The Anglo-Japanese Naval Alliance guarantees naval security in east Asia
- **1904** *Entente Cordiale* signed between Britian and France
- **1907** Agreement between Britain and Russia results in a Triple Entente in Europe
- **1914** Germany pledges total support ("Blank Check") for Austrian actions in Balkans

Crises and rearmament

- **1875–78** Eastern crisis begins when Bosnia and Herzegovina rebel against Turks
- **1877–78** Russo-Turkish War ends; Russia gains much from the Treaty of San Stefano
- **1878** The Congress of Berlin compels Russia to reduce its recent gains in the Balkans
- **1885–86** Tension between Austria and Russia over Bulgaria destroys the *Dreikaiserbund*
- **1889** Britain guarantees dominance of the Royal Navy
- **1898** Fashoda crisis: a clash between French and British military missions in Sudan causes mutual hostility
- **1900** Second German Naval Law (First 1898) confirms growth of the Imperial Navy
- **1905–06** German colonial ambitions spark the first Morocco crisis
- **1906** HMS *Dreadnought* revolutionizes warship design
- **1908** Austria–Hungary annexes Bosnia–Herzegovina
- **1911** The visit of a German gunboat to Agadir causes the second Morocco crisis
- **1914** The Sarajevo crisis leads to Austrian bombardment of Belgrade, Russian mobilization and war

1890 · 1910

Britain had stood aloof from these alliances but after the death of Queen Victoria in 1901 the new king Edward VII made overtures to France that culminated in the *Entente Cordiale* of 1904. A similar agreement was made with Russia in 1907, forming a Triple Entente (of what became known as the "Allied powers" in 1914) to balance the Triple Alliance.

Several international incidents occurred that tested the commitment of the European powers to peace. Germany's claims to Morocco ran into opposition from both Britain and France, and resulted in the Tangier crisis (1905), settled at the Algeciras conference, and the Agadir crisis of 1911, which resulted in German recognition of France's claim to Morocco. The Balkans, too, continued to provide a highly charged arena. The Balkan peoples tried to organize

1 The Treaty of San Stefano concluded between Russia and Turkey in 1878 envisaged the creation of a large new Bulgarian state beholden to Russia.

2 In France in 1886–89, a vociferous *revanche* ("revenge") movement arose over Alsace-Lorraine, headed by war minister Georges Boulanger.

3 From 1887–89, British prime minister Lord Salisbury resisted Bismarck's requests for an Anglo-German alliance. Salisbury described Britain's disdain for alliances as "splendid isolation."

4 One of the greatest European industrial complexes was the Skoda Works in Pilsen, built to produce a new machine-gun for the Austrian army in 1890.

5 Britain transferred sovereignty of the North Sea island of Heligoland (Helgoland) to Germany in return for Zanzibar in 1890. Germany developed Helgoland into a major naval base.

6 The *Entente Cordiale* was tested in 1905, when Wilhelm II spoke in Tangier in favor of Moroccan independence. The Algeçiras conference in 1906 upheld French claims to the territory.

into nation-states and the Balkan Wars of 1912 and 1913 radically transformed the map of southeast Europe, arousing the hostility of Austria–Hungary.

Throughout this period, plans were made for war. The most ambitious was devised by the German chief of staff, Alfred von Schlieffen, for a war on two fronts. The Schlieffen plan required a surprise push through neutral Holland, Belgium and Luxembourg to isolate Paris from the coast and encircle the French armies. Troops would then be transferred by rail to reinforce the eastern front against Russia, which was expected to attack near Königsberg .

Rapid developments were also made in armaments. Germany produced medium and heavy artillery of high quality, France excelled in rapid-fire field guns, while all countries were perfecting the machine-gun. At sea, the British *Dreadnought* class of battleship, begun in 1906, inaugurated a new era of naval design. Heavily armored, equipped entirely with big guns and driven by steam turbines, these ships started a race to build ever more powerful fleets. Wilhelm II was especially keen to develop the navy to challenge the might of Britain's Royal Navy.

Conscription swelled the size of the continent's armies. Most German youth served for three years in the army corps; French conscripts served for two. Both these countries (and Italy) could mobilize a million men within days. Austria and Russia could call on three times this number, though more slowly. The threat of war had loomed for so long over Europe that by 1914 all countries had arsenals and forces of unparalleled size and efficiency.

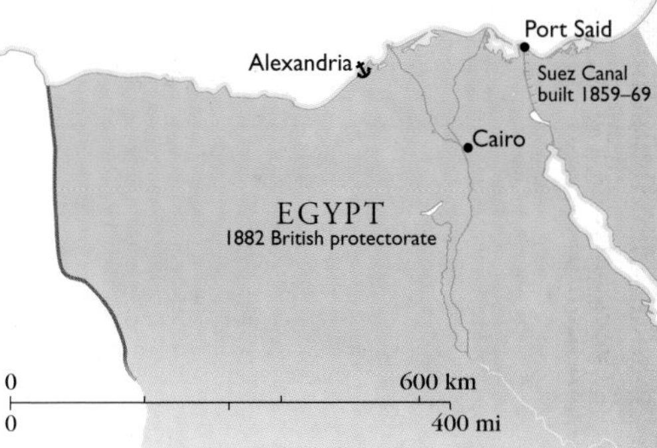

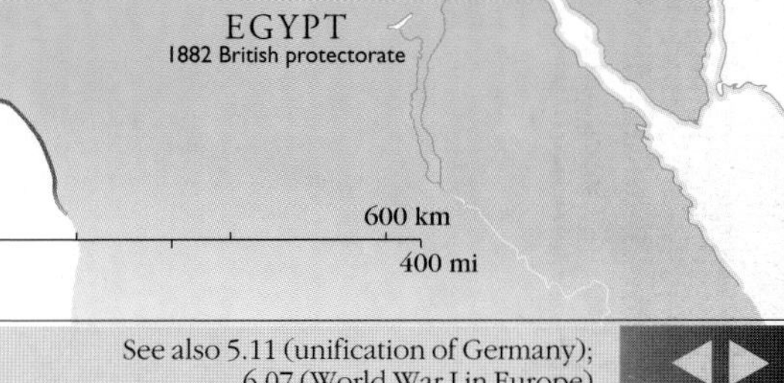
Port Said
Alexandria
Suez Canal
built 1859–69
Cairo
EGYPT
1882 British protectorate
0
600 km
0
400 mi

See also 5.11 (unification of Germany); 6.07 (World War I in Europe)

5.14 The decline of Ottoman power • 1783 – 1923 •

In the late 18th century the Europeans continued to encroach on the Ottoman empire. In a second war against the Turks (1787–92), Catherine II of Russia failed to partition the Ottoman empire, but still extended Russian control of the northern Black Sea coast. Further losses were incurred in 1806–12, when Russia gained Bessarabia. Insurrections also broke out in Serbia in 1804 and 1817. Later attempts by the Ottomans to regain control of Serbia and the Principalities (Wallachia and Moldavia) resulted in the Russo-Turkish war of 1828–29, and the concession of Serbian autonomy.

Yet the most serious threat to the empire's survival during this period came from its vassal state of Egypt. Napoleon's invasion of 1798 profoundly altered Egypt's internal politics: Mehmet Ali, an Albanian officer of the force sent by Sultan Selim III to expel the French, seized control of the moribund state, becoming viceroy in 1805. At first, this dynamic modernizing ruler aided the Ottomans, ending the occupation of the Muslim holy sites of Arabia by the fanatical Wahhabi sect and acceding to Sultan Mahmud II's request in 1825 for help in the Greek War of Independence. However, in 1831 Mehmet Ali and his son Ibrahim Pasha (commander of the Egyptian force in Greece) invaded Syria to assert their authority against the sultan. Ottoman power was almost broken by defeats in 1832 at Konya in Anatolia, and in 1839 at Nezib (northern Syria), but the empire was saved by the Austrians and the British, who feared that a power vacuum in the region would threaten their links with India.

Further western support for the Ottomans appeared during the Crimean War. This arose from a Russian claim to protect Orthodox Christians in Ottoman European territories, and was fueled by disagreements between Russia and France over the administration of holy sites in Jerusalem. Russia invaded Moldavia and Wallachia, and in response Turkey (supported by Britain and France) declared war. Turkey's naval defeat at Sinope was followed by British and French assaults on the Crimea. The outcome of the war was a united Romania (in 1861) and a great power agreement to preserve the diminishing Ottoman empire.

French influence in the Levant grew after France sent an expedition to Syria in 1860 to halt a massacre of Maronite Christians. France had also gained the concession to build the Suez Canal in 1854 (completed in 1869). However, the debt-ridden *khedive* (the Ottoman viceroy of Egypt's new title) sold his canal shares to Britain in 1875. Arab nationalists led by Urabi Pasha now began to agitate against European influence in Egyptian affairs. France and Britain gradually adopted a more interventionist approach toward Ottoman survival. France established a protectorate in Tunisia in 1881, and Egypt, nominally still an autonomous viceroyalty of the Ottoman empire, was occupied by Britain.

North Sea
SWEDEN
DENMARK
Baltic
Elbe
Berlin
Oder
NETHERLANDS
GERMAN EMPIRE
BELGIUM
LUXEMBOURG
Karlsruhe
Stuttgart
Danube
Rhine
Paris
Vienna
Munich
Loire
LIECHTENSTEIN
SWITZERLAND
FRANCE
Bosnia–Herzegovina
1908 to Austro-Hungarian empire
SAN MARINO
MONACO
ITALY
MONTENEGRO
1878 independence
Marseille
Toulon
Rome
ANDORRA
Corsica
Douro
Ebro
SPAIN
Madrid
Tagus
Guadiana
PORTUGAL
1830
1881
Sardinia
Balearic Islands
2
Sicily
Algiers
Bone
Bizerte
Tunis
Gibraltar
to Britain
Tangier
Oran
Tunisia
1871 autonomous
1881 French protectorate
Malta
Spanish Morocco
1912 Spanish protectorate
1852
Algeria
1830/48 to France
4
Casablanca
French Morocco
1912 French protectorate
Laghouat
Tripoli
Tripolitania
1912 to Italy
2
Fezzan
1842 to Ottoman empire
Murzaq
Ottoman empire, 1800
Ottoman territory lost, 1805–1914
Wahhabi influence
Wahhabi attack
"Big Bulgaria" devised by Russia, 1878
borders, 1914
Ottoman empire, 1914
Austro-Hungarian empire, 1914
British territory, 1914
British sphere of influence, 1907
French territory, 1914
Italian territory, 1914
Russian empire, 1914
Russian sphere of influence, 1907
Spanish territory, 1914
Turkey, 1923
revolt or uprising
known oilfield, 1914
Orient Express railroad, 1800
extension of Orient Express to Berlin and Baghdad
Hejaz railroad
campaign of Mehmet Ali and Ibrahim
French campaign
Italian campaign
Russian campaign, 1877–78

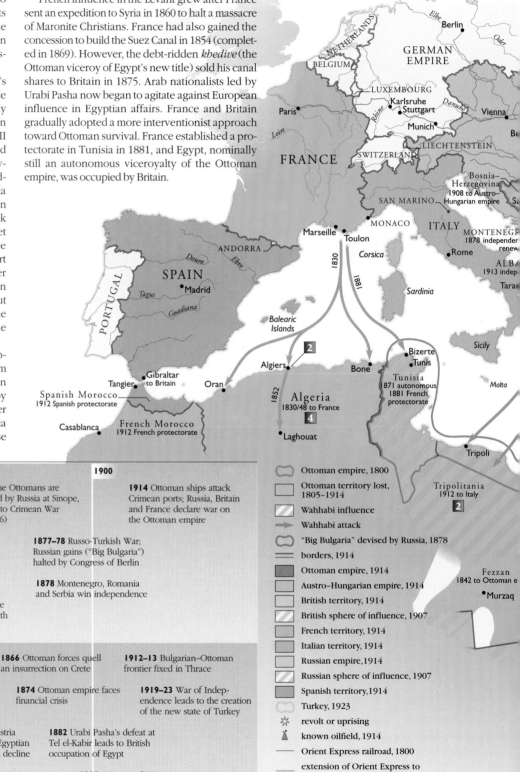

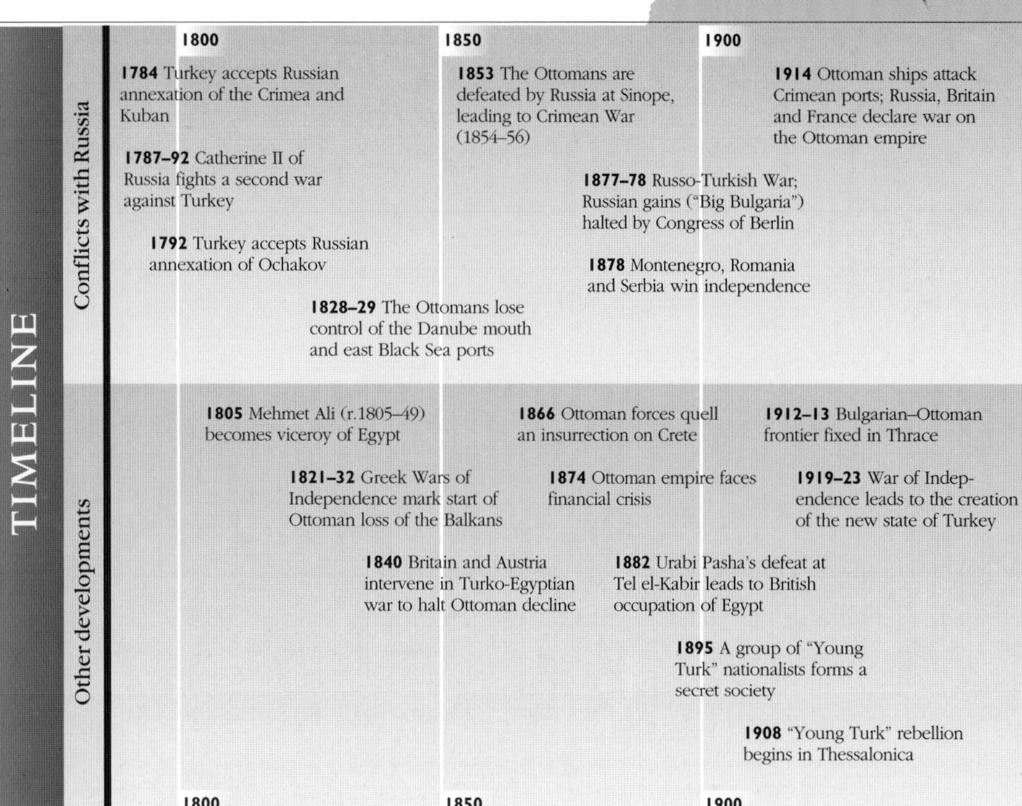
TIMELINE
Conflicts with Russia
1800
1850
1900
1784 Turkey accepts Russian annexation of the Crimea and Kuban
1787–92 Catherine II of Russia fights a second war against Turkey
1792 Turkey accepts Russian annexation of Ochakov
1828–29 The Ottomans lose control of the Danube mouth and east Black Sea ports
1853 The Ottomans are defeated by Russia at Sinope, leading to Crimean War (1854–56)
1877–78 Russo-Turkish War; Russian gains ("Big Bulgaria") halted by Congress of Berlin
1878 Montenegro, Romania and Serbia win independence
1914 Ottoman ships attack Crimean ports; Russia, Britain and France declare war on the Ottoman empire
Other developments
1805 Mehmet Ali (r.1805–49) becomes viceroy of Egypt
1821–32 Greek Wars of Independence mark start of Ottoman loss of the Balkans
1840 Britain and Austria intervene in Turko-Egyptian war to halt Ottoman decline
1866 Ottoman forces quell an insurrection on Crete
1874 Ottoman empire faces financial crisis
1882 Urabi Pasha's defeat at Tel el-Kabir leads to British occupation of Egypt
1895 A group of "Young Turk" nationalists forms a secret society
1908 "Young Turk" rebellion begins in Thessalonica
1912–13 Bulgarian–Ottoman frontier fixed in Thrace
1919–23 War of Independence leads to the creation of the new state of Turkey
1800
1850
1900

Nationalist rebellions in Bosnia–Herzegovina, Serbia, Bulgaria and Montenegro provoked yet another Russian invasion of the Ottoman empire (1877); the ensuing Peace of San Stefano created a pro-Russian "Big Bulgaria". Yet a Congress of European powers at Berlin in 1878 revised these frontiers to check Russian expansion. The Ottomans' last foothold in Bulgaria – eastern Rumelia – was lost when this province rebelled and merged with Bulgaria in 1885–88

In 1898, a surprise visit to Constantinople by Kaiser Wilhelm II consolidated a growing Ottoman association with Germany. Turkey and Germany agreed to extend the Orient Express railroad across Asia Minor to Baghdad. Subsequently Sultan Abdul Hamid II raised Muslim subscriptions to build the Hejaz railroad between Damascus and Medina.

Fears for the continuing demise of the Ottoman empire led disaffected army officers under Enver Pasha – the "Young Turks" – to overthrow Abdul Hamid in 1909. The reformers promoted westernization, but foreign encroachment began again. Austria annexed Bosnia–Herzegovina in 1908, Italy took Tripolitania in 1912, and two Balkan wars (1912–13) were precipitated, further reducing the Ottoman empire. Apart from eastern Thrace, all the European and north African provinces had now vanished.

In 1914 Turkey's new rulers staked its future on a secret alliance with Germany. The Treaty of Sèvres (1920), signed upon the defeat of the Central powers, stripped the Ottoman empire of all its non-Turkish regions. After capitulation, a war of independence was waged by nationalists under Kemal Atatürk from 1919–23, which drove foreign forces from Anatolia. In 1923 the Ottoman empire ceased to exist, after more than six hundred years.

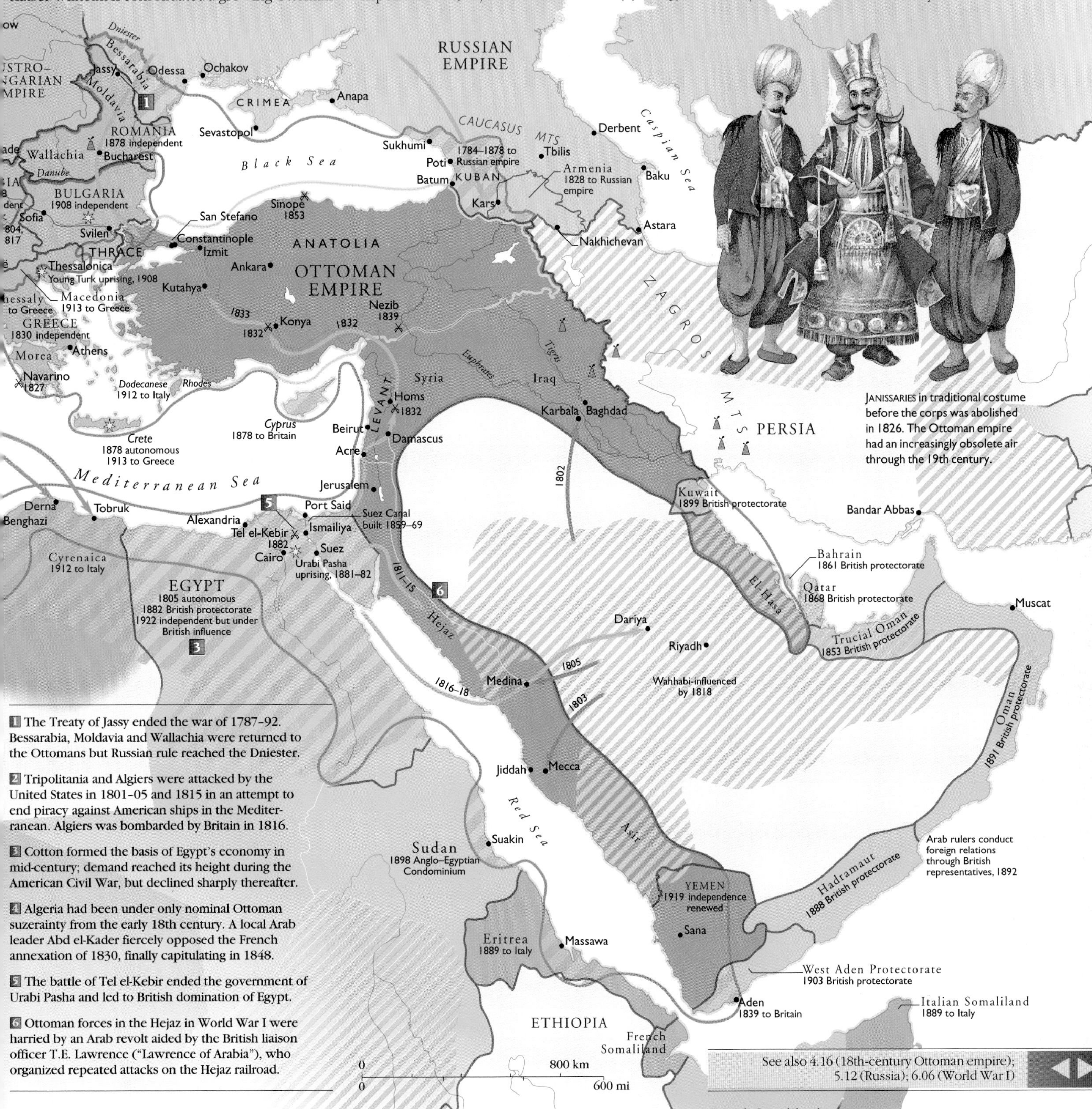
RUSSIAN EMPIRE
Dniester
Bessarabia
Moldavia
Jassy
Odessa
Ochakov
CRIMEA
Anapa
Sevastopol
ROMANIA
1878 independent
Wallachia
Bucharest
Danube
BULGARIA
1908 independent
Sofia
Svilen
THRACE
San Stefano
Constantinople
Izmit
Black Sea
Sinope
1853
CAUCASUS MTS
Sukhumi
Poti
1784–1878 to Russian empire
Batum
KUBAN
Kars
Tbilisis
Armenia
1828 to Russian empire
Derbent
Baku
Caspian Sea
Astara
Nakhichevan
ANATOLIA
OTTOMAN EMPIRE
Ankara
Kutahya
Konya
1833
1832
Nezib
1839
Thessalonica
Young Turk uprising, 1908
Macedonia
1913 to Greece
Thessaly
to Greece
GREECE
1830 independent
Morea
Athens
Navarino
1827
Dodecanese
1912 to Italy
Rhodes
Crete
1878 autonomous
1913 to Greece
Cyprus
1878 to Britain
Syria
Euphrates
Tigris
Iraq
LEVANT
Homs
1832
Beirut
Damascus
Acre
Karbala
Baghdad
ZAGROS MTS
PERSIA
Mediterranean Sea
Jerusalem
Port Said
Suez Canal
built 1859–69
Ismailiya
Suez
Alexandria
Tel el-Kebir
1882
Cairo
Urabi Pasha uprising, 1881–82
Derna
Tobruk
Benghazi
Cyrenaica
1912 to Italy
EGYPT
1805 autonomous
1882 British protectorate
1922 independent but under British influence
1802
Kuwait
1899 British protectorate
Bandar Abbas
Bahrain
1861 British protectorate
Qatar
1868 British protectorate
El-Hasa
Trucial Oman
1853 British protectorate
Muscat
1811–15
Hejaz
Dariya
Riyadh
1805
Medina
1816–18
1803
Wahhabi-influenced by 1818
Oman
1891 British protectorate
Jiddah
Mecca
Red Sea
Asir
Suakin
Sudan
1898 Anglo-Egyptian Condominium
Arab rulers conduct foreign relations through British representatives, 1892
Hadramaut
1888 British protectorate
YEMEN
1919 independence renewed
Sana
Eritrea
1889 to Italy
Massawa
West Aden Protectorate
1903 British protectorate
Aden
1839 to Britain
Italian Somaliland
1889 to Italy
ETHIOPIA
French Somaliland
British Somaliland
1884 to Britain
0
800 km
0
600 mi

JANISSARIES in traditional costume before the corps was abolished in 1826. The Ottoman empire had an increasingly obsolete air through the 19th century.

1 The Treaty of Jassy ended the war of 1787–92. Bessarabia, Moldavia and Wallachia were returned to the Ottomans but Russian rule reached the Dniester.

2 Tripolitania and Algiers were attacked by the United States in 1801–05 and 1815 in an attempt to end piracy against American ships in the Mediterranean. Algiers was bombarded by Britain in 1816.

3 Cotton formed the basis of Egypt's economy in mid-century; demand reached its height during the American Civil War, but declined sharply thereafter.

4 Algeria had been under only nominal Ottoman suzerainty from the early 18th century. A local Arab leader Abd el-Kader fiercely opposed the French annexation of 1830, finally capitulating in 1848.

5 The battle of Tel el-Kebir ended the government of Urabi Pasha and led to British domination of Egypt.

6 Ottoman forces in the Hejaz in World War I were harried by an Arab revolt aided by the British liaison officer T.E. Lawrence ("Lawrence of Arabia"), who organized repeated attacks on the Hejaz railroad.

See also 4.16 (18th-century Ottoman empire); 5.12 (Russia); 6.06 (World War I)

5.15 Africa before the scramble • 1800 – 1880 •

Before the late 19th century European settlement of Africa was mostly confined to French colonization of Algeria, a few Spanish settlements, British and French trading stations in west Africa and Portuguese trade along the coast. Native peoples offered stern resistance, notably the Asante of west Africa. The largest European presence was formed by Afrikaner and British settlers in southern Africa, first in Cape Colony and (after the Great Trek, which began in 1835–36) in the Orange Free State and Transvaal. Disruption was caused by population movements, expansion by indigenous states such as Egypt, holy wars (*jihads*), the continuing slave trade and the emergence of new empires in east, central and west Africa.

Zulu expansion led to an extensive migration of warriors known as the *mfecane*, a condition of almost perpetual conflict. Shaka, who formed the Zulu kingdom from 1816, initiated a period of expansion in southern Africa. Zulu victories caused a chain-reaction among other nations, which surrendered to the Zulu confederacy or came into conflict with other nations as they fled. New states emerged, including Moshoeshoe's Lesotho, Msawati's Swazi kingdom and Mzilikazi's kingdom of Ndebele.

In west Africa, Usman dan Fodio (1754–1816) proclaimed himself the harbinger of the *Mahdi*, the Islamic Messiah, and aimed to create a unified Muslim state in Hausaland. He established the Sokoto caliphate which his successors built into a well-administered empire that survived until the 20th century. To the west, Sheikh Ahmad Lobbo led the Masina *jihad*, with its capital at Hamdallahi; his rival Al Hajj Umar created the Tukulor caliphate with the aid of followers from Futa Toro and Futa Jalon. Another military leader, Samori Toure, brought order, prosperity and Islamic law to a diverse set of peoples torn by commercial and religious conflict where he created the First Samori empire.

The trade in slaves was abolished by Denmark, Britain, France and the United States in the early 19th century, but Portugal allowed it to continue until 1882. Over 50,000 slaves a year were taken from Angola and Madagascar to South America and (up to 1865) illegally into the United States. The trans-Saharan and east African slave trades also flourished.

1 Sierra Leone was established by philanthropists as a home for freed British slaves in 1787. It became a British colony in 1808.

2 The conquests of the Zulu king Shaka (r.1816–28) were based on his of effective tactics of encirclement and on the new *assegai*, a deadly stabbing spear.

3 Kazembe was envied for its prosperity and subjected to constant attacks by Utetera, Yeke Katanga and Bemba.

4 In 1820, an army under the formidable Egyptian commander Ismail Pasha conquered Nilotic Sudan in search of gold and slaves.

5 The American explorer-journalist H.M. Stanley created the direct link between exploration and colonization. In 1874, he journeyed into central Africa to discover suitable colonies for Leopold II of Belgium.

A permanent settlement of the Omani Arabs in Zanzibar guaranteed a demand for African slaves in the Middle East and Asia. Not until 1873 did Britain manage to persuade the sultan of Zanzibar to close the slave market. Many African peoples became closely involved in the slave trade; the Yao and Nyamwezi, for example, depopulated much of east Africa in search of slaves for their plantations.

The presence of Muslim slave traders – Swahilis, Arabs, Egyptians and Sudanese – led to a spate of African state-building. Commercial empires such as Tippu Tip's Sultanate of Utetera emerged. This was at its peak by 1880, dealing in slaves and ivory throughout east central Africa. The Nyamwezi formed the trading empires of Urambo, Ukimbu and Unyanyembe. One outstanding leader, Mirambo (or Mbulya Mtelala), expanded Urambo and commanded a professional army of 50,000 riflemen. On the floodplain of the upper Zambezi was the rich, centralized Lozi empire, while to the northeast lay Kazembe, a prosperous agricultural state. In Angola Cokwe hunters successfully expanded their ivory exports and developed rubber plantations.

African leaders who had abandoned the slave trade now depended on export of commodities. In west Africa exports of timber, gum, gold, beeswax, ivory and hides doubled 1808–80. There was also a growing interior trade in kola nuts. Everywhere, Africans and Europeans were in conflict over trade and access to raw materials; the ensuing rivalries created the conditions for partition. The Africans' confidence that they could stop Europeans from advancing inland, though, proved to be misplaced.

European explorers increased in number and ambition. In 1827–28, the Frenchman René-Auguste Caillé traveled through west Africa, an area also charted by the German Heinrich Barth on behalf of the British in the 1850s. The greatest explorer was the Scottish missionary David Livingstone, who journeyed extensively in central and southern Africa from 1840 and fought to destroy the slave trade. With the discovery of mineral wealth in southern Africa in the 1870s there began the "scramble" for Africa, a more systematic encroachment; the continent was almost totally colonized by 1900.

David Livingstone combined geographical, religious, commercial, and humanitarian goals in his exploration journeys.

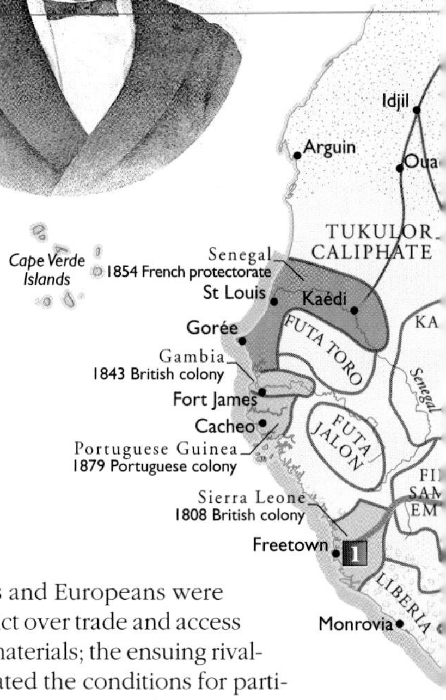

TIMELINE

1800 · 1825 · 1850 · 1875

West Africa

- **1783** France recovers Senegal at the end of the American War of Independence
- **1787** 400 freed slaves are settled in Sierra Leone
- **1804** Usman dan Fodio begins a *jihad*
- **1821** Hamdallahi becomes capital of a new Masina state
- **1822** Liberia is founded for freed US slaves
- **1826** The Asante are defeated by British in the first of four wars (to 1896)
- **1841** The Ibadan empire begins its expansion in quest of slaves and tribute
- **1849** France founds Libreville for freed slaves
- **1861** Britain annexes Lagos and begins to suppress the Sokoto caliphate
- **1865** Samori Toure (1830–90) founds his first Madinka empire

N. & E. Africa

- **1806** Sayyid Said rebuilds Omani power in east Africa
- **1820** Ismail Pasha begins his invasion of Sudan
- **1830** The French conquest of Algeria begins
- **1840** Death of Kazembe IV, with his empire at its peak
- **1850** Tippu Tip introduces large trading caravans in east Africa
- **1855** Emperor Tewedros revives Ethiopian empire
- **1873–76** Britain persuades the sultan Barghash of Zanzibar to suppress slavery
- **1875** Egypt moves into the Horn of Africa

South Africa

- **1810** The kingdom of Merina gains control of Madagascar
- **1816** Shaka is made *Inkosi*, king of the Zulus
- **1835–36** The Great Trek begins to leave Cape Colony
- **1840** Mzilikazi founds the Ndebele kingdom
- **1868** French commercial treaty with Madagascar signed
- **1879** Britain defeats the Zulu kingdom

1800 · 1825 · 1850 · 1875

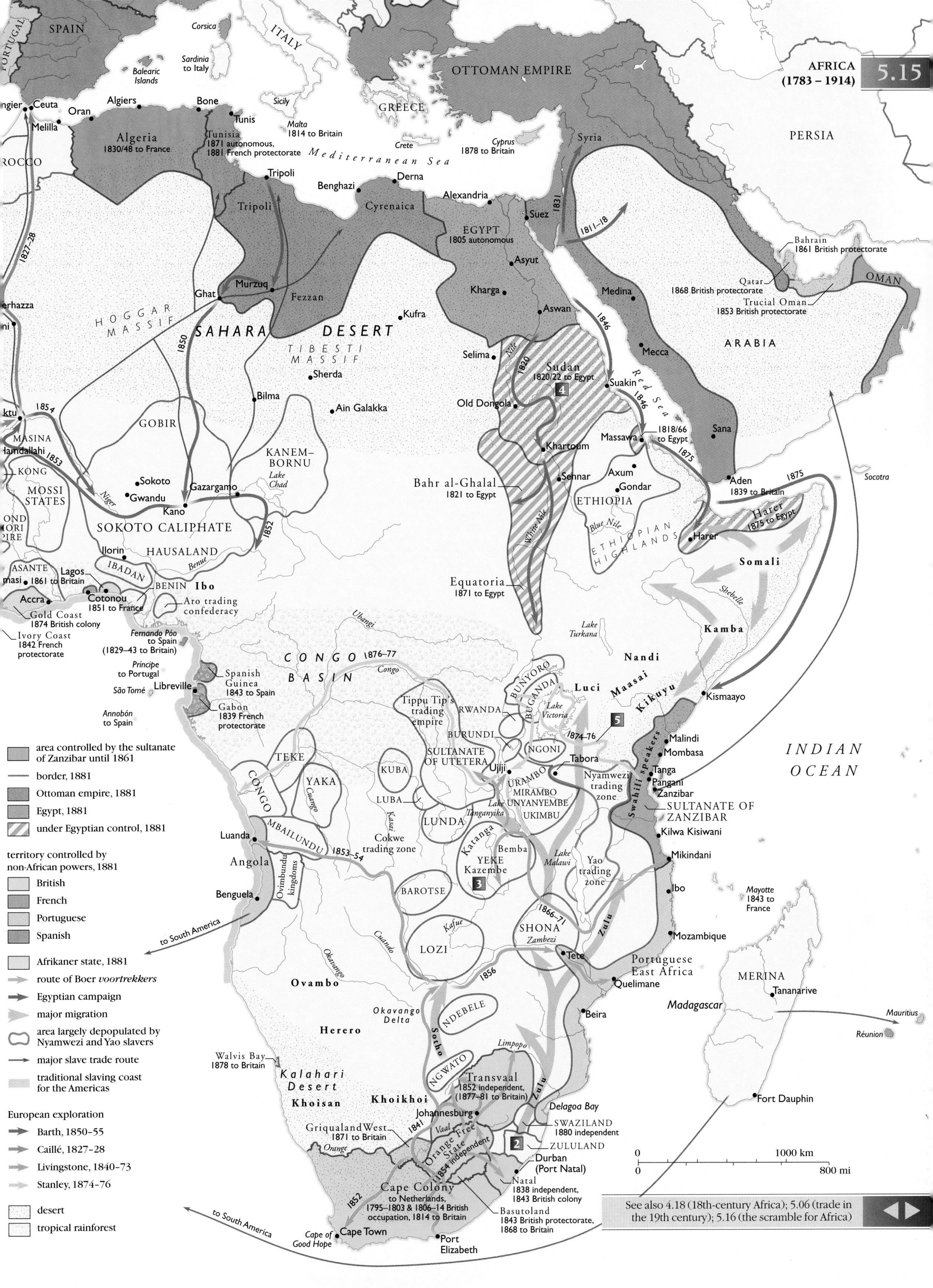
AFRICA
(1783 – 1914)
5.15
SPAIN
PORTUGAL
Corsica
ITALY
Sardinia to Italy
Balearic Islands
OTTOMAN EMPIRE
Tangier
Ceuta
Melilla
Oran
Algiers
Bone
Tunis
Sicily
GREECE
Malta 1814 to Britain
Crete
Cyprus 1878 to Britain
PERSIA
Algeria 1830/48 to France
Tunisia 1871 autonomous, 1881 French protectorate
Mediterranean Sea
Syria
MOROCCO
Tripoli
Derna
Benghazi
Cyrenaica
Alexandria
Suez
1831
1811–18
EGYPT 1805 autonomous
Asyut
Bahrain 1861 British protectorate
Qatar 1868 British protectorate
Trucial Oman 1853 British protectorate
OMAN
1827–28
Ghat
Murzuq
Fezzan
Kharga
Medina
Aswan
1846
HOGGAR MASSIF
SAHARA DESERT
Kufra
TIBESTI MASSIF
1850
Mecca
ARABIA
Selima
Nile
1820
Sudan 1820/22 to Egypt
4
Suakin
Red Sea
1846
Sherda
Bilma
Ain Galakka
Old Dongola
GOBIR
1854
MASINA
Hamdallahi
1853
KANEM-BORNU
Lake Chad
Khartoum
Massawa
1818/66 to Egypt
1875
Sana
KONG
MOSSI STATES
Sokoto
Gwandu
Niger
Gazargamo
Kano
Bahr al-Ghalal 1821 to Egypt
Sennar
Axum
Gondar
ETHIOPIA
Aden 1839 to Britain
1875
Socotra
SOKOTO CALIPHATE
1852
Harer 1875 to Egypt
Harer
Blue Nile
ETHIOPIAN HIGHLANDS
White Nile
Ilorin
HAUSALAND
Benue
ASANTE
1861 to Britain
Lagos
IBADAN
BENIN
Ibo
Somali
Accra
Cotonou 1851 to France
Aro trading confederacy
Equatoria 1871 to Egypt
Shebelle
Gold Coast 1874 British colony
Ivory Coast 1842 French protectorate
Fernando Póo to Spain (1829–43 to Britain)
Ubangi
Lake Turkana
Kamba
CONGO BASIN
1876–77
Congo
Nandi
Principe to Portugal
São Tomé
Spanish Guinea 1843 to Spain
Libreville
Gabon 1839 French protectorate
Annobón to Spain
BUNYORO
BUGANDA
Luci
Maasai
Kikuyu
Kismaayo
Lake Victoria
Tippu Tip's trading empire
RWANDA
BURUNDI
5
1874–76
NGONI
Malindi
Mombasa
INDIAN OCEAN
SULTANATE OF UTETERA
Ujiji
Tabora
Tanga
Pangani
Zanzibar
TEKE
CONGO
YAKA
Cuango
KUBA
LUBA
Kasai
URAMBO
MIRAMBO
UNYANYEMBE
UKIMBU
Lake Tanganyika
Nyamwezi trading zone
Swahili speakers
SULTANATE OF ZANZIBAR
Luanda
MBAILUNDU
1853–54
LUNDA
Cokwe trading zone
Katanga
Bemba
YEKE
Kazembe
3
Lake Malawi
Yao trading zone
Kilwa Kisiwani
Mikindani
Angola
Ovimbundu kingdoms
Benguela
BAROTSE
Ibo
Mayotte 1843 to France
1866–71
to South America
Cuando
Kafue
SHONA
Zambezi
Zulu
Mozambique
LOZI
Okavango
1856
Tete
Portuguese East Africa
Quelimane
MERINA
Tananarive
Ovambo
NDEBELE
Okavango Delta
Madagascar
Beira
Mauritius
Réunion
Herero
Sotho
Limpopo
Walvis Bay 1878 to Britain
NGWATO
Transvaal 1852 independent, (1877–81 to Britain)
Zulu
Kalahari Desert
Khoisan
Khoikhoi
Delagoa Bay
Fort Dauphin
Johannesburg
SWAZILAND 1880 independent
1841
Vaal
Griqualand West 1871 to Britain
Orange Free State 1854 independent
2
ZULULAND
Orange
Durban (Port Natal)
0 1000 km
0 800 mi
Cape Colony to Netherlands, 1795–1803 & 1806–14 British occupation, 1814 to Britain
Natal 1838 independent, 1843 British colony
1852
Basutoland 1843 British protectorate, 1868 to Britain
Cape of Good Hope
Cape Town
Port Elizabeth
to South America
area controlled by the sultanate of Zanzibar until 1861
border, 1881
Ottoman empire, 1881
Egypt, 1881
under Egyptian control, 1881
territory controlled by non-African powers, 1881
British
French
Portuguese
Spanish
Afrikaner state, 1881
route of Boer voortrekkers
Egyptian campaign
major migration
area largely depopulated by Nyamwezi and Yao slavers
major slave trade route
traditional slaving coast for the Americas
European exploration
Barth, 1850–55
Caillé, 1827–28
Livingstone, 1840–73
Stanley, 1874–76
desert
tropical rainforest
See also 4.18 (18th-century Africa); 5.06 (trade in the 19th century); 5.16 (the scramble for Africa)

5.16 Africa and the European empires • 1880 – 1914 •

In 1884–85 representatives of fifteen European nations met in Berlin to settle rival claims to Africa. The Berlin Conference did not designate specific regions as colonies; rather it established the broad principles of the "scramble for Africa". The hinterland of a coast occupied by a European power was defined as a sphere of influence. To claim it, a power had to show itself capable of protecting "existing rights" and "freedom of trade and transit". This doctrine of "effective occupation" meant the process of colonization was conducted violently. Although the partition of Africa occurred quickly, it was the climax of years of activity by traders, administrators, soldiers and missionaries.

Africans were confronted with sudden piecemeal colonization. Some European governments worked through commercial ventures such as the Portuguese Niassa Company, the German South West and East Africa Companies, the Imperial East Africa Company, the Royal Niger Company and the British South Africa Company. By crudely imposing western practices – abolishing existing currencies, introducing hut taxes and removing middlemen from established trade patterns – these companies sowed the seeds of confrontation and armed resistance. In other cases companies conquered territory without reference to their governments. Sometimes, though, Africans invited the Europeans in, then found them impossible to remove.

The Europeans brought changes in modes of life and work. To pay the new taxes, Africans had to undertake wage labor. Imperial enterprises created a vast demand for unskilled labor: railroads, rubber, sugar and cocoa estates, and mining operations in central and southern Africa were all highly labor-intensive. By forcing Africans into these jobs, Europeans took away their culture and independence.

The response was varied. Some – such as the Bugandans who helped the British take over the states between the Great Lakes and form Uganda in 1903 – collaborated with the invaders. Others put their faith in religion: in the Sudan, Muhammad Ahmed (the *Mahdi*) rebelled against Anglo-Egyptian rule and founded a strict Islamic state. Yet apart from the Mahdist revolt and the defiance of the west African Asante, most African resistance was short-lived. Artillery and rapid-fire maxim guns brought many uprisings to a swift end: the Ijebu surrendered in 1892, the Matabele in 1896, the Mandinka (under Samori Toure) in 1898 and the Zulu in 1908.

The Swazi branch of the Zulu nation was never defeated in battle; their state was guaranteed independence by the Transvaal and the British, before becoming a British protectorate in 1905. Only one state successfully defied the Europeans: Ethiopia, led by a modernizing Emperor Menelik II, crushed the Italian army at the Battle of Adowa in 1896. The freed-slave state of Liberia also survived despite losing parts of its territory to Britain and France.

By 1914,virtually the whole continent had come under European control. African raw materials and human resources were exploited for the benefit of European industry and commerce. Portugal shipped thousands of indentured laborers to the cocoa plantations on São Tomé and Príncipe, where they lived and died in appalling conditions. Leopold II of Belgium, who took the Congo Free State as his personal possession in 1885, amassed a fortune in revenues from rubber and ivory. By 1908 when the Belgian state annexed the Congo, its population was half what it had been in 1891. Conditions then improved only marginally: thousands of people were moved forcibly to work the copper mines.

With footholds in the west, south and north of Africa, Britain was well placed to acquire half of the new colonies and protectorates during the "scramble". Its Gold Coast colony was the world's top rubber producer by 1895. Threatened by competitors in southeast Asia, the colony switched to cocoa and became world leader in this crop by 1914.

Germany came late to colonization. Among its African possessions was Togoland, where medical reforms, support for missionary schools, new roads and rail links brought some benefits of modern life.

1 The British general Charles Gordon, appointed governor of the Sudan by Khedive Ismail Pasha in 1873, was killed when Mahdist forces overran Khartoum in 1885.

2 In an uprising in 1905–07, Kinkjikitele Ngwale promised his followers that magic water (*maji-maji*) would protect them against machine-guns.

3 The Uganda railroad was built from 1896–1901, and was the most important factor in opening up the landlocked but fertile area north of Lake Victoria.

4 German colonization of Africa was characterized by foreign minister Bernard von Bülow in 1897 as the country claiming its right to "a place in the sun".

5 In 1898, at Fashoda on the White Nile, a confrontation between a French expeditionary force sent from west Africa and British troops almost led to war. The French ultimately withdrew.

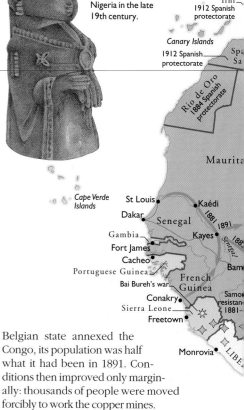

QUEEN VICTORIA of Britain, as visualized by a Yoruba craftsman in Nigeria in the late 19th century.

TIMELINE

European colonial policy

- **1881** Bey of Tunis accepts a French protectorate
- **1883** French culture is imposed on African colonies
- **1883** France begins its conquest of Madagascar
- **1884** The Berlin Conference on Africa opens
- **1889** Italy establishes its first colony in Eritrea
- **1890** Britain gives Germany Heligoland in exchange for Pemba and Zanzibar
- **1894** Britain occupies Uganda
- **1898** Britain creates the West African Frontier Force
- **1904** *Entente Cordiale* settles the Anglo-French disputes over Morocco, Egypt, the Suez Canal and Madagascar
- **1904** France creates a federal structure for its African empire, based at Dakar
- **1906** Control of Morocco split between Spain and France
- **1912** Italy annexes Tripolitania and Cyrenaica
- **1914** Amalgamation of Northern and Southern provinces into Nigeria

Wars and conflicts

- **1884** Samori Toure proclaims his Islamic theocracy
- **1885** British relieve Khartoum from Mahdist attack
- **1889** Chief Abushiri, leader of the Swahili peoples, is executed
- **1890** Hendrik Witbooi leads the first Nama rebellion against Germans in South-West Africa
- **1892** France destroys the Tukulor empire (Mali)
- **1893** French suppress the Fon warriors of Dahomey
- **1896** Ndebele massacre whites and their African supporters in Matebeleland
- **1898** Kitchener defeats the Mahdists at Omdurman and defuses the Fashoda incident
- **1900** Death of Samori Toure, two years after his capture
- **1900** Britain finally subjugates the Asante of west Africa
- **1905–07** Maji-Maji rebellion in German East Africa leads to an estimated 75,000 deaths
- **1906–08** Chief Bambata leads the last Zulu revolt
- **1911** German gunboat *Panther* creates international incident at Agadir
- **1914** European warfare transfers to all the German colonies in Africa

AFRICA (1783 – 1914)
5.16
Mahdist state, 1881–98
border, 1914
territory controlled by non-African powers, 1914
Belgium
France
Germany
Italy
Ottoman empire
Portugal
Spain
United Kingdom
European routes of expansion, 1880–1914
Belgian
British
French
German
Italian
Portuguese
major African resistance
oasis
gold
diamonds
copper
coal
railroads by 1914
0 1000 km
0 800 mi
See also 5.15 (Africa in the early 19th-century); 5.17 (southern Africa); 6.24 (early 20th century)

5.17 The making of southern Africa • 1800 – 1914 •

By 1800 there were 15,000 Afrikaner (Dutch-origin) colonists at the Cape. British influence then began to grow; a brief occupation of the Cape to secure Britain's trade routes during the French Revolutionary Wars was followed by the construction of a naval base in 1806 and formal annexation of the area in 1814. Tension rose with the original settlers a decade later as unpopular land reforms were introduced. In response, Cape Boers (Afrikaners) embarked on the Great Trek, a migration into the interior to escape British administration. Some of these *voortrekkers* (pioneers) went north, others east into Natal. Violent clashes sometimes occurred with the native peoples they encountered.

Britain annexed Natal in 1843 and the Boers moved on again, crossing the Drakensberg mountains and heading into the high veld, where they founded the republics of Orange Free State and Transvaal. Britain recognized the independence of the Boer republics in the early 1850s. Their economies developed without staple crops or plantations as vast estates were rented out to African farmers who paid their dues in kind or labor. House slaves were commonly held by Boer families, who based their prestige on land ownership, superior weapons and a belief in racial supremacy.

Diamonds were discovered at Kimberley in Griqualand in 1871, revolutionizing the history of southern Africa and beginning a flood of European immigration. By 1880 diamond exports from here, increasingly in the hands of Cecil Rhodes' De Beers Mining Company Ltd, were worth over US$20 million annually. Then a gold boom started in 1886 in Witwatersrand, and was even more spectacular; *Uitlanders* (mainly British immigrants) poured into the Transvaal to make their fortunes. Rhodes financed settler expeditions traveling north into Bechuanaland and Zambesia, where they encountered Lobengula's Ndebele armies in Matabeleland, Lewanika's Lozi kingdom and the declining Kazembe kingdom northwest of Lake Malawi.

New roads and railroads transformed the countryside. Migrants from Mozambique and India came to work in the deep extractive mines. Soon the Witwatersrand was the world's biggest goldfield, attracting foreign investment and expertise, and transforming the Transvaal into a modern nation-state. To assert their predominance in the region and forestall German and Portuguese expansion, the

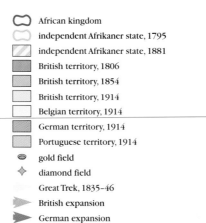

- African kingdom
- independent Afrikaner state, 1795
- independent Afrikaner state, 1881
- British territory, 1806
- British territory, 1854
- British territory, 1914
- Belgian territory, 1914
- German territory, 1914
- Portuguese territory, 1914
- gold field
- diamond field
- Great Trek, 1835–46
- British expansion
- German expansion

Anglo–Boer War, 1899–1902

- territory captured by Afrikaners, 1899
- Afrikaner campaign
- British campaign
- Afrikaner victory
- British victory
- under siege by Afrikaners, 1899–1900
- railroad by 1914
- borders, 1914

0 300 km
0 400 mi

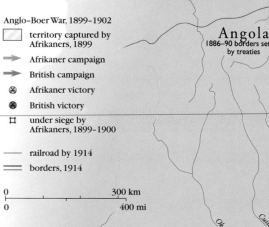

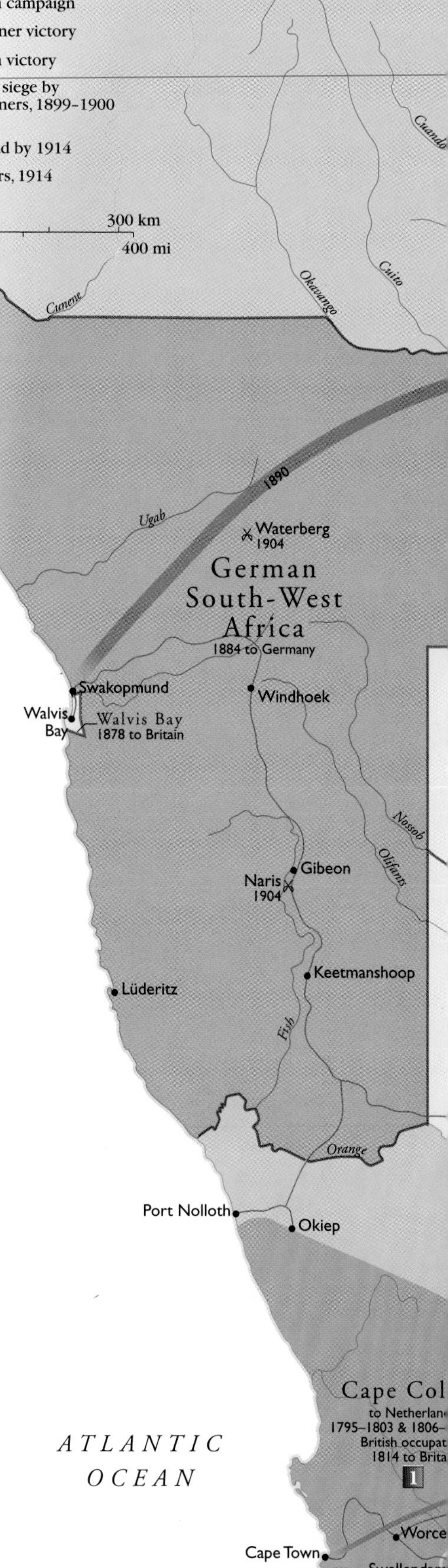

Angola
1886–90 borders settled by treaties
Cuando
Cuito
Okavango
Cunene
1890
Ugab
Waterberg 1904
German South-West Africa
1884 to Germany
Swakopmund
Walvis Bay
Walvis Bay 1878 to Britain
Windhoek
Nossob
Olifants
Gibeon
Naris 1904
Keetmanshoop
Lüderitz
Fish
Orange
Port Nolloth
Okiep
ATLANTIC OCEAN
1
Cape Town
Simonstown
Swellendam
SWELLENDAM

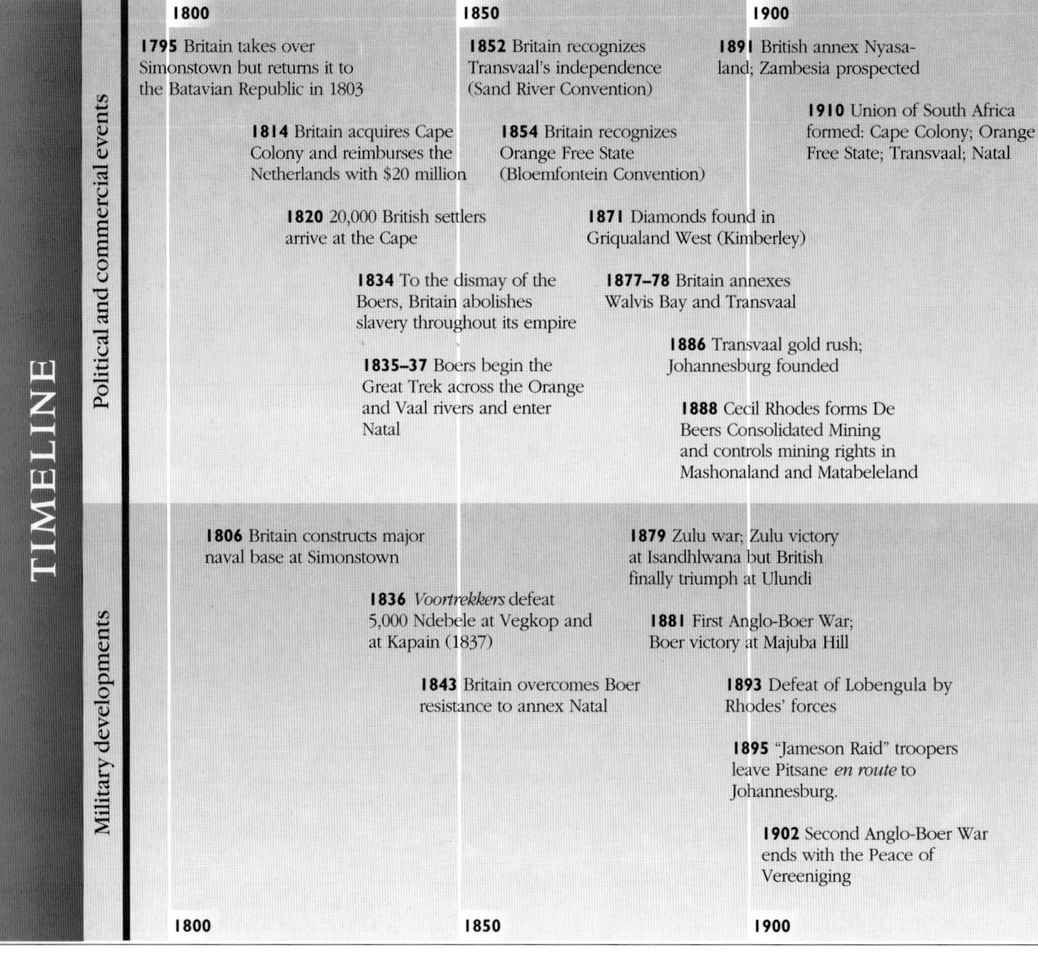

TIMELINE
Political and commercial events
1800
1850
1900
1795 Britain takes over Simonstown but returns it to the Batavian Republic in 1803
1814 Britain acquires Cape Colony and reimburses the Netherlands with $20 million
1820 20,000 British settlers arrive at the Cape
1834 To the dismay of the Boers, Britain abolishes slavery throughout its empire
1835–37 Boers begin the Great Trek across the Orange and Vaal rivers and enter Natal
1852 Britain recognizes Transvaal's independence (Sand River Convention)
1854 Britain recognizes Orange Free State (Bloemfontein Convention)
1871 Diamonds found in Griqualand West (Kimberley)
1877–78 Britain annexes Walvis Bay and Transvaal
1886 Transvaal gold rush; Johannesburg founded
1888 Cecil Rhodes forms De Beers Consolidated Mining and controls mining rights in Mashonaland and Matabeleland
1891 British annex Nyasaland; Zambesia prospected
1910 Union of South Africa formed: Cape Colony; Orange Free State; Transvaal; Natal
Military developments
1806 Britain constructs major naval base at Simonstown
1836 Voortrekkers defeat 5,000 Ndebele at Vegkop and at Kapain (1837)
1843 Britain overcomes Boer resistance to annex Natal
1879 Zulu war; Zulu victory at Isandhlwana but British finally triumph at Ulundi
1881 First Anglo-Boer War; Boer victory at Majuba Hill
1893 Defeat of Lobengula by Rhodes' forces
1895 "Jameson Raid" troopers leave Pitsane en route to Johannesburg.
1902 Second Anglo-Boer War ends with the Peace of Vereeniging
1800
1850
1900

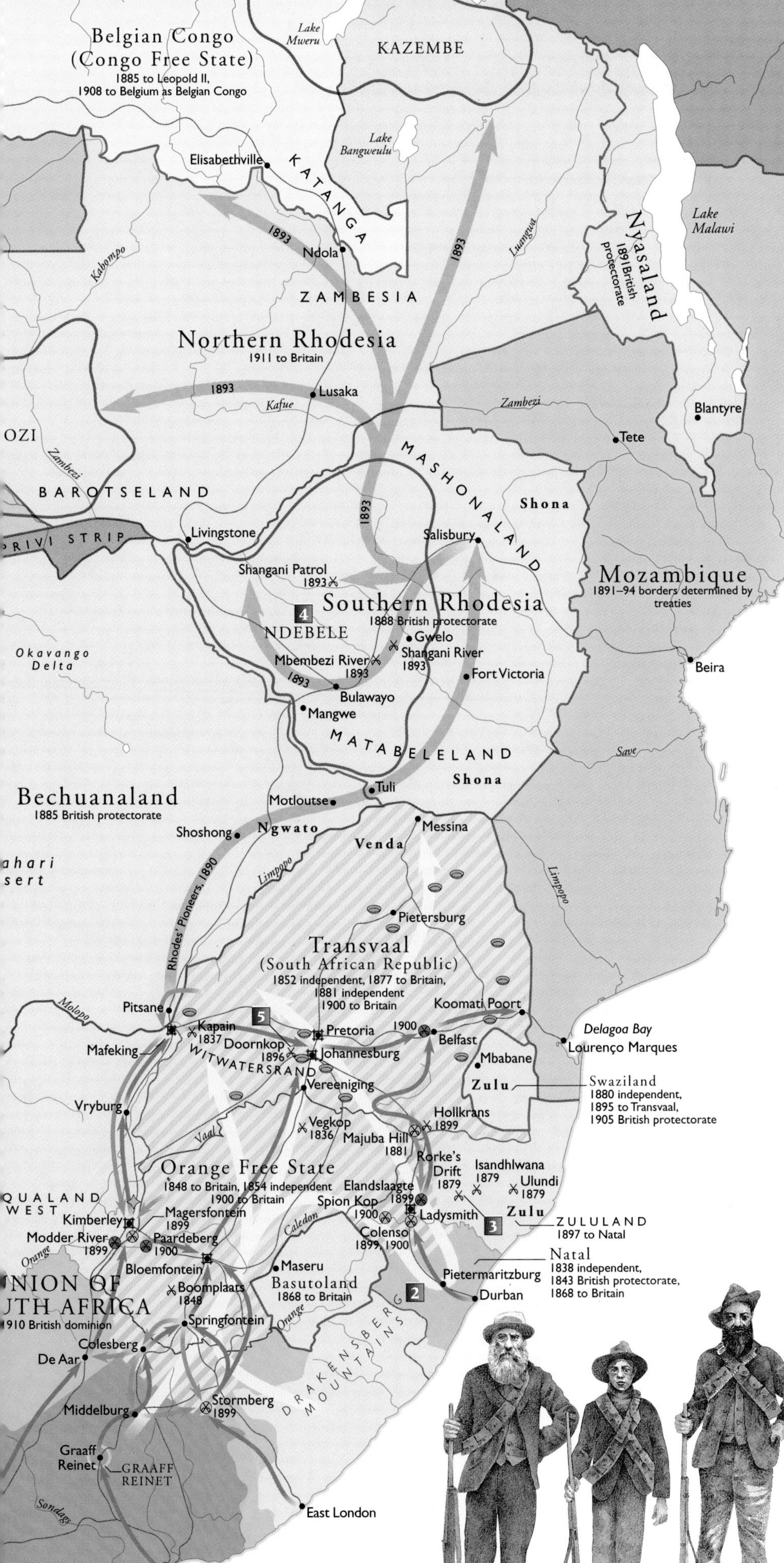
Belgian Congo
(Congo Free State)
1885 to Leopold II,
1908 to Belgium as Belgian Congo
Lake Mweru
KAZEMBE
German
East Africa
1885 to Germany
Lake Bangweulu
Elisabethville
KATANGA
1893
Ndola
Kabompo
Luangwa
Nyasaland
1891 British protectorate
Lake Malawi
ZAMBESIA
Northern Rhodesia
1911 to Britain
1893
Lusaka
Kafue
Zambezi
Blantyre
Tete
OZI
Zambezi
MASHONALAND
BAROTSELAND
Shona
Livingstone
Salisbury
Shangani Patrol
1893
Mozambique
1891–94 borders determined by treaties
Southern Rhodesia
1888 British protectorate
NDEBELE
Gwelo
Shangani River
1893
Okavango
Delta
Mbembezi River
1893
Fort Victoria
Beira
Bulawayo
Mangwe
MATABELELAND
Save
Shona
Bechuanaland
1885 British protectorate
Motloutse
Tuli
Shoshong
Ngwato
Messina
Venda
Limpopo
Limpopo
Rhodes' Pioneers, 1890
Pietersburg
Transvaal
(South African Republic)
1852 independent, 1877 to Britain,
1881 independent
1900 to Britain
Molopo
Pitsane
Komati Poort
Kapain
1837
Doornkop
1896
Pretoria
1900
Belfast
Delagoa Bay
Lourenço Marques
Mafeking
WITWATERSRAND
Johannesburg
Mbabane
Vereeniging
Zulu
Swaziland
1880 independent,
1895 to Transvaal,
1905 British protectorate
Vryburg
Vegkop
1836
Majuba Hill
1881
Hollkrans
1899
Vaal
Rorke's
Drift
1879
Isandhlwana
1879
Ulundi
1879
Orange Free State
1848 to Britain, 1854 independent
1900 to Britain
Elandslaagte
1899
Spion Kop
1900
Ladysmith
Zulu
ZULULAND
1897 to Natal
Kimberley
Magersfontein
1899
Modder River
1899
Paardeberg
1900
Caledon
Colenso
1899, 1900
Natal
1838 independent,
1843 British protectorate,
1868 to Britain
Bloemfontein
Maseru
Basutoland
1868 to Britain
Pietermaritzburg
Durban
Boomplaats
1848
Springfontein
Orange
DRAKENSBERG MOUNTAINS
Colesberg
De Aar
Stormberg
1899
Middelburg
Graaff
Reinet
GRAAFF
REINET
Sondags
East London
Port
Elizabeth

AFRIKANERS defended their homeland stubbornly against the British, using guerrilla tactics in 1899–1902.

British annexed the Transvaal and invaded Zululand. The Zulu War of 1879 began with a crushing defeat for the British at Isandhlwana but victory at Ulundi was followed with the capture of the Zulu leader Cetshwayo. The following year, the Transvaal Boers rebelled; they defeated the British at Majuba Hill in the first Anglo-Boer War and regained independent status as the South African Republic.

Cecil Rhodes ultimately hoped to extend British rule from the Cape to Cairo. To gain control of the strategically and economically vital Transvaal, he sent an armed party commanded by Leander Starr Jameson to overthrow its government in 1895–96. The "Jameson Raid" was a fiasco, souring Anglo-Boer relations. Three years later, the Second Anglo-Boer War broke out. Initially Boer forces besieged Ladysmith, Mafeking and Kimberley and won victories at Magersfontein, Colenso and Stormberg during December 1899. Led by generals Roberts and Kitchener, the British relieved the besieged towns and invaded the two Boer republics. The Boers switched to guerrilla warfare and Kitchener resorted to armored trains to counter the Boer commandos. Boer farms were destroyed and displaced families interned in hastily built concentration camps. This, together with the British use of African troops and a steady flow of British reinforcements (to 300,000 by 1901) forced the Boers to surrender in 1901.

The Peace of Vereeniging (1902) incorporated the Boer republics within the British empire. Britain granted US$12 million to rebuild the Afrikaner homesteads and introduced responsible government to the Transvaal (1906) and to the Orange Free State (1907). The Union of South Africa was formed in 1910; Louis Botha, the Afrikaner leader, became prime minister of the new state, in which Afrikaners formed the predominant white minority.

In the struggle between Boers and British, the Africans were the real losers. Zulus and many other indigenous peoples were deprived of their lands, forced to live in segregated territories and to become migrant workers in mining and industrial centers. The new South African state immediately enacted systematic racial discrimination. The Natives' Land Act (1913) decreed that no African might own land except in prescribed and often unproductive areas.

1 The humane treatment of the native population by British missionaries who had arrived at the Cape in 1816, followed by abolition of slavery throughout the British empire, was strongly opposed by the Boers.

2 The first Indians in Africa were indentured laborers imported to work on Natal sugar plantations in 1860.

3 At Rorke's Drift (23 January 1879), a British garrison of around 100 troops held off an assault by thousands of Zulu *impi*. After losing 350 men, the Zulus withdrew out of respect for British bravery.

4 Lobengula of the Ndebele (or Matabele) granted mining concessions to Cecil Rhodes. When the British aimed to annex the kingdom, Lobengula vainly resisted in 1893 and committed suicide.

5 After the defeat of the Jameson Raid at Krugersdorp (1 January 1896), a congratulatory telegram sent by Kaiser Wilhelm II to president Kruger of the Transvaal created a crisis in Anglo-German relations.

See also 5.16, 5.17 (19th-century Africa); 6.28 (20th-century southern Africa)

5.18 The European settlement of Australia and New Zealand • 1788 – 1914 •

European settlement in Australia began when the British government, faced with severe overcrowding in its jails, resolved in 1786 to found a penal colony there. The first convict transports arrived at Botany Bay in 1788; prisoners were subsequently transferred to settlements at Sydney (Port Jackson) and on Norfolk Island. The young colony began to expand as discharged soldiers and freed convicts cultivated their own parcels of land. Conflict arose with the Aboriginal inhabitants whose raids on settlements brought reprisals culminating in the massacre of Myall Creek (1838). In the 1830s settlers on Van Diemen's Land (Tasmania) attempted a wholesale expulsion of Aboriginals to Flinders Island; those who resisted were massacred.

The free Swan River colony established at Perth and Fremantle in the west attracted over a thousand people by 1831; again, hostilities developed with local peoples. The British government helped sustain the western Australian colony with convict labor until the practice was discontinued in 1868. By then, some 160,000 prisoners had been transported.

The inhospitable interior meant that the continent was not fully charted for eighty years. Matthew Flinders sailed around Australia in 1802–03; Edward Eyre, with the help of guides, crossed South Australia in 1839–41; Ludwig Leichhardt struck north from Moreton Bay; Burke and Wills crossed from south to north, followed by Stuart on a different route 1861–62; Warburton explored north of Adelaide and reached Port Hedland; Giles traversed the Gibson Desert and Macdonnell Ranges via Perth.

The non-convict populace of Australia rose after 1851, when gold was found at Bathurst, Ballarat, Bendigo and Kalgoorlie. In ten years the population exceeded one million; it doubled during the next decade with a huge influx of Chinese and Asian indentured labor. Racial violence led to strict immigration laws (later emulated in New Zealand). Gold mining played a role in Australian political history: in 1854, the pro-democratic Eureka uprising by Ballarat miners was put down by troops. All the states enjoyed self-government by 1890, and the following year, Australia's population topped three million, nearly a third of them first-generation immigrants.

European settlers first arrived in New Zealand's Bay of Islands during 1792, exchanging muskets with the indigenous Maoris for land. This trade caused "musket wars" between Maori tribes from 1818. Australian whalers also established coastal settlements on South Island. Disputes between the Maoris and the settlers led to the Treaty of Waitangi, which confirmed the Maoris' right to their land. However, settlers soon violated its terms, and the First Maori War (1843–48) saw fierce fighting at Ohaeawai *pa* (fortified site). Maori unity appeared in the "King Movement" of 1858 and then in the "Fire in

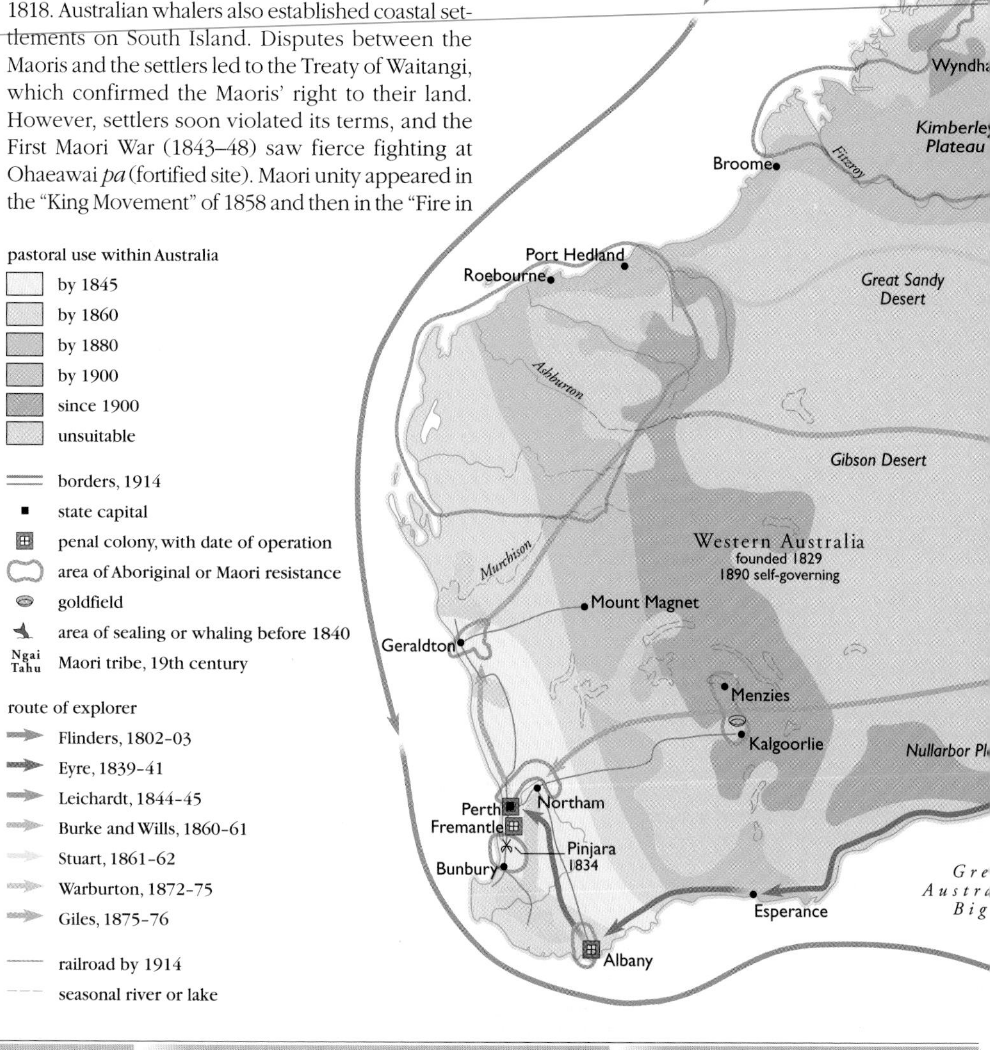

pastoral use within Australia
by 1845
by 1860
by 1880
by 1900
since 1900
unsuitable
borders, 1914
state capital
penal colony, with date of operation
area of Aboriginal or Maori resistance
goldfield
area of sealing or whaling before 1840
Ngai Tahu
Maori tribe, 19th century
route of explorer
Flinders, 1802-03
Eyre, 1839-41
Leichhardt, 1844-45
Burke and Wills, 1860-61
Stuart, 1861-62
Warburton, 1872-75
Giles, 1875-76
railroad by 1914
seasonal river or lake
Timor Sea
Wyndha
Kimberley Plateau
Broome
Fitzroy
Port Hedland
Roebourne
Great Sandy Desert
Ashburton
Gibson Desert
Western Australia
founded 1829
1890 self-governing
Murchison
Mount Magnet
Geraldton
Menzies
Kalgoorlie
Nullarbor Pl
Perth
Northam
Fremantle
Pinjara
1834
Bunbury
Esperance
Albany

TIMELINE

Australia

1788 Captain Arthur Phillip enters Botany Bay with 750 British convicts

1790 The Aboriginal guerrilla leader, Pemulwy, begins raids on British settlements

1803 A penal settlement is set up on Van Diemen's Land

1804 Transported Irish nationalists lead an anti-colonial revolt at Castle Hill

1827 Capt Stirling chooses the site for Perth

1830 Many Aboriginals on Van Diemen's Land are killed

1848 Leichhardt vanishes in attempting east–west crossing

1851 Gold is discovered at Bathurst, New South Wales

1854 Miners' uprising at the Eureka Stockade, Ballarat

1855 Responsible government is granted to most states

1859 Queensland is set up as a separate colony

1872 A submarine cable to Java is connected to the Darwin–Adelaide telegraph

1885 New South Wales troops assist British in Sudan

1901 The Commonwealth of Australia is proclaimed

1902 Immigration Restriction Act; "White Australia" policy

1911 An Australian expedition explores the Antarctic

1914 Australian troops are committed to the Allied cause

New Zealand

1792 The first European settlements at Bay of Islands

1814 New South Wales claims New Zealand as a dependency

1840 Five hundred Maori chiefs sign Treaty of Waitangi

1843 Wairau River incident leads to the First Maori War

1852 Britain passes the New Zealand Constitution Act.

1860 Disputes over Waitara land purchase lead to the Second Maori War

1865 The capital is moved from Auckland to Wellington

1872 The Maoris end their guerrilla war in North Island

1880 Decline in wool trade brings a temporary slump

1882 Refrigerated ships begin to transport New Zealand produce

1907 New Zealand is given Dominion status

1911 New Zealand urges the formation of an Imperial Parliament to ensure defense of the British empire

1800 1850 1900

the Fern", a guerrilla war that began in 1860. Resistance to European settlers died out in 1870–72, but peace was not formally concluded until 1881.

Discovery of gold in Otago in 1861 stimulated immigration to New Zealand. Yet the main incentives to emigrate to Australia or New Zealand were cheap fares offered by shipping lines and unusually high standards of living. Both countries were enriched by the export of wool and foodstuffs; the introduction of refrigerated holds on steamships in 1882 enabled the bulk transportation of meat and dairy products. A minimum wage and generous welfare benefits attracted migrants, whose adopted countries gained self-government when Australia became a Commonwealth in 1901 and New Zealand a Dominion in 1907. Both retained emotional ties with Britain, and committed large forces to aid the "mother country" in 1914.

A transcontinental telegraph system was quickly established in Australia, though deserts and mountain ranges presented obstacles to a railroad system and different gauges were adopted by different states. The Trans-Australia railroad was completed in 1912–17, with the Kalgoorlie–Port Augusta link across the Nullarbor Plain. New Zealand's railroads were also slow to develop. Christchurch and Invercargill were linked in 1880, and the regular services began between Wellington and Auckland in 1908.

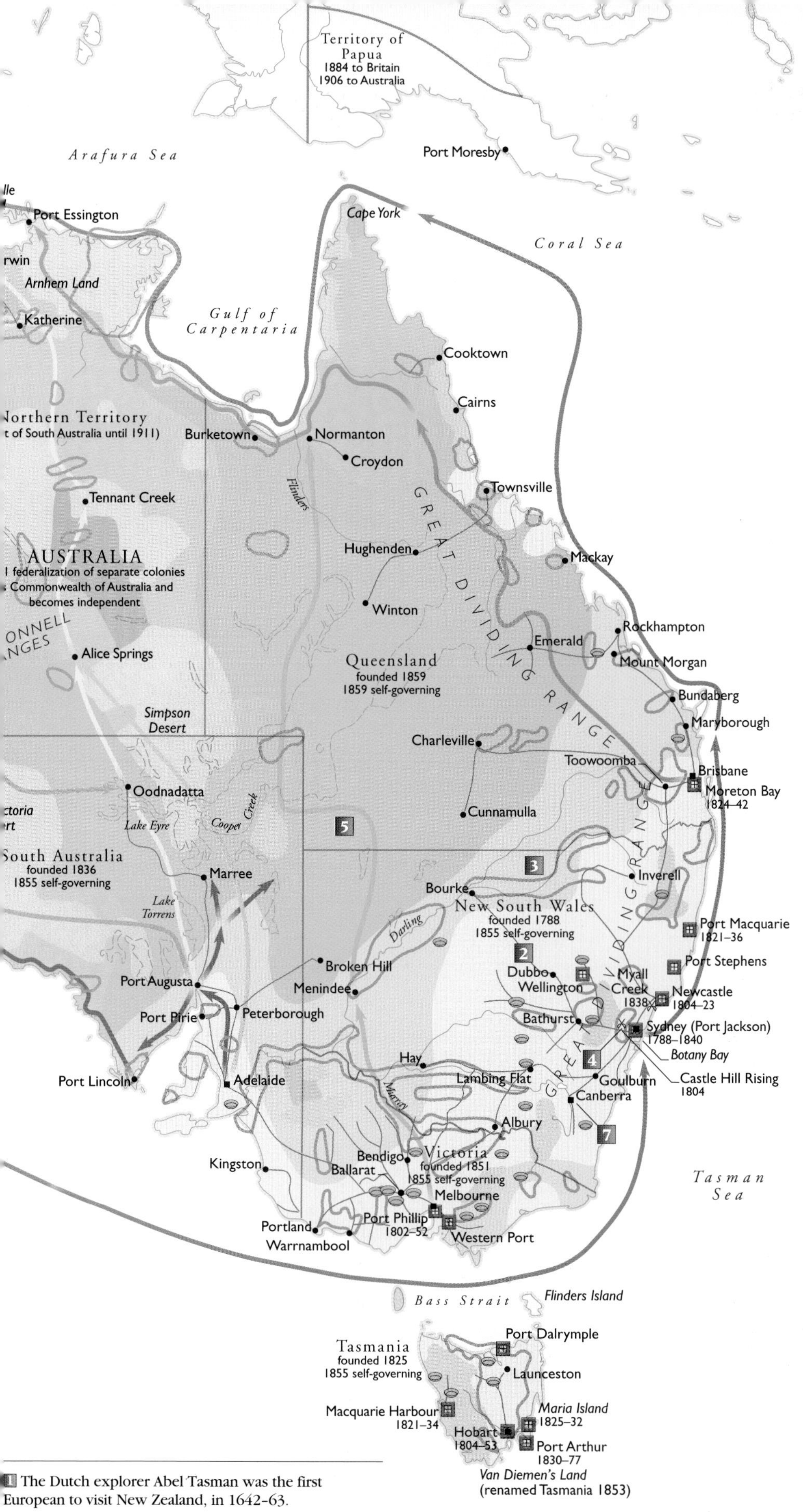

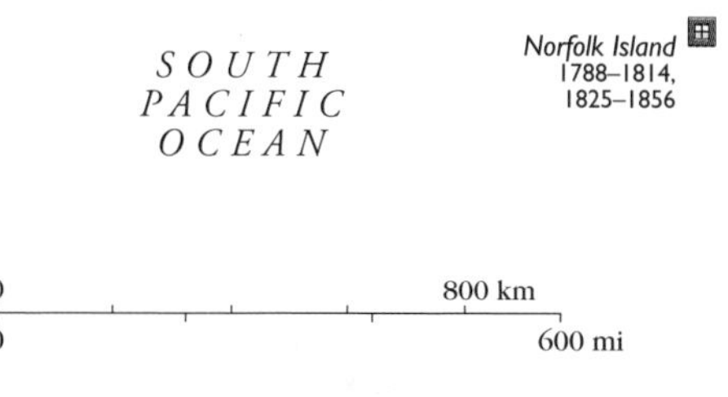
SOUTH PACIFIC OCEAN
Norfolk Island
1788–1814,
1825–1856
0
800 km
0
600 mi

Bay of Islands
Ohaeawai
1845
Russell
Waitangi
Ngapuhi
North Island
Auckland
center of "King Movement"
Thames
Waikato
Ngati Toa
Ngati Raukawa
New Plymouth
Te Ati Awa
Gisborne
NEW ZEALAND
1814 to Britain
1907 British dominion
Napier
Wanganui
Ngati Toa
Palmerston North
Te Ati Awa
Te Ati Awa
Nelson
Wellington
Westport
Greymouth
Ngati Toa
South Island
Christchurch
Lyttleton
Queenstown
Cromwell
OTAGO
Ngai Tahu
Dunedin
Invercargill
Stewart Island
0
600 km
0
400 mi

1 The Dutch explorer Abel Tasman was the first European to visit New Zealand, in 1642–63.

2 In 1794, John Macarthur began farming Merino sheep (a breed noted for its wool) in New South Wales, thus establishing Australia's future prosperity.

3 Aboriginals numbered c.300,000 when European colonization began. This figure declined drastically with exposure to disease and settler violence.

4 Irish political prisoners, transported after the anti-British rising of 1798, staged the Castle Hill uprising (1804). It was ruthlessly suppressed.

5 Burke and Wills' expedition of 1860–61 ended tragically; they narrowly missed a relief party and starved.

6 One form of Maori opposition to European settlement from 1865 onward was the Hau-hau movement, a blend of Christianity and native mythology.

7 Canberra was the site selected for the Australian Commonwealth capital in 1908. Its Parliament building was opened in 1927.

See also 2.26 (pre-European Australia and New Zealand); 6.18 (Australasia in the 20th century)

5.19 The decline of Manchu China • 1783 – 1912

Under the expansionist Manchu (Qing) dynasty, China enjoyed unrivaled power in east Asia. By 1783, emperor Qianlong (r.1736–96) had settled colonists in Xinjiang and imposed tributary status on Burma and Annam. He restricted foreign merchants to Guangzhou and shunned the industrial innovations offered by western "barbarian" traders. After his abdication, however, imports of opium from British India increased steadily, and eventually led to two "Opium Wars" with China (1839–42; 1856–60). The outcome of the first was the 1842 Treaty of Nanjing, which confirmed Britain's gain of Hong Kong and right to trade through five "treaty ports"; the second resulted in two agreements (in 1858 and 1860) for more western commercial footholds.

Russian ambitions focussed on acquiring strategically important Chinese territory. Russian forces annexed the valuable Ili region and advanced into Xinjiang, from which they withdrew in return for cash compensation in 1881. Russia also annexed eastern Siberia (1858–60) to secure ice-free waters in the Sea of Japan. A similar policy of territorial acquisition was adopted by Britain, France and Japan, which began to encroach on the tributary states beyond the Manchu borders. Britain moved into Lower Burma in 1852 and annexed the entire country in 1886. France, entrenched in southern Indo-China, was anxious to open trade with the southern Chinese province of Yunnan; it therefore fought a brief war with China to establish a protectorate over Tongking by 1885. Between 1875 and 1880, Japan annexed the Chinese tributary of the Ryukyu islands and began to weaken Chinese influence in another tributary, Korea. Taiwan and the Pescadores were also lost by China in 1894–95. These concessions and defeats represented unprecedented humiliation for the Qing dynasty.

While foreign powers eroded its frontiers, China faced even greater dangers from within. Official corruption, high taxation and continuing internal migration caused local uprisings. Many were caused by secret societies with political aspirations. The White Lotus sect vowed to overthrow the Qing and restore the Ming dynasty. Their rebellion raged through central China 1796–1804, though some unrest continued to 1813. After 1850 these revolts became so serious as to threaten the survival of the Qing. Hong Xiuquan led the Taiping rebellion, proclaiming the end of Manchu rule and the advent of the "Heavenly Kingdom of the Great Peace". This insurrection and its suppression by Qing forces cost up to 20 million lives. Disaffection with Manchu rule also brought rebellion in Taiwan, Muslim revolts in Xinjiang and Yunnan, Nian peasant risings in Henan and Miao tribal unrest in Guizhou.

The short-lived "self-strengthening movement" instigated by the statesman Li Hongzhang in the 1860s attempted to construct a modern military and industrial state. Yet his plan to purchase foreign armaments and build arsenals and factories met with little support from the dowager empress Cixi (r.1862–1908) and her court at Beijing. Meanwhile, the western clamor for land concessions, mining rights, railroad, building and trade facilities continued. In Cixi's reign, anti-western sentiment took on a republican flavor, and crystallized into the nationalist movement led by Sun Yixian (Sun Yat-sen).

The shame of further territory losses in 1898 led to the Boxer Uprising of 1900–01. This major revolt engulfed several provinces but concentrated chiefly on attacking the foreign legations in Beijing. The outcome of this rebellion, which was supported by the dowager empress, was the International Protocol of 1901, which gave the powers yet more trade concessions and a huge indemnity payment from the Qing. Western soldiers guarded the civilian settlements, while gunboats patrolled the rivers. Merchant and missionary activity increased. Foreign

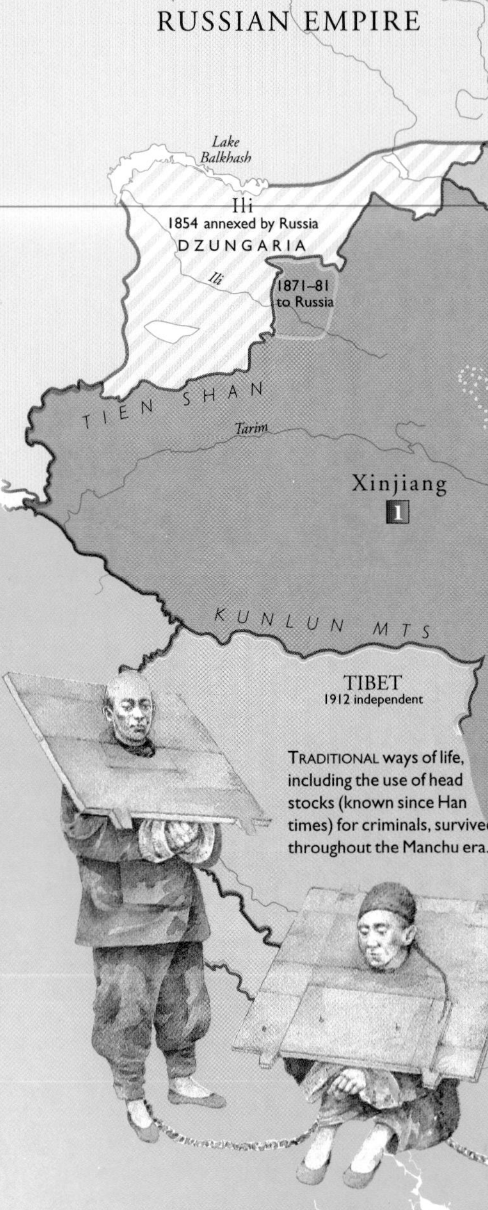

Omsk
RUSSIAN EMPIRE
Lake Balkhash
Ili
1854 annexed by Russia
DZUNGARIA
Ili
1871–81 to Russia
TIEN SHAN
Tarim
Xinjiang
1
KUNLUN MTS
TIBET
1912 independent

TRADITIONAL ways of life, including the use of head stocks (known since Han times) for criminals, survived throughout the Manchu era.

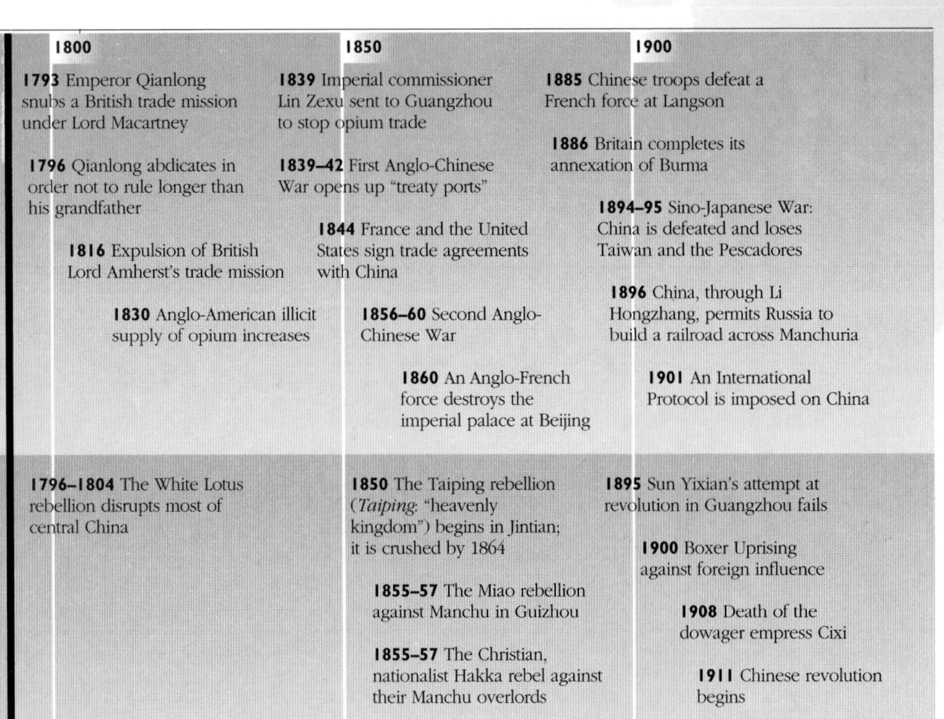

TIMELINE
Trade and politics
1800
1850
1900
1793 Emperor Qianlong snubs a British trade mission under Lord Macartney
1796 Qianlong abdicates in order not to rule longer than his grandfather
1816 Expulsion of British Lord Amherst's trade mission
1830 Anglo-American illicit supply of opium increases
1839 Imperial commissioner Lin Zexu sent to Guangzhou to stop opium trade
1839–42 First Anglo-Chinese War opens up "treaty ports"
1844 France and the United States sign trade agreements with China
1856–60 Second Anglo-Chinese War
1860 An Anglo-French force destroys the imperial palace at Beijing
1885 Chinese troops defeat a French force at Langson
1886 Britain completes its annexation of Burma
1894–95 Sino-Japanese War: China is defeated and loses Taiwan and the Pescadores
1896 China, through Li Hongzhang, permits Russia to build a railroad across Manchuria
1901 An International Protocol is imposed on China
Rebellions
1796–1804 The White Lotus rebellion disrupts most of central China
1850 The Taiping rebellion (Taiping: "heavenly kingdom") begins in Jintian; it is crushed by 1864
1855–57 The Miao rebellion against Manchu in Guizhou
1855–57 The Christian, nationalist Hakka rebel against their Manchu overlords
1863–73 Muslim rebellion in Gansu, Qinghai and Shanxi
1895 Sun Yixian's attempt at revolution in Guangzhou fails
1900 Boxer Uprising against foreign influence
1908 Death of the dowager empress Cixi
1911 Chinese revolution begins
1912 Yuan Shikai president of the new Chinese Republic
1800
1850
1900

1 With acquisitions of new territories such as Xinjiang by the Manchu, the Chinese population rose to over 400 million by the mid-19th century.

2 Opium was imported to China not as a narcotic, but as a pharmaceutical. Its addictive properties led to imperial decrees against its import and cultivation from 1800 onward.

3 Hong Kong was ceded to Britain by China in 1841 (confirmed in 1842); in 1898, the British signed a 99-year lease on the territory.

4 Shanghai was one of the first treaty ports, opened to western trade in 1842. In these ports, westerners were free from all aspects of Chinese jurisdiction, including taxation.

5 The Taiping rebellion of 1850–64 took its egalitarianism from Christianity brought by western missionaries. Its leader Hong Xiuquan claimed to be the younger brother of Jesus Christ.

6 The Boxers – or "League of Righteous Harmonious Fists" – were an anti-foreigner, anti-Christian secret society originating in the Shandong peninsula.

7 Germany sent a force to occupy the port of Qingdao in 1897. Thereafter the site was heavily industrialized; with the outbreak of war in 1914, Japan (an Allied country) captured the city.

Krasnoyarsk
Angara
Lena
Trans-Siberian railroad
completed 1916
Amur
Amur
1858 annexed by Russia
Nikolayevsk
founded 1850
Sakhalin
1875 to Russia,
1905 southern half
to Japan
Kuril Islands
1875 northern islands to Japan
Lake Baykal
Irkutsk
Chita
Nerchinsk
Aigun
Khabarovsk
founded 1858
Ussuri
1860 annexed by Russia
Tannu Tuva
protectorate
1911 independent,
1914 to Russia
completed 1915
Selenga
Manzhouli
Manchuria
1900–05 under Russian influence,
1905–45 under Japanese influence
Songhua
Ussuri
Sapporo
Hokkaido
Ulan Bator
Inner Mongolian Plateau
Harbin
Suifenhe
Lake Khanka
Hakodate
MONGOLIA
1912 independent
Changchun
Hunchun
Vladivostok
founded 1860
Gobi Desert
Mukden
(Shenyang)
Yalu
KOREA
1905 Japanese protectorate,
1910 Japanese colony
Sea of Japan
Honshu
Kwangtung Territory
1898–1905 to Russia,
1905 to Japan
Niuzhuang
Dandong
Yalu River
1894
Beijing
capital city,
focus of Boxer
Uprising
Qinhuangdao
Tokyo
Yokohama
JAPAN
rebellion
62–73
Gansu
Ordos Desert
Tianjin
Lushun
(Port Arthur)
Dalian
Seoul
Dengzhou
Weihaiwei
1895
Ganzhou
Pingluo
Yulin
Longkou
Chefoo
Shandong
Shanxi
Pusan
Yellow
Jinan
Weihaiwei
1898 to Britain
Shimonoseki
Shikoku
Lake Qinghai
Hegang
Qingdao
1898 to
Germany
Qingdao
Muslim rebellion
1862–73
Yellow Sea
Nagasaki
Kyushu
Hezhou
Nian rebellion
1853–68
Kagoshima
QIN MTS
Henan
Zhenjiang
IMPERIAL CHINA
Yanguan
Han
Huai
Nanjing
Shanghai
Taiping
rebellion
1850–64
Wuhu
Suzhou
DABA MTS
Hangzhou
Wanxian
Yichang
Hankou
Wuhan
Wuchang
Anqing
Ningbo
(Mingzhou)
Lichuan
Shasi
Jiujiang
Taiping
rebellion
1850–64
Assam
1826 annexed by
Britain
Mingshan
Chongqing
Yangtze
Yeuyang
Nanchang
Lake Pengli
Wenzhou
Luzhou
Lake Dongting
Yalong
Jinsha
Mianning
Tanzhou
Santuao
Taiping
rebellion
1850–64
Upper Burma
1886 annexed by Britain
Guizhou
Miao rebellion
1855–57
Fuzhou
Tan-shui
Aboriginal
rebellion
1862–63
Dali
Muslim
rebellion
1855–73
Xiamen
(Amoy)
Tengyueh
Yunnan
Hakka rebellion
1855–57
Pescadores
1895 to Japan
Tainan
Mengzi
Jintian
Wuzhou
Guangzhou
(Canton)
Shantou
(Swatow)
Taiwan
1895 to Japan
Manhao
Nanning
Xi
Sanshui
Kowloon
Hong Kong
Simao
Longzhou
Macao
to Portugal
Salween
Linan
Langson
Pakhoi
Hong Kong
1841 to Britain
Tongking
1884–85 French protectorate
Hanoi
Zhanjiang
Zhanjiang
1898 to France
Laos
1899 French
protectorate
Qiongzhou
Hainan
Lower Burma
created 1862
Mekong
Philippine Islands
1571–1898 to Spain,
1898 to United States
FRENCH
INDO-CHINA
1887–98 united by
France
Annam
1883–85 French
protectorate
South China Sea
SIAM
Manila
Manchu empire, mid-19th century
former Manchu tributary state
British India, mid-19th century
Japanese empire, mid-19th century
Russian empire, mid-19th century
borders, c.1912
Manchu /Chinese empire, 1912
former Manchu state gaining independence
Manchu territory lost to Britain by 1912
Manchu territory lost to France by 1912
Manchu territory under Japanese control
at some time before 1912
Manchu territory lost to Russian empire by 1912
temporary Russian territorial gain
area leased by China to foreign power
spheres of influence
British
French
German
Japanese
port open to foreign trade under the
Treaty of Nanjing, 1842
treaty port opened from 1858
Taiping marches, 1850–64
anti-Manchu rebellion, with date
center of Boxer Uprising, 1900–01
railroad by 1914
Trans-Siberian railroad sector completed in 1915
Trans-Siberian rail link to Vladivostok,
completed 1916
0
1000 km
0
800 mi

banks virtually ran China's economy, funding such projects as the rail link across Manchuria between the Trans-Siberian railroad and Vladivostok.

In 1911, an army mutiny in the industrial conurbation of Wuhan was exploited by Sun Yixian's Revolutionary Alliance Party, or Guomindang (KMT), which proceeded to seize power in central and southern China and overthrow the Qing dynasty. Sun Yixian returned from overseas exile to Shanghai, proclaimed the Three Principles of the republican revolution – nationalism, democracy and people's livelihood – and was duly appointed provisional president of China. On 1 January 1912 the Chinese Republic was founded. However, when the Manchu boy-emperor Pu Yi abdicated on 13 February, General Yuan Shikai was named as president. For the sake of national unity, Sun Yixian voluntarily relinquished the presidency. Yet Yuan Shikai's desire to found a new imperial dynasty led to suppression of the Guomindang. In 1913, Sun Yixian established the first of a series of provisional governments at Guangzhou.

See also 4.22 (the rise of Manchu China); 5.12 (19th-century Russia); 6.17 (China to 1949)

5.20 Japan in the 19th century • 1800 – 1914 •

Irkutsk
Lake Baykal
Trans-Siberian railroad
RUSSI
EMPIR
Mongolia
1912 independent

The military bureaucracy (*bakufu*) that had been established at Edo by Tokugawa Ieyasu at the beginning of the 17th century held sway over Japan until the mid-19th century. Under this system, the governor (*shogun*) exercised absolute power and kept close control of the provincial barons (*daimyo*) and the increasingly poverty-stricken *samurai* warrior class. The emperor remained a remote, divine figurehead, residing at Kyoto some 480 kilometers (280 miles) from Edo.

Contact with foreigners was abhorred by this closed society. Russian and American ships that attempted to trade with Japan in 1791–92 were repelled. However, the opening up of California and the 1849 gold rush made the United States conscious that the Pacific offered unexplored commercial opportunities. The arrival at Uraga in 1853 of US Commodore Matthew Perry's "black ships" – a naval expedition to open trade with Japan – brought the question of contact with the outside world to the fore. Perry's return to Edo Bay the following year with a squadron of warships and 4,000 marines forced the *bakufu*'s hand, and the first limited concessions were granted to westerners to trade through the small ports of Shimoda and Hakodate.

The years following Perry's expedition saw resistance to foreign influence, organized by young samurai. Attacks on shipping caused a multinational naval force to bombard the forts at Kagoshima and Shimonoseki in 1863–64. Anti-foreign sentiment grew into concerted opposition to the shogunate. During 1867–68 civil war led to the the shogun being replaced with the emperor, in a development known as the Meiji ("enlightened rule") restoration. The emperor moved to Edo, now renamed Tokyo.

Under the new imperial regime, Japan resolved to compete with the west by industrializing, building a modern army and navy and adopting an aggressive foreign policy. In this way, it was intended that Japan should become the dominant power in east Asia. A pragmatic line was now taken toward foreign influence; western expertise was harnessed to build Japan's first light industrial enterprise, a silk-reeling factory. The growth of heavy industry also required the import of western plant and materials – steel, steam engines, and railroad rolling stock were all purchased from overseas. Through the offices of a samurai financier, Masayoshi Matsukata, the Japanese government borrowed money from the four giant *zaibatsu*, (financial organizations) that dominated banking, industry and commerce – Mitsui, Mitsubishi, Sumitomo and Yasuda.

Between 1871 and 1914 Japan achieved dominance in east Asia; the country acquired the Ryukyu Islands, the Bonin Islands (Ogasawara), southern Sakhalin and the Kuril Islands. In 1894 the Tonghak revolt in Korea reflected a growing socio-economic crisis at home but this provoked Chinese and Japanese intervention, with war erupting between the two powers the same year. Japanese ships destroyed the Chinese navy at the Battle of the Yellow Sea, while its army crushed the Chinese in Manchuria. The Japanese took Taiwan and the Pescadores; Korea became briefly independent. Yet intervention by the great powers subsequently deprived Japan of Port Arthur and the Liaodong Peninsula. When Russia was granted a lease of Port Arthur by China and attempted to expand its influence in Korea, Japanese fears grew stronger. Japan negotiated an alliance with Britain in 1902 that effectively neutralized Russia's ally, France, in the event of war, and then resolved to confront and overcome its chief rival in the region.

In 1904 Japanese troops landed in Korea and moved north toward the Yalu. Japanese warships attacked and then blockaded the Russian fleet at Port Arthur. On 1 January 1905 the Russian base surrendered. At Mukden Japan defeated the Russian army. Meanwhile the Russian Baltic Fleet, having sailed halfway around the world, arrived in Tsushima Straits too late to relieve Port Arthur. In one of the most important sea victories in history, Admiral Togo annihilated the obsolescent Russian fleet. In 1905 by the Treaty of Portsmouth (USA), Russia surrendered south Sakhalin and leases on Port Arthur and the South Manchurian railroad (completed in 1904). In 1910 Japan annexed independent Korea. By 1914 Japan had a major sphere of influence in east Asia.

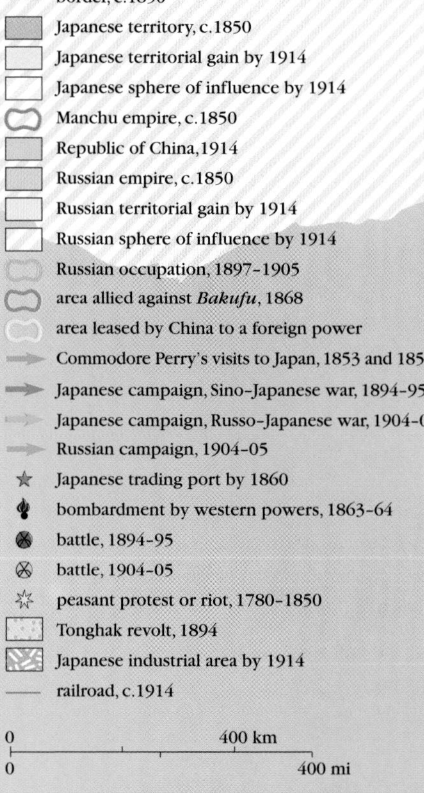
border, c.1850
Japanese territory, c.1850
Japanese territorial gain by 1914
Japanese sphere of influence by 1914
Manchu empire, c.1850
Republic of China, 1914
Russian empire, c.1850
Russian territorial gain by 1914
Russian sphere of influence by 1914
Russian occupation, 1897–1905
area allied against *Bakufu*, 1868
area leased by China to a foreign power
Commodore Perry's visits to Japan, 1853 and 1854
Japanese campaign, Sino-Japanese war, 1894–95
Japanese campaign, Russo-Japanese war, 1904–05
Russian campaign, 1904–05
Japanese trading port by 1860
bombardment by western powers, 1863–64
battle, 1894–95
battle, 1904–05
peasant protest or riot, 1780–1850
Tonghak revolt, 1894
Japanese industrial area by 1914
railroad, c.1914
0 400 km
0 400 mi

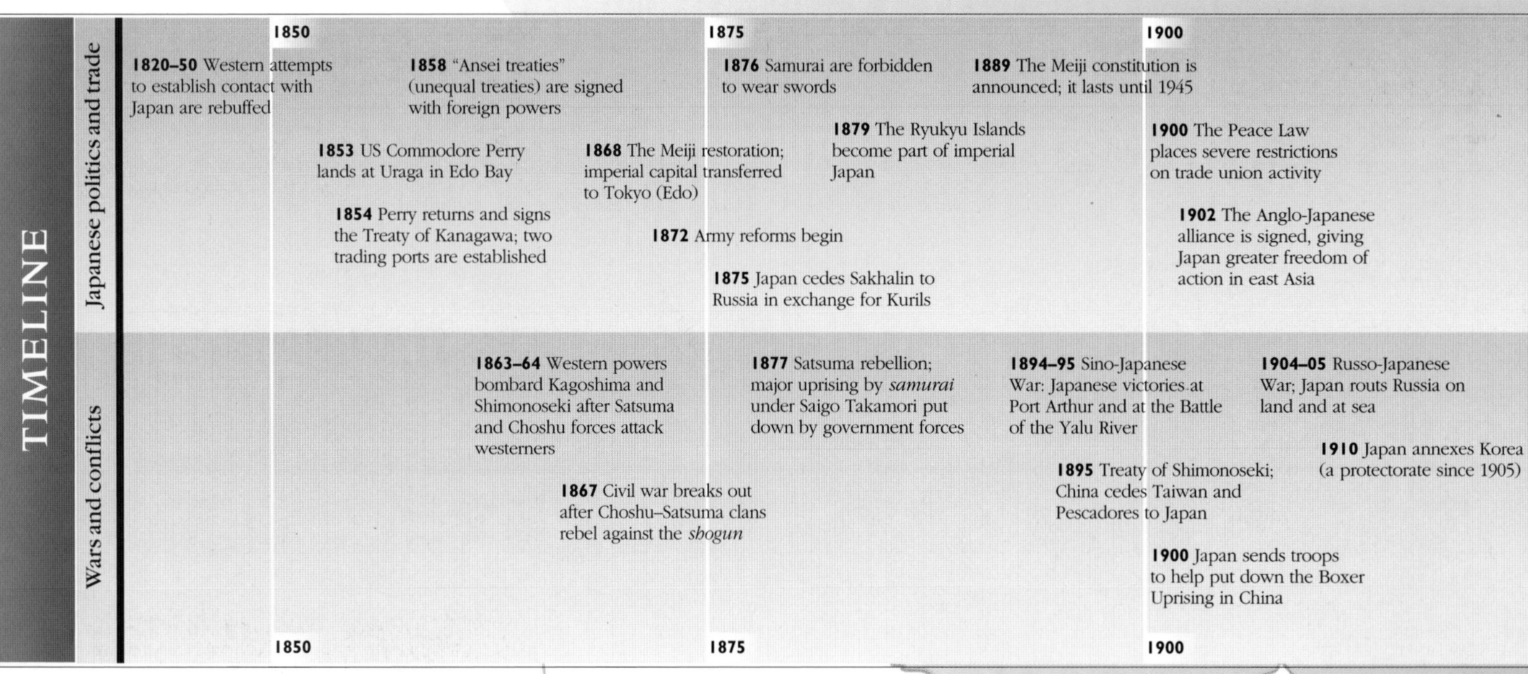

TIMELINE

Japanese politics and trade

1850 — 1875 — 1900

1820–50 Western attempts to establish contact with Japan are rebuffed

1853 US Commodore Perry lands at Uraga in Edo Bay

1854 Perry returns and signs the Treaty of Kanagawa; two trading ports are established

1858 "Ansei treaties" (unequal treaties) are signed with foreign powers

1868 The Meiji restoration; imperial capital transferred to Tokyo (Edo)

1872 Army reforms begin

1875 Japan cedes Sakhalin to Russia in exchange for Kurils

1876 Samurai are forbidden to wear swords

1879 The Ryukyu Islands become part of imperial Japan

1889 The Meiji constitution is announced; it lasts until 1945

1900 The Peace Law places severe restrictions on trade union activity

1902 The Anglo-Japanese alliance is signed, giving Japan greater freedom of action in east Asia

Wars and conflicts

1863–64 Western powers bombard Kagoshima and Shimonoseki after Satsuma and Choshu forces attack westerners

1867 Civil war breaks out after Choshu–Satsuma clans rebel against the *shogun*

1877 Satsuma rebellion; major uprising by *samurai* under Saigo Takamori put down by government forces

1894–95 Sino-Japanese War: Japanese victories at Port Arthur and at the Battle of the Yalu River

1895 Treaty of Shimonoseki; China cedes Taiwan and Pescadores to Japan

1900 Japan sends troops to help put down the Boxer Uprising in China

1904–05 Russo-Japanese War; Japan routs Russia on land and at sea

1910 Japan annexes Korea (a protectorate since 1905)

1850 — 1875 — 1900

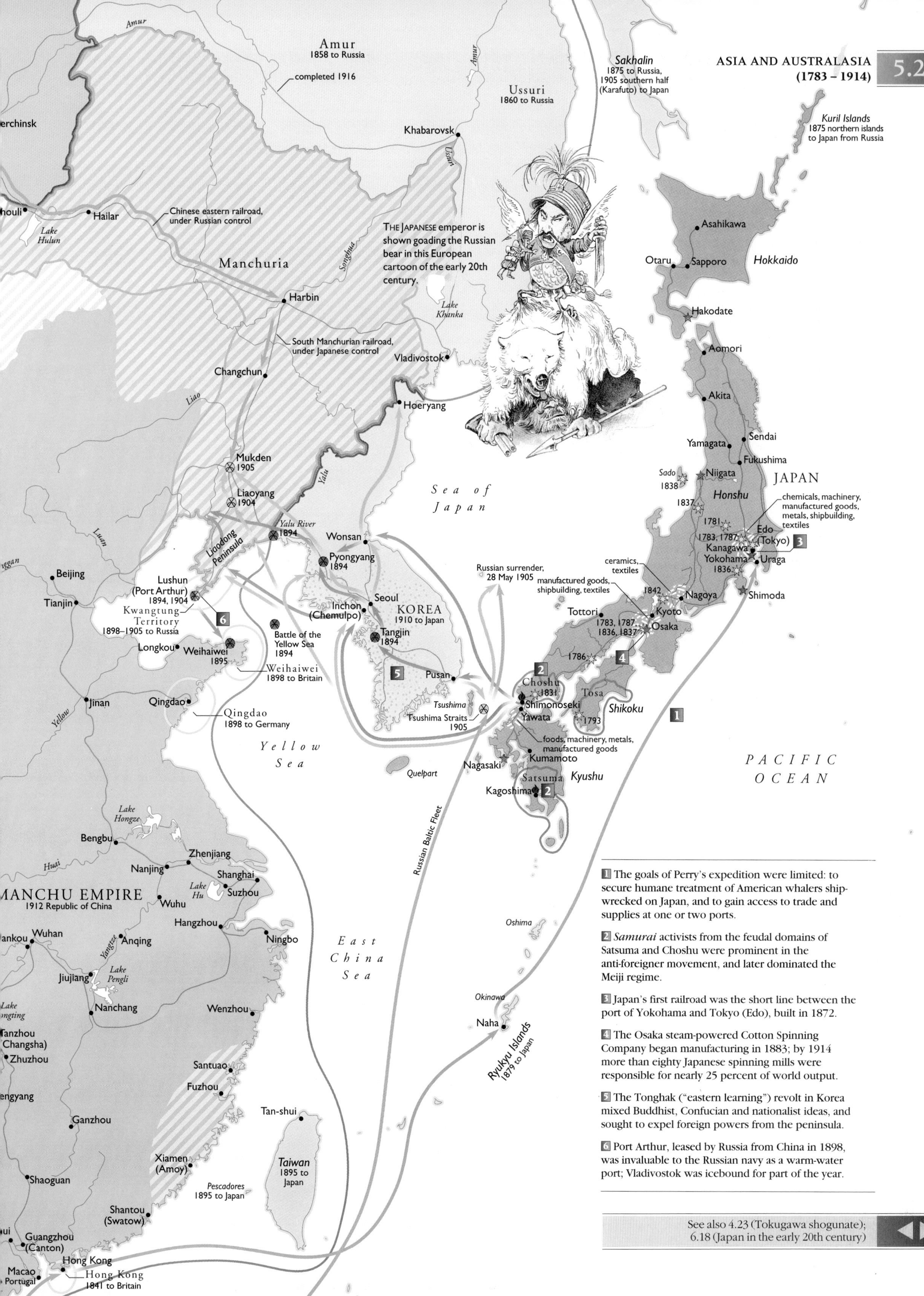
Amur
Amur
1858 to Russia
completed 1916
Amur
Sakhalin
1875 to Russia,
1905 southern half
(Karafuto) to Japan
Ussuri
1860 to Russia
Khabarovsk
Ussuri
Kuril Islands
1875 northern islands
to Japan from Russia
erchinsk
houli
Hailar
Lake Hulun
Chinese eastern railroad,
under Russian control
THE JAPANESE emperor is shown goading the Russian bear in this European cartoon of the early 20th century.
Manchuria
Songhua
Harbin
Lake Khanka
South Manchurian railroad,
under Japanese control
Vladivostok
Changchun
Liao
Hoeryang
Asahikawa
Otaru
Sapporo
Hokkaido
Hakodate
Aomori
Akita
Sendai
Yamagata
Fukushima
Sado
1838
Niigata
JAPAN
Honshu
1837
chemicals, machinery,
manufactured goods,
metals, shipbuilding,
textiles
1781
1783, 1787
Edo
(Tokyo)
3
Kanagawa
Yokohama
1836
Uraga
Shimoda
Mukden
1905
Liaoyang
1904
Yalu
Sea of Japan
Luan
Liaodong Peninsula
Yalu River
1894
Wonsan
Pyongyang
1894
Beijing
Tianjin
Lushun
(Port Arthur)
1894, 1904
Kwangtung
Territory
1898–1905 to Russia
6
Seoul
Inchon
(Chemulpo)
KOREA
1910 to Japan
Tangjin
1894
Battle of the
Yellow Sea
1894
Russian surrender,
28 May 1905
ceramics,
textiles
manufactured goods,
shipbuilding, textiles
1842
Nagoya
Kyoto
Osaka
Tottori
1783, 1787,
1836, 1837
1786
4
Longkou
Weihaiwei
1895
Weihaiwei
1898 to Britain
5
Pusan
2
Choshu
1831
Tosa
Shikoku
Tsushima
Shimonoseki
Yawata
1793
1
Jinan
Qingdao
Qingdao
1898 to Germany
Tsushima Straits
1905
Yellow
Yellow Sea
foods, machinery, metals,
manufactured goods
Nagasaki
Kumamoto
Quelpart
Satsuma
Kyushu
Kagoshima
2
PACIFIC OCEAN
Lake Hongze
Bengbu
Zhenjiang
Huai
Nanjing
Shanghai
Lake Hu
Suzhou
MANCHU EMPIRE
1912 Republic of China
Wuhu
Russian Baltic Fleet
Hangzhou
ankou
Wuhan
Yangtze
Anqing
Ningbo
Oshima
East China Sea
Jiujiang
Lake Pengli
Nanchang
Wenzhou
Okinawa
Naha
Ryukyu Islands
1879 to Japan
anzhou
Changsha)
Zhuzhou
Santuao
Fuzhou
engyang
Ganzhou
Tan-shui
Xiamen
(Amoy)
Taiwan
1895 to
Japan
Pescadores
1895 to Japan
Shaoguan
Shantou
(Swatow)
Guangzhou
(Canton)
Hong Kong
Macao
Portugal
Hong Kong
1841 to Britain

1 The goals of Perry's expedition were limited: to secure humane treatment of American whalers shipwrecked on Japan, and to gain access to trade and supplies at one or two ports.

2 *Samurai* activists from the feudal domains of Satsuma and Choshu were prominent in the anti-foreigner movement, and later dominated the Meiji regime.

3 Japan's first railroad was the short line between the port of Yokohama and Tokyo (Edo), built in 1872.

4 The Osaka steam-powered Cotton Spinning Company began manufacturing in 1883; by 1914 more than eighty Japanese spinning mills were responsible for nearly 25 percent of world output.

5 The Tonghak ("eastern learning") revolt in Korea mixed Buddhist, Confucian and nationalist ideas, and sought to expel foreign powers from the peninsula.

6 Port Arthur, leased by Russia from China in 1898, was invaluable to the Russian navy as a warm-water port; Vladivostok was icebound for part of the year.

See also 4.23 (Tokugawa shogunate); 6.18 (Japan in the early 20th century)

5.21 Britain and India • 1783 – 1914 •

Despite its territorial acquisitions toward the end of the 18th century, the British East India Company still saw its role in the subcontinent as primarily commercial. This was enshrined in the India Act passed by the British Parliament in 1784, which forbade further annexation. Nevertheless, British rule (*raj*) in India continued to grow, as successive governors-general felt obliged to occupy hostile territory or form protectorates to prevent disruption to trade. Thus, when Tipu Sultan of Mysore attacked Travancore in 1789, he saw half his dominions annexed by Lord Cornwallis (governor-general 1786–93) in the ensuing war. Warfare was resumed against the Marathas of central India in 1803.

The fear of an assault on India by Napoleon radically altered British policy. A far more aggressive approach was adopted, in which independent principalities such as Hyderabad were reduced to dependencies by the stationing of British troops there. After the French threat had passed, Company interest turned toward countering Burmese aggression in the east and guarding against Russian incursions from the north. Assam, Arakan, and Tenasserim were acquired from Burma in 1824–26. On the northwest frontier, the First Afghan War (1839–42) was begun against Dost Muhammed; in both this and a later conflict (1878–80), the British occupied Kabul but failed to dominate the country. An attack on Sind secured the Bolan Pass in 1843, while two bloody wars against the Sikhs brought control of the Punjab. Lord Dalhousie (governor-general 1848–56) now evolved the doctrine of "lapse" (when a Hindu prince had no natural heirs his lands passed to the Company) and, on the pretext of ineffective government, annexed Muslim Oudh in 1856.

The East India Company also instituted administrative reforms. These began with revision of land revenue collection (the principal source of public finance) and a reorganization of the judicial system along British lines. Despite a Parliamentary directive urging respect for the people's rights and customs, the Company often disregarded religious and cultural sensitivities – particularly under governor-general Lord Bentinck (1828–35) who tried to ban *suttee* (the immolation of Hindu widows), *thuggee* (ritual robbery and murder) and infanticide. Continuing Christian conversion, plans to extend roads and railroads and an insistence on English as the language of education and commerce all threatened the traditional ways of life of both Hindus and Muslims.

Opposition to British rule was not, however, anticipated among the Company's *sepoy* (native) armies. Three such armies had been raised in India; those based at Madras and Bombay were largely untroubled by questions of caste and religion, but the Bengal *sepoys* – high-caste Hindus and Shi'ite Muslims – were offended by a rumor that new rifle cartridges (which had to be bitten before use) were greased with pork and beef fat. This violated the dietary proscriptions of their religions. Thus began the most serious challenge to British rule in India.

The Indian mutiny (also known as the First War of Independence) arose in January 1857 among troops stationed at Meerut and rapidly spread through north central India. The army revolt acted as a catalyst to a number of other grievances, and the mutineers were supported by peasant uprisings and some isolated *jihads*. The capture of Delhi and the besieging of the cities of Kanpur and Lucknow were serious blows to British authority. However, the Bombay and Madras armies remained largely loyal, and there was no strategy for a national revolt.

Though brief, the mutiny changed the face of British India; suspicion was now widespread on both sides. The 1858 Government of India Act transferred sovereignty from the East India Company to the British monarch and ended the doctrine of lapse, but other reforms were never instituted. Theoretically, racial impartiality operated in recruitment to the Indian civil service; in practice few Indians were admitted. The insular community of Anglo-Indians shunned contact with the indigenous population and became ever more prosperous, partly through investment in plantations in southeast Asia and Africa. Gurkha and Sikh troops from the northwest of India now formed the backbone of the army.

The British policy in frontier regions continued to be determined by fear of Russian expansion; this led to the Second Afghan War of 1878–80, which ended with the recognition that Afghanistan could not be incorporated within the Indian empire. Similarly, in 1903 the British under Colonel Younghusband invaded Tibet. After a year's conflict Tibet agreed not to concede territory to a foreign power.

Excluded from the administration of their country, educated Indians turned increasingly toward nationalism. The Indian National Congress was founded in 1885 and Gopal Gokhale, its president in 1905, worked for peaceful constitutional progress towards responsible government. The All-India Muslim League, a similarly constitutional organization, was founded in 1906. The Morley–Minto constitutional reforms (1909) brought in a measure of representative government, but Indians were still denied true legislative and financial power.

territory under direct Maratha rule, 1785
British territory, 1805
British territorial gains by 1838
British territorial gains by 1857
British territorial gains by 1914
British sphere of influence, 1914
princely state or protectorate, 1914
border of princely state or protectorate
border, 1914
battle in the second Maratha War, 1803–05
disruption to British administration during the Indian mutiny, 1857–59
Sepoy army base remaining loyal to Britain, 1857
center of rebellion
naval station
coal source of commodity
British campaign
railroad by 1914

AFGHANISTAN
Kandahar
Quetta
PERSIA
1893 to Britain
Baluchistan
1876 British protectorate

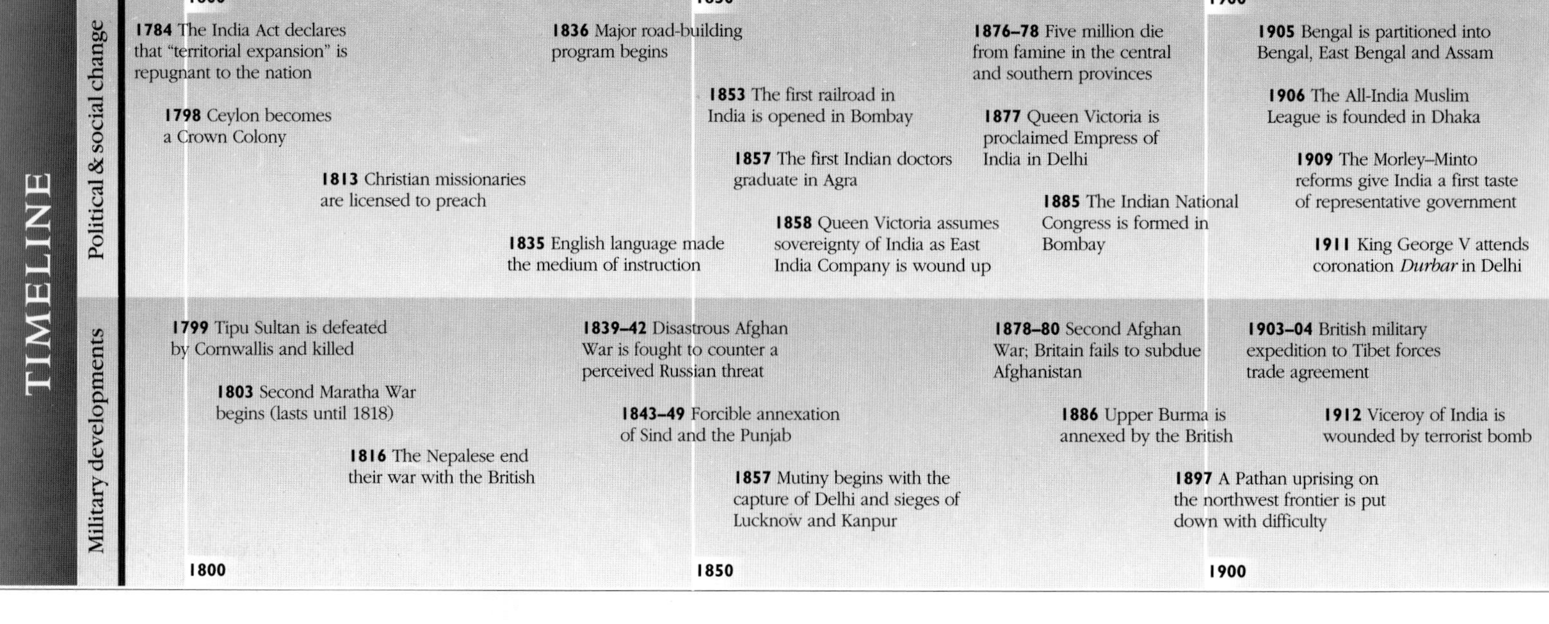
TIMELINE
Political & social change
Military developments
1800
1850
1900
1784 The India Act declares that "territorial expansion" is repugnant to the nation
1798 Ceylon becomes a Crown Colony
1813 Christian missionaries are licensed to preach
1835 English language made the medium of instruction
1836 Major road-building program begins
1853 The first railroad in India is opened in Bombay
1857 The first Indian doctors graduate in Agra
1858 Queen Victoria assumes sovereignty of India as East India Company is wound up
1876–78 Five million die from famine in the central and southern provinces
1877 Queen Victoria is proclaimed Empress of India in Delhi
1885 The Indian National Congress is formed in Bombay
1905 Bengal is partitioned into Bengal, East Bengal and Assam
1906 The All-India Muslim League is founded in Dhaka
1909 The Morley–Minto reforms give India a first taste of representative government
1911 King George V attends coronation *Durbar* in Delhi
1799 Tipu Sultan is defeated by Cornwallis and killed
1803 Second Maratha War begins (lasts until 1818)
1816 The Nepalese end their war with the British
1839–42 Disastrous Afghan War is fought to counter a perceived Russian threat
1843–49 Forcible annexation of Sind and the Punjab
1857 Mutiny begins with the capture of Delhi and sieges of Lucknow and Kanpur
1878–80 Second Afghan War; Britain fails to subdue Afghanistan
1886 Upper Burma is annexed by the British
1897 A Pathan uprising on the northwest frontier is put down with difficulty
1903–04 British military expedition to Tibet forces trade agreement
1912 Viceroy of India is wounded by terrorist bomb
1800
1850
1900

1 Tipu Sultan of Mysore, the East India Company's greatest adversary in south India from the early 1780s, tried to ally himself with the French and was killed at the siege of Seringapatam in 1799.

2 Gurkha warriors from the hill tribes of Nepal fought fiercely against the British from 1814–16. From 1860 to the present day, Gurkhas have been recruited to form an elite infantry unit of the British Army.

3 The First Afghan War ended with a humiliating retreat from Kabul to Jalalabad (1842); only 121 men of the entire 20,000-strong British force survived.

4 Atrocities were committed by both sides during the mutiny; British reprisals included executing mutineers by strapping them to the muzzles of artillery pieces.

5 Tea has been cultivated as a major commercial crop since the mid-19th century, particularly in the fertile, rainy upper Brahmaputra valley in Assam.

6 The northwest frontier of India proved the most troublesome to defend for the British. In 1897, 35,000 troops were needed to quell a rising by Pathan tribes.

7 The British briefly invaded Tibet in 1903–04, to counter Russian influence there by imposing a trading agreement on the Dalai Lama.

8 Bombay was the site of the Gateway to India, an arch erected in Mughal style in 1911.

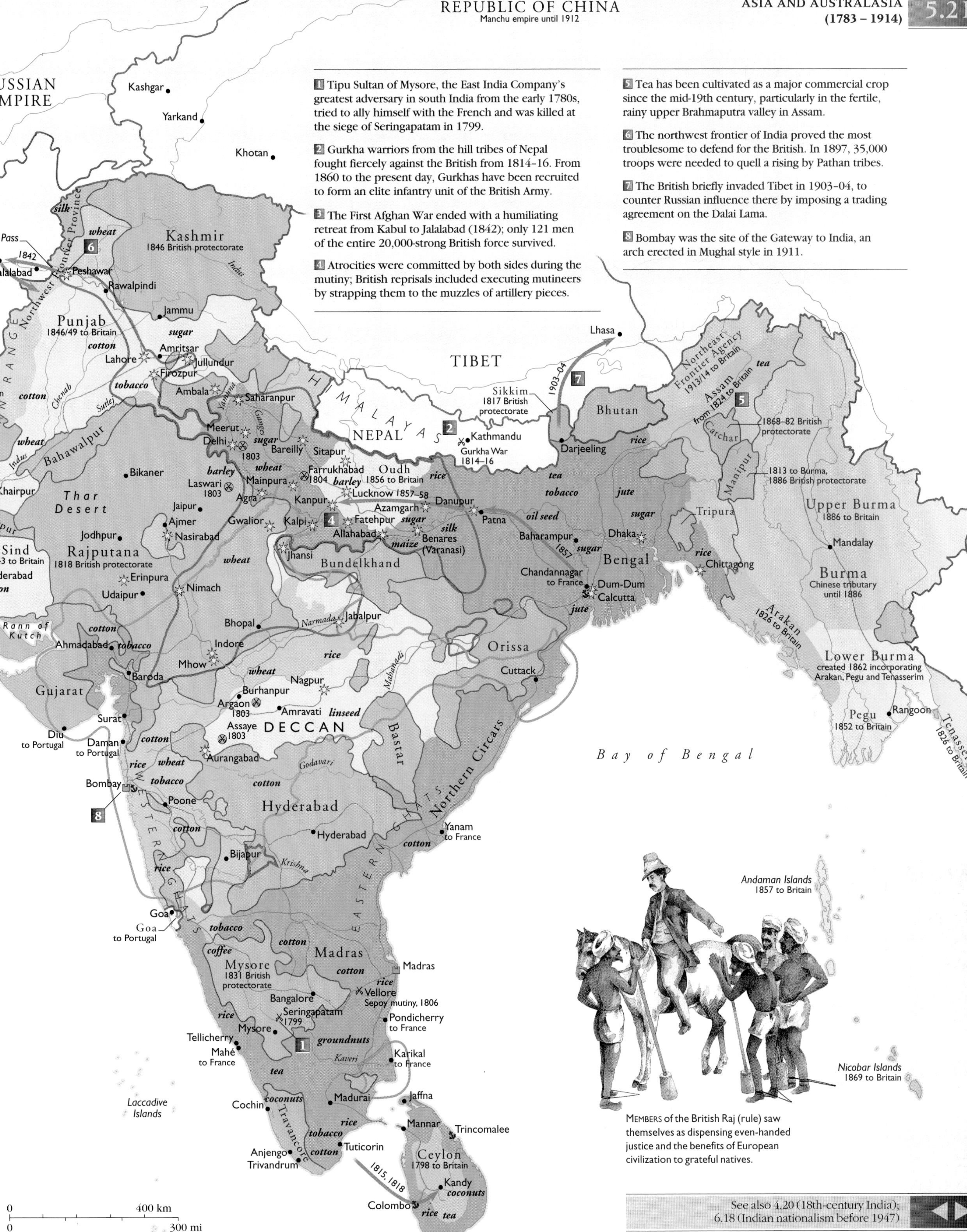
REPUBLIC OF CHINA
Manchu empire until 1912
USSIAN
MPIRE
Kashgar
Yarkand
Khotan
Kashmir
1846 British protectorate
Northwest Frontier Province
Pass
1842
alalabad
Peshawar
Rawalpindi
Jammu
Punjab
1846/49 to Britain
Lahore
Amritsar
Jullundur
Firozpur
Ambala
Saharanpur
Meerut
Delhi
1803
Bareilly
Sitapur
Farrukhabad
1804
Oudh
1856 to Britain
Lucknow 1857–58
Kanpur
Azamgarh
Danupur
Patna
Mainpura
Laswari
1803
Agra
Bikaner
Bahawalpur
Thar Desert
Khairpur
Jaipur
Ajmer
Nasirabad
Gwalior
Kalpi
Fatehpur
Allahabad
Benares (Varanasi)
Jhansi
Bundelkhand
Jodhpur
Sind
Rajputana
1818 British protectorate
Erinpura
Udaipur
Nimach
Rann of Kutch
Ahmadabad
Bhopal
Jabalpur
Indore
Mhow
Baroda
Gujarat
Nagpur
Burhanpur
Argaon
1803
Amravati
Assaye
1803
DECCAN
Surat
Diu
to Portugal
Daman
to Portugal
Aurangabad
Bombay
Poone
Hyderabad
Bijapur
Goa
to Portugal
Madras
Mysore
1831 British protectorate
Bangalore
Vellore
Sepoy mutiny, 1806
Seringapatam
1799
Pondicherry
to France
Tellicherry
Mahé
to France
Karikal
to France
Cochin
Travancore
Madurai
Jaffna
Mannar
Trincomalee
Anjengo
Trivandrum
Tuticorin
Ceylon
1798 to Britain
1815, 1818
Kandy
Colombo
Laccadive Islands
Yanam
to France
Bastar
Northern Circars
Western Ghats
Eastern Ghats
Orissa
Cuttack
Bengal
Chandannagar
to France
Dum-Dum
Calcutta
Baharampur
1857
Dhaka
Chittagong
Tripura
Manipur
1813 to Burma,
1886 British protectorate
Carchar
1868–82 British protectorate
Assam
from 1824 to Britain
Northeast Frontier Agency
1913/14 to Britain
Bhutan
Darjeeling
Sikkim
1817 British protectorate
1903–04
Lhasa
TIBET
HIMALAYAS
NEPAL
Kathmandu
Gurkha War
1814–16
Upper Burma
1886 to Britain
Mandalay
Burma
Chinese tributary until 1886
Arakan
1826 to Britain
Lower Burma
created 1862 incorporating Arakan, Pegu and Tenasserim
Pegu
1852 to Britain
Rangoon
Tenasserim
1826 to Britain
Bay of Bengal
Andaman Islands
1857 to Britain
Nicobar Islands
1869 to Britain
silk
wheat
sugar
cotton
tobacco
barley
rice
tea
jute
oil seed
maize
linseed
coffee
groundnuts
coconuts
Indus
Chenab
Sutlej
Yamuna
Ganges
Narmada
Mahanadi
Godavari
Krishna
Kaveri
0
400 km
0
300 mi

MEMBERS of the British Raj (rule) saw themselves as dispensing even-handed justice and the benefits of European civilization to grateful natives.

See also 4.20 (18th-century India); 6.18 (Indian nationalism before 1947)

5.22 Colonialism in southeast Asia • 1800 – 1914 •

Southeast Asia had suffered extensive foreign intervention by the end of the 18th century. While the Dutch seaborne empire in island southeast Asia remained the major European presence, British entrepreneurs had also set up bases for trade with China. French missionaries and traders, interested in Vietnam since the 17th century, were given more leeway through a 1787 treaty. However, the first major French expedition did not occur until 1858–59, when the empire-building aspirations of Napoleon III resulted in the capture of Saigon. Despite resistance in the Mekong delta area, the French made further gains, establishing a protectorate over the Buddhist state of Cambodia and opening Hanoi and Tourane (Da Nang) as treaty ports. In an undeclared war with China (1883–85), France tried to win control of the whole of Indo-China, a goal achieved in 1887 with the merging of Cochin China, Cambodia, Annam and Tongking as the Indo-Chinese Union (French Indo-China). In 1893 it was extended to include Laos.

At first the French in Indo-China concentrated on modernizing and maximizing profits. Peasants were urged to sell land to boost rice production, so undermining traditional large viable villages. Landless peasants took jobs in salt and opium factories or worked for landlords.

British involvement in mainland southeast Asia began with the purchase of the island of Penang from the sultan of Kedah in 1786. During the Napoleonic Wars (when the Netherlands was under French control), Britain attacked Batavia to win control of Java and safeguard its trade routes to China through the island channels. The administrator Sir Stamford Raffles founded the free port of Singapore in 1819, which rapidly became the commercial center of the region, stimulating demand for British cotton manufactures in southeast Asia and China. In 1824 Britain ceded Benkulen and its claims to Sumatra in exchange for Dutch recognition of British sovereignty over Penang, Port Wellesley, Singapore and Malacca (collectively known as the Straits Settlements). Britain became involved in combating piracy and slavery, and settling disputes among the Malay princely states and sultanates on

Calcutta
Chittagong
tea
Yandabu
Mandalay
tin
Upper Burma
1886 to Britain
Arakan
1826 to Britain
1825, 52, 85
Tongking
1885 to France
Langson
1885
Nannin
Zhanjia
Hanoi
rice
Haiphong
1882–83
Hai
Chiang Mai
Laos
1893 to France
silk
rice
Lower Burma
created 1862
tobacco
Rangoon
rice
French Indo-China
founded 1887
rubber
Hue
Tourane
(Da Na
SIAM
6
ivory
tin
1824
Tenasserim
1826 to Britain
rice
tobacco
Bangkok
3
Annam
1883 to France
Andaman Islands
1857 to Britain
tin
rubber
Cambodia
1863 to France
Mekong
rice
Tenasserim
rubber
tin
Phnom Penh
rubber
Andaman Sea
Plain of Reeds
Saigon
Cochin China
1867 to France
rice
1859
tin
Nicobar Islands
1869 to Britain
rubber
sultanate of Aceh, 1873
Federated Malay States, 1896
Unfederated Malay States, 1909
borders, 1914
British territory, 1914
British sphere of influence
Dutch East Indies, 1914
French Indochina, 1914
German territory, 1914
Portuguese territory, 1914
United States territory, 1914
area of piracy
area of resistance by indigenous peoples
British campaign
French campaign
United States campaign
gold source of commodity
trade route through Malacca Straits
0 600 km
0 400 mi
Kutaraja
tobacco
Aceh
Aceh War, 1873–1903
rubber
5
tin
Simeulue
Barus
rubber
rubber
Sarawak
Sambas
Nias
rice
ivory
spices
oil
Padri War, 1830–39
Tiku
Indragiri
tin
1811
Padang
Sumatra
Minangkabau
Painan
Jambi
Siberut
Batang
ivory
Indrapura
spices
Sukadana
Bangka
tin
tin
Belitung
INDIAN OCEAN
Palembang
Benkulen
1824 to Netherlands
spices
rubber
Bantam
Batavia
(Jakarta)
bauxite
Tegal
Java War, 1825–3
Yogyakarta

TIMELINE

Indo-China

1800

1782–1809 Rama I founds Bangkok and increases Siam's influence in Chiangmai, the Lao states and Cambodia

1786 Britain acquires Penang from Sultan of Kedah

1795 Britain takes Malacca from the Dutch

1802 Nguyen Anh unifies Vietnam and rules from Hue as the first Nguyen emperor

1819 Founding of Singapore by Sir Stamford Raffles

1820–42 Vietnamese emperor Minh-Manh revives Confucianism and persecutes Christians

1824 The Anglo-Dutch Treaty confirms British dominance in Malaya (and Singapore)

1824–25 The British take Rangoon in First Burmese War

1850

1852–53 Second Burmese War; British gains reduce Burma to an inland state

1855 King Mongkut (r.1851–68) opens Siam to British trade

1858–59 French and Spanish naval force bombards Tourane and occupies Saigon

1873 France begins the occupation of Tongking

1883 The Treaty of Hué leads to the creation of French protectorates in Annam and Tongking

1886 Britain annexes Upper Burma in Third Burmese War

1887 The Indo-Chinese Union is created by France

1896 Malay states of Perak, Selangor, Negri Sembilan and Pahang are federated

1900

1909 Anglo-Siamese Treaty; Britain controls Kedah, Perlis, Kelantan and Trengganu

1914 100,000 Vietnamese go to France to serve in labor battalions in World War I

Island southeast Asia

1811 The Dutch surrender Java to a British invasion force

1814–16 The Netherlands regains Sumatra and Java

1841 The sultan of Brunei cedes Sarawak to Brooke

1859 The Dutch and Portuguese agree to partition island of Timor

1873 The Dutch attack the Aceh sultanate (to 1907)

1884 Germany annexes northern New Guinea and the Bismarck Archipelago

1898–99 US takes Philippines in the Spanish-American War

1901 Filipino leader Emileo Aguinaldo is captured

1800 **1850** **1900**

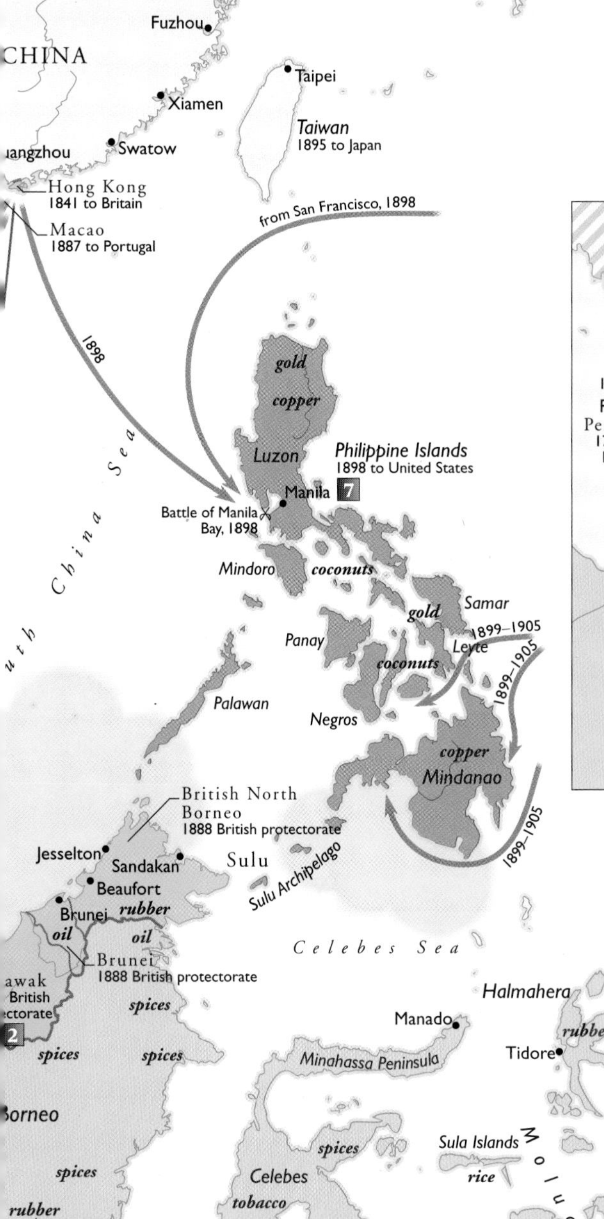

CHINA
Fuzhou
Xiamen
Swatow
Taipei
Taiwan
1895 to Japan
Hong Kong
1841 to Britain
Macao
1887 to Portugal
from San Francisco, 1898
1898
South China Sea
gold
copper
Luzon
Philippine Islands
1898 to United States
Manila
7
Battle of Manila Bay, 1898
Mindoro
coconuts
Samar
gold
Panay
Leyte
1899–1905
coconuts
Palawan
Negros
copper
Mindanao
British North Borneo
1888 British protectorate
Jesselton
Sandakan
Beaufort
Sulu
Sulu Archipelago
Brunei
rubber
oil
Brunei
1888 British protectorate

0 300 km
0 200 mi
Perlis
1909 to Britain
Port Wellesley
1800 to Britain
Kelantan
Kedah
1909 to Britain
Penang
Penang
1786 to Britain
Kelantan
1909 to Britain
Kuala Trengganu
Trengganu
1909 to Britain
Perak
Perak
1875 to Britain
Pahang
1887 to Britain
Pahang
Selangor
1874 to Britain
Kuala Lumpur
Negri Sembilan
1874 to Britain
Malacca
Johore
1885 to Britain
Johore Bahru
Malacca
1795 to Britain
Singapore
1819 to Britain
Celebes Sea
Halmahera
Manado
rubber
Tidore
Minahassa Peninsula
spices
Borneo
Sula Islands
Moluccas
rice
Celebes
tobacco
nickel
Ceram
oil
Amboina
Buru
Banjarmasin
Macassar
Bone
Dutch East Indies
(Netherlands India)
Banda Sea
Kai Islands
Aru Islands
Hollandia
Bismarck Archipelago
Dutch New Guinea
1828 to Netherlands
German New Guinea
1884 to Germany
New Guinea
Territory of Papua
1884 to Britain
1888 British colony
1906 to Australia
4
Merauke
Port Moresby
Wetar
rice
Tanimbar Islands
Bali
Flores
Alore
coconuts
1881–94
Bima
copra
Dili
East Timor
to Portugal
Lombok
Sumbawa
copra
rubber
Timor
Sumba
Arafura Sea
Melville Island

1 The first of several revolts against Dutch rule on Java took place in 1825–30 under Dipo Negora, and was only suppressed with great difficulty.

2 As a reward for helping the sultan of Brunei put down a revolt in Sarawak in 1841, the British adventurer James Brooke was made *rajah* of the area. The Brooke "White Rajahs" ruled Sarawak for a century.

3 In 1858–59, a joint French and Spanish naval force bombarded Tourane and sailed south to take Saigon.

4 The Australian state of Queensland's attempt to annex the east of New Guinea in 1884 to forestall German expansion was repudiated by the British government. By the time the British acted, Germany had already established control of the north.

5 Rubber began to be commercially grown in Malaya from 1896 onward, when plants cultivated in England from South American stock were planted there.

6 In 1896, France and Britain agreed that Siam should remain an independent buffer state between their respective possessions in Indo-China and Burma.

7 To take the Philippines from the Spanish in 1898, the United States dispatched 10,000 troops from San Francisco, while the US Asiatic squadron under Admiral Dewey left Hong Kong for Manila.

the peninsula. In 1896 Federated Malay States was set up under a British resident-general. Thirteen years later other states were acquired from Siam; these formed the Unfederated Malay States. Tin exports increased after mining was mechanized in the early 1900s. Rubber also became a major export; by 1911 nearly half a million hectares of rubber was being grown, mainly on large, European-owned estates. The 1824 treaty had also provided a case for the "white rajah" James Brooke to gain British protection for the state he created in Sarawak in 1841. In North Borneo commercial competition for concessions from Brunei and Sulu led eventually to an 1881 royal charter for a British North Borneo Company, which undertook the exploitation of the territory.

To protect India's borders, Britain also annexed Burma in the course of three brief wars. The first (1824–26) was in response to a Burmese invasion of Bengal, and resulted in Burma surrendering large tracts of territory. Lower Burma was secured by the British in the second war (1852–53), and Upper Burma in the third (1885–86). The British administered the country as part of India.

Germany and the United States were late beginning their colonial ventures in southeast Asia. Rival claims to the eastern part of New Guinea eventually saw Germany occupy the northeast and the adjacent islands (renamed the Bismarck Archipelago), and a British protectorate over the southeast of the island. A crown colony in 1888, British New Guinea became a territory of the Australian Commonwealth in 1906. The United States acquired its first and most important southeast Asian colony in 1898, when Admiral Dewey destroyed a Spanish fleet in Manila Bay to secure the Philippines. Filipino nationalists, who had been encouraged by the United States to fight for their independence against Spanish rule, now felt betrayed by US actions and fierce fighting ensued on Mindanao during 1902–05. The conflict wrecked the fragile economy and, in addition to military casualties, 100,000 people died from famine.

After the withdrawal of the British from Sumatra, the Dutch faced opposition from indigenous people in the East Indies. Prince Dipo Negoro's rebellion led to the Java War of 1825–29; Tuanku Imam, Minangkabau's militant leader, fought the Dutch 1830–39; and persistent attacks on merchant shipping by the state of Aceh led the Dutch to declare war in 1873. Thirty years of conflict drained the Dutch reserves so that effective occupation of the islands was still incomplete by 1914, although the governor-general J.B. Van Heutsz (1904–09) strove relentlessly to govern the East Indies as a single state from Batavia.

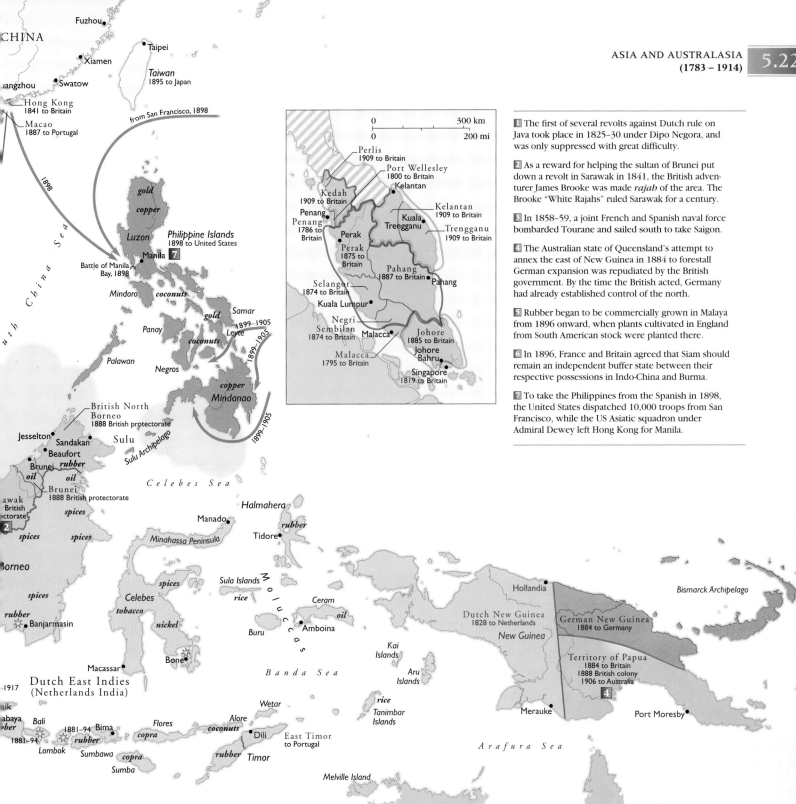

See also 4.24 (southeast Asia in the 18th century); 6.12 (southeast Asia 1914–41)

Latin America • 1783 – 1914 •

Napoleon's invasion of the Iberian peninsula in 1808–09 was the catalyst to the independence movements in the American colonies of Spain and Portugal. In the Spanish territories, wars of liberation broke out when Napoleon's brother Joseph Bonaparte took the Spanish throne. Brazil played host to Portugal's prince regent, later JoãoVI, who fled there in 1807 after the French occupied Portugal. When he returned home in 1822, his son Pedro became emperor of an independent Brazil. The new state was recognized by Portugal in 1825.

Mexico's war of independence, led by the priest Miguel Hidalgo, began in 1810. Hidalgo was executed, but his conservative successor Agustín Iturbide united Mexican society and in 1822–23 formed the Mexican empire with himself as emperor. At the same time, the Spanish colonies in Central America proclaimed a Confederation of the United Provinces, which lasted until 1838, when its constituent parts became individual sovereign states.

The principal figure of South American independence, Simón Bolívar (the "Liberator"), began his fight to free his native Venezuela and adjoining territories from Spanish rule in 1811. Bolívar's victory at Boyacá in 1819 heralded the proclamation of the Republic of Gran Colombia, and his defeat of the royalists at Carabobo in 1821 led to the fall of Caracas and to Venezuelan independence. In Argentina, revolutionary forces were led by José de San Martín, a veteran of the Peninsular War. San Martín trained an army and led it across the Andes in 1817 to take Lima in 1821. He proclaimed Peru's independence, then gave up control to Bolívar who established a revolutionary government at Lima. With the final battle of the wars of liberation at Ayacucho in 1824, all Spanish possessions in the Americas were independent, except Cuba and Puerto Rico.

The new states not only inherited the frontiers of the former Spanish and Portuguese administrative regions; social divisions also remained intact. There was no tradition of pluralistic government, and color was still decisive. Spanish-born whites or peninsulares (and reinóis, the Portuguese equivalent in Brazil) were dominant. The majority of the people (mestizos or Indian–Europeans) had limited power

UNITED STATES
1783
Fort Leavenworth
St Louis
Memphis
Atlanta
Birmingham
Jacksonville
New Orleans
Florida 1810/19 to US
Mississippi
Arkansas
Salt Lake City
Denver
Kearney 1845
Fremont 1846
Fremont 1845–46
Colorado
Sacramento
San Francisco
Monterey
Santa Barbara
Stockton 1846
Los Angeles
1848 to US under Treaty of Guadalupe Hidalgo
Kearney 1846
1836–1845 to Texas, 1850 sold to US
1836–45 to Texas
cattle
Texas
1836–45 independent republic, 1845 to US
San Diego
Mexicali
1853 sold to US under Gadsden Purchase
Sloat 1846
Ciudad Juárez
San Antonio
Alamo 1836
San Jacinto 1836
Scott 1846
Doniphan 1847
Rio Grande
Chihuahua 1847
Resaca de la Palma 1846
Taylor 1846
Palo Alto 1846
Fort Brown
Gulf of Mexico
Havana
sugar
Ciudad Obregón
Monterrey
Buena Vista 1847
Padilla
oil
Tampico
Scott 1847
Mérida
Yucatan 1835–48 independent
British Honduras to Britain
Mazatlán
San Luis Potosí
silver
sugar
Cerro Gordo 1847
Veracruz
Mexico City
Chapultepec 1847
MEXICO 1821
coffee
GUATEMALA 1838
HONDURAS 1838
Tegucigalpa
bananas
Guatemala City
San Salvador
EL SALVADOR 1838
Managua
NICARAGUA 1838
San José
COSTA RICA 1838
PANAMA 1821 to Colombia, 1903
Galapagos Islands 1832 to Ecuador
Portuguese colony c.1800
Spanish colony c.1800
Republic of Gran Colombia, 1819–30
united with Mexico 1821–23, independent as United Provinces of Central America 1823–38
Confederation of Peru & Bolivia 1836–39
1838 date of independence as a nation-state
territory gained by former Spanish colony since independence, with date
territory gained by the United States from Mexico, with date
campaign by Simón Bolívar 1819–24
campaign by José de San Martín 1817–22
campaign by United States forces, 1846–48
battle fought by José de San Martín
battle fought by Bolívar or de Sucre
battle during the Mexican–American War, 1846–48
battle during the Paraguayan War (War of the Triple Alliance), 1864–70
battle during the War of the Pacific 1879–83
border c.1840
other border
railroad within Latin America by 1914
oil trade commodity
movement of peoples

SIMON BOLIVAR was a remarkable military leader, and is the only individual to have a state named for him today.

TIMELINE

Wars and revolutions

1810–11 Miguel Hidalgo leads an unsuccessful popular revolt in Mexico

1810–14 An attempted revolution in Chile is defeated

1819 Simón Bolívar routs the Spanish at Boyacá and founds Republic of Gran Colombia

1821 Battle of Carabobo; independence of Venezuela

1836 Texas gains its independence from Mexico at the Battle of San Jacinto

1836–39 Bolivia and Peru form a brief confederation

1846–48 Mexican–American War following US annexation of Texas (1845); Mexico loses all its northern territories

1863 Ill-fated attempt by Mexican conservatives and French to install emperor (Maximilian I; executed 1867)

1864–70 War of the Triple Alliance is fought by Paraguay against Argentina, Uruguay and Brazil.

1879–83 War of the Pacific between Chile and Bolivia and Peru

1903 A revolution in Panama brings independence from Colombia

1910 The Mexican Revolution begins; forces under Francisco Madero oppose dictatorship of Porfirio Diaz (1876–1911)

1914 United States Marines occupy Veracruz to safeguard US interests

Social and political change

1807 The Braganzas (Portuguese royal family) flee to Brazil under British escort

1823 US recognizes newly independent states and proclaims the "Monroe Doctrine"

1829–52 Dictatorship of Juan Manuel Rosas in Argentina

1831 Emperor Pedro I of Brazil abdicates and his son Pedro II succeeds

1853 Mexico sells the Mesilla Valley to the United States in the "Gadsden Purchase"

1870–88 Liberal Guzman Blanco is president in Venezuela; many social and political reforms are instituted

1879 French company under Ferdinand de Lesseps is set up to build the Panama Canal

1889 The Brazilian empire is succeeded by Republic of the United States of Brazil

1904 US engineers begin cutting the Panama Canal (completed 1914)

1830 · 1860 · 1890

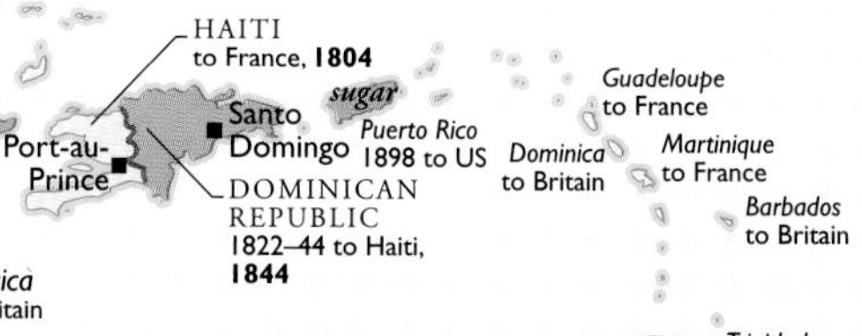
HAITI
to France, 1804
sugar
Santo
Domingo
Puerto Rico
1898 to US
Port-au-
Prince
DOMINICAN
REPUBLIC
1822–44 to Haiti,
1844
Guadeloupe
to France
Dominica
to Britain
Martinique
to France
Barbados
to Britain

while the *mulattoes* (African–Europeans), *zambos* (Indian–Africans), blacks and Indians all suffered discrimination. Sectional interests, such as the military, the church, industrialists, bankers and landlords were often in conflict, and power was frequently seized by *caudillos*, dictators who ruled through patronage and private armies.

The *caudillo* José Francia helped lead Paraguay's struggle for independence and was "el supremo" 1814–40. Bernardo O'Higgins was prominent in Chile's revolution and became "supreme director" 1817–23. The Mexican Antonio de Santa Anna, after a period as an elected president (1833–36), intermittently took dictatorial powers. During his rule Mexico fought, largely unsuccessfully, against the United States, and ceded large tracts of land by 1850.

Intervention by European powers in Latin American affairs was effectively preempted by the Monroe doctrine of 1823, which signaled US hostility toward any attempt to colonize the region. Most territorial changes that occurred did so as a result of wars between the new sovereign states. Major conflicts of the period were the War of the Pacific, in which Chile defeated Peru and Bolivia, and the War of the Triple Alliance), involving Paraguay, Brazil, Argentina and Uruguay. The 1910–11 Mexican revolution led to chaos, mass slaughter and eventual US intervention, as US president Wilson supported General Huerta who exterminated the nationalist Zapata rebels while Pancho Villa's bandits ran riot in the north. Wilson sent warships to Tampico and troops to Veracruz in 1914.

Economic change came swiftly to Latin America. Foreign capital funded railroad and harbor construction; the Panama Canal was completed by US engineers in 1914 after an earlier French venture had failed. British firms exploited the natural phosphates and nitrates of Peru and northern Chile, for use in fertilizers and explosives. US investment turned coffee exports into a vital element in Brazil's economy. In Argentina, revenue from wool, leather and beef exports brought a sharp rise in the standard of living; meat exports grew after refrigerated sea transport was introduced in the 1880s; but a decline in world trade in the 1890s ended the boom years.

Immigrants were among the region's greatest assets. Initially they entered Chile and Argentina (which saw a huge influx of Italian immigrants from the 1850s), but Brazil became the preferred destination after slavery was abolished there in 1888. Over one million Europeans arrived in Brazil by 1898; they were favored over the original inhabitants for educational and work opportunities. Chinese and Japanese laborers were also imported in large numbers to work on the railroads and in the mines.

1 Peruvian *guano* (seabird droppings used as fertilizer) was a major source of foreign revenue after independence, but deposits were exhausted in 20 years.

2 At the Alamo in 1836, during the Texan War of Independence from Mexico, 180 defenders resisted Mexican forces but were eventually overcome.

3 The War of the Triple Alliance was the bloodiest conflict in Latin American history. Paraguay lost over 60 percent (300,000) of its population.

4 Costa Rica was the first Central American republic to export coffee beans. The United Fruit Company developed the country, building its railroad and port facilities. The first elections were held there in 1885.

5 Manaus, in the Amazon basin, saw great prosperity in the rubber boom of 1890–1920; the town's lavishly appointed opera house was built in 1896.

6 Mechanization (railroads, steam excavators) and medical provision against malaria were crucial in the success of the US Panama Canal project (1904–14).

See also 4. 25 (the Spanish–American empire); 5.26 (expansion of the United States)

5.24 The Caribbean • 1783 – 1914 •

In the late 18th century, British and French Caribbean cane sugar plantations became extremely lucrative ventures. Profits were particularly high on the French islands: St Domingue (Haiti), where 37,000 white planters and 450,000 slaves farmed some of the richest and most extensive estates in the Caribbean, provided 85 percent of France's foreign trade. Yet the heart of the French Caribbean empire was destroyed by the slave insurrection that began on St Domingue in 1791. Under the leadership of Toussaint L'Ouverture and Jean-Jacques Dessalines, the slaves established the independent state of Haiti and repelled French attempts to retake the island. Rebellions among maroons (escaped slaves) in Jamaica and slaves in Guadeloupe, Grenada, St Vincent, Dominica and Barbados failed to repeat the success of the Haitian rebellion.

After the Napoleonic Wars, Britain emerged as the dominant power in the Caribbean. Britain secured St Lucia and Tobago from France; Trinidad from Spain; and Demerara, Essequibo and Berbice from Holland (forming British Guiana). West Indian cane sugar remained the most valuable element of British overseas commerce until the early 1820s.

The prosperity of British Caribbean plantations faced both internal and external threats as the 19th century progressed. The growing presence of Christian missions (first established on Jamaica in 1783) was opposed by planters as contributing to the cause of slave emancipation. Moreover, British West Indian cane sugar faced competition from Mauritius and India, French and German beet sugar and (most serious of all) the huge plantations being developed in Spanish Cuba, independent Brazil and Louisiana, all of which relied heavily on slave labor. In 1834 the abolition of slavery throughout the British empire realized the planters' worst fears. The government paid compensation and set a transitional period during which freed slaves would work the land for wages until 1838, but the industry declined steadily.

On the slave plantations of other countries, industrialization brought increased production. Spanish Cuba constructed the first railroad in the region and invested in new refineries. Brazil was equally progressive. No longer able to compete in the sugar trade, some Caribbean islands began to diversify. Jamaica exported its first bananas to New York in 1870, thus inaugurating a thriving trade. As well as new products, many colonies needed fresh labor to remain viable. Although the remaining French islands did not emancipate their slaves until 1848, they had to attract indentured workers from the Congo. The Dutch imported Javanese laborers, while Cuba and Puerto Rico brought in 125,000 Chinese. Over 430,000 Indians arrived before 1914, adding a new Asian element to the Guianas, Trinidad, Guadeloupe, Martinique and Jamaica.

A rebellion that broke out in 1865 among smallholders at Morant Bay on Jamaica profoundly changed the way the British colonies were governed. The brutal suppression of the uprising by the island's governor persuaded Britain to introduce direct crown colony government to most of its Caribbean possessions, in an effort to improve colonial government, modernize sugar production and promote social welfare. The remaining sugar

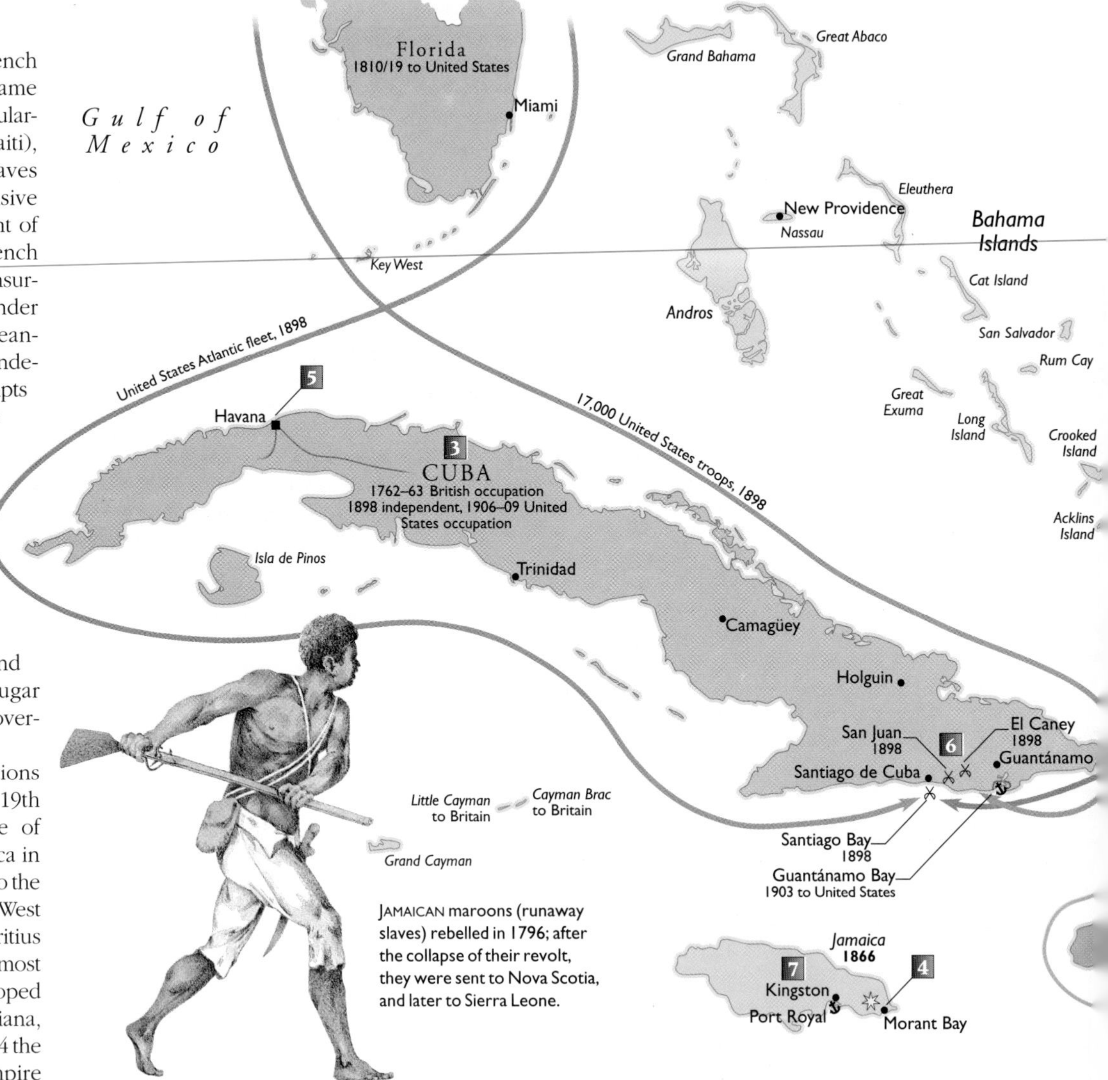

Tampa
Florida
1810/19 to United States
Miami
Gulf of Mexico
Key West
Grand Bahama
Great Abaco
Eleuthera
New Providence
Nassau
Bahama Islands
Andros
Cat Island
San Salvador
Rum Cay
Great Exuma
Long Island
Crooked Island
Acklins Island
United States Atlantic fleet, 1898
17,000 United States troops, 1898
5
Havana
3
CUBA
1762–63 British occupation
1898 independent, 1906–09 United States occupation
Isla de Pinos
Trinidad
Camagüey
Holguin
San Juan 1898
6
El Caney 1898
Guantánamo
Santiago de Cuba
Little Cayman to Britain
Cayman Brac to Britain
Grand Cayman
Santiago Bay 1898
Guantánamo Bay 1903 to United States
Jamaica 1866
7
4
Kingston
Port Royal
Morant Bay

JAMAICAN maroons (runaway slaves) rebelled in 1796; after the collapse of their revolt, they were sent to Nova Scotia, and later to Sierra Leone.

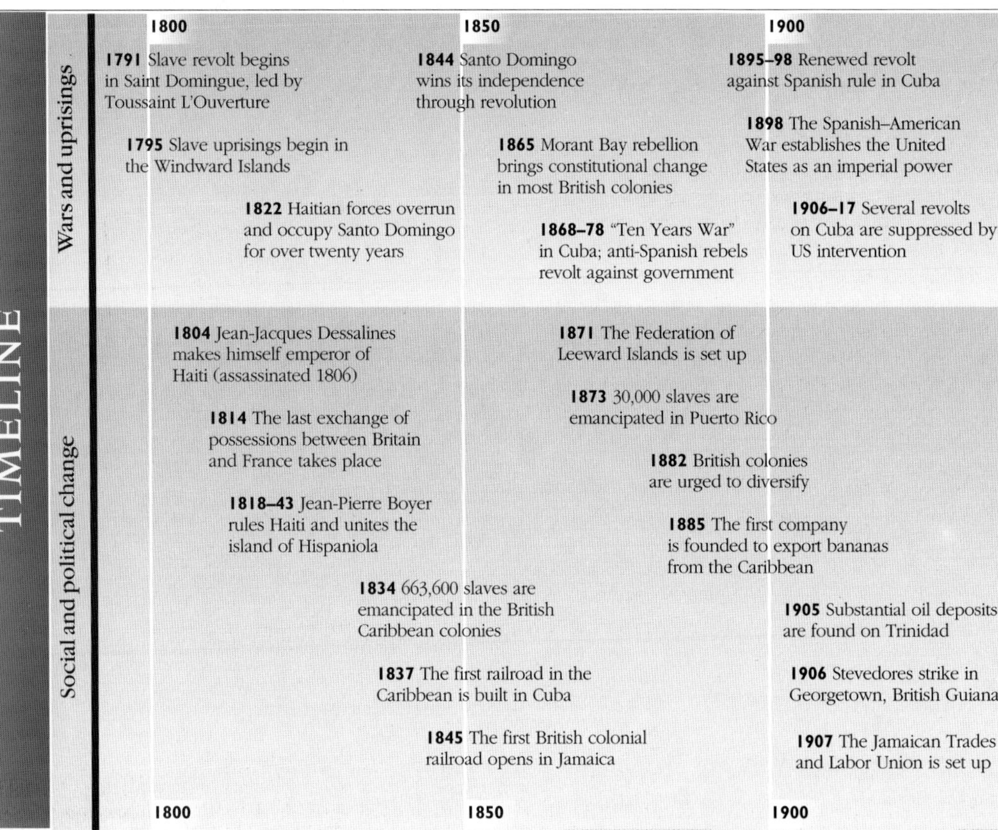

TIMELINE

1800 | 1850 | 1900

Wars and uprisings

1791 Slave revolt begins in Saint Domingue, led by Toussaint L'Ouverture

1795 Slave uprisings begin in the Windward Islands

1822 Haitian forces overrun and occupy Santo Domingo for over twenty years

1844 Santo Domingo wins its independence through revolution

1865 Morant Bay rebellion brings constitutional change in most British colonies

1868–78 "Ten Years War" in Cuba; anti-Spanish rebels revolt against government

1895–98 Renewed revolt against Spanish rule in Cuba

1898 The Spanish–American War establishes the United States as an imperial power

1906–17 Several revolts on Cuba are suppressed by US intervention

Social and political change

1804 Jean-Jacques Dessalines makes himself emperor of Haiti (assassinated 1806)

1814 The last exchange of possessions between Britain and France takes place

1818–43 Jean-Pierre Boyer rules Haiti and unites the island of Hispaniola

1834 663,600 slaves are emancipated in the British Caribbean colonies

1837 The first railroad in the Caribbean is built in Cuba

1845 The first British colonial railroad opens in Jamaica

1871 The Federation of Leeward Islands is set up

1873 30,000 slaves are emancipated in Puerto Rico

1882 British colonies are urged to diversify

1885 The first company is founded to export bananas from the Caribbean

1905 Substantial oil deposits are found on Trinidad

1906 Stevedores strike in Georgetown, British Guiana

1907 The Jamaican Trades and Labor Union is set up

1800 | 1850 | 1900

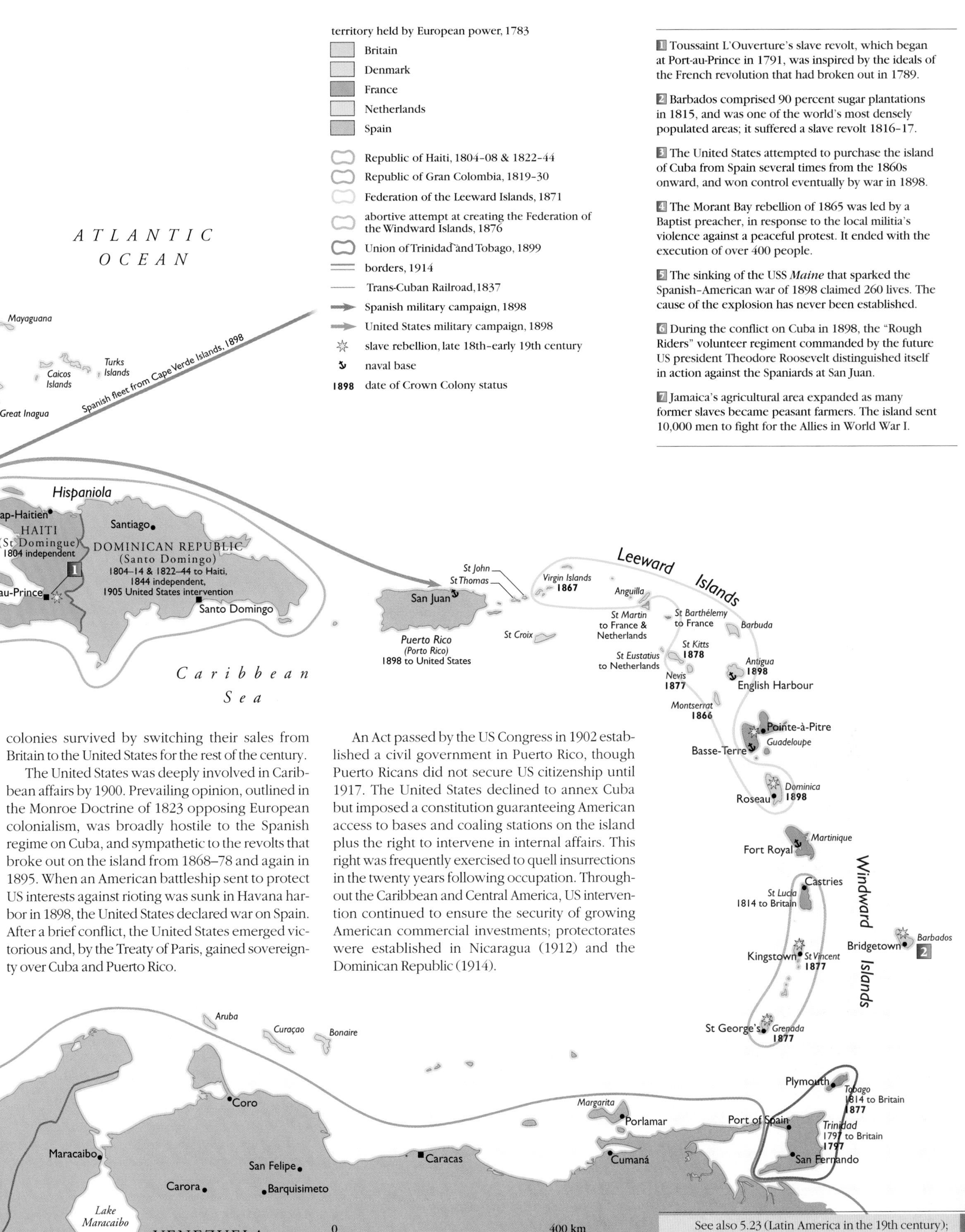
territory held by European power, 1783
Britain
Denmark
France
Netherlands
Spain
Republic of Haiti, 1804–08 & 1822–44
Republic of Gran Colombia, 1819–30
Federation of the Leeward Islands, 1871
abortive attempt at creating the Federation of the Windward Islands, 1876
Union of Trinidad and Tobago, 1899
borders, 1914
Trans-Cuban Railroad, 1837
Spanish military campaign, 1898
United States military campaign, 1898
slave rebellion, late 18th–early 19th century
naval base
1898 date of Crown Colony status
ATLANTIC OCEAN
Mayaguana
Turks Islands
Caicos Islands
Great Inagua
Spanish fleet from Cape Verde Islands, 1898
Hispaniola
Cap-Haitien
HAITI (St Domingue) 1804 independent
Santiago
DOMINICAN REPUBLIC (Santo Domingo) 1804–14 & 1822–44 to Haiti, 1844 independent, 1905 United States intervention
-au-Prince
Santo Domingo
Caribbean Sea
St John
St Thomas
San Juan
Puerto Rico (Porto Rico) 1898 to United States
St Croix
Virgin Islands 1867
Leeward Islands
Anguilla
St Martin to France & Netherlands
St Barthélemy to France
Barbuda
St Kitts 1878
St Eustatius to Netherlands
Nevis 1877
Antigua 1898
English Harbour
Montserrat 1866
Pointe-à-Pitre
Guadeloupe
Basse-Terre
Dominica 1898
Roseau
Martinique
Fort Royal
Windward Islands
Castries
St Lucia 1814 to Britain
Barbados
Bridgetown
Kingstown
St Vincent 1877
St George's
Grenada 1877
Aruba
Curaçao
Bonaire
Plymouth
Tobago 1814 to Britain 1877
Coro
Margarita
Porlamar
Port of Spain
Trinidad 1797 to Britain 1797
Maracaibo
San Felipe
Caracas
Cumaná
San Fernando
Carora
Barquisimeto
Lake Maracaibo
VENEZUELA 1821 to Gran Colombia, 1830 independent
0 400 km
0 300 mi

1 Toussaint L'Ouverture's slave revolt, which began at Port-au-Prince in 1791, was inspired by the ideals of the French revolution that had broken out in 1789.

2 Barbados comprised 90 percent sugar plantations in 1815, and was one of the world's most densely populated areas; it suffered a slave revolt 1816–17.

3 The United States attempted to purchase the island of Cuba from Spain several times from the 1860s onward, and won control eventually by war in 1898.

4 The Morant Bay rebellion of 1865 was led by a Baptist preacher, in response to the local militia's violence against a peaceful protest. It ended with the execution of over 400 people.

5 The sinking of the USS *Maine* that sparked the Spanish–American war of 1898 claimed 260 lives. The cause of the explosion has never been established.

6 During the conflict on Cuba in 1898, the "Rough Riders" volunteer regiment commanded by the future US president Theodore Roosevelt distinguished itself in action against the Spaniards at San Juan.

7 Jamaica's agricultural area expanded as many former slaves became peasant farmers. The island sent 10,000 men to fight for the Allies in World War I.

colonies survived by switching their sales from Britain to the United States for the rest of the century.

The United States was deeply involved in Caribbean affairs by 1900. Prevailing opinion, outlined in the Monroe Doctrine of 1823 opposing European colonialism, was broadly hostile to the Spanish regime on Cuba, and sympathetic to the revolts that broke out on the island from 1868–78 and again in 1895. When an American battleship sent to protect US interests against rioting was sunk in Havana harbor in 1898, the United States declared war on Spain. After a brief conflict, the United States emerged victorious and, by the Treaty of Paris, gained sovereignty over Cuba and Puerto Rico.

An Act passed by the US Congress in 1902 established a civil government in Puerto Rico, though Puerto Ricans did not secure US citizenship until 1917. The United States declined to annex Cuba but imposed a constitution guaranteeing American access to bases and coaling stations on the island plus the right to intervene in internal affairs. This right was frequently exercised to quell insurrections in the twenty years following occupation. Throughout the Caribbean and Central America, US intervention continued to ensure the security of growing American commercial investments; protectorates were established in Nicaragua (1912) and the Dominican Republic (1914).

See also 5.23 (Latin America in the 19th century); 6.14 (Caribbean in the 20th century)

The growth of Canada • 1763 – 1914 •

The demographic composition of Canada changed markedly with Britain's loss of its thirteen American colonies in the late 18th century. After this conflict loyal colonists, having no wish to be citizens of the new United States, migrated northward. Thousands of white loyalists from New York and South Carolina, together with the Mohawks who had fought alongside the British, settled in Nova Scotia, New Brunswick, Cape Breton and Prince Edward Island. Ontario (Upper Canada) saw an influx of new arrivals. In addition, the numbers of immigrants from Britain, especially Scotland, continued to rise. French settlers, most of whom had remained in Canada after Britain gained control in 1763 (and whose rights and customs had been enshrined in the 1774 Quebec Act), now found themselves overwhelmed. To reflect this change, in 1791 the Canada Act provided for a governor and two deputies to oversee the interests of Quebec (Lower Canada) and Ontario. Expansion westward began in 1812, when the Red River Colony, the nucleus of what later became Manitoba, was founded by Thomas Douglas, Easl of Selkirk. Yet further growth in this direction was hampered by the rocky terrain of the Canadian Shield.

Trouble between British North America and the United States flared up in the 1812 Anglo-American War. A United States invasion of Canada was followed by a British attack on Washington (1814) and the Battle of New Orleans (1815). The major effect of this brief war was to foster a new Canadian patriotism, founded on fear of American encroachment. Thereafter, border issues were settled peacefully: the 1818 agreement on the 49th Parallel created an undefended US–Canadian frontier from the Lake of the Woods to the Rockies, which the 1846 Oregon Treaty then extended to Vancouver.

Two rebellions in 1837 – Papineau's attempt to break Quebec's links with the British empire and Mackenzie's protest in Toronto against elitist government – resulted in the drafting of a report that recommended unifying Upper and Lower Canada and introducing responsible government. Though this was duly awarded in 1840–47, the American Civil War (1861–65) proved to be the decisive factor in Canadian unification. The Federal victory in 1865, attacks by the Fenian Brotherhood on Canadian territory (1866–70) and the inexorable westward expansion of the United States together caused Canada to press for a coast-to-coast union to ensure national security. The British North America Act of 1867 united Nova Scotia, New Brunswick, Quebec and Ontario in the Dominion of Canada. Manitoba joined in 1870, British Columbia in 1871 and Prince Edward Island in 1873. The first government of the new dominion promoted a "national policy" aimed at peopling the Canadian Shield and the Far West, building a transcontinental railroad and introducing tariffs to protect farm prices.

The rights and claims of indigenous peoples were largely ignored by the new Canadian state. Many Iroquois, Crees and Algonquins entered reservations, and were joined by refugees from the American Indian wars. Some Ojibwa, on the other hand, took the option of moving into uncharted territories. The Métis of Manitoba (Franco–Indians of

1 Loyalist settlers in Upper Canada in the years following the American War of Independence were given US$30 million by the British government.

2 William Mackenzie's unsuccessful Toronto rebellion of 1837 was directed against the "Family Compact", a system of patronage that benefited the privileged classes.

3 In 1866–70, the Fenian Brotherhood, an American arm of the Irish Republican Brotherhood, carried out raids in Canada, trying to change British policy on Irish independence. The first attack was at Fort Erie.

4 British Columbia joined the Dominion of Canada in 1871, on the condition that the Canadian Pacific Railway would be built across its territory in ten years.

5 The gold rush that began in 1896 on the Klondike river in Canada's Yukon territory lasted five years and Dawson, established to cater for the influx of prospectors, had a population of 30,000 by 1900.

6 Hardy new wheat strains boosted grain production on the prairies so that by 1914 Canada was one of the world's greatest wheat-exporting nations.

Banks Island
Alaska
to United States
Yukon
Kutchin
Inuit
Athabascan
5
Dawson
Yukon
Yukon Territory
1895–98 district of Northwest Territories
Mackenzie
Great Bear Lake
Whitehorse
Yellowknife
Tlingit
Liard
60th Parallel
Juneau
Slav
Kwakiutl
ROCKY MTS
COAST MTS
Peace
Alberta
1882 district of Northwest Territories
1905
Prince Rupert
British Columbia
1871
Sekani
Queen Charlotte Island
Haida
4
Athabasca
Edmonton
Sarcee
Fraser
Tlingit
Vancouver Island
Blackfoot
Calgary
Nootka Sound
Nootka
Vancouver
lead, silver, zinc
Trail
Victoria
Chinese and Japanese
Seattle
Spokane
Portland
Columbia
PACIFIC OCEAN
Oregon Country
1818–46 joint Canadian and United States occupation, 1846 to United States
Boise
PROSPECTORS panning for gold flooded to the Canadian west in the later 19th century.

TIMELINE

Constitutional change

- **1784** New Brunswick is founded to accommodate British loyalists
- **1791** Representative government is established in Ontario and Quebec
- **1812** The Red River Colony is founded
- **1818** Agreement is reached on siting the US–Canadian frontier on the 49th Parallel
- **1839** Lord Durham, governor-general of British North America, plans a unified state
- **1842** The Ashburton Treaty defines the southern limits of Quebec and New Brunswick
- **1846** Oregon Treaty is signed and the Pacific coast frontier extended along 49th Parallel
- **1867** Dominion of Canada is set up: Quebec, Ontario, New Brunswick and Nova Scotia

Other developments

- **1763** French forces evacuate Canada after defeat by Britain
- **1783** Peace of Paris ends War of American Independence
- **1789** The explorer Alexander Mackenzie (1755–1820) reaches the Beaufort Sea
- **1793** Mackenzie crosses the Rockies to reach the Pacific
- **1812–14** United States at war with Britain; Canada attacked
- **1837** Papineau in Montreal and Mackenzie in Toronto attempt to separate Canada from the British empire
- **1858** Fraser River gold rush; British Columbia becomes a Crown Colony
- **1869–70** Méti revolt under Louis Riel fails in Manitoba
- **1885** Méti revolt fails in Saskatchewan
- **1885** Completion of the Canadian Pacific Railway
- **1896** Discovery of gold in the Yukon; Klondike gold rush
- **1908** Anti-Asian riots in British Columbia

1800 1850 1900

Cree Native American nation
exploration route
Hearne, 1770–71
Mackenzie, 1789–93
Thompson, 1789–1811
expansion of Canada
Canadian provinces, 1867
territory added 1870
province added by 1873
territory added 1880
British crown colony
Canadian territorial claim surrendered to the United States, with date
1867 date of achieving provincial status
Métis' rebellion under Louis Riel
Red River, 1869–70
Northwest (Saskatchewan), 1885
other rebellion, 1837
goldfield
other metal deposit
oil or gas field
fertile belt of the Canadian prairies
Canadian Pacific Railway, 1881–85
other railroad by 1914
migration of Mohawk and colonists loyal to Britain, 1783
other migration of peoples
borders, 1914
state capital
provincial capital
0 1000 km
0 700 mi
Greenland
to Denmark
Ammassalik
Thule
Ellesmere Island
Baffin Bay
Devon Island
Somerset Island
Prince of Wales Island
Baffin Island
Foxe Basin
Inuit
Southampton Island
Back
Northwest Territories
organized into districts 1882–95
CANADIAN SHIELD
Hudson Bay
Churchill
Chipewyan
Port Nelson
Reindeer Lake
Nelson
CANADA
Manitoba
1870
Churchill
Saskatchewan
1882 district of Northwest Territories
1905
Cree
Saskatoon
Regina
Lake Winnipeg
Lake Winnipegosis
Lake Manitoba
Winnipeg
Assinboine
49th Parallel
Minot
Red River Colony
1818 to United States
Missouri
Bismarck
Moorhead
Duluth
Minneapolis
St Paul
Mississippi
UNITED STATES
Rapid City
Des Moines
Omaha
Platte
Ojibwa
Round Lake
Ontario
(Upper Canada)
1867
Lake Nipigon
Mandan
Fort William
Lake Superior
Sault Ste Marie
Timmins
cobalt, silver
Cobalt
Huron
nickel
Sudbury
Ottawa
Michigan
1783 to United States
Lake Huron
Toronto (York)
Lake Michigan
Milwaukee
Chicago
Detroit
Lake Erie
Fort Erie
Buffalo
Cleveland
Pittsburgh
Ohio
Columbus
Indianapolis
Cincinnati
Lake Ontario
Mackenzie's protest, 1837
Rochester
James Bay
Quebec
(Lower Canada)
1867
Algonquin
Papineau's rebellion, 1837
Montréal
Québec
St Lawrence
LABRADOR
1809 to Newfoundland
NEWFOUNDLAND
Newfoundland
St John's
St Pierre & Miquelon
to France
Anticosti Island
Abenaki
Prince Edward Island
1873
Cape Breton Island
Charlottetown
Europeans
New Brunswick
1867
Nova Scotia
1867
Fredericton
St John
Halifax
1842 to US
extension to Canadian Pacific Railroad, 1889
Boston
New York
Philadelphia
Baltimore
Washington
Norfolk
ATLANTIC OCEAN
Bermuda Islands
to Britain

mixed-blood) saw their buffalo-hunting culture threatened by immigrants, a process exacerbated by the surrender of the province to the Crown by the Hudson's Bay Company in 1869. The ensuing Red River Rebellion (1869–70) and the Northwest Rebellion in Saskatchewan (1885) – both led by Louis Riel – were vain attempts to preserve the traditional way of life of the Métis.

The long-promised Canadian Pacific Railway was completed in 1885 and the first transcontinental services began in 1886. This was a crucial element in the unification of Canada; the railroad consolidated the western frontier, created new towns along its route and provided a tangible link between British Columbia and the east.

Canada's frontiers continued to expand to the north. In 1912 Manitoba advanced to the 60th Parallel (to match Saskatchewan and Alberta). In the same year Quebec and Ontario were extended to the Hudson Bay and the Arctic. Another frontier developed as Canada's northernmost territories, home to the Inuit, were encroached upon first by fur-trappers and then thousands of gold prospectors (notably at the Yukon in the far northwest in 1896). Petroleum companies arrived in Alberta when oil reserves were found there in 1912–14.

The first French-Canadian and Catholic prime minister of Canada was the Liberal Wilfred Laurier (1896–1911). Laurier maintained the policy of expansion by encouraging American and eastern European immigrants to settle the prairies. During his premiership, the annual immigration figure rose to almost 400,000. Among them were Japanese and Chinese who worked in railroad construction, timber industries and in mining for coal and gold.

See also 4.27 (18th-century North America); 5.26 (expansion of the United States)

Two decisions made by the Congress of the embryonic United States of America set up the conflict between white settlers and native Americans that characterized the country's expansion. In 1787 the indigenous peoples were promised that their lands and property could only be ceded with their consent. Yet four years later, George Washington authorized expansion westward along the Ohio. Initially the growth of the United States was limited by Spain's (from 1800, France's) possession of lands beyond the Mississippi. However, even at this stage, strong trade links existed between the thirteen eastern states of the Union and the Pacific; in time, these would spur westward expansion.

Expeditions into native territories began in the late 18th century. The Shawnee and Piankashaw succeeded in repelling a group led by General St Clair in 1791. Yet by 1795, in the Treaty of Greenville, the pattern of substantial territorial gains by the whites and displacement of native Americans to vacant lands in the west was set. The process was hastened by Thomas Jefferson's purchase of Louisiana from France in 1803, when, at a stroke, the territory of the United States was doubled.

In the ensuing decades further territories were gained by the United States, through purchase or conflict: Florida, Texas, Oregon, the Mexican cession and the Gadsden Purchase. Some 400,000 native people were confronted by the westward thrust of settler culture across the Great Plains, enforced by troops stationed west of the Mississippi.

In Florida, the Seminole people conducted a sustained resistance that was only ultimately suppressed in the 1840s. The forcible removal of the Cherokee to the unsettled "Indian Territory" of Oklahoma in 1838–39, after gold was found in their original homelands, cost four thousand lives (the "Trail of Tears"). The Delaware, Wichita and many others suffered a similar fate. Settlers annexed native American lands with the support of the US government: a succession of bills enacted by Congress offering free land in return for minimal investment encouraged claims to be staked to territories on the Great Plains. Railroads further threatened the Plains peoples' main food source, the vast buffalo herds, already depleted by indiscriminate hunting. Atrocities peaked when the families of Arapaho and Cheyenne warriors who had assembled to sign a treaty at Sand Creek in Colorado in 1864 were slaughtered by a US cavalry contingent.

The Federal government tried to end the killing with an Indian peace commission. The Kiowa, Comanche and Arapaho reluctantly accepted reservation status at the Medicine Lodge Creek Conference (1867), while Sitting Bull's Dakota Sioux

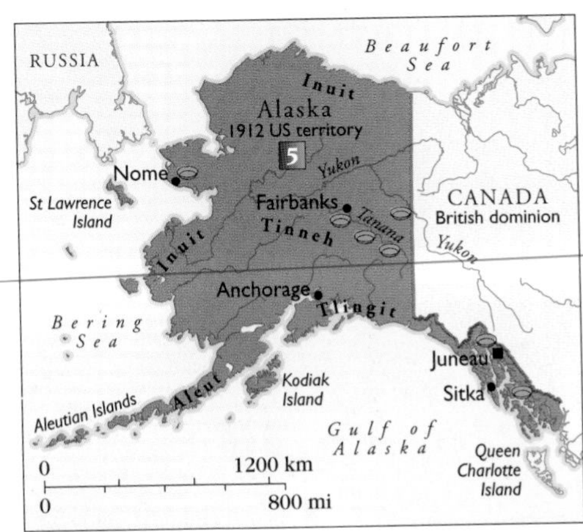
RUSSIA
Beaufort Sea
Inuit
Alaska
1912 US territory
5
Nome
Yukon
St Lawrence Island
Fairbanks
Tinneh
Tanana
CANADA
British dominion
Yukon
Inuit
Anchorage
Tlingit
Bering Sea
Juneau
Sitka
Aleut
Kodiak Island
Aleutian Islands
Gulf of Alaska
Queen Charlotte Island
0 1200 km
0 800 mi

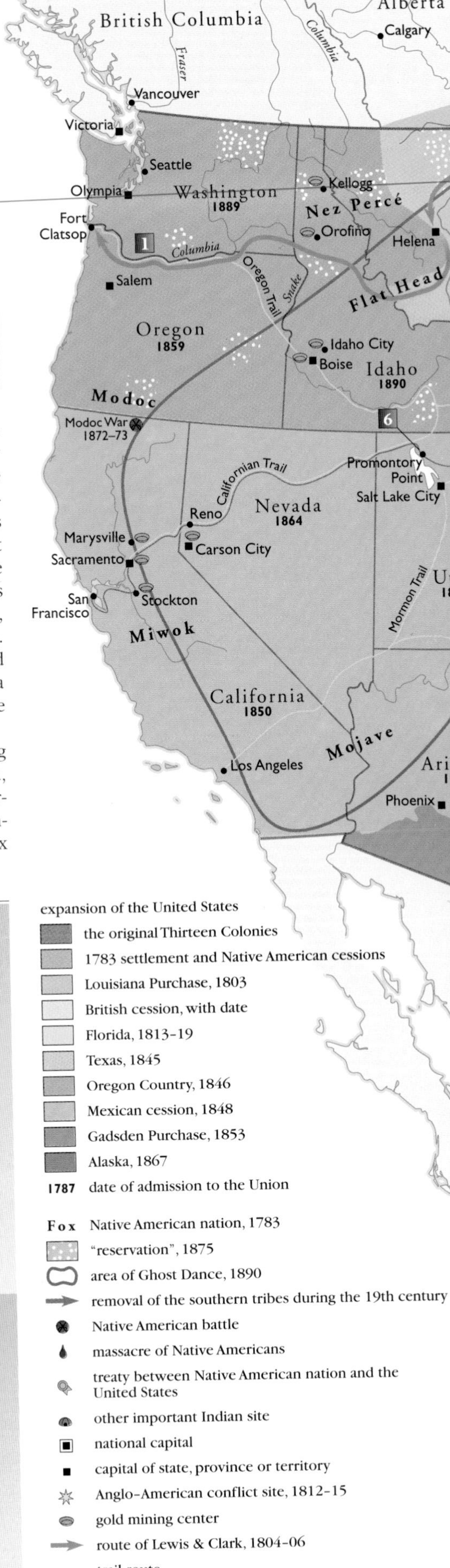
British Columbia
Alberta
Calgary
Fraser
Columbia
Vancouver
Victoria
Seattle
Olympia
Washington
1889
Kellogg
Nez Percé
Fort Clatsop
Orofino
Helena
1
Columbia
Salem
Oregon Trail
Snake
Flat Head
Oregon
1859
Idaho City
Boise
Idaho
1890
Modoc
Modoc War
1872–73
6
Californian Trail
Promontory Point
Salt Lake City
Reno
Nevada
1864
Marysville
Sacramento
Carson City
San Francisco
Stockton
Mormon Trail
Utah
1896
Miwok
California
1850
Mojave
Los Angeles
Arizona
1912
Phoenix
expansion of the United States
the original Thirteen Colonies
1783 settlement and Native American cessions
Louisiana Purchase, 1803
British cession, with date
Florida, 1813–19
Texas, 1845
Oregon Country, 1846
Mexican cession, 1848
Gadsden Purchase, 1853
Alaska, 1867
1787 date of admission to the Union
Fox Native American nation, 1783
"reservation", 1875
area of Ghost Dance, 1890
removal of the southern tribes during the 19th century
Native American battle
massacre of Native Americans
treaty between Native American nation and the United States
other important Indian site
national capital
capital of state, province or territory
Anglo-American conflict site, 1812–15
gold mining center
route of Lewis & Clark, 1804–06
trail route
Union Pacific and Central Pacific railroads
borders, 1914

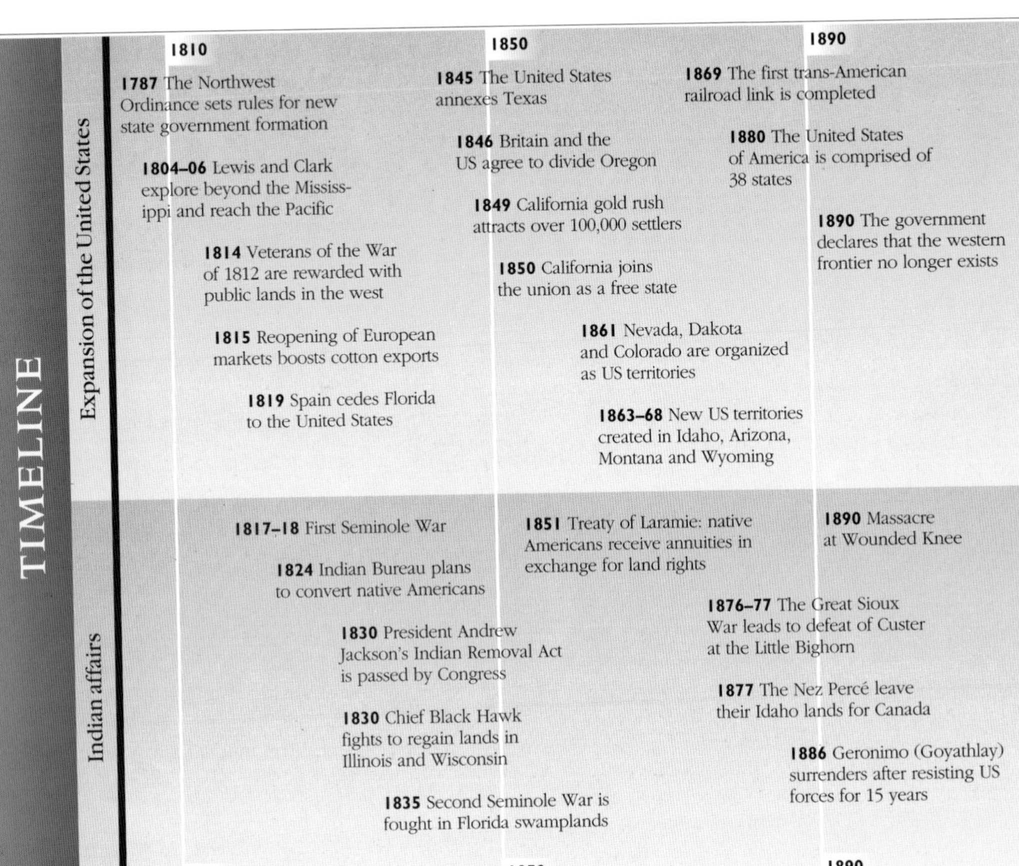
TIMELINE
Expansion of the United States
1810
1850
1890
1787 The Northwest Ordinance sets rules for new state government formation
1804–06 Lewis and Clark explore beyond the Mississippi and reach the Pacific
1814 Veterans of the War of 1812 are rewarded with public lands in the west
1815 Reopening of European markets boosts cotton exports
1819 Spain cedes Florida to the United States
1845 The United States annexes Texas
1846 Britain and the US agree to divide Oregon
1849 California gold rush attracts over 100,000 settlers
1850 California joins the union as a free state
1861 Nevada, Dakota and Colorado are organized as US territories
1863–68 New US territories created in Idaho, Arizona, Montana and Wyoming
1869 The first trans-American railroad link is completed
1880 The United States of America is comprised of 38 states
1890 The government declares that the western frontier no longer exists
Indian affairs
1817–18 First Seminole War
1824 Indian Bureau plans to convert native Americans
1830 President Andrew Jackson's Indian Removal Act is passed by Congress
1830 Chief Black Hawk fights to regain lands in Illinois and Wisconsin
1835 Second Seminole War is fought in Florida swamplands
1851 Treaty of Laramie: native Americans receive annuities in exchange for land rights
1876–77 The Great Sioux War leads to defeat of Custer at the Little Bighorn
1877 The Nez Percé leave their Idaho lands for Canada
1886 Geronimo (Goyathlay) surrenders after resisting US forces for 15 years
1890 Massacre at Wounded Knee
1810
1850
1890

ceased hostilities in return for permanent occupation of the Black Hills reservation. However, incursion by gold prospectors in 1874 provoked resistance by the Sioux aided by the Northern Cheyenne in 1876–77. They annihilated General Custer and 200 troopers at the Battle of the Little Bighorn, but their leaders Sitting Bull and Crazy Horse could not capitalize on this victory and were eventually forced to surrender.

The Blackfoot and Crow in Wyoming and Montana, the Modoc in Oregon, and the Nez Percé in Idaho met similar fates. Cochise and Geronimo of the Chiricahua Apaches in Arizona and New Mexico conducted guerrilla campaigns until forced to surrender (1872 and 1886 respectively).

Geronimo's surrender marked the end of the Indian Wars. For the first time in over a century the United States was at peace. However,despair at their situation led many native Americans to follow Wovoka, a Paiute religious leader. Wovoka conducted ghost dances which, he claimed, would make his disciples immune to gunfire, and he promised that Sitting Bull would expel the whites. Sitting Bull was murdered while in custody and the US Seventh Cavalry massacred Sioux ghost dancers and their families at Wounded Knee Creek in December 1890.

Throughout this period the United States thrived. The northeast saw a stream of immigration from Europe, and new industries arose to feed, house and clothe the growing population. In the south, the high export prices of cotton brought the development of large plantations. The invention of the cotton gin in 1792 to separate cotton fiber from seeds stimulated production. Yet the plantation system relied on slavery, a growing point of contention between North and South. In the 1820s, many had hoped to liberate the plantation slaves, but three decades later the rising value of slaves made this less attractive. A compromise was reached when California was allowed to join the Union as a "free" state in 1850 in return for harsh laws against fugitive slaves, but the issue soon exploded into civil war.

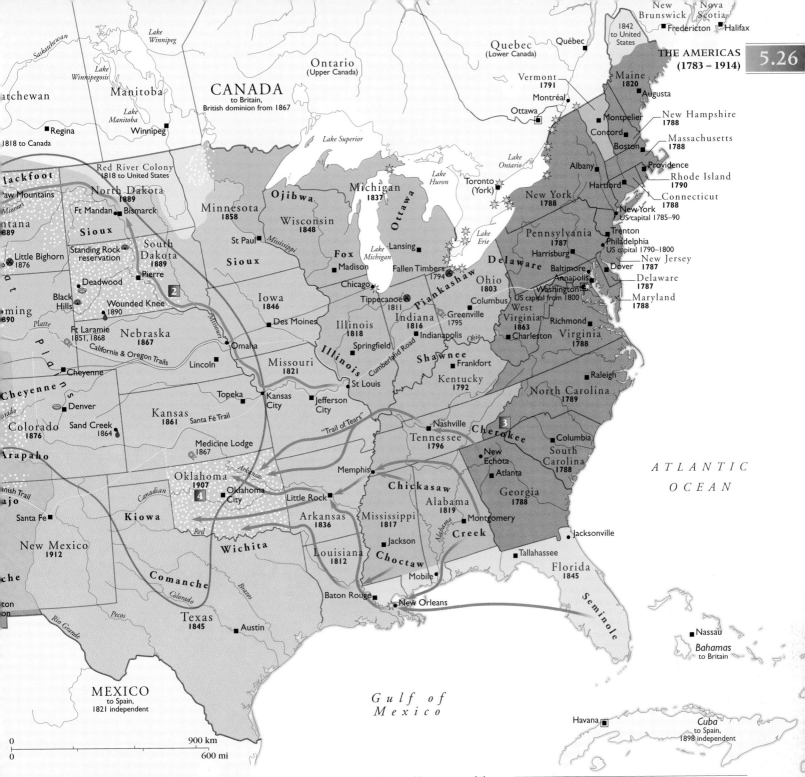

1 The Columbia River was explored by Capt Robert Gray in 1792, who claimed it for the United States.

2 Meriwether Lewis and William Clark were commissioned by Thomas Jefferson to explore beyond the Mississippi in 1804.

3 The "Five Civilized Tribes" of the southeast United States – Choctaw, Cherokee, Chickasaw, Creek, and Seminole – were socalled for their adaptation to white culture. Even so, they were forcibly relocated in 1830.

4 The Indian Territory was set up as a homeland for native Americans in the 1830s, but the territory was shrunk in 1854 and 1890 and abolished in 1907.

5 Alaska was bought from czarist Russia in 1867 for US$7.2 million.

6 In 1869, the Union Pacific and the Central Pacific railroads met at Promontory Point in Utah.

See also 4.27 (colonial North America); 5.27 (American Civil War); 5.28 (US society to 1914)

5.27 The American Civil War • 1850 – 1865 •

The demand for cotton as an export crop made the economy of the states south of the Mason–Dixon line (the border between Pennsylvania and Maryland) dependent on the systematic exploitation of humanity. On plantations and farms and in cities and towns, four million black slaves were denied their rights to a family, education and citizenship. Slavery became a political issue during the westward expansion of the United States. In deference to southern interests, the Constitutional Convention of 1787 prohibited the importation of slaves, but protected slavery in the states from federal interference. In the Missouri compromise of 1820, which admitted Maine and the Louisiana Purchase lands (except Missouri) as free and proclaimed all states above latitude 36° 30' as free, a convention of balancing abolitionist and slave-owning interests was established.

Attitudes toward slavery were polarized; some demanded complete and immediate abolition, while others saw good economic and racial reasons for its retention. The issue was made even more divisive by a number of legislative decisions in the 1850s. The 1850 compromise admitted California as a free state, but took no action to curb slavery in the other territories ceded by Mexico after the war of 1846–48 (Utah and New Mexico). The Kansas–Nebraska Act (1854) gave settlers the right to decide whether or not to permit slavery in a new territory, a situation that led to open warfare between rival groups in "bleeding Kansas". Finally a Supreme Court ruling of 1857 – the "Dred Scott" case – declared that neither Congress nor the people of a territory could abolish slavery in the territories. This meant the Missouri compromise was unconstitutional and destroyed the artificial balance between free and slave states. This decision threatened the entire democratic foundation of the Union. Meanwhile, fugitive slaves escaped to the north via the "Underground Railroad" (a network of abolitionist households). In the 1860 presidential elections all the free states – except New Jersey – returned the Republican Abraham Lincoln, who refused to extend slavery to new territories.

On 20 December 1860 South Carolina seceded from the Union. Georgia, Alabama, Texas, Florida, Mississippi and Louisiana soon followed, creating a Confederacy and electing Jefferson Davis as their president. On 12 April 1861 Confederate forces began hostilities with a bombardment of Fort Sumter. Lincoln called for 75,000 northern volunteers, prompting Virginia, North Carolina, Tennessee and Arkansas to join the Confederacy. Yet not all the slave states seceded: Kentucky declared itself neutral; Delaware, Maryland and Missouri remained loyal, as did the northwestern counties of Virginia (which became the state of West Virginia in 1863).

The civil war that erupted was a devastating conflict: a quarter of all those who saw combat lost their lives. Confederate strategy was to defend itself and win international recognition as an independent state. The Union government thus had no option but to attack the south and restore the rebel states to the Union. The Union had a larger population, less vulnerable railroads and far greater industrial resources than the Confederacy. Lincoln was confident of achieving his two main objectives: to blockade the Confederate coastline and capture Richmond, the Confederate capital. However, superior Confederate generalship caused Union armies several early setbacks, notably their defeat at the two Battles of Bull Run, and their failure to take the key town of Fredericksburg. In January 1863, Lincoln espoused outright abolition in his emancipation proclamation, freeing all slaves in the Confederacy. Meanwhile, Confederate armies pushed north into Pennsylvania to take the war to the enemy. This aim was thwarted at the Battle of Gettysburg in July 1863, which marked a turning point in Union fortunes.

At the same time, Union armies were victorious in the west. Under the command of Ulysses Grant, they advanced down the Mississippi; after gaining control of the area through the battle of Shiloh and the siege of Vicksburg, they succeeded in cutting off Arkansas, Louisiana and Texas from the Confederacy. William Sherman's campaign in Georgia saw the destruction of Atlanta and the capture of Savannah. Grant fought a series of battles (Wilderness, Spotsylvania, Cold Harbor and Petersburg) against the Confederate commander Robert E. Lee, which left the south with barely 60,000 troops. Richmond fell on 3 April 1865 and Lee surrendered the Confederate army at Appomattox Court House on 9 April. Five days later, Lincoln was assassinated.

Northwest Territory (slavery forbidden, 1787)
Mason-Dixon line
Missouri Compromise line, 1820
borders, 1861
Confederate state, 1861, with date of secession
slave state loyal to the Union
Union state, 1861
United States territory, 1861
Confederate campaign
Union campaign
deployment of Confederate troops by rail
deployment of Union troops by rail
Confederate victory
Union victory
Confederate fort
Union fort
burned by Union troops
coast blockaded by Union Navy
capital
state or provincial capital
Mobile slave port
population density over 18 per sq km, 1860
cotton growing area, 1860
1865 date of abolition of slavery

Minnesota 1858
Des Moines
Kansas 1861
Fort Scott
Missouri Compromise line
Pea Ridge 1862
Indian Territory 1862
Dallas
Texas seceded Feb 1861 1865
Brazos
Colorado
Austin
San Antonio
Houston
Louisiana seceded Jan 1861 1865
Baton Rouge
0 400 km
0 300 mi

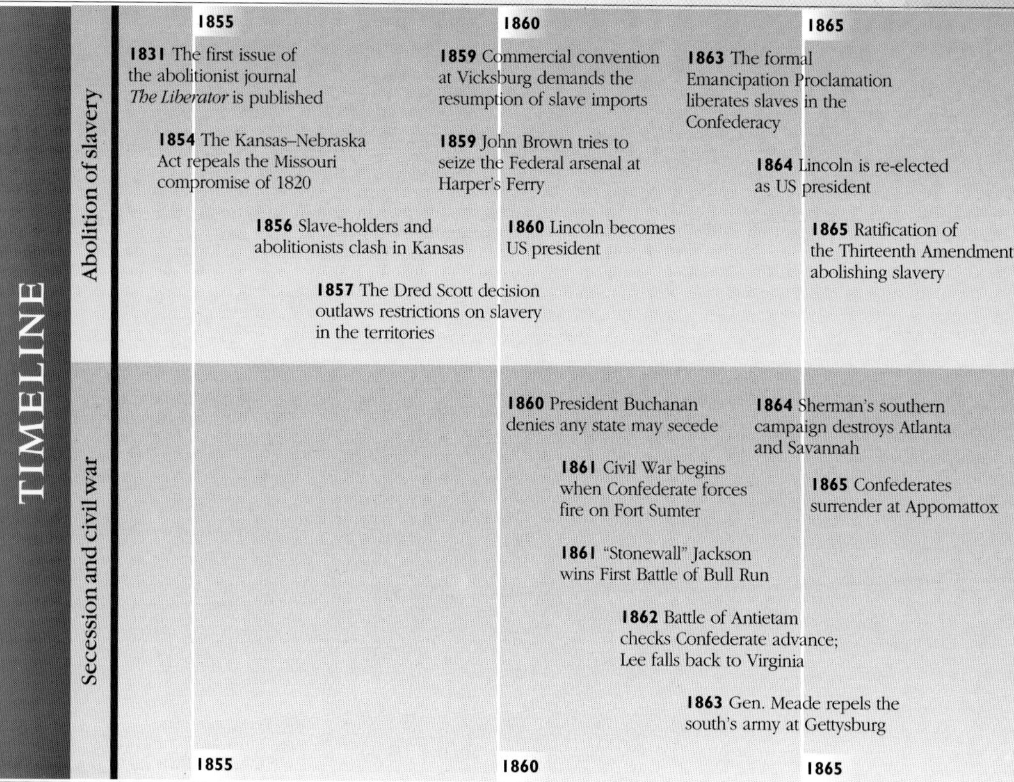
TIMELINE
Abolition of slavery
1855
1860
1865
1831 The first issue of the abolitionist journal The Liberator is published
1854 The Kansas–Nebraska Act repeals the Missouri compromise of 1820
1856 Slave-holders and abolitionists clash in Kansas
1857 The Dred Scott decision outlaws restrictions on slavery in the territories
1859 Commercial convention at Vicksburg demands the resumption of slave imports
1859 John Brown tries to seize the Federal arsenal at Harper's Ferry
1860 Lincoln becomes US president
1863 The formal Emancipation Proclamation liberates slaves in the Confederacy
1864 Lincoln is re-elected as US president
1865 Ratification of the Thirteenth Amendment abolishing slavery
Secession and civil war
1860 President Buchanan denies any state may secede
1861 Civil War begins when Confederate forces fire on Fort Sumter
1861 "Stonewall" Jackson wins First Battle of Bull Run
1862 Battle of Antietam checks Confederate advance; Lee falls back to Virginia
1863 Gen. Meade repels the south's army at Gettysburg
1864 Sherman's southern campaign destroys Atlanta and Savannah
1865 Confederates surrender at Appomattox
1855
1860
1865

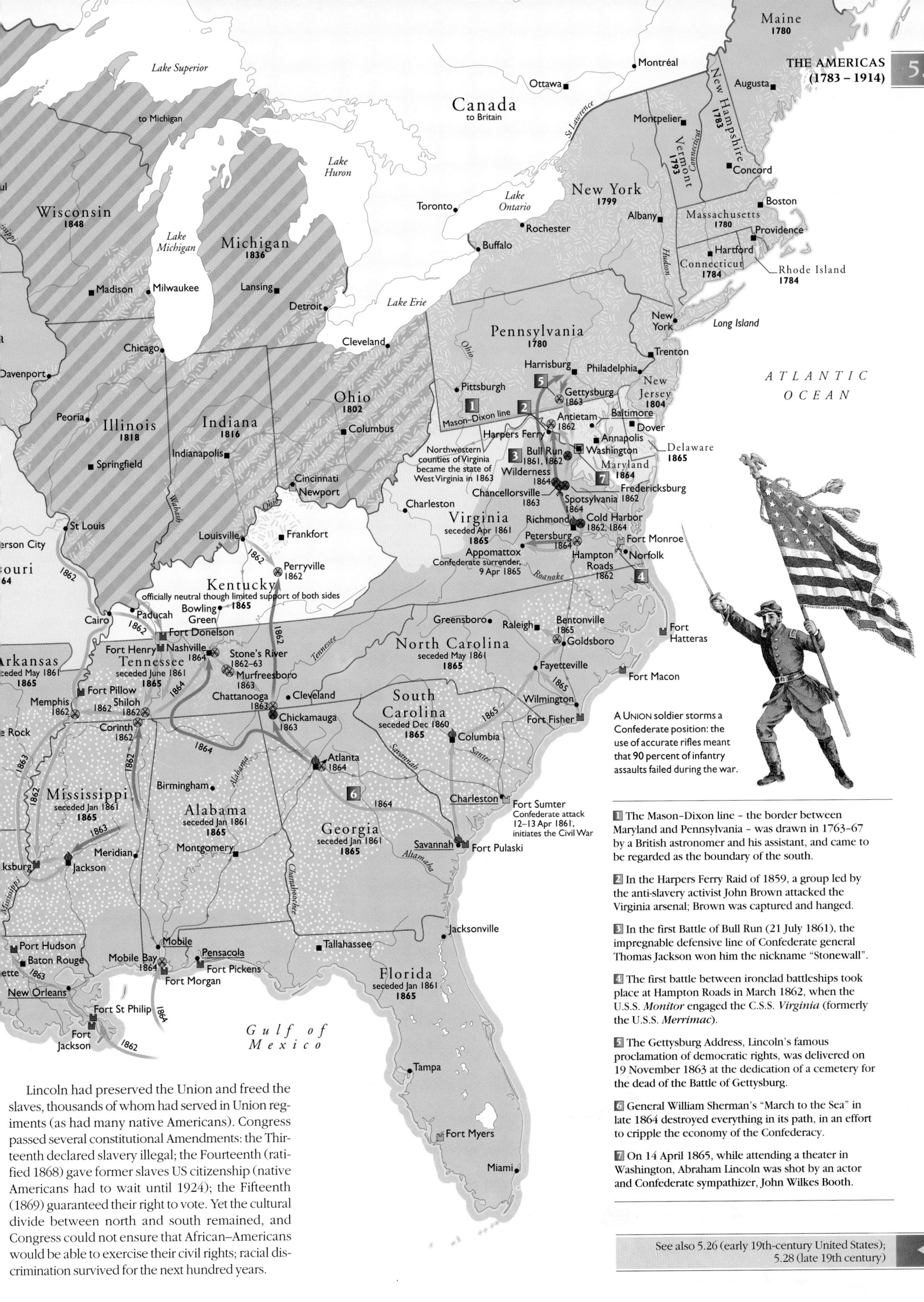

Lake Superior
Canada
to Britain
to Michigan
Lake Huron
Lake Ontario
Lake Michigan
Lake Erie
Maine 1780
Montréal
Ottawa
Augusta
St Lawrence
Montpelier
New Hampshire 1783
Vermont 1793
Connecticut
Concord
New York 1799
Toronto
Rochester
Albany
Boston
Massachusetts 1780
Providence
Buffalo
Hartford
Connecticut 1784
Rhode Island 1784
Hudson
Wisconsin 1848
Michigan 1836
Madison
Milwaukee
Lansing
Detroit
New York
Long Island
Pennsylvania 1780
Chicago
Cleveland
Trenton
Davenport
Harrisburg
Philadelphia
ATLANTIC OCEAN
Pittsburgh
Gettysburg 1863
New Jersey 1804
Ohio 1802
Mason–Dixon line
Antietam 1862
Baltimore
Dover
Peoria
Illinois 1818
Indiana 1816
Columbus
Harpers Ferry
Annapolis
Northwestern counties of Virginia became the state of West Virginia in 1863
Bull Run 1861, 1862
Washington
Delaware 1865
Maryland 1864
Indianapolis
Springfield
Wilderness 1864
Fredericksburg 1862
Cincinnati
Newport
Chancellorsville 1863
Spotsylvania 1864
Wabash
Charleston
Virginia seceded Apr 1861 1865
Richmond
Cold Harbor 1862, 1864
St Louis
Louisville
Frankfort
Petersburg 1864
Fort Monroe
Appomattox Confederate surrender, 9 Apr 1865
Hampton Roads 1862
Norfolk
Perryville 1862
Roanoke
Kentucky officially neutral though limited support of both sides
Bowling Green 1865
Paducah
Cairo
Fort Donelson
Greensboro
Raleigh
Bentonville 1865
Goldsboro
Fort Hatteras
Fort Henry
Nashville 1864
Stone's River 1862–63
Murfreesboro 1863
North Carolina seceded May 1861 1865
Arkansas seceded May 1861 1865
Tennessee seceded June 1861 1865
Fort Pillow
Memphis 1862
Shiloh 1862
Chattanooga 1863
Cleveland
Fayetteville
Fort Macon
Wilmington
Corinth 1862
Chickamauga 1863
South Carolina seceded Dec 1860 1865
Fort Fisher
Columbia
Atlanta 1864
Savannah
Santee
Birmingham
Mississippi seceded Jan 1861 1865
Alabama seceded Jan 1861 1865
Charleston
Fort Sumter Confederate attack 12–13 Apr 1861, initiates the Civil War
Georgia seceded Jan 1861 1865
Meridian
Montgomery
Jackson
Savannah
Fort Pulaski
Altamaha
Chattahoochee
Jacksonville
Port Hudson
Baton Rouge
Mobile
Mobile Bay 1864
Pensacola
Fort Pickens
Fort Morgan
Tallahassee
Florida seceded Jan 1861 1865
New Orleans
Fort St Philip
Fort Jackson
Gulf of Mexico
Tampa
Fort Myers
Miami

A UNION soldier storms a Confederate position: the use of accurate rifles meant that 90 percent of infantry assaults failed during the war.

Lincoln had preserved the Union and freed the slaves, thousands of whom had served in Union regiments (as had many native Americans). Congress passed several constitutional Amendments: the Thirteenth declared slavery illegal; the Fourteenth (ratified 1868) gave former slaves US citizenship (native Americans had to wait until 1924); the Fifteenth (1869) guaranteed their right to vote. Yet the cultural divide between north and south remained, and Congress could not ensure that African–Americans would be able to exercise their civil rights; racial discrimination survived for the next hundred years.

1 The Mason–Dixon line – the border between Maryland and Pennsylvania – was drawn in 1763–67 by a British astronomer and his assistant, and came to be regarded as the boundary of the south.

2 In the Harpers Ferry Raid of 1859, a group led by the anti-slavery activist John Brown attacked the Virginia arsenal; Brown was captured and hanged.

3 In the first Battle of Bull Run (21 July 1861), the impregnable defensive line of Confederate general Thomas Jackson won him the nickname "Stonewall".

4 The first battle between ironclad battleships took place at Hampton Roads in March 1862, when the U.S.S. *Monitor* engaged the C.S.S. *Virginia* (formerly the U.S.S. *Merrimac*).

5 The Gettysburg Address, Lincoln's famous proclamation of democratic rights, was delivered on 19 November 1863 at the dedication of a cemetery for the dead of the Battle of Gettysburg.

6 General William Sherman's "March to the Sea" in late 1864 destroyed everything in its path, in an effort to cripple the economy of the Confederacy.

7 On 14 April 1865, while attending a theater in Washington, Abraham Lincoln was shot by an actor and Confederate sympathizer, John Wilkes Booth.

See also 5.26 (early 19th-century United States); 5.28 (late 19th century)

Population and economy of the United States • 1865 – 1914 •

At the end of the Civil War, the northern states experienced unprecedented prosperity as American and foreign speculators rushed to invest in a new wave of industrialization. Railroad construction drove the economy. The completion of the first transcontinental link in 1869 encouraged the development of other lines across America; three more were in operation by 1883. Urban centers and rural areas alike benefited; millions of cattle were transported to slaughterhouses in the new cities of Chicago and Kansas City. By opening up the west to profitable farming, railroads also hastened political change; by 1890 most of the western territories had been admitted as fully-fledged states of the Union. Yet the railroad boom was not without its negative aspects. Corrupt share-dealing provoked a panic and withdrawal of foreign capital in 1873.

The south had been devastated by the civil war. Its principal towns lay in ruins and its economic life destroyed. Opinion in the north was divided on how the rebel states should be treated. President Andrew Johnson (Lincoln's successor) favored reconciliation, while hardliners counseled repression. After a period of radical administration, conservatives reasserted white rule in the south, circumventing the constitutional rights guaranteed by Congress to freed blacks. Reconstruction proceeded slowly, and states were gradually readmitted to the Union.

Towns and cities grew with astonishing rapidity; by 1914, the United States had an urban population of 45 million, most of whom were immigrants. On five occasions the annual total of immigrants – from every corner of Europe – exceeded one million. Desperate for work and willing to take low-paid employment, the newcomers were quickly absorbed into the factories of New York, Chicago, Buffalo, Pittsburgh, Cleveland, Milwaukee, Cincinnati and St Louis. Appalling conditions prevailed in the crowded cities, polluted factories, primitive mining communities and harsh lumber camps. Immigrants often faced discrimination; as early as 1871, the Chinese who had entered through California to work in mining and on the railroads were the

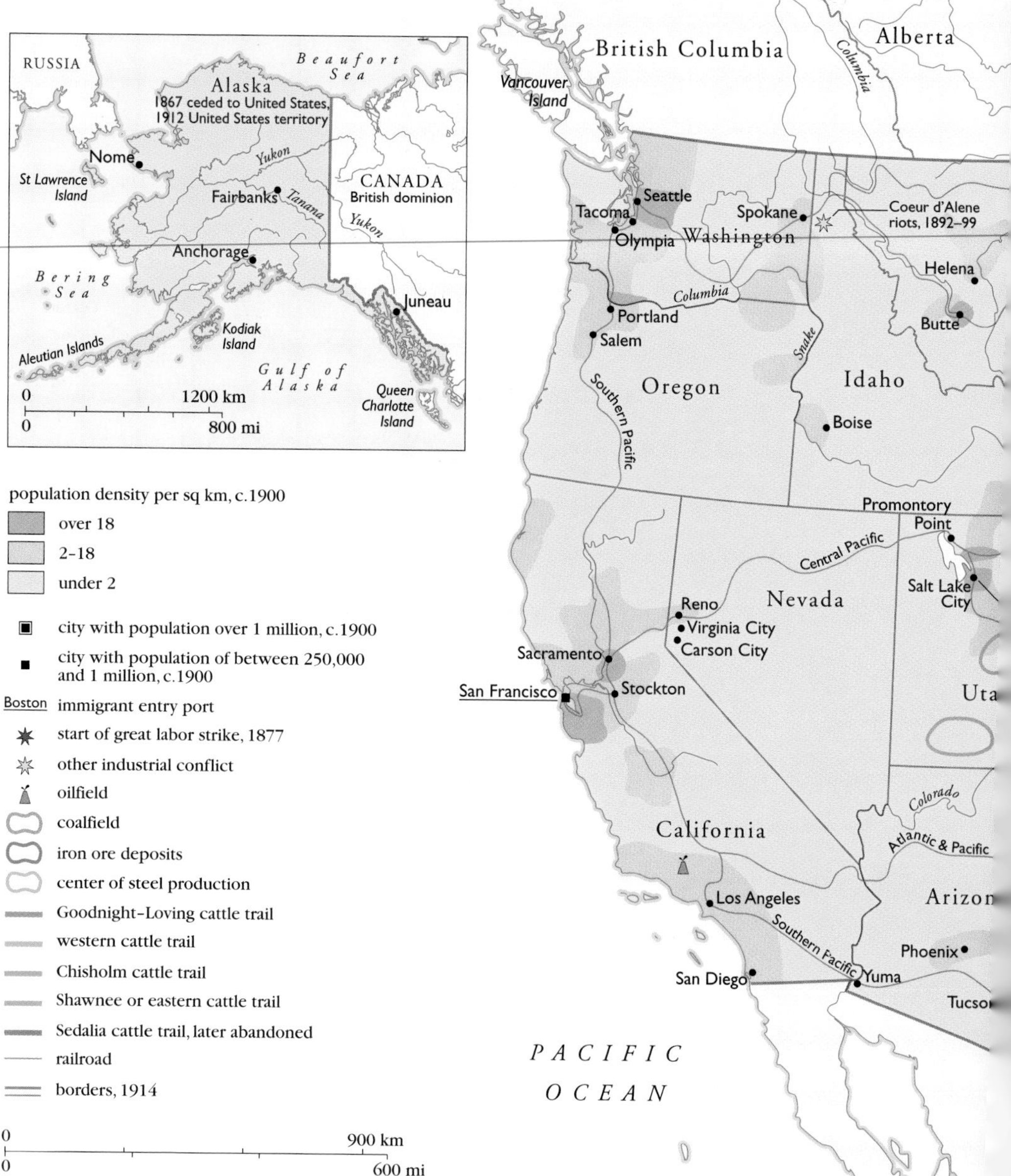
RUSSIA
Beaufort Sea
Alaska
1867 ceded to United States,
1912 United States territory
Nome
Yukon
St Lawrence Island
Fairbanks
Tanana
CANADA
British dominion
Anchorage
Bering Sea
Juneau
Kodiak Island
Aleutian Islands
Gulf of Alaska
Queen Charlotte Island
0 1200 km
0 800 mi
population density per sq km, c.1900
over 18
2–18
under 2
city with population over 1 million, c.1900
city with population of between 250,000 and 1 million, c.1900
Boston immigrant entry port
start of great labor strike, 1877
other industrial conflict
oilfield
coalfield
iron ore deposits
center of steel production
Goodnight–Loving cattle trail
western cattle trail
Chisholm cattle trail
Shawnee or eastern cattle trail
Sedalia cattle trail, later abandoned
railroad
borders, 1914
0 900 km
0 600 mi
British Columbia
Alberta
Columbia
Vancouver Island
Seattle
Tacoma
Olympia
Washington
Spokane
Coeur d'Alene riots, 1892–99
Helena
Butte
Columbia
Portland
Salem
Snake
Oregon
Idaho
Boise
Southern Pacific
Promontory Point
Central Pacific
Salt Lake City
Reno
Nevada
Virginia City
Carson City
Sacramento
San Francisco
Stockton
Uta
Colorado
California
Atlantic & Pacific
Los Angeles
Arizon
Southern Pacific
Phoenix
San Diego
Yuma
Tucso
PACIFIC OCEAN

TIMELINE

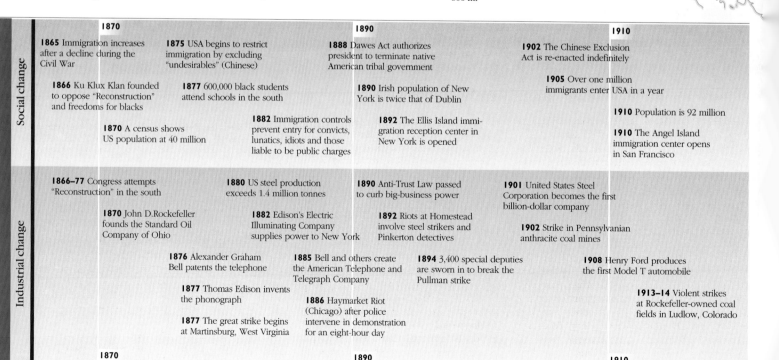

Social change

1865 Immigration increases after a decline during the Civil War

1866 Ku Klux Klan founded to oppose "Reconstruction" and freedoms for blacks

1870 A census shows US population at 40 million

1875 USA begins to restrict immigration by excluding "undesirables" (Chinese)

1877 600,000 black students attend schools in the south

1882 Immigration controls prevent entry for convicts, lunatics, idiots and those liable to be public charges

1888 Dawes Act authorizes president to terminate native American tribal government

1890 Irish population of New York is twice that of Dublin

1892 The Ellis Island immigration reception center in New York is opened

1902 The Chinese Exclusion Act is re-enacted indefinitely

1905 Over one million immigrants enter USA in a year

1910 Population is 92 million

1910 The Angel Island immigration center opens in San Francisco

Industrial change

1866–77 Congress attempts "Reconstruction" in the south

1870 John D.Rockefeller founds the Standard Oil Company of Ohio

1876 Alexander Graham Bell patents the telephone

1877 Thomas Edison invents the phonograph

1877 The great strike begins at Martinsburg, West Virginia

1880 US steel production exceeds 1.4 million tonnes

1882 Edison's Electric Illuminating Company supplies power to New York

1885 Bell and others create the American Telephone and Telegraph Company

1886 Haymarket Riot (Chicago) after police intervene in demonstration for an eight-hour day

1890 Anti-Trust Law passed to curb big-business power

1892 Riots at Homestead involve steel strikers and Pinkerton detectives

1894 3,400 special deputies are sworn in to break the Pullman strike

1901 United States Steel Corporation becomes the first billion-dollar company

1902 Strike in Pennsylvanian anthracite coal mines

1908 Henry Ford produces the first Model T automobile

1913–14 Violent strikes at Rockefeller-owned coal fields in Ludlow, Colorado

1870 1890 1910

victims of race riots. Further Chinese immigration was blocked by the Chinese Exclusion Act of 1882.

The depression that affected Europe in the late 19th century had little effect on the vibrant US economy. This period saw the rise of magnates who made the United States into the world's great industrial power. John D. Rockefeller dominated the oil industry while Philip D. Armour controlled a meat-packing empire, the financier J. Pierpont Morgan underwrote railroads, and Andrew Carnegie was the leading figure in the steel industry. These men took advantage of low interest rates, cheap labor and a largely unregulated market. However, though employers used ruthless business methods and dealt summarily with discontent among their workforces, the age of American high capitalism had its benefits. The essential symbol of American enterprise and democracy was the Model T automobile, first made in 1908 by the Detroit mechanic Henry Ford. Also some multimillionaires, such as Carnegie, were philanthropists who gave away their fortunes.

Industrial growth brought labor problems. The job losses resulting from the 1873 economic crisis made labor unions hostile to further immigration. Strikes were common, the most damaging in 1877. Railroad employees, enraged by a pay cut, withdrew their labor and were supported in their grievances by a large army of unemployed. Unrest spread to Pittsburgh, Chicago, St Louis, Kansas City, Galveston and San Francisco before militiamen were called out to suppress it. Although this dispute, the first general strike in American history, involved millions and even spread to Canada, its most significant feature was the Federal administration's use of troops. In 1892, workers at the Carnegie steel mill in Homestead were beaten by the state militia; two years later president Cleveland sent soldiers to put down a strike of railroad workers in Chicago.

The economy, though, stayed buoyant. By 1914, with a population over 97 million, the United States led the world in the manufacture of steel and lumber products, in meat-packing and precious metal extraction, and had the most telephones, telegraphs, electric lights and automobiles in the world.

1 Between 1867 and 1871, about 1.5 million head of cattle were herded on "long drives" along the Chisholm Trail to the railhead at Abilene, Kansas.

2 Atlanta had been razed by fire during the Georgia campaign of the civil war, but became the center of Federal government activity during reconstruction.

3 During the great strike of 1877, Pittsburgh was devastated by three days of rioting that destroyed much railroad property and almost leveled the city.

4 Oklahoma was opened to settlement in 1889; settlers raced across the prairie to stake their claims.

5 Ellis Island in New York Bay became the country's principal immigration station from 1892 onward.

6 Utah was admitted to the Union as a state in 1896, after its Mormon inhabitants had promised to relinquish the practice of polygamy.

See also 5.27 (American Civil War); 6.12 (the Americas in the early 20th century)

Part 6

FROM WORLD WAR TO

Many of those who went into battle in August 1914 expected the war to be glorious. However, World War I proved long and arduous, testing human endurance to the limit. A century of industrial development had provided the combatant governments with the ideological, bureaucratic and technological capabilities to mobilize vast human and material resources.

The postwar settlement was built on the principle of national self-determination. But the settlement was partial and temporary: the harsh treatment of Germany, an American retreat into isolationism, the rise of the revolutionary Soviet Union and the depression of the 1930s all undermined the peace. The result was the emergence of totalitarian governments in Germany, Italy and Russia, employing the resources of the state to foster a virulent nationalism.

Germany's invasion of Poland in September 1939 led to a war that became truly global. Like its counterpart of 1914–18, World War II was an "absolute" or total war. Each side sought the unconditional surrender of the other, and the distinction between soldier and civilian collapsed as air power provided the means to strike at the enemy's heartland. This strategy culminated in the atomic destruction of the Japanese cities of Hiroshima and Nagasaki, and the devastation of Germany. Meanwhile six million Jews and others perished in the Holocaust, a demonstration of the ability of the totalitarian state to combine ideology, technology and bureaucracy in order to undertake systematic mass extermination.

The two great wars had one positive outcome: the recognition that the propensity of states to destroy one another had to be restrained, by the establishment of international institutions for reinforcing the rule of law. The League of Nations, created in 1919, failed, but its successor the United Nations raised expectations that a concert of victorious

WAR I

THE PRESENT

great powers could deter and defend against aggressive state behavior. Power was now expected to confer responsibility for keeping the peace.

The Cold War between the United States and the Soviet Union dominated the postwar years. It was perhaps a product of misperception: each assumed the other was bent on aggression, and each built alliances – NATO in 1949, the Warsaw Pact in 1955 – to counter the other. A precarious order ensued, at times threatened over three decades by crises in Korea, Cuba, the Middle East, and elsewhere, in which nuclear disaster was sometimes only narrowly averted.

There were, in addition, other trends in the postwar years, the influence of which shaped international relations for many years. First, the United States committed itself to restoring western Europe's battered economies, and equally to the defense of Europe – a reversal of its isolationism after 1919. NATO's protective umbrella gave western Europe the confidence to begin the work of economic integration as the European Economic Community was set up in 1957–58.

Second, the postwar independence of India, Pakistan and Ceylon from British rule set a precedent for anticolonial struggle elsewhere. By 1968 fifty African states had joined the United Nations. China, too, began a long march to great power status after the Communist victory in 1949, despite a long, acrimonious ideological dispute with the Soviet Union for the leadership of the Communist world.

Third, the principle of domestic jurisdiction, which had offered legal protection to a state's internal arrangements, now dissolved. This brought an expansion in the legal competence of bodies such as the UN to intervene when human rights were abused. South Africa's policy of *apartheid* was the catalyst; a series of UN-sponsored declarations claimed the right of the international community to assert human rights.

The apparent stability offered by the threat of "mutually assured destruction" in east–west relations was bought at the expense of the Third World. Initially leaders such as Nehru in India, Sukarno in Indonesia, Nkrumah in Ghana and Nasser in Egypt aspired to build a third force in international affairs, mediating between east and west, and committed to redressing the inequalities between the rich northern states and their poor counterparts in the south. There was a scramble for votes and prestige in the General Assembly of the UN, where African and Asian states had a large, vociferous majority. Some victories were won: the legal establishment of human rights; the isolation of *apartheid*-ridden South Africa; the recognition that Third World states needed aid and technical assistance to provide a decent life for their peoples.

The Cold War years also saw wars by proxy fought in Third World states such as Angola, Ethiopia, Somalia and Vietnam, as the superpowers supported rival factions in civil wars. The result was prolonged conflict and devastation. As détente, or relaxation of superpower tension, took hold, the influence of the "nonaligned movement" began to wane, especially as many Third World states failed to deliver social and economic benefits to their people. The Test Ban Treaty (1963) and the Non-Proliferation Treaty (1968) heralded substantial agreements in the 1970s and 1980s.

Meanwhile, led by Japan, the "tiger" economies – South Korea, Singapore, Taiwan, Malaysia, Hong Kong – underwent an economic miracle via export-led growth and a mix of government intervention and private enterprise. China, too, encouraged market liberalization, though under the control of the Communist Party. The Pacific rim economic powerhouse all but exploded in 1997-98 with the collapse of stock markets and currencies; but there were signs of recovery in the early years of the 21st century.

SINGAPORE, a city founded by the British less than two hundred years earlier, was typical of the high-rise commercial centers of the late 20th century, when former imperial capitals and their colonial counterparts came together to compete for a share of the single global market.

It was clear that the Soviet Union could not deliver both "guns and butter" to its people. The economy was hamstrung by state controls, and the arms race of the 1980s placed great burdens on the economy just when conservative western governments – especially in the United States and Britain – were successfully using free market solutions to boost productivity. Mikhail Gorbachev tried to reform the Soviet Union, but this led to revolt against Russian rule in several of the republics and the satellite states of east and south Europe. The fall of the Berlin Wall – symbol of Cold War division – in 1989 heralded a new global era in which free-market capitalism was enshrined as the chief ideology for economic development throughout the world. Aid or investment became available only to governments willing to demonstrate a commitment to liberalization and the principles of "good governance". Many former command economies were forced to postpone the satisfaction of their people's needs until the painful adjustments to market conditions had been achieved. Even when the "rules" were followed, however, as they were in Argentina – including privatization of industries and strict fiscal policies – the hoped-for rewards did not materialize; the result for Argentina was political turmoil and debt default.

All governments were constrained by the impact of global economic forces. Conventional attack often seemed less threatening than organized crime, drugs and arms trafficking, illegal migration, environmental degradation, and terrorism. In response, pressure mounted for the establishment of wider groupings of states. Such regional associations as the European Union, the North Atlantic Free Trade Association and the Asian-Pacific Economic Community seemed to be potential building blocks for a "new world order" for the third millennium. Environmental concerns that surfaced included global warming. The 1997 Kyoto Treaty committed UN member-states to reducing their greenhouse gas emissions, but it was rejected by the United States in 2001 as unscientific and unworkable.

On September 11, 2001, the World Trade Center in New York was destroyed and the Pentagon damaged by Islamic Al Qaeda terrorists who hijacked four US civilian passenger jets and crashed three of them into their intended targets. Al Qaeda was established as early as 1988 by the Saudi billionaire and member of the ***Mujahideen*** (Afghan resistance to the Soviet invasion) Osama bin Laden. Based first in the Sudan and later in Afghanistan, Al Qaeda was already implicated in terrorist attacks in Yemen, Somalia, Ethiopia, Kenya and Tanzania before the events of 9/11; and perhaps even the first bomb attack on the World Trade Center in February 1993.

Bin Laden's declaration of ***jihad***, or "holy war", against the United States and its allies reconfigured world politics at the beginning of the new millennium. New international alliances were formed – and old ones tested – in what the US president Bush described as the war on terrorism. The first targets were the ruling Taliban, Islamic fundamentalists in Afghanistan, and the Al Qaeda training camps they sheltered. The aggressive policy of the United States against Iraq, principally justified by the desire to prevent its president Saddam Hussein developing weapons of mass destruction, and generally supported by the UN, gained fresh impetus from claims that Iraq was a state sponsor of terrorist organizations. Many feared that the US-led invasion of Iraq in 2003 might destabilize the entire Islamic region, from the Indian subcontinent to Saudi Arabia. In Iraq itself, the downfall of Saddam Hussein signalled the start of a prolonged insurgency conducted mainly by Sunni Muslims against occupying forces. Elsewhere the reduction of tension in Israel after the death of Palestinian leader Yasser Arafat seemed to offer grounds for hope that unrest could be limited to Iraq itself. Even there, the successful holding of elections in early 2005 promised a more optimistic future. A "surge" by U.S. troops helped restore order to the point that by 2009 both Britain and the United States announced their intention to withdraw their troops. Both, however, considered sending more troops to Afghanistan, where the tribal border lands with Pakistan harboured Taliban and Al Qaeda terrorists who launched attacks in both countries and in neighboring India.

The 2009 inauguration of Barack Obama, the first black U.S. president, seemed to promise a new phase in global relations as he sought to engage with traditional opponents of America, including Iran. However, a global economic downturn and credit crisis threatened to dominate the attention of the new president and the world's other rulers, as did the threat in 2009 of a global pandemic of swine flu.

Singapore Telecom

At the beginning of the 20th century the world was dominated by Europe's imperial powers, many of them in the hands of ancient, autocratic monarchies. World War I shattered much of this, and by its end revolutions had swept away several monarchies, to be replaced in some states, such as Germany, by fragile democracies and others (such as Russia) by revolutionary dictatorships (▷ *6.06*). Among the factors driving change were the introduction of new technologies, particularly in the field of communications. Continental and oceanic transit networks were completed, and wireless telegraphy and radio were developed. Horse- and steam-power began to give way to gasoline- and diesel-driven transportation systems and the war brought a rapid advance in air transport, for civilian as well as military purposes.

Challenges to Europe's empires were already evident before 1914. In the east, Japan was industrializing rapidly and had defeated Russia and advanced into Manchuria as the Manchu dynasty in China collapsed (▷ *6.18*). Europe's most formidable challenge, however, came from the United States which, following the defeat of Spain in 1898, became the only power capable of determining the development of the American continent. As a result, the United States built its own informal empire, enforcing its will if necessary by military intervention (▷ *6.12*).

During World War I, Britain and France relied on their colonies and on the United States for men and materiel; when they came to make peace in 1919, they could not dictate the settlement alone. The United States was now the world's leading financial, industrial and, potentially, military power, thanks to the boost given to its industry by Allied orders at a time when the European economies were drastically disrupted. While Britain almost bankrupted itself funding the Allied war effort, the United States took over as the world's banker.

The American president Woodrow Wilson used this power to alter the conduct of international relations. On his initiative the League of Nations was set up, an organization of nation-states dedicated to preventing war by substituting mediation for military action. Wilson was also committed to the principle of national self-determination, and promoted the creation of new states such as Czechoslovakia, Yugoslavia and an independent Poland (▷ *6.07*). He also tried to discourage imperialism, arguing that Germany's colonies should not be seized as the spoils of war. Instead, he persuaded the victorious powers to mandate these territories to Britain (whose empire thereby achieved its greatest territorial extent), France,

A. Albania
AU. Austria
B. Belgium
C. Czechoslovakia
D. Denmark
E. Estonia
H. Hungary
KS. Kingdom of Serbs, Croats, and Slovenes
L. Luxembourg
LI. Lithuania
N. Netherlands
PG. Portuguese Guinea
S. Switzerland
T. Transjordan
YE. Yemen

TIMELINE: The Americas · Europe · Middle East · Africa · Asia and Australasia · 1914 · 1916 · 1918

1914 (Aug) Opening of the Panama Canal under US auspices

1914 (Aug) Outbreak of general European war as Germany invades France and attacks Russia

1914 Japan takes over many German colonies in the Pacific

1914 Australia takes over the German colony of Kaiser Wilhelmsland

1915 (Apr) Italy, formerly a member of the Central Powers, joins the Allies

1915 (Apr) The Allies attempt to seize control of the Dardanelles by landing at Gallipoli

1915 Allied armies advance through Mesopotamia

1916 Battles of Verdun and the Somme on the Western Front

1916 (Jun) An Arab revolt against the Ottomans begins in the Hejaz

1917 (Apr) The United States declares war on the Central Powers

1917 (Nov) Bolshevik revolution in Russia, leading to civil war (to 1921)

1917 (Nov) The Balfour Declaration commits Britain to the creation of a Jewish state in Palestine

1917 (Dec) British forces occupy Jerusalem

1918 (Mar) Treaty of Brest-Litovsk yields much of western Russia to Germany

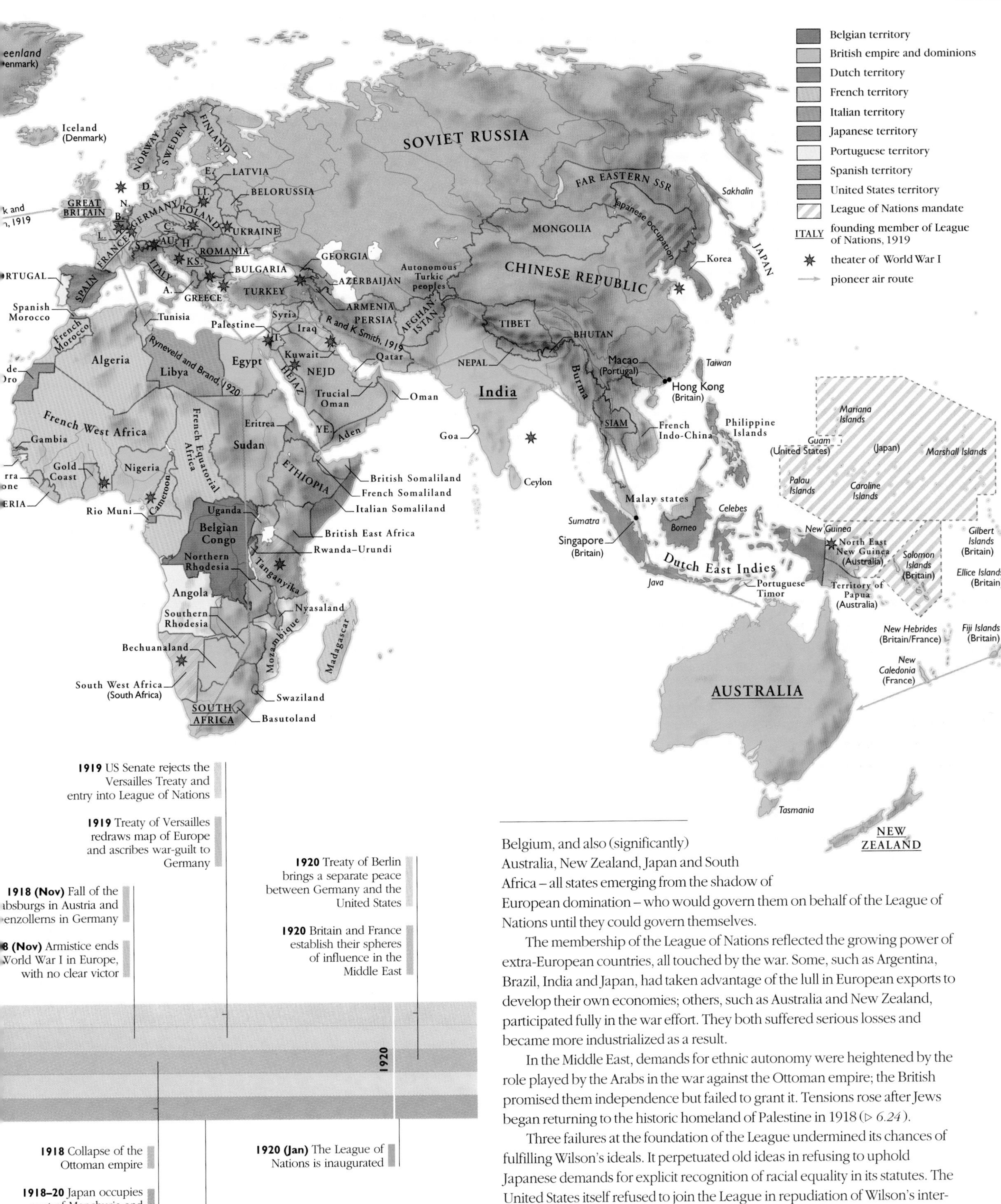
Belgian territory
British empire and dominions
Dutch territory
French territory
Italian territory
Japanese territory
Portuguese territory
Spanish territory
United States territory
League of Nations mandate
ITALY founding member of League of Nations, 1919
theater of World War I
pioneer air route
SOVIET RUSSIA
FAR EASTERN SSR
Japanese occupation
Sakhalin
MONGOLIA
CHINESE REPUBLIC
Korea
JAPAN
Iceland (Denmark)
NORWAY
SWEDEN
FINLAND
LATVIA
BELORUSSIA
UKRAINE
POLAND
GERMANY
GREAT BRITAIN
FRANCE
SPAIN
ITALY
ROMANIA
BULGARIA
GREECE
TURKEY
GEORGIA
AZERBAIJAN
ARMENIA
Autonomous Turkic peoples
PERSIA
AFGHANISTAN
R and K Smith, 1919
Syria
Iraq
Palestine
Kuwait
NEJD
HEJAZ
Qatar
Trucial Oman
Oman
YE.
Aden
Tunisia
Spanish Morocco
French Morocco
Algeria
Libya
Egypt
Ryneveld and Brand, 1920
French West Africa
Gambia
Gold Coast
Nigeria
Cameroon
Rio Muni
French Equatorial Africa
Sudan
Eritrea
ETHIOPIA
British Somaliland
French Somaliland
Italian Somaliland
Uganda
Belgian Congo
British East Africa
Rwanda–Urundi
Northern Rhodesia
Tanganyika
Angola
Nyasaland
Southern Rhodesia
Mozambique
Madagascar
Bechuanaland
South West Africa (South Africa)
Swaziland
SOUTH AFRICA
Basutoland
TIBET
BHUTAN
NEPAL
India
Goa
Ceylon
Burma
Macao (Portugal)
Hong Kong (Britain)
Taiwan
SIAM
French Indo-China
Philippine Islands
Malay states
Sumatra
Singapore (Britain)
Borneo
Celebes
Dutch East Indies
Java
Portuguese Timor
Mariana Islands
Guam (United States)
(Japan)
Marshall Islands
Palau Islands
Caroline Islands
New Guinea
North East New Guinea (Australia)
Territory of Papua (Australia)
Solomon Islands (Britain)
Gilbert Islands (Britain)
Ellice Islands (Britain)
New Hebrides (Britain/France)
Fiji Islands (Britain)
New Caledonia (France)
AUSTRALIA
Tasmania
NEW ZEALAND

1919 US Senate rejects the Versailles Treaty and entry into League of Nations

1919 Treaty of Versailles redraws map of Europe and ascribes war-guilt to Germany

1918 (Nov) Fall of the ...absburgs in Austria and ...enzollerns in Germany

...8 (Nov) Armistice ends World War I in Europe, with no clear victor

1920 Treaty of Berlin brings a separate peace between Germany and the United States

1920 Britain and France establish their spheres of influence in the Middle East

1920

1918 Collapse of the Ottoman empire

1918–20 Japan occupies part of Manchuria and Siberia

1919 (Jun) British aviators Alcock and Brown cross the Atlantic nonstop

1920 (Jan) The League of Nations is inaugurated

Belgium, and also (significantly) Australia, New Zealand, Japan and South Africa – all states emerging from the shadow of European domination – who would govern them on behalf of the League of Nations until they could govern themselves.

The membership of the League of Nations reflected the growing power of extra-European countries, all touched by the war. Some, such as Argentina, Brazil, India and Japan, had taken advantage of the lull in European exports to develop their own economies; others, such as Australia and New Zealand, participated fully in the war effort. They both suffered serious losses and became more industrialized as a result.

In the Middle East, demands for ethnic autonomy were heightened by the role played by the Arabs in the war against the Ottoman empire; the British promised them independence but failed to grant it. Tensions rose after Jews began returning to the historic homeland of Palestine in 1918 (▷ *6.24*).

Three failures at the foundation of the League undermined its chances of fulfilling Wilson's ideals. It perpetuated old ideas in refusing to uphold Japanese demands for explicit recognition of racial equality in its statutes. The United States itself refused to join the League in repudiation of Wilson's internationalism, and after 1919 distanced itself from international politics. Finally, Soviet Russia – engaged from 1917–21 in a destructive revolution and civil war – was excluded from the peace-making and membership of the League ■

The international order which emerged from World War I failed to match the intentions of allowing for national self-determination for all, and left a deep resentment in Germany, which was made to carry the blame for the war. As a result, stability was not achieved, and the post-Versailles order was overturned by extremist powers which by 1942 dominated much of the globe. The Axis powers, Germany and Japan, exploited the political vacuum left by the withdrawal of the United States and Russia from world affairs after the war, and by the effects of the depression on Britain and France. However, although 1942 marked the zenith of Axis power, their attacks on the two nascent superpowers made their eventual victory unlikely.

Soviet Russia emerged from its civil war of the early 1920s and turned in on itself as Stalin tried to build "socialism in one country" (▷ *6.15*). The attempt to entrench Soviet power and catch up with the west was partially successful but extremely costly, as Stalin unleashed famine and terror on the Soviet Union.

In Europe, economic recovery was built on American loans. The US stock exchange crash of 1929 precipitated the global economic collapse known as the Great Depression. Its effect was to increase the appeal of fascist or extreme rightwing schemes of national regeneration in countries dissatisfied with the outcome of the peace settlements of 1919–23 (notably Germany). Governments everywhere looked to protect their interests by erecting tariff barriers and closed trading blocs, which further depressed the world economy.

The United States became isolated from international affairs as it tried to resolve its internal problems, and Britain and France were left to try to contain fascist expansion. But, although the depression began to lift in the late 1930s, both were economically too weak and too preoccupied by their global commitments to act effectively (▷ *6.07*). They feared the prospect of fighting on three fronts – against Germany in Europe, Italy in the Mediterranean, and Japan in Asia. Their empires were potentially unstable – especially British India, where the nationalist Congress Party was growing in strength (▷ *6.18*) – as were their domestic economies and societies.

The League of Nations reacted impotently to a series of crises in the 1930s – an Italian invasion of Ethiopia and German invasions of the Rhineland, Austria, Czechoslovakia – and thereby lost its credibility. France and Britain tried but failed to preserve peace through negotiation, alliances

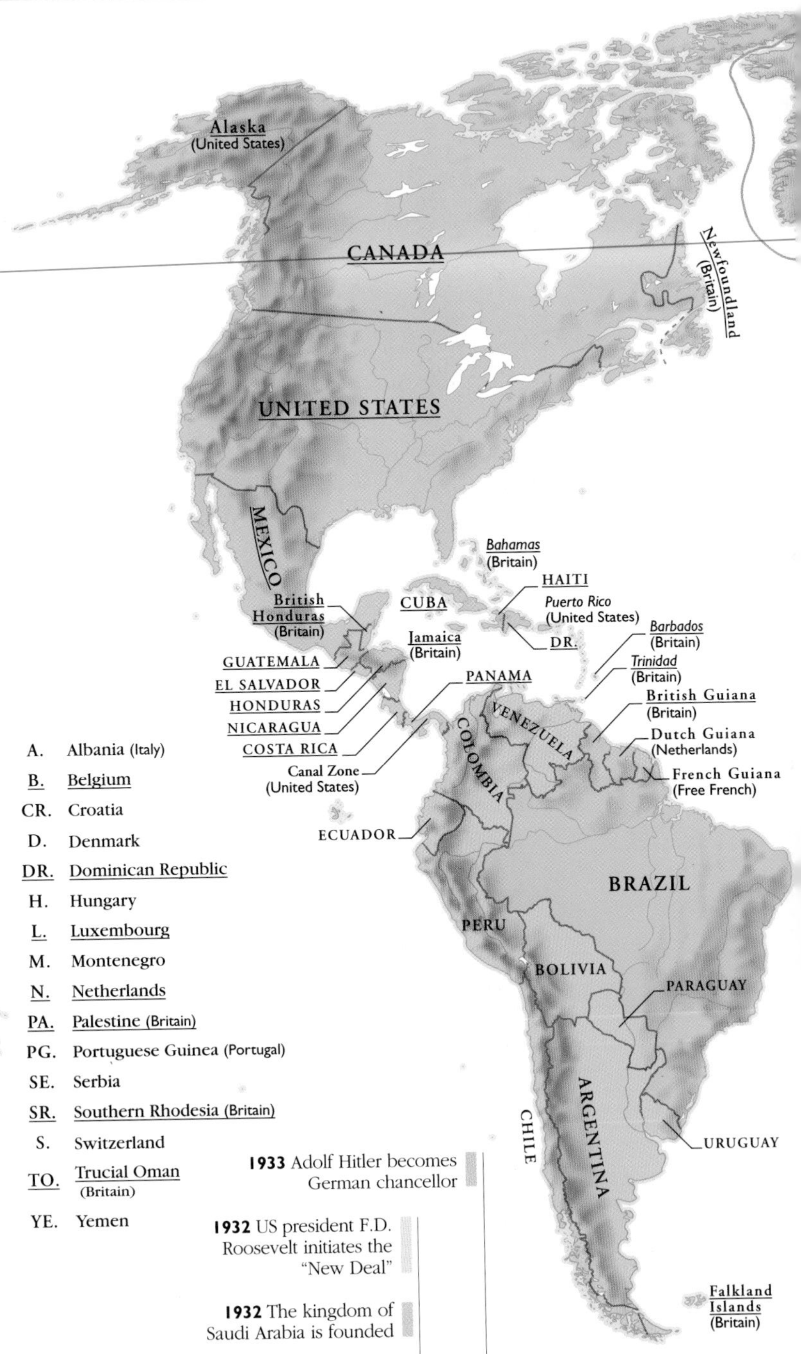

Hawaiian Islands (United States)
French Polynesia (Free French)
Alaska (United States)
CANADA
Newfoundland (Britain)
UNITED STATES
MEXICO
Bahamas (Britain)
HAITI
Puerto Rico (United States)
British Honduras (Britain)
CUBA
Barbados (Britain)
Jamaica (Britain)
DR.
Trinidad (Britain)
GUATEMALA
EL SALVADOR
HONDURAS
NICARAGUA
COSTA RICA
Canal Zone (United States)
PANAMA
VENEZUELA
COLOMBIA
British Guiana (Britain)
Dutch Guiana (Netherlands)
French Guiana (Free French)
ECUADOR
BRAZIL
PERU
BOLIVIA
PARAGUAY
CHILE
ARGENTINA
URUGUAY
Falkland Islands (Britain)

A. Albania (Italy)
B. Belgium
CR. Croatia
D. Denmark
DR. Dominican Republic
H. Hungary
L. Luxembourg
M. Montenegro
N. Netherlands
PA. Palestine (Britain)
PG. Portuguese Guinea (Portugal)
SE. Serbia
SR. Southern Rhodesia (Britain)
S. Switzerland
TO. Trucial Oman (Britain)
YE. Yemen

TIMELINE

The Americas
Europe
Middle East
Africa
Asia and Australasia

1920
1930

1921 The Russian civil war ends with a Bolshevik victory

1922 Mussolini marches on Rome, establishing the first Fascist government

1922 Washington Naval Agreement limits Japanese naval power in the Pacific

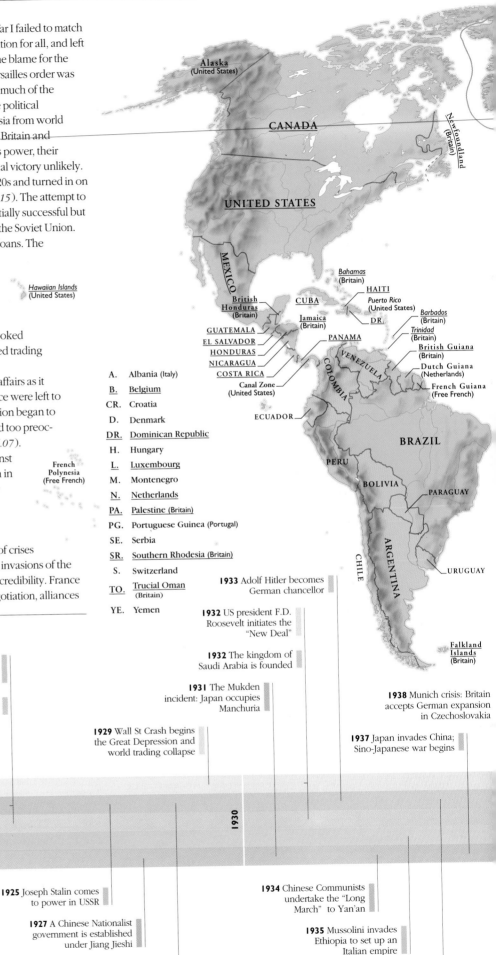

1923 France occupies the Ruhr; hyperinflation results in Germany

1923 Foundation of the modern republic of Turkey

1925 Joseph Stalin comes to power in USSR

1927 A Chinese Nationalist government is established under Jiang Jieshi

1928 Russia's first Five Year Plan of industrialization is introduced

1929 Wall St Crash begins the Great Depression and world trading collapse

1931 The Mukden incident: Japan occupies Manchuria

1932 US president F.D. Roosevelt initiates the "New Deal"

1932 The kingdom of Saudi Arabia is founded

1933 Adolf Hitler becomes German chancellor

1934 Chinese Communists undertake the "Long March" to Yan'an

1935 Mussolini invades Ethiopia to set up an Italian empire

1936 Civil war in Spain after a rightwing uprising against the government

1937 Japan invades China; Sino-Japanese war begins

1938 Munich crisis: Britain accepts German expansion in Czechoslovakia

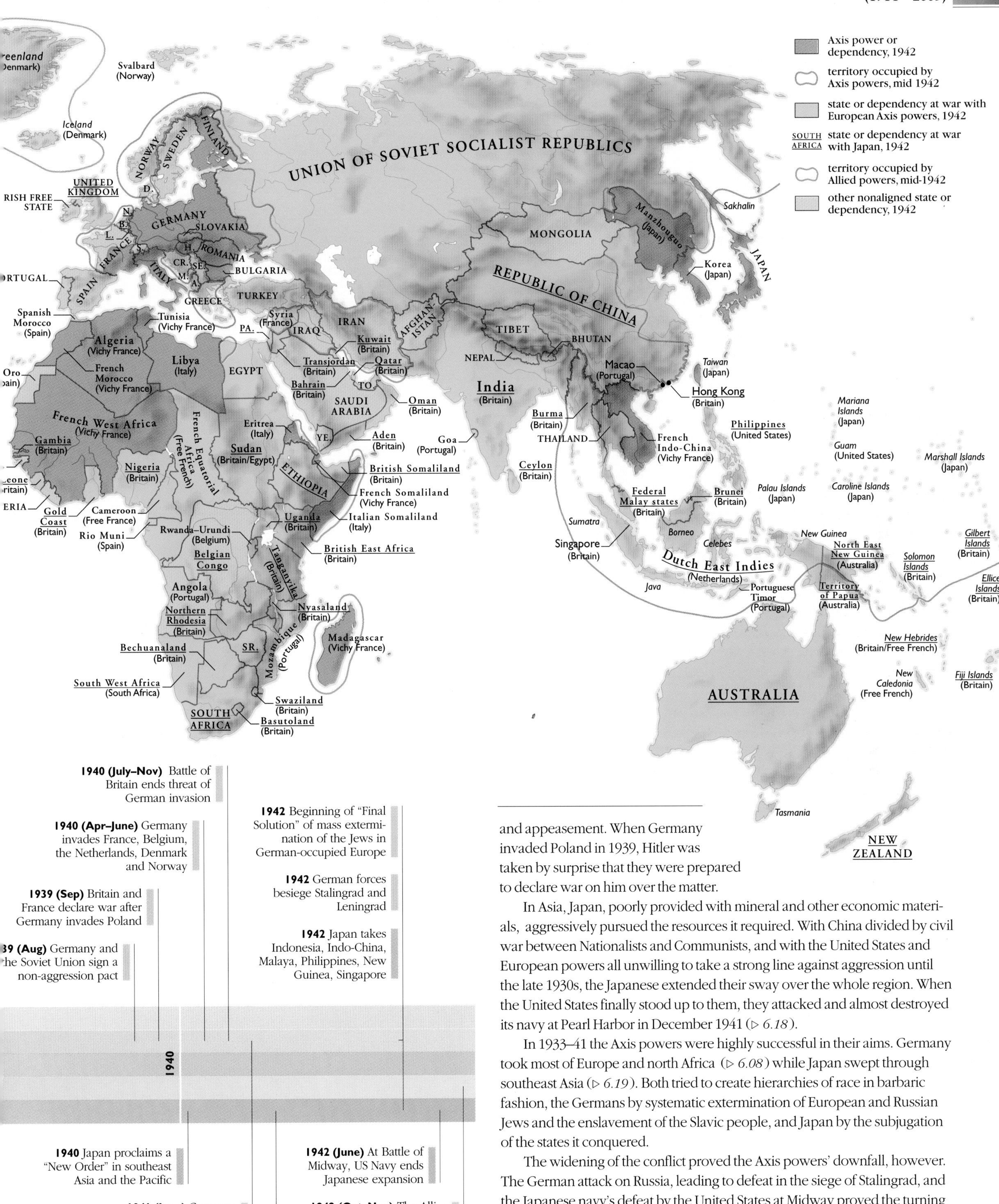
Axis power or dependency, 1942
territory occupied by Axis powers, mid 1942
state or dependency at war with European Axis powers, 1942
SOUTH AFRICA state or dependency at war with Japan, 1942
territory occupied by Allied powers, mid-1942
other nonaligned state or dependency, 1942
Svalbard (Norway)
Iceland (Denmark)
UNITED KINGDOM
NORWAY
SWEDEN
FINLAND
D.
N.
B.
L.
GERMANY
SLOVAKIA
FRANCE
H.
ROMANIA
CR.
SE.
M.
A.
ITALY
SPAIN
BULGARIA
GREECE
TURKEY
UNION OF SOVIET SOCIALIST REPUBLICS
Spanish Morocco (Spain)
Tunisia (Vichy France)
Syria (France)
PA.
IRAQ
IRAN
AFGHANISTAN
Algeria (Vichy France)
French Morocco (Vichy France)
Libya (Italy)
EGYPT
Transjordan (Britain)
Kuwait (Britain)
Qatar (Britain)
Bahrain (Britain)
TO.
SAUDI ARABIA
Oman (Britain)
French West Africa (Vichy France)
Gambia (Britain)
Eritrea (Italy)
YE.
Aden (Britain)
Goa (Portugal)
French Equatorial Africa (Free French)
Sudan (Britain/Egypt)
Nigeria (Britain)
ETHIOPIA
British Somaliland (Britain)
French Somaliland (Vichy France)
Italian Somaliland (Italy)
Gold Coast (Britain)
Cameroon (Free France)
Rio Muni (Spain)
Rwanda-Urundi (Belgium)
Uganda (Britain)
British East Africa (Britain)
Belgian Congo
Tanganyika (Britain)
Angola (Portugal)
Nyasaland (Britain)
Northern Rhodesia (Britain)
Madagascar (Vichy France)
Mozambique (Portugal)
Bechuanaland (Britain)
SR.
South West Africa (South Africa)
Swaziland (Britain)
SOUTH AFRICA
Basutoland (Britain)
MONGOLIA
Manzhouguo (Japan)
Sakhalin
Korea (Japan)
JAPAN
REPUBLIC OF CHINA
TIBET
BHUTAN
NEPAL
India (Britain)
Macao (Portugal)
Taiwan (Japan)
Hong Kong (Britain)
Burma (Britain)
THAILAND
French Indo-China (Vichy France)
Philippines (United States)
Mariana Islands (Japan)
Guam (United States)
Marshall Islands (Japan)
Ceylon (Britain)
Federal Malay states (Britain)
Brunei (Britain)
Palau Islands (Japan)
Caroline Islands (Japan)
Sumatra
Borneo
Celebes
New Guinea
North East New Guinea (Australia)
Solomon Islands (Britain)
Gilbert Islands (Britain)
Singapore (Britain)
Dutch East Indies (Netherlands)
Java
Portuguese Timor (Portugal)
Territory of Papua (Australia)
Ellice Islands (Britain)
New Hebrides (Britain/Free French)
New Caledonia (Free French)
Fiji Islands (Britain)
AUSTRALIA
Tasmania
NEW ZEALAND
1940

1940 (July–Nov) Battle of Britain ends threat of German invasion

1940 (Apr–June) Germany invades France, Belgium, the Netherlands, Denmark and Norway

1939 (Sep) Britain and France declare war after Germany invades Poland

39 (Aug) Germany and he Soviet Union sign a non-aggression pact

1942 Beginning of "Final Solution" of mass extermination of the Jews in German-occupied Europe

1942 German forces besiege Stalingrad and Leningrad

1942 Japan takes Indonesia, Indo-China, Malaya, Philippines, New Guinea, Singapore

1940 Japan proclaims a "New Order" in southeast Asia and the Pacific

1941 (June) Germany invades the Soviet Union

1941 (Dec) Japanese attack on Pearl Harbor leads USA to enter the war

1942 (June) At Battle of Midway, US Navy ends Japanese expansion

1942 (Oct–Nov) The Allies invade north Africa; Battle of El Alamein

and appeasement. When Germany invaded Poland in 1939, Hitler was taken by surprise that they were prepared to declare war on him over the matter.

In Asia, Japan, poorly provided with mineral and other economic materials, aggressively pursued the resources it required. With China divided by civil war between Nationalists and Communists, and with the United States and European powers all unwilling to take a strong line against aggression until the late 1930s, the Japanese extended their sway over the whole region. When the United States finally stood up to them, they attacked and almost destroyed its navy at Pearl Harbor in December 1941 (▷ *6.18*).

In 1933–41 the Axis powers were highly successful in their aims. Germany took most of Europe and north Africa (▷ *6.08*) while Japan swept through southeast Asia (▷ *6.19*). Both tried to create hierarchies of race in barbaric fashion, the Germans by systematic extermination of European and Russian Jews and the enslavement of the Slavic people, and Japan by the subjugation of the states it conquered.

The widening of the conflict proved the Axis powers' downfall, however. The German attack on Russia, leading to defeat in the siege of Stalingrad, and the Japanese navy's defeat by the United States at Midway proved the turning points of the war. The two new superpowers decisively defeated their adversaries, and marshalled their greater array of resources to follow up their victories. In doing so they forged the shape of the postwar world ■

6.03 THE WORLD • AD 1950 •

The United States had entered World War II at the end of 1941 to prevent the domination of Europe and Asia by totalitarian regimes. Yet by 1950 the world was again polarized. The split of the wartime Allies (the United States, the Soviet Union and Britain) created power blocs whose rivalry was consolidated by the outbreak of war in Korea, a conflict by proxy between the democratic capitalist "west" and authoritarian Communist "east".

The Axis powers were in retreat from 1942. Japan was pushed across the Pacific by American military and naval might (▷ *6.19*); Germany was beaten by the Soviet Union at Stalingrad and Kursk; British and American troops landed in Italy and Normandy as their airforces pounded German cities (▷ *6.09*). When the war ended after the dropping of atomic bombs on Hiroshima and Nagasaki, 50 million people, mostly civilians, had died.

As the tide of war turned, the patterns of the postwar world were being laid down. The United Nations Organization (UNO), a new body for resolving international disputes, was set up, but it was clear that the United States and Soviet Union would be the world's strongest powers. The United States and Britain tried to win the trust of the USSR, which had forced the Germans from eastern Europe. They also accepted the incorporation of the Baltic states into the Soviet Union, the annexation of Polish territory and the forced repatriation of Soviet prisoners of war.

The Soviet Union soon become involved in the internal affairs of the states of eastern Europe, however, and the wartime lines of demarcation became the boundaries of a divided postwar Europe. The United States supplied massive aid to prevent the devastated countries of western Europe from succumbing to Communism. In response the Soviet Union created Comecon, a system of interstate economic planning designed to strengthen its hold on eastern Europe. Germany remained divided, a division reinforced by the Soviet blockade of the western zones of Berlin in 1948–49, when Britain and the United States kept the city supplied by air (▷ *6.10*).

American aid to Europe followed the Truman doctrine of 1947, which committed the United States to supporting "free peoples" in the struggle against totalitarianism. Initially the struggle against Communism was a European one: in much of Asia, the immediate struggle was for independence from colonial rule.

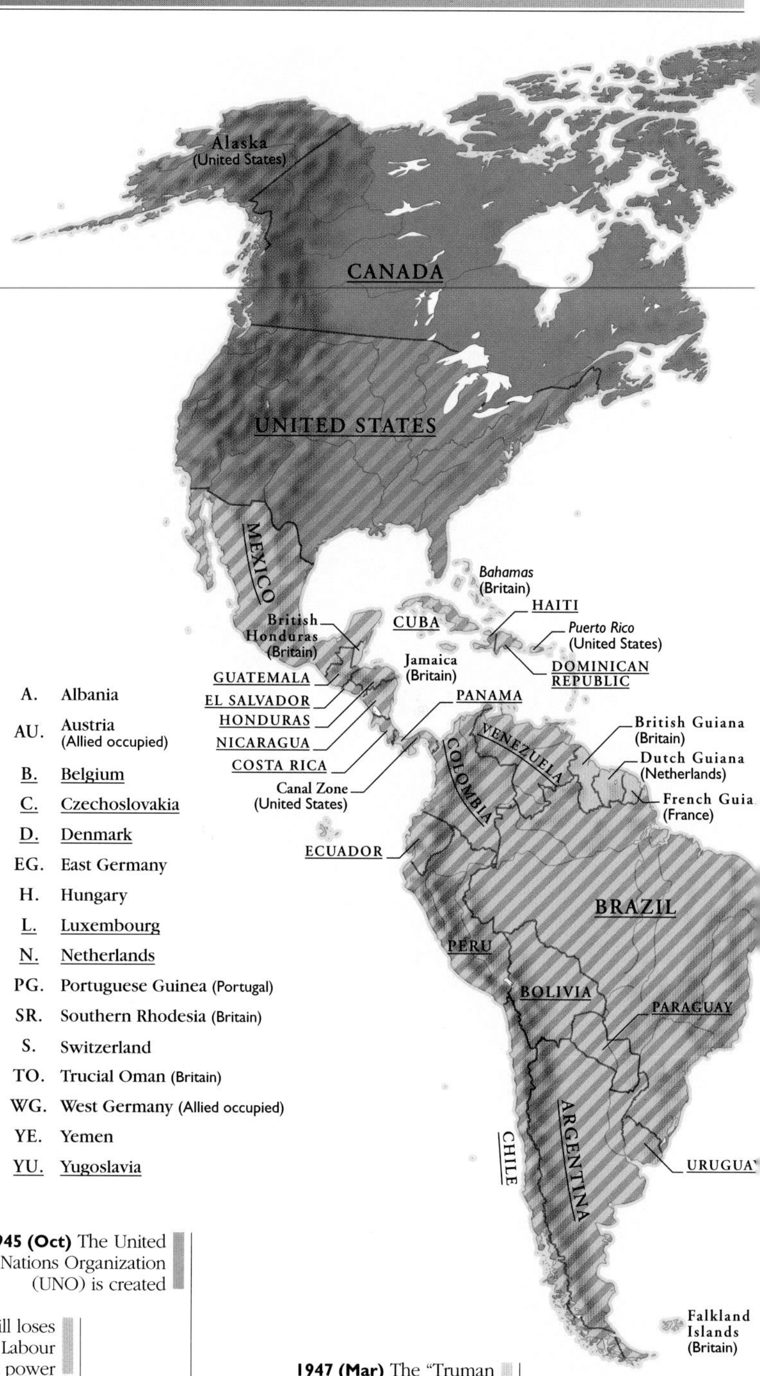

Alaska (United States)
CANADA
UNITED STATES
MEXICO
Hawaiian Islands (United States)
Bahamas (Britain)
HAITI
CUBA
British Honduras (Britain)
Puerto Rico (United States)
Jamaica (Britain)
DOMINICAN REPUBLIC
GUATEMALA
EL SALVADOR
HONDURAS
NICARAGUA
COSTA RICA
Canal Zone (United States)
PANAMA
VENEZUELA
COLOMBIA
British Guiana (Britain)
Dutch Guiana (Netherlands)
French Guia (France)
ECUADOR
BRAZIL
PERU
BOLIVIA
PARAGUAY
French Polynesia (France)
CHILE
ARGENTINA
URUGUA
Falkland Islands (Britain)
A. Albania
AU. Austria (Allied occupied)
B. Belgium
C. Czechoslovakia
D. Denmark
EG. East Germany
H. Hungary
L. Luxembourg
N. Netherlands
PG. Portuguese Guinea (Portugal)
SR. Southern Rhodesia (Britain)
S. Switzerland
TO. Trucial Oman (Britain)
WG. West Germany (Allied occupied)
YE. Yemen
YU. Yugoslavia

TIMELINE

The Americas | Europe | Middle East | Africa | Asia and Australasia

1944 · 1946 · 1948

1942–43 (Jan) Defeat at Stalingrad ends German expansion to the east

1943 June) Allied forces land in Italy

1943 (May) Axis forces are evacuated from north Africa

1943 (July) Soviet forces defeat Germans at Kursk

1944 (June) D-Day: a huge Allied force invades northern France

1944 (July) The International Monetary Fund (IMF) is founded

1945 (May) Germany surrenders, ending war in Europe

1945 (July) Churchill loses British election; Labour wins power

1945 (Aug–Sep) Japan surrenders after atomic bombs are dropped at Hiroshima and Nagasaki

1945 (Sep) North and South Korea independent

1945 (Oct) The United Nations Organization (UNO) is created

1945 (Oct) The Arab league is founded

1946 (July) The Philippines gain their independence

1947 The United States withdraw from China

1947 (Mar) The "Truman Doctrine" is announced

1947 (June) US "Marshall Aid" to assist recovery in western Europe proposed

1947 (Aug) India and Pakistan gain independence from Britain

1948 (Feb) A Communist coup takes place in Czechoslovakia

1948 (Apr) Organization of American States is founded

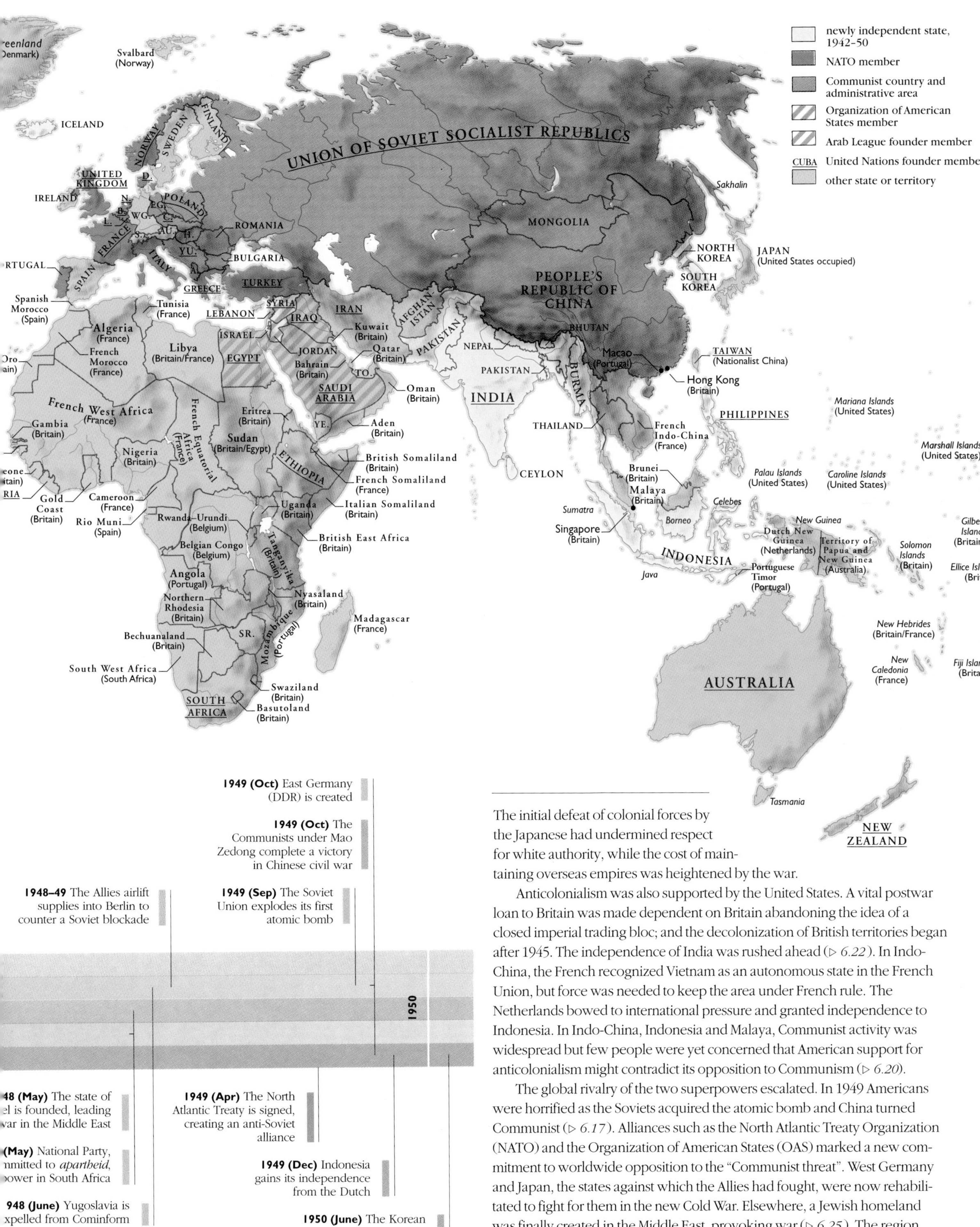
newly independent state, 1942–50
NATO member
Communist country and administrative area
Organization of American States member
Arab League founder member
CUBA United Nations founder member
other state or territory
Svalbard (Norway)
ICELAND
UNITED KINGDOM
IRELAND
NORWAY
SWEDEN
FINLAND
UNION OF SOVIET SOCIALIST REPUBLICS
Sakhalin
MONGOLIA
ROMANIA
BULGARIA
GREECE
TURKEY
SYRIA
LEBANON
IRAQ
IRAN
ISRAEL
JORDAN
EGYPT
SAUDI ARABIA
Kuwait (Britain)
Qatar (Britain)
Bahrain (Britain)
Oman (Britain)
Aden (Britain)
AFGHANISTAN
PAKISTAN
NEPAL
BHUTAN
INDIA
CEYLON
BURMA
THAILAND
PEOPLE'S REPUBLIC OF CHINA
NORTH KOREA
SOUTH KOREA
JAPAN (United States occupied)
TAIWAN (Nationalist China)
Macao (Portugal)
Hong Kong (Britain)
PHILIPPINES
French Indo-China (France)
Brunei (Britain)
Malaya (Britain)
Singapore (Britain)
Sumatra
Borneo
Celebes
Java
INDONESIA
Portuguese Timor (Portugal)
New Guinea
Dutch New Guinea (Netherlands)
Territory of Papua and New Guinea (Australia)
Mariana Islands (United States)
Marshall Islands (United States)
Palau Islands (United States)
Caroline Islands (United States)
Gilbert Islands (Britain)
Solomon Islands (Britain)
Ellice Islands (Britain)
New Hebrides (Britain/France)
New Caledonia (France)
Fiji Islands (Britain)
AUSTRALIA
Tasmania
NEW ZEALAND
Spanish Morocco (Spain)
Tunisia (France)
Algeria (France)
French Morocco (France)
Libya (Britain/France)
French West Africa (France)
Gambia (Britain)
Nigeria (Britain)
French Equatorial Africa (France)
Sudan (Britain/Egypt)
Eritrea (Britain)
ETHIOPIA
British Somaliland (Britain)
French Somaliland (France)
Italian Somaliland (Britain)
Gold Coast (Britain)
Cameroon (France)
Rio Muni (Spain)
Uganda (Britain)
Rwanda-Urundi (Belgium)
Belgian Congo (Belgium)
British East Africa (Britain)
Tanganyika (Britain)
Angola (Portugal)
Northern Rhodesia (Britain)
Nyasaland (Britain)
Mozambique (Portugal)
Madagascar (France)
Bechuanaland (Britain)
South West Africa (South Africa)
Swaziland (Britain)
Basutoland (Britain)
SOUTH AFRICA
1949 (Oct) East Germany (DDR) is created
1949 (Oct) The Communists under Mao Zedong complete a victory in Chinese civil war
1948–49 The Allies airlift supplies into Berlin to counter a Soviet blockade
1949 (Sep) The Soviet Union explodes its first atomic bomb
1950
48 (May) The state of el is founded, leading var in the Middle East
(May) National Party, nmitted to apartheid, power in South Africa
948 (June) Yugoslavia is xpelled from Cominform
1949 (Apr) The North Atlantic Treaty is signed, creating an anti-Soviet alliance
1949 (Dec) Indonesia gains its independence from the Dutch
1950 (June) The Korean War begins as Communist troops invade the south

The initial defeat of colonial forces by the Japanese had undermined respect for white authority, while the cost of maintaining overseas empires was heightened by the war.

Anticolonialism was also supported by the United States. A vital postwar loan to Britain was made dependent on Britain abandoning the idea of a closed imperial trading bloc; and the decolonization of British territories began after 1945. The independence of India was rushed ahead (▷ 6.22). In Indo-China, the French recognized Vietnam as an autonomous state in the French Union, but force was needed to keep the area under French rule. The Netherlands bowed to international pressure and granted independence to Indonesia. In Indo-China, Indonesia and Malaya, Communist activity was widespread but few people were yet concerned that American support for anticolonialism might contradict its opposition to Communism (▷ 6.20).

The global rivalry of the two superpowers escalated. In 1949 Americans were horrified as the Soviets acquired the atomic bomb and China turned Communist (▷ 6.17). Alliances such as the North Atlantic Treaty Organization (NATO) and the Organization of American States (OAS) marked a new commitment to worldwide opposition to the "Communist threat". West Germany and Japan, the states against which the Allies had fought, were now rehabilitated to fight for them in the new Cold War. Elsewhere, a Jewish homeland was finally created in the Middle East, provoking war (▷ 6.25). The region would grow ever more unstable as the value of the oil it exported rose ■

By 1974 rivalry between the Soviet Union and the United States still dominated international affairs. The USSR guarded its European satellite states jealously. When, in 1956, Hungary tried to break free from the Soviet-dominated Warsaw Pact, the Red Army crushed the revolution. In 1961 the Berlin Wall was erected to enforce Soviet control over East Germany. And in 1968, Warsaw Pact forces ended the Czech attempt to introduce "socialism with a human face" (▷ 6.10). Yet Yugoslavia, Albania and Romania all won some independence from Soviet control.

In western Europe, institutions were set up to integrate the economies of the main industrial nations. The European Economic Community (EEC) was seen as a step to political union and the creation of a European superstate, but most countries (France was the main exception) still relied on the United States membership of NATO for security from possible Soviet aggression.

It was in America's "backyard" that superpower rivalry was most apparent. The Cuban missile crisis of 1962 brought a real threat of nuclear war until the Soviet Union withdrew its missiles from within range of the American mainland (▷ 6.14). Anxiety for the spread of Communism also lay behind the United States involvement in southeast Asia. Fearing that neighboring countries would fall to Communism (the "domino effect"), the United States sent men and dollars to prop up an unpopular regime in South Vietnam. It was another war by proxy but, unlike Korea, American withdrawal from Vietnam led to the collapse of South Vietnam and the descent of Cambodia into civil war (▷ 6.21).

Conflict between China and the Soviet Union, underlain by centuries of mutual suspicion, showed that America's opponents were not a unified bloc, however. The Chinese version of Communism was different from the Soviet, as China tried to develop a locally-based economy centered on communes, in contrast to the centralized bureaucracies of the Soviet Union. Chinese Communism was more applicable to non-industrial societies; Communist insurgents worldwide, especially in southeast Asia where rapid decolonization was followed by political upheaval, turned to it for inspiration and support. Eventual American recognition of the Sino-Soviet split led in the early 1970s to an attempt to exploit it and brought a new era of détente (▷ 6.20).

In Africa, opposition to imperial rule was the driving force. The Suez crisis of 1956 showed the weakness of the old imperial powers, and a wave of

Alaska (United States)
CANADA
UNITED STATES
MEXICO
Hawaii (United States)
BAHAMAS
HAITI
CUBA
Puerto Rico (United States)
British Honduras (Britain)
JAMAICA
DR.
GRENADA
PANAMA
BARBADOS
TRINIDAD & TOBAGO
GUATEMALA
EL SALVADOR
HONDURAS
NICARAGUA
COSTA RICA
Canal Zone (United States)
VENEZUELA
COLOMBIA
GUYANA
Dutch Guiana (Netherlands)
French Guiana (France)
ECUADOR
BRAZIL
PERU
French Polynesia (France)
BOLIVIA
PARAGUAY
CHILE
ARGENTINA
URUGUAY
Falkland Islands (Britain)

A.	Albania
AU.	Austria
B.	Belgium
CAR.	Central African Republic
C.	Czechoslovakia
D.	Denmark
DR.	Dominican Republic
DY.	People's Democratic Republic of Yemen
EG.	East Germany
H.	Hungary
LE.	Lebanon
L.	Luxembourg
N.	Netherlands
NV.	North Vietnam
S.	Switzerland
U.	United Arab Emirates
WG.	West Germany
YA.	Yemen Arab Republic
YU.	Yugoslavia

TIMELINE

The Americas / Europe / Middle East / Africa / Asia and Australasia

1955 · 1960 · 1965

1951 USA, Australia and New Zealand, sign a defense treaty

1954 Algerian uprising begins against French rule

1954 Laos, Cambodia, South and North Vietnam gain independence

1955 The Warsaw Pact is created as a Soviet-bloc opponent of NATO

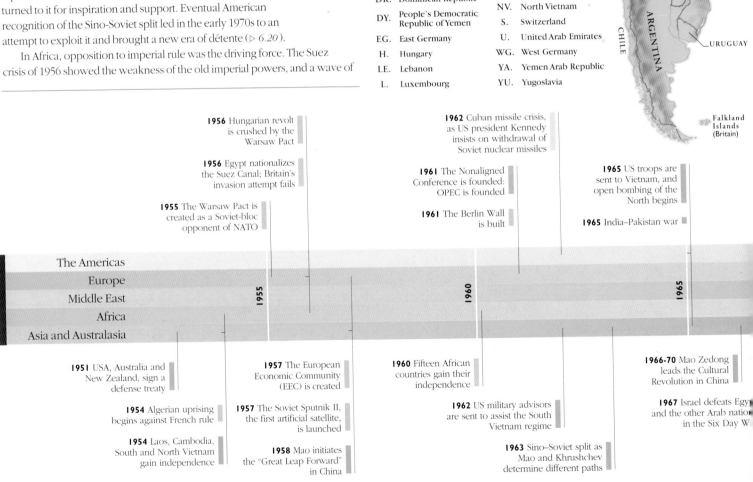

1956 Hungarian revolt is crushed by the Warsaw Pact

1956 Egypt nationalizes the Suez Canal; Britain's invasion attempt fails

1957 The European Economic Community (EEC) is created

1957 The Soviet Sputnik II, the first artificial satellite, is launched

1958 Mao initiates the "Great Leap Forward" in China

1960 Fifteen African countries gain their independence

1961 The Nonaligned Conference is founded: OPEC is founded

1961 The Berlin Wall is built

1962 Cuban missile crisis, as US president Kennedy insists on withdrawal of Soviet nuclear missiles

1962 US military advisors are sent to assist the South Vietnam regime

1963 Sino–Soviet split as Mao and Khrushchev determine different paths

1965 US troops are sent to Vietnam, and open bombing of the North begins

1965 India–Pakistan war

1966-70 Mao Zedong leads the Cultural Revolution in China

1967 Israel defeats Egy[pt] and the other Arab natio[ns] in the Six Day W[ar]

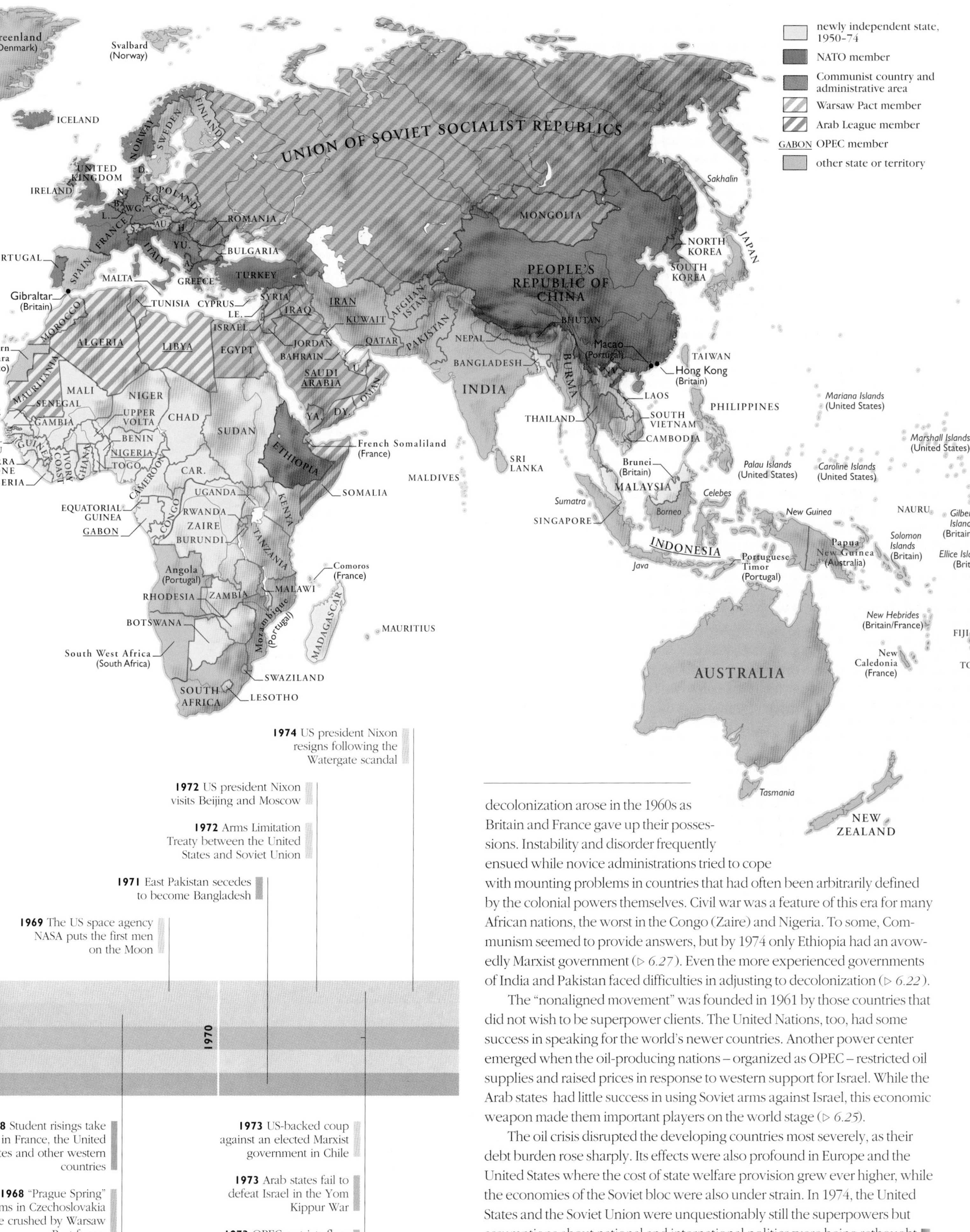
newly independent state, 1950–74
NATO member
Communist country and administrative area
Warsaw Pact member
Arab League member
GABON OPEC member
other state or territory
Svalbard (Norway)
ICELAND
UNITED KINGDOM
IRELAND
UNION OF SOVIET SOCIALIST REPUBLICS
FINLAND
SWEDEN
NORWAY
POLAND
ROMANIA
BULGARIA
FRANCE
ITALY
SPAIN
GREECE
TURKEY
MALTA
Gibraltar (Britain)
MOROCCO
ALGERIA
TUNISIA
LIBYA
EGYPT
CYPRUS
SYRIA
IRAQ
IRAN
ISRAEL
JORDAN
KUWAIT
BAHRAIN
QATAR
SAUDI ARABIA
OMAN
AFGHANISTAN
PAKISTAN
NEPAL
BHUTAN
BANGLADESH
INDIA
MONGOLIA
PEOPLE'S REPUBLIC OF CHINA
NORTH KOREA
SOUTH KOREA
JAPAN
Sakhalin
TAIWAN
Macao (Portugal)
Hong Kong (Britain)
BURMA
LAOS
THAILAND
SOUTH VIETNAM
CAMBODIA
PHILIPPINES
SRI LANKA
MALDIVES
Brunei (Britain)
MALAYSIA
Sumatra
SINGAPORE
Borneo
Celebes
INDONESIA
Java
Portuguese Timor (Portugal)
New Guinea
Papua New Guinea (Australia)
Mariana Islands (United States)
Marshall Islands (United States)
Palau Islands (United States)
Caroline Islands (United States)
NAURU
Gilbert Islands (Britain)
Solomon Islands (Britain)
Ellice Islands (Britain)
New Hebrides (Britain/France)
FIJI
New Caledonia (France)
TONGA
AUSTRALIA
Tasmania
NEW ZEALAND
MAURITANIA
MALI
NIGER
SENEGAL
GAMBIA
UPPER VOLTA
CHAD
SUDAN
BENIN
NIGERIA
TOGO
GHANA
IVORY COAST
GUINEA
CAR.
CAMEROON
ETHIOPIA
French Somaliland (France)
SOMALIA
EQUATORIAL GUINEA
GABON
CONGO
UGANDA
KENYA
RWANDA
ZAIRE
BURUNDI
TANZANIA
Angola (Portugal)
ZAMBIA
MALAWI
RHODESIA
Mozambique (Portugal)
Comoros (France)
MADAGASCAR
MAURITIUS
BOTSWANA
South West Africa (South Africa)
SWAZILAND
SOUTH AFRICA
LESOTHO
1970

1974 US president Nixon resigns following the Watergate scandal

1972 US president Nixon visits Beijing and Moscow

1972 Arms Limitation Treaty between the United States and Soviet Union

1971 East Pakistan secedes to become Bangladesh

1969 The US space agency NASA puts the first men on the Moon

[19]68 Student risings take in France, the United [Sta]tes and other western countries

1968 "Prague Spring" [refor]ms in Czechoslovakia [ar]e crushed by Warsaw Pact forces

1973 US-backed coup against an elected Marxist government in Chile

1973 Arab states fail to defeat Israel in the Yom Kippur War

1973 OPEC restricts flow of oil to world markets

decolonization arose in the 1960s as Britain and France gave up their possessions. Instability and disorder frequently ensued while novice administrations tried to cope with mounting problems in countries that had often been arbitrarily defined by the colonial powers themselves. Civil war was a feature of this era for many African nations, the worst in the Congo (Zaire) and Nigeria. To some, Communism seemed to provide answers, but by 1974 only Ethiopia had an avowedly Marxist government (▷ *6.27*). Even the more experienced governments of India and Pakistan faced difficulties in adjusting to decolonization (▷ *6.22*).

The "nonaligned movement" was founded in 1961 by those countries that did not wish to be superpower clients. The United Nations, too, had some success in speaking for the world's newer countries. Another power center emerged when the oil-producing nations – organized as OPEC – restricted oil supplies and raised prices in response to western support for Israel. While the Arab states had little success in using Soviet arms against Israel, this economic weapon made them important players on the world stage (▷ *6.25*).

The oil crisis disrupted the developing countries most severely, as their debt burden rose sharply. Its effects were also profound in Europe and the United States where the cost of state welfare provision grew ever higher, while the economies of the Soviet bloc were also under strain. In 1974, the United States and the Soviet Union were unquestionably still the superpowers but assumptions about national and international politics were being rethought ■

THE WORLD • AD 2008

The years from 1975 saw seismic shifts in world politics. With the end of the Cold War, fears of imminent disaster abated, though the shape of the world was still uncertain. Central to these changes was the collapse of the Soviet Union. Under Leonid Brezhnev, the country stagnated and the *détente* of the 1970s came to an end with the invasion of Afghanistan (1979–89). The United States emerged from its post-Vietnam crisis of confidence under President Ronald Reagan, who changed the nation's mood in the early 1980s. A new leader, Mikhail Gorbachev, tried to liberalize the Soviet system, but he unleashed forces that he could not control. Gorbachev did not resist demands for more independence from many of the USSR's eastern European satellites and, in 1989–90, the people took the chance to overthrow their Communist governments. In the Soviet Union itself the separate republics seceded to form the Commonwealth of Independent States. By the end of the century, several had joined their former enemy NATO. The old order was not so easily replaced in Yugoslavia, which was ripped apart by ethnic conflict. The UN was unable to resolve conflicts in Bosnia and elsewhere, though military action in Kosovo restored some credibility.

Meanwhile, greater centralization was occurring in western Europe, where the European Community (later the European Union) expanded (including the admission of several countries from the former Soviet bloc), abolished many border restrictions and initiated moves toward political and economic union.

The collapse of the Soviet Union led to change in Africa, where superpower conflict had exacerbated problems of decolonization and debt. South Africa's role in opposing the spread of Communism vanished and, in 1994, the country achieved majority rule under the charismatic Nelson Mandela. Civil wars and famine continued to dominate African countries such as Sudan, where unrest in the Darfur region in 2003 created a huge humanitarian crisis. An AIDS/HIV pandemic in sub-Saharan Africa added to the death toll in many of these impoverished countries (▷ *6.28*).

In the Middle East, the Islamist takeover of Iran in 1979 complicated the politics of the region: Iraq fought a long war with its neighbour through the 1980s, only to itself emerge soon after as a major threat to stability by invading Kuwait. In a remarkable example of cooperation, an international force led by the US and Saudi Arabia defeated Iraq (▷ *6.26*).

A.	Albania	RO.	Romania
AR.	Armenia	S.	Switzerland
AU.	Austria	SK.	Saint Kitts-Nevis
AZ.	Azerbaijan	SV.	Saint Vincent & the Grenadines
B.	Belgium	SL.	Slovakia
BO.	Bosnia-Herzegovina	SLV.	Slovenia
CAR.	Central African Republic	SM.	Serbia and Montenegro
CR.	Croatia	U.	United Arab Emirates
C.	Czech Republic		
D.	Denmark		
DR.	Dominican Republic		
GE.	Georgia		
GER.	Germany		
H.	Hungary		
LE.	Lebanon		
L.	Luxembourg		
M.	Macedonia (Former Yugoslav Republic of)		
N.	Netherlands		

TIMELINE: The Americas · Europe · Middle East · Africa · Asia and Australasia — 1975 · 1985 · 1995

1975 The Helsinki Agreement between the USA and USSR establishes an atmosphere of détente

1975 Angola and Mozambique gain independence

1975 The US-backed South Vietnam regime falls

1977 Egypt's president Sadat visits Israel, initiating the Middle Eastern peace process

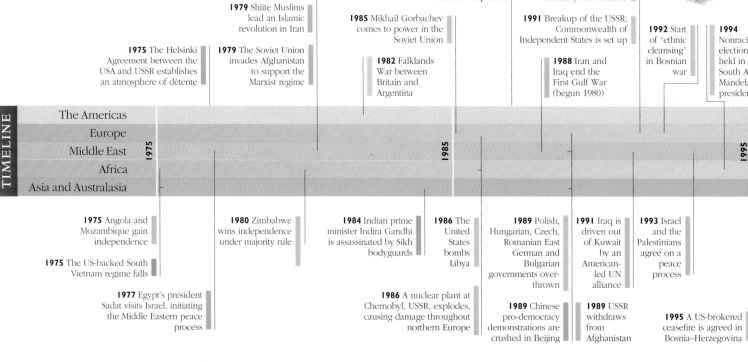

1979 China and the United States establish diplomatic relations

1979 Shiite Muslims lead an Islamic revolution in Iran

1979 The Soviet Union invades Afghanistan to support the Marxist regime

1980 Zimbabwe wins independence under majority rule

1982 Falklands War between Britain and Argentina

1984 Indian prime minister Indira Gandhi is assassinated by Sikh bodyguards

1985 Mikhail Gorbachev comes to power in the Soviet Union

1986 The United States bombs Libya

1986 A nuclear plant at Chernobyl, USSR, explodes, causing damage throughout northern Europe

1987 The USA and USSR agree to limit intermediate nuclear weapons

1988 Iran and Iraq end the First Gulf War (begun 1980)

1989 Polish, Hungarian, Czech, Romanian East German and Bulgarian governments overthrown

1989 Chinese pro-democracy demonstrations are crushed in Beijing

1989 USSR withdraws from Afghanistan

1991 East and West Germany are reunited

1991 Breakup of the USSR; Commonwealth of Independent States is set up

1991 Iraq is driven out of Kuwait by an American-led UN alliance

1992 Start of "ethnic cleansing" in Bosnian war

1993 Israel and the Palestinians agree on a peace process

1994 Nonracial elections held in South Afri[ca]; Mandela [wins] presidenc[y]

1995 A US-brokered ceasefire is agreed in Bosnia–Herzegovina

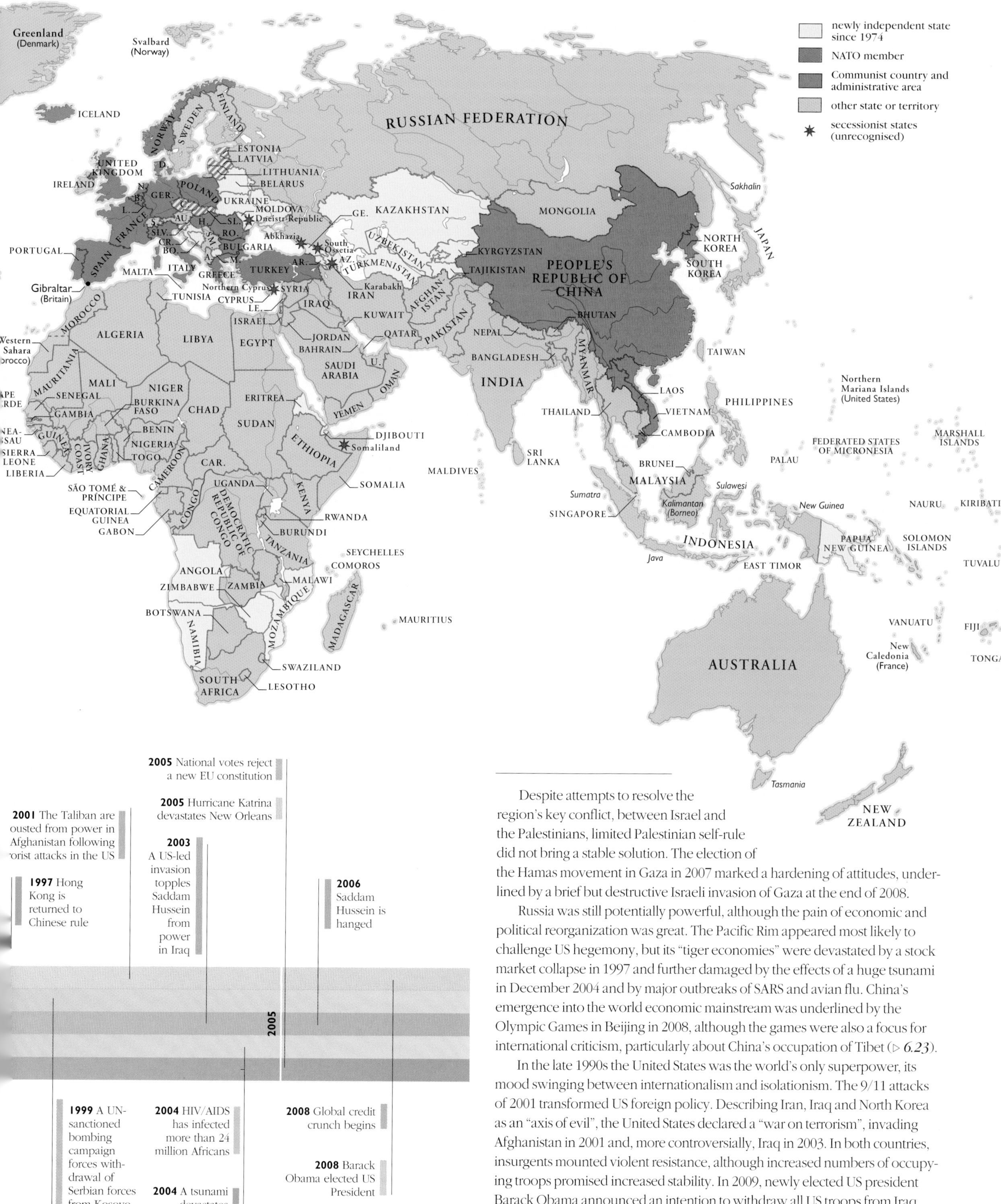
newly independent state since 1974
NATO member
Communist country and administrative area
other state or territory
secessionist states (unrecognised)
Greenland (Denmark)
Svalbard (Norway)
ICELAND
RUSSIAN FEDERATION
NORWAY
SWEDEN
FINLAND
ESTONIA
LATVIA
LITHUANIA
BELARUS
UNITED KINGDOM
IRELAND
POLAND
GER.
UKRAINE
MOLDOVA
Dneistr Republic
FRANCE
SPAIN
PORTUGAL
Gibraltar (Britain)
ITALY
MALTA
GREECE
BULGARIA
RO.
TURKEY
Abkhazia
South Ossetia
AZ.
AR.
Karabakh
Northern Cyprus
CYPRUS
SYRIA
LE.
ISRAEL
JORDAN
IRAQ
IRAN
KUWAIT
BAHRAIN
QATAR
U.
SAUDI ARABIA
OMAN
YEMEN
GE.
KAZAKHSTAN
UZBEKISTAN
TURKMENISTAN
AFGHANISTAN
PAKISTAN
KYRGYZSTAN
TAJIKISTAN
MONGOLIA
PEOPLE'S REPUBLIC OF CHINA
NORTH KOREA
SOUTH KOREA
JAPAN
Sakhalin
NEPAL
BHUTAN
BANGLADESH
INDIA
MYANMAR
TAIWAN
LAOS
VIETNAM
THAILAND
CAMBODIA
PHILIPPINES
SRI LANKA
MALDIVES
BRUNEI
MALAYSIA
Sumatra
SINGAPORE
Kalimantan (Borneo)
Sulawesi
INDONESIA
Java
EAST TIMOR
New Guinea
PAPUA NEW GUINEA
PALAU
FEDERATED STATES OF MICRONESIA
Northern Mariana Islands (United States)
MARSHALL ISLANDS
NAURU
KIRIBATI
SOLOMON ISLANDS
TUVALU
VANUATU
FIJI
New Caledonia (France)
TONGA
AUSTRALIA
Tasmania
NEW ZEALAND
MOROCCO
Western Sahara
ALGERIA
TUNISIA
LIBYA
EGYPT
MAURITANIA
MALI
NIGER
CHAD
SUDAN
ERITREA
DJIBOUTI
Somaliland
ETHIOPIA
SOMALIA
SENEGAL
GAMBIA
BURKINA FASO
BENIN
NIGERIA
TOGO
GHANA
IVORY COAST
GUINEA
SIERRA LEONE
LIBERIA
CAMEROON
CAR.
SÃO TOMÉ & PRÍNCIPE
EQUATORIAL GUINEA
GABON
CONGO
DEMOCRATIC REPUBLIC OF CONGO
UGANDA
KENYA
RWANDA
BURUNDI
TANZANIA
SEYCHELLES
COMOROS
ANGOLA
ZAMBIA
MALAWI
ZIMBABWE
MOZAMBIQUE
MADAGASCAR
MAURITIUS
BOTSWANA
NAMIBIA
SWAZILAND
SOUTH AFRICA
LESOTHO
2005 National votes reject a new EU constitution
2005 Hurricane Katrina devastates New Orleans
2001 The Taliban are ousted from power in Afghanistan following terrorist attacks in the US
2003 A US-led invasion topples Saddam Hussein from power in Iraq
1997 Hong Kong is returned to Chinese rule
2006 Saddam Hussein is hanged
2005
1999 A UN-sanctioned bombing campaign forces withdrawal of Serbian forces from Kosovo
2004 HIV/AIDS has infected more than 24 million Africans
2004 A tsunami devastates nations around the Indian Ocean
2008 Global credit crunch begins
2008 Barack Obama elected US President

Despite attempts to resolve the region's key conflict, between Israel and the Palestinians, limited Palestinian self-rule did not bring a stable solution. The election of the Hamas movement in Gaza in 2007 marked a hardening of attitudes, underlined by a brief but destructive Israeli invasion of Gaza at the end of 2008.

Russia was still potentially powerful, although the pain of economic and political reorganization was great. The Pacific Rim appeared most likely to challenge US hegemony, but its "tiger economies" were devastated by a stock market collapse in 1997 and further damaged by the effects of a huge tsunami in December 2004 and by major outbreaks of SARS and avian flu. China's emergence into the world economic mainstream was underlined by the Olympic Games in Beijing in 2008, although the games were also a focus for international criticism, particularly about China's occupation of Tibet (▷ *6.23*).

In the late 1990s the United States was the world's only superpower, its mood swinging between internationalism and isolationism. The 9/11 attacks of 2001 transformed US foreign policy. Describing Iran, Iraq and North Korea as an "axis of evil", the United States declared a "war on terrorism", invading Afghanistan in 2001 and, more controversially, Iraq in 2003. In both countries, insurgents mounted violent resistance, although increased numbers of occupying troops promised increased stability. In 2009, newly elected US president Barack Obama announced an intention to withdraw all US troops from Iraq within 16 months; he also sent more placatory signals to Iran.

World War I • 1914 – 1918 •

Before 1914, Europe had enjoyed unprecedented prosperity, the fruit of industrialization and a century without a general war. Yet two alliances, the Allied powers (the United Kingdom, France and Russia), and the Central powers (Germany, Austria–Hungary and, later, the Ottoman empire), were preparing for war. The main reason was the ambition and the instability of Germany, Europe's newest, and strongest, industrial and military power.

Germany had enjoyed a period of rapid industrialization, replacing Britain as the main motor of Europe's economy. Furthermore, its strength in iron, steel and coal production, and in the new electrical and chemical industries, was matched by a military machine second to none. In peace, Germany's geographical position enabled it to exploit Europe's extensive rail and sea networks. In wartime, however, it faced the prospect of fighting on two fronts.

Germany's rulers believed that its political standing did not match its commercial and imperial ambitions. One of its oldest ambitions (one which brought it into conflict with Russia) was to expand eastward. Germany believed it was encircled by hostile powers and was intent on protecting its interests, and those of Austria–Hungary, in southern Europe, the Ottoman empire and the Middle East.

In a long war, the strain of fighting on two fronts would inevitably tell. Military planners sought to combat this by launching a knockout blow against France and then transporting troops to the east to face the Russian army. But the plan failed when, in August 1914, war broke out following a crisis over Austrian and Russian influence in the Balkans. The exhausted German army was halted 80 kilometers (50 miles) short of Paris. The French army was swiftly mobilized and the transport network used shrewdly – even the Parisian taxi cabs were pressed into service to take soldiers to the front. Stalemate followed on the Western Front; the war was bogged down in trench warfare, as the defensive capabilities of the machine gun dominated the war until

1914–19
Orkney Islands
Scapa Flow
1918
Bergen
Christiania
SWEDEN
Stockholm
NORWAY
Baltic Sea
Cromarty
Göteborg
North Sea
Jutland May–June 1916
7
DENMARK
Copenhagen
Memel
Gumbinnen Aug 1914
Königsberg
Danzig
Glasgow
Rosyth
Edinburgh
Belfast
Newcastle
Dogger Bank Jan 1915
Heligoland
1914
Kiel
UNITED KINGDOM
9.5m
Hull
Bremerhaven
Wilhelmshaven
Hamburg
Bremen
Stettin
Tannenberg Aug 1914
Dublin
Liverpool
Elbe
Berlin
Warsaw Sep–Nov 1914
5
Birmingham
Amsterdam
NETHERLANDS
Hanover
Oder
Lusitania sunk by U-boat, May 1915
Cardiff
Harwich
Hook of Holland
Essen
GERMAN EMPIRE
13.25m
Gorlice-Tarnow May 1915
Lodz Nov 1914
London
Cologne
Dresden
Plymouth
Portsmouth
Portland
Dover
Dunkirk
Calais
Brussels
BELGIUM
0.38m
Frankfurt
Prague
Limanowa Dec 1914
LUXEMBOURG
Cherbourg
La Havre
Amiens
Reims
AUSTRO–HUNGARIAN EMPIRE
9.0m
1914
Brest
Paris
Rhine
Munich
Vienna
Salzburg
Budapest
Loire
Basel
LIECHTENSTEIN
Nantes
Caporetto Oct–Nov 1917
Danube
SWITZERLAND
Trento 1918
Battles of the Isonzo June 1915–Sep 1917
Geneva
FRANCE
8.2m
Lyon
Milan
Vittorio Veneto Oct–Nov 1918
Venice
Trieste
Bosnia–Herzegovina
Turin
Pola
Bordeaux
Genoa
Bologna
SAN MARINO
Sarajevo
MONTENEGRO capitulated to Central powers Jan 1916
0.05m
Santander
Toulouse
Florence
Bilbao
Ebro
ANDORRA
Marseille
Toulon
ITALY
Allied power Apr 1915
5.6m
Cattaro
Douro
Zaragoza
Corsica to France
Rome
Durazzo
Brindisi
SPAIN
Barcelona
Naples
Taranto
Madrid
PORTUGAL Allied power Mar 1916
Tagus
Guadiana
Valencia
Sardinia to Italy
Lisbon
Balearic Islands to Spain
Palermo
Messina
Sicily
Córdoba
Seville
Algiers
Tunis
Cádiz
1914
Gibraltar to Britain
Malta to Britain
Tangier
Algeria to France
Tunisia French protectorate
Spanish Morocco to Spain

TIMELINE

	1914	1915	1916	1917	1918
General	**1914 (28 June)** Assassination of the Austrian Archduke Franz Ferdinand by a Serb nationalist at Sarajevo **1914 (Aug)** Germany declares war on Russia and France; Britain, France and Russia on Germany and Austria–Hungary	**1915 (Apr)** Allied landings at Gallipoli **1915 (Apr)** Italy joins the Allied war effort **1915 (May)** US liner *Lusitania* is sunk by a German U-boat	**1916 (Apr)** Easter Rising in Dublin against British rule in Ireland **1916 (May)** The British and German fleets meet at Jutland	**1917 (Mar)** Czar Nicholas II abdicates in Russia **1917 (Apr)** The USA declares war on the Central powers **1917 (Nov)** Bolshevik revolution in Russia	**1918 (Jan)** US president Wilson publishes a 14-point peace plan **1918 (Nov)** The Kaiser abdicates and an armistice is signed between Germany and the Allies
Western Front	**1914 (Aug)** Germans launch Schlieffen plan **1914 (Sep)** Germans halted at the Battle of the Marne		**1916 (Feb–Dec)** German offensive at Verdun **1916 (July–Nov)** Expensive British offensive on Somme	**1917 (July)** Third Battle of Ypres (Passchendaele) **1917 (Nov–Dec)** Tanks used by British at battle of Cambrai	**1918 (Mar)** Germans threaten Paris in Ludendorff offensive **1918 (Aug)** Allies break through German lines
Eastern Front	**1914 (Aug)** The Russian advance into Germany is halted at Tannenberg	**1915 (Oct)** Austria-Hungary invades Serbia	**1916 (Sep)** Central powers defeat Romania **1916 (Oct)** The Russian Brusilov offensive ends	**1917 (July)** Last Russian offensive of the war **1917 (Dec)** Bolsheviks sign an armistice with Germany	**1918 (Mar)** Treaty of Brest-Litovsk ends war in Russia

1 The assassination of the Austrian Archduke Franz Ferdinand on 28 June 1914 by a Serbian began the descent into war. Austria declared war on Serbia; Russia mobilized; Germany declared war on Russia and France, and Britain on Germany, by 4 August.

2 The German offensive in the west began with the reduction of the Belgian fortresses around Liège.

3 The French stopped the German advance on Paris on the Marne in September 1914.

4 The unsuccessful Allied landings at Gallipoli were intended to win control of the Dardanelles and secure a sea route to Russia.

5 The sinking of the passenger liner *Lusitania* by a German U-boat in 1915 did much to turn American sentiment in favor of the Allies.

6 The war on the Eastern Front never declined into trench warfare and strategic mobility was preserved; casualties, though, were as heavy as in the west.

7 Although Britain's fleet suffered heavier losses than Germany's, the Battle of Jutland confirmed Britain's control of the seas.

new offensive tactics, using tanks and artillery more intelligently, were developed in 1917. Despite early victories against the Russians, the Germans now had to cope with war on two fronts.

In the Balkans, victories by the Central powers over Serbia and Romania (and the entry of the Ottomans into the war in 1915) seemed to create the kind of central European political and trading empire that Germany wanted. In 1917 czarist Russia collapsed, its economy and political system exhausted by the demands of the war. Early in 1918, its revolutionary Bolshevik government withdrew entirely from the war, leaving Germany in control of much of the Ukraine and southern Russia. German colonial ambitions in Europe seemed satisfied at last.

Yet the Central Powers could not match the Allies for men, materiel, wealth or opportunities. During 1916 Allied economic power began to assert itself. Britain developed a war economy, supplying munitions and other war materiel manufactured at home or imported from the United States and the British empire. Britain's financial superiority allowed it to bankroll the Allied war effort. The German navy tried to break Allied lines of supply by torpedoing British shipping; but when unrestricted submarine warfare began in 1917, the United States was prompted to join the war on the Allied side – though more significantly as a supplier of munitions rather than as a belligerent. The Allies blockaded German ports, intensifying German economic difficulties.

The years 1916–17 saw several desperately costly battles on the Western Front – notably Verdun, the Somme, Ypres – made possible by the huge buildup of arms on the Allied side. The Central powers decided to make a tactical withdrawal on the Western Front and to militarize the economy at home. The result was disastrous. By November 1918, the German army had not retreated to within its own borders (it had in fact made large advances the previous spring), but it was in clear disarray, while food and fuel shortages led to the country collapsing from within. Kaiser Wilhelm II abdicated, as did the emperor of Austria–Hungary. The Allies were clearly in a position to dictate the terms of the peace.

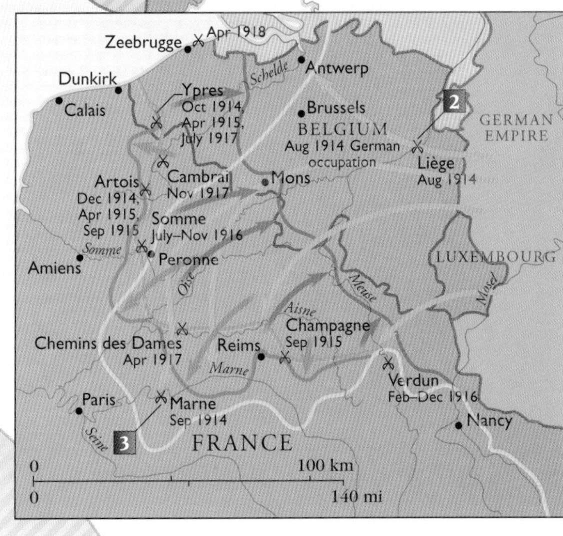
Zeebrugge Apr 1918
Antwerp
Dunkirk
Calais
Ypres Oct 1914, Apr 1915, July 1917
Brussels
BELGIUM
Aug 1914 German occupation
2
GERMAN EMPIRE
Liège Aug 1914
Artois Dec 1914, Apr 1915, Sep 1915
Cambrai Nov 1917
Mons
Somme July–Nov 1916
Peronne
Amiens
LUXEMBOURG
Chemins des Dames Apr 1917
Reims
Champagne Sep 1915
Aisne
Marne
Meuse
Verdun Feb–Dec 1916
Paris
Marne Sep 1914
Nancy
Seine
3
FRANCE
100 km
140 mi

borders, 1914
Allied powers and associates, June 1917
Central powers, June 1917
Central power capitulating before Nov 1918
neutral state
furthest advance of Central powers
furthest advance of Russian forces
Armistice line, 11 Nov 1918

Western Front
front line, 5 Sep 1914
front line, 29 Dec 1914
front line, 11 Nov 1918
German offensive, 16 Aug–5 Sep 1914
German offensive, 5 Apr–17 July 1918
furthest extent of German advance, 17 July 1918
Allied counteroffensive, 26 Sep–10 Nov 1918

Russian territory lost at the Treaty of Brest-Litovsk
main area of U-boat activity, 1915–18
naval base
Allied naval blockade
armaments, engineering and metal industry
chemical industry
shipbuilding industry
9.5m maximum mobilized forces (millions)
railroad
shipping route to United States and Canada

0 600 km
0 400 mi

See also 5.13 (Europe before 1914); 6.01 (the war outside Europe); 6.07 (Europe between the wars)

6.07 Europe between the wars • 1918 – 1939 •

World War I destroyed the old order in central and eastern Europe: the fall of the Romanovs (Russia), Habsburgs (Austria–Hungary) and Hohenzollerns (Germany) brought political instability that compounded the economic and social dislocation of the war. Extremism flourished across central Europe, with Marxist revolutions in several major cities being countered by a rightwing backlash.

The peace treaties failed to create a lasting settlement, and provided instead the grounds for future discontent. United States president Wilson hoped that ethnically homogeneous nation-states could eradicate the nationalist rivalries and squabbling over territory that appeared to have caused the war; but this proved impossible. Two new states (Czechoslovakia and the Kingdom of the Serbs, Croats and Slovenes – later Yugoslavia) and one reconstituted one (Poland) assembled many ethnic groups within arbitrary borders, and nationalist groups were often disappointed in disputed areas. Everywhere populations were on the move. Italy, its promises from the Allies for territory unfulfilled, set out to take the territory it claimed by force, as did Poland.

The Treaty of Versailles forced Germany to admit guilt for starting the war and to pay huge reparations to the Allies. It was forbidden to ally with Austria and was divided by the Polish Corridor, while three million ethnic Germans remained outside the state.

The League of Nations, set up to resolve the disputes that were bound to arise from the settlement, was hamstrung as the United States, the only power capable of giving weight to its decisions, declined to join. With Russia preoccupied with domestic affairs, Britain and France were left to deal with European issues alone. They were faced with the prospect of a renascent Germany avenging its grievances and filling the power vacuum created by the fall of the imperial monarchies. Both Britain and France were economically weak following the war and they sought to keep Germany weak as well. France occupied the Ruhr in 1923 to enforce payment of reparations, but the hyperinflation that ensued provided fertile ground for extremist groups in Germany. With

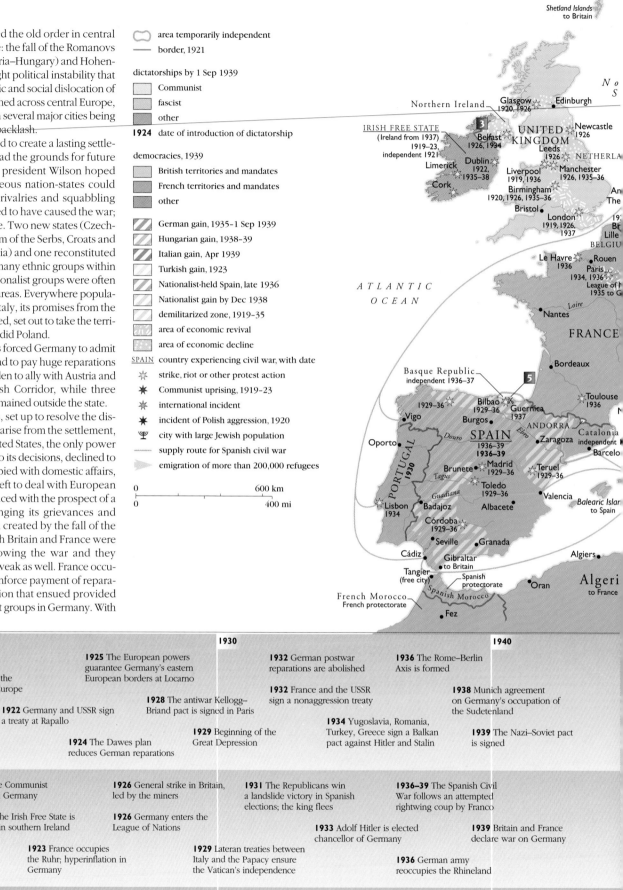

area temporarily independent
border, 1921
dictatorships by 1 Sep 1939
Communist
fascist
other
1924 date of introduction of dictatorship
democracies, 1939
British territories and mandates
French territories and mandates
other
German gain, 1935–1 Sep 1939
Hungarian gain, 1938–39
Italian gain, Apr 1939
Turkish gain, 1923
Nationalist-held Spain, late 1936
Nationalist gain by Dec 1938
demilitarized zone, 1919–35
area of economic revival
area of economic decline
SPAIN country experiencing civil war, with date
strike, riot or other protest action
Communist uprising, 1919–23
international incident
incident of Polish aggression, 1920
city with large Jewish population
supply route for Spanish civil war
emigration of more than 200,000 refugees
0 600 km
0 400 mi
Faroe Islands to Denmark
Shetland Islands to Britain
Northern Ireland
Glasgow 1920, 1926
Edinburgh
IRISH FREE STATE (Ireland from 1937) 1919–23, independent 1921
Belfast 1926, 1934
UNITED KINGDOM
Newcastle 1926
Leeds 1926
Dublin 1922, 1935–38
Limerick
Cork
Liverpool 1919, 1936
Manchester 1926, 1935–36
Birmingham 1920, 1926, 1935–36
Bristol
London 1919, 1926, 1937
Lille
Le Havre 1936
Rouen
Paris 1934, 1936
ATLANTIC OCEAN
Loire
Nantes
FRANCE
Bordeaux
Basque Republic independent 1936–37
Bilbao 1929–36
Guernica 1937
Toulouse 1936
1929–36
Vigo
Burgos
ANDORRA
Catalonia independent
SPAIN 1936–39 1936–39
Douro
Ebro
Zaragoza
Oporto
PORTUGAL 1930
Madrid 1929–36
Brunete
Tagus
Teruel 1929–36
Toledo 1929–36
Guadiana
Valencia
Lisbon 1934
Badajoz
Albacete
Balearic Islands to Spain
Córdoba 1929–36
Seville
Granada
Cádiz
Gibraltar to Britain
Algiers
Tangier (free city)
Spanish protectorate
Oran
Algeria to France
French Morocco French protectorate
Spanish Morocco
Fez

TIMELINE

1920 | 1930 | 1940

International affairs

1919–20 Treaties of Versailles, St Germain, Neuilly, Trianon create the postwar settlement in Europe

1922 Germany and USSR sign a treaty at Rapallo

1924 The Dawes plan reduces German reparations

1925 The European powers guarantee Germany's eastern European borders at Locarno

1928 The antiwar Kellogg–Briand pact is signed in Paris

1929 Beginning of the Great Depression

1932 German postwar reparations are abolished

1932 France and the USSR sign a nonaggression treaty

1934 Yugoslavia, Romania, Turkey, Greece sign a Balkan pact against Hitler and Stalin

1936 The Rome–Berlin Axis is formed

1938 Munich agreement on Germany's occupation of the Sudetenland

1939 The Nazi–Soviet pact is signed

Western Europe

1920 Abortive Communist revolutions in Germany

1921 The Irish Free State is set up in southern Ireland

1923 France occupies the Ruhr; hyperinflation in Germany

1926 General strike in Britain, led by the miners

1926 Germany enters the League of Nations

1929 Lateran treaties between Italy and the Papacy ensure the Vatican's independence

1931 The Republicans win a landslide victory in Spanish elections; the king flees

1933 Adolf Hitler is elected chancellor of Germany

1936–39 The Spanish Civil War follows an attempted rightwing coup by Franco

1936 German army reoccupies the Rhineland

1939 Britain and France declare war on Germany

Eastern Europe

1920–22 War between Greece and Turkey

1920–21 Poland and the Soviet Union are at war

1924–29 Joseph Stalin consolidates his power in USSR

1926 Josef Pilsudski comes to power in Poland

1934 Austrian chancellor Dollfuss is murdered by Nazis

1934 King Alexander of Macedonia is assassinated

1938 German invasion of Austria (*Anschluss*)

1939 Germany and Soviet Union invade Poland

1920 | 1930 | 1940

ESTONIA
FINLAND
LATVIA
UNITED KINGDOM
UNION OF SOVIET SOCIALIST REPUBLICS
BELGIUM
GERMANY
POLAND
FRANCE
AUSTRIA
CZECHOSLOVAKIA
ROMANIA
HUNGARY
ITALY
YUGOSLAVIA
ALBANIA
GREECE
TURKEY
alliance system
French
German
Italian
Locarno treaty, 1925
Balkan Entente, 1934
Baltic Entente, 1922

Germany's prosperity essential for European well-being, reparations were reduced and a limited recovery followed, funded by American loans.

Germany's grievances might have been resolved peacefully. The Locarno pact (1925) guaranteed its western borders and showed that foreign minister Stresemann would work peacefully to revise the Treaty of Versailles while the Kellogg–Briand pact of 1928 officially, if implausibly, renounced war.

The depression of the early 1930s, caused in part by the withdrawal of American loans, shattered the illusion of stability. Democracy was weakly established in many countries: massive unemployment and protest were now seen, followed by a return to authoritarian government. The dictator Pilsudski had upheld Catholicism in Poland since 1926; now Franco did the same in Spain after a three-year civil war. This bloody conflict showed how polarized politics in Europe was, and became a war by proxy between the Soviet-supplied republic and German- and Italian-supported right. Royal dictatorships also flourished in Bulgaria, Romania and Yugoslavia.

The radical new phenomenon of fascism now threatened the peace. Promising national renewal and fueled by grievances over the peace settlement, Mussolini's movement in Italy had established itself as a totalitarian regime in 1925. Fascist parties formed across Europe and in 1933 Hitler's Nazi party won power in Germany, its appeal magnified by mass unemployment and fear of Communism.

The British and French governments continued to be cautious. In Germany the Nazis eliminated unemployment by means of public work schemes, but in Britain the principles of classical economics still applied. Some economists, led by J.M. Keynes, advocated kick-starting the economy through government spending, but heavy industry did not recover until the armaments boom at the end of the 1930s (newer industries, such as electronics, motor and aircraft production did, however, show rapid growth).

The same caution applied to foreign policy. Unwilling to destabilize the international economy with wars or sanctions, the League proved unable to take a firm line with Germany and Italy in the 1930s. Britain and France tried to buy them off by conceding small territorial claims (the policy of "appeasement"), but the dictators demanded more. Italy escaped virtually unpunished for invading Ethiopia in 1935 as Britain and France tried (unsuccessfully) to preserve Mussolini as an ally against Germany. Hitler, as well as initiating his anti-Jewish policies, began to challenge the Treaty of Versailles: in 1935 Germany began to rearm and then reoccupied the Rhineland. Further steps to extend German power and territory followed, with the *Anschluss* with Austria (1938) and the partition of Czechoslovakia (agreed with Britain and France at Munich in 1938).

By now Britain and France had lost all credibility. Germany invaded Czechoslovakia in 1939 and the French and British guaranteed the security of several other European states, but to little avail. A French strategy of fencing the Germans in with the "Little Entente" in eastern Europe had already been weakened by a German–Polish non-aggression treaty in 1934. The democracies failed to secure an alliance with the Soviet Union and Stalin, believing Britain and France to be encouraging Hitler to expand to the east, signed a Nazi–Soviet pact in August 1939. Hitler and Stalin partitioned Poland between them, but Hitler failed to anticipate a sea-change in British and French opinion after his annexation of Czechoslovakia. Unexpectedly he had to fight in the west before pursuing his primary objectives in the east.

1 Budapest saw a Communist takeover in March 1919 under Bela Kun. Hungary then invaded Slovakia and Transylvania; Kun fled abroad in August 1919.

2 Following a plebiscite in 1920, Schleswig was divided between Germany and Denmark.

3 Ireland was divided in 1921: the mainly Protestant north elected to stay in the United Kingdom, the south became the Irish Free State. Civil war ensued in the south (1922–23), where many rejected partition.

4 The Saar became a League of Nations mandate under French rule in 1919, but returned to Germany by plebiscite in 1935.

5 The town of Guernica was destroyed by German bombers in the first massive aerial attack on civilians.

6 The Sudetenland of northwest Czechoslovakia, which had a large German minority, was annexed by Hitler following the Munich agreement in 1938.

See also 6.06 (World War I); 6.08 (World War II); 6.15 (the Soviet Union to 1941)

The declaration of war on Germany by Britain and France in 1939 took Hitler by surprise; he was now forced to deal with the threat to Germany's western flank in order to avoid fighting the war on two fronts. His primary objective, though, remained the conquest of the Soviet Union.

Germany and the Soviet Union divided Poland between them as they had agreed in the Nazi–Soviet pact of 1939, both sides deporting large numbers of people. The USSR later absorbed the Baltic states with the exception of Finland, which preserved its independence in the "Winter War" of 1939–40. A "phoney war" ensued, the first break in the inactivity being the German invasion of Denmark and Norway in April 1940. The Allies had planned to seize Narvik to deny Germany access to the only port capable of handling the exports of vital Swedish iron ore; however, the rapid and well-planned German advance resulted in a hurried Allied withdrawal.

Soon after, Winston Churchill took over as British prime minister, but Allied resistance was ineffectual during the German attack on the Low Countries and France in May. France surrendered within six weeks. Germany occupied the north, while a collaborationist regime at Vichy controlled the south; Belgium and the Netherlands became satellites in the German industrial complex. Britain evacuated most of its forces from northern France, but in the Battle of Britain of 1940 (the first decisive battle to be fought in the air) stifled plans for a seaborne invasion by denying air superiority to the Luftwaffe (German air force). Italy chose this point to enter the war. The Mediterranean was closed to British shipping and fighting began in north and east Africa.

While the air offensive continued against Britain and escalated into the Blitz, Hitler turned his attention to the east. By the summer of 1940 he was planning the Barbarossa campaign – an invasion of the Soviet Union which he had planned for the mid-1940s, but which was now brought forward by the success of the German war effort and the rapid rearmament of the other powers.

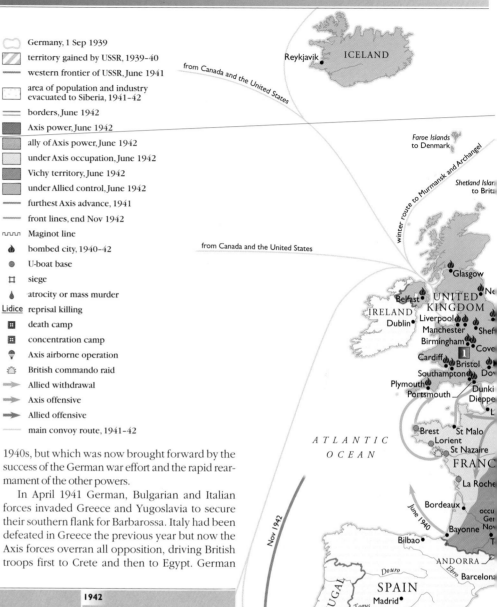

In April 1941 German, Bulgarian and Italian forces invaded Greece and Yugoslavia to secure their southern flank for Barbarossa. Italy had been defeated in Greece the previous year but now the Axis forces overran all opposition, driving British troops first to Crete and then to Egypt. German success had been based on *blitzkrieg* or lightning war. With limited access to raw materials, Germany could not afford a long war. Tanks, dive-bombers and motorized infantry destroyed defenses before reserves could be mobilized or a war of attrition develop. Barbarossa was expected to last six weeks, but by November 1941 the campaign was bogged down by the weather. Hitler had ignored advice to seize Moscow, preferring to advance on all fronts. His forces were now dangerously stretched.

Stalin launched an offensive in the spring of 1942, but the Germans occupied more territory in the summer. It became clear, however, that they could not launch a knockout blow: the vast size of the

- Germany, 1 Sep 1939
- territory gained by USSR, 1939–40
- western frontier of USSR, June 1941
- area of population and industry evacuated to Siberia, 1941–42
- borders, June 1942
- Axis power, June 1942
- ally of Axis power, June 1942
- under Axis occupation, June 1942
- Vichy territory, June 1942
- under Allied control, June 1942
- furthest Axis advance, 1941
- front lines, end Nov 1942
- Maginot line
- bombed city, 1940–42
- U-boat base
- siege
- atrocity or mass murder
- Lidice reprisal killing
- death camp
- concentration camp
- Axis airborne operation
- British commando raid
- Allied withdrawal
- Axis offensive
- Allied offensive
- main convoy route, 1941–42

TIMELINE

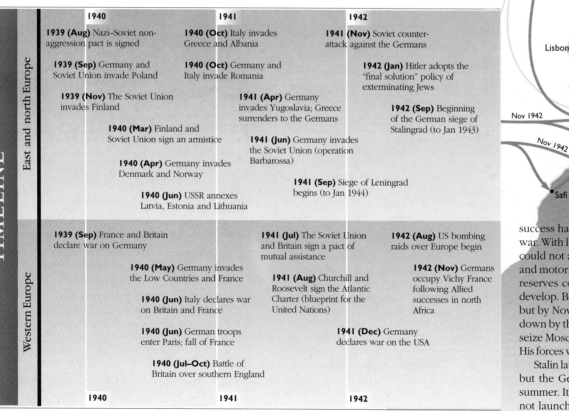

East and north Europe

1939 (Aug) Nazi–Soviet non-aggression pact is signed

1939 (Sep) Germany and Soviet Union invade Poland

1939 (Nov) The Soviet Union invades Finland

1940 (Mar) Finland and Soviet Union sign an armistice

1940 (Apr) Germany invades Denmark and Norway

1940 (Jun) USSR annexes Latvia, Estonia and Lithuania

1940 (Oct) Italy invades Greece and Albania

1940 (Oct) Germany and Italy invade Romania

1941 (Apr) Germany invades Yugoslavia; Greece surrenders to the Germans

1941 (Jun) Germany invades the Soviet Union (operation Barbarossa)

1941 (Sep) Siege of Leningrad begins (to Jan 1944)

1941 (Nov) Soviet counter-attack against the Germans

1942 (Jan) Hitler adopts the "final solution" policy of exterminating Jews

1942 (Sep) Beginning of the German siege of Stalingrad (to Jan 1943)

Western Europe

1939 (Sep) France and Britain declare war on Germany

1940 (May) Germany invades the Low Countries and France

1940 (Jun) Italy declares war on Britain and France

1940 (Jun) German troops enter Paris; fall of France

1940 (Jul–Oct) Battle of Britain over southern England

1941 (Jul) The Soviet Union and Britain sign a pact of mutual assistance

1941 (Aug) Churchill and Roosevelt sign the Atlantic Charter (blueprint for the United Nations)

1941 (Dec) Germany declares war on the USA

1942 (Aug) US bombing raids over Europe begin

1942 (Nov) Germans occupy Vichy France following Allied successes in north Africa

1 London and other cities suffered aerial bombardment from September 1940 to May 1941. The "Blitz" failed to break British industry or civilian morale.

2 A surprise amphibious attack in April 1940 allowed Germany to take Norway before British support could arrive. Only in Narvik did the plan falter temporarily.

3 The defense of Greece in April 1941 was poorly coordinated and quickly overrun; the British forces were evacuated to Crete, and soon after to Alexandria.

4 After the Soviet invasion of November 1939, the Finns caused heavy losses but sued for peace in March 1940. Though nominally neutral, Finland favored Germany against the USSR.

5 Vichy, a spa town, was seat of the collaborationist French government from 1940 to November 1942.

6 Britain's strategic naval base at Malta endured more than 1,200 air raids during World War II.

country and its population, and the safety of the industrial areas evacuated east of the Urals meant that the USSR had huge capacity. By the end of 1942, a turning point was approaching.

The United States had already been supplying Britain and the Soviet Union with materiel through the "lend–lease" scheme, and its entry into the war as a full belligerent in December 1941 gave the Allies a major boost. From then on Allied superiority in men and arms, and Hitler's lack of strategic vision were to lead to German defeat.

Disruption of the supply routes from America had become of central concern to the western Allies. The United States was keen to invade western Europe as quickly as possible, but U-boat attacks on convoys in the Atlantic hampered the transport of men and materiel. A minor invasion of north Africa, occupied by Italian and Vichy forces backed up by General Rommel's Afrika Korps, met with rapid success. If the Battle of the Atlantic could not be won, though, United States numerical and industrial power would count for little in the battle for Europe.

In eastern Europe the Germans undertook the enslavement and murder of the subject populations. Executions of civilians were commonplace in the invasion of Poland, and during Barbarossa mass murder was a tool of occupation policy. Hitler hoped to create a "new order" based on the Nazi idea of the "historic conflict" between the Aryans (Germans) and the other "inferior races". Millions of Slavs and Gypsies were shot, deported, starved or enslaved to create a "living space" for Germans. In what was called the "final solution", mass shootings and gassings were used to exterminate the Jews. Death camps were built and by the end of 1942 almost the entire Jewish population of Poland, the Baltic states, and the USSR as far east as the Caucasus – about three million people – had been killed.

See also 6.07 (Europe between the wars); 6.09 (World War II to 1945); 6.19 (World War II in Asia)

World War II in Europe • 1942 – 1945 •

The end of 1942 marked a turning point, but two more years of fighting were needed before the war in Europe ended. The German surrender at Stalingrad was a major blow to Hitler, who was committed to holding the city and supplying it by air. In July the Soviet army repulsed the Germans at Kursk in the war's biggest land battle; then drove westward, its next victory being at Kharkov.

In May 1943, the Germans capitulated in north Africa. By mid-1943 Germany had also lost the crucial Battle of the Atlantic, where the Allied use of long-range aircraft made Germany's submarine assault on transatlantic convoy routes less effective. The German war effort intensified with the announcement of total war (the complete mobilization of the economy). The Allies invaded Sicily, Mussolini was deposed and the Italians sued for peace; however Germany immediately occupied north and central Italy and made further Allied progress very difficult through the mountainous terrain.

The Allies' Italian campaign was a relatively minor response to success in north Africa, though it dragged on until the end of the war. The main action in the west – the "second front" that Stalin had long demanded – was to be the Allied landing in Normandy, as the Allied leaders had agreed at their meeting in Tehran in November 1943. Even before this was launched, however, Hitler had to withdraw troops from the east to strengthen the western defenses. Allied bombing increased in strength and effectiveness as the US joined the British in attacking German cities in force: the first 1,000-bomber raid took place against Cologne in 1943. The bombing campaign directed German resources from the other fronts and weakened the war economy.

When the Normandy landings finally came in June 1944, they met with stiff resistance. The Allies liberated France and Belgium before halting briefly. Meanwhile in east and southeast Europe the Red Army took advantage of the increased pressure on Germany in the west, and defeated both Romania and Bulgaria. Germany pulled out of Greece but Hungary was kept in the war by a Nazi coup after initially surrendering to the Soviet Union; fierce fighting broke out around Budapest.

Political as well as military considerations had held back United States president Roosevelt from supporting British prime minister Churchill's plan to invade southeast Europe. Unlike Roosevelt, Churchill had little faith in Stalin's postwar intentions, and made an agreement with Stalin which stipulated the influence that Britain and the Soviet Union would each have in the region. Soviet action in Poland and elsewhere did not engender confidence. As the Red Army advanced toward Warsaw, a fullscale rising against the German forces occurred in the city. Despite surrounding the city Stalin did not assist the rebels, and when the Germans eventually quashed the revolt as many as 250,000 people were killed.

Across Europe guerrilla partisan forces fought the Axis powers. Many were divided on ethnic or political lines, and their activities provoked bloody reprisals. A revolt in Slovakia at the same time as the Warsaw rising was brutally put down, but in Yugoslavia the Communist-dominated partisans enjoyed

borders, 1943
Axis power or ally
Axis occupied, Mar 1943
Allied control, Mar 1943
front line, Dec 1943
front line, Aug 1944
front line, Dec 1944
front line, Apr 1945
defensive line
heavily bombed city
siege
area of partisan activity
German reprisal killing
death camp
concentration camp
Allied airborne operation
conference of Allied leaders, with date
London V-weapon target zone
26 Aug 1944 date of capitulation
Axis withdrawal
Axis offensive
Allied offensive
Soviet deportation, 1944–45

CIVILIANS, including women, were universally important to the war effort by working in the factories. This poster was from Britain.

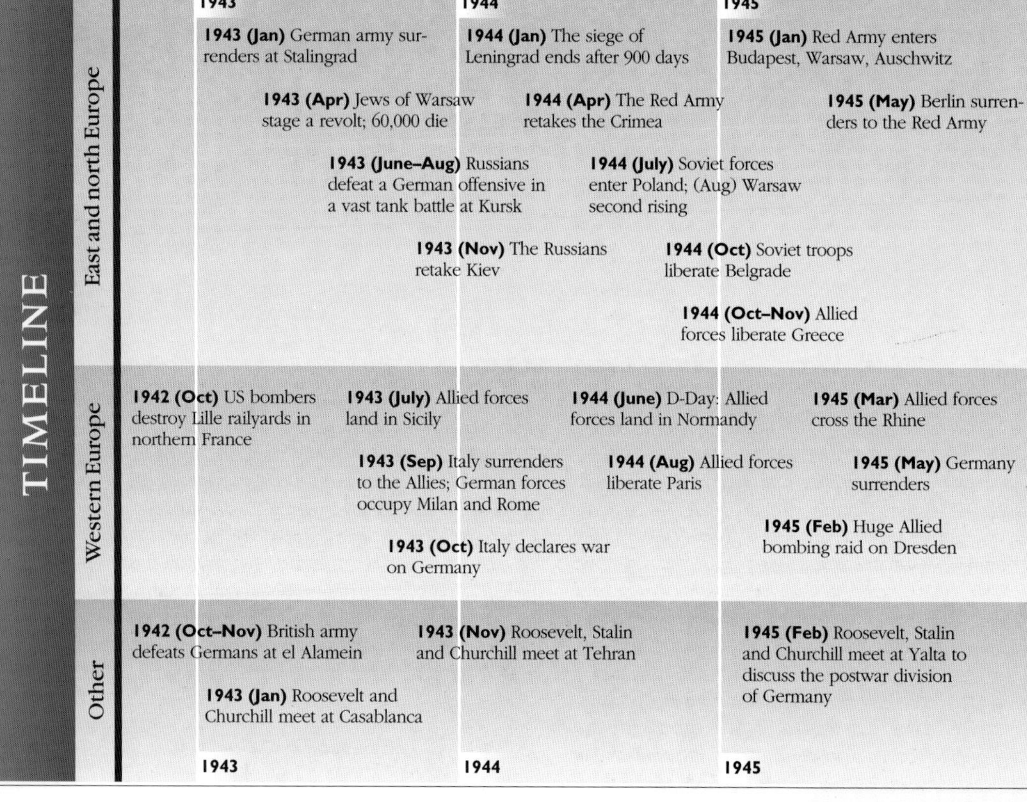
TIMELINE
East and north Europe
1943
1944
1945
1943 (Jan) German army surrenders at Stalingrad
1944 (Jan) The siege of Leningrad ends after 900 days
1945 (Jan) Red Army enters Budapest, Warsaw, Auschwitz
1943 (Apr) Jews of Warsaw stage a revolt; 60,000 die
1944 (Apr) The Red Army retakes the Crimea
1945 (May) Berlin surrenders to the Red Army
1943 (June–Aug) Russians defeat a German offensive in a vast tank battle at Kursk
1944 (July) Soviet forces enter Poland; (Aug) Warsaw second rising
1943 (Nov) The Russians retake Kiev
1944 (Oct) Soviet troops liberate Belgrade
1944 (Oct–Nov) Allied forces liberate Greece
Western Europe
1942 (Oct) US bombers destroy Lille railyards in northern France
1943 (July) Allied forces land in Sicily
1944 (June) D-Day: Allied forces land in Normandy
1945 (Mar) Allied forces cross the Rhine
1943 (Sep) Italy surrenders to the Allies; German forces occupy Milan and Rome
1944 (Aug) Allied forces liberate Paris
1945 (May) Germany surrenders
1945 (Feb) Huge Allied bombing raid on Dresden
1943 (Oct) Italy declares war on Germany
Other
1942 (Oct–Nov) British army defeats Germans at el Alamein
1943 (Nov) Roosevelt, Stalin and Churchill meet at Tehran
1945 (Feb) Roosevelt, Stalin and Churchill meet at Yalta to discuss the postwar division of Germany
1943 (Jan) Roosevelt and Churchill meet at Casablanca
1943
1944
1945

1 Hitler's attack on the Soviet defenses at Kursk (June 1943) led to a conflict between the Soviet light but nimble T-34 tanks, and the heavy German Tiger tanks. Despite huge losses, the Red Army broke through.
2 Some 640 villagers, including 200 women and children, were burned to death in a church at the village of Oradour-sur Glane in June 1944.
3 When the Germans retreated to their prewar defenses – the Siegfried Line – in September 1944, the Allies attacked via the Netherlands. The line was broken in February 1945.
4 Peenemünde was the site of research into rocketry by the Germans under Werner von Braun. Allied intelligence knew of it from 1939.
5 Auschwitz was the largest of the Nazi death camps, established in 1940. Well over a million Jews and Poles died there before liberation in January 1945.
6 Churchill, Stalin and Roosevelt met at Yalta in February 1945 to coordinate strategy and agree spheres of influence in postwar Europe.
Murmansk
Narvik
Archangel
Trondheim
Umeå
Sundsvall
FINLAND
4 Sep 1944
Lake Onega
Lake Ladoga
Kotlas
NORWAY
Gävle
Turku
Helsinki
Tallinn
Leningrad
1941–44
Oslo
SWEDEN
Stockholm
Vänern
Vättern
UNION OF SOVIET SOCIALIST REPUBLICS
Crimean Tatars
Lake Peipus
Pskov
Demyansk
Gorki
Göteborg
Baltic Sea
Riga
Moscow
Oct 1943
DENMARK
Copenhagen
Memel
Reichskommissariat Ostland
liberated by 1945
Vitebsk
Smolensk
Königsberg
Feb–May 1945
Germans and Poles
Minsk
June–July 1944
Orel
Kiel
Peenemünde
Danzig
Rostock
Hamburg
Bremen
Bialystok
June–Aug 1943
Kursk
Bulgarians & Romanians
Berlin
Apr–May 1945
Warsaw
Hanover
Arnhem
Sep 1944
Potsdam
July 1945
GERMANY
8 May 1945
General Government of Poland
Stalingrad
Sep 1942–Feb 1943
Bochum
Essen
Cologne
Leipzig
Dresden
Breslau
Reichskommissariat Ukraine
liberated by spring 1944
Kiev
Kharkov
Kalmyks
Prague
Auschwitz
Krakow
Lvov
Dnieper
Dnepropetrovsk
Frankfurt
Nuremberg
Pilsen
Protectorate of Bohemia–Moravia
SLOVAKIA
Transnistria
Rostov
Stuttgart
Regensburg
Munich
Vienna
Bratislava
HUNGARY
31 Dec 1944
Transylvania
Iasi
Kishinev
Odessa
Caspian Sea
Berne
SWITZERLAND
LIECHTENSTEIN
Innsbruck
Budapest
Dec 1944–Mar 1945
ROMANIA
26 Aug 1944
Sevastopol
Apr–May 1944
Yalta
Feb 1945
Karachais
Meskhetians
Chechens
Grozny
Milan
Trieste
Zagreb
Ploiesti
Bucharest
Black Sea
CAUCASUS MTS
Tbilisi
Baku
Turin
Venice
CROATIA
YUGOSLAVIA
Belgrade
Genoa
Bologna
Zara
Sarajevo
SERBIA
Varna
BULGARIA
28 Oct 1944
Burgas
Florence
Gothic Line
Split
Sofia
Plovdiv
Trabzon
Yerevan
ITALY
8 Sep 1943
MONTENEGRO
Gustav Line
Skopje
Edirne
Istanbul
Corsica
to France
Rome
Cassino
Jan–Mar 1944
Anzio
Tiranë
ALBANIA
liberated by Nov 1944
Ankara
TURKEY
Tehran
Nov 1943
Naples
Salerno
Sardinia
to Italy
GREECE
liberated by Oct 1944
Izmir
Mosul
IRAN
Adana
Patras
Athens
Palermo
Sicily
Syria
Free French
Rhodes
Dodecanese
to Italy
Cyprus
to Britain
Baghdad
IRAQ
Tunis
Sep 1943
Malta
to Britain
Mediterranean Sea
Crete
Heraklion
Beirut
Lebanon
Free French
Damascus
Transjordan
to Britain
Palestine
to Britain
Amman
Jerusalem
Tunisia
liberated by May 1943
Mareth Line
Tripoli
Benghazi
Libya
British protectorate
Alexandria
EGYPT
Cairo
Nov–Dec 1943
Kuwait
British protectorate
600 km
400 mi

considerable success and formed the basis of Tito's postwar government; in Prague, a popular rising helped the Soviet advance on the city. In Greece, the Communists, who dominated the rural resistance movement, defied the British who sought to reestablish the monarchy after the Germans had withdrawn in October 1944; the result was a civil war which ended only with the collapse of the Communists in 1949. Resistance in Poland and countries incorporated into the Soviet Union also continued after the war, but it was now directed against the USSR.

Hitler always believed that providence would save him. He tried to stop the Allied bomber assault on Germany by firing rocket-powered V-bombs at Britain, but the forces ranged against him were too great. The last German offensive, through the Ardennes at the end of 1944, was a failure and after Hitler's suicide, Germany surrendered (8 May 1945).

The implementation of Nazi policies of genocide continued right up until the liberation of the death camps by Allied troops. As the Soviets marched westward, many inmates of camps in Poland were moved to Germany to join prisoners-of-war and other forced foreign labor; by 1944 there were almost eight million foreigners at work in Germany. Some Axis countries – Hungary, Bulgaria and Italy – refused to release many or all of their Jewish population to the Nazis, but the attempt to exterminate the Jews of Europe still proceeded. By the end of the war some six million had been killed, along with millions of other nationalities including Ukrainians, Poles, Balts, Belorussians, Russians and Gypsies.

Of the 5.5 million Soviet soldiers captured by the Germans, 3.3 million had died; as the Red Army advanced it took its revenge. Ten million ethnic Germans were expelled from their homes in central and eastern Europe; perhaps two million died. The USSR deported five million of its subject nationalities for alleged collaboration; returning prisoners-of-war often faced exile or death. By 1945 much of Europe was destroyed, its peoples dead or homeless.

See also 6.08 (World War II to 1942); 6.10 (postwar Europe); 6.19 (World War II in Asia)

The wartime cooperation of the Allies quickly broke down and two blocs emerged: the western democratic countries which were oriented toward the United States, and the eastern Communist countries dominated by the Soviet Union. Europe lived in the shadow of the superpowers.

Blame for the deterioration of international relations and the drawing of the "iron curtain" across Europe has been laid with both sides, and little is known of Soviet motives. It is clear, however, that US hopes of an "open" Europe were misplaced. Stalin never considered giving up the Soviet Union's new influence in eastern Europe and, though he probably did not envisage invading the west either, there was a real fear that the rest of the continent would succumb to Communism. As a result, with Europe devastated and trying to cope with millions of refugees, the United States produced a massive cash injection ("Marshall Aid") in 1947, becoming the counterweight to Soviet power in the east.

Crucial to the division of Europe was the partition of Germany. The economic and military powerbase of the continent was occupied jointly by the Allies, neither side being willing to risk losing overall control to the other. In 1948 the Soviets blockaded western-occupied West Berlin and in 1949 the republics of West and East Germany were formally constituted. The same year the North Atlantic Treaty was signed, binding the western states and America in an anti-Soviet alliance (NATO), and Comecon was formed to incorporate the east European countries in a system of Soviet-dominated interstate economic planning. In 1950 US troops returned to Europe as part of NATO after the outbreak of war in Korea; the Soviet-led Warsaw Pact was founded five years later.

Thereafter west and east Europe developed on different lines. The western countries soon recovered their prosperity, creating economic areas to increase trade. The Benelux Customs Union of 1948 was followed by the creation of the European Coal and Steel Community (ECSC), which laid the basis for the European Economic Community (EEC) in 1958. A looser affiliation, the European Free Trade Area (EFTA), also existed but the EEC was the more important, later becoming the European Community (EC), aspiring to a political as well as economic role.

The EEC was intended to transcend national boundaries, prevent the strife that had characterized Europe's history and assist Europe to become an independent player on the world stage. The French president Charles de Gaulle twice vetoed Britain's application to join, on the grounds of Britain's "special relationship" with the United States. De Gaulle deplored US involvement in Europe, and withdrew France from NATO, yet the idea of an independent European Defense Community proved unworkable. The United States encouraged western European integration but American troops remained essential. Britain and France established independent nuclear capability; West German chancellor Willy Brandt negotiated cooperation agreements between West and East Germany. But given the Soviet Union's military might, Europe could not be independent until the iron curtain was raised.

In eastern Europe the influence of the Soviet Union was deeply resented. Eastern European countries did not enjoy the "economic miracle" seen in West Germany, and felt their national identities to be compromised by Soviet interference. Yugoslavia and Albania preserved their traditions of independent Communism as, to a lesser extent, did Romania. Hungary (1956) and Czechoslovakia (1968) tried more radical escapes from the Soviet bloc but were brought back into line by force.

Following the Helsinki agreement of 1975 under which the borders of the German Democratic Republic (East Germany) were recognized and the governments of eastern Europe accepted the principle of observing human rights, dissident activity grew more intense. In 1980 the Polish trade union Solidarity was set up and long-standing popular resentment (kept alive by the Catholic church and the accession of John Paul II as the first Polish pope) was manifested in widespread industrial disputes.

Protest in western Europe was directed both against the United States (over the Vietnam war or the presence of US-controlled nuclear missiles) or against individual governments. The Paris riots of 1968 were part of a general revolt of youth

TIMELINE

Western Europe

1945 Potsdam conference of the great powers agrees the postwar position in Germany

1947 USA provides Marshall Aid to western Europe

1948–49 The Berlin airlift follows a Soviet blockade of the city's western zone

1949 North Atlantic Treaty is signed; NATO is set up

1955 Allies end occupation of West Germany and Austria; West Germany joins NATO

1957 The Treaty of Rome sets up the European Economic Community (EEC), from Jan 1958

1966 France withdraws from NATO

1967 French president de Gaulle vetoes UK entry to EEC for the second time

1968 Students riot in Paris and almost bring down the government; unrest is felt in West Germany and Britain

1974 Turkey invades northern Cyprus

1974 Portugal's rightwing government is overthrown

1977 Spain's first postwar elections take place following the death of Franco in 1975

1979 Conservative leader Margaret Thatcher is elected prime minister in Britain

1986 Portugal and Spain join the EC

Eastern Europe

1947–48 Sovietization of the governments of eastern Europe

1949 Comecon is set up to integrate eastern Europe's economies

1956 An anti-Soviet revolt takes place in Hungary

1961 The Berlin Wall is built to prevent emigration from East to West Germany

1968 Czechoslovak "Prague spring" ends with Warsaw Pact invasion

1970–72 *Ostpolitik* agreements for East and West German cooperation

1975 Helsinki agreement on Germany's borders and human rights in east Europe

1980 Solidarity, Polish trade union, is founded

1989 The Berlin Wall is taken down; regimes in Hungary, Poland, East Germany, Bulgaria, Czechoslovakia, Romania fall

1950 1970 1990

NORWAY
SWEDEN
FINLAND
Finns
Bergen
Oslo
Gävle
Pori
Tampere
Turku
Helsinki
Leningrad
Lake Ladoga
Dal
Vänern
Vättern
Vasteras
Uppsala
Stockholm
Estonians
Linkoping
Göteborg
Baltic Sea
Tapa
Tallinn
Kopu
Estonians
Estonia
Lake Peipus
Pskov
Yedrovo
Rybinsk Reservoir
Volga
Moscow
Riga
Latvia
Latvians
Liepaja
Lithuania
Lithuanians
Western Dvina
Vitebsk
Smolensk
Russia
DENMARK
1973 EEC member
Århus
Copenhagen
Malmo
Odense
Kaliningrad (Königsberg)
to Russia
Vilna
Minsk
Belorussia
Gdansk (Danzig)
Poles
UNION OF SOVIET SOCIALIST REPUBLICS
Hamburg
Bremen
GERMAN DEMOCRATIC REPUBLIC
1949
Szczecin
Berlin
FEDERAL REPUBLIC OF GERMANY
1945–61
June 1953
June 1956
Poznan
Warsaw
Oct 1956
Belorussians
Lodz
POLAND
1947
Lublin
Ukrainians
Derazhnaya
Kiev
Essen
Cologne
Bonn
Leipzig
Bernsdorf
Dresden
Oder
Vistula
1944–47
Milovice
Krakow
Lvov
Ukraine
Dnieper
Dnepropetrovsk
Frankfurt
Aug 1968
Prague
Temelin
Nuremberg
Brno
CZECHOSLOVAKIA
1948
Dniester
Pervomaysk
Moldavia
Danube
Schwäbisch Gmünd
Neu Ulm
Munich
Linz
Vienna
Bratislava
Nov 1956
Debrecen
Magyars
Iasi
Kishinev
Odessa
Salzburg
AUSTRIA
Oct–Nov 1956
Budapest
HUNGARY
1947
1955 temporarily leaves Warsaw Pact
ROMANIA
1945
Brasov
LIECHTENSTEIN
Graz
Germans
Timisoara
Ploiesti
Bucharest
Sevastopol
Trieste
Zagreb
Sava
Milan
Venice
Belgrade
Turin
Bologna
YUGOSLAVIA
1945
Sarajevo
Black Sea
SAN MARINO
Split
Florence
MONACO
ITALY
BULGARIA
1945
Turks
Varna
Burgas
Albanians, since 1968
Sofia
Plovdiv
Skopje
Dubrovnik
Edirne
Istanbul
Corsicans
Rome
Tiranë
ALBANIA
1945
1968 leaves Warsaw Pact
Thessalonica
Bursa
Gaeta
Bari
La Maddalena
Naples
GREECE
1952–74, 1982 NATO member, 1981 EEC member
1944–1949
TURKEY
1952 NATO member
Izmir
Konya
Gaziantep
Adana
Cagliari
Patras
Athens
since 1974
Aleppo
Euphrates
Palermo
Sicily
Catania
Comiso
Dodecanese 1947 to Greece
TURKISH REPUBLIC OF NORTHERN CYPRUS since 1983
Greeks & Turks
Nicosia
1974
1955–77
Homs
SYRIA
Tunis
TUNISIA
1956 independent
Valletta
MALTA
1964 independent
Mediterranean Sea
Heraklion
Crete
CYPRUS
1960 independent, Northern Cyprus occupied by Turks since 1974
Beirut
LEBANON
1958
Damascus
ISRAEL
1948 independent
pre-war border of Poland
North Atlantic Treaty Organization (NATO), established 1949
Warsaw Pact, established 1955
zones of occupation of Germany and Austria, 1945–55,
American
British
French
Soviet
borders, 1989
NATO nuclear-capable base, 1980s
Warsaw Pact nuclear-capable base, 1980s
nationalist tension or violence, 1945–89
civil war, 1945–89
international dispute, 1945–89
attempted revolution, 1945–89
Soviet military intervention
movement of Germans 1945–50
movement of Russians 1945–50
other movement of peoples 1945–50
mass exodus of refugees, with date
ITALY founding member of EEC, 1957
1945 date of Communist takeover
0 400 km
0 300 mi

against authority, as was the Baader–Meinhof terrorist group in West Germany.

In the 1970s, the economic downturn caused by inflation, high public spending and the rise in oil prices led to unemployment and industrial militancy. British prime minster Margaret Thatcher's response to these problems after 1979 marked a radical departure from the consensus politics of the postwar period, which had stressed cooperation between employers, workers and the state. The introduction of free-market economics and revision of labor legislation brought a year-long miners' strike (1984–85). Elsewhere, terrorism and violence fueled by economic dislocation flared in areas of nationalist tension. Basque separatists mounted a bombing campaign in Spain (where the Catalans gained internal autonomy), and the British province of Ulster simmered on the brink of civil war.

In the late 1980s the disparity in living standards between east and west and the moral and economic bankruptcy of Communism led the new Soviet leader, Mikhail Gorbachev, to slacken the ties binding eastern Europe in an effort to free up the east's economy. It was soon clear that he had unleashed forces beyond his control. Revolutions ensued, first in Poland and then East Germany, Hungary, Czechoslovakia, Bulgaria and Romania. The old order crumbled, with exhilaration mixed with apprehension at the new shape Europe would take.

1 Divided Berlin was a focus for Cold War tension. In 1948–49 the western zone was supplied by air after Soviet forces surrounded the city; in 1961 the Berlin Wall was built to stop refugees leaving the East.

2 The Nuremberg war crimes trials of 1946 indicted many leading Nazis but lesser ones were unpunished; a strong West Germany was needed as a cornerstone of the rebuilding of western Europe.

3 Hungary (1956) and Czechoslovakia (1968) looked to break away from the Communist bloc but both were forced back into line by Warsaw Pact invasions.

4 Yugoslavia remained neutral thanks to its tradition of independent Communism. Its unity was maintained to the 1980s by its Croat leader Tito.

5 The Gdansk shipyards were the center of popular resistance in Poland, which led the way in the later opposition to Communism in eastern Europe.

6 The Treaty of Rome - signed by France, Italy, West Germany, Belgium, the Netherlands and Luxembourg - in 1957 formed the basis for the integration of western Europe under the EEC (later EC and EU).

7 The prolonged attempt by Nikolai Ceauçescu to collectivize the peasantry in Romania was one example of the introduction of Stalinism to eastern Europe, and met with great opposition.

8 The "Forest Brethren" partisans in the Baltic states resisted incorporation into the USSR after 1945.

See also 6.09 (World War II); 6.11 (Europe in the 1990s); 6.16 (the Soviet Union)

6.11 Europe after the Cold War • 1989 – Present •

When Communist control over eastern Europe collapsed in 1989, tension between the North Atlantic Treaty Organization (NATO) and the Warsaw Pact dissolved. However, many former Soviet republics and satellite countries suffered problems of social restructuring, while the western countries faced disagreements over how to cooperate politically and economically.

The rapid reunification of Germany signaled the end of a bi-polar Europe. In the short term, however, the former West Germany paid for taking over East Germany's backward economy. Interest rates rose across Europe, and in 1992 Britain and others were forced to leave the Exchange Rate Mechanism (ERM) intended to guarantee economic stability in the European Union (EU).

Despite the failure to maintain the integrity of the ERM, and doubts about the creation of more unified financial structures within the European Union (EU; formerly EC), monetary union was realized in 2002, when the euro became the currency of 12 EU countries. While some countries stayed out of the euro, others saw vociferous anti-EU campaigns; a referendum on joining led to a "no" vote in Norway. Nevertheless, the EU continued to expand. Ten more countries joined in 2004, most in central and eastern Europe, and Bulgaria and Romania in 2007. Among future candidates for admission is Turkey. The possible unbalancing effects of admitting a largely Islamic nation were in part responsible in 2005 for the rejection of a planned EU Constitution in popular referenda in France and the Netherlands. Another reason for suspicion of closer links within Europe related to the 1995 abolition of border controls. The flow of refugees and economic migrants from eastern Europe was widely perceived in western Europe as a problem.

International tensions increased when Western nations, particularly Spain and Great Britain, suffered Islamic terrorist attacks, such as in Madrid and London in 2004 and 2005, respectively. Meanwhile, domestic terrorism decreased with the end of armed campaigns by the IRA in Britain and ETA in Spain.

Western Europe's internal divisions were heightened by instability in the east, where the governments of eastern Europe and the states of the former Soviet Union faced unprecedented difficulties in developing market-driven economies. The nascent democracies often appeared fragile, not least in Russia itself, where presidents Boris Yeltsin and Vladimir Putin, and Putin's successor, Dmitry Medvedev, faced problems of high unemployment and inflation, organized crime, ethnic conflict, and resurgent Russian nationalism. Separatist terrorists from the province of Chechnya launched attacks in Moscow and elsewhere. In 2009, Medvedev announced a reduction in the Russian military presence within Chechnya. Speaking out became dangerous in Russia. Anticorruption journalists were murdered, including Anna Politkovskaya, while anti-Kremlin campaigner and former spy Alexander Litvinenko was poisoned in London.

Elsewhere, widespread protests in 2003 forced the resignation of Georgian president Edvard Shevardnadze, while in Ukraine in 2004 the so-called "Orange Revolution" overthrew the rigged election of a pro-Russian president in favor of a

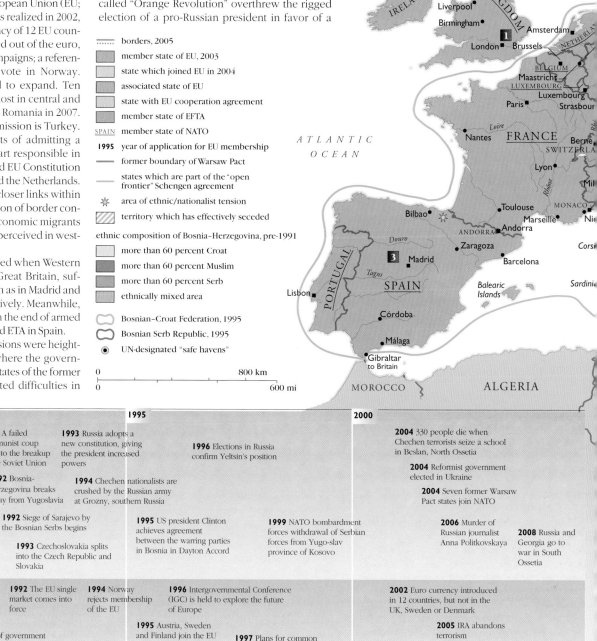

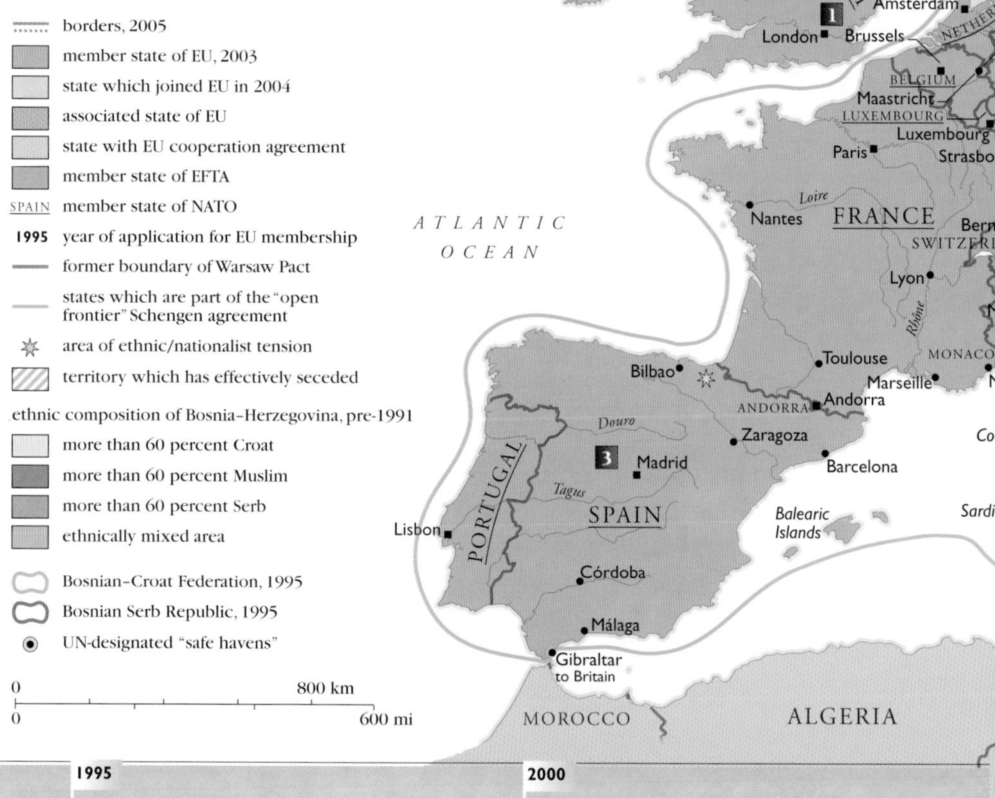
borders, 2005
member state of EU, 2003
state which joined EU in 2004
associated state of EU
state with EU cooperation agreement
member state of EFTA
SPAIN member state of NATO
1995 year of application for EU membership
former boundary of Warsaw Pact
states which are part of the "open frontier" Schengen agreement
area of ethnic/nationalist tension
territory which has effectively seceded
ethnic composition of Bosnia-Herzegovina, pre-1991
more than 60 percent Croat
more than 60 percent Muslim
more than 60 percent Serb
ethnically mixed area
Bosnian-Croat Federation, 1995
Bosnian Serb Republic, 1995
UN-designated "safe havens"
0 800 km
0 600 mi
ICELAND
Reykjavik
Faroe Is to Denmark
Shetland Is to Britain
North Sea
Glasgow
UNITED KINGDOM
Belfast
IRELAND
Dublin
Liverpool
Birmingham
Amsterdam
London
Brussels
BELGIUM
Maastricht
LUXEMBOURG
Luxembourg
Paris
Nantes
Loire
FRANCE
ATLANTIC OCEAN
Lyon
Rhône
Toulouse
MONACO
Marseille
ANDORRA
Andorra
Bilbao
Douro
Zaragoza
Madrid
Barcelona
Tagus
SPAIN
PORTUGAL
Lisbon
Balearic Islands
Córdoba
Málaga
Gibraltar to Britain
MOROCCO
ALGERIA

TIMELINE

1990 · 1995 · 2000

Eastern Europe

1989 Fall of the Communist regimes in Poland, Hungary, Czechoslovakia, Bulgaria, East Germany, and Romania

1989 Ethnic conflicts begin in Azerbaijan and Armenia

1990 Slovenia breaks away from Yugoslavia

1990 Croat-held Dubrovnik is shelled by Serb forces

1991 A failed Communist coup leads to the breakup of the Soviet Union

1992 Bosnia-Herzegovina breaks away from Yugoslavia

1992 Siege of Sarajevo by the Bosnian Serbs begins

1993 Czechoslovakia splits into the Czech Republic and Slovakia

1993 Russia adopts a new constitution, giving the president increased powers

1994 Chechen nationalists are crushed by the Russian army at Grozny, southern Russia

1995 US president Clinton achieves agreement between the warring parties in Bosnia in Dayton Accord

1996 Elections in Russia confirm Yeltsin's position

1999 NATO bombardment forces withdrawal of Serbian forces from Yugo-slav province of Kosovo

2004 330 people die when Chechen terrorists seize a school in Beslan, North Ossetia

2004 Reformist government elected in Ukraine

2004 Seven former Warsaw Pact states join NATO

2006 Murder of Russian journalist Anna Politkovskaya

2008 Russia and Georgia go to war in South Ossetia

Western Europe

1990 The European Bank for Reconstruction and Development is founded

1991 EU heads of government define a strategy for closer political and financial union at Maastricht

1992 The EU single market comes into force

1994 Norway rejects membership of the EU

1995 Austria, Sweden and Finland join the EU

1995 Schengen agreement allows some open frontiers

1996 Intergovernmental Conference (IGC) is held to explore the future of Europe

1997 Plans for common European currency are confirmed

2002 Euro currency introduced in 12 countries, but not in the UK, Sweden or Denmark

2005 IRA abandons terrorism

2005 French and Dutch voters reject proposed EU constitution

2009 Widespread social unrest in Greece

1990 · 1995 · 2000

Zagreb
Virovitica
EASTERN SLAVONIA
Kupa
Sisak
CROATIA
Osijek
Vukovar
Vojvodina
Danube
Sava
Bihac
Banja Luka
Brcko
Sanski Most
Doboj
Tuzla
Una
Bosna
Serbia
Jajce
BOSNIA–HERZEGOVINA
Drina
Knin
Srebrenica
Gornji Vakuf
Zepa
Sarajevo
Pale
Gorazde
5
Split
Mostar
Neretva
Adriatic Sea
Montenegro
Dubrovnik
0 150 km
0 100 mi
SWEDEN
FINLAND
Oulu
Pori
Turku
Helsinki
Tallinn
ESTONIA
NATO member from 2004
Lake Peipus
Lake Ladoga
Lake Onega
St Petersburg
Rybinsk Reservoir
Volga
Moscow
8
Vasteras
Vänern
Stockholm
Vättern
Göteborg
LATVIA
Riga
NATO member from 2004
Western Dvina
Copenhagen
Baltic Sea
LITHUANIA
NATO member from 2004
Kaliningrad
Vilna (Vilnius)
Gdansk
to Russian Federation
Minsk
BELARUS
Vistula
Berlin
POLAND
Warsaw
NATO member from 1999
Elbe
Oder
4
NATO member from 1999
Prague
CZECH REPUBLIC
Krakow
Lvov
Kiev
Kharkov
UKRAINE
Dnieper
SLOVAKIA
NATO member from 2004
Dnepropetrovsk
Donetsk
RUSSIAN FEDERATION
MOLDOVA
Dniestr Republic
Chisinau (Kishinev)
Odessa
Munich
Vienna
Bratislava
AUSTRIA
Budapest
HUNGARY
NATO member from 1999
SLOVENIA
NATO member from 2004
ROMANIA
NATO member from 2004
1995
Ljubljana
Timisoara
Zagreb
CROATIA
2003
Belgrade
Bucharest
Danube
Constanta
BOSNIA-HERZEGOVINA
SERBIA AND MONTENEGRO
BULGARIA
NATO member from 2004
1995
Varna
Sofia
Black Sea
SAN MARINO
Sarajevo
Pristina
Plovdiv
Rome
VATICAN
Tirane
Skopje
ALBANIA
Istanbul
Naples
MACEDONIA (FORMER YUGOSLAV REPUBLIC OF)
Ankara
TURKEY
1987
GREECE
Patras
Athens
Izmir
Sicily
Valletta
MALTA
Mediterranean Sea
Crete
Nicosia
CYPRUS
LEBANON
SYRIA
Adana
Gaziantep
Lake Van
Lake Urmia
IRAN
IRAQ
6
Grozny (Dzhokhar Ghala)
Abkhazia
South Ossetia
GEORGIA
Tbilisi
AZERBAIJAN
Baku
ARMENIA
Yerevan
Karabakh
Caspian Sea
Volga
Aral Sea
KAZAKHSTAN
UZBEKISTAN
TURKMENISTAN

reformer, Viktor Yusyhchenko. After the collapse of Soviet power, resurgent nationalism led to ethnic conflict in Armenia, Azerbaijan, and Yugoslavia. Territories that attempted to secede included Abkhazia and South Ossetia from Georgia, the Dneistr Republic from Moldova, and Karabakh (Ngorno Karabakh) from Azerbaijan. In 2008 Russian and Georgian troops clashed in South Ossetia.

Yugoslavia split into constituent republics, which took no account of ethnic complexities. With the Serbs gripped by militant nationalism, and with Bosnia's population divided among Bosnians, Croats and Serbs, the conflict focused on Bosnia–Herzogovina and its capital Sarajevo. The Yugoslav states – especially Bosnia and Croatia – experienced four years of civil war, which forced hundreds of thousands of civilians to flee their homes. The war revealed the political and military impotence of the rest of Europe, which left the task of peace-keeping to the United Nations; the United States eventually brokered a settlement in 1995. Behind the European failure lay a fear of the war spreading. For this reason, western Europe's economic and military ties with the east continued to grow in importance, with the admission to NATO of former members of the Warsaw Pact. In 1999 NATO intervened in the Yugoslavian province of Kosovo to end Serbian suppression of ethnic Albanians.

The trial of Yugoslav president Milosevic for war crimes began in 2002 but was unfinished at his death in 2008. The arrest that same year of Bosnia Serb leader Radovan Karadzic ensured that high-profile trials would continue.

1 On July 7, 2005, Islamist suicide bombers attacked London's tube and bus systems, killing 52 people and injuring hundreds more.

2 In 1991 at Maastricht the EU agreed to move to common economic and social conditions. Britain rejected Europe-wide provisions on social issues.

3 In March 2004, four bombs blew up on a commuter train in Madrid, killing 191 people and wounding 1,800. The attack was blamed on Islamist supporters of al-Qaeda.

4 Prague, like many cities of eastern Europe, saw a boom in the early 1990s, with tourists and industrialists attracted by new opportunities and low costs.

5 The mainly Muslim inhabitants of Sarajevo, capital of Bosnia, were besieged by Bosnian Serb forces from 1992 to 1995.

6 In 2004 Chechen separatists assassinated the pro-Russian president of Chechnya, Akhmad Kadyrov, in a bomb attack in Grozny.

7 In Northern Ireland the 1998 Good Friday Agreement imposed decommissioning on terrorist groups and created an elected Northern Ireland Assembly; 2003 elections left the Democratic Ulster Unionists and Sinn Fein as the largest parties.

8 Moscow and much of Russia suffered inflation, shortages, gangsterism and unemployment in the early 1990s in the rush to build a market economy.

See also 6.10 (Cold War Europe); 6.16 (decline of the Soviet Union); 6.26 (Middle East)

6.12 The Americas • 1914 – 1945 •

World War I involved many of the American states, despite an original intention to stay out of the conflict. The Caribbean islands and Canada owed direct allegiance to Britain, but most other countries had divided loyalties and were anxious to preserve their own interests; US president Woodrow Wilson advised neutrality. By 1918 Brazil and several Central American states had joined the Allies; the United States itself stayed out until German U-boat (submarine) attacks drove Wilson to declare war in 1917. The nation was put on a war footing: the government took over the railroads and strikers were threatened with the draft. Factories and shipyards converted to warwork, and thousands of African-Americans moved north to the munitions factories.

By the end of the war, there was little enthusiasm for any US involvement in Europe's postwar territorial arrangements. The Treaty of Versailles and the League of Nations, Wilson's brainchild, were both rejected by Congress as Americans sought "normalcy". The "jazz age" of the 1920s brought a quest for consumer goods and material comfort, despite a moral backlash in the form of the Volstead Act which brought Prohibition in 1920, with intoxicating liquor banned across the country. The result was a rise in political corruption and gangsterism.

In 1929, the Wall St stock market crash threw the country into the Great Depression, which had global resonance as US loans and investments had propped up the world's trade. The shadow of the depression was felt throughout the Western Hemisphere. In the United States itself, the crisis was exacerbated by drought and storms that devastated parts of Texas and the Mid-West, and created a dustbowl on the Great Plains. Some 12 million Americans lost their jobs, and shanty-towns (Hoovervilles) sprang up around the main cities. In 1933, Democrat Franklin D. Roosevelt became president, offering a New Deal to alleviate the depression through unprecedented government spending, giving work to millions on infrastructure projects such as dams and airports. The New Deal could not, however, cure all the economic ills of the country: agriculture and heavy industry recovered only after 1940, mainly due to US contributions to Britain's war effort, followed by the outbreak of war with Japan in December 1941.

Canada had suffered in the Great War, and lost 60,000 men by 1918. This experience, followed by the prosperity of the 1920s, encouraged a new spirit of independence; but the country was hit hard by the depression, as it was heavily reliant on the export of wheat and lumber. The great drought of 1934 also wrought havoc on the farmers of the prairies. New political groupings suggested nationalization and the redistribution of income as a cure to national ills, while separatists won a large following in Quebec. The rise in world prices after 1937 and closer economic ties with the United States caused both proposals to be shelved for several decades.

The United States claimed the Caribbean and Central America as its "backyard", intervening to maintain its investments (including the Panama Canal and the oil reserves of Mexico and Venezuela) and building a military base at Guantanamo Bay on Cuba. The region was badly hit by the recession, and strikes and demonstrations were common, especially in the British West Indies. Several countries turned to dictatorships: some, such as Lázaro Cárdenas, ruler of Mexico from 1934–40, tried honestly to improve the condition of their people. Cárdenas restored communal lands to the peasants, and nationalized railroads and oil companies. Venezuela was ruled by Juan Vicente Gómez from 1908–35; he took over the Lake Maracaibo oil reserves but failed to address the weakness of so many Latin American states: the reliance on a single export commodity.

Colombia became the world's second producer of coffee but, like its main rival Brazil (ruled after 1930 by Getúlio Vargas), tried to reduce the economy's dependence on the fragile coffee trade in the 1930s by industrial diversification and import substitution. Argentina, which had flourished since the 19th century on grain and meat exports, now had to endure austerity measures. Chile too suffered with the fall in copper prices, while its nitrate exports were hit by the discovery of new chemical methods of production. Several South American states engaged in border disputes: Chile and Peru clashed over nitrate resources; the Chaco War between Bolivia and Paraguay in the 1930s was the most violent conflict to take place in the world between 1918 and 1939; and Ecuador lost the Amazonian region to Peru in 1942.

World War II brought full employment and high wages to North America: by 1943 the USA was outproducing all the enemy nations combined. Millions moved to the cities; African– Americans flooded to California, Detroit and New York. Convoys took troops and supplies to all main theaters of war, and aid to Britain and the USSR. To counter enemy submarines operating down the Atlantic seaboard and in the Gulf of Mexico, air patrols were maintained far out to sea. For the Latin American countries the war years were eased by Roosevelt's "good neighbor" policy. The Coffee Accords of 1940 guaranteed US markets; in return Roosevelt gained bases and promises of military support.

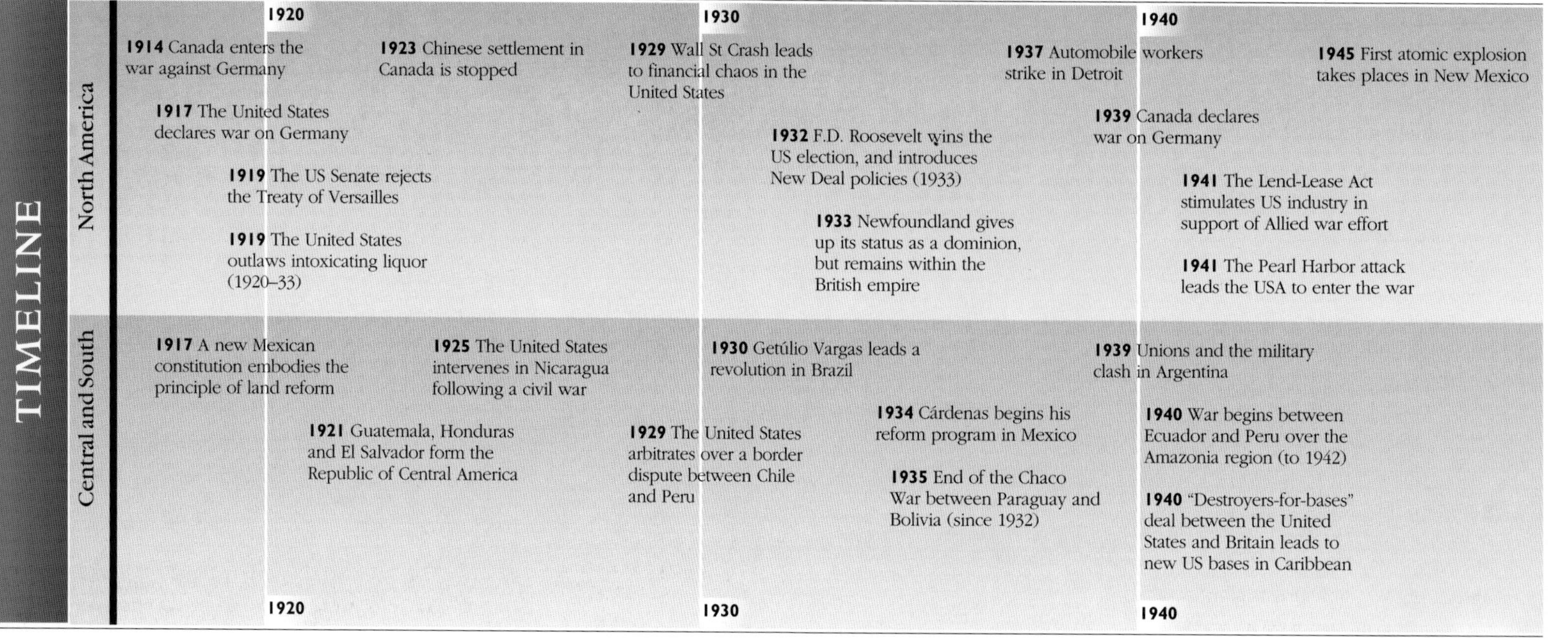

TIMELINE

North America

1914 Canada enters the war against Germany

1917 The United States declares war on Germany

1919 The US Senate rejects the Treaty of Versailles

1919 The United States outlaws intoxicating liquor (1920–33)

1923 Chinese settlement in Canada is stopped

1929 Wall St Crash leads to financial chaos in the United States

1932 F.D. Roosevelt wins the US election, and introduces New Deal policies (1933)

1933 Newfoundland gives up its status as a dominion, but remains within the British empire

1937 Automobile workers strike in Detroit

1939 Canada declares war on Germany

1941 The Lend-Lease Act stimulates US industry in support of Allied war effort

1941 The Pearl Harbor attack leads the USA to enter the war

1945 First atomic explosion takes places in New Mexico

Central and South

1917 A new Mexican constitution embodies the principle of land reform

1921 Guatemala, Honduras and El Salvador form the Republic of Central America

1925 The United States intervenes in Nicaragua following a civil war

1929 The United States arbitrates over a border dispute between Chile and Peru

1930 Getúlio Vargas leads a revolution in Brazil

1934 Cárdenas begins his reform program in Mexico

1935 End of the Chaco War between Paraguay and Bolivia (since 1932)

1939 Unions and the military clash in Argentina

1940 War begins between Ecuador and Peru over the Amazonia region (to 1942)

1940 "Destroyers-for-bases" deal between the United States and Britain leads to new US bases in Caribbean

NRA
MEMBER
U.S.
WE DO OUR PART
The National Recovery Administration (NRA) was set up by Roosevelt to finance New Deal projects in 1933. Its symbol is shown here.
countries with territorial changes, 1914–41
Bolivia, 1914
Canada, 1914
Chile, 1914
Colombia, 1914
Ecuador, 1914
Newfoundland, 1914
Paraguay, 1914
Peru, 1914
border, 1941
region of Oriente claimed by Peru
provincial rebellion in Brazil, 1930
effects of the Depression in North America
area of severe economic decline, 1930–40
area of economic revival, 1930–40
area affected by drought in the early 1930s
seat of Pan-American Congress, with date
West Indian disturbances, 1935–39
strike or labor unrest
United States military intervention
battle of World War I
battle of World War II
Lend-Lease aircraft route, 1941–45
convoy route
area of Allied shipping losses, 1939–45
Antigua United States military base, 1940
center of automobile industry
center of aviation industry
oil field
African-American migration, 1914–18
migration from the "dustbowl states", 1930s
Julianehab
to Reykjavik
Labrador Sea
to Britain
Newfoundland to Britain
Goose
1927 to Newfoundland
Hudson Bay
Gander
St John's
Newfoundland
CANADA
Winnipeg
Québec
Halifax
Montréal
Ottawa
Lake Superior
Lake Huron
Lake Michigan
Boston
Bethpage
Buffalo
Detroit
Cleveland
New York
Philadelphia
Milwaukee
Chicago
Pittsburgh
Columbus
Washington
Indianapolis
Cincinnati
to Gibraltar
Bermuda Islands to Britain
St Louis
Tennessee
Atlanta
Birmingham
Dallas
Jacksonville
New Orleans
Tampa
Miami
Key West
NORTH ATLANTIC OCEAN
Bahamas to Britain
Danish Virgin Islands 1917 to United States
Great Exuma
Mayaguana
St Kitts to Britain
Antigua to Britain
HAITI
1916–24
Puerto Rico to US
St Lucia to Britain
Barbados to Britain
St Vincent to Britain
Gulf of Mexico
Havana
1917, 1921–23, 1933
CUBA
Guantánamo Bay to United States
1915–34
DOMINICAN REPUBLIC
Jamaica to Britain
Caribbean Sea
Trinidad to Britain
to Dakar
to Gold Coast
to Middle East via Cape of Good Hope
Veracruz
1914
British Honduras to Britain
GUATEMALA
HONDURAS
1912–34
NICARAGUA
Guatemala City
EL SALVADOR
COSTA RICA
Panama City
Panama Canal, 1914
PANAMA
Maracaibo
Barranquilla
Cartagena 1939
Caracas
Ciudad Bolivar (Angostura)
Georgetown
Paramaribo
Cayenne
French Guiana to France
Dutch Guiana to Netherlands
British Guiana to Britain
VENEZUELA
Belém
Fortaleza (Ceará)
Pariba
Recife (Pernambuco)
Medellin
Bogotá
Cali
COLOMBIA
1922 to Colombia
Manaus
Amazon Basin
BRAZIL
Quito
ECUADOR
Oriente 1942 to Peru
Guayaquil
Galapagos Islands to Ecuador
Tumbes
Salvador (Bahia)
Brazilian Highlands
Mato Grosso Plateau
Minas Gerais
ANDES
PERU
Lima 1938
BOLIVIA
La Paz
1929 to Peru
Tacna
Arica
Gran Chaco
1938 to Paraguay
PARAGUAY
Asunción
Rio de Janeiro 1906
São Paulo
Santos
SOUTH ATLANTIC OCEAN
SOUTH PACIFIC OCEAN
Rio Grande do Sul
Porto Alegre
ARGENTINA
Córdoba
Rosario
Battle of the River Plate, 1939
URUGUAY
Buenos Aires 1910, 1936
Montevideo 1933
CHILE
Valparaiso
Santiago 1923
Mar del Plata
Bahia Blanca
1914
Patagonia
Falkland Islands (Islas Malvinas) to Britain
1914
0 1500 km
0 1000 mi

1 Seattle, in Washington State, USA, flourished after the opening of the Panama Canal expanded Pacific trade; it became a center of aircraft manufacture.

2 Chicago was a notorious center of gangsterism, built upon the loyalties of existing ethnic communities, in the Prohibition era and into the 1930s.

3 Manaus had been a center of the rubber industry in the 19th century, but was in decline through the early 20th century.

4 The apparent discovery of oil in the disputed Gran Chaco region caused Bolivia to attack Paraguayan positions in 1932. By 1935 Paraguayan control was confirmed; but the oil finds proved illusory.

5 The German East Asian fleet attacked the British coaling station of the Falkland Islands in December 1914, but was defeated by the Royal Navy.

6 Cuba's reliance on United States imports of sugar in the 1920s left the economy defenseless in the 1930s; World War II boosted exports to the United States.

7 The Tennessee Valley Authority built dams and hydroelectric plants which, with flood control and land reclamaion schemes, raised living standards in seven states in the 1930s.

8 Getúlio Vargas used his power base in Minas Gerais to launch a coup in Brazil in 1930.

See also 5.23 (19th-century Latin America); 5.24 (the Caribbean); 6.13 (the postwar Americas)

6.13 The Americas • 1945 – Present •

The United States was the undoubted victor of World War II. With its economy stimulated by the war and its access to the atomic bomb, the country looked forward to prosperity at home and global domination.

In many ways the domestic dream was realized. American families moved away from the field and factory into the rewarding aerospace, automobile, information technology and service industries. Their ambitions led to continuous resettlement in the US itself, a pattern imitated by hopeful immigrants including Hispanics, Filipinos and east Asians. By 1960 almost 40 percent of American families were in the professional or skilled worker classes. Yet the United States failed to abolish poverty, improve health care or to provide real educational opportunity for all. Poverty, especially among black Americans, was a major issue in the Civil Rights campaigns of the 1960s and resurfaced in the 1980s and 1990s.

With the start of the Cold War in the late 1940s, a nuclear arms race ensued that developed into the space race of the 1960s, culminating in putting men on the Moon in 1969. The Cold War affected Americans at home, too, with the McCarthy "witchhunts" against suspected Communists and sympathizers from 1950.

Meanwhile the United States was drawn into costly conflicts across the world. Latin America was one battleground. In Cuba, Soviet support for the socialist-nationalist Castro regime led to a crisis in 1962, when the Soviets threatened to use the island as a base for nuclear missiles. Suspicion and hostility dominated relations between the United States and Cuba. Illness removed Castro from power in 2008, opening the way to a possible reduction in tension.

South America was an area of key US commercial and political involvement as the governments of the region – which ranged from the more or less democratic to out-and-out military dictatorships – wrestled with the problem of having such a rich and powerful neighbor. In Chile in 1973, an elected Marxist government was replaced, with US connivance, by a rightwing dictatorship, characterized by brutal suppression of opposition. In the 1940s the charismatic Juan and Eva Peron were popular in Argentina until unemployment, strikes and inflation brought the army to power. The military regime's attempt to revive falling popularity by invading the Falkland Islands in 1982 failed and led to the election of the civilian "Peronist" government of Carlos Menem.

The interests of the well-off continued to impede social change in South America, and the problems associated with a rapidly growing population worsened. Several countries, including Peru, endured long and violent revolutionary conflicts; others, such as Colombia, were dominated by illegal drug trafficking. In 2002, after eight years of high unemployment, Brazil elected its first left-wing president in 40 years. In Venezuela, the leftist Hugo Chavez became president in 1999 and began what he termed a social "revolution." In 2009 he managed to remove constitutional limits on his maxium term in office.

Many countries joined economic organizations: Venezuela and Ecuador were founder members of the Organization of Petroleum Exporting Countries (OPEC) in 1960; the Latin American Integration Association (1980) and Andean Pact (1969) were attempts at economic cooperation. In 1992 the North American Free Trade Agreement (NAFTA) was extended to include Mexico, which consolidated its position as the second-largest trading partner of the US. Despite economic growth and job creation in Mexico, the country struggled to combat illegal emigration and drug trafficking to its larger neighbor. In 2008, more than 6,000 people were killed in drug-related violence.

Resentment of perceived US imperialism grew in the 1980s and 1990s, combining with Islamic fundamentalism to create a new geopolitical landscape. The US reaction included a growth in fundamentalist Christian pressure and the disputed election in 2001 of Republican George W. Bush. Meanwhile US isolationism was manifest in its refusal to sign up to the Kyoto protocol (the 2001 climate treaty) or to join the International Criminal Court.

In September 2001, the destruction of the World Trade Center in New York and the attack on the Pentagon in Washington DC by Islamic Al Qaeda terrorists provoked the US-led "war on terror". The first target, defeated by a wide coalition of forces, was the ruling Taliban in Afghanistan, hosts to Al Qaeda. The second was Iraq, which, despite the objections of many allies, the US invaded in 2003. Efforts to impose order and democratic rule were dogged by insurgency, until a troop "surge" in 2007 seemed to encourage a reduction in violence and a more stable society.

Barack Obama, who took office as the first black US president in January 2009, announced his intention to withdraw US troops from Iraq within two years. By that time, however, the United States, like the rest of the region, was battling the effects of the global economic downturn. Obama introduced a package of some $800 billion in an attempt to stimulate the national economy.

TIMELINE

North America

1945 The United States develops the first atom bomb at Los Alamos, New Mexico

1949 Newfoundland becomes a province of the Canadian Federation

1961 US president Kennedy launches the manned space program

1963 John F. Kennedy is assassinated in Dallas, Texas

1968 Martin Luther King is assassinated in Memphis Tennessee; youth and antiwar protests across North America

1974 US president Nixon resigns following revelations in the Watergate affair

1988 The North American Free Trade Agreement is signed by the United States and Canada

1992 Mexico joins NAFTA

1995 A terrorist bomb explodes in Oklahoma, USA. American Timothy McVeigh is found guilty and executed

2001 Islamic Al Qaeda terrorists kill 3,000 in New York and Washington DC

2002 A US-led coalition topples Afghanistan's Taliban government

2003 US-led forces invade Iraq; their victory sparks a prolonged insurgency

2005 Hurricane Katrina devastates New Orleans

2007 US forces begin a "surge" in Iraq

2008 Barack Obama elected US president

Latin America

1946 Juan Perón is elected president of Argentina

1954 The pro-American Alfredo Stroessner becomes president of Paraguay

1959 Castro's Marxist revolutionaries take over in Cuba

1967 Bolivian military capture and kill Che Guevara, former associate of Castro

1967 A free-market economic boom in Brazil leads to violent opposition in the early 1970s

1973 Chile's Marxist president Allende is killed in a US-backed coup

1976–82 The "dirty war" is fought between the Argentinian military and guerrilla forces

1982 An Argentinian invasion launches the Falklands War, in which the British confirm their control over the islands

1989 Carlos Menem comes to power in Argentina, introducing economic and political reform

1990 Democracy is restored in Chile under Patricio Aylwin

2002 "Lula" da Silva becomes president of Brazil

2005 Chile's Supreme Court overthrows plans to try former dictator Pinochet

2007 Referendum blocks increased power for Hugo Chavez, president of Venezuela

2008 Fidel Castro is succeeded as president of Cuba by his brother, Raúl

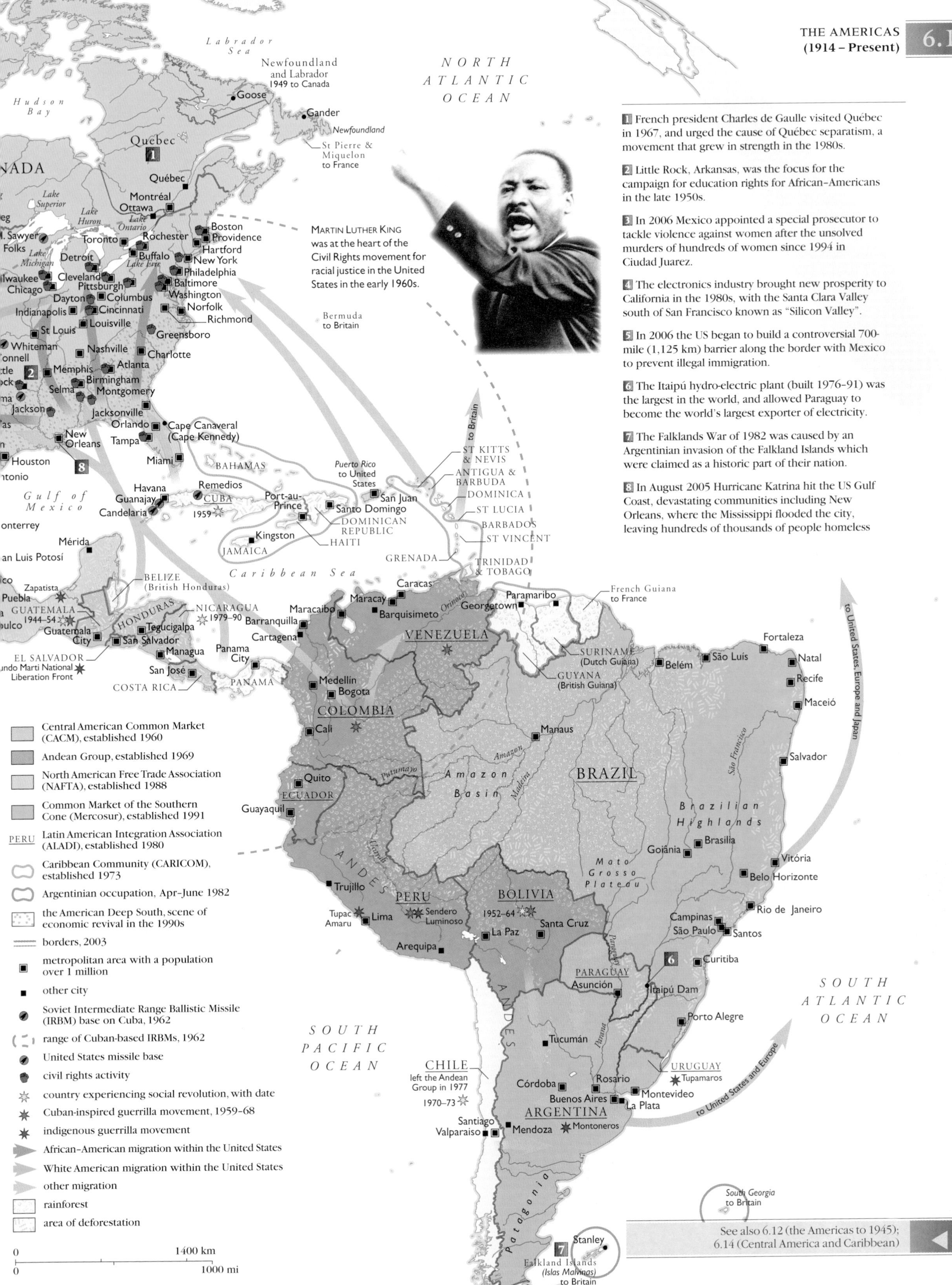
Labrador Sea
Hudson Bay
Newfoundland and Labrador 1949 to Canada
Goose
Gander
Newfoundland
St Pierre & Miquelon to France
NORTH ATLANTIC OCEAN
Québec
Québec
Montréal
Ottawa
Lake Superior
Lake Huron
Lake Ontario
Lake Michigan
Lake Erie
Toronto
Rochester
Boston
Providence
Hartford
Buffalo
New York
Detroit
Philadelphia
Cleveland
Pittsburgh
Baltimore
Chicago
Washington
Dayton
Columbus
Norfolk
Indianapolis
Cincinnati
Richmond
Louisville
St Louis
Greensboro
Nashville
Charlotte
Memphis
Atlanta
Birmingham
Selma
Montgomery
Jackson
Jacksonville
Orlando
Cape Canaveral (Cape Kennedy)
Tampa
New Orleans
Houston
Miami
Bermuda to Britain
to Britain
BAHAMAS
Puerto Rico to United States
ST KITTS & NEVIS
ANTIGUA & BARBUDA
DOMINICA
ST LUCIA
BARBADOS
ST VINCENT
GRENADA
TRINIDAD & TOBAGO
Havana
Remedios
Guanajay
Candelaria
CUBA
1959
Port-au-Prince
Santo Domingo
San Juan
DOMINICAN REPUBLIC
HAITI
Kingston
JAMAICA
Gulf of Mexico
Mérida
Caribbean Sea
BELIZE (British Honduras)
Zapatista
Puebla
GUATEMALA 1944–54
Guatemala City
HONDURAS
Tegucigalpa
San Salvador
NICARAGUA 1979–90
Managua
EL SALVADOR
Liberation Front
San José
COSTA RICA
Panama City
PANAMA
Barranquilla
Cartagena
Maracaibo
Maracay
Caracas
Barquisimeto
Orinoco
Georgetown
Paramaribo
French Guiana to France
VENEZUELA
SURINAME (Dutch Guiana)
GUYANA (British Guiana)
Medellín
Bogota
COLOMBIA
Cali
Belém
São Luís
Fortaleza
Natal
Recife
Maceió
Manaus
Amazon
Amazon Basin
Madeira
Putumayo
São Francisco
BRAZIL
Salvador
Quito
ECUADOR
Guayaquil
Brazilian Highlands
Brasília
Goiânia
Mato Grosso Plateau
Vitória
Belo Horizonte
to United States, Europe and Japan
ANDES
Ucayali
Trujillo
PERU
Sendero Luminoso
BOLIVIA
1952–64
Tupac Amaru
Lima
Santa Cruz
La Paz
Arequipa
Rio de Janeiro
Campinas
São Paulo
Santos
Curitiba
PARAGUAY
Asunción
Paraguay
Itaipú Dam
SOUTH ATLANTIC OCEAN
Porto Alegre
SOUTH PACIFIC OCEAN
Tucumán
Paraná
CHILE left the Andean Group in 1977
1970–73
Córdoba
Rosario
URUGUAY
Tupamaros
Montevideo
Buenos Aires
La Plata
ARGENTINA
to United States and Europe
Santiago
Valparaíso
Mendoza
Montoneros
Patagonia
South Georgia to Britain
Stanley
Falkland Islands (Islas Malvinas) to Britain

MARTIN LUTHER KING was at the heart of the Civil Rights movement for racial justice in the United States in the early 1960s.

1 French president Charles de Gaulle visited Québec in 1967, and urged the cause of Québec separatism, a movement that grew in strength in the 1980s.

2 Little Rock, Arkansas, was the focus for the campaign for education rights for African-Americans in the late 1950s.

3 In 2006 Mexico appointed a special prosecutor to tackle violence against women after the unsolved murders of hundreds of women since 1994 in Ciudad Juarez.

4 The electronics industry brought new prosperity to California in the 1980s, with the Santa Clara Valley south of San Francisco known as "Silicon Valley".

5 In 2006 the US began to build a controversial 700-mile (1,125 km) barrier along the border with Mexico to prevent illegal immigration.

6 The Itaipú hydro-electric plant (built 1976–91) was the largest in the world, and allowed Paraguay to become the world's largest exporter of electricity.

7 The Falklands War of 1982 was caused by an Argentinian invasion of the Falkland Islands which were claimed as a historic part of their nation.

8 In August 2005 Hurricane Katrina hit the US Gulf Coast, devastating communities including New Orleans, where the Mississippi flooded the city, leaving hundreds of thousands of people homeless

- Central American Common Market (CACM), established 1960
- Andean Group, established 1969
- North American Free Trade Association (NAFTA), established 1988
- Common Market of the Southern Cone (Mercosur), established 1991
- PERU Latin American Integration Association (ALADI), established 1980
- Caribbean Community (CARICOM), established 1973
- Argentinian occupation, Apr–June 1982
- the American Deep South, scene of economic revival in the 1990s
- borders, 2003
- metropolitan area with a population over 1 million
- other city
- Soviet Intermediate Range Ballistic Missile (IRBM) base on Cuba, 1962
- range of Cuban-based IRBMs, 1962
- United States missile base
- civil rights activity
- country experiencing social revolution, with date
- Cuban-inspired guerrilla movement, 1959–68
- indigenous guerrilla movement
- African-American migration within the United States
- White American migration within the United States
- other migration
- rainforest
- area of deforestation

0 1400 km
0 1000 mi

See also 6.12 (the Americas to 1945); 6.14 (Central America and Caribbean)

All eight states of Central America, together with several Caribbean islands, shared similar problems in the late 20th century: subsistence agriculture, unfair land distribution and a deprived native peasant class. Tax evasion by the wealthy was endemic, and labor-intensive industries lacking. The states were too poor to fund sufficient welfare to prevent political revolt, so violence and state repression were common. Aid (overwhelmingly from the US) tended to prop up military leaders committed to anti-Communist policies, despite frequent corruption and human rights abuses.

Before its 1959 revolution, Cuba was dominated by United States interests, with their marines stationed at the Guantánamo Bay base (later infamous as the detention center for suspected Afghan Taliban fighters and Al Qaeda members). Fidel Castro's revolution led to hostility from the United States and the International Monetary Fund (IMF). The Soviet Union supported Castro, especially after the abortive US-supported counter-coup at the Bay of Pigs in 1961. The following year, air surveillance revealed that Soviet ballistic missiles had been stationed on the island, and all of eastern and most of the southern US lay within their 3,200-kilometer (2,000-mile) range. US President John F. Kennedy imposed a naval blockade and considered invasion, a step that, it seemed, would lead to nuclear war. The missiles were removed, but Castro became an enduring Soviet ally. The Soviet Union supported Cuba's economy, but after the collapse of the Soviet Union, Cuba went into serious recession in 1990 and faced severe US economic sanctions. In 2004 the Cuban government strengthened its controls over income coming into the economy; illicit migration to the US bcame a growing problem. Castro became seriously sick in 2006, and resigned the presidency in 2008 in favor of his brother Raúl. His modest relaxation of economic controls was met by support from Russia and China, and the lifting of some economic restrictions by the United States.

During the Cold War, the United States believed that Cuba fostered guerrilla revolts in Nicaragua, El Salvador, Guatemala and Honduras. In Nicaragua, Sandinista guerrillas set up a Marxist–Leninist state in 1979. This was subverted by right-wing Contra guerrillas trained by the United States; in 1990, Sandinista leader Daniel Ortega was voted out of office. He was again elected president in 2006, however.

In Mexico, the region's richest country, a devaluation of the peso in late 1994 caused economic turmoil. Trade with the US and Canada tripled after the introduction of NAFTA in 1994, however. Elections in July 2000 marked the first time since the 1910 revolution that the opposition (Alliance for Change) had defeated the Institutional Revolutionary Party (PRI). Mexico faced problems in the north, where in 2006 the US began to construct a controversial border fence to prevent illegal immigration and drug trafficking. In 2008 an upsurge in violence related to the drugs trade killed thousands. Meanwhile, Mexico announced financial measures to mitigate the effects of the economic downturn in the US.

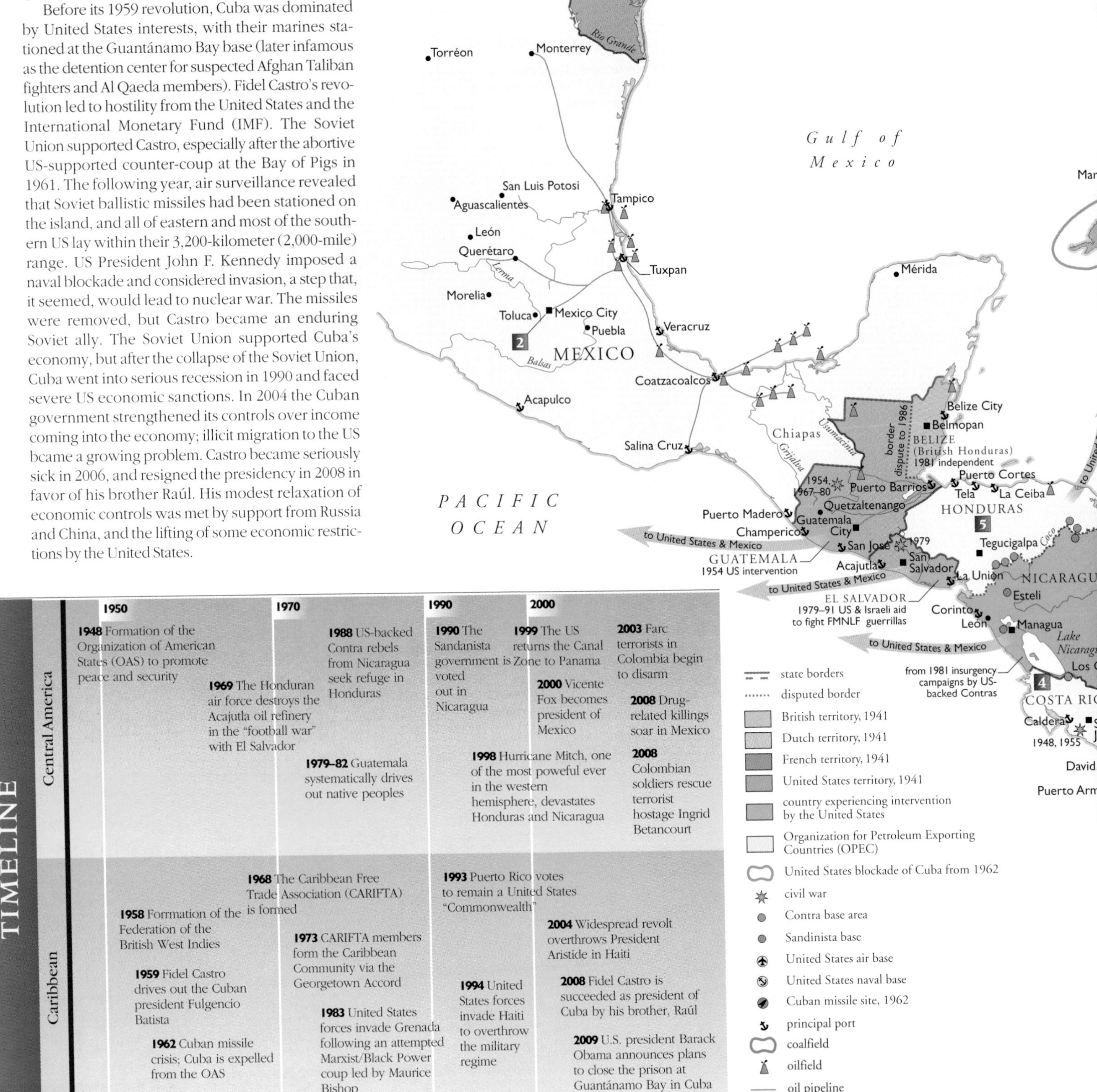
Rio Grande
Torréon
Monterrey
Gulf of Mexico
San Luis Potosi
Aguascalientes
Tampico
León
Querétaro
Lerma
Tuxpan
Mérida
Morelia
Toluca
Mexico City
Puebla
Veracruz
2
MEXICO
Balsas
Coatzacoalcos
Acapulco
Belize City
Belmopan
Chiapas
Usumacinta
border dispute to 1986
BELIZE (British Honduras) 1981 independent
Grijalva
Salina Cruz
1954, 1967–80
Puerto Barrios
Puerto Cortes
Tela
La Ceiba
PACIFIC OCEAN
Quetzaltenango
HONDURAS
Puerto Madero
Guatemala City
5
Champerico
to United States & Mexico
San Jose
1979
Tegucigalpa
GUATEMALA
1954 US intervention
Acajutla
San Salvador
La Unión
NICARAGUA
to United States & Mexico
Esteli
EL SALVADOR
1979–91 US & Israeli aid to fight FMNLF guerrillas
Corinto
León
Managua
Lake Nicaragua
to United States & Mexico
from 1981 insurgency campaigns by US-backed Contras
4
COSTA RICA
Caldera
1948, 1955
David
Puerto Armuelles
state borders
disputed border
British territory, 1941
Dutch territory, 1941
French territory, 1941
United States territory, 1941
country experiencing intervention by the United States
Organization for Petroleum Exporting Countries (OPEC)
United States blockade of Cuba from 1962
civil war
Contra base area
Sandinista base
United States air base
United States naval base
Cuban missile site, 1962
principal port
coalfield
oilfield
oil pipeline
major migration since 1945

TIMELINE

Central America

1948 Formation of the Organization of American States (OAS) to promote peace and security

1969 The Honduran air force destroys the Acajutla oil refinery in the "football war" with El Salvador

1979–82 Guatemala systematically drives out native peoples

1988 US-backed Contra rebels from Nicaragua seek refuge in Honduras

1990 The Sandanista government is voted out in Nicaragua

1998 Hurricane Mitch, one of the most poweful ever in the western hemisphere, devastates Honduras and Nicaragua

1999 The US returns the Canal Zone to Panama

2000 Vicente Fox becomes president of Mexico

2003 Farc terrorists in Colombia begin to disarm

2008 Drug-related killings soar in Mexico

2008 Colombian soldiers rescue terrorist hostage Ingrid Betancourt

Caribbean

1958 Formation of the Federation of the British West Indies

1959 Fidel Castro drives out the Cuban president Fulgencio Batista

1962 Cuban missile crisis; Cuba is expelled from the OAS

1968 The Caribbean Free Trade Association (CARIFTA) is formed

1973 CARIFTA members form the Caribbean Community via the Georgetown Accord

1983 United States forces invade Grenada following an attempted Marxist/Black Power coup led by Maurice Bishop

1993 Puerto Rico votes to remain a United States "Commonwealth"

1994 United States forces invade Haiti to overthrow the military regime

2004 Widespread revolt overthrows President Aristide in Haiti

2008 Fidel Castro is succeeded as president of Cuba by his brother, Raúl

2009 U.S. president Barack Obama announces plans to close the prison at Guantánamo Bay in Cuba

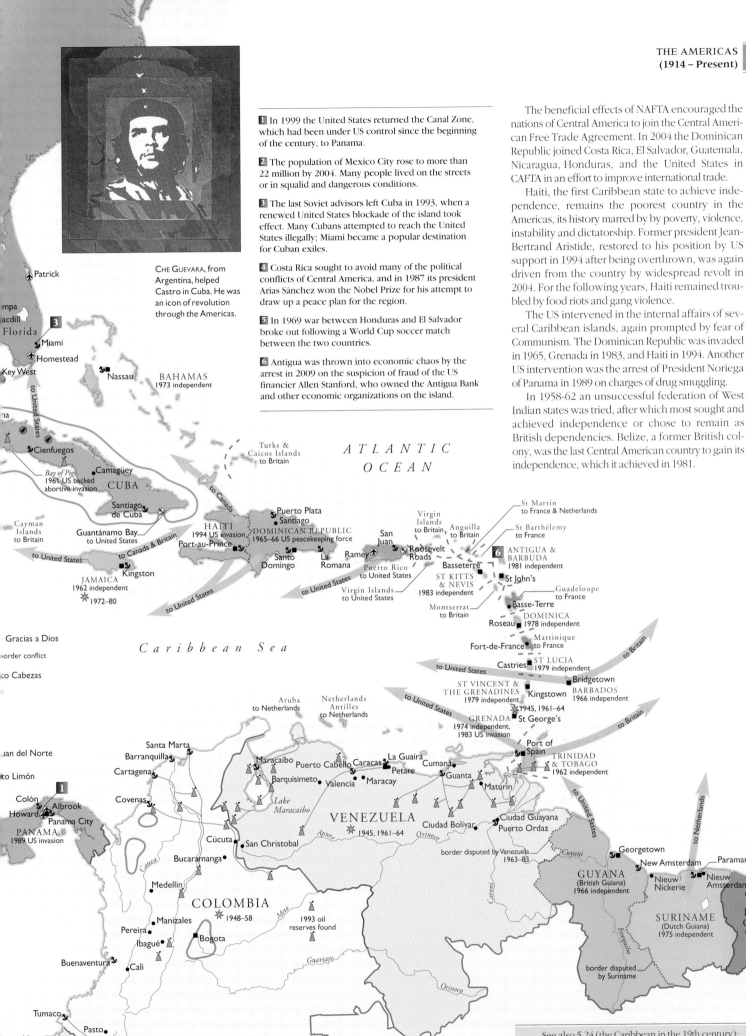

CHE GUEVARA, from Argentina, helped Castro in Cuba. He was an icon of revolution through the Americas.

1 In 1999 the United States returned the Canal Zone, which had been under US control since the beginning of the century, to Panama.

2 The population of Mexico City rose to more than 22 million by 2004. Many people lived on the streets or in squalid and dangerous conditions.

3 The last Soviet advisors left Cuba in 1993, when a renewed United States blockade of the island took effect. Many Cubans attempted to reach the United States illegally; Miami became a popular destination for Cuban exiles.

4 Costa Rica sought to avoid many of the political conflicts of Central America, and in 1987 its president Arias Sánchez won the Nobel Prize for his attempt to draw up a peace plan for the region.

5 In 1969 war between Honduras and El Salvador broke out following a World Cup soccer match between the two countries.

6 Antigua was thrown into economic chaos by the arrest in 2009 on the suspicion of fraud of the US financier Allen Stanford, who owned the Antigua Bank and other economic organizations on the island.

The beneficial effects of NAFTA encouraged the nations of Central America to join the Central American Free Trade Agreement. In 2004 the Dominican Republic joined Costa Rica, El Salvador, Guatemala, Nicaragua, Honduras, and the United States in CAFTA in an effort to improve international trade.

Haiti, the first Caribbean state to achieve independence, remains the poorest country in the Americas, its history marred by by poverty, violence, instability and dictatorship. Former president Jean-Bertrand Aristide, restored to his position by US support in 1994 after being overthrown, was again driven from the country by widespread revolt in 2004. For the following years, Haiti remained troubled by food riots and gang violence.

The US intervened in the internal affairs of several Caribbean islands, again prompted by fear of Communism. The Dominican Republic was invaded in 1965, Grenada in 1983, and Haiti in 1994. Another US intervention was the arrest of President Noriega of Panama in 1989 on charges of drug smuggling.

In 1958-62 an unsuccessful federation of West Indian states was tried, after which most sought and achieved independence or chose to remain as British dependencies. Belize, a former British colony, was the last Central American country to gain its independence, which it achieved in 1981.

See also 5.24 (the Caribbean in the 19th century); 6.13 (the Americas from 1945)

6.15 The making of the Soviet Union • 1917 – 1941 •

World War I imposed unbearable social and economic strain on Russia. The czar, who had assumed personal command of the armed forces in 1915, was held responsible for many of the failures of the war, and abdicated following a revolution in Petrograd in March (February in the Russian calendar) 1917. A provisional government took power but its decision to continue the war combined with fear of counterrevolution led to increasing radicalization. Local *soviets* – committees of workers, soldiers and sailors – sprang up in industrial areas. Many were dominated by the radical socialist parties, among whom the anti-war Bolsheviks (led by Vladimir Ilych Lenin since his return in April from exile in Berne) won growing influence. In November (October) 1917, the Bolsheviks overthrew the government.

The Bolsheviks were heavily outnumbered in the Constituent Assembly by the Socialist Revolutionaries representing the peasantry. Lenin therefore dissolved the Assembly and fought a bloody civil war to secure his position. Non-Bolshevik socialists, liberals, aristocrats, national minorities and the peasantry all opposed the regime, and several foreign powers also intervened. Nevertheless, the "Whites" (anti-Bolshevik forces) were too divided geographically and politically to depose the government. Nineteen independent governments were formed but, although at one point the Whites were within 400 kilometers (250 miles) of Moscow, the Bolsheviks ("Reds") recaptured the Ukraine, Caucasus, central Asia and Siberia. They ceded territory to Poland and recognized the independence of the Baltic states, but in 1923 the Union of Soviet Socialist Republics (USSR) was created, comprising the republics of Russia, Ukraine, Belorussia and Transcaucasia.

During the civil war the Bolsheviks adopted a policy of "war communism" and requisitioned food for the army and cities. This brought an arduous struggle with the peasantry which culminated in widespread revolts in 1920–22 and a famine in the Volga region that killed five million people. With the end of the civil war in 1921 Lenin adopted the "new economic policy" (NEP). This reintroduced limited

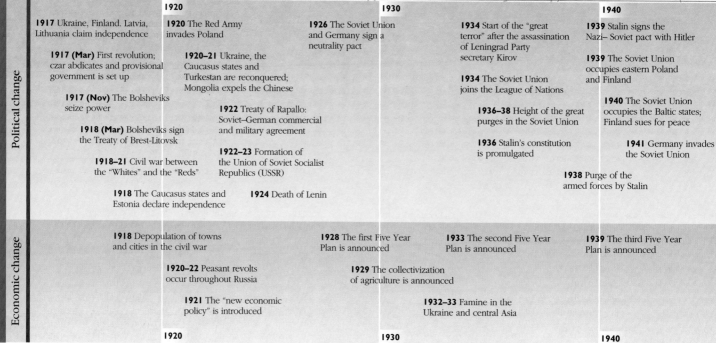

SWEDEN
GERMANY
Stockholm
LITHUANIA 1940 to USSR
LATVIA 1940 to USSR
FINLAND 1917 independent
Murmansk
British, French Canadian, Italian, Serbian, American
Danzig
Tallinn
ESTONIA 1940 to USSR
Vienna
to Germany
Riga
Finns
Lithuanians
Latvians
Warsaw
POLAND
Pskov
Leningrad (Petrograd)
1
SLOVAKIA
HUNGARY
YUGOSLAVIA
Minsk
Belorussia 1919–21 independent
Poles
Archangel
Novaya Zemlya
Zhitomir
Smolensk
Shenkursk
ROMANIA
Romanians
Danube
2
Kiev
Kaluga
Moscow
Volga
Kotlas
Ukraine 1917–20 independent
Orel
BULGARIA
Odessa
Poltava
Kharkov
Vorkuta
French
Nikolayev
Gorki
Novyy Port
Yekaterinoslav
6
Istanbul
Voronezh
Tambov
Sevastopol
Kazan
Czechs
Simferopol
Mariupol
TURKEY
Black Sea
Rostov
Novocherkassk
Saratov
Simbirsk
Perm (Molotov)
British
Novorossisk
Samara (Kuybyshev)
Kolchak 1918–19
Ufa
Stalingrad
Yekaterinburg (Sverdlovsk)
Armenia 1918–21 independent
Cossacks, Ukrainians, White Russians
Cossacks
Chelyabinsk
Tobolsk
Orenburg
Tyumen
Batumi
Astrakhan
Magnitogorsk
URAL MOUNTAINS
Irtysh
Tbilisi
Georgia 1918–21 independent
Guryev
4
Azerbaijan 1918–20 independent
Omsk
Ob
Tigris
Euphrates
Tabriz
Baku
Caspian Sea
Tomsk
Kazalinsk
Akmolinsk
Novosibirsk
Aral Sea
British
Krasnovodsk
Karaganda
5
Stalinsk
Tehran
Amu Dar'ya
Lake Balkhash
Ashkhabad
Bukhara
Merv
IRAN
Tashkent
Frunze
Samarkand
Alma-Ata
Kushka
Herat
TIEN SHAN
AFGHANISTAN
Kabul

TIMELINE

Political change

1917 Ukraine, Finland. Latvia, Lithuania claim independence

1917 (Mar) First revolution; czar abdicates and provisional government is set up

1917 (Nov) The Bolsheviks seize power

1918 (Mar) Bolsheviks sign the Treaty of Brest-Litovsk

1918–21 Civil war between the "Whites" and the "Reds"

1918 The Caucasus states and Estonia declare independence

1920

1920 The Red Army invades Poland

1920–21 Ukraine, the Caucasus states and Turkestan are reconquered; Mongolia expels the Chinese

1922 Treaty of Rapallo: Soviet–German commercial and military agreement

1922–23 Formation of the Union of Soviet Socialist Republics (USSR)

1924 Death of Lenin

1926 The Soviet Union and Germany sign a neutrality pact

1930

1934 Start of the "great terror" after the assassination of Leningrad Party secretary Kirov

1934 The Soviet Union joins the League of Nations

1936–38 Height of the great purges in the Soviet Union

1936 Stalin's constitution is promulgated

1938 Purge of the armed forces by Stalin

1940

1939 Stalin signs the Nazi– Soviet pact with Hitler

1939 The Soviet Union occupies eastern Poland and Finland

1940 The Soviet Union occupies the Baltic states; Finland sues for peace

1941 Germany invades the Soviet Union

Economic change

1918 Depopulation of towns and cities in the civil war

1920–22 Peasant revolts occur throughout Russia

1921 The "new economic policy" is introduced

1928 The first Five Year Plan is announced

1929 The collectivization of agriculture is announced

1933 The second Five Year Plan is announced

1932–33 Famine in the Ukraine and central Asia

1939 The third Five Year Plan is announced

1920 1930 1940

free trade to encourage the peasants to produce more while the Bolsheviks (soon to be called Communists) tried to modernize the country.

Lenin died in 1924 without leaving an obvious successor, but Joseph Stalin used his post as general-secretary of the Communist Party to secure control of the state. The Communists now had to face the contradiction that they were a workers' government in a peasant country. In 1929 Stalin addressed this issue by ordering the collectivization of agriculture. Private trade was abolished and peasants forced to give up their private holdings and work on collective farms. Many responded by slaughtering their livestock and planting only enough grain to feed themselves. When this was requisitioned famine ensued, and millions were deported to the *gulag* (prison camps), resulting in around 14.5 million deaths.

Collectivization was intended to cow the peasantry and provide sufficient grain to support a massive program of industrialization as the Soviet Union was built into a modern economic power. Even during the famine, grain was being used to feed the city population and sold abroad to buy western technology. In 1928 Stalin announced the first Five Year Plan, with which he proposed that the Soviet Union should catch up with the west which, he claimed, was "50 to 100 years ahead". Production grew quickly, especially in the heavy and defense industries as old industrial centers were expanded and new ones created in remote regions.

Industrial development was undermined by the purges that Stalin unleashed in 1934. "Subversives" (in the first instance, old Bolsheviks) appeared in show trials, were convicted of fantastic crimes and shot, while millions of others faced deportation to labor camps. Stalin's war with his own population extended across the Soviet Union as he sought scapegoats for the failures of collectivization and industrialization to achieve the targets set out in the Plan. Fear and suspicion led to mass denunciations and the decimation of the upper levels of bureaucracy and Party.

By 1938 a purge of the army and navy began and the country lost most of its officer corps. The following year Stalin agreed the Nazi–Soviet pact with Hitler and subsequently occupied eastern Poland and the Baltic states. Stalin apparently believed that Hitler would not invade Russia until France and Britain were defeated; he also thought that fascism, which he saw as the highest form of capitalism, must presage the Communist revolution in Europe.

In 1941, though, Hitler did invade. The Soviet Union was in a better position to resist than Russia had been in 1914, despite the depredations of the purges. Communism had been established against all the odds in what had been Europe's most backward country. Stalin's policies, which were mainly an extension of those used by Lenin to win the civil war, were pursued at massive human cost and allowed the Communist Party to prevail.

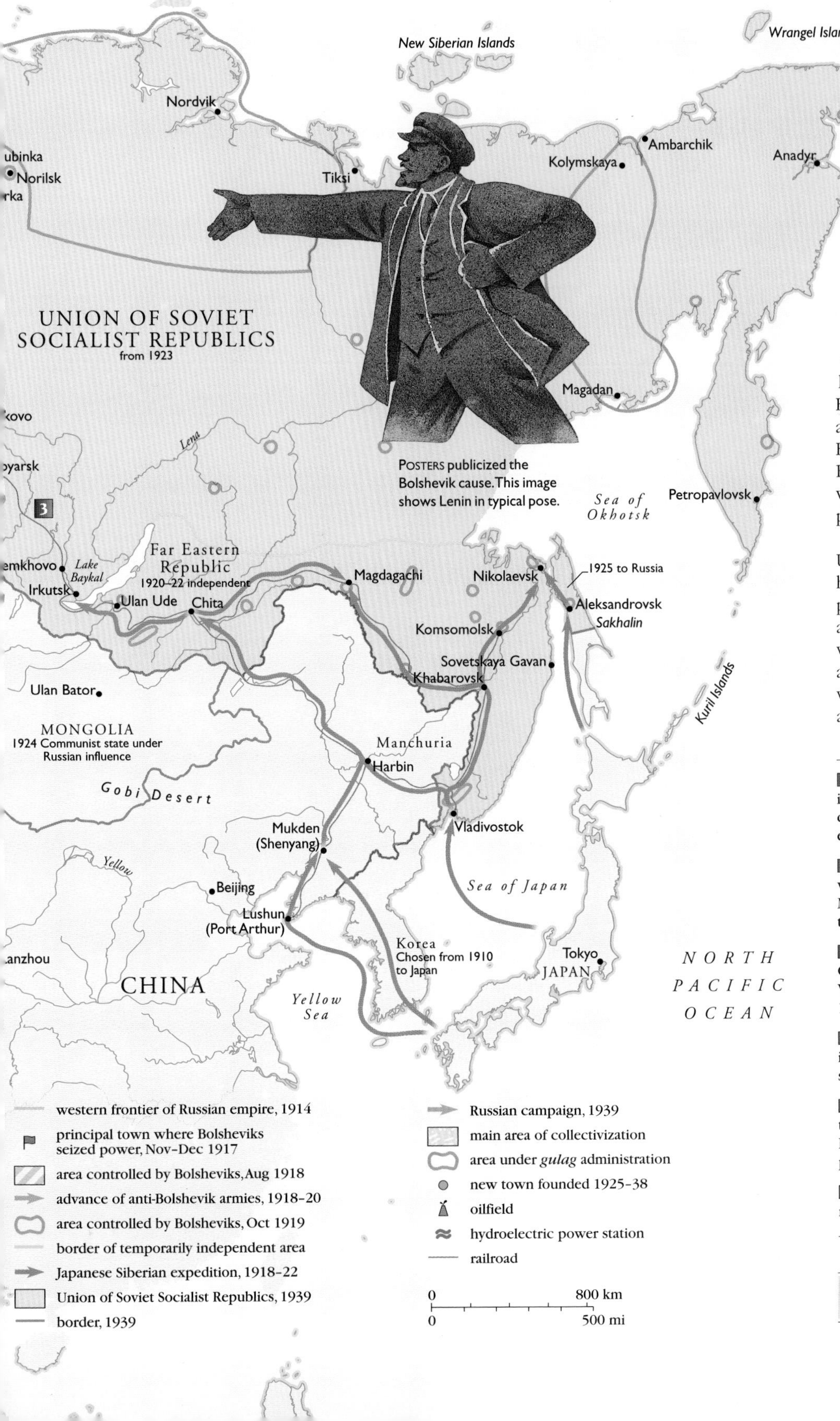

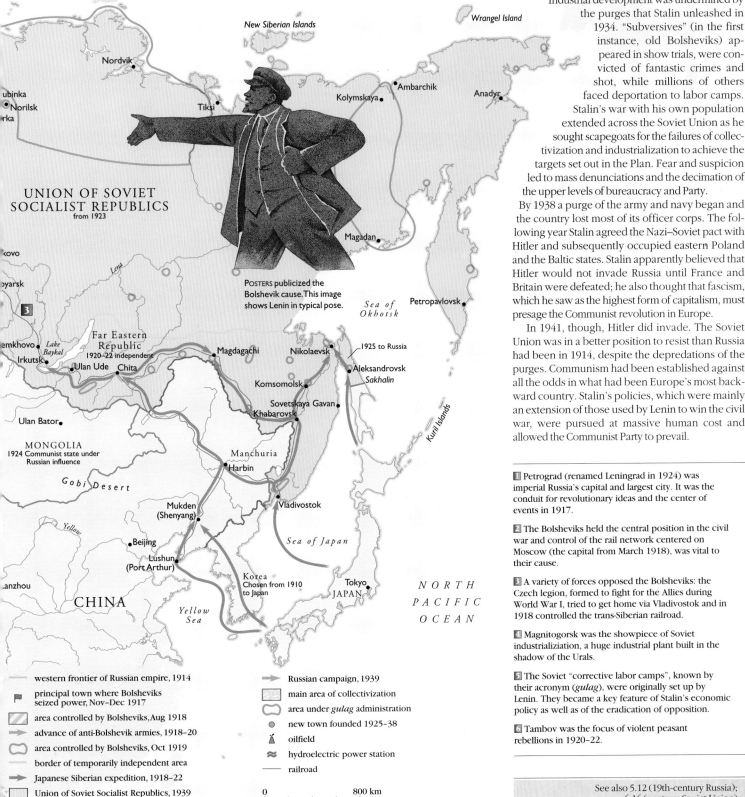

Posters publicized the Bolshevik cause. This image shows Lenin in typical pose.

- western frontier of Russian empire, 1914
- principal town where Bolsheviks seized power, Nov–Dec 1917
- area controlled by Bolsheviks, Aug 1918
- advance of anti-Bolshevik armies, 1918–20
- area controlled by Bolsheviks, Oct 1919
- border of temporarily independent area
- Japanese Siberian expedition, 1918–22
- Union of Soviet Socialist Republics, 1939
- border, 1939
- Russian campaign, 1939
- main area of collectivization
- area under *gulag* administration
- new town founded 1925–38
- oilfield
- hydroelectric power station
- railroad

0 – 800 km
0 – 500 mi

1 Petrograd (renamed Leningrad in 1924) was imperial Russia's capital and largest city. It was the conduit for revolutionary ideas and the center of events in 1917.

2 The Bolsheviks held the central position in the civil war and control of the rail network centered on Moscow (the capital from March 1918), was vital to their cause.

3 A variety of forces opposed the Bolsheviks: the Czech legion, formed to fight for the Allies during World War I, tried to get home via Vladivostok and in 1918 controlled the trans-Siberian railroad.

4 Magnitogorsk was the showpiece of Soviet industrializiation, a huge industrial plant built in the shadow of the Urals.

5 The Soviet "corrective labor camps", known by their acronym (*gulag*), were originally set up by Lenin. They became a key feature of Stalin's economic policy as well as of the eradication of opposition.

6 Tambov was the focus of violent peasant rebellions in 1920–22.

See also 5.12 (19th-century Russia); 6.16 (postwar Soviet Union)

6.16 The decline of the Soviet Union and Russia • 1941 – Present •

The German army took full advantage of the depradations wrought by the purges to advance far into Russia. Yet after the defeat of the Germans at Stalingrad and Kursk, the Soviet forces advanced to Berlin by April 1945. At the cost of 20 million lives, the Soviet Union emerged from the war a superpower; it took back the lands it had lost in 1918 and liberated most of east Europe, then incorporated the region into what was effectively an empire. In 1949 it became a nuclear power.

However, the basic problems of the Soviet Union remained: agricultural production was costly and weak, bureaucracy was rampant in state and industry, and order (especially over national minorities) was enforced by terror. The Red Army took some years to put down partisan armies in Ukraine and Poland, while the annexed Baltic states were also hostile to Soviet rule. The western republics had sustained the highest casualty rates of the war, yet Stalin dealt with resurgent nationalism by deporting some subject nationalities for alleged collaboration. An anti-Jewish campaign was begun in 1948 to widespread dismay; many greeted Stalin's death in 1953 with relief rather than sorrow.

Many political prisoners were freed shortly after and, in another sign of change, only Lavrenti Beria, head of the security forces, was executed after wrangling over the succession. Eventually Nikita Khrushchev emerged as the new Soviet head and he tried to rectify the problems of the Soviet Union, attacking Stalin in 1956. Khrushchev tried to enthuse, rather than coerce, the Soviet people, launching a "race to Communism" to be completed by 1980. He sought to improve the sluggish economy by producing consumer goods and the bureaucratic administration by decentralizing economic planning. Two notable failures in foreign policy were the Cuban missile crisis and the Sino-Soviet split. Planning for the possibility of war with NATO and China simultaneously proved a huge drain on Soviet resources. Heavy industry and rocket

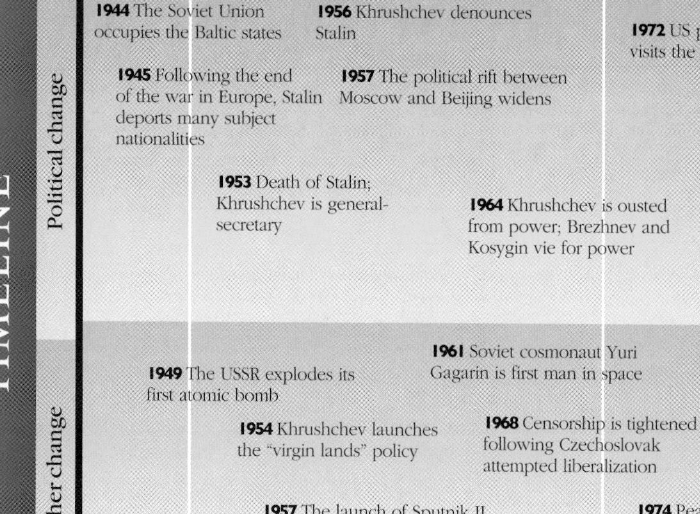

TIMELINE

Political change

1950 · 1970 · 1990

1944 The Soviet Union occupies the Baltic states

1945 Following the end of the war in Europe, Stalin deports many subject nationalities

1953 Death of Stalin; Khrushchev is general-secretary

1956 Khrushchev denounces Stalin

1957 The political rift between Moscow and Beijing widens

1964 Khrushchev is ousted from power; Brezhnev and Kosygin vie for power

1972 US president Nixon visits the USSR

1977 The "Brezhnev constitution" is introduced; Brezhnev becomes president

1982 Yuri Andropov becomes Soviet general secretary on death of Brezhnev

1985 Mikhail Gorbachev becomes Soviet leader

1989 The USSR withdraws from the war in Afghanistan

1990 Under a more liberal constitution, Gorbachev is elected president

1991 Gorbachev resigns after an attempted coup

1991 Dissolution of the USSR, formation of the CIS

2000 Vladimir Putin wins presidential election

2005 Viktor Yushchenko wins disputed presidential election in Ukraine

2008 Russia and Georgia go to war in South Ossettia

2008 Dmitry Medvedev bcomes president; Putin becomes prime minister

Other change

1949 The USSR explodes its first atomic bomb

1954 Khrushchev launches the "virgin lands" policy

1957 The launch of Sputnik II initiates the space race

1961 Soviet cosmonaut Yuri Gagarin is first man in space

1968 Censorship is tightened following Czechoslovak attempted liberalization

1974 Peasants are granted limited freedom of movement

1986 Chernobyl nuclear power plant blows up

1988 Nationality disturbances in Nagorno-Karabakh

1989 Miners' strikes in Donbass region threaten the Soviet regime

1999 After years of contraction the Russian economy improves following higher oil prices and a weakened ruble

2004 Chechen president Akhmad Kadyrov killed in terrorist attack

2004 School siege at Beslan in North Ossettia ends with 330 hostages dead

2006 Murder of campaigning Russian journalist Anna Politkovskaya

2006 Outspoken Kremlin critic Alexandr Litvinenko assassinated in London

2009 Russia interrupts gas supplies to Ukraine and Europe

1950 · 1970 · 1990

1964 Subsidies are paid to peasant farmers

technology (the Soviet Union astonished the world by launching the world's first artificial satellite, in 1957) absorbed money earmarked for other areas. Khrushchev could not remedy the problems of agriculture. Artificial fertilizers increased the yield of existing farms and helped cultivate untilled soil – the "virgin lands" campaign. The overfarming of land led to poor harvests and soil erosion; in 1963 the USSR was forced to import grain. Shortly thereafter, Khrushchev was deposed in a palace coup.

Under his successor Leonid Brezhnev, the Soviet Union atrophied. Brezhnev reversed Khrushchev's administrative policies and gave the bureaucracy the security it craved. Corruption became endemic and growth rates slowed. The climate of international détente evaporated with the Soviet invasion of Afghanistan and the election of the hawkish Ronald Reagan as president of the United States in 1980. Arms spending soared and the technological gap became ever more apparent. In 1985 Mikhail Gorbachev became the youngest general-secretary of the Party since Stalin. Gorbachev aimed to reduce arms spending and introduce reform. His policies of *Glasnost* ("openness") and *perestroika* ("restructuring") failed to bring a reformed Soviet system. Instead, the relaxation of censorship allowed grievances – social, economic and national – to surface.

The crucial area of dispute proved to be the nationalities question. The republics fixed onto the idea of independence, the Baltic states and the Caucasus leading the way; and the state was undermined in its heartland by the opposition of the Moscow-based reformist Boris Yeltsin. Elections took Gorbachev's reforms further than he had envisaged and led to the dissolution of the Soviet Union, despite a coup in 1991 by reactionaries. The Union was replaced by a loosely-based Commonwealth of Independent States (CIS). These faced drastic reorganization into market economies, and several – including the Russian Federation – faced civil war over nationality issues.

Vladimir Putin won the Russian presidency in 2000 partly on the promise of tough measures against Islamic Chechen separatists. More than 230,000 Chechens fled from the Russian army. Chechen rebels launched terrorist attacks on Russian targets, notably a Moscow theater in 2002 and a school at Beslan in 2004. After Putin stood down as president in 2008 – to become prime minister – his successor, Dmitry Medvedev, announced intentions to reduce Russian military operations in Chechnya. Medvedev also signalled his readiness to take a hardline stance when Russian troops fought Georgian forces in South Ossetia in support of the Ossetian majority. Within Russia, economic upheaval led to a rise in organized crime and gangsterism. Critics of corruption and the government were killed, including the journalist Anna Politkovskaya and the former spy Alexander Litvinenko, whose murder in London was denied by the Russian secret service.

New Siberian Islands
Wrangel Island
Taimyr (Dolgan–Nenets)
RUSSIAN FEDERATION
from 1991
Evenki
Bilibino
Chukot
Koryak
Magadan
Lena
ladkaya
asnoyarsk
Kansk
Ust Ordyn Buryat
Lake Baykal
Irkutsk
Chita
Agin Buryat
Olovyannaya
Svobodnyy
Sea of Okhotsk
Sakhalin
Kuril Islands
Ulan Bator
MONGOLIA
Birobijan Jewish Autonomous Region
Khabarovsk
Harbin
CHINA
Gobi Desert
Vladivostok
Mukden
Yellow
Beijing
NORTH KOREA
Pyongyang
Seoul
SOUTH KOREA
Sea of Japan
JAPAN
Tokyo
NORTH PACIFIC OCEAN
border of USSR, 1945
border, 2003
CIS member states
autonomous state within Russian Federation
border of autonomous ethnic area
territory disputed with China
uprising against Soviet intervention
ethnic unrest
area under Soviet influence at some time between 1945-91
ICBM base
cosmodrome
nuclear power station
area of "virgin land" policy
wheat production area
1991 date of independence from USSR
A. Albania
B-H. Bosnia-Herzegovina
C. Croatia
M. Macedonia (former Yugoslav Republic of)
S. Slovenia
S.M. Serbia and Montenegro (formerly Yugoslavia)
0 800 km
0 500 mi

YURI GAGARIN, in 1961 the first man in space, provided a propaganda coup worldwide for Khrushchev's USSR.

1 The murder of Politburo member Andrei Zhdanov in 1948 gave Stalin a chance to purge the Leningrad Communist Party. In 1991 the city rejected its Soviet past and reverted to its former name of St Petersburg.

2 Chernobyl's aging nuclear reactor exploded in 1986, causing much of west and north Europe to be exposed to radiation. The Soviet bureaucracy was blamed for allowing the accident to occur.

3 Demonstrations in Estonia in 1980–81 followed the success of the Solidarity movement in Poland, which was reported on Finnish television.

4 Chechen separatists seized more than 1,100 hostages at a school at Beslan, North Ossetia, in 2004. In the army rescue operation 334 hostages were killed, including 186 children.

5 In 2005 Victor Yuschenko became president of Ukraine after the "Orange Revolution," a popular movement that overturned the disputed election of a pro-Moscow president.

6 Bulgaria and Romania became the latest former members of the Warsaw Pact to join the EU, in 2007.

See also 6.08, 6.09 (World War II in Europe); 6.15 (USSR to 1941); 6.11 (Europe since 1991)

6.17 China: chaos to Communism • 1911 – 1949 •

The sudden but relatively bloodless revolution of 1911 led to the abdication of the Manchu emperor; the new republic was headed first by Sun Yixian (Sun Yat-sen) and then by Yuan Shikai (from 1912). Yuan used terror to consolidate his power and banned the Guomindang (KMT – Nationalist Party); the disillusioned Sun Yixiang sought refuge in Japan which was allied with Britain and France against Germany. Japanese troops landed on the Shandong peninsula, seized the German base at Qingdao and demanded concessions from Yuan. Yuan, seeing China threatened by Japan and by continuing uncertainty, planned a new dynasty with himself as emperor. After another rebellion, Yuan retreated to Beijing where he died in 1916.

China drifted into a state of chaos. Warlords pillaged the countryside. When floods or famine struck, there was no administration available to alleviate the effects. China sided with the Allies in World War I, but gained nothing at the Versailles peace conference. Japan kept its foothold in Shandong, while foreign governments held concessions along the coast as well as those bordering the Yangtze river. Chinese sovereignty and territorial rights were ignored. Students receptive to the teachings of Marx led nationalist demonstrations and helped form the Chinese Communist Party (CCP) in Shanghai.

The Soviet Union assisted in the formation of the CCP but supported Sun Yixiang's Guomindang and provided military and political guidance to emerging Guomindang leaders such as Jiang Jieshi (Chiang Kai-shek), who succeeded Sun Yixiang, and who built up a powerful base in Guangdong province. Jiang moved against the warlords in the north and devised the "white terror" to eliminate the Communists. The survivors fled into Jiangxi province where they soon came under Guomindang attack.

The Japanese invasion of Manchuria transformed the situation. Jiang was unwilling to commit himself to a major war against Japan, regarding the Japanese as a "disease of the skin" but the Communists as a "disease of the heart". He continued his war of extermination against the Communists and forced them to break out from their Jiangxi soviet. From here they began their Long March to Yan'an in Shaanxi province, during which Mao Zedong emerged as the CCP leader. Their retreat left Jiang master of the rich valley of the lower Yangtze. Here he attempted to force through an industrial and communications revolution, bringing in expertise from Fascist Italy, Nazi Germany and the United States.

In 1937 Japan launched a fullscale invasion of China from Manchuria, and Jiang shifted his capital from Nanjing to Chongqing. Since Jiang could hold out as long as he received supplies from the western Allies, Japan moved into French Indo-China to cut the rail link with Chongqing. Jiang used conscripted armies equipped with American materiel, and cajoled and bribed warlords to fight on his behalf. His supplies arrived via the Burma Road (until the Japanese cut it in 1942), via the Ledo Road during 1945 and by Allied transport aircraft flying over the mountains east of the Brahmaputra. In the north Mao Zedong organized a guerrilla war against the Japanese but the fighting remained local. When the Americans built up a bomber force in west China, the Japanese overran a great deal of China in an attempt to destroy the US bases.

For the Chinese people, World War II was merely an interruption in the protracted civil war. The Japanese surrender gave the Communists and the Nationalists the chance to compete for Manchuria. At this point, however, the US terminated all aid to both sides. Inflation, corruption and food shortages soon wrecked civilian morale and despair transferred to the Nationalist soldiers. In 1948, when US president Truman agreed to restore aid supplies, the Communist People's Liberation Army (PLA) was already moving south. The PLA crossed the Yangtze in 1949 and, as Nationalist armies crumbled, began a triumphal march through the cities of southern China. By September the civil war was virtually over and Mao Zedong announced the final victory over foreign and domestic enemies, and the establishment of the People's Republic of China with himself as chairman of the central government.

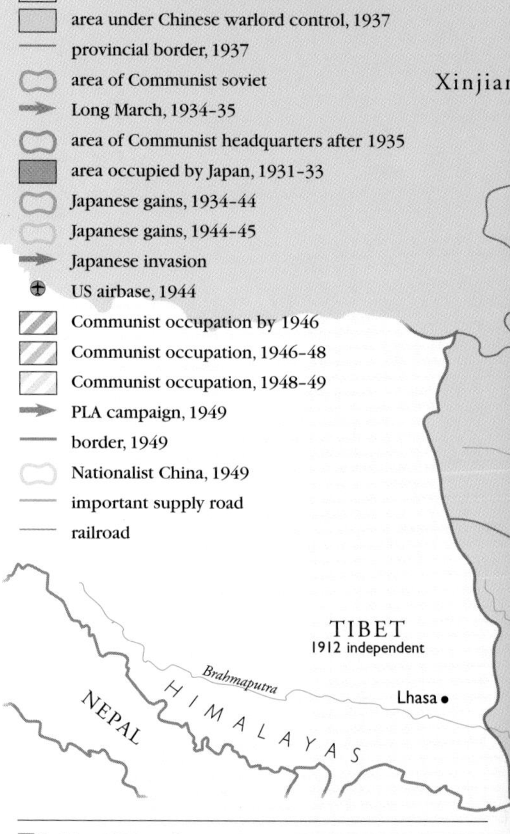
strike or demonstration, 1919
Nationalist and pro-Nationalist "Northern Expedition", 1926–28
area under Nationalist China control, 1937
area under Chinese warlord control, 1937
provincial border, 1937
area of Communist soviet
Long March, 1934–35
area of Communist headquarters after 1935
area occupied by Japan, 1931–33
Japanese gains, 1934–44
Japanese gains, 1944–45
Japanese invasion
US airbase, 1944
Communist occupation by 1946
Communist occupation, 1946–48
Communist occupation, 1948–49
PLA campaign, 1949
border, 1949
Nationalist China, 1949
important supply road
railroad
Xinjiang
TIBET
1912 independent
Brahmaputra
Lhasa
NEPAL
HIMALAYAS

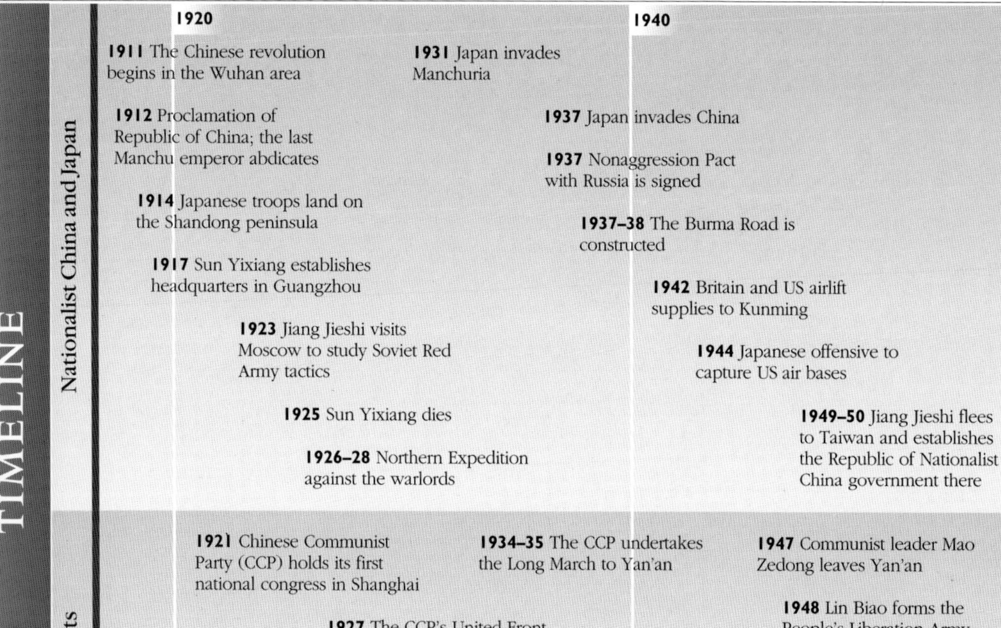
TIMELINE
Nationalist China and Japan
1920
1940
1911 The Chinese revolution begins in the Wuhan area
1912 Proclamation of Republic of China; the last Manchu emperor abdicates
1914 Japanese troops land on the Shandong peninsula
1917 Sun Yixiang establishes headquarters in Guangzhou
1923 Jiang Jieshi visits Moscow to study Soviet Red Army tactics
1925 Sun Yixiang dies
1926–28 Northern Expedition against the warlords
1931 Japan invades Manchuria
1937 Japan invades China
1937 Nonaggression Pact with Russia is signed
1937–38 The Burma Road is constructed
1942 Britain and US airlift supplies to Kunming
1944 Japanese offensive to capture US air bases
1949–50 Jiang Jieshi flees to Taiwan and establishes the Republic of Nationalist China government there
Communists
1921 Chinese Communist Party (CCP) holds its first national congress in Shanghai
1927 The CCP's United Front with the Guomindang against the warlords collapses with the start of the "white terror"
1930–31 The CCP survives three Nationalist attacks
1934–35 The CCP undertakes the Long March to Yan'an
1947 Communist leader Mao Zedong leaves Yan'an
1948 Lin Biao forms the People's Liberation Army (PLA) and campaigns successfully in Manchuria
1949 PLA captures Beijing
1949 Mao Zedong proclaims the People's Republic of China
1920
1940

1 In May 1919 students at Beijing University protested fruitlessly against the disregard of Chinese interests at the Versailles peace conference.

2 The Communists set up a Peasants' Union in 1922 near Haifeng in eastern Guangdong to mobilize rural hatred of landlords and to build a peasants' army.

3 Nanjing was the capital of Jiang Jieshi's Guomindang government from 1928–37; Jiang presented himself as "China's Hitler or China's Stalin".

4 More than 100,000 Communists under Mao Zedong trekked over 8,000 km (5,000 miles) between October 1934 and October 1935 in order to escape Guomindang encirclement.

5 At Xuzhou in December 1948 to January 1949, the Communists achieved a decisive victory over a larger, better equipped Nationalist army.

6 The Battle of Kaifeng in 1948 (a brief Nationalist victory) was the first "positional" battle between the Nationalists and Communists.

7 Jiang Jieshi planned his final stand against the Communists at Xichang in 1949, but then decided to flee to Taiwan.

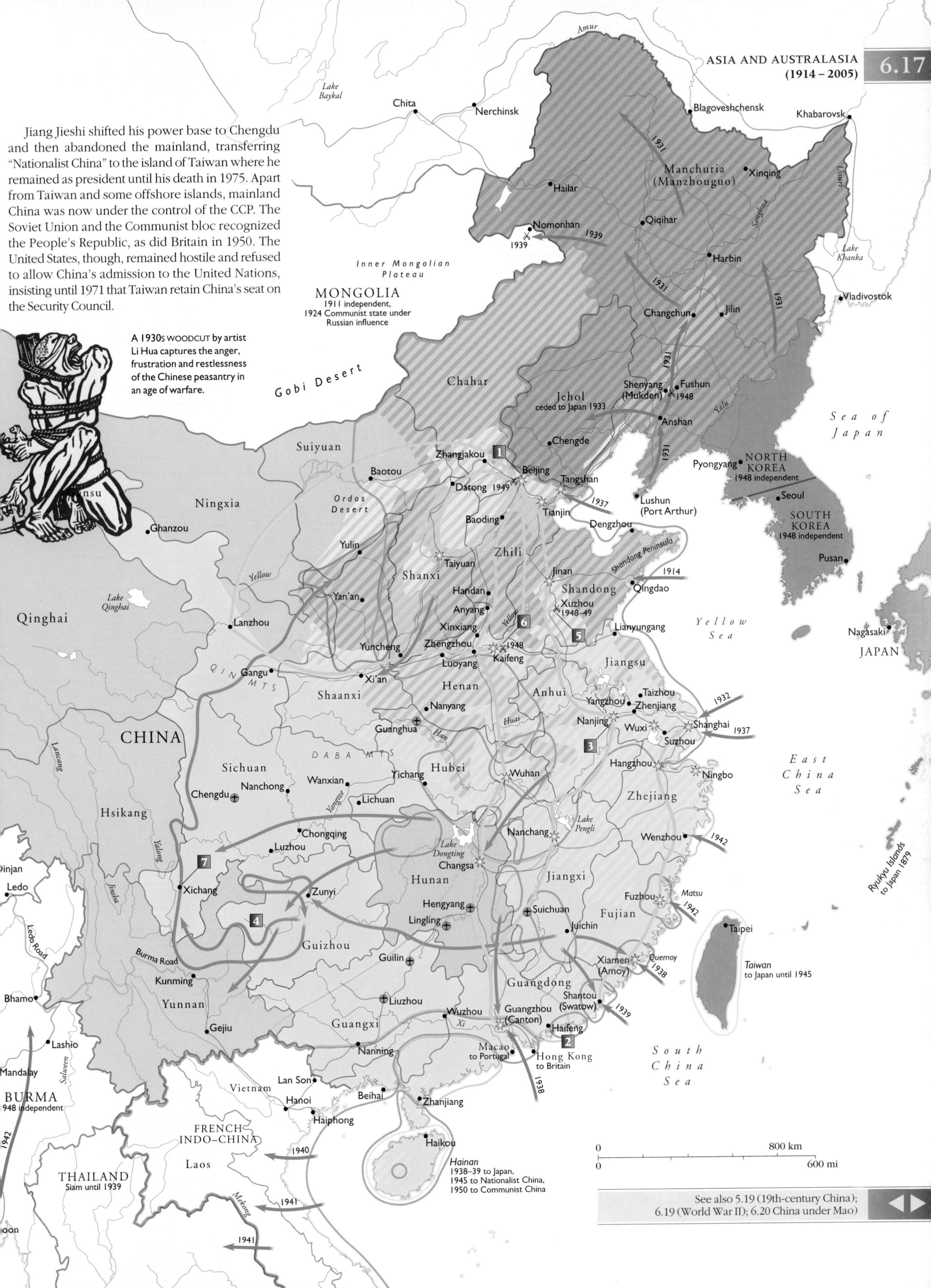

Amur
Lake Baykal
Chita
Nerchinsk
Blagoveshchensk
Khabarovsk
Manchuria (Manzhouguo)
Xinqing
Ussuri
Hailar
Qiqihar
Songhua
Nomonhan
1939
1931
Harbin
Lake Khanka
Inner Mongolian Plateau
MONGOLIA
1911 independent,
1924 Communist state under Russian influence
Changchun
Jilin
Vladivostok
Gobi Desert
Chahar
Jehol
ceded to Japan 1933
Shenyang (Mukden)
Fushun
1948
Yalu
Anshan
Sea of Japan
Chengde
Suiyuan
Zhangjiakou
Baotou
Beijing
Tangshan
Pyongyang
NORTH KOREA
1948 independent
Datong
1949
Tianjin
1937
Lushun (Port Arthur)
Seoul
Ningxia
Ordos Desert
Baoding
Dengzhou
SOUTH KOREA
1948 independent
Ghanzou
Yulin
Zhili
Shandong Peninsula
Pusan
Taiyuan
Yellow
Shanxi
Jinan
Shandong
1914
Qingdao
Lake Qinghai
Yan'an
Handan
Xuzhou
1948–49
Qinghai
Lanzhou
Anyang
Yellow Sea
Xinxiang
Lianyungang
Nagasaki
JAPAN
Yuncheng
Zhengzhou
Kaifeng
Luoyang
Jiangsu
Gangu
QIN MTS
Xi'an
Henan
Shaanxi
Anhui
Taizhou
Yangzhou
Zhenjiang
1932
Nanyang
Nanjing
Wuxi
Shanghai
Huai
Guanghua
Han
Suzhou
CHINA
Lancang
DABA MTS
Sichuan
Hubei
Hangzhou
Ningbo
East China Sea
Nanchong
Wanxian
Yichang
Wuhan
Chengdu
Lichuan
Zhejiang
Hsikang
Yangtze
Lake Pengli
Nanchang
Chongqing
Wenzhou
1942
Luzhou
Yalong
Lake Dongting
Changsa
Ryukyu Islands to Japan 1879
Ledo
Xichang
Hunan
Jiangxi
Zunyi
Matsu
Fuzhou
Jinsha
Hengyang
Suichuan
Fujian
Lingling
Juichin
Taipei
Ledo Road
Guizhou
Guilin
Xiamen (Amoy)
Quemoy
1938
Burma Road
Taiwan
to Japan until 1945
Kunming
Guangdong
Bhamo
Yunnan
Liuzhou
Shantou (Swatow)
Guangzhou (Canton)
Wuzhou
Xi
Guangxi
Gejiu
Haifeng
Lashio
Nanning
Macao to Portugal
Hong Kong to Britain
South China Sea
Salween
Mandalay
Lan Son
BURMA
1948 independent
Vietnam
Hanoi
Beihai
Zhanjiang
Haiphong
FRENCH INDO-CHINA
Haikou
1940
Laos
THAILAND
Siam until 1939
Hainan
1938–39 to Japan,
1945 to Nationalist China,
1950 to Communist China
1941
Mekong
0
800 km
600 mi

Jiang Jieshi shifted his power base to Chengdu and then abandoned the mainland, transferring "Nationalist China" to the island of Taiwan where he remained as president until his death in 1975. Apart from Taiwan and some offshore islands, mainland China was now under the control of the CCP. The Soviet Union and the Communist bloc recognized the People's Republic, as did Britain in 1950. The United States, though, remained hostile and refused to allow China's admission to the United Nations, insisting until 1971 that Taiwan retain China's seat on the Security Council.

A 1930s WOODCUT by artist Li Hua captures the anger, frustration and restlessness of the Chinese peasantry in an age of warfare.

See also 5.19 (19th-century China); 6.19 (World War II); 6.20 China under Mao)

The Russo-Japanese War of 1904–05 gave Japan protectorate authority over Korea and the lease of Chinese territory in south Manchuria. From these bases the army looked to consolidate its influence in Manchuria and north China. By this time, a new and increasingly militant anti-imperialist nationalism was developing among young Chinese intellectuals, merchants and soldiers. This development was echoed elsewhere in the region, for example in the growth of Indian and Vietnamese national movements. In the case of China, resentment after 1905 was clearly focussed on Japan as the other western powers were preoccupied with European politics and hoped merely to hold onto their Asian interests.

Tokyo's decision to enter World War I was driven as much by interests in China – where the Manchu dynasty had finally fallen three years earlier – as by the desire to help its ally Britain. In August 1914 Japan issued an ultimatum to Germany to hand over territories in Shandong province. Japan then took the German outpost of Qingdao; the whole province was eventually occupied.

As one of the victorious nations, Japan was invited to attend the Versailles peace conference in 1919 and retained the former German territory in Shandong. However, this conference marked a turning point in the position of the European powers in east Asia – Britain, France, the Netherlands, and, to a lesser extent, Portugal. All had been weakened by the war, while the revolution of 1917 ended Russia's imperialism. The League of Nations, created in the aftermath of war, adopted a policy generally critical of colonialism. In the interwar years Britain, while publicly supporting its empire, privately explored ways to enable the Asian colonies to achieve self-governing Dominion status (like New Zealand, since 1907) or Commonwealth status (like Australia). The Dutch, too, were beginning to consider ways of passing power to the native populations.

Nationalist movements in the colonies were given impetus by the severe effects of the worldwide depression of the 1930s and the collapse of European prestige wrought by the carnage of World War I. In India, the Indian National Congress, led by Jawaharlal Nehru and Mohandas "Mahatma" Gandhi, organized a mass self-rule movement in the 1920s and 1930s. In Burma, which was separated from India and given a form of responsible government in 1937, nationalist demands were heightened by the depression. The Dutch East Indies experienced a Communist uprising in 1926–27, and French Indo-China also saw Communist-inspired strikes and rural unrest with the overall objective of national independence. Neither the French nor the Dutch made significant concessions, and – except in India – the nationalist movements appeared divided and unable to make a lasting impression. The United States, though, appeared to support the nationalists, and in 1935 promised independence for its own colony in the Philippines within ten years.

The general unrest in east and southeast Asia led Japan into further military expansion from 1931. After establishing the puppet state of Manzhouguo in Manchuria, however, Japan was criticized by the League of Nations and quit this body in protest. The resulting international isolation made Japan turn for new allies to Germany and Italy and, in China, to pursue an even more aggressive and uncompromising policy toward the Nationalist government which was already engaged in civil war with Chinese Communists. In mid-1937 Japan and China engaged unofficially in a war which Japanese generals confidently promised would be over by the end of the year. Japan's bombing of cities and the massacre of civilians as its forces took the Nationalist cities of Shanghai and Nanjing brought the war to the attention of the world, heightening criticism in the west.

In 1939 Japanese forces landed in French Indo-China to cut off supply routes to the Chinese Nationalists. After the fall of France to Hitler in 1940, the Japanese went on to occupy most of the colony, while maintaining a French administration. Politically, the Japanese exploited the anti-European feeling among the nationalist groups, promising a form of independence such as Burma had been given. Economic prosperity was similarly promised in the Japanese-sponsored Greater East Asian Co-Prosperity Sphere. Some – such as the Indian leader

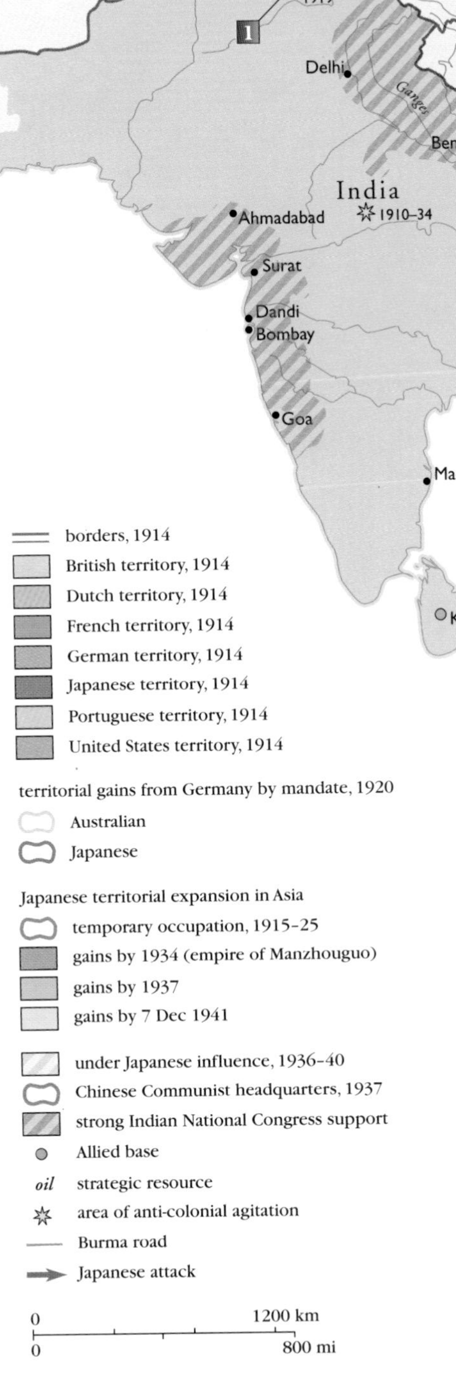
Amritsar 1919
TIBET
1
Delhi
NEP
Ganges
Benares
India
1910–34
Ahmadabad
Surat
Dandi
Bombay
Goa
Madras
Kandy
borders, 1914
British territory, 1914
Dutch territory, 1914
French territory, 1914
German territory, 1914
Japanese territory, 1914
Portuguese territory, 1914
United States territory, 1914
territorial gains from Germany by mandate, 1920
Australian
Japanese
Japanese territorial expansion in Asia
temporary occupation, 1915–25
gains by 1934 (empire of Manzhouguo)
gains by 1937
gains by 7 Dec 1941
under Japanese influence, 1936–40
Chinese Communist headquarters, 1937
strong Indian National Congress support
Allied base
oil strategic resource
area of anti-colonial agitation
Burma road
Japanese attack
0 1200 km
0 800 mi

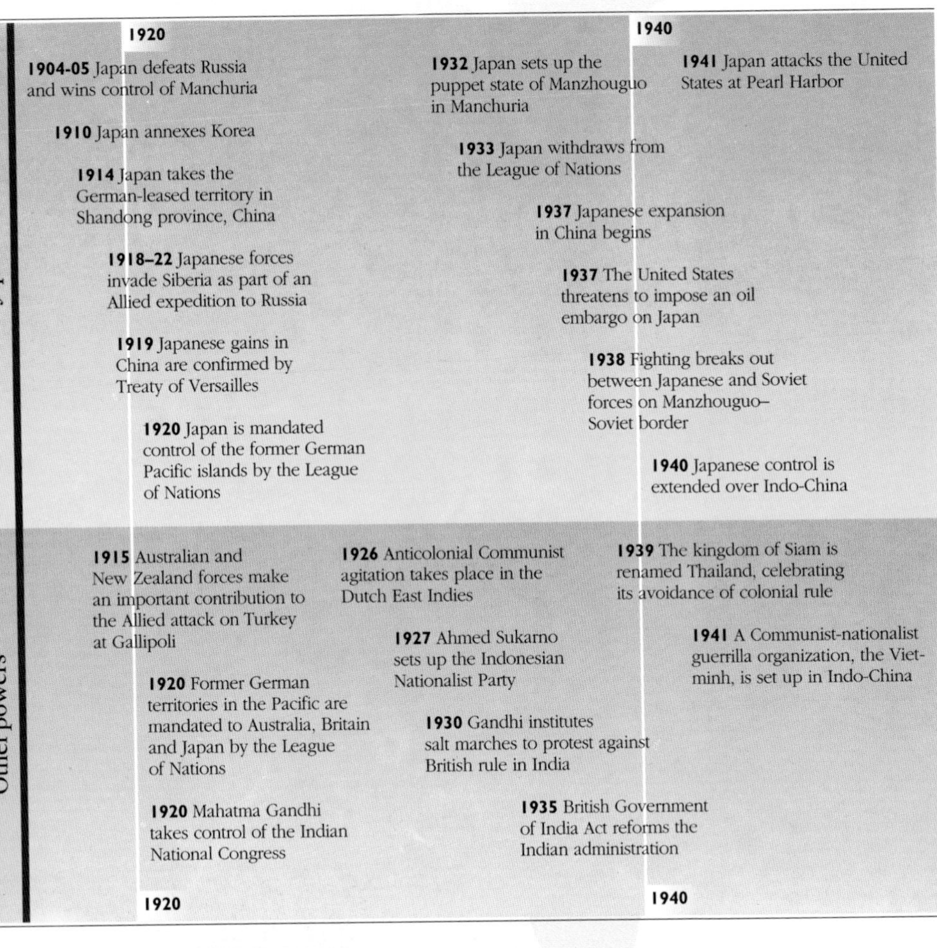
TIMELINE
1920
1940
Japan
1904-05 Japan defeats Russia and wins control of Manchuria
1910 Japan annexes Korea
1914 Japan takes the German-leased territory in Shandong province, China
1918–22 Japanese forces invade Siberia as part of an Allied expedition to Russia
1919 Japanese gains in China are confirmed by Treaty of Versailles
1920 Japan is mandated control of the former German Pacific islands by the League of Nations
1932 Japan sets up the puppet state of Manzhouguo in Manchuria
1933 Japan withdraws from the League of Nations
1937 Japanese expansion in China begins
1937 The United States threatens to impose an oil embargo on Japan
1938 Fighting breaks out between Japanese and Soviet forces on Manzhouguo–Soviet border
1940 Japanese control is extended over Indo-China
1941 Japan attacks the United States at Pearl Harbor
Other powers
1915 Australian and New Zealand forces make an important contribution to the Allied attack on Turkey at Gallipoli
1920 Former German territories in the Pacific are mandated to Australia, Britain and Japan by the League of Nations
1920 Mahatma Gandhi takes control of the Indian National Congress
1926 Anticolonial Communist agitation takes place in the Dutch East Indies
1927 Ahmed Sukarno sets up the Indonesian Nationalist Party
1930 Gandhi institutes salt marches to protest against British rule in India
1935 British Government of India Act reforms the Indian administration
1939 The kingdom of Siam is renamed Thailand, celebrating its avoidance of colonial rule
1941 A Communist-nationalist guerrilla organization, the Viet-minh, is set up in Indo-China
1920
1940

Subhas Chandra Bose – were persuaded by this message; others thought that European imperialism was being replaced by a Japanese variety.

The United States proposed an embargo on imports from Japan in 1937, and banned exports to Japan of scrap iron (1940) and oil (1941). The British and Dutch supported the oil embargo, whereupon Japan viewed the oil-rich Dutch East Indies, and the tin- and rubber-producing British colonies of Burma and Malaya as alternative sources of raw materials. Japan realized that any aggression against these would lead to war with the United States itself, but when diplomacy failed Japan attacked the United States naval base of Pearl Harbor and the Philippines in December 1941, then swept down into Dutch and British colonial southeast Asia.

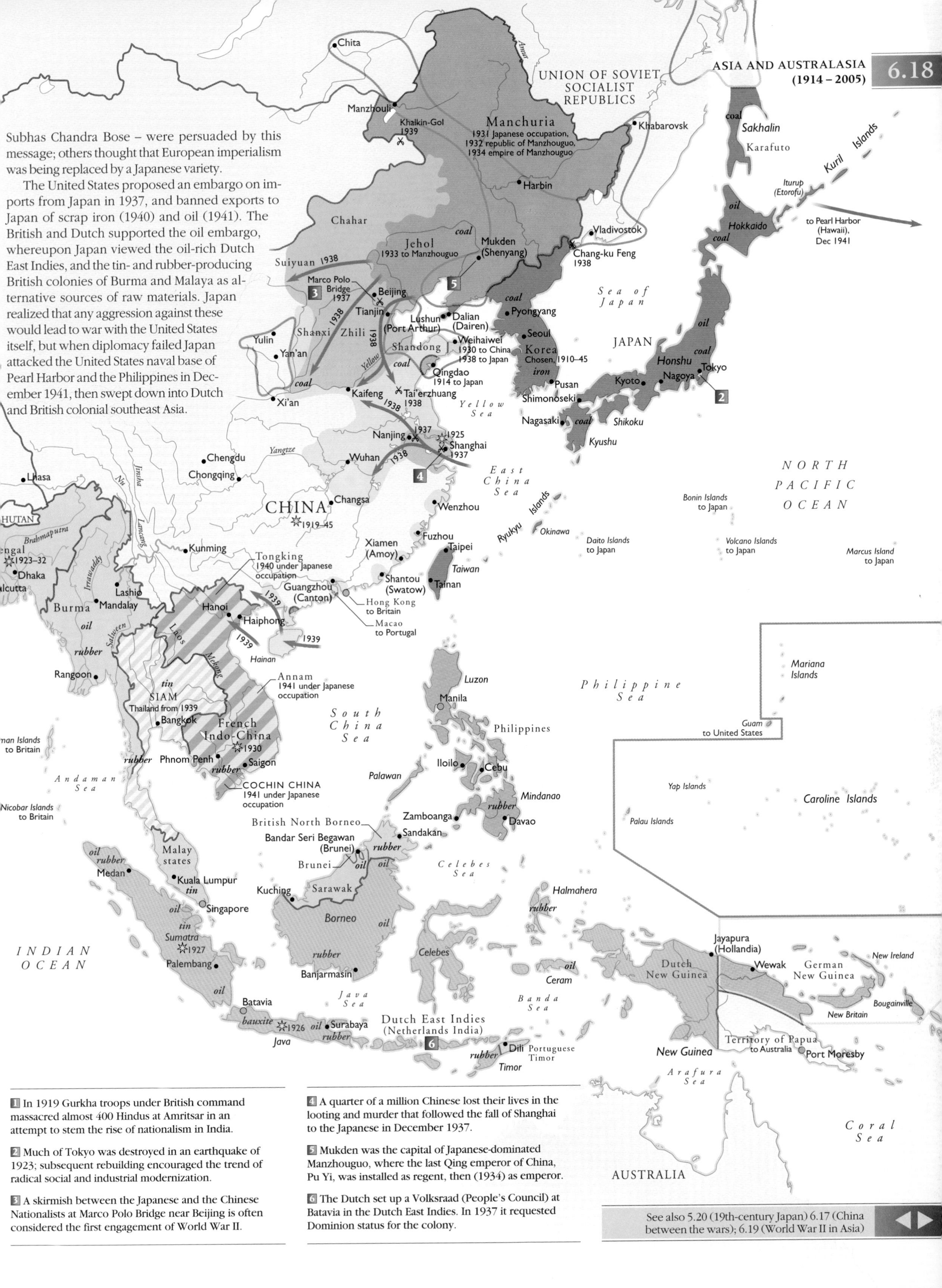

Chita
UNION OF SOVIET SOCIALIST REPUBLICS
Amur
Manzhouli
Khalkin-Gol 1939
Manchuria
1931 Japanese occupation, 1932 republic of Manzhouguo, 1934 empire of Manzhouguo
Khabarovsk
Sakhalin
Karafuto
coal
Kuril Islands
Iturup (Etorofu)
Harbin
Chahar
Jehol
1933 to Manzhouguo
Mukden (Shenyang)
Vladivostok
Chang-ku Feng 1938
Hokkaido
oil
to Pearl Harbor (Hawaii), Dec 1941
Suiyuan 1938
Marco Polo Bridge 1937
Beijing
Tianjin
Lushun (Port Arthur)
Dalian (Dairen)
Pyongyang
Seoul
Sea of Japan
JAPAN
Yulin
Yan'an
Shanxi
Zhili
Shandong
Weihaiwei 1930 to China 1938 to Japan
Korea Chosen, 1910–45
iron
Honshu
Tokyo
Nagoya
Kyoto
Qingdao 1914 to Japan
Pusan
Shimonoseki
Xi'an
Kaifeng
Tai'erzhuang 1938
Yellow Sea
Nagasaki
Shikoku
Kyushu
Nanjing
1937
1925
Shanghai 1937
Chengdu
Yangtze
Wuhan
Chongqing
Lhasa
Jinsha
Nu
East China Sea
NORTH PACIFIC OCEAN
CHINA
1919–45
Changsa
Wenzhou
Ryukyu Islands
Okinawa
Bonin Islands to Japan
BHUTAN
Brahmaputra
Bengal 1923–32
Dhaka
Calcutta
Kunming
Lancang
Tongking 1940 under Japanese occupation
Xiamen (Amoy)
Fuzhou
Taipei
Taiwan
Tainan
Daito Islands to Japan
Volcano Islands to Japan
Marcus Island to Japan
Irrawaddy
Lashio
Mandalay
Burma
Guangzhou (Canton)
Shantou (Swatow)
Hong Kong to Britain
Macao to Portugal
Hanoi
Haiphong
Laos
1939
Hainan
Salween
Mekong
rubber
tin
Rangoon
Annam 1941 under Japanese occupation
Luzon
Manila
Philippine Sea
Mariana Islands
SIAM Thailand from 1939
Bangkok
French Indo-China
1930
South China Sea
Philippines
Guam to United States
Andaman Islands to Britain
Phnom Penh
Saigon
Palawan
Iloilo
Cebu
Andaman Sea
COCHIN CHINA 1941 under Japanese occupation
Mindanao
Yap Islands
Caroline Islands
Nicobar Islands to Britain
British North Borneo
Zamboanga
Davao
Palau Islands
Bandar Seri Begawan (Brunei)
Sandakan
Malay states
Medan
Brunei
Celebes Sea
Kuala Lumpur
Kuching
Sarawak
Halmahera
Singapore
Borneo
Sumatra 1927
INDIAN OCEAN
Palembang
Celebes
Banjarmasin
Jayapura (Hollandia)
Wewak
German New Guinea
New Ireland
Dutch New Guinea
Ceram
Java Sea
Banda Sea
Bougainville
New Britain
Batavia
bauxite
1926
Surabaya
Java
Dutch East Indies (Netherlands India)
Dili
Portuguese Timor
Timor
New Guinea
Territory of Papua to Australia
Port Moresby
Arafura Sea
Coral Sea
AUSTRALIA

1 In 1919 Gurkha troops under British command massacred almost 400 Hindus at Amritsar in an attempt to stem the rise of nationalism in India.

2 Much of Tokyo was destroyed in an earthquake of 1923; subsequent rebuilding encouraged the trend of radical social and industrial modernization.

3 A skirmish between the Japanese and the Chinese Nationalists at Marco Polo Bridge near Beijing is often considered the first engagement of World War II.

4 A quarter of a million Chinese lost their lives in the looting and murder that followed the fall of Shanghai to the Japanese in December 1937.

5 Mukden was the capital of Japanese-dominated Manzhouguo, where the last Qing emperor of China, Pu Yi, was installed as regent, then (1934) as emperor.

6 The Dutch set up a Volksraad (People's Council) at Batavia in the Dutch East Indies. In 1937 it requested Dominion status for the colony.

See also 5.20 (19th-century Japan) 6.17 (China between the wars); 6.19 (World War II in Asia)

In late 1941 the Japanese planned a series of synchronized attacks to secure control in the Pacific and Asia. Prime minister Hideki Tojo and Isoroko Yamamoto, head of the navy and mastermind behind the attack on the United States naval base of Pearl Harbor in Hawaii, sought to create a defense perimeter from the Kurils to the Dutch East Indies and containing all the oil, rubber and rice Japan would need for survival. Yamamoto promised a string of victories in the first six months.

The surprise attack on Pearl Harbor on 7 December 1941 destroyed the US Pacific battlefleet, but all the large aircraft carriers were at sea. Their survival was to be of crucial significance. By the spring of 1942 Japan had taken the Philippines (attacked the same day as Pearl Harbor), ejected the Dutch from the East Indies, driven the British from Hong Kong, Malaya (including the great naval base of Singapore) and most of Burma, and forced the Americans to surrender Guam, Wake Island, Attu and Kiska. At this point, Japan suffered a setback at the Battle of the Coral Sea as the Japanese attempted to take the Allied base at Port Moresby on New Guinea (thus isolating Australia). Further advances across the Pacific were decisively halted when their fleet was defeated by the US Navy at the Battle of Midway.

Allied strategy for the destruction of Japan's new empire depended upon the immense resources and manpower that the United States could bring to bear. The plan required the British, who had suffered during their long retreat in Burma, to block a Japanese invasion of India, undertake offensives in the Arakan and recapture Rangoon. They would have limited US assistance and cooperation from Chinese Nationalist armies from Yunnan. These forces came under a new southeast Asia command headed by Lord Louis Mountbatten. US forces in the south and southwest Pacific under General Douglas MacArthur and Admiral William Halsey were planned to retake New Guinea and the Solomons. Admiral Nimitz would assemble fresh task forces at Pearl Harbor and attack Japanese-held islands in the central and north Pacific. Key bases would be established on the islands and in China for an air assault upon Japan.

In the north Pacific, US and Canadian troops attacked in the Aleutians and forced the Japanese back. In the central Pacific, US marines assaulted the tiny coral atoll of Tarawa, 5,000 kilometers (3,000 miles) from Japan. They wiped out its Japanese and Korean defenders, but only after three days of bitter fighting. After this experience, the Americans decided to ignore unimportant islands and by-pass many Japanese bases. They fought and won the Battle of the Philippine Sea and then targeted Kwajalein and Eniwetok in the Marshalls. They went on to occupy Saipan, Guam and Tinian, the bases from which in 1944–45 US B-29 bombers undertook their raids on Japanese cities.

US forces returned to the Philippines and fought the Battle of Leyte Gulf, during which the Japanese navy was effectively destroyed. The Battle of Iwo Jima, the fiercest of the war, provided the Americans with a base for their fighter aircraft capable of escorting the bombers to Japan and back. About 500,000

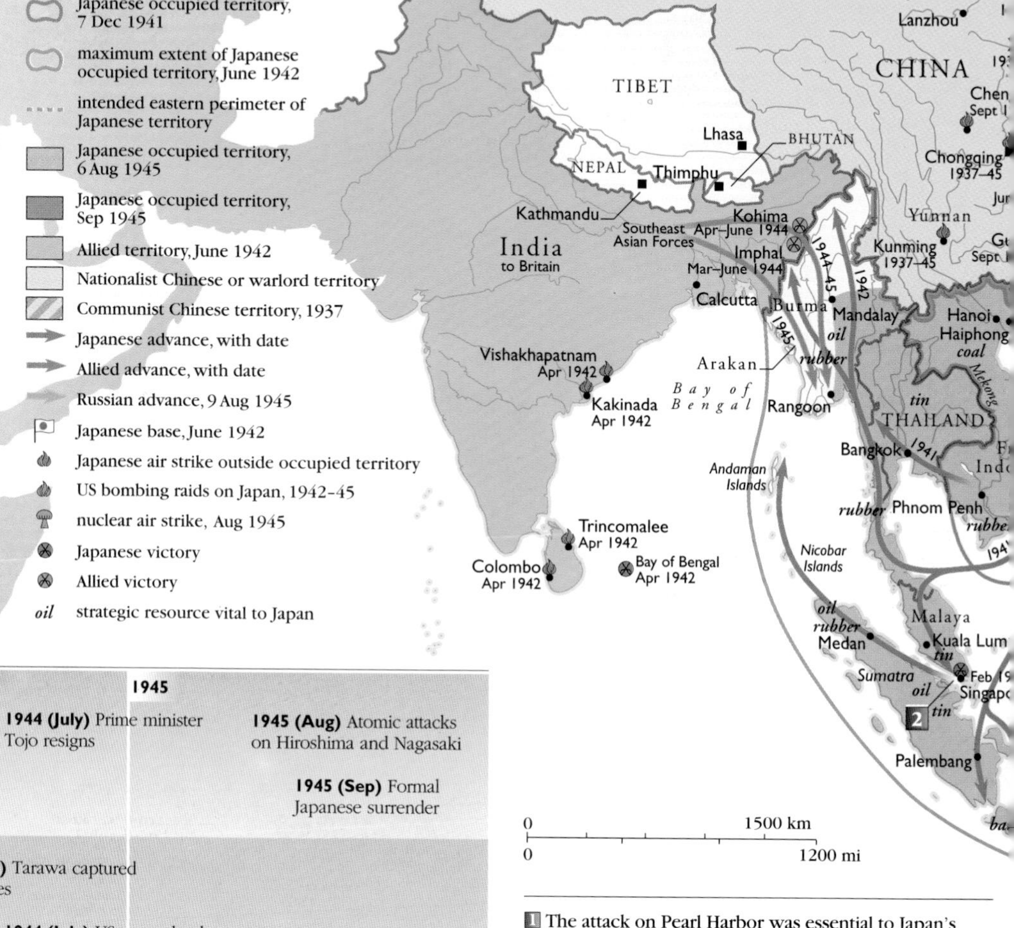
borders, 7 Dec 1941
Japanese occupied territory, 7 Dec 1941
maximum extent of Japanese occupied territory, June 1942
intended eastern perimeter of Japanese territory
Japanese occupied territory, 6 Aug 1945
Japanese occupied territory, Sep 1945
Allied territory, June 1942
Nationalist Chinese or warlord territory
Communist Chinese territory, 1937
Japanese advance, with date
Allied advance, with date
Russian advance, 9 Aug 1945
Japanese base, June 1942
Japanese air strike outside occupied territory
US bombing raids on Japan, 1942–45
nuclear air strike, Aug 1945
Japanese victory
Allied victory
oil strategic resource vital to Japan
TIBET
CHINA
Lanzhou
Chen Sept
Lhasa
BHUTAN
NEPAL
Thimphu
Chongqing 1937–45
Kathmandu
Kohima
Southeast Asian Forces
Apr–June 1944
Yunnan
India
to Britain
Imphal Mar–June 1944
Kunming 1937–45
Calcutta
Burma
Mandalay
oil
Hanoi
Haiphong
coal
Vishakhapatnam Apr 1942
Arakan
rubber
Bay of Bengal
Kakinada Apr 1942
Rangoon
tin
THAILAND
Bangkok
Andaman Islands
rubber
Phnom Penh
Trincomalee Apr 1942
Colombo Apr 1942
Bay of Bengal Apr 1942
Nicobar Islands
oil
rubber
Medan
Malaya
Kuala Lum
tin
Sumatra
oil
tin
Singapo
Palembang
0 1500 km
0 1200 mi

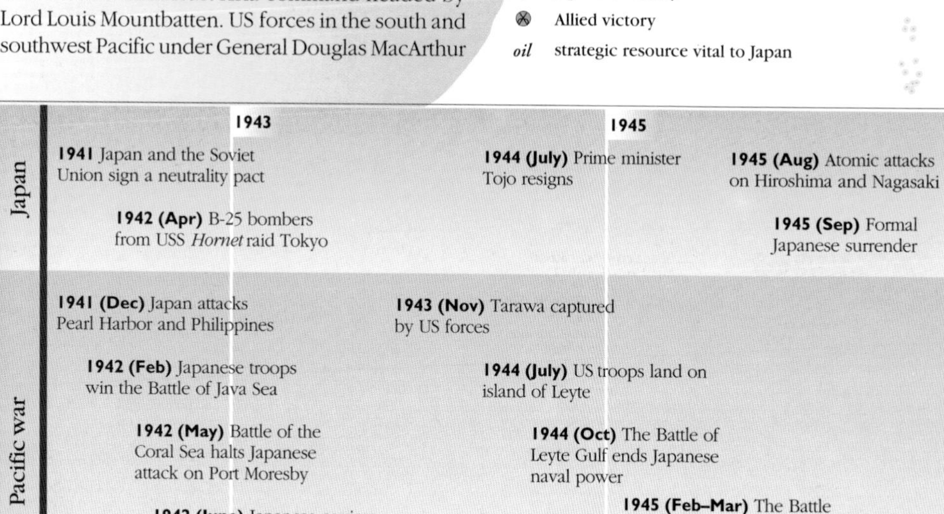

TIMELINE

Japan

- **1941** Japan and the Soviet Union sign a neutrality pact
- **1942 (Apr)** B-25 bombers from USS *Hornet* raid Tokyo
- **1944 (July)** Prime minister Tojo resigns
- **1945 (Aug)** Atomic attacks on Hiroshima and Nagasaki
- **1945 (Sep)** Formal Japanese surrender

Pacific war

- **1941 (Dec)** Japan attacks Pearl Harbor and Philippines
- **1942 (Feb)** Japanese troops win the Battle of Java Sea
- **1942 (May)** Battle of the Coral Sea halts Japanese attack on Port Moresby
- **1942 (June)** Japanese carriers are destroyed at Midway
- **1942 (Aug)** US marines land on Guadalcanal
- **1943 (Nov)** Tarawa captured by US forces
- **1944 (July)** US troops land on island of Leyte
- **1944 (Oct)** The Battle of Leyte Gulf ends Japanese naval power
- **1945 (Feb–Mar)** The Battle of Iwo Jima is followed by the invasion of Okinawa

Southeast Asia

- **1941 (Dec)** Japan attacks Hong Kong and Malaya
- **1942 (Feb)** British forces in Singapore surrender to Japan
- **1942 (Mar)** The Dutch surrender the East Indies
- **1942** British retreat from Burma
- **1943** Nationalists stem the Japanese offensives in China
- **1944** Japanese invasion of India; sieges of Imphal and Kohima (Mar–June)
- **1944** Chinese Communists and Japan stop fighting
- **1945 (May)** The Burma Road reopened and Rangoon recaptured
- **1945 (Aug)** The Soviet Union declares war and attacks in Manchuria and Korea

1943 1945

1 The attack on Pearl Harbor was essential to Japan's plans to control the Pacific. Eight battleships were destroyed but dockyard facilities remained intact.

2 Singapore was Britain's foremost and most recently equipped naval base in the region, but it fell to a surprise land attack in February 1942.

3 The Bataan peninsula in the Philippines was the scene of an incident in April 1942, when the Japanese forced 35,000 men to march 100km (60 miles) in six days; more than 10,000 died.

4 The Japanese invasion of the Dutch East Indies was welcomed by Ahmed Sukarno, leader of the Indonesian Nationalist Party (PNI).

5 Darwin and other north Australian towns were bombed, and the east coast was blockaded by submarines in 1943; the country was a key base for US operations in the southwest Pacific.

6 Saipan was a major air base, used by the US Air Force for bombing Japan from November 1944.

7 Hiroshima suffered the world's first atomic bomb attack on 6 August 1945; 80,000 people died instantly.

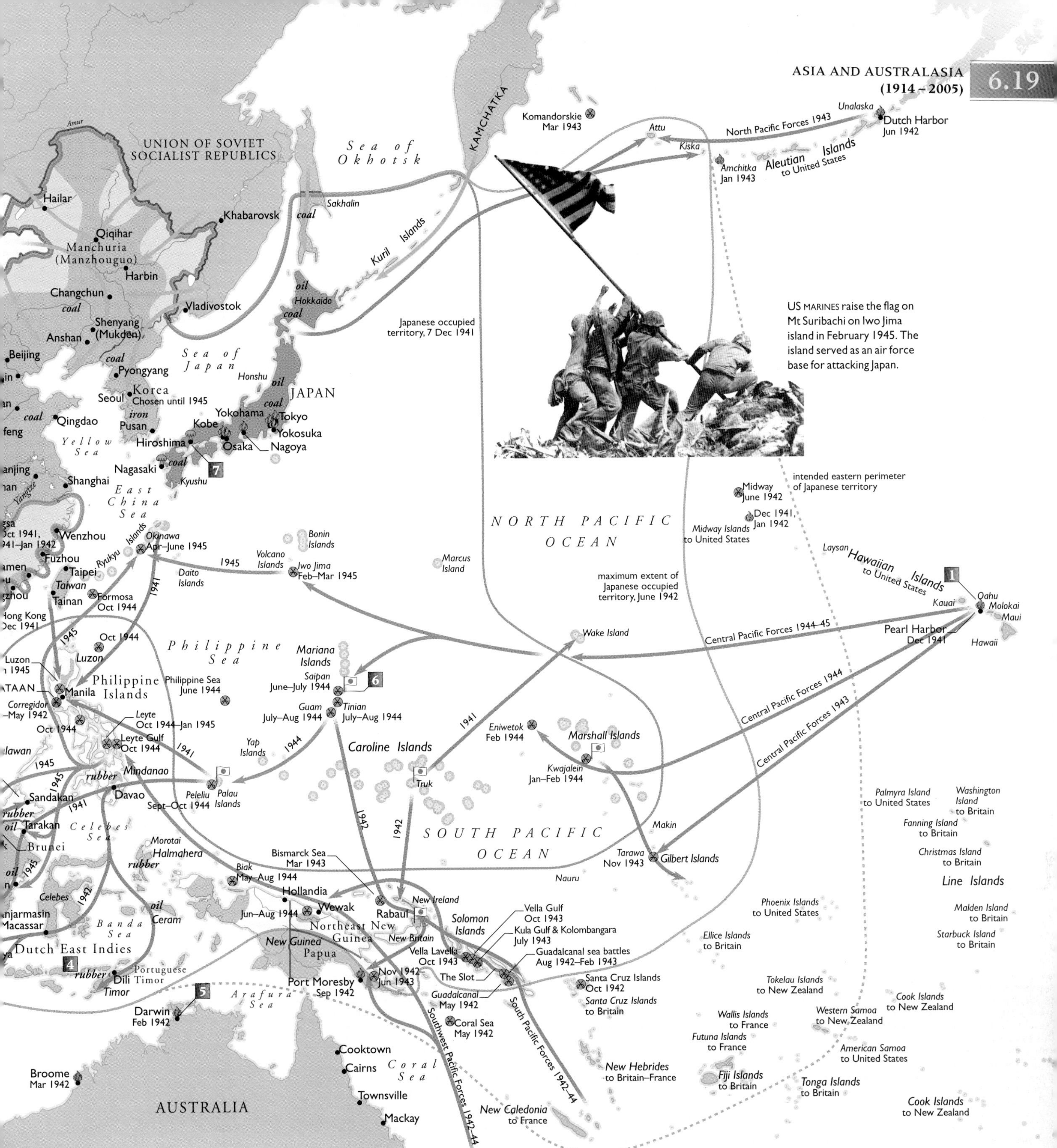

US MARINES raise the flag on Mt Suribachi on Iwo Jima island in February 1945. The island served as an air force base for attacking Japan.

troops were then committed to attack Okinawa; the Japanese defenders employed *kamikaze* aircraft and piloted bombs against American and British ships.

Before and during the Iwo Jima and Okinawa campaigns the Americans subjected Japan to ruthless bombing. Tokyo, Nagoya and Osaka were devastated and the Tokyo firestorm of May 1945 is considered to be the most destructive air raid in history. In the Philippines, the Battle of Luzon was still in progress and in Burma the British, Indian, African, Chinese and US troops, after great battles at Kohima and Imphal, were slowly pushing down the Irrawaddy toward Mandalay and Rangoon.

Despite near universal defeat, the Japanese had no desire to surrender and all sides anticipated a fight to the finish. Allied planning for an amphibious attack on Japan went ahead. Stalin promised that the Soviet Union would enter the war against Japan three months after the total surrender of Nazi Germany. President Truman assessed the likely scale of casualties involved in an invasion (approximately one million fighting men), and compared this with the enemy civilian deaths that would result from the use of the new atomic bomb being tested in New Mexico. He chose the atomic weapon: the bombs fell on Hiroshima and Nagasaki in August 1945. After the first strike Stalin declared war and Soviet troops invaded Manchuria and Korea. As Japan reeled, carrier aircraft harried Honshu and Kyushu and a giant bombing raid savaged the remains of Tokyo. On 15 August 1945, Emperor Hirohito asked the Japanese people to "endure the unendurable and suffer the insufferable." Japan formally signed the surrender document on the battleship USS *Missouri* on 2 September 1945.

See also 6.07, 6.08 (World War II in Europe); 6.18 (east Asia between the wars);

The end of World War II left the United States dominant but the Soviet Union was also moving strongly into east Asia. The Chinese civil wars were soon to be resolved, while the European colonies had been decisively altered by the experience of Japanese occupation and US liberation.

In September 1945 US forces landed at Inchon on the former Japanese colony of Korea, in response to the presence of Soviet troops in north Korea. No formula could be found for unifying the country and the UN approved an American plan to hold elections in the south. Syngman Rhee's Republic of Korea (South Korea) emerged in 1948, followed shortly by Kim Il Sung's Communist Democratic Republic of Korea (North Korea). The Soviet Union and United States withdrew in 1948 and 1949 respectively, leaving Korea divided.

Many US troops withdrew to Japan, where America was responsible for its military occupation and the repatriation of three million Japanese servicemen. The United States and its Commonwealth Allies met with unexpected cooperation from Japanese police and local officials. Emperor Hirohito remained, though only as titular ruler, and real power was in the hands of General MacArthur, Supreme Commander of Allied Powers. MacArthur introduced a democratic constitution, ensured that the United States shipped in adequate food supplies and generally charmed the Japanese with his dignity and benevolence. The Japanese came to admire Americans and their way of life. By 1949 Japan was willingly drawn inside America's defense perimeter.

By 1950 Mao Zedong had succeeded in unifying China, partly by demonstrating that the PLA was no warlord army. Soldiers, workers, the Party hierarchy (cadres) and the government were united. Mao assured the people that China was no longer isolated: the Sino–Soviet Treaty (1950) guaranteed their membership of a international socialist brotherhood. He promised land reform and development plans, and protection for China's frontiers. His first move was to invade Tibet in the winter of 1950–51 to recover what China considered a historic province.

North Korea invaded South Korea in 1950. This provoked a major United Nations response and an army from sixteen nations, spearheaded by the Americans, was sent to Korea to resist the invaders. UN forces attacked across the 38th Parallel dividing North from South, and a few reached the border with China on the Yalu River. At this point the PLA entered the war and forced a UN retreat. A static war ensued, with both sides digging in. An armistice was agreed at Panmunjom in 1953 and five years later the PLA left Korea, although a UN presence remained. After the war, North Korea remained a Stalinist state, while the South began to rebuild its shattered economy. Heavy industry and infrastructure, as well as electronics and consumer industries, were all constructed from scratch as Korea, like Japan, used the opportunity of war to build a new prosperity.

Chinese armed forces were also involved in 1954 when PLA gunners shelled the two small islands of Quemoy and Matsu that were claimed by the Nationalist government based in Taiwan. PLA forces landed on other Nationalist islands and in 1958 resumed the shelling of Quemoy. America mobilized a massive fleet in the Taiwan Straits in support of Jiang Jieshi, who still claimed to be the legitimate ruler of the whole of mainland China. In 1962 PLA forces attempted to push across the Indian border and were poised to enter Assam. After brief fighting against ill-prepared Indian troops, the Chinese withdrew. Along the Ussuri River Chinese patrols clashed with Soviet troops in 1969.

In the 1950s and 1960s, Mao Zedong attempted to forge a Chinese version of Marxism, based on a drive toward establishing economic modernization (especially in the chaotic "Great Leap Forward" of 1958–60) and the collectivization of agriculture. From the mid-1960s he fomented "permanent revolution" by encouraging the youthful Red Guards to challenge all forms of authority, especially in education, administration, industry and the Party itself, and to send many intellectuals to work on communes. China was almost totally cut off from the outside world until after Mao's death in 1976.

former colony, c.1939
British
Dutch
French
United States
North Korea, 1948
South Korea, 1948
People's Republic of China (Communist), 1950
Republic of China (Nationalist), 1950
Tibet prior to the Chinese invasion, 1950
North Vietnam, 1954
South Vietnam, 1954
Japan, 1972
Indonesia, 1949
United Nations Trust Territory
1946 date of independence as a nation-state
LAOS Communist state by 1976
insurgency, with date
clash between Red Guards and the Army or workers, 1965–69
disruption caused by Red Guards, 1965–69
urban youth sent to Chinese provinces, 1974–76
main center from where urban youth were removed
Chinese troop movements, with date
Nationalist Chinese attacks, 1954–55
Nationalist Chinese evacuation to Taiwan, 1950
borders, 1976
disputed border, 1976
Korean War, 1950–53
United Nations airbase
Chinese and North Korean airbase
North Korean advance, June–Sep 1950
United Nations advance, July–Sep 1950
Chinese and North Korean advance, Nov 1950–Jan 1951
limit of North Korean advance, Aug–Sep 1950
limit of United Nations advance, Nov 1950
limit of Chinese and North Korean advance, Jan 1951
Islamabad
PAKISTAN
West Pakistan until 1971
1947

TIMELINE

China, Korea and Japan

1945 The United States occupy Japan (to 1952)

1948 The states of North and South Korea are established

1949–50 Chinese Nationalists evacuate to Taiwan

1950 North Korea invades the South

1953 Korean armistice is signed in Panmunjom

1958–60 Mao's "Great Leap Forward" establishes agrarian and industrial communes

1958 Agricultural collectivization in North Korea

1962 China challenges India in the Himalayas

1962 Start of policy of export-led growth in South Korea

1966–70 The Cultural Revolution to prevent revisionism causes internal disruption in China

1968 Japan is the world's second largest economy

1969 China confronts the Soviet Union in east Asia

1971 People's Republic of China is admitted to the United Nations

1975 Death of Jiang Jieshi

1976 Death of Mao Zedong

Indo-China

1946 French forces return to Indo-China

1954 The French surrender at Dien Bien Phu

1954 Laos and Cambodia become independent states; Vietnam is divided

1964 The US assert that "all measures will be taken to resist aggression" in Vietnam

1965 US ground troops in action against the Viet Cong

1970 US troops enter Cambodia

1973 US troops leave South Vietnam

1976 Vietnam is reunited

Southeast Asia

1946 The Philippines become an independent republic

1948 Burma is independent

1956 Indonesia's last links with the Dutch crown are severed

1963 Federation of Malaysia set up, including Malaya, North Borneo, Sabah and Sarawak, Singapore (to 1965)

1971 The British military presence in Singapore is ended

1950 1960 1970

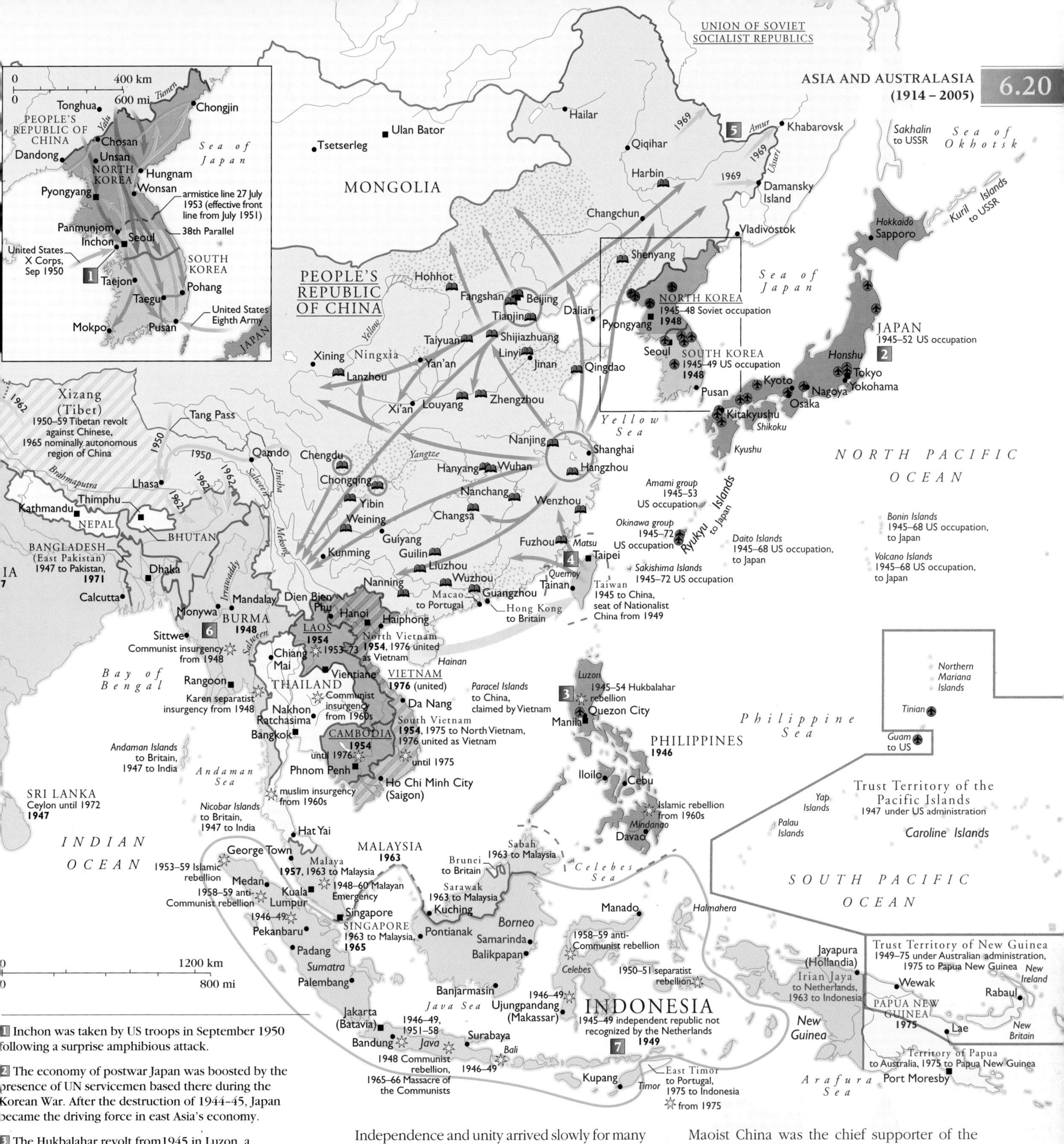
UNION OF SOVIET SOCIALIST REPUBLICS
400 km
600 mi
Tonghua
Chongjin
PEOPLE'S REPUBLIC OF CHINA
Chosan
Unsan
Dandong
Sea of Japan
NORTH KOREA
Hungnam
Pyongyang
Wonsan
armistice line 27 July 1953 (effective front line from July 1951)
Panmunjom
Seoul
38th Parallel
United States X Corps, Sep 1950
Inchon
SOUTH KOREA
Taejon
Pohang
Taegu
United States Eighth Army
Mokpo
Pusan
JAPAN
Hailar
Ulan Bator
Tsetserleg
MONGOLIA
Amur
Khabarovsk
Qiqihar
Harbin
1969
Damansky Island
Ussuri
Sakhalin to USSR
Sea of Okhotsk
Kuril Islands to USSR
Hokkaido
Sapporo
Changchun
Vladivostok
Shenyang
Sea of Japan
PEOPLE'S REPUBLIC OF CHINA
Hohhot
Fangshan
Beijing
Tianjin
Dalian
NORTH KOREA
1945–48 Soviet occupation
1948
Pyongyang
JAPAN
1945–52 US occupation
Taiyuan
Shijiazhuang
Linyi
Jinan
Seoul
SOUTH KOREA
1945–49 US occupation
1948
Honshu
Tokyo
Yokohama
Xining
Ningxia
Yan'an
Lanzhou
Qingdao
Pusan
Kyoto
Nagoya
Osaka
Kitakyushu
Shikoku
Xi'an
Louyang
Zhengzhou
Xizang (Tibet)
1950–59 Tibetan revolt against Chinese,
1965 nominally autonomous region of China
Tang Pass
Yellow Sea
Nanjing
Shanghai
Kyushu
NORTH PACIFIC OCEAN
Qamdo
Chengdu
Yangtze
Hangzhou
Brahmaputra
Lhasa
Chongqing
Hanyang
Wuhan
Amami group 1945–53 US occupation
Ryukyu Islands to Japan
Kathmandu
Thimphu
NEPAL
BHUTAN
Yibin
Nanchang
Wenzhou
Changsa
Weining
Okinawa group 1945–72 US occupation
Bonin Islands 1945–68 US occupation, to Japan
Daito Islands 1945–68 US occupation, to Japan
Guiyang
Fuzhou
Matsu
BANGLADESH (East Pakistan) 1947 to Pakistan, 1971
Kunming
Guilin
Taipei
Volcano Islands 1945–68 US occupation, to Japan
Sakishima Islands 1945–72 US occupation
Liuzhou
Dhaka
Wuzhou
Quemoy
Tainan
Taiwan 1945 to China, seat of Nationalist China from 1949
Calcutta
Nanning
Macao to Portugal
Guangzhou
Hong Kong to Britain
Mandalay
Dien Bien Phu
Hanoi
Haiphong
Monywa
BURMA 1948
Irrawaddy
Salween
Mekong
LAOS 1954
North Vietnam 1954, 1976 united as Vietnam
Sittwe
Communist insurgency from 1948
Chiang Mai
1953–73
Hainan
Bay of Bengal
Rangoon
Vientiane
VIETNAM 1976 (united)
Paracel Islands to China, claimed by Vietnam
Northern Mariana Islands
THAILAND
Karen separatist insurgency from 1948
Communist insurgency from 1960s
Da Nang
Luzon
1945–54 Hukbalahar rebellion
Quezon City
Tinian
Nakhon Ratchasima
South Vietnam 1954, 1975 to North Vietnam, 1976 united as Vietnam
Manila
Philippine Sea
Bangkok
CAMBODIA 1954
Guam to US
PHILIPPINES 1946
Andaman Islands to Britain, 1947 to India
until 1976
until 1975
Andaman Sea
Phnom Penh
Iloilo
Cebu
Ho Chi Minh City (Saigon)
Trust Territory of the Pacific Islands 1947 under US administration
Yap Islands
SRI LANKA Ceylon until 1972 1947
muslim insurgency from 1960s
Nicobar Islands to Britain, 1947 to India
Islamic rebellion from 1960s
Mindanao
Davao
Palau Islands
Caroline Islands
INDIAN OCEAN
Hat Yai
MALAYSIA 1963
Sabah 1963 to Malaysia
George Town
1953–59 Islamic rebellion
Malaya 1957, 1963 to Malaysia
Brunei to Britain
Celebes Sea
SOUTH PACIFIC OCEAN
Medan
1958–59 anti-Communist rebellion
Kuala Lumpur
1948–60 Malayan Emergency
Sarawak 1963 to Malaysia
Kuching
1946–49
Singapore
SINGAPORE 1963 to Malaysia, 1965
Manado
Halmahera
Borneo
Pekanbaru
Pontianak
Samarinda
1958–59 anti-Communist rebellion
Padang
Balikpapan
Celebes
1950–51 separatist rebellion
Jayapura (Hollandia)
Irian Jaya to Netherlands, 1963 to Indonesia
Trust Territory of New Guinea 1949–75 under Australian administration, 1975 to Papua New Guinea
New Ireland
1200 km
800 mi
Sumatra
Palembang
Wewak
Rabaul
Banjarmasin
1946–49
Java Sea
Ujungpandang (Makassar)
INDONESIA
1945–49 independent republic not recognized by the Netherlands
1949
PAPUA NEW GUINEA 1975
New Guinea
Lae
New Britain
Jakarta (Batavia)
1946–49, 1951–58
Java
Surabaya
Bandung
Bali
1948 Communist rebellion, 1965–66 Massacre of the Communists
Kupang
Timor
East Timor to Portugal, 1975 to Indonesia
from 1975
Territory of Papua to Australia, 1975 to Papua New Guinea
Arafura Sea
Port Moresby

1 Inchon was taken by US troops in September 1950 following a surprise amphibious attack.

2 The economy of postwar Japan was boosted by the presence of UN servicemen based there during the Korean War. After the destruction of 1944–45, Japan became the driving force in east Asia's economy.

3 The Hukbalahar revolt from1945 in Luzon, a peasant uprising over land ownership, was crushed by the government in 1953–54.

4 In 1958 US president Eisenhower sent "the most powerful fighting force in history" to confront the Communist Chinese in the Taiwan Straits.

5 Tension between the Soviet Union and Maoist China on the Amur River border from 1969 emphasized the rift between these former allies.

6 Burma, which pursued a neutral foreign policy after independence under U Nu, was under a socialist military regime led by Ne Win from 1962.

7 East Timor, a Portuguese colony until the Portuguese revolution of 1975, was invaded by Indonesia the same year, and annexed in 1976.

Independence and unity arrived slowly for many east Asian nations. The Philippines became an independent republic in 1946; Burma in 1948; after the partition of India in 1947, East Pakistan became Bangladesh in 1971. But the former French Indo-Chinese colonies of Laos, Cambodia and Vietnam became embroiled in the longest war of the century. During World War II the French had accepted Japanese domination of the area; only the Communist Vietminh forces led by Ho Chi Minh resisted, and declared independence in 1945. The return of the French led to a long guerrilla war in which the French initially drove the Vietminh from the major cities, but in 1953–54 the Vietminh general Giap won a remarkable and decisive victory over the French at Dien Bien Phu.

Maoist China was the chief supporter of the insurgents in Indo-China, and also of the Communists in Malaya who inspired a long guerrilla campaign against the British; eventually independence was achieved by the anti-Communist, Malay-led nationalists in 1957. Indonesia, which claimed its independence after the war and won Dutch acceptance of the fact in 1949 after a bitter struggle, also suffered Communist, regionalist and Islamist activity. To a lesser extent, the Philippines (where United States' influence was still paramount), Burma and Thailand also saw Communist movements.

See also 6.19 (World War II in Asia); 6.21 (Vietnam War); 6.23 (the Pacific Rim after 1976)

.21 The Indo–China wars • 1954 – 1976 •

Following the victories of Ho Chi Minh's Vietminh guerrilla forces in 1943–54, France withdrew from most of Indo-China. The subsequent Geneva Conference ruled that Vietnam would be divided between the North, ruled from Hanoi by the Vietminh, and the non-Communist South, with its capital in Saigon. Two neutral states, Laos and Cambodia, would also be formed and within two years the Vietnamese would hold free elections and be united under a government of their own choice.

The elections were never held. Vietnam stayed divided and weak: the North by being cut off from the rich rice-fields of the Mekong delta, and the South by the presence of the Vietminh. Land reform was a key issue in the Mekong delta where two million peasants were landless, with many more paying high rents to absentee landlords. Saigon was reluctant to redistribute the land, whereas the Vietminh soldiers gave land to the peasants and also handed over responsibility for food production and local government. The Communists thus began to win the hearts and minds of the people, who were alienated by the anti-Buddhist president Diem in Saigon. Coercion, too, was rife on the Communist side in intimidating or eliminating anti-Communists.

John Foster Dulles, US secretary of state from 1953, had never endorsed the Geneva agreements. He intended to save all of southeast Asia from Communism and to this end set up the South-East Asia Treaty Organization (SEATO) to prevent subversion within member states. When guerrilla uprisings began in Vietnam during 1955–56, the United States sent military advisers to train the ARVN (Army of the Republic of South Vietnam). Gradually the guerrillas, now termed the Viet Cong (Vietnamese Communists or VC), won control of half of Diem's provinces. Disillusioned ARVN officers killed him.

A succession of Saigon governments followed. For the United States, the war against North Vietnam (NVN) became "the great issue" of the 1960s. America's leaders accepted the "domino theory": if South Vietnam (SVN) succumbed to Communism, the same fate would in turn befall Laos, Cambodia, Thailand, Burma and Pakistan. After Kennedy's assassination in 1963, president Johnson left the conduct of the war in the hands of defense secretary Robert McNamara. More American troops arrived in the South as VCs and their supplies swarmed down the "Ho Chi Minh Trail". In an effort to halt the flow of war materiel from China and Russia via Hanoi, the US provoked the Tongking crisis in 1964: an attack by patrol boats on US destroyers became an excuse for bombing North Vietnam 1965–70.

Air attack failed to reduce VC activity. US soldiers (and others from Australasia and South Korea) were sent to fight an elusive enemy hiding in the hamlets, jungles and paddy fields. They had enormous firepower; but the fundamental issue – how to defeat well-armed, well-supplied nationalists operating in an agrarian economy – was never resolved. The Central Intelligence Agency (CIA) did not penetrate the VC high command; it did not warn of the Tet offensive of 1968 when Viet Cong battle-squads entered Saigon, Hue and other towns, and failed to reveal the buildup around the US base at Khe Sanh.

With antiwar sentiment growing in the United States, president Johnson authorized negotiations with North Vietnam in Paris. His successor Richard Nixon pledged to scale down US troop involvement and to "vietnamize" the war by boosting the ARVN military contribution. Even as US troops were quitting Vietnam, he backed the invasions of Cambodia and Laos plus Operation Linebacker II, a resumption of the air war designed to destroy the transportation systems of North Vietnam. US air power now proved irresistible, destroying bridges, truck factories and harbor installations. Linebacker II encouraged Le Duc Tho, the NVN delegation leader, to sign the Paris peace agreement with Henry Kissinger (US national security adviser). South Vietnam's president Thieu reluctantly agreed to the ceasefire, and the last American combat troops left Vietnam in 1973.

Nixon's subsequent resignation and the decline of US aid encouraged Le Duan (Ho Chi Minh's successor) to attempt the reunification of Vietnam. The Ho Chi Minh Trail now provided unhindered access to the south, and China and the Soviet Union had re-equipped the regular NVN Army so that it could put infantry divisions, armored brigades and artillery regiments into the field. These advanced from the north and the west, fighting the kind of war that the Americans had always wanted them to fight. In 1975 SVN's president Thieu fled to Taiwan; American helicopters ferried their remaining personnel from the capital as NVN tanks entered Saigon. At the same time Laos and Cambodia, both destabilized by Viet Cong activity and by constant US air attack, also fell to the Communists: Pathet Lao guerrillas set up a People's Democratic Republic in Laos, while the Khmer Rouge captured Cambodia's capital, Phnom Penh. Vietnam was reunited as the Socialist Republic of Vietnam under the leadership of Le Duan.

- border, 1954
- Communist control within Indo-China, 1954
- under Vietnamese Communist control, 1970
- Vietnamese Communist gains by Jan 1975
- Vietnamese Communist gains by Apr 1975
- Khmer Rouge control, 1975
- Pathet Lao control, 1975
- Communist guerrilla activity in Thailand, 1975
- US carrier fleet on permanent station
- US air base in South Vietnam and Thailand
- North Vietnamese air base
- Tet Offensive assault, Jan–Feb 1968
- major combat area
- interdiction by US Air Force
- VI A zoned target area (Route Packages) of the US Air Force within North Vietnam
- border of zoned target area
- forbidden target for US air strikes until Operation Linebacker II, 1972
- Vinh harbor mined by the US Navy
- Viet Cong supply route
- US and South Vietnamese offensive, 1970
- Vietnamese Communist advance, Jan–Apr 1975
- Vietnamese invasion of Cambodia, 1978–79
- Chinese invasion of Vietnam, 1979
- US evacuation, with date
- railroad

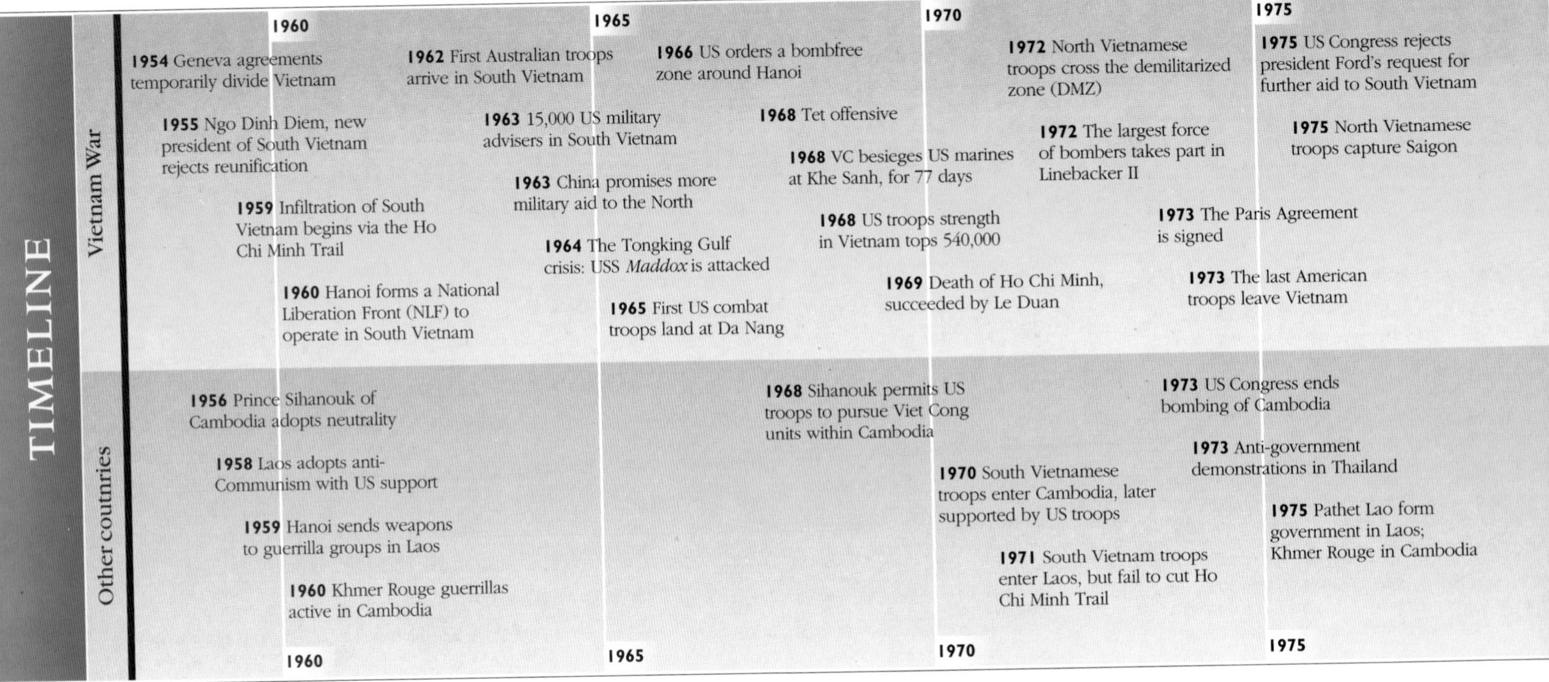
TIMELINE
Vietnam War
1960
1965
1970
1975
1954 Geneva agreements temporarily divide Vietnam
1955 Ngo Dinh Diem, new president of South Vietnam rejects reunification
1959 Infiltration of South Vietnam begins via the Ho Chi Minh Trail
1960 Hanoi forms a National Liberation Front (NLF) to operate in South Vietnam
1962 First Australian troops arrive in South Vietnam
1963 15,000 US military advisers in South Vietnam
1963 China promises more military aid to the North
1964 The Tongking Gulf crisis: USS Maddox is attacked
1965 First US combat troops land at Da Nang
1966 US orders a bombfree zone around Hanoi
1968 Tet offensive
1968 VC besieges US marines at Khe Sanh, for 77 days
1968 US troops strength in Vietnam tops 540,000
1969 Death of Ho Chi Minh, succeeded by Le Duan
1972 North Vietnamese troops cross the demilitarized zone (DMZ)
1972 The largest force of bombers takes part in Linebacker II
1973 The Paris Agreement is signed
1973 The last American troops leave Vietnam
1975 US Congress rejects president Ford's request for further aid to South Vietnam
1975 North Vietnamese troops capture Saigon
Other countries
1956 Prince Sihanouk of Cambodia adopts neutrality
1958 Laos adopts anti-Communism with US support
1959 Hanoi sends weapons to guerrilla groups in Laos
1960 Khmer Rouge guerrillas active in Cambodia
1968 Sihanouk permits US troops to pursue Viet Cong units within Cambodia
1970 South Vietnamese troops enter Cambodia, later supported by US troops
1971 South Vietnam troops enter Laos, but fail to cut Ho Chi Minh Trail
1973 US Congress ends bombing of Cambodia
1973 Anti-government demonstrations in Thailand
1975 Pathet Lao form government in Laos; Khmer Rouge in Cambodia
1960
1965
1970
1975

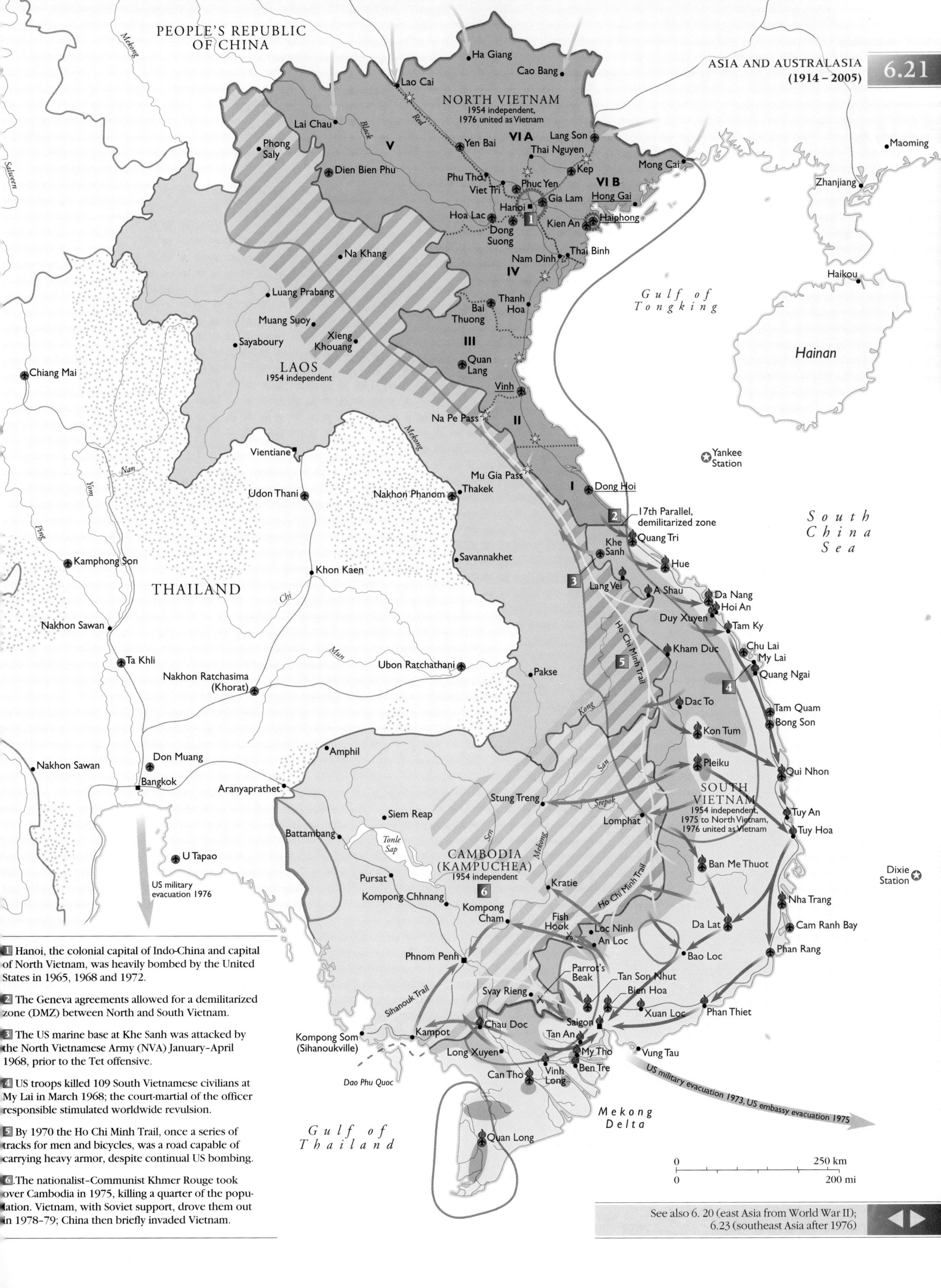

PEOPLE'S REPUBLIC OF CHINA
NORTH VIETNAM
1954 independent, 1976 united as Vietnam
LAOS
1954 independent
THAILAND
CAMBODIA (KAMPUCHEA)
1954 independent
SOUTH VIETNAM
1954 independent, 1975 to North Vietnam, 1976 united as Vietnam
Gulf of Tongking
South China Sea
Gulf of Thailand
Hainan
Mekong Delta
Ha Giang
Cao Bang
Lao Cai
Lai Chau
Phong Saly
Yen Bai
Lang Son
Thai Nguyen
Kep
Mong Cai
Dien Bien Phu
Phu Tho
Viet Tri
Phuc Yen
Gia Lam
Hong Gai
Hanoi
Hoa Lac
Dong Suong
Kien An
Haiphong
Thai Binh
Nam Dinh
Na Khang
Luang Prabang
Muang Suoy
Xieng Khouang
Sayaboury
Thanh Hoa
Bai Thuong
Quan Lang
Vinh
Na Pe Pass
Mu Gia Pass
Dong Hoi
Chiang Mai
Vientiane
Udon Thani
Nakhon Phanom
Thakek
17th Parallel, demilitarized zone
Quang Tri
Khe Sanh
Hue
Savannakhet
Kamphong Son
Khon Kaen
Lang Vei
A Shau
Da Nang
Hoi An
Duy Xuyen
Tam Ky
Nakhon Sawan
Ta Khli
Kham Duc
Chu Lai
My Lai
Quang Ngai
Ho Chi Minh Trail
Ubon Ratchathani
Nakhon Ratchasima (Khorat)
Pakse
Dac To
Tam Quam
Bong Son
Kon Tum
Pleiku
Qui Nhon
Don Muang
Bangkok
Amphil
Aranyaprathet
Stung Treng
Lomphat
Siem Reap
Battambang
Tonle Sap
Tuy An
Tuy Hoa
U Tapao
US military evacuation 1976
Ban Me Thuot
Pursat
Kompong Chhnang
Kratie
Kompong Cham
Nha Trang
Dixie Station
Yankee Station
Fish Hook
Loc Ninh
An Loc
Da Lat
Cam Ranh Bay
Phnom Penh
Bao Loc
Phan Rang
Parrot's Beak
Tan Son Nhut
Svay Rieng
Bien Hoa
Xuan Loc
Phan Thiet
Sihanouk Trail
Chau Doc
Saigon
Tan An
Kampot
Kompong Som (Sihanoukville)
Long Xuyen
My Tho
Ben Tre
Vung Tau
Can Tho
Vinh Long
Dao Phu Quoc
Quan Long
US military evacuation 1973, US embassy evacuation 1975
Zhanjiang
Maoming
Haikou
0 250 km
0 200 mi

1 Hanoi, the colonial capital of Indo-China and capital of North Vietnam, was heavily bombed by the United States in 1965, 1968 and 1972.

2 The Geneva agreements allowed for a demilitarized zone (DMZ) between North and South Vietnam.

3 The US marine base at Khe Sanh was attacked by the North Vietnamese Army (NVA) January–April 1968, prior to the Tet offensive.

4 US troops killed 109 South Vietnamese civilians at My Lai in March 1968; the court-martial of the officer responsible stimulated worldwide revulsion.

5 By 1970 the Ho Chi Minh Trail, once a series of tracks for men and bicycles, was a road capable of carrying heavy armor, despite continual US bombing.

6 The nationalist-Communist Khmer Rouge took over Cambodia in 1975, killing a quarter of the population. Vietnam, with Soviet support, drove them out in 1978–79; China then briefly invaded Vietnam.

See also 6. 20 (east Asia from World War II); 6.23 (southeast Asia after 1976)

In India, expectations of political change were high after World War II. By 1945, however, enmity between Muslims and Hindus caused rioting in Calcutta and Delhi and the British decided to withdraw. Two independent republics were carved out of the subcontinent in 1947. Partition brought renewed civil conflict plus mass migration as millions of Muslims moved from India to East and West Pakistan, and Hindus and Sikhs made their way to India.

The two republics continued to dispute Kashmir, and a war in 1948–49 led to a UN truce line across Kashmir. The truce lasted until 1965, when troops from both sides crossed the ceasefire line. Hostilities flared up again in 1971, when Indian troops invaded East Pakistan in support of separatist guerrillas against West Pakistan; the region gained its independence as Bangladesh. The Kashmir dispute continued into the new century, stoked by separatist guerrillas. In 2005, Indian, Pakistani and Kashmiri leaders agreed a tenative peace deal, and improved trade and transportation in the disputed region. In October the same year, a huge earthquake left 80,000 dead, mainly in Pakistani Kashmir. Despite cooperation over disaster relief, mutual suspicion remained. In 2008 India blamed Pakistan for terrorist attacks on prominent targets in Bombay (Mumbai).

As a secular state, India tried to change long-established customs through parliamentary legislation. When Congress Party leader Indira Gandhi became prime minister in 1966, she invested heavily in industry, food-grain production and family planning. She made many enemies and was assassinated in 1984 by her own Sikh bodyguard.

By this time India was an industrial and military power, which had acquired nuclear military technology in 1974. During the 1990s, India's economy was steadily liberalized and measures of positive discrimination taken in favor of people of lower castes and minorities. Prime minister Rajiv Gandhi was assassinated in 1991 and riots continued to blight cities as Hindu fundamentalism began to challenge the consitutional assumptions of the state. The Bharatiya Janata Party (BJP) swept to electoral victory in 1998 on the promise of *Hindutva*, a militant Hindu nationalism. Elections in 2004, however, returned the Congress Party to power.

In Pakistan in the 1960s, Zulfikar Ali Bhutto tried to initiate a program of nationalization, but his ruthless approach led to his execution. His daughter, Benazir, then began a stormy political career and was prime minister in the early 1990s. President Pervez Musharraf, who took power in 1999, angered Islamic militants with his support for US military operations in Afghanistan in 2001 and 2002 and his commitment to defeat Islamic terrorists. He resigned in 2008 to try to halt a breakdown of order, which included the assassination of Benazir Bhutto in late 2007. Pakistan's tribal homelands, however, were widely suspected of continuing to provide a base for al-Qaeda and other Islamist terrorists.

Bangladesh, one of the poorest countries in the world, is subject to cyclones that flood huge regions. The country's first prime minister, Sheikh Mujibur, was assassinated, as was president Zia Rahman. Neighboring Burma (now Myanmar) experienced little of the democracy promised after General Aung San led it to independence in 1948. His daughter, prodemocracy campaigner Aung San Suu Kyi, languished under house arrest through the 1990s, despite winning a landslide victory in elections in 1990. Mass protests against the military government by Buddhist monks in 2007 were violently suppressed, and a future return to democracy remains uncertain.

Sri Lanka, independent since 1948, was racked by civil war between the minority Tamils and the Sinhalese from 1983. The Tamils tried to establish an independent state in the north of the island and captured Jaffna in 1991. The government retook the city in 1996 as Tamil bomb squads resorted to terrorism. A ceasefire and political agreement reached in late 2002 raised hopes for a settlement; but peace talks stalled. In 2009 the government claimed to be close to the final military defeat of the terrorists.

In December 2004, the Indian Ocean tsunami devastated southern and eastern coastlines of Sri Lanka, which suffered more than anywhere apart from Indonesia. The tidal wave continued to India, where Tamil Nadu was badly affected.

communal rioting in British India, 1946–47

independent state formed by the partition of British Indian territory, 1947

India

Pakistan

cession of princely state or protectorate between 1947 and 1950

to India

to Pakistan

refugee movement, 1947–50

Hindu

Muslim

other migration

other former British territory gaining independence in 1948

People's Republic of China, 1950

Tibet, 1950

Union of Soviet Socialist Republics, 1950

Soviet occupation, 1979–89

Mujihadeen activity, 1979–88

territory disputed between China and India from 1947 until 1993

Chinese offensive

Pakistani offensive

Indian offensive

Indian airfield bombed by Pakistan, 1971

strikes on Taliban/Al Qaeda targets by US-led coalition, 2001

separatist movement

Burmese road linking China with Bay of Bengal

Chinese military base

United Nations truce line, 1949

borders, 2003

disputed border

0 400 km

0 300 mi

UZBEKIST
to Soviet Unic
1991 independ

TURKMENI
to Soviet Unic
1991 independ

Ashkha

IRAN

Muscat

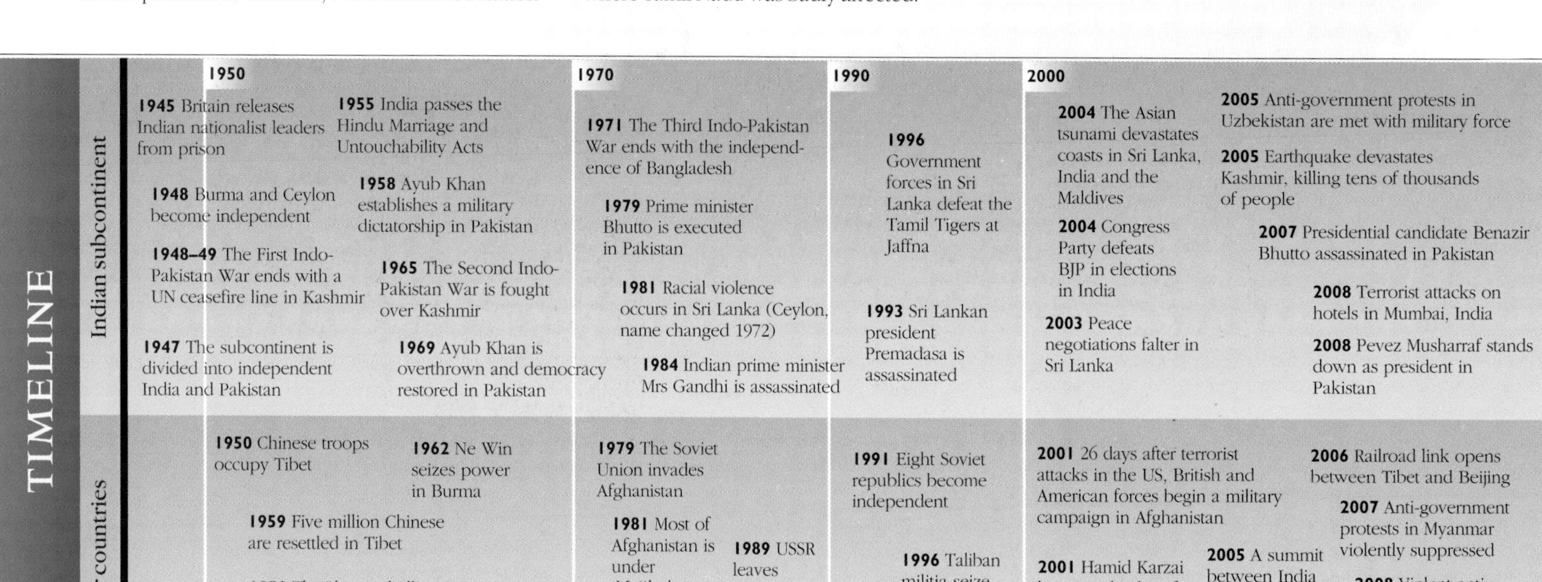
TIMELINE
Indian subcontinent
1950
1970
1990
2000
1945 Britain releases Indian nationalist leaders from prison
1955 India passes the Hindu Marriage and Untouchability Acts
1948 Burma and Ceylon become independent
1958 Ayub Khan establishes a military dictatorship in Pakistan
1948–49 The First Indo-Pakistan War ends with a UN ceasefire line in Kashmir
1965 The Second Indo-Pakistan War is fought over Kashmir
1947 The subcontinent is divided into independent India and Pakistan
1969 Ayub Khan is overthrown and democracy restored in Pakistan
1971 The Third Indo-Pakistan War ends with the independence of Bangladesh
1979 Prime minister Bhutto is executed in Pakistan
1981 Racial violence occurs in Sri Lanka (Ceylon, name changed 1972)
1984 Indian prime minister Mrs Gandhi is assassinated
1996 Government forces in Sri Lanka defeat the Tamil Tigers at Jaffna
1993 Sri Lankan president Premadasa is assassinated
2004 The Asian tsunami devastates coasts in Sri Lanka, India and the Maldives
2004 Congress Party defeats BJP in elections in India
2003 Peace negotiations falter in Sri Lanka
2005 Anti-government protests in Uzbekistan are met with military force
2005 Earthquake devastates Kashmir, killing tens of thousands of people
2007 Presidential candidate Benazir Bhutto assassinated in Pakistan
2008 Terrorist attacks on hotels in Mumbai, India
2008 Pevez Musharraf stands down as president in Pakistan
Other countries
1950 Chinese troops occupy Tibet
1962 Ne Win seizes power in Burma
1959 Five million Chinese are resettled in Tibet
1959 The Lhasa rebellion is followed by the escape of the Dalai Lama to India
1979 The Soviet Union invades Afghanistan
1981 Most of Afghanistan is under *Mujihadeen* control
1989 USSR leaves Afghanistan
1988 Pro-democracy riots flare in Rangoon
1991 Eight Soviet republics become independent
1996 Taliban militia seize power in Afghanistan
2001 26 days after terrorist attacks in the US, British and American forces begin a military campaign in Afghanistan
2001 Hamid Karzai becomes leader of Afghanistan; he becomes president in 2002
2005 A summit between India and Pakistan reduces tension in Kashmir
2006 Railroad link opens between Tibet and Beijing
2007 Anti-government protests in Myanmar violently suppressed
2008 Violent anti-Chinese protests in Tibet
2008 Nepal becomes a republic; the monarchy is abolished
1950
1970
1990
2000

Tibet, occupied by China in 1950, experienced military rule after the failure of the Lhasa rebellion and the flight of Tibet's spiritual leader, the Dalai Lama, to India in 1959. The Chinese installed a puppet ruler. Mass immigration of Han Chinese to the region threatened to swamp the indigenous population; a rail link between Lhasa and China opened in 2007. The Beijing Olympics of 2008 were the focus for worldwide pro-Tibet demonstrations.

In 1973 Afghanistan's constitutional monarchy was ousted by Communists who in 1979 sought Soviet assistance against Muslim *Mujihadeen* guerrillas. Soviet forces suffered heavy losses against guerrillas and withdrew in 1988. Civil war ensued, and in 1996 the Taliban captured Kabul.

Following the Al Qaeda attacks in the United States in 2001, a US-led coalition in alliance with Afghan warlords began the UN-mandated destruction of terrorist training camps and the removal of the Taliban from power. Hamid Karzai, whose presidency was confirmed by elections in 2004, struggled to restore order. In 2009, faced by a resurgent Taliban, new US president Barack Obama announced plans to increase US forces in the country.

1 The nizam of Muslim Hyderabad had to be forced to join India in 1949.

2 Despite the presence of US and British troops, the Taliban remained active in Afghanistan. Al-Qaeda leader Osama bin Laden was believed to be hiding in tribal homelands along the Afghan–Pakistan border.

3 Dharamsala became the center for the Dalai Lama and the Tibetan government in exile after fleeing from the Chinese in 1959.

4 Bangladesh and India engaged in a long dispute over water resources after India built the Farakka dam over the Ganges in 1989.

5 An explosion at a chemical factory in Bhopal in 1984 killed about 2,500 people as a consequence of poor administration and planning.

6 In Nepal, Maoist rebels joined the government in 2007; in 2008 the monarchy was abolished and a republic took power.

7 Islamist terrorists shocked South Asia in 2009 when they attacked the visiting Sri Lankan cricket team in Lahore, killing seven people.

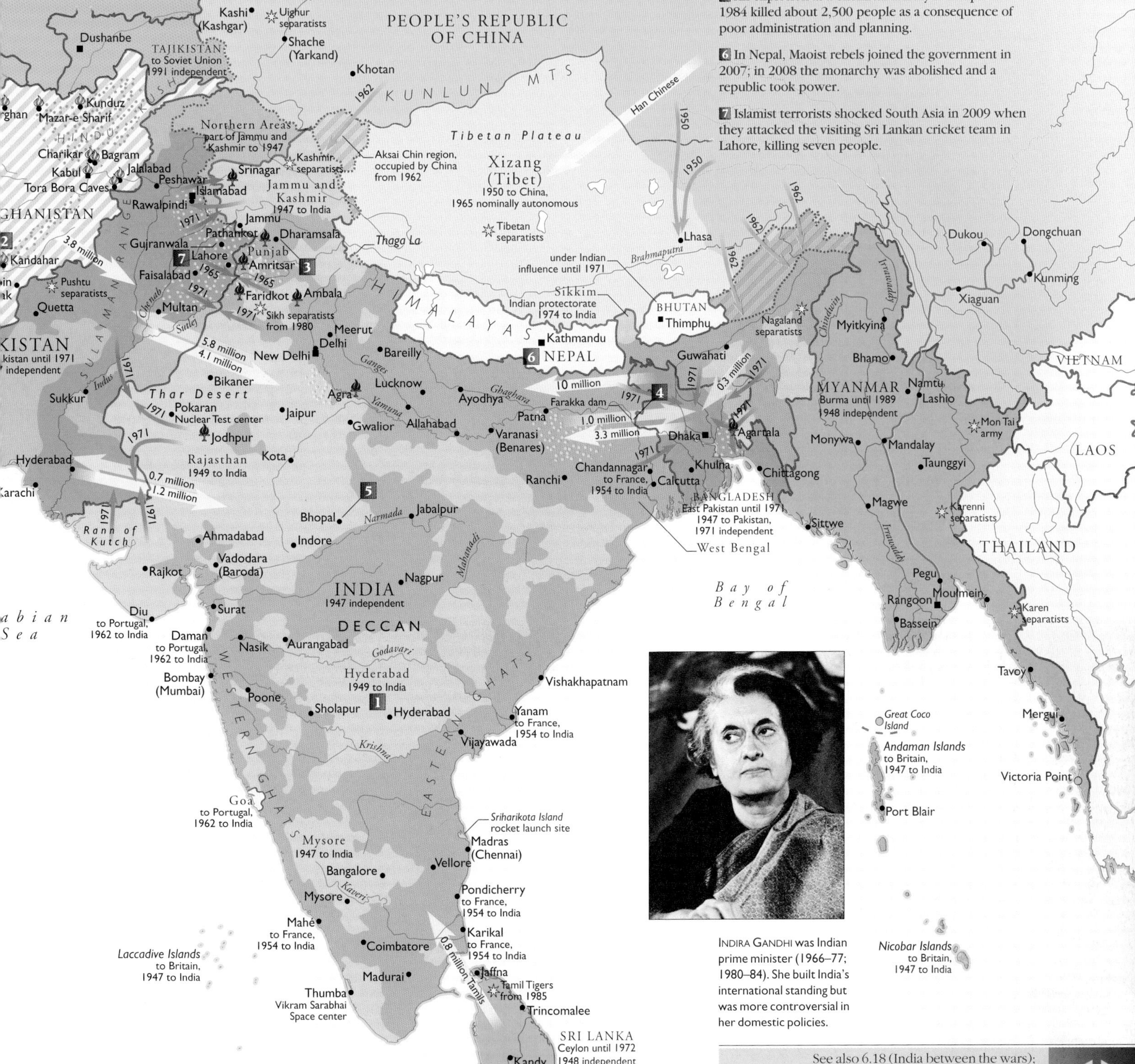
PEOPLE'S REPUBLIC OF CHINA
Kashi (Kashgar)
Uighur separatists
Shache (Yarkand)
Khotan
Dushanbe
TAJIKISTAN to Soviet Union 1991 independent
Kunduz
Mazar-e Sharif
HINDU KUSH
KUNLUN MTS
Han Chinese
Northern Areas part of Jammu and Kashmir to 1947
Charikar
Bagram
Kabul
Jalalabad
Tora Bora Caves
Peshawar
Islamabad
Rawalpindi
Srinagar
Kashmir separatists
Jammu and Kashmir 1947 to India
Jammu
Aksai Chin region, occupied by China from 1962
Tibetan Plateau
Xizang (Tibet) 1950 to China, 1965 nominally autonomous
Tibetan separatists
Lhasa
Thaga La
Brahmaputra
under Indian influence until 1971
Dukou
Dongchuan
Kunming
Xiaguan
AFGHANISTAN
3.8 million
Kandahar
Pushtu separatists
Quetta
Gujranwala
Pathankot
Dharamsala
Lahore
Punjab
Amritsar
Faisalabad
Faridkot
Ambala
Multan
Chenab
Sutlej
Sikh separatists from 1980
SULAIMAN RANGE
HIMALAYAS
Sikkim Indian protectorate 1974 to India
BHUTAN
Thimphu
Nagaland separatists
Irrawaddy
Chindwin
Myitkyina
PAKISTAN
Pakistan until 1971 independent
5.8 million
4.1 million
New Delhi
Meerut
Delhi
Kathmandu
NEPAL
Bareilly
Ganges
Guwahati
0.3 million
Bhamo
VIETNAM
Bikaner
Lucknow
10 million
Indus
Sukkur
Thar Desert
Pokaran Nuclear Test center
Agra
Yamuna
Ayodhya
Ghaghara
Farakka dam
Jaipur
Gwalior
Allahabad
Patna
1.0 million
3.3 million
Varanasi (Benares)
Dhaka
Agartala
MYANMAR Burma until 1989 1948 independent
Namtu
Lashio
Mon Tai army
Monywa
Mandalay
Taunggyi
LAOS
Jodhpur
Hyderabad
Rajasthan 1949 to India
Kota
0.7 million
1.2 million
Karachi
Ranchi
Chandannagar to France, 1954 to India
Calcutta
Khulna
Chittagong
BANGLADESH East Pakistan until 1971 1947 to Pakistan, 1971 independent
West Bengal
Magwe
Karenni separatists
Sittwe
THAILAND
Bhopal
Narmada
Jabalpur
Mahanadi
Rann of Kutch
Ahmadabad
Indore
Vadodara (Baroda)
Rajkot
Nagpur
INDIA 1947 independent
Pegu
Rangoon
Moulmein
Bassein
Karen separatists
Bay of Bengal
Arabian Sea
Diu to Portugal, 1962 to India
Surat
DECCAN
Daman to Portugal, 1962 to India
Nasik
Aurangabad
Godavari
Bombay (Mumbai)
Poone
Hyderabad 1949 to India
Sholapur
Hyderabad
WESTERN GHATS
EASTERN GHATS
Vishakhapatnam
Yanam to France, 1954 to India
Vijayawada
Krishna
Tavoy
Mergui
Great Coco Island
Andaman Islands to Britain, 1947 to India
Victoria Point
Port Blair
Goa to Portugal, 1962 to India
Sriharikota Island rocket launch site
Mysore 1947 to India
Madras (Chennai)
Vellore
Bangalore
Mysore
Kaveri
Pondicherry to France, 1954 to India
Mahé to France, 1954 to India
Karikal to France, 1954 to India
Coimbatore
0.8 million Tamils
Laccadive Islands to Britain, 1947 to India
Madurai
Jaffna
Tamil Tigers from 1985
Trincomalee
Thumba Vikram Sarabhai Space center
SRI LANKA Ceylon until 1972 1948 independent
Kandy
Colombo
Nicobar Islands to Britain, 1947 to India
MALDIVES 1965 independent

INDIRA GANDHI was Indian prime minister (1966–77; 1980–84). She built India's international standing but was more controversial in her domestic policies.

See also 6.18 (India between the wars); 6.20 (east Asia after 1945)

6.23 The rise and fall of the Pacific rim • 1976 – Present •

The balance of world power was dramatically altered by the rise of the Asian economies in the last quarter of the 20th century. The region had plentiful supplies of cheap labor able to take on work of a highly technical nature.

The economic power driving this development was Japan, which trebled its investments in many of the east and southeast Asian countries after 1985. By the late 1990s, countries such as Malaysia, Hong Kong, Taiwan and, increasingly, China had overtaken the United States as Japan's main trading partner.

As the region developed, new countries, such as Vietnam, opened up for development. These newly industrializing economies (NIEs) had a number of characteristics in common: none had significant raw materials and so turned to export-oriented small light industries in the 1960s and 1970s. Like Japan, they had lost the advantage of low labor costs by the mid-1990s, and moved to invest in their neighbors with reserves of cheap labor, notably China. By the 1980s South Korea had shifted its manufacturing base toward high technology, transport and heavy industry, and growth continued at a high rate. South Korean firms slowly opened trading links with the Communist regime in North Korea.

The foundations for Taiwan's economy were laid from the late 1970s by Jiang Ching-kuo, who developed shipbuilding, petrochemicals and electronic industries, especially computers. By the mid-1990s this small island, remarkably, was the eighth largest trading power in the world. The dominant political issue, however, continued to be the question of eventual unification with China.

Hong Kong, a small offshore island leased to Britain in 1898, returned to Chinese rule in 1997, having moved economically toward trade and banking while retaining its textile and other labor-intensive industries. By contrast, Singapore, another former British trading colony, pursued high-technology manufacture in conjunction with finance and business services.

In 1975, China had little or no foreign investment and little direct trade with non-Communist states other than Japan. In 1978, vice-premier Deng Xiaoping embarked on economic and educational reforms, with the goal of economic modernization. Political reform, however, was not pursued and a prodemocracy movement that arose in the wake of economic reform was crushed in 1989. Despite worldwide condemnation of China's human rights record, China actively sought investment, trade and technology from overseas. The tiger economies that did most in China were those with the strongest political or ethnic ties with the country – notably Singapore and Taiwan. From 1984 Hong Kong increasingly shifted its production to nearby Chinese provinces to take advantage of lower labor costs.

Japan retained its status as an economic superpower thanks to its technological superiority, even though its growth was slowing and other Asian countries were industrializing fast. Thailand, Malaysia and Indonesia – which has large reserves of oil and gas to finance the growth of heavy industries – were growing. The Philippines, too, opted in the mid-1990s for policies modeled on the successes of other economies of the region.

A few countries did not form part of the "Asian miracle": notably Cambodia and Myanmar (formerly Burma), where oppressive regimes deterred foreign investment, and Laos, which had poor infrastructure.

border, 2005
original newly industrializing economies
emergent newly industrializing economies
Chinese special economic zone
little industrialization
Organization for Economic Cooperation and Development
ASEAN member state (Association of Southeast Asian Nations), 1967
Japanese investment flow
population over 1,000,000
Manila major international port
Chinese prodemocracy demonstration 1989
separatist movement
fiber-optic cable, 1996
source of major resource
gold
copper
nickel
tin
other metal
oilfield
0 1200 km
0 800 mi
BHU
NEPAL
BANGLAD
INDI

TIMELINE

East Asia

1975 In Taiwan, Jiang Ching-kuo plans for rapid growth

1978 In China, Deng Xiaoping advocates economic reforms; China and Japan sign a trade agreement

1979 China and the United States normalize relations

1984 The NIEs begin to invest in China

1987 Democratic elections are held in Taiwan, and martial law is lifted for the first time since 1949

1989 In China, the prodemocracy movement led by students is crushed at Tiananmen Square, Beijing

1993 Japan's Liberal Democratic Party loses power for the first time since 1955

1994 Kim Il Sung, Stalinist president of North Korea, dies

1997 Death of Deng Xiaoping; Hong Kong returns to Chinese rule

2002 182 people (most tourists) killed in bomb attack on Bali, Indonesia, by Islamic extremist group possibly financed by Osama bin Laden

2003 SARS virus hits China, Hong Kong and Vietnam

2005 First meeting of Chinese and Taiwanese leaders since 1945

2008 Widespread international protests against China's presence in Tibet follow Olypic flame to Beijing

2008 The United States removes North Korea from the Axis of Evil

Southeast Asia

1975 The Khmer Rouge take over Cambodia, leading to mass killings

1975 Collapse of South Vietnam and creation of a single Vietnamese state

1976 Indonesia annexes Portuguese East Timor

1978–79 Vietnam invades Cambodia to crush Khmer Rouge regime; China invades northern Vietnam

1986 Prodemocracy candidate Corazon Aquino takes over from Ferdinand Marcos after the Philippines presidential elections

1986 Laos signs an economic development agreement with Thailand

1987 Democratic elections are held in South Korea

1988 A military junta seizes power in Burma

1989 Australia initiates the Asia Pacific Economic Cooperation Forum

1991 Burmese prodemocracy leader Aung San Suu Kyi is imprisoned by the military government

1992 Vietnam opens a free-trade zone, funded by Taiwan

1999 Australian referendum rejects change from a British commonwealth country to an independent republic

2002 East Timor wins independence from Indonesia

2004 A huge tsunami devastates countries around the Indian Ocean

2005 Anti-immigrant violence in Australia

2009 Forest fires devastate communities in Victoria, Australia

Politically, despite the intrusion of global market forces, the region saw the survival of Communism as the dominant ideology in China, Vietnam and North Korea. Security in east Asia was threatened by a stand-off between the US and North Korea: however, after North Korea halted its nuclear programme in 2008, it was removed from what US president George Bush had termed the "axis of evil."

It was in the Pacific rim (specifically Thailand) that a run on the national currency in 1997 signalled world recession. The crisis spread to Hong Kong and then to the rest of the region. Japan, economically stagnant from 1989, could no longer invest in its neighbors economies, and China began to suffer from production overcapacity. Recovery was strong in 2002, however; by 2004 China was having to make efforts to cool its booming economy.

China's increasing involvement in the global economy brought increased international attention. Criticism of political repression and human rights abuses rose, as did environmental protest against the huge Three Gorges Dam, completed on the Yangtze River in 2008. In western China, many Muslim Uighurs fled persecution. During the build-up to the Beijing Olympic Games in 2008, Tibet was the focus of international criticism. Protests followed the Olympic flame around the world.

A collapsing Indonesian economy forced President Suharto from power in 1998 and led indirectly – following further loss of life in a bitter conflict – to the creation of the new state of East Timor in 2002. Islamic separatists waged continuing terrorist campaigns in various parts of Indonesia.

1 Taiwan's economic success was based on heavy investment in human resources: in 1995, four-fifths of 18-year-olds were in higher education.

2 Shanghai led China's economic boom in the early 2000s, becoming one of the world's fastest-growing cities. In 2005 it became the world's largest cargo port.

3 In the late 1990s Japan endured ongoing recession for the first time sine 1945.

4 East Timor finally achieved independence in 2002, 25 years after Portugal's withdrawal and Indonesia's subsequent invasion and brutally repressive regime.

5 The seabed surrounding the Spratly Islands — disputed by Vietnam, China, Malaysia, the Philippines, Taiwan and Brunei — contains the world's fourth largest oil reserves.

6 In 2009 Australia's worst bushfires devastated communities and killed around 100 people in Victoria.

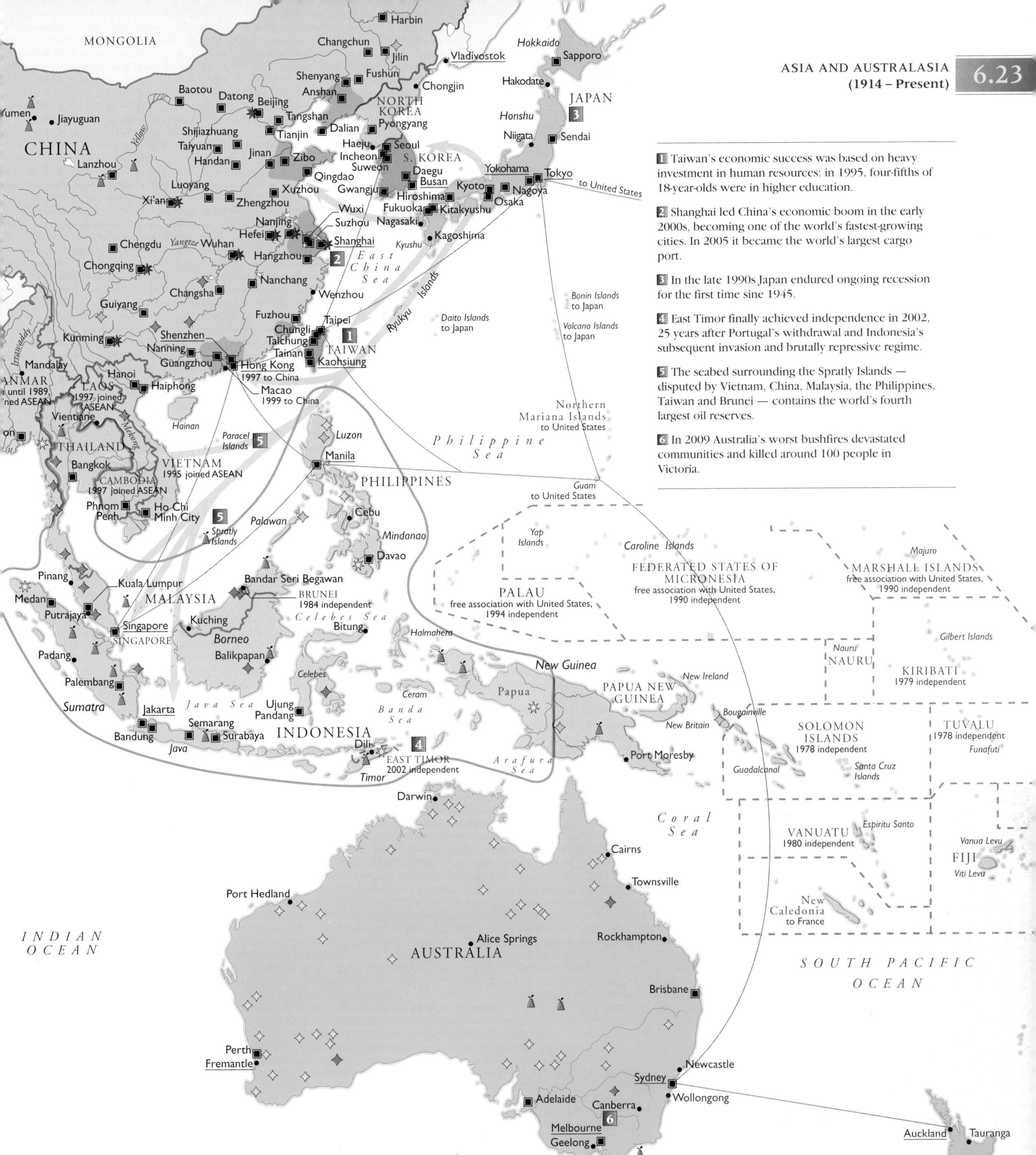

Economic and social progress in Asia was seriously damaged in the first years of the new millenium by natural disasters. In December 2004, a devastating tsunami (unleashed by a massive earthquake off the coast of northwest Sumatra) spread across the Indian Ocean, destroying everything in its path and taking the lives of nearly 300,000 people, in countries as far apart as Indonesia, Thailand, the Maldives, Sri Lanka and Somalia. As well as local residents, casualties included many European tourists.

Tourism and the wider economies of the region were also damaged by two significant new diseases. The appearance of SARS (severe acute respiratory syndrome) and avian (bird) flu raised fears of global infection, but both appeared to be contained by extensive public health campaigns.

In 2008, economic growth throughout Southeast Asia was undermined by the global credit crunch. Millions of Chinese jobless workers left the cities to return to their rural homes. Japan's Toyota, the largest motor manufacturer in the world, meanwhile, announced the first loss in its history.

See also 6.14 (the Americas); 6.20 (east Asia to 1976); 6.21 (southeast Asia to 1976)

6.24 The Middle East and north Africa • 1914 – 1948 •

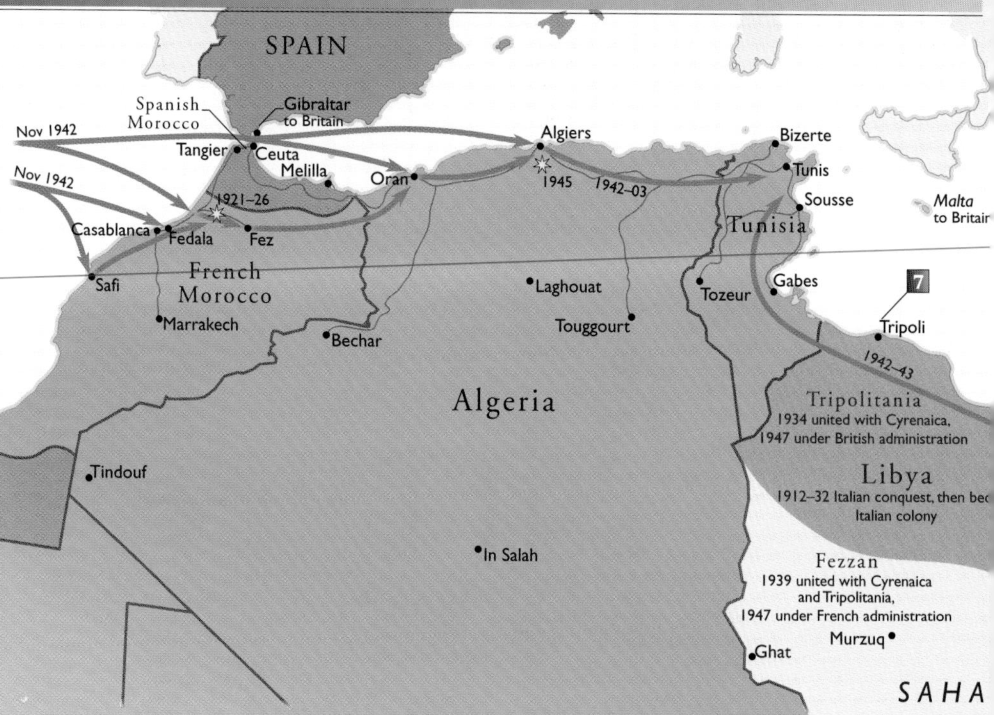

SPAIN
Spanish Morocco
Gibraltar to Britain
Nov 1942
Nov 1942
Tangier
Ceuta
Melilla
Oran
Algiers
1945
1942–03
Bizerte
Tunis
Sousse
Malta to Britain
Tunisia
1921–26
Casablanca
Fedala
Fez
French Morocco
Safi
Marrakech
Bechar
Laghouat
Touggourt
Tozeur
Gabes
7
Tripoli
1942–43
Algeria
Tripolitania
1934 united with Cyrenaica,
1947 under British administration
Tindouf
Libya
1912–32 Italian conquest, then bec
Italian colony
In Salah
Fezzan
1939 united with Cyrenaica and Tripolitania,
1947 under French administration
Murzuq
Ghat
SAHA

In 1914 the Allies decided to carry the war into every German colony in Africa. Military operations in Togoland, Cameroon and South-West Africa were completed by 1916; the campaigns in German East Africa (later Tanganyika) continued until 1918, a week after the armistice was signed on the Western Front. Turkey's alliance with Germany led to assaults on the Suez Canal and Basra, both repelled by Allied forces. The British supported the Arab revolts against the Turks: they took Jerusalem in 1917, and a more general assault on Turkish control of the Middle East followed as the British raced to occupy the Mesopotamian oilfields. Britain ensured its hold over the oilfields of southern Persia, too, claiming a *de facto* protectorate in 1918.

The Covenant of the League of Nations required the peacemakers to help underdeveloped peoples to cope with the "strenuous conditions of the modern world". The colonies of the defunct German and Turkish empires were administered under the mandate system. Some ex-colonies were scheduled for rapid independence: on this understanding Britain was awarded a mandate over Palestine, Iraq (formerly Mesopotamia) and Transjordan; France gained Syria and Lebanon. Less advanced areas could not expect independence in the near future; these included the Cameroons and Togoland, shared between Britain and France; Britain acquired Tanganyika, Belgium was awarded Ruanda-Urundi.

This redistribution of territory meant that the British and French colonial empires grew substantially; the indigenous peoples were not consulted about their aspirations for independence. The notable exception was in Palestine where, the British government declared in 1917, it favored the establishment of a national home for the Jews. This conflicted with an earlier promise to the Arabs that their new lands would include Palestine, where the population was 90 percent Muslim. Jewish immigration to the area was limited through the 1920s, but grew substantially in the 1930s, when the British first proposed the division of Palestine into separate Jewish and Arab states. After World War II, with the world horrified by the Holocaust and the Jews and Arabs in Palestine engaged in civil war, the United Nations supported partition and approved the state of Israel which came into being in 1948.

Britain, by 1918 the dominant power in the region, held back from interfering in central Arabia, permitting the Saudi kingdom to emerge in 1932. Britain's mandate in Iraq ended in 1932 but the right to protect oil and military interests was retained, notably by means of two airforce bases. A native Pahlavi dynasty seized control of Persia in 1925, renaming it Iran in 1935. By the outbreak of war, Iran produced more oil than the rest of the Middle East, and the shah's ties with Nazi Germany led the Allies to occupy the country again in 1941; the shah was forced to abdicate and his son Mohammed Reza Pahlavi installed in his place. The market for Middle Eastern oil grew in the interwar years, but the oilfields were not fully developed until the 1950s. French rule in Syria and Lebanon was benevolent, but was compromised by the fall of France in 1940; both countries were occupied during the war by Free French and British troops, and their independent status was recognized in 1946.

North and east Africa, too, were caught up in the conflicts of the European powers. The British confirmed Egyptian independence in 1922 but maintained the right to use Egypt's facilities in time of war, to defend the Suez Canal and maintain the Anglo-Egyptian condominium in the Sudan. The British in Egypt and Italians in Libya began a conflict in 1940 which drew in the German army the following year; by 1943 the entire North Africa littoral was involved. Meanwhile indigenous independence movements were beginning to emerge, though most did not bear fruit until after World War II.

Ethiopia had retained its independence from colonial rule since defeating the Italians in 1896, and from 1935 was ruled by Haile Selassie (formerly Ras Tafari), who faced an invasion from Italy's Fascist dictator Mussolini. After using mustard gas on the Ethiopians, the Italians took Addis Ababa in 1936; a resistance movement continued to harry the Italians until World War II, when the British invaded and drove the Italians out once more, restoring Haile Selassie in 1941 and making Ethiopia the first African country to be liberated. Britain now took over the adminstration of the former Italian colonies of Eritrea and Somaliland.

French colonization of north Africa had failed to create a settler class comparable with the traditional peasantry of France. Settlers tended to be large farmers engaged in speculative agriculture for

TIMELINE

1920 — 1940

Middle East

- **1916** Arab revolt in the Hejaz against Ottoman rule
- **1917** "Balfour Declaration" promises a national homeland for the Jews in Palestine
- **1918** Iraq is brought under British rule
- **1922** The League of Nations approves Palestinian mandate
- **1924** Britain insists on control of Transjordan's affairs
- **1930** Standard Oil and Texas Oil form Bahrain Petroleum Company
- **1932** The British mandate in Iraq ends
- **1933** Ibn Saud permits Standard Oil to prospect in Saudi Arabia
- **1941** Britain and Soviet Union invade Iran
- **1946** Transjordan wins independence, annexes the West Bank and becomes kingdom of Jordan
- **1948** Proclamation of the state of Israel

North Africa

- **1914** Egypt is proclaimed a British protectorate
- **1921-26** A nationalist revolt against French and Spanish rule in Morocoo
- **1922** Egypt gains independence under King Fuad I
- **1928** Muslim Brotherhood founded in Egypt
- **1934** Formation of Moroccan nationalist party
- **1936** Britain is granted use of Egyptian facilities in wartime
- **1941** Germans conquer north Libya and invade Egypt
- **1943** Allied forces defeat the Germans in Tunisia

Sub-Saharan Africa

- **1914** African, French and British forces take Togoland and German East Africa
- **1920** Old German colonies mandated to Britain, Belgium, France and South Africa
- **1935–36** Italian invasion of Ethiopia
- **1941** Italy surrenders Ethiopia, Eritrea, and Somaliland

1920 — 1940

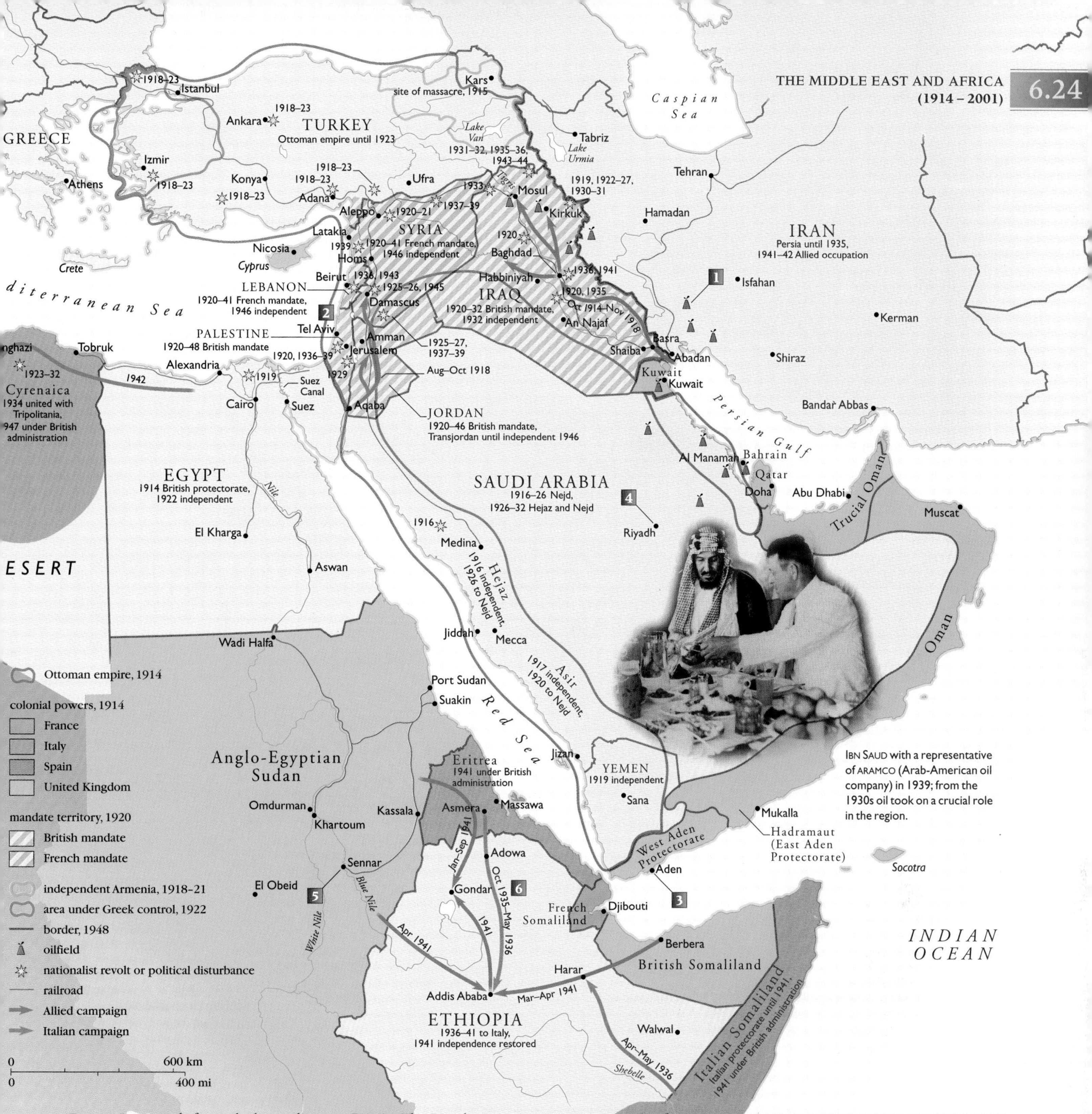

Ottoman empire, 1914

colonial powers, 1914
- France
- Italy
- Spain
- United Kingdom

mandate territory, 1920
- British mandate
- French mandate

- independent Armenia, 1918–21
- area under Greek control, 1922
- border, 1948
- oilfield
- nationalist revolt or political disturbance
- railroad
- Allied campaign
- Italian campaign

0 600 km
0 400 mi

IBN SAUD with a representative of ARAMCO (Arab-American oil company) in 1939; from the 1930s oil took on a crucial role in the region.

export to France. Intensively farmed wheat, olives and vines required capital investment but between 1914 and 1935 these produced spectacular yields, strong exports and brought about the development of the north African workforce. In the same way control of mineral resources by French managers meant that virtually all the production of iron ore and phosphates, and the zinc, lead and cobalt deposits, went to France. The depression of the 1930s led to the collapse of much of this activity, and a rise in unemployment.

Libyan resistance to Italian colonization persisted until 1932. Italy's Fascist government encouraged large estates worked by Italian settlers, but there was little investment in infrastructure and barely 90,000 Italians had settled in Libya by 1939.

British policy toward Egypt and the Sudan was very different, with little or no settlement from Britain. The British saw Egypt as a major source of cotton, and encouraged Egyptian financial institutions to support local industry and cotton-related projects in the Sudan. By 1939 Egypt was approaching self-sufficiency in a range of manufactured goods; production rose further during the war years.

1 Masjed-Suleyman was the site of the first oil find in the Middle East, in 1908. Oil was found in Libya in the 1920s, and in Kuwait in 1932.

2 Tel Aviv was founded in 1909 by Zionist idealists as a suburb of the ancient city of Jaffa; the Turks cleared the settlement in 1916–17, but it became the focus for Jewish immigration in the 1920s and 1930s.

3 Aden, an important British coaling station on the route to India, was ruled from India until 1937 when it became a crown colony.

4 Abdul Aziz Ibn Saud (r.1901-53) took Riyadh in 1901, consolidated his hold over Nejd by 1906 and Hejaz (1926) and set up the kingdom of Saudi Arabia in 1932. Oil reserves were found there in 1938.

5 The Sennar Dam was completed in 1925, marking the beginning of a plan to irrigate the Sudan and develop the cotton industry for export.

6 Italy's invasion of Ethiopia in October 1935 began with a land and air attack on Adowa, the scene of an Italian defeat in 1896.

7 Tripoli was the center of Mussolini's Libyan industrial program: more than 700 factories were in operation there by 1939.

See also 5.14 (decline of the Ottoman empire); 6.25 (postwar Middle East); 6.26 (Africa)

6.25 Arab–Israeli conflict • 1948 – 1977 •

Only a few hours after the proclamation of the independent state of Israel on 14 May 1948, the armies of Syria, Jordan, Egypt and Iraq invaded, expecting to crush the Jewish state and establish an Arab Palestine. The Jews drew on reserves of experienced soldiers from around the world, defeated the Arabs and conquered territory as far as West Jerusalem. When East Jerusalem and the West Bank of the Jordan became part of the territory of Jordan the following year, Palestine ceased to exist. No Arab state would recognize the permanence of the new frontiers, though they received *de facto* acceptance at armistice talks in 1949. Israel's victory meant that the new state attracted thousands of Jewish immigrants to a new homeland, while more than a million Palestinians became refugees in their own land – a potentially explosive force in the politics of the region and of Jordan in particular.

Defeat led to a nationalist revolt in Egypt in 1952, when the British-sponsored ruling family was expelled and a republic instituted by a group of army officers. Colonel Nasser, president from 1954, relied on American dollars to subsidize the massive Aswan Dam project, regarded as essential for Egypt's economic and industrial development. When the United States withdrew in response to Nasser's increasingly anti-western foreign policy, he nationalized the Suez Canal, long seen as a strategic key to the east by Britain and France. These two old colonial powers decided to invade. Israel's support was secretly secured and Israeli forces invaded Sinai in October 1956, with Anglo-French troops arriving a week later. American pressure brought about a withdrawal and a United Nations force was sent in, while Nasser blocked the canal with sunken ships.

Widespread condemnation of Britain and France was followed by increased superpower involvement in the region: Arab states turned to the Soviet Union for weaponry while the United States became Israel's arsenal. Nasser was convinced that Egypt, allied with Syria (the two were united as the United Arab Republic in 1958–61), would defeat Israel. He assembled an alliance of Arab states and provoked a crisis by closing the Gulf of Aqaba. Israel, however, launched the most effective pre-emptive strike in history, attacking all of Egypt's air bases in June 1967. Most Egyptian combat aircraft were destroyed; Syria and Jordan suffered similar devastation.

When a ceasefire was agreed six days later, Israeli forces had occupied Gaza and the entire Sinai east of Suez, Jordan surrendered East Jerusalem, Bethlehem and Hebron, and Syria lost the Golan Heights, an area dominating the north of Israel.

The United Nations, however, passed resolutions requiring Israel to evacuate the occupied territories, deploring the loss of Palestinian civil rights, and confirming the Palestinian right to selfdetermination. These pointed to the deep divisions within Israel, where the Palestinians were treated as second-class citizens, many of them – particularly in the areas recently occupied by Israel – condemned to a life in refugee camps. The Palestinian Liberation Organization (PLO) was founded in 1964, and by the early 1970s had won, through a combination of terrorist tactics and moral pressure, a powerful and independent voice in the politics of the region. Seeming to endanger the fragile stability of Jordan, the PLO was evicted from the kingdom in 1970 and settled in Lebanon. The growing numbers of refugees there, most with little to lose, proved destabilizing to that country as well and contributed to the outbreak of civil war in Beirut in 1975.

In October 1973 Egypt's new president Anwar Sadat broke through into Israeli-held territory without warning on the Jewish Day of Atonement (Yom Kippur). The Israelis concentrated on holding the Golan Heights against Syrian tanks, but three weeks later Israel had defeated both attacks comprehensively while the two superpowers refused to intervene actively to support the protagonists.

In response to the United States' supply of military materiel to the Israelis, Saudi Arabia (where oil revenues had grown dramatically since 1945 and which was the leading member of the Organization of Petroleum Exporting Countries, OPEC) imposed oil sanctions on the west, restricting OPEC exports and causing a sharp price rise. Despite this, the governments of Saudi Arabia and the Gulf states, including Iran (where the Allied occupation in World War II had left a legacy of popular bitterness toward "imperialists"), remained close to the United States and rejected the growing influence of the Soviet Union in the region. The main oil-producing states were reluctant to give military support to the anti-Israeli effort, and tensions developed between Saudi Arabia and Egypt over Egyptian policy in the southern Arabian peninsula. Syria and Iraq, however, were both under the control of the "anti-imperialist" and Arab nationalist Ba'ath Party, from 1963 and 1968 respectively. Libya too, another important oil producer, was in the control of a strongly anti-American regime inspired by the success of Nasser and led by Muammar Qadhafi from 1969.

Following the Yom Kippur War, Menachem Begin became prime minister of Israel, and realized that, like himself, Sadat was now interested in reducing Arab–Israeli tensions. Begin invited Sadat to Jerusalem, and a peace process was initiated which was formalized in the United States in 1979.

1 Jerusalem, a holy city to Jews, Muslims and Christians, was divided after the failure of the Arab attack of 1948; the Israelis took the whole city in 1967, but disputes continued into the 1990s.

2 In 1953 the CIA (US intelligence agency) backed a coup against Iranian prime minister Mohammed Moussadeq, who had tried to nationalize the oil industry in 1951. The exiled shah returned to power.

3 Sharm el-Sheikh, a cove on the Sinai peninsula controlling entry to the Straits of Tiran, was captured by the Israelis in 1956 and controlled by the United Nations Emergency Force 1957–67.

4 This neutral zone between Kuwait and Saudi Arabia was partitioned between the two countries in 1966.

5 Israel bombed Palestinian bases in Jordan in 1968 and its troops defeated the Al Fatah (PLO military wing) guerrillas at the Battle of Karama.

6 Jordan expelled the Al Fatah guerrillas in 1970; many established new bases in southern Lebanon.

7 After ethnic conflict in Cyprus through the 1950s and UN intervention from 1964, a Turkish invasion in 1974 divided the island into Greek and Turkish zones.

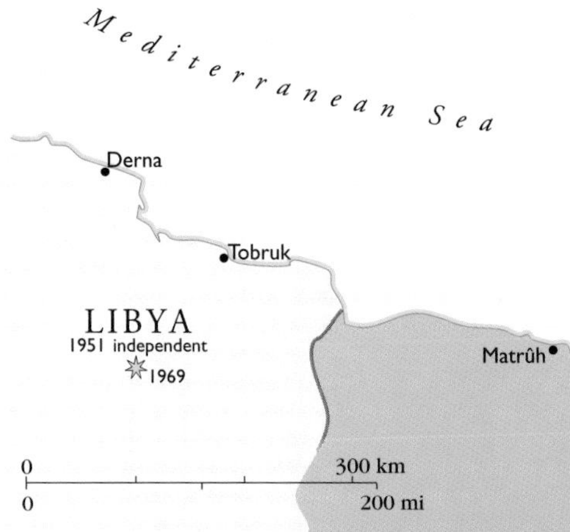

Mediterranean Sea
Derna
Tobruk
LIBYA
1951 independent
1969
Matrûh
0
300 km
0
200 mi

TIMELINE

Arab–Israeli Wars

(1955 / 1965 / 1975)

- **1948** Israel's foundation is followed by an Arab attack
- **1949** One million Palestinians flee Israel
- **1956** Nasser's nationalization of the Suez Canal leads to British, French and Israeli invasions of Egypt
- **1958** Nationalist revolution in Iraq overthrows the monarchy
- **1964** Palestinian Liberation Organization (PLO) is founded in Jerusalem
- **1967** Six-Day War ends with Israeli control over Sinai
- **1969** Yassir Arafat becomes PLO chairman
- **1970** The PLO are driven out of Jordan and settle in Lebanon; terrorist hijacking of civilian aircraft begins
- **1973** Sadat launches the fourth war against Israel
- **1977** Egypt's president Sadat offers Israel peace in return for a Palestinian state

Other developments

- **1951** Moussadeq becomes Iranian prime minister and nationalizes the oil industry
- **1952** The Egyptian monarchy is overthrown
- **1953** The CIA sponsor a coup in Iran and reinstate Reza Khan Pahlavi as shah
- **1961** Kuwait gains its independence, though it is claimed by Iraq
- **1965** Iran exiles Islamic leader Ayatollah Khomeini
- **1968** Ba'ath leader Saddam Hussein takes power in Iraq
- **1970** General Asad seizes power in Syria
- **1973** OPEC countries raise the price of oil to exert political influence on the west
- **1975** Civil war breaks out in Beirut

(1955 / 1965 / 1975)

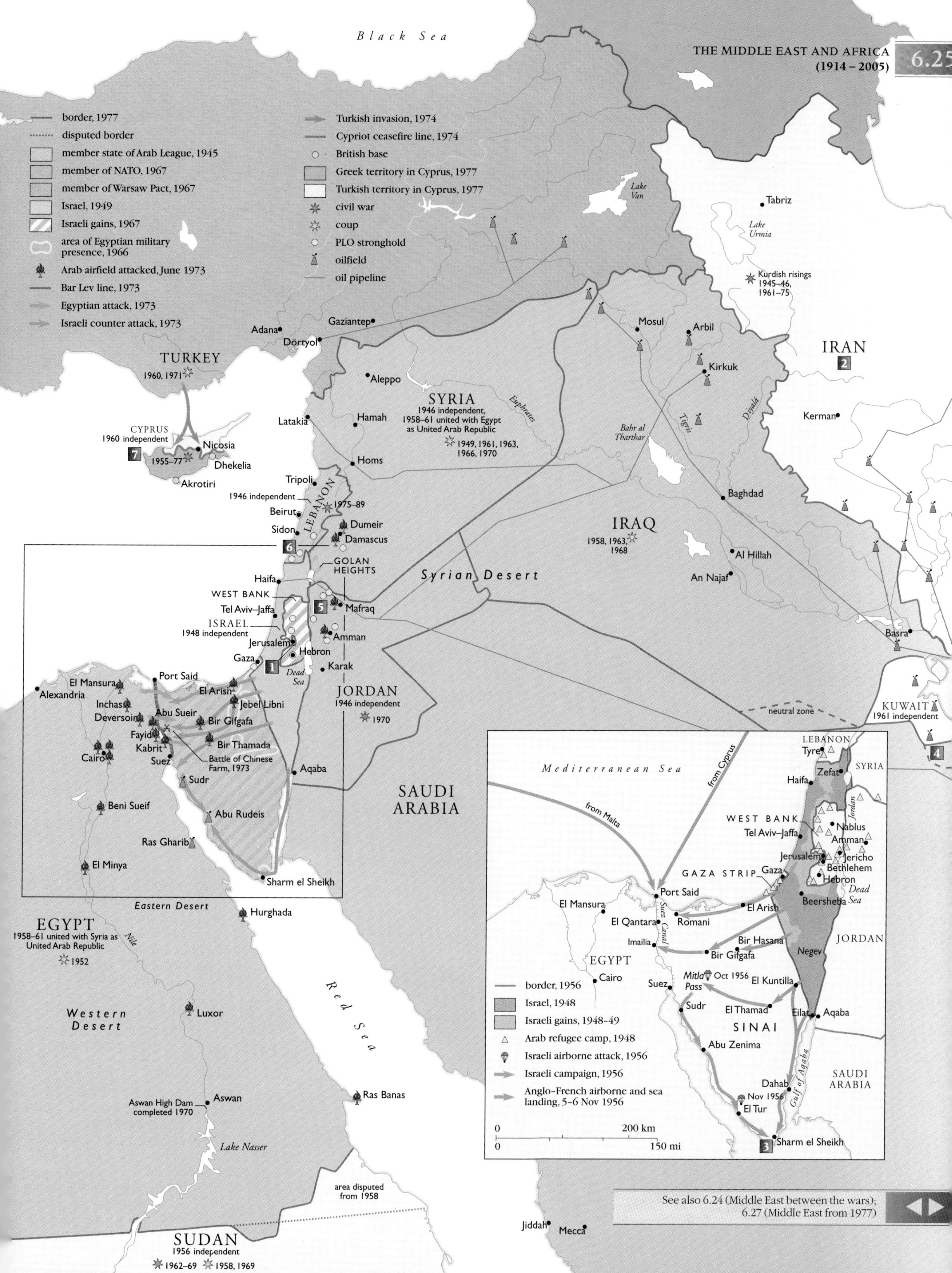
Black Sea
border, 1977
disputed border
member state of Arab League, 1945
member of NATO, 1967
member of Warsaw Pact, 1967
Israel, 1949
Israeli gains, 1967
area of Egyptian military presence, 1966
Arab airfield attacked, June 1973
Bar Lev line, 1973
Egyptian attack, 1973
Israeli counter attack, 1973
Turkish invasion, 1974
Cypriot ceasefire line, 1974
British base
Greek territory in Cyprus, 1977
Turkish territory in Cyprus, 1977
civil war
coup
PLO stronghold
oilfield
oil pipeline
Lake Van
Tabriz
Lake Urmia
Kurdish risings 1945–46, 1961–75
TURKEY
1960, 1971
CYPRUS
1960 independent
1955–77
Nicosia
Dhekelia
Akrotiri
Adana
Dörtyol
Gaziantep
Aleppo
SYRIA
1946 independent, 1958–61 united with Egypt as United Arab Republic
1949, 1961, 1963, 1966, 1970
Euphrates
Latakia
Hamah
Homs
Tripoli
LEBANON
1946 independent
1975–89
Beirut
Sidon
Dumeir
Damascus
GOLAN HEIGHTS
Haifa
WEST BANK
Tel Aviv–Jaffa
ISRAEL
1948 independent
Jerusalem
Hebron
Gaza
Dead Sea
Mafraq
Amman
Karak
JORDAN
1946 independent
1970
Aqaba
Mosul
Arbil
Kirkuk
IRAN
Kerman
Tigris
Diyala
Bahr al Tharthar
Baghdad
IRAQ
1958, 1963, 1968
Al Hillah
An Najaf
Syrian Desert
Basra
KUWAIT
1961 independent
neutral zone
SAUDI ARABIA
Port Said
El Mansura
Alexandria
El Arish
Inchas
Jebel Libni
Abu Sueir
Deversoir
Bir Gifgafa
Fayid
Kabrit
Bir Thamada
Cairo
Suez
Battle of Chinese Farm, 1973
Sudr
Beni Sueif
Abu Rudeis
Ras Gharib
El Minya
Sharm el Sheikh
Eastern Desert
Hurghada
EGYPT
1958–61 united with Syria as United Arab Republic
1952
Nile
Western Desert
Luxor
Red Sea
Ras Banas
Aswan
Aswan High Dam completed 1970
Lake Nasser
area disputed from 1958
SUDAN
1956 independent
1962–69
1958, 1969
Jiddah
Mecca
Mediterranean Sea
from Malta
from Cyprus
LEBANON
Tyre
Zefat
SYRIA
Haifa
Jordan
WEST BANK
Nablus
Tel Aviv–Jaffa
Amman
Jerusalem
Jericho
Bethlehem
Hebron
GAZA STRIP
Gaza
Dead Sea
Port Said
Beersheba
El Mansura
El Arish
El Qantara
Romani
Suez Canal
Imailia
Bir Hasana
JORDAN
Bir Gifgafa
EGYPT
Negev
Cairo
Mitla Pass
Oct 1956
El Kuntilla
Suez
Sudr
El Thamad
Eilat
Aqaba
SINAI
Abu Zenima
border, 1956
Israel, 1948
Israeli gains, 1948–49
Arab refugee camp, 1948
Israeli airborne attack, 1956
Israeli campaign, 1956
Anglo-French airborne and sea landing, 5–6 Nov 1956
SAUDI ARABIA
Dahab
Gulf of Aqaba
Nov 1956
El Tur
Sharm el Sheikh
0 200 km
0 150 mi
1
2
3
4
5
6
7

See also 6.24 (Middle East between the wars);
6.27 (Middle East from 1977)

6.26 The Middle East • 1977 – Present •

The Camp David Accords of 1979 between Israel and Egypt (the first Arab state to take such a step) recognized the state of Israel, promised autonomy to the Palestinians in Gaza and the West Bank, and returned the Sinai to Egypt. The Palestine Liberation Organization (PLO) took on the task of fighting Israel from its bases in Lebanon, where civil war was raging between Christian Phalangist and Islamic forces and where, since 1976, Syria had provided the main authority. In 1978 Israel invaded and UN forces struggled to keep apart the armies of Israel, Syria and the Christian militia. Lebanon's civil war continued until Syria restored peace in the early 1990s; the Syrian occupation ended only in 2005, in the face of popular Lebanese opposition.

The political force of Islam had been dramatically seen in Iran, where the shah was overthrown in 1979 by demonstrations in support of Ayatollah Khomeini, who became president of a new theocratic republic. Khomeini's resurgent Shiite Islam and apparent intention to dominate the region led Saddam Hussein, Ba'athist leader of mainly Sunni Iraq, to invade Iran in 1980. War between the two states continued for eight years; neither won a clear victory despite almost a million casualties. After the ceasefire in 1988, Saddam revived an old Iraqi claim on the rich emirate of Kuwait, and invaded in 1990. Saudi Arabia, fearing further Iraqi expansion, permitted its territory to be used as a base for an attack. The United Nations sanctioned the use of force, and war broke out in January 1991. A US-led UN coalition (including Egypt and Syria) won a quick victory. Civil war broke out in Iraq as Shiites in the south and Kurds in the north both sought to secede. Saddam remained in power, however, destroying the Shiite power base and forcing two million Kurds to flee to Iran and Turkey, before the UN enforced no-fly zones and imposed sanctions on Iraq.

Meanwhile, the Camp David agreements failed to materialize, as Jewish settlers continued to encroach on the West Bank. In 1987 Gaza and West Bank Palestinians began an *intifada* (uprising) against Israel. Eventually a peace process led to recognition of a Palestinian National Authority under Yasser Arafat. Israel faced a rightwing backlash. Prime minister Rabin was murdered in 1995 and under his sucessors moves toward Palestinian self-rule slowed. Ariel Sharon, elected in 2001, hardened the Israeli position and oversaw the building of a security barrier to prevent suicide bombers entering the country. The barrier was widely condemned, including by Israel's own Supreme Court. The death in 2004 of Palestinian leader Yasser Arafat, and the election of Mahmoud Abbas (Abu Mazewn), promised a chance for renewed peace initiatives, particularly when Sharon removed all Israeli settlements from the Gaza Strip in 2005. However, a stroke that left Sharon in a permanent coma, together with the election of a Hamas government in Gaza in 2007, again derailed peace initiatives. In 2006 Israel fought an inconclusive war in Lebanon after the kidnap of two of its soldiers. In late 2008, bomb attacks on Israeli settlements were met by a brief but large-scale military attack on Gaza.

In 2002 the United States argued that Iraq had broken UN resolutions concerning weapons of mass destruction. Despite international protest, the United States, Britain and their allies invaded Iraq in March 2003, quickly toppling Saddam, who was captured later that year, tried, and hanged in 2006. Elections in January 2005 saw Kurdish leader Jalal Talabani become president, but Iraq remained torn by an ongoing insurgency until a huge increase in US forces in 2008, termed a "surge," seemed to promise increased stability. The announcement that the US intended to withdraw its troops by the end of 2010 left Iraq's future uncertain.

Western attention turned again to Iran, where tensions were raised by the 2004 election of a conservative parliament and international concern over apparent Iranian moves to develop a nuclear program. Hawkish US opposition was softened by new president Barack Obama in 2009. In Saudi Arabia, the government cracked down on radicals protesting against its pro-Western attitudes, who had attacked foreign interests in the country.

- border of Soviet Union to 1991
- member of OPEC
- member of NATO
- Egypt, 1983
- Israel, 1983
- territory restored to Egypt, May 1979–Apr 1982
- area occupied by Israel
- territory captured by Iraq, Sep–Dec 1980
- territory captured by Iran, Oct 1984
- Qom center of Islamic revolution in Iran, 1970s
- PLO diaspora, 1982
- Iran–Iraq war air strike, 1980–88
- area of Shiite population, 1983
- area claimed by Kurds as national homeland
- Anti-Iraq coalition state, 1990–91
- Coalition air base, 1990–91
- Coalition offensive, 1991
- UN-imposed Iraqi "no-fly" zone
- UN peace-keeping force
- movement of refugees
- migrant labor
- border, 2005
- oilfield
- oil pipeline
- desert

TIMELINE

Arab–Israeli conflict

1978 First Israeli invasion of Lebanon

1978 The Camp David agreements are signed

1981 Assassination of president Sadat of Egypt

1982 Second Israeli invasion of Lebanon: Christians massacre Palestinian refugees

1985 Israel agrees to withdraw from Lebanon

1987 *Intifada* by Palestinians in occupied territories begins

1992 Lebanese elections mark the end of the civil war

1993 In the Oslo Declaration, Israel and PLO agree on the formation of a Palestinian state

1995 Israel agrees to begin withdrawal from West Bank towns; premier Yitzhak Rabin is assassinated

1996 Israel attacks Hizbollah strongholds in south Lebanon

2000 Likud Party leader Ariel Sharon's tour of the Temple Mount in Jerusalem provokes second *Intifada*

2002 Israel begins to build controversial security barrier on boundary of West Bank

2003 U.S.-sponsored roadmap lays plans for a peace agreement

2003 The United States and its allies invade Iraq and overthrow Saddam

2004 Death of Yasser Arafat; Mahmoud Abbas is elected Palestinian prime minister. Israel announces plans to withdraw from Gaza

2005 Israel withdraws settlements from Gaza

2006 Ariel Sharon enters a coma after a stroke; Hamas wins Palestinian elections; Israel war with Lebanon

2007 Hamas takes control of Gaza

2008 Israel attacks Gaza

The Gulf

1979 Islamic forces in Iran oust the shah; Khomeini comes to power

1980 Iraq invades Iran; Iraqi oil terminals are damaged by Iranian attacks

1988 Iraq uses chemical weapons on the Kurds of northern Iraq

1988 The UN arranges a ceasefire between Iran and Iraq

1990 Iraq invades and annexes Kuwait

1991 An American-led UN coalition defeats Iraq and liberates Kuwait

2004 Attacks on Western targets rise in Saudi Arabia

2004 Saudi Arabia begins crackdown on Al Qaeda militants

2005 Iraqis vote in their first election after the fall of Saddam

2005 Syrian troops withdraw from Lebanon

2006 Saddam Hussein hanged in Iraq

2007 UN imposes sanctions to prevent Iran developing nuclear power

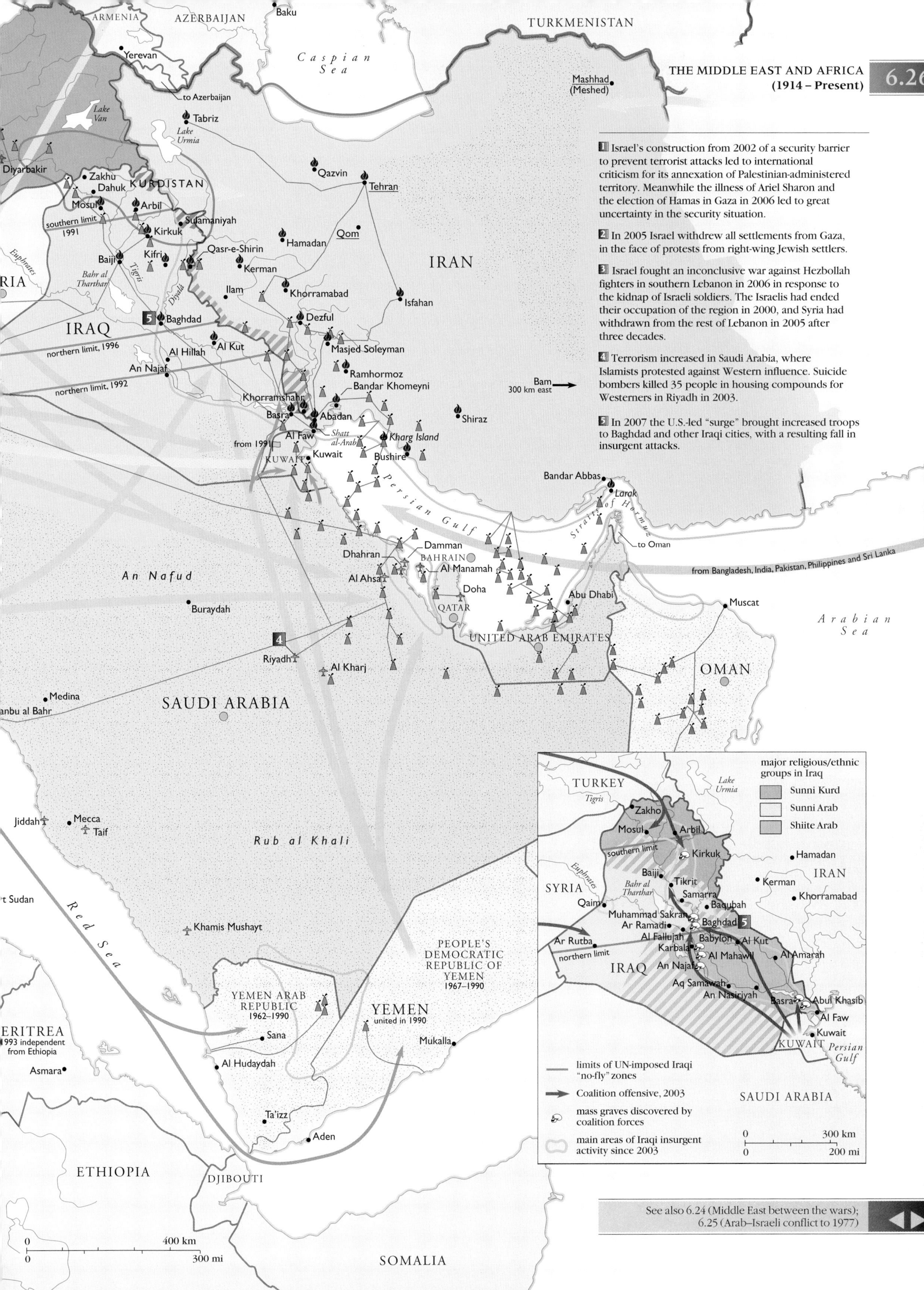
ARMENIA
AZERBAIJAN
Baku
TURKMENISTAN
Yerevan
Caspian Sea
Mashhad (Meshed)
to Azerbaijan
Tabriz
Lake Van
Lake Urmia
Diyarbakir
Zakhu
Dahuk
KURDISTAN
Qazvin
Tehran
Mosul
Arbil
southern limit 1991
Sulamaniyah
Kirkuk
Hamadan
Qom
Euphrates
Baiji
Kifri
Qasr-e-Shirin
Kerman
IRAN
Bahr al Tharthar
Tigris
Diyala
Ilam
Khorramabad
Isfahan
Baghdad
Dezful
IRAQ
northern limit, 1996
Al Kut
Al Hillah
Masjed Soleyman
An Najaf
Ramhormoz
northern limit, 1992
Bandar Khomeyni
Khorramshahr
Bam 300 km east
Basra
Abadan
Shiraz
Al Faw
Shatt al-Arab
Kharg Island
from 1991
KUWAIT
Kuwait
Bushire
Persian Gulf
Bandar Abbas
Larak
Strait of Hormuz
to Oman
Damman
Dhahran
BAHRAIN
Al Manamah
from Bangladesh, India, Pakistan, Philippines and Sri Lanka
An Nafud
Al Ahsa
Doha
Abu Dhabi
Muscat
QATAR
Buraydah
Arabian Sea
UNITED ARAB EMIRATES
Riyadh
Al Kharj
OMAN
Medina
Yanbu al Bahr
SAUDI ARABIA
Jiddah
Mecca
Taif
Rub al Khali
Sudan
Red Sea
Khamis Mushayt
PEOPLE'S DEMOCRATIC REPUBLIC OF YEMEN 1967–1990
YEMEN ARAB REPUBLIC 1962–1990
YEMEN united in 1990
ERITREA 1993 independent from Ethiopia
Sana
Mukalla
Asmara
Al Hudaydah
Ta'izz
Aden
ETHIOPIA
DJIBOUTI
SOMALIA
0 400 km
0 300 mi
major religious/ethnic groups in Iraq
Sunni Kurd
Sunni Arab
Shiite Arab
TURKEY
Lake Urmia
Tigris
Zakho
Mosul
Arbil
southern limit
Kirkuk
Hamadan
Euphrates
Baiji
Tikrit
Kerman
IRAN
SYRIA
Bahr al Tharthar
Samarra
Khorramabad
Qaim
Baqubah
Muhammad Sakran
Ar Ramadi
Baghdad
Al Fallujah
Babylon
Al Kut
Ar Rutba
Karbala
Al Mahawil
Al Amarah
northern limit
IRAQ
An Najaf
Aq Samawah
An Nasiriyah
Basra
Abul Khasib
Al Faw
Kuwait
KUWAIT
Persian Gulf
limits of UN-imposed Iraqi "no-fly" zones
Coalition offensive, 2003
mass graves discovered by coalition forces
main areas of Iraqi insurgent activity since 2003
SAUDI ARABIA
0 300 km
0 200 mi

1 Israel's construction from 2002 of a security barrier to prevent terrorist attacks led to international criticism for its annexation of Palestinian-administered territory. Meanwhile the illness of Ariel Sharon and the election of Hamas in Gaza in 2006 led to great uncertainty in the security situation.

2 In 2005 Israel withdrew all settlements from Gaza, in the face of protests from right-wing Jewish settlers.

3 Israel fought an inconclusive war against Hezbollah fighters in southern Lebanon in 2006 in response to the kidnap of Israeli soldiers. The Israelis had ended their occupation of the region in 2000, and Syria had withdrawn from the rest of Lebanon in 2005 after three decades.

4 Terrorism increased in Saudi Arabia, where Islamists protested against Western influence. Suicide bombers killed 35 people in housing compounds for Westerners in Riyadh in 2003.

5 In 2007 the U.S.-led "surge" brought increased troops to Baghdad and other Iraqi cities, with a resulting fall in insurgent attacks.

See also 6.24 (Middle East between the wars); 6.25 (Arab–Israeli conflict to 1977)

Africans played an active part in World War II, fighting on behalf of the Allies and identifying with the democratic freedom for which they fought. War meant that independence could not long be denied. In British West Africa, the transfer of power was swift and peaceful. The Gold Coast (now Ghana) became independent in 1956 and, by 1965, Britain had granted independence equally readily to Nigeria, Sierra Leone and the Gambia.

In French West Africa, "colonies" were replaced by "overseas territories," with all Africans becoming French citizens. While many Africans accepted French control, Algeria began its fight for independence on the day that World War II ended in Europe. In 1958, nationalist freedom fighters were confronted by settlers, causing a crisis that brought Charles de Gaulle back to the French presidency. By 1960 most French colonies had been given independence but this was not achieved in Algeria until 1962.

In Kenya, where white settlers controlled the best farming land, the Mau Mau movement instigated reprisals. Some 20,000 people, mostly Kikuyu sympathetic to their white masters, were murdered before independence was granted in 1963. In contrast, independence came relatively peacefully in Uganda, Tanganyika, Nyasaland and Northern Rhodesia.

The ends of both the Belgian and Portuguese empires were violent. When Congo became independent, the Congolese army mutinied and thousands of Belgian citizens became refugees. Belgian paratroopers went to their aid, and the copper-rich province of Katanga declared independence. Eventually, General Mobutu crushed the Katangans and their mercenary supporters, creating a unified state, which he renamed Zaire.

Portugal bitterly opposed nationalists in Guinea, Angola and Mozambique. By 1975, though, when Portugal underwent its own political convulsions, the colonies became sovereign states.

Few African states found that independence brought stability or prosperity. Many faced ethnic conflict, a legacy of colonial borders that had little relevance to physical, social or economic realities. Most had impoverished, poorly educated, rapidly growing populations, and their economies proved vulnerable to multinationals keen to exploit natural resources. With institutions of government weak, much of the continent has experienced civil war, dictatorship and corruption, accompanied by a series of humanitarian crises.

The experience of Nigeria was typical: a civil war in the late 1960s led to widespread famine and resulted in a cycle of weak civilian governments replaced by military strong men. In the early 21st century, militants in the Niger Delta continued a terrorist campaign against oil companies. Marxist forces fought tenaciously in many countries including Mozambique and Angola, and won control of Ethiopia in 1974. Elsewhere, dictators such as Jean-Bédel Bokassa in the Central African Republic and Idi Amin in Uganda ruled by terror with few aims beyond personal aggrandizement. Robert Mugabe, leader of Zimbabwe since 1980, encouraged his followers to drive white farmers from their land; the economic effect, combined with drought, was that by 2005 the country could no longer feed its people.

Elsewhere, too, natural problems were often exacerbated by human activity. Environmental degradation continued as the Sahara moved southward and the continent faced shortages of wood and fresh water. From the 1980s into the new millennium sub-Saharan Africa was gripped by an HIV/AIDS epidemic. By 2007 the continent was home to well over two-thirds of the world's AIDS sufferers, 22 million Africans were infected, and the disease killed around 4,000 people every day. The fight against AIDS was limited by a lack of political will, an unwillingness to acknowledge the problem, or a lack of funds. Meanwhile, a general recognition in the West of the need to help Africa tackle its problems yielded initiatives to cancel international debt in the poorest countries, but also a complex debate about what conditions should be placed on debt relief to encourage reform.

Rwanda, where old ethnic rivalries overflowed into genocide in 1994, causing a flood of refugees into neighboring Zaire, made substantial economic progress though it continued to receive substantial aid. At the start of the new millennium civil wars continued to create turmoil in African countries, including the Democratic Republic of Congo, Liberia, Ivory Cost, Sierra Leone and Sudan, where unrest in the Darfur region killed some 180,000 people and displaced 2 million more, creating a refugee crisis in neighbouring Chad. Ceasefires and the presence of UN peacekeepers failed to halt the violence. In 2009 the International Criminal Court issued a warrant for the arrest of Sudanese president Omar al-Bashir for crimes against humanity in Darfur. Famine meanwhile struck across the continent, including Chad, Sudan, Zimbabwe, Eritrea, Ethiopia, Democratic Republic of Congo, Sudan, Swaziland, Lesotho, Somalia and Malawi.

Western Sahara
1979 to Morocco
1957
from 1975
Nouadhibou
Atar
MAURITANIA
1960 independent
1960, 1971–74, 1983
CAPE VERDE
1975 independent
1963–74
1983
Praia
Nouakchott
Senegal
St Louis
Kiffa
Kaédi
SENEGAL
1960 independent
Dakar
1971–74
Kayes
GAMBIA
1965 independent
1973
Banjul
GUINEA-BISSAU
1974 independent
Bissau
1959–74
Bamako
GUINEA
1958 independent
Kankan
Conakry
SIERRA LEONE
1961 independent
1997 coup
1991–2002
Freetown
Kenema
Monrovia
LIBERIA
1985–95, 2000–03

1 Libya's international rehabilitation culminates in 2008 with its temporary presidency of the United Nations Security Council.

2 Eritrea was annexed by Ethiopia in 1952, but won its independence in 1993 following a bitter civil war.

3 Uganda was among 17 countries worst-hit by heavy rain and flooding that left 600,000 people homeless across central Africa in 2007.

4 1.5 million refugees fled Darfur (Sudan) in 2003 as pro-government Arab militia launched campaign of ethnic cleansing against rebels fighting for autonomy.

5 In 2003, the Sudanese civil war ended, leaving 1.5 million dead and many more displaced. A 2005 peace deal provides for autonomy for South Sudan.

6 In 2009 Ethiopian troops withdrew from Somalia, where they had been fighting Islamist rebels.

TIMELINE

1950 · 1970 · 1990 · 2000

North & east Africa

- **1946** Houphouet-Boigny of Liberia founds African Democratic Federation
- **1949** Mau Mau movement founded in Kenya
- **1954** Algerian National Liberation Front (FLN) declares war on French
- **1962** End of war in Algeria against French rule
- **1963** State of emergency ends in Kenya with independence
- **1974** Marxists oust emperor Haile Selassie in Ethiopia
- **1977–88** Somali forces clash with Ethiopia in a claim over the Ogaden area
- **1984–85** Civil war in Eritrea leads to widespread famine in Ethiopia
- **1992** Civil war in Algeria between Islamic fundamentalists and government
- **2003** Libya abandons weapons of mass destruction; UN lifts sanctions on Libya
- **2005** First national government created in Somalia since 1991
- **2005** Terrorists attack tourist resorts in Egypt
- **2006** Warring parties in Sudan sign peace deal
- **2007** Violence breaks out following elections in Kenya; floods hit a million people across Africa
- **2008** Peace accords in Somalia

West & central Africa

- **1954** Gold Coast's National Liberation Movement begins
- **1956** Representative government promised to Nigeria
- **1958** French colonies hold referenda on independence
- **1961** Wars of liberation begin in Portuguese colonies
- **1965** Southern Rhodesia's whites declare unilateral independence (UDI)
- **1967–70** Biafran war brings famine to eastern Nigeria
- **1975** Civil war breaks out in Angola immediately after independence
- **1994** Ethnic conflict in Rwanda results in mass slaughter and a refugee crisis
- **1999** After 16 years of military rule, President Obasanjo heads civilian government in Nigeria
- **2003** Ethnic unrest in Darfur region of Sudan displaces 1.5 million refugees
- **2003** Charles Taylor quits as president of Liberia
- **2004** HIV/AIDS infects more than 24 million Africans

1950 · 1970 · 1990 · 2000

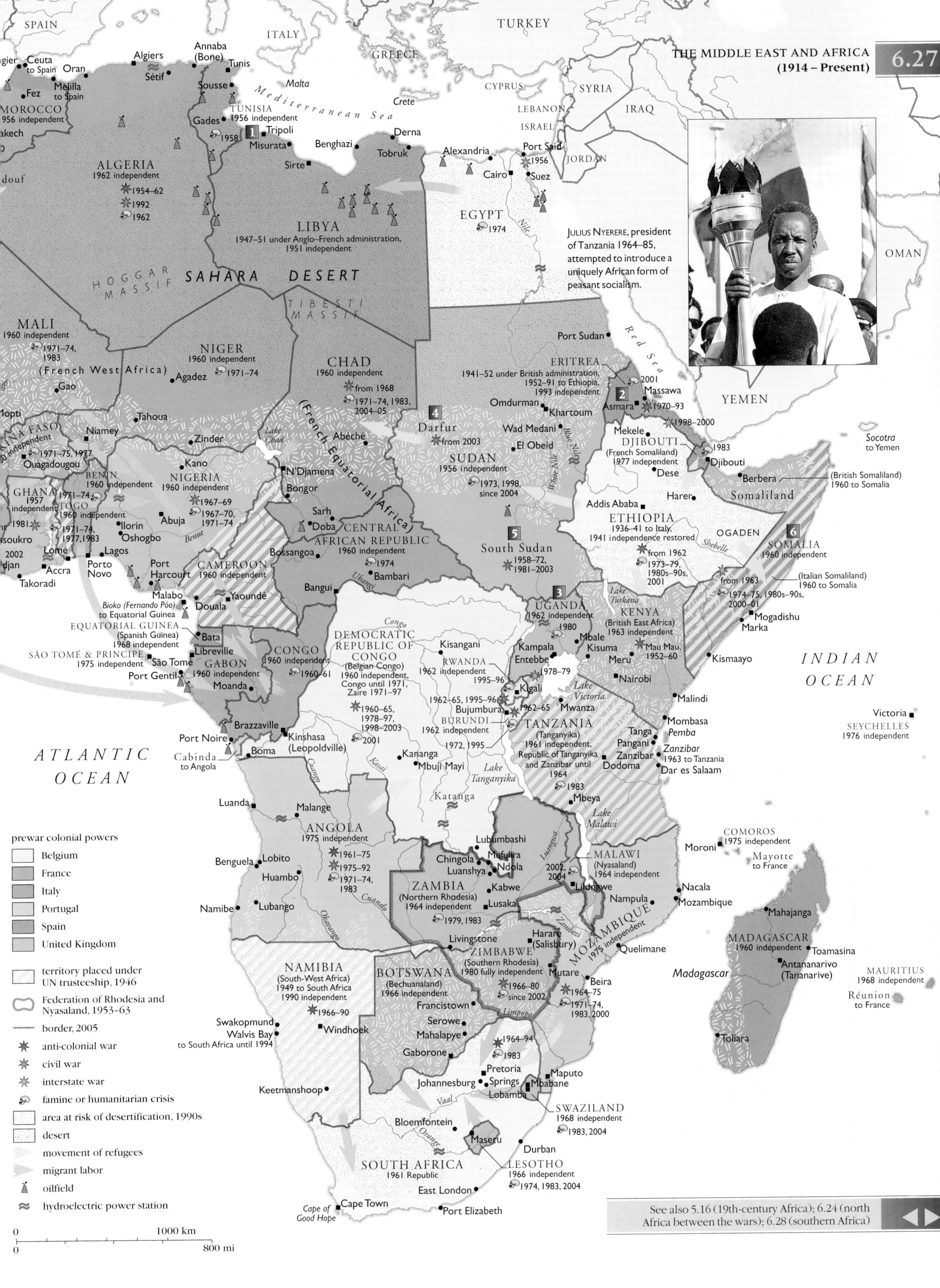
SPAIN
ITALY
GREECE
TURKEY
CYPRUS
SYRIA
IRAQ
LEBANON
ISRAEL
JORDAN
Malta
Crete
Mediterranean Sea
Ceuta to Spain
Oran
Melilla to Spain
Fez
MOROCCO
1956 independent
Algiers
Sétif
Annaba (Bone)
Tunis
Sousse
TUNISIA
1956 independent
Gades
1958
Tripoli
Misurata
Benghazi
Derna
Tobruk
Sirte
Alexandria
Port Said
1956
Cairo
Suez
ALGERIA
1962 independent
1954–62
1992
1962
LIBYA
1947–51 under Anglo-French administration,
1951 independent
EGYPT
1974
Nile
HOGGAR MASSIF
SAHARA DESERT
TIBESTI MASSIF
MALI
1960 independent
1971–74,
1983
(French West Africa)
Gao
NIGER
1960 independent
1971–74
Agadez
CHAD
1960 independent
from 1968
1971–74, 1983,
2004–05
(French Equatorial Africa)
Tahoua
Niamey
Zinder
Lake Chad
Abéché
Darfur
from 2003
Port Sudan
Red Sea
ERITREA
1941–52 under British administration,
1952–91 to Ethiopia,
1993 independent
2001
Massawa
Asmara
1970–93
1998–2000
Omdurman
Khartoum
Wad Medani
El Obeid
Blue Nile
White Nile
SUDAN
1956 independent
1973, 1998,
since 2004
Mekele
DJIBOUTI
(French Somaliland)
1977 independent
1983
Djibouti
Dese
Ouagadougou
1971–75, 1977
Kano
BENIN
1960 independent
NIGERIA
1960 independent
1967–69
1967–70,
1971–74
N'Djamena
Bongor
GHANA
1957 independent
TOGO
1960 independent
1971–74
1981
1971–74,
1977, 1983
Ilorin
Oshogbo
Abuja
Benue
Sarh
Doba
CENTRAL AFRICAN REPUBLIC
1960 independent
1974
Bambari
Bossangoa
Bangui
Ubangi
Lomé
Accra
Takoradi
Lagos
Porto Novo
Port Harcourt
CAMEROON
1960 independent
Malabo
Yaoundé
Douala
Bioko (Fernando Póo)
to Equatorial Guinea
EQUATORIAL GUINEA
(Spanish Guinea)
1968 independent
Bata
SÃO TOMÉ & PRINCIPE
1975 independent
São Tomé
Libreville
GABON
1960 independent
Port Gentil
Moanda
CONGO
1960 independent
1960–61
Brazzaville
Port Noire
Cabinda to Angola
Boma
Kinshasa (Leopoldville)
DEMOCRATIC REPUBLIC OF CONGO
(Belgian Congo)
1960 independent,
Congo until 1971,
Zaire 1971–97
1960–65,
1978–97,
1998–2003
2001
Congo
Kisangani
Kananga
Mbuji Mayi
Kasai
Cuango
Katanga
Addis Ababa
ETHIOPIA
1936–41 to Italy,
1941 independence restored
from 1962
1973–79,
1980s–90s,
2001
Harer
Berbera
Somaliland
(British Somaliland)
1960 to Somalia
OGADEN
Shebelle
SOMALIA
1960 independent
from 1963
1974–75, 1980s–90s,
2000–01
(Italian Somaliland)
1960 to Somalia
Mogadishu
Marka
Kismaayo
South Sudan
1958–72,
1981–2003
UGANDA
1962 independent
1980
Lake Turkana
KENYA
(British East Africa)
1963 independent
Mau Mau,
1952–60
Mbale
Kisuma
Meru
Kampala
Entebbe
1978–79
Nairobi
RWANDA
1962 independent
1995–96
Kigali
1962–65, 1995–96
Bujumbura
1962–65
BURUNDI
1962 independent
1972, 1995
Lake Victoria
Mwanza
TANZANIA
(Tanganyika)
1961 independent,
Republic of Tanganyika
and Zanzibar until
1964
1983
Dodoma
Tanga
Pangani
Zanzibar
Pemba
Zanzibar
1963 to Tanzania
Dar es Salaam
Mbeya
Lake Tanganyika
Lake Malawi
Malindi
Mombasa
INDIAN OCEAN
Socotra
to Yemen
YEMEN
OMAN
Victoria
SEYCHELLES
1976 independent
ATLANTIC OCEAN
Luanda
Malange
ANGOLA
1975 independent
1961–75
1975–92
1971–74,
1983
Benguela
Lobito
Huambo
Namibe
Lubango
Cuando
Okavango
Lubumbashi
Chingola
Mufulira
Ndola
Luanshya
Kabwe
ZAMBIA
(Northern Rhodesia)
1964 independent
1979, 1983
Lusaka
Luangwa
MALAWI
(Nyasaland)
1964 independent
2002,
2004
Lilongwe
Moroni
COMOROS
1975 independent
Mayotte
to France
Nacala
Mozambique
Nampula
Quelimane
MOZAMBIQUE
1975 independent
Zambezi
Livingstone
Harare (Salisbury)
ZIMBABWE
(Southern Rhodesia)
1980 fully independent
1966–80
since 2002
Mutare
Beira
1964–75
1971–74,
1983, 2000
Mahajanga
MADAGASCAR
1960 independent
Toamasina
Antananarivo (Tananarive)
Madagascar
Toliara
MAURITIUS
1968 independent
Réunion
to France
NAMIBIA
(South-West Africa)
1949 to South Africa
1990 independent
1966–90
Windhoek
Swakopmund
Walvis Bay
to South Africa until 1994
BOTSWANA
(Bechuanaland)
1966 independent
Francistown
Serowe
Mahalapye
Gaborone
Limpopo
1964–94
1983
Pretoria
Springs
Johannesburg
Lobamba
Mbabane
Maputo
SWAZILAND
1968 independent
1983, 2004
Keetmanshoop
Vaal
Bloemfontein
Orange
Maseru
Durban
SOUTH AFRICA
1961 Republic
LESOTHO
1966 independent
1974, 1983, 2004
East London
Cape Town
Cape of Good Hope
Port Elizabeth
prewar colonial powers
Belgium
France
Italy
Portugal
Spain
United Kingdom
territory placed under UN trusteeship, 1946
Federation of Rhodesia and Nyasaland, 1953–63
border, 2005
anti-colonial war
civil war
interstate war
famine or humanitarian crisis
area at risk of desertification, 1990s
desert
movement of refugees
migrant labor
oilfield
hydroelectric power station
0 1000 km
0 800 mi

JULIUS NYERERE, president of Tanzania 1964–85, attempted to introduce a uniquely African form of peasant socialism.

See also 5.16 (19th-century Africa); 6.24 (north Africa between the wars); 6.28 (southern Africa)

6.28 Southern Africa • 1914 – Present •

In 1910, the Union of South Africa was set up with Louis Botha as premier. Tension between Afrikaners and the British continued, but attempts to unify the two were made during the world depression of the 1930s. Elsewhere, the colonial authorities continued to develop southern Africa for their own benefit, although South Africa's mining companies dominated the region economically.

The denial of African hopes of self-determination was accompanied by land expropriation, racial legislation and enforced urbanization. Opposition was slow to form politically and strikes or rebellions were often brutally crushed. Founded in 1912, the African National Congress (ANC) fought against racial segregation, but neither the Afrikaner-dominated National Party, led by James Hertzog, nor Jan Smuts' South Africa Party was moved.

In 1945, every other country south of the Zambezi was still an externally governed colony. In 1948, the National Party came to power in the wake of white anxiety at the number of blacks moving into white areas and South Africa sought to institutionalize white control by creating the system of *apartheid*. Their vision was that blacks and whites would eventually live in different states. People were removed *en masse* to the so-called black "homelands" – nominally independent countries, often with no territorial integrity, natural resources or employment possibilities beyond those offered by white South Africa.

By 1960, South Africa was opposed worldwide. When the British signaled their intention to transfer power to its colonies throughout Africa, South Africa left the Commonwealth. Movements for black rights formed terrorist wings and became more violent.

Decolonization began relatively peacefully with Tanganyika (Tanzania) in 1961 but, in 1965, the

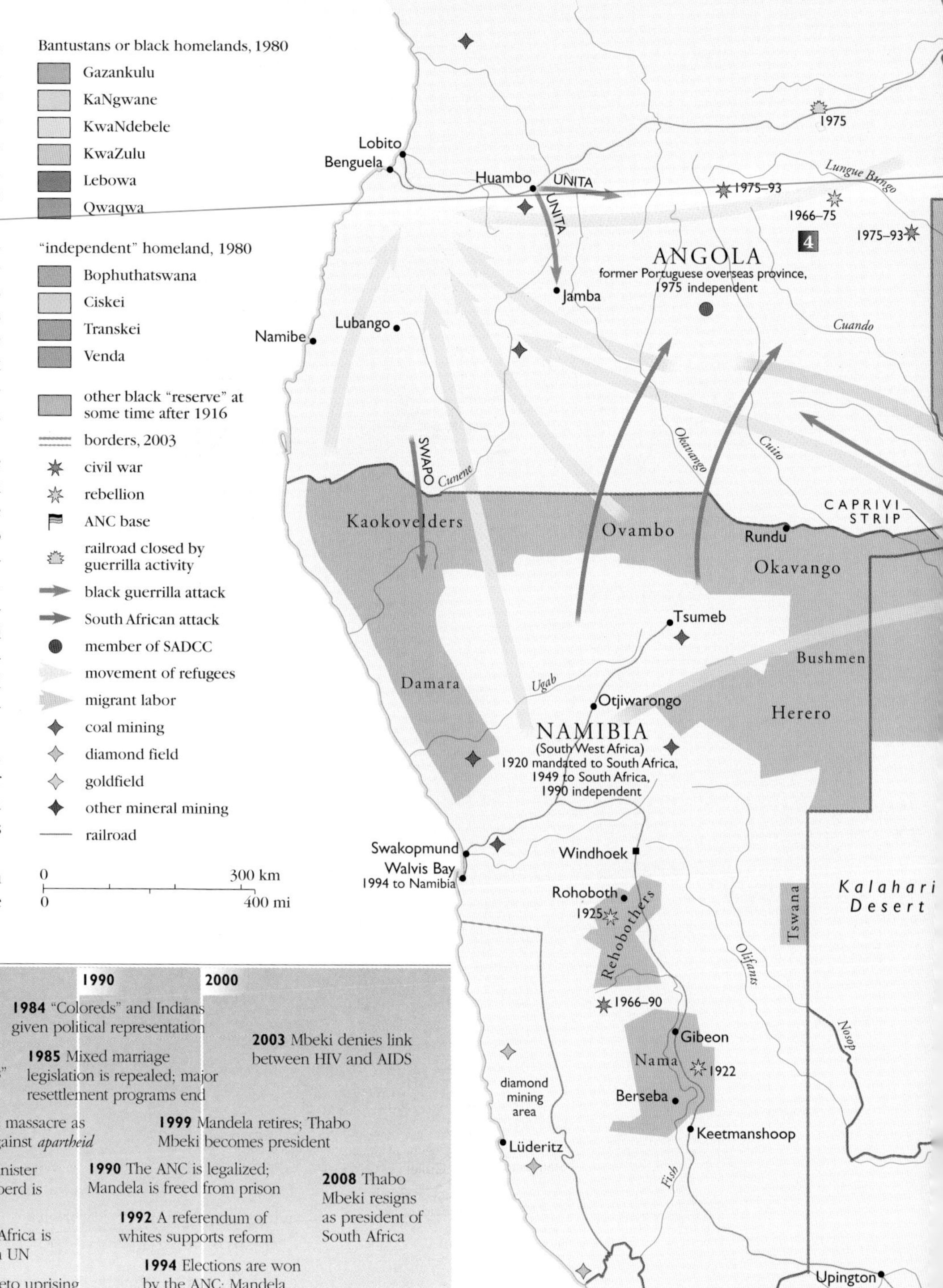

Bantustans or black homelands, 1980
Gazankulu
KaNgwane
KwaNdebele
KwaZulu
Lebowa
Qwaqwa
"independent" homeland, 1980
Bophuthatswana
Ciskei
Transkei
Venda
other black "reserve" at some time after 1916
borders, 2003
civil war
rebellion
ANC base
railroad closed by guerrilla activity
black guerrilla attack
South African attack
member of SADCC
movement of refugees
migrant labor
coal mining
diamond field
goldfield
other mineral mining
railroad
0 300 km
0 400 mi
Lobito
Benguela
Huambo
UNITA
UNITA
1975
1975–93
1966–75
1975–93
Lungue Bungo
ANGOLA
former Portuguese overseas province, 1975 independent
Jamba
Cuando
Lubango
Namibe
SWAPO
Cunene
Okavango
Cuito
CAPRIVI STRIP
Kaokovelders
Ovambo
Rundu
Okavango
Tsumeb
Bushmen
Damara
Ugab
Otjiwarongo
Herero
NAMIBIA
(South West Africa)
1920 mandated to South Africa,
1949 to South Africa,
1990 independent
Swakopmund
Walvis Bay
1994 to Namibia
Windhoek
Rohoboth
1925
Rehobothers
Tswana
Kalahari Desert
Olifants
1966–90
Gibeon
Nama
1922
Nosop
diamond mining area
Berseba
Keetmanshoop
Lüderitz
Fish
Orange
Upington
Northern Cape
SOUTH AFRIC
former British dominion, 1961 became a Republic
ATLANTIC OCEAN
Beaufort West
Western Cape
Robben Island
Cape Town
Worcester
Oudtshoo
Strand
Mosselb

TIMELINE

South Africa

1930 · 1960 · 1990 · 2000

- **1926** ANC conventions are held in Bloemfonte and Kimberley
- **1934** The Nationalist and South African parties join to form the United Party
- **1948** Pro-apartheid National Party wins election
- **1949** Apartheid is intro-duced; mixed marriages and inter-racial sex are banned, franchise restricted to whites
- **1955** Group Areas Act restricts areas of black residence
- **1959** Black "homelands" (Bantustans) are set up
- **1960** Sharpeville massacre as blacks protest against *apartheid*
- **1966** Prime minister Hendrik Verwoerd is assassinated.
- **1974** South Africa is banned from UN
- **1976** Soweto uprising leads to other township riots
- **1984** "Coloreds" and Indians given political representation
- **1985** Mixed marriage legislation is repealed; major resettlement programs end
- **1990** The ANC is legalized; Mandela is freed from prison
- **1992** A referendum of whites supports reform
- **1994** Elections are won by the ANC; Mandela becomes state president
- **1999** Mandela retires; Thabo Mbeki becomes president
- **2003** Mbeki denies link between HIV and AIDS
- **2008** Thabo Mbeki resigns as president of South Africa

Rest of region

- **1920** South-West Africa is mandated to South Africa
- **1922** Jan Smuts sends forces into South-West Africa
- **1924–27** 60,000 Africans are evicted from prime farmland in Northern Rhodesia
- **1947** South Africa refuses to allow South-West Africa to be put under UN trusteeship
- **1965** Whites in Rhodesia declare independence (UDI)
- **1975** South Africa invades Angola but MPLA wins power
- **1979** Internal settlement in Rhodesia/Zimbabwe ends white rule
- **1980** Mugabe is elected premier of Zimbabwe
- **1990** Namibia becomes Africa's last country to gain independence
- **2000** Zimbabwean government targets 25 million acres of white-owned farms for expropriation to black settlers
- **2005** The number of people living with HIV/AIDS in sub-Saharan Africa is estimated to be near 25 million
- **2005** Zimbabwean elections are condemned as neither free nor fair; Mugabe remains in power
- **2006** Joseph Kabila wins first elections in DR Congo for decades
- **2008** Robert Mugabe to share power after contested election in Zimbabwe

1930 · 1960 · 1990 · 2000

Lake Mweru
DEMOCRATIC REPUBLIC OF CONGO
(Belgian Congo)
1960 independent,
Congo until 1971,
Zaire 1971–97
TANZANIA
(Tanganyika)
former British territory,
1961 independent
Kolwezi
Likasi
Lake Bangweulu
Lubumbashi
Lake Malawi
Mzuzu
MALAWI
(Nyasaland)
former British protectorate,
1964 independent
FRELIMO
Lugenda
Luangwa
Chingola
Mufulira
Kitwe
Ndola
Luanshya
Kabompo
1964–75
Lilongwe
ZAMBIA
(Nothern Rhodesia)
former British protectorate,
1964 independent
Kafue
Kabwe
Lusaka
Zomba
Zambezi
Blantyre
ZANU
1966–80
Lake Kariba
East Caprivians
Livingstone
1986
Quelimane
Harare
(Salisbury)
Hwange
ZAPU
1966–80
MOZAMBIQUE
former Portuguese overseas province,
1975 independent
ZANU
Mutare
ZIMBABWE
(Southern Rhodesia)
former British protectorate,
1965 unilaterally independent,
1980 fully independent
Gweru
1966–80
1981
Beira
Bulawayo
Francistown
Save
BOTSWANA
(Bechuanaland)
former British protectorate,
1966 independent
Bobonong
Serowe
Messina
Limpopo
Thohoyandou
Mahalapye
Northern Province
1984
1964–75
Inhambane
1964–75
Pietersburg
Gaborone
Gauteng
Mpumalanga
Xai-Xai
Mmabatho
Middelburg
Johannesburg
Pretoria
Barberton
Maputo
Lichtenburg
Springs
Mbabane
WITWATERSRAND
SWAZILAND
former British territory,
1968 independent
North-West
Soweto
Vereeniging
Lobamba
Vryburg
Standerton
Gollel
Vaal
Kroonstad
Vryheid
Odendaalsrus
Bethlehem
Dundee
Free State
Ladysmith
Kimberley
KwaZulu-Natal
Caledon
Bloemfontein
Maseru
LESOTHO
(Basutoland)
former British colony,
1966 independent
Orange
Durban
Springfontein
De Aar
to Eastern Cape
Eastern Cape
Umtata
Queenstown
Reinet
East London
Port Elizabeth

white population of Southern Rhodesia declared independence and seized power.

South Africa relied on the Portuguese colonies of Mozambique and Angola as well as Southern Rhodesia to isolate black South Africa from the changes in the north. However, in all these countries, guerrilla organizations grew rapidly and, in 1975, Mozambique and Angola gained independence following the fall of the government in Portugal. Civil war erupted between rival factions.

South Africa pursued a strategy of undermining the new black states. In Angola,the South Africans fomented civil war by maintaining bases in the south of the country and funding the UNITA resistance group; in Mozambique they supported the anti-government MNR.

White rule ended in Rhodesia in 1980. The same year the black countries of southern Africa formed an association for development coordination (SADCC) to reduce their dependence on South Africa. South Africa responded with raids allegedly targeting ANC bases on its neighbours' land, and forced Mozambique and Swaziland to sign non-aggression treaties. The costs of *apartheid* grew, however. From 1984, sanctions were widely imposed on South Africa and multinational companies pulled out. Proposals for limited electoral reform met with mass protests in the mid-1980s.

In 1990, National Party president F.W. de Klerk announced negotiations for a new democratic constitution. Despite opposition from the Zulus and white extremists, the transition to multiparty democracy was made in April 1994 with the election of ANC leader Nelson Mandela as state president. The first years of the new "rainbow nation" proved optimistic as Mandela fostered reconciliation and restored the prestige of the state overseas. But the task of raising the living standards of the historically disadvantaged groups remained a daunting one.

A decade after the end of white rule, South Africa faced major problems, but its democratic culture appeared to be taking hold. Thabo Mbeki, Mandela's successor, won his second five-year term in April 2004 with his ruling ANC party. Mbeki caused controversy with his opposition to anti-AIDS drugs and was also implicated in 2008 of interfering in the trial of his former deputy and potential opponent for the presidency, Jacob Zuma.

In 2003, six countries faced famine in southern Africa. In 2005 United Nations food agency representatives opened negotiations with Zimbabwe, where eight million people faced shortages that were exacerbated by seizure of almost all white-owned commercial farms by the government of Robert Mugabe. By 2008 Zimbabwe faced ruin. Inflation reached 2 million percent, food and fuel were scarce and there were outbreaks of cholera. Thousands of Zimbabweans fled to neighboring South Africa. Morgan Tsvangirai, leader of the MDC party, won the first round of the presidential election in 2008 but refused to take part in the second round, alleging intimidation. Mugabe and Tsvangirai eventually reached a power-sharing agreement, which saw the MDC leader sworn in as prime minister in 2009. Although relations between the two men remained wary, there were signs that the period of hyperinflation was beginning to end.

1 Soweto (South Western Township) was the largest squatter township for blacks near Johannesburg and the focus of unrest after the Sharpeville and Soweto massacres (1960 and 1976).

2 Poor in agricultural and industrial resources, Basutoland continued to provide huge numbers of migrant workers for South Africa even after its national independence in 1966 as Lesotho.

3 Millions of refugees fled to South Africa to escape economic chaos and disease in Zimbabwe in 2008 and 2009.

4 South Africa fomented civil war in its neighbors to destabilize them. As a result, millions of refugees were forced to flee war and famine, especially from Mozambique and Angola.

5 ANC leader Nelson Mandela was imprisoned in 1964 on terrorist charges, and spent many years in the prison on Robben Island.

See also 5.17 (19th-century South Africa); 6.27 (decolonization in Africa)

Acknowledgements

Text, timelines and maps

The authors and publishers readily acknowledge the work of a large number of scholars and published works, on which they have drawn in the preparation of this atlas. Many of these works remain in print, and can be used as reliable secondary reading on the many topics covered in this atlas. Among them are the following:

Adams, A.E., Matley, I.M. and McCagg, W.O. *An Atlas of Russian and East European History* (London 1967)

Ajayi, J.F.A. and Crowder, Michael (eds) *Historical Atlas of Africa* (Cambridge and New York 1985)

Allchin, B. and R. *The Birth of Indian Civilization: India and Pakistan before 500 BC* (2nd ed., London 1994)

Almond, M., Black, J. McKitterick, R., and Scarre, C. *The Times Atlas of European History* (London and New York 1994)

Ardagh, John with Jones, Colin *Cultural Atlas of France* (London and New York 1991)

Ashdown, P. *Caribbean History in Maps* (London and New York 1979)

Bagot Glubb, J. *The Great Arab Conquests* (London 1963)

Bahn, Paul G. (ed) *Cambridge Illustrated History of Archaeology* (Cambridge and New York 1996)

Baines, John and Malek, Jaromir *Atlas of Ancient Egypt* (Oxford and New York 1980)

Barraclough, G. (ed) *The Times Atlas of World History* (4th ed., London 1993 and New York 1994)

Bartlett, R. *The Making of Europe: Conquest, Colonisation and Cultural Change 950–1300* (London 1993)

Bayley, Christopher (ed) *Atlas of the British Empire* (London and New York 1989)

Black, C. and others *Cultural Atlas of the Renaissance* (London and New York 1993)

Black, Jeremy *The Cambridge Illustrated Atlas of Warfare: Renaissance to Revolution 1492–1792* (Cambridge and New York 1996)

Blunden, Caroline and Elvin, Mark *Cultural Atlas of China* (London and New York 1986)

Bolton, Geoffrey (ed) *The Oxford History of Australia* (Oxford and Melbourne 1994)

Braudel, Fernand *Civilization and Capitalism* (3 vols, revised ed., Princeton 1992)

Brown, Dee *The American West* (New York 1994)

Campbell, John (ed) *The Experience of World War II* (London and New York 1989)

Chadwick, Henry and Evans, Gillian R. (eds) *Atlas of the Christian Church* (London and New York 1987)

Champion, T., Gamble, C., Shennan, S. and Whittle, A. *Prehistoric Europe* (London 1984)

Chang, K.C. *The Archaeology of Ancient China* (Yale 1977)

Chard, C.S. *Northeast Asia in Prehistory* (Madison, USA 1974)

Coe, Michael, Snow, Dean and Benson, Elizabeth *Atlas of Ancient America* (London and New York 1986)

Coe, Michael *Mexico: from the Olmecs to the Aztecs* (4th ed., London and New York 1994)

Cohn-Sherbok, D. *Atlas of Jewish History* (London and New York 1994)

Collcutt, Martin, Jansen, Marius and Kumakura, Isao *Cultural Atlas of Japan* (London and New York 1988)

Connah, G. *African Civilizations: Precolonial cities and states in tropical Africa* (Cambridge and New York 1987)

Cook, J.M. *The Persian Empire* (London 1983)

Cornell, Tim and Matthews, John *Atlas of the Roman World* (London and New York 1982)

Cotterell, A. *East Asia* (London 1993, New York 1995)

Crawford, M. *The Roman Republic* (London 1978, Cambridge, Mass 1993)

Cunliffe, Barry (ed) *The Oxford Illustrated Prehistory of Europe* (Oxford and New York 1994)

Darby, H.C. and Fullard, Harold *The New Cambridge Modern History Atlas* (Cambrdge 1970)

Davies, R.H.C. *A History of Medieval Europe* (2nd ed., London and New York 1988)

Davis, Norman *Europe: a History* (Oxford and New York 1996)

Dear, I.C.B. and Foot, M.R.D. (eds) *The Oxford Companion to the Second World War* (Oxford and New York 1995)

de Lange, Nicholas *Atlas of the Jewish World* (London and New York 1984)

Elliott, J.H. (ed) *The Hispanic World* (London and New York 1991)

Fagan, Brian M. *The Journey from Eden: the Peopling of our World* (London and New York 1990)

Fagan, Brian M. *Ancient North America* (London and New York 1995)

Fage, J.D. and Oliver, R. (eds) *The Cambridge History of Africa* (Cambridge and New York 1975–)

Fernández-Armesto, Felipe (ed) *The Times Atlas of World Exploration* (London and New York 1991)

Fiedel, S.J. *Prehistory of the Americas* (2nd ed., Cambridge and New York 1992)

Freedman, Lawrence *Atlas of Global Strategy* (London and New York 1985)

Freeman-Grenville, G.S.P. *Historical Atlas of the Middle East* (New York 1993)

Frye, R.N. *The Heritage of Persia* (2nd ed., London 1976)

Gamble, C. *The Palaeolithic Settlement of Europe* (Cambridge 1986)

Gamble, C. *Timewalkers: the Prehistory of Global Colonization* (Stroud 1993, Cambridge, Mass. 1994)

Gaur, A. *A History of Writing* (London 1984, New York 1994)

Gilbert, Martin *The Atlas of Jewish History* (5th ed., London and New York 1996)

Graham Campbell, James (ed) *Cultural Atlas of the Viking World* (London and New York 1994)

Green, M.J. *The Celtic World* (London and New York 1995)

Griffiths, Ieuan L. *The Atlas of African Affairs* (London 1984)

Grosser Historischer Weltatlas (3 vols, Munich 1981)

Hall, D.G.E. *A History of South-east Asia* (4th ed., London 1981)

Handlin, O. *The History of the United States* (New York 1967)

Hartman, Tom *A World Atlas of Military History 1945–1984* (New York 1985)

Haywood, John *Historical Atlas of the Vikings* (London and New York 1995)

Haywood, John *Dark Age Naval Power* (London and New York 1991)

Holt, P.M., Lambeth, A.K.S. and Lewis, B. (eds) *The Cambridge History of Islam* (Cambridge 1970–)

Homberger, E. *Historical Atlas of North America* (London and New York 1995)

Hooper, Nicholas and Bennett, Matthew *The Cambridge Illustrated Atlas of Warfare: The Middle Ages 768–1487* (Cambridge and New York 1996)

Hosking, G. *A History of the Soviet Union* (London 1985)

Johnson, Gordon, Bayly, C. and Richards J.F. *The New Cambridge History of India* (Cambridge 1987–)

Johnson, Gordon *Cultural Atlas of India* (London 1995, New York 1996)

Kemp, B.J. *Ancient Egypt* (London 1989, New York 1992)

Kinder, H. and Hilgemann, W. *Atlas of World History* (2 vols, Munich, London and New York 1974)

King, P.D. *Charlemagne* (London 1986)

Kuhrt, A. *The Ancient Near East* (London and New York 1995)

Kulke, H. and Rothermund, D. *A History of India* (London 1990)

Langer, William L. *An Encyclopedia of World History* (5th ed., London and New York 1973)

Lee, K. *A New History of Korea* (Cambridge, Mass 1988)

Levi, Peter *Cultural Atlas of the Greek World* (London and New York 1984)

Lynch, J.H. *The Medieval Church* (Harlow 1992)

Mallory, J.P. *In Search of the Indo-Europeans* (London 1989, New York 1991)

Matthew, Donald *Atlas of Medieval Europe* (London and New York 1989)

McEvedy, Colin and Jones, Richard *Atlas of World Population History* (London 1978)

Milner, C.A., O'Connor, C.A. and Sandweiss, M. *The Oxford History of the American West* (Oxford and New York 1994)

Milner-Gulland, Robin with Dejevsky, Nikolai *Cultural Atlas of Russia and the Soviet Union* (London and New York 1989)

Moore, R.I. (ed) *The Hamlyn Historical Atlas* (London 1981)

Morgan, D. *The Mongols* (Oxford 1986, Cambridge, Mass 1990)

Moseley, M.E. *The Incas and their Ancestors* (London and New York 1993)

Murray, Oswyn *Early Greece* (2nd ed., London 1993)

Nile, R. and Clerk, C. *Cultural Atlas of Australia, New Zealand and the South Pacific* (London and New York 1995)

Ostrogorsky, G. *History of the Byzantine State* (revised ed., New Brunswick 1986)

Parker, W.H. *An Historical Geography of Russia* (London 1968)

Paxton, John *The Statesman's Yearbook Historical Companion* (London 1988)

Phillipson, D.W. *African Archaeology* (Cambridge 1993)

Pitcher, D.E. *An Historical Geography of the Ottoman Empire* (Leiden 1972)

Porter, A.N. (ed) *Atlas of British Overseas Expansion* (London 1991)

Pounds, Norman J.G. *An Historical Geography of Europe* (Cambridge 1990)

Reid, Anthony (ed) *Southeast Asia in the Early Modern Era: Trade, Power and Belief* (New York 1993)

Riasanovsky, N.V. *A History of Russia* (5th ed., Oxford and New York 1993)

Riley-Smith, Jonathon *The Atlas of the Crusades* (London and New York 1991)

Roaf, Michael and Postgate, Nicholas *Cultural Atlas of Mesopotamia* (London and New York 1990)

Roberts, J.M. *The Hutchinson History of the World* (London 1976)

Robinson, Francis *Atlas of the Islamic World since 1500* (London and New York, 1982)

Rogerson, John *Atlas of the Bible* (London and New York 1985)

Scammell, G.V. *The World Encompassed: the First European Maritime Empires c.800–1650* (London 1981)

Scarre, Dr Chris *Past Worlds: The Times Atlas of Archaeology* (London and New York 1988)

Schmidt, K.J. *An Atlas and Survey of South Asian History* (New York and London 1995)

Schwartzberg, Joseph E. (ed) *A Historical Atlas of South Asia* (revised ed., Chicago and London 1992)

Segal, Aaron *An Atlas of International Migration* (London and New Jersey 1993)

Sharer, R.J. *The Ancient Maya* (5th ed., Stanford Ca. 1994)

Shepherd, William R. *Shepherd's Historical Atlas* (9th ed., New York and London 1974)

Sinclair, Keith (ed) *The Oxford Illustrated History of New Zealand* (Oxford and Auckland 1990)

Sinor, D. (ed) *The Cambridge History of Early Inner Asia* (Cambridge 1990)

Smith, B.D. *The Emergence of Agriculture* (New York 1995)

Spence, J. *The Search for Modern China* (London and New York 1990)

Spence J.E. (ed) *The World Today* (London 1994)

Taylour, W. *The Mycenaeans* (2nd ed., London and New York 1990)

The Times Atlas of the World (8th ed., London and New York 1990)

Thornton, John K. *Africa and Africans in the Formation of the Atlantic World 1400-1680* (Cambridge and New York 1992)

Tindall, G. and Shi, D.E. *America, a Narrative History* (New York 1996)

Todd, M. *The Early Germans* (Oxford and Cambridge, Mass. 1992)

Twitchett, D. and Fairbank, J. (eds) *The Cambridge History of China* (15 vols, Cambridge and New York 1978–91)

Vincent Mary and Stradling, R.A. *Cultural Atlas of Spain and Portugal* (London 1994, New York 1995)

Walbank F.W. *The Hellenistic World* (3rd ed., London 1992, Cambridge, Mass. 1993)

Wallace-Hadrill, J.M. *The Barbarian West 400–1000* (5th ed., Oxford and Cambridge, Mass. 1996)

Waller, Philip (ed) *Chronology of the 20th Century* (Oxford 1995)

Webster's New Geographical Dictionary (Springfield, Mass. 1984)

Whittle, A. *Neolithic Europe: a Survey* (Cambridge and New York 1985)

Winter, J.M. *The Experience of World War I* (London and New York 1988)

Wintle, J. *The Vietnam Years* (London 1991)

Photographs

Introductions: *Part 1:* Hutchison Library; *Part 2:* Images Colour Library; *Part 3:* Hutchison Library; *Part 4:* Images Colour Library; *Part 5:* Robert Harding Picture Library; *Part 6:* R. Ian Lloyd/Hutchison Library;

Maps: *6.09:* ZEC/Dalkeith Poster Cards; *6.13:* Popperfoto; *6.14:* Andromeda Oxford Limited; *6.16:* Corbis; *6.19:* Corbis-Bettmann/UPI; *6.22:* Hulton Getty; *6.24:* Saudi Aramco; *6.27:* Hulton Getty.

Artwork references have been assembled from a wide variety of sources. Any individual or institution who can demonstrate that copyright may have been infringed is invited to contact Andromeda Oxford Ltd.

Figures refer to map numbers; **bold** type indicates major references.

A

D

E

J

K

L

N

O

Q

R

S

T

W

X

Y

Z